1981

1981

AN INTRODUCTION TO TAXATION
ADVANCED TOPICS

AN INTRODUCTION TO TAXATION ADVANCED TOPICS

RAY M. SOMMERFELD
The University of Texas at Austin

HERSHEL M. ANDERSON
North Texas State University

HORACE R. BROCK
North Texas State University

RICHARD BOLEY
University of Michigan

JAMES H. BOYD
Arizona State University

ANNA C. FOWLER
The University of Texas at Austin

JOHN L. KRAMER
University of Florida

SANDRA S. KRAMER
University of Florida

SILVIA A. MADEO
Washington University

MICHAEL L. MOORE
University of Southern California

G. FRED STREULING
Brigham Young University

JAMES E. WHEELER
University of Michigan

HARCOURT BRACE JOVANOVICH, INC.
New York   San Diego   Chicago   San Francisco   Atlanta
London   Sydney   Toronto

Printed in the United States of America
Library of Congress Catalog Card Number: 80-81452
ISBN: 0-15-546315-2

preface

An Introduction to Taxation: Advanced Topics is designed to provide current text material for a second—and, possibly, a third—course in federal taxation. The material is appropriate at either the upper division undergraduate or the graduate level. The amount of technical material included clearly is greater than that which most professors will desire to cover in one three-semester-hour course. Our general approach, therefore, is deliberately eclectic.

The general topics included in this text and their depth of coverage may be summarized as follows:

PART	GENERAL TOPIC	NO. OF CHAPTERS
One	Tax Research	3
Two	Corporate/Shareholder Taxation	6
Three	Partnership Taxation	3
Four	Fiduciary Income Taxation	2
Five	Estate and Gift Taxation	4
Six	Miscellaneous Taxes (Accumulated Earnings Tax; Personal Holding Company; FICA Tax)	2
Seven	International Taxation	3

This topical coverage is patterned quite closely after the core subjects studied in most graduate tax programs. Consequently, by using this text, a student can become acquainted with the important general rules that ordinarily control the tax consequences in the most important areas of federal taxation.

Tax research methodology is, of course, common to all areas of taxation. Because good basic tax research skills are critical to success in any tax practice, we have placed this material at the front of the volume. We recommend that all who adopt this book assign Chapters 1 through 3 in their entirety at the start of the course.

The universal importance of other parts and chapters is far less certain. In some instances, you may elect to omit one or two chapters, even though you assign the remainder of a part. For example, in Part Two, Chapter 8 (Consolidated Tax Returns) and Chapter 9 (Subchapter S Corporations) are obviously not essential to the general subject of corporate/shareholder taxation. In other instances, you may wish to include Chapter 9 (Subchapter S Corporations) with study of Part Three (Partnership Taxation). In summary, we have tried to provide maximum flexibility for each professor in his or her design of the second and third tax courses.

Each of the contributing authors was selected because of his or her special expertise in one or more areas of taxation. The authors and their respective chapters are: G. Fred Streuling, Chapters 1–3; Ray M. Sommerfeld, Chapter 4; Richard Boley, Chapters 5 and 6; John L. Kramer, Chapters 7 and 8; Horace R. Brock, Chapter 9; James H. Boyd, Chapters 10–12; Michael L. Moore, Chapters 13 and 14; Anna C. Fowler, Chapters 15–17; Hershel M. Anderson, Chapter 18; Silvia A. Madeo, Chapter 19; James E. Wheeler, Chapter 20; and John L. Kramer and Sandra S. Kramer, Chapters 21–23.

Although such a multiplicity of authors may sometimes result in minor differences in style, we believe that any style problems will be more than offset by the additional insight made possible through each author's depth of technical competence. In short, we have tried to make available to you a highly authoritative text in a condensed treatise.

Several features of *An Introduction to Taxation: Advanced Topics* are designed to make the book useful to both student and instructor. An Instructor's Manual provides solutions for all the problems in the text. The problems are divided into three categories: those that can be solved or answered by using text material; those that require research; and those that require the completion of tax returns.

The book contains a complete glossary of important words and phrases. Two indexes appear at the back of the book. One lists all court cases cited in the text; the other is the usual subject index.

Each chapter is replete with examples illustrating situations in which tax regulations are applied. These examples are designed to clarify the abstractions contained in the tax laws.

Because the subjects included in this volume are restricted to the more advanced and less frequently amended topics in taxation, this book will be revised every other year. Updates, when necessary, will be provided to users at the beginning of the academic year in which the book is not revised. Keyed to the text, these updates will provide the latest material available.

An Introduction to Taxation: Advanced Topics is designed as a companion volume to *An Introduction to Taxation,* the basic text, which deals with basic concepts of taxation. The books share joint authorship and are physically and pedagogically similar. *An Introduction to Taxation: Advanced Topics* is a more technical volume, more rule oriented, than *An Introduction to Taxation,* as befits a second course, which is more likely to be taken by accounting majors. Consequently, although the two volumes work well together as volumes for first and second courses in taxation, they are independent and each may be used alone.

A number of reviewers read portions of the manuscript and made suggestions. We would like to thank Kathryn Buckner and Gary Winkle, Georgia State University; Jane Burns and Ronald Ross, Indiana University; Grover Cleveland and Frederick Jacobs, University of Minnesota; and Allan Ford, University of Kansas for their assistance. Any errors of omission or commission are, of course, ours.

An Introduction to Taxation: Advanced Topics represents the work of twelve authors. Editing and reviews have made it a unified work. We invite your comments and suggestions addressed to individual authors, to us as coordinating authors, or to the publisher.

Hershel Anderson
Horace Brock
Ray Sommerfeld
June 1980

contents

PART TWO

the income taxation of corporations

PART THREE
partnership taxation

PART FOUR
estates and trusts

PART FIVE
wealth transfer taxes

PART SIX
other business–related taxes

PART SEVEN
international taxation

PART

ONE

tax
research

1

the nature of tax research

We assume in this book that you have had some prior exposure to the field of income taxation. During your first tax course, you should have observed numerous limitations in the wording of the Internal Revenue Code. Frequently, even after you have located and read the pertinent code section, the tax answer relevant to a specific set of facts is not obvious. The architects of a tax statute and the related regulations are unable to predict all the situations that may arise in connection with the affairs of millions of taxpayers. Consequently, attempts are made continually by Congress, the Treasury Department, the I.R.S., and the courts to clarify and interpret the statute, adding volumes of authority to the already complex maze of the Code. Thus, every successful tax advisor must be proficient in quickly locating, from among the volumes upon volumes of potential authority, a defensible solution to the tax questions that arise from specific facts. The process of locating and articulating good tax answers is called tax research.

The first three chapters of this book serve as an introduction to tax research as defined in the above paragraph. We shall introduce you to the research methodology commonly used by accountants and lawyers as they perform tax-related work. Upon completion of these three chapters and the associated problems, you should be able to perform basic tax research by yourself. At the same time, however, you should realize that the ability to do good tax research quickly is a skill; and, as with every other skill, your ability to perform well will increase with practice. This introduction can be a good starting point for years of experience.

In compliance work, a tax advisor's primary objective is to be certain that the client has done whatever the law demands, that is, has complied with the law. In planning engagements, an advisor's primary objective generally is to arrange the client's affairs in such a way as to minimize the tax liability. The research methodology used for both tax compliance and tax planning is basically the same. It consists of locating, interpreting, and applying the appropriate tax laws to particular facts. Unfortunately, these are not easy tasks. Although much publicity has been given to the simplification of our tax laws, the opposite has occurred. Every recent tax act has, in fact, added complexities to laws that are already quite complex. Consequently, more and more taxpayers seek assistance from "tax experts" to assure correct compliance at minimum tax costs.

Tax research consists of five basic steps: (1) determining accurate facts; (2) identifying the issues or questions; (3) searching for defensible and authoritative solutions; (4) resolving incomplete and sometimes conflicting authority, evaluating those authorities, and reaching a conclusion; and (5) communicating the conclusion. In Chapter 1 we shall consider the process of gathering sufficient and accurate facts in conjunction with a tax problem. Identifying the pertinent question or questions from a set of facts will also be discussed. In Chapter 2, we shall deal with the creation, location, and interpretation of appropriate authority. In Chapter 3, we shall examine the proper methods of communicating research conclusions and provide an example that will demonstrate the steps to follow in searching for and documenting a defensible position for a given set of facts.

THE IMPORTANCE OF FACTS

The first task that a tax advisor must master is that of properly gathering facts. The assimilation of facts is a skill that can only be learned with experience. An inexperienced tax advisor may be embarrassed upon returning from a conference with a client and realizing that one or more pertinent questions were never raised. Sometimes obtaining the necessary facts can be costly. For example, assume that you have a client who entered the United States on an immigrant visa, and subsequently returned to his native country to oversee personal business matters. He remains outside the United States for a period in excess of 12 months, including one complete tax year. Because your client is not a U.S. citizen and because he was absent from the United States during a complete tax year, it might appear that, for that tax year, he should be considered a *nonresident* alien. Judicial law, however, seems to imply that his status may be that of a resident alien if he intends to return to the United States at some future date on his immigrant visa.[1] The fact that his absence is temporary and that he intends to return to the United States as an immigrant could account for such a status. The tax consequences of such a situation could be far-reaching. Income earned by the taxpayer from services rendered in his native country and potential disposition of property in that country just could be taxable under U.S. tax laws. Obviously, therefore, your ability to reach a correct tax answer will depend to a great degree on your understanding of all the facts. And gathering those facts, especially from an overseas client, may be quite expensive. Knowledge of the law is important, but without a full knowledge of the facts, even a thorough knowledge of the law may be of little value in specific cases.

The critical role of facts can also be demonstrated in less exotic areas such as computing bad debts, selecting depreciation lives, deducting losses, and determining travel and entertainment expenses. In each area, the tax statutes appear to be precise. Consequently, specific facts are frequently the most relevant criteria to tax situations. Section 165(c) of the Internal Revenue Code, for example, limits loss deductions by an individual taxpayer to those incurred in a trade or business, those arising from a transaction entered into for profit, and those considered to be a casualty or theft loss. Assume that your client intends to claim a theft loss deduction. In order to satisfy the definition of theft loss given in the Code, your client must establish that a

theft actually occurred. The courts have held on a number of occasions that a mysterious disappearance of property does not constitute a casualty or theft loss.[2] Thus, an actual police report verifying the theft, depositions of witnesses who observed a break-in, or photographs helping to establish that a break-in occurred may be needed to provide sufficient factual evidence of a casualty loss to sustain the deduction claimed. Once again, *the facts* are important.

Documentation of facts, as indicated by the foregoing example, is another important skill to be learned by every tax advisor. In the case of a casualty loss deduction, the tax advisor should impress on the client the importance of gathering and retaining such documents as accident reports and written statements of witnesses. Purchase invoices and insurance policies can also serve as evidence that the damaged or stolen property existed and belonged to the taxpayer. An appraisal report or pictures or both can help to establish the condition of property before and after a casualty.

A closely related question concerns the proper time to prepare documentation in support of a deduction. Should documentation be made in the year in which the loss is claimed, or should the tax advisor wait to see if the deduction is challenged by the Internal Revenue Service? Audits are usually made two to three years after a return is filed. After considerable time has elapsed, it may be quite cumbersome to assemble evidence and documentation to support a deduction. Often prospective witnesses have died or moved, and important documents are no longer available. On the other hand, collecting documents does cost something, and the I.R.S. may never challenge the return. After all, fewer than 3 percent of all returns filed are audited. In sum, needed documentation generally will be much less costly to gather and preserve at an early date; therefore, some effort to do so is warranted because the risk of an I.R.S. challenge is always present.

TWO CASES OF FACT COMPARED

To further illustrate the important role of facts in the resolution of tax questions, let us examine two court decisions. Both cases deal with the same question: Does the invasion of a house by termites and the resulting destruction constitute a deductible casualty loss under Section 165(c)? Although neither case is a benchmark decision, each one demonstrates the importance of facts in the resolution of a tax question.

---

[1] *J.J. Friedman*, 37 TC 539 (1961).

[2] See for example *Edgar F. Stevens*, 6 TCM 805 (1947).

As you read the decisions of both cases, note the similarities and differences. The first case, involving Joseph and Roselle Shopmaker, was decided in 1953 by the U.S. District Court for the Eastern District of Missouri. The decision, rendered by District Judge Hulen, reads in part as follows:

FINDINGS OF FACT

In December, 1949, plaintiffs purchased the residence which is the subject matter of the claim. It had been constructed some twelve years prior. Its expectancy is fifty years. At time of purchase, plaintiff, Joseph Shopmaker, and the real estate agent testified that he had made a number of inspections of houses and knew how to detect termites. No evidence of termites was found at the time plaintiffs purchased the residence. No termites were found during the year 1950. On February 8, 1951, termites swarmed in the kitchen. Witness Ralph Hoener examined the house and found extensive damage from termites. He has been in the termite business for twenty-one years. As an expert he testified he could not tell when the termites invaded the house for the first time. On February 8 he found swarms in two locations.

Installation of termite controls is an occupation for experts, but the presence of termites can be determined by non-experts. They are detected by the runways on the ground and across material that they do not attack, by swarming and piercing the wood, which after termite destruction remains only a hollow shell. The real estate agent who examined the property at the time plaintiffs made the purchase testified he was informed on the manner of detecting termites. He found no runways or swarms at the time of his inspection. He used a penknife to pierce the wood joints in the basement. This is substantial evidence that the residence was free of termites at the time plaintiffs purchased in December, 1949. The facts bring this case within the *Rosenberg* case.

OPINION

We are impressed with the argument of plaintiffs that the casualty is the invasion of the premises by termites. This is a comparatively quick or sudden operation. The resultant damage which may extend over a period of months or years flows from the casualty. The damage and the time it takes for the termites to effect it should not be confused with their initial invasion and determining what is the casualty. The case of *Burkett* 10 TCM 948, (1951), referred to in the *Rosenberg* opinion, illustrates this observation. In the Burkett case, sand from wooden foundations under a house was washed away during a hurricane. The result was that foundation posts gradually sank over a period of two years, eventually requiring the replacement of many of the posts in order to level the floors.

The commissioner held this was a loss by casualty. The casualty was the washing away of the sand during the hurricane. The damage developed over a period of years from that casualty.

The evidence is undisputed that if plaintiffs are entitled to recover, judgment should be for a refund of $1,476.56.

Let judgment be settled and submitted accordingly.[3]

The second case, involving Joseph and Margaret Austra, was heard by the Tax Court in 1960. The decision, rendered by Judge Tannenwald, reads in part as follows:

FINDINGS OF FACT

The petitioners are husband and wife and reside in Germantown, Maryland. They filed their joint federal income tax return for the year 1960 with the district director of internal revenue, Baltimore, Maryland.

Petitioners completed construction of a home in Germantown in 1954. They lived in the house through the taxable year involved herein.

The house was one-story and of wood frame construction. There was an open or "crawl" between the ground and the base of the house under the kitchen and dining area.

In July 1958, termite infestation was discovered in supporting wooden beams and posts in the crawl space, and the damage was repaired. The repairs consisted of replacing the damaged wooden posts which had been in contact with the ground with posts of steel and adding a cement wall capped with concrete to the base of the house under the kitchen and dining area. The contractor who made the repairs did not check the remainder of the house for termite infestation.

After the repairs in 1958 and through May 1960, no exterminator inspected the house for termites, although petitioners themselves made periodic examinations of the house. The contractor who made the 1958 repairs applied preventative spray to the house twice in 1959.

In June 1960, termite infestation, consisting of both live and dead channels, were discovered in the portion of the house not checked for infestation in 1958. There was no infestation discovered in the primary supports of the house which the contractor had checked and repaired in 1958. The damage was repaired and the repairs were paid for in 1960.

Termite infestation may be present notwithstanding the absence of outward signs of such infestation. It may not be apparent from visual inspection of the interior and exterior of a building.

[3]*Shopmaker*, 54-1 USTC 9195 (DC, ED MO; 1953)

Petitioners in 1960 had the house repaired and remodeled and paid therefor a total of $4,200. Of this amount, $2,565 represented the cost of repairing the termite damage.

In their 1960 return petitioners deducted $2,500 as a loss from termite damage. In an amended return for that year they increased the amount of the claim deduction to $2,789.22.

OPINION

The sole issue in the instant case is whether the hole drilled in the petitioners' pocketbook by termites in 1960 gave rise to a deductible casualty loss. Petitioners contend that the termite infestation occurred between 1958 and 1960 and thus met the requirement of "suddenness" which the decisions have incorporated in subsection (c)(3). Respondent argues that petitioners have not proved that the infestation discovered in 1960 had not begun before July 1958, and, even if the infestation began on or after July 1958, petitioners have still not established the requisite suddenness. We agree with respondent.

In prior cases, we have construed "casualty" as used in section 165(c)(3) to mean "an accident, a mishap, some sudden invasion of a hostile agency; it excludes the progressive deterioration of property through a steadily operating cause."

The instant case is strikingly similar to *Rudolph Lewis Hoppy,* supra. In that case, a professional exterminator in 1956 discovered and repaired damage to the substructure of the taxpayer's residence caused by a fungus infestation commonly known as "dry rot." The exterminator's inspection of the premises was limited to the substructure.

After the repairs and through November 1959, taxpayer, from time to time, personally inspected the substructure of the house. In November 1959, infestation was discovered entirely above the substructure. We held that the taxpayer had failed to prove that the areas first discovered in 1959 to be infested were free of such infestation at the time of the exterminator's inspection in 1956 and that, as a consequence, he had not shown the suddenness necessary to support a deduction in 1959. Compare *E.G. Kilroe,* supra.

Although the instant case involves termite damage and Hoppy involved damage from dry rot, petitioners in both cases failed to prove that the damage did not occur substantially earlier than its discovery, and the decision in Hoppy is controlling in the instant case.[4]

Comparing these cases, we find a number of identical facts. In both instances the taxpayers claimed a casualty loss deduction in their income tax returns for a loss incurred through the invasion of their personal

[4]*Joseph A. Austra,* 66,028 P-H Memo TC (1966).

residences by termites. The question, therefore, is whether or not the invasion of a personal residence by termites constitutes a casualty loss. In *Shopmaker,* the taxpayers were able to establish to the satisfaction of the court that their home had been free of termites at a specific date. The taxpayers' proof relied heavily on the testimony of two expert witnesses. A real estate agent testified that he had made an inspection in December of 1949 and had found the home free of termites. Further evidence was introduced to show that a termite inspection can be performed by one not regularly in the business of pest extermination. Detailed procedures of the initial inspection were explained. These facts were corroborated by a second expert witness whose profession was that of termite control. This evidence indicated that termites were first discovered in February 1951. Finally, the period from December 1949 to February 1951 was determined by the courts to satisfy the suddenness test, which is an essential ingredient for a casualty loss deduction.

In *Austra,* the facts presented did not prove to the satisfaction of the court that in July 1958, when a termite infestation was first discovered in a portion of the house, the rest of the home was completely free of termites. In fact, the findings indicate that in June of 1960 termites were discovered in a portion of the house that had not been checked for infestation in 1958. Observe also that no expert testimony was presented; hence, many of the facts introduced by the taxpayers were not independently corroborated.

As indicated previously, neither of these decisions is a particularly important judicial determination. In fact, the Internal Revenue Service has announced that a deduction for termite damage will be routinely challenged. In the opinion of the I.R.S., termite infestation cannot meet the suddenness test. Nevertheless, these two cases demonstrate the importance of facts. They also suggest the importance of presenting facts; the way facts are assembled and substantiated frequently influences a court's decision. An expert understanding of the tax laws alone will not make anyone a good tax advisor. The ability to delineate, assimilate, and interpret the facts in each situation is an equally necessary and important quality for a successful tax researcher.

IDENTIFYING THE QUESTIONS

Once the researcher has gathered and identified all the pertinent facts, he or she must then enumerate the appropriate questions so that the necessary authority can be located. Consider the following example. Tracy Field is the proprietor of a small ski resort on the western slopes of the Rocky Mountains. In 19X1 he sold five acres of unimproved real estate to a famous movie star, Ray Gunn, for a total price of $100,000. Tracy acquired the property as an investment six years earlier at a cost of $20,000. The arrangements call for Mr. Gunn to assume a $20,000 mortgage. In addition, Tracy will receive four 10 percent interest-bearing notes of $20,000 each, with one note maturing annually beginning in 19X2.

This year, 19X2, Ray Gunn starred in a hit science fiction release. With his new-found wealth, he decided to pay off all four notes immediately. He approaches your client, Tracy Field, with the proposal. Tracy thereupon inquires of you what tax consequences will result from the receipt of the $80,000 lump-sum payment plus accrued interest. He had intended to report the transaction on the installment basis, and you had originally advised him that the transaction would qualify for installment reporting. A proper election was made on Tracy's 19X1 tax return.

Because 19X1 was a fantastic ski season, the resort's operating income amounted to $150,000. So far, however, 19X2 has been a dismal year. Consequently, Tracy anticipates that the lump-sum receipt of $80,000 can be sheltered with an operating loss of around $120,000. Tax returns for years before 19X1 show that operating losses cannot be carried back past 19X1.

Generating the appropriate questions (or "issues") is another critical tax skill that can be developed through practice. Typically, the form in which the issues are stated varies with experience. A tax advisor with limited experience and only a passing knowledge of the Internal Revenue Code might assemble the following questions from the example:

1. Can Field defer recognition of a gain until he collects the cash?

2. What methods of deferral are available to the taxpayer?

3. What is the installment method of reporting?

4. What requirements must be met to elect the installment method of reporting income?

The initial search for satisfactory conclusions to tax questions ordinarily raises additional questions (issues) in the mind of the tax advisor. Sometimes questions that should be raised completely escape the attention of an inexperienced researcher. In order to reach a supportable solution to this example problem, the researcher must enumerate all of the requirements for electing the installment sales method. Thus, even if overlooked initially, a tax advisor should eventually reach at least two additional questions; namely:

5. Does the installment sale method require more than one payment?

6. If more than one payment is required, must they occur in more than one tax year?

These questions must be examined if Ray Gunn proceeds to make a lump-sum payment in the year after the sale.

A more experienced tax advisor might phrase the original questions in an entirely different way. The fact that he or she has greater knowledge of the Code is likely to result in a question that includes a direct reference to a specific Code section. For instance, a more seasoned advisor might ask the following question:

1. Does the transaction between Gunn and Field qualify for an election under Section 453?

The advisor's familiarity with Sec. 453 quite possibly includes an implicit recognition of the significance of the facts that this transaction involves real estate, qualifies as a casual sale, and exceeds the $1,000 minimum sales price requirement. The more experienced researcher might well recognize that one or more additional tests must also be satisfied. That knowledge could give rise to the following question:

2. Does the transaction between Gunn and Field satisfy the 30 percent requirement of Section 453(b) (2)(B)?

Experience and a careful reading of Sec. 453(a) might also make a more experienced advisor aware of a second critical issue. Because Sec. 453(a) refers to installment *payments,* a veteran researcher would soon ask this key question:

3. Does an election under Sec. 453 require more than one payment?

Anyone with business experience will probably realize that an installment transaction can easily be arranged to include two or more payments. If only two payments are required, however, and if the two represent the entire transaction, will a tax advantage remain for the taxpayer? Thus, experience may help a tax advisor formulate the final question:

4. If Sec. 453 requires more than one payment, must such payments be made in two separate tax years?

The seasoned tax researcher realizes that lengthy periods of contemplative thought may be necessary before the complex tax issues implicit in many business transactions become obvious. In addition, a good imagination and considerable creativity are important traits of every successful tax advisor. Experience, of course, cannot be overrated. Familiarity with tax provisions enables a researcher to ignore potential issues for which he or she already knows the answers. Research of similar issues on previous occasions is an important item of inventory to the tax advisor. On the other hand, too much experience can sometimes stunt one's ability to be imaginative. Too often a researcher may simply say, "Yes, that looks familiar. We'll handle it the same way we did in previous situations." Whenever that happens, the tax advisor obviously forfeits the opportunity to investigate alternatives that may be even more advantageous to a particular client.

Before-the-facts research

In the foregoing discussion we have emphasized the methodology appropriate for after-the-fact research. Research before all of the critical events of a transaction have actually occurred is known as tax planning. Tax planning involves carefully structuring facts before they have occurred. As a first step, the tax advisor must determine what desired outcome the client has in mind. Once the desired result is established, the question is one of identifying the alternatives available to reach the desired outcome. The process is much the same as identifying a point on a road map and then examining the various ways of getting there. Some routes will turn out to be more efficient; that is, they may be shorter or have fewer obstacles such as rugged mountains, narrow

bridges, or roads in need of repair. Tax planning carries with it considerable risk; seldom will the tax advisor find a client situation that duplicates, in every respect, the facts implicit in prior authority. Thus, the objective of the tax planner is to reduce the risk inherent in the plan proposed to a client. An advisor should explain to the client any risks involved in each alternative. Because nontax considerations may frequently outweigh tax objectives, the client may not always elect the safest and most efficient alternative. In the end, the client must make the final decision as to which alternative should be pursued.

After a decision has been made to adopt a particular course of action to achieve a desired tax result, the advisor should exercise sufficient care and offer constant encouragement to implement the facts assumed in the original plan. Even a slight variation in facts can often introduce additional issues and undesired results. Sufficient documentation should be preserved to substantiate that the desired course of action was followed. Finally, every tax plan must have as an underlying objective a business purpose other than that of tax avoidance. If no business purpose exists, the I.R.S. is likely to challenge the plan and invoke the judicial "substance over form" doctrine. Accordingly, the good tax advisor will also ensure that every tax plan has a well documented business purpose.

In this chapter, we have examined the critical role that facts play in tax research. Appropriate issue(s) can be identified only if all the facts are known and can be substantiated. In the next chapter, we shall examine the task of locating appropriate authority to prepare a defensible position for specific tax questions.

PROBLEMS

1. As defined in Chapter 1, tax research involves a sequence of five steps. List them in order.

2. Research in connection with tax planning is frequently referred to as before-the-fact research. Explain what is meant by tax planning and contrast it with after-the-fact research.

3. a. Locate and read the two cases cited below. If you don't know how to locate tax court cases, see Volume 1, Appendix A to Chapter 4. The format of judicial citations is also discussed in detail in Chapter 2 of this book. Table 2-3 should be helpful.
   Robert N. Hewitt, 16 TCM 468, TC Memo 1957–112.
   John Thomas Blake, 29 TCM 513, TC Memo 1970–117.
   b. Enumerate, in outline form, the important facts of each case.
   c. Suggest, in outline form, the facts that you feel most influenced the judges to reach opposite conclusions in the two cases.

4. a. Locate and read the two cases cited below:

   FS Services, Inc., 413 F2d 548, 69-2 USTC ¶9539 (Ct.Cl., 1969).

   Dearborn Company, 444 F2d 1145, 71-1 USTC ¶9478 (Ct.Cl., 1971).

   b. Enumerate, in outline form, the important facts of each case.

   c. Suggest, in outline form, those facts that you feel most influenced the judges to reach opposite conclusions in the two cases.

5. a. Locate and read the two cases cited below:

   Martha S. Cowarde, 35 TCM 1066, TC Memo 1976-246.

   C.E.R. Howard, 28 TCM 1435, TC Memo 1969-277.

   b. Enumerate, in outline form, the important facts related to casualty losses in each case.

   c. Suggest, in outline form, those facts that you feel most influenced the judges to reach opposite conclusions in the two cases.

6. On January 2, 19X1, Paul Daniels sold a parcel of land to John Pope. Paul acquired the parcel several years ago at a cost of $6,200. At the time of the acquisition, his intentions were to hold the land for appreciation. The city commission, however, recently voted to locate the new city dump adjacent to his property. Fortunately, Paul heard that John, who operates a scavenger and antique business, was searching for a piece of land near the new dump site. Paul arranged the sale on an installment contract. The arrangement called for four $1,500 installment notes (noninterest bearing) due in consecutive years on the last day of the year. The first note is due on December 31, 19X1. In connection with the filing of Paul Daniel's 19X1 tax return, what questions should be raised based on the foregoing facts? Do not search for solutions at this time. Just enumerate those issues that you feel require further investigation.

7. A CPA firm reimburses its employees for expenses related to educational pursuits that are either directly or indirectly related to the performance of their duties in the firm. As a result, two of its employees are working toward law degrees at two different institutions. Tom Layton is enrolled at Future State University and will graduate next year with a law degree. He plans to sit for the bar exam at that time but intends to remain with his present employer. Rick Simpson did not do well on the LSAT exam and, therefore, could not obtain acceptance at Future State. He enrolled at Night Tech College. The college is not accredited; consequently, Rick will not be able to sit for the bar exam. After graduation, however, he plans to look for a position as an assistant controller or controller and feels that the law degree will make him more marketable. Also, the firm wishes to further formalize the educational benefits program and plans to publish a pamphlet that will answer questions employees such as Tom and Rick may raise concerning the tax treatment of the educational benefits. What questions should be examined relative to the payments made by the CPA firm? Do not search for solutions at this time. Simply enumerate those issues you feel require further investigation.

8. Alice Mariyou is a junior at Golden West University, where she has been enrolled on a full-time basis since her freshman year. Alice is employed on a part-time basis by the student bookstore. According to the W-2 form issued by the bookstore, she earned gross wages of $3,400 for 19X1, which she used entirely for her own support. In November of 19X1 Alice married Tom Ready, a first-year law student. For 19X1 Tom earned $1,200 from a summer job. Tom and Alice filed a joint return and were refunded all income taxes withheld.

   Alice's parents have assisted with her educational expenses. In past years, however, Alice has usually earned more at the bookstore than the total amount furnished by her parents. For example, in 19X1 Alice's parents paid $800 toward tuition and $200 for books. Tom and Alice have moved into a one-bedroom apartment located within walking distance of campus. The monthly rent, including utilities, totals $300. Before her marriage, when school was in session, Alice lived in her sorority house. During the summer and on weekends, however, she usually stayed with her parents. Even now, Tom and Alice frequently visit Alice's parents on weekends. Alice's parents have stated that her former bedroom will always be available for them to use. Recently, someone inquired about the possibility of renting Alice's bedroom as a sleeping room and offered $100 per month. Although Alice's parents are not wealthy and could use the extra income at this time, the offer was declined. They are still smarting from the November wedding which cost a total of $2,400 (wedding dress, $280; flowers, $220; reception, $1,800; contribution to the minister, $100). Alice's parents feel that taking in a renter would jeopardize the visits from Tom and Alice, which they look forward to.

List all possible tax questions that come to mind for the tax year 19X1. Do not search for solutions at this time, but enumerate those issues that you feel require further investigation.

9. Earl and Ellice are married but have for various good reasons filed separate tax returns during the last five years. Recently, an early winter storm caused considerable damage to their personal residence. Earl paid all the expenses necessary to restore the property to its condition immediately before the casualty. The storm had been forecast by the National Weather Service, and Earl and Ellice had plenty of time to prepare for the onslaught. Despite all their preparations, however, the storm caused approximately $2,400 in damages, which were not covered by insurance. Earl and Ellice own their personal residence under state law as tenants by the entireties. You have been asked to prepare Earl and Ellice's separate returns for the current year. List the tax questions that you feel warrant research. Do not search for solutions at this time. Just enumerate those issues that you feel require further investigation.

finding, interpreting, and assessing potential authority

Unlike some other areas of the law, most questions about income taxation have a statutory base. Consequently, the first step in locating potential authority in tax matters often consists of identifying the pertinent Code sections. Although the current statute is found in the Internal Revenue Code of 1954 (as amended), many provisions of that law were carried over from the 1939 Revenue Code; some even go back to the numerous Revenue Acts that predate the 1939 Code. In addition to locating the pertinent Code section, a tax researcher may have to examine the legislative history of relevant section(s). This process is simplified if one understands clearly how a tax law comes into existence. Therefore, we shall begin this chapter with a brief review of the legislative process.

THE LEGISLATIVE HISTORY OF A TAX ACT

The U.S. Constitution requires that all revenue measures be initiated by the House of Representatives. After a bill is passed by the House, it is transmitted to the Senate. Although not occurring simultaneously, the progress of a bill through both bodies of Congress is similar. First, the bill is sent to committee—in the House, the Ways and Means Committee and in the Senate, the Finance Committee. Next, the committees schedule hearings and allow interested parties to testify. When a bill is passed by the committee, it is sent to the larger bodies of Congress where the full membership votes on the proposed legislation. Bills passed by the House and the Senate usually vary significantly. Differences between two versions of the same bill must be ironed out by a *Conference Committee,* whose members are appointed by the Speaker of the House and the President of the Senate. After the Conference Committee reconciles the differences between the House and the Senate versions, the bill is returned to both the House and the Senate for a final vote. If approved, the bill is sent to the White House for the President's signature.

The work of the House Ways and Means, Senate Finance, and conference committees is recorded in official documents known as committee reports. These reports are usually the primary means of determining the underlying rationale for a specific provision and the intent behind action taken by either house. Changes or amendments are sometimes made on the floor of either house, most frequently the Senate. Such action is recorded and preserved as part of the *Congressional Record* but does not otherwise become part of a committee report.

A tax bill passed by Congress is usually issued as a Revenue Act that amends the existing Internal Revenue Code. Some Revenue Acts are named to reflect a specific objective of Congress, for example, the Tax Reform Act of 1976 and the Tax Reduction and Simplification Act of 1977. Officially, however, a revenue bill is signed into law as a public law. For example, the Tax Reduction and Simplification Act of 1977 is officially known as Public Law 95-30.

THE ADMINISTRATION OF THE TAX STATUTES

The Internal Revenue Service, an arm of the Treasury Department, is responsible for the administration of the income tax statutes. The administrative process consists of both interpreting and enforcing the law. The I.R.S. interprets the law by issuing Treasury Regulations, Revenue Rulings, Revenue Procedures, and Private Letter Rulings requested by individual taxpayers. The I.R.S. enforces the law through systematic audits of returns, the administration of an appeals mechanism for taxpayers to arbitrate disagreements with audit adjustments, and a collection process designed to collect overdue taxes.

The taxpayer has little control over the process that selects tax returns for audit. If additional assessments are levied by revenue agents, however, a taxpayer may appeal the assessment to a Regional Conferee, who has administrative authority to settle the grievance. A conference between a taxpayer (or the taxpayer's legal representative such as a CPA or lawyer) and a regional conferee constitutes an informal meeting during which the views of the taxpayer and the I.R.S. are presented. A written appeal by the taxpayer delineating his or her complaints is not required unless the tax deficiency in question exceeds $2,500. A regional conferee is authorized, based on the evidence presented, to administratively (i.e., outside the formal judicial system) reach a settlement with the taxpayer. A settlement could mean a cancellation of the previously assessed tax deficiency or a compromise reduction in the amount of additional tax assessed during the audit. Should the parties reach no agreement, the taxpayer may seek further recourse through the judicial system.

Note that files and correspondence generated during an audit or appellate conference have no legal precedential value because they are not publicly released unless they subsequently become a part of a formal court record. In fact, administratively resolving the tax treatment of a particular transaction with the I.R.S. does not prohibit the I.R.S. from taking a contrary position in a subsequent year, even with the same taxpayer. Precedent-setting authority, such as Treasury Regulations, Revenue Rulings and Revenue Procedures, is of great importance in a self-assessment tax system (a system in which taxpayers are responsible for figuring and paying their own taxes), because it provides greater certainty for taxpayers who must interpret the tax laws. For example, using a revenue ruling as a "precedent" means that a taxpayer with a fact situation identical to one enunciated in that ruling can

expect with reasonable certainty that his or her case will receive the same treatment by the I.R.S. as announced in the ruling. The absence of useful precedential authority compels the I.R.S. to formulate precedent-setting authority in the form of regulations, revenue rulings, revenue procedures, and so on, which may be contrary to the interpretation hoped for by the taxpayer. If the taxpayer's interpretation is contrary to the position taken by the I.R.S., either the government or the taxpayer may file suit in a federal court to resolve the disagreement.

THE JUDICIAL PROCESS

When disagreements between the I.R.S. and a taxpayer cannot be settled through the administrative appeals process, the taxpayer may seek relief through the judicial system. The taxpayer may select one of three courts in which to initiate litigation with the I.R.S.—the Tax Court, a U.S. District Court, or the Court of Claims. The selection of a court depends largely on when the taxpayer makes payment of the contested tax deficiency. If the tax deficiency is paid *before* litigation is begun, a taxpayer must sue for a refund in either the District Court or the Court of Claims. If the taxpayer refuses to or is unable to make payments of the alleged deficiency, the question must be litigated in the Tax Court.

Decisions rendered by both the Tax Court and the District Court may be appealed by either the taxpayer or the I.R.S. to one of the 11 Circuit Courts of Appeals. To appeal a decision of the Court of Claims or the Circuit Courts of Appeals requires a *Writ of Certiorari* (a request for review) to the U.S. Supreme Court. The Supreme Court is selective in granting *certiorari* and usually will review a lower court decision only when a conflict of opinion exists between two or more courts or when an issue is deemed to be of major significance. Figure 2-1 depicts the judicial process available to a taxpayer in a tax dispute.

U.S. Tax Court

The Tax Court is an official court of the United States with jurisdiction over deficiencies in income, excess profits, self-employment, estate, and gift taxes. Before 1943, the Tax Court was known as the Board of Tax Appeals. The 16 judges of the Tax Court are appointed by the President of the United States for 15-year terms each. Functioning under the direction of a chief judge, with administrative offices in Washington, D.C., the Tax Court conducts hearings in most major cities of the

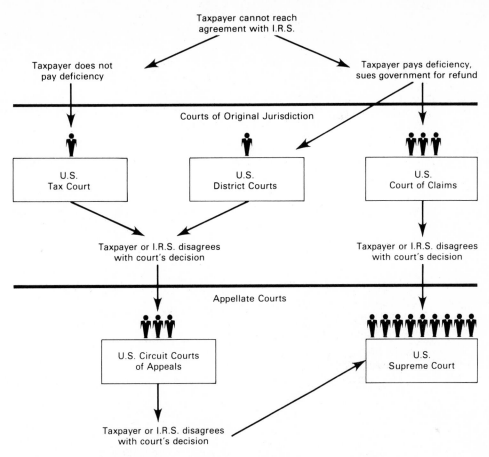

FIGURE **2-1**   The Taxpayer and the U.S. Court System

United States. Hearings are conducted by a single judge who submits findings to the chief judge. The chief judge then determines if the subject matter is sufficiently important or controversial to be considered for a review by the full court. A decision by the Tax Court that has been heard by either one judge or by the full court must be further classified by the chief judge as either a "memorandum" or a "regular" decision. Cases in which the law, in the opinion of the chief judge, is well established—and which, therefore, require only a determination of facts—are classified as "memorandum" decisions. "Regular" decisions concern points of law that are either less well established or about which considerable disagreement exists among the judges.

Concern about the expense of litigation, particularly issues involving relatively small amounts of tax, prompted Congress to establish a Small Tax Case Division as part of the Tax Court. The Small Tax Case Division hears disputes involving alleged tax deficiencies of $5,000 or less. Presided over by commissioners who report to one of the Tax Court judges, the hearings are conducted in the same cities in which the regular court

meets. The Small Tax Case Division differs from the regular Tax Court in the following ways. A taxpayer may appear in the Small Case Division without being represented by counsel. No formal record is maintained of these proceedings, and the decisions have no precedential value. Furthermore, no appeal is possible from a decision by the Small Tax Case Division.

The District and Circuit Court system

The U.S. federal court system consists of 11 circuits, each circuit divided into several districts. District Courts are presided over by a District Judge, who may hear a case either with or without a jury. The District Court is the only tribunal in which a taxpayer may request a jury trial. As noted above, appeals from both the District Court and the Tax Court must be directed to the Circuit Court of Appeals having jurisdiction. A panel of three circuit court judges ordinarily reviews cases appealed from a lower court. The geographical division of the Circuit Courts of Appeals is shown in Figure 2-2.

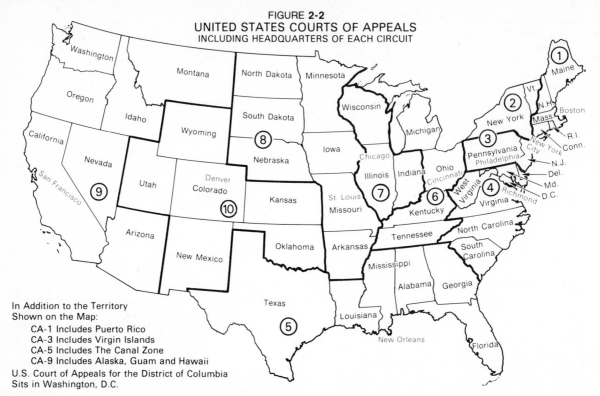

FIGURE 2-2
UNITED STATES COURTS OF APPEALS
INCLUDING HEADQUARTERS OF EACH CIRCUIT

In Addition to the Territory
Shown on the Map:
   CA-1 Includes Puerto Rico
   CA-3 Includes Virgin Islands
   CA-5 Includes The Canal Zone
   CA-9 Includes Alaska, Guam and Hawaii
U.S. Court of Appeals for the District of Columbia
Sits in Washington, D.C.

SOURCE: *CCH Standard Federal Tax Reporter*, Vol. '79(10), p. 70,604. Reproduced with permission from *Standard Federal Tax Reporter*, published and copyrighted by Commerce Clearing House, Inc., 4025 W. Peterson Avenue, Chicago, Illinois 60646.

In resolving tax issues or questions, a researcher must locate, interpret, and evaluate all the numerous authorities relevant to the particular situation, including the statutes and interpretations by the I.R.S. and the courts. Ordinarily, the search should begin with statutory authority. From that point, the procedures become less well defined. Some good researchers go next to administrative authority, then to judicial authority, and finally to secondary references. Other good researchers contend that one should avoid reading administrative authority as long as possible because it represents the I.R.S.'s point of view. They argue that it is too easy to become closed minded early in the research process, and hence, they would defer the government's position until the end.

STATUTORY AUTHORITY

The federal tax statutes are compiled in the Internal Revenue Code of 1954 (I.R.C.). Commercial companies—such as Commerce Clearing House (CCH), Prentice-Hall (P-H), Research Institute of America (RIA), and West Publishing Company—publish paperback editions of the Code, which are typically used by tax professionals as their working copy. The official copy of the Internal Revenue Code is found in Title 26 of the United States Code.

The Internal Revenue Code of 1954 is divided into Subtitles, Chapters, Subchapters, and Parts. Table 2-1 lists the Subchapters and Parts of Chapter 1. Besides Subtitle A—Income Taxes, the I.R.C. contains seven additional Subtitles, including, for example, Subtitle C—Employment Taxes, and Subtitle F—Procedures and Administration. The Subtitle divisions are broken into Chapters, designated by Arabic numerals. As shown in Table 2-1, Chapter 1 is titled Normal Taxes and Surtaxes. Within each Chapter, a Subchapter designation is used for further organization. Chapter 1 contains Subchapters A through U. Because Subchapter R was repealed in 1969, only 20 Subchapters are currently operative.

Note that each Subchapter is divided into Parts—each Part designated by a Roman numeral. Two further divisions, not shown in Table 2-1, are Subparts and Sections.

Nearly all the "popular" income-tax literature refers only to sections of the Code. Thus, for instance, "Section 301" refers (without specific mention) to the 1954 Code, Subtitle A, Chapter 1, Subchapter C, Part

TABLE 2-1

(continued on page 2/6)

TABLE **2-1** (continued)

Subchapter Q (continued)					
Part II	Mitigation of effect of limitations and other provisions			Subchapter R was repealed, effective January 1, 1969.]	
Part III	Involuntary liquidation and replacement of LIFO inventories		Subchapter S	Election of certain small business corporations as to taxable status	
Part IV	War loss recoveries		Subchapter T	Cooperatives and their patrons	
Part V	Claim of right		Part I	Tax treatment of cooperatives	
Part VI	Other limitations		Part II	Tax treatment by patrons of patronage dividends	
Part VII	Recoveries of foreign expropriation losses				
Subchapter R	Election of certain partnerships and proprietorships as to taxable status. [Note:		Part III	Definitions; special rules	
			Subchapter U	General stock ownership plans	

1, Subpart A. We know this because section designations get progressively larger. For example, section numbers 1 through 1561 are used in Subtitle A—Income Taxes; section numbers 2001 through 2621 are found in Subtitle B—Estate and Gift Taxes; Subtitle F—Procedure and Administration—is designated by section numbers 6001 through 7851. Note that not all section numbers within each set belonging to a Subtitle are currently in use. This allows Congress to insert (or delete) changes in the law without renumbering the entire Code.

Because most of the tax literature refers only to a section number, it is important to understand what a reference, such as "Sec. 301(b)(1)(A)," means. Suppose you read this citation in connection with a discussion on "distributions by a corporation to individual shareholders." Obtaining a copy of the 1954 Code, you find in Section 301, Subsection (b), Paragraph (1), Subparagraph (A) that a distribution by a corporation to a noncorporate shareholder includes the amount of money distributed plus the fair market value of any additional property received by the shareholder. A portion of Section 301, reproduced in Figure 2-3, shows that

the organizational division of a code section entails subsections, paragraphs, subparagraphs, and sub-subparagraphs.

As mentioned earlier, as a tax law proceeds through Congress, a number of committee reports are prepared. These reports can usually shed considerable light on the intent of Congress in passing a particular law. Although all the commercial publishers cited above reprint various portions of committee reports, the reports are also published in their entirety by the Government Printing Office (GPO), and the full reports can be found in the government documents section of any research library.

ADMINISTRATIVE PRONOUNCEMENTS

The responsibility for interpreting the tax statutes is delegated to the Secretary of the Treasury by Sec. 7805 of the Internal Revenue Code. The Internal Revenue Service discharges this responsibility by issuing various documents. Treasury Regulations inform tax-

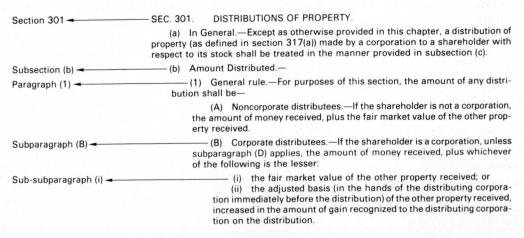

FIGURE 2-3

payers how the government interprets various segments of the Code without reference to any specific taxpayer's situation. Again, the publishing companies previously noted print paperback editions of the regulations. Usually, regulations are first issued in proposed form in the *Federal Register,* which is published twice a month by the Government Printing Office (GPO). Interested parties ordinarily have 30 days to comment on their content. Eventually, final regulations are issued as Treasury Decisions (TDs). The TDs also appear in the *Federal Register.* Thereafter, the Treasury Regulations are formally embodied in Title 26 in the Code of Federal Regulations.

The numerical reference number of each regulation, which consists of three critical parts, identifies its relationship to the Code. For example, Treas. Reg. Sec. 1.162-5(b)(2)(ii) can be segmented into three parts, as follows:

Treas. Reg. Sec. 1.162-5(b)(2)(ii)

1 2   3

The first part, the number before the decimal, indicates which tax the regulation interprets. Number 1 refers to an income tax provision of the Code; 31 indicates an employment tax interpretation; 301 refers to an administrative and procedural interpretation. The number immediately after the decimal designates which specific I.R.C. section is being interpreted; in this case it is Sec. 162. The final set of numbers and letters [in this example, -5(b)(2)(ii)] depicts the organizational scheme used to make reference to the regulation. No direct correlation exists between the organizational scheme of part three in the regulations and the organizational scheme of the reference numbers found in the I.R.C.

Although regulations are intended to be interpretive, in a few instances they are almost "statutory" in nature. In Sec. 1502 of the I.R.C., Congress delegated to the Secretary of the Treasury the responsibility of prescribing rules for filing consolidated tax returns. In conformity with the regulations promulgated under Sec. 1502, corporations filing a consolidated tax return are required to execute a consent form in which they agree to abide by the rules stipulated in the regulations. Because the taxpayers' consent enjoins them from subsequently taking issue with the regulations, the regulations are therefore considered to be nearly statutory. The Supreme Court has also held that the reenactment of a statute without disapproval of the regulations gives the regulations the force of law.[1] At the other extreme, however, the courts occasionally will overrule regulations if they are found to be contrary to the statute.[2]

In addition to the Treasury Regulations, which provide nonspecific interpretations, the I.R.S. regularly publishes Revenue Rulings that provide taxpayers with interpretations for a specific set of facts. Frequently, the facts explained in the Revenue Ruling are taken from actual inquiries received by the I.R.S. If officials of the I.R.S. feel that the subject matter may be of a general interest, they publish that Revenue Ruling in the weekly *Internal Revenue Bulletin* (IRB). The published Revenue Rulings are reissued twice a year in a permanently bound Cumulative Bulletin (CB). Revenue Rulings are chronologically numbered. Thus, the 474th Revenue Ruling issued in 1980 will be Rev. Rul. 80-474. When referring to the weekly *Internal Revenue Bulletin,* in which that ruling first appeared, the citation will be: Rev. Rul. 80-474, IRB 49, 11, indicating that the text can be found on page 11 of the 49th weekly *Bulletin.* A later reference to the more permanent cumulative bulletin would be: Rev. Rul. 80-474, 1980-2 CB 134. This signifies that the full text of the ruling can be found in volume 2 of the 1980 *Cumulative Bulletin,* page 134.

Revenue Procedures are issued to publicize how the I.R.S. will conduct certain administrative matters. For example in Rev. Proc. 79-38, the I.R.S. set forth rules relating to the reporting of wages and payment of taxes with respect to seamen. The same general mechanism for publishing relevant rulings is used for Revenue Procedures. Therefore, citations to Revenue Procedures are written in the same format as citations to Revenue Rulings, except for the prefix "Rev. Proc."

Other interpretive materials furnished by the I.R.S. are Information Releases (IRs), private letter rulings, technical advice memoranda, and determination letters. Only the IRs (formerly known as Technical Information Releases, or TIRs), which are initially issued in the form of news releases and then occasionally reissued as Revenue Rulings or Revenue Procedures, are of general application. The private letter rulings and advice memoranda have precedential value only for those taxpayers for whom they were issued and then only to the fact situation for which they were issued. Both CCH and P-H, however, have begun to publish a loose-leaf service that contains private letter rulings,

---

[1] *R.J. Reynolds Tobacco Company,* 306 U.S. 110 (1938).
[2] *M.E. Blatt Company,* 305 U.S. 267 (1938).

technical advice memoranda, and determination letters, which are now being released under the Freedom of Information Act. Publication of these rulings helps taxpayers to determine the attitude of the I.R.S. with respect to certain types of transactions even though the rulings do not constitute authority with precedential value. Before releasing the rulings, the I.R.S. "sanitizes" the documents to eliminate all means of identifying the actual taxpayer who requested the information.

JUDICIAL AUTHORITY

Litigated disagreements between the I.R.S. and taxpayers create yet another authoritative source of tax law. Because judicial decisions are so numerous and are published in so many (often duplicative) sources, retrieving them is quite complicated.

Looking first at the Tax Court, the GPO publishes only the regular decisions of the Tax Court, not memorandum decisions. Between 1924 and October 1942, this hard-bound government publication was called the *United States Board of Tax Appeals Reports* (BTA); from 1942 until 1969 it was known as *The Tax Court of the United States Reports* (TC); since 1970, it has been called the *United States Tax Court Reports* (TC). A typical reference to the Tax Court Reports appears as follows: *Thomas Miller,* 19 TC 1046 (1953). This tells us that the 1953 case of Thomas Miller versus the commissioner of the Internal Revenue Service can be found on page 1046 of the 19th volume of the Tax Court Reports. Occasionally, a Tax Court citation is followed by "a." or "n.a." These two abbreviations indicate whether or not the I.R.S. has *acquiesced* or *non-acquiesced* to the decision in the case. In this manner the I.R.S. announces, in the weekly IRB, whether or not it will follow a particular Tax Court decision in subsequent cases with comparable facts. This acquiescence policy does not apply to Tax Court Memorandum Decisions or to decisions of any other court. Although great significance is placed on this policy, the I.R.S. is not bound by its pronouncements and may take a position contrary to an announced acquiescence.[3] The Supreme Court also has upheld the right of the commissioner to retroactively withdraw a prior acquiescence.[4]

Tax Court Memorandum Decisions are published by the government only in mimeograph form. Because these decisions do have precedential value, two publishing companies (CCH and P-H) publish all memoran-

[3]*H.B. Quinn,* 524 F2d 617 (CA-7, 1975).
[4]*W. Palmer Dixon,* 381 U.S. 68 (1965).

dum decisions, first in loose-leaf "advance sheets" and, at the end of each year, in hard-bound copy. The CCH publication is titled *Tax Court Memorandum Decisions* (cited _____ TCM _____; the P-H edition is titled *Prentice-Hall Memorandum Decisions* (cited _____ PH Memo TC).

Decisions of the federal district courts, the Court of Claims, and the various circuit courts of appeals are published by West Publishing Company in two reporter services: *The Federal Reporter* (cited either _____ Fed. _____ or _____ F2d _____ for all decisions since 1925) and *The Federal Supplement* (cited _____ F. Supp _____). The Court of Claims decisions are published by the GPO in the *U.S. Court of Claims Reports* (cited _____ Ct.Cls. _____). West Publishing Company also publishes Court of Claims decisions. For a long time, Court of Claims decisions were published in the *Federal Supplement*. Since 1960, however, they have appeared in the *Federal Reporter, 2d Series* (cited _____ F2d _____). Supreme Court Decisions are published in West's *Supreme Court Reporter* (cited _____ S.Ct. _____); the GPO's *United States Reports* (cited _____ U.S. _____); and the Lawyers' Cooperative Publishing Company's *United States Supreme Court Reports, Lawyers' Edition* (cited _____ L.Ed. _____).

Except for the Tax Court decisions (both regular and memo), the court reporters mentioned above contain not only tax cases but all decisions rendered by the respective courts. Thus, to reduce the potential cost and size of a tax library, CCH and P-H each publish a Tax Reporter Service that contains *only* tax-related cases (other than Tax Court decisions). These services are popular with professionals who are interested only in tax cases. Commerce Clearing House publishes the reporter service as the *United States Tax Cases* (cited _____ USTC _____). *The American Federal Tax Reports* (cited _____ AFTR _____ or _____ AFTR2d _____ for cases since 1952) are marketed by Prentice-Hall.

Table 2-2 summarizes the various publications that contain judicial tax decisions and presents an acceptable form of citation of cases in written communication.

LOCATING COURT DECISIONS

The researcher frequently relies on a citator to locate pertinent judicial authority. A citator is a reference that directs a researcher to the appropriate judicial reporter service in which a particular case can be located.

TABLE 2-2

PUBLICATION SUMMARY OF COURT DECISIONS

Courts		Publisher	Title	Citations
TAX COURT				
Regular Decisions:				
1924–1942	Pa	GPO	U.S. Board of Tax Appeals Reports	*Nellie G. Dodge*, 40 BTA 209 (1939)
1943–Present	P	GPO	Tax Court of U.S. Reportsb	*Lester Crown*, 67 TC 1060 (1977)
Memorandum Decisions:				
1924–1942	P	P-H	P-H BTA Memorandum Decisions	*R. Olsen*, 38 BTA 1531, Dock 86970 (Memo) Aug. 16, 1938, 1938 P-H ¶ 6.413
1943–Present	P	P-H	P-H TC Memorandum Decisions	*John C. Kenny*, 1966 P-H TC Memo 66-1027
1942–Present	P	CCH	Tax Court Memorandum Decisions	*John C. Kenny*, 25 TCM 913 (1966)
DISTRICT COURT				
1924–1932	P	West	Federal Reporter 2nd	*Obispo Oil Co.* v. *Welch*, 48 F2d 872 (DC Cal., 1931)
1932–Present	P	West	Federal Supplement	*Armstrong* v. *O'Connell*, 451 F.Supp 817 (DC Wisc., 1978)
1900–Present	S	P-H	American Federal Tax Reports	*Nickerson* v. *Gilbert*, 42 AFTR2d 78-5886 (DC RI, 1978)
1913–Present	S	CCH	United States Tax Cases	*Nick* v. *Dunlap*, 50-2 USTC ¶ 9436 (DC Tex., 1950)
COURT OF CLAIMS				
1932–1960	P	West	Federal Supplement	*Hall* v. *U.S.*, 43 F.Supp 130 (Ct.Cls., 1932)
1929–32; 1960–Present	P	West	Federal Reporter 2nd	*Bell* v. *U.S.*, 591 F2d 647 (Ct.Cls., 1979)
1900–Present	S	P-H	American Federal Tax Reports 2nd	*Bell Intercont. Corp.* v. *U.S.*, 20 AFTR2d 5153 (Ct.Cls., 1967)
1913–Present	S	CCH	United States Tax Cases	*Bell Intercont. Corp.* v. *U.S.*, 67-2 USTC ¶ 9574 (Ct.Cls., 1967)
CIRCUIT COURT OF APPEALS				
1900–Present	P	West	Federal Reporter 2nd	*Vishnevsky* v. *U.S.*, 581 F2d 1249 (CA-7, 1978)
1900–Present	S	P-H	American Federal Tax Reports 2nd	*Vishnevsky* v. *U.S.*, 42 AFTR2d 78-5681 (CA-7, 1978)
1913–Present	S	CCH	United States Tax Cases	*Vishnevsky* v. *U.S.*, 78-2 USTC ¶ 9640 (CA-7, 1978)
SUPREME COURT				
1900–Present	P	West	Supreme Court Reporter	*Comr.* v. *Kowalski*, 984 S.Ct. 315 (1977)
1900–Present	P	GPO	United States Reports	*Comr.* v. *Kowalski*, 434 US 77 (1977)
1900–Present	S	P-H	American Federal Tax Reports 2nd	*Comr.* v. *Kowalski*, 40 AFTR2d 78-5681 (S.Ct., 1977)
1913–Present	S	CCH	United States Tax Cases	*Comr.* v. *Kowalski*, 77-2 USTC ¶ 9748 (S.Ct., 1977)

a "P" = Primary Citation; "S" = Secondary Citation.
b After 1969, "Tax Court of the U.S. Reports" is referred to as "United States Tax Court Reports."

The most important function of a citator, however, is to identify subsequent cases that are related with respect to facts and issues to the primary case.

Three major citator services are available. Shepard's Citations, Inc. publishes a comprehensive legal citator that references all federal and state cases, tax and nontax alike. Consisting of numerous volumes requiring extensive space, *Shepard's Citations* is not found in the typical tax library. Both CCH and P-H publish citator services that focus entirely on tax cases. The CCH edition is a one-volume, loose-leaf service that contains case names in alphabetical order. The judicial history of each case is shown, including the court of original jurisdiction and subsequent appeals. In addition, most subsequent cases in which the original case was cited are listed after that specific case. The CCH citator does not, however, communicate the disposition of the subsequent cases. If a later case deals with an issue considered in the original case, the researcher must actually read the later case to determine whether or not the subsequent case followed the former case, overruled the former case, or was distinguished from the former case.

The P-H citator consists of four bound volumes and one loose-leaf binder. Each volume covers a specific period of time. The most recent volume, the loose-leaf, covers cases handed down from 1978 to the present. Thus, the judicial history of relatively current cases (those handed down after 1977) can be determined by referring only to the current volume. The judicial history of cases that were adjudicated before 1942, however, requires an examination in each of the 5 volumes,

because volume 1 covers all citations made during the period 1919 to 1941, volume 2 covers citations from 1942 to 1948; and so on. For example, a case decided in 1948 will initially be cited in volume 2. Subsequent developments regarding the case—such as appeals to a higher court, use as precedent in a new case, or a new case with similar facts for which a court renders an opposing opinion and effectively overrules the original case—will be located in subsequent volumes of the citator. Disclosure of each case citation is similar to that found in the CCH citator with two major exceptions. Case citations of subsequent cases in the P-H citator disclose whether they followed, overruled, or modified the original case or issue. In addition, subsequent cases in which the original case is cited are listed in order of specific issues enumerated in the original case. Consequently, even though the CCH citator is more convenient to work with, the P-H citator provides more complete information pertaining to a particular case.

EDITORIAL SOURCES

Several publishing companies have created tax services that conveniently assemble, in one set of reference works, the necessary research materials relating to a specific tax topic. Table 2-3 identifies the most popular services currently available.

All the tax services mentioned in Table 2-3 are published in a loose-leaf format. Source materials are found in each service either through a topical index or by reference to a Code section. Learning to use the in-

TABLE **2-3**

LIST OF MAJOR TAX SERVICE PUBLICATIONS

Title of Services	Publisher	Organization according to—	Arrangement of content
Federal Taxes	Prentice-Hall	Code Section	Code Section, Regs., Editorials, Synopsis of Cases & Rev. Rul.
Mertens Law of Federal Income Taxation	Callaghan & Co.	Topic	Editorial treatise with footnotes
Rabkin & Johnson, Federal Income, Gift & Estate Taxation	Matthew Bender & Co.	Code Section	Editorial discussion with references in body of text
Standard Federal Tax Reporter	Commerce Clearing House, Inc.	Code Section	Code Section, Regs., Editorials, Synopsis of Cases & Rev. Rul.
Tax Coordinator 2d	Research Institute of America	Topic	Editorial discussion with footnotes
Tax Management Portfolios	Bureau of National Affairs	Topic	Editorial discussion with footnotes

dex of a particular service is the key to using it effectively. A good tax library necessarily includes more than one tax service and possibly contains all available services. Because each service may emphasize a different facet of a particular tax law and each service has a unique indexing system, a researcher should check a tax problem through several services to assure that he or she has located and defined all aspects of a defensible position.

Other potential editorial sources for locating answers to tax research problems are books, magazines, and newsletters. One example of a widely respected treatise is Bittker and Eustice's *Federal Income Taxation of Corporations and Shareholders,* published by Warren, Gorham & Lamont. Numerous other reference works can be found in any tax library.

Tax magazines—for example, *The Journal of Taxation, The Tax Adviser, TAXES—The Tax Magazine, Taxation for Accountants*—as well as various law journals are an excellent source of discussion on current tax topics that can assist a researcher in finding a solution to a difficult tax issue. Most tax professionals personally subscribe to one or more of these journals; all of them are standard items in a good tax library.

A number of tax newsletters are also published on a monthly, biweekly, weekly, and even daily basis. For instance, both CCH and P-H provide weekly updates titled *Taxes on Parade* and *Accountant's Weekly Report,* respectively. Because tax advisors work in a dynamic field, newsletters are an important means of keeping informed of recent developments at the congressional, administrative, and judicial levels.

INTERPRETING AND ASSESSING POTENTIAL AUTHORITY

In searching for a defensible solution to a tax problem, the researcher must keep in mind that the primary authority ordinarily consists of the tax statute—the Internal Revenue Code of 1954 as amended. Frequently, however, the specific problem with which the researcher is wrestling is not explicitly addressed in the Code. Consequently, the next line of authority to be considered might be the Treasury Regulations. Yet, as students soon discover, even the regulations are limited in many respects when explaining the application of the law. Another step in seeking a solution is to consider revenue rulings or revenue procedures. If the researcher is unable to locate a ruling or procedure that is "on all fours" (that is, identical with the given facts), potential judicial authority might be investigated. Note

that the sequence suggested here agrees with the format found in both the CCH and P-H tax services; that is, statute first, regulations next, and other administrative and judicial authority last.

Consideration of judicial decisions should include a review of the court that rendered the decision, the year in which the decision was rendered, and subsequent cases on similar facts. Because Supreme Court decisions cannot be appealed further, they are final authority and may even hold that the statute and regulations are unconstitutional. A decision by one of the circuit courts of appeals is controlling only in that respective circuit. That is, neither the I.R.S. nor the Tax Court is obliged to follow a fifth circuit decision in a ninth circuit dispute. Any taxpayer may attempt to take a position contrary to that rendered by a circuit court in a circuit in which he or she does not reside. Obviously, however, the risks are high that in the event of litigation, the local circuit court may follow its sister court. A similar philosophy applies to district court decisions. No general application of a district court decision is required outside its immediate jurisdiction. Court of Claims decisions are hard to assess; unless a conflicting decision by one or more of the circuit courts exists, however, a request to the Supreme Court for *certiorari* is not likely to be granted. Thus, a Court of Claims decision may constitute a final authority—at least for the taxpayer involved in that litigation.

Tax Court decisions have general application. The commissioner, through his acquiescence policy, however, has taken the liberty of putting taxpayers on notice that he will either follow a decision or take a hard-line position in opposing a Tax Court decision. A Tax Court case to which the commissioner has not publicly announced an acquiescence or nonacquiescence is nevertheless an important precedent. The Tax Court is not required to follow a circuit court decision that overturned an earlier Tax Court decision. The Tax Court has held in *Jack E. Golsen,* 54 TC 742 (1970), however, that it will consider itself bound by a circuit court decision, *but only for other cases litigated in that particular circuit.*

A formal citation to a judicial decision should specify the year in which the case was litigated. The age of a case may signal to the researcher that the authority may be outdated. In a few instances, however, older cases have become benchmark decisions, and such cases have unusually strong precedential authority. One can usually detect the importance of a case by noting how often it has been cited in subsequent decisions. (The CCH citator can furnish such information to the researcher at a glance.) As indicated earlier, it is also essential to trace a case through a citator to assure that subsequent court decisions did not overturn the law on which the researcher intends to rely.

On relatively rare occasions, a tax researcher may encounter a situation for which he or she is absolutely unable to locate any applicable authority. In such cases, authority from a set of related but not identical facts may be used. For example, a Tax Court decision or Revenue Ruling dealing with the valuation process of stock in a closely held corporation may help to determine the value of a partnership interest. Without any authority, a researcher may need to apply creativity or some logical methodology from another related field, such as accounting. In this way, if the I.R.S. accepts the treatment, new authority may be created.

Another obstacle may be encountered when the researcher finds conflicting authority. This can happen in the form of disagreements between courts or between the courts and the I.R.S. Disagreements between courts are usually resolved in favor of the conclusion rendered by the court of highest authority. Conflicting decisions between the Tax Court and a district court, between two district courts, or between the Tax Court and a circuit court of appeals must be considered temporary authority. In those instances there is a high probability of further litigation on similar facts that

will be appealed to a higher court for clarification. The risk of receiving an adverse decision, therefore, is higher than normal.

Finally, a researcher may be faced with a situation such as the two cases dealing with casualty losses that resulted in opposing judicial opinions that we presented in Chapter 1. Because the law pertaining to casualty losses is well established, the divergent opinions resulted from a difference in the underlying facts. Thus, if the law is specific and clear but the facts are uncertain or unsubstantiated, the tax advisor must do everything possible to bring order to whatever factual information is available. The researcher must be careful, however, that in a desire to create a favorable situation for a client, he or she does not modify any existing facts. Facts can only be changed in a planning situation, that is, before they occur. Changing facts after an event has occurred could constitute fraud. Thus, the advisor must try to clarify and substantiate facts through verifiable evidence such as testimony, pictures, appraisals, and so on.

Much of what has been discussed in this chapter can be fully appreciated only through experience in a tax library. It is critical, therefore, that you supplement your reading with considerable time in a tax library. Only in that way will the foregoing pages come to life.

PROBLEMS

1. Indicate whether each of the following statements is true (T) or False (F).
   a. Tax proposals for consideration by Congress may be introduced in either the House or Senate.
   b. The House Ways and Means Committee and the Senate Finance Committee hold separate hearings on the same proposed tax bill.
   c. Committee Reports are the only general source from which interested parties can obtain an understanding of the underlying reasons for passage of a particular tax provision.
   d. Amendments to a tax bill, made during the bill's debate on the floor of either the House or Senate, are reported in the Congressional Committee Reports.
   e. Treasury Regulations are published by the Treasury Department to assist taxpayers with a general interpretation of the Internal Revenue Code.
   f. Since passage of the 16th amendment, Congress has passed only two Internal Revenue Codes. The most recent Code is known as the Internal Revenue Code of 1954.
   g. Revenue Rulings are issued regularly by the I.R.S. Taxpayers may rely on rulings when their fact situations are identical with those mentioned in the published rulings.
   h. Revenue Rulings are similar to Revenue Procedures except that rulings apply to income tax issues while procedures apply to gift and estate tax issues.
   i. Private letter rulings issued to taxpayers by the I.R.S. are published by commercial publishers like CCH and P-H. They have no precedential value,

however, other than for the taxpayer by whom the ruling was requested and only for the identical fact situation mentioned in the ruling request.

j. If a taxpayer cannot reach an agreement through the normal appeals process with the I.R.S. over a tax issue, he or she must pay the contested tax liability. The taxpayer may then file suit in the United States Tax Court and request a refund.

k. Decisions rendered by the United States Tax Court are published by CCH in a publication titled *U.S. Tax Cases*.

l. The I.R.S. publishes Revenue Rulings and Revenue Procedures in a weekly publication titled *Internal Revenue Bulletin*. The weekly bulletins are then compiled in an annual publication of two to three volumes under the title *Cumulative Bulletin*.

m. The Tax Court issues both regular and memorandum decisions. Only the regular decisions are published, however, while *memorandum* decisions are only informally announced to interested parties. Memorandum decisions therefore have no precedential value.

n. A number of commercial publishers produce tax services that are a helpful tool to tax professionals.

o. Each publisher uses a unique system of organizing the various tax resource materials. Consequently, most tax professionals subscribe to that one tax service with which they can most readily identify. Subscription to more than one tax service is an unnecessary expense that most tax professionals can ill afford.

p. The I.R.S. is required by law to comply with decisions handed down by the Tax Court and to dispose of subsequent fact situations by other taxpayers in the same manner.

q. Decisions by the Tax Court can be appealed by either the taxpayer or the I.R.S. to a Circuit Court of Appeals.

r. *The Journal of Taxation* is a highly respected tax magazine read by most competent tax professionals.

s. Most tax services are updated weekly. It is therefore a waste of money to subscribe to any of the many tax newsletters available on a weekly, biweekly, or monthly basis.

t. The sign of a true professional is her desire to keep up to date with knowledge developed in her field. It is therefore understood that a tax advisor must maintain her professional competence by being aware of new developments and changes in the law that may be of importance to clients even if it means that she has to do it on her own time.

2. Visit your campus library and determine which of the following publications it includes:
   a. Standard Federal Tax Reporter (CCH)
   b. Federal Taxes (P-H)
   c. Law of Federal Income Taxation (Mertens)
   d. Tax Management Portfolios (BNA)
   e. United States Tax Court Reports (GPO)
   f. United States Tax Cases (CCH)
   g. The American Federal Tax Reports (P-H)
   h. Prentice-Hall T.C. Memorandum Decisions (P-H)
   i. Tax Court Memorandum Decisions (CCH)
   j. Cumulative Bulletin (GPO)

3. Locate the case cited at 77-2 USTC ¶9536.
   a. What court heard the case?

    b.   Name the judge who issued the opinion.

    c.   How many issues were enumerated in this case?

    d.   Can you give a primary citation for the case?

4.   Locate Volume 67 of the *Tax Court of the United States Reports* (TC).

    a.   What is the time period covered by this volume?

    b.   How many regular judges served on the Tax Court for the period covered by Volume 67?

    c.   List the various indexes found in Volume 67.

    d.   Locate the case cited at 67 TC 352 and indicate how many issues were presented in the case.

5.   Locate *1976-1 Internal Revenue Cumulative Bulletin (CB)*.

    a.   What time period is covered by Volume 1?

    b.   What do you find on page 1?

    c.   What items are printed in Part I of the bulletin?

    d.   In what order are the items presented in Part I?

    e.   What items are printed in Part II?

    f.   What items are printed in Part III?

6.   Locate the case cited at 28 AFTR 2d 71-5676.

    a.   What court heard the case?

    b.   List the judge(s) who heard the case.

    c.   Who wrote the opinion?

    d.   Name the court of original jurisdiction.

    e.   What is the primary citation for this case?

    f.   Where did you find the primary citation?

    g.   Write the complete citation to a CCH publication in which the same case is located.

7.   Locate the *Tax Management Portfolios* (BNA) in your library.

    a.   Examine Volume 274 and list the title of the portfolio.

    b.   Examine Volume 5 and list the title of the portfolio.

    c.   Examine Volume 132 and list the title of the portfolio.

    d.   Notice that a different color ink was used for the title of each of the portfolios you examined. What significance does the color have?

        (1)   Red

        (2)   Black

        (3)   Green

    e.   Each portfolio is organized in three main sections. List the three sections.

    f.   How can the researcher find material in the respective portfolios?

8.   Locate Prentice-Hall's *Federal Taxes* and Commerce Clearing House's *Standard Federal Tax Reporter*. Then for each tax service, answer the following questions:

    a.   In which volume is the index located?

    b.   Is the index arranged by topic or Code section?

    c.   If all you have is a Code section, how do you locate additional material?

    d.   Each service has a volume designated as New Matters. What does it contain?

    e.   Each service uses tabs to facilitate indexing. How is the material between the tabs organized?

9.   Locate Merten's Law of Federal Income Taxation in your library.

    a.   Which volume contains the index?

    b.   Is the index arranged by Code section or topic?

    c.   Can access be obtained to the treatise volume if the researcher only knows a code section?

    d. Examine the loose-leaf "Rulings" volume and indicate what is found under the tab designated "Code-Rulings Table."

    e. What type of information is available under the tab designated "Rulings Status Table"?

    f. Examine one of the treatise volumes. In what form is the material in the volumes presented?

    g. Can you locate the complete text of the Internal Revenue Code of 1954 in any of the treatise volumes or in one of the other volumes?

10. In your library locate the bound volumes that contain the Tax Court Memorandum Decisions.

    a. Indicate the publisher of the service in your library:

        (1) CCH

        (2) P-H

        (3) Both

Answer the remaining questions with respect to either the CCH or P-H publication, and indicate which publication you used.

    b. How are Tax Court Memorandum Decisions cited?

    c. What time period is covered by Volume 35?

    d. In what order are the cases presented in each volume?

tax research and communication

Knowledge can benefit society only if it is properly communicated. This fact is particularly critical for persons engaged in a service profession. For example, the most competent physician will never build more than a mediocre practice unless he or she learns to communicate with patients. Similarly, a tax researcher has gained little after locating a defensible answer to a research problem unless the conclusion can be communicated to associates, clients, and the I.R.S.

Communication, of course, consists of both verbal and written forms of disseminating information. In this chapter, we shall limit ourselves to the methodology employed by tax professionals as they convey in writing the facts and conclusions of their tax research.

THE CLIENT FILE

Law firms and CPA firms typically maintain files on their clients in which they retain copies of correspondence, selected documents, and possibly tax returns. In some instances, tax returns are kept in annual files, while other documents—such as articles of incorporation, partnership agreements, and special research projects—are retained in a master file spanning a number of years. Regardless of the system employed, client files are an important source for storing and disseminating information.

The starting point for a tax research project is a set of facts. A tax researcher may receive the necessary facts directly from the client or through a superior. If the information is obtained orally, the researcher should prepare a memo setting forth his or her understanding of the facts and place that memo in the client file. Of course, information obtained in written form,

either from a superior or directly from the client, is also filed in the client file. Additional communications elaborating or clarifying existing information are retained in the same manner.

As a researcher begins the task of locating authority for the pertinent questions identified from the facts, copies of relevant source material—Code sections, regulations, judicial decisions, and revenue rulings—are systematically arranged by issue in the client file. The process of organizing the pertinent materials will be demonstrated through an example later in the chapter.

When the researcher has reached a defensible solution to a research problem, that conclusion is usually communicated via an office memorandum to the researcher's superior or superiors or to a colleague who has authority for review and approval. Frequently, a partner or manager may request that all pertinent information be set forth in the form of a draft client letter (or protest letter to the I.R.S.). These letters also become part of the client file.

A properly maintained client file is extremely important to a smoothly operating tax practice. The file should be systematically indexed and cross-referenced to allow the reviewing authority to move quickly through the material. The old adage "time is money" is especially true for the tax professional. In preparing a client file, therefore, the researcher must leave sufficient tracks so that persons who follow can easily understand the methodology employed and line of reasoning pursued.

In addition to facilitating the reviewing process, a client file is important for subsequent I.R.S. audits, which usually occur several years after the research was performed. At that time, the client research file becomes a significant source of information for purposes of recalling the authority used in support of the position taken on the tax return under audit.

Because staff assignments in both CPA and law firms change frequently due to promotion and personnel turnover, a client file is an important source of information for the newly assigned staff person. The file reveals all prior research performed and the authority on which conclusions were based. Without a good client file, each new staff person would have to repeat much of the work previously performed in order to be comfortable with the treatment of certain transactions on a current tax return. A client file can also save significant time when another client of the same office or the same firm presents a fact situation similar to one already researched for another client.

THE CLIENT LETTER

A tax advisor can sell only time and expertise. Clients frequently measure the quality of the service they receive on the basis of a tangible end product. In connection with a tax compliance engagement, such a product may constitute the completed tax return and possibly the amount of additional tax the client must pay (or the size of the refund the client will receive). In tax planning engagements, the end product is usually a conference and a letter to the client summarizing the research undertaken. Thus, because the client letter is the product for which the client is billed, it should be representative of the effort expended.

The style of a client letter will vary from firm to firm. Some firms believe that the contents of a client letter should depend on the degree of the client's sophistication in the field of taxation or law. Other firms feel that the letter should contain considerable detail—including citations to appropriate Code sections, regulations, court decisions, and revenue rulings—regardless of the client's expertise, in order to demonstrate the degree of research performed. Some firms prepare two letters: One letter spells out the technical detail of the research findings, complete with citations, and the second serves as a transmittal letter, conveying in layperson's terms the gist of the research findings and recommendations.

The reasons for preparing both a technical and a transmittal letter may be twofold. First, if a firm espouses the philosophy that a client letter should be written with the technical expertise of the client in mind, more often than not it becomes a document that deals in generalities rather than specific technical details. If the research conclusions are subsequently chal-

lenged by an I.R.S. audit, a technical letter containing the basis for the conclusion will serve to substantiate the original advice given. In a more serious situation, such as a potential lawsuit from a client who claims that the tax advisor gave erroneous advice, a technical letter may be the only evidence the tax advisor has to protect his or her reputation. A second reason for preparing two separate letters is that client letters have a tendency of falling into the wrong hands at the wrong time. If a client letter is examined during an I.R.S. audit, the agent has the advantage of preparing a case based on the specific authority set forth in the client letter. Consequently, some firms feel that the technical letter should be kept in the client file in the tax advisor's vault. If a firm sends both the transmittal and technical letter to the client, the tax advisor may request that the client return or destroy the technical letter.[1]

Every client letter should follow a specific format. The letter should include a restatement of the facts on which the research was based. Applicable facts should be accompanied by a disclaimer similar to the following:

> The conclusions reached in our research are based on the above facts. If these facts are incorrect or incomplete, no matter how insignificant they may appear to you, please bring it to our attention immediately, because different facts may require a different conclusion.

The foregoing statement is appropriate in conjunction with an "after-the-fact" engagement. In a planning engagement, the wording may cover the following points:

> The conclusions reached in our research are based on the above facts. It is, therefore, important that you implement the tax plan exactly as stated. Any deviation from the suggested plan, no matter how insignificant it may appear to you, may jeopardize the result. In addition, future changes in the tax law may also adversely affect our conclusion.

After a concise restatement of facts and the appropriate disclaimer, the client letter should enumerate the various issues that were examined. Conclusions are then presented. The letter may end with a summary, which can range from a brief statement to a detailed discussion, setting forth reasons and authorities on which the conclusions are based.

---

[1] Tax accountants, unlike attorneys, are not protected by privileged communication. Thus, the I.R.S. may issue a summons for specific documents in the possession of the accountant that are pertinent to an examination. Sometimes, however, a district court judge will not enforce the I.R.S. summons unless serious violations on the part of the client are suspected.

PROTEST LETTERS, DETERMINATION LETTERS, AND REQUESTS FOR RULINGS

A considerable portion of the services rendered by a tax advisor consists of the settlement of disagreements between taxpayers and the I.R.S. The tax laws are replete with areas of uncertainty, which frequently result in divergent interpretations. If a revenue agent, as a result of an audit, makes a deficiency assessment to which the taxpayer and the advisor take exception, in most cases a written protest must be prepared. The format of a *protest letter* is similar to that of a technical client letter. The protest should contain an accurate summary of the facts and an enumeration of the issues contested. In addition, the protest should set forth the reasons why the taxpayer is taking issue with the revenue agent's report (RAR) as well as the authority on which the taxpayer relies.

A *determination letter* is a request for technical advice on an issue raised by a revenue agent during an audit. The taxpayer and the revenue agent may seek advice from the national I.R.S. office with respect to a specific issue for which little or no authority is available. Again, the format of a determination letter varies little from that of a technical client letter or a protest letter. It will contain facts, issues or points of disagreement, authoritative discussion, and tentative conclusions reached by the opposing parties.

Both the protest letter and the determination letter result from after-the-fact situations. Frequently, however, a taxpayer wishes to understand the full impact of potential tax considerations before the events have occurred. In such a case, the taxpayer—through a tax advisor—may request an advance ruling from the I.R.S. A request for an advance ruling sets forth all the facts and circumstances surrounding the proposed transaction, the possible issues for which additional advice is needed, the tentative conclusion the client or the advisor has reached, and the appropriate supporting authority. It can be seen that a ruling request resembles both a protest letter and a determination letter in format and content.

AN EXAMPLE

In the remaining pages of this chapter, we present an example showing the general format of a client file. Certain features, such as the indexing, will vary from firm to firm. The general concept, however, should be universal in application. The importance of a well-organized client file cannot be overstated.

The fact situation we use in our example is that depicted in Chapter 1: Tracy Field sells real estate to Ray Gunn on the installment plan. Notice that we are dealing with an open-fact situation, since Mr. Field, our client, has not as yet accepted the lump-sum payment of $80,000 plus interest. The facts of the case are restated below.

Example: Tracy Field is the proprietor of a small ski resort on the western slopes of the Rocky Mountains. In 19X1 he sold five acres of unimproved real estate to a famous movie star, Ray Gunn, for a total price of $100,000. Tracy acquired the property as an investment six years earlier at a cost of $20,000. The arrangements call for Mr. Gunn to assume a $20,000 mortgage. In addition, Tracy will receive four 10 percent interest-bearing notes of $20,000 each, with one note maturing annually beginning in 19X2.

This year, 19X2, Ray Gunn starred in a hit science fiction release. With his new-found wealth, he decided to pay off all four notes immediately. He approaches Tracy Field with the proposal. Tracy, thereupon inquires of his tax advisor what tax consequences will result from the receipt of the $80,000 lump-sum payment plus accrued interest. He had intended to report the transaction on the installment basis, and his advisor had originally told him that the transaction would qualify for installment reporting. A proper election was made on Tracy's 19X1 tax return.

Because 19X1 was a fantastic ski season, the resort's operating income amounted to $150,000. So far, however, 19X2 has been a dismal year. Consequently, Tracy anticipates that the lump-sum receipt of $80,000 can be sheltered with an operating loss of around $120,000. Tax returns for years before 19X1 show that operating losses cannot be carried back past 19X1.

The client file in this case contains a client letter, a memo to the file, a general summary of the tax research problem, and a detailed summary of the problem. An index to the file appears in Figure 3-1.

Note that the client letter, shown in Figure 3-2, contains a disclaimer before the restatement of facts. The memo to the file (Figure 3-3) records information received by telephone.

Figure 3-4 is the general summary of research questions, and Figure 3-5 is a detailed summary containing copies of and citations to relevant authoritative documents.

FIGURE 3-1

Tracy Field
Tax File
June 19X2

Index to Working Papers

Item	Page Ref.
Client Letter	I-1 & 2
Memo to File - Paul Advisor	I-3
General Summary - Tax Research Problem	A-1
Detailed Summary - Tax Research Problem	B-1, B-2, B-3; C-1, C-2

FIGURE 3-2

PAUL ADVISOR & CO.
CERTIFIED PUBLIC ACCOUNTANTS
1313 High Rise Court
Professional City, USA 11111

June 30, 19X2

Mr. Tracy Field
777 Easy Street
Snow Mountain, CO 81652

Dear Mr. Field:

This letter acknowledges our oral agreement of June 13, 19X2, to investigate the tax implication of one of your proposed business transactions. Set forth in this letter are the results of the research we performed in connection with your inquiry.

Before stating the results of our investigation, I would like to restate the important facts as we understand them. Please review these facts carefully. If any of the following facts are incomplete or incorrect, please bring it to my attention immediately, no matter how insignificant the difference may appear to you.

In 19X1 you sold five acres of unimproved real estate to Mr. Ray Gunn for $100,000. As part of the agreement, Mr. Gunn assumed a $20,000 mortgage and also issued four 10 percent, interest-bearing notes of $20,000 each, with one note maturing annually beginning in 19X2. You acquired the real property six years ago at a cost of $20,000. Recently, Mr. Gunn inquired if you are willing to accept payment for all four notes immediately. Since you are expecting an operating loss for the tax year 19X2, you are currently inclined to agree to Mr. Gunn's proposal. You plan to shelter the $80,000 lump-sum payment with operating losses of approximately $120,000.

Assuming that the foregoing is a complete and accurate summary of the facts, we report the following. Should you decide to accept the full $80,000 in notes, it would disqualify the initial 19X1 election to report the receipt of the notes on the installment basis. Therefore, an amended return must be filed for 19X1, which includes the receipt of $80,000 in capital gains. If the anticipated operating loss for 19X2 of $120,000 materializes, however, the inclusion of both the $80,000 capital gain and the $120,000 net operating loss carryback on the 19X1 tax return will result in a refund of $51,370 for 19X1.

If you refuse to accept all four notes in 19X2 and only receive one, as originally contracted, the net operating loss for 19X2, which can be carried back to 19X1, will amount to $100,000 ($120,000 operating loss less $20,000 capital gains from receipt of installment note). The $100,000 net operating loss carryback to 19X1 will result in a refund with respect to the 19X1 tax return of $56,902. You will

FIGURE 3-2 (continued)

Mr. Tracy Field
Page 2
June 30, 19X2

be taxed in each of the next three years, when the remaining notes
fall due, on $8,000 ($20,000 - 60 percent LTCGD) each year at your
respective marginal tax rate of 19X3, 19X4, and 19X5.

If you have additional questions, please contact me. I recommend
that before you implement one of the alternatives examined, we discuss
the content of this letter. Please telephone me so we can arrange an
appointment.

Sincerely,

Paul Advisor

PA:sc

FIGURE 3-3

3
7

PAUL ADVISOR & CO.
CERTIFIED PUBLIC ACCOUNTANTS
1313 High Rise Court
Professional City, USA 11111

June 13, 19X2

MEMO TO FILE

FROM: Paul Advisor

SUBJECT: Tracy Field - Real Estate Transaction

Mr. Field called this morning to inquire about a proposal he
received from Mr. Ray Gunn to whom he sold a parcel of real property in
19X1. The total sales price of the property amounted to $100,000, including
an assumption by Mr. Gunn of a $20,000 mortgage. For the remaining
$80,000 Mr. Field accepted four 10 percent, interest-bearing notes of
$20,000 each, with one note maturing annually beginning in 19X2. The
property had been acquired by Mr. Field as an investment six years
earlier for $20,000. Owing to a recent windfall, Mr. Gunn intends to
pay off all four notes plus the accrued interest in the current year
(19X2).

The sale of the real property was reported on Mr. Field's 19X1 tax
return via a proper election as an installment sale. While 19X1 turned
out to be a rather prosperous year for Mr. Field as a result of the
exceptionally long skiing season, 19X2 looks rather bleak due to
drought conditions. Mr. Field feels it might be a good idea to accept
the full $80,000 in 19X2 and shelter the resulting gain with the anti-
cipated operating loss of approximately $120,000. It is clear from
prior years' returns that operating losses cannot be carried back to
years before 19X1.

19X1 Real Property Transaction:

Amount realized		
4 notes	$ 80,000	
Debt transferred	20,000	
Total	$100,000	
Less: Basis	20,000	
Gain realized	$ 80,000	
Gain recognized	-0-	Sec. 453 election
Gross Profit Percentage	$ 80,000 / $ 80,000 = 100%	

FIGURE 3-4

Tracy Field
General Summary of Research Questions

June 19X2

<u>W.P. Index</u>

I. *Does the receipt of a lump-sum payment of $80,000 plus accrued interest in 19X2 violate any of the requirements under Sec. 453?*

Conclusion: Yes; Sec. 453 requires that the seller receive at least two installment payments; one in each of two separate tax years. The transfer of the mortgage in the year of sale does not constitute a payment for this purpose.

B-1 – B-3

II. *Is it advantageous to accept the lump-sum payment in 19X2 and report it as income taxable in 19X1?*

Conclusion: No; on a short-run basis it will be better to refuse the lump-sum payment and only collect $20,000 for 19X2. As the remaining three notes are collected, however, $8,000 ($20,000 less 60% LTCGD) must be added to the taxable income of Mr. Field.

C-1, C-2

A-1

FIGURE 3-5

3
—
9

Tracy Field
Detailed Summary of Research Questions

June 19X2

Question I-1:   Does an election under Sec. 453
                 require more than one payment?

Conclusion: Yes; by definition, an installment
                 contract implies more than one payment.

                 Sec. 453(b) reads as follows:

(b) Sales of Realty and Casual Sales of Personalty
    (1) General rule. -Income from-
         (A) a sale or other disposition
              of real property, or
         (B) a casual sale or other casual
              disposition of personal pro-
              perty (other than property of
              a kind which would properly
              be included in the inventory of
              the taxpayer if on hand at the
              close of the taxable year) for
              a price exceeding $1,000,
    may (under regulations prescribed by the
    Secretary) be returned on the basis and
    in the manner prescribed in subsection (a).

    (2) Limitation. -Paragraph (1) shall apply
         only if in the taxable year of the
         sale or other disposition-
         (A) there are no (payments) or
         (B) the (payments) (exclusive of
              evidence of indebtedness of
              the purchaser) do not exceed
              30 percent of the selling price.

N/A

Qualifies sale of realty by non-dealer for Sec. 453 (a) treatment.

Note plurality of terms

         Also in Baltimore Baseball Club, Inc.,
         73-2 USTC 9549, 481 F2d 1283 (Ct.Cl.,
         1973) the court stated

It is true that in the tax
law the word "installment"
has become, to some extent, a term of art. The
Government does not contend that the contracts
must satisfy sophisticated formulae for periodic
payment on the total. Rather, the Government
urges that multiplicity is at the very heart of
the definition of "installment."

multiple payments

B-1

FIGURE 3-5 (continued)

Tracy Field
Detailed Summary of Research Questions

June 19X2

<u>W.P. Index</u>

For casual sales of personality for a price
exceeding $1,000 and for sales of realty,
a minimum of two payments is the *sine qua non*
for qualification as an installment. Any
lessening of this very minimum requirement would
amount to a holding that deferred lump-sum
payment sales qualify as installments.

at least two payments

See also 10-42 Corporation, 55 TC
593 (1971) for the same conclusion.

Question I-2: *If more than one payment is required,*
must they occur in different tax
years?

Conclusion: *Installment payments must be received*
in at least two separate tax years.
See Rev. Rul. 69-462, 1969-2 CB 107,
which states in a fact situation
similar to Mr. Field's that the
taxpayer

may not elect to report the income from the
sale of real property on the installment
method of accounting since the total amount
to be received for the property is to be received
in a lump sum in a taxable year subsequent to
his taxable year of sale. The installment
method of reporting income is applicable only
to those sales of real property that, by their
terms and conditions, provide for two or more
payments of portions of the purchase price
in two or more taxable years.

more than one payment - at least two t/yr.

B-2

FIGURE 3-5 (continued)

Tracy Field
Detailed Summary of Research Questions

June 19X2

<u>W.P. Index</u>

<u>Question I-3</u>: Does the assumption of the mortgage by Ray Gunn (the buyer) constitute a payment received in 19X1?

<u>Conclusion</u>: The assumption of a mortgage by the buyer in connection with the sale of property is not considered a payment received in the year of sale.

See Rev. Rul. 71-543, 1971-2 CB 223. Also David Burnet, 3 USTC 1064, 288 US 406 (1932).

Sales price vs. Contract price

<u>Summary</u>: If Mr. Field accepts the $80,000 lump-sum payment in 19X2, the original election to report on the installment will be invalid and the full gain ($80,000) must be reported as income in 19X1.

B-3

FIGURE 3-5 (continued)

Tracy Field
Detailed Summary of Research Questions

June 19X2

Question II-1: What are the consequences to Mr. Field if he accepts the lump-sum payment of $80,000 in 19X2?

Conclusion: Because the installment election will be voided and the $80,000 capital gain must be included on the return for the year of sale, that is, 19X1, Mr. Field's 19X1 tax return as initially filed compared with amended return--

Original*		Amended*
$150,000	Operating income (1)	$150,000
-0-	NOL from 19X2	(120,000)
-0-	Capital gain	80,000
-0-	Less: LTCG deduction	(48,000)
	Excess itemized	
(8,000)	deductions	(8,000)
(2,000)	Exemptions	(2,000)
$140,000	Taxable income	$ 52,000
$ 67,128	Tax liability	$ 15,758

$51,370
Refund

Est. Refund
on 19X1 amended return

(1) includes interest income from four installment notes.

Question II-2: What are the consequences to Mr. Field if he does not accept the lump-sum payment in 19X2 but only the one $20,000 that is due?

Conclusion: The $20,000 realized gain will be offset against the $120,000 estimated operating loss for 19X2 resulting in the following NOL carryback to 19X1:

19X2 Operating loss	$(120,000)
Capital gain	20,000
NOL carryback	$(100,000)
Amount of tax due	$ -0-

FIGURE 3-5 (continued)

Tracy Field
Detailed Summary of Research Questions

June 19X2

Mr. Field's 19X1 tax return
as initially filed compared
with amended return

Original*		Amended*
$150,000	Operating income (1)	$150,000
-0-	NOL from 19X2	(100,000)
	Less: Excess itemized	
(8,000)	deductions	(8,000)
(2,000)	Exemptions	(2,000)
$140,000	Taxable income	$ 40,000
$ 67,128		$ 10,226

$56,902
Refund

Est. Refund
on 19X1 amended return

(1) includes interest income from four installment notes.

Over the next three years,
however, as the remaining three
notes become due, Mr. Field
must add each year $8,000
($20,000 less 60% capital gain
deduction) to his taxable income.
The amount of additional tax due
will, of course, depend on his
respective marginal tax rate for
each of those respective years.

*The foregoing computations assumed that the LTCG
deduction for both 19X1 and 19X2 is 60% and the
exemption is $1,000 per qualifying individual.
It also assumes as applicable the tax rate
tables established with the 1978 Revenue Act.

C-2

The detailed summary (Figure 3-5) should be assembled in successive steps as the researcher identifies issues and subissues and locates solutions to the issues raised. Producing the detailed summary entails a lot of cutting and pasting; that is, pertinent authority such as Code sections, regulations, revenue rulings, and court decisions are located, and selected segments are then xeroxed and pasted into the working papers. Subsequently, key words or phrases are highlighted to focus attention on their significance to the conclusion reached.

As mentioned in Chapter 1, the technique used to identify the important issues or questions for a tax problem cannot be taught in a textbook. To a large extent, the questions that you feel should be investigated will depend on your background and understanding of the tax statutes. Obviously, your ability to think analytically and creatively will play an important role in arriving at satisfactory solutions to a research problem. The following example demonstrates some typical questions a researcher might raise and the sequence in which such questions should come to mind.

PROBLEMS

1. Phillip Hardluck collects antique rugs and wall coverings. Many of his artifacts were acquired years ago at bargain prices and have since increased substantially in value. Recently, the drain-hose of his water softener became disconnected during the softening cycle, flooding both the utility room and Phil's study. As a result, a Chinese rug, constructed of paper cords, was partially immersed in water and completely destroyed. Phil bought the rug 15 years ago for $250. In two recent art shows, however, the rug was appraised by three independent experts at $2,250, $2,500, and $2,450, respectively.

   The loss is covered via a rider on Phil's homeowner's insurance policy, which is written for $200 deductible. Because Phil has already made three claims against his policy during the current calendar year, however, he has decided not to place the claim for the rug. Instead, he wants to deduct the loss on his federal income tax return. For this reason, he has contacted you to assist him in the interpretation of the appropriate casualty loss provisions.
   a. Identify the pertinent issue(s) to be researched.
   b. Compute the appropriate casualty loss deductions.
   c. Write a client letter to Mr. Hardluck in which you set forth the reasons for your conclusions reached in part b.
   d. Prepare a client file that contains the support necessary to substantiate your claim computed in part b.
2. You live in a state that has stiff usury laws. As is the case in most other states, however, corporations are not governed by usury laws. One of your clients, Richard Green, needs a loan for his partnership to develop a new line of business. Several banks are interested lenders but have requested that Green create a corporation for purposes of effecting the loan. One of the bank loan officers, who has a law degree, has suggested that if a corporation is formed to circumvent the usury laws, it will undoubtedly be considered a sham for tax purposes and thus losses sustained by the corporation will still be available as a pass-through to the individual partners.

   The creation of a straw corporation is a commonly used mechanism, and all parties, including the lender, are usually aware of the real intent of the scheme. The new business venture planned by Richard Green and his partners will produce losses for at least four years, and it is important to them that such losses can be offset against other partnership income. A significant portion of the early losses will be the interest expense on the loan.
   a. Identify the pertinent issue(s) to be researched.

b. State your conclusion reached regarding the issue(s) identified above.

c. Write a client letter to Richard Green in which you set forth the reasons for your conclusion reached in part b.

d. Prepare a client file that contains the support necessary to substantiate your conclusion reached in part b.

3. Paul Schussbummer, your client, owns a ski cabin near the Sundance Ski Resort in the Utah Rockies. His permanent residence is in Dallas, Texas, where he is a top-level executive for a manufacturing company that is also your client. Paul and his family take annual skiing vacations in Utah.

During the vacation, the Schussbummers reside exclusively in the ski cabin. Over the years, Paul has enjoyed the annual ski vacations except for one thing. Because the cabin is usually unoccupied for the remainder of the year, a considerable portion of the first week in Utah is wasted on repairs and maintenance to place the cabin into a livable condition. Recently, Paul talked to a cabin neighbor who explained that years ago he had transferred his cabin as a charitable gift to Brigham Young University. Now BYU maintains the cabin year round and uses the cabin for research projects and alumni guests. In addition, BYU guarantees the neighbor use of the cabin for thirty days each year and will not sell the cabin during his or his spouse's lifetime. Paul explained this scheme to his brother-in-law, currently attending law school, whose recollection from his income tax course seemed to be that a taxpayer cannot make a property gift of less than the entire interest. Paul's brother-in-law feels that a guarantee to use the cabin for a specified period of time during the year would constitute a remainder interest, which would disqualify the cabin as a charitable contribution. Paul contacts you for a clarification.

a. Identify the pertinent issue(s) to be researched.

b. State your conclusion reached regarding the issue(s) identified above.

c. Write a client letter to Paul Schussbummer in which you set forth the reasons for your conclusions reached in part b.

d. Prepare a client file that contains the support necessary to substantiate your conclusions reached in part b.

4. Several years ago, Paul Daniels acquired a parcel of land at a cost of $6,400. At the time, he intended to hold the land for appreciation. Recently, however, the city commission voted to locate the new city dump adjacent to his property. Fortunately, Paul heard that John Pope, who operates a scavenger and antique business, was searching for a piece of land near the new dump site. On January 2, 19X1, Paul arranged to sell his land to John on an installment contract. The arrangement called for four $1,600 installment notes (noninterest bearing) due in consecutive years on the last day of the year. The first note is due on December 31, 19X1.

a. Identify the issue(s) to be researched in connection with the foregoing facts.

b. Compute the amount of gain, loss, income, or deduction to be included in the 19X1 tax return of Paul Daniels.

c. Would you change your mind if the property had been sold for $2,000?

d. Assume that John sold Paul certain junk items that Paul intends to use in his business. Cost of the items to John amounted to $4,100. He sold them to Paul for $3,600 and received four noninterest-bearing notes of $900 each. Do the provisions of Section 483 apply?

5. Reed and Susan Jamison were both previously married. Each brought separate property into their current marriage. At the present time, they are both employed in high-paying executive positions and file joint annual federal tax returns. During 19X1 Reed sold some of his separately owned stock to Susan. The broker's advice discloses the following information.

| | Date | | | Net |
Type	Acquired	Sold	Cost	Sales Price
100 Shares ABC common	12-15-U1	1-10-X1	$ 2,200	$ 1,000
2000 Shares XYZ common	6-13-U3	1-12-X1	11,600	32,800

To reduce the immediate tax liability, Reed decided to arrange the second transaction so that it would qualify as an installment sale. Susan has retained the stock from the first transaction but sold the XYZ stock on January 15, 19X1 for $32,900 and later deposited the proceeds in a real estate tax shelter. The agreement between Reed and Susan calls for the transfer of the annual cash flow from the real estate investment to Reed as payment for principal and interest on the installment contract. Reed projects that it will take approximately 10 years to complete the payments for the installment contract.

Because Susan did not buy into the real estate project until January 19X2, she made no payments to Reed until 19X2.

You have been asked to prepare Reed and Susan's joint return for 19X1.

a. Which issue(s) do you wish to examine in connection with the above transactions?

b. Compute the net capital gain or loss to be reported on the 19X1 joint return.

c. Write an office memorandum to the files in which you set forth the reasons for your conclusions reached in part b.

d. Prepare a client file in which you set forth the support necessary to substantiate your conclusions reached in part b.

6. Reacquaint yourself with the facts of Problem 7 in Chapter 1.

a. Determine which issue(s) you wish to examine in connection with the facts of Problem 7.

b. State your conclusions reached regarding the issue(s) identified in part a, above.

c. Write a memo to the files in which you set forth the reasons for your conclusions reached in part b.

d. Prepare a client file that contains the support necessary to substantiate your conclusions reached in part b.

7. Reacquaint yourself with the facts of Problem 8 in Chapter 1.

a. Determine which issue(s) you wish to examine in connection with the facts of Problem 8.

b. State your conclusion reached regarding the issue(s) identified in part a, above.

c. Write a letter to Alice's parents in which you set forth the reasons for your conclusions reached in part b.

d. Prepare a client file that contains the support necessary to substantiate your conclusions reached in part b, above.

8. Reacquaint yourself with the facts of Problem 9 in Chapter 1.

a. Assuming the damage caused to the home qualifies as a legitimate casualty loss and that the I.R.S. will accept the $2,400 as a reasonable amount for the loss sustained, determine which issue(s) you wish to examine in connection with the facts of Problem 9.

b. State your conclusion reached regarding the issue(s) identified in part a, above.

c. Write a memo to the files in which you set forth the reasons for your conclusions reached in part b.

d. Prepare a client file that contains the support necessary to substantiate your conclusions reached in part b, above.

PART
TWO
the income taxation of corporations

4

corporate taxation: basic concepts and the incorporation transaction

Part Two of this book, "The Income Taxation of Corporations," covers seven major topics, namely: (1) basic concepts; (2) the incorporation transaction; (3) nonliquidating distributions; (4) partial and complete liquidations; (5) reorganizations; (6) consolidated tax returns; and (7) Subchapter S corporations. We shall examine the first two topics in this chapter; the five remaining topics are covered in Chapters 5 through 9, respectively. The basic concepts discussed in this chapter are largely a restatement of general rules explained in various chapters of the first volume of *An Introduction to Taxation*. Topics 2 through 5, above, are a substantially expanded explanation of the basic rules introduced briefly in the first volume, and topics 6 and 7 are entirely new subjects.

Although Part Two purports to deal with the income taxation of corporations, an observant student will note that a substantial portion of this part of the book is really concerned with the taxation of the *shareholder* of a corporation rather than the corporate entity itself. Because a shareholder in a corporation may be an individual, an estate, a trust, or another corporation, that portion of our discussion that explains the tax consequences of a transaction involving a shareholder will be concerned with "corporate taxation" only when the shareholder is a corporation. The remainder of this discussion will be concerned with either "personal taxation" (when the shareholder is an individual) or "fiduciary taxation" (when the shareholder is an estate or a trust). In other words, much of what commonly is studied as "corporate income taxation" is not, in fact, corporate taxation at all. Furthermore, as you will soon

discover, much of what commonly is studied as "personal income taxation" is really not unique to individual taxation but applies equally to the taxation of corporations.

BASIC CONCEPTS

Our discussion of basic concepts in the income taxation of corporations can be divided conceptually into two major parts. The first part of this discussion deals with a few important, broad generalizations. The second part deals with specific rules, most of which were introduced in the first volume, *An Introduction to Taxation,* that apply differently to corporate and noncorporate taxpayers.

Corporate taxation: broad generalizations

The first important broad generalization that you should comprehend is that *there is no separate corporate income tax*. The federal government imposes only one income tax, and all the statutory provisions that govern that tax are recorded in Subtitle A of the Internal Revenue Code of 1954 as amended. While it is true that some subdivisions of the Code (for example, certain subchapters, parts, subparts, and sections) address corporate considerations exclusively and other portions individual considerations exclusively, there is no distinct separation of the U.S. federal income tax into two separate taxes. The vast majority of important statutory provisions apply equally to all three taxable entities—individuals, corporations, and fiduciaries. In our opinion, therefore, instructors who artificially separate their federal tax courses into "personal income taxation" and "corporate income taxation" do a disservice to the student. Instead of stressing the many important commonalities of the income taxation of individuals and corporations, the divided approach suggests that the differences are greater than the similarities. Section 1 of the Code imposes a tax "on the taxable income of every . . . individual"; Sec. 11 imposes a tax "on the taxable income of every corporation." Those differences that exist are, therefore, only differences in the technical details that define taxable income and establish tax rates for the different taxable entities.

THE CORPORATION DEFINED   As noted above, Sec. 11 imposes a tax on the taxable income of *every corporation*. But precisely what is a "corporation"? The only statutory answer to that question, found in Sec. 7701(a)(3), is more likely to confuse than to clarify. It reads, in its entirety: "The term 'corporation' includes associations, joint-stock companies, and insurance companies." Therefore, even without further investigation, we know that the federal income tax on corporations may be extended to *unincorporated* "associations," but the Code provides little additional help in defining an association. Judicial and administrative law, however,

help define that term. The benchmark judicial authority is *Morrissey, et al.* v. *Commissioner*, 296 U.S. 344 (1935). The most important administrative authority is Treas. Reg. Sec. 301.7701-2(a), which expands on *Morrissey* and identifies six major characteristics of a corporate entity, as follows: "(i) associates, (ii) an objective to carry on business and divide the gains therefrom, (iii) continuity of life, (iv) centralization of management, (v) liability for corporate debts limited to corporate property, and (vi) free transferability of interests."

A brief comparison of a garden-variety corporation, partnership, sole proprietorship, and trust with regard to these six characteristics can be set forth in the matrix shown in Figure 4-1.

As we can see from this matrix, a substantial amount of overlap and uncertainty exists among the most common forms of business organization with regard to these six characteristics. Accordingly, neither the courts nor the regulations state exactly what combination of characteristics will yield a corporation for federal tax purposes. The regulations merely state:

Whether a particular organization is to be classified as an association must be determined by taking into account the presence or absence of each of these corporate characteristics. The presence or absence of

FIGURE **4-1**

Characteristic	Entity			
	Corporation	Partnership	Proprietorship	Trust
(i) Associates	Yes (but there are corporations with only one shareholder)	Yes	No	Meaning of associates is uncertain in this context
(ii) Objective: to carry on business for gain	Yes	Yes	Yes	No (the purpose of a trust is to protect a property interest)
(iii) Continuity of life	Yes	No	No	No
(iv) Centralization of management	Yes	No[a]	Yes	Yes
(v) Limited liability	Yes	No[b]	No	Yes
(vi) Free transferability of ownership	Yes	No	Yes	No

[a]Although the classic partnership does not have centralization of management—in other words, every partner can legally act for the entire partnership and thereby obligate every other partner—a centralized form of management is common in large partnerships. For example, consider the management structure of the "Big Eight" public accounting firms.
[b]Again, even though the garden-variety partnership is characterized by the unlimited liability of every partner, limited partnerships are quite common today.

these characteristics will depend upon the facts in each individual case.... An organization will be treated as an association if the corporate characteristics are such that the organization more nearly resembles a corporation than a partnership or trust.[1]

At this point, we need not resolve the definitional issue. It is sufficient to understand that *the federal income tax on corporations may, in unusual circumstances, be extended to an unincorporated business venture.*

Perhaps the most interesting, large-scale, recent controversy in the taxation of unincorporated businesses as corporations concerns the practice of medicine. Although the details of that story are too long to be detailed here, in summary, the controversy concerned physicians who wanted to have their medical practices treated as corporations in order to take advantage of the tax benefits of corporate pension plans. To do this, they originally created "associations" with characteristics more typical of corporations than of partnerships.[2]

The judicial decisions on this issue eventually led to major tax reform in two distinct areas. First, every state was forced to adopt a professional corporation act, giving physicians, dentists, accountants, lawyers, and other professionals the right to incorporate their professional practices. Second, Congress dramatically improved the tax benefits available through noncorporate pension plans in an attempt to stem the national tide toward the incorporation of all professionals.

THE SUBCHAPTER S CORPORATION   Just as an unincorporated business may, in unusual circumstances, be taxed as a corporation, so also a legal corporation may be taxed in a manner similar to an unincorporated business. The most common explanation for the latter event is the Subchapter S election. A Subchapter S corporation is a tax hybrid—part corporation, part partnership—based on a veritable jungle of tax rules. A detailed investigation of the statutory provisions found in Subchapter S of the Code is provided in Chapter 9. It is sufficient to observe here that not every legal corporation is taxed according to the usual corporate rules; many special federal income tax rules apply to corporations that properly make a Subchapter S election.

THE CORPORATE SHAM   On rare occasions, the courts have held that a legally incorporated entity should be ignored for federal income tax purposes. The circumstances that compel a court to reach such a drastic conclusion are, to say the least, unusual. Generally, the facts that support such a decision show beyond any doubt that the corporate shell was a mere sham. Although the stockholder went to the trouble of incorporating, he or she continued to ignore all other corporate realities. In addition, some "grand" tax plan is usually involved in these cases.[3]

CLOSELY RELATED CORPORATIONS   Two or more corporations that are entirely separate *legal* entities may, under certain circumstances, be treated to some extent as a single corporation for federal income tax purposes. This treatment can usually be attributed to one of two factors: Either the multiple corporations elect to file a consolidated corporate tax return, or multiple corporations are owned by so few persons that to tax them in the normal way would yield unintended and substantial tax benefits. Some of the more important details of consolidated corporate taxation are considered in Chapter 8.

In summary, not every separate corporate entity is treated as a separate corporate entity for federal income tax purposes. A wholly unincorporated business venture may be taxed as a corporation; a legally incorporated business venture may be taxed in a hybrid fashion—partly as a corporation and partly as a partnership—by making the Subchapter S election; a legal corporate entity may be completely ignored if it is considered to be a sham for tax purposes; and multiple corporate entities may be taxed to some extent as a single corporation either because they elect to file a consolidated corporate tax return or because they are a closely owned group of controlled corporations.

FOREIGN CORPORATIONS   The United States purports to have a global income tax. This means that the federal income tax applies to both foreign and domestic taxable entities. The rules governing the taxation of individual taxpayers are divided between those for citizens and those for aliens. Furthermore, the tax rules that apply to aliens are further separated into those applying to resident aliens and those applying to nonresident aliens. Generally, all U.S. citizens (whether or not they reside in the United States) and all *resident aliens* are treated the same way for purposes of federal in-

---

[1] Reg. Sec. 301.7701-2(a)(1).
[2] If you are interested in this issue, see one or all of the four following judicial decisions: *United States* v. *Kintner*, 216 F.2d 418 (CCA-9, 1954); *United States* v. *Empey*, 406 F.2d 157 (CCA-10, 1969); *O'Neill* v. *United States*, 418 F.2d 888 (CCA-6, 1969); and *Kurzner* v. *United States*, 413 F.2d 97 (CCA-5, 1969).

[3] Persons interested in the corporate sham phenomenon might read *Johansson* v. *United States*, 336 F.2d 809 (CCA-5, 1964) or *Paymer* v. *Commissioner*, 150 F.2d 334 (CCA-2, 1945).

come taxation. Only nonresident aliens are subject to special treatment: Generally nonresident aliens pay the U.S. income tax only on income derived from U.S. "sources." Corporate taxpayers are similarly divided into two classes: namely, "domestic" and "foreign" corporations. Domestic corporations generally are those chartered by one of the 50 states or by the U.S. government; foreign corporations are those chartered by some other (foreign) government. Ordinarily, foreign corporations, like nonresident aliens, are subject to the U.S. income tax only to the extent that they earn income from U.S. "sources." Because of widespread tax avoidance schemes, however, the general rule just stated was severely modified a few years ago. A "controlled foreign corporation" (or "CFC") is a corporation chartered by a foreign government but under the control of U.S. citizens; accordingly, it may be subject to the full and immediate U.S. federal income tax. The more important details of multinational taxation are reviewed in Chapters 22 and 23.

OTHER SPECIAL CORPORATIONS   In addition to the puzzling exceptions already noted, the Code contains a number of provisions intended to apply only to certain special types of incorporated businesses. For example, Subchapter H provides unique income tax rules for banking institutions; Subchapter L, for insurance companies; and Subchapter M, for regulated investment companies and real estate investment trusts. In addition, Subchapter G imposes some additional non-income taxes on corporations that are designed to avoid the income tax on shareholders, most notably the Personal Holding Company Tax and the Accumulated Earnings Tax. Finally, Subchapter F provides an entirely separate set of federal income tax rules for certain tax-exempt organizations, including many corporate entities.

In summary, remember that our discussion in Part Two, "The Income Taxation of Corporations," is both incomplete and at least partially misleading. The Code does *not* specify one set of income tax rules for corporations and another set for individuals. Rather, within a single document, the Code contains a multiplicity of rules, some unique to individuals, some unique to "routine" corporations, and some unique to quite special entities, but most applying equally to all entities. These general rules are the ones that we stressed in the first volume of *An Introduction to Taxation*. Even in that general introduction, we had to deal with different corporate and individual provisions in a limited number of situations. Before we consider additional special provisions, let us briefly review the limited differences.

Specific differences between corporate and individual income taxation

Although a majority of the general concepts as well as the detailed rules of our federal income tax apply equally to individual and corporate taxpayers, there are a number of special cases in which corporate and individual taxpayers receive different treatment. Because the more important differences were explained in reasonable detail in the first volume, they will be mentioned only briefly in this review. In addition, we shall not discuss patently obvious differences, such as that only an individual may claim a deduction for alimony, only an individual may claim the personal and dependent exemption, and only an individual may receive Social Security benefits.

THE ITEMIZED DEDUCTIONS   As you know, corporate taxpayers do not divide their income tax deductions into the "for A.G.I." and "from A.G.I." categories in the same way that individual taxpayers do. Nevertheless, many itemized deductions (or deductions from A.G.I.) common among individual taxpayers may also be deducted by the corporate taxpayer. For example, individuals and corporations both may incur a "medical expense." In the case of the corporation, however, a medical expense is an amount expended on behalf of its employees. Individuals and corporations both may incur a "moving expense." For a corporation, this expense might be related to either the movement of corporate property directly or the movement of the personal property of an employee. And individuals and corporations both may claim deductions for taxes, interest, and charitable contributions. Although corporate and individual taxpayers both may incur and deduct what we know as "itemized deductions," the statutory authority for those deductions is quite different. In the case of an individual taxpayer, the authority to deduct "personal" items generally stems from one of the sections included in Subchapter B (titled "computation of taxable income"), Part VII ("additional itemized deductions for individuals"). In the case of a corporate taxpayer, the authority to deduct a similar item is usually Sec. 162: The deduction is allowed because the expenditure is an ordinary and necessary expense of conducting a trade or business. Consequently, many of the limitations that apply to the itemized deductions claimed by individual taxpayers have no counterpart for corporate taxpayers.

In addition to the different statutory basis for itemized deductions, the fact that a corporation is ordinarily deemed to be engaged in a trade or business makes many corporate expenditures almost automatically deductible. For example, a corporate taxpayer may deduct almost automatically the total amount that it pays for gasoline, tires, liquor, airline tickets, telephone calls, and a host of other items that an individual taxpayer would have to examine and document carefully before he or she could determine whether or not they were deductible for tax purposes. Before 1979, for example, an individual taxpayer could deduct the cost of the state tax on all gasoline purchases (even if the gasoline were consumed in purely personal pursuits) but could deduct neither the remaining cost of the gasoline nor the cost of tires, liquor, airline tickets, or telephone calls *unless* those expenditures were either (1) an ordinary and necessary expense of carrying on a trade or business (Sec. 162), or (2) an expense incurred for the production of income (Sec. 212). Because a corporate entity is generally deemed to be constantly and solely engaged in a trade or business, nearly all expenditures for these and many other items are deductible under Sec. 162. Corporate taxpayers have no need for Sec. 212.

In a closely held corporation, however, the I.R.S. is always suspicious that the purely personal expenses of an owner or manager may be disguised as corporate business expenses. Therefore, supporting documentation often becomes of greater significance in the tax audit of a closely held corporation than it does in the case of a large publicly owned and independently managed corporation in which a better system of internal checks and balances is presumed to exist. We do not intend to imply, however, that large corporations may keep sloppy records for income tax purposes. Rather, we only mean to suggest that the I.R.S. is well aware that corporations owned by one or a few individuals are especially capable of manipulation and, therefore, the I.R.S. deals with them accordingly.

The trade-or-business presumption common to the corporate entity may also be important to the application of other Code sections. For example, the loss deduction authorized by Sec. 165 is much more severely restricted for the individual taxpayer than it is for the corporate taxpayer. Losses incurred by individuals on purely personal (that is, nonbusiness related) properties are deductible only if due to a casualty or a theft. Because corporations ordinarily own no purely personal property, no comparable limitation exists. Another example of the same difference is found in Sec. 166(d), which requires that the *nonbusiness bad debts* of individual taxpayers be treated as short-term capital losses. Because corporations ordinarily have only business bad debts, they have no comparable restriction.

THE DIVIDENDS-RECEIVED DEDUCTION   Corporate taxpayers generally are entitled to deduct 85 percent of the amount of dividends they receive from other *domestic* corporations under the provisions of Sec. 243. In the case of certain related or "affiliated" corporations, the amount of this deduction may be increased to 100 percent of the dividends received. Individual taxpayers, on the other hand, may exclude from gross income only up to $200 in dividends received each year (Sec. 116); they are not entitled to claim any dividend-received deduction. Part VIII of Subchapter B (Secs. 241 through 250) authorizes a few other special corporate deductions, most of which relate to the payment or receipt of dividends, but these are generally of limited interest.

CAPITAL GAINS AND LOSSES   The taxation of capital gains and losses differs in important respects for corporate and noncorporate taxpayers. A corporation may pay a tax on the net capital gain realized and recognized in any year at a 28 percent alternative tax rate; an individual may claim a deduction equal to 60 percent of the net capital gain realized and recognized. Furthermore, corporations may *not* deduct any amount of net capital loss from ordinary income (individuals may deduct up to $3,000 per year in that manner). Corporations, however, may carry a net capital loss back and offset it against capital gains realized and recognized in the three prior years. If the corporation's net capital loss in the current year is greater than the sum of recognized capital gains in the three prior years, any remainder may be carried forward for five additional years. All capital loss carrybacks and carryforwards are treated as short-term capital losses by corporate taxpayers.[4]

CHARITABLE CONTRIBUTIONS   The maximum charitable contribution deduction that may be claimed by a corporate taxpayer is equal to 5 percent of its taxable income determined without reference to the net operating loss deduction, the charitable contribution deduction itself, or any of the deductions related to *corporate dividends* received by or paid by a corporation (see Sec. 170(b)(2)). The limits of charitable contribution deductions for individual taxpayers differ in many respects from those just stated. In general, individuals may deduct up to 50 percent of their A.G.I. for contributions made to public charities.

---

[4]Individual taxpayers are not entitled to any capital loss carrybacks. On the other hand, individuals may carry capital losses forward for an indefinite period. Finally, individual capital losses always retain their original character (as long- or short-term) in carryforward years.

TAX RATES   The tax rate applied to the tax base (taxable income) differs in important respects for corporate and individual taxpayers. The corporate tax rate consists of a five-step progressive tax, as follows:

17 percent on the first $25,000 of taxable income;

20 percent on the second $25,000 of taxable income;

30 percent on the third $25,000 of taxable income;

40 percent on the fourth $25,000 of taxable income;

46 percent on any taxable income in excess of $100,000.

Thus, the corporate tax rate of Sec. 11 has significantly fewer tax brackets and less progression than the individual tax rates contained in Sec. 1. (Those marginal rates range from a minimum of 14 percent to a maximum of 70 percent; the exact number of brackets and the rate of progression differ for single persons, heads of households, and married persons filing joint returns.)

OTHER DIFFERENCES   This brief restatement of specific differences between a determination of the federal income tax liability of corporations and noncorporate taxpayers is by no means exhaustive. It does, however, capture the more important differences of general interest. Rather than belabor other differences—for example, Sec. 108 and the income from discharge of indebtedness; Sec. 171 and the rules for amortizing bond premiums; and Sec. 248 and the rules for the amortization of organization expenses—we turn now to a second topic: the tax consequences of an incorporation transaction. The "birth" of a corporation represents the first of many transactions that occur between a corporation and its shareholders. These initial transactions receive special attention in Subchapter C of the Code. Other transactions that become commonplace as the corporation matures (for example, distributions, redemptions, liquidations, and reorganizations) are discussed in the next three chapters. The special provisions of Subchapter C are often implicit in a reference to "corporate income taxation."

THE INCORPORATION TRANSACTION

After all legal prerequisites have been satisfied, a corporation is ready to begin its financial existence. The first financial transaction of a new corporation ordinarily consists of an exchange between the corporation and its shareholders. We may refer to this initial financial exchange as "the incorporation transaction." In its most elementary form, the incorporation transaction is depicted in Figure 4-2. A corporation's shareholders may be divided into three distinct classes of taxpayers, as follows: (1) Individual persons, represented in the figure by "I"; (2) Other corporations (that is, corporations other than X Corporation itself), represented by the rectangle "C"; and (3) Fiduciaries (estates and trusts), represented by the diamond "T." Shareholders ordinarily exchange some of their cash, other property, services, or some combination, for some portion or all of X Corporation's previously authorized but unissued stock and, possibly, long-term debt obligations (a "security") of X Corporation.

The wide range of tax questions inherent in an incorporation transaction can be illustrated by the example depicted in Figure 4-3. Four individual taxpayers (A, B, C, and D) each exchange something with a fair market value of $25,000 for 100 shares of X Corporation's common stock. Eight fundamental tax questions inherent in this example can be separated into four questions at the stockholder level and four at the corporate level, as follows:

Stockholder questions

1. Has A, B, C, or D realized any gross income because of this incorporation transaction?

2. If A, B, C, or D has realized gross income, must that income be recognized for tax purposes?

3. If A, B, C or D must recognize gross income, what type or kind of income is it? (Ordinary income? Capital gain? Sec. 1231 gain? Earned income?)

4. What tax basis do A, B, C, and D have in their 100 shares of X Corporation common stock?

Corporate questions

1. Has X Corporation realized any gross income because of this incorporation transaction?

2. If X Corporation has realized gross income, must that income be recognized for tax purposes?

3. What tax basis does X Corporation have in the assets it receives?

4. Is X Corporation entitled to any tax deductions because of this incorporation transaction?

Before reading further, try to answer these eight questions and thereby review your comprehension of the general rules of our federal income tax, as explained in the first volume of *An Introduction to Taxation*.

General rules: a review

The general rules pertinent to the fundamental tax issues detailed in Figure 4-3 can be paraphrased as follows.

FIGURE **4-2**   The Incorporation Transaction

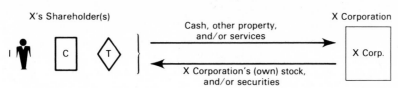

1. Unless there is specific authority to the contrary, all income is gross income (Sec. 61(a));

2. (a) Realization of income generally requires only the consummation of an external transaction; (b) "any significant change in the form or the substance of any property or property right" constitutes a transaction; and (c) an external transaction is simply one involving more than one entity;

3. Income must be recognized for tax purposes at the time it is realized, unless authority for a contrary treatment exists (see Sec. 1001); and

4. Nothing is deductible unless it is specifically authorized by the Code or regulations.

Applying these four general rules to the tax questions inherent in Figure 4-3 would seem to suggest that: (1) B, C, D, and X have all realized some amount of gross income that must be recognized immediately (unless there is specific authority to the contrary); and (2) X is not entitled to a deduction (unless there is specific authority authorizing it). Before the incorporation transaction, each taxpayer (A, B, C, D, and X) owned something that was different from that owned after the exchange. An external (second) taxpayer was involved in each exchange. Consequently, unless some authority to the contrary can be cited, each taxpayer must apply the general rule of Sec. 1001 and immediately recognize as gross income the difference between (a) the

amount realized (that is, the value received) and (b) the adjusted basis given up in this exchange. To be more specific:

☐ A would recognize no gross income (but only because the apparent $25,000 value of the 100 shares of X stock received is equal to A's tax basis in the $25,000 cash surrendered);

☐ B would recognize a $10,000 gross income (that is, $25,000 amount realized less $15,000 adjusted basis);

☐ C would recognize a $15,000 gross income (that is, $25,000 amount realized less $10,000 adjusted basis);

☐ D would recognize a $25,000 gross income (that is, $25,000 amount realized less no basis in the services rendered); and

☐ X would recognize a $100,000 gross income (that is, $100,000 amount realized less little or no tax basis in the shares surrendered).

Before 1921 there was no contrary authority, and the tax consequences suggested above, at least as far as the four stockholders are concerned, would be in effect.[5] Such consequences obviously discourage the incorporation of American businesses. Few taxpayers would be

[5] See *Jefferson Livingston*, 18 B.T.A. 1184 (1930).

FIGURE **4-3**   Tax Questions Inherent in an Incorporation Transaction for X's Shareholders

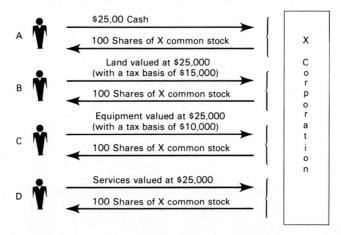

willing to pay an income tax on the increased value of any assets transferred to a new corporate entity, especially if the stock in that corporation were held by the same person or persons who previously owned the assets outside the corporation. In order to facilitate business readjustments that *usually* involve a mere change in legal form, with little or no change in economic substance, Congress in 1921 passed the predecessor of the present Code Sec. 351. Sec. 351 provides a special nonrecognition rule that might apply to Taxpayers B and C in Figure 4-3 above.

Section 351—an overview

In general, Sec. 351 provides that *no gain or loss shall be recognized by the transferors of property to a corporation if those transferors control, immediately after the transfer, at least 80 percent of the recipient corporation's stock.*[6] Applying this statutory test to our illustration in Figure 4-3 suggests that whether or not Taxpayers B and C must recognize any gain depends on the meaning of the word "property." If both the cash and the services contributed by Taxpayers A and D, respectively, may be counted as property, then no gain will be recognized because the transferors (A, B, C, and D) collectively control 100 percent of X Corporation. On the other hand, if either the cash or the services are *not* to be included as property, then the transferors of property would, at best, control only 75 percent of X Corporation immediately after the exchange. And if the property transferors have less than 80 percent control, Sec. 351 does not apply. In that event, the general rule of Sec. 1001 (requiring the immediate recognition of any gain realized) will apply, and B and C must pay the income tax on $10,000 and $15,000, respectively. The last sentence of Sec. 351(a) specifically states that "stock or securities issued for services shall not be considered as issued in return for property." Consequently, it would appear that B and C must recognize taxable income in the transaction illustrated in Figure 4-3. Although this cursory review of the general rule of Sec. 351(a) may seem simple enough, a more careful examination of that Code section will reveal many interesting questions of interpretation. We shall examine some of the more common questions encountered in the incorporation transaction in the remaining pages of this chapter.

[6]The exact words of Sec. 351(a) are as follows:
General rule.—No gain or loss shall be recognized if property is transferred to a corporation by one or more persons solely in exchange for stock or securities in such corporation and immediately after the exchange such person or persons are in control (as defined in Section 368(c)) of the corporation. For purposes of this section, stock or securities issued for services shall not be considered as issued in return for property.

Section 351—some problem areas

A thorough review of all the tax issues encountered in the incorporation of a business is beyond the scope of this book. A brief review of the more common issues, however, will illustrate the diversity and complexity of this relatively routine business event. A few problems may be easily resolved with minimal research. For example, we asked above whether or not cash or services should be considered "property" for purposes of interpreting Sec. 351(a). Because the Code explicitly states that stocks or securities issued for services are not to be considered as issued for property, we did not investigate further the right to include stocks issued for cash in making the 80 percent test. If we were to search for an answer to that question in a tax library, it should not take long to locate either Rev. Rul. 69-357, 1969-1 CB 101, or *George M. Holstein*, 23 TC 923 (1955). Both authorities clearly support the conclusion that cash is property within the meaning of Sec. 351(a). Other questions are less easily resolved.

SERVICES AND PROPERTY   What if a transferor contributes both services and property? Would all or only a part of that transferor's shares be counted in determining whether or not the transferors of property had 80 percent control immediately after the transfer? In other words, if in Figure 4-3, Taxpayer D had transferred both services and property, with an *aggregate* value of $25,000, for 100 shares of X Corporation's common stock, would Taxpayers B and C still have to recognize gross income of $10,000 and $15,000, respectively?

The answer to this question is not as quickly determined. Treas. Reg. Sec. 1.351-1(a)(1)(ii) states only that "stock or securities issued for property *which is of relatively small value* in comparison to the value of the stock and securities already owned (or to be received for services) by the person who transferred such property, shall not be treated as having been issued in return for property if the *primary purpose* of the transfer is to qualify under this section the exchanges of property by other persons transferring property." (Emphasis added.) Before we can convert the words of this regulation into an operative managerial rule, we must, of course, define the phrases "relatively small value" and "primary purpose." Unfortunately, these interpretations do not come easily.

The need for precaution on the part of the Treasury Department can, however, be readily demonstrated. Returning to Figure 4-3, if there were no ambiguity in interpretation, Taxpayer D would seem to be entirely in control of the tax fate of Taxpayers B and C. In other words, if Taxpayer D were to substitute $1 (cash) in the exchange as originally diagramed (and correspondingly reduce the value of his or her services from $25,000 to $24,999), then—if the contribution of *any* property means that all shares are to be counted for purposes of satisfying the 80 percent control test—Taxpayers B and C escape taxation. If, on the other hand, Taxpayer D refuses to include $1 in cash, Taxpayers B and C must recognize the gain they realized. Obviously, such a conclusion would clearly elevate the importance of form over substance in matters of taxation. And, in general, the courts do not choose to place undue importance on form. At least theoretically, the economic substance of a transaction should be more important than its apparent form.[7]

Whether or not a taxpayer wishes to recognize the tax consequences of a realized gain or loss depends on a host of sometimes diverse factors. Note, for example, that the general rule of Sec. 351(a) applies to *both gains and losses*. Ordinarily, a taxpayer will prefer to recognize any deductible losses at the earliest possible moment. It seems unlikely, therefore, that the I.R.S. would be willing to allow the inclusion or exclusion of $1 cash by Taxpayer D to determine whether or not some other taxpayer (for example, B or C) may recognize a loss. (To see this more clearly, return to Figure 4-3 and assume that Taxpayer C's property had a basis of $40,000, rather than $10,000 as originally stated. Would the mere substitution of $1 in cash for $1 in the value of services by Taxpayer D be sufficient economic substance to allow Taxpayer C to recognize $15,000 loss—and concurrently to force Taxpayer B to recognize a $10,000 gain? We think not, and that is, of course, the general conclusion of Treas. Reg. Sec. 1.351-1(a)(1)(ii), quoted above.) In addition to situations involving losses, the transferor taxpayers may opt for a taxable event (rather than a nontaxable event) if their gain is capital gain and recognition of that gain would allow the transferee (X Corporation) the right to larger depreciation deductions in the future. If a transferor had a net operating loss that was about to expire, that fact might also be sufficient reason to trigger an otherwise deferable income. Given the many reasons taxpayers may have to either defer or accelerate the recognition of gain or loss, it is easy to see why the Treasury Department and the I.R.S. are unwilling to allow form to control over substance in every instance. On the other hand, there must be a limit as to how far even a court may go in making arbitrary decisions on what is of "relatively small value" or what is a "primary purpose."

In an attempt to reduce uncertainty, the I.R.S. has issued safe-haven rules to answer many of the questions posed by the transfer of services *and* property by a single transferor. For advanced ruling purposes, the I.R.S. requires that the value of the property transferred be equal to or greater than 10 percent of the value of the shares received if all of the transferor's shares are to be counted as issued for property in determining whether or not the 80 percent control requirement has been satisfied.[8] Returning once again to Figure 4-3, we see that this means Taxpayer D would have to substitute for services property valued at $2,500 or more before D's combined transfer of property *and* services would be sufficient to rescue Taxpayers B and C from their obligation to recognize income of $10,000 and $15,000, respectively.

SERVICES EMBODIED IN PROPERTY   A second difficult question to resolve concerns the transfer of services that have become embodied in a property. Should such a transfer be considered a transfer of a service or a transfer of property? To illustrate, assume that a cash-basis taxpayer had worked for three years on an oil painting, a copyright, or an account receivable (debt). If that taxpayer were to transfer the painting, the copyright, or the account receivable into a corporation, should that be treated as the transfer of a property or a service? We know that, generally speaking, the sale of such an asset would create ordinary income rather than capital gain by application of the definition contained in Sec. 1221(3). The capital asset definition does not, however, necessarily extend to the meaning of "property" for purposes of Sec. 351(a).

A trip to the tax library might on this occasion prove frustrating to the student who wants unambiguous answers to all questions. There is limited authority to suggest that, for purposes of interpreting Sec. 351(a), services embodied in a property right may sometimes be treated as a property.[9] The number of citations to good authority on this question is, however, surprisingly small. The absence of authority just might imply a "Catch 22" answer. That is, given that so many people incorporate their businesses, and given that so many services are routinely embodied in property rights, the fact that there is so little authority directly in point suggests that services are to be treated as property for purposes of Sec. 351(a). If the I.R.S. were claiming that these assets were not property, it would be reasonable to assume that much more authority on this question would be readily available.

[7]This important judicial doctrine stems largely from *Gregory* v. *Helvering*, 293 U.S. 465 (1935).

[8]See Rev. Proc. 76-22, 1976-1 CB 562.
[9]See, for example, *U.S.* v. *Frazell*, 335 F.2d 487 (CCA-5, 1964).

IMMEDIATELY AFTER THE EXCHANGE   Another series of questions concerns the "immediately-after" test. Sec. 351(a) requires that the transferors of property have 80 percent control *immediately after* the exchange if the property transferor's realized gains and losses are to remain unrecognized for tax purposes. How is one to interpret this immediately after test? At least two distinctly different questions arise relative to this phrase.

First, if there is more than one transferor, how long do the transferors have to complete their several individual transfers of property? May they spread them over one week? One month? Six months? A year? Treas. Reg. Sec. 1.351-1(a)(1) says only that "[t]he phrase 'immediately after the exchange' does not necessarily require simultaneous exchanges by two or more persons, but comprehends a situation where the rights of the parties have been previously defined and the execution of the agreement proceeds with an expedition consistent with orderly procedure." Obviously, the words of this regulation leave a great deal of room for individual interpretation.

A second, wholly unrelated set of problems may also arise from the immediately after test. These questions concern the need for the transferors to retain control for more than a fleeting moment after their transfer of assets to a controlled corporation. Although a narrow reading of the statute might suggest that momentary control of 80 percent is adequate, a review of administrative and judicial authority suggests that something more is required.[10] To oversimplify those authorities, it appears that a *prearranged and mandatory* disposition of sufficient size to reduce the transferors' control to less than 80 percent will remove the incorporation transaction from the nonrecognition rule of Sec. 351(a). On the other hand, a voluntary disposition after such a transaction may be less vulnerable, especially if the subsequent disposition is a noncommercial transaction, for example, a gift to a family member.[11]

SECURITIES   Note that the nonrecognition treatment afforded by Sec. 351(a) applies as long as property is transferred "solely in exchange for stock *or securities* in such corporation. . . ." But what, precisely, is meant by "securities"? Few questions have caused more litigation than a definition of the term "securities." In general, securities refers to *long-term* debt that is

intended to be a relatively permanent part of the capital structure of the corporation. Exactly how long is long term? Is a six-month debt a security? A one-year debt? A five-year debt? As noted in *Camp Wolters Enterprises, Inc.* v. *Commissioner,* 230 F.2d 555 (CCA-5, 1956) *aff'g.* 22 TC 737 (1955), time is an important but by no means the singular test of security status. Thus, in some instances, the tax-free treatment of an incorporation transaction will depend on the ability of a debt instrument received by the transferor to pass muster as a security. If a property transferor receives anything other than the stock or securities of the transferee corporation, some part or all of any realized gain must be recognized per Sec. 351(b).

Section 351(b) and the role of boot

Like most other *nontaxable* transactions, an incorporation transaction may be converted into at least a partially taxable transaction by the transferor's receipt of boot. Subsection 351(b) provides that, if a property transferor receives anything other than the transferee corporation's stock or securities, that transferor must recognize gain equal to the lesser of (a) the value of the boot received or (b) the gain realized.[12] In other words, in an incorporation transaction, *boot* may be defined as anything other than the transferee corporation's stock or securities. Note, however, that Sec. 351(b) applies only to the recognition of *gain;* a realized loss may never be recognized as long as the general conditions of Sec. 351(a) have been satisfied.

To illustrate the rules of Sec. 351(a) and (b), consider Figure 4-4. Assume that individuals E and F each already own 50 percent of the outstanding common stock of the E-F Corporation. Given the situation shown in Figure 4-4, Taxpayer E would *not* be entitled to recognize any of the $10,000 loss realized by the transfer of land to the E-F Corporation. Taxpayer F, on the other hand, would be forced to recognize $5,000 of the $15,000 gain realized on the transfer of the franchise to the E-F Corporation by operation of Sec. 351(b). Even a cursory review of the rules just stated should once again provide you with ample appreciation of the Internal Revenue Service's natural suspicion of

---

[10]See, for example, Rev. Rul 70-140, 1970-1 CB 73 and *American Bantam Car Co.,* 177 F.2d 513 (CCA-3), 1949) *aff'g. per curiam* 11 TC 397 (1948).

[11]See *Stanton* v. *U.S.,* 512 F.2d 13 (CCA-3, 1975) and *Stephens, Inc.* v. *U.S.,* 464 F.2d 53 (CCA-8, 1972).

[12]The exact words of Subsection 351(b) are as follows:
  Receipt of Property.—If subsection (a) would apply to an exchange but for the fact that there is received, in addition to the stock or securities permitted to be received under subsection (a), other property or money, then—
  (1) gain (if any) to such recipient shall be recognized, but not in excess of—
    (A) the amount of money received, plus
    (B) the fair market value of such other property received; and
  (2) no loss to such recipient shall be recognized.

FIGURE **4-4**   The Role of "Boot"

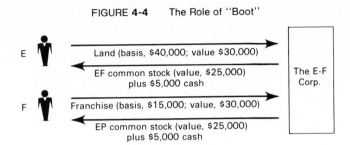

many transactions between the closely held corporation and its stockholders. As you will discover in the next chapter, most distributions of assets by corporations to their shareholders will create a dividend that is fully taxable to the shareholder (and that provides no tax deduction to the distributing corporation). Figure 4-4 seems to present a possible route around the generally unsatisfactory tax consequences of a dividend. What is to keep Taxpayer E from inflating the value of the land transferred to the E-F Corporation? In other words, who is to say exactly what the value of any asset is at any moment in time? Except for stocks and securities regularly traded on the major exchanges, most assets have no readily determined value, which leaves ample room for guessing and even more room for argument. If a taxpayer and an I.R.S. agent cannot agree on valuations, only a court can settle the disagreement. Obviously, if Taxpayer E is successful in inflating the value of the land, he or she may also be successful in extracting cash (or other assets) from the corporation without paying an income tax on a dividend.

To illustrate the limitation of Sec. 351(b)(1), return to Figure 4-4 and assume that Taxpayer F had a basis of $28,000 (rather than a basis of $15,000, as originally stated) in the franchise transferred to the E-F Corporation. What amount of gain must Taxpayer F then recognize? The correct answer is only $2,000. The remaining $3,000 is deemed to be a return of Taxpayer F's capital. In other words, remember that the amount of gain to be recognized by operation of Sec. 351(b) is restricted to the *lesser of* (a) the gain realized or (b) the amount of boot received.

Assumption of debt as boot

Another interesting problem common to many incorporation transactions arises when the transferee corporation assumes a debt of the transferor. Should the assumption of debt be treated as the receipt of boot? Assume, for example, that Taxpayer G decides to incorporate a business that previously was operated as a sole proprietorship. Further assume that Taxpayer G has an outstanding $40,000 mortgage on the real estate (land and buildings) to be transferred to the wholly owned Gee Corporation, and that Gee Corporation agrees to assume that $40,000 debt. The essential elements of this transaction are illustrated in Figure 4-5.

If Taxpayer G owns 100 percent of the stock of Gee Corporation, we know that the general rule of Sec. 351(a) would require that the $25,000 gain realized by G be deferred *unless* the assumption of the $40,000 mortgage debt by Gee Corporation is to be treated as boot. If the assumption of debt is to be treated as boot, then Sec. 351(b) would require that Taxpayer G recognize the $25,000 gain realized in this incorporation transaction.

When the Supreme Court first considered the question of debt as boot (in the context of a corporate reorganization), it concluded, in *U.S.* v. *Hendler,* that the assumption of debt should be treated as boot.[13] The Treasury Department quickly determined, however, that its apparent victory in *Hendler* could create more problems than it solved. Many earlier transactions that

[13]See *U.S.* v. *Hendler,* 303 U.S. 564 (1938).

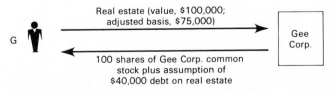

FIGURE **4-5**   The Assumption of Debt

were treated as nontaxable events might now be considered taxable events. And, if the statute of limitations had expired, the taxpayers in those cases might use *Hendler* to their own advantage. Accordingly, the Treasury Department sought relief from Congress through a new law. Eventually, a law was passed that, for all practical purposes, overruled the Supreme Court decision in *Hendler*. This provision is found in Sec. 357(a).

In general, Sec. 357 provides that the assumption of debt should *not* be treated as boot unless either (1) the purpose for the assumption of the debt is the avoidance of the federal income tax, or (2) the liability assumed is greater than the transferor's adjusted basis in the property transferred. The reason for the first exception, found in Sec. 357(b), will become apparent on further reflection.

Recall from your earlier study of income taxation that the act of mortgaging property generally is not treated as a realization event. Presumably, such a conclusion is warranted by the fact that the taxpayer has no income; that is, he or she has no *net* increase in assets after the act of mortgaging a property. In other words, the cash or other property received by the mortgagor via the mortgage is exactly offset by an equal debt owing to the mortgagee; hence, the mortgagor is alleged to have realized no increased net worth. At the same time, however, observe that the mortgagor has indeed changed the form of his or her wealth in a potentially significant way. Before completion of the mortgage, the taxpayer had only an inflated property (perhaps land or stocks) that was not highly liquid; after completion of the mortgage, that same taxpayer had cash in a bank account—the most liquid asset of all. Perhaps the income arose from a prior increase in value. Thus, whether or not a taxpayer mortgaging a property has *realized* any income is largely a matter of definition. Suffice it to observe, however, that the tax authorities have generally concluded that the act of mortgaging a property is not equivalent to the realization of income. This conclusion, combined with the general rule of Sec. 357(a), created a major loophole.

To illustrate the loophole, assume that Taxpayer G paid $75,000 cash five years ago for the real estate noted in Figure 4-5. Today—five years later—that property is worth $100,000. In other words, the real estate has increased in value by $25,000. If Taxpayer G were to sell the property, he or she would, of course, have to recognize the $25,000 gain realized. On the other hand, if Taxpayer G were merely to mortgage the property in exchange for $40,000 cash, the tax authorities would ordinarily hold that no gain had been realized. Suppose, however, that shortly after completing this mortgage, Taxpayer G were to transfer the newly mortgaged real estate to Gee Corporation in the transaction depicted in Figure 4-5. Would not Gee Corporation's assumption of Taxpayer G's mortgage effectively constitute the realization of income via a reduction in debt? In other words, has not Taxpayer G been able to "cash in" on the $25,000 increase in value of the real estate by requiring another taxpayer (Gee Corporation) to pay off the mortgage (debt) just incurred? The apparent answer is "yes," and that is the effect of the exception found in Sec. 357(b). Although the time that elapses between the act of mortgaging a property and its transfer to a controlled corporation is not the only fact that will be considered by an I.R.S. agent or a court, it is a major consideration that may help to sustain a tax-avoidance conclusion.

The second exception to the general rule of Sec. 357(a) is, at least initially, less obtuse. That exception, found in Sec. 357(c), provides that any assumption of debt will be treated as boot if the liability assumed is greater than the basis of the property transferred. Returning to Figure 4-5, assume that Taxpayer G had a basis of only $25,000 in the real estate transferred to Gee Corporation. If all other facts were as originally depicted, Sec. 357(c) would provide that Taxpayer G must recognize $15,000 of the $75,000 gain realized. The $40,000 debt assumed by Gee Corporation exceeds Taxpayer G's $25,000 basis by $15,000; hence, that amount of gain must be recognized.

Even the apparently straightforward exception of Sec. 357(c) has caused a great deal of confusion during the past 15 years. Many small, unincorporated businesses keep books on a cash basis of accounting. Accordingly, these businesses have little tax basis in what is often their major business asset—their accounts receivable. At the same time, however, these businesses often acquire most of their fixed assets (that is, their plant and equipment) by purchasing them on a long-term debt. When these small businesses incorporate, much of their original basis in fixed assets may have disappeared through prior rapid depreciation deductions. Accordingly, it is not unusual for the shareholders' remaining adjusted basis in the assets transferred to a new corporation to be less than the debts of the ongoing business, especially when those debts include both the current liabilities of the business and the long-term debt on the fixed assets previously acquired and depreciated by the shareholders.

The Revenue Act of 1978 put an end to a rapidly growing controversy over the correct interpretation of the word "liabilities" as it is used in Sec. 357(c). In general, the 1978 Act provides that the term liability, as used in Sec. 357(c), does *not* include the current obligations of a newly incorporated business if payment of those obligations would have given rise to a tax deduction had they been paid by the shareholders before the act of incorporation. It is hoped that this change will reduce the number of incorporation transactions that accidentally stumble into a tax trap because of Sec. 357(c).

Collateral tax questions

The preceding discussion is by no means an exhaustive treatment of the many tax questions that may arise in an incorporation transaction. In fact, if you return to Figure 4-3 and review the several questions raised in connection with that illustration, you will note that we have thus far answered only the first two questions pertinent to the stockholder, namely, (1) is any gain or loss realized by the shareholders in an incorporation transaction? And (2) if so, must that gain or loss be recognized immediately upon realization? The other questions noted deserve additional but brief consideration.

"TYPE" OR "KIND" OF GAIN RECOGNIZED   Once we have determined that a shareholder must recognize some amount of gain or loss in an incorporation transaction, we must also determine the "type" or "kind" of gain or loss recognized. To make that determination, we must review many tax rules introduced in Parts Five and Seven of the first volume of *An Introduction to Taxation.* Instead of attempting a comprehensive review, let us consider the specific examples of Taxpayers B, C, and D in Figure 4-3. (Remember, we previously determined that Taxpayer A need not recognize any income because the amount realized by A is exactly equal to the basis surrendered.)

In Figure 4-3, Taxpayer B is exchanging land with a tax basis of $15,000 for common stock in X Corporation with a value of $25,000. Accordingly, unless Taxpayer B is protected by Sec. 351(a), he or she must immediately recognize the $10,000 gain realized by operation of Sec. 1001. To determine what kind of gain Taxpayer B must report, we must further review the definition of capital assets found in Sec. 1221. Recall from your study in Chapter 19 of *An Introduction to Taxation,* that Sec. 1221(2) excludes from the capital asset definition any real or depreciable properties used in a trade or business. Accordingly, before we can determine what kind of gain Taxpayer B must report, we must determine how B used the land before its transfer to X Corporation. If the land was either a property held primarily for resale (Sec. 1221(1)) *or* a property used in a trade or business (Sec. 1221(2)) by Taxpayer

B, then the $10,000 gain realized may *not* be a "pure" capital gain. On the other hand, if the land is neither of the above—if, for example, the land was part of Taxpayer A's personal residence before its transfer to X Corporation—then it will be a capital asset and the gain will be a capital gain. Remember also, however, that many assets excluded from the definition of a "pure" capital asset by Sec. 1221(2) may be treated as if they were capital assets by operation of Sec. 1231. That section, as explained in Chapter 21 of the first volume makes certain assets (often including land) chameleon assets—they may or may not be treated as capital assets, depending on the *net* gain or loss realized from sales or exchanges of all such assets at the end of the year.

In Figure 4-3, Taxpayer C is exchanging equipment with an adjusted tax basis of $10,000 for 100 shares of X Corporation common stock with a value of $25,000. Accordingly, unless Taxpayer C is protected by Sec. 351(a), he or she must also immediately recognize the $15,000 gain realized by operation of Sec. 1001. To determine the kind of gain Taxpayer C must report, we again must review the rules previously discussed in Part Five of the first volume. Recall that Sec. 1245, the recapture section generally applicable to equipment, requires that a taxpayer report as ordinary income any gain realized on the sale or exchange of depreciable nonrealty to the extent that the taxpayer has claimed any depreciation on the property since 1961. If we can determine, therefore, that Taxpayer C has, since 1961, claimed depreciation of $15,000 or more on the equipment being transferred to X Corporation, we can safely conclude that all Taxpayer C's income would be reported as ordinary income by operation of Sec. 1245.

The potential problems of Taxpayer C are really more interesting if we assume that the incorporation transaction is a nontaxable event. In other words, return to Figure 4-3 and change Taxpayer D's contribution from services only to a combined package of property and services. Assume that Taxpayer D exchanged (1) a franchise worth $15,000 and (2) personal services worth $10,000 for 100 shares of X Corporation common stock valued at $25,000. With that one change in facts, all the transferors of property would be protected by Sec. 351(a) because they collectively would then have more than 80 percent control over X Corporation immediately after the exchange. Given that one change, let us now return to the plight of Taxpayer C. Would the recapture rule of Sec. 1245 override the nonrecognition rule of Sec. 351(a)? You may remember that Sec. 1245(d) states that "[t]his section shall apply notwithstanding any other provision of this subtitle." In general, that means, of course, that

Sec. 1245 would override Sec. 351(a). A careful reading of the entire recapture section reveals, however, that a number of exceptions and limitations are stated in Sec. 1245(b). One of the exceptions is the tax-free transaction of Sec. 351. Accordingly, the correct conclusion is that Taxpayer B would *not* (under the revised facts) have to recognize any gain due to the recapture of depreciation as long as he or she received no boot; that is, as long as Sec. 351(a) rather than Sec. 351(b) applied.

In the *original* Figure 4-3, Taxpayer D is exchanging his or her personal services for 100 shares of X Corporation common stock with a value of $25,000. Because there is little chance that income from services can be capital gain, and because Sec. 61 seems to require that all ordinary income be recognized immediately, the only question to be resolved concerns the classification of such income as *earned* income. A review of the rules presented in Chapter 27 of the first volume suggests that D's income would be earned income as long as it was intended as compensation for personal services rendered (or to be rendered) by Taxpayer D. In other words, the $25,000 in gross income would be eligible for the 50 percent maximum tax on earned income if Taxpayer D has sufficient earned income from other sources to otherwise qualify him or her for that alternative.

Tax basis in stock received

The tax basis that shareholders have in the stock they receive in an incorporation transaction depends on whether that transaction is a taxable or a nontaxable event. If it is a taxable event, the normal rule will apply—that is, the basis of the property received will be equal to its cost, as provided in Sec. 1012. In other words, as originally diagrammed in Figure 4-3, Taxpayers A, B, C, and D will *each* have a basis of $25,000 in their 100 shares of X Corporation common stock. If we again modify Figure 4-3 so that Taxpayer D exchanges (1) a franchise worth $15,000 and (2) services worth $10,000 for 100 shares of X Corporation common stock (worth $25,000), then the transaction becomes a wholly nontaxable event for Taxpayers B and C. And if the transaction is wholly nontaxable by operation of Sec. 351(a), then the applicable basis rules are found in Sec. 358(a)(1). If no boot is received, the rules are simple: The taxpayer takes a basis in the stock or securities received equal to the basis he or she had in the property surrendered. In other words, if the facts implicit in the original Figure 4-3 were modified for Taxpayer D in order to make this a nontaxable transaction, then Taxpayer B would have a tax basis of

$15,000 in his or her 100 shares of X Corporation's common stock, whereas Taxpayer C would have a basis of only $10,000.

If a taxpayer receives boot in an incorporation transaction, the basis rules become somewhat more complex. In general, however, the revised rules can be paraphrased as follows:

Basis of property given up in the exchange
+ Gain recognized
− Boot received
= Basis of stock or securities received

If you wish to test your ability to apply the above rule, return to the facts suggested in Figure 4-4. As the facts were *initially* presented in that illustration, Taxpayer E would have a tax basis of $35,000 in the E-F common stock that he or she received while Taxpayer F would have a basis of $15,000. And in the modified version of Figure 4-4 (in which F's original basis was increased from $15,000 to $28,000), Taxpayer F's basis in the E-F stock would be $25,000.

If a shareholder is relieved of a debt—that is, if the corporation either assumes a shareholder's prior debt or takes a property subject to a prior debt—then the shareholder must reduce the basis of any stocks or securities received by the amount of the debt. This last modification to the general carryover basis rule is found in Sec. 358(d).

Corporate realization and recognition

Our discussion thus far of the tax problems in an incorporation transaction has been from the point of view of the stockholders. We have not considered in detail the same transaction from the standpoint of the newly created corporation. As suggested earlier in this chapter, the corporation is faced with four basic tax questions, namely:

1. Does the corporation realize any gross income in an incorporation transaction?
2. If the corporation does realize gross income, must it be recognized at the time it issues stocks or securities?
3. What basis does the corporation have in any assets it receives in an incorporation transaction?
4. Is the corporation entitled to any deduction because of the shares it issues for services?

Application of the general rules suggested earlier implies that a corporate entity may well have realized income in an incorporation transaction. That is, (1) a significant change in the form of the corporation's property rights takes place, and (2) an external taxpayer is involved. Consequently, the essential elements of income realization are present. We need not ponder long the measurement of such income, however, because Sec. 1032 clearly provides an operative nonrecognition provision. That section provides that "[n]o gain or loss shall be recognized to a corporation on the receipt of money or other property in exchange for stock (including treasury stock) of such corporation." As to any issue of securities, one could argue that there is no income because the corporation's outstanding debt is increased by an amount equal to any increase in assets as far as a securities-for-property transaction is concerned. In summary, the corporation need *not* recognize any income either in the original incorporation transaction or in a subsequent contribution to capital by the shareholders.

Corporation's tax basis

What is the recipient corporation's tax basis in any property it receives in an incorporation transaction? Specifically, returning to Figure 4-3, what is X Corporation's tax basis in the land it receives from Taxpayer B and in the equipment it receives from Taxpayer C? The answer to this question is similar to the answer that applies to the shareholders. If the transaction is a fully taxable transaction—as originally diagramed in Figure 4-3—then the corporation takes a cost basis (via Sec. 1012) in any assets it receives. In that event, X Corporation would have a tax basis of $25,000 in the land and $25,000 in the equipment. If, however, we once more modify Figure 4-3 and change it into a nontaxable transaction—for example, if we have Taxpayer D contribute a franchise worth $15,000 and services worth $10,000—then X Corporation will determine its basis in any property received via the rules of Sec. 362. Section 362 provides that the corporation will take as its basis whatever basis the transferor had, increased, possibly, by the amount of any gain recognized by the transferor. In other words, the corporation normally

takes a *carryover basis* from the transferor. Thus, if Figure 4-3 is modified to make it a wholly nontaxable transaction, X Corporation will have a tax basis of $15,000 in the land and $10,000 in the equipment.

Corporate deduction for services received

One final question remains: Can the corporation deduct as an ordinary and necessary business expense the value of any stocks or securities that it issues to shareholders in exchange for services rendered (or to be rendered) by the shareholder? The answer is not affected by the medium of payment. In other words, if the corporation could have deducted the payment had it been made in cash—that is, if the services rendered were of a type that would have given rise to a deduction under Sec. 162—then it would also be entitled to that same deduction if the payment were made in stock or securities. An investigation of which services yield deductible expenses and which yield only capitalized costs is beyond the scope of this chapter. Suffice it to observe that many start-up costs may be subject to capitalization and, possibly, subsequent amortization.

This concludes our discussion of the tax consequences commonly associated with the birth of a corporation. In Chapters 5–7, we shall pursue the tax problems that accompany the growth years of the corporate entity. The *successful* corporation typically desires to distribute some of its assets to its shareholders either as a dividend, a stock redemption, or a partial liquidation. In the next two chapters, we devote special attention to these three transactions. The death of a corporate entity is known as a complete liquidation. In one sense, it is the mirror image of the incorporation transaction discussed in this chapter. As you will discover, however, the tax consequences of a complete liquidation are often different from those of an incorporation transaction. And the tax problems associated with corporate mergers and reorganizations—which can be thought of as the corporate equivalent of marriage— are even more complex. Accordingly, mergers and reorganizations are given special treatment in Chapter 7 of Part Two.

PROBLEMS

1. Repeat Corporation's income and expenses for the current year are summarized below:

    Income:

        Sales of merchandise $975,000

        Interest:

            From customers' accounts $2,300

From AT&T bonds	4,000	
From New York State bonds	3,400	9,700
Life insurance (from policy carried on life of recently deceased corporate president)		100,000
Refund of federal income tax from previous year		12,000
Dividends on GE stock held as an investment		22,000
Expenses:		
Cost of goods sold		$500,000
Salaries		122,000
Advertising and promotion expenses		28,000
Depreciation		64,000
Taxes (real estate, payroll, etc.)		32,000
Interest		4,000
Amortization of organization expense		500
Office expenses, postage, etc.		80,000
Other business expenses		116,000

a. What is Repeat Corporation's
   (1) Gross income?
   (2) Taxable income?
   (3) Gross tax liability?
b. What one major difference would exist in the determination of taxable income if this problem were rewritten for a sole proprietorship?

2. Backward Corporation (BC) reports a taxable income of $100,000. In determining its taxable income, BC deducted charitable contributions of $2,000 and dividends-received deductions of $8,000. Given this information, what is the legal maximum amount that BC could have deducted as a charitable contribution had it actually made charitable contributions in some amount greater than the maximum limit?

3. Four unrelated corporate taxpayers recognized the taxable income detailed below:

	Corporate taxpayer			
Income components	W	X	Y	Z
Ordinary taxable income	$27,200	$40,200	$73,200	$173,200
Net short-term capital gain (loss)	(5,000)	6,000	(28,000)	30,000
Net long-term capital gain (loss)	11,000	10,000	20,000	60,000

a. Determine *by inspection only* which of these corporations will
   (1) Receive no special capital-gain treatment.
   (2) Pay the 28 percent alternative tax.
b. Which of the above explanations was difficult to make "by inspection only"? Why? Explain briefly.

4. During years 19X1 through 19X4, Over Corporation recognized the following ordinary incomes and capital gains and losses:

Year	Ordinary income	Net long-term capital gain (or loss)*	Net short-term capital gain (or loss)*
19X1	$ 80,000	$ 20,000	$ 5,000
19X2	100,000	10,000	20,000
19X3	120,000	15,000	-0-
19X4	140,000	(35,000)	10,000

*Excluding any losses carried back or forward

a. Explain the correct tax treatment of the $35,000 net long-term capital loss incurred in 19X4.

b. Compute Over Corporation's tax refund for 19X4; use the current tax rates for all years.

5. Adam Close and his sister, Eve, each own 50 percent of the outstanding stock of Brother Corporation and of Sister Corporation. During the current year, Brother Corporation and Sister Corporation each recognize a taxable income of $100,000. If no special elections are filed, what is the gross tax liability of each corporation? Briefly explain your solution.

6. Tom, Dick, and Harry decided early in 19X1 to join efforts and form the TDY Corporation. The three men agreed to an initial transfer of the following assets to TDY:

Transferor	Asset	Fair market value	Transferor's basis	Debt assumed by TDY Corporation
Tom	Cash	$10,000	$10,000	$ -0-
Tom	Land	21,000	8,000	6,000
Dick	Equipment	14,000	3,000	5,000
Dick	Services	1,000	-0-	-0-
Harry	Services	5,000	-0-	-0-

In exchange for these assets, TDY Corporation issued the following stocks and securities (20-year, 15% bonds):

Recipient	TDY stock		TDY bonds	
	No. of shares	Value	No. of bonds	Value
Tom	150	$15,000	10	$10,000
Dick	50	5,000	5	5,000
Harry	50	5,000	0	NA

The land transferred by Tom had been held as an investment property for six years before this transfer. The equipment transferred by Dick had been used in Dick's business for four years before transfer; straight-line depreciation had been claimed in the amount of $12,000 during these four years.

a. (1) What amount of gross income must be recognized in 19X1 by each of the three men because of their transfer of assets to TDY? Is that income "ordinary income" or "capital gain"?

(2) What amount of gross income must be recognized in 19X1 by TDY Corporation because of its acquisition of these assets for its own stock and securities?

(3) What amount of tax deduction, if any, may TDY Corporation claim in 19X1 because of the stocks and securities it transferred to Tom, Dick, and Harry?

(4) What is each stockholder's tax basis in his TDY stock and securities?

(5) What is TDY's basis in the land and the equipment?

b. Assume that between 19X1 and 19X3 there is no change of TDY's ownership and that in 19X3 Harry and Barry (who is unrelated to any of the three original owners) transfer additional assets to TDY Corporation in an expansion of corporate operations, as follows.

Transferor	Asset	Fair market value	Transferor's basis	Debt assumed by TDY Corporation
Harry	Land	$20,000	$ 7,000	$ -0-
Barry	Land	20,000	14,000	10,000

In exchange for the land transferred to TDY, the corporation issued Harry an additional 100 shares of its stock and issued Barry 50 shares.

    (1)   What amount of gross income must be recognized in 19X3 by Harry and Barry because of the transfer of the land to TDY Corporation?

    (2)   Assuming that Barry originally bought the land transferred to TDY on August 10, 19X0, what is Barry's cost and date basis in the TDY shares he received in 19X3?

    (3)   What is TDY Corporation's basis in the land it acquired in 19X3 from Harry and Barry?

7.   Jim Furst began raising hogs in 19X0. He enjoyed his work but became increasingly frustrated with the wide fluctuations in prices for hogs. Jim observed that the price of pork did not vary nearly as much in the retail meat markets as it did in the wholesale markets. Although his farming business had been profitable overall, he wished that he could reduce the boom-and-bust atmosphere in which he was forced to operate. One night, while drinking beer in Luckenback, Jim began to expound on his unhappiness over the fluctuations in the wholesale price of hogs. One of the persons listening to Jim was Tom Wurst, a fellow who had recently inherited one-third of the outstanding common stock of Pork Pack Corporation (PPC).

    PPC was founded 30 years ago by Tom's father, who had recently died. For the past 30 years, PPC had remained a small processor of pork products with one small retail outlet. PPC was a modest financial success, having accumulated approximately $200,000 in earnings and profits since its inception. Tom's father (whose tax basis in the 3,000 outstanding shares of PPC was only $30,000) left 1,000 shares of PPC common to each of his three children, Tom, Dick, and Harriet. Of the three children, only Tom was interested in the management of PPC, and since he was too young to know the business very well, he thought that he certainly could use Jim's help in running it. His brother, Dick, was a career officer on the local police force, and his sister, Harriet, was married to John Beef, a local reporter, and involved with raising a family.

    To make a long story just a little shorter, Jim and Tom became close friends and decided to join their two businesses in a new corporation, Furst Wurst (FW). Because of their sentimental attachment to PPC and because they could see some good business reasons for keeping the meat packing and retailing aspects of their business separate from the pork production aspects, Jim and Tom decided not to eliminate PPC in the new venture. Instead, on July 1, 19X4, Jim agreed to transfer all his hog-raising assets (detailed below) to FW in exchange for 25 shares of FW common and 225 shares of FW 10 percent preferred stock. Finally, FW agreed to assume the mortgage that Jim had incurred on the real estate used in his hog farm business, which had been operated as a sole proprietorship.

    Specifically, Jim transferred to FW the following properties:

Asset	Fair market value	Adjusted tax basis
Inventories	$ 50,000	$10,000
Equipment	60,000	30,000
Real estate*	100,000*	80,000

*FW assumed the $60,000 mortgage outstanding against this property.

On the same date, Tom, Dick, and Harriet transferred their 3,000 shares of PPC stock to FW in exchange for 75 shares of FW common and 75 shares of FW preferred stock. The 3,000 shares of PPC common (which had been valued for estate tax purposes at $240,000) were agreed to be worth $250,000 on July 1, 19X4. All parties agreed that FW common was worth $3,000 per share; FW preferred, $333.33 per share.

In answering the questions, assume that:

    1. All valuations stated in the problem are reasonable and *not* subject to challenge by the I.R.S. or the courts.

    2. Tom, Dick, and Harriet divided their shares of FW stock equally. (That is, each person received 25 shares of common and 25 shares of preferred.)

    3. FW preferred stock is nonvoting stock.

a. Does the transfer of assets on July 1, 19X4, constitute a taxable event for:

    (1) Jim Furst? (Explain briefly.)

    (2) Tom, Dick, or Harriet? (Explain briefly.)

    (3) PPC? (Explain briefly.)

    (4) FW? (Explain briefly.)

b. What is FW's tax basis in:

    (1) Inventories?

    (2) Equipment?

    (3) Real estate?

    (4) PPC stock?

c. What is Jim Furst's basis in:

    (1) His 25 shares of FW common stock?

    (2) His 225 shares of FW preferred stock?

d. What is Tom Wurst's basis in:

    (1) His 25 shares of FW common stock?

    (2) His 25 shares of FW preferred stock?

e. If you had been consulted by Jim, Tom, Dick, or Harriet for tax advice in conjunction with the formation of FW, what *major reasons* might you have for suggesting an alternative capital structure? In other words, why might you have suggested that FW be capitalized in some manner other than by issuance of 100 shares of common and 300 shares of preferred stock?

SUPPLEMENTAL PROBLEM

8. Bill I. Grande (BIG), Harold E. Planner (HEP), and Mary P. Abyss (MPA) decided on October 31, 19X9, to form a new corporation, Grand Plan Abyss (GPA), to design, manufacture, and sell various products related to solar energy. Although none of these three unrelated persons had any special expertise in solar energy, each was personally convinced that it was the "wave of the future" and believed that a personal fortune could be made in the field.

Bill and Harold had known each other for eight years. Bill, a building subcontractor, had hired Harold to work on various construction projects. When Harold was not working for Bill, he was engaged in the sale and installation of solar window coverings, solar heating panels, and solar skylights. The fact that Harold was willing to join Bill in this new corporate venture was somewhat surprising because Bill still owed Harold approximately $10,000 for work he had done in the past two years.

The real explanation for the three getting together was Mary. Mary met Bill and Harold at an antinuclear demonstration in Texas. Mary (B.S.E.E., Rice, 'X0;

M.P.A. in Tax, Texas, 'X2) was the brains behind the new corporation. She had worked in public accounting for seven years and was anxious to try putting together a corporate venture on her own. Bill and Harold seemed like ideal partners because they had prior building experience, were intelligent, hard working, and interested in solar energy.

After many hours of deliberation, the three agreed to the following:

Person	Property/services transferred	Value	Stock/securities received	
			No. of shares [c]	No. of securities [d]
BIG	Land[a]	$40,000	100	10
HEP	Equipment[b]	20,000	200	10
MPA	Services ($10,000) and cash			
	($10,000)	20,000	100	10

[a]BIG paid $25,000 for this land in 19X0; he still owed $10,000 on the original mortgage, which GPA assumed.
[b]HEP purchased this equipment for $30,000 in 19X4 and claimed straight-line depreciation of $15,000 before transferring it to GPA. The original estimated life was 10 years.
[c]The 400 shares of GPA stock originally issued were no-par common stock.
[d]The 30 GPA bonds (securities) each had a maturity value of $1,000. They call for a stated interest of 15 percent per annum and are to mature in 15 years.

a. What amount and kind of income must each of the three shareholders recognize in 19X9 because of the incorporation transaction on October 31, 19X9? Explain.

b. What tax basis does each shareholder have in the GPA stocks and securities received?

   (1) BIG:

      (a) In the 100 shares?

      (b) In the 10 bonds?

      (c) What is the statutory authority for the two answers, above?

   (2) HEP:

      (a) In the 200 shares?

      (b) In the 10 bonds?

   (3) MPA:

      (a) In the 100 shares?

      (b) In the 10 bonds?

c. What is GPA's basis in

   (1) The land? What is the statutory authority for this answer?

   (2) The equipment?

d. Do the security owners have any "original issue discount" (OID), which must be amortized over the 15-year life of the bonds? Explain and cite statutory authority.

e. Because of the October 31, 19X9 property transfer to GPA, must Harold (HEP) recapture any

   (1) Depreciation? Explain and cite the statutory authority.

   (2) Investment credit? Explain and cite pertinent authority.

corporations: nonliquidating distributions

Transactions that fall under the general heading "nonliquidating distributions" typically fit into one of three broad categories—namely, property distributions, stock distributions, and stock redemptions. A generalized form of the transactions of each of these categories is depicted in Figure 5-1.

FIGURE 5-1   Nonliquidating Distributions

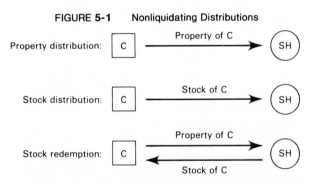

Note in Figure 5-1 that property distributions and stock distributions are both "one-way" transactions; that is, the shareholder returns nothing to the distributing corporation. The need to distinguish between these two categories of nonliquidating distributions is a result of Sec. 317(a), which defines the term "property" as money, securities, and any other property, *except* stock in the corporation making the distribution (or the right to acquire such stock).[1] The general form of a stock redemption is distinguished from distributions of property and stock in that the corporation distributes property *in exchange for* its stock.

Figure 5-1 is only a starting point for the study of nonliquidating distributions. Unfortunately, identifying the form of a transaction is not enough. For example, transactions in all three categories of nonliquidating distributions could cause any one or a combination of three shareholder treatments: as a dividend, a nontaxable event, or a capital gain or loss.

The dichotomy between dividends (that is, ordinary income) and capital gains or losses pervades the entire spectrum of corporate–shareholder transactions.[2] For this reason, we begin with an examination of "earnings and profits," the concept that limits a corporation's *capacity* to pay dividends. We shall follow this discussion with analyses of property distributions, stock distributions, and stock redemptions, respectively. Each of these nonliquidating transactions raises a variety of tax issues for both the distributing corporation and its shareholders.

EARNINGS AND PROFITS

In the preceding paragraph, we referred to earnings and profits (E & P) as a "concept." We did this, in part, because no precise definition of the term exists.

---

[1] Both previously authorized but unissued stock and treasury stock of the distributing corporation are excluded from the definition of "property."

[2] Note that dividend treatment is not necessarily undesirable; because of the dividends-received deduction, a *corporate* shareholder might want a distribution to be characterized as a dividend.

Even though the Code fails to define E & P, Sec. 316(a) clearly states that "the term 'dividend' means any distribution of property made by a corporation to its shareholders ... *out of its earnings and profits*" (emphasis added). Hence, the existence of E & P is a necessary condition for a dividend. Given that requirement, it is surprising that the calculation of earnings and profits may require consideration of an amazing patchwork of statutory, administrative, and judicial pronouncements.[3]

Calculation of earnings and profits

In a general sense, the earnings and profits of a corporation indicate the amount the corporation could distribute to its shareholders without impairing its capital. Accordingly, a computation of the increase in the net fair market value of the corporation's assets since organization would apparently provide a theoretically sound measure of this "excess." Although economists might applaud such a measure, it would represent a major deviation from the transaction-based systems of income realization, which underlie the measurement of both financial and taxable income. Not surprisingly, therefore, the cost of compliance and administrative convenience have caused the measurement of earnings and profits to follow a similar path.

The computation of the increase or decrease in earnings and profits for a particular year usually begins with the taxable income for that year. Although adjustments must often be made to convert taxable income into earnings and profits, Treas. Reg. Sec. 1.312-6(a) provides that the method of accounting (for example, cash, accrual, or installment) employed in computing taxable income will also apply in determining earnings and profits. All three components of net income—gross income, losses, and expenses—create issues to be resolved in the computation of earnings and profits and specific adjustments that are necessary to convert taxable income to earnings and profits.

GROSS INCOME   The definition of *income* for purposes of earnings and profits appears to follow closely the definition for income tax purposes—that is, "all income from whatever source derived" (Sec. 61). The primary difference concerns exclusions. All income that is exempt for federal income tax purposes is in-

cluded in earnings and profits (Treas. Reg. Sec. 1.312-6(b)). This means that when converting from taxable income to earnings and profits, such exempted income as municipal bond interest and life insurance proceeds must be added. Note that this treatment conforms with the previously developed theory underlying earnings and profits—that is, a measurement of income concerned with the protection of capital. Municipal bond interest, for example, represents economic income that could be distributed without impairing the corporation's capital. The fact that municipal bond interest is not taxable (to the corporation) is not germane to the objectives of the E & P measurement.

The sale or other disposition of property ordinarily results in a realized gain or loss that is recognized in the computation of taxable income (Sec. 1001). Postponement of recognition is allowed (or required) only in such limited cases as like-kind exchanges (Sec. 1031), involuntary conversions (Sec. 1033), and transfers to controlled corporations (Sec. 351). While the theory supporting earnings and profits might justify the immediate recognition of tax-deferred gains for the computation of earnings and profits, the Code specifies that E & P recognition shall be the same as taxable income (Sec. 312(f)(1)). Thus, no special adjustment is required for the "nontaxable exchange" transactions. This consistency can be explained more in terms of convenience than theory.

LOSSES   The earnings and profits treatment of postponed losses parallels that of postponed gains; that is, earnings and profits recognition is the same as the income tax treatment of such losses. Transactions for which realized losses are not initially recognized are like-kind exchanges (Sec. 1031), transfers to controlled corporations (Sec. 351), and wash sales (Sec. 1091). No adjustment to taxable income is required for these transactions.

Two types of losses, however, require an adjustment. The first concerns realized losses that are subject to carryover deduction rules in the computation of taxable income. Corporate capital losses may only be deducted in years with recognized capital gains, while net operating losses offset any positive taxable income. Such losses are deemed to reduce a corporation's capacity to pay dividends in the year of realization and, therefore, they must be deducted in full in computing E & P in that year. This also means that when computing the earnings and profits for a year to which a net capital or net operating loss has been carried (for taxable income purposes), the taxable income of such carryover year will have to be adjusted by "adding back"

---

[3]In addition to Sec. 312 and the related regulations, you might also review Rev. Proc. 75-17, 1975-1 C.B. 677; Englebrecht and Banham, "Earnings and Profits: The Income Tax Dilemma," *Journal of Accounting,* February 1979, pp. 58–64; and Bittker and Eustice, *Federal Income Taxation of Corporations and Shareholders* (4th ed., 1979) paragraph 7.03.

the carryovers utilized in the computation of taxable income in such year.

The second category of losses that require adjustment are those that are never deductible for federal income tax purposes. In keeping with the idea that realized losses reduce a corporation's capacity to make distributions without invading capital, losses permanently disallowed for income tax purposes—such as those under Sec. 267(a)(1) involving sales or exchanges of property between related taxpayers—reduce earnings and profits in the year realized.

EXPENSES   The basic definition of an *expense* for purposes of earnings and profits does not vary from that used to determine taxable income. Capital expenditures may not initially be expensed. Rather, they must be recovered through use (depreciation expense) or upon disposition of the asset (capital recovery). The major definitional difference between deductions for taxable income and earnings and profits purposes concerns the "artificial" dividends-received deduction that is allowed in computing taxable income. Because there is no actual expense involved (and therefore no reduction in the receiving corporation's capacity to pay dividends), this deduction must be "added back" to convert taxable income to earnings and profits.

The treatment of expenses disallowed in the computation of taxable income generally conforms to the basic theory of earnings and profits. These actual expenditures reduce dividend capacity and are, therefore, deducted in the computation of earnings and profits. Examples of such expenses that must be subtracted from taxable income to arrive at E & P are federal income taxes (net of credits), expenses disallowed under Sec. 265 (relating to tax-exempt income), losses denied by Sec. 267(a)(2) (transactions between related parties), and nondeductible life insurance premiums (Sec. 264).[4]

The treatment of expenses that are disallowed in the computation of taxable income for public policy reasons—for example, illegal payments, political contributions, fines and penalties under Sec. 162(c), (e), (f), and (g)—is currently uncertain. The conflicting theories behind earnings and profits and proper implementation of public policy seem to be irreconcilable.

Historically, the E & P theory has prevailed and such items generally have been thought to reduce earnings and profits. Since the Tax Reform Act of 1976, however, certain foreign corporations have explicitly been denied a reduction in earnings and profits for expenses disallowed under Sec. 162(c) (Sec. 964(a)). The possibility that Congress, the I.R.S., or the courts might apply this treatment to a wider range of public policy situations leaves the proper treatment of this category of expenses greatly in doubt.

Charitable contributions reduce earnings and profits without regard to the 5 percent limitation that is imposed in the computation of taxable income. Therefore, two types of adjustments must be made to taxable income. First, in the year of "excess contributions," the excess is subtracted from taxable income to arrive at earnings and profits. Second, in the carryforward year, the excess must be "added back." These adjustments result in a full deduction in the year of the charitable contribution and prevent any second deduction in taxable income carryover years.

Accelerated depreciation and percentage depletion are two specific accounting procedures that are disallowed in the computation of E & P. For E & P purposes, depreciation must generally be based on the straight-line method, calculated from date of acquisition (Sec. 312(k), applicable to years beginning after June 30, 1972). Depletion is only allowed on the cost method (Treas. Reg. Sec. 1.312-6(c)). The use of accelerated depreciation and percentage depletion for determining taxable income is often justified in terms of investment incentives. This is not an objective of earnings and profits. Congress evidently views straight-line depreciation and cost depletion as more realistic measures of the flow of cost recovery.[5]

Two types of adjustments concerning depreciation and depletion must be made to convert taxable income to earnings and profits. First, in any year accelerated depreciation or percentage depletion is used in computing taxable income, the difference between these methods and straight-line or cost depletion must be "added back" (if greater) or subtracted (if less). The second type of adjustment takes place in the year the depreciable or depletable asset is disposed of. Because two different methods of depreciation or depletion exist (one for taxable income and the other for earnings and profits), a different adjusted basis is likely to exist under each method. Therefore, taxable income in the year the asset is sold will have to be adjusted to reflect

---

[4]The treatment of life insurance premiums disallowed under Sec. 264 appears to vary between term and whole life policies. Disallowed premiums on term insurance are fully deductible for E & P, and any related proceeds are fully included in E & P. The treatment of whole life premiums and proceeds is not settled. Current practice appears to reduce E & P for only the excess of annual premiums over the increase in cash surrender value. Proceeds up to the cash surrender value at death are considered a return of capital, with only the excess treated as an increase in E & P.

[5]To the extent that percentage depletion may be deducted in excess of cost basis, it may also be viewed as "artificial" and therefore not an expense.

any difference in the earnings-and-profits gain or loss compared with taxable-income gain or loss from the sale. Typically, an asset's adjusted basis will be lower when accelerated depreciation or percentage depletion is used. This would cause the taxable-income gain to be greater (or loss to be less) than that for purposes of earnings and profits. Thus, the adjustment would normally be in the form of a subtraction from taxable income.

Earnings and profits: summary

Few, if any, corporations maintain a completely separate set of books for the calculation of earnings and profits. Most corporations convert taxable income to earnings and profits only when such determination appears necessary. An exact determination *may* never be necessary for the corporation that clearly limits its annual shareholder distributions to amounts less than the earnings and profits for the year. Situations do arise, however, in which a precise calculation of both current and accumulated earnings and profits is required. Always keep in mind that earnings and profits for a year may not be assumed to equal the year's taxable income; nor may "book" retained earnings be assumed to equal accumulated E & P. Finally, note that earnings and profits may be positive or negative.[6] A deficit may exist from a cumulative standpoint (accumulated deficit in earnings and profits) as well as for a specific year (deficit in earnings and profits for a year).

PROPERTY DISTRIBUTIONS

When a corporation distributes property to its shareholders, we must examine the provisions of Subchapter C to determine the appropriate tax treatment of that distribution. The generalized form of the transaction we are interested in at this point is shown in Figure 5-2.

FIGURE **5-2**   Property Distribution

One caution with respect to Figure 5-2 is in order. A "shareholder" may also be a creditor or an employee of C Corporation. In determining the tax consequences of a distribution, we must be sure that the distribution is being made because of stock ownership and not because of some other relationship. Both Sec. 301 (effect

---

[6]The same is true for "taxable income." See Sec. 63(a), which does not impose a lower limit of zero on "taxable income."

on shareholder) and Sec. 311 (effect on corporation) refer to distributions by a corporation *with respect to its stock*. Distributions to employees and creditors are not covered in Subchapter C; these transactions are controlled by the general rules covered in the first volume of *An Introduction to Taxation*.

Once we have determined that the distribution is to a shareholder with respect to such shareholder's stock ownership, we may address the following questions.

1. Does the shareholder recognize any income, gain, or loss on the distribution?
2. What is the tax character of the income, gain, or loss recognized by the shareholder?
3. What is the basis of the property received by the shareholder?
4. Does the corporation recognize any income, gain, or loss on the distribution?
5. What is the tax character of the income, gain, or loss recognized by the corporation?
6. What is the tax effect of the distribution on the corporation's earnings and profits?

Tax treatment to shareholders

Section 301 prescribes the tax consequences of a property distribution to the shareholder. It provides, in part, that the "portion of the distribution which is a dividend . . . shall be included in gross income" (Sec. 301(c)(1)). The term "dividend" is defined in Sec. 316(a) as any distribution of property made by a corporation to its shareholders.

1. Out of its earnings and profits accumulated after February 28, 1913 (accumulated E & P), *or*
2. Out of its earnings and profits of the taxable year (current E & P).

Section 316(a) further provides that distributions are first considered to come out of the most recent earnings and profits and that current year earnings and profits are to be computed as of the close of the year, without reduction for distributions to shareholders during the year.

Assuming that the distributing corporation has ample E & P, the measure of the dividend is the "amount distributed" (Sec. 301(b)). If the property distributed is cash, the "amount distributed" obviously equals the face value of the cash. If noncash property is distributed, the rules differ for corporate and noncorporate shareholders. For noncorporate shareholders, the fair market value of the property (as of the date of the distribution) is the proper measure of the amount distributed (Secs. 301(b)(1)(A) and 301(b)(3)). For corporate shareholders, the amount distributed is the lesser of:

1. The fair market value of the property as of the date of the distribution; or

2. The adjusted basis of the property (to the *distributing* corporation), plus any gain recognized (by the *distributing* corporation) (Secs. 301(b)(1)(B) and 301(b)(3)).

The corporate shareholder is required to use the lesser of fair market value or adjusted basis because, otherwise, the potential would exist for "stepping-up" the basis of property at a low tax cost. The possibility may be illustrated as follows:

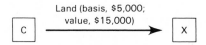

Land (basis, $5,000; value, $15,000)

C ⟶ X

Corporation C distributes to X Corporation land with a basis of $5,000 and a fair market value of $15,000. If X Corporation used the fair market value to determine the "amount distributed," X would report a dividend of $15,000 and would also be entitled to claim a dividends-received deduction of $12,750 (that is, 85 percent of $15,000). Only the net amount of $2,250 would be included in X's taxable income. The real "tax cost" would depend on X's marginal tax rate, which could vary from zero to 46 percent. According to Sec. 301(d), the shareholder's tax basis in the property received is not reduced by the dividends-received deduction. Consequently, if there were no special rule for corporate taxpayers, X's basis on the land would be $15,000. The end result would be a step-up in basis from $5,000 (C's basis) to $15,000 (X's basis) at a quite low tax cost. The rule that corporate taxpayers

must use the lesser of (a) basis or (b) fair market value as the measure of the amount received obviously serves to stop this ploy. As discussed below, X's basis in the land will also be $5,000.

Two further rules have an impact on the calculation of the amount distributed. First, if in addition to receiving property, a shareholder assumes the distributing corporation's liability or takes a property subject to a liability, the amount distributed is reduced, but not below zero, by the amount of liability (Sec. 301(b)(2)). Second, if the property distributed is the distributing corporation's own debt (that is, C's securities, such as bonds) then the recipient shareholder—corporate as well as noncorporate—generally must treat the fair market value of the debt as the measure of the amount received.

A summary of the rules determining the amount distributed appears in Table 5-1. Five examples follow.

Example 1: C Corporation distributes $5,000 in cash and land (previously held as an investment) to A, an individual shareholder of C. The land had an adjusted basis to C of $15,000 and a fair market value of $25,000 at the time of distribution. Shareholder A agrees to assume an existing mortgage on the land of $12,000. The amount distributed to A is $18,000 ($5,000 + $25,000 − $12,000).

Example 2: Same facts as in Example 1, except that A is a corporation. The amount distributed to A is $8,000 ($5,000 + $15,000 − $12,000). (As we shall explain, C will not recognize its $10,000 gain on the land.)

Example 3: C Corporation distributes its own bond to Shareholder A. The principal (face) amount of the bond is $10,000; its fair market value is $10,100 at the time of the distribution.

TABLE **5-1**
PROPERTY DISTRIBUTIONS—DETERMINATION OF AMOUNT DISTRIBUTED

Property	Amount distributed[a]	
	Noncorporate shareholder	Corporate shareholder
Cash	Amount of cash	Amount of cash
Obligation of distributing corporation	Fair market value	Fair market value
Other property	Fair market value	Lesser of: 1. Fair market value 2. Basis to distributing corporation (plus gain recognized by the distributing corporation, if any)

[a]The amount distributed to a shareholder is reduced, but not below zero, by the liabilities of the distributing corporation such shareholder assumes (or takes the property subject to) in connection with the distribution.

The amount distributed is $10,100 regardless of whether Shareholder A is an individual or a corporation.

Example 4: C Corporation distributes a machine that it has used in its business to Shareholder A, an individual. The machine cost C $8,000 three years ago. At the time of the distribution, the machine had a fair market value of $10,000; C had deducted $3,000 of depreciation before this distribution.

The amount distributed to A is $10,000, the fair market value.

Example 5: Same facts as in Example 4, except that A is a corporation. The amount distributed to A is $8,000 ($5,000 basis + $3,000 gain recognized by C). The $3,000 gain recognized by C is a result of depreciation recapture under Sec. 1245.

We have indicated that *assuming* the distributing corporation has ample E & P, the measure of the dividend is the "amount distributed." What happens if that assumption is not valid? In that event, Sec. 301(c) requires that the amount distributed be allocated as follows:

1. Dividend income to the extent out of current or accumulated E & P;
2. Reduction of stock basis;
3. Tax-free distribution to the extent the distribution is out of an increase in value accrued before March 1, 1913; and, finally,
4. Gain from the sale of stock

It should be emphasized that the above ordering procedure must be followed; that is, a distribution may not be allocated to the second "level" (reduction of stock basis) until the first "level" (dividend income) has been applied to the maximum extent possible. As a final observation, note that a shareholder may not recognize a loss on a property distribution. The only possibilities on which a taxpayer may recognize a loss on a property distribution are *dividend income, reduction of basis, exempt income,* and *gain on sale.*

SHAREHOLDER'S BASIS IN PROPERTY RECEIVED   The basis of property received by a shareholder in a property distribution is identical to the "amount distributed," except that basis is *not* reduced by any liabilities the shareholder assumes or subject to which the shareholder takes the property (Sec. 301(d) and

Treas. Reg. Sec. 1.301-1(h)). Thus, the calculation of basis will depend on the kind of property distributed and the corporate or noncorporate status of the receiving shareholder. To illustrate, refer to the five examples on pages **5**/5–6. The basis of the property received in each case would be:

	Kind of property	*Basis*
Example 1	Cash	$ 5,000
	Land	13,000
Example 2	Cash	5,000
	Land	3,000
Example 3	Bond	10,100
Example 4	Machine	10,000
Example 5	Machine	8,000

In addition to the determination of basis, a shareholder may also be concerned with the characterization of the property as capital or noncapital, its depreciable or nondepreciable status, and the "date basis" of the property received. Sections 167 (depreciation) and 1221 (capital asset defined) consider only the current owner's use. The rules to apply, therefore, are those detailed in the first volume of *An Introduction to Taxation.* The holding period of property received in a corporate distribution generally begins with the date of the distribution. The Internal Revenue Service has ruled, however, that when a corporate shareholder takes a carryover basis from the distributing corporation, such corporation's date basis also carrys over to the corporate shareholder (Rev. Rul. 70-6, 1970 C.B. 172).

Tax treatment to the distributing corporation

The notion that a corporation making a property distribution might be required to recognize income may at first appear unusual because we tend to think of income in terms of receipts rather than disbursements. Section 1001 provides, however, the general rule that gain or loss must be recognized whenever a sale *or other disposition of property* takes place. Distribution of property to a shareholder clearly represents a disposition of property. Section 1001 indicates that the gain or loss is to be measured by the difference between the amount realized and the adjusted basis of the property surrendered. But what is the "amount realized" when a corporation makes a one-way distribution of property to a shareholder? Quite possibly, the amount realized is the value of the property distributed. This answer follows the assumption that the distribution represents the satisfaction of a debt to the shareholder.

By authorizing a distribution, the corporate Board of Directors creates an obligation, and that obligation is settled when the distribution takes place. The amount realized is the value of the obligation, which presumably is the fair market value of the distributed property.[7]

In summary, without any exception to the general principle of Sec. 1001, any difference between fair market value and adjusted basis of property at date of distribution must be recognized. An exception exists, however, in Sec. 311(a), which begins with the general rule that no gain or loss shall be recognized by a corporation on the distribution of property to a shareholder. This general rule is, alas, also subject to several exceptions. Some of the exceptions are included in Sec. 311; others are found in sections that have priority over Sec. 311; and still others arise from judicial doctrines of uncertain application.

Section 311(b), which is one of the exceptions to the general rule of Sec. 311(a), provides that any distribution to shareholders of inventory accounted for under the LIFO (last in, first out) method will cause the distributing corporation to recognize ordinary income equal to the excess of the LIFO basis over the basis that would have obtained had a non-LIFO (usually FIFO) method been used.

Section 311(c) provides another exception. Gain must be recognized if, in connection with a property distribution, (a) a shareholder assumes a liability of the corporation or takes the property subject to a liability, *and* (b) the amount of such liability exceeds the distributing corporation's adjusted basis in the distributed property.[8] The amount of the gain to be recognized by the distributing corporation will generally equal the excess determined above. If, however, the shareholder does not personally assume the liability (that is, if he or she takes the property only subject to the liability) *and* the liability exceeds the property's fair market value, the corporation recognizes gain only to the extent of any excess of the property's fair market value over its adjusted basis.

In addition to the provisions of Secs. 311(b) and (c), other exceptions to the general rule of Sec. 311(a) may be found in other parts of the Code. For example, Sec. 453(d)—as noted in Sec. 311(a)—provides that a corporation distributing installment obligations will have to recognize gain. And the depreciation recapture

sections—such as Secs. 1245, 1250, and 1254—also override the general nonrecognition rule of Sec. 311(a). Hence, if a corporation distributes depreciable personal property—for example, a car or an office desk—it will have to recognize gain on the distribution in an amount equal to what it would have recognized had it sold the same property to a third party in an arm's-length transaction. (It may also have to recapture the investment credit.)

In addition to the several statutory provisions requiring corporate recognition on shareholder property distributions, the judicial doctrine prohibiting any assignment of income has also occasionally been considered by the courts to trigger that recognition. The cases that have been decided provide little basis for generalization other than an uneasiness that the courts might look unfavorably on a situation that combines both tax avoidance and lack of a clear business purpose.[9]

EFFECT OF PROPERTY DISTRIBUTIONS ON EARNINGS AND PROFITS   Two important relationships exist between property distributions and earnings and profits. First, to the extent gain (or loss) is *recognized* by the distributing corporation, earnings and profits are increased (or decreased). The upper limit on dividend income to the shareholders receiving the distributions is, therefore, directly affected. Any realized but unrecognized income arising from property distributions is generally *not* considered to be "exempted income" that must be included in earnings and profits. Any other conclusion would make the special treatment prescribed for inventory assets totally unnecessary. Section 312(b) specifically provides that earnings and profits are to be increased by the excess of fair market value over adjusted basis when inventory assets are distributed to shareholders. Except for distributions of LIFO inventory, none of this increase is included in taxable income. As previously noted, when LIFO inventory is distributed, the excess of fair market value over (usually) the FIFO basis is recognized. The increase in earnings and profits under Sec. 312(b) usually ensures sufficient earnings and profits to create a dividend when inventory is distributed to shareholders.

The second relationship between property distributions and earnings and profits concerns the amount by which E & P is to be reduced because of the distribution. That reduction will directly affect the maximum extent to which shareholder distributions in subsequent years may be considered dividends. Table 5-2 summa-

---

[7]To argue that there is no amount realized on a property distribution would lead to the untenable conclusion of a realized loss equal to the adjusted basis of the property distributed.

[8]Note that the determination of "liability in excess of basis" is calculated by examining each recipient shareholder separately.

[9]See Bittker and Eustice, *op. cit,* paragraph 7.21, for a review of the case law in this area.

TABLE 5-2

EXTENT TO WHICH PROPERTY DISTRIBUTIONS REDUCE EARNINGS AND PROFITS

Type of Property	*Amount of E & P Reduction*
Cash	Amount of cash
Obligation of distributing corporation	Principal amount of obligation
Appreciated inventory	Fair market value
Other property	Corporation's adjusted basis
Special Adjustments	
Subtract: liabilities transferred (both "assumed" and "subject to")	(Amount of liability)
Add: any gain recognized by the distributing corporation	Amount of gain recognized
	Reduction in E & P

rizes the amount by which property distributions generally reduce earnings and profits. Note, however, that:

1.   Property distributions may reduce earnings and profits to zero but they may not create or add to a *deficit* in earnings and profits.

2.   The reduction in earnings and profits due to a property distribution is not necessarily equal to the "amount distributed" (or to the dividend income recognized by the shareholder receiving the distribution).

The following examples illustrate the computation of the reduction in E & P as a result of property distributions:

Example 1:   C Corporation distributes $10,000 cash to its shareholders during 19X8. C's accumulated earnings and profits at the beginning of 19X8 were zero, and current 19X8 earnings and profits are $5,000.

Accumulated E & P at January 1, 19X9, will be zero.

Example 2:   Same facts as in Example 1, except that current 19X8 earnings and profits are a deficit of $5,000.

Accumulated earnings and profits at January 1, 19X9, will also be a deficit of $5,000.

Example 3:   During 19X8, C Corporation distributed to its sole shareholder a vacant lot that was not an inventory asset. When distributed, the lot had a fair market value of $5,000 and was subject to a mortgage of $2,000. The adjusted basis of the lot was $3,100. Accumulated earnings and

profits at January 1, 19X8, were $20,000, and 19X8 current earnings and profits, before considering the distribution, were $10,000.

Neither taxable income nor current earnings and profits are increased because of the distribution. Current earnings and profits are reduced by $1,100 ($3,100 − $2,000) and accumulated earnings and profits at January 1, 19X9, will be $28,900 ($20,000 + $10,000 − $1,100).[10]

Example 4:   Same facts as in Example 3, except that the mortgage to which the property was subject was $4,000.

Current earnings and profits are $10,900 ($10,000 + $900). The $900 recognized gain arises because the liability to which the property was subject ($4,000) exceeds its basis ($3,100). The reduction in earnings and profits because of the distribution is zero ($3,100 basis − $4,000 liability + $900 gain recognized). Accumulated earnings and profits at January 1, 19X9, will be $30,900 ($20,000 + $10,900 − zero).[11]

Example 5:   During 19X8, C Corporation distributed to its shareholders inventory assets that had a LIFO basis of $46,000; the FIFO basis would have been $50,000. Assume that the inventory had a fair market value of $55,000 and was subject to a liability of $35,000. Also assume that accumulated earnings and profits at January 1, 19X8 were $100,000, and current earnings and

[10]This example was adapted from Treas. Reg. Sec. 1.312-4, Example (1).

[11]Adapted from Treas. Reg. Sec. 1.312-4, Example (2). This explanation disregards any decrease in earnings and profits that would arise because of an increase in federal income taxes resulting from the $900 recognized gain.

profits before considering the distribution were $30,000.

Current earnings and profits are $39,000 ($30,000 + $4,000 + $5,000). The $4,000 increase represents the excess of FIFO valuation over actual LIFO basis, which must be recognized in computing 19X8 taxable income. The $5,000 excess of fair market value over FIFO valuation increases current earnings and profits but is not recognized in computing 19X8 taxable income. The reduction in earnings and profits because of the distribution is $20,000 ($55,000 fair market value − $35,000 liability). Accumulated earnings and profits at January 1, 19X9 will be $119,000 ($100,000 + $39,000 − $20,000).[12]

STOCK DISTRIBUTIONS

In the preceding discussion of property distributions, we excluded any consideration of a "stock dividend"; that is, of a transaction in which C Corporation distributes some of its own stock (either previously authorized but unissued shares or treasury stock) to its shareholders in their role as shareholders. The essence of a stock dividend transaction is illustrated in Figure 5-3.

FIGURE 5-3   Stock Distribution

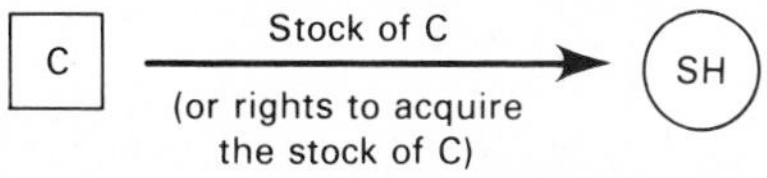

Section 305(a) sets forth the general rule that stock distributions are *not* to be included in the gross income of the recipient shareholder. This general rule, however, is followed by five "exceptions" in Sec. 305(b). If a stock distribution is classified as an exception to Sec. 305(a), it is to be *treated as* a property distribution. Thus, instead of being nontaxable to the shareholder, a taxable stock distribution results in dividend income to the shareholder to the extent the distribution is considered to come out of the distributing corporation's current or accumulated earnings and profits. Our discussion of stock distributions is divided into four major sections. In the first two sections, we shall examine the tax consequences of nontaxable and taxable stock distributions to both the shareholders and the distributing corporation. In the third section, we shall review the criteria for determining which stock distributions are

taxable. In the fourth section, we shall look at Sec. 306—a particular subset of stock distributions—which may cause adverse tax consequences when the shareholder later disposes of certain tax-free stock-dividend stocks.

Treatment of nontaxable stock distributions

If a stock (or stock right) distribution falls under the general rule of Sec. 305(a), nothing is included in the gross income of the recipient shareholder. Further, if the recipient shareholder is a corporation, there is no increase in its own earnings and profits (Sec. 312(f)(2)). The receipt of a nontaxable stock distribution, however, does have basis implications for the shareholder. If stock is distributed, part of the shareholder's basis in the original stock that gave rise to the stock dividend distribution is reallocated to the shares received (Sec. 307(a)). This allocation is based on the relative fair market values of the "old" and the "new" stock at the date of the distribution (Treas. Reg. Sec. 1.307-1). The date basis (holding period) of the share that gave rise to the distribution carrys over (or tacks on) to the newly distributed shares (Sec. 1223(5)). To illustrate these rules, consider the following example.

Example: On January 19, 19X3, Jones purchased 40 shares of ABC common stock for $1,000 ($25 per share). Four years later, on April 15, 19X7, ABC distributed one additional share of ABC common for every four common shares owned on April 1, 19X7. Jones received 10 shares. The fair market value per share of ABC common was $40 on April 15, 19X7. Assuming the distribution is nontaxable, Jones recognizes no income on receipt of the 10 shares of ABC common. Jones's total basis in the 10 shares will be $200 ($20 per share); that is,

$$\frac{\$400 \text{ (FMV of 10 new shares)}}{\$2,000 \text{ (FMV of 10 new + 40 old shares)}} \times \$1,000 \text{ (Basis of old shares)}$$

The $200 basis allocated to the new shares reduces the basis in the old shares from $1,000 to $800. The date basis of both the old and new shares is January 19, 19X3.

If, in the prior example, the 10 shares received by Jones had been ABC preferred, rather than ABC common, and if the fair market value of ABC preferred

[12]Adapted from Treas. Reg. Sec. 1.312-4, Example (3). This explanation disregards any decrease in earnings and profits that would arise because of an increase in federal income taxes resulting from the $4,000 recognized gain.

was $20 on April 15, 19X7, Jones would still not have to recognize any income on receiving the 10 shares of ABC preferred.[13] Jones's basis in the 10 shares of ABC preferred, however, would now be $111.10 ($11.11 per share), calculated as follows:

$$\frac{\substack{\$200 \\ \text{(FMV of 10 preferred shares)}}}{\substack{\$1,800 \\ \text{(FMV of 10 preferred + FMV of 40 common)}}} \times \substack{\$1,000 \\ \text{(Basis of} \\ \text{common)}}$$

Jones's basis in the 40 shares of ABC common would have been reduced to $888.90 ($1,000 − $111.10), or $22.22 per share. The date basis (holding period) of *both* the old common and the new preferred is January 19, 19X3.

The shareholder treatment of a distribution of nontaxable *stock rights* generally parallels our preceding discussion of nontaxable stock distributions. The following qualifications, however, should be noted:

1. No basis may be allocated to rights that are allowed to lapse (Treas. Reg. Sec. 1.307-1(a)). (This rule prevents the possibility of a recognized loss on such occurrence.)

2. If the fair market value of the rights, when distributed, is less than 15 percent of the fair market value at date of distribution of the stock that gave rise to the rights (the old stock), no basis is allocated to the rights unless the shareholder elects to do so. Any election must be attached to the shareholder's return for the year in which the rights are received (Sec. 307(b) and Treas. Reg. Sec. 1.307-2).

3. The holding period (or date basis) of the old stock carries over and tacks on to any rights that are *sold* (Sec. 1223(5)).

4. The basis of any shares acquired by exercising stock rights includes any basis allocated to the rights plus the exercise price. The holding period of such stock starts with the date the right to acquire was exercised (Sec. 1223(6)).

The three following examples illustrate these rules.

Example 1: On June 30, 19X3, Smith purchased 10 shares of ABC common stock for $600 ($60 per share). On September 15, 19X8, ABC distributed nontaxable stock rights to its common shareholders. Smith received 10 rights. Each right entitled Smith to acquire one additional share of ABC common stock for $80. Immediately after

the rights were issued, ABC common had a fair market value, *ex-rights*, of $100 per share and the rights had a fair market value of $20 each. On October 15, 19X8, when ABC common had a fair market value, *ex rights*, of $110 a share, Smith sold the 10 rights for $300.

Smith *must* allocate basis between the rights and the old stock (the stock in respect of which the rights were acquired):

$$\frac{\substack{\$200 \text{ (FMV of 10 rights)} \\ \$1,200 \text{ (FMV of 10 rights}} }{\text{+ FMV of 10 old common)}} \times \substack{\$600 \text{ (basis of} \\ \text{old common)}}$$

= $100 basis allocated to the 10 rights received

$$\frac{\substack{\$1,000 \text{ (FMV of 10 old common)} \\ \$1,200 \text{ (FMV of 10 rights}} }{\text{+ FMV of 10 old common)}} \times \substack{\$600 \text{ (basis of} \\ \text{old common)}}$$

= $500 basis for 10 old common

Smith must recognize a $200 long-term capital gain on the sale of the rights. Smith will still have a $500 basis in the 10 ABC common shares that he purchased on June 30, 19X3.

Example 2: Same facts as in Example 1, except that Smith exercises the 10 rights on October 15, 19X8, and receives 10 shares of ABC common for $800.

Smith will have a cost basis in the 10 old common shares of $500 (as calculated above) and a date basis in such stock of June 30, 19X3. The 10 shares received on the exercise of the rights will have a cost basis of $900 ($100 from the allocation plus $800 exercise price) and a date basis of October 15, 19X8.

Example 3: Same facts as in Example 1, except that Smith neither sells nor exercises the rights; in other words, they are allowed to lapse.

No loss is recognized. Smith retains the original $600 basis in the old common stock.

A nontaxable distribution of stock (or stock rights) has no tax effect on the distributing corporation. No gain or loss is recognized, and earnings and profits are not reduced (Secs. 311(a) and 312(d)).

Treatment of taxable stock distributions

When one of the exceptions to Sec. 305(a) applies to a distribution of a corporation's own stock (or stock rights), a potentially taxable transaction occurs. This

---

[13]Adverse tax consequences may arise on the eventual disposition of this preferred stock. See the discussion of Section 306 stock on page 5/16.

results from the requirement in Secs. 305(b) and (c) that such transactions be treated as property distributions. For *both* corporate and noncorporate shareholders, the amount distributed is the fair market value of the stock (or rights) as of the date distributed (Treas. Reg. Sec. 1.305-1(b)). In accordance with our earlier discussion of property distributions, the amount distributed to a shareholder will first be dividend income (to the extent of current or accumulated earnings and profits); any remaining amount distributed will next reduce the basis of the stock that gave rise to the distribution, with any excess treated as gain on sale of such stock. Both corporate and noncorporate shareholders take a cost basis equal to the fair market value of the taxable stock (or rights) as of the date distributed (Treas. Reg. Sec. 1.301-1(d)). The holding period of such stock or rights begins on the date of the distribution.

A corporation making a taxable distribution of stock (or stock rights) does *not* recognize any gain or loss (Sec. 311(a)). The distributing corporation does, however, reduce its earnings and profits by the fair market value, at the date of distribution, of the taxable stock (or rights) (Treas. Reg. Sec. 1.312-1(d)).

Taxable stock distributions

The question whether or not stock dividends should be taxable has a long history. In a landmark case, *Eisner* v. *Macomber* (252 U.S. 189 (1920)), the Supreme Court found that a stock dividend was nontaxable. Based on the conclusion that "a stock dividend really take(s) nothing from the property of the corporation and add(s) nothing to that of the shareholder," the court held that *no income had been realized* and, therefore, the transaction constitutionally could not be taxed. The stock dividend in *Eisner* v. *Macomber* was common stock distributed to existing common shareholders. No other classes of stock existed. Because the scope of the decision might prove to have limitations, Congress provided in the Revenue Act of 1921 that *all* stock dividends were nontaxable to shareholders.

The current Internal Revenue Code reflects the gradual shift that has taken place from the extreme position adopted in 1921. As indicated previously, Sec. 305 provides a general rule that stock and stock right distributions are nontaxable, but this general rule is followed by five exceptions that require certain transactions to be treated as property distributions. The most recent major changes in Sec. 305 occurred under the Tax Reform Act of 1969. New regulations reflecting these amendments were issued in T.D. 7281, filed July 11, 1973.

The discussion and examples that follow are intended to provide an overview of *taxable* distributions of stock and stock rights under Sec. 305, as amended by the Tax Reform Act of 1969. In certain situations, some of the changes found in the 1969 Act become effective as late as January 1, 1991! An examination of the effective date rules and the "pre-1969" Sec. 305 is beyond the scope of this book.

DISTRIBUTIONS IN LIEU OF MONEY   If *any* shareholder has the right to an election or option whether a distribution shall be made either in money or any other property, or in stock of the distributing corporation, then, with respect to *all* shareholders, the *distribution of stock is treated as a property distribution* (Sec. 305(b)(1) and Treas. Reg. Sec. 1.305-2).[14] It should be emphasized that to the extent *any* shareholder may elect to receive stock or property, *all* shareholders receiving stock are treated as receiving property distributions. This is true even if no shareholder elects to take property.

DISPROPORTIONATE DISTRIBUTIONS   A distribution by a corporation of its stock is treated as a distribution of property if the distribution (or a series of distributions of which such distribution is one) has the result of (1) the receipt of money or other property by some shareholders, and (2) an increase in the proportionate interests of other shareholders in the assets or earnings and profits of the corporation (Sec. 305(b)(2) and Treas. Reg. Sec. 1.305-3(a)).

In interpreting the term "distribution" and the phrase "a series of distributions," Treas. Reg. Sec. 1.305-3 indicates that "distribution" includes a deemed distribution of stock, and "a series of distributions" encompasses all distributions of stock made or deemed made by a corporation that have the result of the receipt of cash or property by some shareholders and an increase in proportionate interests of other shareholders. Further, it is not necessary that the stock distribution(s) and cash or property distribution(s) be steps in an overall plan unless they are separated by more than 36 months.

The following examples are from Treas. Reg. Sec. 1.305-3(e).

> *Example 1:*   Corporation X is organized with two classes of common stock, class A and class B. Each share of stock is entitled to share equally in the assets and earnings and profits of the corporation.

---

[14]For purposes of this and the following categories of taxable stock distributions, the term *shareholder* includes a holder of rights or of convertible securities and the term *stock* includes rights to acquire such stock.

Dividends may be paid in stock or in cash on either class of stock without regard to the medium of payment of dividends on the other class. A dividend is declared on the class A stock payable in additional shares of class A stock, and a dividend is declared on class B stock payable in cash. Since the class A shareholders as a class will have increased their proportionate interests in the assets and earnings and profits of the corporation and the class B shareholders will have received cash, the additional shares of class A stock are distributions of property to which Sec. 301 applies. This is true even with respect to those shareholders who may own class A stock and class B stock in the same proportion.

Example 2: Corporation Y is organized with two classes of stock, class A common, and class B, which is nonconvertible and limited and preferred as to dividends. A dividend is declared on the class A stock payable in additional shares of class A stock, and a dividend is declared on the class B stock payable in cash. The distribution of class A stock is not one to which Sec. 301 applies because the distribution does not increase the proportionate interests of the class A shareholders as a class.

DISTRIBUTIONS OF COMMON AND PREFERRED STOCK
If a distribution (or a series of distributions) by a corporation results in the receipt of preferred stock (whether or not convertible into common stock) by some common shareholders and the receipt of common stock by other common shareholders, *both* the preferred and the common stock are treated as property distributions (Sec. 305(b)(3) and Treas. Reg. Sec. 1.305-4(a)).

The following example from Treas. Reg. Sec. 1.305-4(b), Ex. (1) illustrates this rule:

Example: Corporation X is organized with two classes of common stock, class A and class B. Dividends may be paid in stock or in cash on either class of stock without regard to the medium of payment of dividends on the other class. A dividend is declared on the class A stock payable in additional shares of class A stock, and a dividend is declared on class B stock payable in newly authorized class C stock, which is nonconvertible and limited and preferred as to dividends. Both the distribution of class A shares and the distribution of new class C shares are distributions to which Sec. 301 applies.

DISTRIBUTIONS ON PREFERRED STOCK Distributions of stock (common or preferred) by a corporation, made (or deemed made) *with respect to* its preferred stock, are generally treated as property distributions (Sec. 305(b)(4) and Treas. Reg. Sec. 1.305-5(a)). The only exception, found in Sec. 305(b)(4), concerns convertible preferred stock. An increase in the conversion ratio of convertible preferred stock, made solely to take account of a stock dividend or stock split with respect to the stock into which such convertible stock is convertible, does *not* result in a deemed distribution on preferred stock that must be treated as a property distribution.

Treas. Reg. Sec. 1.305-5(a) provides some guidance on what constitutes preferred stock. The term *preferred stock* generally refers to stock that, in relation to other classes of stock outstanding, enjoys certain limited rights and privileges (generally associated with specified dividend and liquidation priorities) but does not participate in corporate growth to any significant extent. The classification of *participating* preferred stock as preferred stock for purposes of Sec. 305(b)(4) is highly subjective. If, taking into account all the facts and circumstances at the time of a stock distribution on participating preferred stock, it is reasonable to anticipate little or no likelihood of such participating preferred stock *actually* participating in current and anticipated earnings (and upon liquidation) beyond its preferred interest, such participating preferred stock will be considered preferred stock. On the other hand, if it is likely that such preferred stock will significantly participate in current and anticipated earnings (and upon liquidation) beyond its preferred interest, it will *not* be considered preferred stock. The determination of whether convertible stock is preferred is made without reference to the characteristics of the stock into which it may be converted. The term preferred stock does not include convertible debentures.

Example 1: Corporation Q is organized with 10,000 shares of class A stock and 1,000 shares of class B stock. The terms of the class B stock require that the class B stock have a preference of $5 per share with respect to dividends and $100 per share with respect to liquidation. In addition, upon a distribution of $10 per share to the class A stock, class B participates equally in any additional dividends. The terms also provide that upon liquidation, the class B stock participates equally after the class A stock receives $100 per share. Corporation Q has no accumulated earnings and profits. In 1971, it earned $10,000, the highest earnings in its history. The corporation is in an industry in which it is reasonable to anticipate a growth in earnings of 5 percent per year. In 1971, the book value of Corporation Q's assets totaled $100,000. In that year, the corporation paid a dividend of $5 per share to the class B stock and $0.50 per share to the class A stock. In 1972, the corporation had no earnings and, in lieu of a $5 dividend, distributed one share of class B stock for each outstanding share of class B stock. No distribution was made to the class A stock. Because, in 1972, it was not reasonable to anticipate that the class B stock would participate in the current and anticipated earnings and growth of the corporation beyond its preferred interest, the class B stock is preferred stock and the distribution of class B shares to the class B shareholders is a distribution to which Secs. 305(b)(4) and 301 apply.[15]

Example 2: Corporation P is organized with 10,000 shares of class A stock and 1,000 shares of class B stock. The terms of the class B stock have a preference of $5 per share with respect to dividends and $100 per share with respect to liquidation. In addition, upon a distribution of $5 per share to the class A stock, class B participates equally in any additional dividends. The terms also provide that upon liquidation, the class B stock participates equally after the class A receives $100 per share. Corporation P has accumulated earnings and profits of $100,000. In 1971, it earned $75,000. The corporation is in an industry in which it is reasonable to anticipate a growth in earnings of 10 percent per year. In 1971, the book value of Corporation P's assets totaled $5 million. In that year, the corporation paid a dividend of $5 per share to the class B stock, $5 per share to the class A stock, and it distributed an additional $1 per share to both class A and class B stock. In 1972, the corporation had earnings of $82,500. In that year, it paid a dividend of $5 per share to the class B stock and $5 per share to the class A stock. In addition, the corporation declared stock dividends of one share of class B stock for every 10 outstanding shares of class B stock and one share of class A stock for every 10 outstanding shares of class A stock. Because, in 1972, it was reasonable to anticipate that both the class B stock and the class A stock would participate in the current and anticipated earnings and growth of the corporation

beyond their preferred interests, neither class is preferred stock and the stock dividends are not distributions to which Sec. 305(b)(4) applies.[16]

DISTRIBUTIONS OF CONVERTIBLE PREFERRED STOCK   A distribution of *convertible* preferred stock will be treated as a property distribution unless the corporation can establish that it will *not* result in a disproportionate distribution (Sec. 305(b)(5) and Treas. Reg. Sec. 1.305-6(a)). Treasury Regulation Sec. 1.305-6(a)(1) presumes that a distribution of *convertible* preferred stock is likely to result in a disproportionate distribution when both of the following conditions exist:

1.   The conversion right must be exercised within a relatively short period of time after the date of distribution of the stock.
2.   Taking into account such factors as the dividend rate, the redemption provisions, the marketability of the convertible stock, and the conversion price, it may be anticipated that some shareholders will exercise their conversion rights and some will not.

The above conditions imply a disproportionate distribution because some shareholders would increase their proportionate interest (those who convert to common stock) while others would receive property (those who sell or redeem their convertible preferred stock). On the other hand, when the conversion period extends over many years and the dividend rate is consistent with market conditions at the time the convertible preferred stock is distributed, there is no way to predict the extent to which shareholders will or will not convert, and thus a disproportionate distribution is not considered to have taken place.

Although the conversion time period is clearly an important factor, the regulations do little to distinguish between "a relatively short period of time" and "many years." In the two examples provided, a four-month period results in a taxable distribution, while 20 years does not. Plenty of room for disagreement apparently remains!

CERTAIN TRANSACTIONS TREATED AS DISTRIBUTIONS
When Congress amended Sec. 305 in the Tax Reform Act of 1969, there was concern about the possibility that the five exceptions to the general rule of Sec. 305(a) would not cover all transactions that should be taxable. In response to this concern, Sec. 305(c) was

---

[15]This example is taken from Treas. Reg. Sec. 1.305-5(d), Ex. (8).

[16]Example taken from Treas. Reg. Sec. 1.305-5(d), Ex. (9).

created. This section directs the Treasury to prescribe regulations under which a broad variety of transactions may be treated as property distributions even though, in form, they do not fit one of the five exceptions of Sec. 305(b).

The thrust of Sec. 305(c) is that a change in conversion ratio, a change in redemption price, a difference between redemption price and issue price, a redemption, or a recapitalization may have the effect of increasing a shareholder's proportionate interest in the earnings or assets of a corporation. The Treasury was charged with developing regulations to indicate when such transactions should be treated as property distributions to the shareholder whose proportionate interest is increased by such transactions. A few examples follow.

Example 1: Corporation M is organized with two classes of stock outstanding, class A and class B. Each class B share may be converted, at the option of the holder, into class A shares. During the first year, the conversion ratio is one share of class A stock for each share of class B stock. At the beginning of each subsequent year, the conversion ratio is increased by 0.05 share of class A stock for each share of class B stock. Thus, during the second year, the conversion ratio would be 1.05 shares of class A stock for each share of class B stock; during the third year, the ratio would be 1.10 shares, and so on.

Corporation M pays an annual cash dividend on the class A stock. At the beginning of the second year, when the conversion ratio is 1.05 shares of class A stock for each share of class B stock, a distribution of 0.05 shares of class A stock is deemed made under Sec. 305(c) with respect to each share of class B stock, since the proportionate interests of the class B shareholders in the assets or earnings and profits of Corporation M are increased and the transaction has the effect described in Sec. 305(b)(2). Accordingly, Secs. 305(b)(2) and 301 apply to the transaction.[17]

Example 2: Corporation T has outstanding 1,000 shares of $100 par 5 percent cumulative preferred stock and 10,000 shares of no-par common stock. The corporation is four years in arrears on dividends to the preferred shareholders. The issue price of the preferred stock is $100 per share. Pursuant to a recapitalization under Sec.

368(a)(1)(E), the preferred shareholders exchange their preferred stock, including the right to dividend arrearages on the basis of one old preferred share for 1.20 newly authorized class A preferred shares. Immediately after the recapitalization, the new class A shares are traded at $100 per share. The class A shares are entitled to a liquidation preference of $100. The preferred shareholders have increased their proportionate interest in the assets or earnings and profits of corporation T, because the fair market value of 1.20 shares of class A preferred stock ($120) exceeds the issue price of the old preferred stock ($100). Accordingly, the preferred shareholders are deemed under Sec. 305(c) to have received a distribution in the amount of $20 on each share of old preferred stock, and the distribution is one to which Secs. 305(b)(4) and 301 apply.

The same result would occur if the fair market value of the common stock immediately after the recapitalization were $20 per share and each share of preferred stock were exchanged for one share of the new class A preferred stock and one share of common stock.[18]

Example 3: Corporation W issues preferred stock for $100 per share. The stock pays no dividends but is redeemable at the end of five years for $185 with yearly increases thereafter of $15. There are no facts to indicate that a call premium in excess of $10 is reasonable. Because the difference between redemption price and issue price exceeds the reasonable call premium to the extent of $75, that amount is considered to be a distribution of additional stock on preferred stock that is constructively received over the five-year period. Therefore, the shareholder is deemed under Sec. 305(c) to have received on the last day of each year during the five-year period a distribution on the preferred stock in an amount equal to 15 percent of the issue price. Each $15 increase in the redemption price thereafter is considered to be a distribution on the preferred stock at the time each such increase becomes effective.[19]

Section 306 stock

Although the Tax Reform Act of 1969 expanded the category of taxable stock (or stock right) distributions, the general rule of Sec. 305(a) retains considerable vi-

[17]Example taken from Treas. Reg. Sec. 1.305-3(e), Ex. (6).

[18]Taken from Treas. Reg. Sec. 1.305-5(d), Ex. (1).
[19]Taken from Treas. Reg. Sec. 1.305-5(d), Ex. (5).

FIGURE **5-4**

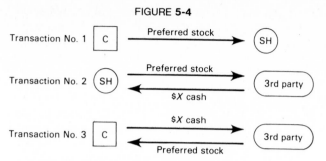

Net result: SH receives $X cash but does not surrender
any common stock equity or control.

tality. Pro rata distributions of common stock (or non-convertible preferred stock) by a corporation with only common stock outstanding would clearly be nontaxable, assuming no cash option or convertible debentures existed. In that situation, the shareholder really has nothing extra after the distribution, other than "more pieces of paper," to represent ownership interest.

The fact that preferred stock may be distributed tax free to common shareholders does, however, raise a potential problem. Consider the three transactions portrayed in Figure 5-4.

In transaction No. 1, all common shareholders receive a nontaxable *pro rata* distribution of preferred stock. Transaction No. 2 represents a sale of this preferred stock to an outside party. In accordance with the preceding discussion on nontaxable stock dividends, it would *appear* that any difference between the sales price and basis allocated to the preferred stock should be treated as capital gain (or loss). Then, in the redemption of transaction No. 3, the outside party surrenders that same preferred stock for cash and reports as capital gain the excess (if any) of redemption price over cost. Some premium on redemption of the preferred stock would provide the necessary incentive to attract a willing outside party to play the intermediary role.

The net result of the three transactions is that the shareholders have indirectly received a cash distribution but *appear* to be able to treat it as a sale of stock rather than dividend income.[20] The net effect is a "bail-out" of earnings and profits at capital gains rates.

A bail-out of the type shown in Figure 5-4 was accomplished in *Chamberlin*, 207 F.2d 462 (6th Cir. 1953). In response to this potential "end run" around property distributions and dividend treatment, Congress enacted Sec. 306. The thrust of Sec. 306 is to

impose special rules in cases in which the shareholder disposes of preferred stock originally received as a nontaxable stock dividend. Section 306 addresses three important questions: (1) Exactly which stock is Sec. 306 stock? (2) What special rules apply when a taxpayer disposes of Sec. 306 stock? (3) What exceptions allow dispositions of Sec. 306 stock under "normal" rules?

DEFINITION: SECTION 306 STOCK   The label "Sec. 306 stock" is applied in three situations. In the first and most general case, it applies to preferred stock a shareholder receives as a stock distribution if *any* part of such distribution was not income under the general rule of Sec. 305(a) (Sec. 306(c)(1)(A)). For this purpose, common stock that is convertible into preferred stock or property is considered preferred stock and thus would be "tainted" Sec. 306 stock if distributed as a nontaxable stock distribution (Sec. 306(e)(2)). For example, the preferred stock distributed to common shareholders in transaction No. 1 of Figure 5-4 would not be included in gross income and thus would be Sec. 306 stock.[21]

The second situation in which stock is classified as Sec. 306 stock concerns corporate reorganizations and divisions. (For a discussion of reorganizations and divisions, see Chapter 7.) Preferred stock received by a shareholder in a reorganization or division is Sec. 306 stock if the transaction was at least partially nontaxable and had substantially the same effect as the receipt of a stock dividend, or the stock was received in exchange for Sec. 306 stock (Sec. 306(c)(1)(B)).[22]

In the final situation, any stock (preferred or com-

---

[20]A critical element in the transactions portrayed in Figure 5-4 is the sale of the preferred stock to a third party. As will be explained later, a direct redemption of the preferred stock runs the risk of being treated as a dividend.

[21]One exception applies to this first category of Sec. 306 stock. If, at the time of the nontaxable distribution of preferred stock, a distribution of money would not have been characterized as a dividend, such preferred stock is not Sec. 306 stock (Sec. 306(c)(2)). For this exception to apply, there generally must be *no* current or accumulated earning and profits.

[22]The same exception exists for this category as the first, that is, stock will not be Sec. 306 stock if no part of a distribution of money in lieu of the preferred stock would have been a dividend.

mon), the basis of which is determined by reference to Sec. 306 stock is classified as Sec. 306 stock (Sec. 306(c)(1)(c)). This includes:

1. Stock held by a donee if the stock was Sec. 306 stock in the hands of the donor;
2. Stock received by a shareholder under Sec. 1036, which defines certain nontaxable stock for stock exchanges, if the stock exchanged was Sec. 306 stock; and
3. *Both* the stock transferred to a corporation *and* the stock received in exchange by the shareholder in a Sec. 351 transaction if the stock transferred by the shareholder was Sec. 306 stock.

Section 306(d) provides that stock rights are to be treated as stock and that stock acquired through the exercise of stock rights is to be treated as stock distributed at the time of the distribution of the stock rights. Thus, subject to the exceptions noted above, stock rights and stock acquired through the exercise of stock rights are considered Sec. 306 stock if they fall into any of the three categories previously described.

Stock will no longer be classified as Sec. 306 stock when one of the following events occurs:

1. A taxable disposition, upon which harsh tax consequences usually apply;
2. The death of the shareholder if the heir's basis is determined by reference to the stock's fair market value at death or alternate valuation date; or
3. The stock's exchange for common stock in the same corporation from which it was originally issued.

DISPOSITION OF SECTION 306 STOCK   The bail-out potential is eliminated by the disposition rules of Sec. 306. Dispositions of Sec. 306 stock may be divided into two categories: (1) redemptions (the corporation directly acquires the stock from the shareholder in exchange for property) and (2) sales to third parties.[23]

When a corporation redeems its own Sec. 306 stock from a shareholder in exchange for property, the amount realized by the shareholder is treated as a property distribution (Sec. 306(a)(2)). This means that the fair market value of the entire proceeds (amount realized) is considered to be the amount distributed and is first dividend income (to the extent of current or accumulated earnings and profits); next, a return of

basis; and any remainder as capital gain.[24] Any of the shareholder's basis in the Sec. 306 stock that is not recovered reverts to the basis of the stock with respect to which the Sec. 306 stock was originally distributed.

Example: P Corporation is owned entirely by Mr. Jones. In 19X4, P distributed a nontaxable stock dividend of 10 shares of P preferred stock to Mr. Jones. When distributed, the 10 shares had a total fair market value of $10,000 and P had earnings and profits of $5,000. A total basis of $3,000 was properly allocated to the 10 shares. In 19X7, P redeemed the 10 shares from Jones for $11,000. As of 19X7, current and accumulated earnings and profits totaled $9,000.

Mr. Jones is treated as receiving a property distribution in 19X7 of $11,000, of which $9,000 is dividend income and $2,000 is return of basis. The remaining $1,000 basis in his Sec. 306 stock is added to his basis in the stock on which the Sec. 306 stock was distributed.

Adverse tax consequences also apply if a shareholder sells Sec. 306 stock. The rules, however, are different from the redemption situation described above. Upon sale, Sec. 306(a)(1) provides that the amount realized is:

1. Ordinary income to the extent, at the time such Sec. 306 stock was distributed, a distribution of money (in lieu of the Sec. 306 stock) equal to the fair market value of such stock would have been a dividend.[25]
2. If the amount realized on the sale exceeds the amount that must be characterized as ordinary income, the excess next reduces the basis of the Sec. 306 stock sold. Any portion of such basis that is not recovered is added back to the basis of the stock with respect to which the sold Sec. 306 stock was distributed.
3. If the amount realized exceeds both the amount that must be characterized as ordinary income and the basis of the Sec. 306 stock sold, any remainder is treated as gain on sale of such stock (usually capital gain). No loss may be recognized on the sale of Sec. 306 stock.

Example 1:   In 19X6, when current and accumulated earnings and profits totaled $20,000, P Corporation distributed 10 shares of preferred stock to

---

[23]Section 306 does not impose a tax on dispositions that are otherwise nontaxable, for example, gifts, transfers upon death, exchanges under Secs. 351 and 1036, and corporate reorganizations and divisions. Recall, however, that the Sec. 306 "taint" usually is not purged by a nontaxable disposition.

[24]The regulations are not clear whether the basis to be recovered is just the redeemed Sec. 306 stock basis or the combined basis of the redeemed Sec. 306 stock and the stock upon which the Sec. 306 stock was issued.

[25]Observe that dividend equivalence at the time the Sec. 306 stock was distributed is used to measure the ordinary (*not* dividend) income potential on sale.

each of its two equal common shareholders, Ms. Smith and Mr. Jones. When distributed, each share had a fair market value of $800 and both shareholders properly allocated $300 basis to each share of preferred stock received. In 19X8, when P Corporation had a deficit in both current and accumulated earnings and profits, Ms. Smith sold her 10 shares of preferred stock for $6,000.

The entire $6,000 is ordinary income to Ms. Smith in 19X8. Her $3,000 basis in the preferred stock is added to her basis in her common stock.

Example 2: Same facts as in Example 1, except that Ms. Smith sells the preferred stock for $12,000.

For 19X8, Ms. Smith has $8,000 ordinary income, her entire basis in the preferred stock is recovered, and she will report a $1,000 long-term capital gain.

EXCEPTIONS   The special redemption and sales provisions of Sec. 306 do not apply in all cases. If Sec. 306 stock is sold, the difference between the sales price and shareholder's adjusted basis in the stock will be reported as capital gain or loss (that is, "normal" rules apply) *if the shareholder's entire stock interest has been terminated.* With no remaining stock interest, it is clear that a bail-out is not possible. For this exception to apply, it is necessary that the shareholder have no remaining direct or constructive ownership of stock in the corporation. The constructive ownership rules of Sec. 318(a) indicate the conditions under which stock directly owned by other "related" shareholders is considered "constructively" owned by the selling shareholder. These rules, which we shall discuss in the next section of this chapter, also play an important part in the treatment of stock redemptions.

In two specific situations, a redemption of Sec. 306 stock yields capital gain or loss (measured by the difference between the redemption proceeds and the stock's adjusted basis) rather than the property distribution treatment previously described. These are redemptions meeting the requirements of Sec. 302(b)(3) (termination of shareholder's interest) or Sec. 303 (redemptions to pay death taxes). The provisions of these sections are also covered in the next section of this chapter.

Section 306 also has no application to stock disposed of in a partial or complete liquidation. The Sec. 306 "taint" terminates with the surrender of the stock and the transaction is treated as discussed in Chapter 6.

The final exception to the special disposition rules of Sec. 306 is highly subjective. This exception provides that the usual rules do not apply if the shareholder can prove that the original distribution of Sec. 306 stock and its later disposition "was not in pursuance of a plan having as one of its principal purposes the avoidance of federal income tax" (Sec. 306(b)(4)). Treasury Regulation Sec. 1.306-2(b)(3) provides two examples: (1) isolated dispositions of Sec. 306 stock by minority shareholders; and (2) dispositions of Sec. 306 stock where the stock with respect to which the Sec. 306 stock was issued was previously or simultaneously disposed of.

EFFECT OF DISPOSITIONS OF SECTION 306 STOCK ON THE CORPORATION   Dispositions of Sec. 306 stock that do not directly involve the corporation (for example, gifts and sales) do not cause the corporation to recognize income or adjust its earnings and profits. In the case of a sale, earnings and profits at the time the Sec. 306 stock was distributed are used to measure the shareholder's ordinary income potential, but recognition of such ordinary income by the shareholder does *not* cause a corresponding decrease in earnings and profits (Treas. Reg. Sec. 1.306(b)(1)).

Use of noncash property to redeem Sec. 306 stock may cause gain to be recognized by the corporation. We shall discuss corporate gain or loss recognition in the next section on stock redemptions. The effect of redemptions on earnings and profits depends on how the transaction is treated by the shareholder. If the redemption is treated as a property distribution to the shareholder, the rules summarized in Table 5-2 (page **5**/8 apply. If shareholder treatment is not dictated by Sec. 306 because one of the exceptions applies, earnings and profits are adjusted as described in the following section, which discusses the "normal" tax consequences of redemptions. Similarly, no special rules apply to the corporation upon receipt of Sec. 306 stock in a partial or complete liquidation. We shall discuss these general topics in Chapter 6.

STOCK REDEMPTIONS

Section 317(b) defines a "redemption of stock" as the acquisition by a corporation of its own stock from a shareholder in exchange for property, whether or not the stock so acquired is canceled, retired, or held as **treasury stock. Such transactions have the general form portrayed in Figure 5-5.**

In examining this figure, note:

1. The classification of the transaction as a *stock redemption* is solely dependent upon an examination of what happens at the *shareholder* level;

2. The classification of the transaction as a *partial or complete liquidation* is solely dependent upon an examination of what happens at the *corporate* level; and

3. If a transaction may be classified as both a redemption and a liquidation, the liquidation rules (which will be presented in Chapter 6) are to control. In the remaining portion of this chapter, we shall assume transactions that are not in partial or complete liquidation of the corporation.

FIGURE **5-5** Stock Redemption

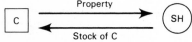

The "property" depicted in Figure 5-5 may be money, securities, or any other property of the distributing corporation; remember, however, that its own stock or rights to acquire its stock are not considered to be a corporate property (Sec. 317(a)). To the redeeming shareholder, a stock redemption has all the characteristics of a "sale" (that is, an exchange of stock for property). If taxable, it would *appear* that the shareholder would recognize gain or loss in an amount determined by subtracting the adjusted basis of the redeemed stock from the fair market value of the property received. Assuming the stock is a capital asset in the hands of the shareholder, the result would be capital gain or loss.

If the apparent treatment described above actually applied to all stock redemptions, a substantial "loophole" would exist in the property distribution rules previously described. Consider the situation in which all 100 shares of the stock of a corporation are owned by one shareholder and the corporation redeems 10 percent of the stock for $10,000. Has the shareholder really given up anything? The shareholder clearly owns 100 percent of the outstanding stock both before and after the redemption. To treat the 10 percent redemption as a sale—when a $10,000 distribution without the surrender of stock would have been a dividend—would allow the tax consequences to be controlled by "form" over substance.

The potential for abuse is not limited to one-shareholder corporations. Whatever the number of shareholders, a pro rata redemption of each shareholder's stock would leave each shareholder's ownership after

the redemption the same as before. Even with redemptions that appear to be non-pro rata, relationships between shareholders may mean there is no "effective" change in ownership. For example, assume a corporation is owned equally by A and B and that all of A's stock is redeemed. The effect of the redemption on A is substantial if A and B are unrelated (the redemption would terminate A's ownership) but could be viewed as minimal if A and B are husband and wife (that is, A-B family continues to own 100 percent).

In the following discussion, we shall examine the variety of tax results that proceed from stock redemptions. The basic issues that must be investigated in the event of a stock redemption are:

1. Does the shareholder recognize any income, gain, or loss on the redemption?

2. What is the tax character of income, gain, or loss recognized by the shareholder?

3. What is the basis of the property received by the shareholder?

4. Does the corporation recognize any income, gain, or loss on the redemption?

5. What is the tax character of income, gain, or loss recognized by the corporation?

6. What is the tax effect of the redemption on the corporation's earnings and profits?

Tax treatment to shareholders

For the shareholder, "sale" treatment will only apply if the redemption meets the requirements of at least one of five situations provided in the Internal Revenue Code (four situations are found in Sec. 302 and one in Sec. 303). If none of these five situations applies, the stock surrender portion of Figure 5-5 is ignored and the transaction is treated by the shareholder as a property distribution. Four of these situations are discussed below.[26]

SUBSTANTIALLY DISPROPORTIONATE REDEMPTION OF STOCK   Section 302(b)(2) provides objective criteria for determining when a redemption is substantially disproportionate. The tests described below must be applied separately to each redeeming shareholder. The basic idea is if a shareholder does not control the corporation after the redemption and has also had a substantial reduction in percentage ownership because of the redemption, the transaction has the characteristics of a sale, *not* a "disguised" property distribution.

With regard to a specific shareholder, a stock re-

---

[26]The fifth, found in Sec. 302(b)(4), involves stock issued by railroad corporations in certain reorganizations and is not covered.

demption is "substantially disproportionate" and, therefore, treated as a sale per Sec. 302(b)(2) if *all* the following criteria are satisfied:

1. Immediately after the redemption, the shareholder owns less than 50 percent of the total combined *voting power* of all classes of stock entitled to vote.

2. Immediately after the redemption, the shareholder's percentage ownership of *voting stock* is less than 80 percent of such shareholder's voting stock percentage ownership immediately before the redemption.

3. Immediately after the redemption, the shareholder's percentage ownership of *common stock* (whether voting or nonvoting) is less than 80 percent of such shareholder's common stock percentage ownership immediately before the redemption. (If more than one class of common stock exists, percentage ownership is to be made by reference to fair market value.)

4. A series of redemptions made pursuant to a plan must be evaluated as a whole. Thus, the first test noted above must apply upon completion of the series of redemptions, and the second and third tests compare ownership immediately before the first redemption and immediately after the last.

The sale treatment provided by Sec. 302(b)(2), as described above, might appear to be potentially available only to redemptions of voting common stock or the simultaneous redemption of both common and voting preferred stock. The regulations, however, specify that otherwise nonqualifying stock (nonvoting preferred) may be redeemed at the same time and receive sale treatment if the other redeemed stock meets the tests of Sec. 302(b)(2). Regulations also provide that stock that does not have voting rights until the happening of an event (such as a default in the payment of dividends on preferred stock) is not "voting stock" until the occurrence of the specified event (Treas. Reg. Sec. 1.302-3(a)(3).

Tests No. 2 and No. 3 require that the specified ownership *percentages* after the redemption be less than 80 percent of such ownership percentages before the redemption. This is *not* the same as requiring the *number* of shares owned after the redemption to be fewer than 80 percent of the number owned before.

Example: Corporation O has outstanding 400 shares of common stock. The shares are owned 200 by A, 120 by B, and 80 by C. A, B, and C are unrelated. Corporation O redeems 50 shares from A, 110 shares from B, and 40 shares from C.

	Before redemption			After redemption		
	No. of shares owned	Percentage ownership	No. of shares redeemed	No. of shares owned	Percentage ownership	80% of prior ownership percentage
A	200	50	50	150	75	40
B	120	30	110	10	5	24
C	80	20	40	40	20	16
Total	400 outstanding shares	—	200	200 outstanding shares	—	—

A, B, and C must each be examined separately to determine if any or all qualify as receiving a substantially disproportionate redemption. Assuming that no plan for a series of redemptions exists, the fourth test noted above may be ignored. Also, the second and third tests will be identical in this example because only one class of stock, voting common, is assumed.

Shareholder A fails the first test because after the redemption A owns 75 percent of combined voting power. A also fails the second and third tests because ownership after the redemption does not fall below 40 percent. Shareholder B meets the requirements of all tests for a substantially disproportionate redemption, that is, less than 50 percent voting power after the redemption (test No. 1) and a decline in stock ownership to less than 24 percent (tests No. 2 and No. 3). Shareholder C meets test No. 1 but not tests No. 2 or No. 3, that is, in this case, ownership after the redemption does not fall below 16 percent. Thus, the full proceeds received by A and C are treated as property distributions, while the difference between B's proceeds and basis in redeemed stock will be capital gain or loss.

TERMINATION OF SHAREHOLDER'S INTEREST Section 302(b)(3) provides for sale treatment to a redeeming shareholder "if the redemption is in complete redemption of all of the stock of the corporation owned by the shareholder." Although sale treatment clearly allows earnings and profits to be "bailed out" at capital gains rates, it is done at the "cost" of the shareholder's entire equity interest. This does not potentially circumvent the property distribution (dividend) rules in the same way that pro rata (or nearly pro rata) redemptions could.

Upon initial consideration, this provision might appear to be a subset of substantially disproportionate redemptions and therefore unnecessary. It does, however, extend sale treatment to three situations not covered by the substantially disproportionate rules, namely:

1. Redemptions of only nonvoting stock that terminate the shareholder's interest;
2. Redemptions of Sec. 306 stock that terminate the shareholder's interest; and
3. Redemptions that terminate the shareholder's interest except for stock constructively owned by reason of family attribution.

In the first situation, redemptions of *only nonvoting stock* may not, by definition, meet the "80 percent *voting stock*" test for substantially disproportionate redemptions because the percentage of voting stock owned obviously could not decrease the required amount. If the redemption of such stock terminates the shareholder's entire stock interest, sale treatment will apply.

In the second situation, recall that the special disposition rules of Sec. 306 generally require that a redemption of Sec. 306 stock is to be treated as a property distribution. As previously noted, one of the exceptions to these rules allows sale treatment if Sec. 302(b)(3) (termination of shareholder's interest) applies.

The third situation indicated above allows sale treatment for certain redemptions that do not qualify as substantially disproportionate because stock is attributed to the redeeming shareholder through family attribution. Further explanation of this aspect of Sec. 302(b)(3) must await later discussion of the constructive ownership rules of Sec. 318 and their relationship to stock redemptions (see page 5/23).

One final aspect of complete terminations concerns a combined sale and redemption. It is not uncommon to find that a party seeking to purchase all the stock of a corporation does not want all the cash or other property that the corporation owns. As long as the two steps (sale of part of the stock and redemption of the rest of the stock for the unwanted assets) are part of a single plan, the redemption should qualify as a complete termination.[27] A redemption of part of a shareholder's stock, followed by a later sale of the rest of the shareholder's stock, could not qualify as a complete termination if the transactions were not part of a single plan.

REDEMPTIONS NOT EQUIVALENT TO DIVIDENDS   Section 302(b)(1) provides that a redemption of stock will be treated as a sale "if the redemption is not essentially equivalent to a dividend." In contrast to the relatively objective requirements of "substantially disproportionate" (Sec. 302(b)(2)) and "complete termination" (Sec. 302(b)(3)) redemptions, Sec. 302(b)(1) is deliberately subjective. Congress clearly wanted to leave room for redemptions that might have "sale" characteristics even though not covered by the more objective provisions.

In examining a redemption to see if it is "not essentially equivalent to a dividend," the Supreme Court, in *Davis*, 397 U.S. 301 (1970), held that the net effect of the redemption on the shareholder's ownership must be determined and that a meaningful reduction in the shareholder's proportionate interest in the corporation must be found. The Court further noted that a "business purpose" for the redemption was not relevant for this classification.

The only example of a Sec. 302(b)(1) redemption provided in the regulations suggests that the redemption of one-half the nonvoting preferred stock (not Sec. 306 stock) owned by a shareholder owning only such stock will "ordinarily" be not essentially equivalent to a dividend (Treas. Reg. Sec. 1.302-2(a)). The I.R.S. has ruled that a redemption of any amount of nonvoting, nonparticipating, non-Section 306 stock is not essentially equivalent to a dividend if the redeemed shareholder owns no common stock, directly or constructively (Rev. Rul. 77-426, 1977-2 C.B. 87).

Other rulings have also held that redemptions that closely approach but do not meet the "80 percent test" of substantially disproportionate redemptions may be considered as not essentially equivalent to a dividend if the shareholder does not control the corporation after the redemption.[28]

The subjective nature of Sec. 302(b)(1) makes "redemptions not equivalent to a dividend" a little-traveled road to sale treatment. Other than for an advance ruling, this approach is typically argued only when a redeeming shareholder has blundered into potential

---

[27]*Zenz v. Quenlivan*, 212 F.2d 914 (6th Cir. 1954) and *Cary*, 289 F.2d 531 (8th Cir. 1961).
[28]Rev. Rul. 75-502, 1975-2 C.B. 111; Rev. Rul. 75-512, 1975-2 C.B. 112; Rev. Rul. 76-364, 1976-2 C.B. 91; Rev. Rul. 76-385, 1976-2 C.B. 92.

property distribution treatment, and all other sale approaches appear inapplicable.

CONSTRUCTIVE OWNERSHIP OF STOCK   A common thread running through paragraphs (b)(1), (b)(2), and (b)(3) of Sec. 302 is some form of stock ownership test. Any shareholder ownership test that considers only direct ownership is subject to potential abuse when family or other relationships exist among shareholders. Congressional awareness of this general problem is reflected by a variety of constructive ownership provisions scattered throughout the Code. For this reason, it is always necessary to determine if any constructive ownership rules apply when stock ownership tests exist.[29]When testing stock redemptions under Secs. 302(b)(1), (b)(2), and (b)(3), it is Sec. 318 that provides rules that indicate when stock directly owned by others is to be attributed to (considered constructively owned by) a shareholder. In the discussion that follows, we shall first summarize the attribution rules of Sec. 318 and then describe their application to Sec. 302(b)(1), (b)(2), and (b)(3) stock redemptions.

Section 318: an overview.   Section 318 sets forth (1) four basic types of attribution and (2) certain operating rules.

1. *Members of family*. An individual constructively owns stock owned by his or her spouse, children, grandchildren, or parents.

2. *Attribution from entities to owners*. Stock owned by a partnership, estate, or trust is constructively owned by its partners or beneficiaries in relation to their proportionate interest in the partnership, estate, or trust.[30] Stock owned by a corporation is only attributed to a shareholder if the shareholder owns 50 percent or more in value of the stock of the corporation. The number of shares attributed to the shareholder is proportionate to the percentage of value of the stock that the shareholder owns.

Example: Assume A Corporation has 100 shares outstanding, 20 owned directly by Mr. Jones, 40 owned by X Corporation, and 40 by the unrelated Mr. Smith. Mr. Jones owns 60 percent of the value of X stock. Because Mr. Jones owns 50 percent or more in the value of X stock, he is considered to constructively own his proportionate interest of any stock owned by X. Mr. Jones therefore "owns"

a total of 44 shares of A Corporation, 20 directly and 24 (60 percent of 40) constructively.

3. *Attribution to entities from owners*. All the stock owned by a partner or beneficiary is constructively owned by the partnership, estate, or trust.[31] If 50 percent or more in value of the stock in a corporation is owned by a shareholder, such corporation constructively owns all stock in other corporations owned by such shareholder.

4. *Options*. Any person who has an option to acquire stock constructively owns such stock.

5. *Operating rules*. With two exceptions, stock that is constructively owned is considered to be actually owned and thus may be reattributed to others under the above procedures.

One exception applies to family attribution. Stock constructively owned by an individual because of family attribution may not be reattributed under family attribution rules from that individual.

Example: Assume grandfather (GF), son (S), and grandson (GS) own directly 50, 30, and 20 shares of X Corporation, respectively. Under the family attribution rules of Sec. 318, GF owns 100 shares of X (50 directly, 30 constructively from S, and 20 constructively from GS), S owns 100 shares (30 directly, 50 constructively from GF, S's father, and 20 from GS, S's son), and GS owns 50 shares (20 directly and 30 constructively from S, GS's father). GS does not constructively own any of GF's shares because the family attribution rules of Sec. 318 extend "upward" only one generation, not two. As indicated above, the 50 shares of GF's stock attributed to S under family attribution rules may not be reattributed under family attribution rules from S to GS.

The second exception to reattribution concerns stock constructively owned by partnerships, estates, trusts, and corporations under the attribution to entities from owners described above. Such stock may *not* be reattributed from the entity to another owner.

Example: Assume P Corporation is owned directly 50 percent by Ms. A and 50 percent by the unrelated Ms. B. A owns directly 100 shares of X Corporation. P constructively owns 100 shares of

[29]Constructive ownership rules generally apply only to an ownership test when made expressly applicable by Code reference or court decision.
[30]"Entity to owner" attribution does not apply to certain employees' trusts (Sec. 318(a)(2) (B)(i)).
[31]Exceptions exist for certain employees' trusts and trust beneficiaries that have only a "remote contingent interest" (Sec. 318(a)(3)(B)).

X under owner-to-entity attribution but none of these shares may be reattributed under entity-to-owner attribution to B.

The final "operating rule" of Sec. 318 provides that any stock that is constructively owned under both family attribution and option attribution is considered owned under the option attribution rules. Reconsider the preceding example concerning GF, S, and GS with the added assumption that S has an option to acquire GF's 50 shares of stock. Because S is considered to constructively own these 50 shares under option attribution and not family attribution, they may be reattributed from S to GS under family attribution. Under these revised assumptions, GS would own 100 shares of X (20 directly and 80 constructively from S). The 80 shares attributed to GS from S represent 30 owned directly by S and 50 constructively owned because of S's option to acquire them.

Sections 318 and 302(b)(2). The tests for determining whether a redemption is substantially disproportionate (Sec. 302(b)(2)) must include stock that is constructively owned under the rules of Sec. 318 as well as directly owned stock.

Example: X Corporation is owned by Father and Son (30 shares each), an unrelated individual, Jones (10 shares), and C Corporation (30 shares). All the stock of C is owned by Jones. X redeems all 10 shares owned by Jones and 20 shares owned by Father. The calculations based on *direct ownership* are shown below:

| | Before redemption | | | After redemption | | |
	No. of shares owned	Percentage ownership	No. of shares redeemed	No. of shares owned	Percentage ownership	80% of prior ownership percentage
Father	30	30	20	10	14	24
Son	30	30	—	30	43	N/A
Jones	10	10	10	0	0	8
C Corp.	30	30	—	30	43	N/A
Total	100 outstanding shares	—	30	70 outstanding shares	—	—

The above calculations would *incorrectly* indicate substantially disproportionate redemptions for both Father and Jones. The *correct calculations*, shown below, include both directly and constructively owned shares.

| | Before redemption | | | After redemption | | |
	No. of shares owned	Percentage ownership	No. of shares redeemed	No. of shares owned	Percentage ownership	80% of prior ownership percentage
Father	60	60	20	40	57	48
Son	60	60	—	40	57	N/A
Jones	40	40	10	30	43	32
C Corp.	40	40	—	30	43	N/A
Total	100 outstanding shares	—	30	70 outstanding shares	—	—

Because Father's ownership did not fall below 48 percent or Jones's below 32 percent, each must treat his entire proceeds as a property distribution.

One obvious implication of the above example is that aggregate share ownership may exceed the number of outstanding shares when both directly and constructively owned shares are counted. There is no prohibition against considering the same shares as being owned by more than one shareholder. It is important to understand, however, that a shareholder's percentage ownership is determined by dividing the number of such shareholder's direct and constructive shares by the actual number of outstanding shares.

The fact that the same shares may be considered to be owned by more than one shareholder does not mean that the same shares may be counted more than once for the same shareholder.

Example: Assume a husband, wife, and daughter each directly own 10 shares of a corporation, and the husband has an option to acquire the wife's 10 shares. The daughter is considered to own 30 shares (10 directly and 20 constructively). The 20 constructive shares may be determined in two ways—10 from each parent by family attribution or 20 from the father alone by family attribution. The father owns 10 directly and the other 10 through option from the mother. The two approaches may not be combined (10 from the mother and 20 from the father) to give the daughter 30 constructively owned shares. To do so would count her as owning 10 of the same shares twice.

Sections 318 and 302(b)(3). The constructive ownership rules of Sec. 318 generally apply in determining whether a redemption qualifies as a termination of a shareholder's interest under Sec. 302(b)(3). If no exceptions existed, the results could be quite harsh for family-owned corporations. For example, consider the situation in which a husband and wife each own one-half the stock of a corporation and the husband wishes to redeem all his stock. The redemption would not be substantially disproportionate under Sec. 302(b)(2)—the husband would be considered to own 100 percent of the stock both before and after redemption because of the application of Sec. 318.

In response to this problem, Sec. 302(c)(2) specifies conditions under which the *family* attribution rules of Sec. 318 will not apply in testing whether a redemption *terminates* a shareholder's interest. Note that this exception potentially can apply only if no direct ownership remains and all constructive ownership is through family attribution rules. The following three requirements must also be met:[32]

1. Immediately after the distribution, the redeemed shareholder has no interest in the corporation (including an interest as officer, director, or employee), other than an interest as a creditor. The regulations caution that if the redeemed shareholder remains a creditor, such claim must not in any sense be proprietary and must not be subordinate to the claims of general creditors.[33]

2. The redeemed shareholder does not acquire any such interest (other than stock acquired by bequest or inheritance) within 10 years from the date of the redemption.

3. The redeemed shareholder files an agreement with the Internal Revenue Service to notify the I.R.S. if a prohibited interest is acquired. The shareholder must also agree to an extended limitation period for possible reassessment and the retention of certain records.

Sections 318 and 302(b)(1). Section 302(b)(1), which prescribes sale treatment if a redemption is "not essentially equivalent to a dividend," makes no direct reference to the attribution rules of Sec. 318. The Supreme Court resolved this uncertainty in *Davis,* 397 U.S. 301 (1970). The Court specified that the constructive ownership rules of Sec. 318 were to be applied in determining whether a "meaningful" reduction in the redeeming shareholder's proportionate interest occurred.

REDEMPTION OF STOCK TO PAY DEATH TAXES Under specified conditions, Sec. 303 provides for sale treatment to the redeeming shareholder even though the redemption does not qualify as substantially disproportionate, a termination of interest, or not essentially equivalent to a dividend. Section 303 originated from Congressional concern that death taxes and funeral and administrative expenses of shareholders of closely held corporations would lead to the forced sales of many family businesses. The requirements and limitations of Sec. 303 are discussed below.

Relationship of stock to decedent's estate. Section 303 applies only if the redeemed stock was included in a decedent's gross estate (for federal estate tax purposes). It is further necessary that the aggregate value of the corporation's stock *included in the decedent's estate* (whether or not redeemed) exceeds 50 percent of the excess of the value of the gross estate over the sum of the expenses, indebtedness, taxes, and losses deductible under Secs. 2053 and 2054.[34] Stock of two or more corporations included in a decedent's estate may be combined to meet the "50 percent test" if the estate includes more than 75 percent in value of *all the outstanding stock* of such corporations.

The qualifying status of stock that meets the above requirements ("old stock") carries over to any "new stock" that has a basis determined by reference to such "old stock." Thus, stock received either as a nontaxable stock dividend or in a tax-free exchange or reorganization may qualify for Sec. 303 treatment as long as such treatment would have applied to the related "old stock."

---

[32] The requirements noted represent only a partial summary of Sec. 302(c)(2). The exceptions that modify these rules (and the exceptions to the exceptions!) are beyond the scope of this book.

[33] Treas. Reg. Sec. 1.302-4(d). For a case in which subordination was allowed, see *Est. of Lennard,* 61 T.C. 544 (1974).

[34] Sections 2053 and 2054 specify the expenses, indebtedness, taxes, and losses that are deductible from the gross estate to arrive at the taxable estate in the computation of a decedent's federal estate tax.

Relationship of shareholder to estate tax. By its terms, Sec. 303 is not limited to stock held by the estate of a decedent. Holders of stock distributed by an estate or given in contemplation of death by the decedent and included in the estate *may* also be eligible. For a shareholder in this group, however, redemption proceeds treated as a sale may not exceed the extent to which such shareholder's interest in the decedent's estate is directly reduced by the taxes and expenses described below.

Limitations on amount distributed as a redemption under Section 303. The amount that may be distributed in redemption of qualified stock and treated as sales proceeds under Sec. 303 may not exceed the sum of:

1. Taxes (estate, inheritance, legacy, and succession) imposed because of the shareholder's death, and
2. Funeral and administrative expenses deductible by the estate under Sec. 2053.

This is the aggregate limit on redemption proceeds that may receive sale treatment under Sec. 303. If more than one shareholder redeems qualified stock, the limit is "used up" chronologically. Redemption proceeds in excess of this limitation are treated as property distributions unless qualifying for sale treatment as substantially disproportionate, termination of interest, or not essentially equivalent to a dividend.

Time period for redemptions under Section 303. Redemptions of stock meeting all the Sec. 303 requirements will generally receive sale treatment if made any time within four years after the shareholder's death. The time period for qualifying a redemption under Sec. 303 may extend beyond four years if a deficiency in the estate tax is being reviewed by the Tax Court or the time period for collecting the estate tax has been extended under Sec. 6166 or 6166A (see Sec. 303(b)). Redemptions made more than four years after a decedent's death, which otherwise qualify under Sec. 303, may receive sale treatment only to the extent that taxes, funeral, and administrative expenses are actually paid during the one-year period following the redemption.

Other considerations. Even though the amount that may be redeemed under Sec. 303 is based on particular death taxes and expenses, there is no requirement that the proceeds be used for these purposes. In qualifying situations, a one-time opportunity may exist for sale treatment on redemptions that would otherwise be treated as property distributions.

The basis the estate or heirs take in the decedent's

stock is important to the significance of Sec. 303. If the basis is fair market value at death, and the stock is redeemed at the estate value, little or no income tax will arise from the redemption. For example, assume that all 100 shares of the stock of a corporation are included in the estate of a decedent; the decedent's basis was $100 per share, the estate's basis (fair market value at death) is $1,000 per share, and the corporation redeems 30 of the shares owned by the estate for $30,000. If Sec. 303 did not exist, the estate would possibly have to recognize $30,000 dividend income. If Sec. 303 applies, however, the redemption is treated as a sale, with no gain recognized by the estate ($30,000 amount realized, $30,000 basis). Although limited by the conditions of Sec. 303, this represents the ultimate in "bail outs"—a distribution of earnings and profits at no income tax cost while potentially giving up no underlying equity or control in the corporation. The necessary condition (death), however, is so final that few are likely to hasten its occurrence.

Other areas in which Sec. 303 may be important are (1) the gain a corporation may have to recognize when using appreciated property to redeem stock, and (2) the accumulated earnings tax. With regard to the first, gain on appreciated property used to redeem stock is generally not recognized by the distributing corporation if the redemption is treated by the shareholder under Sec. 303. In most redemption transactions, the distribution of appreciated property does cause gain to be recognized by the distributing corporation. With regard to the second, Sec. 303 redemption needs of the business are specified in Sec. 537 as one of the "reasonable needs of the business" and, thus, provide one possible defense against imposition of the accumulated earnings tax.

SALES OF STOCK TO RELATED CORPORATIONS (SECTION 304) If a shareholder of X Corporation sells some of his or her X stock to Y Corporation for cash or other property (of Y), the transaction has the form of a sale. It would appear that capital gain or loss on the sale of X stock should be recognized. If, however, the shareholder of X owns all the stock of both X and Y, or if X Corporation owns all the stock of Y Corporation, then it can readily be seen that the "sale" has not actually resulted in any reduction in the shareholder's underlying equity in the X–Y corporate group.

In order to guard against bail-outs of this type, Congress enacted Sec. 304. The basic thrust of Sec. 304 is that certain sales of stock to "related corporations" must be *recast as assumed redemptions.* In their recast form (as redemptions), the transactions are then tested to determine if they are to be treated by the shareholder as sales of stock or property distributions on stock. The "testing" procedure is the same as for other stock redemptions. Sale treatment will apply if, in its recast form, the redemption meets the requirements of a substantially disproportionate redemption (Sec. 302(b)(2)), a termination of interest (Sec. 302(b)(3)), not essentially equivalent to a dividend (Sec. 302(b)(1)), or to pay death taxes (Sec. 303).[35] If none of the preceding applies, the transaction is treated as a property distribution.

The operating rules of Sec. 304 distinguish between sales involving "brother–sister" corporations and "parent–subsidiary" corporations.

Sales to "brother–sister" corporations. If one or more persons sell stock in one corporation to another corporation and such person or persons control both corporations, the transaction is recast under the provisions of Sec. 304(a), which are illustrated in the following example.[36]

Example: Mr. A, who owns 55 of the 100 outstanding shares of X Corporation and 80 of the 100 outstanding shares of Y Corporation, sells 10 shares of X to Y for $10,000. A's basis in the 10 shares of X sold to Y is $1,000. The other shareholders of X and Y are unrelated to A.

The transaction is recast by first assuming A transfers the 10 shares of X to Y as a contribution to the capital of Y. Next, it is assumed that Y issues its own stock to A and then immediately redeems such stock from A for $10,000. The stock of Y that is assumed to be redeemed has a basis to A of $1,000, that is, A's basis in the X stock actually sold to Y.

Recast as a redemption of Y stock, this transaction does not qualify for sale treatment under either Sec. 302 or 303. It is important to understand that in testing for sale treatment under Sec. 302, A's ownership in *X* must be examined because X stock was actually sold. A owned 55 percent (55/100) of X before the transaction and 53 percent [(45 + 8)/100] afterwards. Thus, A must recognize $10,000 dividend income (assuming *Y*

has adequate E & P) and will increase A's basis in the 80 shares of Y by $1,000.

Sales of parent stock to subsidiary. Section 304(b) applies when a shareholder of a parent corporation sells stock of the parent to a subsidiary of the parent corporation. These provisions become operative if the parent owns 50 percent or more of the value or voting power of the subsidiary's stock and a shareholder of the parent sells stock in the parent to the subsidiary.[37] Observe that it is *not* necessary for the shareholder to "control" the parent.

Sales of stock to a subsidiary are recast as redemptions, as illustrated in the following example.

Example: Ms. B owns 70 of 100 outstanding shares of P Corporation. The other shareholders of P are unrelated to B. P owns 100 percent of S Corporation. Ms. B sells 30 shares of P (basis to B of $5,000) to S for $20,000.

It is first assumed that S distributes $20,000 to P. If S has at least $20,000 of E & P, this "deemed" property distribution increases P's E & P by $20,000. (Although the deemed property distribution from S to P may increase P's E & P, it does not trigger recognition of dividend income *by P*.) It is next assumed that P directly redeems its 30 shares of stock from B for $20,000.

Recast as a redemption of P stock, this transaction does not qualify for sale treatment under either Sec. 302 or 303. Note that B owned 70 percent (70/100) of P before the transaction and 52 percent [(40 + 12)/100] afterwards. (The 12 constructively owned shares represent the 30 shares held by S that are first attributed to P and then 40 percent of which are attributed to B.) Thus, B must recognize $20,000 dividend income (assuming *P* has adequate E & P) and will increase her basis in her remaining 40 shares of P by $5,000.

BASIS CONSIDERATIONS   In the preceding discussion of stock redemptions, we have indicated two possible shareholder treatments, namely, (a) sale or (b) property distribution. The basis of any noncash property received by a shareholder in redemption of stock will depend on which treatment is applied to the shareholder. If the redemption is treated as a sale under Sec. 302 or Sec. 303, the shareholder's basis in the property

[35]The only variation required by Sec. 304 for testing the transaction under Sec. 302(b)(1), (2) or (3) is that the owner-to-corporation and corporation-to-owner attribution rules of Sec. 318 are applied without regard to the 50 percent limitations contained in Sec. 318. Thus, for this purpose, a corporation owns all stock owned by its shareholders and shareholders own their percentage of any stock owned by the corporation.

[36]"Control" is defined in Sec. 304(c)(1) as at least 50 percent of total combined voting power or value of shares of all classes of stock. Section 318, modified as indicated in footnote 35, applies in determining if control exists.

[37]The modified attribution rules of Sec. 318 that were noted above also apply to this 50 percent "control" test.

received will be the fair market value of such property when distributed in redemption of the stock (Sec. 1012).

If the redemption does not qualify for sale treatment, it is treated as a property distribution under Sec. 301. In such cases, the shareholder's basis in the property received is determined under the rules discussed in connection with property distributions. These rules are summarized on page 5/6. Note that the basis of property received by a corporate shareholder may be affected by gain recognized by the distributing corporation.

The holding period of property received in a stock redemption generally begins with the date the property is distributed. In the case of a corporate shareholder that receives redemption proceeds treated as a property distribution, the "date basis" of the distributing corporation carries over if its cost basis also carries over.

In addition to the basis of property received in a redemption, issues arise with respect to proper treatment of the basis of the stock redeemed. If the redemption is treated as a sale, the basis of the redeemed stock is offset against the sales price to determine the (usually capital) gain or loss.

If a redemption is treated as a property distribution, the shareholder's basis in the redeemed stock disappears. This does not mean such basis is "lost." Treas. Reg. Sec. 1.302-2(c) indicates that "proper adjustment of the basis of the remaining stock will be made with respect to the stock redeemed." The examples that follow this rather vague statement imply:

1. If the redeemed shareholder retains *any* direct ownership of stock, the entire unrecovered basis of the redeemed stock is added to the basis of the retained stock.

2. If the redeemed shareholder retains no direct ownership, the entire unrecovered basis of the redeemed stock is added to the basis of the stock whose constructive ownership caused the shareholder to receive property distribution treatment. (In this situation, the redeemed shareholder has actually "lost" basis but it is picked up by a "related" shareholder.)

Tax treatment to the distributing corporation

Section 311 provides a general rule that a corporation recognizes no gain or loss on a distribution of property to shareholders with respect to their stock. Exceptions were noted earlier for installment obligations, LIFO inventory, liabilities in excess of basis, and recapture provisions.

It is now necessary to add one additional exception. Section 311(d), added by the Tax Reform Act of 1969, generally provides that *gain* will be recognized by a corporation if it distributes appreciated property (other than an obligation of such corporation) to redeem stock.[38] The gain that must be recognized is any excess of the distributed property's fair market value (on the date distributed) over such property's basis to the distributing corporation.

The "character" of any recognized gain (capital, ordinary, or Sec. 1231) is determined by the corporation's use of the property.[39]

It is extremely important to recognize that Sec. 311(d) is not contingent on the redemption being treated as a sale by the shareholder. The "general rule" of Sec. 311(d) (income recognition on appreciated property) applies to all actual redemptions as well as "deemed" redemptions under Sec. 304, regardless of whether the shareholder treats the redemption as a sale or a property distribution.

Section 311(d)(2) describes seven situations in which the general rule of Sec. 311(d) does not apply. In these seven cases, the distributing corporation will recognize gain or loss only to the extent that the previously discussed rules concerning installment obligations, LIFO inventory, liabilities in excess of basis, or recapture would apply. The three exceptions to Sec. 311(d) of most general interest are:

1. A distribution that terminates the interest of a shareholder who has owned at least 10 percent in value of the corporation's stock for the entire 12-month period ending with the date of distribution. (For this purpose it is not necessary that the terminated shareholder not acquire any interest in the corporation within 10 years after distribution.)

2. A distribution of the stock or obligation of another corporation that is engaged in at least one trade or business if the distributing corporation has owned at least 50 percent in value of such corporation's stock any time within the nine-year period ending one year before the date of distribution. (This exception only applies if a substantial part of the assets of the corporation whose stock or obligation is distributed has *not* been acquired within five years from the distributing corporation in a Sec. 351 or capital contribution transaction.)

---

[38]Section 311(d) does not apply to partial or complete liquidations (Chapter 6) or corporate divisions or reorganizations (Chapter 7).

[39]The potential overlap between Secs. 311(b) (LIFO inventory) and 311(c) (liability in excess of basis) and Sec. 311(d) is resolved by providing priority to the broader Sec. 311(d) when it applies.

3. A distribution to the extent that Sec. 303(a) (relating to distributions in redemption of stock to pay death taxes) applies to such distribution.

EFFECT OF STOCK REDEMPTIONS ON EARNINGS AND PROFITS   Stock redemptions may have two basic effects on earnings and profits of the redeeming corporation. First, to the extent that gain or loss is *recognized* by the distributing corporation, earnings and profits are also increased or decreased. The potential for income recognition is discussed above.

The second effect that redemptions may have on earnings and profits concerns how much earnings and profits are to be reduced because of the redemption. The amount of the reduction will directly affect the maximum extent to which subsequent property distributions may be considered dividends.

The reduction in earnings and profits due to a redemption depends on how the redemption is treated by the shareholder. If the redemption is treated as a property distribution (by the shareholder) because none of the sale provisions of Sec. 302 or 303 apply, earnings and profits are reduced according to the rules for property distributions. (These rules were illustrated in Table 5-2 on page **5**/8 and the related discussion on pages **5**/7–**5**/9.)

If the redemption is treated by the shareholder as a sale of the redeemed stock under Sec. 302 or 303, the amount of the earnings and profits reduction depends on the interpretation of Sec. 312(e). This subsection indicates that the portion of the distribution that is "properly" chargeable to the corporation's capital account shall not reduce earnings and profits. The basic idea of Sec. 312(e) is clear—for redemptions treated as sales by the shareholder, the reduction computed according to the rules illustrated in Table 5-2 first reduces the corporation's capital account. The excess, if any, reduces earnings and profits. Differences between the I.R.S. and the Tax Court over the definition of a corporation's "capital account" and procedures for determining what is "properly" chargeable have only recently been resolved.

In Rev. Rul. 79-376, IRB 47, 6, the I.R.S. acquiesced to the approach originally developed by the Tax Court in *Jarvis*, 43 B.T.A. 439 (1941) affirmed 123 F.2d 742 (4th Cir. 1941).[40] There now appears to be agreement that the capital account represents only amounts paid in to a corporation for its stock (at the adjusted basis for federal income tax purposes). Further, the portion of the distribution that is "properly" chargeable to the capital account is the redeemed stock's ratable share of the capital account.

Example: Smith and Jones form a corporation, to which Smith contributes $75,000 (and receives 75 shares) and Jones contributes $25,000 (and receives 25 shares). At a later date, when E & P of the corporation are $110,000, all 25 of Jones's shares are redeemed by the corporation for $120,000. The redemption qualifies as a termination of Jones's interest, and Jones therefore recognizes a $95,000 ($120,000 − $25,000) capital gain.

The amount properly chargeable to the capital account is $25,000 (25/100 × $100,000). The reduction in E & P is $95,000, that is, the portion of the distribution not chargeable to the capital account ($120,000 − $25,000). Thus, the corporation's E & P after the redemption will be $15,000 ($110,000 − $95,000).

The reduction in E & P due to stock redemptions is only significant to shareholders remaining after the redemption. In the preceding example, Jones will recognize a capital gain of $95,000, regardless of the specific rules applied to reduce E & P. For Smith, however, the maximum extent to which subsequent property distributions may be considered dividends has been permanently reduced by $95,000.

[40]See Rev. Rul. 70-531, 1970-2 C.B. 76 for the I.R.S.'s position before Rev. Rul. 79-376.

PROBLEMS

1. Give examples of some situations involving nonliquidating distributions in which a precise calculation of earnings and profits is necessary.
2. Under what conditions might a shareholder prefer that a stock redemption be treated as a property distribution under Sec. 301 rather than as a sale under Sec. 302? Under what conditions might the redeeming shareholder be indifferent to whether Sec. 301 or Sec. 302 applied?

3. Upon receipt of a property distribution, to what extent do individual and corporate shareholders apply different rules in calculating the amount distributed? Explain why any such differences exist.

4. In what situations does a distributing corporation recognize income, gain, or loss when property is distributed to shareholders and no stock is redeemed? When property is distributed in redemption of stock?

5. What effect do property distributions have on the distributing corporation's earnings and profits?

6. What effect do stock redemptions (treated as sales by the redeeming shareholders) have on the redeeming corporation's E & P?

7. Explain why the retained earnings of a corporation with a history of distributing nontaxable stock dividends would likely be a grossly inaccurate approximation of the corporation's E & P.

8. Most sales of stock have the potential effect of "bailing-out" earnings and profits at capital gains rates. Explain why this bail-out is generally not permitted if the stock is Sec. 306 stock but generally is allowed if it is not Sec. 306 stock.

9. As part of the formation of X Corporation, Jones transfers $20,000 cash to X in exchange for 100 shares of X common stock and 100 shares of X preferred stock. Is the preferred stock Sec. 306 stock?

10. X Corporation redeems 100 of its shares owned by A. Identify the four "paths" to sale treatment that are described in this chapter, and for each "path," indicate additional facts that would allow A to meet its requirements. How does A treat the redemption if it does not qualify for sale treatment?

11. Explain why the constructive ownership rules of Sec. 318 are necessary to prevent potential abuse of the sale treatment available to redeeming shareholders under Sec. 302(b)(1), (b)(2), and (b)(3).

12. Explain why a redemption qualifying under Sec. 303 might be attractive to an estate holding all the stock of a corporation, even though the estate already possessed sufficient cash to pay death taxes and funeral and administrative expenses.

13. What is the effect on the "amount distributed" to a shareholder if, as part of a property distribution, the shareholder assumes liabilities? What is the effect of such liabilities on the shareholder's basis in the property received?

14. For each of the following general categories of adjustments necessary to convert taxable income to E & P, identify specific examples and indicate the "direction" (add or subtract) of the adjustment to taxable income:
    a. Income excluded in the computation of taxable income
    b. Losses and expenses that must be carried over in the computation of taxable income
    c. Losses and expenses permanently disallowed in the computation of taxable income
    d. "Artificial" deductions used in the computation of taxable income
    e. Accounting procedures required in the computation of E & P when a different procedure is used in computing taxable income

15. For 19X8, XYZ Corporation has a taxable income of $60,000. Included in the $60,000 taxable income are depreciation deductions (declining-balance method) of $13,000 on machine No. 1 and $1,000 on machine No. 2 and a $4,000 gain on the sale of machine No. 2 on June 30, 19X8. Straight-line depreciation for 19X8 would have been $5,000 on machine No. 1 (full year) and $2,000 on machine No. 2 (half year). Machine No. 2, which was sold for $7,000 on June 30, 19X8, originally cost $20,000, and as of December 31, 19X7, a total of $16,000 declining-balance depreciation had been deducted. Straight-line depreciation for the period

from purchase to December 31, 19X7 would have been $12,000. Compute XYZ's E & P for the year 19X8.

16. Determine the amount and character of gain or loss recognized by the distributing corporation in each of the following cases:

a. XYZ Corporation has two equal shareholders, John Jones and ABC Corporation. Land No. 1 (FMV = $40,000, basis = $10,000), which was used in XYZ's business for three years, is distributed to Jones, who takes the property subject to (but does not assume) an existing mortgage of $20,000. Land No. 2 (FMV = $5,000, basis = $25,000), which has been held as an investment by XYZ for the last two years, is distributed to ABC, which assumes XYZ's existing mortgage of $30,000.

b. Same as part a, except that Land No. 2 (received by ABC) has a FMV of $20,000, basis equal to $15,000, and no mortgage.

c. Same as part a, except that the mortgage on Land No. 1 is $50,000 and on Land No. 2 is $60,000.

d. MNO Corporation sells for $100,000 a building (adjusted basis of $20,000 after straight-line depreciation), which has been used in its business for eight years. MNO receives the buyer's 9 percent note for $100,000 and elects installment sales treatment. Before any principal collections are received, and at a time the fair market value of the note is $95,000, MNO distributes the $100,000 face value note to its sole shareholder, Smith.

e. DEF Corporation distributes a machine to its sole shareholder. The machine cost $15,000, and $10,000 of straight-line depreciation had been claimed. At distribution the machine was worth $8,000.

f. Same as part e, except that the machine is worth $3,000.

17. The stock of X, a corporation with substantial E & P, is owned 60 percent (60 shares) by A and 40 percent (40 shares) by B. A and B each have a basis in their X stock of $100 per share. On January 15, 19X3, X redeems 25 of A's shares for $200 per share. On August 15, 19X3, X redeems 20 of B's shares, also for $200 per share. How should the January 15, 19X3 redemption be treated by A? How should the August 15, 19X3 redemption be treated by B?

18. A is the sole shareholder of XYZ, a corporation with E & P in excess of $250,000. For each of the following independent situations, determine (1) the amount and character of income or gain recognized by A, (2) A's basis in any noncash property received, (3) the amount and character of income or gain recognized by XYZ, and (4) the effect of the distribution on XYZ's E & P. Assume A is an individual unless otherwise indicated.

a. XYZ distributes its check for $100,000 to A.

b. XYZ distributes unimproved realty with a fair market value of $100,000 and a basis to XYZ of $40,000 to A.

c. Same as part b except that A is a corporation.

d. Same as part b except that A takes the realty subject to XYZ's mortgage of $30,000.

e. XYZ distributes machinery worth $100,000 to A. XYZ's basis in the machinery is $85,000, and $60,000 of depreciation had been taken on it since it was acquired by XYZ.

19. B, an individual, is the sole shareholder of XYZ, a corporation with E & P in excess of $250,000. For each of the following independent situations, determine (1) the amount and character of income or gain recognized by B, (2) B's basis in any noncash property received, (3) the amount and character of income or gain recognized by XYZ, and (4) the effect of the distribution on XYZ's E & P.

a. XYZ distributes 100 shares of IBM stock with a fair market value of $10,000 and a basis to XYZ of $8,000 to B.

b. XYZ distributes its own 10-year 12 percent promissory note to B. The principal amount of the note is $100,000 and its current fair market value is $90,000.

c. XYZ distributes unimproved realty with a fair market value of $150,000 and a basis to XYZ of $60,000 to B. B assumes XYZ's mortgage of $90,000.

d. XYZ distributes to B FIFO inventory with a fair market value of $30,000 and a basis to XYZ of $20,000.

20. All the common stock of MNO, a corporation with substantial E & P, is owned equally by A and B. Unless otherwise indicated, assume no other class of MNO stock is outstanding. For each of the following independent situations, indicate whether or not A or B or both will recognize dividend income. If any dividend income is recognized, indicate the amount or how such amount would be calculated.

a. XYZ authorizes a new class of nonvoting, nonparticipating preferred stock and distributes these shares to A. XYZ distributes additional shares of the common stock to B.

b. Same as part a except that XYZ distributes the preferred stock equally to A and B but does not distribute any additional common stock.

c. Same as part b except that XYZ distributes 25 shares of preferred stock to A and only 15 shares to B.

d. XYZ distributes 50 shares of IBM stock to A and 50 shares of IBM stock to B.

e. XYZ declares a 1 for 5 stock dividend as its common. Each shareholder has the right to accept $25 per 5 shares in lieu of the stock dividend. A and B both elect to take the stock dividend.

f. XYZ distributes 50 shares of IBM stock to A (FMV = $10,000) and 100 shares of XYZ common to B (FMV = $10,000).

g. XYZ has two classes of stock outstanding. One is common stock, which is owned equally by A and B. The other is nonparticipating, nonvoting preferred stock. The preferred, however, may be converted into common at a 1 for 1 rate. XYZ distributes a 25 percent stock dividend on the common.

21. A owns all 100 shares of the outstanding common stock of XYZ Corporation. A purchased her XYZ stock in 19X1 for $120 per share. On December 15, 19X7, XYZ distributes XYZ common stock as a 20 percent (nontaxable) stock dividend. Immediately before the distribution, the fair market value of the XYZ common stock was $480 per share, while immediately after the distribution, the value was $400 per share. On June 30, 19X8, A sells 10 of the shares received on December 15, 19X7, for a total of $4,400. What amount and character of gain or loss is recognized by A on the June 30, 19X8 sale?

22. On June 15, 19X5, DEF Corporation distributed nontaxable stock rights to its common stock shareholders. Shareholder B received 100 rights. For every two rights, B was entitled to purchase one additional share of DEF common for $135. Immediately after the issuance of the rights, DEF common stock had a fair market value of $180 per share and the rights had a fair market value of $20 each. The 100 rights were distributed to B because of his ownership of 100 shares of DEF common stock purchased January 30, 19X2 for $100 per share. On June 30, 19X5, B exercised 50 of the rights and acquired 25 additional shares of DEF common. These 25 shares were sold by B on July 15, 19X5 for $190 per share. On August 15, 19X5, B sold 40 of the rights for $25 per right. The remaining 10 rights lapsed on December 1, 19X5. What amount and character of gain or loss is recognized by B in 19X5 because of these events?

23. A purchased all 100 shares of the outstanding common stock of MNO Corporation in 19X2 for $20,000. On December 31, 19X8, MNO distributed 50 shares of its preferred stock to A as a stock dividend on A's common stock. Immediately after the distribution, the fair market value of the 50 shares of preferred stock and the 100 shares of common stock were $40,000 and $60,000, respectively. MNO's accumulated E & P at December 31, 19X8 was $25,000. On December 31, 19X9, A sold the 50 shares of preferred stock to an unrelated third party for $38,000. MNO's accumulated E & P at December 31, 19X9 was $45,000.
    a. What are the tax consequences to A and to MNO in 19X8 and 19X9?
    b. What would be the tax consequences to A and to MNO in 19X8 and 19X9 if, instead of the sale, MNO redeemed the preferred stock on December 31, 19X9 for $38,000?

24. XYZ Corporation has 100 shares of stock outstanding. It is contemplating a redemption of some of its stock. Considering both direct and Sec. 318 constructive ownership, determine the percent of XYZ stock owned by each shareholder in the following situations:
    a. AA, BB, and CC directly own 50, 30, and 20 shares, respectively. AA, BB, and CC are unrelated individuals.
    b. AA, BB, CC, and DD indirectly own 50, 30, 10, and 10 shares, respectively. AA and BB are husband and wife. CC is their child, and DD is AA's grandparent.
    c. AA directly owns 20 shares and BB Corporation directly owns 80 shares. AA directly owns 100 percent of BB Corporation.
    d. Same facts as part c, above, except that AA directly owns only 10 shares, and CC, his son, directly owns the other 10.
    e. AA directly owns 20 shares. BB Corporation directly owns 70 shares. CC, who is unrelated to AA, directly owns the remaining 10. AA directly owns 60 percent of the BB stock, while CC directly owns 40 percent.

25. AA and BB (unrelated individuals) are shareholders of XYZ Corporation. XYZ has one class of stock and has 100 shares outstanding. AA owns 60 shares and BB owns 40 shares. AA's basis in the 60 shares of XYZ is $10,000. XYZ redeems 30 shares of AA's stock for $500 per share. XYZ's E & P is greater than $50,000.
    a. What are the tax consequences to AA?
    b. Assume all the above facts except that XYZ redeems 20 shares of AA's stock. What are the tax consequences to AA?

26. AA and BB (unrelated individuals) and CC Corporation are shareholders of XYZ Corporation. XYZ has 100 shares of stock outstanding. AA and BB own 40 shares each, while CC Corporation owns the remaining 20. CC Corporation is owned by AA and BB. AA owns 60 percent of CC Corporation's stock, while BB owns the remaining 40 percent. XYZ redeems all of BB's stock in 19X1 for $60,000. XYZ's accumulated E & P is in excess of $100,000 at the time of distribution. AA's basis in the stock redeemed is $30,000. What are the tax consequences to BB?

27. XYZ Corporation has 200 shares of stock outstanding. AA and BB both own 90 shares. The remaining 20 shares are owned by MM Corporation, whose shareholders are CC and AA. AA and CC each own 50 percent of MM's stock. AA, BB, and CC are unrelated individuals. XYZ redeems 30 shares of AA's stock (basis, $10,000) for $1,000 per share. XYZ's E & P is in excess of $100,000. What are the tax consequences to AA?

28. XYZ Corporation distributes land that was purchased five years earlier and that has been held as an investment (basis, $10,000; fair market value, $20,000) to one of its shareholders. Indicate the amount, if any, and character of gain or loss XYZ would recognize, assuming the following.

a. The land is distributed in redemption of some of the shareholder's stock, and the redemption qualifies as substantially disproportionate under Sec. 302(b)(2).

b. The land is distributed in redemption of some of the shareholder's stock and the redemption qualifies under Sec. 303 (redemption of stock to pay death taxes).

c. The land is distributed in redemption of all of the shareholder's stock and the redemption qualifies as a termination of the shareholder's interest under Sec. 302(b)(3). The shareholder owned 40 percent of XYZ's stock for the last seven years.

d. The land is distributed in redemption of some of the shareholder's stock but does not qualify the shareholder for sale treatment under Sec. 302 or 303.

e. The land is distributed to the shareholder as a dividend; no stock is redeemed.

29. AA was the sole shareholder of XYZ Corporation when he died in 19X1. The total value of his 100 shares of XYZ stock ($100,000) was included in his gross estate. AA's gross estate was equal to $200,000. AA's will directed XYZ to redeem 50 percent of the stock from the estate for $50,000. Total estate and inheritance taxes on AA's estate amounted to $15,000. Another $10,000 was allowed as funeral and administration expenses, which were deductible against the gross estate under Sec. 2053. XYZ redeems the 50 shares from AA's estate in 19X2. Assume that XYZ's E & P is in excess of $60,000 and that the estate's basis in the XYZ stock is $1,000 per share. Determine the tax consequences of the redemption to AA's estate.

30. A and B organized DEF Corporation in 19X1; each contributed $50,000 in exchange for 50 shares of DEF common stock. In 19X8, when its E & P was $70,000, DEF redeemed 40 of A's shares for $90,000. What effect does the redemption have on DEF's E & P if:

a. A and B are husband and wife.

b. A and B are unrelated individuals.

31. Individual A owns 120 of the 200 outstanding shares of P Corporation. P owns 100 percent of S Corporation. A sells 30 shares of P (basis, $20,000) to S for $80,000. Without regard to this transaction, S's E & P is $100,000 and P's E & P is zero. What are the tax consequences to A, P, and S?

32. The 100 outstanding shares of X Corporation are owned by A (40), B (20), and C Corporation (40). A and B are unrelated individuals. C is owned 40 percent by A and 60 percent by B. A and B also own all the stock of Y Corporation—70 percent by A and 30 percent by B. Assume the E & P of X is $100,000 and that of Y is $30,000. A sells 20 shares of X stock (basis, $10,000) to Y for $50,000.

a. What are the tax consequences of the sale to A?

b. Assume that B sells 10 shares of X stock (basis, $5,000) to Y for $25,000 and that A does *not* sell any X stock. What are the tax consequences of the sale to B?

SUPPLEMENTAL PROBLEMS

33. For each of the following independent situations, determine how much of the amount distributed would be recognized as dividend income. Assume all the stock of the distributing corporation is owned by one shareholder, and one distribution takes place during 19X9.

	19X9 current E & P	Accum. E & P at begin. of 19X9	Amount distributed	Date distributed
a.	$2,000	$3,000	$1,000	Jan. 15
b.	2,000	3,000	4,000	Jan. 15
c.	2,000	3,000	6,000	Jan. 15
d.	2,000	(4,000)	1,000	Jan. 15
e.	2,000	(4,000)	3,000	Jan. 15
f.	(2,000)	(4,000)	3,000	April 1
g.	(2,000)	4,000	1,000	April 1
h.	(2,000)	4,000	4,000	July 1

Research aids: Rev. Rul. 74-164, 1974-1 CB 74
Treas. Reg. Sec. 1.316-2 (b)

34. The following information applies to X Corporation, which has 100 shares outstanding:

Accumulated E & P, beginning of year	$15,000
Current year E & P	$9,000

Stock ownership:
   Ms. A—50 shares for entire year
   Mr. B—50 shares Jan. 1–March 31
   Mr. C—50 shares April 1–Dec. 31
Distributions:
   Feb. 15—$5,000 to Ms. A
        5,000 to Mr. B
   Aug. 15—$10,000 to Ms. A
        10,000 to Mr. C

What amount of dividend income is recognized by A, B, and C?
Research aid: Treas. Reg. Sec. 1.316-2(b)

35. ABC, a calendar-year, accrual basis corporation, has accumulated earnings and profits of $20,000 at January 1, 19X6 and current 19X6 earnings and profits of $14,000 before considering property distributions to shareholders. X Corporation purchased all the stock to ABC in 19X3 for $75,000 and sold its entire ownership in ABC to Mr. Jones on June 15, 19X6 for $200,000. ABC made two nonliquidating distributions during 19X6. On January 15, 19X6, a machine that had been used in ABC's business for five years was distributed to X Corporation. The machine cost ABC $25,000, was worth $50,000 on January 15, 19X6, and has been subject to $20,000 straight-line depreciation. On October 1, 19X6, land that had been purchased six months earlier for $45,000 was distributed to Jones. The fair market value of this land on October 1, 19X6 was $65,000. Jones assumed ABC's mortgage of $15,000. Determine the:
   a. effect of the distributions on ABC's 19X6 taxable income.
   b. effect of the distributions on ABC's 19X6 current E & P.
   c. treatment of the distributions by the shareholders.
   d. shareholders' cost and date basis in the property received.
   e. effect of the distributions on ABC's January 1, 19X7 accumulated E & P.
Research aid: Treas. Reg. Sec. 1.316-2(b)

36. The following information applies to Y Corporation, which has 50 shares of common and 50 shares of preferred stock outstanding:

Accum. E & P, beginning of year	$ -0-
Current year E & P	10,000

Stock ownership:
   Ms. A—50 shares common

Mr. B—50 shares preferred

Distributions:

June 30—$6,000 to Ms. A

6,000 to Mr. B

What amount of dividend income is recognized by A? by B?

Research aid: Rev. Rul. 69-440, 1969-2 CB 46

37. A owns three shares of stock in XYZ Corporation, two of common and one of preferred. XYZ distributes $500 cash per share to each holder of common stock. Assume that only $200 of the $1,000 received by A is considered to come out of the E & P of XYZ and A's stock basis is:

Common No. 1	$300
Common No. 2	600
Preferred No. 1	400

What amount and character of income, gain, and/or loss is recognized by A, and what is A's basis, after the distribution, in Common No. 1, Common No. 2, and Preferred No. 1?

Research aids: *Wm H. Kinch,* ¶42, 613 P-H Memo T.C. (1942)

Johnson, 435 F.2d 1257 (4th Cir. 1971)

38. In 19X1, X Corporation was organized by the unrelated A (40 percent of X stock for $20,000) and B (60 percent of X stock for $30,000.) X's accumulated E & P at December 31, 19X7 was $10,000. Current E & P for 19X8, before considering redemptions and distributions to shareholders, was $20,000. On March 15, 19X8, X redeemed all of A's stock for $50,000 and on June 15, 19X8, X distributed $25,000 to B. What amount and character of income, gain, or loss is recognized by A and B? What is X's accumulated E & P at December 31, 19X8?

Research aids: *Baker,* 460 F.2d 827 (8th Cir. 1972)

Rev. Rul. 74-338, 1974-2 CB 101

Rev. Rul. 74-339, 1974-2 CB 103

Rev. Rul. 79-376, IRB 47, 6

39. All the stock of MNO, a corporation with substantial E & P, is owned by A. B is interested in purchasing all the MNO stock but believes MNO currently holds more cash than is necessary to operate its business. B insists that A get the excess cash out of MNO before the purchase takes place. A plan is worked out under which part of A's stock is redeemed for the excess cash, and a month later all of A's remaining MNO stock is sold to B. What tax treatment does A receive on the redemption? Would the tax treatment be different if A first sold part of the MNO stock to B and then redeemed the rest for the excess cash? Why might A want to structure the transactions differently if A were a corporation? Why would B not want to purchase MNO with all its assets and then redeem part of its MNO stock for the excess cash?

Research aids: *Zenz* v. *Quinlivan,* 213 F.2d 914 (6th Cir. 1954)

Rev. Rul. 55-745, 1955-2 CB 223

Carey, 289 F.2d 531 (8th Cir. 1961)

40. Three sisters, Sarah, Sally, and Sue, each own one-third of the outstanding stock of X Corporation. All of Sarah's stock, which has a basis to her of $30,000, is redeemed for $20,000. After the redemption, Sarah continues to be employed by X on a full-time basis at a substantial salary. Although it has recently operated at a loss, X's accumulated E & P is substantial. What amount of income, gain, or loss is recognized by Sarah on the redemption? What gain or loss is recognized by X, if eight years later the stock redeemed from Sarah is reissued for $40,000?

Research aids: Secs. 302, 267, 1032

McCarthy v. *Conley, Jr.,* 341 F.2d 948 (2nd Cir. 1965)

Rev. Rul. 57-387, 1957-2 CB 225

41. The following transactions took place between Mr. Jones and ABC, a corporation with substantial E & P and owned 60 percent by Mr. Jones.
    a. ABC sold land with a basis to ABC of $10,000 and a fair market value of $22,000 to Jones for $15,000.
    b. ABC leased equipment to Jones for $3,000. Similar equipment was also leased to regular (nonshareholder) customers for $7,000.
    c. ABC made an interest-free loan of $50,000 to Jones. A "fair" rate of interest would have been 15 percent. Jones repaid the $50,000 12 months later as scheduled in the loan agreement.

    For each transaction, discuss the tax treatment to Jones.

    > Research aids: Treas. Reg. Sec. 1.301-1(j)
    > Rev. Rul. 58-1, 1958-1 CB 173
    > *J. Simpson Dean,* 35 TC 1083 (1961)

42. Individual A owns all the stock of X and Y corporations. A transfers all her X stock to Y in exchange for additional shares of Y and $20,000 cash. Explain why the transaction appears to meet the requirements of both Secs. 351 and 304. Which section has priority? Why is the question of priority important?

    > Research aids: *Haserot,* 41 TC 562 (1964), 355 F.2d 200 (6th Cir. 1965), 46 TC 864 (1966), sub nom. *Stickney,* 399 F.2d 828 (6th Cir. 1968)
    > Rev. Rul. 73-2, 1973-1 CB 171
    > Rev. Rul. 78-422, 1978-2 CB 129
    > *Rose Ann Coates Trust,* 480 F.2d 468 (9th Cir. 1973), cert. denied, 414 US 1045 (1973)

43. Smith is the sole shareholder and primary employee of X, a corporation with substantial E & P. X pays Smith a $100,000 salary in the current year. A comparable amount of compensation would have been necessary to employ someone else with Smith's skills to take over his various employment responsibilities. X has paid no dividends since its formation by Smith 10 years ago. Is it possible that part of the $100,000 could be treated as a property distribution, taxable to Smith, under Sec. 301?

    > Research aids: *McCandless Tile,* 422 F.2d 1336 (Ct.Cl. 1970)
    > *Nor-Cal Adjusters,* 503 F.2d 359 (9th Cir. 1974)
    > *Laure,* 20 TC 97 (1978)
    > Rev. Rul. 79-8, 1979-1 CB 92

44. ABC Corporation is owned 40 percent by Jones, Sr. and 60 percent by his adult son, Jones, Jr. Jones, Sr. and Jones, Jr. have had personal differences in the past and, in fact, have not spoken to each other for a number of years. ABC redeems 200 of the 400 shares of ABC owned by Jones, Sr. Does Jones, Sr. qualify for sale treatment under Sec. 302(b)(2)? Sec. 302(b)(1)?

    > Research aids: Treas. Reg. Secs. 1.302-2 and 1.302-3
    > *Robin Haft Trust,* 510 F.2d 43 (1st Cir. 1975)
    > *Niedermeyer,* 62 TC 280 (1974)
    > Rev. Rul. 77-218, 1977-1 CB 81

45. A father and a trust own all the stock of a corporation. The father's daughter is the sole beneficiary of the trust. The corporation redeems all of its stock owned by the trust. Is the redemption "substantially disproportionate"? May the family attribution rules of Sec. 318(a)(1) be waived so that the trust will qualify for sale treatment under Sec. 302(b)(3)?

    > Research aids: Rev. Rul. 59-233, 1959-2 CB 106
    > Rev. Rul. 72-472, 1972-2 CB 202
    > *Crawford,* 59 TC 830 (1973)
    > *Rickey,* 427 F.Supp. 484 (W.C. La. 1977)
    > *Robin Haft Trust,* 62 TC 145 (1974)

corporations: distributions in partial and complete liquidations

In this chapter, the same basic questions that were raised in connection with nonliquidating distributions will be examined with regard to partial and complete liquidations:

1. Does the shareholder recognize any income, gain, or loss?
2. What is the tax character of the income, gain, or loss recognized by the shareholder?
3. What is the basis of the property received by the shareholder?
4. Does the corporation recognize any income, gain, or loss?
5. What is the tax character of the income, gain, or loss recognized by the corporation?
6. What is the effect on the corporation's earnings and profits?

If a distribution of property by a corporation—usually in exchange for some or all of its outstanding stock—qualifies as a partial or complete liquidation, the shareholders are generally accorded sale treatment and the corporation usually recognizes no gain or loss on the distribution. In this chapter, we shall examine in detail the specific requirements for this treatment as well as the inevitable exceptions.

In order to distinguish between a nonliquidating distribution and a partial or complete liquidation, it is necessary to focus on the effect of the property distribution at the corporate level. The term "liquidation"

implies that the asset transfer is in conjunction with the cessation of some or all of the corporation's business activities. Consequently, liquidating distributions generally are viewed as a return of capital on the shares surrendered. If the property distribution is not in conjunction with the cessation of some part or all of the corporation's business activities, it closely resembles a return *on* capital—that is, a distribution of the earnings and profits of a continuing, unchanged corporation.

The classification of a distribution as a partial liquidation may be particularly troublesome because of its similarity to a dividend distribution. In the section that follows, we shall discuss partial liquidations. In the next major section, we shall examine complete liquidations. We shall conclude this chapter with an overview of the problems associated with "collapsible corporations."

PARTIAL LIQUIDATIONS

Figure 6-1 portrays in generalized form a partial liquidation involving exchanges with two shareholders. Note in this figure that the transaction has the same form as a stock redemption involving two shareholders. Because of this similarity in form, it is important to understand that in order to classify the transaction as a partial liquidation, we must focus on what is happening at the corporate level. This contrasts with the stock redemption rules discussed in Chapter 5, which applied tests at the shareholder level.

FIGURE **6-1**   Partial Liquidation

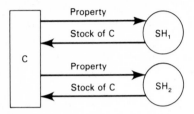

If the transaction portrayed in Figure 6-1 meets the requirements of either one of the two categories of partial liquidations defined in Sec. 346, then both SH$_1$ and SH$_2$ will receive sale treatment. If the transaction does not qualify as a liquidation, then SH$_1$ and SH$_2$ must separately test their redemptions under Sec. 302 or 303 or both to see if either, both, or neither qualifies for sale treatment.

If a transaction meets the technical requirements of both a partial liquidation and a stock redemption treated as a sale, the partial liquidation rules have priority (Treas. Reg. Sec. 1.346-2). Although the shareholder receives sale treatment in both cases, this priority could be important in at least two situations:

1.   A complete termination of a shareholder's interest (Sec. 302(b)(3)) that requires waiver of family attribution, may be retroactively treated as a property distribution if a forbidden interest is reacquired within 10 years. If the transaction qualifies as a partial liquidation, however, the initial sale treatment will not be retroactively changed by later events.

2.   A distribution of appreciated property in exchange for stock is less likely to trigger income recognition to the corporation when the transaction is a partial liquidation than when considered a redemption not in liquidation. Such reduced potential for income recognition by the distributing corporation is discussed in more detail later.

Partial liquidation defined

Before we examine the consequences of a partial liquidation, we must first review its definition. As indicated above, Sec. 346 sets forth two types of partial liquidations. The first, found in Sec. 346(a)(1), provides that a distribution shall be treated as a partial liquidation of a corporation if:

> the distribution is one of a series of distributions in redemption of all of the stock of the corporation pursuant to a plan.

The reason for classifying the above transaction as a partial liquidation is not clear. It appears to overlap the definition of a complete liquidation. As a practical matter, however, this overlap has apparently not raised any significant problems. The existence of a "plan" is a factual question. Assuming one exists, a series of distributions in redemption of *all* the stock of a corporation under such a plan will be considered a series of partial liquidations.

The second category of partial liquidations is found in Sec. 346(a)(2), which provides that a distribution shall be treated as a partial liquidation of a corporation if:

> the distribution is not essentially equivalent to a dividend, is in redemption of a part of the stock of the corporation pursuant to a plan and occurs within the taxable year in which the plan is adopted or within the succeeding taxable year.

It is unfortunate that both Sec. 346(a)(2) and Sec. 302(b)(1) use the phrase "not essentially equivalent to a dividend." The different focuses (that is, what is happening at the corporate level versus what is happening to the shareholder) result in entirely different meanings for the same phrase. For a distribution to be "not essentially equivalent to a dividend" under Sec. 346(a)(2), a genuine contraction of the corporate business must take place. This second category of partial liquidation exists if, under a plan to contract or "cut back" its business, a corporation redeems part of its stock in either the year the plan is adopted or the following year. The property used to redeem the stock may be either the actual assets of the contracted business or the proceeds arising from the corporation's disposition of such assets.

Congress faced particular difficulty in drafting this second definition of a partial liquidation. Every dividend and every stock redemption clearly "contracts" the corporation's net worth. The problem is in identifying those transactions that represent a meaningful contraction of "the business," sufficient to justify the label "partial liquidation." Congress derived a two-pronged solution to this problem, namely, the quite subjective general definition of Sec. 346(a)(2) and the slightly more objective standards of Sec. 346(b).

Section 346(b), which defines a termination of a business, is essentially a "safe harbor" provision. If its requirements are met, the distribution is automatically deemed to be a partial liquidation. Even though Sec. 346(b) was originally drafted as only an objective subset of partial liquidations, qualifying under the general definition of Sec. 346(a)(2), it appears that without the security of Sec. 346(b), Sec. 346(a)(2) is a little-traveled road. Few cases or rulings provide guidance. The regulations give only the example of the distribution of unused insurance proceeds recovered as a result of a fire that destroyed part of the business, causing a part of its activities to cease.[1]

Section 346(b) provides that a distribution in redemption of stock shall be treated as not essentially equivalent to a dividend (thereby meeting one of the requirements of the second category of partial liquidations) if:

1. The distribution is attributable to the corporation's ceasing to conduct, or consists of the assets of, a trade or business which has been actively conducted throughout the 5-year period immediately before the distribution, which trade or business was not acquired by the corporation within such period in a transaction in which gain or loss was recognized in whole or in part, *and*
2. Immediately after the distribution the liquidating corporation is actively engaged in the conduct of a trade or business, which trade or business was actively conducted throughout the 5-year period ending on the date of the distribution and was not acquired by the corporation within such period in a transaction in which gain or loss was recognized in whole or in part.

The complexity of the above requirements is caused by the need to draft the statute so that an intended objective safe harbor does not become an unintended but legislatively sanctioned "loophole." The basic thrust of Sec. 346(b) is that a termination of one active trade or business by a corporation conducting two or more active trades or businesses results in a partial liquidation if the corporation distributes all the assets (or the disposition proceeds) from the terminated business to its shareholders in redemption for part of its stock. A distribution in redemption of stock related to a contraction of a single trade or business could also be a partial liquidation but not under the safe harbor of Sec. 346(b). Such contractions would have to find authority under Sec. 346(a)(1) or the general (and uncertain) provisions of Sec. 346(a)(2).

The requirements that both the terminated and retained trades or businesses have a five-year history and that neither be acquired in a taxable transaction within the five-year period are intended to prevent the corporate bail-out of unwanted assets or excess accumulation of earnings as capital gains. The five-year history may include periods during which the business was owned by others but only if the acquisition transaction was not a taxable transaction. Corporate reorganizations, which are discussed in Chapter 7, allow for such nontaxable acquisitions.

Determining what constitutes an active trade or business is frequently difficult. The regulations under Sec. 346 refer to Sec. 355 which uses quite similar language (Treas. Reg. Sec. 1.346-1(c)). For this reason, we shall consider this issue in Chapter 7. Observe, however, that lack of agreement on the meaning of "actively conducted trade or business" often creates the necessity of an advance ruling before a partial liquidation is attempted under the "safe harbor" of Sec. 346(b).

Two additional considerations concerning partial liquidations require further discussion. The first relates to the percentage of the distributed assets transferred to each shareholder. Both pro rata and non-pro rata transfers may qualify as partial liquidations. The preceding definitions impose no requirements on the relative percentage of assets received by each shareholder.

Refer to Figure 6-1. Assuming that SH_1 and SH_2 each initially owned 50 percent of C, the portrayed transaction is *potentially* a partial liquidation regardless of whether SH_1 and SH_2 each receive 50 percent of the distributed property (pro rata), SH_1 receives 75 percent and SH_2 receives 25 percent (non-pro rata), or SH_1 receives 100 percent and SH_2 is not involved (also non-pro rata).

The last consideration relates to the necessity of surrendering stock in exchange for the distributed property. Although both definitions refer to distributions in *redemption* of stock, the courts have allowed pro rata property distributions not involving the surrender of any stock to be treated as partial liquidations when all other definitional requirements were met.[2] This apparent leniency is attributable to the fact that a pro rata surrender of stock by shareholders of a corporation having only one class of stock causes no relative change in the interests of the shareholders. Thus, the absence of a pro rata surrender of shares may be regarded as insignificant in a transaction otherwise qualifying as a partial liquidation. This should be viewed as a possible "after-the-fact" argument for partial liquidation status. In seeking to minimize potential problems, the professional advisor would normally insist on the physical surrender of stock as one step in any planned partial liquidation.

Treatment to shareholder— income, gain, or loss recognized

Section 346 merely defines the term partial liquidation; otherwise it has no operative effect. With respect to the

---

[1] Treas. Reg. Sec. 1.346-1(a); see also, *Joseph W. Imler*, 11 TC 836 (1948).

[2] See *Fowler Hosiery Co.*, 301 F.2d 394 (7th Cir., 1962).

shareholder, it is Sec. 331(a)(2) that provides that amounts distributed in partial liquidation of a corporation shall be treated as payment in exchange for the stock. Because the stock surrendered typically will be a capital asset in the hands of the shareholder, a partial liquidation usually causes the shareholder to recognize capital gain or loss. Whether it is long- or short-term capital gain or loss will depend on the holding period of the stock at the time of the liquidation distribution.

Under the first category of partial liquidations (that is, a series of distributions in redemption of all the stock of a corporation), the physical surrender of stock may take place at the beginning, during, or at the end of the series of distributions. Regardless of the timing of the stock surrender, the I.R.S. has ruled that a portion of each distribution must be applied to each "block" of stock held by the shareholder. Gain is recognized after basis in the "block" is recovered. Loss is recognized for any basis still not recovered after the last distribution (Rev. Rul 68-348, 1968-2 CB 141).

Example: Shareholder A owns 20 shares of X Corporation, 15 shares that were acquired in 19X1 at a cost of $25,000 and the remaining five shares in April 19X8 at a cost of $14,000. Shareholder A receives $40,000 in November 19X8 as one of a series of distributions in redemption of all the stock of X. A second and final distribution of $10,000 is received by A in January of 19X9.

Regardless of the timing or order ("old" versus "new") of stock surrendered, 75 percent (15 ÷ 20) of each distribution is allocated to the 19X1 block of stock, and 25 percent (5 ÷ 20) is allocated to the April 19X8 block. Thus, $30,000 of the November 19X8 distribution is allocated to the 15 shares acquired in 19X1. This fully recovers the $25,000 basis and results in a $5,000 long-term capital gain to be reported for 19X8. A $10,000 allocation to the five shares acquired in April 19X8 reduces the unrecovered basis of these shares to $40,000. No loss is recognized on these five shares in 19X8. The $10,000 final distribution in January 19X9 is allocated $7,500 to the 15 shares acquired in 19X1 and $2,500 to the five shares acquired in April 19X8. The entire $7,500 must be reported as long-term capital gain recognized in 19X9 on the 15 19X1 shares. The $2,500 allocated to the five shares acquired in April 19X8 reduces their unrecovered basis to $1,500. This $1,500 is recognized as a short-term capital loss in 19X9.

Under the second category of partial liquidations (that is, not essentially equivalent to a dividend), a shareholder will usually compute capital gain or loss by comparing the fair market value of the property distributed to the basis of the stock surrendered. Whether it is short- or long-term capital gain or loss will depend on the holding period of surrendered stock.

Example: In a transaction qualifying as a partial liquidation, O Corporation distributes property with a fair market value of $20,000 to Jones in exchange for 10 of the 100 outstanding shares of O. The total fair market value of the net assets of O before the distribution was $200,000. Jones surrenders eight shares acquired 10 months earlier that have a basis of $2,000 per share and two shares acquired 10 years ago for $500 per share.

Jones recognizes no gain or loss on the eight "new" shares; 80 percent (8 ÷ 10) of the distribution, $16,000, equals his basis in these shares. Jones recognizes a $3,000 long-term gain on the two "old" shares [(20% × $20,000) − (2 × $500)].

Assuming that a shareholder can identify specific shares with differing bases, the selection of which shares to surrender is up to the shareholder. In this way, the shareholder might have some control over the gain or loss recognized. If Jones in the above example owned an additional 10 shares with a basis of $3,000 per share, these shares could be surrendered (and the other 10 retained) and, in that event, a $10,000 capital loss could be recognized.

Note that in the preceding example the 1:10 ratio between the number of shares surrendered and the total shares outstanding is the same as the ratio between the value of the property distributed and the total net assets of the corporation. A number of interesting issues are raised if the percentage of outstanding stock surrendered by a shareholder does not equal the percentage of total net assets distributed to such shareholder. In the following examples, we assume that the basic definitional requirements of a partial liquidation have been met.

Example 1: X Corporation has three shareholders, 100 shares of stock outstanding, and net assets with a fair market value of $300,000. X Corporation redeems 20 shares owned by Smith for $80,000.

This *might* be viewed as $60,000 (20 percent of $300,000) received in partial liquidation and $20,000 as a property distribution to Smith. Alternatively, the $20,000 "excess" *could* be viewed as income or a gift paid by the other shareholders to

Smith. Additional facts could support other interpretations. No definite answer can be given.

Example 2: A and B each own 50 of the 200 outstanding shares of O Corporation, which has assets with a net fair market value of $400,000. O redeems 10 of A's shares for $15,000 and 10 of B's shares for $25,000.

Additional facts *might* suggest that this be viewed as A and B each first receiving $20,000 in partial liquidation, followed by a gift or payment of income of $5,000 from A to B.

The preceding examples illustrate discrepancies between the percentage of assets received and the percentage of stock surrendered. In a non-pro rata partial liquidation, the relative ownership of the shareholders changes. Assuming the shareholders are completely independent, their competing interests would normally lead to a correspondence between percentage of assets distributed and percentage of stock redeemed. As previously observed, pro rata redemptions are not subject to this constraint.

In actual situations, considerable difficulty may arise in determining the "proper" number of shares to redeem. Reasonable people may easily disagree on the value of corporate assets. While this can be frustrating, it does provide some flexibility in determining the number of shares to be redeemed. Certainly, much more flexibility exists than the preceding examples might imply. This flexibility has an impact on the gain or loss the shareholder will recognize and should be considered in planning a partial liquidation.

Treatment to shareholder— basis of property received

The basis of property received by a shareholder in a partial liquidation is the fair market value of such property at the time of the distribution. This treatment applies to corporate shareholders as well as noncorporate shareholders (Sec. 334(a)).

Treatment to corporation— income, gain, or loss recognized

For partial liquidations, Sec. 336 sets forth a general rule that no gain or loss is recognized by a corporation on the distribution of property in partial liquidation. The two major exceptions are installment obligations and recapture property. Section 336 clearly indicates that its general rule of nonrecognition does not apply to the distribution of an installment obligation and states

that Sec. 453(d) (which requires gain or loss to be recognized) is to have priority. Although not directly mentioned in Sec. 336, the depreciation recapture provisions of Secs. 1245 and 1250, intangible drilling and development costs recapture of Sec. 1254, and investment credit recapture of Sec. 47 also have priority over Sec. 336. Section 453(d) and the recapture provisions raise the same recognition potential for both nonliquidating distributions and distributions in partial liquidation. In the former, they are exceptions to the general rule of Sec. 331(a); in the latter, they represent exceptions to the general rule of Sec. 336.

Effect of partial liquidations on earnings and profits

Partial liquidations may have two basic effects on the earnings and profits of the liquidating corporation. First, to the extent that gain or loss is *recognized* by the corporation, earnings and profits are also increased or decreased. We have already discussed the potential for income recognition. The second effect concerns the amount by which earnings and profits are to be reduced because of the distribution. The appropriate reduction in earnings and profits depends on the interpretation of Sec. 312(e). This subsection implies that when property is distributed in a partial liquidation, the distribution first reduces the capital account. Any excess over the amount "properly chargeable to the capital account" reduces earnings and profits. This is the same calculation required for the earnings and profits reduction of stock redemptions that are treated as sales. In this regard, recall that the unsettled status of the definition of a corporation's "capital account" (and the procedures for determining what is "properly chargeable") were resolved in 1979 when the I.R.S. acquiesced to the *Jarvis* case. The discussion in Chapter 5 concerning the earnings and profits reduction for stock redemptions treated as sales also applies to partial liquidations.

COMPLETE LIQUIDATIONS

Code Secs. 331, 332, 333, 334, 336, 337, and 381 set forth a rather complex structure for the taxation of complete liquidations. Interestingly, none of these sections provides a definition of the term "complete liquidation." Congress apparently assumed that a generally recognized and accepted meaning existed and no statutory definition was necessary. This "common sense" approach assumes that a decision has been made to cease all corporate activities and that the property of the corporation is to be distributed to shareholders in complete cancellation or redemption of all outstanding stock. Figure 6-2 illustrates a complete liquidation of a corporation with two shareholders.

FIGURE **6-2**   Complete Liquidation

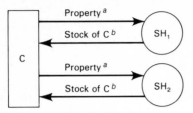

[a] All property of C
[b] All stock of C

Additional insight into the meaning of "complete liquidation" is provided in Treas. Reg. Sec. 1.332-2, which states in part:

> A status of liquidation exists when the corporation ceases to be a going concern and its activities are merely for the purpose of winding up its affairs, paying its debts, and distributing any remaining balance to its shareholders. A liquidation may be completed prior to the actual dissolution of the liquidating corporation. However, legal dissolution of the corporation is not required. Nor will the mere retention of a nominal amount of assets for the sole purpose of preserving the corporation's legal existence disqualify the transaction . . . If a transaction constitutes a distribution in complete liquidation within the meaning of the Internal Revenue Code . . . it is not material that it is otherwise described under local law.

The classification of a distribution as a complete liquidation usually poses no special problems.[3] Once so

[3]Note, however, that lack of proper documentation in corporate minutes or failure to complete the liquidation process could cause the transactions to be treated as property distributions or nonliquidating stock redemptions.

classified, the pattern of taxation becomes more complex. From the point of view of the shareholder, four possible treatments exist. These treatments are summarized in Table 6-1 and discussed separately in more detail.

Shareholder treatment— Sections 331(a)(1) and 334(a)

Section 331(a)(1) may be viewed as providing the "general rule" for shareholder treatment on the complete liquidation of a corporation. It specifies that "amounts distributed in complete liquidation of a corporation shall be treated as in full exchange for the stock." This means that the fair market value of the distributed property at the date of distribution must be compared with the shareholder's basis in the stock of the liquidating corporation, with any difference resulting in recognized gain or loss on the stock. If the stock is a capital asset in the hands of the shareholder, as it usually is, the gain or loss will be a capital gain or loss.

As indicated in Table 6-1, the rules for determining the basis of property received in complete liquidation of a corporation depend on the recognition procedures used by the shareholder. When a shareholder's gain or loss is determined under the "general rule" of Sec. 331(a)(1), the basis of the property received is its fair market value at the time of the distribution. This result, provided by Sec. 334(a), is consistent with tax logic; that is, by recognizing any gain or loss on the liquidating distribution, the shareholder has paid the "tax price" necessary to receive a fair market value basis in the distributed property.

Example: In complete liquidation of C Corporation, land with a fair market value of $15,000 is

TABLE **6-1**
COMPLETE LIQUIDATIONS: SHAREHOLDER TREATMENT

Category	Recognition	Basis of property received
General rule	Recognize gain or loss on stock (Sec. 331(a)(1))	Fair market value (Sec. 334(a))
Special rule—liquidation of subsidiary	No gain or loss recognized on subsidiary's stock (Sec. 332)	Subsidiary's property basis carrys over to parent (Sec. 334(b)(1))
Special rule—liquidation of recently purchased subsidiary	No gain or loss recognized on subsidiary's stock (Sec. 332)	Parent's basis in subsidiary's stock allocated to property received (Sec. 334(b)(2))
Special rule—election re gain on stock	No gain recognized on stock (Sec. 333)	Shareholders' stock basis allocated to property received (Sec. 334(c))

distributed to Jones on August 15, 19X7. C acquired the land five years earlier for $8,000. All of Jones's stock in C is surrendered—10 shares acquired June 15, 19X1 for $1,000 and five shares acquired December 1, 19X6 for $7,000. The 15 shares are all the same class of stock and all were purchased as investments.

Jones will recognize a $9,000 [(10/15) × $15,000 − $1,000 basis] long-term capital gain on the 10 shares of C acquired June 15, 19X1 and a $2,000 [(5/15) × $15,000 − $7,000 basis] short-term capital loss on the five shares acquired December 1, 19X6. The basis of the land to Jones will be $15,000 and Jones's holding period will start August 15, 19X7.

Shareholder treatment— Sections 332 and 334(b)(1)

The preceding general rules of Secs. 331(a)(1) and 334(a) do not apply to distributions in complete liquidation of subsidiary corporations. Section 332 provides a *mandatory* rule that certain parent corporations recognize no gain or loss when the property of a qualifying subsidiary is distributed to its parent in complete liquidation of the subsidiary.

The rationale for this nonrecognition treatment is that the tax law should not interfere with mere changes in the corporate structure used to conduct business activities. The liquidating transfer of property from a subsidiary to its parent is considered a change in form only. The transferred property remains under the same controlling corporate ownership. In this sense, no external transaction has taken place and recognition of gain or loss is not permitted.

Specific requirements for liquidations that must be treated under Sec. 332 are discussed below. Observe that any shareholders not meeting these requirements—for example, individuals or minority corporate shareholders—do not come under Sec. 332, and they, therefore, must look to the general rules of Secs. 331(a)(1) and 334(a) (or to the special election of Secs. 333 and 334(c)) for the appropriate treatment.

Nonrecognition of gain or loss on distributions in complete cancellation or redemption of all the stock of a subsidiary corporation applies to a (parent) *corporate* shareholder if both the following tests are met:

1. *Ownership.* The parent must continuously own (1) at least 80 percent of the voting power and (2) at least 80 percent of the number of shares of nonvoting stock of the subsidiary, from the date of the adop-

tion of the plan of liquidation until the property is received. Stock that is nonvoting and limited and preferred as to dividends is not included in this test.

2. *Time period for distributions.* Either (1) all distributions of the subsidiary's property must occur within one taxable year or (2) the plan of liquidation must specifically provide for (and result in) distribution of all property within three years of the close of the taxable year during which the first liquidating distribution under the plan is made.

If the ownership test is not met at the time of all liquidating distributions, or if any distribution is made after expiration of the maximum time period, *none* of the distributions qualifies under Sec. 332. The apparently objective nature of the preceding tests might encourage intentional avoidance by a parent corporation that would prefer recognition of a capital gain or capital loss to nonrecognition treatment. A parent corporation might want to recognize a capital gain, for example, to offset an about-to-expire capital loss or to establish a fair market value basis in the assets received. On the other hand, it might prefer a capital loss to offset existing capital gains. The I.R.S. would be likely to challenge any attempt to narrowly fail either the ownership or time period tests if the primary objective appeared to be avoidance of Sec. 332. If Congress wished Sec. 332 to be elective, directly providing for such an election would have been preferable.

Determining that a corporate shareholder recognizes no gain or loss under Sec. 332 does not give us sufficient information to identify the rules for calculating the basis of property received. As noted in Table 6-1, one of two different procedures, provided in Secs. 334(b)(1) and 334(b)(2), may potentially apply to property received in a Sec. 332 liquidation. Section 334(b)(1), under which the subsidiary's basis in the distributed property carries over to the parent, may be thought of as the "general rule." This treatment applies unless the additional requirements (to be discussed next) of Sec. 334(b)(2) are met. The logic of Sec. 334(b)(1) is simple: The parent corporation is just "stepping into the shoes" of the subsidiary, it recognizes no gain or loss under Sec. 332, and thus it should take the subsidiary's basis in the distributed assets.

Example: On November 15, 19X7, S Corporation adopts a plan of complete liquidation. On February 15, 19X8, S distributes all its property in complete cancellation of its 100 outstanding shares. P Corporation, which has owned 80 shares of S (basis $50,000) for 10 years, receives:

	Fair market value on February 15, 19X8	Basis to S
Land	$45,000	$10,000
Building	70,000	40,000
Equipment	30,000	35,000
Cash	15,000	15,000

M Corporation, which has owned 10 shares of S (basis $12,000) for five years, receives:

	Fair market value on February 15, 19X8	Basis to S
Land	$15,000	$8,000
Cash	5,000	5,000

Ms. Smith, who has owned 10 shares of S (basis $22,000) since June 1, 19X7, receives:

	Fair market value on February 15, 19X8	Basis to S
XYZ stock	$18,000	$15,000
Cash	2,000	2,000

P Corporation meets both the ownership and time period tests of Sec. 332 and therefore recognizes no gain or loss on the February 15, 19X8, distribution. P's basis in the land, building, and equipment will be $10,000, $40,000, and $35,000, respectively. S's "date basis" in these properties will also carry over to P. P's $50,000 basis in the 80 shares of S stock "disappears" at this time and thus the $110,000 ($160,000 − $50,000) "paper gain" on the stock will never be recognized.

Section 332 does not apply to either M Corporation or Ms. Smith. Under the general rules of Secs. 331(a)(1) and 334(a), in 19X8 M will recognize an $8,000 ($20,000 − $12,000) long-term capital gain and Smith will recognize a $2,000 ($20,000 − $22,000) short-term capital loss. M's basis in the land will be $15,000 and Smith's basis in the XYZ stock will be $18,000. The date basis of both properties will be February 15, 19X8.

Shareholder treatment— Sections 332 and 334(b)(2)

When the ownership and time period tests of Sec. 332 are met on the complete liquidation of a subsidiary, the qualifying parent corporation recognizes no gain or loss. If the additional requirements of Sec. 334(b)(2) are also met, however, the subsidiary's basis in the dis-

tributed property does *not* carry over to the parent. Instead, the parent's basis in the subsidiary's stock is allocated to the property received.

Section 334(b)(2) is intended to apply to those situations in which a corporation apparently acquired a majority shareholder interest in a subsidiary primarily as a means to acquire the assets held by the second corporation. In substance, this two-step process is considered to be equivalent to a direct purchase of assets. In the case of a direct purchase of assets, the *acquiring* corporation recognizes no gain or loss on the purchase and receives a fair market value basis in the assets received. Sections 332 and 334(b)(2) provide this same result—that is, no gain or loss to the parent on liquidation of the subsidiary and a fair market value basis in the distributed assets. This fair market value basis is accomplished by allocating the purchase price of the subsidiary's stock (parent's basis in the subsidiary's stock) to the property distributed in liquidation to the parent. The purchase price of the stock presumably reflects the fair market value of the parent's share of the property of the subsidiary.[4]

The additional requirements of Sec. 334(b)(2) are:

1. The parent corporation must have acquired *by purchase* at least 80 percent of the subsidiary's stock (except nonvoting stock that is limited and preferred as to dividends) during a 12-month period beginning with the date of the first purchase of stock. "Purchase" does not include stock received through gift, inheritance, contribution to capital, tax-free reorganization, or a Sec. 351 exchange. It also does not generally include stock, however acquired, from an entity "related" under the attribution rules of Sec. 318. An exception is provided for subsidiaries of purchased subsidiaries. For example, if M purchases the stock of N and N has an existing subsidiary O, M is considered to have purchased O at the same date. If N is liquidated first, followed by the liquidation of O, M may potentially qualify for Secs. 332 and 334(b)(2) treatment for both liquidations. In the absence of this exception, M would be considered to have acquired the O stock from N, a "related" entity, at the time of N's liquidation.

2. The plan of liquidation must be adopted not more than two years after the date by which at least 80 percent of the subsidiary's stock has been acquired by purchase. The time period for completing the plan is controlled by the requirements of Sec. 332, which were previously discussed.

---

[4] The approach utilized in Sec. 334(b)(2) was first developed by the courts in *Kimbell-Diamond Milling Co.*, 187 F.2d 718 (CCA-5, 1951).

Example 1: P Corporation purchases 90 percent of the outstanding stock of S Corporation on January 15, 19X7, for $99,000 and the remaining 10 percent on January 5, 19X8, for $11,000. On January 6, 19X8, a plan of complete liquidation is adopted and the following properties and liabilities of S are distributed to P:

	Fair market value on January 6, 19X8	Basis to S
Cash	$10,000	$10,000
Land	40,000	20,000
Building	50,000	40,000
Equipment	30,000	25,000
Accounts payable	(20,000)	

Under Sec. 332, P recognizes no gain or loss on the liquidation of S. Observe that, in this example, if recognition were required there would be neither gain nor loss because the stock basis ($110,000) equals the net fair market value received. Because the requirements of Sec. 334(b)(2) are also met, S's basis in the property does not carry over to P. P is considered to have "paid" $130,000 for the cash, land, building, and equipment. The $130,000 represents P's basis in S stock ($110,000 total purchase price) plus the $20,000 liabilities assumed. The $10,000 cash received is first subtracted from the $130,000 and the remaining $120,000 is allocated among the noncash assets in accordance with their relative fair market values at January 6, 19X8:

		Basis to P
Land	($40,000/$120,000 × $120,000)	$40,000
Building	($50,000/$120,000 × $120,000)	50,000
Equipment	($30,000/$120,000 × $120,000)	30,000

Example 2: Assume the same facts as in Example 1, except that 50 percent of S is acquired on January 15, 19X7, for $55,000 and the remaining 50 percent is acquired on February 15, 19X8, also for $55,000. The plan of liquidation is adopted, and transfer takes place on February 16, 19X8. (Values at February 16, 19X8 are the same as previously given for January 6, 19X8.)

The liquidation qualifies under Sec. 332 but not under Sec. 334(b)(2) because 80 percent of S was not purchased within 12 months after January

15, 19X7. P will recognize no gain or loss and, under Sec. 334(b)(1), will carry over S's basis in the land ($20,000), building ($40,000), and equipment ($25,000).

It is important to recognize the deceptive simplicity of the preceding examples. Although they illustrate the basic thrust of Sec. 334(b)(2), "real world" situations often produce additional complexities. Consideration of the problems associated with liabilities, goodwill, and continued operations between stock acquisition and liquidation is beyond the scope of this book.

Treatment of shareholder— Sections 333 and 334(c)

Of the four possible shareholder treatments on complete liquidation of a corporation, the provisions of Secs. 333 and 334(c) find the least use. In the discussion that follows, you should focus not only on the "mechanics" of these provisions but also consider when and why they would be useful (or detrimental) to a shareholder. Although Sec. 333 potentially allows gain to go unrecognized at the time of complete liquidation, many pitfalls exist along the way. The provisions of Secs. 333 and 334(c) are summarized below.

QUALIFIED ELECTING SHAREHOLDERS   Only *qualified electing shareholders* (QES) may receive Secs. 333 and 334(c) treatment. Shareholders at the date the plan of liquidation is adopted must be divided into three groups: excluded corporate shareholders, other corporate shareholders, and noncorporate shareholders.

An excluded corporate shareholder may never be a QES. An excluded corporate shareholder is any corporate shareholder that has owned, at *any time* since January 1, 1954, 50 percent or more of the stock entitled to vote on adoption of the plan of liquidation.

Other corporate shareholders may receive Secs. 333 and 334(c) treatment, but only if shareholders representing at least 80 percent of the voting power entitled to vote on the plan of liquidation in this other-corporate-shareholder group file written elections. If this 80 percent test is met, all "other corporate shareholders" that filed elections (whether or not entitled to vote on the plan) are qualified electing shareholders.

The same 80 percent test must be applied separately to the noncorporate shareholder group. If met, all noncorporate shareholders who filed elections (whether or not entitled to vote on the plan) are QES.

Example: X Corporation has two classes of stock outstanding. Class A is entitled to vote on the adoption of a plan of liquidation, class B is not. At the time of the adoption of a plan of liquidation, the stock ownership of X was:

Class A:

     M Corporation   60 shares
     N Corporation   25 shares
     O Corporation   5 shares
     Ms. Jones   10 shares

Class B:

     Mr. Smith   90 shares
     P Corporation   10 shares

Written elections for Secs. 333 and 334(c) treatment are filed by N, P, and Smith. (N and P have never owned 50 percent or more of the class A stock.) As an excluded corporation, M may not file an election. Jones and O chose not to file. (O has never owned 50 percent or more of the class A stock.)

In the "other corporate shareholders" group, 30 shares (N and O) are entitled to vote on the plan of liquidation. Because an election was made on 25 of these shares by N, the "80 percent test" is met. Therefore, N and P, the other corporate shareholders that filed elections, are QES.

In the noncorporate shareholders group, 10 shares (Jones) are entitled to vote on the plan of liquidation. Because an election was not made on any of these shares, the "80 percent test" for this group is not met. Smith, therefore, is not a QES.

TIME PERIOD REQUIREMENTS OF SECTION 333   Section 333 imposes two time requirements that are strictly interpreted. First, the written elections must be filed within 30 days of the date of the adoption of the plan of liquidation. Second, the distributions in complete cancellation or redemption of all the stock must occur within one calendar month (which is *not* the same as any 30-day period). If these requirements are met, all QES will be treated under Secs. 333 and 334(c), as described below. Other shareholders will look to Secs. 331(a)(1) and 334(a), 332 and 334(b)(1), or 332 and 334(b)(2) for the appropriate tax treatment.

TREATMENT OF QES   The special election of Sec. 333 applies only to shares on which there is a realized gain. If a loss is realized on any shares, the QES must (1) recognize that loss under the general rule of Sec. 331(a)(1), and (2) take a fair market value basis in the property received for those shares, under Sec. 334(a). When shares have been acquired at different times and different costs, loss on some of the shares may not be offset against gain on others (Treas. Reg. Sec. 1.333-4(a)).

Noncorporate QES.   If the liquidating corporation has (1) no earnings and profits *and* (2) distributes neither any money nor any stock or securities acquired after December 31, 1953, to a noncorporate QES, then any gain realized is not recognized. If the distributing corporation has earnings and profits at the time of liquidation, then any gain realized is first recognized *as dividend income* to the extent of such stock's ratable share of earnings and profits (but the dividend income may not exceed the gain realized). If money or stock or securities is distributed to a noncorporate QES, any portion of the gain realized that is not treated as dividend income must still be recognized—*as capital gain*—to the extent that the fair market value of the money, stock, and securities received exceeds the liquidated stock's ratable share of earnings and profits.[5]

The basis of property received under Sec. 333 is determined under rules provided in Sec. 334(c). That basis will be the same as the shareholder's basis in the stock (for which the property was received) minus any money received, plus any gain recognized by the shareholder.[6] The holding period of the liquidated stock will carry over to the acquired property.

Example: Mr. Jones owns 10 of the 100 outstanding shares of X Corporation. The 10 shares were acquired 20 years ago for $2,000. In a liquidation qualifying under Sec. 333, Jones, a QES, receives the following:

	Fair market value	Basis to X
Money	$ 3,000	$3,000
Stock of Z	10,000	4,000
Land	20,000	5,000

Earnings and profits of X, before reduction for liquidating distributions, were $50,000.

Jones has a gain realized of $31,000 ($33,000 − $2,000). Dividend income of $5,000 (10 percent of $50,000) must be recognized and $8,000 ($13,000 − $5,000) must be recognized as long-term capital gain. Jones's total basis in the Z stock and land will be $12,000 ($2,000 − $3,000 + $13,000). This $12,000 basis will be allocated on relative fair market values; that is, $4,000 (1/3 of $12,000) to the Z stock and $8,000 (2/3 of $12,000) to the land. Jones's date basis in the X

---

[5]Stock or securities acquired by the liquidating corporation before January 1, 1954, are not treated as "stock or securities" for this purpose.

[6]See Treas. Reg. Sec. 1.334-2 for additional adjustments to arrive at the basis of property received when the shareholder assumes liabilities or takes property subject to liabilities.

stock will carry over to both the Z stock and land received.

Corporate QES. Corporate QES treatment is similar to noncorporate QES treatment in that any gain realized is not recognized if the liquidating corporation has no earnings and profits and no money, stock, or securities are distributed to the corporate QES. If (1) earnings and profits exist and/or (2) money, stock, or securities are distributed, the recognition rules differ for corporate QES. The corporate QES recognizes any realized gain to the extent of the greater of (1) the stock's ratable share of the earnings and profits, or (2) the fair market value of the money, stock, and securities received for the liquidated stock.[7] This recognized gain is *not* converted into dividend income. If the canceled or redeemed stock was a capital asset in the hands of the corporate QES, the recognized gain is a capital gain. The basis of property received by a corporate QES is determined under Sec. 334(c). These rules were previously discussed in connection with noncorporate QES.

Example: Assume the same facts as in the preceding example for noncorporate QES but change Mr. Jones to S Corporation.

Of S Corporation's $31,000 realized gain, $13,000 will be recognized as a long-term capital gain. All other aspects of the prior solution apply.

SUMMARY After struggling with the mechanics of Secs. 333 and 334(c), it seems reasonable to ask two questions: (1) Why do these provisions exist? (2) Why spend time learning the rules if they are seldom used? To answer the first question, provisions similar to the current Secs. 333 and 334(c) were originally enacted to encourage the liquidations of corporations that were made personal holding companies by changes in the tax law. The belief that these provisions remain appropriate in some situations and that they do not create potential for unintended tax avoidance have allowed them to survive. With regard to the second question, the provisions are discussed because they sometimes can be quite useful and because it is important to understand their pitfalls. The generalization that Sec. 333 may be used to avoid recognition of gain on liquidation is dangerous.

The preceding review of Sec. 333 suggests that it is most applicable to corporations with appreciated property but with no earnings and profits and little or no

cash, stock, or securities. In addition, the shareholders ordinarily have a low basis in their stock, wish to terminate the corporation, and desire to acquire direct ownership of the assets held by the corporation. Sometimes, although not frequently, these circumstances do occur!

Some of the potential pitfalls of Secs. 333 and 334(c) are:

1. The time period requirements for election and liquidation are strictly applied by the I.R.S. An inadvertent timing error may disqualify the liquidation and make it taxable to shareholders who were relying on nonrecognition.

2. A precise calculation of earnings and profits is required. Many subtleties exist in this area. The possible creation of earnings and profits on the liquidating distributions is but one example. "Book" retained earnings should never be assumed to approximate earnings and profits.

3. Once a shareholder files a written election under Sec. 333, it generally cannot be withdrawn (Treas. Reg. Sec. 1.333-2(b)(1)). The courts have usually supported this view.

4. The character of gain on a later sale of the property by the shareholder may be less desirable than the character that would have been recognized on liquidation if Sec. 333 had not applied. For example, the gain on undeveloped but appreciated land, distributed under Sec. 333, which is subsequently developed and sold by the shareholder, will be entirely ordinary income. Alternatively, a liquidation under Secs. 331(a)(1) and 334(a) would necessitate the recognition of capital gain and step up the basis in the land to fair market value at date of distribution. Under this alternative, only the appreciation due to development would be taxed as ordinary income.

5. Section 334(c) frequently results in a low basis for the property received because it is determined by reference to the shareholder's ("old") basis in the stock surrendered. Liquidations under Secs. 331(a)(1) and 334(a) yield a ("new") fair-market-value basis. When depreciable property is involved, the benefit of larger depreciation deductions in the future, resulting from Sec. 334(a), may exceed the cost of any capital gain that must be recognized under Sec. 331(a)(1).

Treatment of corporation— sales during liquidation

In many cases, when a decision to liquidate a corporation has been made, the shareholders do not desire to receive directly the various operating properties and in-

[7]Stock or securities acquired by the liquidating corporation before January 1, 1954, are not treated as "stock or securities" for this purpose.

vestments of the corporation, but rather they prefer to receive cash equal in value to the corporation's assets. For this reason, it is often convenient for the corporation to sell its noncash assets during the liquidation process and distribute cash to the shareholders in exchange for their stock. The corporation is often in a better position to negotiate and arrange for the sale of its noncash properties than the shareholders would be if the properties were distributed directly to them. This situation could raise significant tax problems when appreciated properties are involved.

> *Example:* Assume Mr. Smith, a taxpayer in the 70 percent marginal tax bracket, owns all the stock (basis of $10,000) of X Corporation, which now holds one property, investment land with a basis to X of $5,000 and a fair market value of $30,000. X has substantial earnings and profits from prior operations. Smith wants the land sold and X liquidated. If X sells the land, is taxed on the sale, and then distributes the after-tax proceeds to Smith in exchange for his stock, Smith will receive $25,750 ($30,000 sales prices − 17% tax on $25,000 gain to X). This will cause Smith to recognize a $15,750 ($25,750 − $10,000) gain on the liquidation. If Smith's effective tax rate on the gain is 28 percent,[8] he will pay a tax of $4,410 and be left with a net of only $21,340 ($25,750 − $4,410). On the other hand, if X directly distributes the land to Smith in exchange for his stock and Smith then sells the land, he will end up with a net of $24,400. As will be explained later, X would not recognize any income on the distribution of the land in complete liquidation. Smith would recognize a gain of $20,000 ($30,000 − $10,000) on the liquidation, pay a tax of $5,600 (28 percent effective rate on $20,000), and have a basis in the land of $30,000. He would recognize no gain or loss on the sale of the land ($30,000 − $30,000) and end up with a net of $24,400 ($30,000 sales price − $5,600 tax on liquidation).

Remember that the preceding example deals with appreciated property. If X Corporation held depreciated property and could utilize the loss, Smith would benefit from a recognized loss on a sale *by the corporation* of the depreciated property. A direct distribution of such property to Smith would yield a fair-market-

value basis, and therefore no loss would be recognized by Smith on a subsequent sale of the property.

The critical element in the discussion to this point is the assumption that a corporation *is* taxed on sales of property that take place during the process of liquidation. In this setting, as the preceding example illustrates, the factual question of who sold the property (the corporation or the shareholder) can be quite significant. It is essentially a "facts and circumstances" question that can be extremely difficult to resolve.[9] Both mechanical form and underlying substance are important. In closely held corporations, in which the same persons are both corporate officers and shareholders, it is rather esoteric to ask who negotiated and set the terms of the sale—the "corporation" or the shareholders. In an attempt to resolve this problem, Congress enacted Sec. 337. The thrust of Sec. 337 is that neither gain nor loss will be recognized on sales of property by corporations in the process of complete liquidations. In situations in which it applies, Sec. 337 causes shareholders to be treated the same, regardless of whether the corporation sells the property and distributes the proceeds in liquidation or the property is directly distributed to the shareholders and the property is subsequently sold by them. To illustrate, consider the preceding example concerning Smith and X Corporation with the assumption that X would not recognize any gain if it sells the property. Under this assumption, which reflects Sec. 337 treatment, Smith ends up with a net of $24,400 under *both* fact situations given in that example.

It was previously noted that Sec. 337 results in no recognized gain or loss on sales of property by corporations in the process of certain complete liquidations. Before turning to some of the specific requirements of Sec. 337, a few important generalizations are necessary. First, even in those complete liquidations to which it applies, Sec. 337 has nothing to do with distributions to shareholders in exchange for their stock. The potential for income recognition by the corporation on these distributions is covered in the next portion of this chapter. Section 337 applies only to *sales* of property in connection with certain complete liquidations.

Second, you should understand that Sec. 337 has no counterpart that provides for nonrecognition on *sales* in connection with nonliquidating or partially liquidating distributions to shareholders. If a corporation wishes to make a property distribution, stock redemption, or partial liquidation, and it sells property so that

---

[8]The 28 percent effective tax rate reflects the 70 percent marginal rate of Mr. Smith applied to 40 percent of the gain that remains after subtracting the 60 percent long-term capital gain deduction.

[9]See *Court Holding Co.,* 324 U.S. 331 (1945) and *Cumberland Pub. Serv. Co.,* 338 U.S. 451 (1950).

cash may be distributed, gain or loss *is* recognized on the sale. If, instead, the property is directly distributed to the shareholder, the potential for gain or loss recognition by the corporation is substantially reduced. Because the combined tax cost to corporation and shareholder may vary depending on who sells the property, an incentive exists to structure the transactions in the least-cost manner. Thus, the question "who sold the property" remains important in many situations not covered by Sec. 337. Appreciated property that is nominally sold by a shareholder shortly after its distribution by the corporation is likely to invite I.R.S. attention.

Section 337

Section 337(a) provides the "general rule," which states:

> If, within the 12-month period beginning on the date on which a corporation adopts a plan of complete liquidation, all of the assets of the corporation are distributed in complete liquidation, less assets retained to meet claims, then no gain or loss shall be recognized to such corporation from the sale or exchange by it of property within such 12-month period.

The major issues related to the application of Sec. 337 concern what qualifies as "property," the time period requirement, rules related to complete liquidations for which there is limited or no application of Sec. 337, and recognition provisions that outrank Sec. 337.

DEFINITION OF PROPERTY   For purposes of Sec. 337, "property" means all property of the corporation *except*:

1.   Inventory or property held by the corporation primarily for sale to customers in the ordinary course of its trade or business.
2.   Installment obligations arising from the sale of inventory or property held primarily for sale to customers.
3.   Other installment obligations arising from sales *before* the date of the adoption of the plan of liquidation.

In limited circumstances, items 1 and 2 *may* be considered "property" and therefore receive nonrecognition treatment if sold. If, within the time period specified in Sec. 337(a), substantially all (determined at the time of sale) the property described in 1, above—which is attributable to any one trade or business of the corporation—is sold or exchanged with *one person in one*

transaction, such inventory or property held for sale is "property" for purposes of Sec. 337. An installment obligation arising from such a bulk sale is also considered property, so that, if it were later sold within the 12-month time period, no gain or loss would be recognized on its sale. Note that a corporation may have more than one trade or business. Thus, more than one bulk sale may qualify under Sec. 337.

TIME PERIOD REQUIREMENT   Section 337 extends nonrecognition treatment to only those sales of property that occur during the 12-month period beginning on the date on which the plan of complete liquidation is adopted. Sales of any property before that date are taxable as well as any sales of nonqualifying property during the 12-month period. If the liquidation process is not completed during the 12-month period, *all* sales are taxable. The process is considered complete if the only assets retained are to meet claims against the corporation.

By its terms, Sec. 337 is mandatory. If a corporation wishes to avoid the application of Sec. 337, extending the liquidation process for more than 12 months after the date of adoption of the plan is generally effective.

More typically, corporations consider the possibility of selling any depreciated (or loss) properties before formal adoption of the plan and then selling appreciated (or gain) properties after the plan is adopted. The intent, of course, is to get the best of both worlds: the benefit of recognized losses but not the tax on realized gains.

The regulations indicate that, ordinarily, the date of the adoption of a plan of complete liquidation is the date of adoption by the shareholders of the resolution authorizing the distribution of all the assets of the corporation (other than those retained to meet claims) (Treas. Reg. Sec. 1.337-2(b)). It is further specified that this date (that is, the shareholder resolution date) will be accepted if the corporation sells substantially all its Sec. 337 property either before or after such date. Thus, if a corporation is willing to have substantially all its gains and losses on sales of Sec. 337 property either recognized or unrecognized, it may time these sales either before or after the date of the formal shareholder resolution.

If the corporation attempts to straddle the shareholder resolution date—with loss sales of Sec. 337 property occurring before and gain sales occurring after "the date on which the corporation adopts a plan of complete liquidation"—the tax result becomes a factual question. The I.R.S. may argue that the date of adoption was really some date before the loss sales took place. This could either cause both losses and gains to go unrecognized under Sec. 337 *or* full recognition of all gains and losses on sales, if the liquidation process extended more than 12 months beyond this date. The I.R.S. has not had a great deal of success with this approach in the courts. The "straddle technique" appears to be alive and well.

The decision to liquidate a corporation is sometimes made after an involuntary conversion has occurred. If a gain is realized, the shareholders might want nonrecognition under Sec. 337 but the date of realization may cause a problem. If the date of realization is considered to be the date the involuntary conversion occurred, a timely shareholder resolution for complete liquidation may be impossible. Stories exist of shareholders frantically trying to meet while a factory is burning! To alleviate this problem, Sec. 337(e) was added to the Code. It provides that realized gain or loss on an involuntary conversion within 60 days of the start of the 12-month liquidation period will be considered as occurring within the 12-month period if the corporation so elects.

COMPLETE LIQUIDATIONS TO WHICH SECTION 337 HAS LIMITED OR NO APPLICATION   If Secs. 333 and 334(c) apply to *any* shareholder, Sec. 337 does not apply to sales by the liquidating corporation. The conditions of Sec. 333 are such that a minority shareholder might be able to elect and qualify for Sec. 333 treatment. This could adversely affect the remaining shareholders. Congress evidently did not want to extend to any shareholders the opportunity for the combined nonrecognition of Sec. 337 and deferred recognition of Secs. 333 and 334(c). The approach taken is effective but rather harsh.

Section 337 also will not generally apply to a corporation being liquidated under Secs. 332 and 334(b)(1). From the standpoint of the parent shareholder, this nonapplication is usually appropriate. If Sec. 337 did apply, there would be no recognition either on sales by the liquidating subsidiary or on receipt of the liquidating distributions by the parent. Congress intended Sec. 337 to cause recognition at the shareholder level—not recognition at both the corporate *and* shareholder level—but it did not intend to avoid recognition at both levels. An exception applies if the parent corporation is also being liquidated in the same 12-month period. Nonrecognition under Sec. 337 is then allowed on sales by the subsidiary because, in this case, the related liquidation of the parent will be a taxable event for its shareholders.

When a parent corporation is not also being liqui-

dated and Sec. 337, therefore, may not apply, an unfairness could exist for any minority shareholders. Section 337 treatment is denied to prevent the parent from going untaxed, but minority shareholders face a potential double tax. In order to mitigate this problem, Sec. 337(d) provides a special rule for minority shareholders. If Sec. 337 nonrecognition is denied solely because a parent shareholder treats the liquidation under Secs. 332 and 334(b)(1), the other shareholders treat the liquidation as though Sec. 337 had applied. This is done by increasing the amount realized on liquidation by their share of the tax imposed on the corporation because Sec. 337 did not apply and by allowing a tax credit in the amount of such increase.

Example: S Corporation is owned 90 percent by P Corporation and 10 percent by Mr. Smith. A plan of liquidation of S is adopted, and within 12 months S sells all its properties and, after paying taxes and other liabilities, distributes $90,000 to P and $10,000 to Smith in complete liquidation. P will treat the liquidation under Secs. 332 and 334(b)(1) and, therefore, Sec. 337 may not apply to the sales after the adoption of the plan of liquidation. Assume that federal income taxes paid by S during this period were $10,000. If Sec. 337 had applied, these taxes would have been only $2,000. Smith has a basis in S stock of $4,000.

Smith's distribution (amount realized) is considered to be $10,800 ($10,000 plus 10 percent of $8,000). He recognizes a $6,800 ($10,800 − $4,000) capital gain on the liquidation and is entitled to a tax credit of $800 (10 percent of $8,000). With regard to federal income taxes, this treatment leaves Smith with the same net cash as if Sec. 337 had applied, that is, a $10,800 actual distribution and no credit to apply against the tax liability on the $6,800 gain.

Section 337 has only limited application to sales in connection with liquidations under Secs. 332 and 334(b)(2). Recall that the intent of Secs. 332 and 334(b)(2) is to treat certain stock purchases as though assets were acquired directly by allocating the purchase price of the stock to the basis of the assets. If the acquired subsidiary sells any of its properties before liquidating, this basis adjustment has not yet taken place. This means that the gain or loss realized is determined by the subsidiary's basis in the property. If the liquidation otherwise qualifies under Sec. 337, the gain realized on sales of property is unrecognized to the extent a Sec. 334(b)(2) allocation would have exceeded the subsidiary's basis.

An exception to this limited Sec. 337 treatment occurs when the parent is also being liquidated within the same 12-month period. In this case Sec. 337 has full application to realized gains *and* losses on sales of property by the subsidiary. In all other situations, in which the parent is being treated under Secs. 332 and 334(b)(2), only the limited nonrecognition of gain described above applies. Losses are fully recognized, and no special rules exist for minority shareholders.

> *Example:* All the stock of S Corporation is purchased by P Corporation for $100,000. After this purchase but before S is liquidated under Secs. 332 and 334(b)(2), S sells investment land that cost $4,000 for $11,000. Of P's $100,000 stock purchase price, $10,000 would be allocated under Sec. 334(b)(2) to this land.
>
> Assuming that Sec. 337 otherwise applies to the land sale, S will recognize $1,000. The realized gain of $7,000 ($11,000 − $4,000) goes unrecognized under Sec. 337 to the extent the Sec. 334(b)(2) allocation of $10,000 exceeds S's basis of $4,000.

RECOGNITION PROVISIONS THAT OUTRANK SECTION 337 Before relying on any nonrecognition provision, the provision's relationship to the recapture Code sections should always be reviewed. Section 337 is but one of many nonrecognition provisions that make no direct reference to the recapture sections. The depreciation recapture provisions of Secs. 1245 and 1250, the intangible drilling and development cost recapture of Sec. 1254, and the investment credit recapture of Sec. 47 all are worded in a manner to give them priority over Sec. 337.

> *Example:* A building is sold for $80,000 in a transaction meeting the general requirements of Sec. 337. The adjusted basis of the building is $30,000, and excess depreciation per Sec. 1250 (at the time of the sale) is $20,000. In that event, $20,000 out of the total realized gain of $50,000 must be recognized under Sec. 1250 (Sec. 1250(a)). The remaining $30,000 gain realized goes unrecognized under Sec. 337.

Treatment of corporation— liquidating distributions

Corporations quite often do not convert all their properties into money during the liquidation process. Noncash distributions to shareholders in cancellation of their stock raise the issue whether or not the corporation treats the difference between the distributed property's adjusted basis and fair market value as recognized gain or loss. Obviously, this is of interest to the shareholders in that an increase or decrease in the corporation's tax liability will directly affect the total amount that the corporation can distribute to them.

Section 336 provides a general rule that no gain or loss shall be recognized to a corporation on the distribution of property to shareholders in complete liquidation.[10] There are no exceptions to this general rule in situations in which the shareholder receiving the property is treating the liquidation under Secs. 332 and 334(b)(1). The carryover of the subsidiary's basis ensures that normal income, gain, or loss recognition rules will eventually apply to the property. The parent has simply "stepped into the shoes" of the subsidiary.

Certain exceptions to the general nonrecognition rule of Sec. 336 apply when property is distributed to shareholders who treated the liquidation under Secs. 331(a) and 334(a), 332 and 334(b)(2), or 333 and 334(c). Of most general importance in these situations is the application of the depreciation recapture provisions of Secs. 1245 and 1250, the intangible drilling and development cost recapture of Sec. 1254, and the investment credit recapture of Sec. 47. Gain or loss is also recognized under Sec. 453(d) if an installment obligation is distributed, unless a sale of such installment obligation would have qualified for nonrecognition under Sec. 337. Finally, the judicial doctrine prohibiting any assignment of income and the statutory requirement of Sec. 446(b) (that an accounting method "clearly reflect" income) have occasionally been raised by the I.R.S. in support of income recognition.

Treatment of corporation—earnings and profits

A precise calculation of the earnings and profits of a corporation that is being completely liquidated is usually not necessary because (1) the shareholders do not look to earnings and profits to determine their treatment, and (2) the corporation's earning and profits disappear upon completion of the liquidation process. In two situations, however, a calculation of earnings and profits is necessary. Under Sec. 333, a qualifying electing shareholder's treatment is determined, in part, by reference to earnings and profits at the end of the liquidation process. Also, when a subsidiary is liquidated under Secs. 332 and 334(b)(1), its earnings and profits are inherited by the parent corporation (see Secs. 381(a)(1) and (c)(2)). Gains and losses realized but not recognized under Secs. 336 and 337 do not increase or decrease earnings and profits (Sec. 312(f)(1)).

---

[10]As previously discussed, Sec. 336 also applies to partial liquidations.

COLLAPSIBLE CORPORATIONS

The final pages of this chapter are a brief introduction to the pitfalls associated with collapsible corporations. Section 341, which deals with this topic, is among the more complex sections to be found in the Code. It comprises approximately seven pages of sight-destroying, mind-numbing text. As with the making of sausage, it is questionable how much one really wants to know about Sec. 341! A general understanding of the topic, however, is essential and should not prove unduly painful. The tax practitioner needs to know considerably more.

The typical abuse at which Sec. 341 is aimed is easily understood. Without such a provision, a corporation could be formed for a one-time project, such as making a movie or constructing a building. After completion of the project but before its sale, the shareholders would liquidate (or "collapse") the corporation by taking its completed property in exchange for their stock. Under the rules of Secs. 331(a)(1) and 334(a), a capital gain would be recognized on the liquidation and the shareholders would receive a fair-market-value basis in the property distributed. The property could be sold immediately thereafter at little gain or loss. The same results could be achieved with a property distribution (assuming no earnings and profits), stock redemption, partial liquidation, or sale of the stock. If, on the other hand, the corporation had sold the property and then liquidated, there would be two gains: one (ordinary) to the corporation and one (capital) to the shareholders, instead of one (capital) gain to the shareholder.

Section 341 was drafted in a manner that gives it much broader application than the classic example just described. Section 341(b) defines a collapsible corporation as a corporation formed or availed of principally for the manufacture, construction, or production of property, or purchase of certain property, with a view to realization by the shareholders of gain attributable to such property before the corporation has realized a substantial part of the taxable income to be derived from such property. The most common examples of purchased property that may trigger Sec. 341 are inventory and property held primarily for sale to customers.

The following generalizations may be made about the above definition:

1. Almost all corporations are formed or availed of principally for the manufacture, construction, or production of property, or for the purchase of inventory or property held for sale to customers.

2. The regulations take the position that the forbidden view exists if the persons who are or were in a position to control the actions of the corporation contemplated or recognized the possibility of shareholder recognition before corporate recognition some time during manufacture, construction, production, or purchase of the property (Treas. Reg. Sec. 1.341-2(a)(2) and (3)).

3. The I.R.S., following *Kelley*, 293 F.2d 904 (CCA-5, 1961), has ruled that realization by the corporation of one-third of the taxable income to be derived from the property *is* "substantial" (Rev. Rul. 72-48, 1972-1 CB 102). This represents the most lenient interpretation of any aspect of the basic definition of a collapsible corporation.

Treatment of shareholder

Unless one of the exceptions of Sec. 341(d), (e), or (f) applies, gain recognized by a shareholder on a property distribution by a collapsible corporation—or on a sale, partial liquidation, or complete liquidation of the stock of a collapsible corporation that would otherwise be long-term capital gain—is treated as ordinary income (Sec. 341(a)). It is only *recognized long-term capital gain* that is converted into *ordinary income* by Sec. 341. Gain that is realized but not recognized under other Code provisions is not affected by Sec. 341(a), nor are recognized capital losses or short-term capital gains.

The consequences of Sec. 341(a) (conversion of long-term capital gain into ordinary income) are so harsh that shareholders would seldom, if ever, prefer its results over those of some alternative course of action. This is, of course, precisely what Congress intended.

Other aspects of Section 341

In addition to the definition of a collapsible corporation (contained in Sec. 341(b)) and the shareholder treatment (provided in Sec. 341(a)), other subsections set forth certain presumptions and limitations. Section 341(c) specifies an objective test that, if met, indicates a presumption that the corporation is collapsible. This presumption is rebuttable but presumably places a greater burden of proof on the corporation. Congress apparently felt the basic definition of a collapsible corporation was so subjective that some additional objective criteria were necessary to make Sec. 341 effective. The presumption applies if the fair market value of the corporation's "Sec. 341 assets" (inventory and property held for sale to customers are two examples) is (1) 50 percent or more of the fair market value of its total assets, and (2) 120 percent or more of the adjusted basis of such Sec. 341 assets.[11]

Sections 341(d), (e), and (f) provide exceptions that allow shareholders to recognize long-term capital gain rather than ordinary income, even though the corporation is a collapsible corporation. Under Sec. 341(d), the ordinary income treatment of Sec. 341(a) does not apply to:

1. Certain shareholders who own 5 percent or less of the stock of the corporation;

2. Gain recognized by a shareholder during a year when 70 percent or less of the gain is attributable to manufactured, constructed, or produced property or certain purchased property; or

3. Gain realized by a shareholder more than 3 years after the completion of the manufacture, construction, production, or purchase of property.

With regard to the third exception, note that the three-year time period does not start until the *completion* of the manufacture or construction, for example. Suffice it to say that the I.R.S. often perceives a continuation of manufacture long after the taxpayer has viewed the process as complete.

Section 341(e) allows long-term capital gain to be recognized by shareholders on certain sales of stock and complete liquidations of otherwise collapsible corporations when only a minimal percentage of the corporation's net worth relates to assets that would produce ordinary income if sold directly by the corporation. Similar tests under Sec. 341(e) also permit the corporation to utilize Sec. 337 or the shareholder to elect Sec. 333 upon liquidation of the corporation. The nonrecognition provisions of Secs. 337 and 333 are normally not available on the liquidation of a collapsible corporation.

The final exception to ordinary income recognition under Sec. 341(a) is found in Sec. 341(f). Long-term capital gain may be recognized by a shareholder on the *sale* of stock of a collapsible corporation if the corporation consents to recognize gain on later disposition of certain of its assets in situations that would otherwise not be taxable dispositions. These assets are referred to as "subsection (f) assets" and generally consist of non-capital assets and certain real estate.

Some examples of potentially nontaxable dispositions that we have discussed in Chapters 5 and 6 are nonliquidating property distributions (Sec. 311), distributions in partial and complete liquidation (Sec. 336), and sales in connection with certain liquidations (Sec. 337). A corporation that has consented to Sec. 341(f), so that a shareholder can sell stock and recognize long-term capital gain, may not later distribute or sell an appreciated "subsection (f) asset" and receive nonrecognition under Secs. 311, 336, or 337. The corporation's realized gain would be recognized.

---

[11] "Section 341 assets" are described in Sec. 341(b)(3), and total assets are defined in Sec. 341(c)(2).

PROBLEMS

Note: Assume corporations are not "collapsible" unless so indicated in the problem.

1. X Corporation distributes cash to shareholders Jones and Smith in exchange for part of their X stock. Explain why *both* Jones and Smith *will* receive sale treatment if the transaction is a partial liquidation, while *either, both, or neither might* qualify for sale treatment if the transaction is not a partial liquidation.

2. Z Corporation plans to distribute appreciated property to its shareholders in exchange for part of their Z stock. Assume the transaction may be structured to qualify either as a partial liquidation or as a nonliquidating stock redemption qualifying the shareholders for sale treatment.
   a. Is there any advantage in structuring the transaction as a partial liquidation? Discuss.
   b. What requirements would have to be met to qualify the transaction as a partial liquidation?

3. Y Corporation has been engaged in the active conduct of two different businesses for 10 years. A decision to terminate one of the businesses has been reached, and three different plans are under consideration:
   Plan No. 1: Y will sell all the assets of the terminated business and distribute the proceeds to its shareholders in exchange for part of their Y stock.

Plan No. 2: Y will sell some of the assets of the terminated business and distribute the proceeds and unsold assets to its shareholders in exchange for part of their Y stock.

Plan No. 3: Y will distribute all of the assets of the terminated business to its shareholders in exchange for part of their stock.

Under Plans No. 2 and No. 3 it is assumed that some shareholders would immediately sell the noncash assets received while others would not.

While most of the assets of the business to be terminated have a fair market value in excess of their adjusted basis to Y, for some assets, Y's adjusted basis exceeds fair market value.

   a.   Do any of the plans qualify for partial liquidation treatment? Explain.
   b.   Discuss both favorable and unfavorable aspects of Plans No. 1 and No. 3.
   c.   What issue is raised by the immediate sale by some shareholders of the noncash assets under Plans No. 2 and No. 3?

4.   Describe how the definition of "complete liquidation" contrasts with that of "legal dissolution." Why might this distinction be important?

5.   Table 6–1 summarizes four possible shareholder treatments that may arise from complete liquidations. For each category, briefly provide a logical explanation for the indicated recognition and basis rules.

6.   Section 332 provides a mandatory rule that certain parent corporations recognize no gain or loss when the property of a qualifying subsidiary is distributed to its parent in complete liquidation of the subsidiary. Why might a parent corporation seek to avoid Sec. 332 treatment? How might this be accomplished?

7.   Identify factors that would suggest an election under Sec. 333 (election concerning recognition of gain in certain liquidations) might be unwise.

8.   a.   Briefly summarize the tax treatment prescribed by Sec. 337.
   b.   Section 337 was aimed at resolving what problem?
   c.   What application does Sec. 337 have to distributions of property to shareholders by corporations in the process of complete liquidation?
   d.   What application does Sec. 337 have to the sales of property by corporations, where the sales proceeds will be distributed in the process of partial liquidation?
   e.   Is Sec. 337 elective or mandatory?
   f.   How might a corporation avoid Sec. 337 treatment?
   g.   Explain the "straddle technique" used in connection with Sec. 337. What risks are associated with this technique?

9.   a.   Section 341 (collapsible corporations) is aimed at closing what potential "loophole" in the tax law?
   b.   Considering the Sec. 341(b) definition of collapsible corporation, what factors could prevent a corporation from being "collapsible"?
   c.   Assuming a corporation is considered collapsible and no exceptions apply, summarize the tax treatment prescribed by Sec. 341(a).

10.   Ten shareholders each own 10 of the 100 outstanding shares of P Corporation, which has assets with a net fair market value of $500,000. P distributes $5,000 to each shareholder in exchange for each surrendering 9 shares of P. Assume the transaction qualifies as a partial liquidation and each shareholder's basis in the P stock is $2,000 per share. What gain or loss will each shareholder recognize?

11.   Ninety percent of Corporation S, which has only common stock outstanding, is owned by Corporation P and 10 percent by individual A. Both P and A have owned their stock in S for more than three years. The sole assets of S are two buildings, each having a fair market value of $100,000 and a basis to S of $50,000. A's basis for her stock is $10,000. P's basis for its stock is $60,000. On

August 1, 19X8, S adopts a plan of complete liquidation. On September 1, 19X8, S sells building No. 1 for $100,000 and, during October 19X8, S makes a pro rata distribution of building No. 2 and the net of tax proceeds from the sale of building No. 1.

a. What is S's realized gain on the sale of building No. 1?

b. What, if any, is S's recognized gain on the sale of building No. 1?

c. If gain is recognized by S, determine the income tax S would pay. (Use current corporate rates and assume no other transactions for the year.)

d. Determine the amount, if any, and character of gain recognized by P on the liquidation of S and P's basis in building No. 2. (Note: After the liquidation of S, P directly owns 90 percent of building No. 2.)

e. Determine the amount, if any, and character of gain recognized by A on the liquidation of S and A's basis in building No. 2. (Note: After the liquidation of S, A directly owns 10 percent of building No. 2.)

f. If A's nominal marginal tax rate is 70 percent, what fair market value of property and money will A have, after tax, from the liquidation of S?

12. Big Wheels has owned 10 percent of Circle Corporation since Circle was organized in 19X0. On October 15, 19X9, pursuant to a plan to complete liquidation, Circle distributed all of its properties (other than some cash needed to pay liabilities) to its shareholders. Each shareholder received a pro rata share of each type of property distributed. The *total* distribution was:

	Fair market value	Basis to Circle
Cash	$ 40,000	$ 40,000
Land	350,000	130,000
Building	50,000	60,000
Equipment	140,000	150,000
XYZ stock	60,000	20,000

Circle's total accumulated earnings and profits, immediately before the liquidating distribution, were $60,000. Big's stock basis was $24,000.

In parts a–e, assume Sec. 333 does *not* apply to Big Wheels.

a. What is Big's realized gain?

b. What is Big's recognized gain and its character?

c. What is Big's cost basis and date basis in the noncash properties received?

d. Explain how Circle and Big would be affected if immediately before the October 15, 19X9 distribution it was discovered that the equipment's basis was $100,000 rather than $150,000. (No calculations are required.)

e. With regard to your answers to parts a–d, does it matter whether Big is an individual or a corporation?

In parts f–h, assume Sec. 333 *does* apply and Big Wheels is an individual.

f. What is Big's recognized gain and its character?

g. What is Big's cost basis and date basis in the noncash properties received?

h. Explain how Circle and Big would be affected if immediately before the October 15, 19X9 distribution it was discovered that the equipment's basis was $100,000 rather than $150,000. (No calculations are required.)

In parts i and j assume Sec. 333 *does* apply and Big Wheels is a corporation.

i. What is Big's recognized gain and its character?

j. Review your answers to parts f and i. Does the corporate qualified electing shareholder receive preferential treatment compared with the treatment accorded the noncorporate qualified electing shareholder? Explain.

13. Pursuant to a plan of liquidation, Willoughby Corporation transferred all of its properties during May 19X7 to its shareholders in cancellation of all 1,000 shares of its outstanding stock. The stock, all shares of which were entitled to vote on the plan of liquidation, was owned as follows:

	No. of shares
A Corporation	100
B Corporation	300
C Corporation	200
Ricky Individual	80
Lucy Individual	200
Fred Individual	120
	1,000

B, C, Ricky, and Lucy filed timely elections under Sec. 333.
  a. Based on the above facts, which shareholders are qualified electing shareholders under Sec. 333?
  b. Which shareholders are qualified electing shareholders if it is further assumed that B had owned 600 of Willoughby's 1,000 shares from 19X0 to 19X5?

14. Even though a valid election under Sec. 333 has been made, a qualified electing shareholder must recognize income or gain if earnings and profits exist or if cash or marketable securities (acquired after December 31, 1953) are distributed. Briefly present logical explanations why each of these three factors triggers recognition, that is, for each, identify an argument that supports its treatment as an exception to the general (nonrecognition) rule of Sec. 333.

15. Individual A has owned all the stock of Corporation X for more than three years. During this time, X has also owned 90 percent of the stock of Corporation Y. The remaining 10 percent of Y has been owned by individual B. A desires the complete liquidation of both X and Y and wants Sec. 337 to apply to both liquidations.
  a. In meeting A's objective, does the order (X first, then Y or Y first, then X) of the liquidations matter? Explain.
  b. Assume B wants to elect Sec. 333 on the liquidation of Y. Does this pose any threat to A's objective of having Sec. 337 apply to the liquidation of Y? How could A prevent Sec. 333 from applying to B if X is liquidated first? If Y is liquidated first?

16. X Corporation was formed in 19X3 by the unrelated individuals A, B, and C. In exchange for $1,000 cash per share, 100 shares of common stock were issued (A, 60; B, 30; and C, 10). In 19X9, after accumulating substantial earnings and profits, X redeemed 30 shares from A for $45,000 cash and 20 shares from B for business-use land with a fair market value of $30,000 and a basis to X of $5,000.
  Assuming the redemptions *qualify* as a partial liquidation of X:
  a. What amount, if any, and character of gain or loss is recognized by A, B, C, and X?
  b. What basis will B have in the land?
  c. What is the effect on X's E & P?
  Assuming the redemptions do *not* qualify as a partial liquidation of X:
  d. What amount, if any, and character of gain or loss is recognized by A, B, C, and X?

e. What basis will B have in the land?

f. What is the effect on X's E & P?

Considering your answers to parts a–f:

g. Indicate which shareholders should prefer partial liquidation status, which should prefer that the redemptions not be classified as a partial liquidation, and which (considering their self-interests) would be indifferent. Explain.

17. Z Corporation was organized on January 15, 19X1. Z purchased land to be used in its business on February 1, 19X2 for $20,000. On August 12, 19X8, when the land was worth $35,000, Z adopted a plan of partial liquidation. As part of this plan, on June 3, 19X9, when the land had a fair market value of $40,000, it was distributed to shareholder Jones in exchange for Z stock purchased by Jones on September 1, 19X7.

a. In determining his gain or loss on the partial liquidation, what value does Jones use for the land?

b. Will gain or loss recognized by Jones be short-term or long-term?

c. What cost basis will Jones have in the land?

d. What date basis will Jones have in the land?

e. Will the land be a capital or noncapital asset to Jones? Explain.

18. In 19X7, after operating both a retail furniture store and a local moving and storage business for 10 years, DEF Corporation decided to get out of the moving and storage business. On October 15, 19X7, under a plan adopted in July 19X7, DEF distributed all of the properties of the moving and storage business, except a warehouse, to its shareholders in exchange for 30 percent of their DEF stock. The warehouse was retained to store inventory for DEF's growing furniture business.

a. Identify each requirement that must be met to qualify a distribution as a Sec. 346(a)(2) partial liquidation under the safe harbor of Sec. 346(b).

b. Do any of the requirements appear vulnerable to I.R.S. attack as not having been met by DEF? Explain.

c. What restructuring of the transactions would have been necessary to minimize the possibility of I.R.S. objections while still meeting DEF's objectives?

19. J.W. and D.S. own 40 shares and 60 shares, respectively, of Taxiland Corporation. Taxiland has operated an amusement park, Taxiland, Michigan, since 19X1. It also operates a successful driving school. On December 31, 19X8, J.W. and D.S. approved a plan that calls for the sale of Taxiland, Michigan in July of 19X9. One-third of the proceeds of the sale are to be used to redeem 20 shares of J.W.'s stock and two-thirds to redeem 40 shares of D.S.'s stock. How would the redemptions be characterized if:

a. The driving school was started on July 1, 19X6?

b. The driving school was started on July 1, 19X3?

c. The driving school was started on July 1, 19X3, *and* no stock was surrendered by either J.W. or D.S.?

20. Girder, Inc. has the following shareholders:

	No. of shares	When acquired	Basis
A	60	March 14, 19X2	$ 5,000
	80	August 10, 19X5	30,000
B	80	December 4, 19X6	60,000
C	40	July 15, 19X7	15,000
	40	August 31, 19X7	80,000

On January 1, 19X8, the shareholders approved a plan of complete liquidation. On June 30, 19X8, a pro rata distribution of $150,000 was made, and on January 31, 19X9 a final pro rata distribution of $240,000 was made.

What gain or loss (and character) is recognized by A, B, and C in 19X8? In 19X9?

21. On June 1, 19X7, a plan of complete liquidation was adopted for Zip, a calendar-year accrual basis corporation. During the period June 1, 19X7 through December 31, 19X7, Zip discontinued its operations, paid its liabilities, and sold certain of its properties. From January 1, 19X8 to March 1, 19X8, its only activity consisted of paying the balance due on its 19X7 federal income tax. On March 15, 19X8, the remaining properties of Zip, less any cash needed to pay its 19X8 federal income tax, will be distributed to its sole shareholder in redemption of all its stock. At March 14, 19X8, the properties of Zip are:

	Fair market value	Basis
Cash	$35,000	$35,000
Building (Note 1)	40,000	30,000
Equipment No. 1 (Note 2)	12,000	10,000
Equipment No. 2 (Note 3)	15,000	20,000
Land (Note 4)	60,000	40,000
XYZ stock (Note 5)	10,000	4,000
Note receivable No. 1 (Note 6)	35,000	(See Note 6)
Note receivable No. 2 (Note 7)	20,000	(See Note 7)

Note 1: The building was purchased for $60,000 10 years ago and has been depreciated on the straight-line method.

Note 2: Equipment No. 1 was purchased 10 years ago for $30,000. Straight-line depreciation over a 15-year life has been used.

Note 3: Equipment No. 2 was purchased two years ago for $25,000. Straight-line depreciation over a 10-year life has been used.

Note 4: The land was acquired six years ago and was used in Zip's business.

Note 5: The XYZ stock was acquired July 15, 19X7 as an investment.

Note 6: Note receivable No. 1 was received by Zip on Februauy 15, 19X6, when Zip sold investment land it had owned for five years for $35,000. The land cost Zip $20,000. The first collections on the note are scheduled to start in 19X9. Zip elected installment sale treatment.

Note 7: Note receivable No. 2 was received by Zip on August 15, 19X7, when Zip sold its entire inventory to one buyer for $20,000. Zip's basis in the inventory was $8,000. The first collections on the note are scheduled to start in 19X9. Zip elected installment sale treatment.

What amount of cash should be retained by Zip in order to pay its 19X8 federal income tax, assuming the income tax provisions currently in effect would apply, and:

a. Zip's sole shareholder is an individual *not* electing Sec. 333.

b. Zip's sole shareholder is an individual who properly elects and qualifies for Sec. 333 treatment.

c. Zip's sole shareholder is a corporation that meets the requirements of Secs. 332 and 334(b)(1).

d. Zip's sole shareholder is a corporation that meets the requirements of Secs. 332 and 334(b)(2).

22. A Corporation owns the following assets:

	Basis	Fair market value	Date acquired
Cash	$20,000	$20,000	
Land	30,000	50,000	December 26, 19X1
Equipment	35,000	30,000	July 10, 19X8

A is owned by four individuals:

	No. of shares	Date acquired	Basis
W	25	July 4, 19X5	$10,000
	25	December 2, 19X8	20,000
X	40	December 15, 19X7	18,000
Y	50	December 15, 19X8	40,000
Z	60	June 28, 19X3	28,000

On June 30, 19X9 the following distributions are made in complete liquidation of A:

W	$25,000 fair market value of land
X	$20,000 cash
Y	$25,000 fair market value of land
Z	$30,000 fair market value of equipment

For each shareholder, determine any gain or loss recognized (including its character), the basis of any noncash property received, and the date basis for such property.

23. Stork Corporation manufactures chimney gratings. It has three classes of stock: (1) nonvoting preferred (500 shares); (2) voting preferred (5,000 shares); and (3) voting common (5,000 shares). Neither class of preferred stock is entitled to participate in dividends or liquidation beyond its preferred interests. Upon liquidation, the nonvoting and voting preferred are entitled to $50 and $20 per share, respectively, before any remaining properties may be distributed to the common shareholders. The stock ownership of Stork, which has remained unchanged for the last 10 years, is:

	Penguin Corp.	Robin Corp.	Alabaster
Nonvoting preferred	100	100	300
	(basis, $3000)	(basis, $3000)	(basis, $9000)
Voting preferred	4720	none	280
	(basis, $47,200)		(basis, $2800)
Voting common	3500	1500	none
	(basis, $20,000)	(basis, $25,000)	

On July 1, 19X8, the shareholders of Stork Corporation voted to liquidate the company. Operations immediately stopped. Stork Corporation's assets and liabilities as of July 1, 19X8, were as follows:

Assets	Fair market value	Basis	Liabilities
Cash	$ 35,000	$30,000	Accounts payable $20,000
Accounts receivable	60,000	60,000	
Inventory	110,000	60,000	
Equipment	80,000	50,000	
Land:			
Lot No. 1	35,000	20,000	
Lot No. 2	60,000	50,000	

On July 15, 19X8, in redemption of all its stock, Stork made the following distributions.

Penguin Corp.: All the inventory and equipment
             $50,000 of the accounts receivable
             $400 cash

Robin Corp.: Lots No. 1 and No. 2
             $4,000 cash

Alabaster: $10,000 of accounts receivable
             $10,600 cash

The remaining $20,000 cash was retained by the corporation to pay the accounts payable as they came due.

a. Compute the gain or loss (if any) recognized by Penguin Corporation, Robin Corporation, Alabaster, and Stork Corporation.

b. Compute the bases in the property received in the liquidating distribution by Penguin Corporation, Robin Corporation and Alabaster.

24. Zenon Corporation adopted a plan of complete liquidation on July 1, 19X5. The fact that Zenon was owned by many different shareholders, none owning more than 10 percent of its stock, caused a direct distribution of its properties to be impractical. Therefore, it was decided to sell all the assets and on December 15, 19X5, in redemption of all the stock, to distribute cash to the shareholders. The following transactions (in chronological order) occurred between July 1, 19X5 and December 15, 19X5:

1. Equipment with a basis of $5,000 was sold for $3,000. The equipment was purchased two years earlier, and $2,000 of depreciation had been claimed.

2. Land with a basis of $40,000, which had been used in the business for 10 years, was sold for $60,000.

3. Inventory with a basis of $8,000 was sold for $12,000. Although the purchaser of this inventory had been a regular customer of Zenon's, the amount involved in this purchase greatly exceeded prior transactions, and the $12,000 reflected a substantial "volume discount."

4. An installment note receivable (which had originally been received in 19X3 when investment land owned for three years was sold) was sold for $30,000. The note's face amount was $35,000. Zenon's basis in the note was $26,000.

5. All remaining inventory (basis $54,000) was sold to a competitor for $60,000.

6. Equipment purchased 10 years earlier for $47,000 was sold for $11,000. Basis at time of sale was $10,000.

7. Accounts receivable with a face amount and basis of $30,000 were sold to a bank for $27,000. All of these accounts were considered to be fully collectible.

Determine the amount (and character) of gain or loss recognized by Zenon as a result of each of the above transactions.

25. On December 31, 19X5, P Corporation purchased all the outstanding stock of S Corporation for $70,000 cash. At the time of this purchase, S had E & P of $8,000, liabilities of $20,000, and the following assets:

	Basis	Fair market value	Date acquired
Cash	$30,000	$30,000	
Accounts receivable	10,000	10,000	
Inventory	7,000	14,000	
Equipment	18,000	16,000	June 30, 19X5
Land	5,000	20,000	December 1, 19X1

On January 1, 19X6, a plan for the complete liquidation of S was adopted and all of P's assets, except $20,000 cash retained to pay the liabilities, were distributed to P.

a. What amount, and character, of gain or loss is recognized by S? by P?

b. What is P's basis in each of the noncash properties received?

c. What is P's date basis in the equipment and land?

d. What happens to S's E & P?

   In parts e–h, assume P purchased 50 percent of S's stock on June 30, 19X4 for $35,000 and the remaining 50 percent on December 31, 19X5 for $35,000.

e. What amount, and character, of gain or loss is recognized by S? by P?

f. What is P's basis in each of the noncash properties received?

g. What is P's date basis in the equipment and land?

h. What happens to S's E & P?

i. How would you modify your answers to parts a and e if S's basis in the equipment had been $14,000 rather than $18,000? Assume accumulated depreciation on the equipment at December 31, 19X5 was $6,000.

26. On August 15, 19X7, under a plan of complete liquidation adopted March 15, 19X7, Rigid Corporation distributed 100 shares of Ajax Corporation stock to shareholder Flexible. Rigid originally purchased the stock in 19X3. Flexible sold the Ajax stock on June 30, 19X8. Assume the sale resulted in a capital gain. Indicate whether the gain will be short-term or long-term and explain why, assuming Flexible's basis in the Ajax stock was determined under:

a. Sec. 334(a)

b. Sec. 334(b)(1)

c. Sec. 334(b)(2)

d. Sec. 334(c)

27. P and S are both calendar-year corporations. P purchased 100 percent of S's stock on January 15, 19X1. P plans to liquidate S and wants its basis in S's assets to be determined under Sec. 334(b)(2).

a. What is the latest date a plan for S's liquidation could be adopted?

b. If S is to be liquidated in a series of distributions to P, what is the latest year the first distribution in the series could be made?

c. Assuming the first distribution is made on June 15, 19X3, what is the latest date the final distribution could be made?

SUPPLEMENTAL PROBLEMS

28. A liquidation under Sec. 331 requires a valuation of all properties distributed. Could it be argued that a determination of fair market value is not possible? What view does the I.R.S. take and why?

Research aids: *Burnet* v. *Logan,* 283 US 404 (1931)

Rev. Rul. 58-402, 1958-2 CB 15

29. S Corporation transfers property with a fair market value of $10,000 and a basis of $6,000 to a creditor in payment of a $10,000 debt. For each of the following situations, indicate what gain, if any, S will recognize and the basis the creditor will take in the property:

a. The creditor is unrelated to S, and S is not in the process of liquidation.

b. The creditor is unrelated to S, and S is liquidating in a manner that meets the general requirements of Sec. 337.

    c. The creditor is S's parent corporation, and S is liquidating in a manner that meets the general requirements of Secs. 332 and 334(b)(1).

    d. The creditor is S's parent corporation, and S is liquidating in a manner that meets the general requirements of Sec. 332 and 334(b)(2).

        Research aids: Secs. 1001, 1002, 1012, 332(c), 334(b)(1), 334(b)(2)

        Rev. Rul. 69-426, 1969-2 CB 48

30. Individual A owns all the stock of X Corporation and has also loaned X $5,000. A's basis in the X stock is $40,000. In complete liquidation of X and in payment of the loan, X transfers land (X's only asset) with fair market value of $30,000 to A. X's basis in the land is $36,000. What is X's *realized* loss on (1) the portion of the land used to pay the $5,000 debt, and (2) the portion of the land used to redeem the X stock? What is A's *realized* loss on the X stock? For each of these losses, indicate whether or not it will be *recognized* and the Code section that supports recognition or nonrecognition.

        Research aid: Rev. Rul. 76-175, 1976-1 CB 92

31. S Corporation, a wholly owned subsidiary of P Corporation, is liquidated. Owing to S's insolvency, the creditors of S receive all of S's assets and P receives nothing upon surrender of all of its S stock. P's basis in S's stock is $10,000. What amount, if any, and character of gain or loss is recognized by P? What Code section authorizes the treatment indicated?

        Research aids: Treas. Reg. Sec. 1.332-2(b)

        Spaulding Bakeries, Inc., 252 F.2d 693 (2d Cir. 1958)

32. X Corporation holds accounts receivable with a face amount of $20,000 and a related reserve for bad debts of $4,000. As part of a Secs. 331 and 334(a) liquidation meeting the general requirements of Sec. 337, X sells the accounts receivable for $17,000. What amount, if any, and character of gain or loss will X recognize? What would your answer be if the receivables were distributed directly to X shareholders as part of the liquidation? (Assume a fair market value of $17,000.)

        Research aids: Rev. Rul. 78-278, 1978-2 CB 134

        Rev. Rul. 78-279, 1978-2 CB 135

        Coast Coil Co., 422 F.2d 402 (9th Cir. 1970)

corporate divisions and reorganizations

The provisions of the Internal Revenue Code concerning corporate divisions and reorganizations are among the more complex provisions in the Code. In this chapter, we introduce these provisions and assess their impact on American business. The provisions on corporate reorganizations and divisions apply equally to closely held and publicly traded corporations. An understanding of these provisions permits the owners of large and small businesses alike to take advantage of a legal, tax planning device that enables them to retain their capital intact while changing the form of their investment.

This chapter is divided into four parts. In the first part, we present an overview of the basic principles of corporate reorganizations and divisions, discuss their development, and examine the statutory provisions governing each type of transaction. In the second part, we examine the amount and character of the gain recognized by the parties to each type of transaction and the basic rules applying to the property received. In the third part, we review the various problem areas associated with reorganization transactions, including the restrictions imposed by various judicial doctrines. In the final part, we examine the ability of the acquiring corporation to use the tax attributes of the acquired corporation.

HISTORY OF THE REORGANIZATION PROVISIONS

Before the passage of the Revenue Act of 1918, the restructuring of a business enterprise that involved an exchange of stock in one corporation for stock in a sec-

ond, successor corporation generally resulted in a gain that was taxable to the shareholder. A taxable gain resulted when the market value of the stock received exceeded the cost of the original stock *and* when the stock that was received constituted a different business interest from the original investment. This occurred even though the successor corporation may have been formed under the laws of another state and carried on the activities of the first corporation.[1]

When considering the Revenue Act of 1918, Congress approved an exception to the general gain or loss recognition rules involving reorganization and merger transactions in order to permit corporations to restructure their activities without incurring any tax liability. This exception, found in Sec. 202(b) of the Act, provided . . .

> but when in connection with the reorganization, merger, or consolidation of a corporation a person receives in place of stock or securities owned by him new stock or securities of no greater aggregate par or face value, no gain or loss shall be deemed to occur from the exchange, and the new stock or securities received shall be treated as taking the place of the stock, securities, or property exchanged.
>
> When in the case of any such reorganization, merger or consolidation the aggregate par or face value of the new stock or securities received is in excess of the aggregate par or face value of the stock or securities exchanged, a like amount in par or face value of the new stock or securities received shall be treated as taking the place of the stock or securities exchanged, and the amount of the excess in par or face value shall be treated as a gain to the extent that the fair market value of the new stock or securities is greater than

[1] See, for example, *Walter L. Marr* v. *U.S.*, 268 U.S. 536 (1924) *aff'g.* 58 Ct. Cls. 658 (1923).

the cost (or if acquired prior to March 1, 1913, the fair market value as of that date) of the stock or securities exchanged.[2]

The 1918 Act dealt only with a case in which the stockholders or security holders of one company received new stock or securities in exchange for old stock or securities. These nonrecognition rules did not extend tax-free reorganization treatment to other types of corporate adjustments, such as an exchange of assets by one corporation for stock or securities of another corporation.

This original definition of a tax-free reorganization was substantially expanded and modified in the 1921 and 1924 Revenue Acts to include a number of additional forms of transactions, including the exchange by a corporation of property for stock or securities of a second corporation pursuant to a plan of reorganization. In addition, the predecessors to our current rules regarding the receipt of "boot" in a tax-free reorganization were introduced. Although further technical changes to the tax-free reorganization rules have been made, the basic transactions covered by this portion of the Code are quite similar to these "early" provisions. The transaction forms that are covered by the tax-free reorganization rules are discussed in the next two sections.

OVERVIEW OF THE BASIC REORGANIZATION PRINCIPLES

Corporate reorganizations may be either divisive or nondivisive. A divisive reorganization is one in which a single corporation is divided into two or more corporations, one of which may be the original corporation. Thus, in a divisive reorganization, A Corporation may be divided into A Corporation and a new entity known as B Corporation, or two new entities, known as B Corporation and C Corporation, may be created. Nondivisive reorganizations may be of two types: acquisitive and nonacquisitive reorganizations. An acquisitive reorganization takes place when the assets or stock of one or more corporations is acquired by another corporation. For example, A Corporation may acquire the assets or stock of B Corporation. Alternatively, two independent corporations, A Corporation and B Corporation, may be "merged" into a single, continuing corporation (either A Corporation or B Corporation), or A Corporation and B Corporation may be "consolidated"

into a single, new corporation known as C Corporation. A nonacquisitive reorganization ordinarily involves only (1) a change in the capital structure of a single corporation that remains in existence, or (2) a change in the identity, form, or place of incorporation of a single corporation whereby the "new" corporation formed represents a continuation of a corporation that goes out of existence.

A reorganization transaction thus generally involves one or more corporate entities. Some reorganizations involve both the corporation and its shareholders; other reorganizations involve a corporation and the shareholders of one or more other corporations. Common to each transaction, however, is the *exchange* of assets or stocks or both by the parties to the reorganization in a transaction in which a gain or loss may be realized. The question facing the parties to the reorganization is: Will the *realized* gain or loss need to be *recognized* for tax purposes?

Recognition of realized gains and losses

Section 1001(c) provides the general rule regarding the need to recognize the amount of a realized gain or loss:

> (c) Recognition of Gain or Loss.—Except as otherwise provided in this subtitle, the entire amount of the gain or loss, determined under this section, on the sale or exchange of property shall be recognized.

A transaction qualifying under the corporate reorganization provisions of Secs. 354–368 represents an exception to the general rule of Sec. 1001(c).[3] The gain or loss on the reorganization transaction is not permanently excluded from taxation but only deferred until a subsequent event occurs that causes the deferred gain or loss, as well as any other subsequent change in value, to be recognized under Sec. 1001(c). The theory behind the deferral of the gain or loss in a corporate reorganization is similar to that found in the Sec. 351 corporate formation provisions, the Sec. 1031 "like-kind" exchange provisions, or any one of a number of other nonrecognition provisions. The various *parties* to the reorganization are deemed only to have changed the form of their investments, and the new properties received are treated essentially as continuations of the old investments. Such a change in the nature of an investment is considered to provide the parties to the re-

---

[2]Rev. Act of 1918, 40 Stat. 1057, Sec. 202(b).

[3]The Sec. 1031 "like-kind" exchange rules, though permitting the nonrecognition of gain or loss on the exchange of investment property, do not generally apply to a corporate reorganization because of the specific prohibition against stocks, bonds, notes, and other securities or evidences of indebtedness from qualifying under those nonrecognition rules.

organization no funds with which to pay an income tax; therefore, the tax is assessed when these "new" investments are disposed of in a taxable transaction.[4] The reorganization provisions thus act to prevent a taxpayer from having to liquidate part or all of his or her capital investment in order to pay the income taxes resulting from a change in the form in which the investment is held. Only to the extent that, as part of the reorganization, the taxpayer receives property different from the original investment (otherwise known as "boot") is part of the deferred gain required to be recognized. Similar to the "like-kind" exchange rules, deferred losses are not triggered by the receipt of boot.[5]

Preservation of the deferred gain or loss is accomplished by using a substituted basis for any stocks, securities, or properties other than boot received in the reorganization. This substituted basis procedure causes the basis of any stocks and securities received by a shareholder or security holder to equal the basis of the stock, securities, or property the taxpayer transfers plus the amount of the realized gain that the taxpayer recognizes. This substituted basis is reduced by the amount of any boot that is received. Because of the use of a substituted basis different from the fair market value of the stocks and securities received, any deferred gain (loss) is presumed to be recouped at the time that a subsequent event involving the stocks or securities triggers recognition of a gain or loss under Sec. 1001(c).

Similar substituted basis rules apply to property received by a transferee corporation in exchange for its stocks or securities. The transferor's basis is carried over to the transferee corporation and is increased by the amount of the transferor's recognized gain. Use of the substituted basis here reduces the amount of the expense recognized when the asset is utilized, or increases (decreases) the amount of the gain (loss) recognized when the asset is sold or exchanged.

DEFINITIONAL REORGANIZATION PROVISIONS

Code Sec. 368(a)(1) specifies the six types of corporation reorganizations as follows.

---

[4]The repeal of the "carryover basis" rules (discussed in Volume 1, Chapter 19) by the Crude Oil Windfall Profit Tax Act of 1980 (P.L. 96-223) now permits a permanent deferral of the gain because of the operation of the Sec. 1014 stepped-up basis rules for property transferred at death.

[5]Because the tax-free reorganization provisions allow nonrecognition of both gains and losses, a taxpayer may be in a situation in which a loss has been incurred but cannot be recognized if the transaction falls within the definition of one of the reorganization forms. In order to recognize the loss, the transaction must be structured in such a manner as to fall outside the reorganization rules.

(A) A statutory merger or consolidation;
(B) The acquisition by one corporation, in exchange solely for all or part of its voting stock (or in exchange solely for all or a part of the voting stock of a corporation which is in control of the acquiring corporation), of stock of another corporation if, immediately after the acquisition, the acquiring corporation has control of such other corporation (whether or not such acquiring corporation had control immediately before the acquisition);
(C) The acquisition by one corporation, in exchange solely for all or part of its voting stock (or in exchange solely for all or a part of the voting stock of a corporation which is in control of the acquiring corporation), of substantially all of the properties of another corporation, but in determining whether the exchange is solely for stock the assumption by the acquiring corporation of a liability of the other, or the fact that property acquired is subject to a liability, shall be disregarded;
(D) A transfer by a corporation of all or a part of its assets to another corporation if immediately after the transfer the transferor, or one or more of its shareholders (including persons who were shareholders immediately before the transfer), or any combination thereof, is in control of the corporation to which the assets are transferred; but only if, in pursuance of the plan, stock or securities of the corporation to which the assets are transferred are distributed in a transaction which qualifies under Section 354, 355, or 356;
(E) A recapitalization; or
(F) A mere change in identity, form, or place of organization, however effected.

These six types of corporate reorganizations are commonly referred to by tax practitioners by the subparagraph of Sec. 368(a)(1) that contains the applicable definitional rule (for example, a "Type A" reorganization is either a statutory merger or a consolidation). Using the classification scheme developed earlier (divisive or nondivisive; acquisitive or nonacquisitive), the Type D reorganization is the only one of the six that may be a divisive reorganization. The remaining reorganizations may be classified as nondivisive. Of these, Types A, B, and C may be classified as acquisitive reorganizations. The nondivisive Type D and Types E and F are considered nonacquisitive reorganizations because they primarily mean the continuation of an existing corporation that, as a result of the transaction, may take on a new capital structure, identity, name, or state of incorporation, but essentially retains the same assets it held before the transaction.

Not all reorganization transactions fit neatly into one of the six classifications, and in fact, a reorganization may fit into two or more of the six classifications. In a number of these cases, the Code or the I.R.S. has indicated which reorganization rules shall prevail. In still other transactions, a reorganization may satisfy the literal requirements of one of the classifications, but because it lacks a business purpose, an entirely different tax treatment may result. Further discussion of the overlap of the reorganization provisions, their interaction with other types of transactions, and the problems encountered with various judicial doctrines is presented below.

Although Sec. 368 defines the six classifications for reorganization transactions, a number of other Code provisions apply to the determination of the taxability of the transaction to the various parties, the character of the gain, the basis for any property received, and whether the tax attributes of the acquired corporation are assumed by the acquiring corporation. These provisions are outlined in Figure 7-1.

REORGANIZATIONS DEFINED

In this section, we shall discuss in greater detail the definitional requirements for each of the six types of reorganizations.

"Type A" reorganizations

To qualify as a Type A reorganization, a transaction must be structured as either a merger or a consolida-

tion that satisfies the corporation laws of the United States, a state, or the District of Columbia[6] (Treas. Reg. Sec. 1.368-2(b)(1)). A merger transaction, illustrated in Figure 7-2, consists of one corporation acquiring the stock of one or more other corporations (Step 1) and then liquidating the acquired corporation (Step 2). The acquiring corporation acquires all of the acquired corporation's assets and liabilities, after which the acquired corporation goes out of existence.

A consolidation transaction (Figure 7-3) occurs when a newly created corporation's stock is used to acquire the stock of two or more corporations (Step 1), each of which is then liquidated (Step 2). The newly created corporation thus acquires all the assets and liabilities of the acquired corporations, which then proceed to go out of existence.

In a Type A reorganization, the acquiring corporation holds all the acquired corporation's assets and liabilities immediately after the liquidation is completed. Section 368(a)(2)(C) permits the acquiring corporation to transfer all or part of these assets to a corpora-

---

[6]In *Edward H. Russell* v. *Commissioner,* 345 F.2d 534 (CCA-5, 1965) *aff'g.* 40 TC 810 (1963), the failure of the taxpayer to comply with the Mississippi law regarding a merger cost him tax-free treatment for the transaction.

FIGURE **7-1**   Taxation of Reorganization Transactions

Code Section		Description of Provision
1. Recognition of Gain:	354(a)	Permits the nonrecognition of gains and losses when pursuant to a plan of reorganization; stocks or securities[a] of a corporation that is a party to the reorganization are exchanged solely for stocks or securities of that corporation or another corporation that is a party to the reorganization.
	355	Permits a distributee to receive stocks or securities of a corporation that is controlled by the distributing corporation without having to recognize any income.
	357	Provides that the assumption of a taxpayer's liability as part of a reorganization transaction is not to be treated as the receipt of money or other property unless a tax avoidance purpose exists or the liabilities assumed exceed the basis of the property exchanged.
	361	Permits the nonrecognition of gain or loss when, pursuant to a plan of reorganization, a corporation that is a party to the reorganization exchanges property solely for stocks or securities of another corporation that is also a party to the reorganization.
2. Character of Recognized Gain:	356	Determines the amount and character of the gain recognized when boot is received as part of a reorganization.
3. Basis Rules:	358	Determines the basis of stocks and securities received by a transferor as part of the reorganization transaction.
	362	Determines the basis of property acquired by a transferee corporation as part of a reorganization transaction.
4. Assumption of Tax Attributes:	381-383	Provides for the carryover of certain tax attributes of the transferor corporation to the acquiring corporation as part of a tax-free reorganization. Sections 382 and 383 act to limit the acquiring corporation's ability to use these attribute carryovers if the equity interest of the transferor corporation's shareholders in the acquiring corporation falls below certain levels.

[a]Section 354's nonrecognition rules apply only to debts that are considered to be securities. Perhaps the leading case addressing whether an indebtedness is a security is *Camp Wolters Enterprises, Inc.* v. *Commissioner,* 230 F.2d 555 (CCA-5, 1956) *aff'g.* 22 TC 737 (1954). In this case, the Tax Court said, "The test as to whether notes are securities is not a mechanical determination of the time period of the note. Though time is an important factor, the controlling consideration is an overall evaluation of the nature of the debt, degree of participation and continuing interest in the business, the extent of proprietary interest (compared with the similarity of the note to a cash payment), the purpose of the advances, etc." (22 TC 737 at 751). Indebtednesses failing to qualify as securities are classified as "other property" to which the "boot" rules of Sec. 356 apply.

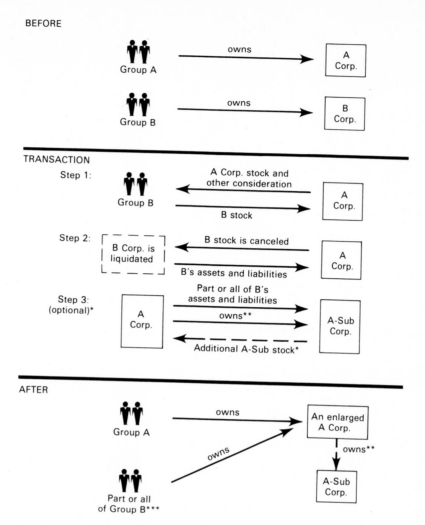

BEFORE

Group A — owns → A Corp.

Group B — owns → B Corp.

TRANSACTION

Step 1:

Group B ← A Corp. stock and other consideration

→ B stock — A Corp.

Step 2:

B Corp. is liquidated ← B stock is canceled

B's assets and liabilities → A Corp.

Step 3: (optional)*

A Corp. → Part or all of B's assets and liabilities

→ owns** → A-Sub Corp.

← Additional A-Sub stock*

AFTER

Group A — owns → An enlarged A Corp.

Part or all of Group B*** — owns →

owns** → A-Sub Corp.

*This step may or may not take place. No additional benefits accrue if A Corporation receives additional A-Sub Corporation stock if it already owns 100% of A-Sub's stock.
**80% control (as defined by Sec. 368(c)) must be held by A Corporation.
***Some or part of the acquired corporation(s) shareholders are required to maintain a "continuity of their equity interest" through ownership of stock of the acquiring corporation.

FIGURE 7-2   Type A Reorganization: Merger

tion that it controls.[7] This arrangement, for example, could permit the acquiring corporation to acquire the assets of a corporation and then to transfer them immediately to a newly created subsidiary corporation whose activities would be conducted separately from those of the parent corporation. (See Step 3 of the merger transaction in Figure 7-2.)

The Type A reorganization permits the acquiring corporation a great deal of flexibility in the types of consideration used to effect the reorganization transaction. The acquiring corporation may use not only its common stock, but also its preferred stock, its debt instruments, cash, and other property to acquire the stock of the acquired corporation. The only restriction placed on the use of nonstock consideration is that the former shareholders of the acquired corporation must maintain a minimum continuing interest in the acquired corporation through stock ownership. We shall examine this judicial doctrine of continuity of interest in the final pages of this chapter.

Nonrecognition of gain or loss is required of the

[7]The minimum level of control required is defined in Sec. 368(c) as the ownership of "80 percent of the total combined voting power of all classes of stock entitled to vote," and 80 percent of the total number of shares of each additional class of stock. The 80 percent test is applied separately to each class of nonvoting stock (Rev. Rul. 59-259, 1959-2 CB 115). Control as used in this chapter will refer to Sec. 368(c) unless otherwise indicated.

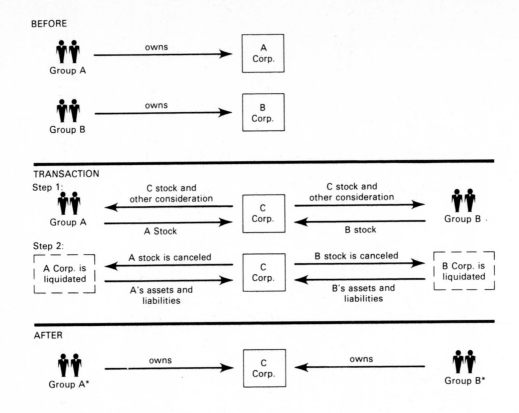

*Some or part of the acquired corporation(s) shareholders are required to maintain a "continuity of their equity interest" through ownership of stock of the acquiring corporation.

FIGURE 7-3   Type A Reorganization: Consolidation

shareholders in the Type A reorganization under Sec. 354(a)(1). Section 354(a)(1) provides that:

> No gain or loss shall be recognized if stock or securities in a corporation a party to the reorganization are, in pursuance of the plan of reorganization, exchanged solely for stock or securities in such a corporation or in another corporation a party to the reorganization.

Thus, the shareholders of the acquired corporation in a Type A reorganization may exchange their stock or securities for those of the acquiring corporation without recognizing any gain or loss on the transaction. Section 354(a)(2), however, restricts tax-free exchanges of securities to situations in which the principal amount of the securities received is equal to or less than the principal amount of the securities surrendered. Otherwise, the fair market value of the excess principal amount of the securities received is considered to be "boot" under Sec. 356 and triggers the recognition of all or part of the realized gain. The receipt of money, other property, and indebtedness not classified as securities by the

acquired corporation's shareholders also constitutes boot under Sec. 356. We shall discuss the characterization of any gain recognized by the shareholders in a later section of this chapter.

Two other Type A reorganization forms—the triangular merger and the reverse triangular merger—act as alternatives, transferring the assets to a controlled corporation under Sec. 368(a)(2)(C) (Figure 7-4). In the triangular merger transaction, stock of the acquiring corporation's parent corporation is transferred to the acquiring corporation as a capital contribution (Step 1); that stock is then used by the acquiring corporation to acquire the stock of the acquired corporation (Step 2). The acquired corporation is then merged with the subsidiary that acted as the acquiring corporation (Step 3). Although the subsidiary acts as the acquiring corporation, the merger transaction still must comply with both the requirements of Sec. 368(a)(1)(A) and applicable state laws as if the parent corporation had been the acquiring corporation. Furthermore, two additional requirements apply to the

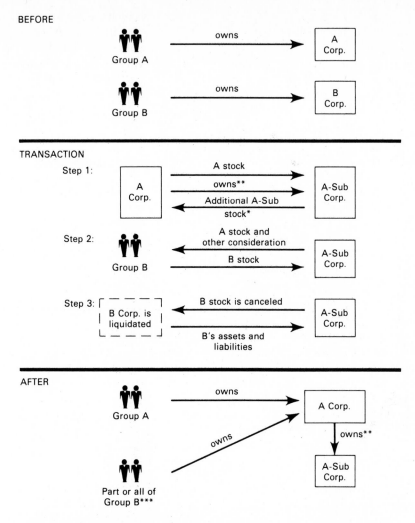

BEFORE

TRANSACTION

AFTER

*This step may or may not take place. No additional benefits accrue if A Corporation receives additional A-Sub Corporation stock if it already owns 100% of A-Sub's stock.

**80% control (as defined by Sec. 368(c)) must be held by A Corporation.

***Some or part of the acquired corporation(s) shareholders are required to maintain a "continuity of their equity interest" through ownership of stock of the acquiring corporation.

FIGURE 7-4   Type A Reorganization: Triangular Merger

triangular merger that do not apply to a regular merger transaction. First, the stock used to effect the acquisition must *only* be that of the parent corporation. None of the acquiring corporation's stock may be used in the transaction, although the acquiring corporation may contribute cash and other property to the transaction. Second, the acquiring corporation must receive "substantially all" the properties of the acquired corporation (Sec. 368(a)(2)(D)). "Substantially all" the properties has been defined by the I.R.S. as "assets representing at least 90 percent of the fair market value of the net assets and at least 70 percent of the fair market value of the gross assets held by the corpo-

ration immediately prior to the transfer."[8] All payments that are made to dissenting stockholders, any stock redemptions, and all other distributions (other than regular, normal distributions made by the corporation immediately before the transfer as part of the reorganization plan) are considered to be part of the

[8]Rev. Proc. 79-14, 1979-1 CB 496, Sec. 3.01. The "substantially-all" requirement that was promulgated in Revenue Procedure 79-14 is one of the Internal Revenue Service's guidelines for issuing ruling letters. This minimum requirement (as well as the other Revenue Procedure 79-14 guidelines cited later) are not binding upon the courts, which have in various cases been both less restrictive and more restrictive than the Service's guidelines in applying the "substantially-all" requirement. Further discussions on the "substantially-all" requirement appear in connection with a Type C reorganization.

asset base to which the "substantially-all" requirement is applied.[9] Thus, if a large number of shareholders of the acquired corporation dissent from a triangular merger, the subsequent transaction could fail the "substantially-all" requirement and create a taxable exchange.

An alternative form of the triangular merger is permitted under Sec. 368(a)(2)(E). In this reverse triangular merger, the acquired corporation remains in existence as a subsidiary of the parent corporation whose voting stock is used to effect the merger. This form of the Type A reorganization transaction is less common than the three forms discussed above, and a detailed review of its coverage is not presented in this book.

Although the Type A reorganization permits the acquiring corporation a great deal of flexibility in the consideration that may be used, four major disadvantages act to restrict its usage. First, the state corporation laws may limit the types of transactions that qualify as a merger, thereby restricting tax planning. Second, under state law, a majority of the shareholders of both the acquiring and the acquired corporations generally must approve the transaction.[10] Obtaining this approval can be costly and time consuming, particularly if both corporations are publicly traded and their stock is held by a large number of shareholders (or a large block of dissenting shareholders exists). For example, shareholders' meetings may be required and proxy materials must be prepared. Because of the need to obtain voting approval of the shareholders of both corporations, the statutory merger is usually thought of as an acquisition rather than a "takeover" transaction. Third, many states permit the dissenting shareholders of both corporations to assert the right to have their shares appraised and purchased for cash. This appraisal and purchase process may involve a substantial cash outlay, and if a large enough block of shares is involved, the dissenters may prevent the transaction from qualifying as a reorganization. The purchase of the dissenting shareholders' stock, however, eliminates any minority interests. Finally, the acquiring corporation assumes all the acquired corporation's assets *and liabilities*. Included in the liabilities may be a number of liabilities that are either unknown to the acquiring party at the time of the merger or that are contingent upon the occurrence of a future event. Such liabilities will act to reduce the value of the net assets received in the reorganization. Each of these problems may be avoided or reduced by using one of the alternative forms of reorganization discussed below.[11] In general, solving these problems requires a trade-off, because the other reorganization forms generally place greater restrictions on the types and amounts of consideration that may be used by the acquiring party. We shall discuss these advantages and disadvantages in greater detail below.

"Type B" reorganization

A Type B reorganization (illustrated in Figures 7-5 and 7-6) is defined as an exchange transaction in which one corporation acquires the stock of a second corporation in such a way that the acquiring corporation has control of the acquired corporation immediately after the acquisition (Sec. 368(a)(1)(B)). The definition of control is found in Sec. 368(c), which was described ear-

[11]Alternatively, when the possibility of incurring such liabilities is substantial, part or all of the consideration given may be placed in escrow, or a contingent stock arrangement developed that permits the consideration to be delivered when the conditions established in the exchange agreement relating to the amount of the liabilities have been satisfied.

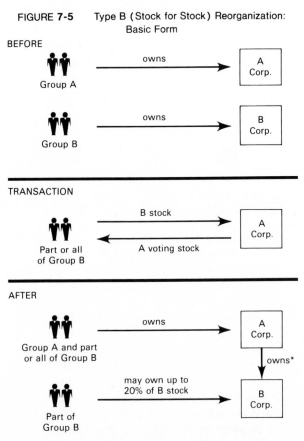

FIGURE **7-5**   Type B (Stock for Stock) Reorganization: Basic Form

*80% control (as defined by Sec. 368(c)) must be held by A Corporation.

[9]The redemption of the shares of the dissenting shareholders may be taxable under Sec. 302 as either a dividend or a capital gain (Rev. Rul. 75-83, 1975-1 CB 112).

[10]Some states require the approval of as many as two-thirds of both corporation's shareholders.

FIGURE 7-6   Subsidiary Corporation Acts as Acquiring Corporation

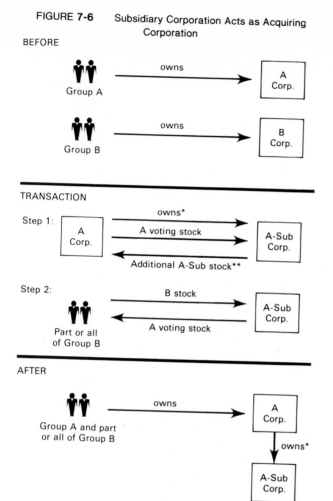

BEFORE

Group A — owns → A Corp.

Group B — owns → B Corp.

TRANSACTION

Step 1:

A Corp. — owns* / A voting stock → A-Sub Corp.

← Additional A-Sub stock**

Step 2:

Part or all of Group B — B stock → A-Sub Corp.

← A voting stock

AFTER

Group A and part or all of Group B — owns → A Corp.

A Corp. — owns* → A-Sub Corp.

A-Sub Corp. — owns* → B Corp.

Part of Group B — may own up to 20% of B stock → B Corp.

*80% control (as defined in Sec. 368(c)) must be held by A Corporation.
**This step may or may not take place. No additional benefits accrue if A Corporation receives additional A-Sub Corporation stock if it already owns 100% of A-Sub's stock.

lier (page 7/5). Control of the acquired corporation may be achieved in a number of ways. It may be acquired in the reorganization transaction either through a single stock acquisition or through a series of stock acquisitions. Alternatively, control of the acquired corporation may be held by the acquiring corporation both before and after a stock acquisition. Thus, once control has been attained, additional acquisitions of minority stockholders' shares that are made using the acquiring corporation's voting stock may be accomplished tax free as a Type B reorganization.

Section 368(a)(1)(B) limits the consideration that may be given by the acquiring corporation to "solely voting stock." This voting stock may be that of the ac-

quiring corporation or the acquiring corporation's parent corporation, but not a mixture of the voting stock of both corporations. (See Figure 7-6.) No other consideration, such as preferred stock, cash, securities, or other property, may be used in the acquisition. The "solely voting stock" requirement, however, does not prevent the acquiring corporation from using cash or other consideration to acquire debt obligations or other property of the acquired corporation in a transaction *separate* from the reorganization transaction.[12]

The Type B reorganization is generally employed when it is desirable for the acquiring corporation to maintain the separate identity of the acquired corporation for such reasons as to use the corporate name, to maintain customer goodwill, or perhaps to take advantage of a nonassignable lease, franchise, license, or other privilege owned by the acquired corporation.[13] As a separate entity, all the acquired corporation's tax attributes remain in its possession. The maintenance of the acquired corporation as a subsidiary may be either permanent or temporary. For as long as it retains separate entity status, the parent and subsidiary corporations may elect to file either consolidated or separate tax returns (see Chapter 8). At some time subsequent to the reorganization date, it may be desirable to liquidate the acquired corporation into the acquiring corporation. If this occurs shortly after the reorganization, the economic result is quite difficult to distinguish from either a Type A or a Type C reorganization.

The solely-for-voting-stock requirement permits the use of either common stock or voting preferred stock in the reorganization. This stock may be either previously unissued stock or treasury stock. Consideration that in the past has been excluded from the definition of voting stock (and will disqualify a transaction from being a Type B reorganization) includes stock rights or warrants,[14] convertible debentures, convertible securities, and stock options. Cash may be used only in a limited fashion. It may be used to acquire stock in lieu of issuing fractional shares to the acquired corporation's shareholders. The use of cash, however, must be a "mechanical rounding-off of the fractions in the exchange, and not be a separately bargained for consideration."[15] Cash may not be used by the acquiring corporation to

[12]See, for example, the exchange of the acquiring corporation's voting stock for the outstanding bonds of the acquiring corporation that did not disqualify a stock-for-stock exchange from being treated as a Type B reorganization when it was separate from the bond-for-stock exchange (Rev. Rul. 70-41, 1970-1 CB 77).
[13]Acquisition of the acquired corporation's stock in a Type B reorganization carries with it the problem of acquiring "hidden" or "contingent" liabilities that was discussed in connection with the Type A reorganization.
[14]*Helvering* v. *Southwest Consolidated Corp.*, 315 U.S. 194 (1942) and Treas. Reg. Sec. 1.354-1(e).
[15]Rev. Rul. 66-365, 1966-2 CB 116.

acquire shares held by the dissenting minority share-holders as part of the reorganization without violating the solely-for-voting-stock requirement. A common technique employed to acquire these shares is to have the acquired corporation redeem the shares held by the dissenters for cash in a transaction separate from the reofganization transaction.[16] When a paper loss is inherent in a situation that would otherwise qualify as a Type B reorganization, the use of cash or other consideration may generally cause the transaction to be disqualified as a tax-free reorganization. As long as the transaction does not qualify as another type of reorganization, this disqualification permits any paper loss to be recognized by the shareholders of the acquired corporation.

Expenses incurred in connection with the reorganization that are directly related to the stock acquisition may be paid in cash by the acquiring corporation without violating the solely-for-voting-stock requirement of a Type B reorganization. Acceptable costs of the reorganization include legal fees, appraisal fees, and administrative costs incurred by the acquiring corporation in order to obtain the stock. In general, payment by the acquiring corporation of costs incurred by the acquired corporation's shareholders violates the solely-for-voting-stock requirement.[17]

The Type B reorganization may involve the acquisition of the necessary stock from either the acquired corporation or its shareholders in a single transaction or in a series of transactions that take place over a relatively short period of time, such as 12 months (Treas. Reg. Sec. 1.368-2(c)). The acquisition is permitted to take place tax free even though the acquiring corporation may already own some of the acquired corporation's stock.[18] Thus, as illustrated in the examples below, the tax-free treatment of a reorganization may apply to part but not all of the stock transactions used to acquire a "controlling interest."

[16]Rev. Rul. 68-285, 1968-1 CB 147.
[17]Rev. Rul. 73-54, 1973-1 CB 187.
[18]The time period between a cash payment for stock and the acquisition of a controlling interest in a corporation may be quite small. For example, in the *C.E. Graham Reeves* case (71 TC 727 (1979)), International Telephone and Telegraph Co. (ITT) purchased for cash a 6 percent (block) interest in the Hartford Insurance Co. in November 1968, and purchased for cash additional Hartford shares between November 1968, and January 1969. In early 1970, ITT acquired additional shares of Hartford stock that satisfied the Sec. 368(c) control requirement. The Tax Court disregarded ITT's earlier cash purchases in determining whether the 1970 acquisition qualified as a Type B reorganization. See, however, two recent Appeals Court decisions in *Arden S. Heverly* v. *Commissioner*, 80-1 USTC para. 9322 (CCA-3, 1980) *rev'g.* 71 TC 727 (1979) and *John L. Pierson* v. *U.S.*, 472 F.Supp. 957 (D.C.-Del., 1979) and *Eldon S. Chapman* v. *Commissioner*, 80-1 USTC para. 9330 (CCA-1, 1980) *rev'g.* 71 TC 727 (1979), which disallowed the use of nonstock consideration in a Type B reorganization. These cases, involving the ITT acquisition of the Hartford Insurance Company, were remanded to the Tax Court and District Court for a determination of whether the cash acquisition was part of a reorganization.

Example (1): A Corporation acquires all the outstanding stock of B Corporation in four separate transactions that took place as follows: 50 percent interest, June 19X1; 25 percent interest, June 19X3; 15 percent interest, January 19X6; and 10 percent interest, June 19X7. Only the last two acquisitions would qualify for reorganization treatment because only immediately after each of these last two acquisitions would A Corporation control B Corporation. If all four acquisitions occurred in a single 12-month period, all acquisitions would most likely receive tax-free treatment by being considered a single series of related transactions.

Example (2): A Corporation purchased for cash 30 percent of the B Corporation stock in 19X0. In 19X9, A Corporation exchanged its own common stock for an additional 60 percent interest in the B Corporation. No gain or loss is recognized by B's shareholders when they exchange their B Corporation stock for the A Corporation common stock because after the transaction A owned a controlling interest in B. The fact that A acquired a 30 percent interest for cash is immaterial to the tax treatment accorded the second transaction because the cash acquisition was considered separate from the reorganization plan. Generally, a cash purchase of stock may be disregarded if it precedes the reorganization transaction by more than 12 months.

The Type B reorganization presents a tax planner with a definite disadvantage in the limited types of consideration that may be used. Generally, however, this type of reorganization may be accomplished without the need to obtain the formal approval of the shareholders of the acquired and acquiring corporations, or of the acquired corporation's directors or management.[19] Thus, the time from the initial offer to acquire the shares to the completion of the transaction may be quite short. In fact, many of these reorganizations are accomplished by having the acquiring corporation issue a tender offer whereby it agrees to exchange its shares for shares of the acquired corporation tendered by a given date. Included in this tender offer may be a statement indicating that if a certain minimum number of

[19]When a takeover is attempted by a second corporation, both the management and director groups of the acquired corporation may resist the actions of the acquiring corporation. They cannot prevent the reorganization by voting against the exchange of stock by the corporation's shareholders, however, except in their capacity as shareholders, or unless the actions of the acquiring corporation violate federal or state laws. See, for example, the opposition of the management and board of directors in the recent unsuccessful attempted acquisition of McGraw-Hill Inc. by the American Express Company (*The Wall Street Journal*, January 16, 1979, p. 5).

shares (usually the number to achieve "control") are not tendered, then the offer will be withdrawn.

In addition, because a Type B reorganization may occur when only 80 percent of the voting stock has been acquired, a 20 percent minority interest may be left with those who refuse to exchange their stock in the acquired corporation for stock of the acquiring corporation. Such a minority shareholder group may prove to be a passive investor group or may be quite bothersome to the parent corporation.

"Type C" reorganization

The Type C, asset-for-stock, reorganization is defined as the acquisition by one corporation of "substantially all" the assets of a second corporation. The consideration permitted to be used to effect a Type C reorganization includes the acquiring corporation's voting stock, the voting stock of the acquiring corporation's parent corporation, the assumption or acquisition of the acquired corporation's liabilities, and a limited amount of cash or other property (Secs. 368(a)(1)(C) and 368(a)(2)(D)). The Type C reorganization is illustrated in Figures 7-7 and 7-8.

The "substantially-all" requirement of a Type C reorganization, like the similar requirement for a triangular Type A reorganization, is not defined in the Code. The I.R.S. provides the same operating rule for defining "substantially all" for both the triangular Type A and the Type C reorganization. The courts have not indicated any minimum percentage of assets that must be transferred in order to satisfy the substantially-all requirement; they generally rely on the facts and circumstances of the situation with particular emphasis on the amount and types of assets transferred and retained, the need for retention of the assets, and whether or not the assets were distributed to the shareholders.[20] Although the Code requires a transfer of substantially all the assets, the acquired corporation is not required to be liquidated in order for the transaction to qualify as a Type C reorganization (Optional Step 2). The acquired corporation may be kept alive for any one of a number of purposes, including: to retain liquid assets in order to satisfy creditor claims, to hold the stock of the acquiring corporation received in the reorganization, to prevent others from using the

[20]Rev. Rul. 57-518, 1957-2 CB 253; *Charles S. Payson v. Commissioner,* 166 F.2d 1008 (CCA-2, 1948) *aff'g.* 6 TCM 590 (1947); *American Foundation Co. v. U.S.,* 120 F.2d 807 (CCA-9, 1941) *rev'g.* unreported D.C. decision; *Daniels Buick, Inc. v. Commissioner,* 251 F.2d 528 (CCA-6, 1958) *aff'g.* 26 TC 894 (1956); *James E. Armour, Inc.* 43 TC 295 (1964); and *John G. Moffatt v. Commissioner,* 363 F.2d 262 (CCA-9, 1966) *aff'g.* 42 TC 558 (1964).

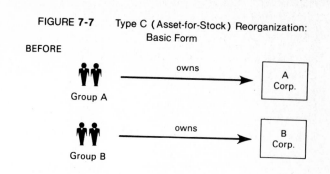

FIGURE 7-7   Type C (Asset-for-Stock) Reorganization: Basic Form

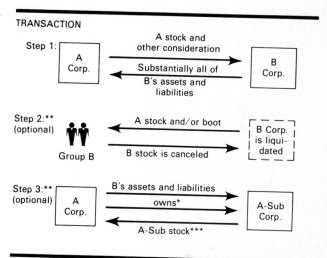

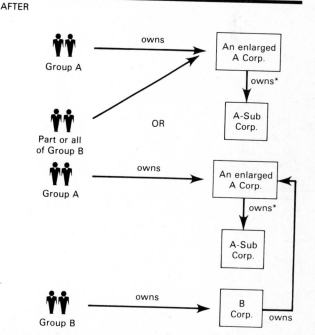

*80% control (as defined by Sec. 368(c)) must be held by A Corporation.
**Optional steps—the stock and/or boot may be distributed, but the acquired corporation does not need to be liquidated. Similarly, A Corporation may transfer part or all of B's assets and liabilities to a subsidiary corporation under Section 368(a)(2)(C).
***This step may or may not take place. No additional benefits accrue if A Corporation receives additional A-Sub Corporation stock if it already owns 100% of A-Sub's stock.

FIGURE 7-8   Subsidiary Corporation Acts as Acquiring Corporation

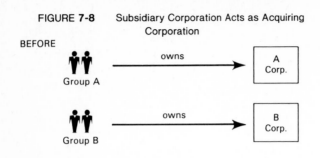

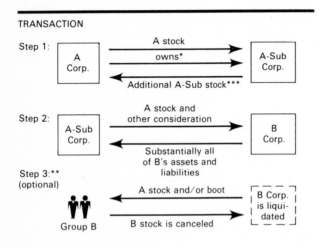

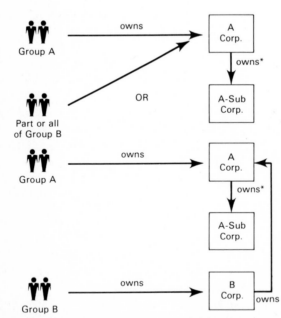

*80% control (as defined by Sec. 368(c)) must be held by A Corporation.
**Optional steps—the stock and/or boot may be distributed, but the acquired corporation does not need to be liquidated. Similarly, A Corporation may transfer part or all of B's assets and liabilities to a subsidiary corporation under Section 368(a)(2)(C).
***This step may or may not take place. No additional benefits accrue if A Corporation receives additional A-Sub Corporation stock if it already owns 100% of A-Sub's stock.

corporate name, and to retain liquid assets with the intention of using the assets to conduct a new trade or business.[21] Although the minimum outlined earlier for the "substantially-all" requirement represents only an I.R.S. guideline for advance ruling purposes, the retention by the acquired corporation of more than a minimal amount of operating assets would probably lead to an I.R.S. challenge and subsequent litigation.

The acquiring corporation may not want to acquire all the assets of the corporation. As a result, the acquired corporation may make a disposition of the unwanted assets before effecting the reorganization transaction. If the amount of unwanted assets is large (compared with the assets transferred in the reorganization), this may lead to the application of the "substantially-all" requirement before the disposition of the unwanted assets, and the transaction may be disqualified from being a Type C reorganization.[22]

The liquidation of the acquired corporation in a Type C reorganization results in a similar situation to a Type A reorganization; that is, the acquiring corporation acquires the assets of the acquired corporation, which goes out of existence. The nonrecognition rules of Sec. 354 permit the acquired corporation's shareholders to defer the recognition of any gains and losses realized when the stock of the acquiring corporation that is received in the reorganization is distributed in exchange for its outstanding shares. An exception to the nonrecognition rules applies when the acquired corporation distributes either securities of the acquiring corporation (in excess of its securities that are surrendered by the acquired corporation's security holders), cash or other property received in the exchange, or some of the acquired corporation's assets that were not transferred to the acquiring corporation. Such payments are considered boot and result in the recognition of gain (but not loss) under Sec. 356.

The bulk of the consideration used to acquire the assets in a Type C reorganization must be either voting stock of the acquiring corporation *or* voting stock of the corporation that controls the acquiring corporation (but not a mixture of both). The definition of voting stock is similar to that outlined earlier in connection with a Type B reorganization (see page 7/9). Cash and other property may be part of the consideration, providing the acquiring corporation acquires solely-for-voting-stock properties of the acquiring corporation having a fair market value of at least 80 percent of the

[21]Rev. Ruls. 68-358, 1968-2 CB 156 and 73-552, 1973-2 CB 116.

[22]*Helvering v. Elkhorn Coal Co.,* 95 F.2d 732 (CCA-4, 1937) *rev'g.* 34 BTA 845 (1936) and 33 BTA 995 (1935). A similar problem may exist with Type A and D reorganizations.

total fair market value of all acquired properties. Thus, when cash and other property are part of the consideration package and exceed 20 percent of the total consideration given, the transaction is prevented from qualifying for tax-free treatment as a Type C reorganization (Sec. 368(a)(2)(B)).

The acquiring corporation may also assume the acquired corporation's liabilities or acquire some of the acquired corporation's properties subject to a liability. The assumption or acquisition of these liabilities is generally not treated as boot under Sec. 357(a). Consequently, an assumption of debt by the acquiring corporation will not trigger the recognition of any part of the gain realized. Section 357(b), however, may result in the assumed or acquired liability being treated as money if the principal purpose of the assumption was the avoidance of federal income taxes or the assumption lacked business purpose. The acquired corporation's assumption or acquisition of the acquired corporation's liabilities is, however, considered to be money for one purpose, namely, for applying the 20 percent limitation on the cash and other consideration that may be included as part of the consideration transferred. Because the liabilities are considered to be money when applying the 20 percent limitation, the acquired corporation's assumption or acquisition of any liabilities reduces (by an equal amount) the maximum amount of cash and other consideration that may be transferred. Once the liabilities assumed or acquired exceed the 20 percent limitation, the transaction may not include any cash or other property in the consideration exchanged and still be a Type C reorganization. No limit exists on the proportion of the total gross assets that may be acquired by having the acquiring corporation assume the acquired corporation's liabilities when cash and other property are not part of the consideration given by the acquiring corporation. The courts have said in some cases, however, that when only a small portion of the total gross assets were acquired for voting stock (with the bulk of the assets being acquired by the acquiring corporation's assuming various liabilities), the shareholders have failed to maintain a sufficient continuity of their equity interest and prevented the transaction from qualifying as a Type C reorganization (Treas. Reg. Sec. 1.368-2(d)(2)(ii)).

An illustration of the rules regarding the use of cash and other consideration is presented below:

Example (1): Corporation A owns properties with a fair market value of $100,000 and liabilities of $12,000. Corporation B intends to acquire A's assets and liabilities in a Type C reorganization in

which stock and money are exchanged by B in the amount of the "net" assets transferred, $88,000 ($100,000 − $12,000 = $88,000). The maximum amount of money and other property that B may exchange is $20,000 ($100,000 × 0.20 = $20,000). The assumption of the $12,000 of A's liabilities, however, restricts B's actual cash and other property payments to $8,000 ($20,000 − $12,000 = $8,000) or less.

Example (2): Assume the same facts as in the preceding example, except that A's liabilities equal $48,000 and B agrees to exchange $52,000 of consideration for A's assets and liabilities. B is only permitted to exchange voting stock for A's assets and liabilities and still qualify under the Type C reorganization provisions because the liabilities assumed already exceed the 20 percent other consideration limitation.

Section 361(a) permits a corporation that is a party to a reorganization to exchange its property pursuant to a plan of reorganization solely for stock or securities of a second corporation that is a party to the reorganization and avoid recognizing any gains or losses. An exception to the nonrecognition rule applies when money and other property is received for the property along with the stocks and securities. The amount of gain recognized equals the lesser of the acquired corporation's gain realized or the "boot" received. The acquired corporation may avoid recognizing the gain by distributing the boot to its shareholders as part of the reorganization plan. In such a case, only the boot that is retained by the acquired corporation triggers the recognition of a gain (Sec. 361(b)(1)). The receipt of boot does not trigger the recognition of losses, however. A further discussion of the gain and loss recognition is presented below.

The acquired corporation is permitted to transfer the assets it acquires to a subsidiary corporation as part of the reorganization (Sec. 368(a)(2)(C)). Alternatively, the rules permit a Type C reorganization to take place with a controlled subsidiary corporation acting as the acquiring corporation and using the stock of the acquiring corporation's parent corporation as the bulk of the consideration given (see Figure 7-8). The consideration given is subject to two restrictions. First, the 20 percent limitation outlined above still applies. In addition, a mixture of the voting stock of the parent corporation and of the acquiring subsidiary corporation may not be used as consideration (Sec. 368(a)(1)(C)).

The Type C reorganization provides a number of advantages and disadvantages compared with a Type A or Type B reorganization. First, the consideration permitted in the Type C reorganization is less restricted than is the solely-for-voting-stock requirement of the Type B reorganization. The consideration is, however, more limited than the Type A reorganization. Second, the acquiring corporation in a Type C reorganization does not acquire all the acquired corporation's liabilities. Only those liabilities that are specified in the purchase agreement are assumed or acquired. Third, majority approval by the shareholders of the acquired or the acquiring corporation generally is not required under state corporation law. Such a vote of the acquired corporation's shareholders may be required in order to effect the sale and is definitely required in order to liquidate the acquired corporation. Dissenting shareholders generally do not have the right to have their shares valued and purchased for cash, as in the Type A reorganization. Finally, the portion of the purchase price allocated to each of the assets ordinarily may be specified in the purchase agreement so that the buyer and seller may take advantage of any favorable tax consequences resulting from a specific allocation.

A number of disadvantages may also exist in a Type C reorganization. First, the title to substantially all the various assets must be transferred to the purchaser, which may produce a significant cost. Second, certain assets may not be assignable to the purchaser, so that the seller may have to be retained as a separate entity in order to take advantage of these assets. Third, the shareholders of the acquired corporation generally end up holding a minority ownership interest in the acquired corporation. A cash acquisition of the assets, however, would not introduce any new outside ownership interests to the acquiring corporation.

"Type D" reorganization

A Type D reorganization is defined as the transfer by a corporation of either part or all of its assets to a second corporation, which immediately after the transfer is controlled by the transferor, by one or more of its shareholders, or by a combination thereof. In addition, the stocks and securities of the controlled corporation must be distributed in a transaction coming under Sec. 354, 355, or 356 (Sec. 368(a)(1)(D)). Accordingly, the Type D reorganizations may be either a "divisive" or "nondivisive" type of transaction. The nondivisive Type D reorganization (Figure 7-9) involves the transfer by one corporation of substantially all its assets to a single, controlled transferee corporation (Steps 1 and 2), followed by the liquidation of the transferor corporation (Step 3) (Secs. 368(a)(1)(D) and 354(b)). The non-

FIGURE 7-9 Nondivisive Type D Reorganization (Secs. 368(a)(1)(D) and 354(b))

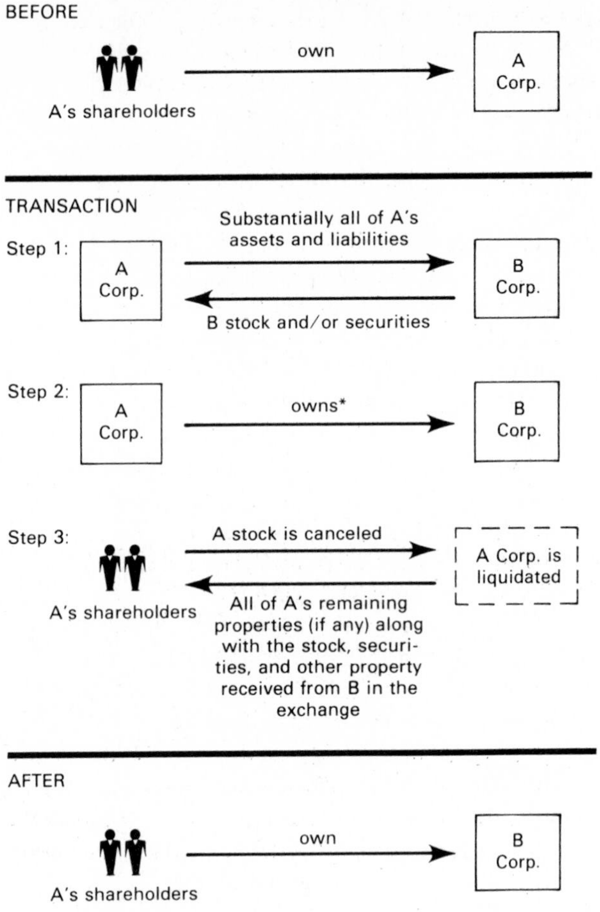

*80% control (as defined by Sec. 368(c)) must be held by A Corporation.

divisive Type D reorganization takes its name from the fact that the properties of a single corporation (the transferor) become the properties of a second corporation (the controlled corporation), which is the only corporation to survive the reorganization. The nondivisive reorganization may provide a result quite similar to either the Type E or Type F reorganization, in which a corporation changes its capital structure or its identity, or a Type C acquisitive reorganization.[23] The divisive Type D reorganization, on the other hand, involves the transfer by one corporation of part or all of its assets to one or more controlled transferee corporations, followed by a distribution or exchange coming under Sec. 354 or 355. In any of the three divisive Type D reorganizations, at least two corporations survive the reorganization (see Figures 7-10, 7-11, and 7-12).

[23]In the case of an overlap of a Type C and Type D reorganization, Sec. 368(a)(2)(A) provides that the Type D reorganization provisions will prevail.

FIGURE 7-10   Type D Divisive Reorganizations: Spin-Off
Transaction (Secs. 368(a)(1)(D) and 355)

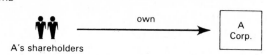

BEFORE

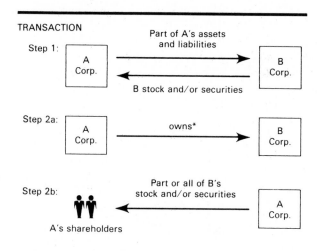

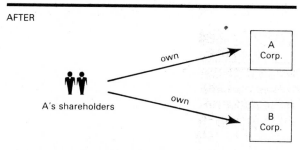

AFTER

*80% control (as defined in Sec. 368(c)) must be held by A Corporation (or A Corporation in combination with its shareholders).

FIGURE 7-11   Type D Divisive Reorganizations: Split-Off
Transaction (Secs. 368(a)(1)(D) and 355)

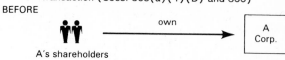

BEFORE

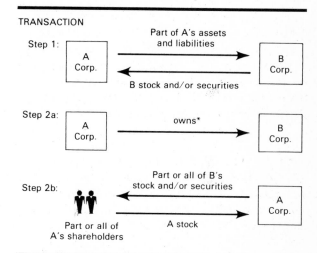

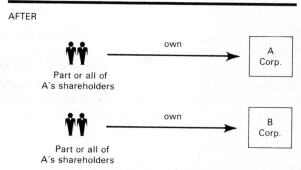

*80% control (as defined in Sec. 368(c)) must be held by A Corporation (or A Corporation in combination with its shareholders).

No matter what form Type D reorganization is used, a transfer of part or all the assets to the controlled corporation is required. The consideration received in exchange for the assets must be stock or securities (or both) of the controlled corporation. No stock need be included as part of the consideration, however, if before the transfer, the transferor already controls the transferee corporation. Control of the transferee corporation is measured by the provisions of Sec. 368(c), discussed above. No gains or losses are generally recognized by the transferor corporation because of the Sec. 361 nonrecognition rules. Sec. 357(c), however, may require the recognition of a gain by the transferor corporation if the basis of the assets transferred is less than the amount of liabilities assumed.[24]

[24] The Type D reorganization is the only asset exchange coming under Sec. 361 that is subject to the gain recognition requirement of Sec. 357(c) (basis of assets transferred are less than the liabilities purchased or assumed by the transferee).

In that event, the gain recognized by the transferor equals the sum of the liabilities assumed (and acquired) by the transferee minus the aggregate adjusted basis of all property transferred to the transferee in the exchange. The gain recognized will be characterized as capital gain or ordinary income, as previously discussed in connection with Sec. 351 (see Chapter 4).

Note that a Type D reorganization requires the distribution of the stock and securities of the controlled corporation under either Sec. 354 or Sec. 355 (and Sec. 356 as it applies to either of these sections). If the transferor does not make the necessary distribution, then the nonrecognition rules of Sec. 351 (instead of Sec. 361) generally apply to the asset transfer.

The general nonrecognition of gain or loss under Sec. 354 was discussed earlier. Two additional require-

FIGURE 7-12   Type D Divisive Reorganizations: Split-Up
Transaction (Secs. 368(a)(1)(D) and 355)

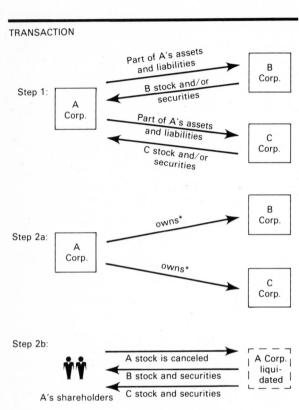

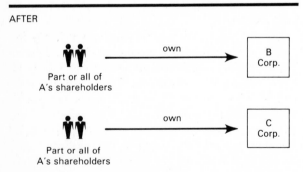

*80% control (as defined in Sec. 368(c)) must be held by A Corporation (or A Corporation in combination with its shareholders).

ments must be satisfied by an exchange of stocks or securities that is part of a Type D reorganization. These requirements are:

1. The controlled corporation must acquire substantially all of the transferor corporation's assets. This "substantially-all" requirement is interpreted by the I.R.S. in the same manner as previously outlined for the Type A and Type C reorganizations.

2. The transferor corporation must distribute all its remaining properties (if any) and the stock, securities, and other properties received in the exchange to the holders of its stock and securities as part of the plan of reorganization (Sec. 354(b)(1)).

Not all properties need to be distributed. Some of the properties that have been retained by the transferor, including some of those that were received by the transferor in exchange for its assets, are permitted to be retained and used to satisfy liabilities incurred by the transferor corporation in the conduct of its business before the reorganization (Treas. Reg. Sec. 1.354-1(b)).

Although Sec. 354 does not specify that the transferor corporation must be liquidated, the need to distribute all its properties leaves, for all practical purposes, only the corporate shell. Only the stocks and securities that are distributed may be received tax free by the transferor's shareholders and creditors. When securities are distributed with a principal amount in excess of those securities that are surrendered (if any), the fair market value of the excess principal amount is considered boot. If no securities are surrendered, then the entire principal amount of the securities received is considered boot (Sec. 356(d)(2)). Boot is also deemed received when shareholders receive money, non-securities indebtedness of the controlled corporation, or other property.

Section 355 distribution or exchanges

Section 355 provides for the separation of one or more existing businesses operated either directly by a corporation or indirectly as a subsidiary corporation, without the recognition of a gain or loss to the holders of the corporation's stocks or securities. These nonrecognition provisions concern two general types of corporate divisions:

1. The distribution of the stock of an existing subsidiary corporation.[25]

2. The distribution of the stock of a new subsidiary corporation that holds the assets of a business pre-

[25]Only Sec. 355 may apply to the distribution or exchange of the stock or securities of an existing subsidiary corporation that takes place outside of the reorganization rules. In order for Sec. 354 to apply, the exchange of the stock or securities must take place pursuant to a plan of reorganization.

viously operated by the distributing corporation (Treas. Reg. Sec. 1.355-1(b)).[26]

In the second type of corporate division, the acquisition of the distributing corporation's assets by the corporation whose stock is being distributed generally represents the first part of a Type D reorganization. As we can see by the other type of corporate division (Type 1, above), however, Sec. 355 may be used to effect a tax-free distribution or exchange of stocks and securities previously owned by the distributing corporation without invoking the reorganization rules (Treas. Reg. Sec. 1.355-3(c)). The discussion of the Sec. 355 provisions presented here applies to both types of separations.

The following six general requirements must be satisfied for Sec. 355 to apply:

1.   The distributing corporation must distribute stock to a shareholder—or distribute stock or securities to a security holder (in exchange for some or all of the distributing corporation's securities)—of a corporation that it controls immediately before the distribution.

2.   The distributing corporation must distribute all the controlled corporation's stocks and securities that it holds immediately before the distribution, *or* it must distribute a sufficient amount of stock to constitute control under Sec. 368(c).

3.   The distribution must not be used principally as a device for distributing the earnings and profits of the distributing corporation, the controlled corporation, or both.

4.   Both the distributing corporation and the controlled corporation must be engaged in the active conduct of a trade or business immediately after the distribution. In addition, each trade or business must have been actively conducted throughout the five-year period ending on the date of the distribution.

5.   The distribution must have a substantial business purpose to the corporation.

6.   The direct or indirect owners of the business or businesses that existed before the distribution are expected to maintain a continuity of their equity interests in part or all of the business enterprises that exist after the distribution.

We shall describe each of these requirements in greater detail below.

[26]This type of corporation division may take place under the distribution rules of Sec. 354 or Sec. 355. When the transaction comes under the Type D reorganization rules, the Sec. 355 distribution rules may be easier to satisfy because the transfer of "substantially all" the transferor corporation's properties and the distribution of all stocks, securities, and other property requirements do not have to be satisfied.

DISTRIBUTION OF CONTROLLED CORPORATION'S STOCKS OR SECURITIES   Three types of distributions—the *spin-off,* the *split-off,* and the *split-up*—are permitted under the nonrecognition rules of Sec. 355 (see Figures 7-10, 7-11, and 7-12). Although the spin-off (Figure 7-10) and split-off (Figure 7-11) transactions are depicted as part of a Type D reorganization (in which a *new* subsidiary corporation is created, the stock of which is distributed or exchanged by the controlled corporation), the Sec. 355 rules also permit the stock of an existing subsidiary corporation to be distributed or exchanged. In that event, the previously extant parent-subsidiary relationship is replaced by direct shareholder ownership of both corporations.

The *spin-off* transaction involves the transfer by the distributing corporation of part of its assets (and possibly some liabilities) to a controlled corporation (Step 1) followed by distribution of the controlled corporation's stocks and securities (Step 2). None of the distributing corporation's stocks and securities is surrendered as part of the transaction. The *split-off* transaction is similar to the spin-off transaction except that in Step 2 the distributing corporation's shareholders—that is, those receiving stocks and securities of the controlled corporation—surrender part or all their stocks and securities in the distributing corporation. The *split-up* transaction results in the transfer of all the assets of an existing corporation to two new controlled corporations (Step 1), the stocks and securities of which are then exchanged by the distributing corporation for all its outstanding stocks and securities (Step 2). The transferor corporation is liquidated, and the two new subsidiary corporations carry on the transferor's business activities.

Stock distributions made under Sec. 355 may involve both common and preferred stock. In addition, the distributions do not need to be made on a pro rata basis to all the distributing corporation's shareholders. As a result, a split-off transaction involving a Type D reorganization may effectively be used to divide up two business activities, operated by a single corporation, between two dissenting shareholders.

Example: Individuals A and B each own 50 percent of the Old Corporation stock. Old Corporation operated both a manufacturing business and a construction business. Because the shareholders have not been able to agree on business decisions for a number of years, they decide to divide up the business, with each shareholder taking one of the business activities. The Type D reorganization rules permit the assets of the construction business to be transferred to New Corporation in exchange for all its stock. The New stock could then be distributed tax free under Sec. 355 to A by Old Corporation in exchange for all of A's Old Corporation stock. As a result of this split-off transaction, A and B each become the sole owner of a single corporation without being required to recognize any gain on the transaction.

If the corporate division does not qualify under Sec. 355 because it fails any of the six requirements outlined above, then the applicable tax treatment depends on the nature of the distribution. The Sec. 301 dividend distribution rules generally apply to all distributions of stocks, securities, and other property for a nonqualifying spin-off transaction. The Sec. 302 (redemption of stock) or Sec. 346 (partial liquidation) rules generally apply to provide either dividend income or sale-or-exchange treatment for the stock received in a nonqualifying split-off transaction. And, because the distributing corporation is liquidated in a split-up transaction, the Sec. 331 (complete liquidation) rules provide sale or exchange treatment for the stock surrendered in a nonqualifying split-up transaction.

MINIMUM DISTRIBUTION AMOUNT   The amount of stock that must be distributed in order to avoid recognizing a gain or loss must equal or exceed one of the following:

1.   All the stock and securities of the controlled corporation that are held immediately preceding the distribution; or
2.   An amount of the controlled corporation's stock necessary to constitute control (as defined by Sec. 368(c)), generally 80 percent of the outstanding stock of the controlled corporation.

Under the second requirement, the distributing corporation may thus retain up to 20 percent of the controlled corporation's stock that is outstanding immediately preceding the distribution. To prevent the distributing corporation or its shareholders, or both, from taking undue liberties with this ability to retain stock, however, the distributing corporation is required to establish to the satisfaction of the I.R.S. that the retention of any stock (and possibly securities) of the controlled corporation was not part of a plan that had as one of its principal purposes the avoidance of federal income taxes (Sec. 355(a)(1)(D)). The Sec. 355 regulations also indicate that the business reasons supporting a distribution require the distribution of *all* the stock and securities (Treas. Reg. Sec. 1.355-2(d)(2)).

The nonrecognition rules of Sec. 355 do not apply to the distribution of the following: stock of a controlled corporation acquired in a transaction in which a gain or loss is recognized within five years of the date of distribution; near-stock items, such as stock rights;[27] and securities, where the principal amount of the securities distributed exceeds the principal amount of the securities surrendered by the security holder (or where no securities are surrendered by the security holder). In each of these cases, the boot (recognition) rules of Sec. 356 (relating to securities and other property described earlier) apply. When securities of the controlled corporation are surrendered in exchange for controlled corporation stock, no gain or loss is required to be recognized by the security holder on the exchange (Treas. Reg. Sec. 1.355-2(e)).

THE DEVICE REQUIREMENT   The prohibition against the distribution being "a device" for distributing earnings and profits results from the potential for tax avoidance available when a distribution may be made tax free. Tax avoidance may occur if the shareholders are able to avoid the dividend income provisions of Sec. 301 (and receive those same earnings and profits at capital gains rates) by first receiving the stock of the controlled corporation in a tax-free distribution and then selling the stock (or causing either the distributing corporation or the controlled corporation to liquidate). Whether a transaction is a device for distributing earnings and profits depends on the facts and circumstances surrounding the distribution. In general, a pro rata or substantially pro rata distribution has, because of its near equivalence to a dividend distribution, the greatest potential for being considered a device for distributing earnings and profits. Fact situations that result in a distribution being considered a device for distributing earnings and profits include (but are not limited to) the following:

1.   The sale or exchange of either the distributing corporation's or the controlled corporation's stock shortly after the tax-free distribution. [For example, the proposed Treasury regulations indicate that a device for distributing the earnings and profits of the distributing corporation, the controlled corporation, or both, *exists* if 20 percent or more of the stock of either the distributing corporation or the controlled corporation is to be sold or exchanged pursuant to an arrange-

27 *Irving Gordon* v. *Commissioner*, 424 F.2d 378 (CCA-3, 1970) *aff'g.* 51 TC 1032 (1968) (stock rights); *Oscar E. Baan*, 451 F.2d 198 (CCA-9, 1971) *aff'g.* 51 TC 1032 (1968) (stock rights); *William H. Bateman*, 40 TC 408 (1963) N.A. 1965-2 CB 7 (warrants); and *Estate of Charles A. Smith*, 63 TC 722 (1975) (stock rights), A. 1976-2 CB 2.

ment negotiated or entered into before the distribution. If, pursuant to such an arrangement, part or all of the securities, or less than 20 percent of the stock of either corporation is to be sold or exchanged after the distribution, then *substantial evidence* will exist that the transaction was a device for the distribution of earnings and profits.]

2. The transfer of cash or liquid assets to a transferee corporation (unrelated to the reasonable needs of the transferee's business) followed by the distribution of the stock of the transferee corporation to the transferor corporation's shareholders.

Excluded from the "device" category, however, are split-off or split-up transactions that are otherwise eligible for exchange treatment under Sec. 302(b) and distributions made when the distributing corporation does not have any earnings and profits on the date of the distribution (Prop. Reg. Sec. 1.355-2(c)).

THE ACTIVE TRADE OR BUSINESS REQUIREMENT Section 355 requires that both the distributing corporation and the controlled corporation be engaged in the "active conduct of a trade or business" immediately after the distribution of the controlled corporation's stock or securities (Sec. 355(b)(1)(A)). An exception to this requirement exists if the distributing corporation, immediately preceding the distribution, had no assets other than stocks and securities in two or more controlled corporations and each controlled corporation was engaged in the active conduct of a trade or business immediately after the distribution.[28] (In other words, an exception exists for distributions made by certain parent holding companies.)

The following two requirements must be satisfied for a corporation to be engaged in the active conduct of a trade or business for purposes of Sec. 355:

1. The corporation must be engaged in the conduct of a trade or business (as outlined below), or substantially all of the corporation's assets must consist of stock or securities of a controlled corporation that is engaged in the conduct of a trade or business.

2. The trade or business must have been conducted throughout the five-year period ending on the distribution date. The same trade or business is considered to have been conducted throughout the period, even if changes have been made in the method of operating the business, provided these changes do not constitute the acquisition of a new or different business.

According to one leading commentator, the purpose behind the five-year requirement is to prevent taxpayers from making a temporary investment of liquid assets in a new business preparatory to engaging in one of the tax-free corporation division transactions included under Sec. 355.[29]

Two exceptions to the five-year requirement exist. The first exception permits the acquisition of a new trade or business by either the distributing or the controlled corporation in a transaction whereby no gain or loss was recognized *and* the basis of the acquired assets is determined by reference to the basis such assets had in the transferor's hands. Thus, a new trade or business that is acquired in a transaction other than a purchase—for example, an acquisitive tax-free reorganization involving either the distributing or controlled corporation—does not violate the five-year requirement. The second exception permits the control of a corporation (that conducts a properly aged trade or business) to be acquired during the five-year period in a transaction in which a gain or loss went unrecognized and still not violate the minimum time requirement for conducting a trade or business (Sec. 355(b)(2)).

The regulations specify that a corporation is considered to be engaged in a trade or business when:

a specific group of activities are being carried on by such corporation for the purpose of earning income or profit from such group of activities, and the activities included in such group include every operation which forms part of, or a step in, the process of earning income or profit from such group. Such group of activities ordinarily must include the collection of income and the payment of expenses (Prop. Reg. Sec. 1.355-3(b)(2)(ii)).

Whether a corporation is actively conducting a trade or business is a question of fact. In general, for a corporation to be actively conducting a trade or business, it must perform active and substantial management and operational functions. Excluded from the active conduct of a trade or business are:

1. The holding of stocks, securities, land, or other property solely for investment purposes; and

2. The ownership and operation (including leasing) of real or personal property used in a trade or business unless the owner performs significant services with respect to the operation and management of the property (Prop. Reg. Sec. 1.355-3(b)(2)(iv)).

The following examples illustrate the application of the active conduct of a trade or business requirement.

---

[28]A *de minimus* rule does exist that permits the holding of a small amount of assets other than stocks and securities.

[29]Boris I. Bittker and James S. Eustice, *Federal Income Taxation of Corporations and Shareholders* (Boston: Warren, Gorham and Lamont, 1979), pp. 13–30.

Example (1): Corporation A is engaged in the manufacture and sale of soap and detergents and also owns investment securities. Corporation A proposes to place the investment securities in a new corporation and distribute the stock of such new corporation to its shareholders. The new corporation's holding of investment securities does not qualify as the active conduct of a trade or business immediately after the distribution (Prop. Reg. Sec. 1.355-3(c) Ex. (1)).

Example (2): Corporation F is engaged in the retail grocery business and owns all the stock of Corporation G. Corporation G has for the past 10 years derived all its gross income from the rental of its land and building to F, under a lease in which G's principal activity consists of the collection of rent from the building. Corporation F proposes to distribute the G stock to its shareholders. Corporation G will not be engaged in the active conduct of a trade or business immediately after the distribution because it has not actively conducted a trade or business throughout the five-year period ending on the date of the distribution (Prop. Reg. Sec. 1.355-3(c) Ex. (6)).

Example (3): Corporation D, a bank, has for the past seven years owned an 11-story downtown office building, the ground floor of which the corporation has occupied in the conduct of its banking business. The remaining 10 floors are rented to various tenants, and the building is managed and maintained by employees of the bank. Corporation D proposes to transfer the building to a new corporation and to distribute the stock of such new corporation to the bank's shareholders. The new corporation will manage the building, negotiate leases, seek new tenants, and repair and maintain the building. Immediately after the distribution, the activities in connection with banking will constitute the active conduct of a trade or business, as will the activities connected with the rental of the building (Prop. Reg. Sec. 1.355-3(c) Ex. (4)).

Although the corporate division provisions for many years contemplated the separation of two distinct trade or business activities, the courts, in *Coady* and in *Marrett,* found no restriction that prevented the division of a single business activity into two separate parts.[30] In *Coady,* the courts permitted a "vertical" di-

[30]*Edmund P. Coady* v. *Commissioner,* 289 F.2d 490 (CCA-6, 1961) *aff'g.* 33 TC 771 (1960) A. 1965-2 CB 4, and *W.W. Marett* v. *Commissioner,* 325 F.2d 28 (CCA-5, 1963) *aff'g.* 63-2 USTC para. 9567 (D.C.-Ga., 1963).

vision of a single business, whereby one-half the assets representing each activity of a construction company were transferred to a new corporation, and the existing corporation kept the remaining assets. The stock of the new corporation was received by one of the two shareholders in exchange for all his stock in the existing corporation, so that at the completion of the transaction, each shareholder owned all the stock of one of the corporations and one-half the original pool of assets. Even though the courts permitted vertical divisions of a corporation, the regulations maintained a steadfast position against a corporate division that involved the distribution of selected functions of a trade or business. The regulations insisted that the activities being distributed "include every operation which forms a part of, or a step in, the process of earning income or profit for such a group." This position has been relaxed in the proposed Sec. 355 regulations, which permit (1) the vertical division of a single business into two separate parts without requiring that all functions be divided between the owners *and* (2) the separation of an individual activity as a trade or business, even though it operates solely to serve the parent corporation's needs, provided the activity constitutes a trade or business as defined above.

Example (1): Division of two activities: For eight years, Corporation K has been engaged in the manufacture and sale of steel and steel products. For six years, K's wholly owned subsidiary, Corporation L, has owned and operated a coal mine for the sole purpose of meeting K's coal requirements in the manufacture of steel. It is proposed that the stock of L be distributed to the shareholders of K. Immediately after the distribution, the activities of L in connection with the operation of the coal mine constitute the active conduct of a trade or business. The activities of K in connection with the manufacture and sale of steel products immediately after the distribution also constitute the active conduct of a trade or business (Prop. Reg. Sec. 1.355-3(c) Ex. (9)).

Example (2): Separation of a department of a single trade or business: Corporation S had been engaged in the manufacture and sale of household products for eight years. Throughout this period, in connection with such manufacturing, it has maintained a research department for its own use. The research department has 30 employees actively engaged in the development of new products. Corporation S proposes to transfer the research department to a new corporation and to distribute the stock of the new corporation to its shareholders. After the distribution, the new corporation will continue its research operations on a contractual basis with several corporations, including S. Immediately after the distribution, the activities of the new corporation in connection with research will constitute the active conduct of a trade or business, as will the activities of S in connection with manufacturing (Prop. Reg. Sec. 1.355-3(c) Ex. (14)).

Example (3): Division of all parts of a single business equally between two shareholders: Corporation M has for more than five years been engaged in the single business of constructing sewage disposal plants and other facilities. Corporation M proposes to transfer one-half its assets to Corporation N. These assets will include a contract for the construction of a sewage disposal plant in State X, construction equipment, cash, and other tangible assets. Corporation M will retain a contract for the construction of a sewage disposal plant in State Y, construction equipment, cash, and other intangible assets. The N stock is then to be distributed to one of the M shareholders in exchange for all of her M stock. Both corporations will be engaged in the active conduct of the construction business immediately after the distribution (Prop. Reg. Sec. 1.355-3(c) Ex. (10)).

BUSINESS PURPOSE REQUIREMENT   The distribution of stock or securities under Sec. 355 is permitted to be carried out tax free only if "real and substantial nontax reasons germane to the business of the corporation" exist (Treas. Reg. Sec. 1.355-2(c)). Although not indicated in the Code, this requirement has evolved through judicial decisions. (Further elaboration on the judicial restraints appears at the end of the chapter.) The required business purpose has been found to exist when a corporate division is accomplished in order to satisfy an antitrust judgment, to divide the ownership of a business among dissenting shareholders, and to satisfy a loan covenant (Prop. Reg. Sec. 1.355-2(b)(1)). When a transaction is motivated solely by the shareholders' personal desires, it apparently fails to qualify under Sec. 355 because it is not carried out for reasons germane to the conduct of the *corporation's* business. Thus, a distribution undertaken solely to assist in a controlling shareholder's personal tax planning fails to qualify under Sec. 355. The Sec. 355 regulations, however, do not rule out the possibility that a shareholder and the distributing corporation may have similar nontax avoidance reasons for engaging in a

transaction, and in this case, the required business purpose may be found to exist.[31]

CONTINUITY OF INTEREST REQUIREMENT   The business purpose and continuity of interest requirements are closely related. Like the business purpose requirement, the need for a continuity of interest arose from judicial decisions (which we shall further discuss at the end of the chapter). When taken together, the two requirements are designed to limit the application of Sec. 355 to a "readjustment of corporate structures as is required by business exigencies" and that "effect only a readjustment of continuing interests in property under modified corporate forms" (Treas. Reg. Sec. 1.355-2(c)). These regulations indicate that the person (or persons) who directly or indirectly owned the enterprise before the distribution or exchange is expected to retain an interest in part or all of the business enterprise (or enterprises) after the transaction takes place. Thus, a shareholder need not maintain an equity interest in both the distributing corporation and the controlled corporation after the transaction but should maintain an equity interest in at least one of the entities.

"Type E" reorganization

The Type E reorganization is defined in Sec. 368(a)(1)(E) as a recapitalization. Although not found in the Code, the meaning of recapitalization has evolved through a series of government promulgations and judicial decisions. In *Helvering* v. *Southwest Consolidated Corporation,* the term was defined as "the reshuffling of the capital structure within the framework of an existing corporation."[32] The recapitalization transaction generally involves only the corporation and its shareholders, creditors, or both. The corporation generally does not increase or decrease its assets and does not modify its tax attributes (for example, net operating loss carryover); it will, however, reshuffle the equity side of its tax "balance sheet."

Five forms of recapitalization transactions are identified in the Treasury regulations, as follows:

1.   The discharge of a corporation's outstanding bonds by having the corporation issue preferred stock to the bondholders in exchange for their bonds;

2.   The exchange by the corporation of no-par common stock for 20 percent of its outstanding preferred stock;

[31.]*Estate of Moses L. Parshelsky* v. *Commissioner,* 303 F.2d 14 (CCA-2, 1962) *rev'g.* and *rem'g.* 34 TC 946 (1960) and *Joseph V. Rafferty* v. *Commissioner,* 452 F.2d 767 (CCA-1, 1972) *aff'g.* 55 TC 490 (1970).
[32.]315 U.S. 194 (1942).

3. The exchange by the corporation of previously authorized but unissued preferred stock for outstanding common stock;

4. The exchange by the corporation of its outstanding preferred stock having a preference with respect to the amount and time of dividend payments and the distribution of corporate assets on liquidation, for a new common stock issue of the corporation having no such rights; and

5. The exchange by the corporation of its outstanding preferred stock having a dividend arrearage for another class of its stock (Treas. Reg. Sec. 1.368-2(e)).

The taxability of the recapitalization transaction to the corporation's shareholders or creditors depends on the type of consideration given and received. A summary of these tax treatments is presented below.

1. STOCK-FOR-STOCK EXCHANGE   Two provisions govern these exchanges: First, the Sec. 354(a)(1) rules discussed above permit a shareholder to exchange a corporation's stock for other stock of the same corporation without being required to recognize a gain or loss, provided the transaction takes place as part of a reorganization plan. Second, Sec. 1036 permits common stock (preferred stock) in a corporation to be exchanged for common stock (preferred stock) in the same corporation without requiring the transaction to qualify as a reorganization. The Sec. 1036 rules apply even though voting stock is exchanged for nonvoting stock, or vice versa. The Sec. 1036 rules, however, do not apply when stock is exchanged for bonds, preferred stock is exchanged for common stock, common stock is exchanged for preferred stock, or a liability of the taxpayer is assumed by the other party to the exchange (Treas. Reg. Sec. 1.1036-1(a) and (c)).

With two exceptions, the conversion of preferred stock of one corporation into common stock of the same corporation causes no gain or loss to be recognized (Sec. 354(a)(1)). The first exception is that dividend income is recognized when (1) the preferred stock has dividends in arrears, (2) the exchange transaction results in common stock being exchanged for the preferred stock and the defaulted dividend claim, *and* (3) the exchange results in an increase in the preferred stockholders' proportionate interest in the assets (or earnings and profits) of the corporation. The amount of dividend income recognized under this exception equals the difference between (a) the greater of the fair market value, or the liquidation preference, of the stock received in the exchange, and (b) the issue price of the

preferred stock surrendered. In no case, however, may the amount of such dividend income exceed the amount of the dividends that are in arrears. In the second exception, a recapitalization results in dividend income being recognized when the stock exchange is part of a plan to increase periodically a shareholder's proportionate interest in the assets or earnings and profits of the corporation (Treas. Reg. Sec. 1.305-7(c)(1)).

The conversion of outstanding common stock into preferred stock is permitted to occur tax free when it takes place pursuant to a reorganization plan and the fair market value of the preferred stock received equals that of the common stock surrendered (Sec. 354 (a)(1)). An excess of the fair market value of the preferred stock received over the fair market value of the common stock surrendered, or an excess of the fair market value of the common stock surrendered over the fair market value of the preferred, causes the difference between these two amounts to be "treated as having been used to make a gift, pay compensation, satisfy obligations of any kind, or for whatever purposes the facts indicate."[33]

A recapitalization transaction in which common stock is exchanged for preferred stock may be used to convert an individual's interest in a business from one in which he or she participates in the operation of the business (and owns common stock) to one in which he or she occupies the role of a passive investor and receives a fixed profit distribution based on the amount of the preferred stock held. Thus, an individual in anticipation of retirement may exchange part or all of his or her common stock interest in a corporation for part or all of the corporation's preferred stock, and at the same time surrender operating control of the corporation to his or her successors.[34]

2. BONDS-FOR-STOCK EXCHANGE   Creditors may exchange debt obligations classified as securities for either common stock or preferred stock and avoid recognizing gains and losses on the transfer because the exchange qualifies as a recapitalization[35] (Treas. Reg. Sec. 1.368-2(e)(1)). If the outstanding bonds carry an original issue discount (Sec. 1232), this discount is also permitted to go unrecognized.[36] Similarly, the corporation is unable to recognize losses incurred when it is required to exchange bonds that have been sold for a

[33]Rev. Rul. 74-269, 1974-1 CB 87.
[34]The receipt of preferred stock or common stock may trigger the Sec. 306 preferred stock bailout provisions. A discussion is presented later on the interaction of the Sec. 306 provisions and the reorganization provisions.
[35]*Neville Coke and Chemical Co.* v. *U.S.*, 148 F.2d 599 (CCA-3, 1945) *aff'g.* 3 TC 113 (1944), A. 1944 CB 21.
[36]Rev. Rul. 75-39, 1975-1 CB 272.

discount for preferred stock having a greater value; likewise, a corporation is not required to recognize income from the discharge of indebtedness when stocks are exchanged that have a value less than the principal amount of the indebtednesses surrendered by the creditors.

3. BONDS-FOR-BONDS EXCHANGE   The exchange of securities of one corporation that is a party to a reorganization, pursuant to the reorganization plan, for securities of a second corporation that is a party to the reorganization may take place tax free under Sec. 354(a)(1) as a recapitalization if the principal amount of the securities received is equal to or less than that of the securities surrendered. If the principal amount of the securities received exceeds the principal amount of the securities surrendered, then the fair market value of such an excess is treated as other property and is subject to the rules of Sec. 356 regarding boot (Sec. 356(d)(2)(B)).

4. STOCK-FOR-BONDS EXCHANGE   Most attempts to exchange stock of a corporation for its debt obligations will result in the exchange producing boot that would be taxable as ordinary income to the shareholders. Such an outcome is based on Sec. 354(a)(2), which denies the use of the nonrecognition rules of Sec. 354(a)(1) when securities are received by a taxpayer and no such securities have been surrendered. In such a case, Sec. 356(d)(2)(B) requires the full principal amount of the securities received to be recognized as other property. To the extent that this transaction has the effect of a dividend distribution, such as in the case of a pro rata distribution, the shareholder who receives the securities must recognize the boot as dividend income[37] (Sec. 356(a)(2)). Alternatively, the exchange might be treated as a redemption of the surrendered stock that results in ordinary income or capital gains under Sec. 302 if, for example, the bonds were distributed only to certain shareholders in exchange for their stock (Treas. Reg. Sec. 1.354-1(d) Ex. (2)).

"Type F" reorganization

The Type F reorganization is defined as a "mere change in identity, form, or place of organization, however effected" (Sec. 368(a)(1)(F)). This type of reorganization is commonly used to effect a change in a corporation's name or state of incorporation, whereby the stocks and securities of the "old" corporation are exchanged for stocks and securities of the "new" corporation that have been issued pursuant to a reorganization plan. The Type F reorganization, like the Type E reorganization, generally does not result in a net increase or decrease in corporate assets but in a transfer of all (or substantially all) the assets of the "old" corporation to the "new" corporation and the "new" corporation continuing to conduct the trade or business of the "old" corporation. Similarly, the creditors and shareholders of the "old" corporation generally continue as the creditors and shareholders of the "new" corporation, having substantially the same or identical debt and equity interests as before the reorganization. As a result, a Type A, Type C, or nondivisive Type D reorganization may, in many cases, also fit the statutory definition of a Type F reorganization. In the event of such an overlap, the I.R.S. has held that the transaction will be treated as a Type F reorganization.[38]

The combination of two or more corporations may also be considered a Type F reorganization if the following requirements are satisfied:

1.   There must be complete identity of shareholders and their proprietary interests in the transferor corporations and acquiring corporations;
2.   The transferor corporations and the acquiring corporations must be engaged in the same business activities or integrated activities before the combination; and
3.   The business enterprise of the transferor corporation and the acquiring corporations must continue unchanged after the combination.[39]

In a Type F reorganization, the shareholders are permitted to exchange their stocks and securities tax free under the nonrecognition rules of Sec. 354. Boot is recognizable under Sec. 356 if the principal amount of the securities received from the new corporation exceeds the principal amount of those securities (if any) of the "old" corporation that are surrendered, or if money or other property retained by the "old" corporation is distributed.

Because the "new" corporation is considered to be a continuation of the "old" corporation, the "old" corporation is permitted under Sec. 361 to transfer its assets to the "new" corporation without recognizing any gains or losses. Similarly, the "new" corporation's basis for the properties is considered to be the basis that the

---

[37]*J. Robert Bazley* v. *U.S.*, 332 U.S. 567 (1947) *aff'g.* 155 F.2d 237 (CCA-3, 1946) *aff'g.* 4 TC 897 (1945).

[38]Rev. Rul. 57-276, 1957-1 CB 126.
[39]Rev. Rul. 75-561, 1975-2 CB 129.

properties had in the hands of the "old" corporation. A Type F reorganization also does not affect the various tax elections of the "old" corporation. For example, elections to file consolidated tax returns, to be taxed under Subchapter S, or to have stock treated as Sec. 1244 stock all remain intact. All the tax attributes of the "old" corporation carry over to the "new" corporation under the provisions of Sec. 381. The limitations on the use of these carryovers found in Secs. 382 and 383 generally do not apply because substantially the same equity interests in both the "old" and "new" corporations are held by the shareholders.

Holding that the "new" corporation is a continuation of the "old" corporation allows two important benefits for any carryovers. First, the taxable year in which the reorganization falls is considered to be a single taxable year instead of broken up into two separate, short taxable years for the "old" and "new" corporations. Second, postreorganization losses of the acquired corporation may be carried back and offset against profits accruing in prereorganization taxable years. Such carrybacks are *not* permitted for the Type A, C, or D reorganizations. These two advantages are fairly strong reasons for attempting to have any combination of two or more companies that qualify under any one of these provisions or under the Type F reorganization rules to be treated as a Type F reorganization.[40]

DEFINITIONAL TERMS

In this section, we shall define or explain a number of terms that we have been using to define the types of reorganizations.

Party to a reorganization

The term "party to a reorganization" is found in both Sec. 354 and Sec. 361. These sections require, as a condition for nonrecognition, that certain parties to the transaction be "party to a reorganization." As Sec. 368(b) defines this term, it includes a corporation resulting from the reorganization or both corporations in a reorganization transaction in which one corporation acquires the stock or assets of a second corporation. An acquiring corporation is considered to be a party to a reorganization even though it subsequently transfers part or all of the acquired corporation's assets to a subsidiary corporation under Sec. 368(a)(2)(C). Likewise, the parent corporation is a party to a reorganization in which its stock is used by a subsidiary corporation to acquire the stock or assets of a second corporation in a triangular Type A, B, or C reorganization (Treas. Reg. Sec. 1.368-2(f)).

Plan of reorganization

A "plan of reorganization" is also a requirement for the nonrecognition of gain or loss under Secs. 354 and 361. This term, however, is not defined in the Code. The accompanying Treasury regulations indicate that a plan of reorganization refers to a consummated transaction that satisfies any one of the six reorganization definitions contained in Sec. 368(a) and limits the application of the nonrecognition provisions to exchanges and distributions that (1) are part of such a transaction, and (2) were "undertaken for reasons germane to the continuance of the business of a corporation that is a party to the reorganization" (Treas. Reg. Sec. 1.368-2(g)). A plan of reorganization need not be prepared in any particular form, nor does it need to be a written document. Failure to prepare a plan, however, may render the exchanges or distributions taxable events.[41] Consequently, a written plan is generally desirable.

RECOGNITION AND CHARACTERIZATION OF GAINS AND LOSSES

Transferor corporation

The transferor corporation is generally protected by the nonrecognition rules of Sec. 361 when it exchanges its own property for stocks and securities of a second corporation, providing both it and the transferee corporation are parties to the reorganization and the exchange is made pursuant to a plan of reorganization (Sec. 361(a)). If money or other property is received by the transferor corporation, in addition to the stocks and securities, then any gain realized on the exchange must be recognized in an amount equal to the lesser of the gain realized or the boot received. The gain recognized may be eliminated if the boot is distributed by the

[40]See, among others, *J.E. Davant v. Commissioner,* 366 F.2d 874 (CCA-5, 1966) *aff'g.* and *rev'g.* 43 TC 540 (1965); *Reef Corp. v. Commissioner,* 368 F.2d 125 (CCA-5, 1966) *aff'g.* 24 TCM 379 (1965); *Eastern Color Printing Co.,* 63 TC 27 (1974) A. 1975-2 CB 1; *Aetna Casualty and Surety Co. v. Commissioner,* 568 F.2d 811 (CCA-2, 1977) *rev'g.* 403 F.Supp. 498 (D.C.-Conn., 1975); and *Home Construction Corp. of America v. Commissioner,* 439 F.2d 1165 (CCA-5, 1971) *aff'g.* 311 F.Supp. 830 (D.C.-Ala., 1970).

[41]*C.T. Investment Co. v. Commissioner,* 88 F.2d 582 (CCA-8, 1937) *rev'g.* BTA Dec. 9026-E (July 6, 1935).

transferor to its shareholders pursuant to the plan of reorganization. Although any amount of boot retained by the transferor will trigger the recognition of a gain, neither the receipt nor the retention of boot will trigger the recognition of a loss (Sec. 361(b)).

The transferor corporation is also exempt from recognizing a gain under any of the recapture provisions when the asset exchange comes within the purview of Sec. 361. (See Secs. 617(d)(3), 1245(b)(3), 1248(a), 1250(d)(3), 1251(d)(3), 1252(b), 1254(b), and 1255(b)(1).) In each case, the recapture potential carries over to the transferee corporation and is recognized when a subsequent taxable event occurs. If the exchange qualifies under Sec. 361, the transferor corporation is also permitted to be exempt from the investment tax credit recapture provisions of Sec. 47. If the transferred property ceases to qualify under Sec. 38 before the passage of the estimated useful life used by the transferor in determining its investment tax credit, then the investment tax credit recapture provisions will apply to the transferee corporation using the combined holding periods of the transferor and transferee corporations as the actual useful life (Sec. 47(b)(2)).

Transferee corporation's recognition of gain

The transferee corporation is generally protected by the nonrecognition rules of Sec. 1032 when it exchanges its own stock for money or property of the transferor corporation as part of a reorganization transaction (Sec. 1032(a)). These nonrecognition rules apply whether previously unissued stock or treasury stock is used to effect the exchange. The precise authority for a subsidiary's tax-free issuance of its parent's stock is less obvious, although the tradition of such tax-free exchanges in a triangular reorganization is clearly established.

Distributing corporation

A distribution or exchange of stock coming under Sec. 355 that is not part of a tax-free reorganization generally does not result in the recognition of a gain or loss by the distributing corporation because of the application of the nonrecognition rules of Sec. 311(a) or (d)(2). Such a distribution will result in a reduction in the earnings and profits of the distributing corporation according to the rules of Treas. Reg. Sec. 1.312-10, even though the distribution or exchange is tax free to the shareholders.

Stockholders and security holders

Stockholders and security holders are generally protected under Sec. 354 from the recognition of gain or loss when exchanging stocks or securities or both in corporations that are a party to a reorganization or when receiving a stock distribution, provided the transaction qualifies as a reorganization and the exchange or distribution takes place as part of the plan of reorganization. If the transaction fails to qualify as a reorganization, then the full amount of the realized gain or loss will be recognized.[42] In addition, a realized gain may have to be recognized under Sec. 356 if cash or other property is received by the shareholders or security holders as part of the reorganization.

Sec. 356 provides that the recognized gain on a transaction otherwise qualifying under Sec. 354 or 355 is limited to the lesser of the gain realized or the sum of the amount of money received and the fair market value of the other property received. The receipt of boot does not trigger the recognition of a realized loss. Any gain recognized may be characterized as either dividend income or "gain from the sale of exchange of property." Any dividend income is limited to the shareholder's ratable share of the distributing corporation's post-1913 accumulated earnings and profits. Any remaining realized gain is characterized as "gain from the sale or exchange of property" (Sec. 356(a)(2)).

An exchange of stocks does not necessarily trigger the recognition of dividend income even though the distributing corporation whose stock is surrendered has a positive earnings and profits balance.[43] Characterization of boot as dividend income occurs only if the exchange "has the effect of the distribution of a dividend," (Sec. 356(a)(2)). In most situations, the equivalency of a distribution to a dividend rests on the facts and circumstances of the situation. If a meaningful reduction in stock ownership is found per Sec. 302(b)(2)—that is, a substantially disproportionate stock redemption has occurred—the result should be a capital gain.[44] If the amount of boot received is not considered to be the equivalent of a dividend, then the gain recognized is generally accorded capital gain

---

[42]*Grover D. Turnbow* v. *U.S.*, 368 U.S. 332 (1962) *aff'g.* 286 F.2d 669 (CCA-9, 1961) *rev'g.* 32 TC 646 (1959).

[43]Rev. Ruls. 74-515, 1974-2 CB 118; 74-516, 1974-2 CB 121; and 75-83, 1975-1 CB 112. See also: *King Enterprises, Inc.* v. *U.S.*, 418 F.2d 511 (Ct. Cls., 1969); *William F. Wright* v. *U.S.*, 482 F.2d 600 (CCA-8, 1973) *aff'g.* 72-2 USTC para. 9495 (D.C.-Ark., 1972); *Mandell Shimberg, Jr.* v. *U.S.*, 577 F.2d 283 (CCA-5, 1978) *rev'g.* 415 F.Supp. 832 (D.C.-Fla., 1976).

[44]Rev. Rul. 74-515, 1974-2 CB 118. The Fifth Circuit Court of Appeals in *Shimberg* (footnote 43) used a slightly different test to see whether a pro rata distribution of boot among a group of shareholders had the effect of being a dividend distribution.

treatment. The eligibility of boot for capital gain treatment is illustrated below:

> *Example:* X Corporation had common and preferred stock outstanding. The preferred stock represented less than 10 percent of the value of all the outstanding stock. Some shareholders owned common stock, others owned preferred stock, and still others owned both classes of stock. X Corporation was merged into Y Corporation under Sec. 368(a)(1)(A) with X's shareholders receiving Y common stock for their common stock and cash for their preferred stock. Shareholders of X owning only common stock are required to apply the nonrecognition rules of Sec. 354(a)(1) to their exchange. Those shareholders owning only preferred stock could not apply the reorganization rules but are permitted to treat the exchange as a redemption producing capital gain treatment under Sec. 302(b)(3) because their interest in X has been completely terminated. Shareholders of X owning both classes of stock come under the reorganization rules with respect to their exchanges of both classes of stock. The Sec. 354(a)(1) nonrecognition rules apply to the exchange of the X common stock, and Sec. 356(a) boot rules apply to the exchange of the X preferred stock. The preferred stock exchange was not considered to be the equivalent of a dividend and triggered the recognition of a gain only to the extent that the cash received exceeded the adjusted basis of the preferred stock.[45]

When Sec. 355 applies to a nonexchange transaction—such as a distribution occurring as part of a spin-off transaction—the receipt of money or other property by the shareholder triggers the recognition of income under Sec. 356(b). The amount of money and the fair market value of the other property received is treated as a distribution to which Sec. 301 applies. The shareholder recognizes dividend income to the extent that the portion of the distribution coming under Sec. 356 is treated as coming out of the distributing corporation's earnings and profits (Sec. 356(b)). The portion of this boot taxable to a corporate shareholder as dividend income under Sec. 356 is eligible for the dividends-received deduction.[46]

As previously mentioned, the distribution of securities, or the exchange of securities having a larger principal amount than the securities surrendered,

causes part or all of the securities to be considered to be "other property" (Sec. 356(d)). The fair market value of the securities classified as "other property" is treated as dividend income if the security holder is not required to surrender any securities. If securities are surrendered, then the fair market value of the excess principal amount of the securities that are distributed is treated as either dividend income or gain from the sale or exchange of property according to the dividend equivalency rules outlined above.

BASIS OF PROPERTIES RECEIVED IN A CORPORATE DIVISION OR REORGANIZATION

The same general basis rules that apply to a Sec. 351 exchange apply to a corporate division or reorganization.

Transferee corporation's basis for property received

The basis rules of Sec. 362 apply to the property received by the transferee corporation when the nonrecognition rules of Sec. 361 apply to an exchange transaction that is part of a reorganization. The basis of the property received equals its basis in the transferor corporation's hands plus the amount of any gain recognized by the transferor on the exchange (Sec. 362(b)). Thus, no increase in basis is permitted unless the transferor corporation receives boot as part of the consideration paid by the transferee, *and* some or all of the boot is retained by the transferor (Sec. 361(b)(1)(B)). If the exchange transaction falls outside the reorganization area, then the transferee acquires a basis equal to cost, as determined by Sec. 1012.

Transferor corporation, shareholders, and security holders

The Sec. 358 basis rules apply to the stock and securities received by the transferor corporation, its shareholders, or its security holders when the nonrecognition rules of Sec. 354, 355, 356, or 361 apply to a distribution or exchange. The following general rule applies to the stocks and securities (nonrecognition property) received in the exchange:

> Basis of the property exchanged (in the transferor's hands)
>
> + Amount of dividend income and/or gain recognized by the transferor on the exchange

[45]Rev. Rul. 74-515, 1974-2 CB 118.
[46]*King Enterprises, Inc. v. U.S.*, 418 F.2d 511 (Ct. Cls., 1969).

- (1) Fair market value of nonmoney, other property received;
- (2) Amount of money received;
- (3) Amount of loss recognized on the exchange; and
- (4) Amount of the taxpayer's liabilities assumed or acquired as part of the exchange

= Basis of the nonrecognition property received

When a transferor corporation exchanges property solely for stocks or securities as part of a reorganization, therefore, the basis of the stocks or securities received exactly equals that of the property surrendered. Other property that is received by the taxpayer in a transaction coming under one of the nonrecognition rules mentioned above receives a basis equal to its fair market value (Secs. 358(a) and (b)).

The total basis for the nonrecognition property may need to be allocated between various classes of stocks or securities received in an exchange. The allocation rules found in Treas. Reg. Sec. 1.358-2 will apply.

SECTION 306 AND THE REORGANIZATION PROVISIONS

Section 306 ordinarily converts the proceeds from the sale or redemption of stock that is classified as Sec. 306 stock into ordinary income. An exception to the Sec. 306 income recognition rules occurs when Sec. 306 stock is exchanged solely for stock in connection with a reorganization (or in a distribution or exchange transaction qualifying under Sec. 355 or 1036) and a gain or loss is not recognized by the shareholder (Sec. 306(b) (3)). If Sec. 306 stock is exchanged in a transaction controlled by the boot recognition rules of Sec. 356, however, then the amount of money and the fair market value of any other property received is treated as a dividend under Sec. 301 without regard to the amount of gain actually recognized by the taxpayer (Sec. 356(e)).

Section 306 stock includes any noncommon stock received by a shareholder in a reorganization transaction (or a Sec. 355 distribution or exchange) in which gain or loss went unrecognized, provided the transaction has substantially the same effect as the receipt of a stock dividend or the stock is received in exchange for Sec. 306 stock (Sec. 306(c)(1)(B)). In addition, common stock received in exchange for Sec. 306 stock as part of a reorganization (or a Sec. 355 exchange) will be considered Sec. 306 stock unless it is common stock

received pursuant to a recapitalization coming under Sec. 368(a)(1)(E), which receives a special exemption. Noncommon stock received as part of one of the aforementioned transactions is generally classified as Sec. 306 stock if, had cash been received in lieu of such stock, it would have resulted in dividend income being recognized under the boot recognition provisions of Sec. 356 (Treas. Reg. Sec. 1.306-3(d)). Even though the stock received in a reorganization or exchange is classified as Sec. 306 stock, ordinary income or dividend income treatment may still be avoided if one of the Sec. 306(b) exceptions applies to a subsequent sale or exchange of the stock in question. (See the discussion of Sec. 306 stock in Chapter 5, pages **5/14–17**.)

RULING REQUESTS

Because the area of tax-free reorganizations is quite complex, a taxpayer may want to initiate a private letter ruling request with the I.R.S. in order to ascertain whether a proposed transaction will be accorded the anticipated tax treatment when it is consummated and provide the taxpayer with the expected tax benefits. If the ruling fails to accord a proposed transaction the anticipated tax treatment, the taxpayer, aware of the possible cost of completing the transaction in its proposed form, may proceed in one of two directions. The transaction may be restructured in a manner that will provide the anticipated outcome, or the taxpayer may proceed with the transaction and anticipate a possible challenge by the I.R.S.

The I.R.S.'s Reorganization Branch will ordinarily issue an advance ruling if the proposed transaction fits within the operating rules of Revenue Procedure 79-14.[47] Although these operating rules do not carry any weight in a court of law, they do provide guidance to a taxpayer on the I.R.S.'s position with respect to various areas of the law. A transaction that lies outside the operating rules is more likely to be challenged by the I.R.S. The operating rules specified in Revenue Procedure 79-14 seem to reflect a higher standard for certain requirements—such as the "substantially all" requirement associated with an asset transfer and the minimum continuity of interest required by the acquired corporation's shareholders—than has been accepted by the courts in certain instances. These higher standards may, in fact, represent an attempt by the I.R.S. to discourage taxpayers from engaging in questionable transactions.

[47]Rev. Proc. 79-14, 1979-1 CB 496.

JUDICIAL RESTRICTIONS ON THE USE OF REORGANIZATIONS

In many cases, a taxpayer will devise a transaction that fits into one of the six statutory definitions of a tax-free reorganization but that is subsequently disqualified from tax-free treatment by the courts because it fails to satisfy the basic Congressional intent and purpose of the reorganization provisions. Five of these judicial modifications, which act as restrictions on the use of the reorganization rules, are discussed below.

Business purpose

Section 368 does not mention the need for a reorganization to have a business purpose. The Treasury regulations, however, contain such a requirement, which represents an outgrowth of the Supreme Court's denial in *Gregory* v. *Helvering*[48] of tax-free treatment to a transaction that satisfied the minimum statutory requirements for a tax-free reorganization but that served no real business purpose. Treasury Reg. Sec. 1.368-1(c) states:

> A plan of reorganization must contemplate the bona fide execution of one of the transactions specifically described as a reorganization in section 368(a) and for the bona fide consummation of each of the requisite acts under which nonrecognition of gain is claimed. Such transaction and such acts must be an ordinary and necessary incident of the conduct of the enterprise and must provide for a continuation of the enterprise. A scheme, which involves an abrupt departure from normal reorganization procedure in connection with a transaction on which the imposition of tax is imminent, such as a mere device that puts on the form of a corporate reorganization as a disguise for concealing its real character, and the object and accomplishment of which is the consummation of a preconceived plan having no business or corporate purpose, is not a plan of reorganization.

In general, the issue of a purported business purpose is brought up by the I.R.S. in an attempt to require the recognition of a gain by the corporation or shareholders in question.

Continuity of shareholder interest

Like the business purpose requirement, Sec. 368 fails to mention the need for the shareholders of the acquired corporation to maintain a continuing equity participation in the acquiring corporation. The need for a continuing equity participation is the result of a series of judicial decisions. The continuity of interest doctrine, as applied by the courts, denies tax-free treatment to transactions satisfying the statutory requirements for a reorganization if the consideration received by the acquired corporation, its shareholders, or both, is primarily cash and short-term securities, so that the transaction overall more closely resembles a sale than a reorganization.[49] In *Pinellas Ice and Cold Storage Co.* v. *Commissioner*[50] and *LeTulle* v. *Scofield*,[51] the Supreme Court held that the acquired corporation must acquire a proprietary interest in the acquiring corporation and that cash and short-term notes or bonds fail to provide such an interest. The need for a continuing proprietary interest has found its way into Treas. Reg. Sec. 1.368-1(b), which states:

> Requisite to a reorganization under the Code are a continuity of the business enterprise under the modified corporate form, and (except as provided in section 368(a)(1)(D)) a continuity of interest therein on the part of those persons who, directly or indirectly, were the owners of the enterprise prior to the reorganization. The Code recognizes as a reorganization the amalgamation (occurring in a specified way) of two corporate enterprises under a single corporate structure if there exists among the holders of the stock and securities of either of the old corporations the requisite continuity of interest in the new corporation, but there is not a reorganization if the holders of the stock and securities of the old corporation are merely the holders of short-term notes in the new corporation.

Though a continuity of the proprietary interest is a necessity, neither Congress nor the courts have been ready to determine what minimum equity participation is required. The I.R.S., however, has adopted a guideline for the continuity of interest requirement that applies to taxpayers preparing ruling requests. This guideline indicates that the minimum equity participation in the acquiring (or transferee) corporation by the former shareholders of the acquired (or transferor) corporation exists when at least 50 percent of the value of all of the formerly outstanding stock of the acquired (or transferor) corporation is acquired for stock of the acquiring (or transferee) corporation.[52] These guide-

---

[48]293 U.S. 465 (1935) *aff'g.* 69 F.2d 809 (CCA-2, 1934) *rev'g.* 27 BTA 223 (1932).

[49]*Phillip J. Cogan v. Commissioner,* 97 F.2d 996 (CCA-2, 1937) *aff'g.* 36 BTA 639 (1937); *Wortham Machinery Co. v. Commissioner,* 521 F.2d 160 (CCA-10, 1975) *aff'g.* 375 F.Supp. 835 (D.C.-Wyo. 1974); *American Bronze Corporation,* 64 TC 1111 (1975); *Estate of Moses L. Parshelsky v. Commissioner,* 303 F.2d 14 (CCA-2, 1962) *rev'g.* 34 TC 946 (1960); and *Harriet S.W. Lewis v. Commissioner,* 176 F.2d 646 (CCA-1, 1949) *aff'g.* 10 TC 1080 (1948).

[50]287 U.S. 462 (1933) *aff'g.* 57 F.2d 188 (CCA-5, 1932) *aff'g.* 21 BTA 425 (1930).

[51]308 U.S. 415 (1940) *aff'g.* 103 F.2d 20 (CCA-5, 1939) *rev'g.* unreported D.C. decision.

[52]Rev. Proc. 79-14, 1979-1 CB 496, Sec. 3.01.

lines also specify that not all shareholders are required to satisfy this 50 percent minimum, as long as the 50 percent minimum is satisfied for the total consideration used in the reorganization.[53] Sales, redemptions, and other dispositions of stock that occur before or after the exchange, but that are part of the plan of reorganization, are considered in determining whether the 50 percent minimum has been satisfied as of the effective date for the reorganization. This judicial restriction thus has the effect of increasing the minimum equity participation required in the reorganization.

The continuity of interest requirement generally presents a problem only with the Type A reorganization, in which a substantial degree of freedom exists as to the amount of consideration (other than stock) that will be used. The requirement also holds in a Type F reorganization, in which substantially all the shareholders must participate in the new corporation. The Type B solely-for-voting-stock requirement and the Type C restrictions on the use of nonstock consideration generally provide a much more difficult standard than that found in the I.R.S. guidelines. There is a special continuity-of-interest requirement for divisive Type D reorganizations that necessitates continuing equity participation in only one of the two surviving corporations. (See the earlier discussion of this point under Type D reorganizations and corporate divisions on page 7/21.

Continuity of business enterprise

The continuity-of-business-enterprise requirement is founded on the basic restriction of tax-free reorganizations to "exchanges incident to readjustments of corporate structure ... as are required by business exigencies and which effect only a readjustment of continuing interest in property under modified corporate forms" (Treas. Reg. Sec. 1.368-1(b)). The courts and the I.R.S. have generally interpreted this regulation as requiring only that the acquiring (or transferee) corporation continue some form of business activities. These business activities may be the same as originally conducted by the acquiring corporation as part of the reorganization.[54] When the new corporation is a shell

formed to facilitate a sale or exchange, however, the requisite continuity of business enterprise may not be found.[55]

Step transaction doctrine

A taxpayer may find it advantageous to take a transaction that in its entirety would qualify as a tax-free reorganization and break it down into a series of separate transactions that, when accounted for on an individual basis, fail to qualify as a tax-free reorganization. Accomplishing the end result in a series of individual steps may permit the taxpayer to obtain a tax result that is unavailable under the reorganization rules. For example, splitting the transfer of assets to a controlled corporation (a Type D reorganization) into two parts—a sale transaction and a tax-free transfer (followed by an exchange of the controlled corporation's shares)—may be designed to permit a taxpayer to recognize a loss that would otherwise be subject to the nonrecognition rules of Sec. 361 or to increase the transferee's basis in some assets to its market value, rather than being required to use the carryover basis rules of Sec. 362 that apply to a tax-free transfer. The treatment of these two transactions as a single transaction by the I.R.S. through the use of the step transaction doctrine may negate any advantage otherwise associated with the use of separate transactions.

Conversely, treating the two separate steps that a taxpayer may utilize as a single, integrated transaction may disqualify a transaction from tax-free treatment as a reorganization. For example, treating as a single transaction a sale of some assets, unwanted by an acquiring corporation, and the exchange of the remaining assets to an acquiring corporation in exchange for its stock may disqualify a potential Type C reorganization because (as a single transaction) it fails to satisfy the consideration restrictions or the substantially-all requirement.[56] Similarly, treating a cash purchase of some of a corporation's stock as related to a subsequent acquisition of the same stock in exchange for the voting stock of the acquiring corporation may disqualify a transaction from being a Type B reorganization because it fails to satisfy the solely-for-voting-stock requirement.[57]

[53]The 50 percent requirement may also be measured in terms of the stock of the corporation that controls the acquiring corporation. The 50 percent operating rule does not carry the weight of law, and the courts have permitted tax-free treatment for transactions in which the continuing proprietary interest falls below this minimum. See, for example, *John A. Nelson Co.* v. *Helvering*, 296 U.S. 374 (1935) *rev'g.* 75 F.2d 696 (CCA-7, 1935) *aff'g.* 28 BTA 529 (1933).

[54]Rev. Rul. 63-29, 1963-1 CB 77.

[55]*Standard Realization Co.*, 10 TC 708 (1948) A. 1948-2 CB 3; *Donald L. Bentsen* v. *Phinney*, 199 F.Supp. 363 (S.D.-Tex., 1961); *Atlas Tool Co., Inc.* v. *Commissioner*, 80-1 USTC para. 9177 (CCA-3, 1980) *aff'g.*70 TC 86 (1978); *Ernest F. Becher* v. *Commissioner*, 221 F.2d 252 (CCA-2, 1955) *aff'g.* 22 TC 932 (1954); and *Adkins-Phelps, Inc.* v. *Commissioner*, 400 F.2d 737 (CCA-8, 1968) *aff'g.* 67-1 USTC para. 9289 (D.C.-Ark., 1966).

[56]*Helvering* v. *Elkhorn Coal Co.*, 95 F.2d 732 (CCA-4, 1937) *rev'g.* 34 BTA 845 (1936).

[57]Rev. Rul. 75-360, 1975-2 CB 110.

Whether each individual transaction is viewed as part of a larger transaction generally depends on the degree of continuity that exists between the individual steps. To the extent that the individual transactions can be seen as parts of a whole, the ultimate goal of the taxpayer's individual transactions may not be achieved.

Liquidation and reincorporation

The owners of a highly profitable corporation sometimes attempt to take advantage of the capital gains treatment accorded the liquidation of a corporation under Sec. 331, and the nonrecognition of gain or loss permitted under Sec. 351, to withdraw excess funds from a corporation as a capital gain while continuing the business activities. The excess funds would be withdrawn by liquidating a profitable corporation and incurring a capital gains tax on the difference between the fair market value of the properties received and the owner's adjusted basis for the stock. The necessary operating assets of the business would then be transferred to a new corporate shell, where they would have a basis equal to their fair market value (rather than their old adjusted basis). Because the old corporation was liquidated under Sec. 331, the new corporation would not assume its earnings and profits, or any of its other tax attributes. Provided the fair market value of the assets exceeded their adjusted basis in the hands of the liquidated corporation, the new corporation would be able to claim an increased amount of depreciation on the operating assets at the expense of a mere capital gains tax to the shareholders. The I.R.S. has used a number of different approaches to prevent the use of these tax planning tactics, including:

1. Court-imposed restrictions such as the step transaction doctrine, the failure of the transaction to have a sound business purpose, or the treatment of the transaction as a sham.

2. The treatment of the assets retained by the shareholders after the liquidation and second incorporation transactions as a dividend (Treas. Reg. Sec. 1.331-1(c)).

3. The characterization of the transaction as a Type D, E, or F reorganization with the assets retained by the shareholders treated as boot under Sec. 356.[58]

The successful application of any one of these defenses usually prevents the withdrawal of earnings at capital gains rates, preserves the asset's original adjusted basis, and allows a carryover of the earnings and profits and other tax attributes.

The liquidation-reincorporation trap can apparently be avoided by several means, including but not limited to: (1) separating the two transactions by a sufficient time period; (2) involving sufficiently different owners in the "old" and "new" corporations; (3) having owners that are common to the two corporations maintain different ownership interests in the two corporations; (4) having the new corporation conduct a business different from that of the old corporation; (5) having less than substantially all the old corporation's total assets or operating assets or both received by the new corporation; and (6) possessing a satisfactory business purpose for the transaction.[59]

TAX ATTRIBUTE CARRYOVERS

One of the factors ordinarily considered in the acquisition of one corporation by another is the value of any loss, deduction, or credit carryovers owned by the acquired corporation. Section 381 permits the acquiring corporation—or the distributee corporation in certain tax-free transactions—to assume the tax attributes of the acquired corporation. Because of the potential economic value of these tax attributes, three statutory restrictions exist that may limit the ability of a corporation to use a tax attribute carryover. These limitations are found in Sec. 382 (Special Limitation on Net Operating Loss Carryovers), Sec. 383 (Special Limitations on Carryovers of Unused Investments Credits, Work Incentive Program Credits, New Employee Credits, Foreign Taxes, and Capital Losses), and Sec. 269 (Acquisitions Made to Evade or Avoid Income Taxes).

Transactions covered by Section 381

Section 381(a) specifies two types of transactions—tax-free liquidations and tax-free reorganizations—that *require* the acquired corporation's tax attributes to be carried over to the acquiring corporation. In a tax-free liquidation, the tax attributes of a liquidated subsidiary corporation carry over to a domestic parent corporation whenever Sec. 332 permits nonrecognition of gain or loss by the distributee and Sec. 334(b)(1) provides a carryover basis for the assets. The tax at-

---

[58]Rev. Rul. 61-156, 1961-2 CB 62; *J.E. Davant v. Commissioner,* 366 F.2d 874 (CCA-5, 1966) *aff'g.* and *rev'g.* 43 TC 540 (1965); *Reef Corp v. Commissioner,* 368 F.2d 125 (CCA-5, 1966) *aff'g.* 24 TCM 379 (1965); *American Manufacturing Co., Inc.* 55 TC 204 (1970); and *Atlas Tool Co. Inc. v. Commissioner,* 80-1 USTC para. 9177 (CCA-3, 1980) *aff'g.*70 TC 86 (1978).

[59]*Ross M. Simon Trust* v. *U.S.,* 402 F.2d 272 (Ct. Cls., 1968); *Commissioner* v. *Hyman H. Berghash,* 361 F.2d 257 (CCA-2, 1966) *aff'g.* 43 TC 743 (1965); *Joseph C. Gallagher,* 39 TC 144 (1962); and *Pridemark, Inc.* v. *Commissioner,* 345 F.2d 35 (CCA-4, 1965) *aff'g.* and *rev'g.* 42 TC 510 (1964).

tribute carryover rules do *not* apply when a purchase has occurred, even if the subsidiary corporation is liquidated in a tax-free transaction, as long as the Sec. 334(b)(2) rules permit the basis of the property received to equal the parent corporation's adjusted basis for the liquidated corporation's stock (Sec. 381(a)(1)).

Four types of tax-free reorganizations *require* the acquired corporation's tax attributes to be carried over (Sec. 381(a)):

1. A Type A reorganization—that is, a statutory merger or consolidation;
2. A Type C reorganization—that is, an asset-for-stock acquisition;
3. A nondivisive Type D reorganization—that is, a reorganization that qualifies under both Sec. 368(a)(1)(D) and Sec. 354(b)(1); and
4. A Type F reorganization—that is, a change in identity, form, or place of incorporation.

The following types of tax-free reorganizations are excluded from the list of transactions invoking the tax attribute carryover rules (Sec. 381(a)):

1. A Type B reorganization—that is, a stock-for-stock reorganization;
2. A divisive Type D reorganization—that is, a reorganization qualifying under Secs. 368(a)(1)(D), 355, and 356;
3. A Type E reorganization—that is, a recapitalization;
4. Corporate divisions controlled by Sec. 355;
5. Tax-free asset acquisitions by a controlled corporation, controlled by Sec. 351; and
6. Partial and complete liquidations controlled by Secs. 331 and 333.

The Sec. 381(a) rules fail to apply to transactions (1) and (3) because, after the exchange, the original corporate entity remains in existence without undergoing a substantive change in its asset composition. Even though transactions (2), (4), and (5) do not invoke the Sec. 381(a) tax attribute carryover rules, Treas. Reg. Secs. 1.312-10 and -11 may require an allocation of earnings and profits between the transferor corporation and the controlled corporation. Further discussion of these rules is beyond the scope of this text.

Tax attributes that are carried over

Section 381(c) provides for the carryover of the following 23 tax attributes of a regular corporation:

1. Net operating losses;
2. Earnings and profits;
3. Capital losses;
4. Accounting method(s);
5. Inventory method(s);
6. Depreciation method(s);
7. Installment method election for an obligation;
8. Amortization of bond discount or premium election;
9. Election for deduction of certain deferred mining development and exploration expenditures (Sec. 616);
10. Unused contributions to pension plans, employee annuity plans, and stock bonus and profit-sharing plans;
11. Recovery of bad debts, prior taxes, or delinquency amounts;
12. Election to defer gain on an involuntary conversion;
13. Personal holding company (PHC) dividend carryover;
14. Amounts set aside to pay qualified PHC indebtedness;
15. Deduction for obligations relating to expense or allowance items;
16. PHC, regulated investment company, and real estate investment trust deficiency dividends;
17. Percentage depletion on mine tailings;
18. Excess charitable contributions;
19. Certain insurance company attributes;
20. Unused investment tax credit carryovers and recapture potential;
21. Unused Work Incentive (WIN) tax credit carryovers;
22. Unused new jobs tax credit carryovers; and
23. Unused alcohol fuels usage credit carryover (Sec. 381(c)(1)–(27)).

Because each of these areas is potentially complex, and because each one is relatively significant in most reorganizations, we shall limit our discussion of tax attributes to net operating loss carryovers. The operating rules for the other tax attributes may be found in Treas. Reg. Sec. 1.381(c)(2)-1.381(c)(23).

Net operating loss carryovers

A number of operating rules exist for net operating loss (NOL) carryovers, which in general also apply to other types of tax-attribute carryovers. When a tax-free liquidation or reorganization (other than a Type F reorganization) occurs, the taxable year of the liquidated (or acquired) corporation ends on the date that the distribution (or transfer) is completed. An income tax return must be filed by the liquidated (or acquired) corporation for the taxable year that ends on this date. The net operating losses of the liquidated (or acquired) corporation incurred before this date are required to be carried back to the preceding taxable years (unless an election is made under Sec. 172(b)(3)(C) to forego the carryback period) before being carried over to offset profits accruing in a subsequent taxable year of the acquiring corporation (Sec. 381(b)). An exception to the general rule just stated exists for a Type F reorganization. The acquiring corporation in a Type F reorganization is treated for purposes of Sec. 381 as a continuation of the acquired corporation; hence, no break in the taxable year of the two corporations is required (Treas. Reg. Sec. 1.381(b)-1(a)(2)).

The acquired corporation's net operating loss carryover must be carried over to the first taxable year of the acquiring corporation that ends after the date of transfer. The amount of the net operating loss carryover for a given taxable year of the acquired corporation is determined by applying the carryover rules of Secs. 172(c) and (d). The entire amount of the net operating loss carryover is assumed by the acquiring corporation even though the tax-free transaction does not cause the acquiring corporation to receive all the acquired corporation's assets (Sec. 381(c)(1)).

The amount of the net operating loss deduction claimed in the first taxable year ending after the date of transfer is limited to the portion of the acquiring corporation's taxable income for the carryover year that accrues after the date of transfer (Sec. 381(c)(1)(B)). The net operating loss carryover limitation for the first postdistribution year is determined as follows:

$$\text{NOL Carryover Limitation} = \begin{array}{c}\text{Taxable income} \\ \text{of the acquiring} \\ \text{corporation} \\ \text{for first} \\ \text{postacquisition} \\ \text{taxable year*}\end{array} \times \frac{\begin{array}{c}\text{Number of days in the} \\ \text{acquiring corporation's} \\ \text{taxable year after the} \\ \text{date of acquisition}\end{array}}{\begin{array}{c}\text{Total number of days} \\ \text{in the acquiring corpo-} \\ \text{ration's taxable year}\end{array}}$$

*Excluding any NOL deduction, but including other Sec. 381 carryovers.

No such limitation applies to the acquiring corporation's second or succeeding taxable years ending after the date of transfer. The above limitation applies to each net operating loss carryover when the losses are incurred in two or more taxable years of the acquired corporation. If a net operating loss carryover arises from net operating losses incurred in two or more taxable years, these losses are applied by the acquiring

corporation in a first in, first out (FIFO) manner, beginning with the earliest sustained losses.

The carryover period for the losses of the acquired corporation is based on the general rules applying to all corporations found in Sec. 172(b)(1). The acquired corporation's taxable year ending with the date of transfer, and the carryover portion of the acquiring corporation's first posttransfer taxable year, both count as full taxable years for carryover purposes, even though each generally consists of a shorter period than 12 months. Thus, the time for absorption of the net operating loss carryover usually is shortened for a Sec. 381(a) transaction (other than a Type F reorganization) to something less than seven calendar years. In a Type F reorganization, generally, no such shortening of the time period occurs because the taxable year of transfer is not interrupted at the date of transfer (Treas. Reg. Sec. 1.381(c)(1)-1(e)(3)).

Any net operating losses of the acquiring corporation incurred in a taxable year ending after the date of transfer are prohibited from being carried back to an earlier taxable year of the acquired corporation. An exception to this general rule applies to net operating losses incurred by the acquiring corporation after a Type F reorganization. These losses may be carried back to the earlier taxable years of the acquired corporation subject only to the normal Sec. 172(b) restrictions. Similarly, losses incurred by the acquiring corporation may be carried back to offset profits of *its* earlier taxable years subject only to the Sec. 172(b) restrictions (Sec. 381(b)(3)). In some reorganization transactions (such as Type C reorganizations), the acquired corporation does not need to be liquidated after the transfer of its assets. Postacquisition losses of an acquired corporation that remains in existence may be carried back or over to *its* other taxable years (Treas. Reg. Sec. 1.381(c)(1)-1(b)).

Section 382 net operating loss carryover limitation

The Sec. 382 limitation rules are an attempt to restrict the use of net operating loss carryovers in situations in which an acquisition has been undertaken primarily to enable the acquired or acquiring corporations to take greater advantage of the tax benefits associated with the carryover. Net operating loss carryovers of corporations that undergo normal changes in ownership associated with the conduct of a going business generally are unaffected by the Sec. 382 rules.

The rules in effect before the Tax Reform Act of 1976 may be divided into two parts: (1) Sec. 382(a) rules, applying to purchase transactions; and (2) Sec. 382(b) rules, applying to certain forms of tax-free reorganizations. These rules govern reorganization transactions in which the plan was adopted before January 1, 1982, and for other changes in stock ownership occurring in taxable years beginning before July 1, 1982.[60]

The Sec. 382(a) rules deny the tax benefits associated with a net operating loss carryover to the current taxable year or to a subsequent taxable year if:

1. Any one or more of the 10 shareholders owning the largest amount of stock (in terms of fair market value) of the loss corporation have increased their stock ownership in the current or preceding taxable year by a total of 50 percentage points in a "purchase" transaction (as defined by Sec. 382(a)(1)(B)); *and*
2. The loss corporation fails to conduct a trade or business that is substantially the same as it conducted before any change in the stock ownership.

Thus, the purchase of all a loss corporation's stock by one or more shareholders, followed by a major shift in its business operations, would prevent the new owners from taking advantage of the tax benefits of any of the net operating loss carryovers.

Section 382(b) partially or entirely eliminated the net operating loss carryover of a loss corporation that had been involved in certain types of tax-free reorganizations. A reduction of the net operating loss carryover occurred when:

1. A Type A, C, nondivisive D, or F reorganization had occurred;[61]
2. The acquired or acquiring corporation had a net operating loss that could be carried over to the acquiring corporation's first taxable year ending after the acquisition date; *and*
3. The loss corporation's shareholders (who owned stock immediately preceding the reorganization) ended up owning less than 20 percent of the fair market value of the acquiring corporation's stock immediately after the reorganization (Sec. 382(b)(1)).

A reorganization satisfying these three requirements caused the net operating loss carryover amount to be reduced by the percentage resulting from multiplying by five the amount that the loss corporation's shareholders' stock ownership percentage in the acquiring corporation (immediately after the reorganization) fell below 20 percent (Sec. 382(b)(2)). Thus, the loss corporation's shareholders could assume a minority position in the acquiring corporation, providing it did not fall below a 20 percent level, without jeopardizing the net operating loss carryover.

The new Sec. 382(a) rules in general parallel the old Sec. 382(a) rules, except that:

1. The 50 percentage point increase in stock ownership has been increased to 60 percentage points.
2. The number of shareholders whose ownership change is examined has been increased from 10 to 15.
3. The ownership comparison is applied between the last day of the current taxable year and the beginning of the current, first preceding, and second preceding taxable years.
4. The requirement that the corporation substantially change its trade or business, before Sec. 382(a) is invoked, has been deleted. (Now only a sufficient change in the continuity of ownership is required before the net operating loss carryover is reduced.)

Section 382(a) now requires a minimum continuity of interest by the shareholders of the loss corporation of 40 percent (rather than 50 percent). If Sec. 382(a) is invoked, the net operating loss carryover is no longer completely eliminated, but it is reduced by the sum of:

1. 3½ percent times the aggregate increase in ownership percentage occurring for the 15 (or fewer) principal shareholders above 60 percentage points (but not in excess of 80 percentage points); plus
2. 1½ percent times the aggregate increase in ownership percentage occurring for the same shareholders above the 80 percentage point level.

The Sec. 382(b) requirements for invoking a reduction in the amount of a net operating loss carryover after the occurrence of a tax-free reorganization have also changed. The changes include:

1. Certain Type B reorganizations now trigger a net operating loss reduction.
2. The minimum ownership level of the acquiring corporation's stock by the loss corporation's shareholders has been increased to 40 percent of the fair market value of such stock.

---

[60]The Sec. 382 changes that were enacted in the Tax Reform Act of 1976 (P. L. 94-455) were originally scheduled to go into effect four years earlier than indicated here. Section 368 of The Revenue Act of 1978 (P. L. 95-600), however, delayed these changes for two years so that the rules were to be effective two years earlier than indicated here. P.L. 96-167 (approved December 29, 1979) further delayed these changes until the effective dates indicated.

[61]The reorganization transactions covered here are the same as governed by the Sec. 381 attribute carryover rules.

If Sec. 382(b) is invoked, the net operating loss carryover is reduced by the sum of:

1. 3½ percent times the number of percentage points (including fractions thereof) that the ownership level falls below 40 percent (but not below the 20 percent level); plus
2. 1½ percent times the number of percentage points (including fractions thereof) that the ownership level falls below 20 percent (Sec. 382(b)(2)).

Secs. 382(a) and (b) contain other technical changes, but a discussion of these points is left to subsequent tax courses.

Sections 383 and 269

Section 383 provides that reductions in the amount of certain credit and loss carryovers, similar to those described earlier for net operating losses, occur when a change in corporate ownership of a nature described in either Sec. 382(a) or (b) takes place. Credit carryovers subject to reduction are unused investment tax credits, work incentive program credits, new employee credits, alcohol fuels usage credits, and foreign tax credits. Also subject to reduction under Sec. 383 are net capital loss carryovers available under Sec. 1212.

Section 269 may also apply to deny a taxpayer the benefits of a deduction, allowance, or credit that it would otherwise enjoy when the control of a corporation is acquired with the intention of increasing the usability of these tax benefits. For Sec. 269 to apply to a tax attribute, the following conditions must be met.

1. A person must acquire direct or indirect control[62] of a corporation; *or*
2. A corporation must acquire direct or indirect control of a corporation that (a) immediately preceding the acquisition was not controlled by the corporation or its shareholders; and (b) a carryover basis applies to the acquired property in the acquiring corporation's hands;
and
3. The *principal purpose* of the acquisition is the evasion or avoidance of federal income taxes through the acquisition of the benefits of deductions, credits, or other allowances that would not otherwise be available to the acquiring person or corporation (Sec. 269(a)).

Section 269 may thus be invoked in any situation that is not covered under Sec. 382 or 383.[63] It calls for a *complete* denial of tax benefits rather than a reduction in the amount of a carryover. Because of the principal purpose requirement, it is generally harder for the I.R.S. to apply successfully.[64]

SUMMARY

In our introduction to the topic of corporate reorganizations presented here, we have attempted to demonstrate some of the economic advantages to using such a device to alter the nature of the corporate structure or activities or the form of an individual's investment in a corporate entity. When attempting to take advantage of the corporate reorganization provisions, one should be careful to avoid encountering any of the legislative or judicial restrictions that apply to reorganization transactions and the associated problems and penalties. One should also be cognizant of the advantages that may be available to a taxpayer by structuring a transaction that falls outside the purview of the reorganization rules. These advantages, which in many cases are more difficult to achieve than is compliance with the reorganization rules, should be examined when contemplating any potential transaction.

---

[62]Control here is defined as 50 percent ownership of the acquired corporation's stock, rather than the 80 percent minimum for Sec. 368(c).

[63]Staff of the Joint Committee on Taxation, *General Explanation of the Tax Reform Act of 1976*, p. 203. The mutual exclusion of Secs. 269, 382, and 383 only applies in taxable years to which the "new" Sec. 382 rules apply.
[64]Compare, for example, *Canaveral International Corp.* 61 TC 520 (1974), where Sec. 269 was successfully applied by the I.R.S. with *Rocco, Inc.*, 72 TC 140 (1979) where the I.R.S. was unable to successfully establish the principal purpose motive.

PROBLEMS

1. Classify each of the following transactions according to its reorganization designation (that is, Type A, B, C).
    a. Ace Corporation exchanges two shares of its common stock for each of the 1,000 shares of Beta Corporation's single class of outstanding stock.
    b. Ace Corporation exchanges two shares of its common stock and $10 cash for each of the 1,000 shares of Beta Corporation's single class of outstanding

stock. Beta, a Delaware corporation, is subsequently liquidated into Ace. The transaction satisfies the merger statute requirements of the state of Delaware.

c. The shareholders of Ace Corporation, a New York corporation, exchange all their outstanding shares for shares of New Corporation, also a New York corporation. The Ace shares are retired by the Ace management. New Corporation continues all Ace's activities.

d. Ace Corporation exchanges $100,000 of its common stock and $25,000 cash for all of Beta Corporation's assets. Beta uses the cash to pay off its liabilities and is then liquidated.

e. Ace Corporation's preferred stockholders exchange each share of the $100 par 8 percent preferred stock that is outstanding for 10 shares of $10 par Ace Corporation common stock.

f. Ace Corporation transfers one-half its assets to the newly created Beta Corporation in exchange for all of Beta's stock. Ace distributes the Beta stock to one of its shareholders in exchange for all of her Ace stock.

g. Ace Corporation exchanges two shares of its common stock for each outstanding share of Beta Corporation's single class of stock. Ace also exchanges three shares of its common stock for each outstanding share of Charlie Corporation's single class of stock. Shortly thereafter, Beta and Charlie are liquidated into Ace Corporation. The transaction satisfies the merger statute requirements of the state of Texas.

2. a. Classify each of the following corporate division transactions according to its designation.

   (1) Parent Corporation distributes, on a pro rata basis, all the stock of the wholly owned Subsidiary Corporation to its shareholders.

   (2) Parent Corporation distributes all the stock of the wholly owned Subsidiary Corporation to two of its four shareholders in exchange for their stockholdings in Parent Corporation.

   (3) Parent Corporation transfers all its assets to two newly created subsidiaries in exchange for all their outstanding stock. Parent Corporation exchanges the stock of these two subsidiaries for all the outstanding Parent Corporation stock.

   b. If the above transactions fail to satisfy one or more of the Sec. 355 requirements, indicate how they would be taxed.

3. Alpha Corporation is seeking to acquire the assets of Bravo Corporation by utilizing a statutory merger. The total consideration to be transferred to Bravo's sole shareholder for all the Bravo stock is $200,000. This shareholder's adjusted basis in his stock is $125,000. Indicate the amount of gain that is to be recognized by Bravo's sole shareholder in each of the following independent situations.

   a. Alpha transfers only its common stock for Bravo's common stock. Bravo's former shareholder owns 50 percent of Alpha after the merger.

   b. Assume the same facts as in part a, except the Alpha stock is publicly traded and Bravo's former shareholder owns 0.01 percent of the stock after the merger.

   c. Alpha exchanges only its preferred stock for the Bravo common stock.

   d. Alpha exchanges $175,000 of its common stock and $25,000 cash for the Bravo common stock.

   e. Alpha exchanges $120,000 of its common stock and $80,000 cash for the Bravo common stock.

   f. Alpha exchanges $152,000 of its common stock and $50,000 of its 9 percent bonds (having a market value of $48,000) for the Bravo stock.

g. Alpha exchanges $75,000 of its common stock and $125,000 of its 10 percent bonds (having a market value of $125,000) for the Bravo stock.

4. MKH Enterprises exchanges, in a transaction satisfying the Florida merger statutes, 2,000 shares of its common stock having a market value of $280,000 and $20,000 cash for all the single class of stock of GKW Corporation. GKW's shareholder has a basis of $175,000 in her shares.

   a. What is the shareholder's realized gain? Her recognized gain?
   b. What is the character of the recognized gain?
   c. What is the shareholder's basis in the MKH Enterprises stock that is received?
   d. Does MKH Enterprises recognize a gain on issuing previously unissued stock to acquire the GKW stock? Would your answer change if treasury stock that cost $100 per share had been used in the acquisition?
   e. How would your answers to parts a and b change if the sole shareholder's basis in the GKW Corporation shares were $400,000? Is there any alternative way to achieve a better tax result?

5. The sole shareholder of DAS, Inc. agrees to exchange, on August 1, 19X6, all his common stock for a combination of preferred stock and bonds that will be issued by JVB Corporation as part of a statutory merger coming under the Michigan merger statutes. JVB Corporation will issue $80,000 of JVB preferred stock and $20,000 of 10 percent JVB bonds (having a market value equal to their face amount) in exchange for the DAS stock that was acquired for $30,000 on April 1, 19X4.

   a. What is the realized gain on the exchange of the DAS shares? The recognized gain?
   b. What is the character of the recognized gain?
   c. What is the shareholder's basis in the JVB preferred stock?
   d. What is the shareholder's basis in the JVB bonds?

6. High Corporation is planning to acquire all the single class of Low Corporation stock. Which of the following types of consideration, if given by High Corporation to Low's shareholder, would permit the exchange to qualify under Sec. 368(a)(1)(B)?

   a. High Corporation common stock, where the former Low Corporation shareholders end up owning 60 percent of the acquiring corporation's common stock.
   b. High Corporation common stock, where the former Low Corporation shareholders end up owning 1 percent of the acquiring corporation's common stock.
   c. High Corporation preferred stock.
   d. A combination of High Corporation common stock and preferred stock.
   e. High Corporation voting preferred stock.
   f. High Corporation common stock to the shareholders that vote to approve the acquisition. Shareholders who dissent to the acquisition will have their shares purchased by High Corporation for $35 each.

7. Smithco is attempting to acquire American Transfer Company by exchanging its common stock for American's outstanding common and preferred stock. American Transfer has 100,000 shares of $1 par common stock and 20,000 shares of $100 par preferred stock outstanding.

   a. What is the minimum number of shares of American Transfer stock that Smithco must acquire for the transfer to qualify under Sec. 368(a)(1)(B)?
   b. If Smithco acquires all of American's stock, what options exist for the filing of tax returns by Smithco and American?

c. If the stock acquisition is followed by a prearranged liquidation of American Transfer into Smithco, these two steps are the equivalent of what other types of reorganizations?

d. Assume Johnny Dee owns 10,000 shares of American Transfer common stock, which he acquired at a cost of $20 per share, and that as part of the reorganization, three shares of Smithco stock trading at $20 are exchanged for each share of American Transfer common stock. Mr. Dee sells 1,000 shares of the Smithco stock six months after the reorganization for $25,000. What is the amount of his recognized gain? What is the character of the gain?

8. Three independent transactions involving potential Type B stock-for-stock reorganizations are presented below. Which of these independent events should actually result in nonrecognition of gain for Delta's shareholders?

a. Echo Corporation exchanges cash for 20 percent of the single class of the Delta stock on March 1, 19X1. On November 1, 19X1, Echo exchanges additional common stock for 70 percent more of Delta stock.

b. On March 1, 19X2 Echo Corporation exchanges some of its common stock for 80 percent of the Delta stock. On April 15, 19X3, Echo purchases for cash 15 percent of the Delta stock from minority shareholders who originally did not desire to exchange their stock.

c. Echo Corporation acquires for cash on July 1, 19X3 10 percent of the Delta stock. On October 1, 19X5 Echo exchanges some of its common stock for 85 percent of the Delta stock.

9. RWA Corporation is considering acquiring all the assets of FEC Corporation in a tax-free reorganization qualifying under Sec. 368(a)(1)(C). FEC's total assets are worth $100,000. Determine which of the following "packages" RWA could transfer to FEC for its assets and still permit FEC to avoid recognizing any gain.

a. $80,000 of RWA common stock and $20,000 of RWA preferred stock.

b. $80,000 of RWA common stock and $20,000 of RWA 10 percent bonds.

c. $80,000 of RWA common stock and the assumption of $20,000 of FEC's liabilities.

d. $70,000 of RWA common stock, $10,000 cash, and the assumption of $20,000 of FEC's liabilities.

e. $70,000 of RWA common stock and the assumption of $30,000 of FEC's liabilities.

f. $80,000 of common stock of RWA's parent corporation and $20,000 cash.

10. Section 368(a)(1)(C) requires the acquiring corporation to obtain "substantially all" of the acquired corporation's assets in the reorganization transaction. RLS Corporation reports the following assets and liabilities on January 1, 19X1.

	Situation 1	Situation 2
Gross assets (at market value)	$250,000	$250,000
Liabilities	40,000	$100,000

a. What is the minimum level of assets that must be transferred in each of the above situations?

b. Is it possible for RLS to remain in existence after the reorganization to hold the stock of the acquiring corporation? To conduct a new trade or business?

11. DOD Corporation desires to acquire all the assets of the CLM Corporation in a tax-free reorganization. Determine the amount of gain realized and recognized in each of the following alternative transactions. What is the basis of the assets in the hands of DOD Corporation?

a. *Transaction 1:* CLM agrees to transfer assets having a market value of $700,000 and $125,000 of liabilities to DOD in exchange for $575,000 of DOD common stock. The assets have an adjusted basis of $475,000 in CLM's hands.

b. *Transaction 2:* Assume the same facts as in Transaction 1, except that CLM retains its liabilities and instead receives $575,000 of DOD stock and $125,000 in cash, which is used to pay the liabilities.

What is the basis of the DOD stock in the hands of CLM Corporation's shareholders, assuming that CLM exchanges its outstanding common stock (having an adjusted basis of $150,000) for the DOD stock it receives in the reorganization?

12. Ruby Corporation exchanges all its assets having a market value of $125,000 (and an adjusted basis of $80,000) and liabilities in the amount of $5,000 to Diamond Corporation for $100,000 of its common stock and $20,000 in cash. The boot and stock are retained by Ruby Corporation.

a. Does the transaction qualify as a tax-free reorganization under Sec. 368(a)(1)(C)?

b. What is Ruby Corporation's realized gain? Its recognized gain?

c. What is Ruby Corporation's basis in its Diamond stock?

d. What is Diamond Corporation's basis in the acquired assets?

e. How would your answers to parts a through d change if Ruby Corporation distributed the cash to its shareholders?

13. Hill Corporation has owned and operated a printing plant in Austin, Texas, and another in Dearborn, Michigan, for 10 years. Each factory is managed separately. All of Hill's stock is owned equally by individuals A and B. Each shareholder purchased his stock for $30,000 when Hill was organized. Hill organizes a new corporation (the Still Corporation) and transfers the Dearborn plant and certain liquid assets to Still in exchange for Still stock valued at $150,000. Shareholder A then surrenders all his Hill stock for the Still stock and $10,000 cash. The earnings and profits of Hill immediately preceding the transfer were $180,000.

a. What are the tax consequences of the transaction to A, Still, and Hill?

b. How would the tax consequences to A change if the Dearborn factory had been acquired in a taxable transaction only three years ago?

14. Individual A owns 100 percent of the stock of Rocky Mountain Investment Company (RMI), which holds a number of highly appreciated securities. A causes RMI to transfer 1,000 shares of ABC Industries stock to a newly created subsidiary, XYZ Investment Company, in exchange for all its single class of stock. The ABC stock had a market value of $100,000 and a basis of $10,000 at the time of transfer. One week after the transfer, RMI distributes all the XYZ stock to A. Shortly thereafter, A causes XYZ to liquidate, thereby receiving the ABC Industries stock.

a. What are the tax consequences of the liquidation of XYZ?

b. Do you think that the I.R.S. will permit A to use this arrangement to receive the ABC Industries stock at capital gains rates?

15. Old Company has engaged in the manufacture of electronic components for a number of years. Because of some financial difficulties in earlier years, Old decides to transfer most of its assets to New Company as part of a plan of reorganization. Old transfers assets having a $350,000 market value (and a $275,000 adjusted basis) and $50,000 in liabilities to New in exchange for all of New's single class of stock. Old then distributes the New stock and $30,000 cash that it had retained to its shareholders in exchange for their Old stockholdings.

a. Within what reorganization classification would this transaction most likely fall?

b. Does the transfer of assets to New satisfy the "substantially-all" requirements for this type of transfer?

c. Is it possible for Old to retain any of the assets in question and still have the transaction qualify as a tax-free reorganization under Secs. 368(a)(1)(D) and 354(a)?

d. What is the maximum amount of gain that would be recognized by Old's shareholders, assuming the transaction qualifies as a tax-free reorganization?

e. Will Old's tax attributes carry over to New as part of this transaction?

16. Individual A operates a small manufacturing business as a sole proprietorship. A larger corporation, X, wants to acquire A's sole proprietorship. Individual A would like to minimize the tax consequences of making the transfer of the assets to X. His tax accountant tells him that he should incorporate his business and then at some later date transfer either his stock interest in the new corporation, or the assets of the new corporation to X in a tax-free reorganization. Discuss the merits of such a plan versus a direct sale or transfer of the proprietorship's assets to X.

17. What is the "continuity of shareholder interest" judicial doctrine? Describe the standard that the I.R.S. uses in applying this doctrine.

18. a. Beta Corporation acquires all the assets and liabilities of Xenon Corporation by giving up 1,000 shares of its common stock having a market value of $125,000. Xenon's assets have a market value of $275,000, an adjusted basis of $100,000, and carry with them liabilities in the amount of $150,000, which were assumed by Beta. Xenon ends up owning 30 percent of Beta's common stock after the reorganization. Calculate the amount of gain recognized by Xenon and its basis in the Beta stock.

b. SSK Corporation decides to place its two manufacturing activities into separate entities to diversify the risk associated with them. SSK transfers part of its assets to Sub Corporation in exchange for all its stock. The assets had a market value of $200,000, an adjusted basis of $60,000, and carried with them $100,000 of liabilities that were assumed by Sub. Calculate the amount of gain recognized by SSK Corporation and its basis in the Sub stock.

19. Determine the amount of gain (or loss) that must be recognized by each of the parties in the following two independent situations. Also, indicate the shareholder's basis for the stocks and securities that she receives.

a. A Corporation has $250,000 of 8 percent bonds outstanding that mature on October 1, 19X4. On the maturation date, A Corporation, through an agreement with its bondholders, exchanges one $1,000 bond for 10 shares of unissued preferred stock. Each share of preferred stock has a $100 par amount and a similar market value. Individual X holds 10 bonds that she acquired on February 1, 19X1 for $8,800. No amortization of any of the bond discount has occurred.

b. B Corporation is owned by two individuals—A.J. and her daughter, A.J., Jr. A.J. holds 80 percent of the outstanding common stock. A.J., Jr. owns the remaining 20 percent. A.J. decides to retire and agrees to exchange her 800 shares of common stock that she had acquired on January 3, 19X0, for $10 per share, for 500 shares of $100 par B Corporation preferred stock having a market value of $52,000 and fifty $1,000 face amount B Corporation bonds having a market value of $48,000.

20. Which transactions result in the carryover of tax attributes from an acquired or distributing corporation to an acquiring or distributee corporation?

a. Liquidation of a subsidiary corporation coming under Secs. 332 and 334(b)(1)?

    b.   A Type A corporate reorganization?

    c.   A Type B corporate reorganization?

    d.   A Type C corporate reorganization?

    e.   A tax-free corporate formation coming under Sec. 351 in which the sole transferor is a corporation?

    f.   A Type E corporate reorganization?

    g.   A Type F corporate reorganization?

21. Able Moses is contemplating acquiring the Amalgamated Buggy Whip Company that has incurred a substantial net operating loss during the period 1980–1982. It is estimated that a $2,000,000 net operating loss carryover would be available on the June 30, 1983 proposed acquisition date. Able is considering a number of alternative acquisition methods that have been proposed by Amalgamated's owners. Comment on the availability of the net operating loss carryovers under each of the alternatives and its effect on Able's purchase price.

    a.   *Alternative A:* Able will purchase 100 percent of Amalgamated's common stock for cash.

    b.   *Alternative B:* Able will exchange Able Moses, Ltd. common stock for 100 percent of Amalgamated's common stock as part of a statutory merger in which Amalgamated will be liquidated into Able Moses, Ltd. Amalgamated's shareholders will own 35 percent of Able Moses after the reorganization.

    c.   *Alternative C:* The same consideration will be given as in Alternative B, except that Able Moses will acquire all of Amalgamated's assets. Amalgamated plans to hold the Able Moses, Ltd. stock and Amalgamated will not be liquidated.

22. Alpha Corporation acquired all the assets of Omega Corporation at the close of business on May 26, 19X4 as part of a tax-free merger transaction coming under the purview of Sec. 368(a)(1)(A). The taxable income that has been reported by Alpha and Omega for the period 19X1–19X9 is as follows:

Year [a]	Omega	Alpha
19X1	$(50,000)	$(15,000)
19X2	(35,000)	10,000
19X3	(20,000)	15,000
19X4 [b]	(10,000)	20,000
19X5		5,000
19X6		7,000
19X7		10,000
19X8		45,000
19X9		50,000

[a] Assume all taxable years begin after December 31, 1975.
[b] Not a leap year.

    a.   May Alpha use Omega's net operating loss carryover? If so, what is the amount of Omega's net operating loss carryover, assuming Sec. 382(b) does not apply?

    b.   In what years may Omega's net operating loss carryover be utilized?

23. Kraco, a domestic corporation that uses the calendar year as its taxable year, manufactured parts for use in the automotive industry while incurring substantial net operating losses during the period 1978–1980. During August 1982, Individual A purchased 49 percent of the outstanding Kraco stock from Individual Y. A had previously acquired 21 percent of the Kraco stock, in June 1981, from

Individual X. Even though A had purchased a majority interest in Kraco, and loaned the firm additional monies, Kraco conducted its manufacturing and sales activities in much the same fashion as it had prior to A's purchases.

a. Does the acquisition of the Kraco stock restrict the use of the net operating losses in 1981 to offset current profits? In 1982?

b. If Kraco changed the nature of its business activities in 1982, would this change the availability of its net operating loss carryovers?

c. Would Sec. 382(a) act to restrict the availability of a carryover for a net operating loss incurred in 1981 or 1982?

d. Would your answers to parts (a)–(c) change if A had instead purchased the Kraco stock in July 1982 and August 1983?

24. ABC Corporation has incurred substantial net operating losses over a number of years. The Very Public Corporation (VPC) approaches ABC's management in July 1981 with an offer to exchange some of its unissued common stock for all of ABC's assets. ABC's management intends to liquidate ABC and exchange the VPC shares for the outstanding ABC shares after the asset-for-stock tax-free reorganization occurs. What portion of the ABC net operating loss carryovers would be able to be used by VPC if the former ABC shareholders ended up owning the following percentages of VPC's single class of stock?

a. 50 percent

b. 35 percent

c. 12 percent

d. Would your answers to parts (a)–(c) change if the reorganization took place in July 1982 pursuant to a plan adopted in the same month?

SUPPLEMENTAL PROBLEMS

25. The tax-free reorganization provisions were not part of the original income tax laws that were enacted in 1913. Explain why they were added shortly thereafter and have become a cornerstone of corporate taxation.

26. Ace Duncan owned a small manufacturing enterprise that was operated as a sole proprietorship. On the advice of his attorney, Ace decided to incorporate his business to reduce his potential legal liability from product liability suits. On April 1, 19X0, Ace transferred assets having an adjusted basis of $175,000 and $35,000 of liabilities to Ace Corporation in exchange for $200,000 of Ace's stock. The Ace Corporation prospered and Duncan decided he would sell out the business to Very Public Corporation (VPC). On August 31, 19X4, Ace Corporation transferred in a Type C reorganization, assets having a market value of $600,000 (and an adjusted basis of $275,000) and $150,000 of liabilities to VPC in exchange for stock having an equal value. Shortly after the asset transfer, Ace Corporation was liquidated as part of the reorganization. After holding the VPC stock for a few years, Ace Duncan exchanged all his VPC stock for $1,000,000 of Amalgamated Conglomerate stock (0.001 percent of the total Amalgamated stock) as part of a Type B reorganization.

a. Determine Ace's realized and recognized gain in each of the transactions.

b. What is Ace's basis in his Amalgamated Conglomerate stock?

c. Has the nature of Ace Duncan's investment changed from his original investment in the sole proprietorship?

d. Does Ace now have the wherewithal to pay? Should he pay taxes on his acquisition of the VPC or Amalgamated stocks?

27. Rice Corporation is owned equally by two shareholders—DXS Corporation and William Rice, an individual. DXS Corporation has a large capital loss carryover that expires at the end of the current taxable year. Rice Corporation holds a building that has been fully depreciated but that is worth $1,000,000. The two shareholders, each of whom has a $100,000 basis in his stock, would like to be able to claim additional depreciation on the building by liquidating Rice Corporation and then transferring the building in a tax-free transaction to a new corporation that would be owned equally by DXS and William Rice. At the time of liquidation, it is anticipated that Rice Corporation will have $200,000 of cash and earnings and profits of $1,000,000. The cash will be retained by DXS and William Rice. What will be the tax consequences of the proposed transaction? Do you think the proposed transaction will succeed? If not, what will be the likely tax consequences?

28. XYZ Corporation is formed as a result of the consolidation of X Corporation, Y Corporation, and Z Corporation, each of which was equally owned by individuals A, B, C, and D. Each of these four shareholders received 25 percent of the stock of XYZ Corporation. The operating results of X, Y, Z and XYZ corporations for the period 19X1–19X4 is presented below:

Year ending	Taxable income			
	X	Y	Z	XYZ
12/31/X1	$40,000	$(10,000)*	$30,000	xx
12/31/X2	30,000	(10,000)	40,000	xx
12/31/X3	20,000	20,000	50,000	xx
12/31/X4	xx	xx	xx	$(150,000)**

* Excluding any net operating loss carryback or carryover. These losses cannot be carried back to pre-19X1 taxable years.
**Two-thirds of this loss is attributable to X's former business activities and one-third to Y's former activities.

a. What are the benefits of this transaction qualifying as a Type F reorganization (instead of a Type D reorganization)? Does this transaction qualify as a Type F reorganization?

b. How much of XYZ's loss may be carried back to prior taxable years?

29. Comment on the following statement: Section 382(b) acts to limit the size of the profitable corporation that may acquire, through the use of a tax-free reorganization, a corporation that has a loss carryover.

30. Chris Vaughan acquires all the stock of LBM Corporation, which has been engaged in the business of operating retail drug stores. At the time of the acquisition, LBM has a net operating loss carryover of $1,000,000 and its net worth is $1,000,000. After the acquisition, LBM continues to operate its retail drug stores, but these stores fail to produce sufficient profits to absorb a sufficient portion of the net operating loss carryover. Shortly after the acquisition, Vaughan transfers the assets of a hardware business he previously controlled to LBM Corporation. The hardware business produces profits sufficient to absorb a substantial portion of LBM's net operating loss carryovers. Is Vaughan likely to encounter any problem under either Sec. 269 or 382?

8

consolidated tax returns

A group of corporations that are affiliated with one another (a parent corporation and one or more subsidiaries) has three options for filing federal income tax returns. Such a group may file (1) a consolidated tax return; (2) separate tax returns for each member; or (3) separate tax returns for each member with a 100 percent dividends-received deduction election made under Sec. 243. In this chapter, we compare the advantages and disadvantages of filing a consolidated tax return and discuss the basic requirements for computing the consolidated tax liability.

HISTORY OF THE CONSOLIDATED TAX RETURN

Consolidated tax returns date back to the World War I excess profits regulations issued in 1917. The Commissioner of the Internal Revenue Service was given the power to require a corporation to file a consolidated tax return if it had attempted to avoid the excess profits tax by arbitrarily shifting income or by increasing the number of affiliated corporations. In 1918, consolidated tax returns became part of both the income tax laws and excess profits tax laws and were required of all affiliated groups as a means of preventing the avoidance of taxes.[1] Three years later, in 1921, consolidated tax returns were no longer required of affiliated groups. Once an affiliated group elected to file a consolidated tax return, however, the election became binding on subsequent taxable years unless the Commissioner of

Internal Revenue authorized a change. The Senate Finance Committee stated that the repeal of the mandatory requirement for the filing of consolidated tax returns by affiliated groups occurred for two reasons. First, with the scheduled repeal of the excess profits tax in 1922, consolidated tax returns were no longer necessary to prevent the evasion of high excess profits tax rates. Second, while a number of firms would elect the tax-saving advantages of a consolidated return, many other firms would prefer to avoid the complexity of the consolidated tax return regulations by filing separate tax returns.[2]

From 1934 to 1942, consolidated tax returns were prohibited for income tax purposes for nearly all taxpayers except railroad and railway corporations and Pan American trade corporations.[3] This general rejection of the affiliated group as a taxpaying entity resulted from objections to losses of one group member offsetting the profits of other group members. The retention of the election for railroads and certain other special types of corporations occurred because railroads were frequently required by state and federal regulatory agencies to maintain separate corporate structures in the several states in which they operated, although for all general business and accounting purposes, they formed a single operating system.[4] Since 1942, consolidated income tax returns have generally been an option for most affiliated groups. Certain "special tax status corporations"—for example, foreign corporations, life insurance corporations, U.S. possessions

---

[1] S.Rept. No. 617, 65th Cong., 3d Sess., Dec. 6, 1918. A group of corporations that join together in filing a consolidated tax return is known as an "affiliated group."

[2] S. Rept. No. 275, 67th Cong., 1st Sess., Sept. 26, 1921.
[3] For the period 1940 to 1942, the consolidated tax return election was available for most corporate groups when determining their excess profits tax liability even though it was generally unavailable for income tax purposes.
[4] H. Rept. No. 704, 73rd Cong., 2d Sess., Feb. 12, 1934.

corporations, and tax-exempt organizations—have at various times been prohibited from being part of a consolidated tax return. The exclusion of these special tax entities generally results from either (1) the entirely different tax treatments afforded these special entity forms (compared with regular, domestic corporations), which could lead to additional complexity in the consolidated tax return regulations, or (2) a desire to prevent the avoidance of federal income taxes that could result from the inclusion of these special corporation forms in a consolidated tax return.

In the early years of consolidated tax returns, no specific measure of stock ownership was required of the parent corporation. In order to file a consolidated tax return, a single (parent) corporation had to own "substantially all" the stock of a corporation, or a partnership or an individual had to have control of substantially all the stock of two corporations.[5] In 1924, the "substantially-all" requirement was replaced by the "95-percent-of-the-voting-stock" requirement. In 1926, a minor technical revision occurred, causing the wording of this requirement to change so that all the stock except "nonvoting stock which is limited and preferred as to dividends" was included in the ownership test. In 1928, because of the heavy burden of litigation regarding consolidated tax returns, and as a compromise to a House proposal to abolish consolidated tax returns altogether, the option of filing consolidated tax returns was repealed for "brother-sister" corporations; hence only the parent–subsidiary requirement remained.[6] In 1954, the 95 percent requirement was reduced to the currently required minimum stock ownership of 80 percent.

Because filing a consolidated tax return has particular benefits, affiliated groups of corporations have at various times been forced to pay additional taxes for the privilege. For example, from 1932 to 1935, the additional taxes were in the form of a penalty tax of up to 1 percent, which was levied in addition to the regular corporate income tax. The reenactment of the consolidated tax return election in 1942 brought with it a 2 percent penalty tax levy that lasted through 1963.[7]

In recent years, affiliated groups have developed a renewed interest in filing consolidated tax returns because the Tax Reform Act of 1969 eliminated the advantage of multiple surtax exemptions. Many affiliated groups that formerly filed separate tax returns in order to take advantage of additional surtax exemptions now file consolidated tax returns.

SOURCE OF THE CONSOLIDATED TAX RETURN RULES

Sections 1501–1505 and 1552 (and the supporting Treasury regulations) embody the consolidated tax return provisions. Section 1501 specifies that an affiliated group is permitted to file a consolidated tax return and also that, by filing such a return, the affiliated group consents to the consolidated tax return regulations found in Sec. 1502.

> Sec. 1501. Privilege to File Consolidated Returns.
> An affiliated group of corporations shall, subject to the provisions of this chapter, have the privilege of making a consolidated return with respect to the income tax imposed by chapter 1 for the taxable year in lieu of separate returns. The making of a consolidated return shall be upon the condition that all corporations which at any time during the taxable year have been members of the affiliated group consent to all the consolidated return regulations prescribed under section 1502 prior to the last day prescribed by law for the filing of such return. The making of a consolidated return shall be considered as such consent. In the case of a corporation which is a member of the affiliated group for a fractional part of the year, the consolidated return shall include the income of such corporation for such part of the year as it is a member of the affiliated group.

Section 1502 permits the Secretary of the Treasury to prescribe any regulations deemed necessary to permit an affiliated group to file a consolidated tax return.

> Sec. 1502. Regulations.
> The Secretary shall prescribe such regulations as he may deem necessary in order that the tax liability of any affiliated group of corporations making a consolidated return and of each corporation in the group, both during and after the period of affiliation, may be returned, determined, computed, assessed, collected, and adjusted, in such manner as clearly to reflect the income-tax liability and the various factors necessary for the determination of such liability, and in order to prevent avoidance of such tax liability.

Because of the breadth of Sec. 1502, the Secretary of the Treasury has practically legislative authority to prescribe the regulations required to permit an affiliated group of corporations to file a consolidated tax return.

These "statutory" regulations may be contrasted with the "interpretive" regulations associated with most other sections. Statutory regulations generally are treated as statutory law; that is, they are law unless the

---

[5] The latter ownership is currently known as a "brother–sister" group of controlled (but not affiliated) corporations.

[6] S. Rept. No. 960, 70th Cong., 1st Sess., May 1, 1928.

[7] A detailed history of the consolidated tax return election may be found in: Jacob Mertens, Jr., *Law of Federal Income Taxation* (Chicago: Callaghan and Company, 1971), Chapter 46.02, pp. 6–14.

courts overturn them on the grounds that they exceed the scope of the authority delegated, are contrary to statute, or are unreasonable.[8] Interpretive regulations, on the other hand, are promulgated primarily "to clarify the language of the code as passed by Congress." Interpretive regulations also have the force of law, but whenever they are found by the courts to contradict the intent of Congress, they are overturned.[9]

Section 1503 contains two special provisions relating to the computation of the consolidated tax liability and payment of taxes due. Section 1503(a) says that the tax is to be "determined, computed, assessed, collected, and adjusted" in accordance with the regulations prescribed before the last day for the timely filing of the return. The other provision, Sec. 1503(c), concerns the treatment of net operating losses incurred by noninsurance company members of an affiliated group.

Section 1504 defines the term "affiliated group" and specifies the special tax status corporations that are eligible to join in filing a consolidated tax return.

Section 1552 provides the rules for allocating the consolidated tax liability among the members of the affiliated group in order to determine each member's earnings and profits (E & P) for the taxable year.

WHY FILE A CONSOLIDATED TAX RETURN?

A group of separate but affiliated corporate entities may be treated as a single taxpaying entity by filing a consolidated tax return. Filing a consolidated tax return offers a number of advantages and disadvantages, some of the more important of which are discussed below.

Advantages of filing a consolidated tax return

Some of the advantages that may be gained by filing a consolidated tax return are the following:

1. Net operating losses of one affiliated group member may be offset against the operating profits of other group members in the current taxable year. Such losses provide an immediate tax benefit by reducing the tax due on other ordinary income, eliminating the need to carry a loss to a subsequent taxable year or to offset it against a net capital gain.[10]

2. Capital losses of one affiliated group member may be offset against the capital gains of other members in the current taxable year. Again, this avoids having to carry these losses to subsequent taxable years.

3. The various credit and deduction limitations are computed on a consolidated basis, which may permit group members to use in the current taxable year "excess" credits or "excess" deductions that would otherwise have to be treated as a carryover.

4. Gains on intercompany transactions are deferred. Similarly, the depreciation and other recapture provisions (for example, Secs. 1245 and 1250) do not apply to intercompany transactions. Such gains are deferred until a subsequent "restoration event" occurs. (Restoration event is defined in a later portion of the chapter.)

5. No investment tax credit recapture occurs when an asset is transferred between group members. Recapture, however, may be required at the time the property is transferred outside the group.

Disadvantages of filing a consolidated tax return

Some disadvantages of filing a consolidated tax return are the following:

1. A consolidated return election is binding on all subsequent taxable years unless the group is terminated or the I.R.S. grants the group permission to discontinue filing a consolidated return.

2. Losses on intercompany transactions are deferred until a subsequent restoration event occurs.

3. Restrictions are placed on the recognition of income and expense items when intercompany transactions occur between group members that do not use the same overall method of accounting (cash or accrual method).

4. Section 1231 losses of one group member that might have been eligible for ordinary loss treatment if a separate tax return had been filed must be offset against Sec. 1231 gains of other group members.

5. Net operating losses and net capital losses of group members may reduce (or eliminate) the ability of profitable group members to take advantage of credits or deductions by lowering the applicable credit or deduction limitation.

6. The initial consolidated tax return contains as part of gross income any intercompany profits included in the portion of one group member's beginning inventory balance that (1) were received from another group member and (2) have been sold outside the affili-

[8]*Joseph Weidenhoff, Inc.*, 32 TC 1222 (1959), Acq. 1960-2 CB 7.
[9]See Ray M. Sommerfeld and G. Fred Streuling, *AICPA Tax Study No. 5*, "Tax Research Techniques" (New York: AICPA, 1976), pp. 94–95 for a comparison of the authority of statutory and interpretive regulations.
[10]*Foster Lumber Co., Inc.* v. *U.S.*, 429 U.S. 32 (1976) *rev'g.* 500 F.2d 1230 (CCA-8, 1974) *aff'g.* unreported District Court decision.

ated group during the initial "consolidated return year."[11] This inclusion, known as the initial inventory adjustment, occurs even though the profit on the original sale had been reported in the selling member's tax return for a preceding "separate return year." Recovery of this amount as a deduction occurs in a later taxable year when the total intercompany profit included in inventories decreases below the initial inventory adjustment or the selling corporation ceases to be a group member. Until this occurs, a double counting of income, as well as a double payment of taxes, is required.

7. Additional administrative costs may be incurred in maintaining the necessary records to account for deferred intercompany transactions and the initial inventory adjustments.

There is no general rule that can be applied to determine whether an affiliated group should elect to file a consolidated tax return. Each group should examine the long- and short-run advantages and disadvantages of filing a consolidated tax return and make the appropriate decision.

FILING A CONSOLIDATED TAX RETURN

When the initial decision is made to file a consolidated tax return, there are two areas of concern to the corporation. First, the eligible affiliated group must be determined. Second, the necessary election must be made. These two areas are discussed below.

Eligibility to file a consolidated tax return

Only affiliated groups may file consolidated tax returns. For an affiliated group to exist, the following requirements must be satisfied:

1. A common parent corporation must own directly stock having 80 percent or more of the voting power of all classes of stock entitled to vote and 80 percent or more of each class of nonvoting stock of at least *one* other "includible" corporation.

2. Stock having 80 percent or more of the voting power of all classes of stock entitled to vote and 80 percent or more of each class of nonvoting stock of *each*

other corporation eligible to be included in the affiliated group must be owned directly by the common parent corporation and the other group members.[12]

More than one parent–subsidiary chain of includible corporations may be in the affiliated group, provided each chain is connected through stock ownership with a common parent corporation. The term stock, as used above, does not include nonvoting stock limited and preferred as to dividends, nor does it include "employer securities" that are held under an employee stock ownership plan (Sec. 1504(a)).

As few as two corporations may satisfy the definition of affiliated group. In many of the nation's largest companies, however, the number of related corporations runs into the hundreds. Some of these corporate groups may have a number of subsidiary corporations that are not eligible to join in filing a consolidated tax return because Sec. 1504(b) does not consider them to be *includible corporations*. The following are not considered includible corporations:

1. Foreign corporations;[13]
2. Corporations exempt from tax under Sec. 501;
3. Domestic corporations electing the U.S. Possessions and Puerto Rican tax credit under Sec. 936 (see Chapter 23);
4. Domestic International Sales Corporations (DISCs) or "former" DISCs (see Chapter 23);
5. Regulated investment companies;
6. Real estate investment trusts;
7. Insurance companies subject to tax under Secs. 802 and 821 (Life Insurance Companies and Mutual Insurance Companies);[14] and
8. Subchapter S corporations.[15]

---

[11]A "consolidated return year" is defined as a taxable year for which a consolidated return is filed or is required to be filed by the affiliated group. A "separate return year" is defined as a taxable year of a corporation for which it files a separate return or for which it joins in the filing of consolidated tax return with a different affiliated group (Treas. Reg. Sec. 1.1502-1(d) and (e)).

[12]A *controlled* group of corporations is defined in Sec. 1563. Under Sec. 1561, a controlled group is restricted to a single reduction in tax rates under Sec. 11(b) for the first $100,000 of taxable income, a single $150,000 accumulated earnings credit, and a single $25,000 small business deduction for life insurance companies. An affiliated group of corporations is defined in Sec. 1504. Certain corporations that are includible in a controlled group may not be includible in an affiliated group. When an affiliated group files a consolidated tax return, and it does not include all of the members of a controlled group, the amount of each of these special limitations needs to be allocated between the corporations included and excluded from the affiliated group. Only that portion that is allocated to the affiliated group members may be used by them to determine their tax liabilities. A further discussion of the controlled group concept is found in Chapter 4 of this volume and in Chapter 9 of the first volume.

[13]A limited exception for foreign corporations (incorporated in Canada or Mexico) is found in Sec. 1504(d).

[14]For taxable year 1980 and before, two or more Sec. 802 or 821 domestic insurance companies may join together to form an affiliated group. Beginning with taxable year 1981, these firms may be included in affiliated groups containing other types of corporations.

[15]The election made under Subchapter S terminates at the beginning of the taxable year in which affiliation first takes place and applies to all subsequent taxable years.

We shall illustrate the rules defining the affiliated group in the following three examples. Each example is diagrammed in Figure 8-1.

Example (1): P Corporation[16] owns 90 percent of the single class of stock of S_1 Corporation. S_1, in turn, owns 80 percent of the voting stock of S_2 Corporation. P, S_1, and S_2 are members of the P-S_1-S_2 affiliated group (illustrated in Figure 8-1) because P's ownership exceeds the 80 percent minimum required for the common parent corporation and S_1's ownership of S_2 stock equals the 80 percent minimum required for S_2's inclusion in the affiliated group. (Note: No minimum level of indirect ownership of S_2's stock by P exists.)

Example (2): P Corporation owns 100 percent of the single class of stock of S_1 and S_2 Corporations. S_1 and S_2 each own 40 percent of the single class of stock of S_3 Corporation. The remaining 20 percent of the S_3 stock is owned by minority shareholders. P, S_1, S_2, and S_3 are all members of the P-S_1-S_2-S_3 affiliated group because, although neither S_1 nor S_2 directly owns 80 percent of S_3's voting stock, together they own the necessary minimum amount.

Example (3): P Corporation owns 100 percent of the single classes of stock of S_1 and S_3 Corpora-

---

[16]Unless otherwise indicated, all corporations used in our examples are domestic corporations that are includible in a consolidated tax return. Also, when an affiliated group is used in the example, P Corporation is considered to be the common parent corporation and all corporations are considered to use the calendar year as their taxable year.

tions. S_1 and S_3 own 100 percent of S_2 and S_4 Corporations, respectively. S_2 and S_4 own 20 and 80 percent, respectively, of S_5 Corporation. Both S_1 and S_2 are incorporated in France. P, S_3, S_4, and S_5 are members of the P-S_3-S_4-S_5 affiliated group. S_1 and S_2 are excluded from the affiliated group because they are not domestic corporations, or foreign corporations eligible under Sec. 1504(d) for inclusion in the affiliated group. The ownership of S_5 stock by the S_1-S_2 chain is not counted in determining if the 80 percent minimum ownership level is satisfied. S_5 is still includible in the affiliated group because S_4 owns directly the 80 percent minimum amount required to permit S_5's inclusion.

Election to file a consolidated tax return

A group may elect to file an initial consolidated tax return if each corporation that has been a member of the affiliated group for any portion of the taxable year for which the return is to be filed consents to the election. The common parent corporation consents to the election by filing the consolidated tax return (Form 1120). Each subsidiary consents to the election by filing a Form 1122 (Authorization and Consent of Subsidiary Corporation to Be Included in a Consolidated Income Tax Return) and attaching it to the return.

The privilege of filing a consolidated tax return is exercised by filing such a return not later than the due date for the common parent corporation's tax return (taking into consideration any permitted extensions) (Treas. Reg. Sec. 1.1502-75(a)(1)). The group may not withdraw the consolidated tax return and file separate

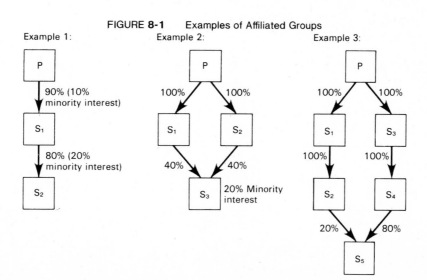

FIGURE 8-1   Examples of Affiliated Groups

tax returns after the last day for filing the consolidated tax return. The group may decide, however, at any time before this last day to change from a consolidated tax return to separate tax returns or from separate tax returns to a consolidated tax return.[17]

DISCONTINUING THE CONSOLIDATED RETURN ELECTION

An affiliated group that filed, or was required to file, a consolidated tax return for the immediately preceding taxable year must continue to exercise the election unless permission is granted to discontinue filing on a consolidated basis *and* the group members begin to file separate tax returns or the group's existence has been terminated.

Revocation of the election

Permission to discontinue filing a consolidated tax return is usually granted (1) in response to a "good cause" request for discontinuing an election that has been initiated by the taxpayer, or (2) as part of blanket permission granted all affiliated groups to discontinue filing consolidated tax returns. Such blanket permission is usually granted when an amendment to the Code or regulations occurs that could have a substantial adverse effect on the filing of consolidated tax returns (relative to the filing of separate tax returns) for all affiliated groups. Some "good cause" reasons for discontinuing the consolidated tax return election are a "substantial adverse effect" on the consolidated tax liability for the taxable year (relative to what the aggregate tax liability would be if the group members filed separate tax returns) originating from amendments to the Code or regulations; a substantial reduction in the consolidated net operating loss or consolidated unused investment tax credit (relative to what the total of such amounts would have been had the individual group members filed separate tax returns) originating from amendments to the Code or regulations; and changes in the law or circumstances—including ones that do not affect federal income tax liabilities (Treas. Reg. Sec. 1.1502-75(c)(1)(iii)).

To elect to discontinue filing a consolidated tax return, the common parent corporation need only file a separate tax return for the taxable year for which permission has been granted. The separate return must be filed on or before the last day prescribed by law (including any extensions) for filing the separate tax return (Treas. Reg. Sec. 1.1502-75(c)(3)).

Termination of the affiliated group

An affiliated group continues in existence if the common parent corporation and at least one subsidiary corporation remain affiliated. The same subsidiary corporation need not have been in existence for the entire taxable year, nor must the subsidiary corporation have been in existence at the beginning of the taxable year. The necessity for the affiliated group to continue to file a consolidated tax return is illustrated below:

> *Example:* On January 1, 19X1, P Corporation owned 100 percent of the single class of stock of S_1 Corporation. On September 1, 19X1, P purchased for cash 100 percent of the voting stock of S_2 Corporation. On October 1, 19X1, P sold its entire holding of S_1 stock. An affiliated group, with P as the common parent corporation, may file a consolidated tax return because at all times during the taxable year P has remained the parent corporation of at least one subsidiary corporation (first S_1, later S_2). Had the two transactions been reversed—that is, had the sale of S_1 stock occurred one month before the acquisition of the S_2 stock—no consolidated tax return could be filed because a one-month period existed during which P failed to own the stock of at least one subsidiary (Treas. Reg. Sec. 1.1502-75(d)(1)).

An affiliated group generally is terminated when a parent corporation either terminates its existence or is acquired by another affiliated group. Three exceptions to this rule exist. First, the common parent corporation may continue as the head of an affiliated group if its identity has changed, provided the change occurs as a result of a Type F reorganization (see Chapter 7). Second, an affiliated group may remain in existence even though the parent corporation goes out of existence, provided substantially all its assets have been acquired by one or more of its subsidiary corporations (Treas. Reg. Sec. 1.1502-75(d)(2)). The third exception is a "reverse acquisition" (as defined in Treas. Reg. Sec. 1.1502-1(d)(3)), whereby a parent corporation is acquired by the common parent corporation of another group, but the parent corporation's shareholders own a majority of the acquiring corporation's stock after the transaction.

[17]Rev. Ruls. 56-67, 1956-1 CB 437 and 76-393, 1976-3 CB 255.

The termination of an affiliated group affects the affiliated group's former members in several ways, namely:

1. Any gains and losses that have been deferred on intercompany transactions generally must be recognized.

2. Consolidated tax attributes—such as net operating loss carryovers, capital loss carryovers, tax credit carryovers, and excess charitable contributions—must be allocated among the former group members.

3. The amount of any negative investment account ("excess loss account") attaching to an investment in a lower-tier corporation may have to be taken into income.

THE CONSOLIDATED TAX RETURN

The affiliated group's tax liability for a consolidated return year is the sum of the following separate tax liabilities:

1. The federal income tax imposed by Sec. 11 on consolidated taxable income;[18]

2. The alternative tax on capital gains (imposed by Sec. 1201 on the excess of consolidated net long-term capital gains over consolidated net short-term capital losses);

3. The minimum tax (imposed by Sec. 56 on the affiliated group's tax preference items);

4. The personal holding company (PHC) tax [imposed by Sec. 541 on the consolidated undistributed personal holding company income (UPHCI)];[19]

5. The accumulated earnings tax (imposed by Sec. 531 on the consolidated accumulated taxable income)[20] (Treas. Reg. Sec. 1.1502-2).

No provisions exist for the filing of consolidated payroll tax returns or excise tax returns.

An affiliated group must file a consolidated estimated tax declaration if it has filed a consolidated tax return for two or more consecutive taxable years. When determining the need for an estimated tax declaration and the payment of the estimated tax amounts, the affiliated group is treated as a single entity. Until the two-year period passes, the affiliated group may make its estimated tax deposits on the basis of either a separate return or a consolidated return, or it may switch from one method of making the deposits to the other (Treas. Reg. Sec. 1.1502-5).

Taxable years

An affiliated group's consolidated tax return must be filed using the taxable year of the common parent corporation. Each subsidiary corporation must adopt the parent corporation's annual accounting period for the initial consolidated return year for which it is includible in the consolidated tax return. The requirement for a common taxable year applies to affiliated group members both when an initial consolidated tax return is being filed and when the stock of a new member is acquired. Special rules exist for group members using the 52–53 week taxable year or an includible insurance company (Treas. Reg. Sec. 1.1502-76(a)).

Income included in the consolidated tax return

The consolidated tax return includes the common parent corporation's income for its entire taxable year, except for any portion of the year that it was a member of another affiliated group that filed a consolidated tax return. The income of each subsidiary corporation is included in the consolidated tax return only for the portion of the affiliated group's taxable year for which it was a group member and for which it did not elect to be excluded from the affiliated group under the "30-day rule" (Treas. Reg. Sec. 1.1502-76(b)(1)). When the income of a corporation is included in a consolidated tax return for only a portion of its taxable year, then the member's income for the remainder of the taxable year is included in a separate tax return or the consolidated tax return of another affiliated group (Treas. Reg. Sec. 1.1502-76(b)(2)).

The two income inclusion rules are illustrated below:

Example (1): P and S Corporations file separate tax returns for taxable year 19X1. At the close of business on June 30, 19X2, P Corporation acquires 100 percent of the single class of stock of S Corporation. If the P-S affiliated group files a consolidated tax return for taxable year 19X2, P's income is included in the consolidated tax return for the entire taxable year, and S's income is includible

---

[18]Special rules are found in Secs. 594(a), 802(a), and 831(a) for income derived by an affiliated group member from insurance activities.

[19]If the Sec. 541 rules relating to consolidated UPHCI do not apply, the PHC tax is the sum of the separate PHC taxes imposed on each affiliated group member that is classified as a PHC.

[20]The accumulated earnings tax does not apply if the PHC penalty surtax applies to the consolidated UPHCI.

only for the period July 1 through December 31, 19X2. S must file a separate tax return to report its income for the period January 1 through June 30, 19X2.

Example (2): P and S Corporations have filed consolidated tax returns for a number of taxable years. At the close of business on August 31, 19X1, P Corporation sells 100 percent of the single class of stock of S Corporation. In the consolidated tax return that is required for the P-S affiliated group for 19X1, P's income is included for the entire taxable year, and S's income is includible only for the period January 1 through August 31, 19X1. S must file a separate tax return to report its income for the period September 1 through December 31, 19X1.

Two "30-day rules" exist. The first permits a corporation to be a member of an affiliated group from the beginning of its taxable year if, within the first 30 days of its taxable year (determined without regard to any change in taxable year that may be required), it becomes a member of an affiliated group that files a consolidated tax return for a taxable year including such time period. Using this 30-day rule, a corporation does not have to file a short-period (separate) tax return for the period of time from the beginning of its taxable year to the date it joins an affiliated group. The short taxable year otherwise required would count as a full taxable year when determining the number of carryover years in which various deduction and credit carryovers could be utilized, and could cause an "early" expiration of these carryovers. (See Chapter 7, page 7/32, for a more detailed discussion of the "short" taxable year problem.) The second 30-day rule permits a corporation that has been a group member for 30 or fewer days out of the consolidated return year to be considered a nonmember of the group for the entire year. As a nonmember, the corporation may file a single tax return for a calendar year in which two or more tax returns may otherwise be required. In addition, as a nonmember, the corporation would not be held liable for part or all the consolidated tax liability for the taxable year (Treas. Reg. Sec. 1.1502-76(b)(5)).

Methods of accounting

The accounting methods used by each affiliated group member are determined by using the Sec. 446 rules as if the member had filed a separate tax return (Treas.

Reg. Sec. 1.1502-17(a)). When a consolidated tax return election is made, the group members continue to use the accounting methods employed when separate tax returns were filed unless the I.R.S. grants permission for a change in accounting method. Thus, one group member may use the cash method of accounting while a second group member uses the accrual method of accounting. Special rules exist, however, to prevent the inconsistent reporting of income or deduction items that originate in intercompany transactions because two group members use different accounting methods (Treas. Reg. Sec. 1.1502-13(b)(2)). We discuss these rules further below.

Common parent as agent for the affiliated group

The common parent corporation acts as the sole agent for each subsidiary corporation and the affiliated group. As agent for each subsidiary, the common parent corporation is authorized to act in its own name in all matters relating to the affiliated group's tax liability for the consolidated return year (Treas. Reg. Sec. 1.1502-77(a)). The common parent corporation is prohibited from acting on behalf of the subsidiary corporation only when the initial consent to file a consolidated tax return is made, an election for the subsidiary corporation to be treated as a Domestic International Sales Corporation (DISC) is made, or a change in the annual accounting period required by the DISC provisions is made. No subsidiary corporation is permitted to act in its own behalf with respect to a consolidated return year except to the extent that the parent corporation is prohibited from acting in its behalf.

Liability for taxes due

The common parent corporation and every other corporation that was a group member for any part of the consolidated return year are severally liable for that year's consolidated taxes (Treas. Reg. Sec. 1.1502-6(a)). Thus, the entire consolidated tax liability may be collected from one group member if, for example, the other group members are unable to pay their allocable portion. The I.R.S. is allowed to disregard attempts made by the group members to limit their share of the liability by entering into agreements with one another or with third parties.

An exception to this several liability principle occurs when a subsidiary corporation ceases to be a group member as a result of its stock being sold or exchanged prior to the date of the assessment of a deficiency against the affiliated group. This exception permits the I.R.S. to make an assessment of a deficiency against a former subsidiary corporation only for its allocable portion of the total deficiency, provided it believes that the assessment and collection of the balance of the deficiency from the other group members will not be jeopardized.

CONSOLIDATED TAXABLE INCOME

The calculation of *consolidated taxable income* is the heart of the computation of consolidated federal income tax liability. First, each group member's *separate taxable income* is determined. From the aggregate of these amounts, a number of adjustments are required to determine consolidated taxable income. Consolidated taxable income then is multiplied by the appropriate rates of Sec. 11 or the alternative capital gains rate of Sec. 1201 (or both) to determine the consolidated gross tax liability. Various consolidated credits and estimated tax payments are subtracted from the gross tax liability to determine the consolidated net tax liability.

Separate taxable income

A group member's separate taxable income is computed as if the group member were filing a separate tax return except for the series of adjustments outlined below (Treas. Reg. Sec. 1.1502-12). In this computation, the group member uses the accounting methods that it has adopted or its common parent corporation has adopted for the group under Treas. Reg. Sec. 1.1502-17. The following adjustments to the member's income, deductions, and losses are required as the first step in the separate taxable income computation.

1. Intercompany transactions between group members are to be accounted for according to Treas. Reg. Sec. 1.1502-13. In general, this step requires the deferral of intercompany gains and losses and the recognition of certain previously deferred intercompany gains and losses.

2. Transactions involving stocks, bonds, and other obligations of group members are to be accounted for according to Treas. Reg. Sec. 1.1502-14. In general, this step requires the elimination of intercompany dividend distributions by the distributee group member.

3. Any "built-in deductions" [defined in Treas. Reg. Sec. 1.1502-15(a)(2)] claimed by the subsidiary are deductible only up to the subsidiary's limitation.

4. Mine exploration expenditures claimed by the subsidiary are deductible only up to the limit established in Treas. Reg. Sec. 1.1502-16.

5. Inventory adjustments must be made according to Treas. Reg. Sec. 1.1502-18. Income or deductions must be recognized by a selling group member according to the level of deferred intercompany profits accruing as a result of the inventory held by a second, purchasing group member.

6. Excess loss amounts (defined by Treas. Reg. Sec. 1.1502-19) are included in income.

A second adjustment is required to eliminate from the separate taxable income calculation any income, deduction, or loss item that must be reported on a consolidated basis. These include a group member's:

1. Net operating loss deduction;
2. Capital gains and losses;
3. Section 1231 gains and losses (including casualty and theft gains and losses);
4. Charitable contribution deduction; and
5. Dividends-received and dividends-paid deductions.

The resulting amount is the group member's *separate taxable income.*[21]

Determining separate taxable income

Once the separate taxable income of each group member has been determined, the consolidated taxable income may be found. The affiliated group's consolidated taxable income is the aggregate of:

1. The separate taxable income of each group member;
2. The consolidated net operating loss deduction;
3. The consolidated net capital gain (including any consolidated capital loss carrybacks or carryovers);
4. The consolidated net Sec. 1231 loss;
5. The consolidated casualty and theft loss;
6. The consolidated charitable contributions deduction; and
7. The consolidated dividends-received and dividends-paid deduction.[22]

[21]The Western Hemisphere Trade Corporation (WHTC) deduction is omitted because it was repealed for taxable years after December 31, 1979.
[22]The consolidated Western Hemisphere Trade Corporation deduction is no longer in effect.

INTERCOMPANY TRANSACTIONS

Major differences between financial and tax accounting exist in the treatment of transactions between members of an affiliated group. Our discussion of intercompany transactions is divided into three areas: a definition of intercompany transactions, the treatment of deferred intercompany transactions, and the treatment of other intercompany transactions.

Definition of intercompany transactions

For tax purposes, an intercompany transaction is defined as "a transaction during a consolidated return year between corporations which are members of the same group immediately after such transaction" (Treas. Reg. Sec. 1.1502-13(a)(1)). Specifically excluded from this definition are distributions by one group member to a second group member with respect to the distributing corporation's stock and capital contributions on which no gain is realized. Dividend distributions made with respect to, or distributions in redemption or liquidation of, a group member's stock are not considered intercompany transactions. Also excluded are sales of, exchanges and redemptions of, and the worthlessness of obligations of other group members.

Intercompany transactions may be divided into deferred intercompany transactions and other intercompany transactions. A *deferred intercompany transaction* is an intercompany transaction involving (1) a sale or exchange of property; (2) the performance of services in which the acquiring party capitalizes the amount of the expenditure for the services; and (3) any other transaction involving an expenditure that is capitalized by the acquiring party (Treas. Reg. Sec. 1.1502-13(a)(2)). Any intercompany transaction not classified as a deferred intercompany transaction falls into the "other" intercompany transaction classification. We shall discuss other intercompany transactions first.

Other intercompany transactions

Any gain or loss on *other intercompany transactions* is included in the income and expense classifications in the taxable year in which the transaction is ordinarily reported. Both parties report their side of the transaction in determining separate taxable income (Treas. Reg. Sec. 1.1502-13(b)(1)). When the transaction results in the recognition of income by one group member and a deduction by a second group member, both amounts are included in the determination of the consolidated taxable income; obviously, these amounts net to zero. This procedure may be contrasted with financial accounting, in which the consolidation process requires the elimination of both sides of the transaction in preparing the consolidated financial statements.

A special rule exists for "other" intercompany transactions in which, because of the accounting methods used by the group members, one group member reports an income or deduction item for a consolidated return year earlier than the taxable year (whether a consolidated or separate tax return is being filed) for which a second group member reports the corresponding income or deduction item. In this situation, both group members report the income and deduction items in the later taxable year. The special rule does not apply to a situation in which one group member reports an income or deduction item in a *separate return year* that is earlier than the consolidated return year in which the second group member reports the corresponding income or deduction item. In this case, each group member reports the income and deduction items in the taxable year that is appropriate under its respective accounting method.

> *Example:* P and S Corporations are members of the P-S affiliated group. P Corporation uses the cash method of accounting and S Corporation uses the accrual method of accounting. P lends S $100,000 on January 1, 19X1; this debt and the related interest are unpaid at the end of 19X1. Interest is charged by P at an annual rate of 10 percent. Ordinarily, P would report no interest income and S would report $10,000 of interest expense in the computation of their separate taxable incomes for 19X1. Because there is a timing difference in reporting the intercompany transaction, S is required to defer the reporting of the interest expense until the consolidated return year in which P reports the interest income (19X2). Thus, the income and expense items are "matched" within the consolidated tax return.

Deferred intercompany transactions

Any gain or loss realized on a *deferred intercompany transaction* must be deferred by the selling group member (Treas. Reg. Sec. 1.1502-13(c)(1)(i)). The selling member recognizes all or a portion of the deferred gain or loss at the time a restoration event (see page **8**/11) occurs, regardless of the accounting method it employs.

The portion of the deferred gain or loss recognized depends on the nature of the restoration event.[23]

The amount and character of the deferred gain or loss is generally determined at the time the intercompany transaction takes place as if the transaction had occurred in a separate return year. The amount of the deferred gain or loss includes all direct and indirect costs that are part of the cost of goods sold, the cost of the services performed, or the cost of the property sold (Treas. Reg. Sec. 1.1502-13(c)(2)). There are two exceptions to the rule that determines the character of the gain or loss at the time the transaction takes place. Deferred gains and losses are treated as ordinary income and loss if they are recognized (1) when the depreciation, depletion, or amortization of a property is the restoration event, or (2) as a result of the acquiring group member claiming an abandonment loss (Treas. Reg. Sec. 1.1502-13(c)(4)).

The basis of the property received in a deferred intercompany transaction is determined in the same way it would be if separate tax returns were filed. Thus, the adjusted basis for an asset is the property's acquisition cost if the property is purchased by a group member for cash from a second group member. Alternatively, a carryover basis from the selling group member is used if the property is acquired in a "like-kind" exchange. No reference is made in either case to the basis that the property had in the selling group member's hands (Treas. Reg. Sec. 1.1502-31(a)). Similarly, the holding period for such property is not required to include the period of time that the property was held by the selling member (Treas. Reg. Sec. 1.1502-13(g)).

An affiliated group is not required to defer intercompany gains and losses. The affiliated group may elect current recognition of gains and losses on deferred intercompany transactions either involving all properties or only specific classes of property. This election is binding until the I.R.S. grants permission to revoke it (Treas. Reg. Sec. 1.1502-13(c)(3)).

Restoration events

A number of events involving the selling and acquiring group members are treated as restoration events and thereby result in the triggering of a deferred gain or loss. The restoration event date is the earliest of the following.

1. The claiming of a depletion, depreciation, or amortization deduction with respect to property, capital expenditures made for services, or any other form of capital expenditure made by the acquiring group member.

2. The collection, satisfaction, discharge, or disposition (outside the affiliated group) of an installment obligation of a nonmember of the group originating from a group member's disposition of property (acquired in a deferred intercompany transaction) outside the affiliated group in a transaction in which the installment method of accounting was elected.[24]

3. The collection, satisfaction, or worthlessness of an installment obligation of a nonmember of the group that has been transferred between group members in an intercompany transaction.

4. The disposition of property acquired in a deferred intercompany transaction outside the affiliated group.[25]

5. The writing down of inventory that is accounted for by the lower of the cost or market method to its market value.[26]

6. The redemption or worthlessness of the stock of a member or nonmember of the affiliated group.

7. The selling member, or the member of the group that acquires the property, ceases to be a group member.

8. The first day of a separate return year for the common parent corporation (Treas. Reg. Sec. 1.1502-13(f)(1)).

In situation 8, the selling member is required to recognize only those deferred gains and losses relating to inventory and property held primarily for sale to customers on the first day of its (or the member that owns the property) first separate return year, provided consolidated tax returns have been filed for at least the three consecutive taxable years preceding a separate return year for the common parent corporation. Under this exception to the general rule requiring all deferred gains and losses to be recognized, deferred gains and losses attaching to the other properties are recognized in the selling member's separate return years *only* when another of the restoration events has occurred.

Three rules relating to the restoration of a deferred gain or loss are illustrated below:

---

[23]In a deferred intercompany transaction, the selling member is not permitted to use the installment method of reporting the deferred gain (or loss). The deferred gain (or loss) is required to be reported according to the rules applicable to restoration events (Treas. Reg. Sec. 1.1502-13(c)(1)(ii)(a)).

[24]This event also includes the selling member's repossession of the property.

[25]This event also includes the acquiring member's abandonment of the property.

[26]Restoration occurs only to the extent of the gains and losses relating to the markdown.

Example (1): P and S Corporations form the P-S affiliated group. The P-S group has filed consolidated tax returns since 19X1. In 19X2, P acquired some land adjacent to its manufacturing plant in anticipation of the possible expansion of these facilities. The land cost P $75,000. In 19X5 P sold this land to S for $125,000. The P-S group, in filing its 19X5 consolidated tax return, would defer the $50,000 gain with respect to the sale. S takes as its basis for the land the $125,000 purchase price. Its holding period commences with the date of acquisition in 19X5. The deferred gain is recognized by P in 19X7 when S sells the land to a third party for $150,000. In the P-S group's 19X7 consolidated tax return, P reports $50,000 of Section 1231 gain that represents the restoration of the 19X5 deferred gain, and S reports $25,000 of Section 1231 gain [$150,000 (proceeds) minus $125,000 (adjusted basis)] representing the postacquisition price appreciation.

Example (2): P and S Corporations form the P-S affiliated group. On January 1, 19X1, P pays $6,000 to a nonmember of the group for machinery having a useful life of four years. The machinery is depreciated by P using the double-declining balance method with the following depreciation deductions being claimed:

Year	Depreciation
19X1	$3,000
19X2	1,500
19X3	750

On January 1, 19X4, the machinery is sold to S for $5,000. The $4,250 Sec. 1245 gain [$5,000 (proceeds) minus $750 (adjusted basis)] is deferred by P until S commences depreciating the asset. The amount of the deferred gain that P recognizes each year is determined by the following formula:

$$\frac{\text{Amount of depreciation deduction claimed in the taxable year}}{\text{Depreciable basis (less salvage value) of the property in the hands of the acquiring group member}} \times \frac{\text{Deferred gain (or loss)}}{} = \frac{\text{Restored gain (or loss)}}{}$$

S depreciates the asset's $5,000 adjusted basis over a four-year useful life beginning in 19X4. The amount of depreciation claimed by S and the re-

stored gain or loss recognized by P during S's holding period for the asset is as follows:

Year	Depreciation	P's restored Sec. 1245 gain
19X4	$2,500[27]	$2,125.00 ($2,500/$5,000 × $4,250)
19X5	1,250	$1,062.50 ($1,250/$5,000 × $4,250)
19X6	625	$531.25 ($625/$5,000 × $4,250)

On January 1, 19X7, S sells the asset to a third party for $500, thereby realizing a $125 Sec. 1231 loss [$500 (proceeds) minus $625 (adjusted basis)]. At this time P reports $531.25, the remainder of the deferred Sec. 1245 gain.

Example (3): P and S Corporations form the P-S affiliated group with P as the common parent corporation. On July 1, 19X1, P sells land to S for $200,000 that it had acquired a number of years earlier for $50,000. S holds the land until July 1, 19X5, when it sells it to a third party for $400,000. The sales price is payable in four equal installments, beginning September 1, 19X5, plus interest at 6 percent annually on the unpaid balance. Immediately after selling the land, S elects to report the sale under the installment sale provisions of Sec. 453. P is required to defer the gain on the sale of the land to S and recognize it as S collects the amounts due under the installment contract. The formula used to determine the amount of P's recognized gain is as follows:

$$\frac{\text{Amount of the installment payment received}}{\text{Total contract price}} \times \frac{\text{Deferred gain}}{} = \frac{\text{Restored gain}}{}$$

P will restore $37,500 of the deferred gain ($50,000/$200,000 × ($200,000 − $50,000)) in each of the taxable years 19X5–19X8. S likewise reports its $200,000 gain over the life of the contract plus any interest that is earned on the unpaid balance.

INVENTORY ADJUSTMENTS

Inventory sales between group members are treated as deferred intercompany transactions. Gain or loss on these sales is deferred until a restoration event occurs

---

[27]Treasury Reg. Sec. 1.1502-12(g) permits "new" property acquired in an intercompany transaction to retain this status in the transferee's hands.

such as the inventory being sold, the inventory being treated as having been disposed of outside the affiliated group owing to the purchasing member's departure from the affiliated group, or the inventory being written down to its market value (Treas. Reg. Sec. 1.1502-13(f)(1)).

A series of special inventory adjustments may be required of a corporation if it (1) is a member of an affiliated group that files a consolidated tax return for the current taxable year, (2) was a member of the affiliated group for its immediately preceding taxable year, (3) filed a separate tax return for the preceding taxable year, and (4) sold inventory to other group members during the separate return year. These adjustments provide that the selling member's intercompany profit on the goods that make up "initial inventory amount" for the separate return year is added to its income for the consolidated return year(s) during which such goods are disposed of outside the group, or in which the selling member leaves the affiliated group. Thus, the special inventory adjustments are generally required only if: (1) inventory sales occurred between group members during the separate return year immediately preceding the initial consolidated return year, (2) the inventory remains unsold at the beginning of the initial consolidated return year, and (3) the inventory is considered disposed of during a consolidated return year.

The inventory adjustment procedures enable a group member to defer from taxation only the additional intercompany profits arising after the beginning of the initial consolidated return year. When inventory is sold between group members in a separate return year, any intercompany profit originating on the transaction is reported by the selling group member. The purchasing member uses the inventory's cost as its carrying value. When the inventory is sold outside the group during a consolidated return year, the group member that purchased the inventory within the group includes this amount in its cost of goods sold. During this initial consolidated return year, the intercompany profit included in the purchasing group member's inventory balance at the beginning of the year must be recognized by the selling member as ordinary income to the extent that it is attributable to inventory that the purchasing member transfers outside the group. An example should make this clearer.

Example: P and S form the P-S affiliated group. P and S both use the first in, first out (FIFO) inventory valuation method. During 19X1, a separate return year for P and S, S sells P goods that remain in P's 19X1 ending inventory and that rep-

resent an intercompany profit of $50,000. This profit is included in S's 19X1 tax return. During 19X2, the initial consolidated return year for the P-S affiliated group, the goods in P's initial inventory were sold, and sufficient additional goods were purchased by P and included in P's 19X2 ending inventory to produce an intercompany profit of $80,000. S, the selling group member, must recognize $50,000, the profit on the *initial inventory amount,* as ordinary income in 19X2. S, however, is permitted to defer the $80,000 intercompany profit. As a result, the net intercompany profit that is deferred is the additional $30,000 of intercompany profit accruing since the beginning of the initial consolidated return year (19X2).

This example illustrates that the inventory adjustment process results in a double counting of the initial inventory amount until a reversal of this adjustment is permitted by a decline in the level of intercompany profits or until the selling member encounters a separate return year and an ordinary loss may be claimed for part or all of the initial inventory amount. If inventory sales between group members continue at a level permitting the amount of intercompany profits to remain at or above the initial inventory amount, then the exemption from current taxation for intercompany profits is available for the selling member's total intercompany profits minus its initial inventory amount that has been taken into income.

INTERCOMPANY PROFIT AMOUNT   For a taxable year, the "intercompany profit amount" is the amount of intercompany profit that has risen with respect to goods that are included in the inventories of other group members at the close of the selling group member's taxable year. Excluded from this amount are (1) any amounts for which an election not to defer intercompany profits has been made, and (2) amounts that have been included in gross income as a result of a restoration event (Treas. Reg. Sec. 1.1502-18(a)).

INITIAL INVENTORY AMOUNT   A group member's initial inventory amount is its intercompany profit amount for the separate return year immediately preceding the affiliated group's first consolidated return year (Treas. Reg. Sec. 1.1502-18(b)).

UNRECOVERED INVENTORY AMOUNT   The unrecovered inventory amount for any consolidated return year is the lesser of the intercompany profit amount for the taxable year or the initial inventory amount. A corporation that ceases to be a group member during a consolidated return year is considered to have an unrecovered inventory amount of zero (Treas. Reg. Sec. 1.1502-18(c)(1)).

RECOGNITION OF INVENTORY ADJUSTMENTS   The initial inventory amount is recognized in the consolidated return year(s) during which the goods representing the initial inventory amount are disposed of outside the affiliated group. Initially, only a portion of the initial inventory amount may be included in the selling member's gross income if some of the purchasing member's beginning inventory is not disposed of by the end of the first consolidated return year. This will be true, for example, if the purchasing member uses the last in, first out (LIFO) inventory method.

The selling group member may take an ordinary loss deduction, which reverses the income recognition required for the initial inventory amount. During consolidated return years, a deduction is permitted for the amount of the reduction in the unrecovered inventory amount that has taken place when the current year's unrecovered inventory amount is less than such amount for the immediately preceding year. As a result, when the level of intercompany profits falls below the initial inventory amount, the selling group member is permitted to offset part or all of its positive inventory adjustments that were made earlier. If the unrecovered inventory amount increases in the next consolidated return year, then the selling group member recognizes ordinary income equal to the difference between the unrecovered inventory amount for the preceding year and the lesser of the current year's unrecovered inventory amount or the initial inventory amount. If a corporation ceases to be a group member during a consolidated return year, its unrecovered inventory amount is considered to be zero, thus permitting a full recovery of previously reported income items.

The selling member may reverse any remaining double counting of income in its first separate return year. To do this, it claims a deduction equal to the unrecovered inventory amount minus any portion of the initial inventory amount that has not been previously recognized as ordinary income.

The following examples illustrate the operation of the inventory adjustment rules.

Example (1):   P and S Corporations form the P-S affiliated group. Both corporations use the FIFO inventory valuation method. During 19X1, P and S filed separate tax returns. Beginning in 19X2, the P-S group filed a consolidated tax return. P's inventory at the end of 19X1 included $26,000 of intercompany profits on items acquired from S since the affiliated group was created. P sold all these goods outside the group in 19X2. During taxable years 19X2–19X6, consolidated tax returns were filed using the following initial inventory amounts, intercompany profit amounts, and unrecovered inventory amounts. Necessary inventory adjustments are shown below.

Year	Initial Inventory Amount	Intercompany Profit Amount	Unrecovered Inventory Amount	S's Inventory Adjustment Income	Deduction
19X2	$26,000	$24,000	$24,000	$26,000	$2,000
19X3	26,000	16,000	16,000		8,000
19X4	26,000	22,000	22,000	6,000	
19X5	26,000	40,000	26,000	4,000	
19X6	26,000	31,000	26,000		-0-

During 19X2, the first consolidated return year, the entire initial inventory amount is included in S's income because P disposed of outside the group all the purchases from S that were included in its beginning inventory. As the intercompany profit amount falls below $26,000 at the end of 19X2 and 19X3, recovery of $2,000 and $8,000, respectively, as a deduction is permitted. The increase in the intercompany profit amount from $16,000 to $40,000 in 19X4 and 19X5 requires the unrecovered inventory amount to be restored to the $26,000 initial inventory amount. In 19X6, even though the intercompany profits declined, no deduction is permitted because the intercompany profit amount remained above the $26,000 initial inventory amount.

Example (2):   Assume the same facts as in the preceding example. If in 19X7 P sold its investment in S, then S would begin filing separate tax returns. P and S would include a $26,000 deduction representing the recovery of the unrecovered inventory amount in the 19X7 consolidated tax return that included P's income earned prior to its departure from the group. Had P and S instead discontinued filing consolidated tax returns, the income would have been recognized in S's first separate tax return, covering the portion of 19X7 following its departure from the group.

NET OPERATING LOSSES

One advantage of filing a consolidated tax return is the ability of an affiliated group to offset one member's current year net operating loss (NOL) against the profits of other members. Should these losses cause the affiliated group to report a consolidated net operating loss, then these losses may be carried to the affiliated group's other consolidated return years or the individual member's separate return years.

Current year net operating losses

When determining consolidated taxable income, each member's separate taxable income is combined before any adjustment is made for net operating loss deductions resulting from losses originating in other taxable years (Treas. Reg. Sec. 1.1502-12). Such a combining process requires the net operating loss of an unprofitable group member to offset the positive taxable income of a profitable group member. A group member is thus unable to carry back or carry over its separate net operating loss from a consolidated return year to one of its profitable separate return years. Only the group's consolidated net operating loss, not the separate net operating losses, may be carried back or over. The consolidated net operating loss may be used by a member to offset profits accruing in a separate return year only to the extent that part or all of the group's total loss is apportioned to it. In a similar fashion, none of an individual group member's separate return year net operating loss carryovers or carrybacks may be used in a taxable year for which the affiliated group reports a consolidated net operating loss.

Example: P and S Corporations form the P-S affiliated group, with P as the common parent corporation. During 19X1, the initial year of operation, P and S Corporations filed separate tax returns. Beginning in 19X2, the P-S group elected to file a consolidated tax return. The following results were reported by P and S.

	19X1	*19X2*
P	$(15,000)	$28,000
S	25,000	(15,000)
Consolidated taxable income	$ xxx	$13,000

P's 19X1 net operating loss may not be used to offset the profits reported by S. The 19X1 net operating loss may only be used to reduce the $13,000 of consolidated taxable income otherwise reported after S's net operating loss is offset against P's separate taxable income. S is unable to carry its 19X2 net operating loss back against its 19X1 profits.

The net operating loss from a subsidiary's activity can be included in determining consolidated taxable income (or consolidated net operating loss) and consolidated capital gain net income (or consolidated net capital loss) only to the extent that the loss does not exceed the amount that the parent is at risk under Temporary Reg. Sec. 5.1502-45(b) in the activity at the close of the subsidiary's taxable year.

Carrybacks and carryovers of consolidated net operating losses

The consolidated net operating loss rules are similar to those net operating loss rules applying to a corporation filing a separate tax return. The consolidated net operating loss may be carried back to the three consolidated return years preceding the loss year. A consolidated net operating loss may also be carried over to the seven consolidated return years following the loss year.[28] The affiliated group may also elect to relinquish the entire carryback period for a loss incurred in a taxable year beginning after December 31, 1975 and use the consolidated net operating loss only as a carryover to succeeding taxable years (Sec. 172(b)(3)(C)).

The affiliated group's absorption of net operating loss carrybacks or carryovers takes place in the normal FIFO manner, whether the loss was incurred in a separate return year or a consolidated return year. Thus, all net operating losses that may be carried to a taxable year are absorbed in the order of the taxable years in which the losses were incurred, beginning with the taxable year that ends earliest. When more than one tax-

---

[28] If the loss is eligible for a special carryover time period, such as in the case of a regulated transportation company, the consolidated tax return regulations also permit this extended carryover period to be used (Treas. Reg. Sec. 1.1502-21(b)(2)(i)).

able year ends on the same date, the losses from each of these years are considered to be absorbed on a pro rata basis (Treas. Reg. Sec. 1.1502-21).

Consolidated net operating loss is determined as follows:

Separate taxable income
Plus: Consolidated net capital gain
Minus: Consolidated Sec. 1231 loss
Consolidated charitable contributions deduction
Consolidated dividends-received deduction
Consolidated dividends-paid deduction
Equals: Consolidated net operating loss

A carryback or carryover of the consolidated net operating loss to a taxable year in which the members of the affiliated group have not changed poses no real problem. The amount of the consolidated net operating loss that is absorbed is determined according to the Sec. 172 rules.

The common parent corporation applies for the refund on Form 1139 (Corporation Application for Tentative Refund from Carryback of Net Operating Loss, Net Capital Loss, Unused Investment Tax Credit, or Unused Work Incentive (WIN) Program Credit). The refund is paid only to the common parent corporation, not to any subsidiaries (Treas. Reg. Sec. 1.1502-78(b)(1)).

Determining the amount of the consolidated net operating loss that may be absorbed in a taxable year is more difficult when the group members are not the same in the carryback or carryover year. In such a case, the consolidated net operating loss is apportioned to each corporation that was both a member of the affiliated group *and* incurred a "separate net operating loss" during the loss year. When a "loss" corporation is not a group member in the carryback or carryover year, the rules relating to carrybacks and carryovers to separate return years (discussed below) must be applied.

Special rules apply to the absorption of a consolidated net operating loss carryover in a consolidated return year in which a major change in the ownership of the common parent corporation's stock occurs *and* a new corporation is added to the affiliated group. In such a situation, the "consolidated return change of ownership" (CRCO) limitation rules restrict the ability of an affiliated group to carry over a consolidated net operating loss as well as certain credits.

A CRCO occurs during any taxable year (a "CRCO year") of the common parent corporation to which the tax attribute is to be carried when:

1. Any one or more of the 10 (or fewer) persons owning the greatest percentage of the fair market value of the common parent corporation's stock at the end of the taxable year in question owns a percentage of the fair market value of the outstanding stock that is more than 50 percentage points greater than they owned at (a) the beginning of the taxable year or (b) the beginning of the preceding taxable year; and

2. The increase is attributable to (a) a purchase[29] by such person(s) of stock of the common parent corporation (or an interest in a partnership or trust that owns stock of the common parent corporation); or (b) a decrease in the amount of the common parent corporation's outstanding stock (or in the amount of the outstanding stock of a second corporation that owns stock in the common parent corporation)[30] (Treas. Reg. Sec. 1.1502-1(g)(1)(i)).

If a CRCO has occurred, a special limitation applies to net operating loss carryovers (but not carrybacks). Net operating losses that are carried over to a CRCO year or to a subsequent taxable year may not exceed the lesser of:

1. The consolidated taxable income for the taxable year (including any net operating loss deduction), as determined by including only the gross income and deductions of the old members of the affiliated group; or

2. The unused net operating losses attributable to the old group members originating in taxable years ending before the CRCO year.

This limitation prevents the affiliated group from acquiring profitable new members in order to fully utilize the net operating loss carryovers of the original group.

The term "old members" of an affiliated group applies only to corporations that were members of the group immediately preceding the first day of a CRCO year. When the CRCO occurs in the affiliated group's first taxable year, the "old members" include only the common parent corporation for the taxable year to which the tax attribute is carried (Treas. Reg. Sec. 1.1502-1(g)(3)). As a result of this definition, the occurrence of a CRCO does not restrict the use of a net operating loss carryover when no new members have been added to the affiliated group because all members constitute old members of the affiliated group.

[29] As defined by Sec. 382(a)(4).
[30] An exception to this rule (regarding the amount of stock of the common parent corporation's stock that is outstanding) occurs when the decrease is a result of a redemption to pay death taxes coming under Sec. 303. The Sec. 318 constructive ownership rules are applied with certain modifications to determine if stock ownership has increased. The term stock as used in the CRCO rules excludes nonvoting stock that is limited and preferred as to dividends (Treas. Reg. Sec. 1.1502-1(g)(2)).

The CRCO limitation on the use of a net operating loss carryover is illustrated below.

Example: P Corporation is formed on January 1, 19X1, and on the same day it forms a 100 percent owned subsidiary corporation known as S. The P-S affiliated group files a consolidated tax return for 19X1 showing a consolidated net operating loss of $500,000. On January 10, 19X2, all of P's outstanding stock is acquired by a third party who immediately contributes additional funds to P that are used to purchase all the stock of T Corporation. Affiliated group P-S-T files a consolidated tax return for 19X2 that reports the following results (excluding the consolidated net operating loss deduction):

	Taxable income
P	$275,000
S	75,000
T (since acquisition)	250,000
Total	$600,000

Because a CRCO occurred in 19X2 (a more than 50 percent increase in ownership percentage for P's new shareholder), the amount of the consolidated net operating loss deduction is limited to $350,000 ($275,000 + $75,000)—P's and S's contribution to the consolidated taxable income. A similar limitation applies to 19X3 and later loss carryover years.

Carryback of consolidated net operating loss to separate return year

A consolidated net operating loss may be carried back and absorbed against a member's taxable income from a preceding separate return year. In order to effect such a carryback, part or all of the consolidated net operating loss must be apportioned to the member. To the extent that a member uses its allocable share of the consolidated net operating loss, such an amount is not available to the remaining members as a carryback or carryover to a consolidated return year (Treas. Reg. Sec. 1.1502-79(a)(1)(i)). Thus, if a member files a separate tax return in its third taxable year preceding the loss year, and a portion of the consolidated net operating loss is apportioned to this member, then this member carries the loss back to its separate return year.[31] This portion of the consolidated net operating loss is

[31]Such a carryback would not be required if the affiliated group elected under Sec. 172(b)(3)(E) to forego the carryback privilege.

not available to the affiliated group for a carryback to its third preceding taxable year.

The consolidated net operating loss is apportioned to a loss member in the following manner.

$$\frac{\text{Separate NOL of the individual member}}{\substack{\text{Sum of the separate} \\ \text{NOLs incurred by} \\ \text{all members having} \\ \text{such losses}}} \times \substack{\text{Consolidated} \\ \text{NOL}} = \substack{\text{Portion of} \\ \text{consolidated} \\ \text{NOL attributable} \\ \text{to member}}$$

The member's separate net operating loss is determined in a manner similar to the calculation of separate taxable income except for a series of adjustments prescribed in Treas. Reg. Sec. 1.1502-79(a)(3) to account for the member's share of the consolidated charitable contributions and dividends-paid and dividends-received deductions, the member's net capital gain or loss, the member's net Sec. 1231 loss, and the member's share of the consolidated net capital loss that was absorbed currently.

When the consolidated net operating loss is apportioned to a member and carried back to a separate return year of the member, then a special rule *may* permit the remaining affiliated group members to carry this portion of the loss back to *their* equivalent separate return or consolidated return year if the member corporation with the carryback loss did not yet exist in the carryback year. If the loss member was a member of the affiliated group immediately after its organization, then the portion of the consolidated net operating loss that is attributable to it is carried back as part of the consolidated net operating loss carryback (or separate net operating loss carryback) to the *equivalent* consolidated return year (or separate return year). An equivalent consolidated return year is generally defined in the regulations as a similarly numbered preceding taxable year (for example, the third preceding taxable year of the individual group member is considered equivalent to the third preceding taxable year of the affiliated group). If the loss corporation is not a member of the affiliated group immediately after its organization, then that member's portion of the consolidated net operating loss is carried back only to *its* prior separate return years.

The carryback of a net operating loss to a preceding taxable year in which a separate tax return was filed is illustrated below.

Example: Corporations P, S, and T make up the P-S-T affiliated group. Before 19X3, P and S had been affiliated for 19X1 and 19X2, during which time they filed consolidated tax returns. P acquired all of T's stock on January 1, 19X3. Before this time, T had filed separate tax returns. The following results were reported by P-S-T for the period 19X1–19X4.

	Taxable income			
	19X1	*19X2*	*19X3*	*19X4*
P	$ 500	$ 750	$ 250	$2,000
S	750	750	250	500
T	1,000	1,000	750	(7,500)
Consolidated taxable income[32]	$1,250	$1,500	$1,250	$(5,000)

All the $5,000 consolidated net operating loss of 19X4 is attributable to T. Two options are available with respect to this loss: (1) the loss may be carried initially back to the period 19X1–19X3; or (2) the loss may be carried over to subsequent taxable years. If the first alternative is selected, T must first carry the loss back and offset its profits from separate return years 19X1 and 19X2. Of the remaining $3,000 ($5,000 − $1,000 − $1,000) loss, $1,250 may be used against 19X3's consolidated taxable income. The final $1,750 must be carried over to the first seven consolidated return years occurring after 19X4.

The member carrying the loss back to its separate return year applies for a refund on Form 1139, and the refund is paid to the member (Treas. Reg. Sec. 1.1502-78(b)(1)).

Carryover of consolidated net operating loss to separate return year

If a corporation ceases to be a member of the affiliated group during the current year, then any available consolidated net operating loss carryover must be absorbed in the current consolidated return year. This requirement exists even though part or all of the carryover may be attributable to the departing member. Any portion of the member's share of the carryover that remains after the consolidated return year may then be carried to the departing member's first separate return year.

Carryover of a departing group member's portion of the consolidated net operating loss is illustrated below.

Example: Corporations P, S, and T make up the P-S-T affiliated group. During 19X1, 19X2, and 19X3, the group files consolidated tax returns. On

June 30, 19X3, P sells its investment in T. T files a separate tax return covering the period July 1, 19X3 through December 31, 19X3. The operating results of the corporations for the 19X1–19X3 period are presented below:

	Taxable income		
	19X1	*19X2*	*19X3*
P	$ 10,000	$10,000	$10,000
S	(25,000)	5,000	5,000
T—			
1/1/X3–6/30/X3	(50,000)	5,000	5,000
7/1/X3–12/31/X3			15,000[33]
Consolidated taxable income	$(65,000)	$20,000	$20,000

The 19X1 consolidated net operating loss is apportioned at the end of the loss year using the formula outlined earlier:

$$S = \frac{\$25,000}{\$75,000} \times \$65,000 = \underline{\$21,667}$$

$$T = \frac{\$50,000}{\$75,000} \times \$65,000 = \underline{\$43,333}$$

The pro rata absorption of S's and T's net operating losses takes place in the following manner for the two consolidated return years:

	19X2	*19X3*	*Total absorbed*	*NOL carryover*
S	$ 6,667	$ 6,667	$13,334	$ 8,333
T	13,333	13,333	26,666	16,667
	$20,000	$20,000	$40,000	$25,000

Of T's original $65,000 loss, only $16,667 ($43,333 − $26,666) remains to be used in separate return years after its departure from the affiliated group. In addition, $8,333 ($21,667 − $13,334) of the consolidated net operating loss that was attributable to S remains to be used by the P-S affiliated group in subsequent taxable years.

CARRYOVER OF NET OPERATING LOSS FROM SEPARATE RETURN YEAR TO CONSOLIDATED RETURN YEAR

A corporation that incurs a net operating loss in a separate return year must carry the loss back to a preceding separate return or consolidated return year unless it elects to forego the carryback. If the loss is not fully absorbed as a carryback, and the corporation becomes a member of an affiliated group that files a consolidated tax return, part or all of the net operating loss carryover may be used to reduce the affiliated group's consolidated taxable income.

A member incurring a net operating loss in a separate return year (that is available as a carryover to a consolidated return year) is subject to a limit on the use of the carryover when the loss year is designated a "separate return limitation year" (SRLY).[34] The amount of the member's net operating loss that was incurred in a separate return limitation year that may be used in a consolidated return year equals the excess of the carryover year's consolidated taxable income (excluding the net operating loss deduction) minus consolidated taxable income as recomputed by excluding the loss member's gross income and deductions over the loss member's net operating losses that are carried to the consolidated return year from taxable years ending before the separate return limitation year (Treas. Reg. Sec. 1.1502-21(c)(2)). Any net operating loss carryovers that, because of the SRLY rules, may not be used currently must be carried over to later taxable years. The SRLY rules thus restrict the affiliated group's ability to carry over losses of a member incurred in a separate return year to that member's contribution to the carryover year's consolidated taxable income.

A separate return limitation year is defined as any separate return year *except*:

1. A separate return year of the group member that is designated the common parent corporation for the consolidated return year to which the tax attribute is carried.

2. A separate return year of any corporation that was a group member for each day of such year.

3. A separate return of a predecessor of any group member if the predecessor was a group member for each day of such year.[35]

The application of the SRLY rules to the absorption of a member's loss carryover is illustrated below.

Example: P S, and T Corporations form the P-S-T affiliated group. P and S were formed on January 1, 19X1, and P acquired the stock of T Corporation shortly after its creation in mid-19X1. The P-S-T affiliated group filed separate tax returns for taxable year 19X1 and began filing a consolidated tax return in 19X2. The group's results for the period 19X1–19X5 are presented below:

	Taxable year				
	19X1	*19X2*	*19X3*	*19X4*	*19X5*
P	$ (9,000)	$ 7,000	$ 6,000	$(2,000)	$ 1,000
S	5,000	5,000	2,000	(4,000)	1,000
T	(20,000)	(2,000)	5,000	5,000	17,000
Consolidated taxable income	$ XXX	$10,000	$13,000	$(1,000)	$19,000

T's 19X1 net operating loss was incurred in a separate return limitation year and is subject to the SRLY rules in the carryover years. P's 19X1 loss is not subject to the SRLY rules because it is the common parent corporation in the carryover year. As a result, its $9,000 loss is fully offset against the group's $10,000 19X2 consolidated taxable income. None of T's 19X1 loss may be used because its loss limitation under the SRLY rules for 19X2 is 0. T's 19X1 loss of $5,000—the amount of T's contribution to 19X3 consolidated taxable income—may be used in 19X3. None of the 19X4 loss may be used in 19X5 because a consolidated

net operating loss is reported. In 19X5 the loss limitation under the SRLY rules is $17,000. This permits the $15,000 remainder of T's 19X1 loss to reduce consolidated taxable income. In addition, the $1,000 consolidated net operating loss from 19X4 may be claimed as a net operating loss carryback to 19X2 to offset the remaining $1,000 of taxable income unless an election is made under Sec. 172(b)(3)(C).

We have discussed two separate rules restricting the use of net operating losses—the separate return limita-

---

[34]The SRLY rules apply not only to net operating loss carryovers, but also to net operating loss carrybacks from a separate return limitation year to a consolidated return year (Treas. Reg. Sec. 1.1502-21(c)(1)).

[35]A predecessor corporation is any corporation that is a transferor or distributor of assets to a group member in a tax-free liquidation or reorganization transaction to which the tax attribute carryover rules of Sec. 381(a) apply (see Chapter 7) (Treas. Reg. Sec. 1.1502-1(f)).

tion year rules and the consolidated return change of ownership rules. Both sets of rules may apply to a single net operating loss, and the amount of the net operating loss that is absorbed is limited to the more restrictive of the two sets of rules.

Net operating loss carryback from a separate return year to a consolidated return year

A net operating loss incurred in a separate return year by a former member of an affiliated group may be carried back to a consolidated return year. In that event, the group member incurring the loss files the refund claim on Form 1139. This refund is paid to the corporation that was the common parent corporation for the taxable year to which the loss is carried back (Treas. Reg. Sec. 1.1502-78(c), Example (2)). A former group member may not elect to avoid carrying back a loss to a consolidated return year (for example, the third preceding year) and instead carry it back to a later separate return year (for example, the second or first preceding year). The corporation may, however, elect to forego the net operating loss carryback entirely (Sec. 172(b)(3)(C)).

The SRLY rules limit net operating loss carrybacks from separate return limitation years to consolidated return years in a manner similar to that described earlier for net operating loss carryovers (Treas. Reg. Sec. 1.1502-21(c)(1)). The consolidated return change of ownership rules, however, do not apply to a carryback.

Other loss-related provisions

A number of tax provisions outside the consolidated return sections and the related regulations may affect the use of net operating losses. For example, the rules of Secs. 269 and 381–383 apply to corporations in general, whether or not they are members of an affiliated group. In addition, the consolidated return regulations contain two special loss absorption limitation rules.

The first special provision is similar to Sec. 382(a) and specifies that if at the end of a separate return or consolidated return year (1) there has been an increase in the ownership of the common parent corporation sufficient to trigger Sec. 382(a) (as in existence before the Tax Reform Act of 1976) *and* (2) any member of the group has not carried on a trade or business substantially similar to that conducted before the increase, then the portion of any consolidated net operating loss sustained in prior taxable years and attributable to the member is disallowed as a carryover to the current or subsequent taxable years (Treas. Reg. Sec. 1.1502-21(e)(1)).

The second special provision applies to built-in deductions. A built-in deduction is any deduction or loss that (1) economically accrues in a separate return limitation year, but is not recognized until a consolidated return year or (2) is recognized in a separate return year and is carried over in the form of a net operating loss (or net capital loss) to a consolidated return year (Treas. Reg. Sec. 1.1502-15(a)(2)). The built-in deductions are subject to the SRLY rules and as such may be used by the affiliated group only to the extent of the member's contribution to consolidated taxable income. Amounts that are not currently used are carried over indefinitely to succeeding years (Treas. Reg. Sec. 1.1502-15(a)(1)).

CAPITAL GAINS AND LOSSES

In our earlier discussion of the separate taxable income determination, we excluded discussion of all capital gains and losses, Sec. 1231 gains and losses, and casualty and theft gains and losses. These three types of gains and losses are reported by the affiliated group on a consolidated basis. For a consolidated return year, the affiliated group's consolidated net capital gain is composed of:

1. The aggregate amount of the capital gains and losses of the group members for the year (determined without regard to any Sec. 1231 transactions or net capital loss carryovers);
2. The consolidated Sec. 1231 net gain for the year; and
3. The consolidated net capital loss carryovers to the year (Treas. Reg. Sec. 1.1502-22(a)(1)).

Any consolidated net capital gain that is part of the consolidated taxable income is taxed at either the regular tax rates or the alternative tax rate. Any net capital loss is eligible to be carried back three years or forward five years as a short-term capital loss.

Consolidated net capital gain

The amount of any group member's capital or Sec. 1231 gains or losses excludes any such gains realized in deferred intercompany transactions. These gains are reported at the time a restoration event occurs. In addition, any capital or Sec. 1231 losses that originate as a result of a built-in deduction are subject to the built-in deduction limitations outlined above.

Once the recognized gains and losses of each group member have been determined, then each member's short-term and long-term transactions are combined into separate net gain or net loss positions. The sum of these separate short-term and long-term net gain or loss positions then determines the affiliated group's aggregate capital gain or loss amounts that enter into determining the consolidated net capital gain.

Consolidated Section 1231 gain or loss

The consolidated Sec. 1231 net gain or loss for the taxable year is determined by taking into account the aggregate of the group member's Sec. 1231 transactions. Two combining processes are required to determine the consolidated Sec. 1231 net gain or loss. First, the aggregate amount of the casualty and theft-related gains and losses must be determined for the entire affiliated group. If the affiliated group's aggregate gains exceed its aggregate losses, then the net gain from these transactions is combined with the gains and losses originating from its other Sec. 1231 transactions. If the group's aggregate casualty and theft losses exceed its aggregate casualty and theft gains, then its net loss from these transactions is treated as an ordinary loss and is deductible in determining consolidated taxable income.

Similarly, if the group's total Sec. 1231 gains (including any net gain from casualty and theft occur-rences) exceed similar losses, then the net gain from these transactions is considered to be the consolidated net Sec. 1231 gain and is eligible for long-term capital gain treatment. If the group reports a net loss from the Sec. 1231 transactions, however, then the net Sec. 1231 loss is treated as an ordinary loss and is deductible in determining consolidated taxable income.

Absorption of net capital losses

The affiliated group's consolidated net capital loss equals the sum of the group's capital losses and the consolidated net Sec. 1231 gain for the consolidated return year. The consolidated net capital loss carryovers available in a consolidated return year equals the sum of (1) the affiliated group's consolidated net capital losses and (2) any unused net capital losses of individual group members arising in separate return years that may be carried back or carried over to the consolidated return year. These capital loss carrybacks and carryovers are absorbed in a FIFO manner, beginning with the capital losses sustained in the taxable year that ends the earliest. The losses are absorbed on a pro rata basis when more than one taxable year ends on the same date.

The consolidated net capital gain or loss determination is illustrated below.

Example: P, S, and T Corporations form the P-S-T affiliated group. The P-S-T affiliated group has filed consolidated tax returns since its inception in 19X1. During 19X3 the affiliated group reported the following property transaction results:

| | Capital gains and losses | | Section 1231 | |
Member	Short-term	Long-term	Noncasualty and theft	Casualty and theft
P	$ 2,000	$(1,000)	$(2,500)	-0-
S	(1,000)	4,000	2,000	$ 1,500
T	(2,000)	3,000	2,000	(1,000)
	$(1,000)	$ 6,000	$ 1,500	$ 500

In addition, the group carried over a consolidated net capital loss of $3,000 from 19X2. The P-S-T affiliated group reports a $2,000 ($500 + $1,500) consolidated net Sec. 1231 gain in 19X3 because net gains were reported in both Sec. 1231 subdivisions. This amount is then merged with the $5,000 aggregate amount of capital gains and losses and the $3,000 consolidated net capital loss carryover to determine the 19X3 consolidated net capital gain of $4,000. This entire amount is eligible to be taxed at the alternative tax rates.

Net capital loss carrybacks and carryovers

Consolidated net capital loss carrybacks and carryovers are treated similarly to net operating losses. The losses that are carried back or forward to other consolidated return years are treated as short-term capital losses and serve as a component of the consolidated net capital gain or loss position.

The consolidated return change of ownership rules apply to consolidated and separate return year net capital loss carryovers as they apply to the consolidated net operating loss carryovers. The amount of the consolidated net capital loss carryover from a specific taxable year that may be carried over by the affiliated group's old members is limited to the old members' contribution to the consolidated net capital gain. This contribution equals the current year's consolidated net capital gain for the old members (excluding any net capital loss carryovers) minus any net capital losses of the old members originating in earlier loss years that are carried over to the current year (Treas. Reg. Sec. 1.1502-22(d)).

Carrybacks of a member's apportionment of a consolidated net capital loss to one of its preceding separate return years are required when capital gains are available in the carryback year against which the loss may be offset. No election is available, as was the case with a net operating loss, which permits a member to forego the carryback and use the loss only as a carryover. When the group member did not exist in the carryback year, but became a group member immediately after its creation, Treas. Reg. Sec. 1.1502-79(b)(1) also permits a carryback of the capital loss to the other group members' equivalent consolidated or separate return years. The portion of the group's consolidated net capital loss that is apportioned to a member is calculated as follows:

$$\frac{\text{Group member's}\ \text{separate net}\ \text{capital loss}}{\begin{array}{c}\text{Sum of the group}\\ \text{members' separate}\\ \text{net capital losses}\end{array}} \times \begin{array}{c}\text{Consolidated}\\ \text{net capital}\\ \text{loss}\end{array} = \begin{array}{c}\text{Member's portion}\\ \text{of the}\\ \text{consolidated net}\\ \text{capital loss}\end{array}$$

A member's net capital loss is the sum of: (1) its net capital gain or loss (determined without regard to any net capital loss carryovers) plus (2) the member's Sec. 1231 loss (if any) minus (3) the member's apportionment of the consolidated Sec. 1231 loss (Treas. Reg. Sec. 1.1502-79(b)(2)).

Carryovers or carrybacks of net capital losses from a separate return limitation year invokes the separate return limitation year rules. The amount of the loss carryback or carryover from a separate return limitation year that may be used in any taxable year equals the member's contribution to the group's consolidated net capital gain. This contribution equals the consolidated net capital gain (determined without regard to any capital loss carryovers) minus (1) the consolidated net capital gain that is determined by excluding the member's capital gains and losses and Sec. 1231 gains and losses and (2) any net capital losses of the member that are carried over to the current taxable year from an earlier taxable year.

A member leaving the affiliated group may take with it an apportionment of any consolidated net capital loss carryover and any of its unused capital loss carryovers that originated in a separate return year. These losses may be used in subsequent return years until they expire. The apportionment of the consolidated capital loss carryover to the group member occurs using the formula that we used above to determine the portion of the consolidated net capital loss that a group member could carry back to an earlier separate return year.

In addition to the special capital loss limitations

outlined above for affiliated groups, a general limitation is found in Sec. 1212(a)(1)(A)(ii) that prevents a capital loss that is carried back from creating or increasing a net operating loss for the taxable year to which it is being carried. Thus, the utilization of a capital loss is generally also limited to the corporation's taxable income.

Applications for refunds based on the carryback of net capital losses follow the procedures outlined earlier for net operating losses. The application likewise is filed on Form 1139.

The capital loss carryback and carryover rules are illustrated below.

Example: P, S, and T Corporations form the P-S-T affiliated group. P acquired all the stock of S and T in 19X3, a separate return year for all group members. Beginning in 19X4 the P-S-T affiliated group elected to file a consolidated tax return. During 19X4 a consolidated return change of ownership occurred with respect to P's stock, and P acquired all the stock of X Corporation. The P-S-T-X group reports the following property transactions for 19X4:

| | Capital gains and losses | | Section 1231 gains and losses | |
| | Short- | Long- | Noncasualty | Casualty |
Member	term	term	and theft	and theft
P	$(6,000)	$(2,000)	$ 1,000	$1,000
S	1,000	(2,000)	1,000	
T	1,000	10,000	5,000	
X		15,000	10,000	
	$(4,000)	$21,000	$17,000	$1,000

In addition, T has a $20,000 capital loss carryover from 19X1, a separate return limitation year. All the property transactions (excluding the capital loss carryover) result in a net capital gain of $35,000 ($(4,000) + $21,000 + $17,000 + $1,000). Excluding T, the other group members report a net capital gain of $19,000 ($(5,000) + $11,000 + $12,000 + $1,000). Thus, the SRLY rules restrict the 19X1 capital loss carryover that may be used to T's contribution to the group's net capital gain, or $16,000 ($35,000 − $19,000). The consolidated return change of ownership rules restrict the carryover's usage to $10,000, however, the contribution of the old members (P, S, and T) to the group's net capital gain [$(4,000) + $6,000

+ $7,000 + $1,000]. This limitation is more restrictive and thus permits only $10,000 of T's capital loss carryover to be used.

DIVIDENDS RECEIVED BY GROUP MEMBERS

Dividends received by group members are treated differently depending on whether they come from firms inside or outside the affiliated group. In determining consolidated taxable income, those received from other group members are eliminated, while those received from nonmembers of the group are eligible for an 85 or 100 percent dividends-received deduction. In addition, an alternative to filing a consolidated tax return exists: The members of the affiliated group may file separate tax returns and claim a 100 percent dividends-received deduction under Sec. 243.

Elimination procedure

A dividend distribution from one member to a second member during a consolidated return year is eliminated in determining consolidated taxable income. A dividend is defined as any distribution to the extent of current or accumulated earnings and profits (E & P) whether or not the earnings and profits were accumulated in a separate or consolidated return year (Treas. Reg. Sec. 1.1502-14(a)).

Nondividend distributions—for example, a distribution made when there was no E & P balance—reduce the distributee corporation's adjusted basis in the stock of the distributing corporation. If the amount of the distribution exceeds the distributee's adjusted basis in the stock, the excess creates or increases an existing excess loss account (negative investment account). The distributee corporation, however, does not recognize any gain with respect to the portion of the distribution that exceeds its basis in the distributing corporation's stock, as would be the case with nonaffiliated corporations (Treas. Reg. Sec. 1.1502-14(a)(2)).

Gains realized by the distributing corporation when making a distribution to another group member (including those gains created by the various recapture provisions) are treated as a deferred intercompany transaction. The deferred gain is recognized by the distributing corporation when a restoration event occurs (Treas. Reg. Sec. 1.1502-14(c)).

Special rules exist in Treas. Reg. Sec. 1.1502-14(b) and (d) for distributions made in cancellation or redemption of all or part of the stock of the distributing corporation and the sale or disposition of an obligation of another group member. These rules, however, are beyond the scope of this book.

The consolidated dividends-received deduction

The affiliated group is permitted to claim a consolidated dividends-received deduction for dividends received from nonmembers of the group. No dividends-received deduction, however, is available for any dividends received from other group members during a consolidated return year (Treas. Reg. Sec. 1.1502-26(a) and (b)).

The consolidated dividends-received deduction is the lesser of:

1. The sum of the 85 percent dividends-received deduction permitted under Sec. 243(a)(1) and the special dividends-received deductions permitted under Secs. 244(a) and 245 relating to preferred stock and foreign corporations; or
2. 85 percent of consolidated taxable income computed excluding the consolidated net operating loss deduction, the consolidated dividends-paid deduction (Sec. 247), the consolidated dividends-received deduction, and any consolidated net capital loss carryback.

The limitation based on consolidated taxable income indicated in (2), above, does not apply in any consolidated return year in which a consolidated net operating loss is created (Treas. Reg. Sec. 1.1502-26(a)).

100 percent dividends-received deduction

A 100 percent dividends-received deduction election is permitted by Sec. 243(a)(3), which exempts certain "qualifying dividends" from taxation. This deduction provides one of the major benefits of the consolidated return election without requiring the affiliated group to engage in all the recordkeeping associated with recording the deferred intercompany transactions and restoration events, making the inventory adjustments, and filing the consolidated return itself. This election also may exempt from taxation dividends received by one group member from: (1) a second group member that is not considered to be an includible corporation when making a consolidated return election, or (2) a corporation that elects the benefits of Sec. 936 (U.S. possessions and Puerto Rico tax credit). The election is made for the affiliated group for a taxable year by the common parent corporation and is binding on subsequent taxable years unless revoked. Each corporation that is a member of the affiliated group on the last day of the common parent corporation's taxable year must consent to the election (Sec. 243(b)(2)).

The 100 percent deduction applies to dividends received by a corporation that is a member of the same affiliated group as the distributing corporation on the date of distribution, providing:

1. The necessary election is in effect;

2. The distribution is made out of earnings and profits of a post-December 31, 1963 taxable year of the distributing corporation for which the distributing and distributee corporations were *both* members of the affiliated group on *each* day of the taxable year; and

3. No multiple surtax exemption was in effect for the taxable year (Sec. 243(b)(1)).

Should the dividend fail to qualify for a 100 percent deduction, the regular 85 percent dividends-received deduction rules apply.

The 100 percent deduction is not available without certain costs. The members of the affiliated group are limited to a single reduction in the corporate tax rates under Sec. 11(b), a single estimated tax exemption, a single $150,000 accumulated earnings tax credit, a single $100,000 one year/$400,000 lifetime limitation on deductible mine exploration expenditures under Sec. 617(h)(1), and a single $25,000 limitation on the life insurance companies' small business deduction (Sec. 243(b)(3)).

CONSOLIDATED CHARITABLE CONTRIBUTIONS DEDUCTION

The consolidated charitable contributions deduction is the lesser of: (1) The aggregate of the charitable contributions deductions of the individual group members for the consolidated return year (computed without regard to the limitation imposed on any individual group members) plus any charitable contribution carryovers to the consolidated return year; or (2) 5 percent of adjusted consolidated taxable income (Treas. Reg. Sec. 1.1502-24(a)). Any excess charitable contributions are carried over to the five succeeding taxable years. There are no restrictions on the use of these carryovers or the carryovers of any individual group members, as is the case with a net operating loss or a capital loss.

Adjusted taxable income equals consolidated taxable income computed without regard to any available dividends-received deductions under Secs. 243–245, the consolidated dividends-paid deductions, any consol-

idated net operating loss and capital loss carrybacks, and the consolidated charitable contributions deduction.[36]

The charitable contributions carryover for any consolidated return year equals the sum of (1) any excess consolidated charitable contributions of the group for the year plus (2) any excess contributions of individual group members arising in prior separate return years (Treas. Reg. Sec. 1.1502-24(b)). A member leaving the group takes with it any excess contributions arising in a prior separate return year plus its allocable share of any excess consolidated charitable contributions for a consolidated return year. The excess consolidated charitable contributions are allocated to each group member based on their relative contributions for the consolidated return year (Treas. Reg. Sec. 1.1502-79(e)).

COMPUTATION OF THE AFFILIATED GROUP'S TAX LIABILITY

INCOME TAX LIABILITY   The consolidated income tax liability is determined by applying the tax rates found in Secs. 11 and 1201 (the alternative tax on capital gains) to consolidated taxable income. Section 1561(a) limits a *controlled group* of corporations to a single reduction in the corporate tax rates for the first $100,000 of taxable income under Sec. 11(b), regardless of the number of corporations that make up the *controlled group*. The benefits of the reduced tax rates must be apportioned equally among all the members of the *controlled group* (whether such members are included in or excluded from the consolidated return election) unless the controlled group's members elect to use an unequal method of apportionment[37] (Sec. 1561(a)).

MINIMUM TAX LIABILITY   The minimum tax liability is determined on a consolidated basis for all group members. A single $10,000 statutory exemption from the minimum tax applies to all the members of a controlled group (Sec. 58(b)). This $10,000 exemption is divided evenly among all the members of the *controlled group* unless they elect an unequal method of apportionment.

[36]The consolidated Western Hemisphere Trade Corporation deduction is no longer in effect.
[37]The term "controlled group" is defined in Sec. 1563(a). Two types of controlled groups exist—parent–subsidiary controlled groups and brother–sister controlled groups. While the definitions of an affiliated group (Sec. 1504) and a controlled group are quite similar, it is possible that corporations will be members of a parent–subsidiary controlled group but not belong to an affiliated group. In such a case, the corporations belonging to the affiliated group are permitted to make a consolidated return election while the remaining corporations of the controlled group file separate tax returns.

CONSOLIDATED TAX CREDITS

Seven tax credits—the investment tax credit, the foreign tax credit, the Work Incentive (WIN) Program credit, the targeted jobs credit, the alternative fuels production credit, the alcohol fuels usage credit, and the credit for nonhighway use of gasoline, oils, etc.—are available to an affiliated group. Each of these credits is determined for the affiliated group on a consolidated basis. To date, however, the consolidated return regulations have only been amended to provide special rules for determining the consolidated investment tax credit and consolidated foreign tax credit. We shall examine here only the special consolidated tax return regulations dealing with these credits.

Investment tax credit

The amount of the investment tax credit earned and the investment tax credit limitation based on the amount of the taxpayer's tax liability are both determined on a consolidated basis.

The credit earned by each individual group member is equal to 10 percent of the member's qualified investment (determined under Sec. 46(c)) for the consolidated return year. The aggregate of these individual amounts is the credit earned by the affiliated group.

The amount of the qualified investment for any property acquired from another group member in an intercompany transaction is determined by a special rule. This rule permits a credit to be claimed by the purchasing member equal to the property's purchase price minus any gain (plus any loss) realized by the selling members whether such gain or loss is deferred. An example of this rule is presented below.

> *Example:* P and S Corporations form the P-S affiliated group. P sells Sec. 38 property with an adjusted basis of $60 (a cost of $150) to S for $100. The basis of the property for purposes of computing the purchaser's qualified investment is only $60 [$100 (purchase price) minus $40 (deferred gain)]. This basis is also used when computing the amount of investment tax credit recapture when S disposes of the property. P's $40 deferred gain is excluded from both the initial investment tax credit and the recapture calculations.

A $100,000 used Sec. 38 property limitation applies to a controlled group. The affiliated group's members are permitted to select the used Sec. 38 property

that qualifies under this limitation. Used Sec. 38 property, however, excludes property that was used by another group member before its purchase in an intercompany transaction (Treas. Reg. Sec. 1.48-3(a)(2)).

The consolidated investment tax credit limitation equals the full amount of the first $25,000 consolidated tax liability plus up to 90 percent of the consolidated tax liability in excess of $25,000.[38] When determining the investment tax credit limitation, the consolidated tax liability amount is the affiliated group's federal income tax liability minus its consolidated foreign tax credit. The consolidated tax liability excludes any levies on group members associated with the minimum tax, the accumulated earnings tax, the personal holding company tax, and recoveries of foreign expropriation losses (Treas. Reg. Sec. 1.1502-3(b)(3)). Use of the consolidated tax liability as the basis for the investment tax credit limitation may result in a profitable group member finding its investment tax credit limitation reduced (from the limitation that would have been determined on a separate return basis) because the losses of one group member are permitted to offset the profits earned by other group members. On the other hand, unprofitable members may find their investment tax credit limitations increased so that credits that would otherwise have been carried back or forward may be used currently.

An affiliated group is permitted to increase the amount of the investment tax credit that it earns in a consolidated return year by (1) the amount of the consolidated investment tax credit carryovers and carrybacks to the taxable year, and (2) any investment tax credit carryovers that originate in a group member's separate return years (Treas. Reg. Sec. 1.1502-3 (b)(1)). The absorption of these credit carryovers occurs in a manner similar to the rules applicable to corporations filing separate tax returns. Credit carryovers are absorbed first by the affiliated group, followed by credits originating in the current consolidated return year, and finally, credit carrybacks from subsequent taxable years are utilized. Unused credits, which may be carried to a separate return year or a consolidated return year, are absorbed in a FIFO manner, beginning with the earliest ending taxable year.

Carrybacks and carryovers of unused investment tax credits follow many of the same rules that apply to net operating losses. Generally, the carryback or car-

---

[38]The 90 percent figure represents a change made in the Revenue Act of 1978 that is being phased in over taxable years 1979–1982. The percentage amounts for taxable years within this period are: 1978, 50 percent; 1979, 60 percent; 1980, 70 percent; 1981, 80 percent; and 1982, 90 percent.

ryover of unused credits between consolidated return years follows the rules applying to a corporation filing a separate tax return. A carryback may be made to a group member's separate return year only if the member is apportioned a part of the credit carryback. The apportionment of the carryback between members is based on their relative amounts of earned investment credits.

Similar to the net operating loss and capital loss areas, the Treas. Reg. Sec. 1.1502-79(c)(1) exception to the general carryback rules also applies here. This exception permits a member's apportionment of the carryback to be used in an equivalent consolidated or separate return year if it was not in existence during the carryback year but joined the affiliated group immediately after its organization. A member departing the affiliated group is permitted to take its share of any investment tax credit carryovers and use them in succeeding separate return years. Apportionment of the credit carryover to an individual group member is based on the relative amounts of earned investment credits in the original consolidated return year.

Carryovers and carrybacks from a separate return limitation year are subject to the separate return limitation year rules. These rules are similar to those applying to net operating losses, and basically restrict the carryback or carryover to offset only the individual member's contribution to the affiliated group's investment tax credit limitation (Treas. Reg. Sec. 1.1502-3(c)(1)). Similarly, the consolidated return change of ownership rules apply to an investment tax credit carryover. The credit carryover originating in taxable years before the year in which the CRCO occurs may be used only to the extent of the "old" group members' contribution to the consolidated investment tax credit limitation.

Recapture of previously claimed investment tax credits is required when property on which an investment tax credit has been claimed is disposed of by the affiliated group before the expiration of the useful life that was used in determining the investment tax credit. The recapture occurs by increasing the affiliated group's tax liability for the consolidated return year in which the disposition occurs (Treas. Reg. Sec. 1.1502-3(f)). The affiliated group's tax liability is increased whether the credit was originally claimed in a separate return or a consolidated return year.

The investment tax credit recapture rules for an affiliated group filing a consolidated tax return are similar to those for a corporation filing a separate tax return. An exception to the recapture rules is permitted for transfers of Sec. 38 property between group members during a consolidated return year. If the transferred property is disposed of by the acquiring group member before the expiration of the property's useful life for the original investment tax credit, any investment tax credit recapture increases the tax liability of the affiliated group, provided the disposition occurs in a consolidated return year (or the separate tax liability of the transferee corporation if the disposition occurs in a separate return year). The holding period used in recomputing the credit includes the time that both the transferor and transferee corporations hold the property.

Foreign tax credit

An affiliated group's foreign tax credit for a consolidated return year is determined on a consolidated basis. The common parent corporation elects to claim a deduction or a credit for foreign taxes (Treas. Reg. Sec. 1.1502-4(a)). The affiliated group's foreign tax credit limitation is computed on a consolidated basis, taking into account the group's income from U.S. and non-U.S. sources, the consolidated taxable income, and the consolidated tax liability. Foreign tax credit carryovers and carrybacks are handled in a manner similar to net operating losses; the SRLY and CRCO rules also apply (Treas. Reg. Sec. 1.1502-4(f) and (g)).

EARNINGS AND PROFITS (E & P)

The earnings and profits (E & P) of each group member are computed separately. No consolidated E & P amount is ever calculated for the affiliated group. The E & P amount calculated for each member determines the taxability[39] of a distribution made between group members and to parties external to the affiliated group, and the adjustments that are required to an "investor" group member's investment account to reflect the profits and losses of lower-tier "investee" group members.

The basic E & P calculation is made according to the general Sec. 312 E & P rules. A number of special rules exist for affiliated groups, however, including the following:

1. *Intercompany transactions*—Gains and losses on intercompany transactions are included in the selling member's E & P for the consolidated or separate return year in which the gain or loss is recognized in

---

[39] A dividend made between group members may be included in gross income if, for example, the distributing corporation is not eligible to join in a consolidated return election.

determining taxable income under Treas. Reg. Sec. 1.1502-13. As such, gains and losses on deferred intercompany transactions are included in the selling member's E & P in the taxable year in which a restoration event occurs instead of in the taxable year in which the original intercompany transaction occurred.

2. *Inventory adjustments*—The ordinary income and deductions recognized as inventory adjustments in a consolidated or separate return year are included currently in the E & P determination.

3. *Dividend distributions*—Dividend distributions reduce the E & P of the distributing corporation and increase the E & P of the distributee corporation. Nondividend distributions do not affect the E & P of either corporation.

4. *Excess loss accounts*—The amount of income recognized by a group member when an excess loss account (negative investment account) is restored increases that member's current year E & P.

5. *Allocation of consolidated income tax liability*—A member's allocable share of the consolidated income tax liability reduces its E & P in the year that the taxes are accrued (or when paid if the member uses the cash method of accounting). Section 1552 and the related regulations provide four special allocation methods. In addition, these methods may be used with the complementary methods of allocating the tax liability found in Treas. Reg. Sec. 1.1502-33(d). These complementary methods must be used when the group desires to compensate loss members for the tax benefits, such as net operating losses or investment tax credits, that were used by profitable group members in the course of filing the consolidated tax return.

6. *Disposition of stock or obligations of group members*—These gains and losses (including those related to an excess loss account) are included in E & P in the same taxable year that they enter into the taxable income determination. Thus, when the gain or loss on a stock disposition is deferred under Treas. Reg. Sec. 1.1502-14, it is included in E & P in the year in which the restoration event occurs.

For taxable years beginning after December 31, 1975, each member's E & P account must be increased or decreased to reflect the amount of any adjustments that must be made to the basis of the stock that the member owns in any investee corporations included in the consolidated return election. These positive (or negative) adjustments require the investor corporations to reflect currently any E & P (or E & P deficits) accruing to lower-tier corporations in their E & P accounts as is the case with the investee corporation's

earnings under the equity method used in financial accounting.[40] Before January 1, 1976, the annual adjustment of the E & P account was not required but could be elected by the affiliated group (Treas. Reg. Sec. 1.1502-33(a)(4)).

Dividend distributions made from taxable years in which the E & P accounts are subject to current adjustments are taken into the distributee corporation's E & P. A downward adjustment is required to the distributee's E & P account that corresponds to the basis reduction (described below) that it makes for its holdings of the distributing corporation's stock. Special rules exist for the treatment of distributions received out of E & P accumulated in taxable years in which the E & P were not adjusted currently or were earned in either a preaffiliation taxable year or a separate return year (Treas. Reg. Sec. 1.1502-32(b)(2)(iii)).

INVESTMENTS IN AFFILIATES

The maintenance of investment accounts to determine the adjusted basis for equity investments in subsidiary corporations that join in filing a consolidated tax return is quite similar to the equity method of accounting that is used in financial accounting. The purpose of these adjustments to the tax basis for the equity investments is to prevent (1) double benefits for operating losses that are first used to determine consolidated taxable income and that are recognized again as a capital loss when the investment is disposed of, and (2) double taxation for operating profits that are first included in determining consolidated taxable income and taxed again as a capital gain when the investment is sold.

The initial basis amount for the investment in the subsidiary is determined by applying the basis rules of Secs. 1011, 1012, and 1016. Additional capital contributions made by the investor also act to increase the basis of the investment. Two other positive adjustments to the adjusted basis of the investment may be required to reflect:

1. An allocable portion of the subsidiary's undistributed E & P for the consolidated return year.

2. An allocable portion of any consolidated net operating loss (or consolidated net capital loss) for the taxable year that has been apportioned to the investee corporation but that could not be carried back and utilized in a prior separate return year or consolidated re-

---

[40]Accounting Principles Board, *Opinion No. 18*, "The Equity Method of Accounting for Investments in Common Stock" (New York: AICPA, 1971).

turn year. [This positive adjustment offsets the first negative adjustment described below that reduces the investment account by the total amount of the investor's share of the consolidated net operating loss (or consolidated net capital loss) that was attributable to the investee corporation even though it was unable to be utilized as a carryback.]

Three negative adjustments must be made to the investment to reflect:

1. An allocable portion of the investee's E & P deficit for the consolidated return year.[41]

2. An allocable part of any net operating loss (or net capital loss) incurred by the investee in a prior separate return year or any portion of a consolidated net operating loss (or consolidated net capital loss) incurred in a prior consolidated return year that is attributable to the investee and that is carried over and utilized in the current year. [This negative adjustment reverses the second positive adjustment that is required when the consolidated net operating loss (or consolidated net capital loss) is not completely absorbed as a carryback.]

3. Dividends made by the subsidiary with respect to the investment in question during the current taxable year *and* out of the subsidiary's E & P balance that were accumulated in:
    a. A prior consolidated return year beginning after December 31, 1965; or
    b. A preaffiliation taxable year of the subsidiary (Treas. Reg. Sec. 1.1502-32(b)(2)).

The positive and negative adjustments are made at the end of the consolidated return year. When a number of lower-tier subsidiaries exist, the adjustments to the investment account and E & P begin at the lowest-tier investee corporation and flow up through the various ownership levels to the common parent corporation.

A corporation owning stock in a subsidiary must decrease the amount of its adjusted basis for the investment on the first day of its first separate return year, or the first day of the subsidiary's first separate return year, by the excess of the "positive adjustments" over the "negative adjustments" made with respect to the investment during all consolidated return years (Treas. Reg. Sec. 1.1502-32(g)(2)). The reason for such an ad-

justment is to prevent an investor from decreasing the stock ownership level below that required for affiliation, having the subsidiary pay out a large amount of dividends (without needing to make the downward basis adjustment) and then selling the investment and being required to report little or no capital gains because of the previously made upward adjustments.

The necessity of making a downward adjustment may be avoided if the investor makes a deemed dividend election under Treas. Reg. Sec. 1.1502-32(f)(2). This election is available if all a subsidiary's stock is owned on each day of its taxable year by members of the affiliated group. If such an election is made, the subsidiary is treated as having distributed on the first day of the taxable year all its E & P accumulated through the preceding year. Each member owning stock in the subsidiary is treated as receiving an allocable share of the deemed distribution and having then immediately contributed this amount to the subsidiary's capital. The entire amount of the dividend income is eliminated by the investor corporation when filing the consolidated return. The process of treating the distribution as a negative adjustment to the investment account reduces the amount of any downward adjustment that is required in a separate return year, even though the investment's actual basis is not decreased because of the offsetting effects of the dividend distribution and the capital contribution.

A negative investment account known as an "excess loss account" (ELA) is created if the negative adjustments to the investment account required in a consolidated return year for net operating losses or net capital losses, for distributions made out of preaffiliation-year E & P amounts, or for nondividend distributions, exceed the investment account balance. This ELA balance may be reduced or eliminated if capital contributions are made to the subsidiary (either an actual contribution or a deemed dividend election) or if the subsidiary reports E & P that are retained in the business. The ELA balance must be included in the investor's separate taxable income immediately before any disposition of the subsidiary's stock. The income is treated as gain from the sale of stock and accorded either capital gain or ordinary income status (Treas. Reg. Sec. 1.1502-19(a)).

An investor's ELA balance must be taken into gross income any time that the investor either transfers its stock holdings to any person or receives a distribution in cancellation or redemption of part or all the stock. Only the portion of the ELA that is attributable to the negative adjusted basis of the shares transferred must be recognized. Certain events, however, treat the

---

[41]When the E & P deficit is created by a net operating loss or capital loss that is carried back, the tax refund that is available to an accrual method of accounting taxpayer as a result of the carryback acts to reduce the amount of the E & P deficit. A cash method accounting taxpayer uses the refund to increase the E & P reported in the year that the refund is received.

investor as having disposed of all its shares of stock in the investee corporation, even though an actual disposition did not occur. These include, for example, either the investor or the investee corporation ceasing to be a group member or the affiliated group ceasing to file a consolidated tax return. Transfers of stock within the group, however, do not trigger the recognition of the ELA balance. In a multiple-tier structure, the recognition of an ELA balance commences with the lowest-tier subsidiary and is required at all intermediate ownership levels having ELA balances (after an adjustment for the income already recognized at the lower tier) up to the point at which the disposition is considered to have taken place (Treas. Reg. Sec. 1.1502-19(b) and (c)).

Application of the basic investment account adjustment rules is illustrated in the following examples.

Example (1): P and S Corporations, which both use the accrual method of accounting, form the P-S affiliated group. P initially paid $100,000 for all the S stock in 19X1. Since that date, P and S have filed consolidated tax returns. S's operating results for the 19X1–19X4 period are as follows:

	E & P	Distributions
19X1	$150,000	$80,000
19X2	50,000*	
19X3	250,000	70,000
19X4	(190,000)**	

*Including a $30,000 net capital loss that may not be carried back to any of the three preceding consolidated return years. This carryover is utilized in 19X3.

**Representing the current E & P deficit incurred after an adjustment for the tax refund that is expected to be received as a result of the current year net operating loss.

The adjustments to the adjusted basis for P's investment in S are as follows:

Year	Adjustment	Year-end balance
		$100,000
19X1	+ $ 70,000	170,000
19X2	+ 50,000	
	+ 30,000	250,000
19X3	+ 180,000	
	− 30,000	400,000
19X4	− 190,000	210,000

The subsidiary's $70,000 of undistributed E & P increases the basis of P's investment at the end of 19X1. S's 19X2 E & P balance is a positive adjust-

ment in 19X2. An additional positive adjustment is required in 19X2 because the net capital loss that reduced the E & P balance may not be carried back to an earlier year. In 19X2, both a negative $30,000 and positive $180,000 adjustment are required. The negative adjustment is required to reverse the 19X2 positive adjustment caused by the taxpayer's inability to carry the capital loss back to a prior year. The positive adjustment accrued represents the current E & P that accrued. In 19X4, using the entire net operating loss as a carryback causes a $190,000 downward adjustment to the investment account.

Example (2): P and S Corporations form the P-S affiliated group. P purchased all the S stock in 19X1 for $100. Since that date, negative adjustments in the amount of $300 have been required for the period 19X1–19X4, when S reported net operating losses that were utilized in the P-S consolidated tax return. If the stock of S Corporation were sold in 19X4, then the $200 ELA balance [$100 − $300 = $(200)] must be included in P's gross income immediately preceding the sale. Assuming the S stock were a capital asset, the $200 would be considered a long-term capital gain.

SALE OF A SUBSIDIARY'S STOCK

The sale of an investment in a subsidiary corporation to a nonmember of the group takes place in almost the same manner as if the investor had sold the stock of an unaffiliated corporation. The sale or exchange of the stock triggers the need for the various positive and negative adjustments to the investment account for the portion of the taxable year up to the date of the disposition. Once these adjustments have been made, the determination and characterization of the gain or loss proceeds in the normal manner.

SUMMARY

Although in 1974 consolidated tax returns accounted for fewer than 2 percent of the total corporate income tax returns filed, they accounted for in excess of: 50 percent of total corporate gross receipts reported; 60 percent of the total corporate net income (minus deficits) reported; and 65 percent of the total corporate income taxes reported.[42] The average consolidated tax return included: 4 subsidiary corporations; $47.7 million of gross receipts; $2.7 million of net income; and $1.3 million of federal income taxes.[43] Because of their use by large corporations, consolidated tax returns become important to a tax practitioner, and knowledge of this area and its complexities is essential. Although consolidated tax returns result in a tax savings for a substantial number of corporations, they involve considerable complexity and additional recordkeeping and are not used by many affiliated groups that instead choose to file separate tax returns.

[42]U.S. Department of the Treasury, Internal Revenue Service, *Statistics of Income—1974, Corporate Income Tax Returns* (Washington, D.C.: U.S. Government Printing Office), p. 5. These figures exclude Subchapter S Corporations, Domestic International Sales Corporations, and foreign corporations.
[43]*Ibid.*

PROBLEMS

1. A number of affiliated groups that are eligible to file consolidated tax returns do not make the requisite election. List the advantages and disadvantages of filing a consolidated tax return.

2. Which of the following independent situations results in an affiliated group being created? What corporations are eligible to be included in the making of a consolidated tax return election?
    a. Individual A owns all the stock of domestic corporations X and Y.
    b. Twelve individual shareholders own all the stock of P Corporation. P Corporation in turn owns all the stock of S Corporation. P and S own equally all the stock of T Corporation. P, S, and T are domestic corporations.
    c. P Corporation, a domestic corporation whose stock is publicly traded, owns all the stock of S and T corporations. S Corporation is a domestic corporation. T Corporation is a foreign corporation.
    d. Assume the same facts as in part c, except that S owns 70 percent of the stock of U Corporation.

3. Determine an acceptable minimum ownership level for the following subsidiary corporation(s) to be included as a first-tier subsidiary corporation in the affiliated group having P Corporation as the parent corporation.

	Outstanding shares		
Type of stock	*P Corp.*	*S Corp.*	*T Corp.*
Voting common stock (1 vote/share)	100,000	60,000	50,000
Nonvoting common stock	xx	xx	10,000
Voting preferred stock (4 votes/share)	xx	xx	40,000
Nonvoting preferred stock	xx	15,000	40,000

4. Not all corporations that are members of a "controlled group" (defined by Sec. 1563(a)) are members of an affiliated group (defined by Sec. 1504(a)). Explain.

5. A Corporation acquires all the stock of B Corporation at the close of business on June 30, 19X1. Both corporations have used the calendar year as their taxable year for a number of years. A and B decide to file a consolidated tax return for the A-B affiliated group commencing with taxable year 19X1.
    a. What is the last date on which A and B may make the consolidated tax return election?
    b. What income of A and B corporations must be included in the consolidated tax return for 19X1?
    c. Does the A-B affiliated group need to file a consolidated tax return in 19X2?
    d. What circumstances will permit the A-B affiliated group to discontinue consolidated tax return election?

6. A and B corporations have filed consolidated tax returns (using the calendar year as the taxable year) as the A-B affiliated group for a number of years. During this time, the group has incurred a consolidated net operating loss carryover that may be carried over until 19X5 and a consolidated investment tax credit carryover that may be carried over until 19X3. A Corporation, the parent corporation, sells all its stock in B Corporation at the close of business on April 30, 19X1.

    a. May A and B join in the filing of a consolidated tax return for 19X1? If so, what income must be included in the return?

    b. What happens to the net operating loss and investment tax credit carryovers of the A-B affiliated group?

    c. How would your answer to part a change if the sale occurred at the close of business on January 15, 19X1?

7. Different procedures are used in financial accounting and taxation for income and expense items that result from an intercompany transaction. Compare the procedures used in the preparation of a consolidated financial statement and a consolidated tax return when $10,000 of interest income is earned by the parent corporation, P, as a result of lending money to its subsidiary corporation, S.

8. P and S corporations are members of the P-S affiliated group. P uses the cash method of accounting and S uses the accrual method of accounting. During 19X1, P and S file separate tax returns. Beginning in 19X2, P and S elect to file consolidated tax returns. On December 1, 19X1 P charges S $25,000 for maintenance services that it performed earlier that year. S does not pay the invoice for these deductible expenses until January 19X2.

    a. In which taxable year does P recognize its revenues?

    b. In which taxable year does S recognize its deduction for the expense?

    c. Would your answer change if P and S had elected to file a consolidated tax return for 19X1?

9. Which of the following events results in the recognition of the previously deferred gains and losses by the parent corporation?

    a. Sale to a third party of all of the stock of a 100 percent owned subsidiary corporation.

    b. Sale of property, by a subsidiary corporation to a second subsidiary corporation, that had been acquired from the parent corporation in an intercompany transaction in which a gain was deferred.

    c. The parent corporation of an affiliated group receives permission to discontinue the filing of consolidated tax returns effective with the 19X1 taxable year.

    d. The collection by the parent corporation of the second of five equal installment payments resulting from an intercompany sale of land at a gain to a subsidiary corporation. The subsidiary corporation still owns the land.

    e. The sale of machinery by a subsidiary corporation to a third party. The machinery had been acquired from the parent corporation in an intercompany transaction in which a loss had been deferred.

10. Parent Corporation makes a sale on December 31, 19X1 of some machinery to its subsidiary, Echo Corporation, with which it joins in the filing of a consolidated tax return for 19X1. The sale price for the machine was $40,000. The machine had originally cost Parent $45,000 and had been depreciated by Parent (using the double-declining balance method and a six-year useful life) over its first two years when sold. Parent had claimed the maximum investment tax credit when the machine was acquired. The $40,000 sales price was immediately paid by Echo.

    a. What is the amount of Parent's realized gain?

    b. What is the amount and character of Parent's recognized gain?

    c.   Are any investment tax credits previously claimed by Parent required to be recaptured in 19X1 as a result of the sale (assuming Echo adopts a four-year useful life for the property)?

    d.   What amount of investment tax credit can Echo claim in 19X1?

11.   Refer to the facts in Problem 10. Assume that Echo commences depreciating the property on January 1, 19X2 using a four-year useful life. On January 1, 19X4, Echo sells the property to a third party for $18,000.

    a.   What is Echo's basis for the machine?

    b.   What amount of deferred gain does Parent recognize in 19X2, 19X3, and 19X4? What is the character of these recognized gains?

    c.   What is the amount of Echo's realized gain?

    d.   What is the amount and character of Echo's recognized gain?

    e.   What is the amount of the investment tax credit recapture in 19X4?

    f.   Which corporation's tax liability is increased as a result of the recapture?

12.   Parent Corporation makes a sale on December 31, 19X1 of some land used as a parking lot to its subsidiary, Fox Corporation. The land originally cost Parent $10,000 and the sales price was $15,000. Fox continues to use the land as a parking lot.

    a.   What is the amount of Parent's realized gain?

    b.   What is the amount and character of Parent's recognized gain?

    c.   Assume Fox sells the land in 19X4 to a third party for $30,000. The $30,000 is to be paid in four $7,500 annual installments with 10 percent interest on the unpaid balance. The first installment is collected in 19X4. What is the amount of Fox's realized gain? What amount of gain will Fox recognize over the 19X4–19X7 period?

    d.   What amount of gain will Parent recognize over the 19X4–19X7 period?

13.   P and S corporations were independent entities before 19X1. On January 1, 19X1, P purchases all of the S stock. For taxable year 19X1, P and S file separate tax returns, but for the period 19X2–19X4, the P-S group files consolidated tax returns. S regularly sells widgets to P at its cost plus a 25 percent markup. The inventory balance for P of widgets on January 1 of selected taxable years is as follows:

Year	Amount (using FIFO inventory method)
19X1	$150,000
19X2	70,000
19X3	200,000
19X4	-0-
19X5	120,000

    a.   What is the amount of the initial inventory adjustment? When and how does it appear in the P-S consolidated tax return?

    b.   What income and deduction amounts are subsequently reported by S as inventory adjustments because of the changes in inventory amounts resulting from the intercompany transactions?

    c.   On March 1, 19X5, P sells all of its S stock. How does this transaction affect the previous inventory adjustments, assuming that S files a separate tax return for the remainder of 19X5?

14.   X and Y corporations form the X-Y affiliated group with X Corporation as the parent corporation. The X-Y group, although having been affiliated for a number of years, elects to file a consolidated tax return for the first time in 19X2. X manufactures machines that are sold throughout the United States by Y. At the

close of 19X1, Y's inventory contains 100 machines, which it had purchased from X and with respect to which X had derived $35,000 in profits. During 19X2, X sells 30 machines to Y on which it derives $13,000 in profits and Y sells, outside the group, 25 units that it had on hand at the beginning of the year and on which X had derived a $9,000 profit. (Y uses the specific identification method of inventory valuation.)

    a. Is an inventory adjustment required of the X-Y affiliated group in 19X2?

    b. What is the initial inventory amount?

    c. What is the intercompany profit amount?

    d. What is the unrecovered inventory amount?

    e. What income and loss items must be recognized by X and Y in 19X2?

15. P, S, and T corporations form the P-S-T affiliated group. Each corporation was created by a group of investors in 19X1 with P owning all the stock of S and T. During 19X1–19X3, the P-S-T affiliated group files consolidated tax returns. On August 1, 19X3, P sells one-half its stock in T to a third party. The following profits and losses are reported by the P-S-T group during 19X1–19X3.

	19X1	19X2	19X3
P	$(120,000)	$ 30,000	$ 70,000
S	100,000	(60,000)	30,000
T—1/1/X3–			
7/31/X3	(120,000)	50,000	15,000
—8/1/X3–			
12/31/X3			25,000
Consolidated taxable			
income	$(140,000)	$ 20,000	$115,000[a]

[a]Including T's income only through 7/31/X3.

    a. In what taxable years may the consolidated net operating loss be used?

    b. What portion of the consolidated net operating loss (if any) may be carried over to T's separate tax return years? (Assume all losses were incurred in post-December 31, 1975 taxable years.)

16. P, S, and T corporations form the P-S-T affiliated group. P was formed in 19X1, and S and T corporations were formed in 19X2 when P transferred part of its assets to these corporations in a tax-free transaction coming under Sec. 351. Commencing in 19X2, the P-S-T group elected to file a consolidated tax return. During the period 19X1–19X3, P, S, and T reported the following profits and losses.

	19X1	19X2	19X3
P	$15,000	$ 20,000	$ 25,000
S		(10,000)	15,000
T		(20,000)	15,000
Consolidated taxable			
income	$ xx	$(10,000)	$55,000

    a. What is the P-S-T affiliated group's consolidated net operating loss for 19X2? In what taxable years may the loss be used as a carryback or carryover?

    b. Answer part a, assuming T reported a $120,000 separate operating loss in 19X2.

c. Assume P acquired all the S and T stock on January 1, 19X2 and that these two corporations had filed separate 19X1 tax returns, reporting $1,000 and $7,000 of taxable income, respectively. How would your answer to part a change?

17. P, S, and T corporations began business in 19X1. On January 1, 19X2, P Corporation acquired all the stock of S and T corporations. During 19X1 and 19X2, P, S, and T filed separate tax returns. Beginning in 19X3, the P-S-T group filed consolidated tax returns. During 19X1–19X3, P, S, and T reported the following income and loss amounts.

	19X1	19X2	19X3
P	$(30,000)	$ 20,000	$ 23,000
S	(2,000)	(10,000)	7,000
T	(10,000)	(8,000)	(3,000)
Consolidated taxable income	$ XX	$ XX	$ 27,000

a. What taxable years for P, S, and T are separate return limitation years?
b. Which loss carryovers may be absorbed in 19X2 and 19X3?
c. Which loss carryovers may be carried over to 19X4?

18. P and S corporations were formed on February 1, 19X1. They make up the P-S affiliated group, with P as the common parent corporation. The P-S group has filed consolidated tax returns since its inception. During 19X2, the P-S group added a new member when S purchased all the stock of X Corporation. The profits and losses reported by P, S, and X for 19X1 and 19X2 are presented below:

	19X1	19X2
P	$ (75,000)	130,000
S	(125,000)	(60,000)
X—since acquisition		250,000
Consolidated taxable income	$(200,000)	$320,000

a. What amount of the 19X1 and 19X2 separate losses may be utilized in 19X2?
b. Assume that A Corporation acquired 70 percent of the P stock on April 1, 19X2 from some of P's former owners. Would this change your answer to part a?

19. A and B corporations have for many years filed consolidated tax returns. On April 30, 19X2, B acquires C Corporation. The following table summarizes the property transactions for 19X2 (excluding ordinary gains and losses).

	Capital gain (loss)		Sec. 1231 gain (loss)	
Corp.	Short-term	Long-term	Other	Casualty and theft
A		$ 2,000	$ 2,000	$ (6,000)
B	$ (5,000)	(4,000)	9,000	4,000
C	1,000	6,000	(3,000)	5,000
Total	$ (4,000)	$ 4,000	$ 8,000	$ 3,000

a. Determine the amount and types of property transaction gains and losses reported on the consolidated tax return.

b. If C had capital loss carryovers from its 19X1 and 19X2 (preacquisition) tax returns of $4,000 and $6,000, respectively, how much of the carryover may be used in 19X2?

c. How would your answers to parts a and b change if A's 19X2 casualty and theft loss were $10,000?

20. A and B corporations have for many years filed consolidated tax returns. On January 1, 19X1, B acquires C Corporation. The following results summarize the *property* transactions for 19X1 (excluding ordinary gains and losses).

		Capital gain (loss)		Sec. 1231 gain (loss)	
Corp.	Deferred gain (loss)	Short-term	Long-term	Other	Casualty and theft
A	$(30,000)*	$ 2,000	$ 2,000	$ 1,000	$ (5,000)
B		1,000	(2,000)	12,000	1,000
C		4,000	3,000	(5,000)	1,000
Total	$(30,000)	$ 7,000	$ 3,000	$ 8,000	$ (3,000)

*Sec. 1231 loss.

The A-B-C group reports $200,000 of taxable income other than that indicated from the property transactions.

a. Determine the amount and types of the property transaction gains and losses reported on the consolidated tax return.

b. If C had a $10,000 net capital loss carryover from its 19X0 separate tax return, how much of the carryover may be used in 19X1?

c. If the $30,000 deferred loss could be recognized in 19X1 or in 19X2, a year in which no other property transactions were to be recognized, what would be your choice? Why?

21. P and S corporations form the P-S affiliated group that has elected to file consolidated tax returns. During 19X1, P Corporation received $100,000 in dividends from S and $40,000 from a nonconsolidated foreign subsidiary, T Corporation. S Corporation received $75,000 from its holdings of 40 percent of domestic corporation U. During 19X1, the P-S affiliated group reported taxable income of $100,000, excluding the aforementioned dividends.

a. What is the amount of the P-S group's consolidated dividends-received deduction?

b. How would your answer to part a change if P and S reported separate taxable income amounts (excluding dividends) of $100,000 and $(150,000), respectively?

c. How would your answer to part b change if S had reported a $160,000 loss?

22. P and S Corporations form the P-S affiliated group. The P-S group has filed consolidated tax returns for a number of years. During 19X1 and 19X2, the group members report the following profits and charitable contributions.

	19X1		19X2	
	Separate taxable income*	Charitable contributions	Separate taxable income*	Charitable contributions
P	$200,000	$10,000	$100,000	$ -0-
S	(50,000)	-0-	100,000	8,000
Total	$150,000	$10,000	$200,000	$8,000

*Excluding any charitable contributions.

    a.   Determine the amount of the consolidated charitable contributions deduction for 19X1 and 19X2.

    b.   What is the amount of the excess charitable contributions that may be carried over to 19X3? In what year does it expire?

23.   On January 1, 19X1, P Corporation acquired all the S Corporation stock for $1,000. S's accumulated E & P balance on January 1, 19X1 was $200. S's results of operations (in terms of E & P) and distributions for the period 19X1–19X6 are presented below.

Year	Earnings and Profits	Distributions
19X1	$ -0-	$ 100
19X2	150	-0-
19X3	(30)	200
19X4	(2,000)	-0-
19X5	5,000	1,000
19X6 (1/1–6/20/19X6)	-0-	(2,000)

Assume all distributions are made on the last day of the taxable year. On June 30, 19X6, P sold the S stock to a third party for $3,000. Compute P's gain (or loss) on the sale.

24.   P and S Corporations were created on January 1, 19X1 and form the P-S affiliated group. The P-S affiliated group files consolidated tax returns for 19X1 and 19X2, reporting the following investment tax credit information.

Year	Corporation	Credit earned	Consolidated credit earned	Consolidated limitation based on tax liability
19X1	P	$100,000	$180,000	$200,000
	S	80,000		
19X2	P	125,000	265,000	200,000
	S	140,000		

The consolidated credit represents the sum of the individual credits that were earned.

    a.   Calculate the amount of the investment tax credit carryback and carryover from 19X2.

    b.   Assume P disposes of its investment in S stock on January 1, 19X3. Determine the amount of P's and S's separate investment tax credit carryovers to 19X3.

SUPPLEMENTAL PROBLEMS

25.   The consolidated tax return regulations represent one of a series of "statutory" regulations that are found within the Code. List some of the other statutory regulation provisions. What reasons generally permit these statutory regulations to be overturned?

26.   The consolidated tax return regulations represent an attempt by the taxing authorities to treat a group of separate but affiliated corporate entities as a single taxpaying entity. These regulations also permit the individual group members to retain a large degree of separate entity status. What are some of the tax provisions that indicate each of these two opposing principles?

27.   Refer to Problem 14 and answer the following questions, assuming that Y Corporation used the last-in, first-out (LIFO) inventory method instead of the specific identification method.

a. What portion of X's $35,000 initial inventory amount would be included in its 19X2 income?

b. Assume that in 19X3 Y sold 50 of the units it had on hand at the beginning of 19X3. What amount of income and loss would X recognize in 19X3 as an inventory adjustment?

c. If X sold the Y stock on January 1, 19X4, what amount of income and loss would X recognize as a result of the inventory adjustment process?

28. P Corporation acquires all the stock of X and Y corporations on January 1, 19X1. The P-X-Y affiliated group commences filing consolidated tax returns in 19X1. P Corporation's assets consist only of its holdings of the X and Y stock and about $100,000 cash that represents the remainder of the capital contributed by the shareholders and some bank borrowings made by P. X and Y report the following results for 19X1 and 19X2.

Year	Earnings (E & P)		Distributions	
	X	Y	X	Y
19X1	$100,000	$40,000	$15,000	$-0-
19X2	125,000	60,000	30,000	-0-

On December 31 of 19X1 and 19X2, P Corporation makes a $25,000 distribution to its shareholders. Determine P's E & P balance at the end of each year and the taxability of each $25,000 distribution.

29. P, S, and T Corporations form the P-S-T affiliated group. P Corporation owns all the S Corporation stock and S Corporation owns 90 percent of the T Corporation stock. The P-S-T affiliated group has filed consolidated tax returns for a number of years. On January 1, 19X1, the investment account balances are as follows:

Account	Amount
P in S	$ 8,000
S in T	(1,100)

P sells its investment in S on January 1, 19X1 for $10,000.

a. What income must be included in S's 19X1 separate taxable income as a result of the sale of the S stock? In P's income?

b. What is the character of the income that is recognized in part a?

30. P, S, and T corporations were formed during 19X1. P owns 80 percent of the S and T stock. Together the three corporations form the P-S-T affiliated group, which reports the following results for 19X1 and 19X2.

	Separate taxable income	
	19X1	19X2
P	$ 400,000	$1,000,000
S	800,000	(800,000)
T	(200,000)	-0-
Consolidated taxable income	$1,000,000	$ 200,000

a. What is the group's consolidated tax liability for 19X1 and 19X2?

b. Allocate this liability to P, S, and T, using the tax allocation method described in Treas. Reg. Sec. 1.1552-1(a)(1).

Subchapter S corporations

For decades, individuals operating their businesses as sole proprietorships or partnerships looked longingly at the desirable characteristics of the corporate form of business organization—especially the attributes of limited liability, free transferability of ownership interests, and unlimited life. Even for those individuals initially entering business, these corporate attributes are appealing. Sometimes, however, the tax costs of choosing the corporate form outweigh the nontax advantages, and potential incorporators choose not to incorporate. The tax disadvantages of the corporate form weigh especially heavily when it is anticipated that the profits of the business will be distributed as dividends, with the result that "double taxation" may eat into the earnings finally enjoyed by the corporation's owners. A second negative feature, particularly for a new business venture that is likely to operate at a loss for its first few years, is that losses suffered by the corporation may not be deducted by shareholders on their personal tax returns.

Neither of these unfavorable characteristics applies to a business operated as a sole proprietorship or as a partnership. The ideal business entity, therefore, would be one that encompasses the most desirable tax and nontax attributes of both the corporate and noncorporate forms without the disadvantages of either. Although this ideal is not attainable, many tax scholars and taxpayers have long felt that permitting corporations to be taxed in much the same way as partnerships would go far toward attaining the ideal, and in the 1930s and 1940s various individuals and groups made that recommendation. Some of their suggestions were intended to apply only to small, closely held corporations, while others would have extended to all corporations. Similarly, some of the proposals would have made such treatment optional, and others would have made it mandatory.[1]

The first serious attempt in Congress to permit closely held corporations to escape the corporate income tax resulted in Senate passage in 1954 of a provision that would permit small corporations to be taxed essentially as though they were partnerships.[2] Although this provision was eliminated by a Conference Committee, the idea was obviously one whose time was near. In 1958, Congress enacted Subchapter S (now Secs. 1371 through 1379) of the Internal Revenue Code for the announced purpose of enabling small businesses to choose their legal form without undue influence by tax considerations.[3] The 1958 provisions, although modified a number of times, remain at the heart of Subchapter S today. The popularity of the Subchapter S corporation is shown by the fact that in 1978, out of 2.4 million corporations filing federal income tax returns, almost 400,000 elected to be taxed under the provisions of Subchapter S.

AN OVERVIEW OF SUBCHAPTER S

Unfortunately, because the provisions of Subchapter S are occasionally complex, unwary taxpayers may find themselves in unfavorable tax circumstances because they misunderstand the law. The most obvious tax

---

[1] See, for example, "Final Report of the Committee of the National Tax Association on Federal Taxation of Corporations," *Proceedings of the Thirty-Second Annual Conference on Taxation of the National Tax Association,* pp. 534–99 (1939) and Randolph Paul, *Taxation for Prosperity,* pp. 539–75 (1947). Lorence Bravenec has a good discussion of the background of Subchapter S in *Taxation of Subchapter S Corporations and Shareholders,* pp. 10–11 (1978).

[2] S. Report No. 1622, 83rd Congress, 2d Session, Washington, D.C.: U. S. Government Printing Office, 1954, p. 119.

[3] S. Report No. 1983, 85th Congress, 2d Session, Washington, D.C.: U. S. Government Printing Office, 1958, p. 87.

characteristics of a Subchapter S corporation (one electing to be taxed under the provisions of Subchapter S) are summarized below.

1.   A Subchapter S corporation is not subject to the regular federal corporate income tax.

2.   Even though the Subchapter S corporation does not pay an income tax, it computes "taxable income" in much the same way as does a regular corporation. The corporation's taxable income "flows through" the corporation to the shareholders, and the shareholders report their respective shares of the corporation's income on their personal tax returns, whether or not the income is actually distributed to them. All taxable income of the corporation, except the excess of long-term capital gains over short-term capital losses, is usually treated as ordinary income by the stockholders. Each stockholder's share of the excess of long-term capital gain over short-term capital loss is reported as long-term gain on the shareholder's personal tax return unless the corporation has a net operating loss, in which case the net operating loss is first offset against the excess of long-term gains over short-term losses.

3.   The corporation's net operating loss also flows through to the shareholders. Each shareholder offsets his or her proportionate share of the Subchapter S corporation's net operating loss against other gross income on his or her personal tax return. The amount of loss that a shareholder may deduct is limited to the shareholder's basis in stock and debt of the corporation. The loss is calculated on a daily basis and is allocated pro rata to each shareholder for the number of days during the year that the shareholder owned the stock.

4.   To the extent that earnings for a taxable year are distributed to shareholders during that year, they are reported by the shareholders as dividends (not subject to the $100 exclusion). To the extent that taxable income is *not* distributed during the taxable year, it is allocated as "constructive dividends" to the shareholders in proportion to the number of shares owned by each shareholder on the last day of the corporation's taxable year (again not subject to the dividend exclusion). The undistributed earnings are known as "undistributed taxable income" (UTI).

5.   Undistributed taxable income later distributed in the form of money to a shareholder to whom it was previously taxed is tax free to the recipient if distributed within the first 2½ months after the close of the corporation's taxable year.

6.   After 2½ months have elapsed from the close of a taxable year, any UTI of that year that has not been distributed becomes known as "previously taxed income" (PTI). PTI also may be distributed tax free to shareholders, but only after all current earnings and profits of the tax year in which distributions are made have been distributed.

In this chapter, we shall survey the taxation of Subchapter S corporations, including the requirements for electing to be taxed under Subchapter S, the rules for terminating the election, the flow-through of operating profits, the characteristics of UTI and PTI, cash distributions, property distributions, the flow-through of net operating losses, the flow-through of long-term capital gains, the capital gains tax, and the shareholder's basis in stock and debt of the corporation. The chapter is organized essentially the same as Subchapter S, Secs. 1371 through 1379 of the Code.

CORPORATIONS QUALIFYING TO MAKE THE ELECTION

To initially qualify for electing to be taxed under Subchapter S, a corporation must be classified a "small business corporation." A small business corporation is a domestic corporation that is not a member of an affiliated group and does *not* have: (1) more than 15 shareholders; (2) a shareholder (other than an estate and certain types of trusts) who is not an individual; (3) a nonresident alien as a shareholder; and (4) more than one class of stock.

A corporation that has met the above qualifications as well as elected to file under Subchapter S is referred to as an "electing corporation," or a "Subchapter S corporation." In order to retain that status, the corporation must continue to meet the above qualifications and, in addition, must meet two additional tests, namely:

1.   Not more than 80 percent of the corporation's gross receipts for a taxable year may be from "foreign sources," and

2.   Not more than 20 percent of the corporation's gross receipts may be from "passive investment income sources."

If any of the initial tests is subsequently not met, or if either of the two tests related to the source of the corporation's receipts is not met, the corporation's election terminates retroactively for the current year.

We shall examine these tests in greater detail below.

Qualifying shareholders

Under Sec. 1371(a)(2) of the Code, a corporation qualifies as a small business corporation only if its shareholders are either individuals, estates of decedents, or certain types of trusts. The types of trusts that may be stockholders in a small business corporation, as specified by Sec. 1371(e), include:

1. A trust, all of which is treated as owned by the grantor (who is an individual citizen or resident of the United States);
2. A trust that was treated as owned by the grantor immediately before the grantor's death (but only for the 60-day period beginning on the date of the grantor's death). If the entire corpus of the trust is includible in the grantor's estate, however, the period during which the trust shall qualify after death is extended to two years.
3. A trust created primarily to exercise voting power over stock transferred to it; and
4. A trust with respect to stock transferred to it pursuant to a will, but only for the 60-day period beginning on the date the stock is transferred to it.

Thus, if any one of a corporation's shareholders is another corporation, a partnership, or a disqualified trust, that corporation does not qualify as a small business corporation. (Treas. Reg. Sec. 1.1372-1(a) provides that if a disqualifying shareholder owned shares *prior* to the date of the election, it would not disqualify the corporation if the shareholder terminated such interest before the date of the election.) In addition, per Sec. 1371(a)(3), a nonresident alien may not be a shareholder of a Subchapter S corporation.

Number of shareholders limited to fifteen

For tax years beginning after December 31, 1978, a small business corporation may not have more than 15 shareholders. Before 1979, the general limit was 10 shareholders. For this purpose, a husband and wife (and their estates) are treated as one shareholder. If stock is held in the name of an agent, guardian, or custodian, each person for whom such stock is held is deemed to be a shareholder (Treas. Reg. Sec. 1.1371-1(d)(1). If stock is held in a voting trust, each beneficiary is considered to be a shareholder.

Single class of stock

Section 1371(a)(4) specifies that, in order to qualify as a small business corporation, a corporation may have only one class of stock, each share of which has identical rights. If other shares with rights different from the shares outstanding have been authorized but have not been issued, or if shares with rights different from those outstanding have previously been issued and reacquired, the corporation is not disqualified. The I.R.S. has also agreed that outstanding warrants or options do not constitute a second class of stock.[4]

A degree of controversy exists over whether debt can constitute a second class of stock. Although current regulations (Treas. Reg. Sec. 1.1371-1(g)) state that "debt which is equivalent to equity will be treated as a second class of stock unless the debt is held by stockholders in substantially the same proportion that they own the stock of the corporation," the I.R.S. has, because of several adverse judicial decisions,[5] announced plans to issue proposed regulations (not yet issued) regarding outstanding debt. Until these proposed regulations are issued, in situations in which the facts are similar to those in four related decisions the I.R.S. will not initiate litigation.[6]

Domestic corporation requirement

A small business corporation must be a "domestic" corporation—that is, it must be organized under the laws of the United States or any state or territory.

Prohibition of subsidiaries

Under Sec. 1371(a), a small business corporation may not be a member of an affiliated group, as defined in Sec. 1504. Because a small business corporation may not have another corporation as shareholder, however, the practical impact of this limitation is to prohibit a small business corporation from owning a controlling interest in a subsidiary. Under this provision, there is no attribution of stock ownership, so the restriction merely prohibits the *direct* ownership of 80 percent or more of the stock in another corporation. Because of the nonattribution rule, the shareholders of a small business corporation may own all the shares of another corporation without disqualifying the Subchapter S election. The subsidiary ownership prohibition also will not apply in cases in which the subsidiary corporation has not begun operations before the close of the taxable year and does not have taxable income for the period included in the taxable year.

[4] Rev. Rul. 67-279, 1967-2 C.B. 298.
[5] See, for example, *Amory Cotton Oil Co.* v. *United States*, 468 F. 2d 1046 (CCA-5, 1972) and *Portage Plastics Co., Inc.* v. *United States*, 486 F. 2d 632 (CCA-7, 1973).
[6] T.I.R. No. 1248, July 27, 1973.

Further limitations

In addition to the initial requirements, the Code specifies two additional tests that must be met to maintain the Subchapter S status after the initial election has been properly filed. First, receipts from foreign sources are limited. Second, the corporation's receipts from passive income sources are limited.

LIMITATION ON RECEIPTS FROM FOREIGN SOURCES

Section 1372(e)(4) provides that if more than 80 percent of a corporation's gross receipts for a taxable year are derived from foreign sources (determined under Secs. 861 through 864), the election to be taxed under Subchapter S will be terminated, effective in the taxable year in which such excess occurs.[7]

LIMITATION ON PASSIVE INVESTMENT INCOME

Under Sec. 1372(e)(5), if in any taxable year more than 20 percent of the electing corporation's gross receipts are from "passive investment income," the election will terminate for that year and all future years. The termination does not apply, however, if the taxable year involved is the first taxable year in which the corporation commenced the active conduct of a trade or business (or the next succeeding taxable year) *and* the amount of passive income for the year is less than $3,000.

Passive investment income means gross receipts from royalties, dividends, rents, interest, annuities, and sales or exchanges of stock or securities (up to the amount of gain from such sale or exchange). (If substantial personal services are rendered in earning rents, however, they are not considered passive income.) The time for including "gross receipts" is determined under the general rules related to the taxpayer's method of accounting. According to the regulations, capital losses on the sale or exchange of stocks or securities do not offset gains on such sales or exchanges in measuring passive income. Gains on stocks and securities have been held to be passive income even though the corporation is a regular dealer in stocks.[8]

"Gross receipts" is defined in Treas. Reg. Sec. 1.1372-4(b)(5)(iv) as the total amount received or accrued from sales, services, or investments but does not include amounts received from nontaxable sales or exchanges, borrowed funds, capital contributions, or loan repayments.

MAKING THE ELECTION

In order to be treated as a Subchapter S corporation, a corporation must properly execute a timely election as detailed in Treas. Reg. Sec. 1.1372-4(b)(5)(iii)(b), accompanied by the consent of each shareholder.

Time of election

Section 1372 provides that, in general, the election may be made at any time during the preceding year or at any time during the first 75 days of the year for which an election is to be effective. An election made after the first 75 days of the taxable year shall be treated as having been made for the following taxable year. For example, if a corporation reporting on a calendar year basis files a proper election to be taxed under Subchapter S on March 20, 19X1, the election is treated as having been made for the taxable year beginning January 1, 19X2.

The period during which a new corporation may make the election will usually begin with the first day of its taxable year. No election may be made until the corporation has come into existence under state law.[9] The election may not be made until the earliest of the date on which the corporation (1) has stockholders, (2) acquires assets, or (3) begins doing business.[10]

Consent of each shareholder

All persons who are shareholders in the corporation on the day that the election is made must consent to the election. Detailed rules on who must sign the election are found in Treas. Reg. Sec. 1.1372-3. If stock is owned in joint tenancy, each tenant must sign the election; if it is owned by a husband and wife as community property, both must sign the election; and if stock is owned by an estate, the executor or administrator must sign the election.

TERMINATING A SUBCHAPTER S ELECTION

Once a small business corporation has elected to be taxed under Subchapter S, the election is effective for the taxable year for which it is made and for all suc-

---

[7] See Treas. Reg. Secs. 1.1372-4(b)(4) and 1.1372-4(b)(5)(iv).
[8] *Buhler Mortgage Co., Inc.*, 51 T.C. 971 (1969) *aff'd per curiam*, 443 F.2d 1362 (CCA–9 1971).

[9] *J. William Frentz*, 44TTC 485 (1965) *aff'd per curiam*, 375 F.2d 662 (CCA-6, 1967).
[10] Treas. Reg. Sec. 1.1372-2(b)(1). See also *Nick A. Artukovich*, 61 TC 100 (1970).

ceeding years unless the election is terminated for any such taxable year (Sec. 1372(d)). The election may be terminated either intentionally or unintentionally.

Consent of all shareholders to revoke election

Section 1372(e) controls the termination of a Subchapter S election. After the first year for which an election is effective, the election may be revoked if *all* persons who are deemed to be shareholders in the corporation at the beginning of the day on which the revocation is made consent in writing to the revocation. If the revocation is made before the close of the first month of a tax year, it becomes effective for the year in which it is made. If the revocation is made after the close of the first month of the taxable year, it will become effective in the succeeding taxable year.

Affirmative refusal of new stockholder to consent to the election

A new shareholder who acquires stock in an electing corporation may, on or before the 60th day after the day on which the new shareholder acquires the stock, void the election by affirmatively refusing to consent to the previous election. If the stock is acquired by the estate of a decedent, the period allowed for affirmative refusal to consent to the election expires 60 days after (1) the date on which the executor or administrator of the estate qualifies as such, or (2) the last day of the corporation's taxable year in which the decedent dies, whichever is earlier. A termination resulting from an affirmative refusal of a new shareholder to consent to the election becomes effective for the taxable year in which that person becomes a shareholder in the corporation (or, if later, the first taxable year for which such an election would have otherwise been effective).

Automatic termination

If an electing corporation ceases to meet all the requirements qualifying it as a small business corporation or ceases to meet the requirements related to source of receipts, the election automatically terminates, effective for the taxable year in which the corporation ceases to meet such requirements and remains terminated for all future years. Treas. Reg. Sec. 1.1372-4(b)(3) requires that the corporation immediately notify the I.R.S. and provide specified information if the election is terminated because of failure to meet the initial requirements to qualify as a small busi-

ness corporation. Clearly, terminating a Subchapter S election is a simple matter for the corporation or its shareholder(s).

ELECTION AFTER TERMINATION

If a corporation has elected to be taxed under Subchapter S and the election has subsequently been terminated, the corporation (as well as any "successor corporation") is not eligible to make a new election for any year before the fifth year that begins after the year of termination unless the Commissioner consents to a new election. For example, if an election for a calendar-year corporation was terminated for the year beginning January 1, 19X1, a new election could not be effective for a taxable year beginning before January 1, 19X6, unless the Commissioner gave consent.

Treas. Reg. Sec. 1.372-5 contains detailed rules governing a new election by a corporation, the previous election of which has terminated, including general guidelines for determining when the Commissioner will consent to a new election before the five-year waiting period has expired. In general, consent may be given to a new election before the fifth succeeding year if either (1) 50 percent or more of the corporation's stock is owned by persons who did not own any stock during the year of termination of the previous election, or (2) it can be established that the event that caused the termination was not reasonably within the control of the corporation or shareholders having a substantial interest in the corporation.

As noted, a successor corporation is also ineligible to make a re-election until the fifth succeeding year after termination of a prior election. If 50 percent or more of a corporation's stock is owned directly or indirectly by the same persons who owned 50 percent or more of the stock of a former electing corporation at any time during the year that the former electing corporation terminated its election, the corporation is a successor corporation. Also, a corporation that acquires a substantial portion of the assets of a former Subchapter S corporation that terminated its election is deemed to be a successor corporation.

THE FLOW-THROUGH OF CORPORATE PROFITS TO SHAREHOLDERS

A small business corporation making a Subchapter S election is not subject to the federal corporate income tax. Instead, the corporation's income is taxable to the shareholders. Amounts distributed to shareholders out of current earnings and profits are taxed to the shareholders as dividends not eligible for the $100 exclusion. In addition, Sec. 1373(a) stipulates that undistributed taxable income of an electing small business corporation for any taxable year shall be included in gross income of the individual shareholders of the corporation.

Computing the corporation's undistributed taxable income

The first step in determining the undistributed taxable income (UTI) for a Subchapter S corporation is to compute its taxable income. Section 1378 provides that taxable income for an electing corporation is to be computed in the same way as for a regular corporation, except that:

    1.   There is no deduction for net operating losses of other years, and
    2.   The only "special deduction" allowed is the amortization of organization costs.

The following items are subtracted from taxable income to arrive at UTI:

    1.   Any preference tax under Sec. 56 (page 9/15) and any capital gains tax to be paid for the year under Sec. 1378(a) (pages 9/14–9/15);
    2.   Any distributions of money as dividends during the taxable year, to the extent that the distribution is out of earnings and profits of the current year. Distributions of property, stock, or corporate obligations are *not* deducted in arriving at UTI.

Allocation of UTI to shareholders— the constructive dividend

The corporation's undistributed taxable income is allocated to the shareholders, and each shareholder reports in gross income the allocated amount. The allocation is made in proportion to the number of shares owned by each as of the last day of the corporation's taxable year (Sec. 1373(b)). Under Sec. 1373(c), the amount allocated is treated by the shareholder as an amount distributed as a dividend on the last day of the taxable year of the corporation. Thus, the constructive dividend is reported by the shareholder in the shareholder's taxable year in which or with which the corporation's taxable year ends.

    Note that the allocation is made only to shareholders who own shares at the close of the corporation's taxable year.

Example: Assume that Wilson and Yeager owned 40 and 60 percent, respectively, of an electing corporation's shares on January 1, 19X1, the first day of the corporation's taxable year. On November 12, 19X1, Wilson sold his shares to Zeno, who did not terminate the election. The corporation paid no dividends, and the UTI for the year ending December 31, 19X1, was $30,000. Zeno will be allocated $12,000 of the UTI, and Yeager will be allocated $18,000. No part of UTI will be allocated to Wilson because Wilson was not a shareholder at the close of the taxable year.

Section 1376(a) permits the basis of stock in the hands of the shareholder to be increased by the amount of constructive dividend included in gross income by the shareholder. The constructive dividend decreases the corporation's earnings and profits that might be taxable to the taxpayer on subsequent distributions.

The overall impact of UTI is illustrated in the following example.

Example: University Corporation, an electing small business corporation, began its first taxable year on January 1, 19X1. The corporation's stock is owned by two shareholders. Aaron owns 75 percent of the stock; Beth owns 25 percent. On January 1, 19X1, the basis of Aaron's shares was $200,000; the basis of Beth's shares was $30,000. During 19X1, the corporation's net income from operations was $48,000. In addition, the corporation received dividends of $4,000 on shares of stock owned in other corporations. In November 19X1, the corporation distributed $15,000 cash to Aaron and $5,000 to Beth. Aaron's taxable year is the calendar year; Beth's taxable year is a fiscal year beginning April 1 and ending March 31.

    The corporation's taxable income is $52,000— the sum of the net income from operations and the gross amount of dividends received. The distribution of $20,000 in November is deemed to be a distribution of current earnings and profits and is, therefore, taxable to the shareholders. The undistributed taxable income is $32,000—the amount of taxable income ($52,000) less the distributions of the current year ($20,000). The UTI is allocated on the basis of the number of shares held by each shareholder on the last day of the taxable year of the corporation; thus, Aaron must report a constructive dividend of $24,000 on his personal tax return for the period ending December 31, 19X1, and Beth must report a constructive dividend of $8,000 on her personal tax return for the period ending March 31, 19X2.

The basis of Aaron's stock on December 31, 19X1, is $224,000 (the original basis, plus the constructive dividends of $24,000); the basis of Beth's stock is $38,000.

CASH DISTRIBUTIONS FROM UNDISTRIBUTED TAXABLE INCOME (UTI) AND PREVIOUSLY TAXED INCOME (PTI)

As previously explained, the undistributed taxable income of a Subchapter S corporation is taxed to the shareholders as though it were distributed on the last day of the corporation's taxable year. Obviously, equity dictates that the shareholders should be able subsequently to withdraw, without further tax consequences, amounts on which they have already paid income taxes. If the taxpayer is careful to follow the rules, a tax-free withdrawal is possible. The rules are rather complex, however, and many taxpayers find to their dismay that they have difficulty making a tax-free withdrawal.

First, any distribution of money (but not other property) made by an electing corporation after the close of a taxable year and on or before the 15th day of the third month following the close of that year, to a person who was a shareholder (and therefore was allocated UTI at the end of that taxable year) is treated as a tax-free distribution of UTI to the extent that such distributions do not exceed the taxpayer's share of UTI for that year. This is often referred to as the "2½ month rule." The tax-free distribution reduces the shareholder's basis in the shares. The shareholder's right to receive tax-free distributions out of previously taxed undistributed taxable income is a personal right that cannot be transferred to another person in any manner, even by death (Treas. Regs. Secs. 1.1375-4(e) and 1.1375.6(a)(4)).

Example: Assume that both the corporation and shareholder Cohen are on a fiscal year ending August 31, and that for the electing corporation's taxable year ending August 31, 19X1, Cohen's share of UTI is $14,000. Any cash distributions up to $14,000 made to Cohen by the corporation during the period September 1, 19X1, through November 15, 19X1, will be treated by Cohen as a tax-free distribution of UTI and will reduce Cohen's basis in the shares owned.

Distributions in excess of a stockholder's share

of UTI for a taxable year made in the first 2½ months after close of the year will next be treated as a distribution out of the stockholder's share of taxable income for the year in which the distributions are made. Thus, if Cohen's share of UTI for the corporation's taxable year ending August 31, 19X1, is $14,000, and if during the period September 1 through November 15, 19X1, the corporation distributes $18,000 to Cohen, the first $14,000 is considered to be a tax-free distribution of UTI for the year ending August 31, 19X1 and the remainder is considered to be a distribution of taxable income of the year ending August 31, 19X2 (assuming Cohen's share of taxable income is at least $4,000 in the later year).

After a 2½ month period has elapsed, following the close of the corporation's taxable year, any undistributed taxable income will become known as previously taxed income. Treas. Reg. Sec. 1.1375-4(b) explains that PTI may be distributed tax free only after all current earnings and profits for the year of distribution have first been distributed. Furthermore, PTI may be distributed tax free to the shareholders only *after* it has been included in gross income on the shareholder's personal tax return. As a result, if the corporation and the shareholder are on different fiscal years, in some cases a tax-free PTI distribution may be made only in the shareholder's fiscal year beginning after the close of the year in which the distribution was made.

Example: To illustrate distributions from UTI and PTI, assume again that stockholder Cohen's share of UTI for the electing corporation's taxable year ending August 31, 19X1, was $14,000. Cohen also has a fiscal year ending August 31. During the period September 1 through November 15, 19X1, cash distributions of $8,000 were made to Cohen. On November 16, 19X1, the remaining $6,000 of Cohen's UTI becomes previously taxed income. If $6,000 were distributed to Cohen on November 20, 19X1, it would *not* be considered a tax-free distribution of UTI from the immediately preceding year nor a tax-free distribution of PTI but would be considered a distribution of net taxable income of the taxable year ending August 31, 19X2 (assuming that Cohen's share of taxable income for that year was at least $6,000).

Thus, if there were no further distributions and if Cohen's share of net taxable income for the corporation's fiscal year ending August 31, 19X2, were $10,000, the $6,000 distribution on November 20, 19X1, would be a distribution of current taxable income and Cohen's share of UTI for the year ending August 31, 19X2, would be $4,000. Cohen would still have PTI of $6,000, representing income that was taxed to Cohen for the year ending August 31, 19X1.

If, however, the distribution on November 20, 19X1, were $11,000, Cohen could treat $10,000 as a distribution of taxable income for the current year ending August 31, 19X2, and would treat $1,000 as a distribution from PTI, assuming that current earnings and profits of the corporation do not exceed its taxable income for the year. Thus, for the corporation's year ending August 31, 19X2, Cohen would have no constructive dividend and on that date would have $5,000 of previously taxed income.

As in the case of UTI, during the 2½ month period after the close of the corporation's taxable year, the right to receive a tax-free distribution from PTI is a personal right belonging only to the person to whom the income was previously taxed, and this right may not be transferred to another taxpayer by any method. The corporation must keep detailed records showing each shareholder's PTI. The inability to transfer rights to receive previously taxed income is a major disadvantage of a Subchapter S election because earnings may be taxed at an effective rate of more than 100 percent. For example, if an unmarried shareholder with a marginal tax rate of 70 percent is allocated UTI of $10,000, the shareholder must pay a tax of $7,000 on the UTI. If the UTI is not subsequently distributed and if the taxpayer later dies and the corporate earnings are distributed to the taxpayer's beneficiaries in a subsequent year, the distribution of the $10,000 may be taxed again at a rate of up to 70 percent. Certainly this suggests that current earnings should be distributed in full whenever possible.

OTHER CASH DISTRIBUTIONS

From the above illustrations we can see that the timing and amount of dividend distributions is a crucial element in the taxation of Subchapter S corporations and their shareholders. We shall now examine additional dividend problems, limiting our discussion to distributions in money only and to cases in which there are no long-term capital gain distributions. In later sections of this chapter, we shall discuss situations in which these two assumptions are not valid.

Cash distributions when current earnings and profits exceed taxable income

A Subchapter S corporation, like a regular corporation, may have current earnings and profits in excess of its taxable income. For example, interest received on tax-exempt bonds would not affect taxable income but would create earnings and profits. Similarly, the excess of percentage depletion over cost depletion is not deductible in computing earnings and profits. If the corporation does have current earnings and profits larger than its taxable income, cash distributions made in excess of taxable income are deemed to be out of the excess earnings and profits (and are, therefore, taxable) before they are treated as distributions of PTI.[11] (Section 1377(d), however, provides that for the sole purpose of determining whether a distribution constitutes a distribution of PTI, the current earnings and profits may be reduced by the excess of accelerated depreciation over straight-line depreciation, which is disallowed under Sec. 312(k) in computing current earnings and profits.) Any distributions attributable to the excess of current earnings and profits are subject to the dividend exclusion.

Example: Suppose that shareholder Li had PTI of $10,000 and UTI of $16,000 on January 1, 19X1, the first day of the taxable year of an electing corporation. The only distribution to Li in 19X1 was $18,000 cash on September 1. The corporation's taxable income for 19X1 was $30,000, of which Li's share was $15,000. Because the corporation had tax-exempt interest, however, its current earnings and profits for 19X1 were $34,000, of which Li's proportionate share was $17,000.

Of the $18,000 distributed to Li on September 1, $15,000 is treated as ordinary income not subject to the dividend exclusion. The next $2,000 is attributed to the excess of current earnings and profits over taxable income and is treated by Li as a regular dividend subject to the dividend exclusion of $100. The remaining $1,000 distribution is a distribution of previously taxed income.

Cash dividends in excess of PTI

The amount of a taxpayer's PTI is explained in Sec. 1375(d) as constructive dividends for all prior years, less any deductions for net operating losses and less any amounts previously distributed tax free under Sec. 1375(d). Treas. Reg. Sec. 1.1375-4(g) states that if dis-

---

[11]See *Benderoff* v. *United States,* 398 F.2d 132 (CCA-8, 1968).

9

9

tributions attributed to PTI exceed the shareholder's PTI, the excess is considered to be a distribution of the corporation's earnings and profits of prior years. Distributions from earnings and profits of prior years are ordinary dividends, subject to the dividend exclusion.

Example: Assume that a corporation has accumulated $20,000 in earnings and profits before it became a Subchapter S corporation. On November 1, 19X1, when it made a cash distribution of $80,000, of which $40,000 was shareholder Garcia's share, it had previously taxed income of $42,000 of which Garcia's share was $21,000. The corporation's taxable income and current earnings and profits for the year ending December 31, 19X1, were $30,000, of which Garcia's share was $15,000.

Garcia's distribution of $40,000 is treated as follows:

First $15,000 is out of current taxable income, fully taxable and not subject to dividend exclusion.
Next $21,000 is tax-free return of PTI.
Next $4,000 is ordinary dividend, subject to the dividend exclusion.

Dividends in excess of accumulated earnings and profits

If distributions exceed the total current earnings and profits, PTI, and accumulated earnings and profits, they are considered a nontaxable return of the shareholder's basis in the stock. After the taxpayer's basis has been recovered, all further distributions are treated by the shareholder as capital gain.

If the corporation and the shareholder are on different fiscal years, the shareholder may receive distributions the exact character of which cannot be determined until a later time, when the corporation's fiscal year ends.

Example: Assume that a Subchapter S corporation has a fiscal year ending March 31, 19X2. On November 1, 19X1, the corporation distributed $60,000 to shareholders. The sole shareholder, Ms. Thai, must assume that this is a distribution out of current earnings and profits and report the entire amount as gross income on her tax return for calendar year 19X1. If, however, the taxable income and current earnings and profits of the corporation for the year ending March 31, 19X2, are only $40,000, Thai must file an amended return for

19X1 and show the $60,000 as properly being $40,000 from current earnings and profits (with the balance being from accumulated earnings and profits, distribution of PTI, and so on).

PROPERTY DISTRIBUTIONS

Distributions of noncash property by an electing small business corporation are treated far differently from cash distributions. Most of the special rules concerning property dividends by Subchapter S corporations are found in Sec. 1373.

1. Certain rules of Sec. 301 that apply to property distributions by regular corporations also apply to those made by Subchapter S corporations. For example, the amount of a property distribution is deemed to be the fair market value of the property at the date of the distribution, and that value also becomes the basis of the property to the shareholder. Under Sec. 312(a), the corporation's earnings and profits are reduced by the adjusted basis of the property distributed. The same rules, and exceptions to the rules, relating to nonrecognition of gain on distributions of property[12] apply to both regular corporations and Subchapter S corporations.

2. A property dividend is never considered to be a tax-free distribution of UTI, even though the distribution is made within the first 2½ months after the close of the corporation's taxable year. Nor is a property dividend ever considered to be out of PTI (Treas. Reg. Sec. 1.1375-4(b)).

3. If cash distributions are made that are properly considered to be from current earnings and profits, the current earnings and profits will be allocated to the cash dividends before they are allocated to any property distributed (Treas. Reg. Sec. 1.1373-1(d) and (e)).

Example: Assume that an electing corporation has taxable income and current earnings and profits of $36,000 for the taxable year and that during the year it distributed property with a fair value of $20,000 and an adjusted basis of $8,000. In addition, in the last month of the taxable year, the corporation distributed a cash dividend of $6,000. The earnings and profits are first allocated to the fully taxable cash dividend of $6,000, leaving $30,000 to be allocated between the property distribution and the UTI.

---

[12]For example, in Secs. 311, 341(f), 453(d), and 312(c)(3).

4. Distributions of property during the current taxable year do not reduce the amount of UTI treated as a constructive dividend at the end of the year.

Example: Assume that a corporation's taxable income (and current earnings and profits) for the year is $12,000 and that its accumulated earnings and profits at the start of the taxable year were $40,000. During the year, the corporation distributed property with a fair value of $8,000 and a basis of $5,000 and paid no cash dividends. The shareholders are deemed to have received a property dividend of $8,000.

5. *Current* earnings and profits in excess of actual *money* distributions are allocated between any property distributions and the constructive distribution of UTI in proportion to their relative amounts.

Example: In the preceding example, the amount of *current* earnings and profits (CE&P) allocated to the property distribution and to UTI will be $4,800 and $7,200, respectively, computed as follows:

Property:

$$\frac{\$8,000 \text{ (Prop. value)}}{\$20,000} \times \$12,000 \text{ (CE\&P)} = \$4,800$$
(Prop. value + UTI)

UTI:

$$\frac{\$12,000 \text{ (UTI)}}{\$20,000} \times \$12,000 \text{ (CE\&P)} = \$7,200$$
(Prop. value + UTI)

6. If accumulated earnings and profits of prior years are sufficient to cover both the portion of the *distribution of property* that is not out of current earnings and profits and that portion of the *constructive distribution* that is not out of current earnings and profits, both distributions will be taxable as dividends (Treas. Reg. Sec. 1.1373-1(g)(Example 4)).

Thus, of the $8,000 property distribution in the example above, $4,800 is deemed to be from current earnings and profits and the remaining $3,200 is deemed to be out of accumulated earnings and profits at the beginning of the taxable year. Similarly, the constructive dividend of $12,000 (the entire amount of taxable income) is deemed to consist of $7,200 of current earnings and profits, and $4,800 from earnings and profits of prior years. In summary, the distribution of the property results in the following for the year.

Taxable property dividend from:

Current earnings and profits	$4,800	
Earnings and profits of prior years	3,200	$8,000

Constructive dividend from:

Current earnings and profits	$7,200	
Earnings and profits of prior years	4,800	12,000

Although the property's current value is used to determine whether distributions are covered by current earnings and profits or by accumulated earnings and profits, the property distribution reduces earnings and profits by only the adjusted basis of the property distributed. An analysis of the corporation's earnings and profits in the above example shows the following:

Balance,	beginning of year	$40,000
Add:	current earnings and profits for year	12,000
Deduct:	UTI taxed to shareholder	(12,000)
Deduct:	basis of property distributed	(5,000)
Balance,	end of year	$35,000

7. If earnings and profits are inadequate to cover both the property dividend and the constructive dividend, a portion of the property dividend will be treated as a return of capital, and part of the constructive dividend will be disregarded. This is true because under Treas. Reg. Sec. 1.316-2, accumulated earnings and profits (in contrast to current earnings and profits) are allocated among distributions (both cash and noncash) in the chronological sequence in which distributions are made. Because the constructive distribution of UTI is deemed to have been made at the close of the corporation's taxable year, the UTI is the last distribution to be allocated accumulated earnings and profits.

Example: Assume the following facts:

Taxable income (and current earnings and profits) for year	$12,000
Accumulated earnings and profits on first day of taxable year	2,500
Property dividend (fair value)	8,000
Adjusted basis of property distributed	5,000

Again, current earnings and profits will be allocated in proportion to the value of the property dividend and the amount of the UTI (as illustrated above), with $4,800 being allocated to the property distribution and $7,200 being allocated to UTI. The property distribution will thus be considered as follows.

From current earnings and
profits $4,800 (taxable)
From prior years' earnings
and profits   2,500 (taxable)
Recovery of basis (or capital gain) 700

If the shareholder's basis for the stock is $700 or more, the $700 excess of value over allocated earnings and profits will be treated as a recovery of cost. If the basis is less than $700, the $700 distribution will be treated as a recovery of basis until the entire basis has been recovered, with any excess being treated as capital gain. Thus, if the shareholder's basis in the property were $400, there would be a $300 capital gain.

Although the constructive dividend is measured as $12,000, only that portion out of current earnings and profits ($7,200) will be taxable because there is no balance of earnings and profits to assign to the remaining $4,800. Thus, the $4,800 has no tax effect.

FLOW-THROUGH OF NET OPERATING LOSS

As previously noted, an important reason for a corporation's electing to be taxed under the provisions of Subchapter S is that a net operating loss may, within limits, be allowed as a deduction from gross income of the shareholders of the corporation. Under Sec. 1374 (b), the deduction is considered to be attributable to a trade or business carried on by the shareholder for the stockholder's taxable year in which, or with which, the taxable year of the corporation ends. Any operating loss flow-through may also be carried back or forward as part of the shareholder's own personal net operating loss deduction. This is especially important when owners foresee that losses will be incurred during the first few years of the corporation. In that situation, the owners might wish to operate as an electing corporation in order to get the benefits of the loss flow-through, then terminate the election when operations become profitable. Even an existing corporation may find that a one- or two-year period of operation as a Subchapter S corporation is desirable when a temporary loss situation can be foreseen.

Computing the net operating loss

The net operating loss (NOL) for a Subchapter S corporation is computed in the same general way as it is for a regular corporation. The principal technical difference, under Sec. 1374, is that the Subchapter S corporation is not entitled to the special (strictly corporate) deductions of Secs. 243 through 248 (the most important being the dividends-received deduction), except for amortization of organization costs. Thus, if an electing corporation had dividends received of $5,000, other gross income of $510,000, and routine deductions of $540,000, its net operating loss would be $25,000.

Allocation of net operating loss to shareholders

Each stockholder's share of net operating loss is computed in a manner completely different from that used to allocate UTI. Under Treas. Reg. Sec. 1.1374-1 (b)(3), the corporation's daily net operating loss is determined by dividing the net operating loss by the number of days in the taxable year. This daily operating loss is then allocated on a pro rata basis to each share outstanding on each day. A shareholder's total portion of the corporation's net operating loss is the sum of the amounts allocated to each day of the year. The following example illustrates the net operating loss allocation.

Example: Assume that on January 1, 19X1, Early owned 10,000 of the 100,000 outstanding shares of common stock of S Corporation. Early's basis in the shares was $80,000. On May 27, 19X1, Early sold 2,500 shares to Late, who did not terminate the election. For the taxable year ending December 31, 19X1, S Corporation had a net operating loss of $54,750.

The operating loss is deemed to have been incurred at the rate of $150 per day ($54,750 ÷ 365 days). Early's share of the loss is $4,654, computed as follows:

Jan. 1 through May 26:

$$\frac{10,000 \text{ sh.}}{100,000 \text{ sh.}} \times 146 \text{ days} \times \$150/\text{day} = \$2,190$$

May 27 through Dec. 31:

$$\frac{7,500 \text{ sh.}}{100,000 \text{ sh.}} \times 219 \text{ days} \times \$150/\text{day} = \underline{2,464}$$

$$\text{Total} \quad \underline{\$4,654}$$

Late's share of the net operating loss is $821, computed as follows:

May 27 through Dec. 31:

$$\frac{2,500 \text{ sh.}}{100,000 \text{ sh.}} \times 219 \text{ days} \times \$150/\text{day} = \underline{\$821}$$

The daily loss allocation procedure is used to prevent trafficking in stock of loss corporations that might occur if losses were allocated on the basis of the number of shares held by each shareholder on the last day of the corporation's taxable year.

LIMITATION ON SHAREHOLDER'S DEDUCTIBLE LOSS

Limitations under Subchapter S

Section 1374(c)(2) stipulates that the shareholder's portion of the net operating loss for any taxable year is limited to the sum of (1) the adjusted basis of the shareholder's stock at the close of the taxable year of the corporation (before any adjustment resulting from the current year's loss) and (2) the adjusted basis (before any adjustment resulting from the current year's loss) as of the close of the corporation's taxable year of any indebtedness of the corporation to the shareholder. The debt must be the *direct* debt of the corporation to the shareholder, not indirect debt.[13]

The net operating loss is used first to reduce the shareholder's basis in stock, then the basis of debt. If the net operating loss exceeds the shareholder's basis in both stock and debt, the excess may not be deducted in any year (Treas. Reg. Sec. 1.1374-1(b)(4)(i)) even though the basis is increased in a future year. (Obviously, shareholders faced with this situation might consider the advisability of increasing their investment in the corporation in order to gain the benefit of the net operating loss deduction.) If a net operating loss has eliminated the shareholder's basis in the debt of the corporation, gross income will result if any part of the debt is subsequently repaid.[14] If the basis was eliminated on a debt that was an open account, the later repayment will result in ordinary income;[15] if the debt was evidenced by a formal note, capital gain may result.[16]

If the shareholder has sold or otherwise disposed of any shares during the taxable year, the basis of the shares disposed of on the day before the day of disposition is substituted for the year-end basis of stock in determining the limitation on the deductible loss. Similarly, if the shareholder is no longer a shareholder at the close of the corporation's taxable year, the basis

of any indebtedness of the corporation to the shareholder is determined as of the last day in the taxable year on which the shareholder had shares in the corporation (Sec. 1374(c)(2)).

Limitations under the at-risk provisions

A Subchapter S corporation is not only subject to the special limitations on deductibility of net operating losses under Sec. 1374, but it is also subject to the general at-risk provisions of Sec. 465. The details of the at-risk rules are beyond the scope of this chapter, but we shall review a few of the provisions that particularly involve Subchapter S shareholders.

Before 1979, only certain specified activities were subject to the at-risk provisions. A taxpayer's activity with respect to each film or videotape, Sec. 1245 property, property leased or held for leasing, farm, oil or gas property, and geothermal property was a separate activity subject to the at-risk rules.

Under Sec. 465(c)(2), however, all of a Subchapter S corporation's activities of a particular type (for example, all farming activities) were treated as one activity, and the shareholder's interest in the electing corporation was treated as a single activity to the extent that the corporation was engaged in that activity.

The pre-1979 rules still apply, but in addition, for taxable years beginning after 1978, the at-risk limitations on deductible losses were extended under Sec. 465(c)(3)(a) and (b) to include all trade or business activities not previously covered (except certain real estate holding activities and certain equipment leasing activities by closely held corporations). The newly covered activities must be aggregated and treated as one activity if the trade or business activity is carried on by an electing small business corporation and 65 percent or more of the loss for the taxable year is allocable to persons who actively participate in the management of the trade or business. The Code also provides that the Secretary of the Treasury shall provide regulations under which the covered activities added after 1978 shall be aggregated or treated as separate activities.

The proposed regulations under Sec. 465 make it clear that the at-risk provisions apply at both the corporate and the shareholder level. Therefore, losses from an activity may be deducted by the corporation only to the extent that the corporation is at risk in the activity, and each shareholder will be allowed a loss deduction only to the extent that the shareholder is at risk in the activity (Proposed Reg. Sec. 1.465-10(a)). The amount at risk by the corporation is determined in the same way as that of any other taxpayer, except that an

13*Ruth M. Prasker,* 59 TC 172 (192).

14*George W. Wiebusch,* 487 F.2d 515 (CCA-8, 1973).

15Rev. Rul. 68-537, 1968-2 C.B. 372.

16*Joe M. Smith,* 424 F.2d 219 (CCA-9, 1970); see also Rev. Rul. 64-162, 1964-1 CB 304.

amount borrowed by the corporation from its shareholders may increase the corporation's amount at risk in spite of the fact that the shareholders have an interest in the activity other than that of a creditor.

The amount considered at risk by a shareholder in an electing small business corporation is determined in essentially the same way as the at-risk amounts for other affected taxpayers under Sec. 465(b). The at-risk amount consists of the cash contributed by the taxpayer, the adjusted basis of any property contributed to the activity, and any amount borrowed for use in the activity with respect to which the taxpayer has personal liability or has pledged property (other than property used in the activity) as security for a nonrecourse loan. In addition, under Proposed Reg. Sec. 1.465-10, the shareholder's at-risk amount includes only direct debt of the corporation to the shareholder. The amount at risk is reduced by any loss that is allowed as a deduction with respect to the activity. For a Subchapter S corporation, the at-risk amount is increased by the constructive dividend included in gross income of the shareholder, and is decreased by tax-free distributions of UTI or PTI treated as return of capital by the shareholder.

Under the at-risk provisions of Sec. 465, a loss not allowed in a taxable year—because of the at-risk limitations—may be carried over to future years and allowed as a deduction in those years to the extent that the taxpayer has an amount at risk.

Obviously, the at-risk provisions raise complex questions for the shareholders of an electing corporation. For example, if the corporation is carrying on activities that are subject to the at-risk rules and other activities that are not subject to those provisions, is the taxpayer required to allocate the at-risk amounts between those activities? If so, how? Another unresolved question concerns the relationship between the at-risk limitations and the special net operating loss limitations for Subchapter S corporations under Sec. 1374. For example, under Sec. 1374, losses in excess of the *basis in stock* and debt are permanently disallowed, while under Sec. 465, disallowed losses may be carried to future years and deducted when there is an amount at risk. Presumably, the more stringent rules of Sec. 1374 would prevail in any situation in which they conflict with the rules of Sec. 465.

The application of the at-risk provisions at both the corporate and the shareholder level may actually provide a benefit to the shareholder. For example, if a corporation suffers a loss in excess of its amount at risk in an activity, the loss is disallowed and does not flow through to the shareholders. If the corporation subse-

quently increases its at-risk amount, the loss will be allowed to the corporation at that time. On the other hand, if the loss were allowed at the corporate level and flowed through to the shareholders, the shareholders might never be able to deduct the loss because of the Sec. 1374 limitation.

LONG-TERM CAPITAL GAINS

The excess of an electing corporation's net long-term capital gains over net short-term capital losses passes through to the shareholders under the rules of Sec. 1375(a). A shareholder's dividend (both actual and constructive) from an electing corporation is treated as long-term capital gain to the extent of the shareholder's pro rata share of the corporation's net capital gain for the year. The net capital gain, however, may not exceed the corporation's taxable income for the year. Thus, any operating loss of the corporation for the taxable year reduces the amount of net capital gain that might otherwise pass through.[17] In addition, Sec. 1375(a)(3) stipulates that the electing corporation's long-term capital gain for a taxable year is reduced by the amount of tax on preferences imposed under Sec. 56 and the capital gains tax under Sec. 1378(a), both of which will be discussed later in this chapter.

A shareholder's pro rata share of the net capital gain is the same as the pro rata share of all taxable dividends paid out of current earnings and profits. The following example illustrates the capital gains flow-through rules.

Example: Assume the following facts:

Corporation's net operating income for calendar year 19X1	$100,000
Net long-term capital gain	30,000
Net short-term capital loss	(10,000)
Taxable income and current earnings and profits	120,000
Cash distributions allocable to current earnings and profits	50,000
Shareholder Coda's percentage of stock ownership at end of taxable year	25%

The cash distributions allocable to current earnings and profits ($50,000) are deemed to include long-term capital gain of $8,333 [$20,000/$120,000 × $50,000], and ordinary

---

[17]See *Bryne v. Commissioner*, 361 F.2d 939 (CCA-7, 1968).

income of $41,667 [$100,000/$120,000 × $50,000]. Similarly, the constructive dividend (UTI) of $70,000 includes long-term capital gain of $11,667 [$20,000/$120,000 × $70,000] and ordinary income of $58,333 [$100,000/$120,000 × $70,000].

Because shareholder Coda owns 25 percent of the stock on the last day of the taxable year, she will report capital gains of $5,000, including $2,083 of the cash dividend and $2,917 of the UTI.

If a corporation had an operating loss of $12,000 and a net capital gain of $20,000, its net taxable income would be $8,000 and that would also be the amount of net capital gain that would flow through to the shareholders.

Only the excess of long-term capital gain over short-term capital losses flows through to the stockholders. The component items entering into the excess do not flow through. Thus, if an electing corporation has Sec. 1231 gains on the sale of business property and no capital losses, that gain would flow through to the shareholders as a long-term capital gain rather than as a Sec. 1231 gain (Treas. Reg. Sec. 1.1375-1 (d)). If the corporation has only a net short-term gain, it enters into computation of the corporation's net taxable income and current earnings and profits, and does not flow through to the shareholders as a separate item.

THE CAPITAL GAINS TAX ON SUBCHAPTER S CORPORATIONS

Although Subchapter S corporations are, in general, exempt from income taxes, Sec. 1378 imposes a tax on certain capital gains in order to discourage corporations from electing to be taxed under Subchapter S for short periods in order to secure the benefits of the long-term gain flow-through.[18] The special capital gains "penalty" tax is imposed under Sec. 1.1378(a) if:

1. The net capital gain of the corporation exceeds $25,000 for the taxable year;
2. The net capital gain of the corporation exceeds 50 percent of its taxable income for the year, *and*
3. The taxable income of the corporation for the year exceeds $25,000.

Under Sec. 1378(b), the amount of the tax is the lower of the following.

18See S. Report No. 1007, 89th Cong., 2nd Sess. 6(1966).

1. The capital gain alternative rate (28 percent) applied to the amount by which the net capital gain exceeds $25,000; *or*
2. The regular corporate rates applied to the Subchapter S taxable income for the year.

Sec. 1378(c), however, provides that the capital gains tax does not apply if:

1. The election of the corporation to be taxed under Subchapter S has been in effect for the three immediately preceding taxable years; *or*
2. The electing corporation has been in existence for fewer than four taxable years and the election to be taxed under Subchapter S has been in effect for each of the corporation's taxable years.

To further complicate matters, however, Sec. 1378(c) stipulates that the last two exceptions detailed above will be ignored and the corporate capital gains tax will apply to capital gains on specified property that was acquired by the electing corporation within three years before the first day of the tax year in which the property is sold. The property involved is property that was acquired from another corporation (except a corporation that was an electing Subchapter S corporation throughout the preceding three-year period or throughout its existence if less than three years) in a transaction resulting in a carryover basis to the Subchapter S corporation—for instance, in a transfer of assets to a controlled corporation.

The following example illustrates the computation of the capital gains penalty tax.

Example: From 19X1 through 19X5, Ace Corporation operated as a regular corporation. For the taxable year beginning January 1, 19X6, the corporation elected to be taxed under Subchapter S. The corporation's items of income and loss for the year are:

Net operating income	$30,000
Sec. 1231 gains	60,000
Short-term capital losses	(10,000)

Because Ace Corporation does not meet any one of the tests for exemption, it is subject to the special capital gains tax. The first $25,000 of capital gain is exempt, so the capital gains tax will be $7,000 ($25,000 × 28 percent), because this amount is less than the regular corporate tax would be. (The effect of the tax on capital gains distributions to shareholders and on the corporation's earnings and profits will be discussed later in this chapter.)

MINIMUM TAX ON PREFERENCES

A Subchapter S corporation is normally not subject to the minimum tax on preference items. Under Sec. 58(d)(1), items of preference flow through to the shareholders and are apportioned on a daily basis to shares outstanding in the same way that the corporation's net operating loss is apportioned. If, however, a capital gains penalty tax is imposed under Sec. 1378, the corporation is also subject to the preference tax on that part of the excess of long-term capital gains over short-term capital loss that is subject to the capital gains tax. The capital gains tax preference item that results at the corporate level is not treated as an item of tax preference to the shareholders of the corporation.

The amount of preference item resulting from capital gains is supposedly clarified in Prop. Treas. Reg. Sec. 1.58-4(c)(2); which reads as follows:

(2) The capital gains item of tax preference of an electing small business corporation subject to the tax imposed by section 1378 is the excess of the amount of tax computed under section 1378(b)(2) over the sum of

(i) The amount of tax that would be computed under section 1378(b)(2) if the lesser of the following amounts were excluded:

(a) That portion of the net section 1202 gain of the corporation described in section 1378(b)(1), or

(b) That portion of the net section 1201 gain to which section 1378(c) applies, and

(ii) The amount of tax imposed under section 1378 divided by the sum of the normal tax rate and the surtax rate under section 11 for the taxable year.

The general application of this "clarification" may be illustrated by applying the computational process to the facts of Ace Corporation in the preceding example, in which the following data are pertinent:

Net operating income	$30,000
Net Sec. 1201 gain	50,000
Sec. 1378 tax	7,000

(1) Total tax on taxable income of the corporation, computed as though the corporation were a regular corporation (regular tax on $80,000) $18,750

(2) Less, tax on all taxable income of the corporation except the net 1201 gains subject to the preference tax, computed as though the corporation were a regular corporation (tax on $30,000)   5,250

(3) Regular tax applicable to net Sec. 1201 gains $13,500

(4) Less tax paid on Sec. 1201 gains under Sec. 1378   7,000

(5) "Savings" on preferred treatment of Sec. 1201 gain $6,500

(6) Amount of preference item = $6,500/0.46 $14,130

The corporation's preference tax is 15 percent of the preference item in excess of the larger of: (1) $10,000, or (2) the amount of tax paid under Sec. 1378. Thus, the preference tax on Ace Corporation is 0.15($14,130 − $10,000), or $620.

EFFECT OF CAPITAL GAINS TAX AND PREFERENCE TAX ON DIVIDENDS TO SHAREHOLDERS AND ON EARNINGS AND PROFITS

Example: In the example above, Ace Corporation had the following items for the taxable year ending December 31, 19X6:

Net operating income	$30,000
Net Sec. 1201 gains	50,000
Taxable income and current E & P	80,000
Sec. 1378 capital gains tax	7,000
Sec. 56 tax on preferences	620

Assume further that on January 1, 19X6, the corporation's accumulated earnings and profits were $60,000. During 19X6, the corporation paid cash dividends of $40,000, of which $10,000 was distributed to shareholder Coda who owned 25 percent of the corporation's stock throughout 19X6.

As previously pointed out, the amount of long-term capital gains flowing through to shareholders is reduced by the corporation's capital gains penalty tax under Sec. 1238 and by the tax on preferences under Sec. 56. Consequently, only $42,380 ($50,000 − $7,000 − $620) will be treated as long-term capital gain by the shareholders. Under Sec. 1377(b), any amounts not allowable as a deduction in computing taxable income do not reduce the corporation's *current* earnings and profits, but nevertheless are deductible from the corporation's *accumulated* earnings and profits. Because the capital gains penalty tax is not a deductible item in arriving at the corporation's net income, it does not reduce current earnings and profits but will be deducted from accumulated earnings and profits.[19]

Thus, shareholder Coda will treat her cash distribution of $10,000 as consisting of $4,238 (10% × $42,380) of long-term capital gains; $3,762 ($8,000 − $4,238) of ordinary dividends from current earnings and profits; and $2,000 (10% × $20,000) of dividends from accumulated earnings and profits.

The corporation's accumulated earnings and profits at the end of 19X6 are $12,380, computed as follows:

Balance, January 1, 19X6	$40,000
Current earnings and profits and taxable income	80,000
Distributions from current earnings and profits	(80,000)
Distributions from accumulated earnings and profits	(20,000)
Capital gains tax	(7,000)
Tax on preferences	(620)
Balance, December 31, 19X6	$12,380

Although any capital gains tax paid under Sec. 1378 or any preference tax under Sec. 56 reduces neither the corporation's taxable income for the year nor its current earnings and profits, any such amounts are deducted from taxable income along with cash distributions in computing UTI for the year per Sec. 1373(c). Thus, if the corporation had $20,000 of taxable income for one year, paid a capital gains tax of $600, and made cash distributions of $16,000 out of current earnings and profits, its UTI would be only $3,400.

SHAREHOLDER'S BASIS IN SUBCHAPTER S CORPORATION STOCK

The effects of various transactions and events on the basis of stock owned by a shareholder in a Subchapter S corporation have been described throughout this chapter. Because of the importance of the basis computation (for such purposes as determining gain or loss on sale, the amount of deductible flow-through loss, and the loss on worthless stock), the rules for determining basis are summarized here. The burden of proof is on each stockholder to establish the basis of his or her stock and debt.[20] In general, the initial basis of stock (or debt) of an electing small business corporation is determined in the same manner as the basis of stock in a regular corporation.[21] As you have seen, however, a number of modifications subsequently arise owing to the corporation's status as an electing small business corporation.

First, the shareholder's basis in stock is increased by the UTI included in the shareholder's gross income. Because UTI is deemed to be distributed on the last day of the corporation's tax year, the shares owned by the shareholder on that date (and *only* the shares owned on that date) are affected by this adjustment.

Similarly, the shareholder's portion of the electing corporation's net operating loss reduces the basis of the shareholder's stock (but not below zero). If the shareholder has more than one block of stock, the net operating loss deduction is allocated to the shares on the daily basis previously described. Under the provisions of Treas. Reg. Sec. 1.1376-2(a)(2)(i), if the amount of basis reduction applicable to any share exceeds the basis of that share, the excess is then allocated as a reduction of each other share owned, in proportion to the remaining adjusted basis of each other share. If the shareholder's portion of operating loss for a year is greater than the adjusted basis of all shares owned, the excess will be applied to reduce the basis of any indebtedness of the corporation to the shareholder. If there is more than one debt from the corporation to the shareholder, each debt is reduced by an amount proportionate to the ratio of that debt's basis to the total basis of all debts (Treas. Reg. Sec. 1.1376-2(b)(3)).

Under Treas. Reg. Sec. 1.1375-6(a)(1), tax-free distributions received by the shareholder out of the immediately preceding year's UTI reduce the basis of shares owned. Treas. Reg. Sec. 1.1375-4(a) allows similar treatment for all distributions of PTI. Distributions treated as return of capital because they exceed current and accumulated earnings and profits also reduce the basis of the shares (Sec. 301(c)(2)).

OTHER CONSIDERATIONS FOR SUBCHAPTER S CORPORATIONS

In the preceding pages, we have discussed the major questions surrounding the tax treatment of Subchapter S corporations. A number of other frequently encountered problems are worthy of mention.

[19]See Rev. Rul. 73-590, 1973-2 C.B. 313.

[20]*George T. Wise,* T.C. Memo Dec. 1978-38.
[21]*Joe E. Borg,* 50 TC 257(1968).

Qualified retirement plans

Although the general rules governing retirement plans established by regular corporations also apply to Subchapter S corporations, restrictions have been instituted by Sec. 1379 to prevent abuses. For example, contributions to a qualified plan made on behalf of a shareholder-employee (an officer or employee who directly and constructively owns more than 5 percent of the outstanding stock on any day of the tax year) in excess of $7,500, or 15 percent of the shareholder-employee's covered compensation for the year, whichever is lower, must be included in gross income of the shareholder-employee. Also, forfeitures under a profit-sharing plan may not be allocated to shareholder-employees.

Investment tax credit

Under Treas. Reg. Sec. 1.47-4(b), when a regular corporation elects to be taxed under Subchapter S, the election is treated as a disposition of property for purposes of determining whether an investment credit previously taken must be recaptured *unless* the corporation and the shareholders agree to assume joint and several liability for the tax arising from later recapture from premature disposition.

Section 48(a) provides that the investment tax credit on assets bought by a Subchapter S corporation passes through to the shareholders and is allocated on the basis of the number of shares owned on the last day of the corporation's tax year. If an asset is subsequently prematurely disposed of, the tax liability on recapture also must be paid by the shareholders, as specified in Treas. Reg. Sec. 1.47-4(a)(1). In addition, a little-publicized provision in Treas. Reg. Sec. 1.47-4(a)(2)(ii) holds that if a taxpayer disposes of more than one-third of the interest that the shareholder held in the corporation at the time the credit flowed through, credit recapture by the shareholder will be triggered.

SUMMARY

Clearly, the Subchapter S election offers taxpayers opportunities for tax planning in many situations. A newly formed corporation can often anticipate operating losses during the first years of its activities. The Subchapter S election permits shareholders to recognize, within limits, these losses. After the loss period, the shareholders may void the election and return to regular corporation status. If the shareholders are in low personal tax rate brackets, they may wish to use the Subchapter S provisions for a profitable corporation to secure the advantage of the corporate form without the penalty of the federal corporate income tax. In other cases, a corporation may be faced with relatively large capital gains and the shareholders may seek to avoid double taxation on these gains by electing Subchapter S status so that the gains will flow through to the shareholders. (The Subchapter S election also provides a vehicle for allocating income to family members by having bona fide gifts of stock made to those members.)

On the other hand, the Subchapter S vehicle has pitfalls. As we have seen, even though undistributed income is taxed to each shareholder, and the shareholder has a right to withdraw this PTI tax free at a later date, the right to receive tax-free distributions of PTI may not be transferred to another. Thus, if a taxpayer dies before such distributions are made, the taxpayer will have paid a tax on the earnings and the beneficiary of the taxpayer's interest will also have taxable income if the PTI is later distributed. In addition, the distribution of property dividends may result in additional tax liability. Clearly, the Subchapter S election may safely be made for a profitable operation only if it is foreseen that all profits may be quickly distributed as cash dividends. The corporation should make annual cash distributions of all UTI if at all possible. The *caveat* is to think carefully before making a Subchapter S election.

PROBLEMS

1. In each of the following cases, indicate whether a Subchapter S election could be made or continued.
    a. Corporation A has 18 shareholders, consisting of six married couples and six single individuals.
    b. Corporation B has five shareholders, all individuals. Four of the shareholders are U.S. citizens and one is a resident alien.
    c. All the stock of Corporation C is owned by partnership XYZ, which in turn has three equal partners, all of whom are individuals.
    d. Corporation D has five shareholders. Four of them are individuals. The fifth

is the tax-exempt trust of Corporation D's qualified employee profit-sharing plan.

e. Corporation E has four shareholders, consisting of three individuals and the estate of a former shareholder who died two years ago. The estate has 16 beneficiaries to whom the assets will subsequently be distributed.

f. Corporation F has six shareholders, all individuals. Each shareholder owns 200 shares of common stock and 40 shares of $25 par, noncumulative, nonparticipating, nonvoting preferred stock.

g. Corporation G has eight shareholders. One shareholder refuses to sign an election to be taxed under Subchapter S.

h. Corporation H has four shareholders, all individuals. Corporation H owns 1,000 of the 1,200 outstanding shares of National Company, a domestic manufacturing company.

i. Icon Corporation has six shareholders, all individuals. Its gross income has averaged more than $250 million per year for several years, and its net income has been more than $50 million.

j. Corporation J, which uses the accrual method of accounting, has been taxed as a Subchapter S corporation for several years. During the current taxable year, its receipts were as follows:

Sales on account	$400,000
Cash sales	40,000
Collections on accounts	390,000
Cost of goods sold	300,000
Sales price of Sec. 1231 property	80,000
Basis of Sec. 1231 property sold	45,000
Proceeds from bank loans	100,000
Repayment of loans to bank	80,000
Interest income	1,000
Sales price of Sec. 1221 securities	20,000
Basis of Sec. 1221 securities sold	30,000

k. Corporation K has adopted a fiscal year beginning January 1. On January 1 of the current year, the corporation's shareholders included three individuals and Local Corporation. On January 9, one of the individual shareholders of Corporation K purchased from Local Corporation all the shares of Corporation K stock owned by Local.

l. Corporation L was formed on the first day of the current year and the shareholders immediately signed an election to be taxed under Subchapter S. Money paid by stock purchasers was placed in a savings account and earned $8,000 interest during the first six months of the year. At the end of that time, the money was withdrawn and used to purchase operating assets.

2. City Corporation was formed in 19X1 and operated as a regular corporation until it made a proper election to be taxed under Subchapter S for the fiscal year beginning July 1, 19X2. On that date, accumulated earnings and profits were $26,000. Richard Tam owned 25 percent of the outstanding shares on that date and Lev Uris owned 75 percent of the shares. Both Tam and Uris were on a calendar-year basis for tax reporting purposes. On November 1, 19X2, the corporation made a proportionate distribution of $12,000 to the shareholders, and on January 3, 19X3, the corporation made a proportionate cash distribution of $8,000 to the shareholders. For the fiscal year ended June 30, 19X3, the corpora-

tion had net taxable income of $32,000. Discuss the effects of all these facts on the tax situation of the corporation and each shareholder.

3. Assume the same facts as in Problem 2, above, except that the corporation's net taxable income for the year ending June 30, 19X3, was $8,000. Discuss the effects of these facts on the shareholders and the corporation.

4. Assume the same facts as in Problem 2, above, except that for the fiscal year ending June 30, 19X3, the corporation had a net operating loss of $15,000.

5. For its first taxable year beginning January 1, 19X1, Alex Corporation elected to be taxed under Subchapter S. Its two shareholders, Carnes and Doughitt, owned 200 shares and 400 shares, respectively. The basis of Carnes' shares was $31,000 and the basis of Doughitt's shares was $74,000. On April 1, 19X1, the corporation made a cash distribution of $3,000 to Carnes and $6,000 to Doughitt. Carnes sold 50 of his 200 shares to Eason for $22,000 on June 20, 19X1, and Eason did not revoke the Subchapter S election. For the year ending December 31, 19X1, the corporation had net taxable income of $24,000. Discuss the tax effects of these data on the three shareholders, each of whom uses the calendar year as a taxable year.

6. Assume the same facts as in Problem 5, above, except that the corporation reported a net operating loss of $12,000 for the year ending December 31, 19X1. Discuss the tax effects of these facts on the shareholders.

7. In its first taxable year ending December 31, 19X1, Rene Corporation reported taxable income of $16,000. Ms. Rene and Mr. Courtier each owned one-half the stock of Rene Corporation. The basis for Ms. Rene's shares was $40,000, and the basis of Courtier's shares was $42,500. On February 16, 19X2, the corporation made its first cash distribution, totaling $6,000. On July 10, 19X2, it distributed an additional $12,000. For the year ending December 31, 19X2, the corporation's taxable income was $24,000. What are the tax effects of these facts on the shareholders, assuming Rene is a Subchapter S corporation?

8. On January 1, 19X5, Etebari and Amini, who owned 300 shares and 100 shares, respectively, of the 400 outstanding shares of Etam Corporation, had UTI of $6,000 and $2,000, respectively, from the corporation's taxable year ending December 31, 19X4. In addition, Etebari had $9,000 and Amini had $3,000 of PTI from 19X2 and 19X3. Also, the corporation had earnings and profits of $40,000 accumulated before January 1, 19X2, the date on which the corporation was first taxable as a Subchapter S corporation.

On February 1, 19X5, the corporation made a proportionate distribution of $3,000 to its shareholders, and on August 1, 19X5, it distributed an additional $24,000 in cash. The corporation's taxable income for the year ending December 31, 19X5, was $12,000. How do all these facts affect the shareholders and the corporation?

9. Assume the same facts as in Problem 8, above, except that the distribution on August 1 was $12,000. How do these facts affect the shareholders and the corporation?

10. Assume the same facts as in Problem 8, above, except that the distribution on August 1, 19X5, was $48,000. How do these facts affect the shareholders and the corporation?

11. Leison Corporation elected to be taxed under Subchapter S beginning on January 1, 19X1. Before that time, the corporation had accumulated earnings and profits of $40,000. On April 15, 19X1, the corporation made a cash distribution of $10,000 to each of its two shareholders, Lee and Ellison, who owned 500 shares each of the corporation's stock. On July 10, the corporation distributed to each of the shareholders two acres of land that it had purchased three years earlier for

use as a possible business site. The land had cost $10,000, and on the date of distribution it had a fair market value of $30,000. For the year ending December 31, 19X1, the corporation had taxable income of $30,000. Discuss the effects of all these facts on the shareholders and the corporation.

12. Assume the same facts as in Problem 11, above, except that the corporation's taxable income for the year ending December 31, 19X1, had been only $6,000. How do these facts affect the shareholders and the corporation?

13. For its first taxable year, beginning January 1, 19X1, County Corporation elected to be taxed under Subchapter S. During 19X1, the corporation made no distributions and had taxable income of $20,000. On January 15, 19X2, the corporation distributed to its shareholders land with a basis of $18,000 and a fair market value of $30,000. For the year ending December 31, 19X2, the corporation had net taxable income of $8,000, and made no cash distributions. How do these facts affect the shareholders and the corporation?

14. Zaman is the sole shareholder of Zaman Corporation, which is being taxed as a Subchapter S Corporation. The basis of Zaman's shares on January 1, 19X2, was $45,000. On January 1, 19X2, Zaman Corporation has UTI of $10,000 from 19X1, PTI of $34,000 from years before 19X1, and $10,000 of accumulated earnings and profits accumulated prior to the time that the corporation began being taxed under Subchapter S. On May 10, 19X2, the corporation made a cash distribution of $16,000, and on September 1, 19X2, it distributed to Zaman land with a basis of $28,000 and a fair market value of $76,000. For 19X2, the corporation had a net operating loss of $10,000. How do all these facts affect the shareholder and the corporation?

15. For its first taxable year, ending December 31, 19X1, IPEX Corporation, a Subchapter S corporation with a sole shareholder, had taxable income of $18,000, had no transactions involving capital assets, and distributed no dividends. On March 1, 19X2, the corporation distributed a $4,000 cash dividend, and on September 18, 19X2, it distributed a $6,000 cash dividend. For the tax year ending December 31, 19X2, the corporation reported net taxable income, ignoring property transactions, of $12,000. It also had a net loss of $4,000 on Sec. 1231 asset sales and a net gain of $10,000 on the sale of long-term capital assets. On February 15, 19X3, the corporation distributed a cash dividend of $9,000. How are all these facts treated by the shareholder and the corporation?

16. Frequently a Subchapter S corporation is described as "a corporation taxed as a partnership." Discuss the ways in which this statement is correct and the ways it is incorrect.

17. Three individual partners are incorporating their partnership, which has operated profitably for several years. The partnership's business is growing rapidly, and it is anticipated that for several years it will be necessary to retain earnings to finance operations so that dividends will be limited. Discuss the possible tax problems that may result if the Subchapter S election is made.

18. Sioux Corporation was formed in 19W5 by five equal shareholders and was taxed as a regular corporation until 19X1, when it elected to be taxed under Subchapter S. The election was applied for the years 19X1, 19X2, and 19X3. Effective for the tax year beginning January 1, 19X4, all shareholders agreed to revoke the election. In August, 19X5, shareholder Amix died. In January 19X6, the shareholders, including the original four shareholders and Amix's estate, filed a request to be taxed as a Subchapter S corporation for the taxable year beginning January 1, 19X5. Is this request likely to be approved? Explain.

19. Alex Corporation has outstanding 1,000 shares of common stock. Of these shares, 800 are owned by Al Parisch and 200 are owned by Sue Sharpe. The corpora-

tion's net income has averaged approximately $40,000 per year. Al and Sue both have marginal tax rates of approximately 30 percent of their incomes. Several years ago, the corporation purchased several acres of land for $20,000 for possible future expansion. Subsequently, an interstate highway was built on the edge of the property and the corporation has been offered $750,000 for the property. Al and Sue have decided to accept the offer.

Sue has pointed out that the corporation does not need the cash, and that if the land is sold, the corporation will have to pay capital gains tax on the property of $730,000. Then, if the proceeds are distributed as dividends, the shareholders will pay personal income taxes on the distribution as ordinary income, with subsequent rates of up to 70 percent. She suggests that the shareholders elect that the corporation be taxed under Subchapter S for the following year, with the sale of the land to be consummated during that year, and with the Subchapter S election to be terminated during the following year. Comment on her proposal.

20. Subco, Inc. is an electing Subchapter S corporation. Subco's stock is owned as follows: Salmonson, 500 shares; Turner, 200 shares; Ural, 300 shares. During 19X1, the corporation made the following purchases of tangible personal property that qualified for the investment credit:

New assets:		
Life 10 years	$100,000	
Life 5 years	90,000	
Used assets:		
Life 8 years	120,000	

How much, if any, investment credit will flow through to each shareholder for the year?

21. Jason Arcom, president of Arcom Corporation, owns 97 percent of the stock of the corporation. Mary Hornes, vice-president, owns the other 3 percent. The corporation has established a qualified pension plan under which the corporation contributes an amount equal to 15 percent of each employee's and officer's salary. Arcom's salary is $80,000 per year, and Horne's salary is $60,000. The shareholders are considering whether to elect Subchapter S taxation for the corporation. What effects would the election have on the pension plan insofar as the two shareholders are concerned?

22. Weingarten, the sole shareholder of an electing Subchapter S corporation has been advised by his barber that he could reduce his income tax liability by transferring part of his stock to his wife and to each of his four minor children. Weingarten's current salary is $50,000, which is a reasonable amount. Discuss the wisdom of Weingarten's following his barber's suggestions.

23. In what way, if any, would your answer to Problem 22, above, change if the barber also suggested that Weingarten reduce his salary from the corporation to $25,000?

24. Melody Corporation, an electing Subchapter S corporation, has been quite profitable and has grown rapidly. As a result, the corporation has been unable to distribute its net income as dividends. At the present time, each of the two shareholders has previously taxed income of $100,000. The shareholders have discussed the fact that they have "locked-in" earnings and are concerned that the right to recover previously taxable income in a tax-free distribution may not be transferred to another party. They are considering having the corporation borrow $200,000 from a bank to be used to make cash distributions of their previously taxed income to the shareholders. Then they would lend back to the corporation

the $100,000 distributed to them, and the corporation would repay the bank loan. Comment on this plan.

25. All the stock of Stargell Corporation, an electing Subchapter S corporation, is owned by May Stargell. The corporation has been taxed under Subchapter S since its inception two years ago. During 19X1, the corporation had taxable income, other than from property transactions, of $75,000. The corporation had the following property transactions for the year:

Long-term gain on sale of capital assets	$60,000
Short-term loss on sale of capital assets	(10,000)
Gain on sale of land held for three years for business use	25,000
Gain on sale of equipment held three years (depreciation taken in cost, $10,000)	6,000

    a. Determine the effects of these data on the corporation, including computing the corporation's tax liability.

    b. Determine the effects of these data on the shareholder.

26. Chariot Corporation has operated as a regular corporation for five years. During that time its taxable income has increased by about 15 percent per year, reaching $40,000 in 19X1. The corporation has three equal shareholders, whose marginal tax brackets are as follows: Charles, 20 percent; Rita, 40 percent; and Otto, 70 percent. The corporation normally has distributed 50 percent of its taxable income as dividends.

    The shareholders are considering electing to be taxed under Subchapter S. Which of the shareholders would most likely oppose the election? Why?

27. Amelia Haspell and Burke Anthony formed the City Trading Corporation in January, 19X1, each investing $50,000 in cash and receiving 500 shares of the corporation's 1,000 shares of common stock. They elected to be taxed under Subchapter S. On September 10, 19X1, Haspell made a loan of $20,000 to the corporation, receiving the corporation's three-year, 12 percent note. For the taxable year ending December 31, 19X1, the corporation made no distributions and had a net operating loss of $124,000. Explain the impact of this loss on the corporation and the shareholders.

28. Assume, in addition to the facts in Problem 27, that the corporation made no cash distributions during the taxable year ending December 31, 19X2, and that for the taxable year the corporation had net taxable income of $182,000.

    On April 2, 19X3, Anthony sold for $50,000 200 of his 500 shares to Cynthia Charles, who did not void the Subchapter S election. On September 15, 19X3, the corporation made a pro rata distribution totaling $100,000, and for the fiscal year ending December 31, 19X3, the corporation had net taxable income of $60,000. How do all these facts affect the shareholders and the corporation?

29. Alexander, Barnes, and Cyreno formed a Subchapter S corporation in 19X1. During the years 19X1 through 19X3, the corporation grew rapidly and needed to retain its profits for expansion. On January 1, 19X4, the following pertinent information is given:

Shareholder	Shares owned	Basis of shares	UTI from 19X3	PTI from years before 19X3
Alexander	400	$38,000	$ 8,000	$24,000
Barnes	500	60,000	10,000	30,000
Cyreno	100	12,000	2,000	6,000

Alexander, a single individual, died on April 10, 19X4. On May 1, 19X4, the corporation distributed cash of $30,000 to its shareholders, including Alexander's estate. On May 10, 19X4, Alexander's estate sold its 400 shares to Darwin for $82,000. Darwin did not void the Subchapter S election. For the year ending December 31, 19X4, the corporation had net taxable income of $36,500. How do all these facts affect the shareholders and the corporation?

30. C. Fazzi owns all the outstanding shares of Fazzi Corporation, an electing Subchapter S corporation, which was formed eight years ago. The election under Subchapter S was made two years ago. Both the corporation and the shareholder use the calendar year as the taxable year.

During 19X9, Fazzi Corporation had net taxable income, excluding property transactions, of $40,000. In addition, the corporation had Sec. 1231 gains of $100,000 and short-term capital gains of $10,000. The only distribution during 19X9 was a cash dividend of $25,000 on July 15. In addition, the corporation made a cash distribution of $70,000 on March 12, 19Y0. The corporation's net taxable income for the year ending December 31, 19Y0, was $60,000.

a. Compute the corporation's capital gains tax, if any.
b. Compute the corporation's preference tax, if any.
c. Explain how the distribution of $25,000 on July 15, 19X9, should be treated by the shareholder.
d. Compute the constructive dividend to the shareholder on December 31, 19X9.
e. Explain how the distribution of $70,000 on March 12, 19Y0, would be treated by the shareholder.

31. Amos, who has income from several sources, opened a new business corporation on January 1, 19X1, investing $108,000 in the stock of the company as its sole shareholder. The net taxable income of the new business for the first three years was as follows:

19X1	$(68,000)
19X2	(30,000)
19X3	20,000

a. Calculate the combined tax liability of Amos and the corporation for each of the three years if the corporation makes a proper election to be taxed under Subchapter S, assuming that Amos's taxable income from other sources is $123,400 each year and that Amos files a joint return.
b. Calculate the combined tax liability of Amos and the corporation for each of the three years if the corporation does not make a Subchapter S election, assuming that Amos's taxable income from other sources is $123,400 and that Amos files a joint return.

PART

THREE

partnership
taxation

formation of a partnership

A partnership is not a taxable entity. This does not mean, however, that partnership income is not taxed. It simply means that the partnership is not the taxpayer. Partnership income is passed through the partnership to the various partners who report their shares of the income on their own tax returns. The partnership, in effect, acts as a conduit for income that flows through it to the tax returns of the partners. A partner may be a corporation, an estate, a trust, or an individual. Thus, a partnership's income may be reported and taxed on corporate returns, on individual returns, or on fiduciary returns (returns of estates and trusts). The actual tax treatment of each partner's share depends on the tax rules that apply to that partner.

The statutory basis for partnership taxation is prescribed in Subchapter K of the Internal Revenue Code of 1954. Subchapter K comprises Secs. 701–761 of the Code. These provisions permit a large degree of flexibility in the taxation of partnership affairs. Perhaps the most important are those that permit the partner to transfer property in and out of the partnership without recognizing gain or loss. These nonrecognition provisions of Subchapter K give the partnership a degree of operating freedom unmatched by that of corporations and fiduciaries, making the partnership an ideal vehicle for organizing many business operations.

THE NATURE OF PARTNERSHIPS FOR FEDERAL TAXATION

Because the provisions of Subchapter K apply only to those organizations deemed to be partnerships, it is important to be able to recognize the existence of a partnership for tax purposes. Organizations found not to be partnerships are taxed under other provisions of the Internal Revenue Code.

Definition of a partnership

The Uniform Partnership Act defines a partnership as "an association of two or more persons to carry on as co-owners a business for profit." Subchapter K usually applies to organizations that are classified as partnerships under this definition. In addition, the provisions of Subchapter K apply to various other types of organizations that are not classified as partnerships by the Uniform Partnership Act, such as syndicates, groups, pools, joint ventures, and other unincorporated operations through which a business, financial operation, or venture is carried on. Thus, Subchapter K has a much broader application than might be suspected at first. The regulations warn taxpayers not to restrict the application of Subchapter K to those organizations that are common law partnerships or partnerships under state law.

SUPREME COURT DEFINITION   Perhaps the best definitions of a partnership for tax purposes can be found in the decisions of the Supreme Court. The Court concluded that whether or not a partnership exists for tax purposes primarily depends on the partners' intent. In other words, did the partners intend to form a partnership? The intent to form a partnership may be indicated by:

1. Intent of parties to carry on a trade or business;
2. Joint ownership of capital;

3. Joint contribution of capital or services;
4. Sharing of profit and loss;
5. Keeping separate books for the business;
6. Joint control over the business operations;
7. Holding the business out to others as a partnership;
8. Filing partnership returns; and
9. Operating the business in the partnership name.

If a preponderance of these factors exists in a given situation, a partnership will probably be deemed to exist for tax purposes. If not, the organization will be taxed under portions of the Code other than Subchapter K.

For example, the participants in a business venture might establish an organization that is a valid partnership under state law. The organization files a partnership return, and the partners pay tax on their share of the partnership income. The I.R.S. audits the organization and determines that it has more characteristics of a corporation than of a partnership. Thus, it requires the organization to pay taxes as a corporation. The characteristics that would support this position are discussed in Chapter 4. The finding that a corporation exists for tax purposes can be particularly disconcerting to the owners of an organization that fails to produce a profit. Under the tax law, losses, which can be passed through as ordinary losses to a partner, may not be passed through to an owner who is considered to be a shareholder in a corporation. The shareholder must wait until the stock is sold to derive any benefit from the loss. Even then, what benefit is derived is either a lower capital gain or an increased capital loss owing to the effect of the losses on the value of the stock.

CO-OWNERSHIPS   Certain noncorporate organizations are precluded from being taxed as partnerships, even though they may have several owners. The regulations specify that a joint undertaking will not be a partnership for tax purposes if the only joint activity is the sharing of expenses. For example, if two adjacent property owners share the cost of a drainage ditch designed to remove water from both of their properties, no partnership exists. Co-ownership of an apartment building is not a partnership for tax purposes if the co-owners merely rent or lease the property and keep it in good repair. They are not partners because they are not considered to be actively engaged in a trade or business from which they derive profits. If the co-owners of the apartment building supplied maid service, garbage

pick-up, and limousine service for their tenants, however, the operation would probably be considered a partnership for tax purposes. By engaging in such activities the partners indicate that they are actively involved in a trade or business.

If co-owners are found to be partners for tax purposes, some serious consequences may result. For example, an election to defer gain on involuntary conversion of property (Sec. 1033) will not be valid unless it is made by the proper party. If the co-owners do not constitute a partnership, each co-owner makes the election individually. One co-owner may choose to defer the gain while the other co-owner may decide to recognize the gain currently. If the co-ownership is deemed to be a partnership, however, the partnership itself must make the election, and all co-owners will be bound by the partnership election. The courts have held that all the partners must recognize the gain currently if they, rather than the partnership, have made the election under Sec. 1033.

EXCLUSION FROM SUBCHAPTER K   The owners of certain partnerships may elect to have their partnership wholly or partially excluded from being taxed under Subchapter K. This election may be made by organizations that would otherwise be treated as partnerships. Organizations availed of solely for investment purposes may make this election. So may organizations engaged in the joint production, extraction, or use of property. Neither of these types of organizations may be excluded, however, if it is in the business of selling services or selling property invested in, produced by, or extracted by the organization. In addition, neither of these organizations may be excluded from the provisions of Subchapter K unless the income of each participant can be determined without filing an accurate partnership tax return.

WHO IS A PARTNER?   It should now be obvious that the tax law does not adequately define a partnership for tax purposes. Many questions remain regarding the tax status of partnerships, co-ownerships, joint ventures, and similar business organizations. In addition, the tax law fails to define adequately who is a partner. Section 761(b) notes that a partner is a member of a partnership but fails to elaborate any further. The courts have broadened the definition of Sec. 761(b) by finding that an assignee of a limited partner's interest is a partner for tax purposes. An assignee is someone who receives an interest in a partnership but is not accepted into the partnership as a full partner. There are no restrictions on what type of entity may be a partner. A corporation, an estate, a trust, or an individual may all be partners for tax purposes.

Aggregate versus entity concepts

The complexity that arises in taxing partnership affairs results largely from the lack of one cohesive underlying legal theory that explains the relationships between partners and a partnership. Instead, partnership tax law is a mixture of provisions based on two remarkably different legal theories. Some provisions may be understood through application of one of the theories; some through application of the other. The *aggregate* theory, which regards the partners and partnership as the same entity, explains why partnership income may be passed through to the partners. The *entity* theory, which allows the partner to act like an outside party with respect to his or her dealings with the partnership, explains why a partner may buy from or sell assets to the partnership. Much of a student's initial difficulty with partnership taxation can be traced to an inadequate understanding of these theories. Once the appropriate underlying theory can be related to a particular tax provision, the purpose and logic of that provision usually become much clearer.

The aggregate theory regards the partnership as an aggregate of individuals. Under this theory, the partnership itself fails to have any real separate status. The relationship between a partner and his or her partnership is viewed in much the same way as the relationship between a sole proprietor and his or her sole proprietorship. The aggregate theory has its origins in English Common Law and was closely followed by the English courts. In later years, the aggregate theory became less dominant in the English courts. The American Uniform Partnership Act, from which the partnership laws of most states are adopted, reflects a mixture of both the aggregate and the entity theories.

The aggregate theory explains why each partner must report individually his or her distributive share of eight different classes of partnership deductions, gains, losses, and credits. It explains why the partners' bases in the partnership consist partly of their proportionate share of partnership liabilities. This theory also explains why a partnership may elect to increase a new partner's basis in each partnership asset when the new partner purchases an interest in the partnership.

The entity theory, on the other hand, regards the partnership and its partners as separate entities. Transactions governed by this theory are treated much the same as transactions between a shareholder and a corporation. The entity theory explains why the partnership may have a taxable year that is different from that of its partners and why a partner may recognize capital gain or loss on the sale of a partnership interest. It can be argued effectively that the entity theory predominates in the majority of partnership tax situations. As we explain each partnership tax provision in this and the next two chapters, we shall usually note the applicable underlying theory.

Evolution of partnership taxation

Income from partnerships was first taxed in the United States in 1864. Section 117 of the 1864 Revenue Act stated that the gains and profits of partnerships were taxable to the partners. The Federal Income Tax Act of 1913 contained a similar provision. On the whole, however, before 1954, Congress gave scant attention to the taxation of partnerships. The portions of the 1939 Code relating to the taxation of partners and partnerships consisted of nine sections totaling about a thousand words. The 1939 law contained provisions that were supported by both the aggregate and the entity theories. Partners were taxed on their distributive share of partnership income, and the partnership income retained its character as capital gain or ordinary income when it was reported by the partners. These provisions clearly reflect an aggregate concept of the partnership. Other sections provided that net income was computed at the partnership level, partnership books were to be maintained, and the partnership was to file an informational return—all examples of the application of the entity theory. One or the other theory supported other more minor provisions in the 1939 Code.

The 1939 Code probably provided adequate statutory guidelines for most of the partnerships that existed at that time. Partnerships were not widely used for tax shelters, and most partnerships consisted of only a few partners. As the size and sophistication of partnerships grew, it became obvious that the 1939 Code was inadequate to deal with the myriad of special situations that may exist within the partnership framework. Organizations such as the American Institute of Certified Public Accountants and the American Bar Association proposed revisions that would have made the statutory provisions more adequate. Spurred by the recommendations of these groups, Congress passed the revisions that are contained in Subchapter K of the Internal Revenue Code of 1954.

Since 1954, Congress has further modified several

of the provisions contained in Subchapter K. The most recent modifications have been in response to the increasing use of partnerships for tax-shelter purposes. Both the Tax Reform Act of 1976 and the Revenue Act of 1978 contained legislation designed to curb the tax advantages available to taxpayers investing in such partnerships. While these provisions have reduced the advantages formerly available to investors in tax-shelter partnerships, such partnerships continue to provide significant tax relief to high bracket taxpayers.

As currently constructed, Subchapter K attempts to tax partners in a simple, flexible, and equitable manner. Congress recognizes that most of the confusion arising from partnership taxation stems from the failure of either the entity theory or the aggregate theory to provide fully adequate answers to all partnership tax problems. Congress also realizes that flexibility and equity cannot be achieved if one or the other theory were permitted to apply exclusively. Thus, like prior law, the current statute reflects a mixture of entity and aggregate concepts. Several of the more complex provisions in the Code arise from Congressional efforts to provide tax results satisfactory both to the partnership as an entity and to the partners as individuals.

CONTRIBUTIONS FOR AN INTEREST

A partnership interest may be acquired in a variety of ways. A prospective partner may contribute property or services to a partnership in return for an interest in the partnership. A prospective partner may also purchase an interest from an existing partner, receive an interest by gift, or inherit an interest from a deceased partner. The interest received may be an interest in either partnership capital or profits or an interest in both capital and profits. The tax problems generated by the transaction depend on the type of interest received and the way in which the interest is acquired.

Property

The contribution of cash to a partnership and the receipt by the contributor of an interest in that partnership produces no gain or loss to either the partnership or the partner. Section 721 of the Internal Revenue Code provides for this treatment. Similarly, Sec. 721 permits the nonrecognition of gain or loss when property other than cash is contributed to the partnership in exchange for an interest in the partnership. It makes no difference whether the cash or property is contributed when the partnership is formed or later. The nonrecog-

nition of gain or loss applies both to the original partners and to any new partners admitted after the partnership is formed. Note, however, that the partner making the contribution must receive an interest in the partnership. If cash or other property is received, the exchange will be taxable.

At first glance, these rules appear to be simply an application of the aggregate theory of partnership taxation. The contribution of the partner-to-be is treated as merely a contribution to himself or herself. To require the partner to recognize gain or loss on a transfer to himself or herself would be nonsense. When viewed more closely, however, the aggregate theory does not fully explain the entire substance of such transactions. The would-be partner actually transfers only a portion of the property to himself or herself; the rest is contributed to the other partners in return for a portion of their interest in each of the other partnership assets. A pure aggregate approach to this transaction would treat the transfer as tax free only to the extent of the interest retained by the contributing partner in the asset contributed. The transaction would be taxable to the extent of the interest transferred to the other partners. Because the language of Sec. 721 clearly states that none of the transaction is taxable, the underlying justification for the statute can best be explained by the desire of Congress to facilitate business adjustments. Congress recognizes that fewer partnerships would be formed if the prospective partners were required to recognize gain or loss on their formation. Because economic activity is encouraged by the formation of partnerships, Congress chose to pass Sec. 721, despite the lack of a theoretical base that would adequately explain the rationale underlying the statute.

The view of the Internal Revenue Service on this matter has always mirrored the position expressed in Sec. 721. Since 1920, the I.R.S. has publicly stated that no gain or loss should be realized when property is contributed to a partnership. Numerous early judicial decisions supported this position. While Congress failed to include in the 1939 Code a statement that directly stated its position, the I.R.S. interpreted Congressional intent as prescribing no gain or loss on the transaction. Thus, Sec. 721 merely perpetuated the law as it was then understood.

As might be expected, not all transfers of property to a partnership by a partner will be tax free under Sec. 721. Several exceptions exist to the general rule presented above. One exception may occur when the partner's basis in the transferred property is less than the amount of the mortgage that encumbers the property. The transfer may result in the transferor partner being relieved of personal liability on a substantial portion of the mortgage. Section 752(b) treats the relief from liability as a distribution of money from the partnership to the partner. If the amount of this "deemed distribution" of money exceeds the partner's basis in the partnership, the difference is taxable gain to the contributing partner. We shall discuss the computation of this gain more fully in the next section.

The provisions of Sec. 721 also will not protect from immediate taxation a transaction that is essentially an exchange of properties between two partners.

Example: Assume Partner A owned land and Partner B owned stock. The properties were owned individually by each person and were not used in activities of the AB partnership. Further assume that A wanted B's stock and B desired to own A's land. If A and B both contribute their property to the partnership, the transaction would be tax free under Sec. 721. A subsequent distribution by the partnership of the land to B and the stock to A would also appear to be tax free under Sec. 731. Thus, according to a literal interpretation of the statutes, no taxable exchange has occurred. A and B will find, however, that this type of tax subterfuge is not permitted. The I.R.S. will disregard the passage of the properties through the partnership and will hold, instead, that the land and stock were exchanged directly by A and B. The exchange will not fall under the tax-free shield of Secs. 721 and 731 but will be treated as any other taxable exchange.

Several final points should be observed. The transfer to a partnership of installment receivables or property subject to recapture under Secs. 1245 or 1250 will not trigger immediate gain recognition if the consideration received for the transfer is an interest in the partnership. The transfer of property on which investment credit has been taken usually does not trigger a recapture of the investment credit, provided the partnership uses the property as Sec. 38 property and the partner has a substantial interest in the partnership.

Services

One can become a partner in several ways other than by contributing cash or property to a partnership. Often, a partner receives an interest in a partnership as compensation for services rendered. This is not a tax-free transaction because Sec. 721 is inapplicable where services are performed for the partnership. Instead,

Treas. Reg. Sec. 1.61-2(d)(1) requires the partner performing the service to include the fair market value of the partnership interest received as ordinary income. The partnership may deduct this same amount if the services performed are of a deductible nature. If the services are not deductible, they must be capitalized to an asset account. For example, architectural services performed by a partner may be capitalized to the building account. Services performed in the day-to-day management of the partnership, however, are usually deductible.

Although income must be recognized by partners performing services, the recognition of this income may be deferred until a later date. Section 83 provides that income need be recognized only when the service partner's interest is (1) not subject to a substantial risk of forfeiture or (2) freely transferable by the service partner. Thus, if a service partner may not freely transfer his or her interest and may possibly forfeit the interest upon the occurrence of some contingency, no income need be recognized currently. Instead, income will be recognized on the date that one of these restrictions no longer exists. The amount of ordinary income recognized by the service partner is the fair market value of the partnership interest on this later date.

Example: Assume Shelley performed architectural services for the SMB partnership in 19X1. As compensation for these services, she received a partnership interest valued at $10,000. Normally, we would expect her to recognize $10,000 ordinary income in 19X1. If, however, during the subsequent five years, (1) the partnership interest can be sold only to the partnership at a price less than fair market value, and (2) if Shelley will forfeit her entire interest unless she continues to work in the partnership during that period of time, she will recognize ordinary income only when the five-year period has expired. If the fair market value of the partnership interest on that later date is $20,000, Shelley will recognize ordinary income of that amount.

By waiting until the restrictions lapse, Shelley will pay taxes on a greater amount of ordinary income ($20,000) than if she had recognized $10,000 of ordinary income in the year she performed the services. She may be quite unhappy with these tax consequences. Fortunately, Congress has provided her with a way to change this result. Section 83(b) permits her to elect to recognize the $10,000 ordinary income in the year she receives her partnership interest. Although this accelerates the date for income recognition, it also gives her a cost basis of $10,000 for her partnership interest. The interest in the partnership is a capital asset. Thus, if seven years later she sells that interest for $30,000, she will recognize $20,000 long-term capital gain. Had she waited until the restrictions lapsed before she recognized ordinary income, she would have had $20,000 ordinary income and $10,000 long-term capital gain.

A distinction must be made between services performed for a partnership and services performed for others. The transfer to a partnership of receivables generated through the performance of personal services for others is governed by the provisions of Sec. 721. Receivables are regarded as "property," which can be contributed tax free. Thus, an attorney may contribute the receivables from his or her sole proprietorship to a newly formed partnership without having to be concerned about the transaction generating taxable income.

INTEREST IN FUTURE PROFITS ONLY   An unusual problem arises if the service partner receives only an interest in future profits as compensation for his or her services. The regulations provide that "if services are paid for in property the fair market value of the property taken in payment must be included in income." Before 1972, most tax experts had not regarded an interest in future profits as being within the scope of the term "property." An interest in future profits was considered a nebulous interest that had value only as the future profits were earned. The receipt of an interest in future profits, therefore, was nontaxable, and income was recognized only when these future profits were actually received.

The nontaxability of the receipt of a future profits interest was also supported on pragmatic grounds. It is usually quite difficult to predict the income that will be generated by a partnership. An interest in partnership profits often cannot be reasonably valued until the profits are actually earned. Considerable statutory support exists for the proposition that a property right should not be taxed until it can be reasonably valued.

The Department of the Treasury apparently agreed with these arguments. The head of the Treasury staff charged with writing the regulations in this area stated that an interest in future profits was not intended to be taxed until the profits were earned.[1] This rule was not seriously questioned for years. Unfortunately, a single case may now have upset this rule.

In the case of *Sol Diamond*[2], which was first decided in 1971, the I.R.S. successfully taxed a service partner on the receipt of an interest in future profits. The facts in the case were unusual. Mr. Diamond received an interest in future profits for services that he had already performed. He then sold this interest approximately one month after he received it. He claimed that he should be taxed only on the receipt of the sales proceeds and not at the time that the interest in future profits was received. In Mr. Diamond's view, the interest in future profits represented a capital asset, which, when sold, produced a capital gain. The court held that he should be taxed on the value of the interest when the interest was received. Because the interest was not subject to restrictions, it represented current compensation on which Diamond was forced to recognize ordinary income.

The *Diamond* case runs counter to the traditional pattern of Subchapter K. Carried to its extreme, *Diamond* could significantly restructure much of existing partnership tax law. We doubt this will happen. The courts may attempt to tax a receipt of an interest in future profits where the interest is received for past services and is sold shortly after receipt. We do not believe, however, that the I.R.S. will attempt to tax the receipt of a profits interest in a fact situation that differs significantly from *Diamond*.

Basis problems

The contributing partner's basis in the partnership is governed by Code Sec. 722, which reads as follows:

> The basis of an interest in the partnership acquired by a contribution of property, including money, to the partnership shall be the amount of such money and the adjusted basis of such property to the contributing partner at the time of the contribution increased by the amount (if any) of gain recognized to the contributing partner.

This is the Code's way of saying that, in general, the partner's basis in the partnership will equal the partner's basis in the cash and property transferred to the partnership. In tax language, this is termed a "substituted" basis. In cases in which gain is recognized by the partner on the transfer, the partner's basis in the partnership is increased by the amount of the gain. The contribution of property to a partnership rarely creates a recognized gain to the contributing partner.

The substituted basis mandated by Sec. 722 is a natural result of the application of the aggregate theory to tax-free transfers under Sec. 721. The partner is

[1] McDonald, *New Partnership Regulations*, 1957 So. Calif. Inst. 171, 183.

[2] *Sol Diamond*, 56 TC 530 (1971), aff'd 492 F2d 286 (CA-7, 1974).

considered merely to have substituted his or her interest in cash or property for an interest in a partnership. No gain or loss is normally recognized because the transfer is not regarded as an exchange transaction occurring between two different entities. Had the entity theory prevailed in Sec. 721, the transfer of property to the partnership in return for an interest in the partnership would have been taxed as a sale or exchange. Gain or loss would have been recognized by the transferor partner, and the partner would have a cost basis for the partnership interest.

By adopting an aggregate approach in Secs. 721 and 722, Congress may have permitted practical considerations to triumph over theoretical considerations. The entity theory better describes the economic relationships between the partners. The relative fair market value of both the capital contributions and the services performed by the partners largely determines the relative share of ownership each partner will have in the partnership. Financial accounting for partnerships is dominated by the entity theory because of the need to account for these economic relationships. But tax policy makers must be pragmatic. If gain or loss were required to be recognized for tax purposes on each asset transferred by a partner to a partnership, fewer partnerships would be formed and normal business relationships would be discouraged. Congress apparently decided that the formation of partnerships should not be unduly constrained by such tax considerations.

Property may be contributed to a partnership subject to a liability. When such property is transferred, the liability is transferred with it. The transferor partner remains personally liable to the extent of his or her proportionate interest in the partnership. The partner's basis in the partnership, however, is reduced to the extent that the other partners assume personal liability on the rest of the liability. The other partners' assumption of a portion of the liability increases their basis by the amount of the liability assumed.

Example: Assume Albert transfers land to the ABC partnership in exchange for a one-third interest in the capital and profits of the partnership. The land has a basis to Albert of $10,000 and is subject to a mortgage of $9,000. Albert's basis in the partnership will be $4,000 (consisting of the $10,000 substituted basis less the $6,000 mortgage liability transferred to the other partners).

Sometimes a partner may transfer property subject to a mortgage that is substantially greater than the partner's basis in the property. This is not an unusual occurrence in this day of rapidly escalating real-estate prices. In such situations, the portion of the liability regarded as transferred to the other partners may be greater than the transferor's basis in the property. Conceptually, under the substituted basis rules just discussed, the transferor partner would appear to have a negative basis for the partnership interest. Section 704, however, will not permit the partner's basis to be reduced below zero. To ensure that the partner has at least a zero basis, gain must be recognized. The gain equals the difference between the partner's basis in the asset transferred and the liability transferred to the other partners.

Example: Assume in the example above that the land Albert transferred to the ABC partnership was encumbered by an $18,000 mortgage instead of a $9,000 mortgage. Albert is relieved of liability on two-thirds of the mortgage, or $12,000. The initial calculations would produce a negative basis of $2,000 ($10,000 substituted basis less $12,000 mortgage transferred) for Albert's interest in the partnership. Because a negative basis is not permitted, however, Albert's basis must be increased to zero. The $2,000 increase will be taxable gain.

The transferor's holding period for his or her partnership interest depends on how the interest was acquired. Section 1223(1) provides that if the interest is acquired by transferring capital or Sec. 1231 assets to the partnership, the holding period of the interest will include the time the partner held the assets. This is termed a "tacking" of holding periods. If other types of assets are transferred, the partner's holding period begins on the date of transfer. When a partner receives a partnership interest for the performance of personal services, the holding period generally begins from the date the unrestricted interest is received.

The holding period rules reflect primarily the aggregate concept espoused in Secs. 721 and 722. The tacking of holding periods indicates that one form of ownership merely has been substituted for another form. The lack of tacking when noncapital or nonsection 1231 assets are transferred is a loophole closer. If partners were able to obtain a long-term holding period for a partnership interest (a capital asset) by transferring, for example, inventory that had been held for more than one year, potential ordinary income could be converted into long-term capital gain. The holding period rules eliminate this possibility.

The partnership's basis for contributed property is the adjusted basis of the property to the contributing partner. Tax accountants refer to this as carryover basis. If the contributing partner recognized any gain as a result of the transfer, the amount of the gain is added to the carryover basis. In the previous example involving Albert and the ABC partnership, the $2,000 gain would increase the partnership's basis for the land to $12,000.

The partnership's holding period for property transferred by a partner is governed by Treas. Reg. Sec. 1.723-1. The regulation permits the holding period to include the time the property was held by the partner. Figure 10-1 illustrates the application of the holding period rules.

Allocating precontribution gains and losses

In the discussion above, we indicated that a partner may transfer appreciated property to a partnership without triggering the recognition of gain. If you are an observant student, you may be thinking that this is an excellent way for a transferor to avoid paying taxes on some of the gain. Your reasoning might proceed as follows: First, if the transferor partner contributes the property in return for an interest in the partnership, no gain or loss is recognized on the transfer. When the property is sold by the partnership, the general rule of Sec. 704 allocates the gain between the various partners. By allocating the gain among the partners, a portion of the precontribution gain will be taxed to partners other than the transferor. Thus, the transferor partner is able to shift the burden of taxation on some of the precontribution gain. An example may be helpful at this juncture.

> *Example:* Assume Mr. Fox contributes land with a basis of $5,000 and a fair market value of $10,000 to the Fox-Trot partnership. Mr. Fox and Mr. Trot share the profits of the partnership equally. Subsequently, the land is sold by the partnership for $20,000, resulting in a postcontribution gain of $10,000. Section 704(a) provides that both the $5,000 precontribution gain and $10,000 post-

contribution gain will be divided equally between Fox and Trot. Thus, Fox effectively transfers one-half of the $5,000 precontribution appreciation to Trot.

This result stems from the use of different theories to support different portions of the transaction. The aggregate theory explains the tax treatment of property contributed to the partnership. Wanting to ensure that most partnerships are formed in tax-free transactions, Congress provided that none of the precontribution appreciation is taxed at the time of contribution. If the aggregate theory were also followed when the property was eventually sold, all the precontribution appreciation would be taxed to the contributor. Section 704(c)(1), however, states that a partner's distributive share of gain shall "be allocated among the partners in the same manner as if the property had been purchased by the partnership." This means that in an equal partnership of two partners, the total gain will be allocated equally between the two parties. The precontribution appreciation is not specially allocated to the contributing partner. Thus, Sec. 704(c)(1) applies an entity concept to the allocation. This result can produce ill feelings between partners. Many a partner has rued the day he agreed to let his copartner contribute highly appreciated property to the partnership.

The American Bar Association addressed the problem presented by precontribution gain or loss in a symposium held in 1949. Three options were discussed. One option, which was not recommended, was to ignore the problem entirely and allocate all gain or loss on a pro rata basis to each partner. This method produces the result that occurs when the general rule of Sec. 704(a) is applied.

The second method discussed was termed the "ceiling method." This option requires the calculation of a "tentative gain" on the date the property is contributed to the partnership. This gain equals the difference between the property's basis to the contributor and the fair market value of the property on the date of contri-

FIGURE **10-1**

Holding Periods for a Partnership Interest Acquired Through the Transfer of Various Properties.

Property transferred by partner	Date property acquired	Date of transfer	Partner's holding period for partnership interest begins on	Partnership holding period for asset begins on
Cash	1/1/79	1/1/80	1/1/80	1/1/79
Capital asset	1/1/79	1/1/80	1/1/79	1/1/79
Section 1231 asset	1/1/79	1/1/80	1/1/79	1/1/79
Inventory	1/1/79	1/1/80	1/1/80	1/1/79

bution. When the partnership subsequently sells the property, an "actual gain" is recognized. If the actual gain is less than the tentative gain, all the actual gain is allocated to the contributing partner. The remaining tentative gain is disregarded and has no further tax significance. If the actual gain is more than the tentative gain, all the tentative gain is allocated to the contributor. The excess of the actual gain over the tentative gain is allocated to all the partners on a pro rata basis.

The last option discussed at the symposium was the "partnership accounting method." First, a tentative gain is calculated when the property is contributed to the partnership. This gain is calculated in the same manner as the tentative gain discussed under the ceiling method. Unlike the ceiling method, however, the partnership accounting method requires that the entire tentative gain always be recognized by the contributing partner. This entire gain is recognized regardless of the actual gain realized on the sale. Any difference between the actual gain and the tentative gain is allocated to all the partners on a pro rata basis. Thus, the contributing partner may recognize gain on the transaction while the other partners recognize loss.

Both the ceiling and the partnership accounting methods provide reasonable solutions to the problem of allocating precontribution gain. The partnership accounting method is theoretically more acceptable because it allocates the entire tentative gain or loss to the contributor of the property. The ceiling method only allocates to the contributor the lesser of the tentative or actual gain or loss. Congress, for reasons never fully expressed, chose the ceiling method when drafting Sec. 704(c)(2), the current statute dealing with precontribution gains and losses. This section provides that if the partnership elects, the "gain or loss with respect to property contributed to the partnership by a partner shall be shared among the partners so as to take into account the variation between the basis of the property and its fair market value on the date of contribution." Treasury Regulation 1.704-1(c)(1)(i) holds that the ceiling method controls the computation of this allocation. The following example illustrates the application of Sec. 704(c)(2).

Example: Assume that two equal partners, Kit and Kat, contribute cash and property to the KitKat partnership. Kit contributes land with a basis of $40,000 and a fair market value of $60,000; Kat contributes $60,000 cash. After several years, the partners decide to sell the land for $50,000. Kit's tentative gain is $20,000. Because of the ceiling limitation, however, only the $10,000

realized gain ($50,000 − $40,000) may be allocated to Kit. Nothing is allocated to Kat. This causes an injustice to Kat in the amount of one-half the $10,000 paper loss incurred after the property was contributed. The more theoretically correct "partnership income method" would have permitted an allocation of the entire $20,000 precontribution gain to Kit and a pro rata allocation ($5,000 each) of the $10,000 postcontribution loss to Kit and Kat. Congress specifically adopted the ceiling method, however, and the regulations help implement this intent.

The special allocation permitted by Sec. 704(c)(2) must be provided for in the partnership agreement. If it isn't, the gain or loss will be allocated according to the general rule of Sec. 704(c)(1).

Undivided interests

Unless the partnership agreement provides otherwise, gain or loss, depreciation or depletion computed in regard to certain types of partnership property, may be determined as if the property had never been contributed to the partnership. This rule applies when contributed property is owned by two or more partners as joint tenants or tenants in common, and:

1. the partners owned undivided interests in the property before contributing the property to the partnership, and
2. the partners' interests in the partnership correspond (that is, they are identical) with their undivided interests in the property.

This special allocation rule is found in Sec. 704(c)(3). It will apply only if the partnership agreement fails to provide for some other method of allocation. A provision in the agreement that provides for allocating gains, losses, depreciation, or depletion under the general rules of Sec. 704(c)(1) or the exception of Sec. 704(c)(2) will override the statutory presumption of Sec. 704(c)(3).

Example: Assume Mickey and Minnie own as tenants in common a plot of land, which they contribute to the M and M partnership. Mickey's basis in the land is $5,000; Minnie's is $2,000. Each has a 50 percent interest in both the land and the partnership. If the partnership sells the land for $20,000, a $13,000 gain will be recognized ($20,000 sales price less $7,000—Minnie's and

Mickey's bases in the land). If the partnership agreement does not provide otherwise, $5,000 ($10,000 − $5,000) of the gain will be allocated to Mickey and the remaining $8,000 ($10,000 − $2,000) to Minnie. Note that the general rule of Sec. 704(c)(1) would have allocated $6,500 ($13,000/2) of gain to each partner. An allocation under the general rule probably would not have reflected properly the economic results of the transaction.

The regulations provide that the identity of interests must exist not only when the contribution is made but also at all times thereafter. A change in the partner's capital or profits interest usually will terminate the application of Sec. 704(c)(3). After the termination, the general rule of Sec. 704(c)(1) or the allocation rule of Sec. 704(c)(2) will apply. If the partners wish, however, they may agree under Sec. 704(c)(2) to allocate depreciation, gain, and so on, on the property in the same manner as it was allocated before the termination. Thus, the special allocation provided for in Sec. 704(c)(3) may be kept in effect after a change in the relative capital and profits interest of the partners.

Alternatives to property contributions

Sometimes the partners may be unhappy with the tax results that occur when property is contributed to a partnership. They may feel that the tax rules governing property contributions do not reflect adequately the economic realities of their situation.

Example: Assume John owns a plot of land he holds for investment purposes. The adjusted basis and fair market value of the land are $40,000 and $100,000, respectively. The land is a capital asset to John, and any gain he would recognize on the sale of the land would be capital gain. John plans to transfer the land to a partnership that will develop the land. The developed land no longer will be classified as a capital asset to the partnership. Instead, it will be inventory, which, when sold, will produce ordinary income. If John contributes the land to the partnership, the $60,000 unrealized gain at contribution will lose its character as capital gain. Should the developed land be sold for $250,000, the partnership will recognize ordinary income of $210,000. Thus, $60,000 of potential capital gain has been converted to ordinary income.

Fortunately, a partner's property may be acquired by the partnership through means other than by contribution. Perhaps the most obvious alternative is the sales transaction. Rather than contributing the property to the partnership, the partner arranges for the partnership to purchase the property. Section 707(a), which is discussed in detail in Chapter 11, permits the tax recognition of such sales. The partner usually recognizes gain or loss just as if the sale had been made to a third party. The character of the gain or loss depends on the way the asset is used. In certain situations, the character of the gain or the recognition of the loss will be affected by the partner's percentage ownership in the partnership.

A second option to contributing property is to sell some or all of the property to another partner. Immediately after the sale, both the seller and the buyer contribute their interests in the property to the partnership. If the entire property is sold to the other partner, the seller recognizes all the gain at the point of sale. If only a portion of the property is sold to the other partner, the partners may want to allocate any unrecognized preappreciation gain to the seller. This way, if the partnership later sells the property, only postappreciation gain will be allocated between the partners.

A third possibility is to forego contributing or selling the property to the partnership entirely. Instead, the partner leases the property to the partnership. Rent is charged the partnership, and the partner deducts such expenses as depreciation, maintenance, interest, and taxes on the property. Because it permits the partnership to use the property while the owner-partner retains the tax benefits of direct ownership, renting property to a partnership is a relatively common occurrence.

While these three options do not exhaust the various means by which property, or the use of property, may be transferred to a partnership, they indicate that many possibilities exist. The partners must decide which form of transfer will best satisfy their economic and legal requirements.

OTHER PROBLEMS RELATED TO ORGANIZATION

Numerous other decisions must be made by a newly organized partnership. A taxable year must be chosen and various tax elections must be made. Most of these elections are made by the partnership, although certain elections are required to be made individually by each of the partners. One election made by the partnership involves the tax treatment of organization and syndication expenditures.

Organization and syndication expenditures

Amounts spent in organizing and syndicating a partnership are capital expenditures. Before 1976, the partnership could not amortize these costs unless the partnership had a definite limited life. This treatment was a direct result of a 1948 court decision that held that organizational costs are "property of a permanent nature owned by the partnership." Yet, despite this judicial precedent, some taxpayers argued that the Code permitted deduction of such costs if they were paid to partners in the form of guaranteed payments. Congress ended the confusion in 1976 by passing several related pieces of legislation.

First, Congress defined organization expenditures as amounts spent (1) incident to the creation of a partnership; (2) chargeable to a capital account; and (3) which, if expended in creating a partnership having an ascertainable life, would be amortized over such life. This definition limits considerably the type of expenditures that qualify as organization expenditures. Syndication expenditures, which are primarily costs incurred in selling partnership interests, can never satisfy the requirements of this definition. Congress allowed organization expenditures that satisfy this definition to be amortized over five years. Thus, while not permitting an immediate write-off of these costs, Congress does permit them to be amortized over a short period of time.

Only organization expenses paid or incurred in partnership taxable years beginning after December 31, 1976 are eligible for five-year amortization. Organization expenses incurred before that date and all syndication expenses are not eligible for this treatment. If the costs are not amortized or if the partnership is liquidated before all the amounts are amortized, the unamortized amounts may be deducted as a loss in the year of the liquidation.

Selecting the partnership tax year

The partnership tax year is selected as if the partnership were a separate taxable entity. Section 706(b) reads as follows:

(b) Adoption of Taxable Year.—
1) Partnership's taxable year.—The taxable year of a partnership shall be determined as though the part-

nership were a taxpayer. A partnership may not change to, or adopt, a taxable year other than that of all its principal partners unless it establishes, to the satisfaction of the Secretary, a business purpose therefor.
2) Partner's taxable year.—A partner may not change to a taxable year other than that of a partnership in which he is a principal partner unless he establishes, to the satisfaction of the Secretary, a business purpose therefor.
3) Principal partner.—For the purpose of this subsection, a principal partner is a partner having an interest of 5 percent or more in partnership profits or capital.

The intent of this section is to ensure that, as a general rule, both the partnership and the principal partners have the same tax year. The need for such a requirement can be more readily understood when examined in conjunction with Sec. 706(a), which provides:

(a) Year in Which Partnership Income is Includible.—In computing the taxable income of a partner for a taxable year, the inclusions required . . . shall be based on the income, gain, loss, deduction, or credit of the partnership for any taxable year of the partnership ending within or with the taxable year of the partner.

Note that Sec. 706(a) requires the partner to include the partnership income in his or her tax return for the taxable year during which the partnership taxable year ends. If Partner X is a calendar-year taxpayer and the partnership reports on a July 1, 19X0 through June 30, 19X1 fiscal year, tax will not be fully paid on the partnership income until April 15, 19X2 (March 15, 19X2 for a corporate partner) of the subsequent calendar year. This long period between the end of the partnership year and the due date of the partner's return permits the taxpayer interest-free use of tax dollars.

Before 1954, a partnership was free to choose any tax year it desired. Typically, the year chosen was a February 1 through January 31 fiscal year, which maximized the deferral of tax liability for calendar-year partners. Many partnerships were able to satisfy much of their short-term working capital requirements in this way. Section 706(b) was passed to preclude the deferral.

Section 706(b) generally requires the partnership to choose the same taxable year as its "principal partners." This section defines a principal partner as any partner having an interest of 5 percent or more in partnership profits or capital. Some partnerships have many principal partners. In other, larger partnerships, no principal partners exist. Where the latter situation occurs, the Internal Revenue Service has generally preferred that the partnership adopt a calendar year.

Several rules may be derived to govern the selection of the partnership taxable year. If all the principal partners report on the same taxable year, the partnership may:

1. Adopt the tax year of the principal partners.
2. Adopt a tax year different from that of the principal partners, provided the tax year adopted does not result in more than a three-month deferment of income to the partners and a good business purpose can be demonstrated for the partnership year chosen. It is normally not difficult to get I.R.S. approval.[3] For example, a September 30, October 31, or November 30 year end may be selected for a partnership whose principal partners are on a calendar year.
3. Adopt any tax year it wants, provided all the principal partners are willing to change their own tax years to the tax year of the partnership.
4. Apply to the I.R.S. for any fiscal tax year, provided the partnership can demonstrate a good business purpose for selecting that year. It is normally difficult to obtain I.R.S. approval if the deferment of income exceeds three months.

If all the principal partners do not have identical tax years, the partnership may:

1. Adopt a calendar year, or
2. Select a year according to (3) or (4), above.

Partners must annualize their income for any short taxable year created by a change in their tax years. The partnership never annualizes, because it is not a tax-paying entity.

Example: Assume George and Herman, both calendar-year taxpayers, form a partnership. The partnership may adopt a calendar year without I.R.S. approval. It also probably can obtain I.R.S. approval to adopt a September 30, October 31, or November 30 year end. It probably cannot choose any other fiscal year unless George and Herman are willing to change to that same fiscal year.

Now, assume slightly different facts: George is on a calendar year but Herman pays taxes on a July 1 through June 30 fiscal year. The partnership may adopt a calendar year without obtaining ap-

proval from the I.R.S. It also may adopt any fiscal year it chooses if the partners concurrently switch their tax years to that fiscal year. Rarely will the partnership be able to choose any other fiscal year.

Tax elections

Tax elections are formal decisions on how a particular type of transaction or tax attribute should be handled. The choice of the partnership's tax year is an example of an election. The Code provides that certain elections must be made by the partners individually while other elections must be made by the partnership. Elections that must be made by the partnership include:

1. The inventory valuation method (for example, LIFO, FIFO) to be adopted by the partnership;
2. The method of accounting for partnership activities (accrual, cash, or some hybrid method);
3. The taxable year adopted for the partnership (see discussion in previous section);
4. The method for depreciating fixed assets (for example, straight-line, SYD, declining balance);
5. The decision to claim additional first-year depreciation;
6. The decision that sales should be reported on the installment basis; and
7. The method for charging off bad debts (reserve or direct write-off).

Each partner is bound by the decisions made by the partnership in regard to these elections. If the partnership fails to make an election, each partner may not compensate for this error by making the election individually.

While most elections must be made by the partnership, the partners are required to make five specific elections individually. Most of the partners' individual elections are made regarding narrow tax issues. For example, a partner must elect to claim on his or her personal return either a credit or a deduction for foreign taxes generated by partnership activities. This election, while undoubtedly important to some taxpayers, probably need not concern the majority of partnership participants. Most other elections made by the partner are more obscure than the foreign tax election.

Example: To illustrate the importance of making the election at the proper level, consider the case of a two-member partnership that builds and leases a large office building. Several methods are available for depreciating such buildings. One member of

---

[3] Rev. Proc. 72-51, 1972-2 CB 832.

the partnership, Gerald, currently pays a large amount of minimum tax and does not wish to pay more of this tax. Therefore, because accelerated depreciation would increase his minimum tax liability, he prefers to depreciate the building under the straight-line method. The other partner, Hines, wishes to maximize his current depreciation deductions. Thus, he wants the partnership to claim the maximum accelerated depreciation possible. Unfortunately, both partners cannot achieve their desires. The partnership must choose one method for depreciating fixed assets. Whatever method is chosen binds both partners.

Differences between financial and tax accounting

Financial accounting students may have difficulty relating what they have learned in financial accounting to what they have learned in the preceding pages. This is to be expected. The confusion can be eased by examining some of the differences in the theoretical structure underlying financial and tax accounting for partnerships. Under generally accepted financial accounting principles, the partnership is treated primarily as a separate entity. Transactions between the partners and the partnership are viewed as occurring between two different accounting entities. In partnership taxation, however, only some of the transactions between the partner and the partnership are governed by this view. The rest are regarded as occurring between the partner and a partnership composed of an aggregate of partners. When the partnership is viewed as a separate entity for tax purposes, financial and tax accounting are usually identical. When the partnership is regarded as a mere aggregate of individuals (the aggregate theory), however, tax accounting and financial accounting usually differ in their handling of the same transaction.

Example: To illustrate some of the differences that occur between financial and tax accounting, assume M and N organize the MN partnership. M contributes land with an adjusted basis of $4,000 and a fair market value of $10,000. N contributes equipment with an adjusted basis and fair market value of $12,000 and $10,000, respectively. Table 10-1 illustrates the journal entries that would be developed for these transactions. The tax accountant would utilize the aggregate approach of Secs. 721–723 in this situation. The partnership would have a basis of $4,000 in the land and $12,000 in the equipment. M's and N's bases in the partner-

TABLE **10-1**
JOURNAL ENTRIES FOR PARTNERSHIP FORMATION

	D(Cr) Tax	D(Cr) Financial
M's Personal Books:		
Investment in MN Partnership	4,000	10,000
Gain on sale of land		(6,000)
Land	(4,000)	(4,000)
N's Personal Books:		
Investment in MN Partnership	12,000	10,000
Loss on sale of equipment		2,000
Equipment	(12,000)	(12,000)
Partnership Books:		
Land	4,000	10,000
Equipment	12,000	10,000
M, Capital	(4,000)	(10,000)
N, Capital	(12,000)	(10,000)

ship would be $4,000 and $12,000, respectively. No gain or loss would be recognized by M, N, or the partnership on the transaction. The financial accountant, however, would adopt the entity theory as the proper theoretical framework for handling these transactions. M would realize and recognize a gain of $6,000 ($10,000 − $4,000) on the transfer of the land to the partnership. N's realized and recognized loss would be $2,000 ($10,000 − $12,000). The partnership would debit the land and the equipment for $10,000 each and enter a $10,000 credit to each partner's capital account.

The discrepancy between financial accounting and tax accounting should not cause concern. Financial accounting tends to treat each business organization as an entity separate and apart from its owners. Financial accountants are also concerned with computing a "theoretically sound" amount of partnership income. This concept of income requires that income be recognized when it is realized. From this standpoint, it makes no sense to postpone the recognition of M's or N's gain or loss on the contribution of their properties. The gain or loss is a personal gain or loss realized by M and N as individuals.

The tax accountant does not dispute this reasoning. He or she notes, however, that this view is not necessarily relevant for tax purposes. While the calculation of a theoretically correct amount of income may be important for tax purposes, it is not always the most important consideration in developing tax policy. Throughout the history of our income tax laws, Congress has been reluctant to tax transactions that fail to generate cash necessary to pay the tax. The transfer of cash or property in return for a partnership interest does not generate any cash for the partner. If Congress required the partner to pay tax on this transaction, other funds would have to be used for this purpose. Many prospective partners, understandably, would be reluctant to enter into a partnership arrangement under such circumstances.

PROBLEMS

1. Joe and Moe own adjacent lots in a small subdivision. Because of the contour of these lots, water does not drain well from them. The two men decide to share the expense of building a drainage ditch along the property line. Is this undertaking a partnership for tax purposes?

2. Paula Dell is an attorney who is financially quite successful. Bill Mann is a real estate developer who has little cash for investment. The two decide to buy some real estate. Dell will contribute the money to buy the properties and have veto power over decisions regarding which properties to purchase. All other decisions will be made by Mann. Profits and losses from the operation will be shared equally. Is this a partnership for tax purposes? Would your answer change if Dell had no veto power and was to receive a guaranteed 10 percent annual return on her money?

3. The Richmont Oil Company is a joint venture engaged in the extraction of oil from several leases owned by the company in Texas. The company was formed by three businessmen who each own one-third of the operation. The company extracts the oil and sells it to several different refineries. Can the company elect to be excluded from the provisions of Subchapter K? If not, what might be done to ensure that the company could be excluded from tax treatment under Subchapter K?

4. Discuss the difference between the entity and the aggregate theories of partnership taxation. Which theory predominates in financial accounting? Which theory predominates in tax accounting? Enumerate some of the transactions that will be taxed under the aggregate theory of taxation.

5. Mary is a partner in the MNO partnership. She obtained her interest by contributing $3,000 cash and land to the partnership. The land had an adjusted basis of $5,000 and a fair market value of $7,000 at the time of contribution.
   a. Does Mary recognize any taxable gain or loss on the contribution of land to the partnership?
   b. What is the basis of the land to the partnership?
   c. What is Mary's adjusted basis for her partnership interest?
   d. Are your answers to b, c, and d more in accord with the entity theory or the aggregate theory of taxation?

6. The QR partnership wants to build an apartment building. The partnership offers Susie a one-third interest if she will transfer to the partnership a tract of land that she owns. The land has an adjusted basis to Susie of $10,000, a fair market value of $60,000, and is encumbered by a $24,000 mortgage. Assuming Susie contributes the land and mortgage to the partnership, answer the following:
   a. How much gain or loss does Susie recognize on the contribution of the land to the partnership?
   b. What is her basis in the partnership?
   c. What is the partnership's basis in the land?
   d. Now assume the mortgage is $30,000. Answer a, b, and c.
   e. Finally, assuming the mortgage is $45,000, answer a, b, and c.

7. Indicate whether gain or loss is recognized when the following types of properties are contributed to the partnership by a partner.
   a. Land that is not encumbered by a mortgage.
   b. Appreciated land used in farming. The land has an adjusted basis to the partner of $100,000 and is encumbered by a mortgage of $140,000. The partner obtains a 50 percent interest in the partnership.
   c. Installment receivable on which the partnership is not the obligor.
   d. A Sec. 1231 asset subject to Sec. 1245 recapture.
   e. Accounts receivable.

8. William Frye, a certified public accountant, performed accounting services for the ABC partnership. Frye received a one-fourth interest in the partnership as payment for these services. The value of the interest received was $5,000.
   a. Does Frye recognize any income at the time he receives his partnership interest? If so, how much?
   b. Does the partnership obtain a deduction for the $5,000 paid to Frye?
   c. If Frye were to receive only an interest in future profits, would your answer to a or b change? What if Frye sold that interest in future profits to Partner A one month after receiving it?

9. Indicate whether the following statements are true or false.
   a. If a partner contributes a capital asset to a partnership, the partner's holding period for the partnership interest received includes the partner's holding period for the capital asset.
   b. The partnership's holding period for a Sec. 1231 asset contributed by a partner begins on the date of the contribution.
   c. A service partner's interest in a partnership begins when he or she receives an unrestricted interest in the partnership.
   d. The partnership's holding period for inventory contributed by a partner begins on the date of the contribution.

10. Tom, Dick, and Harry formed a partnership in which each of them has a one-third interest. Tom contributed $20,000 cash; Dick contributed land with an adjusted basis of $4,000 and a fair market value of $20,000; and Harry contributed machinery with an adjusted basis of $8,000 and a fair market value of $20,000. Harry had claimed straight-line depreciation amounting to $17,000 on the machinery.
    a. Which partner made the greatest economic contribution?
    b. How can the election under Sec. 704(c)(2) help mitigate the inequities in the economic contribution?
    c. If the machinery has an estimated remaining useful life of 10 years, what is the maximum annual amount of straight-line depreciation that can be allocated to Tom and Dick under Sec. 704(c)(2)? Is this allocation totally equitable?
    d. If the land is sold two years later for $20,000, how much gain should each partner recognize if:
       (1) the general rule of Sec. 704(c)(1) governs the distribution of gain on the sale?
       (2) the special allocation of all precontribution gain has been elected under Sec. 704(c)(2)?

11. Mary and Ann own a plot of land as tenants in common. Ann had originally purchased the entire plot for $10,000 and later sold a half interest in it to Mary for $15,000. The two women contribute the plot to a partnership in which they share profits and losses equally. No provision is written into the partnership agree-

ment regarding the way any gain on the eventual sale of the land should be divided. If the partnership sells the land for $50,000, how should the sale proceeds and the gain be divided between Mary and Ann?

12. Indicate in each of the following cases if the taxpayer can accomplish what is proposed. Give adequate support for your decision.

    a. Joe and Mike, calendar-year taxpayers, form the JM partnership. They would like the partnership to adopt a February 1–January 31 fiscal year because this will maximize their potential tax deferral.

    b. Sally and Rhoda, calendar-year taxpayers, are also equal partners in the calendar-year SR partnership. Sally desires to change her personal taxable year to a July 1–June 30 fiscal year. She likes to vacation in April and finds it inconvenient to file her return (or an extension) on April 15.

    c. Ralph and Walter form the RW partnership. Ralph is a calendar-year taxpayer while Walter pays taxes on a July 1–June 30 fiscal year. A calendar year is elected for the partnership.

    d. Kim and Wendy, both calendar-year taxpayers, form the KW partnership. Because the partnership is involved in a seasonal industry, the partnership adopts a November 1–October 30 fiscal year. October 30 is the low point of the partnership's business year.

13. List an election that must be made by a partner. Also list four elections that must be made by a partnership. Must most partnership elections be made by the partnership or by the partners individually?

14. George and Edna are equal partners in the GE partnership. Each contributed $50,000 in cash to the partnership. The partnership immediately buys some land for $30,000 cash and assumes an outstanding mortgage on the land of $35,000.

    a. What is the basis of the land to the partnership?

    b. What are George and Edna's bases in their partnership interest after the purchase of the land? Would your answer change if the partnership did not assume the mortgage but, instead, purchased the property subject to the mortgage?

SUPPLEMENTAL PROBLEMS

15. Tom and Jerry are equal partners in the TJ partnership. The basis and market value of partnership assets is $50,000. The partnership has no outstanding liabilities. Each partner's capital account is $25,000. In a typical year, the partnership earns $30,000 and each partner withdraws his entire distributive share of the earnings.

    Tom and Jerry hire Donald, a local certified public accountant, to do some sophisticated tax planning for them. Because they do not have the cash to pay Donald, they decide to give him a 10 percent interest in the future profits of the firm instead of his usual fee for the work. Donald estimates that he would normally bill the work out for $20,000.

    The partnership earns $25,000 in the next year and 10 percent of that is distributed to Donald. Two years later, Donald sells his interest in future profits to Mickey, an outside party, for $15,000.

    What are the tax ramifications of this arrangement to Donald, to Tom and Jerry, and to the partnership?

16. Ann, Barbara, and Colleen decide to form the ABC partnership. Ann and Colleen will each contribute $40,000 to the partnership. Barbara contributes a building

that has an adjusted basis to her of $14,000 and a fair market value of $40,000. The building has been depreciated using straight-line depreciation and has a remaining estimated useful life of 10 years, after which time it is expected to have no salvage value.

a. Compute the Sec. 704(c)(2) allocation that can be made in regard to the depreciation.

b. Assume the Sec. 704(c)(2) allocation is made for the depreciation, and the Sec. 704(c)(2) allocation also is made relative to the precontribution gain on the building. The building was contributed to the partnership on January 1, 1977. It was sold on January 1, 1979 after two full years of depreciation had been claimed. Compute each partner's share of the gain, if the building is sold for $47,000.

11

partnership operations and transfers of partnership interests

In Chapter 10, we observed that the formation of a partnership may have significant tax ramifications. After a partnership has been successfully organized, various additional tax problems arise during its operation. Most of the statutory provisions governing the daily activities of a partnership are contained in Secs. 701–708 of the Internal Revenue Code. These rules cover a wide spectrum of tax issues faced by an operating partnership.

Tax problems also arise when a partner transfers his or her interest in the partnership to another party. The selling partner must determine the amount of gain or loss to recognize on the transaction and whether the gain or loss is capital or ordinary. The purchasing partner must determine his or her basis in the newly acquired partnership interest. We shall discuss the proper handling of these tax problems in the last portion of this chapter.

OPERATING THE PARTNERSHIP

Neither the entity theory nor the aggregate theory is followed exclusively in the taxing of partnership operations. Some rules are based on the entity theory; others are based on the aggregate theory. For example, Sec. 701 provides that the partners—and not the partnership—must pay tax on partnership income. This is definitely an aggregate concept. Conversely, Sec. 707(a) permits a partner to be treated as one who is not a partner when that partner sells property to the partnership. Such treatment can be supported only under the entity theory. One of the more difficult problems for students new to the study of partnership taxation is understanding that the law continually shifts between rules based on the entity theory and rules based on the aggregate theory. Thus, an understanding of both theories is essential if partnership taxation is to be mastered.

Partnership income and loss

A partnership is not a tax-paying entity. While all items of partnership revenue, expense, credits, and so on must be reported in the partnership tax return, the partnership pays no tax on these amounts. Instead, such amounts are passed through to the partners and taxed to them on their own tax returns. Section 702(a), which provides the authority for taxing partners on partnership income states:

Section 702. Income and credits of partner
(a) General rule. In determining his income tax, each partner shall take into account separately his distributive share of the partnership's—
  1) gains and losses from sales or exchanges of capital assets held for not more than 12 months,
  2) gains and losses from sales and exchanges of capital assets held for more than 12 months,
  3) gains and losses from sales or exchanges of property described in section 1231 (relating to certain property used in a trade or business and involuntary conversions),
  4) charitable contributions (as defined in section 170(c)),
  5) dividends with respect to which there is provided an

exclusion under section 116 or a deduction under part VIII of subchapter B,

6) taxes, described in section 901, paid or accrued to foreign countries and to possessions of the United States,

7) other items of income, gain, loss, deduction, or credit, to the extent provided by Regulations prescribed by the Secretary, and

8) taxable income or loss, exclusive of items requiring separate computation under other paragraphs of this subsection.

Section 702(a)(7) is a "catch-all" class, permitting the I.R.S. to draft regulations requiring that certain items of partnership income, gain, loss, deduction, and credit be reported separately for tax purposes. Existing regulations include the following among such items:

1. Recoveries of bad debts, prior taxes, and delinquency awards;

2. Gains and loss from wagering transactions;

3. Soil and water conservation expenditures;

4. "Nonbusiness" expenses as defined in Sec. 212;

5. Medical and dental expenses;

6. Expenses for the care of certain dependents;

7. Alimony payments;

8. Taxes and interest paid to cooperative housing corporations;

9. Intangible drilling and development costs;

10. Certain exploration expenditures for minerals;

11. Income, gain, or loss to the partnership under Sec. 751(b);

12. Depreciation, if an estate or a trust is a partner;

13. All items that are part of the tax preference computation;

14. Investment interest;

15. Any item of income, gain, loss, deduction, or credit subject to a special allocation under the partnership agreement that differs from the allocation of partnership taxable income or loss generally; and

16. Any item that, if taken into account separately by any partner, would result in a different tax liability for that partner than would result if the partner did not take that item into account separately

Thus, the Code and Regulations ensure that the partnership will be a conduit through which income, gains, losses, deductions, and credits pass before being reported on the partner's tax return. It is an imperfect conduit, however. While certain classes of partnership tax items, such as net long-term capital gains, are passed through intact, other classes, such as sales revenue and cost of goods sold, are combined on the partnership tax return before being passed through to the partners. Classes that are passed through intact are generally subject to nonroutine tax treatment on at least one of the partner's tax returns.

As noted above, the Code requires that partnership capital gains and losses retain their character when they are passed through to the partner. This treatment is a result of the special tax treatment afforded long-term capital gains. It is important, therefore, to separate capital assets from noncapital assets on the partnership books. Long-term capital gains and losses must be netted by the partnership and passed through to the partners separately from short-term capital gains and losses. Section 1231 gains and losses are also netted by the partnership and passed through separately. The partner will combine the long-term, short-term, and Sec. 1231 items with his or her own items of like kind in the computation of taxable income.

Other classes of tax items are stated separately because tax law excludes certain amounts from the partner's income or limits the amount the partner may deduct. Dividends received and charitable contributions paid are examples. In addition, certain items must be reported separately because limitations apply at both the partnership and the partner level. For example, additional first-year depreciation is limited to 20 percent of $10,000 ($20,000 on a joint return) of the asset's cost. Since 1976, this limitation applies at both the partnership level and the partner level. Thus, a maximum of $10,000 of the cost of these properties is passed through to the partners. The partners claim their proportionate amount of this cost. They, in turn, are each subject to the same limitation on the sum of (1) all assets they purchased during the year, and (2) their share of the partnership's eligible property passed through to them. If they already had purchased eligible property that equaled or exceeded the maximum limitation, the additional cost allocation from the partnership would not provide them with any incremental benefit.

Any items of partnership income, gain, loss, or deduction that are not required to be stated separately are combined into a single amount termed *bottom-line income*. In practice, the bottom-line income and each of the separately stated items are reported on Form 1065 (partnership information return) and on schedule K-1 for each of the partners. The partners transfer the information from schedule K-1 to their own personal tax returns. Examples of Form 1065 and an accompanying schedule K-1 appear at the end of this chapter.

CHARACTER OF PARTNERSHIP INCOME AND LOSS   The Code provides that the character of each item of income, loss, deduction, and credit is determined as if the partner had realized that item directly from the same source as the partnership. We can interpret this statement in two ways. Is the character of the item determined at the partnership level and then passed through to the partner? Or is the character of the item determined in regard to the partner without any concern for its character to the partnership? While there is still some confusion as to what Congress intended by this provision, most courts have decided that the character of an item should be determined at the partnership level. Thus, if a partnership is involved in the business of selling real estate, the partnership's real estate sales will generate ordinary income or ordinary loss. Each partner will report his or her proportionate share of these ordinary gains and losses, even though many of the partners may be mere passive investors in the partnership operations. If these passive investors had invested in the real estate operations individually, they would have reported capital gains or losses from the sales.

The trend toward separately stating many types of income, deductions, losses, and credits is not new. This has been the gradual direction of partnership tax law since it was first enacted in 1913. To see how far the law has come, we need only examine some of the earlier statutes. The most restrictive statute, the Revenue Act of 1913, provided for the pass through of only one class of income. All gains and losses, including capital gains and losses, were combined at the partnership level and passed through to the partner as ordinary income.

The Income Tax Act of 1916 permitted the character of tax-exempt interest and corporate dividends to pass through to the partners. The 1921 Act provided for the pass through of capital gain or loss, although the netting of long- and short-term capital losses occurred at the partnership level. The statute was revised in 1938 to permit capital gains and capital losses to pass through separately to the partners. When Congress wrote the 1954 Code, it provided for the preservation of many more classes of income. Recent revisions to the law have increased further the number of classes. Schedule K of the partnership tax return gives an indication of the large number of separate classes that exist today.

Partner's distributive share of income or loss

Section 704 specifies rules for determining how the items of income, gain, loss, and credit are allocated to each of the partners. Sections 704(a) and (b) read as follows.

Section 704. Partner's distributive share
(a) Effect of Partnership Agreement.—A partner's distributive share of income, gain, loss, deduction or credit shall, except as otherwise provided in this chapter, be determined by the partnership agreement.
(b) Determination of Distributive Share.—A partner's distributive share of income, gain, loss, deduction, or credit (or item thereof) shall be determined in accordance with the partner's interest in the partnership (determined by taking into account all facts and circumstances) if—
1) the partnership agreement does not provide as to the partner's distributive share of income, gain, loss, deduction, or credit (or item thereof), or
2) the allocation to a partner under the agreement of income, gain, loss, deduction, or credit (or item thereof) does not have substantial economic effect.

The partnership agreement usually controls the allocation. Each partner's distributive share of income, gain, loss, deduction, or credit is allocated according to the desires of the partners as expressed in this agreement. The most sophisticated partnership agreement is a formal document drafted by a competent attorney; the least formal is a simple oral understanding.

SPECIAL ALLOCATIONS   Unfortunately, an agreement among the partners as to how they will allocate partnership gain, loss, income, deductions, and credits will not always be honored. Section 704(b) provides that the partnership agreement will not be followed for tax purposes unless the allocations have substantial economic effect. Determining whether an allocation meets this standard is not an easy task. Normally, however, an allocation will have substantial economic effect if:

1.   The allocation can affect the dollar amount of the partner's share of partnership income or loss independently of tax consequences;
2.   The partner's cash flow in liquidation of his or her interest will be affected by the allocation.

In addition, an allocation may not be recognized unless it was made for a good business purpose. Other factors of lesser importance help determine whether a particular allocation will be honored. Several illustrations should help clarify this concept.

Example 1: Assume that the AB partnership earns income from investments in municipal and corporate bonds. The municipal bonds pay $5,000 tax-free interest to the partnership. The corporate bonds generate fully taxable interest income of $10,000. All $5,000 of the tax-free interest is allocated to Partner A, who is in a higher marginal tax bracket than Partner B. An equal amount of taxable interest is allocated to Partner B, with the remaining taxable income being divided equally between Partners A and B. Although each partner receives 50 percent of the partnership income, more tax-favored income is received by the partner in the higher marginal tax bracket. The only reason for making this allocation is to save taxes. Because an equal division of all partnership income would have resulted in each partner receiving the same pretax income, the allocation has no substantial economic effect.

Example 2: Now assume that Partner A is allocated all the tax-exempt income and also the gains or losses that will be recognized when the tax-exempt securities are sold. Partner B is allocated all the interest from the corporate bonds and will recognize the gains or losses generated by the sale of these bonds. Each partner's cash flow on liquidation will be affected by this allocation. Thus, each partner receives all the income, gain, or loss and resulting cash flow in respect to a particular type of investment. Partner B will receive $10,000 of interest while Partner A receives only $5,000. Although A's interest may be more tax-favored than B's, the economic realities of the situation support the validity of the allocation. After all, each partner could withdraw cash, invest it in the respective securities individually, and achieve the same economic results. To forbid this result merely because the partnership holds title to the securities would be a triumph of form over substance.

Sometimes the partnership agreement fails to provide for any allocation of income, gain, loss, deduction, or credit. Moreover, as mentioned above, an allocation may be disregarded if it does not have substantial economic effect. When either of these situations occurs, each partner's distributive share of income, gain, loss, deduction, or credit will be determined according to the partner's proportionate interest in the partnership. Although what constitutes a partner's proportionate interest is open to debate, most tax experts think the partner's proportionate share of bottom-line income is the appropriate measure.

Two final points should be examined with regard to special allocations. Recall from Chapter 10 that Sec. 704(c)(2) permits allocations that take into consideration the difference between the fair market value and the basis of contributed property. In addition, Sec. 704(c)(3) permits treating certain undivided interest in

property as if the partners had never contributed these interests to the partnership. These allocations may always be made. They do not have to satisfy the substantial economic reality test of Sec. 704(b). In fact, they are permitted even though the only purpose for the allocation is tax avoidance.

Effect of partnership operations on the partner's basis

In Chapter 10, we discussed how to compute a partner's adjusted basis when the partnership is formed. We observed that the partner's adjusted basis in the newly formed partnership usually equals (1) his or her adjusted basis in any property he or she contributed to the partnership, *plus* (2) the fair market value of any services he or she performed for the partnership, and (3) the partner's proportionate share of partnership liabilities.

A partnership interest also may be acquired after the partnership has been formed. The method of acquisition controls the way the partner's adjusted basis is computed. If the partnership interest is purchased from another partner, the new partner's basis is the cost of the interest. The basis of a partnership interest acquired by gift is the donor's cost of the interest or the fair market value of the interest at the date of the gift, whichever is lower. Generally, some or all of the transfer taxes paid on the gift may be added to the donee partner's adjusted basis. The basis of a partnership interest acquired through inheritance is usually the fair market value of the interest at the date of death.

PARTNER'S ADJUSTED BASIS—GENERAL RULE   Section 705 provides that the adjusted basis of a partnership interest is increased or decreased by the results of partnership operations. Operating results that increase a partner's adjusted basis are:

1.   The partner's proportionate share of partnership income (including capital gains and tax-exempt income);
2.   The partner's proportionate share of any increase in the partnership liabilities.

Operating results that decrease a partner's basis in the partnership are:

1.   The partner's proportionate share of partnership losses (including capital losses);
2.   The partner's proportionate share of nondeductible expenses;

3. The partner's proportionate share of any decrease in partnership liabilities;

In addition, a partner's adjusted basis is reduced by:

1. The adjusted basis of any partnership property distributed to the partner in a current distribution (this rule is modified in certain circumstances, which we shall discuss in Chapter 12); and
2. The amount of money distributed to the partner.

Once a partner's adjusted basis is reduced to zero, any additional distributions may produce taxable gain to that partner. Under no circumstances may a partner's adjusted basis be reduced below zero.

Generally, a partner is required to compute his or her adjusted basis only at the end of the partnership year. Treasury Regulation 1.731-1(a)(1)(ii) provides that drawings of money or property shall be treated as current distributions made on the last day of the partnership year. Because a reduction in a partner's share of liabilities is treated like a distribution of cash, that reduction also will be determined only at year-end. This relieves the partner from making day-to-day calculations of basis. When a partnership interest is sold, exchanged, or retired, however, the partner must compute his or her adjusted basis as of the date the transaction occurs. Basis must be calculated because these transactions may generate taxable gain or loss. Computation of the gain or loss requires an accurate calculation of the partner's adjusted basis on the date of the transaction.

PARTNER'S ADJUSTED BASIS—SPECIAL RULE   Sometimes partners may not be able to calculate the adjusted basis of their interest according to the rules outlined above. The partnership records may have been lost or stolen, thereby making it impossible to calculate basis directly. Alternatively, a partnership interest may have been received as a gift from a donor who failed to maintain accurate records. Fortunately, a special rule comes to the rescue of such partners. Section 705(b) and its related regulations state that a partner's adjusted basis may be simply his or her proportionate dollar interest in the adjusted basis of partnership property. This special rule may be used when:

1. The partner cannot practicably compute his or her basis under the general rule; or
2. The I.R.S. is satisfied that the calculation of basis under the special rule will not vary substantially from the basis that would have been computed under the general rule.

Example: To illustrate the application of the special rule, assume that Able received his one-third interest in the ABC partnership as a gift from his father. Ten years later, and several years after his father has died, Able decides to sell his interest. Able has never computed his adjusted basis in the partnership and his father's records were destroyed shortly after his death. Able does know, however, that his one-third interest in the basis of the partnership's assets is $20,000. Therefore, under this special rule, Able's adjusted basis for his partnership interest is deemed to be $20,000.

A bill was introduced in Congress in 1960 that would have made the special rule the general rule and the general rule the special rule. According to this bill, a partner's adjusted basis in the partnership generally would be his or her proportionate share of the adjusted basis of the partnership assets. The exact method of computing basis would be utilized only if the partner elected. Although passage of this bill would have made the tax accountant's job much easier, the bill was never made law.

LOSS LIMITATION RULES   A partner may deduct losses only if his or her adjusted basis in the partnership is greater than zero. This basis must exist at the end of the partnership tax year during which the loss was incurred. Specially stated deductions and losses as well as bottom-line loss are subject to this limitation. Any loss that cannot be deducted currently may be deducted at the end of any subsequent year in which the partner's adjusted basis for his or her partnership interest exceeds zero. A partner may carry over the disallowed losses indefinitely, provided he or she maintains an interest in the partnership. Any carryover loss not used before the partner disposes of his or her interest, however, is lost forever and may not be used by the transferee or by the ex-partner in future years.

Example: Assume that on December 31, 1979, Ralph has an adjusted basis of $5,000 in the calendar-year RST partnership. Ralph's proportionate share of partnership losses for 1979 is $12,000. Ralph may claim $5,000 of the loss on his personal return for 1979, thereby reducing his adjusted basis in the partnership to zero. The remaining $7,000 of loss may be used in the first year Ralph obtains some basis. If Ralph has an adjusted basis before the loss carryover of at least $7,000 on December 31, 1980, he may deduct the entire $7,000 on his 1980 tax return.

A thorny technical problem arises when a partner's distributive share of deductions and losses exceeds his adjusted basis in the partnership. Because only some of these deductions and losses may be claimed by him currently, a decision must be made regarding which should be claimed and which should be deferred. Treasury Regulation 1.704-1(d)(4) requires that the partner claim a proportionate share of each loss according to the following formula:

$$\frac{\text{Loss or deduction being claimed}}{\text{Total partnership losses and deductions}} \times \begin{array}{c} \text{Partner's adjusted basis} \\ \text{at the end of the partnership} \\ \text{tax year} \end{array}$$

Example: To illustrate, assume Mary is a one-half partner in the MJ partnership. Her adjusted basis at year end is $20,000. The partnership incurs a bottom-line loss of $15,000 and a net short-term capital loss of $10,000. Mary may claim $12,000 [($15,000 ÷ ($10,000 + $15,000)) × $20,000] of bottom-line loss and $8,000 [($10,000 ÷ ($10,000 + $15,000)) × $20,000] of short-term capital loss on her tax return.

As noted previously, any losses not deducted currently may be carried over indefinitely. Each deduction or loss carried over retains its character for tax purposes. These rules are an excellent example of how the aggregate theory is applied to a partnership tax problem. Losses and deductions pass through to the partners, retain their character when passed through, and keep that character regardless of when they are claimed on the partner's personal return.

Before 1954, the Code did not specifically limit the amount of losses or deductions a partner could claim on his or her return. Because of this lack of statutory authority, several early cases permitted a partner to deduct losses in excess of the partner's basis in the partnership. After the loss limitations were written into the Code, partners sought other ways of maximizing deductions. One way was to specially allocate partnership losses and deductions among the partners. By allocating greater amounts of losses and deductions to certain partners, greater tax benefits could be achieved for the partners as a whole. Because these allocations often were implemented solely for tax avoidance purposes, the I.R.S. was quite successful in persuading courts to overturn such tax-motivated allocations.

Most special allocations may be classified under one of two categories. Special allocations of deduction or loss among existing partners, which were discussed earlier, are now required by the Code to have "substantial economic effect." The other type involves the retroactive allocation of deductions or losses. "Retroactive allocations" are allocations to incoming partners of deductions and losses that were realized by the partnership before the new partner purchased the partnership interest.

RETROACTIVE ALLOCATION OF LOSS   A partnership offering retroactive allocations to an incoming partner was once a favorite investment vehicle for the investor seeking year-end tax relief.

Example: Assume that Peter, a high-bracket calendar-year taxpayer, examines his personal tax situation on December 10, 19X1. He discovers that he will be paying a 70 percent marginal tax rate on $50,000 of his taxable income. Enter the TS partnership. Peter is promised that he will be allocated all the partnership's $50,000 loss for the calendar-year if he will invest $50,000 by December 25, 19X1. Peter invests the cash and claims the loss on his personal return. If the retroactive allocation is not challenged by the I.R.S., Peter saves $35,000 ($50,000 × 0.70) in taxes. Thus, Peter's net investment in the partnership is only $15,000 ($50,000 − $35,000).

Retroactive allocations always appeared risky. It makes little sense to permit an allocation to a new partner of deductions or losses that were realized before the partner obtained the partnership interest. Some tax experts, however, observed that the special allocation of bottom-line income or loss did not appear to be restricted by the literal wording of the Code. Several cases wrestled with the issue. Finally, in 1976, Congress cleared the air by passing an amendment to Sec. 706(c)(2)(B) of the Code, which states that a new partner may obtain a share of the partnership deduction or loss for only that portion of the year that the new partner holds his or her partnership interest. This provision has eliminated retroactive allocations from the list of potential tax benefits available to the investor seeking a tax shelter.

PLANNING LOSS DEDUCTIONS   An interesting tax-planning opportunity arises because of the basis restrictions imposed on the deductibility of partnership losses. These restrictions permit a partner to control—within limits—the timing of the deductions.

Example: Assume Susan's adjusted basis in the partnership is $5,000 at the end of the current year. Her distributive share of the partnership's bottom-line loss is $12,000. She will deduct $5,000 of the loss on her Form 1040, thereby reducing her adjusted basis to zero. The other $7,000 of loss will be held in "suspense" until she has some more adjusted basis at the end of some future partnership year. To a limited extent, how much she may deduct in any particular year is within her control. Her contribution of additional capital will increase her adjusted basis and, thereby, permit her to claim some or all of the loss deductions. Conversely, if Susan withdraws cash or property, her adjusted basis will usually be reduced, and some or all of the loss deduction may be postponed until a later year. Thus, Susan may claim the losses in those tax years that provide her the best after-tax situation. If the transactions that increase or decrease her adjusted basis also have a valid business purpose, the I.R.S. should find little to challenge in her plan.

Changes in taxable years

In Chapter 10, we discussed the problems involved in choosing a partnership's taxable year. Now, we shall focus on changes that may be made in the partnership's taxable year after the partnership has been formed. Section 706(b), which deals with such changes, reads in part as follows:

> Section 706(b)(1). Partnership's taxable year.—. . .A partnership may not change to . . . a taxable year other than that of all its principal partners unless it establishes, to the satisfaction of the Secretary, a business purpose therefor.

In addition, a principal partner is restricted in making changes in his or her tax year. Section 706(b)(2) reads:

> Section 706(b)(2). Partner's taxable year.—A partner may not change to a taxable year other than that of a partnership in which he is a principal partner unless he establishes, to the satisfaction of the Secretary, a business purpose therefor.

A principal partner is one who has at least a 5 percent direct interest in the capital or profits of the partnership.

Congress has good reasons for generally requiring both the partner and the partnership to be on the same taxable year. Before this requirement, calendar-year partners often had the partnership adopt a January 31 year end. This permitted an 11-month deferral of taxes. Partnership income for the February 1, 19X0—

January 31, 19X1 fiscal year was reported on the partner's personal tax return for 19X1. Taxes on this income were not finally due until April 15, 19X2. This deferral of taxes effectively permitted the partners to obtain an interest-free loan from the government. Section 706(b) was an effort to plug this loophole.

In general, once a partnership is established, neither the partnership nor the principal partners may change to a different taxable year unless the change is requested because of a good business need. Normally, the I.R.S. will not scrutinize closely the proposed business purpose if the change results in no more than a three-month deferral of income to a partner. For example, the I.R.S. will usually permit a calendar-year partnership to change to a September 30, October 31, or November 30 year end, provided the principal partners are all calendar-year taxpayers. Establishing a satisfactory business purpose for a change resulting in a greater than three-month deferral of income is much more difficult.

A "satisfactory business purpose" is not easily defined. Neither the committee reports nor the statute elaborate on its meaning. Much depends on the impact of the alleged purpose on the partnership making the request. The regulations provide that a change to a natural business year normally constitutes a good business purpose. Conversely, a change made to benefit the personal schedules of the individual partners will not be a sufficient purpose.

Partner–partnership transactions

Many types of transactions may occur between a partnership and one of its partners. The partner may contribute property to the partnership, perform services for the partnership, or receive distributions from the partnership. The partner may borrow money from or lend money to the partnership. Property may be bought and sold between the partner and the partnership. Because we examined certain of these transactions in the previous chapter, we shall not discuss them further. The remaining types of partner–partnership transactions will be the focus of this section.

Before we can effectively examine the taxation of partner–partnership transactions, however, we must decide whether the aggregate or the entity theory should govern the taxation of these transactions. As early as 1928, the Tax Court held that a bona fide sale should be treated as if made between nonrelated parties, thus applying the entity theory to the entire transaction.

The Bureau of Internal Revenue was not happy with this decision. The General Counsel issued a memorandum in 1932 stating that the aggregate theory should apply to partner–partnership transactions. The partner selling the asset was regarded as having sold a proportionate portion of the asset to each of the other partners. Under this interpretation, the partnership entity was ignored.

It appeared by 1950 that the Treasury might be changing its mind. Because the General Counsel memorandum still stated the official position, however, taxpayers were uncertain of the Treasury's viewpoint regarding such sales. Congress finally settled the issue in 1954. Section 707(a) of the Internal Revenue Code of 1954 provides that a partner may engage in a transaction with a partnership just like any outside party. This is definitely an entity theory concept. On the whole, a partner can be assured that the entity theory primarily will govern the taxation of the following transactions:

1. Sales of property between a partner and the partnership;
2. Cash loans made between a partner and the partnership; and
3. Rents paid between a partner and the partnership.

To illustrate the application of Sec. 707(a), consider the following example.

Example: Alan, a one-third partner in the LMA partnership, owns a tract of land that the partnership wishes to buy. The land has a fair market value of $20,000 and a basis to Alan of $14,000. If he sells the land to the partnership, he will recognize the full $6,000 gain, since he is regarded as having sold the land to a completely separate entity. Had the aggregate theory applied to this transaction, he would have been viewed as selling only two-thirds of the land. Only $4,000 of gain would be recognized under the aggregate concept.

PARTNER–PARTNERSHIP TRANSACTIONS—EXCEPTIONS TO GENERAL RULE   Certain exceptions exist to the general rule of Sec. 707(a). Section 707(b)(1)(A) provides that no loss may be recognized on sales or exchanges between a partner and a partnership in which the partner owns, directly or indirectly, a greater than 50 percent interest in partnership capital or profits. In addition, Sec. 707(b)(1)(B) disallows a loss deduction on sales or exchanges between two or more partnerships where the same partner owns, directly or indirectly, more than a 50 percent interest in partnership capital or profits. The disallowed loss may not vanish

completely, however. If the transferee eventually sells the property at a gain, the disallowed loss reduces the gain that the transferee must otherwise recognize. Apparently, the disallowed loss can neither create nor increase a loss realized by the transferee on the sale or exchange of the asset.

Example: Assume Walter is a two-thirds partner in the WX partnership. He sells to the partnership land that has a basis to him of $5,000 and a fair market value of $3,000. The $2,000 loss realized by Walter will be disallowed under Sec. 707(b)(1)(A). If the partnership later sells the land for $6,000, only $1,000 of the gain will be recognized. Conversely, if the land is later sold for $2,000, the partnership will recognize a loss of only $1,000.

Another exception to the general rule of Sec. 707(a) is described in Sec. 707(b)(2). This exception provides that gain on the sale of an asset that will be a noncapital asset to the transferee will be taxed as ordinary income if the sale is made between certain related parties. Sales governed by this section include those between:

1. A partnership and a partner owning, directly or indirectly, more than 80 percent of the capital or profits interest in the partnership; or
2. Two partnerships in which the same persons own, directly or indirectly, more than 80 percent of the capital or profits interest of the partnerships.

Example: Assume that Fred owns a 90 percent capital interest in the FG partnership. He sells a tract of land to the partnership for $20,000. The land has a basis to Fred of $5,000 and will be used by the partnership as a parking lot. Because the lot is a Sec. 1231 asset to the partnership, Fred will recognize $15,000 ordinary income on the sale. This treatment results even though Fred held the property as an investment and normally would have recognized capital gain on its sale.

Both direct and indirect ownership are relevant in applying the 50 and 80 percent tests. Direct ownership exists when the partner owns the partnership interest in his or her own name. More difficult to define, indirect ownership is primarily ownership that is attributed an individual or entity because of a close relationship to the actual owner. A person is regarded as indirectly owning:

1. The capital or profits interest owned by a partnership, corporation, estate, or trust in proportion to the interest in these entities that is owned by that person; and

2. The capital or profits interest owned by the person's spouse, brothers, sisters, ancestors, and lineal descendants. This includes those interests deemed owned by these relatives because the relatives have an interest in a partnership, corporation, estate, or trust that owns an interest in the partnership.

> *Example:* If Rex owns 40 percent of the RST partnership, and Rex's sister, Susan, owns 20 percent of the partnership, both Rex and Susan are treated as owning 60 percent of the partnership. Neither could recognize loss on a sale of property to the partnership. If Ted, their brother, owned the other 40 percent, all three partners must recognize ordinary income on the sale of Sec. 1231 assets to the partnership.

GUARANTEED PAYMENTS   We have just discovered that sales between a partnership and a partner are governed generally by the entity theory of taxation. We also found that the application of this theory to such transactions is based on longstanding judicial precedents. It is interesting then, that the aggregate theory and not the entity theory provided the basis for the first judicial decisions regarding salaries paid to a partner by the partnership. The Board of Tax Appeals in 1927 held that a partner could not be an employee of his own partnership. If a "salary" is paid, the court decided, it was just one step in the division of partnership profits. The I.R.S. agreed with this position.

When Congress drafted the Internal Revenue Code of 1954, it took exception to these earlier precedents. Congress believed that while a partner may not be able to employ himself, a partnership in which he is only a partial owner should be able to pay him a "salary." Thus, Congress passed Sec. 707(c), which reads as follows:

> Section 707(c). Guaranteed Payments.—To the extent determined without regard to the income of the partnership, payments to a partner for services or the use of capital shall be considered as made to one who is not a member of the partnership, but only for purposes of section 61(a)(relating to gross income) and, subject to section 263, for purposes of section 162(a)(relating to trade or business expenses).

Section 707(c) permits salaries paid to partners to be treated, for purposes of Sec. 61(a) and Sec. 263, as if they were paid to outsiders. It also prescribes the same tax treatment for interest paid to partners on their capital accounts. The statute classifies both types of payments as *guaranteed payments*. The tax treatment prescribed by Sec. 707(c) primarily follows an entity theory approach.

Guaranteed payments do not have all the tax attributes of payments made to nonpartners. The partnership is not required to withhold federal income taxes or pay FICA taxes on them. If capital is a material income-producing factor in the partnership, much of the guaranteed payment may not be eligible for special treatment under the maximum tax provisions of Sec. 1348. Thus, while a guaranteed payment may be regarded as paid to a nonpartner, it is only treated that way for purposes of inclusion in the partners' income (Sec. 61(a)) and for deduction by the partnership (Sec. 162(a)). For other purposes, a guaranteed payment is treated much the same as a distribution of profits.

A guaranteed payment is taxed as income to the partner, even if the partnership does not have sufficient income to cover the payment. All guaranteed payments, if not capitalized, are totally deductible from partnership income. If a partnership earns both ordinary income and capital gain, none of the guaranteed payment is deducted from the capital gain. This can result in a shifting of income between the partners.

> *Example:* Assume the JK partnership earns $30,000 of ordinary income before any guaranteed payments and also recognizes $10,000 of long-term capital gain. The partnership makes a guaranteed payment to Jim, a one-half partner, of $35,000. Jim will recognize ordinary income of $35,000 from the guaranteed payment and the partnership will deduct $35,000 from ordinary income. The resulting $5,000 partnership loss and the $10,000 long-term capital gain will be divided equally between Jim and his copartner.

Before 1976, some tax advisors argued that guaranteed payments were automatically deductible by a partnership. They relied on a statement in a Senate Finance Committee Report stating that guaranteed payments are "deductible by the partnership from its ordinary income as business expenses." Guaranteed payments are clearly deductible when they are ordinary and necessary business expenses. But when they are incurred in organizing the partnership or in acquiring a fixed asset, it is unreasonable to permit the partnership to deduct them. Congress recognized it had unintentionally created a problem and, in 1976, amended Sec. 707(c). Now, any guaranteed payment made for a capitalizable expenditure will have to be capitalized by the partnership.

LOANS BETWEEN THE PARTNER AND THE PARTNER-SHIP   Partners often lend money to their partnerships. Interest on such a loan is deductible by the partnership and is taxable income to the partner. These loans rarely become bad debts in a general partnership, because each general partner has unlimited liability on the loan. If a loan does become uncollectible, however, the bad debt loss should be deductible as an ordinary loss by the partner. This contrasts with the deduction permitted shareholders who make loans to their closely held corporation. Such loans typically are deductible as short-term capital losses under the "nonbusiness" bad debt provisions of Sec. 166(d).

TRANSFERS OF PARTNERSHIP INTERESTS

A partner may transfer his or her partnership interest in a variety of ways. The interest may be sold, exchanged, given away, or transferred to an heir after the partner's death. A partner also may abandon the interest or liquidate the interest by receiving distributions of partnership assets. In this portion of the chapter, we shall focus on those transfers that do not require any distribution of partnership assets. Transfers necessitating a distribution of partnership assets are discussed in Chapter 12.

Sale of a partnership interest

One way to transfer a partnership interest is to sell it. Some or all of the interest may be sold either to a third party or to one or more of the other partners. Section 741 provides that the selling partner will recognize capital gain or loss on the sale except to the extent that some or all of the sales price is paid for Sec. 751 assets. Any gain attributable to this special category of asset is taxed as ordinary income. Initially, our discussion will ignore the effects of Sec. 751. We shall examine the complexities created by this section only after we understand the basic rules relating to transfers of partnership interest.

The amount of capital gain or loss recognized by a selling partner is the difference between the amount realized (selling price) and the selling partner's adjusted basis in the partnership. The amount realized usually is the cash and property (valued at fair market value) received by the seller plus the seller's portion of partnership liabilities that are assumed by the purchaser.

Additionally, any liability created by the purchaser on the sale is added to the amount realized if the purchaser owes that liability to the seller. When the seller's entire interest in the partnership is sold, the seller's proportionate share of partnership income or loss to the date of sale increases or decreases the seller's adjusted basis.

The selling partner's holding period for the partnership interest sold depends on how the seller originally acquired it. If the interest was either purchased or received in return for a cash contribution, the holding period begins when the interest was obtained. If the interest was acquired by contributing capital or Sec. 1231 assets to the partnership, the holding period includes the time these assets were held by the contributor. These rules can cause confusion. A partner may sell a partnership interest that was acquired over several years and, therefore, has several holding periods. Fortunately, most partnership interests are held sufficiently long to be treated as long-term capital gain or loss when they are sold.

Example: Assume Moe sold his interest in the MN partnership to Joe for $50,000 cash and Joe's note for $10,000. Moe's adjusted basis in the partnership is $20,000, of which $5,000 is his proportionate share of partnership liabilities. Moe's share of current partnership income to the date of sale is $3,000. The gain is calculated as follows:

Amount received:

Cash		$50,000
Note from buyer		10,000
Liabilities assumed by buyer		5,000
		$65,000
Adjusted basis:		
Original (including share of partnership liabilities)	$20,000	
Share of income to date of sale	3,000	23,000
Gain on sale		$42,000

Section 741 is grounded in the entity theory. The selling partner is treated as having sold an interest in the partnership entity, rather than a proportionate share of each partnership asset. The decision to base the statute on the entity theory came about after much debate. Before the current statute was written, the Tax Court had applied the entity theory in cases before it. In contrast, the Internal Revenue Service and the Court of Claims held that the aggregate concept should apply. The conflict continued until 1950 when the Internal Revenue Service announced it would tax sales of partnership interests under the entity theory. The I.R.S. capitulated because of "the overwhelming weight of authority ... contrary to the position heretofore taken by the Bureau." The passage by Congress in 1954 of Sec. 741 completed the swing to the entity theory.

Purchase of a partnership interest

In the foregoing discussion, we have been concerned with the tax effects to the seller. What are the tax results to the buyer of a partnership interest? The general rules are relatively easy to understand. The buyer's adjusted basis will be the amount he or she paid for the interest, including the amount of cash transferred, the fair market value of property transferred, and the amount of the liabilities either assumed by the buyer or owed to the seller as a result of the transaction. The buyer's holding period for the partnership interest apparently starts on the day after the sale or exchange.

As a general rule, the adjusted basis of partnership assets will not change because of a sale or exchange. An election is available that permits the adjusted basis of partnership assets to be altered in a manner that reflects the purchase price paid. This election, however, may not be made by the purchasing partner alone. It will be valid only if made by the partnership as a whole. We shall discuss this election later in the chapter.

A partner may obtain his or her partnership interest by contributing money, property, or services to an already existing partnership. Because the old partners have not sold any portion of their partnership interest to the new partner, this transaction is not a sale or exchange. It is no different from a contribution of money, property, or services on the formation of the partnership. Accordingly, it is taxed in the same way. This tax treatment was discussed in Chapter 10.

FINANCIAL VERSUS TAX ACCOUNTING   Substantial differences exist between financial accounting and tax accounting for the admission of a new partner to an existing partnership. When a new partner purchases an interest from one or more existing partners, the financial accounting entry depends on the amount the new partner paid for the interest. If book value is paid, the entry is a debit to the old partner's capital account(s) and a credit to the new partner's capital account. If less than book value is paid, adjustments are often made to reduce the inflated book values of partnership assets.

When an amount greater than book value is paid, implied goodwill may be recognized in the accounts.

As a general rule, the tax accountant is not concerned with recognizing goodwill or reducing overvalued asset accounts. Unless a special election is made, the new partner's adjusted basis is not reflected on the partnership books. The tax accountant merely debits the capital account of the seller and credits the capital account of the purchaser. The amount reflected in this entry will be only coincidentally the amount actually paid for the interest by the new partner.

Optional adjustment to basis

When a partner sells his or her partnership interest, the purchaser receives an interest in the partnership as a whole. In a real sense, the partnership interest is treated in much the same way as a block of stock owned by a corporate shareholder. Congress has permitted the entity theory to dominate the tax treatment of such sales. The aggregate theory explains only the tax treatment required for the transfer of an interest in Sec. 751 assets.

While the entity theory makes sense—both theoretically and practically—it also fosters certain inequities. The purchase price reflects what the purchaser believed the partnership interest was worth. To a large extent, this price indicates the value the purchaser places on each of the partnership assets. But because the purchaser has not purchased the partnership assets directly, the adjusted basis of his interest in the partnership will likely differ from his proportionate share of the adjusted basis of partnership assets. Because of this difference, he will not obtain the same tax results he would have obtained if he had purchased the individual assets directly.

Example: Assume May is a one-third partner in the MDE partnership. Kay wants to purchase May's interest. May's one-third interest in the adjusted basis of partnership assets is $15,000. Because these assets have appreciated in value, Kay has to pay $25,000 for May's interest. Thus, although Kay will have a $25,000 basis for her partnership interest, she will only have a $15,000 interest in the adjusted basis of partnership assets.

Congress attempted to remedy this inequity in 1954. Section 754 permits the purchaser to increase or decrease the adjusted basis of partnership assets to reflect the purchase price paid for them. The rules for determining this basis adjustment are contained in

Secs. 743(b) and 755. Section 743(b), which determines the total amount of the adjustment to be made reads as follows:

Section 743. Optional adjustment to basis of partnership property
(a) . . .
(b) Adjustment to basis of partnership property.—In the case of a transfer of an interest in a partnership by sale or exchange or upon the death of a partner, a partnership with respect to which the election provided in section 754 is in effect shall—
  1) increase the adjusted basis of the partnership property by the excess of the basis to the transferee partner of his interest in the partnership over his proportionate share of the adjusted basis of the partnership property, or
  2) decrease the adjusted basis of the partnership property by the excess of the transferee partner's proportionate share of the adjusted basis of the partnership property over the basis of his interest in the partnership.
     Under regulations prescribed by the Secretary, such increase or decrease shall constitute an adjustment to the basis of partnership property with respect to the transferee partner only. A partner's proportionate share of the adjusted basis of partnership property shall be determined in accordance with his interest in partnership capital and, in the case of an agreement described in section 704(c)(2)(relating to effect of partnership agreement on contributed property), such share shall be determined by taking such agreement into account . . .
(c) Allocation of basis.—The allocation of basis among partnership properties where subsection (b) is applicable shall be made in accordance with the rules provided in section 755.

Section 743(b) states first that a valid election must be made under Sec. 754. Although the purchasing partner may be the only one immediately affected by the election, the election must be made by the partnership. The election applies to all sales of partnership interests made after the election is filed. To be valid, an election must be filed along with the tax return for the taxable year during which the transfer occurs. The election may not be revoked without I.R.S. approval.

Next, Sec. 743(b) authorizes a computation that adjusts the purchasing partner's basis in the partnership property. This adjustment is the difference between the purchasing partner's cost basis for the partnership interest and his or her proportionate share of the adjusted basis of partnership assets. The adjustment affects only the purchasing partner's proportionate share of the partnership assets. The other partners will continue to use the old adjusted basis of the assets in computations affecting them.

Section 743(c) requires that the Sec. 743(b) adjustment be allocated to the various partnership properties according to the rules prescribed in Sec. 755. This latter section requires that the Sec. 743(b) adjustment be allocated to each asset in a manner that reduces the difference between the adjusted basis and the fair market value of the partnership properties. Although various technical rules may complicate the application of Sec. 755 in some situations, for our purposes, the general rule stated here is sufficient.

These rules can best be understood by studying a comprehensive example.

Example: Assume the balance sheet of the XYZ partnership, which is presented in Figure 11-1. X, Y, and Z are all one-third partners, who made a valid Sec. 754 election two years ago. Partner Z sells his partnership interest to Partner A for $11,000 cash. Because A assumes Z's share of the partnership liabilities, A's adjusted basis for his partnership interest will be $13,000 ($11,000 cash plus one-third of the liabilities). A's proportionate share of the adjusted basis of partnership property is $10,000 ($30,000 × ⅓). The Sec. 743(b) adjustment is the $3,000 difference between these two amounts ($13,000 − $10,000). Because A's adjusted basis for his partnership interest is greater than his proportionate share of the adjusted basis of partnership assets, the Sec. 743(b) adjustment will increase A's proportionate basis in these assets. The $3,000 will be allocated to the inventory and capital asset as shown in Figure 11-2. Added to the basis of the inventory is $333, and $2,667 is added to the basis of the capital asset. A's proportionate interest in all the partner-

FIGURE 11-1

XYZ Partnership: Balance Sheet

	Adjusted basis	Fair market value
Assets:		
Cash	$ 6,000	$ 6,000
Inventory	8,000	9,000
Capital asset	16,000	24,000
	$30,000	$39,000
Equities:		
Payables	$ 6,000	$ 6,000
X, capital	8,000	11,000
Y, capital	8,000	11,000
Z, capital	8,000	11,000
	$30,000	$39,000

FIGURE 11-2

XYZ Partnership: Allocation of Sec. 743(b) Adjustment to Partnership Assets

| Partnership assets | A's proportionate share of each partnership asset | | Allocation computation | A's proportionate share of adjusted basis after application of Sec. 743(b) |
	Adjusted basis	Fair market value		
Inventory	$2,667	$ 3,000	$\dfrac{\$333}{\$333 + 2,667} \times \$3,000$	$ 3,000
Capital asset	5,333	8,000	$\dfrac{\$2,667}{\$333 + 2,667} \times \$3,000$	8,000
	$8,000	$11,000		$11,000

ship assets now equals $13,000, the cost of his interest in the partnership.

Now, assume that the partnership sells the inventory at its fair market value. Because A has an increased basis for the inventory, he will recognize no gain or loss on the sale. The effect of this transaction on all three partners is detailed in Figure 11-3. Note that if the partnership had failed to make the Sec. 754 election, A would have recognized ordinary income of $333 on the sale of the inventory. This would have been unfair to A, since he had already paid for that appreciation in the $13,000 purchase price of his partnership interest.

Other shifts of partnership interests

A partnership interest may be transferred in several ways other than those discussed previously. For example, a partner may exchange the interest for another partnership interest, or simply abandon the partnership interest to creditors. Because a detailed study of the unique tax problems created by each of these transfers is beyond the scope of this book, the following discus-

sion will be brief and only summarize the major tax problems created by such transfers.

Gain or loss is normally recognized when a partner abandons an interest in a worthless partnership. The amount recognized is measured by the difference between the amount received by the partner and the partner's adjusted basis for his or her partnership interest. Although most partners probably would contend that they received nothing on abandonment, this is not true in most abandonment situations.

How may a partner abandon his or her partnership interest and receive valuable consideration in return? The answer lies in Sec. 752, which governs the effect of partnership liabilities on a partner's basis. Recall that Sec. 752 requires a partner's adjusted basis in the partnership to be increased by the partner's proportionate share of partnership liabilities. Conversely, Sec. 752 also requires that a reduction in the partner's proportionate share of liabilities reduces the partner's adjusted basis. This reduction in liabilities is deemed a cash distribution to that partner. When a partner abandons a partnership interest, the partner is regarded as having received a cash distribution equivalent to his or

FIGURE 11-3

XYZ Partnership: Sale of Partnership Inventory

| | | Allocation of partnership gain | | |
		X	Y	A
Sales price	$9,000			
Less: Basis of inventory to partnership	8,000			
Gain on sale	$1,000	$333	$333	$333
Less: Additional basis for A due to Sec. 743(b) adjustment				(333)
Gain recognized on sale		$333	$333	$ 0

her former share of the partnership liabilities. This deemed cash distribution makes the abandonment a sale or exchange for tax purposes. Capital gain or loss usually is recognized on such sales or exchanges.

> *Example:* Assume Rollie is a partner in the RST partnership. Rollie's adjusted basis for his partnership interest is $30,000. Included in the adjusted basis is his $20,000 proportionate share of partnership liabilities. On December 1, 1979, Rollie abandons his partnership interest. Although he receives no actual cash on abandonment, he is deemed to have sold his interest for $20,000, the amount of the liabilities he relinquishes. The difference between the $20,000 sales price and the $30,000 adjusted basis is a $10,000 capital loss.

If the partnership has no liabilities that are included in the abandoning partner's adjusted basis, no sale or exchange is deemed to have occurred. Thus, the loss on abandonment will be an ordinary loss. Two tax cases were decided with this result before the Internal Revenue Code of 1954 was written.

The exchange of one partnership interest for an interest in another partnership is treated as a taxable sale or exchange. In general, this transaction produces recognized gain or loss. Some partners, however, have attempted to treat these transactions as nontaxable exchanges under Sec. 1031. They reason that a partnership interest is intangible personal property and, therefore, should be able to be exchanged tax free under the like-kind exchange provisions of Sec. 1031. The Internal Revenue Service has disagreed, using two different arguments. First, it contends that a partnership interest is a security and, therefore, may not be exchanged tax free under Sec. 1031. Secondly, the I.R.S. argues that two different partnership interests are not of like kind. To date, the taxpayer has been somewhat successful in refuting the I.R.S. arguments. Further litigation is necessary to clear up the remaining uncertainty in this area.

The "hot asset" problem

The sale or exchange of a partnership interest creates gain or loss for the seller. We have noted previously that the gain or loss will be capital in character, except to the extent that Sec. 751 overrides this general rule. In all the previous illustrations, we have assumed that Sec. 751 had no application. We shall now observe how Sec. 751 complicates the computation of gain or loss on the sale or exchange of a partnership interest.

Before examining Sec. 751 in detail, let us first examine the tax theory underlying it. As noted previously, the recognition of capital gain or loss on the sale of a partnership interest is an application of the entity theory. The partner is regarded as having sold an interest in the partnership rather than an interest in each partnership asset. Section 751 provides an exception to this general rule. To the extent that Sec. 751 assets are transferred in the transaction, they are taxed under the aggregate theory. This means that they are treated as having been sold in a separate transaction from the sale of the partnership interest. Gain on the sale of these Sec. 751 assets produces ordinary income. When a partnership interest is sold, therefore, both the entity and the aggregate theory may apply to different portions of the same transaction. The application of both these theories to what is essentially the same transaction may require many complex calculations.

Why does Congress require transfers of partnership interests to be taxed in this manner? The answer is simply to close a loophole that might otherwise exist. This problem is illustrated in the following example.

> *Example:* Assume Adam, an attorney, is a partner in the ABC law partnership. The adjusted basis of his partnership interest is $4,000. He wishes to sell his interest in the firm to Donna, another attorney, who will become a full partner in the firm. Donna pays Adam $20,000 for his interest, $15,000 of which is for receivables already billed but not yet collected by the cash basis partnership. According to the aggregate theory, Adam would recognize a $16,000 ($20,000 − $4,000) capital gain. However, $15,000 of that gain results from the sale of Adam's interest in unrealized receivables. If Adam had continued as a partner, all $15,000 would have been taxed to him as ordinary income. Clearly, this conversion of ordinary income to capital gain gives Adam an unfair tax advantage. It is this conversion that Sec. 751 seeks to prevent.

Although Sec. 751 is a fairly lengthy section with numerous paragraphs and subparagraphs, its main provision is as follows:

Section 751. Unrealized receivables and inventory items
(a) Sale or Exchange of Interest in Partnership.—The amount of any money, or the fair market value of any property received by a transferor partner in exchange for all or a part of his interest in the partnership attributable to—
　(1) unrealized receivables of the partnership, or—

(2) inventory items of the partnership which have appreciated substantially in value,

shall be considered as an amount realized from the sale or exchange of property other than a capital asset.

The statute classifies Sec. 751 assets as unrealized receivables and substantially appreciated inventory. Unrealized receivables are defined as rights to payment for goods delivered, or to be delivered, and for services rendered, or to be rendered, provided the receivable was not previously included in partnership income. Adam's right to the $15,000 uncollected billings in the previous example is an obvious example of an unrealized receivable under this definition. Unfortunately, many unrealized receivables are not so easily identified.

Another unrealized receivable is the selling partner's share of any potential Sec. 1245 or 1250 recapture on property owned by the partnership. This is the portion of the gain on the sale of a Sec. 1231 asset that is recapturable as ordinary income. Clearly, such "recapture" is not a receivable within the normal meaning of the term. It is classified as an unrealized receivable to ensure that a selling partner does not avoid recognizing his or her proportionate share of "recapture." Section 651 requires the selling partner to compute his or her share of the potential Sec. 1245 or 1250 gain as if the partnership had sold the Sec. 1231 asset immediately before the partner's interest was sold. Any recapture recognized is taxed as ordinary income.

Inventory items are defined in Sec. 751(d)(2) as:

1. Stock in trade of the partnership;
2. Any other partnership property that, if sold or exchanged by the partnership, would not be a capital asset or Sec. 1231 asset (this includes unrealized receivables);
3. Any other property of the partnership that, if sold or exchanged at a gain by the partnership, would be taxed under subsection (a) of Sec. 1246 (relating to gain on foreign investment company stock); and
4. Any other partnership property that, if held by the selling or distributee partner, would be property described in (1), (2), or (3), above.

This definition is quite broad, encompassing many assets not traditionally regarded as inventory. It is important to recognize, however, that these assets are not necessarily segregated for special treatment under Sec. 751. They will only be regarded as Sec. 751 assets if they have substantially appreciated in value. Inventory is considered to be "substantially appreciated" if its fair market value exceeds the following.

1. 120 percent of the partnership's adjusted basis for the property, *and*
2. 10 percent of the fair market value of all partnership property except money.

Inventory is substantially appreciated only if both tests are met. The second test is met in almost every case. Many accrual basis and some cash basis partnerships, however, do not own inventory that is 120 percent appreciated. If this first test is not satisfied, the problems generated by substantially appreciated inventory can be avoided.

The interaction of Secs. 741 and 751 can be more easily understood by examining an illustration.

Example: The balance sheet of the MNO partnership is shown in Figure 11-4. M, N and O are equal partners with an adjusted basis for their partnership interests of $9,000 each. O decides to sell her interest to P, thereby realizing a $3,000 gain. As shown in Figure 11-5 on page **11/16**, $2,400 of the gain is taxed as ordinary income under Sec. 751; the remaining $600 is taxed as capital gain. Although these calculations are quite involved, the complexity is necessary to ensure the proper tax result.

Tax return illustration

A partnership files an informational tax return on Form 1065. The form must be filed (unless an extension is approved) by the fifteenth day of the fourth month after the partnership year-end. The partnership pays no tax on the income reported in the return. Instead, the partners incorporate the information contained in the Schedule K-1 on their personal returns.

FIGURE **11-4**

MNO Partnership Balance Sheet, December 31, 1979

	Adjusted basis	Fair market value
Assets:		
Cash	$ 9,000	$ 9,000
Merchandise inventory	12,000	19,200
Investment in stock	6,000	7,800
	$27,000	$36,000
Equities:		
M, capital	$ 9,000	$12,000
N, capital	9,000	12,000
O, capital	9,000	12,000
	$27,000	$36,000

FIGURE 11-5

MNO Partnership: Calculation of Gain on the
Sale of O's Interest in the Partnership

Sales price of O's interest		$12,000
Less: O's basis in the partnership		(9,000)
Gain recognized on the sale		$ 3,000

Character of the Gain:

I. Test for substantially appreciated inventory

A. 120% test

(1)	Market value of all inventory owned by the partnership		$19,200
(2)	Adjusted basis of all inventory owned by the partnership		$12,000
(3)	Divide (1) by (2) Because this exceeds 120%, the test is satisfied.		160%

B. 10% test

(1)	Market value of all inventory owned by the partnership		$19,200
(2)	Market value of all partnership property other than money:		
	Merchandise inventory	$19,200	
	Investment in stock	7,800	$27,000
(3)	Divide (1) by (2) Because this exceeds 10%, the test is satisfied.		71.1%

C. Calculation of the Character of the Gain

(1)	A's proportionate share of the fair market value of Sec. 751 assets ($19,200 ÷ 3)	$ 6,400
(2)	A's proportionate share of the adjusted basis of Sec. 751 assets ($12,000 ÷ 3)	4,000
(3)	Subtract (2) from (1). This is the Sec. 751 gain taxed as ordinary income	$ 2,400
(4)	A's proportionate share for the remaining fair market value of his proportionate interest ($12,000 − $6,400)	$ 5,600
(5)	A's adjusted basis in the partnership after subtracting the $4,000 basis of inventory ($9,000 − $4,000)	5,000
(6)	Subtract (5) from (4). This is capital gain	$ 600

A partnership tax return is illustrated in the following pages. To conserve space, only portions of pages 1 and 4 of the return and page 1 of Schedule K-1 are reproduced. The portions of Form 1065 that are not reproduced contain the following information:

☐ Schedule A—Cost of Goods Sold and/or Operations

☐ Schedule D—Capital Gains and Losses

☐ Schedule H—Income from Rents

☐ Schedule I—Bad Debts

☐ Schedule J—Depreciation

☐ Schedule K—Partners' Share of Income, Credits, Deductions, and so on

☐ Schedule L—Balance Sheet

☐ Schedule M—Reconciliation of Partners' Capital Accounts

Page 2 of Schedule K-1 contains information on (1) interest on investment indebtedness; (2) investment credit; (3) property contributed to or distributed by the partnership; and (4) partnership activities in international boycotting.

Lines 1–26 on Form 1065 constitute an income statement. Line 26 is "bottom-line income." This income figure does not take into account any item specially stated under Sec. 702. These items are accounted for by the partnership on Schedule K. Schedules A, H, I, and J provide detailed support for the amounts contained in lines 1–26.

The accompanying forms have been completed for the Quentin–Reynolds partnership. Ms. Quentin and Mr. Reynolds are CPAs operating as partners. The partnership is a general partnership and was in existence throughout 1978. Ms. Quentin is the senior partner and does most of the administrative work. Accordingly, she receives a guaranteed payment of $20,000 to compensate for her additional work and seniority. All remaining profits and losses are divided equally between Quentin and Reynolds. One-half the partnership liabilities are included in each partner's adjusted basis. These liabilities are all full recourse loans, and neither partner is protected against loss by guarantees, stop loss agreements, or other similar arrangements. Quentin's capital account on January 1, 1978 was $60,000; Reynolds's was $40,000. Quentin and Reynolds contributed no personal funds to their capital accounts during the year.

An examination of the partnership accounts provides the following information.

Professional fees earned	$100,000	Supplies	1,500
Interest income on certificate of deposit	1,000	Section 1231 gain on building sold by	
Salary paid to secretary-receptionist	12,000	partnership on January 1, 1978 ($6,000	
Rent paid for office space	6,000	of this gain is attributable to	
Salary paid to Quentin		precontribution appreciation, which is	
(guaranteed payment)	20,000	specially allocated to R under Sec.	
Depreciation on furniture and fixtures:		704(c)(2))	5,000
Regular $10,000		Drawings—Quentin	5,000
Additional first year 2,000	12,000	—Reynolds	17,000

Form **1065**

Department of the Treasury
Internal Revenue Service

U.S. Partnership Return of Income

For calendar year 1979,
or fiscal year beginning ...., 1979, and ending ...., 19.....

1979

A Principal business activity (see page 12 of Instructions) _Accounting_	**Use IRS label. Other-wise please print or type.**	Name _QUENTIN & REYNOLDS, CPAs_	**D** Employer identification no.
B Principal product or service (see page 12 of Instructions) _Accounting_		Number and street _5678 OAK BLVD_	**E** Date business started _1975_
C Business code number (see page 12 of Instructions)		City or town, State, and ZIP code _SOMEWHERE, USA 00000_	**F** Enter total assets from Schedule L, line 13, column (D). $

G Check method of accounting:
(1) ☐ Cash   (2) ☐ Accrual   (3) ☐ Other (attach explanation)

H Is this a final return?
☐ Yes   ☐ No

IMPORTANT—You must fill in all lines and schedules. If more space is needed, see page 2 of Instructions. Enter any items specially allocated to the partners on Schedule K, line 16, and not on the numbered lines on this page or in Schedules A through J.

Income

1a	Gross receipts or sales $ .... **1b** Less returns and allowances $ .... Balance ▶	**1c**	100,000
2	Cost of goods sold and/or operations (Schedule A, line 34)	**2**	
3	Gross profit (subtract line 2 from line 1c)	**3**	
4	Ordinary income (loss) from other partnerships and fiduciaries (attach statement)	**4**	
5	Nonqualifying dividends	**5**	
6	Interest	**6**	1,000
7	Net income (loss) from rents (Schedule H, line 2)	**7**	
8	Net income (loss) from royalties (attach schedule)	**8**	
9	Net farm profit (loss) (attach Schedule F (Form 1040))	**9**	
10	Net gain (loss) (Form 4797, line 11)	**10**	
11	Other income (attach schedule)	**11**	
12	**TOTAL** income (loss) (combine lines 3 through 11)	**12**	101,000

Deductions

13a	Salaries and wages (other than to partners) $ 12,000 **13b** Less Jobs Credit $ -0- Balance ▶	**13c**	12,000
14	Guaranteed payments to partners (see page 4 of Instructions)	**14**	20,000
15	Rent	**15**	6,000
16	Interest	**16**	
17	Taxes	**17**	
18	Bad debts (see page 5 of Instructions)	**18**	
19	Repairs	**19**	
20	Depreciation (Schedule J, line 5)	**20**	12,000
21	Amortization (attach schedule)	**21**	
22	Depletion (other than oil and gas, attach schedule—see page 5 of Instructions)	**22**	
23a	Retirement plans, etc. (see page 5 of Instructions). (Enter number of plans ▶ ....) . . .	**23a**	
23b	Employee benefit programs (see page 5 of Instructions)	**23b**	
24	Other deductions (attach schedule) . SUPPLIES. $1,500	**24**	1,500
25	**TOTAL** deductions (add lines 13c through 24)	**25**	51,500
26	Ordinary income (loss) (subtract line 25 from line 12)	**26**	49,500

Schedule A—COST OF GOODS SOLD AND/OR OPERATIONS (See Page 3 of Instructions)

27	Inventory at beginning of year (if different from last year's closing inventory, attach explanation) . .	**27**	
28a	Purchases $ .... **28b** Less cost of items withdrawn for personal use $ .... Balance ▶	**28c**	
29	Cost of labor	**29**	
30	Materials and supplies	**30**	
31	Other costs (attach schedule)	**31**	
32	Total of lines 27 through 31	**32**	
33	Inventory at end of year	**33**	
34	Cost of goods sold (subtract line 33 from line 32). Enter here and on line 2, above	**34**	

Please Sign Here

Under penalties of perjury, I declare that I have examined this return, including accompanying schedules and statements, and to the best of my knowledge and belief, it is true, correct, and complete. Declaration of preparer (other than taxpayer) is based on all information of which preparer has any knowledge.

▶ Signature of general partner   ▶ Date

Paid Preparer's Information

Preparer's signature and date ▶	Check if self-employed ▶ ☐	Preparer's social security no.
Firm's name (or yours, if self-employed) and address ▶	E.I. No. ▶	
	ZIP code ▶	

Schedule L—BALANCE SHEETS (See Page 10 of Instructions)

ASSETS	Beginning of taxable year		End of taxable year	
	(A) Amount	(B) Total	(C) Amount	(D) Total
1 Cash				
2 Trade notes and accounts receivable				
a Less allowance for bad debts				
3 Inventories				
4 Government obligations: a U.S. and instrumentalities				
b State, subdivisions thereof, etc.				
5 Other current assets (attach schedule)				
6 Mortgage and real estate loans				
7 Other investments (attach schedule)				
8 Buildings and other fixed depreciable assets				
a Less accumulated depreciation				
9 Depletable assets				
a Less accumulated depletion				
10 Land (net of any amortization)				
11 Intangible assets (amortizable only)				
a Less accumulated amortization				
12 Other assets (attach schedule)				
13 Total assets				
LIABILITIES AND CAPITAL				
14 Accounts payable				
15 Mortgages, notes, and bonds payable in less than 1 year				
16 Other current liabilities (attach schedule)				
17 All nonrecourse loans (attach schedule)				
18 Mortgages, notes, and bonds payable in 1 year or more				
19 Other liabilities (attach schedule)				
20 Partners' capital accounts				
21 Total liabilities and capital				

Schedule M—RECONCILIATION OF PARTNERS' CAPITAL ACCOUNTS (See Page 11 of Instructions)
(Show reconciliation of each partner's capital account on Schedule K–1, block M)

a. Capital account at beginning of year	b. Capital contributed during year	c. Ordinary income (loss) from page 1, line 26	d. Income not included in column c, plus non-taxable income	e. Losses not included in column c, plus unallowable deductions	f. Withdrawals and distributions	g. Capital account at end of year

Schedule N—COMPUTATION OF NET EARNINGS FROM SELF-EMPLOYMENT (See Page 11 of Instructions)

1 Ordinary income (loss) (Form 1065, page 1, line 26)	**1**	49,500
2 Guaranteed payments to partners included on Schedule K, lines 1a(1) and 1a(2)	**2** 20,000	
3 Net loss from rental of real estate	**3**	
4 Net loss from Form 4797 (Form 1065, page 1, line 10)	**4**	
5 Total (add lines 2, 3, and 4)	**5**	
6 Add lines 1 and 5. (If line 1 is a loss, reduce line 1 by the amount on line 5)	**6**	20,000
7 Nonqualifying dividends (Form 1065, page 1, line 5)	**7**	
8 Interest	**8** 1,000	
9 Net income from rental of real estate	**9**	
10 Net gain from Form 4797 (Form 1065, page 1, line 10)	**10**	
11 Total (add lines 7, 8, 9, and 10)	**11**	1,000
12 Net earnings (loss) from self-employment (subtract line 11 from line 6). Enter on Schedule K, line 9	**12**	68,500

Additional Information Required

	Yes	No
I Is the partnership a limited partnership (see page 2 of Instructions)?		
J Is this partnership a partner in another partnership?		
K (1) Did you elect to claim amortization (under section 191) or depreciation (under section 167(o)) for a rehabilitated certified historic structure (see page 11 of Instructions)?		
(2) Amortizable basis (see page 11 of Instructions) ▶		

	Yes	No
L Will the character of any liabilities in Schedule L (Balance Sheets), other than line 17, change to nonrecourse or become covered by a guarantee or similar arrangement in the future? . If "Yes," enter the year(s) and amount(s) of the anticipated changes ▶		

	Yes	No
M Has any material regarding the offering of a partnership interest or other security ever been registered or filed with a Federal or State agency or authority? If "Yes," attach a statement giving the name and address of the agency(s)		
N At any time during the tax year, did the partnership have an interest in or a signature or other authority over a bank account, securities account, or other financial account in a foreign country (see page 11 of Instructions)?		
O Was the partnership the grantor of, or transferor to, a foreign trust which existed during the current tax year, whether or not the partnership or any partner has any beneficial interest in it? If "Yes," you may have to file Forms 3520, 3520-A, or 926. (See page 11 of Instructions.)		

Partner's Share of Income, Credits, Deductions, etc.—1979

For calendar year 1979 or fiscal year

beginning ...., 1979, and ending ...., 19........

(Complete for each partner—See instructions on back of Copy C)

Copy A
(File with Form 1065)

Partner's identifying number ▶ | **Partnership's identifying number** ▶

Partner's name, address, and ZIP code

MS. MARGARET QUENTIN
1234 OAK BLVD.
SOMEWHERE, USA   00000

Partnership's name, address, and ZIP code

QUENTIN & REYNOLDS, CPAs
5678 OAK BLVD.
SOMEWHERE, USA   00000

	Yes	No
A (i) Date(s) partner acquired any partnership interest during the year ▶		
(ii) Did partner have any partnership interest before 1/1/77? .		X
B Is partner a nonresident alien?		X
C (i) Is partner a limited partner (see page 2 of Instructions)? .		X
(ii) If "Yes," is partner also a general partner? . . .		X
D (i) Did partner ever contribute property other than money to the partnership (if "Yes," complete line 21)? . .		X
(ii) Did partner ever receive a distribution other than money from the partnership (if "Yes," complete line 22)? .		X
(iii) Was any part of the partner's interest ever acquired from another partner?		X
E (i) Did partnership interest terminate during the year? . .		X
(ii) Did partnership interest decrease during the year? . .		X

Time devoted to business . . . . 100 %

G IRS Center where partnership return filed ▶ ....

H What type of entity is this partner? ▶ ....

I Partner's share of liabilities (see page 8 of Instructions):

(i) Incurred before 1/1/77 | (ii) Incurred after 12/31/76

Nonrecourse . . $............... | $...............

Other . . . . $............... | $ 2500

J Enter total amount of liabilities other than nonrecourse for which the partner is protected against loss through guarantees, stop loss agreements, or similar arrangements of which the partnership has knowledge:

Incurred before 1/1/77 . . . . . . $............... 0

Incurred after 12/31/76 . . . . . $............... 0

K Partner's share of any pre-1976 loss(es) from a section 465(c)(1) activity (i.e. film or video tape, section 1245 property leasing, farm, or oil and gas property) for which there existed a corresponding amount of nonrecourse liability at the end of the year in which loss(es) occurred . . . . $............... 0

F Enter partner's percentage of:

	(i) Before decrease or termination	(ii) End of year
Profit sharing	...............%	50 %
Loss sharing	...............%	50 %
Ownership of capital . .	...............%	50 %

M Reconciliation of partner's capital account:

a. Capital account at beginning of year	b. Capital contributed during year	c. Ordinary income (loss) from line 1b	d. Income not included in column c, plus non-taxable income	e. Losses not included in column c, plus unallowable deductions	f. Withdrawals and distributions	g. Capital account at end of year

---

a. Distributive share item	b. Amount	c. 1040 filers enter col. b amount as shown
1 a Guaranteed payments to partner: (1) Deductible by the partnership . . .	20,000	Sch. E, Part III
(2) Capitalized by the partnership		Sch. E, Part III
b Ordinary income (loss)	24,750	Sch. E, Part III
2 Additional first-year depreciation	1,000	Sch. E, Part III
3 Gross farming or fishing income		Sch. E, Part IV
4 Dividends qualifying for exclusion		Sch. B, Part II, line 3
5 Net short-term capital gain (loss) from transactions entered into: **a** After 10/31/78 . . .		Sch. D, line 2
b Before 11/1/78 . .		Sch. D, line 7
6 Net long-term capital gain (loss) from transactions entered into: **a** After 10/31/78 . .		Sch. D, line 10
b Before 11/1/78 . .		Sch. D, line 19
7 Net gain (loss) from involuntary conversions due to casualty or theft: **a** After 10/31/78 . . .		Form 4797, line 1
b Before 11/1/78 . .		Form 4797, line 1
8 Other net gain (loss) under section 1231 from transactions entered into: **a** After 10/31/78		Form 4797, line 4
b Before 11/1/78	4,000	Form 4797, line 4
9 Net earnings (loss) from self-employment	34,250	Sch. SE, Part I or Part II
10 a Charitable contributions: 50% ...., 30% ...., 20%		Sch. A, line 21 or 22
b Other itemized deductions (attach list)		See Sch. A
11 Expense account allowance		
12 Jobs credit		Form 5884, line 9
13 Taxes paid by regulated investment company		Line 61, add words "from 1065"
14 a Payments for partner to a Keogh Plan (Type of plan ▶..........................) .		Line 26
b Payments for partner to an IRA or Simplified Employee Pension (SEP) . .		Line 25
15 a Foreign taxes paid (attach schedule)		Form 1116
b Other income, deductions, etc. (attach schedule)		(Enter on applicable lines of your return)
c Oil and gas depletion. (Enter amount (not for partner's use) ▶..........................)		
16 Specially allocated items (see attached schedule): **a** Short-term capital gain (loss) . . .		Sch. D, line 2
b Long-term capital gain (loss)		Sch. D, line 10
c Ordinary gain (loss)		Form 4797, line 10
d Other		Sch. E, Part III

PROBLEMS

1. Neither the entity theory nor the aggregate theory is followed exclusively in the taxation of partnership operations. List two types of transactions that are taxed under statutory provisions based on the entity theory and two transactions that are taxed under statutory provisions based on the aggregate theory. How might the statutes be written if the other theory had been used to tax each type of transaction?

2. A partnership is a conduit through which various items of income, gain, loss, deduction, and credit pass to a partner. Below is a list of items that may be found on a typical partnership return. Indicate which ones are passed through intact to the partners and which ones must be combined in computing bottom-line income.

   a. Net short-term capital gains
   b. Salary expense to nonpartners
   c. Salary expense to Partner A
   d. Foreign tax credit
   e. Charitable contributions
   f. Cost of goods sold
   g. Royalty income
   h. Depreciation (neither an estate nor a trust is a partner)
   i. Sales
   j. Soil and water conservation expenses
   k. Interest on loans taken out to hold investments
   l. Dividend income
   m. Repairs expense

3. Sylvia and Janet are unrelated taxpayers who own adjoining tracts of land next to a new sports complex. Because the complex does not provide adequate parking facilities, Sylvia and Janet decide to establish a partnership that will operate a parking lot on their adjoining tracts. Each will sell her land to the newly formed partnership. Sylvia and Janet will divide the land into 200 parking spaces and rent out these spaces to spectators attending games played in the complex. Each tract will be sold to the partnership for $100,000. Each woman has a basis in her tract of $60,000. Both women have held their land for two years as an investment. What are the tax results of the sale of this land to the partnership?

4. Trace the history of the conduit theory in partnership taxation. What trend is evident? Is this trend inevitable? What undesirable consequences might occur as a result of this trend?

5. Which of the following partnership provisions have "substantial economic effect"? For those that have no substantial economic effect, how might they be changed to satisfy this test?

   a. All depreciation will be allocated to Partner X. Upon sale of the depreciable asset, gain will be allocated to X to the extent of any depreciation claimed previously by the partnership on the asset. All cash flow is to be distributed equally.

   b. All intangible drilling costs will be allocated to those partners who contribute cash to pay for these costs. Each partner's share of income, gain, loss, deduction, and drawings will be reflected in the partner's capital account. Upon liquidation of the partnership, the amounts receivable by the partners will be distributed in accordance with their capital accounts.

   c. Partner A will be allocated all the interest income, gain, or loss from the investment in City of Blanksville bonds. Partner B will be allocated all the interest income, gain, or loss from the investment in Flupper Corporation bonds. The partners' capital accounts will reflect these allocations. Upon liquidation of the partnership, the amounts receivable by the partners will be distributed in accordance with their capital accounts.

6. Mildred, a calendar-year taxpayer, has an adjusted basis in the MNO partnership of $70,000 on January 1, 1979. Her share of partnership operations for 1979 is detailed below:

Proportionate share of partnership bottom-line income	$20,000
Net long-term capital gains	6,000
Drawings	(10,000)
Interest paid on loan to buy City of Blanksville bonds	(4,000)
Interest on City of Blanksville bonds	7,000
Decrease in Mildred's share of partnership liabilities	(30,000)

   a. What is Mildred's adjusted basis for her partnership interest on January 1, 1980?
   b. If Mildred's adjusted basis for her partnership interest on January 1, 1979 was $10,000, (1) what is her adjusted basis on January 1, 1980, and (2) how much gain or loss will she recognize in 1979?
   c. Now assume that Mildred does not know what her basis is on January 1, 1979. Does the Code provide an alternative way for her to compute her basis?

7. Kate is a partner in the KLM partnership. Both Kate and the partnership are calendar-year taxpayers. Kate's adjusted basis for her partnership interest on January 1, 19X1 was $12,000. Her proportionate share of partnership income and loss for the next three years is shown below:

Year	Bottom-line income (loss)	Long-term capital gain (loss)
19X1	$ 2,000	$ 10,000
19X2	(20,000)	(10,000)
19X3	15,000	(5,000)

   a. How much bottom-line income (loss) and long-term capital gain (loss) will Kate report on her partnership tax return in each of these three years?
   b. Is there any way she can tax plan to change this result?

8. Dennis is a potential investor in the ZAP partnership. Both Dennis and ZAP report on a calendar year for tax purposes. ZAP offers Dennis two alternative propositions, neither of which he thinks he can refuse. These propositions are:
   a. If Dennis invests $20,000 cash in ZAP by December 31, he will be allocated 50 percent of ZAP's bottom-line loss for the entire year. It appears ZAP will lose $50,000 this year.
   b. Alternatively, Dennis will be allocated $20,000 of deductions that were paid by ZAP in December with his $20,000 investment. ZAP is a cash basis taxpayer and needed Dennis's investment to pay certain liabilities that had accrued as of December 1.

   You are Dennis's tax advisor. Would you advise him to accept either or both of these propositions? Why or why not?

9. Aaron, Bob, and Carol operate as the ABC partnership. All three individuals are on a calendar year for tax purposes. They want a taxable year for the partnership different from the partnership's current December 1–November 30 fiscal year.

Indicate which of the following potential partnership tax years (1) requires I.R.S. approval or (2) requires a satisfactory business purpose, or both

a. January 1–December 31

b. February 1–January 31

c. July 1–June 30

d. October 1–September 30

Assuming that only a weak business purpose is presented to the I.R.S., what are the relative chances, in your opinion, of each of these tax years being approved by the I.R.S.?

10. Rudolph and Roscoe, two unrelated taxpayers, formed the Double-R partnership. Originally, Rudolph owned a 90 percent interest and Roscoe a 10 percent interest in partnership capital and profits. Last year, however, Rudolph transferred one-half his interest to an irrevocable trust for the benefit of his son, Klaus. Indicate the tax treatment given each of the following independent transactions:

a. Sale by Rudolph of investment securities to the partnership for $20,000. The partnership plans to hold the securities as an investment. Rudolph's basis in the securities is $5,000. He has owned the securities for two years.

b. Sale by Roscoe of raw land he held as an investment to the partnership for $30,000. The partnership also plans to hold the land as an investment. Rudolph's basis for the land is $10,000.

c. Sale by the trust of investment securities to the partnership for $10,000. The partnership plans to sell the securities on the open market. The trust's basis in the securities is $25,000.

d. Sale by Rudolph of raw land to the partnership for $60,000. The partnership plans to construct an office building on the land. Rudolph's basis for the land is $20,000.

Assume that the partnership resold each of the properties purchased in parts a–d above for $70,000 fifteen months later. How much gain will be recognized by the partnership on each of these sales? What will be the character of each of these gains?

11. Mr. Sharpie owns a one-third interest in the Shyster, Smoothie, and Sharpie partnership. Mr. Sharpie sells his interest for $30,000. His adjusted basis for his interest is $12,000, and he has held the interest for five years. What are the tax consequences presented in each of the following situations? Treat each situation independently.

a. The partnership has accounts receivable of $10,000. The partnership is on the cash basis.

b. The partnership has Sec. 1231 assets that have a basis of $12,000 and a fair market value of $16,000. Depreciation claimed on the assets is $8,000. The assets are subject to Sec. 1245 recapture.

c. The partnership has an inventory of imitation rubies with a basis of $14,000 and a fair market value of $21,000. The fair market value of all partnership assets (except cash) is $150,000.

12. The balance sheet of the MFT partnership on January 1, 19X9 is shown below:

	Adjusted basis	Fair market value
Cash	$ 6,000	$ 6,000
Land	9,000	12,000
Building (net of straight-line depreciation)	6,000	18,000
	$21,000	$36,000

	Adjusted basis	Fair market value
M, capital	$ 7,000	$12,000
F, capital	7,000	12,000
T, capital	7,000	12,000
	$21,000	$36,000

On January 1, 19X9, M sold her one-third interest in the partnership to Linda for $8,000 cash and Linda's personal note for $4,000. Required:

a. How much gain or loss does M recognize on the sale? What is the character of this gain or loss?

b. Assuming the Sec. 754 election is not made, how much gain or loss will Linda recognize from the sale of the land for $12,000 on January 12, 19X9?

c. Assuming the Sec. 754 election is made, by how much may Linda increase her adjusted basis in the land and building owned by the partnership? Would this change your answer in part b, above?

13. The balance sheet of the HIJ partnership is shown below:

	Adjusted basis	Fair market value
Cash	$ 4,000	$ 4,000
Accounts receivable	-0-	6,000
Building (depreciated using straight-line depreciation)	2,000	5,000
Land (held for investment)	60,000	120,000
	$66,000	$135,000
H, capital	$22,000	$ 45,000
I, capital	22,000	45,000
J, capital	22,000	45,000
	$66,000	$135,000

H sells his interest to K for $45,000.

a. How much gain does K recognize on the sale? What is the character of the gain?

b. If the Sec. 754 election were in effect, how much income would K recognize when the $6,000 accounts receivable are collected?

c. If the building had been depreciated using accelerated depreciation, and the excess of the accelerated depreciation over straight-line depreciation is $1,000, how much ordinary income would H recognize on the sale of his interest for $46,000?

14. JLP is a calendar-year partnership. Profits and losses are shared equally by J, L, and P. Because J was responsible for attracting the majority of the clients during 19x8, the partners agreed to allocate 50 percent of the profits earned during the year to J. The reallocation of profits was agreed to on December 31, 19x8. Will this special allocation be recognized for tax purposes?

15. Wiggly and Biggly agreed to form a partnership and share profits and losses equally. Wiggly contributed $50,000 and Biggly contributed $5,000. The partnership lost $10,000 in the first year, and each partner withdrew $4,000 cash for living expenses. Assume no liabilities are outstanding at year end.

    a.   How much of the loss is allocable to Biggly?

    b.   How much of the loss is deductible by Biggly?

    c.   Can Wiggly use any of Biggly's disallowed loss?

    d.   If Wiggly sells his partnership interest to Swiggly at the end of the year, may Swiggly claim any of Biggly's disallowed loss?

    e.   How might the partners have planned their profit and loss sharing agreement to avoid the loss disallowance problem?

16.   John Trueheart's adjusted basis for his partnership interest is $25,000 on January 1, 1978. During 1978, his share of the partnership taxable income is $7,500, and his share of the partnership tax-exempt income is $1,500. Also during the year, the partnership distributed $6,000 to John. What is John's adjusted basis for his partnership interest at the end of the year?

SUPPLEMENTAL PROBLEM

17.   Lyndon is a general partner in the LBJ partnership. Dick is a general partner in the RMN partnership. Both partnerships invest in real estate. Lyndon's adjusted basis for his partnership interest is $40,000, of which $10,000 represents his proportionate share of LBJ's liabilities. Dick's adjusted basis is $50,000, of which $20,000 represents his proportionate share of RMN liabilities. Both partnership interests are valued at $100, 000. Lyndon exchanges his interest in LBJ for Dick's interest in RMN. What are the tax consequences of this transaction to both Lyndon and Dick?

12

partnership distributions and special problems of limited partnerships

After a partnership is established, most of its day-to-day transactions create no unusual tax problems. Revenues earned and expenses paid by the partnership are typically accounted for in the same way as they are by corporations and sole proprietorships. The transfer or liquidation of a partnership interest, however, is taxed in a manner that has no parallel in any other area of tax law. We examined some of these unique tax rules in Chapter 11. We shall discuss more of them in this chapter. We shall also consider some of the unusual tax problems created by limited partnerships and family partnerships.

TERMINATION OF A PARTNERSHIP

A partnership is a hardy entity under tax law. It typically survives for tax purposes even when it has dissolved under state law. Section 708(a) states that a partnership will remain in existence for tax purposes unless it terminates under the rules presented in Sec. 708(b), which permit termination only when:

1. None of the partnership's business, financial, or venture operations is continued by the partners in a partnership; or
2. There has been a sale or exchange of 50 percent or more of the capital and profits interest of the partnership within a 12-month period; or
3. There has been a merger or consolidation of two or more partnerships, and the members of the old partnership or partnerships do not own an interest of

more than 50 percent in the capital and profits of the resulting partnership; or
4. There has been a division of the partnership into two or more partnerships, and the members of the resulting partnership or partnerships do not own an interest of more than 50 percent in the capital and profits of the original partnership.

Let us examine these rules in more detail. An ongoing business organization ceases to operate as a partnership when the business becomes restructured as a corporation, a business trust, or a sole proprietorship. Operating as a corporation or business trust usually requires some overt action by the partners. A partnership will also terminate on the date it converts to a sole proprietorship. This may occur, for example, when one member of a two-person partnership leaves the business.

A partnership also terminates for tax purposes when it no longer carries on any business, financial operation, or venture in partnership form. What constitutes a valid business, financial operation, or venture is a question that must be decided on the basis of the facts and circumstances of each case. It is sufficient for our purposes to note that the courts are quite reluctant to terminate a partnership for lack of sufficient activity. Almost any business or investment activity will keep a partnership in existence for tax purposes.

A partnership will terminate if there is a sale or exchange of 50 percent or more of the total interest in partnership capital and profits within a 12-month period. A sale and resale of the same interest within the prescribed period is counted as a single sale. Thus, no termination occurs if Art sells a 40 percent interest in capital and profits to Burt, and two months later Burt sells the same interest to Bret. The prescribed period may be any period of 12 consecutive months, starting with the first sale of a partnership interest and ending a year later.

Mergers and consolidations

A partnership may be formed through the merger or consolidation of two or more partnerships. The Code provides that a newly formed partnership will be treated as a continuation of any partnership whose members own a greater than 50 percent interest in its capital and profits. If any partnership terminates because of the merger, all the tax elections made by that partnership also terminate.

Occasionally, members of each of two or more partnerships may own more than 50 percent of the capital and profits interest in the newly formed partnership. This occurs when there is overlapping ownership.

> *Example:* If the JKL and LMN partnerships merge into the JKLMN partnership, and if each of the partners in the newly formed partnership owns a 20 percent capital and profits interest, members of both JKL and LMN will own 60 percent of JKLMN. It would appear that neither of the old partnerships terminates. The regulations create an alternative rule in such situations, however. They provide that the new partnership is a continuation of the old partnership that contributed the greatest dollar value of assets to the new partnership. Thus, if JKL contributed assets valued at $40,000, while LMN contributed assets valued at only $30,000, JKL is the continuing partnership. LMN will terminate despite the large interest its partners own in JKLMN.

All the old partnerships terminate when the partners in each of the old partnerships do not own more than 50 percent of the profits and capital interests in the new partnership.

> *Example:* Assume the MN, OP, QR, and ST partnerships merge. If each partner receives a 12½ percent interest in the MNOPQRST partnership, none of the partners in the merging partnerships will own more than 50 percent of the new partnership. MNOPQRST is treated as a newly created partnership that must make its own tax elections.

The termination of a partnership causes many tax ramifications. All elections made by the partnership are lost, including elections to use maximum accelerated depreciation and to adjust the basis of partnership assets under Sec. 754. Termination also results in closing the partnership tax year, which may cause a bunching of income on the partners' personal tax returns. When a termination occurs, other than a termination caused by a merger or a consolidation, the partnership property is deemed distributed to the partners and then recontributed to the continuing partnership. This may cause one or more of the partners to recognize gain or loss. In many cases, the adjusted bases of the recontributed properties are altered as they pass from the old partnership to the partners. Thus, a loss of basis in depreciable assets may be created with a resultant loss of future depreciation deductions. The continuing partnership also must make new tax elections that may not be as favorable to the partnership as the forfeited elections of the old partnership.

> *Example:* To illustrate the bunching of income problem, assume the MLP partnership is on a July 1–June 30 fiscal year. The partnership terminates on December 1, 19X1. Each calendar-year partner will report on his tax return a proportionate share of partnership income for the entire partnership year ended June 30, 19X1, and for the short year ending December 1, 19X1. Thus, each partner must pay tax on 17 months of income. An unusually high tax payment may result in 19X1 from this income bunching.

PARTNERSHIP DISTRIBUTIONS

Distributions of property by a partnership to its partners fall into two distinct categories: liquidating distributions and partially liquidating distributions. Liquidating distributions, which terminate the partner's entire interest in the partnership, may consist of a single distribution or may be one of a series of distributions designed to terminate a partner's interest. Partially liquidating distributions are defined as all distributions that are not classified as liquidating distributions.

Both cash and property may be distributed in either type of distribution. As we shall discuss later, the amount of any gain or loss recognized in the distribution is highly dependent on the types of assets being distributed. Liquidating distributions may result in the recognition of gain or loss. In partial liquidations, only gains may be recognized. When either type of distribution causes a change in a partner's proportionate share of Sec. 751 assets, ordinary income may result. Otherwise, capital gains or losses are generated by both forms of distributions.

Statutory outline

The taxation of partnership distributions is governed by Secs. 731–736. The general operative rules are found in Secs. 731–735 and Sec. 751(b). These rules apply to all partially liquidating distributions and to liquidating distributions made in conjunction with liquidation of an entire partnership.

Somewhat more complex rules apply to payments made by a continuing partnership to a retiring partner or to a successor in interest of a deceased partner. Section 736 splits such payments into two categories. Payments in exchange for the partner's interest in partnership property are taxed under the general rules of Secs. 731–735 and 751(b). Other payments, referred to as Sec. 736(a) payments, are taxed either as guaranteed payments or as distributive shares of partnership income.

For pedagogical reasons, we shall discuss first the general rules of Secs. 731–735. We shall then examine the impact of Sec. 751(b) on these general rules. Section 736 will be the last topic discussed within this section. Although these discussions will be somewhat compartmentalized, do not forget the close relationship between the various topics. For example, a distribution to a retiring partner by a continuing partnership may be subject to the rules of Secs. 731–735, 751(b), and 736.

Before discussing the various Code sections in detail, it might be valuable to examine the Congressional intent underlying these statutes. Keep in mind that Congress has tried to achieve several goals. In general, Congress has decided that it is not feasible to tax partners when they receive property distributions from the partnership. Distributee partners often have little wherewithal to pay the tax. This is particularly true when nonliquid assets, such as real estate, are distributed. Accordingly, a distribution is regarded first as a return of the partner's capital investment in the partnership, reducing the partner's adjusted basis in the partnership. Gain is recognized only when cash or cash equivalents are received in excess of the partner's adjusted basis. Loss is recognized only when unrealized receivables, inventory, and cash are received, and the basis of those assets is less than the partner's basis in the partnership.

Congress also recognizes, however, that blind adherence to the general rule could lead to tax avoidance in certain cases. Accordingly, some or all of a distribution may be taxable if such treatment is necessary to ensure that (1) income does not escape tax completely and (2) the character of potential income will not change from ordinary income to capital gain. Several special rules implement this intent. Both the general rules and the exceptions are discussed in the following pages.

Partially liquidating distribution

Partial liquidations are, technically speaking, distributions that reduce a partner's interest in partnership capital or profits but do not liquidate the partner's entire partnership interest. *Current distributions* are distributions of current profits. Such distributions neither reduce the partner's interest in capital or profits nor liquidate the partner's interest in the partnership. Both types of distributions are taxed identically. For the sake of readability, we have chosen to refer to both these distributions as *partially liquidating distributions*.

The general statutory scheme consists of reducing the distributive partner's adjusted basis in the partnership by the amount of cash and the adjusted basis of the property distributed to the partner by the partnership. The partner usually takes a carryover basis for the property received. This is clearly an aggregate theory approach. The partner is treated as receiving an asset he or she already owned. All the partner must do is shift some basis from the partnership interest to the asset received.

> *Example:* Assume George has an adjusted basis of $30,000 for his interest in the FGH partnership. George receives a car in a partially liquidating distribution. The car has an adjusted basis to the partnership of $2,000. This amount will become George's basis for the car. George's remaining basis in the partnership is $28,000.

It is possible, of course, in a partially liquidating distribution, that the adjusted basis of the property received exceeds the partner's adjusted basis in the partnership. The same general rule usually applies to such distributions; that is, no gain or loss is recognized. The partner's adjusted basis in the partnership is reduced to zero. The property distributed takes a substituted basis equal to the partner's former adjusted basis in the partnership.

Example: Assume George has an adjusted basis of $1,000 for his interest in the FGH partnership. He receives a partially liquidating distribution of a truck that has an adjusted basis to the partnership of $3,000. George's basis in the partnership is reduced to zero, and the truck will take a substituted basis of $1,000.

The general rule outlined above covers all partially liquidating distributions in which the amount of cash (or cash equivalents) distributed does not exceed the partner's adjusted basis in the partnership. Gain will be recognized, however, if the amount of cash and cash equivalents distributed exceed the partner's adjusted basis. Cash equivalents are considered distributed if a partner's proportionate share of partnership liabilities is reduced. Cancellation of a partner's obligation to repay a loan made by the partnership is also treated as a distribution of cash to the partner. The gain recognized equals the amount that the cash (or cash equivalents) received exceeds the partner's adjusted basis in the partnership. If both cash (or cash equivalents) and property are distributed, the cash is regarded as being distributed first.

Example: Assume Georgette's adjusted basis for her partnership interest is $5,000. She receives a partially liquidating distribution from the partnership, consisting of $4,000 cash and a tract of land with an adjusted basis of $4,000 to the partnership. Her proportionate share of partnership liabilities decreases by $2,000 as a result of the distribution. Georgette's adjusted basis is reduced first by the $6,000 ($4,000 + $2,000) of cash and cash equivalents received. Because these amounts exceed her adjusted basis, she recognizes a $1,000 gain. Since no basis remains to allocate, she will have a zero basis for the land.

Advance drawings of current earnings are treated as current distributions on the last day of the partnership's taxable year. They have no tax effect to the partner until that time. If the partner's adjusted basis (including his or her share of this year's earnings) is greater than the cash (or cash equivalents) distributed, no gain is recognized by the partner.

How is the partnership taxed when a distribution is made to a partner? Fortunately, the partnership faces a much less complicated set of tax rules than does the partner receiving the distribution. No gain or loss generally is recognized by the partnership in either a liquidating or a partially liquidating distribution. The only

exception occurs when a distribution results in a disproportionate distribution of Sec. 751 assets. This exception is discussed later in the chapter.

Liquidating distributions

Liquidating distributions are defined by Sec. 761(d) as a single distribution or a series of distributions that result in the termination of the partner's entire interest in the partnership. Many of the general rules already discussed in regard to partially liquidating distributions also apply to liquidating distributions. In addition, liquidating distributions are also affected by several exceptions to the general rules. Because of the importance of these exceptions, we shall focus much of the following discussion on them. Let us examine the general rules first, however.

Either gain or loss may be recognized on a liquidating distribution. Gain is recognized only if the cash (or cash equivalents) distributed to the partner exceeds the partner's adjusted basis in the partnership. The amount of gain is the difference between money received and the partner's adjusted basis in the partnership. The gain is a capital gain except to the extent that Sec. 751 applies. These are the same rules that apply to gains recognized on partially liquidating distributions.

A distributee partner may also recognize a loss on a liquidating distribution. A loss is recognized if:

1. Only money, unrealized receivables, and inventory are received by the distributee partner, and
2. The partner's adjusted basis in the partnership exceeds the partnership's basis in the items distributed.

The word "only" is important. A distribution of any other property will postpone recognition of the loss.

Example: Assume that Mandy receives a liquidating distribution consisting of $2,000 cash and inventory with a basis to the partnership of $5,000. Mandy's adjusted basis for her partnership interest is $10,000. Mandy reduces her adjusted basis in the partnership by $7,000, the amount of cash ($2,000) and the basis of the inventory ($5,000) received. The remaining $3,000 of Mandy's basis may not be allocated to any assets. Therefore, she will recognize this $3,000 as a loss.

When both cash and property are distributed, the cash (or cash equivalents) is considered to be distributed first. Any inventory and unrealized receivables are regarded as being distributed second. The partner's adjusted basis in the partnership is reduced by these distributions on a dollar-for-dollar basis. The partner's basis in the inventory and the unrealized receivables distributed, however, may not exceed his or her remaining basis in the partnership after reduction for the cash distributed. If the partner has any adjusted basis remaining after the distribution of cash, inventory, and unrealized receivables, the basis is allocated to any other assets distributed. Thus, such property receives a "substituted" basis.

Example: Assume the same facts as in the example above, involving Mandy, except now assume one additional fact. Mandy has a favorite chair that she donated to the partnership years ago. The chair has an adjusted basis to the partnership of $10. Mandy insists that the chair also be distributed to her as part of the liquidating distribution. Applying the rules outlined above to this revised fact situation produces the following set of calculations:

Step 1—Distribute $2,000 cash to Mandy. Her adjusted basis in the partnership is reduced to $8,000 ($10,000 − $2,000).

Step 2—Distribute $5,000 inventory to her. This distribution reduces her adjusted basis in the partnership to $3,000 ($8,000 − $5,000).

Step 3—Allocate Mandy's remaining adjusted basis of $3,000 to the chair.

Mandy has an adjusted basis of $3,000 for her favorite chair. Although the chair was probably a Sec. 1231 asset to the partnership, it may be a purely personal capital asset to Mandy. The Code provides for no loss deduction on the sale of purely personal capital assets. Therefore, if Mandy later sells the chair, she may not be able to deduct any loss realized on the sale!

Holding period for distributed property

Section 735 provides the authority for determining the distributee partner's holding period for any property distributed in either a partially or a completely liquidating distribution. The distributee's holding period will include the partnership's holding period for the property. Two exceptions to this general rule are designed to prevent the conversion of ordinary income into capital gain. If inventory items defined in Sec. 751(d)(2)) are distributed, their holding period begins on the date of distribution. A sale or exchange of the

partnership's inventory by the distributee partner within five years from this date will always generate ordinary income or loss. Although it is not impossible for the distributee partner to recognize capital (or Sec. 1231) gain or loss on the sale of such property, he or she must hold the property for five years from the date of distribution and the asset must be a capital (or Sec. 1231) asset in his or her hands at the time of the sale. Therefore, the sale of most distributed inventory produces ordinary income.

The other modification to the general rules concerns unrealized receivables. Ordinary income or loss will always be recognized on the disposition of unrealized receivables by the distributee partner. This modification is not really an exception to the general holding period rules; it simply states that the holding period is irrelevant. Unrealized receivables will always generate ordinary income or loss for the distributee partner, no matter how long they are held.

Optional adjustments to basis

In the first part of this chapter, we discussed the partner's basis for property distributed in either a partially or a completely liquidating distribution. We ignored the basis of property retained by the partnership after a partially liquidating distribution. At first, it would appear that this property is unaffected by the distribution. This observation is correct, unless the partnership has made an election to adjust the basis of undistributed property under Sec. 754.

Recall that the Sec. 754 election permits the purchaser of a partnership interest to adjust his or her basis in the various partnership assets. Now we shall discover that this same election also permits an adjustment to the basis of property retained by the partnership after either a partially or a completely liquidating distribution. Sec. 734(b), which provides the operating rules for making this adjustment, reads in part as follows:

Section 734(b) Method of Adjustment.—In the case of a distribution of property to a partner, a partnership, with respect to which the election provided in Sec. 754 is in effect, shall—
(1) increase the adjusted basis of partnership properties by—
  (A) the amount of any gain recognized to the distributee partner with respect to such distribution under Section 731(a)(1), and
  (B) in the case of distributed property to which Sec. 732(a)(2) or (b) applies, the excess of the adjusted basis of the distributed property to the partnership immediately before the distribution (as adjusted by Sec. 732(d)) over the basis of the dis-

tributed property to the distributee, as determined under Sec. 732, or

(2) decrease the adjusted basis of partnership property by—

(A) the amount of any loss recognized to the distributee partner with respect to such distribution under Sec. 731(a)(2), and

(B) in the case of distributed property to which Sec. 732(b) applies, the excess of the basis of the distributed property to the distributee, as determined under Sec. 732, over the adjusted basis of the distributed property to the partnership immediately before such distribution (as adjusted by Sec. 732(d)).

These rules provide that the partnership will increase the adjusted basis of its retained property by:

1.   The gain recognized by the distributee partner on the distribution, and

2.   The amount that the partner's adjusted basis for his or her partnership interest immediately before the distribution exceeds the partnership's adjusted basis for the property distributed.

The partnership will decrease the adjusted basis of its retained property by:

1.   The loss recognized by the distributee partner on the distribution, and

2.   The amount that the partner's adjusted basis for his or her partnership interest immediately before the distribution is less than the partnership's adjusted basis for the property distributed.

The application of these rules may be better explained by an illustration.

Example: Assume the balance sheet of the CDE partnership is as follows:

	Adjusted basis	Fair market value
Cash	$18,000	$18,000
Land—Tract No. 1	5,000	11,000
—Tract No. 2	9,000	3,000
Inventory	19,000	22,000
	$51,000	$54,000
C, capital	$17,000	$18,000
D, capital	17,000	18,000
E, capital	17,000	18,000
	$51,000	$54,000

C, D, and E are equal partners. Each has an adjusted basis for his partnership interest of $17,000. Partner E receives a liquidating distribution of $18,000 cash. According to the rules discussed above, E will recognize a $1,000 capital gain. After the distribution, but before any further adjustment, the CD partnership's unbalanced "balance sheet" reads as follows:

	Adjusted basis	Fair market value
Land—Tract No. 1	$ 5,000	$11,000
—Tract No. 2	9,000	3,000
Inventory	19,000	22,000
	$33,000	$36,000
C, capital	$17,000	$18,000
D, capital	17,000	18,000
	$34,000	$36,000

C's and D's capital accounts are $1,000 greater than the partnership's basis for the land and inventory. Even if both their capital accounts were adjusted down to $16,500 each for financial accounting purposes, C's and D's adjusted tax bases for their partnership interests would remain at $17,000. C and D have lost $1,000 of potential tax benefit as a result of the distribution to E. This differential will be restored when they dispose of their partnership interest. Currently, however, this may provide little comfort to them.

The election under Sec. 754 relieves this inequity. The $1,000 will be restored to the adjusted basis of the remaining partnership assets. Treasury Regulation 1.755-1(b)(1)(ii) provides that the $1,000 will be added to the adjusted basis of land—Tract No. 1, thereby increasing the basis of the land to $6,000. After this adjustment, the partnership has been brought back into balance as follows:

	Adjusted basis	Fair market value
Land—Tract No. 1	$ 6,000	$11,000
—Tract No. 2	9,000	3,000
Inventory	19,000	22,000
	$34,000	$36,000
C, capital	$17,000	$18,000
D, capital	17,000	18,000
	$34,000	$36,000

Recall that the Sec. 754 election must be made by the partnership. Sometimes, however, the partnership may not want to make it.

Example: Assume the same original facts as above except that Partner E receives both land—Tract No. 1—and $7,000 cash in liquidation of his interest. According to the tax rules discussed previously, E's basis in the tract will equal $11,000, which is his remaining adjusted basis in the partnership after the adjusted basis is reduced by the $7,000 cash. This results in the following unbalanced balance sheet for the partnership:

	Adjusted basis	Fair market value
Cash	$11,000	$11,000
Land—Tract No. 2	9,000	3,000
Inventory	19,000	22,000
	$39,000	$36,000
C, capital	$17,000	$18,000
D, capital	17,000	18,000
	$34,000	$36,000

C and D are probably quite happy with this result. If the Sec. 754 election has not been made previously, it is doubtful that the CD partnership would choose to make the election now. If the election was made previously and is still in effect, however, the CD partnership must make any adjustments required by the election. In this example, the required adjustment would reduce the basis of land tract No. 2 by $5,000. The balance sheet of the CD partnership after the adjustment is as follows:

	Adjusted basis	Fair market value
Cash	$11,000	$11,000
Land—Tract No. 2	4,000	3,000
Inventory	19,000	22,000
	$34,000	$36,000
C, capital	$17,000	$18,000
D, capital	17,000	18,000
	$34,000	$36,000

In each of the above examples, we assumed that each partner's adjusted basis for his partnership interest equaled the balance in his capital account on the partnership balance sheet. This, of course, is not always the case. When these amounts are not identical, the Sec. 734 adjustment may produce some strange results. After examining all the possible effects of a Sec. 754 election, a tax advisor may find that some of these effects are not beneficial to the clients.

Problem with Section 751 assets

In Chapter 11, we learned that the sale of a partnership interest generally produces capital gain or loss. An exception to this general rule occurs when some of the partnership assets are Sec. 751 assets; that is, unrealized receivables or substantially appreciated inventory. To the extent that the seller is deemed to have sold his or her interest in these assets, the sale is taxed as ordinary income. This exception puts an aggregate theory gloss over the general rules based on the entity theory that otherwise govern sales of partnership interests.

Section 751 also applies to partial and complete liquidations of partnership interests. Special rules apply when the distributee partner acquires either more or less than his or her share of Sec. 751 assets as a result of the distribution. More specifically, the rules provide that a sale or exchange is deemed to occur when a distributee partner:

1. Receives unrealized receivables or substantially appreciated inventory in exchange for part or all of his or her interest in other partnership property (including money); or

2. Receives other property (including money) in exchange for some or all of his or her interest in unrealized receivables or substantially appreciated inventory.

These rules are designed to achieve two goals. First, they attempt to prevent the conversion of ordinary income into capital gain. Second, they also try to ensure that ordinary income is taxed to the proper taxpayer. Both goals are achieved, but only by adding great complexity to Subchapter K. A detailed study of these rules is beyond the scope of this book.

It is interesting to note that other provisions of Subchapter K help achieve these same goals independently of Sec. 751. The application of Sec. 735 requires that a distributee partner recognize ordinary income when he or she sells unrealized receivables distributed by the partnership. The distributee partner's sale of substantially appreciated inventory will produce ordinary income when sold within five years after distribution. In addition, Sec. 732(c)(1) will not permit the distributee's basis in inventory and unrealized receivables to exceed the partnership's basis in those assets. Thus, the exceedingly complex rules of Sec. 751 may not have substantial impact on the tax treatment of a distribution. They are like an ax doing the job required of a jigsaw. As Congress keeps expanding the definition of unrealized receivables, however, these rules will have more impact on partnership distributions.

Alternative adjustments under Section 732

After a partnership interest is purchased, the new partner may believe that his proportionate share of the basis of each partnership asset will be adjusted only if the partnership makes a valid Sec. 754 election. This election may not be attractive to the existing partners, who probably will not benefit immediately from the election. Also, the partnership will have to supply some data from its accounting records to support the informational requirements of the election. Because the election must be made at the partnership level, the existing partners can easily veto the election.

Congress recognized the new partner's vulnerable position. A new partner may not unilaterally elect Sec. 754 treatment and may be unable to convince the other partners to join in the election. To help the new partner out of this dilemma, Congress passed Sec. 732(d). This section applies to distributions of partnership property (other than money) made within two years after the distributee partner acquired his or her partnership interest. If the requirements of this section are satisfied, the distributee partner is provided with the same results that would occur had the Sec. 754 election been in effect on the date the partnership interest was acquired.

Conceptually, Sec. 732(d) is easy to apply. The distributee partner determines the amount of the Sec. 743(b) adjustment that would have been made had the Sec. 754 election been in effect when the partnership interest was acquired. The adjustment is then allocated among the various partnership assets according to the rules of Sec. 755. The basis of the assets distributed includes the effects of this hypothetical Sec. 743(b) adjustment.

REQUIRED APPLICATION OF SEC. 732(d)   In some circumstances, the adjustment under Sec. 732(d) is required by statute. This mandatory application occurs when, at the time of the transfer:

1.   The fair market value of partnership property (other than money) exceeds 110 percent of its adjusted basis to the partnership; and

2.   A shift of basis would occur from property not subject to an allowance for depreciation, depletion, or amortization to property subject to such allowance, if the distributee partner were to have liquidated his interest immediately after the transfer; and

3.   The special basis adjustment under Sec. 743(b) would have resulted in different bases for those distributed assets than would have been determined under the general rules of Sec. 732(c).

Congress does not want a distributee partner to increase his other basis in depreciable, depletable, or amortizable property to an amount greater than the property's fair market value. The required application of Sec. 732(d) prevents such basis increases. Without this provision, such basis increases could otherwise result from distributions made by partnerships owning highly appreciated nondepreciable capital or Sec. 1231 assets.

Example: Assume the following information describes the current financial position of the JKL partnership:

	Adjusted basis	Fair market value
Land	$ 9,000	$ 39,000
Machinery	81,000	81,000
	$90,000	$120,000
J, capital	$30,000	$ 40,000
K, capital	30,000	40,000
L, capital	30,000	40,000
	$90,000	$120,000

No Sec. 754 election is in effect. Partner L sells her one-third partnership interest to M for $40,000. Subsequently, the partnership makes a liquidating distribution to M of one-third of both the land and the machinery. Section 732(d) must be applied in this situation because:

1.   The fair market value of partnership property ($120,000) exceeds its adjusted basis ($90,000) by 133 percent. This is greater than the 110 percent required.

2.   Under Sec. 732(c), M's $40,000 basis in the partnership would be allocated according to the relative adjusted bases of the assets distributed as follows.

Land

$$\$40,000 \times \frac{\$3,000}{\$3,000 + \$27,000} = \underline{\$4,000}$$

Machinery

$$\$40,000 \times \frac{\$27,000}{\$3,000 + \$27,000} = \underline{\$36,000}$$

In actuality, when D purchased the interest, he effectively bought an interest in land for $13,000 (⅓ × $39,000) and in machinery for $27,000 (⅓ × $81,000). Thus, the general allocation rules transferred $9,000 of basis from a nondepreciable to a depreciable asset.

3. If Sec. 754 had been elected, the Sec. 743(b) adjustment would have been:

Purchase price of D's interest	$40,000
Adjusted basis of the property effectively purchased by D	30,000
Sec. 743(b) adjustment	$10,000

All $10,000 of the Sec. 743(b) adjustment is allocated to land. After the allocation, D's basis of interest in the land and machinery is $13,000 and $27,000, respectively. This allocation differs from the results obtained in (2).

Thus, all three tests required by the regulations have been satisfied. D will allocate his basis according to (3), above.

DISTRIBUTIONS TO RETIRING OR DECEASED PARTNERS

Payments made by an ongoing partnership in complete liquidation of a retiring partner's interest are classified as income or property payments by Sec. 736. This section also categorizes payments made to the successor of a deceased partner. Although payments could be made in cash, property, or both cash and property, we shall assume all payments are made in cash. It is imperative to realize that Sec. 736 does nothing more than categorize payments. Other Code sections provide the rules for computing the tax effects of these distributions.

Property payments

Payments made for a partner's interest in partnership property are commonly referred to as Sec. 736(b) payments. Any gain or loss recognized by the distributee partner because of these payments will be capital gain or loss. These payments are taxed according to the rules contained in Secs. 731, 732(b), and 751(b), which have been discussed earlier. When determining the amount of Sec. 736(b) payments, partnership assets should be valued at full fair market value. The Internal Revenue Service normally will accept the valuation reached by the partner and the partnership in an arms-length agreement. For purposes of Sec. 736, payments made for unrealized receivables are excluded from the definition of partnership property.

Payments for partnership goodwill are always property payments to the extent of the partnership's basis for the goodwill. If payments for any additional goodwill are specifically provided for by the partnership agreement, such payments also will be Sec. 736(b) payments. If goodwill is not specifically provided for, however, the payments for the additional goodwill are not treated as property payments. Instead, they are treated as income payments under Sec. 736(a).

The Code provides that, in general, Sec. 736(b) payments will be treated first as a return of the partner's basis in the partnership. No loss will be recognized until all the property payments have been made. Likewise, no gain usually is recognized until the entire basis is recovered. An exception exists, however, to this general rule for gain when the total Sec. 736(b) payments are fixed in amount. The regulations permit the distributee partner to recognize only the pro rata portion of the gain that relates to each payment received.

For example, if the Sec. 736(b) payments consist of $12,000 cash and the partner's basis in the partnership is $9,000, 75 percent ($9,000/$12,000) of each payment is a return of basis. The other 25 percent is taxed as a gain. Thus, a distribution of $2,000 in the first year results in a $500 gain being recognized by the distributee partner. If the partner did not elect the pro rata tax treatment, however, he or she would not recognize any gain until the entire $9,000 basis has been recovered. The last $3,000 of cash received produces taxable gain.

Income payments

All payments that are not classified as Sec. 736(b) payments are categorized as Sec. 736(a) payments. Included in this category are payments made for:

1. Additional goodwill (not provided for in the agreement and not purchased earlier);
2. Unrealized receivables (in excess of their basis to the partnership);
3. Certain annuities paid to retiring partners;

4.   Certain lump-sum amounts paid to successors of deceased partners.

In sum, any payments made in excess of the value of the retiring or deceased partner's proportionate interest in partnership property (including stated goodwill) will be taxed as Sec. 736(a) payments.

Two types of Sec. 736(a) payments may be made. Payments that are determined in regard to partnership income are treated as a distributive share of that income. Payments that are not determined in regard to partnership income are treated as guaranteed payments. Payments that are a distributive share of partnership income reduce the amount of income allocated to the remaining partners. Guaranteed payments are treated as a partnership expense, thereby directly reducing the partnership's income. The guaranteed payments are fully taxable as ordinary income to the distributee partner. The distributive shares are taxed to the distributee according to their character. For example, a distributive share may consist of capital gain or loss as well as ordinary income or loss.

The following comprehensive example illustrates the application of Sec. 736(a).

Example: Assume the balance sheet of the ABC partnership reads as follows:

	Adjusted basis	Fair market value
Cash	$12,000	$12,000
Unrealized receivables	-0-	6,000
Land	3,000	9,000
	$15,000	$27,000
A, capital	$ 5,000	$ 9,000
B, capital	5,000	9,000
C, capital	5,000	9,000
	$15,000	$27,000

Partner A is retiring from the partnership. He will receive $12,000 cash, none of which is stated to be for goodwill. A's proportionate one-third interest in the basis of partnership property is $5,000. Partner A will receive $7,000 for this one-third interest ($\frac{1}{3}$ × [$12,000 + $9,000]). Because these are Sec. 736(b) payments, A will recognize a capital gain of $2,000 ($7,000 received less $5,000 share of basis) on this portion of the liquidating distribution.

The rest of the payments will be taxed as Sec. 736(a) payments. Technically, these payments are for A's proportionate share of the unrealized receivables and the unstated goodwill. Because $7,000 is a Sec. 736(b) payment, $5,000 must be a Sec. 736(a) payment. The $5,000 is taxed as ordinary income.

Often, Sec. 736 payments will be disbursed in installments over a period of years. When these installments consist of both Sec. 736(a) and Sec. 736(b) payments, several possibilities exist regarding the timing of income from each of these payments. If the payments are fixed in amount, the Sec. 736(b) portion of each payment generally is completed according to the following formula:

$$\frac{\begin{array}{c}\text{Total fixed}\\\text{payments for}\\\text{this year}\end{array} \times \begin{array}{c}\text{Total fixed}\\\text{Sec. 736(b)}\\\text{payments under the}\\\text{entire agreement}\end{array}}{\begin{array}{c}\text{Total fixed Sec. 736(a) and (b)}\\\text{payments under the entire agreement}\end{array}} = \begin{array}{c}\text{Sec. 736(b)}\\\text{portion of the}\\\text{payment for}\\\text{this year}\end{array}$$

The portion of each installment not treated as a Sec. 736(b) payment will be taxed as a Sec. 736(a) payment.

When the installment payments are not fixed in amount, all the payments generally are Sec. 736(b) payments until the retiring or deceased partner's interest in Sec. 736(b) property has been fully liquidated. All remaining payments are Sec. 736(a) payments.

In the preceding discussion, the word "generally" plays an important role. Other ways of allocating the payments are possible. In fact, the partners may merely agree among themselves to use a different method of allocation. Any reasonable method of allocation will usually be approved, provided that no more is allocated to Sec. 736(b) payments than would be allocated under the general rule.

LIMITED PARTNERSHIPS

Limited partnerships have increased greatly in number during the past 10 years. This growth has resulted primarily from their increased use as tax shelters. In many ways, limited partnerships operate no differently from general partnerships. Both require a joint contribution of capital or services by the partners. Profits and losses generated by both types of organizations are shared among the partners according to the partnership agreement. Many other similarities exist between both forms of partnerships.

The principal difference between a limited partnership and a general partnership concerns each partner's personal liability for obligations incurred by the partnership. In a general partnership, each partner's personal assets may be tapped to pay partnership creditors. If partnership assets are insufficient to satisfy the legitimate claims of partnership creditors, the creditors may demand payment from any of the partners. In a limited partnership, only the general partners are personally liable for partnership debts. Limited partners are liable for the partnership debts only to the extent of their actual investment in the partnership.

In return for exemption from personal liability, limited partners may not help manage or control the partnership. Any attempt by a limited partner to direct the operations of the partnership will result in the forfeiture of his or her status as a limited partner. Upon losing this status, he or she will be treated as a general partner and, as a result, will have unlimited liability for partnership obligations.

Association (corporate) versus partnership status

A limited partnership incurs a greater risk of being taxed as an association (that is, a corporation) than does a general partnership. A general partnership established under a state law based on the Uniform Partnership Act will always be taxed as a partnership. While limited partnerships are more vulnerable to a finding of corporate status, the Treasury's own regulations almost always require that a limited partnership be taxed as a partnership. The regulations specify four different characteristics of corporations to be used to determine corporate status. A partnership will not be taxed as a corporation unless three of the four characteristics indicate corporate status.

The four corporate characteristics are continuity of life, centralization of management, limited liability, and free transferability of interest. Limited partnerships usually do not have continuity of life. Most state laws require a partnership to dissolve when a general partner retires, dies, or is incapable of performing the duties of a partner. If dissolution may occur in any of these circumstances, the regulations state that the organization will not have continuity of life. Thus, most limited partnerships will not have this corporate characteristic, regardless of how remote the possibility of a general partner's retirement, death, or insanity.

Limited partnerships will not have the corporate characteristic of centralized management unless substantially all the partnership is owned by the limited partners. A general partner who fails to have substantial ownership is regarded as the limited partner's agent. Limited partners typically own almost all the interests in a syndicated tax-shelter partnership. Tax advisors usually assume that centralization of management exists in such partnerships.

A limited partnership will not exhibit the corporate characteristic of limited liability if at least one general partner possesses substantial assets and is not a "dummy." A recent case indicates that this characteristic will almost always indicate partnership status. Finally, a limited partnership will not have freely transferable interests if a complete transfer of a partner's interest may not be made or is subject to approval of the general partner. The general partner, however, is not permitted to withhold this approval unreasonably. Because the regulations require a preponderance (three out of four) of corporate characteristics, few, if any, limited partnerships will be taxed as corporations.

Taxation of limited partners

Because many of the same tax rules apply to both general partners and limited partners, the two types of partners definitely have more similarities than differences. The differences are important, however, because they can make the taxation of a limited partner quite unlike the taxation of a general partner. Therefore, let us examine some of those differences.

Probably the greatest difference concerns the computation of the partner's adjusted basis of interest in the partnership. Section 752(a) provides that each partner will increase his or her basis in the partnership by a proportionate share of partnership liabilities. A partnership may have two types of liabilities—recourse and nonrecourse liabilities. *Recourse liabilities* are those liabilities for which the general partners have unlimited liability. Typically, limited partners are liable on recourse liabilities only to the extent of their capital contribution. Current tax law generally requires that all recourse liabilities be allocated only among the general partners. Recourse liabilities are allocated in the ratio that these partners share losses. The amount allocated to each partner increases the partner's basis in the partnership.

Nonrecourse liabilities are those liabilities for which none of the partners—general or limited—has any personal liability. Such liabilities arise when the lender agrees to hold none of the partners personally responsible for payment. In return for this concession, the lender usually requires the obligation to be collateralized with an asset of substantial value. If the loan is not fully repaid, the lender may seize the collateral to satisfy the unpaid balance.

Nonrecourse debt and tax shelters

Because no partner is personally liable on nonrecourse debt, the regulations provide that all partners may share in the debt. Each partner may increase his adjusted basis in the partnership by the amount of the debt multiplied by the partner's percentage interest for sharing partnership profits. Thus, if a partner owns a 25 percent interest in partnership profits, and the partnership nonrecourse liabilities total $16,000, the partner may add $4,000 to his or her adjusted basis.

The sharing of nonrecourse debt allows all partners a substantial tax-saving opportunity. Recall that partnership losses may be deducted only to the extent of the partner's adjusted basis in his or her partnership interest. The existence of nonrecourse liabilities may permit a partner to obtain large amounts of deductions without risking a great deal of capital. Congress and the courts have acted only recently to reduce this tax-saving opportunity.

An example might help illustrate the advantage of nonrecourse debt.

Example: Assume a limited partner invested $1,000 cash in the limited partnership. The limited partner's share of partnership nonrecourse debt is $5,000, thus giving the limited partner an adjusted basis of $6,000. If the limited partner's share of partnership losses is $6,000, the partner may deduct the full $6,000 on his or her personal return (assuming no "at risk" rule applies). The deduction will generate $3,000 in tax savings for the 50 percent marginal tax bracket partner. Thus, the limited partner has obtained a $3,000 tax savings from a $1,000 cash investment! To many wealthy taxpayers, this might appear to be the ultimate loophole.

Unfortunately, perhaps, there is a darker side to such investments. After the limited partner has claimed the $6,000 deduction on his or her personal tax return, the limited partner's adjusted basis in the partnership is zero. When the partnership liquidates the liabilities, the limited partner will recognize $5,000 of income, since a reduction of partnership liabilities is treated as a deemed distribution of cash to the partner. Although this income may be taxed as capital gain, that fact may be of little comfort to the limited partner.

Tax-shelter abuses are widely publicized in the media. Largely as a result of this adverse publicity, Congress has moved to curtail some of the more flagrant abuses. Several recent tax laws have contained provisions directed primarily at reducing the tax benefits provided by shelters. Perhaps the most important of these is Sec. 465. This statute limits the deductions that may be claimed by investors in all activities except real property investment. Now, these investors may not deduct any more than they have "at risk" in the activity. A partner is usually "at risk" in regard to:

1. The amount of money contributed to the partnership, and
2. The adjusted basis of any property contributed to the partnership, and
3. Amounts borrowed with respect to the activity for which the taxpayer is personally liable or has pledged property to collateralize the borrowings.

Some amounts that might satisfy the above criteria will still not be regarded as "at risk." For example, certain amounts contributed by the partner are not "at risk" if the amounts have been borrowed from a related taxpayer. A partner is also not "at risk" on amounts borrowed through recourse debt, if the partner is protected against loss by guarantees or similar arrangements. Clearly, the tax advantages of nonrecourse debt have been severely limited.

Before the Revenue Act of 1978 was passed, the Sec. 465 limitations applied only to four specific activities: farming, leasing of Sec. 1245 property, oil and gas exploration, and movie and videotape production. When only these four activities were subject to "at risk" limitations, taxpayers would merely invest in other activities that were not so restricted. Congress anticipated this problem and designed another provision of the 1976 Tax Reform Act to prevent it. Section 704(d) was amended to provide "at risk" rules for all partnerships except those primarily invested in real property (except minerals and timber). Although the Sec. 465 and the Sec. 704(d) rules were not identical, a study of the differences are beyond the scope of this volume.

The "at risk" limitations passed in 1976 eliminated much of the advantage once provided investors by limited partnerships. The Revenue Act of 1978 furthered this attack by expanding Sec. 465 to include all activities other than real estate. The 1978 Act eliminated the 1976 amendment to Sec. 704(d). This didn't help the tax-shelter investor, however, because the amendment was unnecessary after the expansion of Sec. 465. The schemes tax-shelter promoters develop in their efforts to avoid these rules will be interesting to observe.

Do not be misled into believing that tax-shelter partnerships are totally dependent on nonrecourse debt. Other factors play an important role in tax shelter. Because the partnership acts as a conduit, investment credit, additional first-year depreciation, and accelerated depreciation may be passed through to the partners. Some tax-shelter partnerships create large deductions in the first year (or years) of operation. Others provide the investors with large amounts of capital gain. Many types of activities may create tax-shelter opportunities. In the following discussion, we shall focus on the tax-shelter benefits provided by two of the more typical types of shelters.

EQUIPMENT LEASING   Equipment leasing has been a favorite of many investors in tax shelters. The basics of the equipment-leasing partnership are relatively easy to understand. A general partner would establish the partnership and sell limited partnership interests to high-bracket taxpayers. The partnership would purchase property to lease, for example, a jet plane. The plane would be purchased with a small down payment provided by the partners and a large nonrecourse note obtained from a financial institution. The limited partners' bases would be increased by their proportionate share of the nonrecourse debt. Thus, in the early years of the partnership, a partner's basis might be several times greater than his or her actual investment.

The plane would generate numerous beneficial tax effects for the partners. The partners would deduct investment credit, additional first-year, and 200 percent declining-balance depreciation. Interest paid on the nonrecourse note would also be deductible. The goal was to ensure that deductible expenses far exceeded the payments on the loan principal. When an equipment-leasing partnership was operating correctly, the limited partners received both a positive cash flow and a tax loss from the partnership. The tax loss generated would often exceed a partner's capital contribution to the partnership.

Congress enacted legislation in 1971, aimed specifically at the equipment-leasing tax shelter, that generally forbade the noncorporate lessor from claiming investment credit on the leased property. Investment credit was available to noncorporate lessors only if they manufactured or produced the property or if the lease itself was not a disguised purchase. Most equipment-leasing partnerships could not satisfy these requirements. Typically, they purchased the leased property and leased that property for almost its entire useful life.

In 1976, the provisions of Sec. 465 effectively eliminated the tax advantage of nonrecourse debt in equipment-leasing operations. Now, the only substantial tax benefit available from an equipment-leasing tax shelter is accelerated depreciation. Even this can be a mixed benefit. Equipment is a Sec. 1231 asset subject to Sec. 1245 recapture. Many investors may not like the trade-off between relatively low current deductions and a large ordinary gain in the future. Clearly, equipment leasing is a less valuable tax shelter now than it was in the past.

REAL-ESTATE SHELTERS   Few shelters were left relatively intact by the recent barrage of legislation. There is at least one, however, that was not severely attacked. This shelter is the real-estate venture. While real estate did not completely escape the efforts of reformers, the real-estate shelter still may produce both substantial tax benefits and large economic rewards.

The principal advantage of the real-estate venture is that it is not subject to the "at risk" rules. An investor may contribute a small amount to a real-estate partnership, increase his or her basis in the investment by a proportionate amount of the partnership's nonrecourse debt, and claim tax deductions greater than his or her actual contribution. The deductions are generated primarily by interest, taxes, maintenance, and depreciation claimed on the real estate. When the investment is sold, capital gains may be generated.

Real-estate partnerships have not been spared totally from the effects of recent legislation. Taxes and interest incurred on the construction of a building must be capitalized and amortized over a period that will eventually span 10 years. Prepaid interest may be deducted only in the period that the interest accrues. When the real estate is sold, ordinary income will be recognized to the extent that Secs. 1245 and 1250 apply. Finally, the excess of accelerated over straight-line depreciation is a tax preference item if the property will be subject to Sec. 1250 recapture. While these reforms reduce the tax benefits available to investors in real estate, they do not appear to affect seriously the decisions of most investors. With the burgeoning market for real estate and the severe restrictions imposed on other forms of tax shelters, real-estate partnerships will probably continue to attract more and more investors.

FAMILY PARTNERSHIPS

A partnership that is owned primarily by members of the same family is termed, for tax purposes, a "family partnership." Such partnerships are established for a variety of reasons. A father may have operated a successful proprietorship for many years and wants his children to participate in the business. A son or daughter might have developed a particular expertise that, when coupled with the father's abilities, will enable them to establish and operate a successful new business. Often, however, the strongest motive for forming a family partnership is the desire to save taxes. If the partners are in a high marginal tax bracket and the children are in lower marginal brackets, many tax dollars may be saved by siphoning off some of the parents' income to the children.

> *Example:* Assume Tom Jones operates a successful small manufacturing business as a sole proprietor. During the past year, Tom earned $70,000 from the business and expects it to generate at least that much income in the foreseeable future. Tom would like to permit his two daughters, Mary and Jane, to share in the profits. Both daughters hold responsible jobs in the business. Tom has no other source of income.
>
> Tom's accountant suggests that he give each daughter a 25 percent interest in the capital and profits of the firm. Tom will receive an annual guaranteed payment of $30,000 for his services. Each daughter will receive a guaranteed payment of $15,000. Any remaining earnings will be divided according to their relative interests in partnership profits. Figure 12-1 illustrates the tax results of this plan. Tom's personal tax liability will be reduced from $25,960 to $7,807. Although each daughter will pay a tax of $3,193, the family's

overall tax liability will be reduced by $11,767 (from $25,960 to $14,193).

With such large tax savings possible, why don't more sole proprietorships become family partnerships? One answer lies in the difficulties encountered in establishing a valid family partnership for tax purposes. The Supreme Court has long maintained that income must be taxed to the person who performs the services or owns the capital that generates the income. Thus, a parent may not simply transfer a profits interest to a child and expect the transfer to be recognized for tax purposes. Because Congress is so concerned with the tax avoidance possibilities inherent in a family partnership, each of the following requirements must be satisfied before a family partnership is recognized for tax purposes:

1. Each partner must own a capital interest in the partnership;
2. Capital must be a material income-producing factor in the partnership;
3. The donor partner must be reasonably compensated for any services provided to the partnership before income may be allocated among the donor and donees;
4. The share of partnership income attributable to each donee's share of capital may not be proportionately greater than the share of income attributable to the donor's capital interest.

It is not sufficient that capital be transferred to the donee. In addition, capital must be a material income-producing item. Capital usually satisfies this test if the business requires substantial inventories or a substantial investment in plant, machinery, or other equipment. Partnerships in which income is earned primarily by performing personal services will normally not sat-

FIGURE **12-1**

Tom's Manufacturing Business: Family Partnership Taxation

	Proprietorship	Partnership		
	Tom	Tom	Mary	Jane
Business income	$70,000			
Guaranteed payments		$30,000	$15,000	$15,000
Distributive shares		5,000	2,500	2,500
Taxable income*a*	$70,000	$35,000	$17,500	$17,500
Tax liability	$25,960	$ 7,807	$ 3,193	$ 3,193

Tax savings is $11,767 [$25,960 − ($7,807 + 3,193 + 3,193)]

*a*Assume each taxpayer has other taxable income equal to the taxpayer's excess itemized deductions. Tom claims two personal exemptions, the daughters each claim one.

isfy this requirement. Thus, doctors, attorneys, CPAs, and other professional people may not use a family partnership to transfer their professional earnings to other family members.

Ownership of a capital interest implies more than the mere possession of legal title to the interest. The donee partner must also have "dominion and control" over the interest. Thus, the donor may not continue to control what he or she has supposedly given away. If too much control is retained, the donor may be treated as the actual owner of the interest. This results in the donee's share of income being taxed to the donor. Controls that, if retained by the donor, may indicate that the donor is still the substantial owner of the interest include:

1. Control over the distribution of partnership income,
2. Control over the right of the donee to sell his or her interest in the partnership,
3. Control over the right of the donee to demand liquidation of his or her interest,
4. Control over the essential assets of the business,
5. Control over the management of the business that is inconsistent with the normal relationships among partners.

Perhaps the family partnership is most valuable when high tax bracket parents are able to give interests in their unincorporated business to their minor children. If the children live at home, they probably are not earning large amounts of taxable income. Valid gifts to minor children, however, are not as easily accomplished as are gifts to children who have attained their majority. The law does not usually consider a minor child to be capable of handling his or her own affairs. Accordingly, valid gifts of partnership interests to minor children must usually be made in one of three ways.

A gift to a minor child may be made to a trust with the child as beneficiary. The parent may serve as trustee. It is best, however, to have an independent trustee so that the donor does not maintain control. Alternatively, the gift may be given directly to the child, provided a court-appointed guardian represents the child on all substantive partnership matters. Finally, the gift may be made under the Uniform Gift to Minors Act, which requires a custodian to be chosen to administer the interest. This Act was passed to permit gifts to minors to be made more cheaply and easily than through a trust or court-appointed guardian. While the custodian functions much like a guardian, he or she is not required to file reports to a court. It is difficult to sustain the validity of a family partnership for tax purposes unless one of these safeguards is present. If one of these safeguards is not present, the transfer probably will not be recognized for tax purposes unless the minor child has the maturity and experience to administer his or her interest in a competent, adult manner. Few minor children satisfy this requirement.

PROBLEMS

1. Several different situations of fact are detailed below. In each situation indicate whether a termination of the partnership has occurred for tax purposes. Be sure to give adequate support for your answer.
   a. Sandy sells her interest in the capital and profits of the BOS partnership. She owns a 65 percent interest in capital and a 48 percent interest in profits of the partnership. No other partnership interests are sold either one year before or one year after this sale.
   b. Mandy and Mindy are equal partners in the M & M partnership. Mandy dies on January 15, 1979. Mindy purchases Mandy's interest from her estate on March 1, 1979. Answer for January 15, 1979.
   c. Answer part b, above, for March 1, 1979.
   d. Abe, Bill, and Carl are equal partners in the ABC partnership. Abe sells his one-third interest to Dave on April 1, 1979. On December 2, 1979, Dave sells this interest to Earl. Bill sells his one-third interest to Fred on January 10, 1980. Answer for 1979.
   e. Answer part d, above, for 1980.
   f. Janet, Karen, and Laurie are partners in a partnership. Their interests in the partnership are as follows.

	Interest in capital	Interest in profits and losses
Janet	20%	25%
Karen	55%	30%
Laurie	25%	45%

Janet sells her interest to Marsha on January 15, 1979. On July 20, 1979, Laurie's interest is sold to Natalie. Marsha is not a compatible partner and sells her interest to Karen on December 1, 1979. On January 20, 1980, Natalie sells her interest to Ophelia. Answer for 1979.

 g. Answer part f, above, for 1980.

2. Several different situations of fact are detailed below. In each situation, indicate which of the partnerships have terminated for tax purposes.

 a. The AB partnership and the CD partnership consolidate into the ABCD partnership. A and B each own a 30 percent interest in ABCD.

 b. Answer part a if each partner owned equal interests in the ABCD partnership.

 c. The ABC and the CDE partnerships merge into the ABCDE partnership. Partner C is the same individual in both the ABC and the CDE partnership. Each individual is an equal partner in the ABCDE partnership. The ABC partnership had assets with a greater fair market value than the assets in the CDE partnership.

 d. The JKLM partnership divides into the JK and LM partnerships. J and K each owned 30 percent interests in the JKLM partnership.

 e. Answer for part d if J and K each owned 25 percent interests in the JKLM partnership.

 f. The NO, PQ, and RS partnerships merge to form the NOPQRS partnership. Each partner has an equal interest in the new partnership.

3. Sally and Sharon operate a successful retail store, which is organized as a partnership. In 1979, The Big Corporation offers to purchase the assets of the store for $1,000,000. Sally and Sharon accept the offer. The purchase price will be paid in installments of $200,000 per year for five years. After the sale is made, the only asset remaining in the partnership is the installment receivable. Does the sale cause the partnership to terminate? Explain your answer.

4. In each of the following independent cases indicate:

 (1) Whether gain or loss is recognized by the partner.

 (2) Whether gain or loss is recognized by the partnership.

 (3) The partner's adjusted basis in the property distributed.

 (4) The partner's adjusted basis for his or her partnership interest after the distribution.

 a. $21,000 cash was distributed to Robert in partial liquidation of his interest in the partnership. Robert's adjusted basis for his partnership interest is $20,000.

 b. Sally received $3,000 cash and land with an adjusted basis to the partnership of $6,000 in partial liquidation of her interest. Sally's adjusted basis for her partnership interest is $8,000.

 c. Answer part b, but assume Sally's adjusted basis for her partnership interest is $13,000.

 d. Mark received $2,000 cash and two tracts of land in partial liquidation of his partnership interest. The two tracts have an adjusted basis to the partnership of $4,000 and $12,000, respectively. Mark's adjusted basis for his partnership interest is $10,000.

e. Vicki received $3,000 cash and receivables valued at $5,000 from the VW partnership. The receivables have an adjusted basis to the partnership of zero. Vicki's basis for her partnership interest is $7,000. Assume no Sec. 751 gain exists.

f. Paul has an adjusted basis for his partnership interest of $10,000. He receives a partially liquidating distribution of $3,000 cash, inventory with a basis to the partnership of $4,000, and land with a basis of $6,000 to the partnership.

5. In each of the following independent cases, indicate:
   (1) Whether gain or loss is recognized by the partner.
   (2) Whether gain or loss is recognized by the partnership.
   (3) The partner's adjusted basis in the property distributed.

   a. $15,000 cash is distributed in complete liquidation of Albert's interest in the partnership. Albert has an adjusted basis for his partnership interest of $12,000.

   b. Answer part a, but assume Albert's adjusted basis for his partnership interest is $20,000.

   c. Barbara receives $2,000 cash and inventory with an adjusted basis to the partnership of $7,000 in complete liquidation of her partnership interest. Her adjusted basis for the interest is $5,000.

   d. Answer part c, but assume Barbara's adjusted basis for her partnership interest is $14,000.

   e. $1,000 cash, receivables, and land are distributed to Carl in complete liquidation of his interest in the partnership. The receivables and land had adjusted bases to the partnership of $2,000 and $20,000, respectively. Carl's adjusted basis for his partnership interest is $16,000.

   f. Answer part e, but assume Carl's adjusted basis for his partnership interest is $36,000.

6. In each of the following independent cases indicate:
   (1) The holding period for each asset distributed to the partner.
   (2) The character of the gain or loss recognized by the partner when he or she resells the asset.

   a. On August 15, 1979, Dottie received land from the partnership in partial liquidation of her partnership interest. The land consisted of five lots that were part of a large tract contributed to the partnership by Ed, another partner, on June 30, 1974. Ed had purchased the property on June 1, 1972. The tract had been subdivided by the partnership into 100 lots, 90 of which were sold to customers. Dottie held the lots for investment purposes. She sold three to Fred on August 15, 1981, and two to Ginny on August 15, 1985. Dottie's adjusted basis for her partnership interest on August 15, 1979 was $10,000 more than the partnership's adjusted basis for the lots distributed to her.

   b. On July 1, 1979, Hal receives a distribution completely liquidating his interest in the partnership. The distribution consists of $3,000 cash and land that takes a substituted basis to Hal of $10,000. The land was held as an investment by the partnership and had been purchased by the partnership on June 1, 1976. Hal also holds the land as an investment until selling it for $15,000 on June 1, 1980.

   c. Ima received a partially liquidating distribution on July 1, 1979. The distribution consists of unrealized receivables with an adjusted basis to Ima and to the partnership of zero. Ima sells the receivables to a bank for $10,000 on August 10, 1979.

7. The balance sheet of the XYZ partnership on December 31, 1979 reads as follows.

	Adjusted basis	Fair market value
Cash	$ 7,000	$ 7,000
Accounts receivable	9,000	9,000
Land—Tract No. 1	12,000	13,000
—Tract No. 2	8,000	13,000
	$36,000	$42,000
Accounts payable	$ 3,000	$ 3,000
X, capital	11,000	13,000
Y, capital	11,000	13,000
Z, capital	11,000	13,000
	$36,000	$42,000

The partnership has a valid Sec. 754 election in effect. In each of the following independent situations, indicate:

(1) Whether any gain or loss is recognized to either the partnership or the partner.

(2) The amount of the Sec. 734(b) adjustment.

a. Land—Tract No. 1 was distributed to X in complete liquidation of her interest in the partnership.

b. All the accounts receivable and $4,000 cash were distributed to Y in complete liquidation of his interest in the partnership.

c. Land—Tract No. 2 was distributed to Z in complete liquidation of her interest in the partnership.

d. All the cash and $5,000 of accounts receivable were distributed to X in partial liquidation of her interest in the partnership.

8. Michelle purchased an interest in the MNO partnership for $20,000 on June 1, 1979. The partnership refuses to make a Sec. 754 election for her. On July 30, 1980, Michelle receives inventory in complete liquidation of her partnership interest. The inventory has an adjusted basis to the partnership of $5,000 and a fair market value of $20,000 on both June 1, 1979, and July 30, 1980. The inventory is the only partnership property other than cash. Assume there is a Sec. 751 problem created by the distribution.

a. Does Michelle or the partnership recognize any gain or loss on the distribution?

b. What is the character of any gain or loss recognized?

c. Assume Michelle sells the inventory for a gain of $20,000. What is the character of this gain?

d. Can Michelle do anything to reduce the tax effects to her of this distribution?

9. The balance sheet of the D & B partnership on July 1, 1979, is as follows:

	Adjusted basis	Fair market value
Cash	$ 7,500	$ 7,500
Government securities	7,500	8,100
Accounts receivable	-0-	3,000
Land	12,000	30,000
	$27,000	$48,600
D, capital	$13,500	$24,300
B, capital	13,500	24,300
	$27,000	$48,600

D decides to retire from the partnership. He is to be paid cash in liquidation of his interest according to the following schedule:

July 1, 1979	$9,000
July 1, 1980	$7,650
July 1, 1981	$7,650

D's adjusted basis for his partnership interest is $13,750. The partnership has never made a valid Sec. 754 election. D acquired his partnership interest in 1970.

a. Compute the amount of each annual payment that is treated as a Sec. 736(b) payment.

b. Compute the amount of each annual payment that is treated as a Sec. 736(a) payment.

c. Would your answer to a or b change if D had died on July 1, 1979, and these payments are being made in liquidation of D's interest in the partnership?

10. The balance sheet of the M & J partnership on December 31, 1979 is as follows:

	Adjusted basis	Fair market value
Cash	$ 4,000	$ 4,000
Accounts receivable	-0-	2,000
Goodwill	6,000	12,000
Land	10,000	20,000
	$20,000	$38,000
M, capital	$10,000	$19,000
J, capital	10,000	19,000
	$20,000	$38,000

M has decided to retire from the partnership. She will be paid cash in liquidation of her partnership interest of $19,000. M's adjusted basis for her partnership interest is $13,000. She bought the interest from J four years ago, and the partnership never made a Sec. 754 election.

a. Compute the amount and character of the gain that M must recognize in 1979, assuming that the partnership agreement provides for the payment of goodwill to M of $12,000.

b. Compute the amount and character of the gain that M must recognize in 1979, assuming that the partnership agreement is silent regarding goodwill.

11. Corporation A and individuals B and C form a limited partnership. Corporation A is wholly owned by B. The corporation's assets consist of $500 cash, which is invested in the partnership. Corporation A is the general partner and B and C are limited partners. B and C are unrelated. Both B and C may transfer their interests to a third party, provided the general partner approves of the transfer. State law requires that the partnership dissolve upon the death, insanity, or bankruptcy of a general partner. The partnership is established in a state that has adopted the Uniform Limited Partnership Act.

Discuss fully whether the limited partnership will be taxed as a partnership or as an association (corporation).

12. Jack is a general partner in the HIJ partnership. His share of partnership capital, profits, and losses is as follows:

Capital	40%
Profits	70%
Losses	30%

Jack invested $10,000 in the partnership on January 1, 1979. During 1979, the partnership incurred losses of $70,000. On December 31, 1979, the partnership had the following liabilities outstanding:

Accounts payable	$ 20,000
Mortgage payable (secured only by the property)	150,000

Assume Jack withdrew nothing from the partnership during 1979.

a. What is the adjusted basis for Jack's partnership interest after taking his share of partnership losses into consideration?

b. What is the maximum loss Jack could deduct in 1979 if the partnership were involved entirely in equipment leasing?

c. What is the maximum loss Jack could deduct in 1979 if the partnership were involved entirely in real estate?

13. What are the current advantages of equipment leasing? What former advantages have been largely eliminated by Congressional action? Do you think the Congressional assault on this "shelter" is justified, considering the crucial impact leasing operations have on our economy?

14. Beth operates a sole proprietorship that generates $100,000 of income per year. She wants to give each of her two children one-third interest in her business. Her children are aged 3 and 5.

a. Assuming Beth is a CPA, can she form a valid family partnership with her children? Why or why not?

b. If Beth operates a manufacturing business, can she form a valid family partnership with her children? Assume Beth's personal services are worth $30,000. How much partnership income could be diverted to each child?

c. What are the different ways gifts may be given to minor children?

15. Guppy bought his interest in the Fishboat partnership from a previous partner, Piranha. He paid $200,000 for the interest. The partnership made an election under Sec. 754. One of the assets of the partnership was a 1948 Packard, which is later distributed to Guppy in a nonliquidating distribution. On the date Guppy purchased his partnership interest, the Packard had an adjusted basis to the partnership of $10,000 and a fair market value of $30,000. The partnership has three partners equally sharing in profits and losses. What are the tax consequences of transferring the Packard to Guppy? What are the tax consequences of transferring the Packard to one of the other partners?

16. George is a general partner and Lippie is a limited partner in the GL partnership. Each contributes $50,000 cash to form the partnership. They share profits equally. The partnership buys some property for $65,000, which is subject to a nonrecourse mortgage of $35,000. Neither the partnership nor any of the partners assumes any liability on the mortgage.

a. What is the basis of the property to the partnership?

b. What are George and Lippie's bases in their partnership interests?

c. What is the tax result if the partnership assumes liability for the mortgage?

SUPPLEMENTAL PROBLEMS

17. The balance sheet of the ABC partnership on December 31, 1979, is as follows:

	Adjusted basis	Fair market value
Cash	$21,000	$21,000
Accounts receivable	-0-	9,000
Land—Tract No. 1	12,000	21,000
—Tract No. 2	15,000	21,000
	$48,000	$72,000
A, capital	$16,000	$24,000
B, capital	16,000	24,000
C, capital	16,000	24,000
	$48,000	$72,000

The partnership has a valid Sec. 754 election in effect. Each partner's adjusted basis for her partnership interest is $16,000. The partners share equally in partnership capital, profits, and losses. On January 1, 1980, Partner A receives a partially liquidating distribution consisting of $12,000 cash. After the distribution, A has a 20 percent interest in partnership capital, profits, and losses.

   a. Determine the gain, if any, recognized by A or the partnership as a result of this distribution.

   b. What is the character of any gain or gains recognized?

   c. What is the partnership's adjusted basis for the accounts receivable after the distribution?

18. Cecille has invested in a real-estate limited partnership. She contributed $20,000 cash to the partnership and obtained a 20 percent interest in partnership profits and losses. The partnership has $500,000 of nonrecourse debt outstanding at all times. She has deducted $75,000 of partnership losses during the two years she has owned the interest. She now is considering either abandoning the interest or selling it for $1 to a friend. As her tax advisor, what would you tell her about the tax ramifications of these alternatives? Assume the partnership has no Sec. 751 assets.

19. Oil and gas investments historically have been one of the most potentially lucrative tax shelters available. In recent years, however, numerous reforms have reduced the tax benefits available to investors in oil and gas.

   a. What tax advantages did oil and gas shelters offer the investor before passage of the Tax Reform Act of 1969?

   b. What changes in the tax law affecting oil and gas shelters were made in 1969?

   c. What changes in the tax law affecting oil and gas shelters were made in 1976 and 1977?

RETURN PROBLEMS

1. Rogers and Hart are attorneys who have been operating as a general partnership for 10 years. In 1979, Rogers receives a guaranteed payment of $50,000 plus 30 percent of the profits after payment of all guaranteed payments. Hart receives a guaranteed payment of $20,000 plus 70 percent of the profits after deducting the guaranteed payments. All guaranteed payments were actually paid to the partners in 1979.

An examination of the partnership accounts reveals the following additional information:

Professional fees earned	$300,000
Rental expense	24,000
Salaries to employees	60,000
Taxes paid on employee salaries	3,000
Pension expense (Keogh plan):	
Contribution for partners	3,000
Contribution for employees	2,400
Office supplies expense	3,600
Depreciation expense:	
Regular (straight-line)	15,000
Additional first year	2,000
Interest earned on municipal bonds	2,000
Drawings, Rogers	60,000
Drawings, Hart	40,000

Both Rogers and Hart had capital accounts of $30,000 on January 1, 1979. No additional capital contributions were made in 1979. Complete the following tax schedules for the partnership:

Form 1065, page 1
Form 1065, Schedule K
Form 1065, Schedule M
Form 1065, Schedule N

2. Using the information in Return Problem 1, above, complete the Schedule K-1 for Rogers.

PART

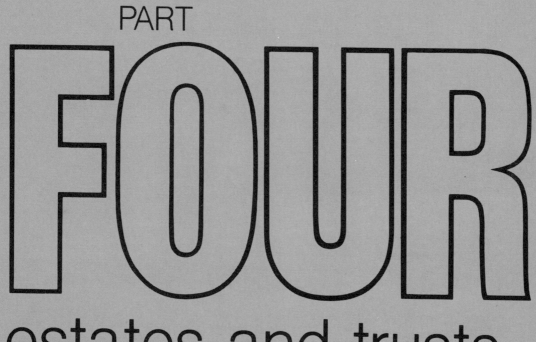

FOUR
estates and trusts

13

income taxation of estates, trusts, and beneficiaries

In Chapters 13 and 14, we shall present the principal rules concerning the income taxation of estates, trusts, and their beneficiaries and of income in respect of decedents. As separate tax entities, estates and trusts exhibit many unique tax attributes. For example, income tax is levied on an estate or trust that accumulates income. Currently distributed income, however, is not taxed to an estate or trust but rather to the beneficiary. The treatment of such problems is specified in Subchapter J of the Internal Revenue Code, which includes the following provisions:

□ Taxation of estates and trusts;
□ Rules relating to trusts that distribute current income only;
□ Estates and trusts that may accumulate income or that distribute corpus (principal);
□ Treatment of excess distributions by trusts;
□ Grantors and other persons treated as substantial owners; and
□ Income in respect of a decedent.

Subchapter J does not apply to an ordinary trust, business trust, or investment trust unless it is classified as a trust for tax purposes. For example, a business trust classified as a corporation for tax purposes will not be treated under Subchapter J. Subchapter J also does not apply to employee trusts or common trust funds. Common trust funds are treated as partnerships and, as such, are legal but not tax entities.

The current provisions of Subchapter J evolved from the original Revenue Act of 1913. Under this Act, trusts and estates were not treated as separate tax entities. The fiduciary (trustee) was required to withhold tax on income received for beneficiaries. If a beneficiary was unborn or unascertained, then no tax was levied because there was no subject to tax. After considerable controversy and attempts to close this loophole, the Revenue Act of 1924 provided that the fiduciary would be primarily responsible for payment of the tax on income received by the estate or trust but could reduce the tax by making distributions to beneficiaries. The current law, although considerably different from the provisions in effect until the 1954 Code, retains the conduit principle; that is, the incidence of tax may be shifted to the beneficiaries to the extent income is distributed to them.

In this chapter, we shall define trust and estate and discuss the taxable income of trusts and estates, income in respect of decedents, and taxation of simple trusts and beneficiaries. In Chapter 14, we shall discuss the taxation of complex trusts and estates.

BASIC RULES FOR TAXATION OF TRUSTS AND ESTATES

In this section, we shall discuss the basic rules for the formation of trusts and estates, definitions, filing and reporting requirements, tax aspects of transfers to a trust or estate, and computing taxable income of a trust or estate.

Formation of trusts and estates

TRUSTS   A trust is a legal entity exhibiting certain characteristics including having a creator or grantor, a trustee, a beneficiary, property, and specific terms. For example, a person (grantor) may create a trust by transferring property to a trustee, who then holds title in the name of the trust. The trustee is responsible for carrying out the wishes of the grantor under the terms of the trust for the benefit of the beneficiary. Trusts may be created for various nontax purposes, such as to build an estate for the grantor; to release the grantor or the grantor's spouse, children, parents, or others from financial responsibility; to provide for the management of a business or of income-producing property; to make special provisions for children, spouse, parents, or others; or to save probate costs, that is, the costs associated with transferring legal title to assets a person owns at death. In addition, there are many tax objectives to creating a trust, which are discussed below.

Generally, an entity will be treated as a trust under the Internal Revenue Code if it can be shown that the purpose of the arrangement is to vest responsibility in the trustee for the protection and conservation of property for beneficiaries who cannot, because of the terms of the instrument, share in the discharge of this responsibility. Even if the person who creates the trust is the beneficiary, it will be recognized as a trust for tax purposes if it was created to protect or conserve the trust property and the creator or beneficiary stands in the same relation to the trust as if the trust had been created by others for him or her (Treas. Reg. Sec. 301.7701-4(a)).

Trusts may be classified as *inter vivos, testamentary, simple,* and *complex.* An *inter vivos trust* (living trust) is formed by a living grantor; a *testamentary trust* is formed under the terms of the grantor's will. A *simple trust* distributes current income only, must distribute all its current income, and has no charitable beneficiaries. A *complex trust* is a trust with charitable beneficiaries or one that distributes corpus or accumulates income.

Because a trust may be a separate entity for income tax purposes, income taxes may be reduced through the use of a trust to split income and maximize deductions and exclusions. A trust may also be used as a vehicle for a charitable contribution deduction.

A trust gives a taxpayer the opportunity to shift income from a high tax bracket to the lower bracket of the trust or the trust beneficiary. If the beneficiary has little or no income before becoming a trust beneficiary, in which case his or her tax bracket is zero, some income may be received without any tax being due because of the $1,000 personal exemption deduction and, except for a person claimed as a dependent with income other than earned income of $1,000 or more, the zero bracket amount. Also, each beneficiary of a trust who receives dividends or interest qualifying for the $200 combined dividend and interest exclusion is entitled to a $200 dividend and interest exclusion on his or her own return.

A trust may also be established for charitable contributions for the charitable contribution deduction. Charitable remainder trusts permit a taxpayer to contribute a remainder interest in property to charity and retain a noncharitable income interest. A charitable contribution deduction is not allowed for a transfer into trust of property with a noncharitable income interest and a charitable remainder interest unless the trust is an annuity trust, a unitrust, or a pooled income fund. An *annuity trust* is a trust that must pay out annually at least 5 percent of the net fair market value of the trust property valued on the transfer date for a term of not more than 20 years or for life. A *unitrust* is subject to the same requirements as an annuity trust except that it must pay out annually at least 5 percent of the net fair market value of the trust assets as valued annually. A *pooled income fund* is a trust to which each donor transfers property, which is then commingled. Income is paid for life to the beneficiary. The amount of annual income each income beneficiary receives is determined by the trust's rate of return for that year.

Trusts also may be formed for a specific function—for example, alimony trusts, insurance trusts, investment trusts, liquidating trusts, and personal trusts.

ESTATES   An estate, which comes into existence when a person dies, consists of all the property to which the decedent holds title at death. It is a separate taxable entity for federal income tax purposes and retains this status until the final distribution of the estate assets to the beneficiaries. The income of an estate is that which the estate receives during the period of administration.

An estate is a taxable entity separate from the beneficiaries (persons to whom property has been bequeathed). If the income in an estate is taxed at a lower rate than it would be if the property had been distributed and its income taxed to the beneficiaries, the executor or administrator may attempt to prolong the estate's existence in order to take advantage of the lower tax bracket of the estate. Rather than distribute income in the year earned, the executor (nominated under the decedent's will) or administrator (appointed by the probate court) could accumulate it in the estate and then distribute it at no tax cost in a later year.

The period of administration or settlement is the time actually required by the administrator or executor to perform the ordinary duties of administration, such as the collection of assets and the payment of debts, taxes, legacies (gifts of personal property under a will), and devises (gifts of real property under a will). For federal income tax purposes, this period may be longer or shorter than the period specified under local law. When the administration of an estate is unreasonably prolonged, the estate will be considered terminated for federal income tax purposes after the executor has had a reasonable period to perform the duties of administration. Further, an estate is considered terminated when all the assets have been distributed except for a reasonable amount set aside for the payment of contingent liabilities and expenses (Treas. Reg. Sec. 1.641(b)-3(a)).

Filing requirements and payment of the tax

REPORTING REQUIREMENTS   A fiduciary is required to make and file an income tax return and pay the tax on the taxable income of an estate or trust. The return, filed on Form 1041, is due the 15th day of the fourth month following the close of the taxable year of the estate or trust. A return must be made:

☐ For each estate for which a fiduciary acts, if the gross income is $600 or more.

☐ For each trust for which a fiduciary acts (except a trust exempt from the income tax under Sec. 501(a)) if the trust has *any* taxable income or has gross income of $600 or more, regardless of the amount of taxable income (Treas. Reg. Sec. 1.6012-3(a)).

☐ For each estate and each trust (except a trust exempt from the income tax under Sec. 501(a)), regardless of the amount of income for the taxable year, of which any beneficiary is a nonresident alien.

If the gross income of an estate or trust is $5,000 or more for any taxable year, a copy of the will or trust instrument must be filed with the return. This will or trust instrument must be accompanied by a written declaration of the fiduciary, under penalty of perjury, that it is a true and complete copy. The fiduciary also must file a statement indicating the provisions of the will or trust instrument that in his or her opinion determine the extent to which the income of the estate or trust is taxable to the estate or trust, the beneficiaries, and the grantor, respectively. Once a will or trust in-

strument and the required statements are filed, they do not have to be filed again as long as future returns state where and when these documents were filed.

If a trust instrument is amended after copies of the trust are filed, the fiduciary must file a copy of the amendment with the return for the taxable year in which the amendment was made. The fiduciary also must file a statement showing the effects of the amendment on the taxation to the estate, the beneficiaries, and the grantor.

LIABILITY FOR PAYMENT OF TAX   The executor or administrator is personally liable for the payment of tax on the taxable income of an estate to the time of and after his or her discharge if, prior to distribution and discharge, the executor or administrator had notice of the tax obligations or failed to exercise due diligence in ascertaining whether or not tax obligations existed.

If a transferor fails to pay a tax due because property is transferred, liability for the tax may follow the assets distributed to the heirs (persons who inherit or are entitled to inherit property of another), devisees, and legatees. These individuals may be required to discharge the amount of the tax due and unpaid to the extent of the distributive shares they receive. This rule is the same for trusts.

An estate or trust, although generally taxed as an individual, is not required to file a declaration of estimated tax. A decedent's estate may elect to pay the estimated income tax in four equal installments.

Transfers to a trust or estate

Property may be transferred to a trust either by gift or by testamentary transfer. An estate is created and property becomes part of the estate upon the death of the person. Neither gain nor loss is recognized on such transfers to trusts or estates. The basis of the property in the trust or estate is computed by following the rules explained below. In addition, investment credit may be recaptured on certain transfers and transferred property may carry a depreciation recapture potential.

BASIS OF PROPERTY IN A TRUST OR ESTATE   To determine the basis of property transferred to a trust by gift, the usual gift rules apply. If the fair market value of the gift property on the date of the transfer is greater than the donor's basis in the property, then the basis of the property in the hands of the trust for computing gain or loss on its sale or exchange or for depreciation purposes is the donor's basis. The donor's basis is increased (but not above fair market value) by the amount of gift tax paid on the transfer related to the appreciation on the gift property to the date of its transfer. If the fair market value of the gift property at the date of transfer is less than the donor's basis, the donor's basis is used to calculate any gain on subsequent sale. Fair market value on the date of the gift is used to calculate losses on subsequent resale. If selling price is between the donor's basis and fair market value as of the date of the gift, an attempt to calculate gain will result in a loss and an attempt to calculate loss will result in a gain. In this situation, no gain or loss is recognized. If the fair market value of the gift property is less than the donor's basis, the donor would be wise to sell the property to realize the loss and make a gift of the proceeds, since the unrealized loss can never be recognized by the trust.

For property transferred by death, the estate or other person (including a trust) who receives the property will usually have a basis equal to the value claimed on the estate tax return. If a return need not be filed or the executor files a return and chooses to value all assets as of the date of death, then the basis equals fair market value as of the date of death. If the executor elects to value the assets as of the alternative valuation date (six months after the date of death), then any assets still on hand at this date are valued at fair market value as of this date. Any assets distributed before the alternative valuation date are valued at their value on the date distributed.

RECAPTURE   Section 47 provides that property that is disposed of before the close of the useful life that was taken into account in computing the investment credit will trigger recapture of part or all of the investment credit taken. A gift is included as a disposition for this purpose. Therefore, the gift of property to a trust could cause the transferor's taxes to be increased by the amount of investment credit recaptured because of any early disposition of the property. Any investment credit taken by a person before death will not be recaptured when the property is disposed of after death.

Neither Sec. 1245 nor Sec. 1250 income is realized to the transferor at the time of a gift in trust. The transferor's Sec. 1245 or Sec. 1250 potential carries over to the trust. Therefore, a gain on a later sale or disposition of property by the trust could result in Sec. 1245 or Sec. 1250 treatment for part or all of the gain.

The depreciation recapture potential under Sec. 1245 and Sec. 1250 is erased at death and is not attached to property inherited.

TRUST USED AS AN EXCHANGE FUND   To cover the possible use of trusts as exchange funds, Sec. 683 provides gains (but not losses) will be recognized to the transferor on a transfer to a trust in exchange for an interest in other trust property where the trust (if a corporation) would qualify as an investment company within the meaning of Sec. 351.

An exchange for an interest in other trust property occurs when numerous persons transfer property to a trust and each person retains a proportionate ownership in all the property held in the trust. A transfer to a trust taxable as an exchange fund results in recognition of the entire amount of gain on all the property transferred to the trust, even though the transferor beneficially owns only a portion of the property transferred to the trust. The amount of gain recognized is determined on a property-by-property basis; that is, losses realized on one property may not be used to reduce the amount of gain recognized on other property transferred to the trust. These provisions apply to normal trusts but not to qualified employee benefit trusts, charitable and other tax-exempt organizations that are organized as trusts, or pooled income funds.

Gain on property transferred to a trust at less than fair market value

Section 644 provides a special rule to cover possible abuse in a situation in which a grantor places property in trust that has unrealized appreciation, to shift payment of tax to the trust, which may be in a lower tax bracket. Basically, Sec. 644 imposes a tax on the trust if:

☐ The property is sold or exchanged at a gain not more than two years after the initial transfer of property in trust by the transferor, and

☐ The fair market value of the initial transfer is greater than the adjusted basis immediately after the property is transferred to trust.

The tax imposed on the trust is equal to the amount of tax, at the transferor's highest marginal bracket, that would have been paid in the year the property was sold. In effect, the transferor is treated as realizing gain and then transferring the after-tax proceeds from the sale to the trust.

The gain taxed to the trust under Sec. 644 is the lesser of the gain realized by the trust or the excess of the fair market value over adjusted basis at the transfer. This amount is excluded from the taxable income of the trust. The tax on the remaining gain is computed without the transferor's gain. The gain taxed under Sec. 644 is not distributable net income and not taxed to the beneficiary when distributed.

The character of the gain taxed under Sec. 644 is

the same as if the transferor had sold the property. Therefore, the gain on the sale will not be entitled to capital gain treatment if the property would not have been a capital asset to the transferor even if the property is a capital asset to the trust.

Example: On April 1, 19X7, property that, if sold, would have been taxed as ordinary income, was transferred to a trust. The property had a basis of $20,000 and fair market value of $45,000 on the date of transfer. On May 15, 19X8, the trust sold the property for $50,000. The transferor, a calendar-year taxpayer, married and filing a joint return, had taxable income of $200,000 and paid a tax of $107,032. The trust, a calendar-year taxpayer, computes the tax on the gain as follows:

Sec. 644 gain ($45,000 − $20,000)	$ 25,000
Transferor's original taxable income	200,000
Taxable income if gain realized in 19X7	$225,000
Tax on adjusted taxable income	124,224
Tax on original taxable income	107,032
Sec. 644 tax	$ 17,192

The $5,000 balance of the gain will be included in the income of the trust and the tax computed on it as part of taxable income.

TAXABLE INCOME OF ESTATES AND TRUSTS

An estate or trust computes its taxable income in the same way as does an individual except for some special features for certain gross income items and deductions. The tax on taxable income for estates and trusts is computed using the rate schedule "Estates and Trusts" (Sec. 1(e)).

In addition, an estate or trust, even though a separate taxable entity, acts as a conduit. In other words, the income passes through to the heirs, legatees, or devisees of the estate or the beneficiaries of a trust for inclusion on their individual income tax returns. A deduction relating to distributions shifts the tax from the estate or trust to the beneficiaries. Amounts that are not paid or payable are taxed to the estate or trust.

Gross income

The gross income of a trust or estate is compiled in the same way as for an individual. In addition to the usual items listed in Sec. 61, the gross income of a trust or estate may also include the following.

1. Income accumulated in trust for the benefit of unborn or unascertained persons or persons with contingent interests;

2. Income accumulated or held for future distribution under the terms of the will or trust;

3. Income that is to be distributed currently by the fiduciary to the beneficiaries and income, collected by a guardian of an infant, to be held or distributed as the court may direct;

4. Income received by an estate of a deceased person during the period of administration or settlement of the estate; and

5. Income that, at the discretion of the fiduciary, may be either distributed to the beneficiaries or accumulated (Treas. Reg. Sec. 1.641(a)-2).

This list is not exhaustive—the regulations state that there may be other items of gross income.

Deductions and credits

Generally, the deductions and credits allowed to individuals are also allowed to estates and trusts. Special rules exist for the computation of certain deductions and for the allocation of certain credits and deductions among the estate or trust and the beneficiaries. These special rules relate to the following items:

1. Personal exemptions
2. Depreciation, depletion, and amortization
3. Charitable contributions
4. Net operating losses
5. Certain double deductions
6. Political contributions
7. Foreign tax credit

In lieu of the $1,000 personal exemption deduction provided by Sec. 151, estates are allowed a personal exemption of $600, a trust that is required to distribute all its income currently is allowed a $300 exemption, and all other trusts are allowed an exemption of $100.

The depreciation, depletion, and amortization deduction associated with property held in trust will be apportioned among the beneficiaries and the trust according to the provisions of the trust instrument. For example, if a trust instrument provides that a beneficiary is to receive one-half the depreciation deduction on property held in the trust, then one-half of such depreciation will be allocated to the beneficiary. If the trust instrument provides that the trust is to receive the depreciation deduction, then the trust will be entitled to the deduction. If no provisions exist for apportionment in a trust instrument or for use of property held by an estate, the depreciation, depletion, or amortization deduction is based on the trust income allocable to each beneficiary or based on estate income allocable to the estate and the heirs, legatees, and devisees on the basis of estate income allocable to each (Treas. Reg. Secs. 1.642(e)-1 and 1.642(f)-1). For example, if a trust instrument is silent with respect to a depreciation deduction on property held in the trust, then the depreciation will be allocated to the beneficiaries based on their allocable income.

An estate or complex trust is allowed a deduction for amounts paid to qualified charities. The rules governing these deductions are in Sec. 642(c), which are in lieu of the normal charitable contribution deduction rules under Sec. 170(a) (Sec. 642(c)(1)). In general, the charitable contribution rules follow the Sec. 170(a) rules, with three main exceptions: First, there is no limit on the deduction or on any deductible amount of gross income paid pursuant to the terms of the estate or trust. Second, for contributions paid after the close of the taxable year but before the last day of the year following the taxable year, an election may be made to treat these contributions as paid during the taxable year (Sec. 642(c)(1)). Third, a special rule allows a deduction for certain amounts permanently set aside for charitable purposes, in limited circumstances (Sec. 642(c)(3)).

The net operating loss deduction allowed by Sec. 172 generally is available to estates and trusts, with certain exceptions and limitations. When computing the gross income and deductions for the net operating loss deduction, the income and deductions attributable to the grantor or other persons because they are treated as substantial owners are excluded (Treas. Reg. Sec. 1.642(d)-1(a)). Also, when computing the net operating loss, an estate or trust may not deduct charitable contributions or distributions to beneficiaries (Reg. 1.642(d)-1(B)). If a trust or estate has an unused net operating loss carryover or capital loss carryover when it terminates, the carryover will be allowed as a deduction to the beneficiaries succeeding to the property of the trust or estate.

Disallowance of double deductions

Estate administrative expenses, such as attorney's fees, probate fees, fiduciaries' commissions, and court costs allowable under Sec. 2053(a)(2), or losses during administration of the estate allowable under Sec. 2054 as deductions in computing the taxable estate of the decedent are not allowed as deductions in computing the taxable income of the estate unless the executor files a statement to the effect that these items will not be deducted on the estate return. In other words, administrative expenses or losses during administration are deductible on the estate tax return or the estate income tax return, but not on both (Treas. Reg. Sec. 1.642(g)-1). The executor should determine on which return the greater tax benefit will be realized, and those expenses should be deducted on that return.

Credits

A trust or estate is entitled to the same tax credits as an individual, such as the investment credit, with two modifications. A trust or estate does not receive the credit against tax for contributions to candidates for public office (Sec. 642(A)(2)). In addition, the trust or estate receives a foreign tax credit only for as much of the properly creditable foreign taxes as are not properly allocable to the beneficiaries (Sec. 642(a)(1)).

Distributable net income

As mentioned above, a deduction of distributions by an estate or trust shifts the tax from the estate or trust to the beneficiaries. This distribution, called distributable net income (DNI), has three functions: first, DNI limits the deduction allowable to estates and trusts for amounts paid, credited, or required to be distributed to beneficiaries; second, DNI is used to determine how much of an amount paid, credited, or required to be distributed to a beneficiary will be part of his or her gross income; third, DNI is used to determine the character of distributions to the beneficiaries (Treas. Reg. Sec. 1.643(a)-0).

DNI is computed using one of two methods. Under the "add back" method, DNI is computed by adjusting taxable income of the estate or trust in the following steps:[1]

1. Add back the deduction for personal exemptions (Treas. Reg. Sec. 1.643(a)-1).
2. Subtract capital gains. Capital gains are not ordinarily considered as paid, credited, or required to be distributed to any beneficiary (Treas. Reg. Sec. 1.643(a)-3(a)).
3. Add back net capital losses (Treas. Reg. Sec. 1.643(a)-3(b)).
4. Subtract extraordinary dividends or taxable stock dividends that are not distributed or credited to a

---

[1] A different set of rules from those for domestic trusts governs the computation of DNI of a foreign trust. These rules are explained in Treas. Reg. Sec. 1.643(a)-6.

beneficiary of a simple trust because the fiduciary determines in good faith that the dividends are allocable to corpus (Treas. Reg. Sec. 1.643(a)-4)).

5. Add back any net tax-exempt interest. The tax-exempt interest is reduced by related expenses that are not deductible for tax purposes. An adjustment also must be made for the portion of the tax-exempt interest deemed to be included in income paid, permanently set aside, or to be used for charitable purposes (Treas. Reg. Sec. 1.643(a)-5).

6. Add back the dividend and interest exclusion. Adjustments must be made for dividends and interest related to charitable contributions (Treas. Reg. Sec. 1.643(a)-7).

DNI may also be calculated using the "worksheet" approach, which, unlike the "add back" method, highlights the differences between income of the trust under the governing instrument and local law, DNI, DNI adjusted for items not included in gross income of the trust, and allocable deductions and taxable income. We shall demonstrate this method in the comprehensive example later in this chapter.

Example: A trust required to distribute all its income currently and allocate all its capital gain to corpus has the following items of income and expenses for the taxable year:

Dividends	$ 8,000
Tax-exempt interest	2,000
Rents	10,000
Rental expenses	1,000
Depreciation of rental property	1,500
Trustee's commissions	2,000
Extraordinary dividends allocated to corpus by the trustee in good faith	1,000
Long-term capital gains	5,000

The distributable net income of the trust is determined as follows:

Dividends		$ 8,000
Rents		10,000
Tax-exempt interest	$2,000	
Less: Expenses allocable thereto ($2,000/ $20,000 × $2,000)	200	1,800
Total		$19,800
Deductions:		
Rental expenses	$1,000	
Depreciation on rental property	1,500	

Trustee's commissions ($2,000 less $200 allocated to tax-exempt interest)	1,800	4,300
Distributable net income		$15,500

In calculating the distributable net income of the trust, the taxable income of the trust was computed with the following modifications.

1. No deductions were allowed for distributions to the beneficiaries.

2. No deduction was allowed for personal exemption of the trust.

3. Capital gains and extraordinary dividends were excluded and no long-term capital gain deduction under Sec. 1202 was taken into account.

4. The dividend exclusion was not taken.

INCOME IN RESPECT OF DECEDENTS

When a person dies, a final income tax return for the short taxable year ending with the death of the taxpayer must be filed. Income, deductions, and credits must be classified and included on the final return or the return of the estate or other person receiving the income. These items are classified according to the accounting method used by the taxpayer. For example, income actually or constructively received or expenses actually paid would be included on the final return of a cash method taxpayer. Income in respect of a decedent (IRD) refers to those amounts to which a decedent was entitled as gross income but not includible in computing taxable income for the taxable year ending with the date of death or for a previous tax year under the decedent's accounting method. IRD includes:

☐ All accrued income of a decedent who reported his or her income using the cash method of accounting;

☐ Income accrued solely by reason of the person's death, if the accrual method of accounting was used;

☐ Income to which the decedent had a contingent claim at the time of death (Treas. Reg. Sec. 1.691 (a)-1).

IRD is included in gross income of the recipient for the taxable year when received, regardless of the accounting method used. Recipients include:

☐ The estate of the decedent, if the right to receive the amount is acquired from the decedent by the decedent's estate;

☐The person who acquires the right to receive the amount, if that right is not acquired by the decedent's estate;

☐The person who acquires from the decedent the right to receive the amount by bequest, devise, or inheritance, if the amount is received after a distribution by the decedent's estate.

The rules with respect to IRD were adopted to prevent avoidance or acceleration of income of the cash method taxpayer. An accrual method taxpayer will not have IRD except with respect to those items that are reported using a cash method of accounting such as installment sale.

The characteristics and basis of IRD

The character of the IRD is the same in the hands of the estate or the person entitled to receive the amount by bequest, devise, or inheritance as the gross income would have been had the decedent lived and received the amount. For example, income that would have been capital gain income to the decedent will be capital gain income to the recipient (Treas. Reg. Sec. 1.691(a)-3). In addition, even though IRD is included in the decedent's estate at fair market value, the basis of the property acquired that represents IRD does not receive a step-up in basis under Sec. 1014 to fair market value as does other property (Sec. 1014(c)).

Transfer of a right to IRD

If a right to IRD is transferred by the estate of the decedent or a person who received the rights to IRD, that estate or person must include in gross income for the year of the transfer the fair market value of the right at the time of the transfer plus any consideration in excess of fair market value. A transfer includes a sale, exchange, or other disposition or the satisfaction of an installment obligation at other than face value. This rule is necessary to prevent transfer of the IRD to a person who may substantially reduce or eliminate income taxes that might otherwise be paid on the IRD. A transfer of IRD does not include transmission to a person's estate upon death or a transfer to a person pursuant to a right to inherit the IRD (Sec. 691(a)(2)).

Treatment of installment obligations

An installment obligation that remains uncollected by a decedent is IRD to the extent of the excess of the face amount of the obligation over the basis of the decedent. The decedent's estate or other person who is entitled to the income from the installment obligation includes, in gross income, the same proportion of any payment as the decedent would have. If an installment obligation is transferred, the amount includible in the gross income of the transferor is the greater of the fair market value of the obligation or the consideration received less the basis of the obligation.

Deductions and credits in respect of a decedent

Expenses, interest, and taxes for which a decedent was liable, but that were not properly allowable as a deduction on his or her final return, are allowed as a deduction when paid. The estate takes these expenses as a deduction if liable, or if not, they are taken by the person who inherited the interest in the property (Sec. 691(b)(1)). Foreign tax credits receive similar treatment (Treas. Reg. Sec. 1.691(b)-1(a)). Incidentally, these expenses are deductible both on the estate tax return and on the estate income tax return or on the income tax return of the person who inherited the property.

In the case of percentage depletion, the person who receives the income to which the deduction relates is allowed the deduction in the taxable year in which the income is received (Sec. 691(b)(2)).

Deduction for estate tax

IRD is included in the gross estate of the decedent at fair market value and is also subject to income tax when paid. To alleviate some of the tax burden on IRD, a person who includes IRD in gross income is allowed a deduction (not a credit) for some of the estate tax paid with respect to the IRD. The deduction is calculated by applying the following formula:

$$\text{Deduction} = \frac{\substack{\text{Net amount} \\ \text{of IRD items}}}{\text{Gross estate value}} \times \substack{\text{Total federal and} \\ \text{state death taxes}}$$

It can be seen that the deduction is determined on the basis of the average death tax liability of the decedent's estate.

TAXATION OF SIMPLE TRUSTS AND BENEFICIARIES

In addition to the usual gross income and deduction rules for computing taxable income, a simple trust is allowed a deduction for the amount of income that the terms of the trust instrument require to be distributed currently to beneficiaries; this is ordinarily the net income of the trust. If the amount of income required to be distributed currently exceeds the distributable net income (DNI), the deduction allowable to the trust is limited to DNI.

A beneficiary of a simple trust includes in gross income for the taxable year the amounts of income required to be distributed for the year, whether distributed, undistributed, or distributed after the close of the taxable year of the trust. Two modifications to this general statement deal with distributions in excess of DNI and the character of the amounts distributed.

If income required to be distributed currently to the beneficiaries is greater than DNI, each beneficiary includes in gross income an amount equivalent to his or her proportionate share of DNI (Treas. Reg. Sec. 1.652(a)-2).

The amounts included in gross income of a beneficiary are of the same character in the hands of the beneficiary as in the hands of the trust. In other words, the character of the amount the trust receives passes through to the beneficiary (Treas. Reg. Sec. 1.652(b)-1). Some common items that retain their character when the income is passed through the trust are:

☐ Tax-exempt interest (Sec. 103);
☐ Dividends and interest for purposes of the combined dividend and interest exclusion (Sec. 116);
☐ Capital gains (if the trust distributes capital gain income) for purposes of special treatment;
☐ Personal service income for 50 percent maximum rate purposes (Sec. 1348).

Amounts that must be included in the gross income of a beneficiary are treated as consisting of the same proportions of each class of items entering into the DNI of the trust (Treas. Reg. Sec. 1.652(b)-2). An exception to the general rule is made if the terms of the trust allocate different classes of income to beneficiaries, or if local law requires such an allocation.

Deductions of a trust that enter into the computation of DNI must be allocated among the items of income according to the following three principles:

1. All deductible items directly attributable to one class of income must be allocated to that class.
2. Deductions not directly attributable to a specific class of income may be allocated to any items of income included in computing DNI. A portion must be allocated to tax-exempt income.
3. Deductions that exceed the income of the class of income to which they are attributable may be allo-

cated to any other class of income included in computing DNI. Excess deductions attributable to tax-exempt income may not be offset against any other class of income.

If a beneficiary has a taxable year different from that of the trust, the income required to be included in the beneficiary's income is based on the income of the trust for the taxable year ending within the beneficiary's taxable year.

The following comprehensive example illustrates a number of the rules and procedures we have just discussed.

Example: Under the terms of the Alice Jones Trust, a simple trust, all the income is to be distributed equally to beneficiaries A and B, and capital gains are to be allocated to corpus. The trust and both beneficiaries file returns on a calendar-year basis. No provision is made in the trust instrument for depreciation. During the taxable year, the trust had the following items of income and expense.

Rents	$15,000
Dividends from domestic corporations	30,000
Tax-exempt interest	10,000
Long-term capital gains	9,000
Taxes and expenses attributable to rents	3,000
Trustee's commissions allocable to the income amount	1,600
Trustee's commissions allocable to the principal account	2,400
Depreciation on rental property	4,000

Income of the trust for fiduciary accounting purposes is $50,400, computed as follows:

Rents		$15,000
Dividends		30,000
Tax-exempt interest		10,000
Total		$55,000
Deductions:		
Expenses directly attributable to rental income	$3,000	
Trustee's commissions allocable to income account	1,600	4,600
Income for fiduciary accounting purposes		$50,400

One-half ($25,200) the income is currently distributable to each beneficiary. Distributable net income of the trust is computed as follows:

Rents		$15,000
Dividends		30,000
Tax-exempt interest	$10,000	
Less: Expenses allocable thereto ($10,000/ 55,000 × 4,000)	727	9,273
Total		$54,273
Deductions:		
Expenses directly attributable to rental income	$3,000	
Trustee's commissions ($4,000 less $727 allocable to tax-exempt interest)	3,273	6,273
Distributable net income		$48,000

The deduction allowable to the trust for distributions to beneficiaries is computed as follows:

Distributable net income	$48,000
Less: Tax-exempt interest as adjusted	9,273
Distributable net income deduction allowed (lesser of $48,000 or $38,727)	$38,727

The taxable income of the trust is determined as follows:

Rents		$15,000
Dividends		30,000
Long-term capital gains		9,000
Gross income		$54,000
Deductions:		
Rental expense	$ 3,000	
Trustee's commissions	3,273	
Capital gain deduction	5,400	
Distributions to beneficiaries	38,727	
Personal exemption	300	50,700
Taxable income		$ 3,300

The same numbers calculated using the worksheet approach are as follows:

ALICE JONES TRUST WORKSHEET FOR CURRENT YEAR END

Accounts	Entries	Adjustments	Trust/local law income	Adjustments	DNI	Adjustments	Deductible/ taxable DNI	Adjustments	Taxable income
Rents	15,000		15,000		15,000		15,000		15,000
Dividends	30,000		30,000		30,000		30,000		30,000
Tax-exempt interest	10,000		10,000	727[d]	9,273	9,273[g]	—		
Long-term capital gains	9,000	9,000[a]	—					9,000[h]	9,000
Taxes and expenses	(3,000)		(3,000)		(3,000)		(3,000)		(3,000)
Trustees' commissions									
—Allocable to income	(1,600)		(1,600)	727[e]	(873)		(873)		(873)
—Allocable to corpus	(2,400)	2,400[b]	—	2,400[f]	(2,400)		(2,400)		(2,400)
Depreciation	(4,000)	4,000[c]	—						
			50,400		48,000		38,727		
DNI deduction									(38,727)[i]
Long-term capital gain deduction									(5,400)[j]
Exemption									(300)[k]
									3,300

[a]Long-term capital gains allocated to corpus under trust instrument.
[b]Trustees' commissions allocable to corpus under trust instrument.
[c]Depreciation allocated to beneficiaries.
[d, e]Trustees' commissions allocable to tax-exempt income $10,000/$55,000 × $4,000.
[f]Trustees' commissions allocable to corpus under local law are deductible to arrive at DNI and taxable income.
[g]Tax-exempt income is not includible in income and is eliminated to arrive at deductible DNI.
[h]Long-term capital gains are part of taxable income of the trust.
[i]DNI deduction.
[j]Long-term capital gain deduction (9,000 × 60%).
[k]Exemption for simple trust is $300.

In determining the character of the amounts includible in the gross income of A and B, it is assumed that the trustee elects to allocate to rents the expenses not directly attributable to a specific item of income other than the portion ($727) of such expenses allocated to tax-exempt interest. The allocation of expenses among the items of income is shown below:

	Rents	Dividends	Tax-exempt interest	Total
Income for trust accounting purposes	$15,000	$30,000	$10,000	$55,000
Less:				
Rental expenses	3,000			3,000
Trustees' commissions	3,273		727	4,000
Character of amounts in the hands of the beneficiaries	$ 8,727	$30,000	$ 9,273	$48,000[a]

[a]Distributable net income

Each beneficiary is deemed to have received one-half of each item of income. In addition, each beneficiary is allowed a deduction of $2,000 for depreciation of rental property attributable to the portion (one-half) of the income of the trust distributed to him.

SUMMARY

In this chapter, we have illustrated the tax complexities involved in transfers to an estate or trust and the taxation of a simple trust and its beneficiaries. Much of the complexity stems from the fact that trusts are taxed differently from other types of tax entities, acting as a conduit for some types of income (DNI) and being taxed on income allocated to corpus.

Trusts play an important role in accomplishing many family tax and nontax objectives. Careful analysis of the income and estate and gift tax provisions is necessary to determine all the tax implications of a plan.

PROBLEMS

1. An estate or trust acts as a conduit for income that is passed through to beneficiaries. Losses, however, are not passed through a trust or estate.
   a. Explain how a beneficiary of a trust or estate might benefit from a net operating loss incurred by the trust or estate.
   b. Explain the treatment of net operating losses when an estate or trust is terminated.
2. C. Lloyd created a trust on January 12, 19X2. On January 18, 19X2, she transferred 100 shares of ABC Corporation stock to the trust, at which time the stock had a fair market value of $18,000. She purchased the stock for $15,000 on June 10, 19X1. A gift tax of $1,500 was paid on the transfer. What is the basis of the property in the trust?
3. Robert Martin purchased a machine for use in his proprietorship business on January 2, 19X1. The machine cost $40,000 and had an estimated useful life of eight years. Because of the purchase, an investment credit of $4,000 was taken on Martin's 19X1 income tax return. The machine was depreciated using the 200 percent declining-balance method for three years.
   a. Martin transferred the property by gift to a trust on January 5, 19X4, at which time the value of the machine was $20,000. No gift tax was due as a result of the transfer. The trustee sold the machine for $20,000 on January 7,

19X4. What are the tax consequences to Martin and the trust as a result of these transactions?

b. Assume instead that Martin died on January 3, 19X4. The machine was valued for estate tax purposes at $21,000. The executor sold the machine on January 5, 19X4 for $21,000. What are the tax consequences to Martin's estate as a result of these events?

4. Under the trust instrument, the Trimble Trust is required to distribute all its income under local law to its beneficiaries. Income under local law is defined as all income except capital gains, which are allocated to corpus. The trust had the following income and expense for the taxable year.

Dividends	$ 2,000
Interest	15,000
Long-term capital gains	3,000
Trustee fees	1,000

Calculate the following:

a. Income under local law
b. Distributable net income

5. Under the trust instrument, the Barlow Trust was required to pay out all its income as determined under local law. Capital gains are not considered part of income under local law but are allocated to corpus. The trust had the following items of income and expenses for the taxable year. No provision was made in the trust instrument or under local law for depreciation.

Rents	$15,000
Tax-exempt interest	1,000
Taxable interest	3,000
Dividends	6,000
Long-term capital gains	2,000
Rental expenses	9,000
Depreciation	4,000
Trustee's commissions—all allocable to income	1,600

Calculate the following:

a. Income under local law
b. Distributable net income
c. The amount deductible as distributable net income
d. Taxable income of the trust

6. What is meant by the term "income in respect of a decedent"? What is meant by the term "deductions in respect of a decedent"? Give examples of both. Explain the tax consequences to the recipient of income and deductions in respect of a decedent.

7. G. Gander, a cash method taxpayer, died on June 18, 19X1. After his death, his estate collected the following amounts.

Broker's commissions due to Gander from real estate sold. The real estate was sold on June 15, 19X1, and payment was due five days after the sale, on June 20, 19X1.	$5,000
Interest credited to Gander's savings account on June 30, 19X1 for the period April 1 to June 30, 19X1. Interest is paid quarterly.	400
Income from an installment note received on September 30, 19X1, the payment due date.	6,000
Salary check mailed to Gander's executor and received by her on June 30, 19X1. The check was issued on June 15, 19X1	

and mailed to Gander's executor when Gander's employer learned of his untimely death.   1,000

Which of the above amounts are to be properly reported as income in respect of a decedent in the estate and which should be included on Gander's final return?

8. On March 15, 19X1, Morris Burns transferred by gift 500 shares of Acme Corporation stock to the Burns Family Trust. The Acme Corporation stock was purchased on February 10, 19X1 for $10,000 and at the time of the transfer to the trust had a fair market value of $18,000. No gift tax was payable as a result of the transfer. On January 8, 19X3, the trustee sold the Acme Corporation stock for $21,000. Mr. Burns paid taxes at a 60 percent marginal rate in 19X1 and 70 percent rate in 19X3. The trust was in the 30 percent marginal tax bracket in 19X3. How much tax under Sec. 644 must the trust pay as a result of the sale of stock?

9. Explain why a trustee or fiduciary might wish to establish a trust or estate year-end that is different from those of the beneficiaries.

10. Explain how the executor determines whether expenses (such as probate fees and administrative expenses) should be deductible on the estate income tax return or estate return.

SUPPLEMENTAL PROBLEMS

11. Under the terms of a testamentary simple trust, all income is to be distributed equally to Albert and Betty. Net capital gains are allocated to corpus. The trust instrument is silent with respect to depreciation. During the taxable year, the trust had the following items of income and expenses:

Rental income from real property	$25,000
Dividends from domestic corporations	10,000
Taxable interest	18,000
Tax-exempt interest	32,000
Long-term capital gains	14,000
Rental expenses	11,000
Trustee's fees	6,000
Depreciation on rental property	9,000

Calculate the following:

a. Income for fiduciary accounting purposes
b. Distributable net income
c. Taxable income of the trust
d. Gross income of Albert and Betty attributable to the distribution from the trust

12. Charles and Dorothy Edwin are contemplating a plan to transfer income-producing property to a trust for the benefit of their four children. The Edwins' sole source of income is portfolio investments (primarily stocks). The total annual taxable income from these investments is $300,000.

The Edwins would like to transfer stocks yielding approximately $60,000 of dividend income to a simple trust with the income divided equally among the four children. None of the trust distributions will be used to satisfy the Edwins' support obligations of the children, aged 13, 15, 17, and 22. The eldest child will no longer qualify as a dependent if trust income is paid to her. The other children will qualify as dependents for several more years. Calculate the total annual tax savings the Edwins can expect because of the plan.

RETURN PROBLEM

Under the terms of the Smith Family Trust, a simple trust, all the income is to be distributed equally to Sarah Jones and Rachel Jones and capital gains are to be allocated to corpus. The trust and both beneficiaries file returns on a calendar-year basis. The trust is entitled to the deductions for depreciation. During the taxable year, the trust had the following items of income and expense:

Rents	$20,000
Dividends from domestic corporations	6,000
Tax-exempt interest	2,000
Long-term capital gains	9,000
Expenses attributable to rents	11,000
Depreciation on rental property	3,000
Trustee's commissions allocable to the principal account	1,000
Trustee's commissions allocable to the income account	1,500

Complete a Form 1041 for the Smith Family Trust.

14

taxation of estates and complex trusts

Recall from Chapter 13 that the taxable income of an estate or a trust is computed in much the same way as it is for an individual. One principal difference is the distributable net income deduction. Because estates and complex trusts may accumulate income, have charitable beneficiaries, and distribute corpus or principal, additional complexities arise in computing distributable net income (DNI) and determining the amount of income and the tax on the income to the beneficiaries.

COMPUTATION OF DNI

Distributable net income is affected by distributions of amounts less than current income and by charitable contributions made from income. DNI must be adjusted in such situations; these adjustments, in turn, affect the treatment of such items in the distribution to the beneficiary. For trusts or estates with tax-exempt income, trustee or executor expenses and charitable contributions must be allocated to the tax-exempt income based on the ratio of tax-exempt income to total trust or estate income. Charitable contributions reduce the DNI deduction in order to prevent the deduction for charitable contributions from being allowed twice—once as a charitable contribution under Sec. 642 and again as part of distributed net income.

Example: Under the terms of a trust, $5,000 a year must be paid out of income to a designated charity. The balance of the income may, at the trustee's discretion, be accumulated or distributed to Beneficiary A. Expenses are allocable against income, and the trust instrument requires a reserve for depreciation. During the current year, the trust contributes $5,000 to charity and, at the trustee's discretion, $4,000 of income to A. The trust has the following items of income and expense for the year:

Dividends	$ 6,000
Tax-exempt interest	5,000
Rents	12,000
Rental expenses	3,000
Depreciation of rental property	1,000
Trustee's commissions	1,500

The distributable net income of the trust is computed as follows:

Dividends			$ 6,000
Rents			12,000
Tax-exempt interest		$ 5,000	
Less: Expenses allocable thereto [($5,000/23,000) × 1,500]	$ 326		
Charitable contributions allocable thereto [($5,000/23,000) × 5,000]	1,087	1,413	3,587
Total			$14,413

Deductions:

Rental expenses	$3,000	
Depreciation of rental property	1,000	
Trustee's commissions ($1,500 less $326 allocated to tax-exempt interest)	1,174	
Charitable contributions ($5,000 less $1,087 allocated to tax-exempt interest)	3,913	9,087
Distributable net income		$ 5,326

The deduction for DNI is limited to $1,739 ($5,326 less $3,587 tax-exempt interest) and $1,739 is the amount the beneficiaries must include in gross income.

TAXATION OF THE BENEFICIARIES OF AN ESTATE OR COMPLEX TRUST

A beneficiary of an estate or complex trust must include in gross income all amounts properly paid, credited, or required to be distributed to him or her by the estate or trust (Treas. Reg. Sec. 1.662(a)-1). These items are subject to several rules concerning currently distributable income, other amounts distributed, and the character of the amounts. When an estate or complex trust has more than one beneficiary, the amounts must be allocated among the beneficiaries. The principal method of allocation is known as the *tier system*. Certain trusts use another method of allocation, known as the *separate share rule*.

Estates and complex trusts may accumulate income. When a distribution is made from the accumulated income of a complex trust, a set of "throwback" rules applies, which provide rules for computing tax on each beneficiary's share of the distributed accumulated income. These throwback rules do not apply to estates. We shall explain these rules later in the chapter.

The 65-day rule

Although a distribution for a trust is ordinarily deductible by the trust and includible by the beneficiary in the year paid or payable, the fiduciary may elect to treat the distribution, if made within the first 65 days after the end of the taxable year, as an amount paid or credited on the last day of the taxable year. In determining the beneficiary's tax liability, if the fiduciary uses the 65-day rule, the beneficiary will include the income on the return for the year it would be included if the amount were paid on the last day of the taxable year.

Beneficiary's gross income

A beneficiary must include in gross income any amount required to be distributed, whether or not it is actually distributed. If the income required to be distributed is greater than DNI computed without consideration of the charitable contribution deduction, DNI is apportioned according to the following formula.

$$\text{Beneficiary's share of DNI} = \text{DNI} \times \frac{\text{Beneficiary's share of currently distributable income}}{\text{Total of all currently distributable income}}$$

Any amount the beneficiary does not include in the above formula is excludable from income unless the distribution is an accumulation distribution and throwback applies.

The amount of income for the taxable year required to be distributed currently includes any amount required to be paid out of income or corpus to the extent the amount is satisfied out of income for the taxable year. For example, an annuity that must be paid out of either income or corpus would qualify in all events as income required to be distributed currently to the extent that income (determined under local law) is not paid, credited, or required to be distributed to other beneficiaries for the taxable year.

Income required to be distributed for the taxable year also includes support payments to a decedent's spouse or other dependents. These amounts must be paid by a decedent's estate during the taxable year out of income or corpus, pursuant to a court order, decree, or local law, as an allowance or award for support of the decedent's spouse or other dependents. Such payments must be made for a limited period during the administration of the estate. Again, the payments are included to the extent there is income of the estate for the taxable year not paid, credited, or required to be distributed to other beneficiaries.

A beneficiary must include in gross income any amount paid, credited, or required to be distributed to the beneficiary for the taxable year, with the following exceptions (Treas. Reg. Sec. 1.662(a)-2):

1. Any income required to be distributed currently that is treated under currently distributable income provisions.

2. Gifts, bequests, and so on.

3. Charitable distributions.

4. Amounts that would result in a double deduction.

5. Amounts in excess of income required to be distributed currently and DNI. These types of payments include:

(a) A distribution made to a beneficiary at the discretion of the fiduciary.

(b) A distribution required by the terms of the governing instrument upon the occurrence of a specific event.

(c) An annuity that is payable only out of corpus.

(d) A distribution of property in kind.

(e) An amount applied or distributed, out of accumulated income in certain circumstances, for the support of a dependent of a grantor or trustee.

(f) A spouse's or dependent's allowance required to be paid out of corpus pursuant to a court order or decree under local law.

If any annuity is paid, credited, or required to be distributed tax free—that is, under a provision whereby the executor or trustee pays an annuitant's income tax that results from the receipt of the annuity—the payment of tax by the executor or trustee will be treated as income paid, credited, or required to be distributed currently, to the extent the payments are made out of income.

The tier system

The tier system of allocating DNI among beneficiaries classifies amounts paid to beneficiaries in two tiers. The first tier is currently distributable income and other amounts required and actually paid from currently distributable income. The second tier is the balance of DNI after allocation to the first tier, including all other amounts paid (except gifts and bequests) to the beneficiary.

Example: A trust instrument requires an annual distribution of $8,000 of income to X. Any remaining income may be accumulated or distributed to Y and Z. The trustee may also invade corpus for X, Y, and Z. The trust has DNI of $15,000. The trustee distributed $8,000 to X, $3,000 to Y, and $3,000 to Z. An additional $6,000 was also distributed to X. X must include $8,000 under Sec. 662(a)(1) because it is a current distribution. The other $12,000 is included in income of X, Y, and Z to the extent of $7,000 (DNI of $15,000 less current distribution of $8,000). X includes $3,500 ($7,000 x $6,000/$12,000). Y and Z each include $1,750 ($7,000 x $3,000/$12,000).

Separate share rule

If a single trust has more than one beneficiary and if different beneficiaries have substantially separate and independent shares, their shares are treated as separate trusts for the sole purpose of determining the amount of DNI allocable to the respective beneficiaries. This treatment is not available for estates. Without the separate share rule, if income were accumulated for Beneficiary A but a distribution of both income and corpus were made to Beneficiary B in an amount exceeding the share of income that would be distributable to B had there been separate trusts, B would be taxed on income that is accumulated for A. The separate share rule divides distributable net income into separate shares, thereby limiting B's tax liability.

Example: Under the terms of a trust, trust income is required to be divided into three equal shares. The income may be accumulated or distributed, and the trustee also has the discretion to invade corpus for the benefit of any beneficiary to the extent of his or her share of the trust estate. The trust has distributable net income of $30,000. The trustee makes a distribution of one-third of DNI to A. She accumulates the other $20,000—$10,000 each for B and C. She also makes a discretionary distribution of $20,000 out of corpus to A. A will be taxed on $10,000. A's taxable share may not exceed the DNI of his trust. The trust will be taxed on the $20,000 accumulated for B and C.

CHARACTER OF INCOME DISTRIBUTED   If an estate or complex trust does not make a charitable contribution, the amounts that are included in the income of the beneficiaries have the same character in the hands of the beneficiary as in the hands of the estate or trust. The amounts are treated as consisting of the same proportion of each class of items entering into the computation of DNI unless the terms of the governing instrument specifically allocate different classes of income to different beneficiaries or unless local law requires such an allocation.

When an estate or trust makes a charitable contribution, the same principles as stated above apply, except that, before allocation of the reductions among items of DNI, the allowed charitable contribution deduction is allocated among the classes of income that enter into the computation of estate or trust income.

When income is required to be distributed currently, charitable contribution deductions may not be fully taken into account for purposes of allocating income and deductions to beneficiaries. The charitable contribution deduction is disregarded to the extent that it exceeds the income of the trust for the taxable year, reduced by amounts required to be distributed currently for the taxable year.

Example: A trust instrument requires that $12,000 of its income be distributed currently to A. The balance of the income may be either distributed to B or to Charity C or accumulated. Accumulated income may be distributed to B and to Charity C. The trust has income of $22,000, consisting of $17,000 royalties and $5,000 tax-exempt income. The trustee distributes $12,000 to A, $7,000 to B, and $20,000 to Charity C.

DNI is $12,000 because the charitable contribution deduction, for this purpose, is taken into account only to the extent of $10,000—the difference between income of the trust for the taxable year ($22,000) and the amount required to be distributed ($12,000).

The $10,000 charitable contribution taken into account is allocated proportionally to items of income in the trust—$7,727 [($17,000/$22,000) × $10,000] to taxable royalties and the $2,273 balance to the tax-exempt income.

B has no gross income from the current distribution. The entire charitable contribution deduction is taken into account to determine B's gross income and, therefore, there is no DNI.

Dividends and interest qualifying for the combined dividends and interest exclusion also retain their character when they are distributed as part of DNI. No deduction is allowed for the portion of excluded dividends and interest deemed to have been distributed to the beneficiary. For example, if a trust received $4,000 of dividends and interest qualifying for the $200 combined dividend and interest exclusion and $1,000 of these dividends and interest were distributed to the beneficiary, the trust would receive a $200 dividend and interest exclusion when computing the gross income of the trust but would receive a DNI deduction as a result of the dividends of $950 ($1,000 less $200 × $1000/$4000). The dividends and interest allocable to the beneficiary are aggregated with other dividends and interest (if any) for purposes of the combined dividend and interest exclusion on the beneficiary's tax return.

Example: Under the terms of a trust, $12,000 a year is required to be paid out of income to a designated charity. The balance of any income may, at the trustee's discretion, be accumulated or distributed to Beneficiary A. Expenses are allocated against income, and the trust instrument requires a reserve for depreciation. During the taxable year, the trustee contributes $12,000 to charity and, at his discretion, distributes $20,000 of income to A. The trust has the following income and expenses for the taxable year.

Dividends	$20,000
Tax-exempt interest	10,000
Rents	30,000
Rental expenses	9,000
Depreciation of rental property	6,000
Trustee's commissions	6,000

For purposes of local law, the income of the trust is $39,000, computed as follows:

Dividends		$20,000
Tax-exempt interest		10,000
Rents		30,000
		$60,000
Less: Rental expenses	$9,000	
Depreciation	6,000	
Trustee's commissions	6,000	21,000
Income under local law		$39,000

The distributable net income of the trust is $27,000, computed as follows:

Rents				$30,000
Dividends				20,000
Tax-exempt interest		$10,000		
Less: Expenses allocable thereto [($10,000/60,000) x $6,000]		$1,000		
Charitable contributions allocable thereto [($10,000/$60,000) x $12,000]		2,000	3,000	7,000
Total				$57,000
Deductions:				
Rental expenses		$ 9,000		
Depreciation of rental property		6,000		
Trustee's commissions ($6,000 less $1,000 allocated to tax-exempt interest)		5,000		

Charitable contributions
($12,000 less $2,000
allocated to tax-exempt
interest)   10,000   30,000
Distributable net income $27,000

The trust DNI is $20,000 ($27,000 less $7,000), which is DNI less the net tax-exempt in-

terest adjusted for expenses and charitable contributions.

In determining the character of amounts distributed, it is assumed that the trustee elected to allocate his commissions to rental income except for the amount required to be allocated to tax-exempt interest.

In computing the amounts deductible by the trust and includible in A's gross income, the

	Rental income	Dividends	Tax-exempt interest	Total
Trust income	$30,000	$20,000	$10,000	$60,000
Less:				
Charitable contributions	6,000	4,000	2,000	12,000
Rental expenses	9,000			9,000
Depreciation	6,000			6,000
Trustee's commissions	5,000		1,000	6,000
Total deductions	$26,000	$ 4,000	$ 3,000	$33,000
Net	$ 4,000	$16,000	$ 7,000	$27,000

$20,000 distribution is composed of the following proportions of the items of income deemed to have been distributed to the beneficiaries by the trust.

Rents [($4,000/$27,000) ×
    $20,000] $ 2,963
Dividends [($16,000/$27,000) ×
    $20,000]   11,852
Dividend exclusion
    [($16,000/$27,000) × $200]   (119)
Tax-exempt interest
    [($7,000/$27,000) × $20,000]   5,185
                    Total $19,881

Taxable income of the trust is computed as follows:

Rental income $30,000
Dividends ($20,000 less $200
    exclusion)   19,800
    Gross income $49,800
Deductions:
    Rental expenses $ 9,000
    Depreciation of rental
        property   6,000
    Trustee's commissions   5,000
    Charitable contributions   10,000
    Distribution to A   14,696
    Personal exemption   100   44,796
        Taxable income $ 5,004

In computing the distributable net income of the trust, the taxable income of the trust was computed with the following modifications.

1. No deductions were allowed for distributions to the beneficiaries.
2. No deduction was allowed for personal exemption of the trust.
3. Capital gains and extraordinary dividends were excluded, and no long-term capital gain under Sec. 1202 was taken.
4. The dividend exclusion was not taken.

Satisfying legal obligations

If the terms of a will or a trust instrument provide for payment of amounts that are used in full or in part to discharge or satisfy a person's legal obligation, that person must include such amounts in gross income as though they were directly distributed to him as beneficiary. A legal obligation to support another person exists if, and only if, the obligation is not affected by the adequacy of the dependent's own resources.

For example, under local law, a parent is legally obligated to support a minor child. Property or income from property owned by the child may not be used for the child's support as long as his parent is able to support him. On the other hand, under local law, the child is not required to support his parent even if the parent's earnings are insufficient for that purpose. No legal obligation exists, regardless of the parent's resources.

In any event, the amount of trust income that is included in the gross income of the person obligated to support another is limited by the extent of the obligation under local law.

Two exceptions exist to the rule that satisfaction of a person's legal obligation will require inclusion of the income on his return. These concern cases relating to alimony payments under Sec. 71 and cases relating to income of a trust in a case of divorce, separate maintenance, or a written separation agreement. In both cases, gross income will not result to the person whose legal obligation is satisfied.

DEDUCTIONS FOR BENEFICIARIES UPON THE TERMINATION OF AN ESTATE OR TRUST

An estate or trust is entitled to the benefits of carrying net operating losses back three years and forward seven years (Sec. 642(d)). An estate or trust also may carry forward capital losses indefinitely. When an estate or trust terminates, any net operating losses carried forward or capital loss carryovers that would otherwise have been allowable are allowed to the beneficiaries who succeed to the property of the estate or trust (Sec. 642(h)). Even an insolvent estate may provide its beneficiaries with some real tax savings.

Net operating losses and capital loss carryovers retain the same character in the hands of the beneficiary as in the hands of the estate or trust. For example, if an estate had a long-term capital loss carryover, the individual beneficiary's carryover also will be long-term. The net operating loss and capital loss carryovers are not itemized deductions but are taken to arrive at adjusted gross income.

The first taxable year of the beneficiary in which the estate or trust terminates is the first one to which the loss is carried over. In computing the number of years to which the net operating loss may be carried over, the last taxable year of the estate or trust (whether or not a short taxable year) and the first taxable year of the beneficiary each count as a taxable year. This does not affect capital loss carryover since the losses are carried over indefinitely for individuals.

When an estate or trust terminates and has deductions in excess of gross income for its last taxable year, the excess is allowed as a deduction to the beneficiaries who succeed to the property of the estate or trust. Such excess deductions do not include the trust or estate personal exemptions or the charitable contribution deduction.

Excess deductions are allowed only in the taxable year of the beneficiary in which the estate or trust terminates. This means that the executor or trustee must plan the termination in such a way that the beneficiary will use these deductions. If the excess deduction causes the noncorporate beneficiary's deductions to exceed his or her income, this condition does not create a net operating loss that may be carried over. The deduction is treated as an itemized deduction on the individual beneficiary's tax return.

TAXATION OF ACCUMULATION DISTRIBUTIONS

A trust is a separate tax entity and is allowed a deduction for distribution of income to beneficiaries. Without some specific provisions in the Code to deal with accumulation distributions, a trustee could accumulate income and pay tax at a relatively low tax rate. At some later year, a tax-free distribution out of this accumulated income could be made to the beneficiaries. For this reason, an accumulation distribution is treated as if it had been received by the beneficiary in the year the trust earned the income. (These rules apply only to trusts and not to estates.)

When a trust accumulates income and makes a distribution of the accumulated income to the beneficiary in a future year, if this distribution is greater than the income of the trust and is an accumulation distribution from a preceding taxable year, it is "thrown back" to determine the tax attributable to the distribution.

The tax attributable to the distribution is computed using an averaging method called the *short-cut method*. The average accumulation distribution, that is, the accumulated distribution divided by the number of years in which the trust earned income, must be added to the beneficiary's taxable income in three years. The beneficiary then computes his taxes attributable to his average increase in income attributable to the average accumulation distribution and multiplies the average increase in taxes by the number of preceding years to determine the total increase in taxes. A credit is allowed up to his additional tax liability for the taxes imposed on the trust attributable to the undistributed net income.

We must define a number of terms in order to be able to compute accurately the accumulation distribution and the tax to the beneficiary. These are:

☐ Undistributed net income
☐ Accumulation distribution

□ Income of the trust
□ Taxes imposed on the trust attributable to undistributed net income
□ Preceding taxable year

Undistributed net income is the excess of distributable net income over (a) the amount of income required to be distributed currently; (b) any amount properly paid or credited or required to be distributed; and (c) the amount of taxes imposed on the trust attributable to distributable net income (Sec. 665(a)).

An *accumulation distribution* is an amount by which the amount paid or credited or required to be distributed exceeds distributable net income for each year reduced (not below zero) by amounts required to be distributed currently (Sec. 665(b) and Treas. Reg. Sec. 1.665(b)-1A(d)). If the amounts properly paid, credited, or required to be distributed by the trust for the taxable year do not exceed the income of the trust, there will be no accumulation distribution for that year (Sec. 665(b)).

The term *income,* when used in this context (as opposed to taxable income, distributable net income, undistributed net income, or gross income) means the amount of income of the trust for the taxable year under the governing trust instrument and applicable local law (Sec. 643(b)). In calculating the amount of income a beneficiary must recognize and the potential tax credit allowed, the taxes imposed on the trust that are attributable to undistributed net income must be computed.

Taxes imposed on the trust attributable to the undistributed net income means the amount of federal income taxes for the taxable year properly allocable to the distributable net income for the taxable year. This amount is computed using the following formula.

$$\text{Taxes imposed on the trust attributable to undistributed net income} = \frac{\text{Total taxes (other than the minimum tax under Sec. 56) of the trust after credits allowed under Sec. 642(a)}}{} = \frac{\text{Taxable income of the trust} - \text{capital gains not included in distributable net income and} - \text{the long-term capital gain deduction}}{\text{Taxable income of the trust}}$$

An accumulation distribution of undistributed net income may not be allocated or thrown back to a taxable year of a trust that is not defined as a *preceding taxable year.* For any distribution made after December 31, 1973, a tax year beginning before January 1, 1969 is not considered a preceding taxable year. For distributions made before January 1, 1974, any taxable year that precedes by more than five years the year in which the accumulation distribution was made is not a preceding taxable year (Treas. Reg. Sec. 1.665(e)-1A).

If the separate share rule is applicable for a trust distribution of an accumulation distribution, the provisions explained above are applied as if each share were a separate trust. Thus, the accumulation distribution, undistributed net income, and taxes imposed on the trust are computed separately for each share.

A domestic trust allocates distribution to the earliest preceding taxable year in which there is undistributed net income, beginning with the earliest of the remaining preceding taxable years of the trust. Again, for distributions made after December 31, 1973, a tax year beginning before January 1, 1969 is not considered a preceding taxable year.

The beneficiary must include in income and pay taxes on amounts that are treated as accumulation distributions; that is, the amount that would have been paid to the beneficiary on the last day of the preceding taxable year of the accumulation. In other words, if the trust had not accumulated the income, the amount that would have been distributed is the undistributed net income plus the taxes imposed on the trust attributable to the undistributed net income. The beneficiary must attach Form 4970, Tax on Accumulation Distribution of Trust, to his or her tax return.

The tax imposed on the beneficiary is computed using the *short-cut method,* which consists of the following six steps.

1. Determine the number of preceding taxable years of the trust on the last day of the year from which the amount is deemed distributed. Divide the deemed distribution by the number of preceding taxable years. If the undistributed net income deemed distributed is less than 25 percent of the amount of the average accumulation distribution (accumulation distribution divided by number of preceding taxable years), this income may be ignored for purposes of the above calculations.

2. Take the five taxable years of the beneficiary preceding the year of the accumulation distribution and eliminate the years with the highest and lowest income. For purposes of the five base years considered for throwback, the taxable income of the beneficiary is deemed to be not less than the zero bracket amount for an individual.

3. Add the average computed in step 1 to the ben-

eficiary's taxable income for each of the three taxable years remaining.

4. Determine the average increase in tax on adjusted taxable income for the three taxable years.

5. Multiply the average increase in tax computed in step 4 by the number of preceding taxable years (step 1).

6. Credit the taxes computed in step 5 by the amount of taxes deemed distributed. This credit may not exceed the amount of tax computed. Also, a trust may not receive a refund or credit for any amount of taxes imposed on the trust.

Example: A trust makes an accumulation distribution of $26,000 in 19X6. For 19X1 through 19X5, the undistributed portion of distributable net income, taxes imposed on the trust, and undistributed net income are as follows:

Year	Undistributed portion of distributable net income	Taxes imposed attributable to distributable net income	Undistributed net income
19X1	$12,100	$3,400	$ 8,700
19X2	16,100	5,200	10,900
19X3	6,100	1,360	4,740
19X4	-0-	-0-	-0-
19X5	10,100	2,640	7,460

The distribution is deemed to be from the earliest preceding taxable year. None of the accumulation years precedes 1969. The distribution is therefore deemed to be $8,700 from 19X1, $10,900 from 19X2, $4,740 from 19X3, and $1,660 from 19X5.

The taxes imposed associated with the distributions are $3,400 from 19X1, $5,200 from 19X2, $1,360 from 19X3, and $566 [($1,600/$7,460) × $2,640] for 19X5. The total distribution, therefore, is $36,526 ($26,000 plus the taxes imposed attributable to distributable net income of $10,526).

The beneficiary had taxable income and taxes paid for the years 19X1 to 19X5 as follows:

Year	Taxable income	Tax paid
19X1	$24,000	$4,337
19X2	28,000	5,593
19X3	26,000	4,953
19X4	25,000	4,633
19X5	30,000	6,238

Step 1: Determine the number of preceding taxable years in the throwback period (for computing 25 percent minimum distribution amount).

Total accumulation distribution	$36,526
Total number of preceding years 19X1–19X5	÷ 5
Average annual amount	$ 7,305
25% of average annual amount	$ 1,826

The lowest undistributed portion of distributable net income in 19X4 is zero. Therefore, the year 19X4 may be disregarded. Now, divide the deemed distribution by the number of preceding taxable years: $36,526 ÷ 4 = $9,132.

Step 2: Eliminate the beneficiary's highest and lowest taxable income years: 19X5, $30,000, and 19X1, $24,000.

Step 3: Add the taxable income for each of the three taxable years to the average from step 1.

Year	Taxable income	Average distribution	Total
19X2	$28,000	$9,132	$37,132
19X3	26,000	9,132	35,132
19X4	25,000	9,132	34,132

Step 4: Compute the average increase in tax for the three taxable years.

	19X2	*19X3*	*19X4*
Recomputed taxable income	$37,132	$35,132	$34,132
Tax on recomputed income	$ 8,993	$ 8,137	$ 7,767
Tax paid on original return	5,593	4,953	4,633
Tax on average distribution	$ 3,400	$ 3,184	$ 3,134

Average increase in tax attributable to the distribution: ($3,400 + $3,184 + $3,134) ÷ 3 = $3,239.

Step 5: Multiply the average increase in tax by the number of preceding taxable years: $3,239 × 4 = $12,956.

Step 6: Credit the tax computed by the amount of taxes deemed distributed ($12,956 − $10,526 = $2,430). The beneficiary must pay a partial tax of $2,430 because of the distribution.

The filled in Form 4970 on page **14/9**, Tax on Accumulation Distribution of Trusts, shows how the above information will look on the beneficiary's tax return.

Form **4970** (Rev. Oct. 1978) Department of the Treasury Internal Revenue Service	# Tax on Accumulation Distribution of Trusts For calendar year 19 **X6**, or other taxable year beginning ...., 19........ and ending ...., 19........	**Attach to Beneficiary's Tax Return**

Name(s) as shown on return	Social security number
Name and address of trust	Identifying number

Type of trust
☑ Domestic ☐ Foreign

Enter number of accumulation distributions received this year.
(See general instruction A) . . . . ▶ | **/**

Part I Average Income and Determination of Computation Years

1 Part of current distribution that represents amounts considered distributed in earlier taxable years. (From Schedule J (Form 1041), line 39, column a.) (see instructions) . . . . | **26,000**

2 Taxes imposed on the trust attributable to amounts on line 1. (From Schedule J (Form 1041), line 39, column b.) (see instructions) . . . . | **10,526**

3 Total accumulation distribution received from trust (add lines 1 and 2) . . . . | **36,526**

4 Tax-exempt interest included in amount on line 3. (From Schedule J (Form 1041), line 39, column c.) . . . | **—**

5 Taxable accumulation distribution (subtract line 4 from line 3) . . . . | **36,526**

6 Number of trust's preceding taxable years in which amounts on line 5 are considered distributed (see instructions) . . . . | **5**

7 Average amount considered distributed (divide line 1 by line 6) . . . . | **7,305**

8 Enter 25% of line 7 . . . . | **1,826**

9 Number of years on line 6 in which amount considered distributed is not less than the amount on line 8 . . . | **4**

10 Average amount for recomputing tax (divide line 5 by line 9). Enter here and in each column on line 13 . . . | **9,132**

11 Enter your taxable income before this distribution for the 5 immediately prior taxable years (see instructions)	19 **X1**	19 **X2**	19 **X3**	19 **X4**	19 **X5**
	24,000	28,000	26,000	25,000	30,000

Part II Computation of Tax Attributable to the Accumulation Distribution

	(a)	(b)	(c)
12 Enter the amounts from line 11, eliminating the highest and lowest taxable income years	28,000	26,000	25,000
13 Enter amount from line 10 in each column	9,132	9,132	9,132
14 Recomputed taxable income (add lines 12 and 13)	37,132	35,132	34,132
15 Income tax on amounts on line 14 (see instructions)	8,993	8,137	7,767
16 Income tax before credits on line 12 income (see instructions)	5,593	4,953	4,633
17 Additional tax before credits (subtract line 16 from line 15)	3,400	3,184	3,134
18 Tax credit adjustment (see instructions)	—	—	—
19 Subtract line 18 from line 17	3,400	3,184	3,134
20 Minimum tax adjustment (see instructions)	—	—	—
21 Combine lines 19 and 20	3,400	3,184	3,134

22 Add amounts in columns (a), (b), and (c), on line 21 . . . . | **9,718**

23 Divide the amount on line 22 by three . . . . | **3239**

24 Multiply the amount on line 23 by the number of years on line 9 . . . . | **12,956**

25 Enter the amount from line 2 . . . . | **10,526**

26 Partial tax (subtract line 25 from line 24). If less than zero, enter zero. Enter here and as indicated in instructions . . . . | **2,430**

27 Interest charge on accumulation distribution from foreign trusts (see instructions) . . . . | **—**

Form **4970** (Rev. 10–78)

GRANTOR TRUSTS

It is an established tax principle that a successful gift for income tax purposes usually may not be made unless a taxpayer gives away all interests in the gift property. A person may wish to transfer property, usually to a trust, and retain some powers over the property. If certain powers over the trust are retained by the grantor or are vested in a person other than the grantor, the tax objectives of the gift plan may be lost because the grantor or other person will be treated as the owner of the trust property and taxed on its income. Such trusts are called *grantor trusts.*

In general, when the grantor or another person is treated as the owner of any portion of a trust, the income and deductions and credits attributable to that income will be included in computing his or her taxable income. Trust income is taxed to a grantor if any of the following conditions are met:

1. A reversionary interest in the trust is retained within specified time limits (Sec. 673).
2. A grantor or a nonadverse party has powers over the beneficial interests of the trust (Sec. 674).
3. Certain administrative powers over the trust exist under which the grantor may or does benefit (Sec. 675).
4. A grantor or a nonadverse party has a power to revoke the trust or return the corpus to the grantor (Sec. 676).
5. The grantor or a nonadverse party has the power to distribute income to or for the benefit of the grantor or the grantor's spouse (Sec. 677).

In addition to powers that a grantor may not retain, a person other than the grantor will be taxed on trust income to the extent he has the sole power to vest corpus or income in himself. That person will receive taxable income for any portion of a trust of which he is treated as the owner. Trusts of this type are called *Mallinckrodt trusts* (see pages **14**/11–12).

The rules under which a grantor or other person will be taxed on trust income, including powers that may and may not be retained, are explained below.

Whenever a person other than a grantor holds a power, that person's status will determine what actions may be attributable to the grantor. This status may be classified as adverse, nonadverse, or related, or subordinate.

An *adverse party* is any person with a substantial beneficial interest in a trust who would be adversely affected by the exercise or nonexercise of a power he or she holds in the trust (Sec. 672(a)). A *nonadverse party* is any person not having an adverse interest (Sec. 672(b)). A trustee is not an adverse party merely because of his interest, but a person having a general power of appointment over the trust property is deemed to have a beneficial interest in the trust (Treas. Reg. Sec. 1.672(a)-1(a)). A beneficiary or remainderman (the person entitled to receive the principal of an estate upon the termination of the intervening life estate or estates) is an adverse party for that part of the income or corpus in which he shares or has rights (Treas. Reg. Sec. 1.672(a)-(b),(c), and (d)).

A *related, or subordinate, party* is any nonadverse party who is the grantor's spouse (if living with the grantor), father, mother, child, brother, sister, or employee of the grantor, or a corporation or any employee of a corporation in which the grantor holds significant voting control or is an executive (Sec. 672(c) and Treas. Reg. Sec. 1.672(c)-1). The related, or subordinate, classifications are relevant for ascertaining if the grantor has powers to control beneficial enjoyment under Sec. 674(c) and the administrative power of borrowing of trust funds under Sec. 675(3). "Power to control beneficial enjoyment" means that the grantor may dispose of the income or corpus of the trust.

Section 673, in general, provides that a grantor is treated as the owner of a trust in which he has a *reversionary interest* in either the corpus or income if he is expected to get the property back within 10 years. This section also provides the principal rules for setting up a Clifford trust, or short-term trust.

In general, a grantor will *not* be treated as the owner of any portion of a trust if his reversionary interest in that portion cannot be returned to him:

1. Within 10 years from the date of transfer of that portion of the trust (Treas. Reg. Sec. 1.673(a)-1(a)).
2. Until the death of the person or persons to whom the income of that portion is payable, regardless of life expectancy (Treas. Reg. Sec. 1.673(a)-(b)).
3. Within 10 years, if the reversionary interest is to take place at the earlier of a specified term of years or death of an income beneficiary (Treas. Reg. Sec. 1.673(a)-1(b)).

A grantor is treated as the owner of any portion of a trust in which he has *power,* exercisable by the grantor, a nonadverse party, or both, without the approval of any adverse party, *to dispose of the beneficial enjoyment* of the corpus of income. Several powers may be retained without tax liability on the trust income to the grantor.

1. Power to apply income to support a dependent.

2. Power affecting beneficial enjoyment, only after the expiration of a 10-year period.

3. Power exercisable by will.

4. Power to allocate among charitable beneficiaries.

5. Power to distribute corpus either to or for beneficiaries, provided that the power is limited by a reasonably definite standard set forth in the trust instrument or, if no standard is provided, to invade corpus held for a particular current-income beneficiary.

6. Power to accumulate income for the beneficiary or his or her estate.

7. Power to withhold income during disability of a beneficiary.

8. Power to allocate between income and corpus.

9. Certain powers of independent trustees.

10. Power to allocate income, if that power is limited by a standard.

These powers and the many exceptions and limitations to them are explained fully in the regulations under Sec. 674.

Section 675 provides, in effect, that a grantor will be treated as the owner of any portion of a trust if he retains *administrative powers* that benefit the grantor rather than the beneficiaries of the trust. The circumstances or powers that cause a grantor to be taxed are:

1. The power to deal with the trust for less than full and adequate consideration (Sec. 675(a)).

2. The power to borrow without adequate interest or security (Sec. 675(2)).

3. The circumstance that the grantor has directly or indirectly borrowed the corpus or income of the trust and has not completely repaid the loan, including interest, before the beginning of the tax year (Sec. 675(3)).

4. Certain general powers of administration, such as a power to vote or direct voting of stock or other securities of a corporation in which the grantor and the trust are significant from the viewpoint of administrative control (Sec. 675(4)).

A grantor will be treated as the owner of any portion of a trust that can be *revoked* by the grantor, a nonadverse party, or both, before a 10-year period expires (Sec. 676(a)).

If, after the 10-year period, the grantor does not relinquish the power to revoke the trust, he will be taxed on the income under his control in the 11th and succeeding years if the exercise of the power may affect the beneficial enjoyment of income received in those years (Sec. 676(b)).

Again, a 10-year period must pass before the income may be used for the benefit of the grantor. After the 10-year period, if the grantor does not relinquish his power, he will be taxed in subsequent years on the income under his control (Sec. 677(a)).

The grantor is treated as owner of any portion of a trust whose income, without the approval or consent of any adverse party or at the discretion of the grantor or a nonadverse party or both may be:

1. Distributed to the grantor or grantor's spouse;

2. Held or accumulated for future distribution to the grantor or the grantor's spouse; or

3. Applied to the payment of premiums on life insurance of the grantor or grantor's spouse (except where insurance is irrevocably payable for a charitable purpose).

The grantor must also report trust income used to satisfy the grantor's or grantor's spouse's legal obligations. Where income may be distributed by a trustee who is not the grantor for the support or maintenance of a beneficiary the grantor is legally obligated to support, the grantor will not report this income.

A person may retain certain powers over a trust without being treated as owner of the trust. This is accomplished through the use of a short-term, or "Clifford" trust (named after a taxpayer whose Supreme Court case prompted the legislation). The Clifford trust provisions permit a grantor to retain a reversionary interest, a power to control beneficial enjoyment, and a power to revoke after a 10-year period and still transfer income to another person.

For example, a grantor may wish to provide for a child's professional education and establishment of a career with income from investment properties but may need to revoke the trust later to provide for retirement. This may be done through a Clifford trust.

Person other than the grantor treated as substantial owner

If a person other than the grantor of a trust has the exclusive power to vest income or corpus in himself, he will be treated as the owner of that portion of the trust in which he has power (Sec. 678(a)(1)). Also, that person will be taxed even if he partially releases or modifies this power so that income or corpus may not be vested in him, but retains other powers that cause the trust to be taxed as a grantor trust if held by a grantor

(Sec. 678(a)(2)). These trusts are commonly called Mallinckrodt trusts (again, named after the person whose case gave rise to the legislation).

SUMMARY

In this chapter, we have seen the complexities of trusts that accumulate income or have charitable beneficiaries in the computation of distributable net income and the amount of tax on the income to the beneficiaries. The tax benefits of complex trusts and the flexibility they provide, however, far outweigh the administrative difficulties involved.

The tax benefits of short-term trusts are also significant. These trusts play an important role in family financial planning because they couple the benefits of income splitting and the flexibility to control the disposition of the trust property and income after a 10-year period.

PROBLEMS

1. How may the 65-day rule be used to plan distributions from a complex trust or estate?

2. The J. Roberts Trust received dividends and interest qualifying for the dividend and interest exclusion of $1,600, of which $1,200 was distributed to the trust beneficiary, J. Roberts III. Calculate the amount of dividend and interest exclusion that may be claimed by the trust. Calculate the amount of dividend and interest exclusion that may be claimed by J. Roberts III.

3. John Michaels, the executor of the William Thompson estate, sold certain securities owned by Mr. Thompson at his death, held in the estate. He paid a broker's commission of $1,000. The gain on the sale of these securities was $15,000. What alternatives are available to Mr. Michaels for the treatment of these commissions?

4. A trust has distributable net income of $40,000, consisting of $10,000 taxable interest, $15,000 royalties, and $15,000 dividends. The trust distributes $20,000 to a beneficiary. Neither the trust instrument nor local law provides for the distribution or accumulation of different classes of income. What is the distributable net income amount and character of the $20,000 received by the beneficiary?

5. The terms of the Miller Family Trust require the distribution annually of $50,000 income to Georgia Miller. If any income remains, it may be accumulated or distributed to Mark, Betsy, or Ann in amounts at the discretion of the trustee. The trustee may also invade corpus for the benefit of Georgia, Mark, Betsy, or Ann. In the taxable year, the trust has $90,000 income after deduction of all expenses. Distributable net income is $90,000. The trustee distributes $50,000 income to Georgia, $12,000 each to Mark, Betsy, and Ann, and an additional $10,000 to Georgia. How much will Georgia, Mark, Betsy, and Ann include in income as a result of the distribution from the trust?

6. The Larson Family Trust provides that $25,000 of its income must be distributed currently to Sally, and the balance may be distributed to Ronald, distributed to State University, or accumulated. Accumulated income may be distributed to Ronald and to State University. For its taxable year, the trust has $42,000 of taxable interest, $8,000 of tax-exempt interest, and no expenses. The trustee distributed $25,000 to Sally, $20,000 to State University, and $10,000 to Ronald. Calculate:
   a. The charitable contribution deduction for the trust.
   b. The amount of income Ronald must recognize as a result of the distribution from the Larson Family Trust.
   c. The amount and character of income that must be recognized by Sally as a result of the distribution from the Larson Family Trust.

7. The Krock Trust provides that $40,000 of current income must be paid annually to Roy Krock and $10,000 per year must be paid to Regina, out of income or

corpus. The trust has distributable income of $45,000. The trustee pays $40,000 of current income to Roy and $10,000 from corpus to Regina. How much income must Regina recognize as a result of the distribution from the Krock Trust?

8. Under the terms of the Jenson Trust, $15,000 of income is required to be distributed currently to Herb Jenson, and the trustee has discretion to make additional distributions to Herb. During the taxable year 19x1, the trust had distributable net income of $40,000, derived from interest and royalties. The trustee made distributions of $25,000 to Herb. Calculate the undistributed net income of the Jenson Trust.

9. Under the terms of the Adams Trust, the trustee has the discretion to either accumulate the trust income or make distributions to Marianne Adams or Ray Sinclair. The trustee may also invade corpus for the benefit of Marianne or Ray. During the taxable year, the trust had income of $14,000 and expenses of $4,500 allocable to corpus. The trustee distributed $8,000 each to Marianne and Ray. Calculate the accumulation distribution that results from these distributions.

10. Explain how short-term trusts provide an advantage over other kinds of trusts. What are some of the uses of short-term trusts?

11. A trust instrument requires the trustee to pay $30,000 annually to W, payable out of income, and $15,000 to X, payable out of income or corpus. DNI was $40,000 during the current year. The trustee paid the $30,000 to W and $15,000 of corpus to X. How much will W and X include in gross income as a result of these distributions?

SUPPLEMENTAL PROBLEMS

12. Tom Raymond created an irrevocable trust. Under the terms of the trust instrument, the ordinary income is payable to Tom for life, and on his death the corpus shall be distributed to Betty Borak, who is not related to Tom. Tom does not retain any other powers that would cause him to be considered an owner of the trust. Under local law, capital gains must be allocated to corpus. During 19X0, the trust had gross income and deductions as follows:

Interest	$ 9,000
Dividends from domestic corporations	4,000
Capital gains	15,000
Expenses allocable to income	800
Expenses allocable to corpus	200

Calculate the amount of income, if any, Tom must include in his income as a result of the income of the trust.

13. The trustee of the Krystal Trust made an accumulation distribution of $70,000 in 19X9 to Jay Krystal. For 19X2 through 19X8, the undistributed portion of distributable net income, taxes imposed on the trust, and undistributed net income were as follows:

Year	Undistributed portion of distributable net income	Taxes imposed attributable to distributable net income	Undistributed net income
19X2	$16,000	$ 4,081	$11,919
19X3	21,300	6,360	14,940
19X4	13,350	3,101	10,249
19X5	10,700	2,253	8,447
19X6	28,400	9,839	18,561
19X7	25,100	8,222	16,878
19X8	30,100	10,557	19,543

Jay Krystal, a single individual, had taxable income and taxes paid for years 19X2 to 19X8 as follows:

Year	Taxable income	Tax paid
19X2	$41,500	$18,392
19X3	46,000	15,867
19X4	50,000	18,067
19X5	48,000	16,967
19X6	55,300	20,982
19X7	60,000	23,943
19X8	54,500	20,542

Calculate on Form 4970 the amount of tax Jay must pay as a result of the distribution.

RETURN PROBLEM

Howard J. Rule died July 9, 1978. A testamentary trust was created that provided that one-half the trust income was to be distributed to Sharon A. Rule, the decedent's wife, for her life. The remaining trust income may, at the trustee's discretion, be paid to Georgia Rule, the decedent's niece, paid to designated charities, or accumulated. Under local law, capital gains are allocable to the principal amount. The trust had the following items of income and deductions for the taxable year:

Dividends from domestic corporations	$15,000
Taxable interest	9,000
Tax-exempt interest	1,000
Long-term capital gains	
—Sale of 100 shares of XYZ Corporation was transferred from the estate and had a basis of $15,000. Selling price was $27,000 on November 25, 1979	12,000
Trustee's commissions allocable to income	1,000
Trustee's commissions allocable to principal	500

The trustee distributes one-half of local law income to Sharon, distributes one-fourth to charity, and accumulates the remaining one-fourth.

Complete Form 1041 and Schedule D. Provide any necessary information.

FIVE

wealth transfer taxes

15

wealth transfer taxes: general concepts

The federal government levies a tax on three selected forms of wealth transfer. Each is an excise tax imposed on the *act* of transferring the property rather than on the property itself. The federal government does not levy any universal wealth tax. Because the Constitution prohibits the federal government from levying direct taxes unless the tax is apportioned among the states in accordance with each state's population,[1] a universal federal wealth tax might be unconstitutional because it might be considered a direct tax. Collection of the greatest portion of a wealth tax from the citizens of the most populous state without regard to the aggregate wealth possessed by that state's citizens would be ludicrous, to say the least.

The three forms of wealth transfer tax imposed at the federal level are the estate tax (levied on the transfer of property by a decedent), the gift tax (which taxes the donor on gifts), and the generation-skipping transfer tax (imposed on the taxable distribution to, or taxable termination in favor of, a younger generation beneficiary). Although the generation-skipping transfer tax was introduced with the Tax Reform Act of 1976, the other two transfer taxes have existed for decades. We shall discuss each of the wealth transfer taxes in some depth in Chapters 16, 17, and 18.

In addition to these federal taxes, all states except Nevada subject transfers by a decedent to some form of death tax—an inheritance tax, an estate tax, or

both. Only 16 states currently tax *inter vivos* transfers (gifts between living persons). To date, California is the only state that has adopted a generation-skipping transfer tax.

Although both estate taxes and inheritance taxes extract a tax for transfers made at death, the computation of the tax base differs for the two taxes. The estate tax base is the aggregate amount, after deductions, transferred by the decedent. With the exception of certain transfers to orphans, the surviving spouse, and charitable organizations, the identity of the recipient is unimportant. Because of the imposition of the estate tax, the amount available for distribution to heirs, legatees, or devisees is smaller.

The tax base for the inheritance tax is the before-inheritance-tax amount that passes to each recipient. Thus, under a progressive tax structure, the aggregate tax is lower if there are 15 recipients instead of two. Generally, different rate schedules apply to different categories of beneficiaries. Surviving spouses and descendants are usually eligible for the lowest rate schedule. In most instances, nonrelatives are subject to the highest rates.

In this chapter, we shall summarize the history of each of the federal wealth transfer taxes. We shall briefly describe each of the three taxes and the manner of computing them. In addition, we shall consider the unification of estate and gift taxes under the 1976 Tax Reform Act and the purposes for this change. We shall also present some statistics concerning the revenue from transfer taxes and the distribution of wealth.

[1] Article I, Section 9, Clause 4 of the U.S. Constitution.

A BRIEF HISTORY OF THE WEALTH TRANSFER TAXES

In the early history of the United States, the federal government levied death taxes on several occasions, primarily during times of war and only for short periods of time. On several occasions, the Populists advocated both a graduated income tax and a graduated estate or inheritance tax. Since its readoption in 1916, a federal estate tax has been levied without interruption, although over the years, Congress has changed the rates and varied the amount of the exemption. Other changes have occurred, such as the introduction of the marital deduction in 1948. The Tax Reform Act of 1976 contained a major overhaul of the estate tax provisions. One aim of the significant alterations was to reduce the disparity in the tax treatment of lifetime transfers and transfers at death.

In 1916, the House Ways and Means Committee decided that an estate tax was preferable to an inheritance tax for two reasons. Because the states relied on inheritance taxes, the committee thought an estate tax would help balance the tax structure. Moreover, the committee viewed the estate tax as simpler to administer, because computing the size of the shares passing to each recipient was unnecessary.[2]

In 1916, Congress was faced with a need to generate additional revenue, and raising revenue is one of the purposes of death taxes. The achievement of social policy goals, such as the breaking up of huge concentrations of wealth, is another goal of death taxation.

In 1935, President Franklin D. Roosevelt proposed that Congress adopt an inheritance tax in addition to the existing estate tax. Roosevelt made the following arguments in favor of additional death taxes:

1. The transmission of vast fortunes from one generation to the next is inconsistent with the ideals and sentiments of U.S. citizens.

2. It is "natural" and "wholesome" for a person to be interested in providing security for himself and for his family. A "reasonable" inheritance, however, will adequately furnish security. The desire to provide security is not a justification for "great" accumulations of wealth. Accumulations of large amounts of wealth perpetuate concentration of control in the hands of relatively few persons.

3. A tax on inherited property is a tax on "static" wealth compared with "dynamic" wealth.[3]

While Congress did not pass the proposed inheritance tax, Roosevelt's justification for the tax sounded again the underlying Populist philosophy that had been used to justify the imposition of the estate tax in 1916.

In 1924, Congress introduced the first federal gift tax. Its life was short, however, as it was repealed in 1926. The 1924 gift tax arose as a result of a dispute between Andrew Mellon, Secretary of the Treasury, and John Nance Garner, a congressman. Garner favored a higher maximum surtax rate for income tax purposes than did Mellon. As a compromise, a small gift tax was adopted and the maximum income tax surtax rates were set at a level below that proposed by Garner and higher than that argued for by Mellon.[4]

When Congress repealed the gift tax in 1926, the estate tax statute was amended to include a conclusive presumption that all gifts made within two years of death were transferred in contemplation of death and, consequently, were subject to the estate tax.[5] The Supreme Court held this provision to be unconstitutional in 1932.[6] Congress responded by reimposing a gift tax that applied to gifts made after June 6, 1932. One purpose of this gift tax, as well as of the original tax, was to prevent persons from avoiding all transfer taxes by giving away all, or most, of their assets during life.

Over the years, the gift tax rates have varied, as have the sizes of the exemption and the annual exclusion. The Tax Reform Act of 1976 included a major revamping of the gift tax. One major alteration was that the gift tax rates were revised to be the same as the estate tax rates, whereas previously they had been only three-quarters as high as the estate tax rates.

Before the generation-skipping transfer tax was imposed, a second transfer tax could be postponed for approximately a hundred years after the death of the first decedent. The Rule Against Perpetuities, which requires that an interest must vest no later that 21 years after the death of some person alive at the time the interest was created, operated to limit the period for which the transfer tax could be postponed. In the following example we shall illustrate how the second transfer tax could be postponed.

---

[2] For a thorough discussion of this matter see Randolph E. Paul, *Federal Estate and Gift Taxation,* Vol. 1 (Boston: Little, Brown and Company, 1942), p. 10.

[3] *Ibid.,* p. 13. By "static" wealth, Roosevelt meant that the person possessing the wealth had not worked to create it.

[4] William C. Warren and Stanley S. Surrey, *Federal Estate and Gift Taxation Cases and Materials,* 1952 ed. (Brooklyn: The Foundation Press, Inc., 1952), p. 5.

[5] *Ibid.*

[6] *Heiner* v. *Donnan,* 285 U.S. 312 (1932).

Example: G's will establishes a trust to pay income to G, Jr., for life, then to G III for life, then to G IV for life, and, upon the death of G IV, to distribute the assets to G IV's descendants.[7] Upon G's death an estate tax would be due. The second estate tax would not be imposed until the death of G IV's descendants.

Similarly, under today's estate tax law, the second estate tax will not be levied until the death of G IV's descendants. A generation-skipping transfer tax, however, will be imposed at each of the following stages: the deaths of G, Jr., G III, and G IV—in other words, once a generation.

Congress adopted the generation-skipping transfer tax to close the gaps in the existing estate and gift tax structure. The tax is referred to as a generation-*skipping* transfer tax because it imposes a transfer tax on transactions in which the donor or decedent *skipped* a generation. That is, the first generation younger than the donor or the decedent does not enjoy outright ownership of the property but has merely a life estate, for example. In fact, more than one younger generation may not have outright ownership. The following points were articulated in support of the generation-skipping transfer tax:

1. The purpose of the federal estate and gift taxes is not simply to raise revenue but to do so with as uniform an effect as possible, generation by generation. The policies of raising revenue and achieving equal treatment are best served when transfer taxes are levied at reasonably uniform intervals.

2. Under current law, transfer taxation occurs at every generation if the property passes directly from the parent to the child or grandchild. When a transferor establishes a generation-skipping trust, however, no estate tax is levied upon the death of the child. Although, theoretically, anyone may establish a generation-skipping trust, such trusts offer the greatest tax savings to wealthier families.

3. Inequities result with respect to transfer taxation because some families use generation-skipping trusts and pay estate taxes only once every several generations. Most families, however, do not use such trusts and consequently incur estate taxes once a generation. The progressive effect of transfer taxes is eroded be-

cause families with a moderate amount of wealth generally may pay as much or more in cumulative transfer taxes over several generations as wealthier families who use generation-skipping trusts and pay taxes only once every few generations.[8]

The Populist political movement was the origin of the estate tax. One of the goals of that movement was to reduce certain other excise taxes by taxing the wealthy. The gift tax and the tax on generation-skipping transfers were enacted to buttress the estate tax. These three taxes, acting in conjunction, ensure that no form of wealth transfer will be totally exempt from taxation.

THE WEALTH TRANSFER TAXES

In Chapters 16, 17, and 18, we shall present detailed rules concerning the transfer taxes on gifts and estates and the tax on generation-skipping transfers. So that you may better appreciate the more detailed rules discussed in these chapters and understand how the detailed provisions fit into the overall taxation scheme, we provide a brief overview of these three transfer taxes here.

The gift tax

The Internal Revenue Code imposes liability for the gift tax on the donor of the property. The tax base is the amount of the donor's taxable gifts. A gift arises when a person makes a transfer for less than adequate consideration. The gift tax, therefore, is not confined to strictly gratuitous transfers. The first step in calculating the amount of gift tax is to determine the fair market value[9] of the property transferred and to deduct from this amount the value of any consideration received by the donor.

If the donee receives immediate use of the property or is immediately entitled to its income, the donor has made a gift of a *present interest*. The significance of this classification is that it entitles the donor to receive an annual exclusion. Just as income tax exclusions lessen taxable income, the gift-tax annual exclusion reduces taxable gifts. The amount of the annual exclusion is $3,000 per donee. Consequently, a donor who

---

[7]The so-called *Rule Against Perpetuities* would require that in a situation such as the one in the example, G IV would have to be alive at the time of G's death for the provisions of G's will to be operative. All states except Wisconsin and Idaho have a Rule Against Perpetuities.

[8]U.S., Congress, House, *Report on Estate and Gift Tax Reform Act of 1976,* 94th Congress, 2d Sess., 1976, Report 94-1380, pp. 429–30, Sec. 2006 of the Act.

[9]The concept of fair market value is discussed in the next chapter. Briefly, it means the price that would be paid by a willing buyer and accepted by a willing seller.

wishes to bestow bounty on 20 persons a year may part with $60,000 each year without suffering any gift tax cost.

The Code authorizes two gift tax deductions—one for certain transfers to one's spouse and one for gifts to charitable organizations. Moreover, spouses may "split" their gifts, that is, gifts made to third parties may be treated as being made equally by each spouse, although in reality only one spouse had owned the transferred property.

The gift tax is a cumulative tax; taxable gifts made in earlier periods affect the marginal rate applicable to the current period's taxable gifts. The rates range from 18 percent on the first $10,000 of cumulative taxable gifts to 70 percent on cumulative taxable gifts in excess of $5,000,000. The gift tax levied on the taxable gifts of the current period is computed as follows:

$$\begin{array}{l} \text{Gift tax on cumulative taxable gifts of this period and all previous periods} \\ - \text{ Gift tax on cumulative taxable gifts of prior periods} \\ \hline = \text{ Gift tax on taxable gifts of current period} \end{array}$$

The current tax rates are used for purposes of these computations, even though the earlier gifts may have actually been taxed at different rates. The unutilized portion of the unified credit is deducted from the gift tax calculated under the process described above.[10] The difference represents the gift tax due with the filing of the return.

The estate tax

Property transfers that are completed by reason of the property owner's death or those made within three years of death are subject to an estate tax, which is paid from the decedent's property. The tax base for the estate consists of the decedent's taxable estate (the calculation of which is explained in Table 15-1 and in the following paragraphs) plus adjusted taxable gifts. The term *adjusted taxable gifts* means all taxable gifts made by the decedent after 1976 unless they have been brought back into the gross estate through another provision of the Code.

The Tax Reform Act of 1976 unified the estate and gift taxes, thereby inaugurating the increasing of the estate tax base by the decedent's post-1976 taxable gifts. This amendment forces the estate into a higher

[10]This credit ranges from $6,000 to $47,000, depending on the date of the transfer. The unified credit is discussed later in the chapter.

TABLE 15-1
COMPUTATION OF ESTATE TAX BALANCE DUE

	Gross estate, valued at fair market value at date of death or alternate valuation date
Less:	Debts, funeral and administrative expenses, losses
Equals:	Adjusted gross estate
Less:	Marital deduction[a] Charitable contribution deduction Orphan's exclusion[a]
Equals:	Taxable estate
Plus:	Adjusted taxable gifts, valued at fair market value on date of gift
Equals:	Estate tax base
	Tentative tax on estate tax base
Less:	Unified credit Post-1976 gift taxes paid by decedent
Equals:	Estate tax balance due[b]

[a]Both the marital deduction and the orphan's exclusion are not available on the same return.
[b]Actually, four additional credits may be available to reduce the balance due. These credits are the state death tax credit, the credit for gift taxes paid on certain pre-1977 gifts, the foreign death tax credit, and the credit for tax on prior transfers.

tax bracket. The estate tax balance due, however, is reduced by the gift taxes paid on post-1976 gifts. Table 15-1 illustrates the computation of the estate tax balance due.

The first step in arriving at the amount of the estate tax is to determine the fair market value of the decedent's gross estate. All items are valued as of the person's date of death or the alternate valuation date (in general, six months after the date of death). Because the estate tax is a transfer tax, it applies to more items than simply those properties that the decedent owned at death. The gross estate also includes interests for which enjoyment or control is shifted at the time of death.

> *Example:* During his lifetime, John created a trust from which he continues to receive income for the rest of his life. Enjoyment of the property is not shifted until he dies. John's gross estate, therefore, includes the trust property.

The probate estate (assets owned by the decedent at the time of death and subject to disposition by the decedent's will) is a possible starting point for determining the amount of the gross estate. This amount is increased by such items as life insurance the decedent owned on his or her life, assets that pass by right of survivorship to a joint owner, assets that the decedent earlier transferred to a trust from which he or she retained the income for life, and property transferred by the decedent within three years of death.

Several deductions from the gross estate are allowed in the computation of the taxable estate. The Code authorizes deductions for such items as mortgages and other debts, funeral expenses, and administration expenses (accountants', attorneys', and executors' fees and court costs). Moreover, deductions are available for certain amounts passing to the surviving spouse, the decedent's minor children (if orphaned), and charitable organizations.

The taxable estate represents the excess of the gross estate over the above deductions. Before 1977, the taxable estate constituted the tax base for the federal death tax. Effective for persons dying after 1976, the taxable estate is increased by the amount of the decedent's adjusted taxable gifts in order to arrive at the estate tax base.

The unified rate schedule

The Tax Reform Act of 1976 slightly revised the rates at which estates are taxed; in addition, it unified the rate schedule for estates and gifts. All taxable gifts made after 1976 are subject to the same rates as those imposed on estates. Before the law was revised, the gift tax rates were only three-fourths as high as the estate tax rates. The unified rates, which apply to all post-1976 taxable transfers of wealth (at death, by gift, or by generation skipping) appear in Appendix A.

A major purpose of unification was to remove most of the previous statutory bias in favor of *inter vivos* transfers. Before 1977, substantial disparity existed in the tax treatment of gifts and transfers at death. Not only were the gift tax rates only three-fourths as high as the estate tax rates, but the gift tax rate schedule was entirely separate from the estate tax rate schedule. Thus, engaging in lifetime transfers enabled a person to take advantage of the lowest rates of two separate rate schedules. A person could give away property while living that would be taxed at quite high rates if retained until death and have it taxed at relatively low gift tax rates, provided he or she had not earlier made substantial gifts. Any gift taxes paid were not included in the estate tax base. Thus, the payment of gift taxes reduced the amount subject to taxation at death. The gift tax statute provided for an exemption and annual exclusions. To the extent that these provisions were not taken advantage of during one's lifetime, they were "wasted."

According to House Committee Reports, "the tax burden imposed on transfers of the same amount of wealth should be substantially the same whether the transfers are made both during life and at death or made only upon death."[11] The report noted that as a practical matter only wealthier individuals can afford to part with property during their lifetimes, and therefore, only certain individuals were able to take advantage of the incentives for lifetime giving.

The 1976 Tax Reform Act removed most of the preferential treatment for gifts. Not only are the gift and estate tax rates now the same, but the death tax base was expanded to include post-1976 taxable gifts made by the decedent. The harshness of this result is lessened somewhat by allowing post-1976 gift taxes paid to be offset against the estate tax liability. For gift taxes paid on transfers within three years of death, the death tax base includes the gift tax paid. The 1976 law did preserve the annual exclusion. Thus, donors may continue to transfer a limited amount of wealth free of taxation. In addition, engaging in lifetime transfers allows individuals to freeze the value of the property taxed to its value on the date of the gift. Post-gift appreciation escapes transfer taxation. The consequences of unification are illustrated in the following example.

Example: In 1981, T made her first and only gift, $503,000 cash to Q. T died in 1985 with a taxable estate of $2,500,000.

Gift Tax Results:	
Gift	$503,000
Less annual exclusion	− 3,000
Taxable gift	$500,000
Tentative gift tax	$155,800
Less unified credit	− 47,000
Gift tax payable	$108,800
Estate Tax Results:	
Taxable estate	$2,500,000
Plus adjusted taxable gift	+ 500,000
Estate tax base	$3,000,000
Tentative estate tax	$1,290,800
Less: unified credit	− 47,000
post-1976 gift taxes paid	− 108,800
Estate tax payable	$1,135,000
Total Transfer Taxes	$1,243,800

[11] U.S., Congress, House, *Report on Estate and Gift Tax Reform Act of 1976,* pp. 11–12, Sec. 2001 of the Act.

The unified credit

Before 1977, the Code allowed an exemption deduction for purposes of computing the amount of the taxable gifts and the taxable estate. The gift tax exemption was $30,000, while the estate tax exemption was $60,000. Use of the gift tax exemption did not foreclose the availability of the estate tax exemption.

The Tax Reform Act of 1976 repealed the exemptions and replaced them with a unified credit. Section 2010 provides an estate tax unified credit as follows:

Date of death	Amount of credit	Credit is equivalent to exemption of
1977	$30,000	$120,666
1978	34,000	134,000
1979	38,000	147,333
1980	42,500	161,563
1981 and later	47,000	175,625

With the exception of the credit for gifts made January 1 through June 30, 1977, the gift tax credit is the same as the estate tax credit shown above (Sec. 2505).

In certain circumstances, the unified credit otherwise available for gift or estate tax purposes must be decreased. A reduction is necessary if the donor used any of the specific exemption (previously available) against gifts made after September 8, 1976. The amount of the adjustment is 20 percent of the amount of the exemption claimed after such date (Secs. 2010(c) and 2505(c)). Because the exemption was $30,000, the maximum reduction is $6,000 (20 percent of $30,000).

From a computational standpoint, the unified credit is available twice; we subtract it once to arrive at the gift tax due and again to determine the estate tax due. As a conceptual matter, however, the benefits of the credit apply only once. Any taxable gifts made after 1976 expand the donor's estate tax base; thus, these amounts are counted twice. The reduction against the estate tax for post-1976 gift taxes reflects only the gift taxes paid, not the amount of taxes before reduction for the gift tax credit.

Congress's purpose in replacing the previous exemptions with credits and raising the amount that may be transferred free of tax consequences was reported as follows:

> The present amount of the estate tax exemption was established in 1942. Since that date, the purchasing power of the dollar has decreased to less than one-third of its value in 1942. . . .
> In addition, since the present estate tax exemption is a deduction in determining the taxable estate, it re-

duces each estate's tax at the highest estate tax brackets. However, a credit in lieu of an exemption will have the effect of reducing the estate tax at the lower estate tax brackets since a tax credit is applied as a dollar-for-dollar reduction of the amount otherwise due. Thus, at a given level of revenue cost, a tax credit tends to confer more tax savings on small- and medium-sized estates, whereas a deduction or exemption tends to confer more tax savings on larger estates. Your committee believes it would be more equitable if the exemption were replaced with a credit.[12]

Congress noted that, as a practical matter, the gift tax exemption was not available to persons who could not afford to make lifetime transfers. Thus, in effect, the transfer tax exemption for gift and estate tax purposes combined was greater for wealthier individuals. According to the House Ways and Means Committee, "it would be more equitable if a unified credit in lieu of an exemption were available . . . without regard to whether the transfers are made only at death or are made both during lifetime and at death."[13]

The tax on generation-skipping transfers

In order for an arrangement to be within the purview of the generation-skipping transfer tax, there must be a transfer to more than one generation of so-called *younger generation beneficiaries.* The tax on generation-skipping transfers was first levied by the Tax Reform Act of 1976. A grandfather clause, however, provides that irrevocable trusts already in existence on June 11, 1976 are exempt from this tax. Moreover, transfers under wills drafted by individuals on or before June 11, 1976 are not subject to the tax, provided the individual dies before 1982. In addition, such individual must not have revised his or her will in a manner that amplifies the size of the generation-skipping transfer. Because of the effective date of this tax, probably little, if any, revenue has been collected from it to date.

In assessing whether the beneficiaries are younger generation beneficiaries, their generation must be compared with that of the grantor (creator). For relatives of the grantor generation, assignments are made in accordance with the family tree. Thus, the grantor's children are the first generation after the grantor, his or her grandchildren the second generation after the grantor, and so on. Persons who are not the grantor's relatives are assigned to generations in accordance with their age compared with the grantor's age. Persons no more

[12]U.S., Congress, House, *Report on Estate and Gift Tax Reform Act of 1976,* p. 406.
[13]*Ibid.*

than 12½ years younger than the grantor are of the grantor's generation. Those who are more than 12½ but less that 37½ years younger than the grantor are considered the first generation after the grantor. Thereafter, a new generation begins every 25 years. In the two following examples, we shall illustrate that the presence of more than one generation of younger generation beneficiaries is necessary for the tax to be imposed.

Example 1: G created a trust and named Mrs. G (his wife) to receive the income for life and Gigi (his daughter) to receive the assets upon Mrs. G's death. There is only one generation of younger generation beneficiaries; the generation-skipping transfer tax does not apply.

Example 2: G established a trust and named G, Jr. (his son) to receive the income for life and G III (his grandson) to possess the assets when G, Jr. died. This arrangement falls within the purview of the generation-skipping transfer tax. Two generations of younger generation beneficiaries exist.

The scope of the generation-skipping transfer tax is not restricted to transfers made in the form of trusts. The tax applies equally to life estates transferred outside of trust as long as there is more than one generation of younger generation beneficiaries.

The most significant event that triggers the generation-skipping transfer tax is the termination of one younger generation beneficiary's interest in favor of another beneficiary assigned to an even younger generation. Perhaps the most common event that results in a termination is the death of a younger generation beneficiary. In the second example above, a termination occurs when G, Jr. dies, survived by G III. The generation-skipping transfer tax is triggered by the death of G, Jr.

The Code authorizes some relief from the tax in the form of the grandchild's exclusion. This provision allows an exclusion from the tax base for certain transfers to grandchildren of the grantor. The amount of the exclusion is $250,000 per so-called "deemed transferor," not per grandchild. Thus, if the creator skipped only his children's generation and created relatively small trusts, the arrangement would be exempt from the generation-skipping transfer tax. The general rule is that a deemed transferor is the parent of the grandchild beneficiary. In particular, the parent who is more closely related to the grantor is the deemed transferor. Thus, for a grantor with only one child, the maximum exclusion is $250,000 regardless of how many grandchildren are beneficiaries.

The tax rate schedule for generation-skipping transfers is the same rate schedule as for taxable gifts and taxable estates. Previous taxable gifts made by the deemed transferor influence the marginal tax rate applicable to generation-skipping transfers. Moreover, if a generation-skipping transfer occurs simultaneously with, or subsequent to, the death of the deemed transferor, the size of the deemed transferor's taxable estate affects the marginal tax rate for the transfer. The detailed rules concerning the computation of the generation-skipping transfer tax are explained in Chapter 18.

In reading the chapters in Part Five concerned with wealth transfer taxes and Chapters 13 and 14 on the income taxation of trusts, keep in mind that while a particular transaction may be subject to the gift tax, this does not guarantee that the gifted property will be excluded from the donor's estate. Similarly, the donor may incur a gift tax cost upon the transfer of property to a trust and nevertheless still be taxed on the trust's income.

ESTATE TAX REVENUE AND THE DISTRIBUTION OF WEALTH

Most decedents are not affected by the estate tax. It is, therefore, a very select tax. The percentages of U.S. decedents for whom an estate tax return was necessary has been estimated for various years as follows:

Year	*Approximate percentage of decedents for whom estate tax return was necessary*[14]
1958	3
1960	4
1962	4½
1965	5
1969	7
1972	9

For the above years, no return was necessary unless the value of the gross estate exceeded $60,000, the amount of the exemption. As discussed earlier, post-1976 law provides for a credit that gradually rises and is the equivalent of an exemption ranging from about $120,000 for 1977 to about $175,000 for 1981 and later years. A return is not necessary unless the value of the decedent's estate exceeds the amount of the exemption equivalent. With the advent of the increased exemption equivalent, the percentage of decedents for whom an estate tax return is mandatory

---

[14]U.S., Treasury Department, *Statistics of Income 1972 Estate Tax Returns* (Washington, D.C.: U.S. Government Printing Office, 1972), p. 1.

should decline, at least for a while. Because of inflation, however, estate tax returns will eventually become mandatory for increasing numbers of decedents.

Approximately 175,000 estate tax returns were filed during 1973, the most recent year for which detailed statistics are available. Of these returns, approximately 121,000 reported a taxable estate. About 3,900 of the taxable returns reflected a gross estate of $1 million or more. The taxable returns reporting a gross estate of $10 million or greater numbered 89.[15]

Although one of the major purposes of the estate tax was to raise substantial revenues from the wealthiest classes and to reduce the taxes of others, it has done little more than add a small supplement to the federal coffers. Total revenue produced by the federal estate tax has not been particularly large. The following figures report federal estate tax revenue for some recent years:

Year	Approximate estate tax revenue
1960	$1.6 billion
1962	1.8 billion
1965	2.4 billion
1969	3.0 billion
1972	4.1 billion[16]

The revenue produced by the gift tax has been lower, in part because before 1977 the gift tax rates were lower than the estate tax rates. Moreover, *inter vivos* transfers, unlike transfers at death, are voluntary. According to I.R.S. Commissioner Jerome Kurtz, during the fiscal year ended September 30, 1976, revenue from gift taxes was approximately $500 million. For the fiscal year ended September 30, 1977, gift tax collections rose to about $1.8 billion. Kurtz speculated that this substantial increase was largely a result of gratuitous transfers made in the last quarter of 1976 to avoid the effects of the impending unification.[17] No statistics are available concerning the amount of revenue from the generation-skipping transfer tax. Because of the grandfather clause concerning the effective date and the structure of the tax, this tax probably has generated little, if any, revenue to date. In general, a younger generation beneficiary of a trust created after June 11, 1976 must die to trigger the generation-skipping transfer tax.

Redistribution of wealth has been voiced as one of the objectives of the taxation of wealth transfers. There is no way to determine the wealth distribution pattern

that would have resulted had there been no transfer taxes. The imposition of such taxes, however, does not seem to have caused significant changes in the distribution of wealth, as illustrated by the following figures.[18]

	Percentage of wealth held by	
Year	Wealthiest 0.5%	Wealthiest 1%
1953	22.0	27.5
1958	21.7	26.9
1962	21.6	27.4
1965	23.7	29.2
1969	20.4	25.6
1972	20.4	25.9

Between 1953 and 1972, therefore, the share of total wealth concentrated in the hands of the wealthiest 0.5 percent of the population changed very little—from 22.0 percent to 20.4 percent.

SUMMARY

In this chapter we have discussed briefly the three wealth transfer taxes levied by the federal government—the gift tax, the estate tax, and the generation-skipping transfer tax. While accounting for only a small percentage of the total federal revenue, these taxes supplement the tax coffers by a few billion dollars a year and add some balance to the federal taxing scheme, which relies heavily on income and Social Security taxes. A small redistribution of wealth possibly occurs as a result of the wealth transfer taxes.

Of the three wealth transfer taxes, the estate tax has the longest history: It has been a continuous part of the tax structure since 1916. The estate tax is levied on transfers that become complete upon a person's death. The gift tax, which has been in continuous effect since 1932, taxes the donor on transfers by gift. The Tax Reform Act of 1976 introduced the generation-skipping transfer tax, which supplements the two earlier taxes by levying a tax on certain transfers of wealth that were formerly tax free. The events that trigger this tax are distributions to or terminations in favor of younger generation beneficiaries. The same rate schedule applies to all three wealth transfer taxes.

Chapter 16 contains a detailed discussion of the gift tax. In Chapter 17, we shall describe in greater depth the various estate tax provisions. The newest transfer tax, the tax on generation-skipping transfers, is the focal point of Chapter 18.

---

[15]*Ibid.*, p. 12.

[16]*Ibid.*, p. 39.

[17]Speech by Jerome Kurtz to University of Southern California Tax Institute, January 17, 1978, reported in BNA *Daily Tax Report,* January 18, 1978, p. J-1.

[18]James D. Smith, "The Impact of the Estate Tax: Only the Wealthy Feel Its Bite," *Tax Notes,* April 26, 1976, p. 20. These data were collected for work Mr. Smith and a colleague did for the Urban Institute under a grant from the National Science Foundation.

PROBLEMS

1. What wealth transfer taxes are imposed by the federal government? Since what dates has each been in effect without interruption?

2. What events cause the federal wealth transfer taxes to be payable?

3. In general terms, compare the tax base for the federal estate tax with the tax base for state inheritance taxes.

4. What were the purposes of levying a federal estate tax? In your opinion, how well has the imposition of the tax achieved these goals?

5. Give an example of a so-called "loophole" that led to the adoption of the generation-skipping transfer tax.

6. In 19X1, Ted Tate deeded real estate with a fair market value of $15,000 to his son Ned. What is the amount of Ted's taxable gift?

7. a. Refer to Problem 6. Later in the year, Ted gave Ned $4,000 in cash. What portion of this gift is taxable?
   b. Same as part a, except Ted gave the $4,000 cash to Fred instead of Ned. What portion of the gift is taxable?

8. a. In 1991, Roberta Reed made taxable gifts aggregating $3 million. Her earlier taxable gifts, all made in 1970, were $1 million. Compute her gift tax payable for 1991.
   b. Same as part a, except that Roberta made the $1 million of taxable gifts in 1981 instead of 1970.

9. As of what date is a decedent's estate valued?

10. Murray, who was never married, died March 13, 1985. His gross estate was valued at $1,200,000. When he died, he owed debts totaling $50,000. His funeral and administrative expenses came to a total of $20,000. His will left $300,000 worth of stock to State University. He made *no* lifetime gifts. Compute his estate tax balance due.

11. Same as Problem 10, except in 1978 Murray made taxable gifts totaling $250,000. By the time Murray died, the value of the gift property had appreciated to $600,000. Compute his estate tax balance due.

12. What is the difference between "gross estate" and "probate estate"?

13. Compare the tax rate schedules for the various federal wealth transfer taxes.

14. Explain the rationale for adopting a unification of estate and gift taxes.

15. If a person dying in 1985 has a taxable estate valued at $200,000, will this estate owe any federal estate taxes? Explain. (Assume the person has made no lifetime transfers.)

16. a. Grandfather (GF) established a trust in 1984. Under the terms of the trust, Mrs. GF (his wife) is to receive the income for the rest of her life. On the death of Mrs. GF, the property will pass to Geraldine, GF's granddaughter. Is this an example of a transfer subject to the generation-skipping transfer tax? Explain.
   b. Assume a certain trust is subject to the generation-skipping transfer tax. G created the trust, which provides that G's daughter H will receive the income for her life. Upon the death of H, the property will pass equally to each of H's three sons—I, J, and K—or their estates. What is the total amount of the grandchild's exclusion available with respect to this trust?

16

the gift tax

As mentioned in Chapter 15, the gift tax was added to the federal tax scheme in 1924, repealed in 1926, and reinstated in 1932. The Supreme Court upheld the constitutionality of the first gift tax, ruling that it was an excise tax and not a direct tax.[1] The Constitution prohibits the federal government from levying direct taxes unless such taxes are apportioned among the states in accordance with their population.

One of the primary reasons Congress readopted the gift tax in 1932 was to make it impossible for persons completely to avoid transfer taxation by giving away their property before death. The Supreme Court had concluded that it was unconstitutional for the estate tax statute to contain a conclusive presumption that all gifts made within two years of death were made in contemplation of death and were, therefore, automatically includible in the estate.[2] Moreover, the gift tax was intended to supplement the income tax revenue. Donors generally transferred property to taxpayers in lower income tax brackets, thereby reducing income tax collections. The readoption of the gift tax ensured that some tax would be collected from individuals transferring income-producing property to family members in lower income tax brackets. Such dispositions would be subject to the gift tax, and the gift tax revenue would help to compensate for the reduction in income tax revenue brought about by the shifting of income to individuals in lower income tax brackets.

The House Ways and Means Committee justified the gift tax as follows:

> The gift tax will supplement both the estate and the income tax. It will tend to reduce the incentive to make gifts in order that distribution of future income from the donated property may be to a number of persons with the result that the taxes imposed by the highest brackets of the income tax are avoided. It will also tend to discourage transfers for the purpose of avoiding the estate tax.[3]

As we shall discover in the next chapter, in which we examine the Code sections that define the gross estate, the payment by the donor of a gift tax does not guarantee that the property is removed from the donor's gross estate. A gift made within three years of the donor's death, for example, is subject to both gift and estate taxation. Under current law, gifts made within three years of death are automatically included in the gross estate, regardless of the donor's motive. Thus, the constitutional problem of the conclusive presumption is avoided. To give another example, a donor creates a trust and names himself to receive the income for life and the assets (the remainder) to pass to another party upon the donor's death. The conveyance of the remainder interest is within the realm of the gift tax. Because the donor retained the income for life, the entire value of the trust assets is taxed to the donor's estate.

Because of certain income tax rules, even though some transfers are subject to a current gift tax, the donor will still be taxed on the income generated by the transferred property. We explored this topic in depth in Chapter 14. The following example illustrates a transaction in which the transferor incurs both gift tax and income tax liability.

Example: X transfers assets to a trust and names A to receive the trust income for nine years. At the

---

[1] *Bromley v. McCaughn,* 280 U.S. 124 (1929).
[2] *Heiner v. Donnan,* 285 U.S. 312 (1932).

[3] U.S., Congress, House, 72nd Congress, 1st Sess., 1932, H.R. Report No. 708, reprinted in 1939-1 C.B. (Part 2), pp. 476–77.

end of the ninth year, the assets will revert (pass back) to X. The amount subject to the gift tax is the present value of an income interest in the assets for nine years. Because A's right to income did not exist for more than 10 years, under the income tax grantor trust rules, the trust income is taxed to X.

In studying this chapter as well as Chapters 13–15 and Chapter 17, keep in mind that income, gift, and estate tax laws are not construed *in pari materia.*[4] In other words, if a transfer is complete for purposes of the gift tax, and thereby subject to the gift tax, this does not automatically mean that the gifted property will be excluded from the donor's estate. Similarly, some dispositions cause the donor to incur a gift tax; nevertheless, because of additional provisions related to the dispositions, the donor continues to be taxed on the income from the transferred property. The income tax and estate tax rules differ concerning what powers or benefits (or both) a donor may retain with respect to transferred property without being taxed on the income or having the property included in his or her estate.

TRANSFERS SUBJECT TO THE GIFT TAX

Determining the amount of gross gifts subject to the gift tax requires two steps: First, one must decide whether the particular transaction under consideration constitutes a gift for purposes of the gift tax. Second, if the transaction is within the purview of the gift tax, one must determine the value of the transferred property.

According to Sec. 2501(a), a gift tax is levied on "the transfer of property by gift." Transfers made after May 7, 1974 to political organizations are exempt. Nowhere, however, does the statute define the term "gift." Section 2511(a) gives some additional assistance to the person concerned with whether a gift has been made by stating that the tax is applicable "whether the transfer is in trust of otherwise, whether the gift is direct or indirect, and whether the property is real or personal, tangible or intangible."

Examples of gifts within the context of the gift tax

The regulations include the following examples of transactions that may be subject to the gift tax: the forgiving of a debt, the assignment of the benefits of a life insurance policy, the transfer of cash, and the transfer of federal, state, or municipal bonds.[5] Thus, even though interest on certain bonds is excluded from gross income, the gratuitous transfer of such bonds generates gift tax consequences.

Donative intent by the transferor is not a prerequisite for levying the gift tax; a donor's motives do not determine taxability. Moreover, the grasp of the gift tax extends beyond those situations in which the transfer was completely gratuitous. If the value of the property transferred exceeds the amount of consideration in money or money's worth received by the transferor, a gift equal to the amount of the excess arises.

> *Example:* A mother sells stock with a fair market value of $50,000 to her son and receives consideration of only $40,000. She has made a $10,000 gift to her son. The mother transferred property worth $10,000 more than the amount of consideration she received.

Relinquishment of dower, curtesy,[6] or other marital property rights is not viewed as consideration in money or money's worth. On the other hand, property settlements in a divorce are deemed to be made for adequate consideration if certain requirements imposed by Sec. 2516 are met.

Some transactions that result in taxable gifts are quite straightforward. For example, transfers subject to the gift tax occur when an individual conveys cash, jewelry, stocks, real estate, or other property outright (outside of trust) to another as the sole owner, and the transferor makes the conveyance for less than adequate consideration in money or money's worth. On the other hand, within families, problems may arise in assessing whether an item purchased for one's spouse or child falls within the legal obligation of support. Transfers classified as support are not transfers subject to the gift tax. As a practical matter, it may be difficult to determine whether certain expenditures for goods and services for one's spouse and children constitute support or a gift. If such amounts do not exceed $3,000 per transferee per year, no taxable gift has taken place, even if a transaction is classified as a gift instead of as a payment for support.

A completed transfer is necessary in order for a taxable event to arise. A gift is complete if the donor "has so parted with dominion and control as to leave in him no power to change its disposition, whether for his

---

[4]If construed *in pari materia,* statutes having the same general purpose are interpreted as if they constitute one law.

[5]Treas. Reg. Sec. 25.2511-1(a).
[6]*Dower* is the interest of a widow in her deceased husband's property; *curtesy* is the interest of a widower in his deceased wife's property.

own benefit or for the benefit of another . . . ."[7] The transfer of assets to a revocable trust is an incomplete transfer, therefore, and not subject to the gift tax. The donor has not parted with control and may revoke the trust and reclaim the assets. A transfer is also incomplete if A conveys property to a trust and names M to receive the trust income for life but reserves the right to terminate M's interest and substitute N to receive the income for life. Again, the donor has not parted with control. In the case of the two trusts just discussed, a completed transfer occurs each year when income is distributed to someone other than the transferor. The amount of the completed gift is the amount of income distributed.

A special set of rules applies to property transferred to the joint ownership of two or more individuals.

Example 1: X deposits cash into a joint bank account in the names of himself and Z. X makes a gift to Z only if and when Z withdraws cash from the account.

Example 2: C purchases land and has it titled in the names of C and D, joint tenants with right of survivorship. C has made a gift to D of one-half the value of the land.

Elective treatment exists if C and D are married to each other, as explained below.

Certain transactions involving life insurance policies and premiums fall within the purview of the gift tax.

Example: K pays a premium on a life insurance policy on his life. K's estate is not the policy beneficiary, and K has no power to change the beneficiary. K, therefore, has made a gift to the owner of the policy. The amount of the gift is the amount of the premium.

When the insured assigns to another party as owner all his rights in a group term life insurance policy paid for by the employer, the I.R.S. has ruled that the insured has not made a gift. The rationale is that one cannot ascertain the value of the policy because the employer may decide to discontinue paying the premiums. Subsequent payments of premiums by the employer, however, are treated as indirect gifts from the employee to the owner of the policy.[8] The value of the gift is the amount of the premium.

If the donor gives away only a partial interest in property, gift tax consequences attach only to the portion of the interest conveyed.

Example 1: Q owns 1,200 acres of land. If Q gives R a one-fifth undivided interest in the acreage, the value of the gift is the value of a one-fifth interest in 1,200 acres.

Example 2: S gives T a remainder interest in a mountain cabin. The subject of the gift is the remainder interest. Its value is a function of the value of the cabin and S's life expectancy, determined from actuarial tables.

Transactions conducted in the ordinary course of business are deemed to have been made for an adequate amount of consideration in money or money's worth. Hence, they are devoid of gift tax consequences. Litigation may address the question whether a transaction arose in the ordinary course of business. One such case concerned the sale of stock to six executives of a firm by major shareholders, who adhered to the opinion that junior executives should own a share of the business. The sales price was an amount less than fair market value. In holding that the transaction was not a gift, the court concluded that the sellers were motivated by "the importance of expert and continuous management."[9] The shareholders wanted younger executives to participate in ownership.

In general, all transfers are subject to the gift tax if they are made for less than adequate consideration in money or money's worth. The transferor's motivation for the transaction is not important. The gift tax does not apply, however, unless the transfer is complete. A transfer is complete if the donor has parted with dominion and control over the property. In one special situation—the acquisition of real property in the joint names of the donor and his or her spouse—it is not mandatory that the donor report the acquisition as a gift.

Special election for gift of joint interest in realty to a spouse

A donor may elect to treat the creation of joint interests in real estate with his or her spouse as a gift. The election is made by reporting the gift of a joint interest in realty on a timely gift tax return. If the donor does not make the special election, the event is not subject to

---

[7] Treas. Reg. Sec. 25.2511-2(b).
[8] Rev. Rul. 76-490, 1976-2 C.B. 300.

[9] *Estate of Anderson,* 8 T.C. 706 (1947).

the gift tax. The two types of joint interests are *joint tenancies with right of survivorship* and *tenancies by the entirety.*[10]

If gift treatment is elected on the creation of joint interests in realty, the amount of the gift is one-half the value of the realty, less the amount of consideration furnished by the spouse providing less than half the consideration. Often one spouse contributes no consideration. Before 1977, actuarial computations based on the spouses' ages were necessary to value each spouse's interest in a tenancy by the entirety. The Tax Reform Act of 1976 authorized actuarial computations to be ignored for tenancies by the entirety in real estate. The 1978 Revenue Act extended this authorization to tenancies by the entirety in personal property. Thus, the amount of each spouse's interest is automatically deemed to be one-half, regardless of whether the property is real or personal. For personal property, however, the acquisition must be reported as a gift if one spouse furnishes more than half the consideration. If the acquisition of the joint interest in real estate is reported as a gift, all additions to the property must likewise be reported as gifts unless the spouses contribute equally to the cost of the additions.

In certain instances the termination of a joint tenancy or a tenancy by the entirety will have gift tax consequences. Creation of the joint interest results in equal ownership between the spouses. If the acquisition was reported as a gift, a subsequent gift will arise upon termination during life of the joint ownership if there is an unequal division of the property or its sales proceeds.

If gift tax treatment was not elected for the acquisition, a termination of joint ownership during life will result in a taxable event if one spouse receives a portion of the property, or its sales proceeds, that exceeds the portion of the consideration he or she furnished. Suppose one spouse provided all the consideration but did not elect to report the acquisition as a gift. Subsequent gift tax consequences may be avoided only if that spouse receives the entire property or proceeds upon termination during that spouse's lifetime of the joint ownership.

The special rules that apply to joint interests between spouses in real estate are illustrated in the following examples. In all instances H denotes the husband and W the wife.

Example 1: W furnished 100 percent of the $100,000 consideration for the acquisition of land that she titled in the names of H and W, joint tenants with right of survivorship. It is not mandatory that she treat this transaction as a gift. If she does elect gift treatment, the amount of her gift to H is $50,000.

Example 2: Same as Example 1, except W furnished $60,000 of the consideration while H furnished $40,000. If W elects gift treatment, the size of the gift is $10,000 ($50,000 − $40,000).

Example 3: Referring to the facts of Example 1, assume W elected to treat that transaction as a gift. Three years later, W spent $80,000 to have a building constructed on the land. Because of the previous gift election, it is mandatory that she now report a $40,000 gift to H.

Example 4: Refer to the facts of Example 1, but disregard those of Example 3. Assume H and W sold the land for $300,000 and divided the proceeds equally. If the acquisition was reported as a gift, no gift tax consequences flow from the equal division of the proceeds. If W did not report the acquisition as a gift, however, she must now report a $150,000 gift to H.

If the proceeds are divided $200,000 to H and $100,000 to W, the results are different. If W elected gift tax treatment for the acquisition, she now must show a $50,000 ($200,000 − $150,000 [H's interest]) gift to H. If gift treament was not elected on the earlier transaction, $200,000 is the amount of the gift to H.

An election after 1976 to treat the creation of a joint interest in realty as a gift affects the amount in-

---

[10]The following definitions are from Henry Campbell Black, *Black's Law Dictionary,* Revised Fourth Edition (St. Paul, Minn.: West Publishing Co., 1968).

Joint tenancy with right of survivorship—An estate in fee-simple, fee-tail, for life, for years, or at will, arising by purchase or grant to two or more persons. Joint tenants have one and the same interest, accruing by one and the same conveyance, commencing at one and the same time, and held by one and the same undivided possession. The grand incident of joint tenancy is survivorship, by which the entire tenancy on the decease of any joint tenant remains to the survivors, and at length to the last survivor.

Tenancy by the entirety—Is created by a conveyance to husband and wife, whereupon each becomes seized and possessed of the entire estate and after the death of one the survivor takes the whole. And is available only to husband and wife. The grand characteristic which distinguishes it from a joint tenancy is that it can be terminated only by joint action of husband and wife during their lives, while "joint tenancy" may be terminated by one tenant's conveyance of his interest.

Both joint tenancies with right of survivorship and tenancies by the entirety have the feature of survivorship. When one joint owner dies, his interest passes by right of survivorship to the remaining joint owner(s). Only spouses may use the tenancy by the entirety arrangement. A joint tenancy with right of survivorship may be severed by the action of any joint owner, whereas a tenancy by the entirety arrangement continues unless severed by the joint action of both joint owners.

cludible in the gross estate of the joint owner who predeceases. Election of gift treatment results in the creation of a "qualified joint interest." We shall explore this matter in the next chapter.

Valuation of the gift

From a practical standpoint, the valuation of a gift is one of the most difficult problems the practitioner faces, especially if the gift is unimproved land, a mineral interest, or stock in a closely held corporation. Although often quite general and sketchy, the regulations provide some guidelines for arriving at values of property. Some of these guidelines are discussed below.

GENERAL VALUATION RULES   All gifts are to be valued at their fair market value on the date the transfer becomes complete. The regulations define fair market value as:

> . . . the price at which such property would change hands between a willing buyer and a willing seller, neither being under any compulsion to buy or to sell, and both having reasonable knowledge of relevant facts.[11]

The regulations add that the price is not to be one that would result from a forced sale situation. If the property subject to valuation is normally obtained at retail (an automobile, for example), the value is to reflect the price that would be paid in a retail market.

VALUATION OF STOCKS AND BONDS   The value of securities that are traded on a stock exchange is the average of their highest and lowest selling price on the day of the gift. If no sales occurred on the day of the gift but sales did occur within a reasonable period of time before and after such date, the value is a weighted average of the high and the low sales prices on the nearest trade date before and after the gift date. The average is weighted inversely in relation to the number of days separating the sales dates and the date of the gift. The following example illustrates these computations.

Example: On May 5, 1979, G gave one share of ABC stock to J. The stock is listed on an exchange, but no sales took place on May 5. The most recent sales occurred two business days before May 5. On that day the shares traded at a high of 500 and a low of 490. The sales after May 5 nearest to that date were three business days later. The high on that day was 492, and the low was 490.

The value of the stock on the day of the gift is computed as follows:

$$\frac{(500 + 490)}{2} = 495 \qquad \frac{(492 + 490)}{2} = 491$$

$$\frac{3(495) + 2(491)}{5} = \frac{1,485 + 982}{5} = 493.40$$

If the actual selling prices do not reflect the fair market value of the stock given, the regulations authorize modification of the general rules:

> In certain exceptional cases, the size of the block of securities made the subject of each separate gift in relation to the number of shares changing hands in sales may be relevant in determining whether selling prices reflect the fair market value of the block of stock to be valued. If the donor can show that the block of stock to be valued, with reference to each separate gift, is so large in relation to the actual sales on the existing market that it could not be liquidated in a reasonable time without depressing the market, the price at which the block could be sold as such outside the usual market, as through an underwriter, may be a more accurate indication of value than market quotations.[12]

The allowance in certain situations of a reduction from the reported sales prices because of the magnitude of the shares to be valued is referred to as the *blockage rule.*

Of course, sales price data for shares of closely held stock are difficult to accumulate because such shares generally are sold infrequently. Additional guidance for valuing closely held shares is provided by a revenue ruling that lists the following items, among others, as factors to be considered in valuing such stock:

1.   The nature and history of the business;
2.   The general economic outlook and the outlook for this specific industry;
3.   The book value of the stock and the business's financial condition;
4.   The firm's earning capacity;
5.   The firm's dividend-paying capacity; and
6.   Market values of actively traded stock of companies engaged in the same business or a similar one.[13]

Implementation of the above guidelines may prove difficult.

[11] Treas. Reg. Sec. 25.2512-1.

[12] Treas. Reg. Sec. 25.2512-2(e).
[13] Rev. Rul. 59-60, 1959-1 C.B. 237.

VALUATION OF MUTUAL FUND SHARES   Shares in open-end investment companies (mutual funds) are to be valued at the public redemption price (the "bid price"). For many years, the I.R.S. maintained that the value was the "asked" price, based on the fact that the asked price, which includes the load factor (similar to a commission), was the price paid. After the Supreme Court held invalid the previous rule calling for valuation at the asked price, the regulations were revised to provide for valuation at the bid price.[14] This was one of the rare instances in which a court overturned a regulation as invalid.

VALUATION OF LIFE INSURANCE POLICIES   When a donor transfers ownership of a life insurance policy to another party, the policy's gift tax value is less than its face value because the policy has not yet matured. The policy is to be valued at the amount that a life insurance company would charge for a comparable contract. This is sometimes referred to as the policy's replacement cost. If this figure cannot be determined and the policy has been in existence for some time and future premiums are to be paid, the value of the policy is its interpolated terminal reserve plus the unexpired portion of the last premium. The interpolated terminal reserve is similar in amount to the cash surrender value.

VALUATION OF ANNUITIES, TERMS FOR YEARS, AND REMAINDERS   The regulations contain special tables for valuation of life estates, remainders, terms for years, and annuities. Predicated upon normal life expectancies, with different figures provided for males and females, these tables assume an earnings rate of 6 percent. Copies of these tables appear in Appendix B. Use of these tables is illustrated with the following examples.

Example 1:   G transferred $100,000 of assets to a trust and named F (a female, age 55) to receive the trust income for her life and M (a male, age 30) to receive the assets upon F's death. In concept, F receives the present value of the income (assumed to be 6 percent), which these assets will produce over her remaining life expectancy. The gift to M is the present value of the assets to be

Table A(2) of Appendix B contains the factors for valuing the two components of the gift. The factor for the life estate for a 55-year-old female is 0.69859. The gift to F, therefore, is $69,859

[14]*Cartwright,* 411 U.S. 546 (1973).

($100,000 × 0.69859). The gift to M of the remainder is valued at $30,141 ($100,000 × 0.30141).

Example 2:   G (a male, age 55) conveyed a remainder interest in his $100,000 personal residence to K (a male, age 28). Even though the residence is non-income producing, we still must use the 6 percent tables. The factor for a remainder interest following the life of a 55-year-old male is 0.38224 (Table A(1) of Appendix B). G's gift to K, therefore, is $38,224 ($100,000 × 0.38224).

Example 3:   G transferred $100,000 of assets to a trust and named B (a male, age 9) to receive the trust income for 11 years. Then the assets will revert to G. Table B of Appendix B is used to value this interest for the term certain—11 years. The factor is 0.473212; the value of the gift to B, therefore, is $47,321 ($100,000 × 0.473212).

VALUATION OF REAL ESTATE   Perhaps surprisingly, the regulations do not specifically address the question of how to value realty. We may see why, however, if we recall the general rule that property is to be valued at a price acceptable to a willing buyer and a willing seller. Appraisal literature discusses three techniques for valuing realty: comparable sales, reproduction cost, and capitalization of earnings.[15] Often there may be no comparable sale. For example, there is but one Mt. Vernon. Arriving at a capitalization rate may prove difficult also. And reproduction cost is not applicable when valuing raw land.

The annual exclusion

Although calculating the amount of the gift tax starts with the valuation of the gift, this value does not necessarily constitute the tax base. In many instances, an annual exclusion reduces the taxable amount. Moreover, the statute also authorizes two types of deductions, which we shall explain in a later section.

Over the years, the amount of the annual exclusion has varied from $3,000 to $5,000 per donee. Currently, the exclusion is $3,000 per donee per year. It is available for an unlimited number of donees. Moreover, each donor receives an exclusion for gifts to the same donee. Consequently, the only limitations are the do-

[15]For a discussion of real estate appraisal techniques, see James C. Bonbright, *The Valuation of Property* (New York: McGraw-Hill Book Company, Inc., 1937).

nor's wealth, generosity, and imagination. The purpose of the exclusion, voiced by the Senate Finance Committee in 1932, is as follows:

> Such exemption . . . is to obviate the necessity of keeping an account of and reporting numerous small gifts, and . . . to fix the amount sufficiently large to cover in most cases wedding and Christmas gifts and occasional gifts of relatively small amount.[16]

Incidentally, the 1932 law authorized a $5,000 exclusion, a relatively high amount compared with today's $3,000 exclusion.

Although the identity of the donee or donees is significant from the standpoint of arriving at the number of exclusions, it may not be particularly obvious. For transfers to a trust, the donees are the beneficiaries. On a transfer by A to X, Y, and Z, joint tenants with right of survivorship, there are three donees: X, Y, and Z.

The annual exclusion is available only for gifts of a present interest. Thus, gifts of a future interest are not eligible for an exclusion. According to Congress, the reason for denying the annual exclusion for gifts of future interest was "dictated by the apprehended difficulty, in many instances, of determining the number of eventual donees and the values of their respective gifts."[17]

The regulations contain the following definitions of future and present interests:

> "Future interest" is a legal term, and includes reversions, remainders, and other interests or estates . . . which are limited to commence in use, possession or enjoyment at some future date or time.
>
> An unrestricted right to the immediate use, possession, or enjoyment of property or the income from property (such as a life estate or term certain) is a present interest in property.[18]

Example: If T transfers a diamond necklace to Mrs. T, he has made a gift of a present interest, eligible for the $3,000 annual exclusion. If T sets up a trust and names U to receive the income for life and V to receive the assets upon U's death, U's interest is classified as present and V's as future.

Section 2503(c) provides a special rule for certain gifts in trust for minor beneficiaries. This provision authorizes the annual exclusion for certain transfers de-

spite the fact that the gift is not actually a present interest. To be eligible for the exclusion, the transfer must meet the following requirements:

The property and the income from the property

1. may be spent by the donee, or for his benefit, before he reaches age 21, and
2. will to the extent not so spent
   (a) pass to the donee when he reaches age 21, and
   (b) if he dies before reaching the age of 21, be payable to the donee's estate or as he appoints under a general power of appointment.

A trust that meets the above criteria is often referred to as a "2503(c) trust."

What if the income is distributable at the trustee's discretion until the beneficiary reaches age 21 and any accumulated income is to be paid out at age 21, but the trust assets are to be retained until the beneficiary reaches a later age, for example, 35? The value of the income interest from the date the trust is created until the beneficiary reaches age 21 is eligible for the annual exclusion. If the beneficiary is 14 years old when a $100,000 trust is created, the value of the seven-year income interest to age 21 is $33,494 ($100,000 × 0.334943); the $3,000 exclusion is allowed.

The donor's judicious use of the annual exclusion beginning at a somewhat early age can go a long way toward sheltering a sizable portion of wealth from transfer taxes. Not only does the exclusion reduce the size of the donor's taxable gifts, it also lessens the magnitude of the adjusted taxable gifts to be added to the tax base at death.

The gift-splitting election

Section 2513 contains gift-splitting provisions that allow the donor and his or her spouse to treat a gift actually made by one spouse to a third party as if one-half the gift had been made by the other spouse. This election offers several advantages. First, if only one spouse makes a gift, it effectively allows a $6,000 per donee annual exclusion, $3,000 to the donor and $3,000 to the spouse. Because of the progressive nature of the rates, gift splitting may lower the marginal rate of taxation. Moreover, each spouse's unified credit may be used to reduce the gift tax balance due. Splitting the gifts results in lower taxable gifts and, consequently, lower adjusted taxable gifts for the donor.

The purpose of the gift-splitting provisions is to achieve more comparable tax treatment between taxpayers of community-property and non-community-property states. For community-property taxpayers, all

[16]U.S., Congress, Senate, 72nd Congress, 1st Sess., 1932, S. Report No. 665, reprinted in 1939-1 C.B. (Part 2), pp. 496, 525–26.

[17]U.S., Congress, House, H.R. Report No. 708, p. 29, and Senate, S. Report No. 665, p. 41.

[18]Treas. Reg. Sec. 25.2503-3(a) and (b).

assets acquired after marriage are community property unless acquired by gift, devise, or descent. Each spouse owns a one-half interest in the community property. Thus, by operation of law, a gift of community property is made equally by each spouse. In a common law state (that is, a non-community-property state), most of the marital wealth usually is concentrated in the hands of one of the spouses. The "poorer" spouse often cannot afford to give away a portion of his or her property. By electing gift splitting, spouses in common law jurisdictions may achieve the same benefits as those automatically available to donors in community property states. If a spouse in a community property jurisdiction conveys an interest in separate property to a third party, this transfer is eligible for gift splitting. If gift splitting is elected for gifts of separate property, it must also be elected for gifts of community property during the same period. Of course, splitting each spouse's gift of community property does not affect the amount of taxable gifts.

Gift splitting may be elected only if each spouse is a U.S. citizen or resident at the time of the transfer. At the time of the gift, the donor must be married to the person who consents to gift splitting. Moreover, the donor must not remarry before the end of the calendar quarter. If gift splitting is elected, it is effective for all transfers to third parties during such part of the quarter as the spouses are married to each other. The preferred method for electing gift splitting is for each spouse to file a gift tax return and to signify his or her consent on the other spouse's return.

DEDUCTIONS AND COMPUTATION OF THE TAX

In the previous section, we have discussed the types of transactions on which the gift tax is imposed and the manner of valuing the gifts. We have also discussed the provisions that allow a small exclusion from the gift tax and the rules that allow, for example, a wife to treat herself as having made half the gifts that were in fact made by her husband. In this section we shall explore the two types of deductions—the marital deduction and the charitable contribution deduction—available in calculating the gift tax base and describe the cumulative nature of the tax.

The marital deduction

The marital deduction has been a feature of gift tax law since 1948. Like the gift-splitting provisions, the rationale for this rule is to provide more uniform treat-

ment of community property and non-community-property donors. As mentioned earlier, community-property law achieves an even split between the spouses with respect to most property acquired during marriage. In general, common law taxpayers may equalize the wealth of the two spouses only by engaging in a gift program. The marital deduction permits some interspousal gifts to escape gift taxation.

Only certain transfers, however, are eligible for the marital deduction. We shall consider the requirements for this deduction later. First, let us examine the dollar amount of the marital deduction.

Before 1977, the marital deduction was equal to one-half the value of the property conveyed in a qualifying manner to the spouse. The Tax Reform Act of 1976 altered the rules for calculating the marital deduction with respect to the first $200,000 of interspousal gifts. As its rationale for allowing a more advantageous marital deduction, the House Ways and Means Committee concluded that previous law tended "to interfere with normal interspousal lifetime transfers."[19]

The first $100,000 of post-1976 gifts to one's spouse is eligible for a 100 percent marital deduction. There is no marital deduction for the next $100,000 of transfers. All transfers in excess of the first $200,000 are eligible for a 50 percent marital deduction. In no event, however, may the marital deduction with respect to a particular gift exceed the amount of the gift to the spouse less the annual exclusion. The following series of examples illustrates the computation of the marital deduction.

Example 1: In October 1977 Mr. G gave Mrs. G $63,000 in cash. This transfer was the first he had ever made to his wife. The gift is eligible for a $3,000 exclusion and a $60,000 marital deduction. There is no taxable gift.

Example 2: In 1978 Mr. G made his second gift to Mrs. G. This time he again gave her $63,000. Now, $40,000 of the 100 percent marital deduction remains, so Mr. G receives a $40,000 marital deduction. He also receives a $3,000 annual exclusion. The taxable gift is $20,000.

Example 3: In 1979 Mr. G made a third gift— $116,000 cash—to Mrs. G. Before 1979 he had made aggregate gifts of $126,000. Of the 1979 gift, $74,000 represents the amount necessary for

[19]U.S., Congress, House, *Report on Estate and Gift Tax Reform Act of 1976,* 94th Congress, 2nd Sess., 1976, Report 94-1380, p. 17, Sec. 2 of the Act.

his gifts to reach the $200,000 threshold. Consequently, $74,000 is ineligible for a marital deduction. The remaining $42,000 ($116,000 − $74,000) is eligible for the 50 percent marital deduction of $21,000. Mr. G also receives a $3,000 exclusion. His taxable gift is $92,000 ($116,000 − $21,000 − $3,000 = $92,000).

The marital deduction is not allowed in several circumstances. The donor and the donee must be married to each other at the time of the conveyance. A transfer of community property does not generate a marital deduction. No deduction is available for transfers that are not treated as gifts. Thus, a marital deduction will not arise when one spouse furnishes all the consideration to acquire realty in joint ownership form with his or her spouse unless he or she elects to treat the transaction as a gift.

The marital deduction also is disallowed when the subject matter of the gift is a "nondeductible terminable interest," a concept explained below. The general idea behind this rule is that in order to enjoy the benefits of the marital deduction, the donor must convey something that will have transfer tax significance to the donee spouse. That is, if the donee spouse transfers it during life, a gift tax will be levied. If kept until death, the item will be included in the donee spouse's estate.

A terminable interest will cease or fail when some event occurs or fails to occur, or upon the passage of time. A terminable interest is ineligible for the marital deduction only if it is a nondeductible terminable interest.

A nondeductible terminable interest (that is, one for which the marital deduction is not available) has one of the following characteristics:

1. The donor has kept an interest or has conveyed an interest to a third party without adequate consideration. In addition, the donor or the third party will possess the property upon the cessation of the donee spouse's interest; or
2. Immediately after making the gift, the donor has the power to name someone to receive an interest in the property and the person named may possess the property once the donee spouse's interest terminates.

A patent is an example of a terminable interest. A patent transferred to a spouse does not constitute a nondeductible terminable interest. Upon expiration of the patent's legal life, a third party will not possess an interest in the patent. On the other hand, if, for example, a donor gives his wife a life estate in land and his son the remainder interest in the land, he will receive no

marital deduction. The wife's interest will cease with her death. The property will then pass to a third party who did not furnish consideration.

The regulations explicitly provide that if a donor makes a gift to his or her spouse in the form of a joint tenancy with right of survivorship or a tenancy by the entirety, the transfer is eligible for the marital deduction. For joint interests in real estate, however, the donor must treat the acquisition as a gift in order to receive a marital deduction. The possibility that the donor may eventually own the property in fee simple (that is, have outright ownership with no restrictions) as a result of surviving his or her spouse does not cause a loss of the marital deduction.

If the donor transfers to his or her spouse a life estate plus a "general power of appointment,"[20] he or she will have conveyed an interest eligible for the marital deduction. The transfer need not be in trust form. The donee must be entitled to receive the income from the property for life, and the income must be payable at least as frequently as annually. The donee must be able to demand that the property be distributed to the donee or to the donee's estate. Such power may be an *inter vivos* or a testamentary power, or both.

The availability of the gift tax marital deduction ensures a no cost, or low cost, method of increasing the wealth of one of the spouses. If the donee spouse predeceases and wills the gift property to the donor, however, the tax advantages will have "gone down the drain."

The charitable deduction

Since the repeal of the $30,000 gift tax exemption, the only deduction other than the marital deduction is the charitable contribution deduction. Consequently, even though charitable contributions in excess of $3,000 must be reported on a gift tax return, those meeting certain requirements do not increase the gift tax base. Claiming an income tax deduction for a charitable contribution does not cause the donor to forego the gift tax charitable contribution deduction. In contrast with the income tax provisions, no percentage limitation exists for the gift tax charitable contribution deduction. The only limit on the deduction is that it may not exceed the amount of the gift to the charitable organization less the amount of the annual exclusion available.

Example: T gives State University cash of $15,000; she receives a $3,000 exclusion and a $12,000 deduction.

[20]A *general power of appointment* is a power that the individual possessing it may exercise in favor of himself, his estate, his creditors, or the creditors of his estate.

Only gifts to "charitable organizations" are deductible. The rules defining charitable organizations are quite similar for income, gift, and estate tax purposes. According to Sec. 2522, a gift tax deduction is available for contributions to:

1.   The United States or any subordinate level of government within the United States as long as the transfer is solely for public purposes;

2.   Corporations, funds, and so on, exclusively for religious, charitable, scientific, literary, or educational purposes, or to foster amateur sports competition, including the encouragement of art and the prevention of cruelty to children or animals;

3.   A fraternal society or similar organization operating under the lodge system if the gifts are to be used only for religious, scientific, literary, or educational purposes; and

4.   War veterans' posts or organizations organized in the United States or its possessions if no part of the net earnings accrue to the benefit of private shareholders or individuals.

Unlike the income tax rules, a gift tax charitable contribution deduction is available for transfers to foreign charitable organizations. No deduction exists, however, for gifts to foreign governments.

Quite specialized rules apply when a donor makes a transfer for both private and public (charitable) purposes, known as a "split-interest" transfer. An example of such a transfer is the gift of a mansion to one's spouse for life and the remainder to the Red Cross. If the gift to the charitable organization is a gift of a remainder interest, the deduction is forfeited unless the remainder takes the form of a remainder interest in a personal residence or a farm, a charitable remainder annuity trust or unitrust, or a pooled income fund.[21] Thus, if X gives an art museum a remainder interest in his art collection, X receives no gift tax (or income tax) charitable contribution deduction. If the split-interest gift to charity is of a present interest, donors who desire to receive a charitable contribution deduction should give the charitable organization a guaranteed annuity interest or a unitrust interest.

[21]In a charitable remainder annuity trust, an individual receives trust distributions for a certain time period or for life. The annual distributions are a uniform percentage (5 percent or higher) of the value of the trust property, valued on the date of the transfer. For a charitable remainder unitrust, the distributions are similar except that they are a uniform percentage (5 percent or higher) of the value of the trust property, revalued at least annually. Thus, the annual distributions from a unitrust, but not an annuity trust, vary from one year to the next. A pooled income fund is similar in concept to a mutual fund. The various individual beneficiaries receive annual distributions of their proportionate shares of the fund's total income.

Cumulative nature of the gift tax

Because the gift tax is cumulative, all the donor's prior taxable gifts plus his or her current taxable gifts affect the marginal rate at which current gifts are taxed. The twofold process for computing the tax levied on current gifts is the following:

Tax on cumulative taxable gifts
− Tax on taxable gifts of previous periods
= Tax on current period's gifts
− Unutilized portion of unified credit

= Amount of tax payable

As mentioned earlier, the Tax Reform Act of 1976 raised the gift tax rates. For purposes of the first computation, above, the current rate schedules are used even though some or all of the gifts may have been made when the lower rates were in effect. This provision, of course, works to the donor's advantage.

The cumulative feature of the gift tax is illustrated in the following example.

Example: In 1975 D made taxable gifts (his first) totaling $2,000,000. In October 1979 D made his first post-1976 taxable gift. The taxable amount was $1,000,000.

The tax payable for 1979 is computed as follows:	
Tax on cumulative taxable gifts of $3,000,000	$1,290,800
Less: Tax on $2,000,000 of taxable gifts of previous periods	− 780,800
Equals: Tax on current period's $1,000,000 taxable gift	$ 510,000
Less: Unutilized portion of unified credit	− 38,000
Equals: Amount of tax payable	$ 472,000

If the gift tax had not been cumulative, a $1,000,000 taxable gift would have been subject to a tax of $345,800 less the unified credit. The cumulative aspect causes the current transfer to be taxed at a 53 percent marginal rate compared with a 39 percent marginal rate if it were not cumulative.

Illustration of the computation of taxable gifts and the gift tax

To compute the taxable gifts for a particular period, we use the following formula.

Fair market value at date of gift of all gifts made by donor during the period

Plus: One-half the value of gifts made by donor's spouse to third parties, but for which donor and spouse elected gift splitting

Less: (1) One-half the value of gifts made by donor to third parties, but for which donor and spouse elected gift splitting
    (2) Annual exclusion of $3,000 per donee
    (3) Marital deduction
    (4) Charitable contribution deduction

Equals: Taxable gifts for the period

Once the amount of taxable gifts for the current period has been determined, the tax payable is computed in the manner described in the previous section.

The following comprehensive example illustrates the computation of the gift tax.

Example: Helen and Walter Welloffski are married to each other. Walter has made no previous gifts. Helen's previous taxable gifts were as follows: $300,000 in October 1976 and $200,000 in October 1978. In 1976 she used the $30,000 exemption then available.

In May 1979 Helen made gifts as follows:

(1)	Cash to Walter (her first gift to Walter)	$53,000
(2)	Cash to son Billy	80,000
(3)	Jewelry to daughter Betsy	4,000
(4)	Cash to Republican Party	12,000
(5)	Cash to State University	20,000
(6)	Life estate in land valued at $10,000 to sister Mabel (age 45); gift is $10,000 × 0.80269	8,027
(7)	Remainder in land valued at $10,000 to nephew Nathan (age 25); gift is $10,000 × 0.19731	1,973

In May 1979 Walter made a gift of $76,000 cash to their son Billy. Walter and Helen elected gift splitting.

Helen's gift tax for the second quarter of 1979 is computed as follows:

Value of all gifts made by donor, items (1)–(3) and (5)–(7), above. (Transfers to political organizations are not gifts.)	$167,000
Plus: One-half of gifts made by spouse to third parties and deemed made by this spouse (½ × $76,000)	38,000
Less:	
(1) One-half of gifts made by donor to third parties and deemed made by spouse (½ × $114,000)	− 57,000

(2) Annual exclusions (Details as follows: Walter—$3,000; Billy—$3,000; Betsy—$2,000; State University—$3,000; Mabel—$3,000; Nathan—0, future interest. Note that the gift deemed made to Betsy was only $2,000; therefore, the exclusion is limited to $2,000. The exclusion is $3,000 per donee *per year;* thus, the exclusion for the two gifts to Billy totals $3,000.)	− 14,000
(3) Marital deduction (100 percent marital deduction for first $100,000 of gifts in excess of exclusion)	− 50,000
(4) Charitable contribution deduction ($10,000, the gift deemed made by Helen, less $3,000 exclusion)	− 7,000
Equals: Taxable gifts for this quarter	$ 77,000
Tax on cumulative taxable gifts of $577,000 ($300,000 + $200,000 + $77,000)	$184,290
Less: Tax on previous taxable gifts of $500,000	− 155,800
Equals: Tax levied on this quarter's gifts	$ 28,490
Less: (1) Unutilized portion of unified credit (1979 credit of $38,000 less adjustment of 20 percent of $30,000 exemption claimed in October, 1976) $32,000	
(2) Less credit utilized in October 1978 ($34,000 less adjustment of 20 percent of $30,000 exemption claimed in October 1976) 28,000	− 4,000
Equals: Tax payable by Helen with return	$ 24,490

The computation of Walter's tax would follow the same general formula. The marital deduction does not apply to Walter, however, because he made no gifts to Helen.

Filing requirements

For a number of years, gift tax returns were required to be filed annually. Currently, in general, returns must be filed quarterly by the fifteenth day of the second month after the end of the calendar quarter. Thus, the return for the first calendar quarter is due by May 15. The gift tax return for the fourth quarter, however, is not due until the fifteenth day of the fourth month after the end of the calendar quarter, the same as the due date for the income tax return for calendar year taxpayers. All gifts that exceed the available annual exclusion (discussed earlier) are reportable on a gift tax return. The gift tax is payable with the filing of the return.

In an exception to the quarterly filing rule, quarterly filing is not mandatory if a donor's taxable gifts for a calendar quarter do not exceed $25,000. A return is necessary by the fifteenth day of the second month after the end of the quarter in which taxable gifts for that quarter plus all previously unreported taxable gifts are greater than $25,000. If, in a particular calendar year, taxable gifts do not exceed $25,000, the return for that year is due by April 15 of the subsequent year. A return need not be filed if there are no gifts in excess of the excludible amount.

CHOOSING GIFT PROPERTIES

The Tax Reform Act of 1976, which unified estate and gift taxes, reduced many of the advantages previously associated with lifetime gifts but by no means eliminated them all. Indeed, valid tax motives still exist for giving away property during life. First, the amount subject to transfer taxation is the value of the property at the date of the gift. Thus, for gifts of appreciating property, post-gift appreciation escapes transfer taxation. In addition, the gift tax paid is not included in the amount subject to the estate tax. To freeze the amount subject to transfer taxation at the property's value on the date of the gift and to keep the gift tax paid out of the estate, the donor must survive the gift by more than three years. Third, the donee will likely pay a smaller amount of income tax than the donor on the income from the property.

The major factor in gift decisions and estate planning, however, must generally be personal considerations. Sizable potential savings of taxes should not override a person's desire to retain control of his or her assets. Once the decision to give away property has been made, the most appropriate gift assets must be chosen.

Both tax and nontax factors should be considered in deciding which assets should be made the subject of a gift. Among the nontax factors are determining the assets with which the donor may conveniently part and for which the donor will have the least need (for in-

come or other reasons) in the future. The remaining discussion will focus on tax considerations.

At this point, a review of the basis rules for gift and inherited property is in order. If the fair market value of the property at the date of the gift exceeds its adjusted basis, the donee's basis is the donor's adjusted basis. The donee may add to the donor's adjusted basis some or all of the gift tax paid. For pre-1977 gifts, all the gift tax may be added. For post-1976 gifts, however, only a portion of the gift tax may be added. The portion is represented by the following fraction:

$$\frac{\text{Amount of appreciation from acquisition}}{\text{date through date of gift}}$$
$$\frac{}{\text{Fair market value on date of gift}}$$

In no event may the donee add so much gift tax that his or her basis in the property exceeds its fair market value on the date of the gift.

If on the date of the gift the property's fair market value is less than the donor's adjusted basis, the rules are more involved. For purposes of computing gain, the donee's basis is the donor's adjusted basis. In computing a loss, the donee must use as his or her basis the fair market value of the property on the date of the gift. The donee may not add any gift tax paid to his or her basis.

"Step-up in basis rules" apply to inherited property. The heir's basis is the amount at which the property is valued on the estate tax return. Thus, the heir's basis is the fair market value of the property on the decedent's date of death or on the alternate valuation date, which is generally six months after the date of death. Thus, any appreciation through the date of death permanently escapes income taxation. The sword cuts the other way too, however. Predeath declines in value do not produce a loss deduction if the property is not sold before death.

If the donor is especially concerned with shifting income to a lower-bracket taxpayer, he or she should give away assets with fairly high yield. Assets that have declined in value should not be given away. The donee's loss on sale will be limited to the excess of the fair market value on the date of the gift over the sales price. A donor who may be expected to survive the gift by more than three years should give away assets that can be expected to appreciate significantly in the future. Such items will be added to the death tax base as adjusted taxable gifts at date of gift values. Thus, further appreciation escapes transfer taxation. A disadvantage of this strategy is that the donee does not receive a step-up in basis for the gift property.

Sometimes gifts are made to a person expected to

die soon in order to take advantage of such person's unified credit. This technique has the added advantage of providing income tax benefits to the person who receives the property as a devise or bequest from the donee. The basis of the property to the recipient of the devise or bequest is the value of the property on the decedent's date of death or on the alternate valuation date. In such situations, highly appreciated property should generally be the subject of the gift.

Example: Assume W is expected to die soon. If she died today, her gross estate would be valued at $20,000. The gross estate of H, her husband, is $600,000. H decides to give property worth $103,000 to W. The property's adjusted basis is $32,000. If H has made no other gifts to W after 1976, this transfer will not produce a taxable gift ($103,000 − $3,000 exclusion − $100,000 marital deduction). Thus, H has reduced the size of his gross estate without incurring a transfer tax. Assume W dies before the assets appreciate further. Because of the unified credit, her estate owes no tax. W wills her property to her daughter. The daughter's basis in the property formerly owned by H is $103,000 under the step-up in basis rules. Hence, $81,000 of appreciation escapes from being subject to income taxation.

Finally, in order to shelter as large an amount as possible with the annual exclusion, timing should be considered. Often this strategy calls for giving a few shares of stock, a few acres of land, or a small undivided interest in realty each year over a series of years. Although this approach increases the probability that an individual will make a transfer within three years of death, it reduces the amount of taxable gifts for a given year.

SUMMARY

Within the context of the gift tax, a transfer of property for less than adequate and full consideration in money or money's worth causes a gift to arise. The motive of the transferor is not determinative. Transfers to political organizations and transactions within the ordinary course of business are exempted from classification as gifts.

The amount of the gift is the excess of the fair market value of the property conveyed over the amount of consideration in money or money's worth that is received. The statute authorizes an exclusion of $3,000 per donee per year. In addition, deductions are available for certain gifts to one's spouse and to charitable organizations. Current taxable gifts represent the excess of the aggregate gifts for the period over the amount of the exclusions, the marital deduction, and the charitable contribution deduction. The gift tax is a cumulative tax; consequently, previous taxable gifts influence the marginal rate applicable to current taxable gifts. Effective for post-1976 gifts, the rates are the same as the estate tax rates.

PROBLEMS

1. Marge Miller engaged in the following transactions during 19X1. Which transactions constitute completed gifts for gift tax purposes?
   a. Marge used $10,000 cash to purchase common stocks registered in the name of her adult nephew and delivered the stock certificates to him.
   b. Marge paid the $1,200 annual premium on a life insurance policy on her life. Her son Arnold owns the policy. Arnold's son Matt is the beneficiary of the policy.
   c. Marge owns coupon bonds on which interest is payable semiannually. Four days before a semiannual payment date, she detached the coupon for the next payment and delivered it to her son Arnold. She informed Arnold that he was to view the cash payment as his own.
   d. She created a revocable trust with First Bank as trustee and funded it with $200,000 of common stock. Her daughter Mildred or Mildred's estate was named to receive the income for 15 years. At the end of the 15th year, the trust property will pass to Mildred's descendants.
   e. She deposited $10,000 into a passbook savings account in the names of herself or her son Archie as joint tenants with right of survivorship.

    f.   Four months later Archie withdrew $740 from the account mentioned in part e.

    g.   Marge purchased land for $140,000 and had the property titled in the names of herself and her husband as joint tenants with right of survivorship.

    h.   She created a trust with Fourth State Bank as trustee and funded it with bonds valued at $300,000. The trust is to last for 14 years; then the property will revert to Marge or her estate. The trustee in its discretion is to decide how much of the annual income is to be distributed to her nieces Peggy, Sandy, and Elaine. All income must be paid out annually to at least one of the nieces, however.

    i.   Same as part h, except Marge named herself trustee.

2.   a.   What is the blockage rule?

    b.   Give an example of a situation in which the blockage rule might apply.

3.   What are some factors that should be considered in arriving at the value of stock in closely held corporations?

4.   On April 4, 19X1, Horace Hertz engaged in the transactions listed below. What is the value of the gift in each of these transactions?

    a.   Horace gave Mindy Hertz 1,000 shares of ABC stock. The shares were traded that day at a high of 37 and a low of 33. The closing quote was 34½.

    b.   Horace gave Mork Hertz a stamp collection recently valued at $12,000.

    c.   He purchased TUV common stock for $160,000 and had it registered in the names of "Horace and Helene Hertz, joint tenants with right of survivorship." Helene is Horace's wife.

    d.   Horace owned a beach cabin and land recently valued at $60,000. He gave a life estate in the property to Avis Hertz, his 40-year-old son. Upon Avis's death the property will revert to Horace.

    e.   Horace created a trust with State Bank as trustee and funded it with common stock valued at $100,000. The income is payable to Amanda White or her estate for 15 years. At the end of the 15th year the property is to pass to Fred Ferth.

    f.   Horace gave Melody Lane 100 shares of FGH Corporation. The stock was not traded on April 4, 19X1. The trades closest to April 4 were as follows:

          2 business days before April 4—high of 104, low of 96, close of 103

          6 business days after April 4—high of 107, low of 105, close of 107

5.   Refer to the facts given in Problem 4.

    a.   Which of the gifts qualify for the annual exclusion?

    b.   Assume Horace had made no previous gifts to Helene. What is the amount, if any, of his gift tax marital deduction?

6.   X owned a $100,000 whole life insurance policy on his own life. He purchased it several years ago. His son is the policy beneficiary. On May 5, 19X1, X transferred the policy to his son's wife as owner. How do you arrive at the value of the policy?

7.   For each of the following transactions, indicate whether a gift within the context of the gift tax arises.

    a.   A sale by a father to his son of land valued at $1,000,000. The sales price was $300,000.

    b.   Prior to marriage, X transferred securities worth $5 million to his fiancee. She, in turn, signed a written agreement to forego her future dower rights, estimated to be worth approximately $5 million.

    c.   A clothing store held a clearance sale at the end of the season. It sold a coat with an original retail price of $350 for $125.

    d.   A mother purchased various toys costing an aggregate of $75 for her minor child.

8. For each of the following situations, indicate whether the annual exclusion is available. Explain.

   a. T created a trust in the amount of $300,000 for the benefit of her 8-year-old daughter V. She named Third National Bank as trustee. Before V reaches age 21, the trustee in its discretion is to pay income or corpus (trust assets) to V or for her benefit. When V reaches age 21, she will receive the unexpended portion of the trust income and corpus. If V dies before reaching age 21, the unexpended income and corpus will be paid to her estate or as she appoints under a general power of appointment.

   b. Same as part a, except T's daughter was age 28 when T created the trust. Substitute age 41 wherever age 21 appears in part a.

9. In 19X1 B made the transfers listed below and did *not* elect gift splitting. How many annual exclusions are available?

   Stock purchased for $300,000 and registered in the names of G, H, and I, joint tenants with right of survivorship, and

   A $500,000 trust fund with First Bank as trustee. For 12 years the income is to be distributed annually, one-half to K or her estate and one-half to J or his estate. At the end of the 12th year the property is to be distributed to L or her estate.

10. Betty married Bob on October 14, 19X1. They were still married at the end of the year. Betty made the following gifts in 19X1:

Cash to Sam on October 1	$116,000
Cash to Sally on October 31	136,000
Cash to Bob on November 7	48,000

    Bob made *no* gifts in 19X1. Assume Betty and Bob elected gift splitting for the fourth quarter of 19X1. Compute the amount of each person's *taxable* gifts.

11. Refer to the facts of Problem 10, and assume the year is 1981. Assume Betty's previous taxable gifts total $150,000 and were made in 1978 and that Bob has made no previous taxable gifts.

    a. Compute the amount of gift tax payable by each.

    b. Compute the amount of gift tax payable by Betty if the couple had not elected gift splitting.

12. a. In November 1971, Carrie Moore made taxable gifts totaling $200,000. In arriving at this taxable amount she claimed the $30,000 exemption then available. This was her first taxable gift. In 1979 she made $300,000 of taxable gifts. In 1989 she made $100,000 of taxable gifts. Compute the amount of her gift tax payable for 1989.

    b. Refer to part a, but change 1971 to 1976. Now compute the amount of Carrie's gift tax payable for both 1979 and 1989.

13. In November 19X4 Hector Garcia made the following gifts:

Cash to his grandson	$200,000
Cash to State University	40,000
Cash to Irma, his wife	70,000

    a. Assume Hector had made no previous gifts to Irma and that he and Irma *did not* elect gift splitting. Compute his taxable gifts.

    b. Same as part a, except Hector and Irma *did* elect gift splitting but she made no gifts.

    c. Same as part b, except Hector and Irma *did* elect gift splitting. Irma's only gift in 19X4 was $36,000 to her daughter in November.

    d. Same as part b, except Hector had made one earlier gift to Irma. In 19X3 he gave her cash of $13,000.

14. In 19X1 Deborah Dubinski provided all the consideration for the purchase of two assets that she titled in the names of herself and her husband as joint tenants with

right of survivorship. She purchased common stock for $600,000 and land for $540,000. What are the gift tax consequences of these two transactions?

15. a. Refer to Problem 14. Assume that Deborah did *not* treat the acquisition of the land as a gift. In 19X9 Deborah and her husband sold the land for $800,000 and divided the sales proceeds equally. What are the gift tax consequences of this transaction?

  b. Refer to part a. Assume that Deborah reported the original transaction as a gift. What are the gift tax consequences of the equal division of the sales proceeds?

  c. Refer to part a. Assume that Deborah reported the original transaction as a gift. What are the gift tax consequences if Deborah's husband receives *all* the sales proceeds?

16. a. In 1972 X made his first taxable gifts, which totaled $500,000. In 1982 he made his next taxable gifts, totaling $1,000,000. Compute the gift tax payable for the 1982 gifts.

  b. Same as part a, except X made his first taxable gift in 1979 and his next taxable gift in 1989. Compute the gift tax payable for each of these two years.

17. In 19X1, Bertha Bruno, a widow, made the following gifts:

January 5	Cash to her son	$ 40,000
May 14	Cash to State University	10,000
July 15	Cash to her brother	100,000
December 4	Cash to her daughter	23,000

By what date(s) must she file a gift tax return? Explain.

18. Before 19X1 neither W nor H (W's husband) had made any taxable gifts. In 19X1 H gave $6,000 cash to each of his 50 nieces and nephews. In 19X2 W gave $6,000 cash to each of these same persons. What is the *minimum* legal gift tax (before subtracting the credit) for 19X1 and 19X2?

19. In 19X1 Merry Sparks (unmarried) gave $7,000 to the campaign fund of Joe Schmore, candidate for governor of her state. This is a political organization. What is the amount of her taxable gift with respect to this transaction?

20. In 19X1 Betty Best (a widow) established a $1 million trust fund with Planters Bank as trustee. For as long as both live, Betty's two children are to share equally in the trust income, which is to be paid out annually. Betty's two children are Carl (age 40) and Carolyn (age 35). Upon the death of each of Betty's children, that child's share is to be distributed equally among his or her children or their estates. Carolyn has five children, and Carl has two. What is the amount of Betty's taxable gifts?

21. In 1991 H and W (who are married) made the gifts listed below. H's previous taxable gifts consist of $200,000 made in 1970 and $800,000 made in 1984. W has made no previous taxable gifts. The only interspousal transfer made by either is a $210,000 gift of cash H made to W in 1984.

W's 1991 gifts were:

| to A | $400,000 |
| to B | 10,000 |

H's gifts for 1991 were:

to L	$800,000
to M, a charitable organization	40,000
to W	20,000

Assume H and W elect gift splitting for 1991. Compute the gift tax liabilities of H and W.

22. a. What is a "present interest"?
    b. What is the significance of the classification of an interest as a present interest?

SUPPLEMENTAL PROBLEMS

23. On July 4, 19X3, Mort Russo created a $200,000 trust with First Bank as trustee. The trust is for the benefit of Mort's 11-year-old daughter, Ruth. The trust is to be terminated in 20 years (that is, when Ruth reaches age 31). Upon the termination of the trust, the trust assets are to be distributed to Ruth or her estate. During the term of the trust, the trustee at its discretion is to pay out income or principal or both to Ruth. According to the trust instrument, before December 31, 19X3, Ruth's guardian may demand in writing that the trustee distribute to Ruth from the trust a maximum of $6,200. No guardian has been appointed for Ruth. Does this transfer qualify for the annual exclusion? Explain your answer and cite appropriate authorities.

24. a. On January 1, 19X1, Grandfather Adams loaned $500,000 to his grandson Ricky (age 26). The purpose of the loan was to enable Ricky to start a gourmet drive-in restaurant. The loan is an interest-free demand loan for which Ricky signed a note. The loan was still outstanding on December 31, 19X2. Grandfather fully intends to demand payment once the restaurant gets firmly established and begins operating "in the black." Are there any gift tax consequences to this transaction? Explain. Cite appropriate authorities.
    b. Refer to part a, but assume the loan was an interest-free term loan payable in full on December 31, 19X8. Answer the question posed in part a.

25. Twelve years ago X died. His will contained the following provision: "The acreage I own in Montana I leave to A for life. Upon the death of A, the acreage is to be divided equally between B and C."

    A, B, and C are males. A is now age 52, B is age 32, and C is age 27. The acreage is currently valued at $330,000. A, B, and C agreed to sell the acreage for $330,000 and to divide the sales proceeds equally. They consulted you to determine whether there are any gift tax consequences associated with the sale of the property and the equal division of the sales proceeds. They also want you to prepare any gift tax returns that may be necessary. Determine the gift tax results of this transaction. Cite appropriate authority.

26. On July 1, 19X1 Albert transferred $200,000 of intangible non-income-producing property to an irrevocable trust, naming Bank of the Northeast as trustee. At the end of 12 years, the trust property is to revert to Albert or his estate. According to the trust agreement, all income is distributable at least annually to the beneficiary—Heidi or her estate. The trust agreement authorizes the trustee at its discretion to invest and reinvest the trust assets as it sees fit in a manner most advantageous to the trust.
    a. What is the value of the gift? Explain. Cite appropriate authority.
    b. If a gift results from this transaction, does it qualify for the annual exclusion? Explain. Cite appropriate authority.

27. H and W (who are husband and wife) were residents of Washington, a community-property state. H died, survived by W and H, Jr., their son. At the time of his death, there were two life insurance policies on H's life. Each policy was a community-property asset. The policies were as follows.

Policy number	Beneficiary	Face value
X987A123Q	W	$100,000
456AB654	H, Jr.	180,000

Assume the insurance companies paid the policy proceeds to the named beneficiaries. Do any gift tax consequences surround the death of H and the transmittal of the policy proceeds?

RETURN PROBLEM

1. Prepare a gift tax return for the last quarter of 1981 for Don Orr (age 57) of Sioux City, Iowa. Don and his wife Soona want to elect gift splitting. Soona will prepare her own return.

Don's gift history is as follows:

Date	Exemption claimed	Taxable gifts
November 1976	$30,000	$100,000
December 1979	—	150,000

During the last quarter of 1981, Don made the following gifts:

(1) Cash to Iowa State University	$28,000
(2) Premium payment on life insurance policy on life of Soona. Don transferred the policy to his son Jimbo as owner in 1979	6,200
(3) Trust established at First Bank and funded with $30,000 cash. Don's mother Helen Orr (age 78) is to receive the income for life. All trust income is to be paid to her in quarterly installments. His sister Maybelline Orr St. Laurent is to receive the remainder	30,000
(4) Land to Soona (In 1979 Don gave her $43,000 cash)	120,000

In the last quarter of 1981, Soona gave her nephew Ernie Tubbs $66,000 cash.

17

the estate tax

In U.S. history, the estate tax predated the gift tax. The federal government imposed an estate tax during several periods in the nineteenth century. In 1916, Congress enacted the estate tax once again, and it has been in existence continuously since that date in somewhat similar form.

At the time the estate tax was introduced, one of its chief objectives was to generate additional revenue. Another purpose was to reduce the concentration of wealth. Indeed, in England in the nineteenth century, Jeremy Bentham and John Stuart Mill had been proponents of death taxes as a device for equalizing wealth.[1] In the United States, Andrew Carnegie voiced his support of increased inheritance taxation in a magazine article published in 1889. In Carnegie's opinion, an inheritance tax was the wisest form of taxation, because by taxing estates heavily at death, the government could express its condemnation of "the selfish millionaire's unworthy life." Carnegie contended that the inheritance tax should be progressive and that "moderate sums to dependents" should be exempt from the tax.[2] In the late nineteenth century, supporters of the Populist movement had advocated both progressive income taxes and progressive estate or inheritance taxes. As pointed out in Chapter 15, the concentration of wealth has remained relatively constant despite the imposition of such taxes.

[1]See Boris I. Bittker and Lawrence M. Stone, *Federal Income Estate and Gift Taxation,* 4th ed. (Boston: Little, Brown and Co., 1972), p. 984.
[2]Reprinted from *North American Review* for June 1889, in Carnegie, *The Gospel of Wealth* 1, 911 (Garden City, New York: Doubleday Doran Co., 1933). See Bittker and Stone, pp. 981–96, for a more thorough discussion.

INCLUSIONS IN THE GROSS ESTATE: GENERAL CONCEPTS

You will more easily understand the rules concerning which items are includible in the gross estate if you bear in mind that the estate tax is a wealth *transfer* tax, not a property tax. The estate tax is levied on transfers that are essentially testamentary in nature. That is, a person's control or enjoyment of the property ceases with death, not before. Property to which the decedent did not hold title at the time of death may be included in the gross estate.

For example, property transferred by gift within three years of the date of death is automatically included in the decedent's gross estate. In another example, before death, a person transferred property to a trust and retained for life the right to receive the trust income. The gross estate then includes the trust property, an item to which the decedent did not hold title at the time of death. The right to income, which passes to another at the transferor's death, is one of the most significant property rights. The estate of the person who retained the lifetime income interest includes such assets. Other instances in which the decedent's estate includes assets to which he did not hold title at death include those over which he had some form of control. A shifting of control occurs upon the person's death.

Later in this chapter, we shall explore in some detail the various statutory provisions concerning inclusions in the gross estate. Before turning to that discussion, however, we shall consider the rules regarding valuation.

Just as is true for valuing gift property, the valuation of items included in the gross estate may prove to be an extremely difficult task. The regulations are quite sketchy concerning how to value components of the gross estate, especially regarding assets other than listed securities and life insurance policies.

General valuation rules

All items included in the gross estate are to be valued either as of the decedent's date of death or as of the alternate valuation date (discussed on page **15/4**). All items must be valued as of the same date. Regardless of which valuation date is chosen, all items are to be valued at fair market value. This rule applies to valuing gifts also. For both gift and estate tax purposes, fair market value is defined as "the price at which the property would change hands between a willing buyer and a willing seller, neither being under any compulsion to buy or to sell and both having reasonable knowledge of relevant facts" (Treas. Reg. Sec. 20.2031-1(b)).

In general, on a given date, values would be identical for estate tax and gift tax purposes. Because we discussed the topic of valuation in some depth in Chapter 16, we shall not repeat the guidelines for how to value certain property interests. Life insurance policies, however, because a policy matures upon the death of the insured, take a different value for gift and estate tax purposes. If the policy is on the life of the deceased and is taxed in his or her estate, it is included at its face amount. When it is the subject of a gift, the same policy would be valued at a lower amount because it has not yet matured. If the decedent owned a policy on another person's life, its estate tax value would be computed in the same manner as if it were a gift.

The alternate valuation method

The Internal Revenue Code authorizes the executor to elect to value all items included in the gross estate at their values on the alternate valuation date. If the executor foregoes this option, date of death values must be used. The alternate valuation date is (1) six months after the date of death, or (2) the date on which the property is disposed of by sale, exchange, distribution, and so on, if such date is earlier.

> *Example:* Assume T died February 5, 1979. If T's executor elects the alternate valuation date, the items in T's estate will be valued as of August 5, 1979, unless they are disposed of before that date.

If a particular asset is sold on June 10, 1979, it is valued at its sales price.

The value of any interest that is affected by the mere passage of time is to be valued at the date of death value, adjusted for changes in value attributable to causes other than mere lapse of time (Treas. Reg. Sec. 20.2032-1(a)(3)). For example, the values of patents and copyrights are affected to some extent by the mere lapse of time. Any property interest arising after death is referred to as excluded property and does not form a part of the gross estate (Treas. Reg. Sec. 20.2032-1(d)). A dividend declared after the decedent's death, for example, is excluded property.

The statute first authorized an alternate valuation date in 1935 in response to the stock market "crash" of 1929. Congress's rationale for such a provision was to foreclose "the danger of complete confiscation of estates due to sudden decline in market values."[3]

If values decline in the period after death, the election of the alternate valuation date permits a reduction of the estate tax base and the corresponding tax liability. Under the "step-up in basis rules," the heir's basis in the inherited property is the same as the value of the property per the estate tax return. Consequently, it is not uncommon for an executor to elect the alternate valuation date even if the values are higher on that date, provided the estate tax rates are estimated to be lower than the projected income tax rates that will apply when the property is subsequently sold. Although such an election will result in higher values and higher estate taxes, the step-up in basis rules will produce a higher basis for computing gain or loss. Thus, gain will be lessened or loss will be increased, resulting in overall tax savings for the family as a unit. This technique is useful, of course, only if a sale of the assets is anticipated in the near future.

Special use valuation

The Tax Reform Act of 1976 inaugurated special valuation rules for certain real estate used for farming or in a closely held business. Section 2032A allows such realty, described as "qualified real property," to be valued in a manner different from the traditional valuation methods that emphasize highest and best use of the property in determining value. Congress expressed the following reason for authorizing special use valuation:

[3] William C. Warren and Stanley S. Surrey, *Federal Estate and Gift Taxation Cases and Materials,* 1952 ed. (Brooklyn: The Foundation Press, Inc., 1952), p. 446, citing Senate Report No. 1240, 74th Congress, 1st Session, p. 9.

[I]t is inappropriate to value the land on the basis of its potential "highest and best use," especially since it is desirable to encourage the continued use of property for farming and other small business purposes.[4]

It added that requiring valuation at highest and best use (such as valuing farm land at an amount for which it could be sold for purposes of subdivision) might sometimes require the heirs to sell the property in order to generate enough cash to pay the estate taxes.[5]

Explicit criteria must be met before special use valuation may be elected. One of the most significant requirements is that farm land must have been farmed for a certain amount of time before the decedent's death. Furthermore, the decedent or a member of the decedent's family must have "materially participated" in the farming operations. Mere passive rental of the land is not sufficient.

In addition, the farm realty must make up a certain portion of the decedent's estate. The realty, after deducting debts against it, must represent 25 percent or more of the value of the gross estate, as reduced by mortgages and other debts.

Section 2032A(e)(7) specifies the following formula for determining special use value:

$$\frac{\text{Average annual gross cash rent for comparable land in the same locality} \quad Less \quad \text{Average annual real estate taxes for comparable land}}{\text{Average annual effective interest rate for all new loans by the Federal Land Bank}}$$

The averages are based on figures from the five calendar years immediately preceding the decedent's date of death. The maximum reduction from fair market value that may be achieved by electing special use valuation is $500,000.

The following example illustrates the computation of special use valuation.

Example: Qualified farm realty has been valued under traditional valuation methods at a fair market value of $1,100,000. The average annual gross cash rent for comparable land is $40,000, and average annual real estate taxes for comparable land are $2,000. The Federal Land Bank's average annual effective interest rate for new loans is 8 percent. Special use value is tentatively $475,000.

[4]U.S., Congress, House, *Report on Estate and Gift Tax Reform Act of 1976*, 94th Congress, 2d Sess., 1976, Report 94-1380, p. 21, Sec. 2003 of the Act.
[5]*Ibid.*

$$\frac{\$40,000 - \$2,000}{8\%}$$

Because the maximum reduction from fair market value is $500,000, the election of special use valuation causes the realty to be valued at $600,000. If the fair market value of the realty were $800,000, for example, the special use value would be $475,000.

If special use valuation is elected and the property is disposed of or ceases to have a qualified use during the first 15 years after the decedent's death, an additional tax will be imposed. In general, the amount of additional tax will be equal to the tax savings that resulted from electing special use valuation.

In certain factual situations, the statutory provisions for special use valuation represent a significant tax planning opportunity. The provisions of Sec. 2032A offer the greatest opportunity for significant estate tax savings when a major portion of the estate consists of a "family farm." In order to reap any tax benefits, a family member must participate in the farming after the former owner dies.

THE GROSS ESTATE: SPECIFICS

The first step in the computation of the estate tax base is to determine the components of the decedent's gross estate. Next, the components must be valued to arrive at the dollar amount of the gross estate. As mentioned earlier, the gross estate encompasses a much wider array of items than merely those to which the decedent possessed title at the date of death. Certain Code provisions, referred to as the *transferor sections,* provide for the gross estate to include items earlier transferred by the decedent. Whether the property is tangible or intangible is immaterial. For other than nonresident aliens, the location of the property has no significance; it is treated the same regardless of its situs (Sec. 2031).

Property in which decedent had an interest

Section 2033 provides that the gross estate includes the value of all the property the decedent beneficially owned at the time of death. This broad language taxes such items as the decedent's personal residence, automobile, stocks, and any other asset titled in the decedent's name. Because the rule refers to "beneficial ownership," however, its scope extends beyond assets to which the decedent held title. For example, such items as remainder interests are also included in the gross estate.[6]

> *Example:* T's will named A to receive trust income for life and B or B's estate to receive the trust remainder upon A's death. B's gross estate, therefore, includes the value of the remainder interest even if B predeceases A. If B does not survive A, the passage of the remainder is controlled by B's will. The transfer is associated with B's death and, hence, is subject to the transfer tax.

Dower or curtesy interest

Certain state laws provide for dower and curtesy interests for surviving spouses. *Dower* is the interest of a widow in her deceased husband's property. *Curtesy* is a widower's interest in the property of his deceased wife. If a man willed all his assets to someone other than his wife, she would be able to receive a certain portion of his property by exercising her dower rights. Section 2034 explicitly states that there is no reduction to the decedent's gross estate for the value of the property in which the surviving spouse had a dower or curtesy interest or some other statutory interest. For example, assume state law gives widows an interest in one-third of the deceased husband's property. Thus, in fact, the husband has absolute control over the devise and bequest of only two-thirds of his property. Regardless of the husband's wishes, his widow will receive at least one-third of his property. Nevertheless, his gross estate is not reduced by the value of the widow's dower interest.

Gifts made within three years of death

One of the major changes made by the Tax Reform Act of 1976 concerned gifts made within three years of death. Under previous law, a rebuttable presumption existed that such gifts were made "in contemplation of death" and were thereby includible in the gross estate. Taxpayer's representatives could overcome this presumption by presenting evidence, such as a history of periodic giving, to support an argument that life-associated motives prompted the gift. Even though the representatives might not be able to overcome the "in contemplation of death" presumption, tax savings could still arise from such gifts. The gift taxes reduced the gross estate if already paid or the taxable estate if still owed at the time of death.

For gifts made after 1976, the Tax Reform Act of

1976 requires that, in general, all gifts made within three years of death are automatically included in the gross estate (Sec. 2035(a)). The motive for the gift no longer has any tax significance. Under an exception to the general rule, if no gift tax return was required to be filed for gifts made within three years of death, there will be no inclusion in the gross estate, even though the property may have escalated in value after the date of the gift. If a gift tax return was necessary, the entire value at the date of death is added to the gross estate. Life insurance policies given away within three years of death will always be added to the gross estate at date of death value, even though the policy might have been valued at $3,000 or less on the date of the gift.

> *Example:* T gave A $2,500 cash in 1978 and died in 1980. Under the exception to the general rule, the gift is not included in T's gross estate. The $2,500 was fully excludable in calculating the 1978 taxable gifts, provided total gifts to A in 1978 did not exceed $3,000. T did not have to report the gift on a gift tax return. If T had given A $90,000 cash in 1978 and died in 1980, the addition to T's gross estate would have been $90,000. If T had given away a life insurance policy on his own life in 1978 and died in 1980, the face value of the policy would automatically be added to his gross estate.

The tax savings from deathbed gifts were foreclosed by amendments to the Code in 1976 that added a "gross-up" rule. For gifts made after 1976 and within three years of death, the decedent's gross estate also includes gift taxes paid by the decedent or the estate on such gifts (Sec. 2035(c)).

Gifts made within three years of death are included in the gross estate at date of death values (or alternate valuation date values, if so elected). Thus, unlike the situation for other gifts, appreciation does not escape the estate tax.

Transfers with retained life estate

The provision concerning retentions of a life estate extends beyond the taxation merely of those transfers in which the transferor retained the income for life. The two chief types of retentions made taxable by this provision (Sec. 2036) are:

1. Those for which the decedent kept possession or enjoyment of the property or the right to its income, and

2. Those for which the decedent retained the

---

[6]A *remainder interest* is an interest that will arise upon the termination of another interest, such as a life estate or an interest for a term certain (a limited, specified amount of time, such as 13 years).

power to designate who is to possess or enjoy the property or to receive its income.

The Tax Reform Act of 1976 expanded the inclusionary provisions so that the retention of voting rights in transferred stock results in an inclusion in the transferor's gross estate. Transfers after June 22, 1976 are subject to these revised rules. The 1978 Revenue Act amended the Code to provide that retention of voting rights results in an inclusion only if the stock is in a "controlled corporation." A controlled corporation is one in which the decedent either owned (directly or indirectly) or had the right to vote stock with at least 20 percent of the voting power.

The retention periods that cause a transfer of the type described above to be included in the gross estate are:

1. For the transferor's life;
2. For a period that may not be determined without referring to the transferor's death (for example, the transferor retained the right to quarterly payments of income, but payments cease with the last quarterly payment prior to the transferor's death); or
3. For a period that in fact does not end before the death of the transferor.

A written retention is not a requisite for inclusion in the gross estate. An implied agreement or understanding is sufficient to trigger taxation. For example, if a mother gives a residence to her daughter and continues to occupy the residence alone and rent free, the residence will likely be included in the mother's estate. The rationale is that there was an implied understanding that the mother could occupy the residence for life.

The second type of retention made taxable by Sec. 2036 causes transferred property to be included in the transferor's estate not because he kept some of the benefits from the property, but rather because he retained some control over others' enjoyment.

Example: Assume T created a trust and named A, B, and C to receive the trust income for their joint lives and D to receive the remainder upon the death of the first among A, B, and C to die. In addition, T reserved the right to designate what portion of the income would go to each particular income beneficiary each year. T predeceased all the other parties. The control over the flow of income did not end before T's death. The date of death value of the trust assets is included in T's estate, because T failed to "cut the string" with respect to his control over the income flow.

Revocable transfers

Another provision affecting transferors taxes "revocable transfers." The statutory language used for the title of Sec. 2038 is overly simplistic: A much more diverse group of transfers than simply "revocable transfers" is taxed. Section 2038 requires the transferor's gross estate to include all the transfers over which at the time of death the transferor had the power to change the enjoyment. The ability to affect enjoyment may arise from the transferor's power to alter, amend, revoke, or terminate an interest. It is not mandatory that the decedent retained these powers. What is crucial is that they were possessed at the time of death, regardless of whether he retained them originally.

The amount taxed under this section is the value of the interest that is subject to change by the decedent. This section and the section taxing transfers with a retained life estate overlap greatly. If one amount is taxable under one section, and a different amount is taxable under the other section, it probably comes as no surprise to learn that the gross estate includes the larger amount. Two types of transfers taxed by Sec. 2038 are illustrated in the following examples.

Example 1: T created a revocable trust and named his son to receive the remainder. While T is alive, he may terminate the trust because it is revocable. The trust becomes irrevocable and the transfer complete upon T's death. T's gross estate includes the date of death value of the trust assets.

Example 2: V created a trust and named A to receive the income for life and B to receive the remainder. V, however, retained the right to substitute C for B as remainderman. When V died, she had the authority to change the enjoyment of the remainder. Thus, the value of the remainder interest is includible in V's estate.

Transfers taking effect at death

Section 2037 taxes an additional form of *inter vivos* transfer made by a decedent. The transferor's gross estate sometimes includes property he or she earlier transferred if another party must survive the decedent in order to own the property. An inclusion occurs only if the possibility remained that the property would be returned to the decedent or his estate or be subject to his disposition. No inclusion arises, however, unless the value of the decedent's "reversionary interest"[7] is

---

[7]A *reversionary interest* is an interest that arises because the transferor did not transfer away the entire interest. For example, if T deeds land "to S for life," the land reverts to T or T's estate upon S's death.

greater than 5 percent of the value of the entire property. Actuarial techniques are used to value the decedent's reversionary interest. The following example illustrates the provisions of Sec. 2037.

> *Example:* T transferred an asset to A for life and then B for life. The asset is to revert to T, if T is alive, upon the death of A or B, whoever dies second. If T is not alive upon the death of the survivor of A and B, the asset is to pass to C, or to a charitable organization if C is not alive. C must survive T in order to receive the property. There will be an inclusion in T's estate if the value of T's reversionary interest exceeds 5 percent. The reversionary interest's value is a function of the present value of the interest T would receive after the deaths of A and B. Valuation also takes into account the probability that A and B will predecease T. The amount included in T's gross estate is not the value of his reversionary interest, but rather the date of death value of the property reduced by the value of A's and B's life estates.

Annuities

Retirement benefits are an asset owned by many decedents. Section 2039 explicitly addresses the estate tax treatment of annuities. If this section did not exist, some annuities probably still would be taxable under the more general definition of the gross estate. For an annuity to be included in the decedent's gross estate, the annuity payments must be made under a contract or an agreement. They must be payable to the decedent, or the decedent must have had a right to collect them either alone or with another person. The annuity must be payable for the decedent's life, for a period that may not be arrived at without referring to the decedent's date of death, or for a period that in actuality does not cease before the decedent's death.

The amount includible in the gross estate is a portion of the value of the annuity or lump-sum payment receivable by the surviving beneficiary. Thus, if the annuity ceases with the decedent's death, nothing is includible in the gross estate. An annuity included in the estate is valued at the cost of a comparable contract. This cost is then multiplied by a fraction that represents the proportion of the purchase price that the decedent contributed. Contributions by the decedent's employer on behalf of the decedent are treated as having been made by the decedent.

Special rules apply to annuities payable under "qualified plans."[8] A portion of such annuities may qualify for exclusion from the gross estate. The fraction eligible for exclusion is that portion of the value attributable to the employer's contributions to the qualified plan. For the exclusion to apply, however, the proceeds must not be payable in a lump sum unless the beneficiary elects to forego the most favorable income tax treatment. Any exclusion otherwise available will be lost if the benefits are payable to the executor.

> *Example:* Assume when D died she was receiving an annuity provided under a qualified plan by her former employer. D's son is to receive an annuity valued at $40,000 as a result of surviving D. The employer made three-quarters of the contributions to the plan, and D made one-quarter. D's gross estate includes only $10,000 if the son collects in the form of an annuity. If the son collects in a lump sum, however, the exclusion is lost unless the son elects to forego the most advantageous income tax treatment. If D had contributed the entire cost of the annuity, her estate would have included $40,000.

Jointly owned property

It is quite common for a decedent to own property jointly with another person. Jointly owned property is property owned with another as a joint tenant with right of survivorship or as a tenant by the entirety. The rules concerning the estate tax treatment of jointly owned property are found in Sec. 2040. An important characteristic of such a form of ownership is that upon the death of one joint owner, the decedent's interest passes automatically to the surviving joint owner. Special rules concerning the taxation of certain joint interests owned by spouses were inaugurated by the Tax Reform Act of 1976 and the 1978 Revenue Act. We shall discuss these rules in later paragraphs.

In general, the estate tax treatment of jointly owned property is controlled by the "consideration furnished test." Property is included in a joint owner's gross estate in accordance with the proportion of the consideration he or she furnished to acquire the interest. For example, if X provided 100 percent of the consideration to acquire land held with Y as joint tenants with right of survivorship, the entire date of death

---

[8] A *qualified plan* is entitled to preferential tax treatment in several areas. Contributions by the employer are tax deductible, and they are not included in the employee's gross income when contributed. Earnings of the plan are tax free. Moreover, the estate tax benefits explained in this chapter are available.

value of the land would be included in X's estate. On the other hand, if X furnished only 25 percent of the consideration, his estate would include only 25 percent of the date of death value of the land.

If part of the consideration furnished by one joint tenant was originally received gratuitously from another joint tenant, such consideration is attributable to the joint tenant who made the gift. If all joint owners acquired their interests by gift, devise, bequest, or inheritance, the decedent joint owner's estate includes his or her proportionate share of the date of death value of the jointly owned property.

Certain property owned jointly by spouses falls within the definition of a *qualified joint interest* and is not governed by the consideration furnished test. Instead, regardless of which spouse provided the consideration, the estate of the first spouse to die includes one-half the value of the jointly owned property. The Code imposes the following four requirements for categorizing an interest as a qualified joint interest:

1. Spouses must own the property as joint tenants or as tenants by the entirety.
2. The decedent, the decedent's spouse, or both must have created the joint interest.
3. Interests in personal property must have been created by gift. If the interest is in realty, the donor must have elected to treat the creation of the interest as a gift.
4. The decedent and the decedent's spouse must be the only joint tenants.

If all the above tests are met, the estate of the first spouse to die includes only one-half the value of the joint tenancy property, regardless of the proportion of consideration furnished by the deceased spouse.

Under an amendment to the Code by the 1978 Revenue Act, yet another rule may apply to certain joint interests of spouses. This provision, which applies only if the executor elects it, offers some opportunities for tax savings in instances in which the surviving spouse furnished little or no consideration but materially participated in operating a jointly owned farm or other business. Only tangible property used for farming purposes or in some other trade or business is eligible for this elective treatment. If the surviving spouse furnished none of the consideration, election of these special rules may cause the inclusion in the decedent's estate to be reduced by 2 percent for every year in which the surviving spouse materially participated in the operations. Two limitations apply: The maximum

reduction to the amount otherwise includible is $500,000, and in no event may the portion excluded exceed 50 percent.

Powers of appointment

Although it may seem surprising on first impression, Sec. 2041 taxes certain interests that the decedent never owned in a legal sense. Such interests are included in the decedent's gross estate if he or she had the power to designate who would eventually own the property. Authority to designate the owner, which is a significant power, is referred to as a *power of appointment*.

Only a "general power of appointment" results in an addition to the gross estate. Furthermore, if the general power was created before October 22, 1942, there is no inclusion unless the decedent exercised the power. A general power of appointment exists if the holder may exercise it in favor of himself, his estate, his creditors, or the creditors of his estate. The power may be exercisable during life, by will, or both.

If the power to appoint is limited by an ascertainable standard, it is not a general power. If appointments of property may be made solely for purposes of the decedent's health, support, maintenance, or education, they are governed by an ascertainable standard, and, therefore, the power is not considered a general power.

> *Example:* T died in 1950; her will created a trust from which D was to receive the income for life. In addition, D may designate by will the person or persons to receive the trust assets. D has a testamentary general power of appointment; the trust assets are included in his gross estate regardless of whether he exercises the power. If T had died in 1940, however, D would have had a pre-1942 power. Such powers are taxed only if exercised. If T's will had merely authorized D to choose from among his descendants which ones are to receive the trust assets, D would have had a special power of appointment because he would not have had the power to leave the property to whomever he so desired. Special powers of appointment, unlike general powers, do not increase the gross estate.

Life insurance

Section 2042 addresses the estate tax treatment of life insurance policies on the life of the decedent. Life insurance policies owned by the decedent on the lives of others are taxed under the more general language of Sec. 2033. A decedent's gross estate includes the value of policies on his or her own life if one of two conditions exists: (1) the proceeds are receivable by the executor or for the benefit of the estate, or (2) the decedent had any "incidents of ownership" at the time of death. The regulations list the following as a partial inventory of incidents of ownership: the powers to change the beneficiary, to surrender or cancel the policy, to borrow against the policy, to pledge the policy for a loan, and to revoke an assignment of the policy (Treas. Reg. Sec. 20.2042-1(c)(2)).

If the decedent could have exercised incidents of ownership only in conjunction with another party, the policy is nevertheless included in the decedent's gross estate. Moreover, it is the legal power to exercise ownership rights, compared with the practical ability, that leads to an inclusion. The Supreme Court emphasized the decedent/insured's legal powers in a case in which the insured was killed in a plane crash and the policies he owned on his life were in his spouse's possession. The Court held that the decedent possessed incidents of ownership and, thus, the policies were includible.[9] Not surprisingly, quite a number of cases have litigated the question whether a decedent possessed any incidents of ownership.

Effect of ownership as community property

In eight states, community property laws determine the ownership of most assets acquired during marriage.[10] Federal tax law recognizes this form of ownership. In these states, in general, all property acquired subsequent to marriage is community property unless acquired by gift, devise, or descent. Property other than community property is referred to as separate property. Each spouse has a currently vested right to a one-half interest in each item of community property. For example, assume only the husband is employed for compensation, and with his earnings, the spouses acquire a residence. The home is community property. Regardless of which spouse predeceases, his or her estate includes the value of his or her one-half interest in the residence. The decedent spouse's interest in the residence passes in accordance with the provisions of his or her will. The surviving spouse continues to own his or her original one-half interest.

For spouses with small amounts of separate property, community-property laws cause practically an even split of the marital wealth. The estate tax cost is practically the same regardless of which spouse predeceases. On the other hand, in the other 42 states (known as common law states) often the wealth is concentrated in the hands of one of the spouses. Proper use of the estate tax marital deduction (discussed later in this chapter) helps to equalize and minimize the combined estate tax burden of the two spouses.

DEDUCTIONS FROM THE GROSS ESTATE: GENERAL CONCEPTS

In the computation of the taxable estate, the Code authorizes five types of deductions from the gross estate. Before it was repealed by the Tax Reform Act of 1976, a specific exemption of $60,000 was deductible also. Two types of deductions cause the tax base to better reflect the net wealth passed to the heirs, devisees, or legatees. These are the deductions for expenses and debts and for losses. Three additional deductions reward the estate with a tax reduction for bequests or devises to certain individuals and organizations. These deductions are the marital deduction, the charitable contribution deduction, and the deduction for bequests to certain minor children (sometimes called the "orphans' exclusion").

Debts and funeral and administrative expenses

Mortgages and all other debts of the decedent are deductible in computing the amount of the taxable estate, provided they represent bona fide contracts for an adequate and full consideration in money or money's worth (Sec. 2053). Some examples of administrative expenses are executors' commissions, attorneys' fees, court costs, accountants' fees, appraisers' fees, and expenses of preserving and distributing the estate. The executor must decide whether to deduct administrative expenses on the estate tax return or the fiduciary income tax return. They are not deductible twice, although some may be deducted on the estate return and others on the fiduciary return.

Losses

Section 2054 authorizes a deduction for losses from theft or casualty incurred while the estate is being settled. Just as in the context of the income tax, casualties include fires, storms, and earthquakes. The amount of the loss takes into consideration the amount of any insurance compensation received. If the alternate valua-

---

[9]*Estate of Noel,* 380 U.S. (1965).
[10]The states are Louisiana, Texas, New Mexico, Arizona, California, Washington, Idaho, and Nevada.

tion date is elected, the loss may not be used to reduce the alternate value and again as a loss deduction. As with administrative expenses, the executor must decide whether to deduct the loss on the estate tax return or the fiduciary income tax return.

Charitable contribution deduction

An unlimited deduction for testamentary transfers to certain charitable organizations is available under Sec. 2055. Moreover, a deduction is available for *inter vivos* transfers to charitable organizations if the value of the property is required to be included in the gross estate. An inclusion would be necessary, for example, for property given away within three years of death.

The requirements for obtaining an estate tax charitable contribution deduction are essentially the same as those for the gift tax charitable contribution deduction, which we discussed in Chapter 16 (see pages **16**/9–10). The estate tax on a multimillion dollar estate may be zero if the decedent willed all, or almost all, of his or her property to charitable organizations or half to charitable organizations and the other half to his or her surviving spouse.

Marital deduction

In an attempt to provide more equal treatment for decedents of community property and common law states, Congress authorized an estate tax marital deduction. Only certain transfers to one's surviving spouse qualify for this deduction. The general idea is that in order for the estate to receive a marital deduction, the interest transferred must be subject to estate tax in the surviving spouse's estate or to gift tax if transferred during life by the surviving spouse. In other words, the surviving spouse may avoid transfer tax consequences only by consuming the property.

To qualify for the marital deduction, the interest must pass from the decedent to the surviving spouse in one of several circumstances. According to Sec. 2056(d), the interest must pass by:

1. Bequest or devise;
2. Inheritance (as a result of an intestate death);
3. Dower or curtesy right;
4. Gift from the decedent within three years of death;
5. Right of survivorship;
6. Appointment from the decedent under a general power of appointment or in default of appointment; or

7. Designation as beneficiary of an annuity or of a life insurance policy on the decedent's life.

In addition, the property must form part of the gross estate in order to generate a marital deduction. Thus, if the wife is the beneficiary of a life insurance policy on the husband's life, but the decedent, or husband, has no incidents of ownership in the policy, the husband's estate receives no marital deduction for the value of the policy. This item is not included in his gross estate.

The interest that passes to the surviving spouse must not be a "nondeductible terminable interest." A *terminable interest* is one that will cease upon the passage of time or the occurrence of some event. Not all terminable interests are ineligible for the marital deduction, however. For example, a patent has a life limited by law, yet it qualifies for the marital deduction. Nondeductible terminable interests have the following features in addition to being terminable:

1. The interest in the property must pass or have passed from the decedent to a person other than the surviving spouse for less than adequate consideration in money or money's worth; and
2. The other person may possess or enjoy any part of the property after the termination of the surviving spouse's interest.

The rules concerning qualification for the estate tax marital deduction are practically the same as those applicable for gift tax purposes. Because we discussed this topic in detail in the preceding chapter, we shall not discuss it in depth here (see pages **16**/8–9).

The Code limits the amount of the marital deduction to $250,000 or one-half the *adjusted gross estate,* whichever is greater. Before the Code was amended by the Tax Reform Act of 1976, the ceiling was simply one-half the adjusted gross estate. The change in the law is advantageous to smaller estates. It is now possible for a decedent whose gross estate slightly exceeds $250,000 to have a taxable estate of zero, provided the decedent leaves all his or her property to his or her spouse. Moreover, if the decedent's adjusted gross estate is approximately $425,000 and at least $250,000 passes to the surviving spouse in a qualifying manner, no estate tax will be due, provided the decedent dies after 1980 and made no adjusted taxable gifts. The tax on the $175,000 taxable estate will be eliminated by the unified credit. (See page **15**/6 for a discussion of unified credit.)

The *adjusted gross estate* is computed by deducting

from the gross estate the amount of debts, funeral and administrative expenses, and losses deducted on the estate tax return. The executor may choose to deduct administrative expenses on the estate tax return or on the fiduciary income tax return or some in each place. Thus, an election to deduct administrative expenses on the fiduciary income tax return may increase the maximum marital deduction. The adjusted gross estate is not reduced for charitable contribution deductions. For community property decedents, a special definition of adjusted gross estate exists, and the computation of the ceiling on the marital deduction is more complicated.

In certain circumstances, the general rule concerning the maximum marital deduction is modified. If a decedent made post-1976 gifts to his or her spouse, the maximum marital deduction may be reduced. The reduction is (a) the amount of the gift tax marital deduction allowed on post-1976 gifts *less* (b) the amount of the gift tax marital deduction that would have been available on post-1976 gifts if the deduction had been restricted to one-half the value of the gifts. No reduction is allowed, however, for gift tax marital deductions claimed on gifts made within three years of death.

Orphans' exclusion

In 1976 Congress expanded the estate tax deductions to include certain bequests and devises to a decedent's minor children. Section 2057(a) authorizes this deduction only if (1) the decedent is not survived by a spouse and (2) the decedent is survived by a minor child with no known living parent. Thus, the deduction is not available in every instance in which a minor child is orphaned.

> *Example:* A child's father dies and his mother remarries. The mother then dies, survived by her second husband. The orphans' exclusion is unavailable.

A minor child is one under the age of 21 at the time of the parent's death. Adopted children are treated as blood children.

The amount of the deduction is the value of the qualifying interest that passed or has passed to the minor child from the decedent. The rules for determining whether an interest passes or has passed from the decedent are the same as for the marital deduction. Just as with the marital deduction, no deduction is available for transfers of nondeductible terminable interests to minor children.

The Code imposes a ceiling on the orphans' exclusion. The deduction per child may not exceed $5,000 times the number of years by which 21 exceeds the age of the child on the decedent's date of death.

> *Example:* T died in 1980 survived by a 7-year-old son but no spouse. T willed assets valued at $200,000 to the son. The deduction for the bequest to the minor child is limited to $70,000 [$5,000 × (21 − 7 = 14)].

COMPUTATION AND PAYMENT OF THE ESTATE TAX

The value of the gross estate is reduced by the deductions discussed in the previous section to arrive at the amount of the taxable estate. Before 1977, the taxable estate was the tax base for the estate tax. Under the unification provisions effective after 1976, the estate tax base consists of the taxable estate plus the adjusted taxable gifts. The addition of the adjusted taxable gifts to the estate tax base probably will cause estates to be taxed at higher marginal rates. (Appendix A contains the unified rates.)

The "tentative estate tax" is calculated on the estate tax base. The unified credit and any gift taxes on post-1976 gifts reduce the tentative estate tax. In addition, the Code authorizes four additional credits: the state death tax credit, the credit for gift taxes paid on pre-1977 gifts, the credit for tax on prior transfers, and the foreign death tax credit. These credits, discussed briefly below, also lessen the estate tax payable.

In general, the estate tax is payable with the filing of the return. Under certain conditions, discussed below, the estate may postpone payment of some of the tax. In this section also, we shall illustrate the computation of the estate tax with an example.

Adjusted taxable gifts

As mentioned previously, adjusted taxable gifts increase the taxable estate. Section 2001(b) defines adjusted taxable gifts as those post-1976 taxable gifts that are not includible in the gross estate. Thus, a taxable gift made within three years of death, because it is automatically added to the gross estate, does not fall within the purview of adjusted taxable gifts. Adjusted taxable gifts are valued at date of gift values. In arriving at their amount, we refer to taxable gifts reported on the decedent's post-1976 gift tax returns. Any post-gift appreciation escapes inclusion in the tax base.

The statute allows some amelioration in the computation of the estate tax due. The tentative estate tax computed on the tax base is reduced by gift taxes paid on post-1976 gifts. Because of the unification of the estate and gift taxes and the requirement that adjusted taxable gifts be added to the estate tax base, the tax base is higher, which may force the estate into a higher marginal estate tax bracket.

The adjusted taxable gifts rule is illustrated with the following example.

Example: In October 1977, T made her first gift by deeding to A land valued at $503,000. Because it qualified for the annual exclusion, T's taxable gift was $500,000. After deduction of the $30,000 unified credit, her gift tax was $125,800. When T died in 1981, she owned stocks worth $600,000 and no other assets. The land given away had appreciated to $800,000. T's estate had no deductions. T's gross estate and taxable estate were $600,000. Her estate tax base was $1,100,000 because it included the $500,000 adjusted taxable gift. T's tentative estate tax of $386,800 (on her $1,100,000 tax base) was reduced by the gift taxes paid on the 1977 taxable gift ($125,800) and by the unified credit ($47,000). The estate tax payable was $214,000.

Gross estate		$600,000
Adjusted taxable gift		500,000
Tax base		$1,100,000
Tentative estate tax		$386,800
Less:		
Post-1976 gift taxes paid	$125,800	
Unified credit	47,000	172,800
Estate tax payable		$214,000

Credits against the estate tax

The Code authorizes five separate credits, which reduce the tax liability dollar for dollar. In addition, the Code allows a subtraction of the post-1976 gift taxes paid. Although, to be precise, this subtraction is not labeled in the Code as a credit, it operates the same way. Except for the unified credit, the purpose of the credits is to ameliorate the effect of taxing the same property twice.

UNIFIED CREDIT   The unified credit was introduced by the Tax Reform Act of 1976, which repealed the $30,000 gift tax exemption and the $60,000 estate tax exemption. The amount of the credit increases over the years. According to Sec. 2010(b), the size varies with the year of the decedent's death, as follows:

Year of death	Amount of unified credit
1977	$30,000
1978	34,000
1979	38,000
1980	42,500
1981 and later	47,000

In certain circumstances, the amount of the unified credit is altered downward. If the decedent claimed any portion of the $30,000 gift tax exemption against gifts made after September 8, 1976, the credit shown above is decreased in the amount of 20 percent of the exemption claimed against those gifts (Sec. 2010(b)).

In terms of the actual computations, the unified credit is available in calculating both the gift tax and the estate tax balance due. As a conceptual matter, however, only one unified credit exists. Any post-1976 taxable gifts not included in the gross estate are added to the taxable estate in computing the estate tax base on which the tentative tax is imposed. The post-1976 gift tax, which is subtracted from the tentative tax, is the amount of gift tax after subtracting the unified credit.

STATE DEATH TAX CREDIT   A credit is available for all types of death taxes (estate, inheritance, and so on) paid to a state or the District of Columbia. Nevada is the only state that does not levy some form of death tax. The amount of the credit may not exceed the smaller of: (1) the state death taxes actually paid, or (2) the credit amount specified in the Code for a given size of "adjusted taxable estate" (Sec. 2011(a) and (b)). Adjusted taxable estate is defined as the taxable estate less $60,000. Thus, adjusted taxable gifts do not affect the maximum state death tax credit.

CREDIT FOR GIFT TAX   Section 2012(a) authorizes a credit for gift taxes paid by the decedent on pre-1977 gifts that are required to be included in the gross estate. Recall that another provision allows a reduction for gift taxes paid on post-1976 gifts. The following transaction is an example of an event that would trigger the gift tax credit.

Example: In 1975 T created a trust from which he is to receive the income for life and T, Jr. is to receive the remainder. T paid a gift tax on the gift of the remainder. Upon T's death in 1980, the date of death value of the trust assets is included in his estate. T's estate will receive a gift tax credit for some or all of his 1975 gift taxes.

In general, the gift tax credit equals the amount of gift tax paid with respect to transfers included in the gross estate, but a ceiling for the credit, which must be computed also, may be lower than the amount of the gift tax paid. A discussion of the computation of the limit and the ceiling on the credits is beyond the scope of this book.

CREDIT FOR TAX ON PRIOR TRANSFERS   The credit for tax on prior transfers reduces the tax impact of property being taxed in more than one estate in quick succession. Without this credit, the overall tax cost could be quite severe if the legatee died soon after the original decedent. The credit applies if the person who transferred the property to the decedent in question died no more than 10 years before or two years after this particular decedent. The potential credit is (1) the federal estate tax of the transferor decedent that is attributable to the transferred interest or (2) the federal estate tax of the transferee decedent that is attributable to the transferred interest, whichever is smaller (Sec. 2013(c)).

To determine the final credit, the potential credit on a prior transfer is multiplied by a percentage that varies inversely with the period of time separating the two dates of death. If the transferor died less than two years before or after the decedent, the percentage is 100 percent. As specified in Sec. 2013(a), the other percentages are as follows:

Number of years by which transferor's death preceded decedent's	*Percentage*
3 or 4	80
5 or 6	60
7 or 8	40
9 or 10	20

FOREIGN DEATH TAX CREDIT   The estate is entitled to a credit for death taxes paid to a foreign country for property located in a foreign country and included in the gross estate. The maximum credit is the lesser of (1) the foreign death tax attributable to the property situated in the foreign country that imposed the tax, or (2) the federal estate tax attributable to the property situated in the foreign country and taxed by such country (Sec. 2014(b)).

Illustration of the computation of the estate tax

Figure 17-1 illustrates the general formula for the computation of the estate tax payable. In the following all-inclusive example, we shall illustrate the computation of the estate tax. Assume Ted, the decedent, made three gifts during life. In 1974 he gave his son $103,000 cash and claimed the $30,000 exemption then available and the $3,000 annual exclusion. In October 1978 Ted gave his daughter cash of $203,000. He gave his grandson land worth $103,000 in June 1979. The land had appreciated in value to $150,000 by the time Ted died in March 1982.

At Ted's date of death, checking accounts and savings accounts in his name had balances of $10,000 and $40,000, respectively. Stocks in Ted's name were worth $200,000 at his date of death. In 1977, his wife provided all the consideration for the purchase of land in the names of Mr. and Mrs. Ted, joint tenants with right of survivorship, and treated the acquisition as a gift. The land was worth $180,000 at the time Ted died. There were two life insurance policies on Ted's life. Policy A was for $100,000; Ted had incidents of ownership, and his wife was beneficiary. The son was owner and beneficiary of Policy B for $40,000. The son had purchased the policy in 1960. Ted's employer provided a qualified pension plan to which the employer made one-third of the contributions and the employees made two-thirds. As a result of surviving Ted, his wife is to receive an annuity valued at $60,000. The personal residence is in the names of Ted and his wife, tenants in common. Its total value is $100,000. Ted's mother, who died in 1950, created a testamentary trust from which Ted is to receive the income for life. Ted was authorized to make a testamentary disposition of the remainder to such of his descendants as he desired. The trust was valued at $225,000 upon Ted's death.

Other data concerning Ted's estate follows. Amount owed on a bank loan, including accrued interest, as of Ted's date of death was $10,200. Balances due on Ted's various charge accounts were $2,000. Ted's funeral expenses were $6,000. Administrative expenses to be deducted on the estate tax return were estimated to be $20,000.

Ted's will contained the following provisions:

(a) To my wife I leave my interest in the residence, my checking and savings accounts, and $100,000 in stocks.

(b) To State University I leave $10,000.

FIGURE **17-1**   Computation of Estate Tax Payable

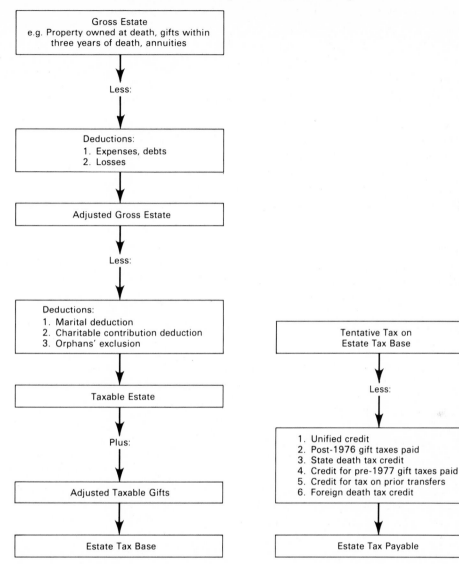

(c) To my grandson I leave the remainder of the trust created by my mother.

(d) To my son and my daughter I leave the residue of my estate in equal shares.

The balance due for Ted's estate tax is $60,383. We show how this tax was computed in Table 17-1 (page **17**/14). Additional tables (pages **17**/14 and **17**/15) illustrate the computation of various items (such as the marital deduction), which have an impact on the tax liability.

Life insurance Policy B was excluded from the gross estate because Ted had no incidents of ownership and his estate was not the beneficiary. The pension ben-

efits were not payable to the estate nor were they payable in a lump sum. Consequently, because the pension is a qualified plan, the contributions attributable to the employer are excluded from the gross estate. The trust created by Ted's mother does not constitute a part of Ted's gross estate. Ted had only a life estate and a special power of appointment. If Ted could have appointed the trust property to himself, his estate, his creditors, or the creditors of his estate, he would have had a general power of appointment and the value of the trust assets would have been included in his gross estate. The mother's testamentary trust is shielded by the grandfather clause from the generation-skipping transfer tax.

TABLE 17-1
COMPUTATION OF THE ESTATE TAX BALANCE DUE

Gross estate:		
Land given to grandson within three years of death (See Table 17-2)		$150,000
Gift tax paid on gift of land to grandson (Table 17-2)		30,000
Checking account		10,000
Savings account		40,000
Stocks		200,000
Land held in joint tenancy with right of survivorship (one-half includible; qualified joint interest)		90,000
Life insurance (Policy A)		100,000
Qualified pension plan (⅔ of $60,000)		40,000
One-half interest in personal residence		50,000
Gross estate		$710,000
Less debts and funeral and administrative expenses:		
Debts	$12,200	
Funeral expenses	6,000	
Administrative expenses	20,000	
Total		38,200
Adjusted gross estate		$671,800
Less marital and charitable contribution deductions:		
Marital deduction (See Table 17-3)	$335,900	
Charitable contribution deduction	10,000	
Total		345,900
Taxable estate		$325,900
Plus adjusted taxable gifts (See Table 17-4)		200,000
Estate tax base		$525,900
Tentative estate tax		$165,383
Less:		
Gift tax paid on post-1976 gifts (Table 17-2)	$58,000	
Unified credit	47,000	
Total		105,000
Balance due		$60,383

TABLE 17-2
COMPUTATION OF GIFT TAX

1974 taxable gift	$ 70,000
1978 taxable gift	$200,000
1979 taxable gift	$100,000
1978 gift tax:	
Tax on $270,000	$ 77,600
Less tax on $70,000	15,600
Tax on $200,000	$ 62,000
Less unified credit	34,000
Amount of gift tax	$ 28,000
1979 gift tax:	
Tax on $370,000	$111,600
Less tax on $270,000	77,600
Tax on $100,000	$ 34,000
Less unused portion of unified credit ($38,000 − $34,000)	4,000
Amount of gift tax	$ 30,000

Total gift tax on post-1976 gifts is $58,000.
The above computations assume that gift splitting was not elected.

SPECIAL RULES FOR CERTAIN INTERESTS IN A CLOSELY HELD BUSINESS Two different Code sections authorize installment payment of the tax if an interest in a closely held business forms a certain portion of the estate. The criteria specified in the two sections are slightly different. The closely held business interest may be in proprietorship, partnership, or corporate form.

The statute defines the exact requirements for clas-

TABLE 17-3
COMPUTATION OF MARITAL DEDUCTION

Property passing to surviving spouse in qualifying manner:	
Residence	$ 50,000[a]
Checking account	10,000[a]
Savings account	40,000[a]
Stocks	100,000[a]
Land in joint tenancy	90,000
Life insurance (Policy A)	100,000
Qualified pension plan (limited to amount included in gross estate)	40,000
Total	$430,000

Maximum marital deduction:
Greater of:
(a) $250,000
   or
(b) One-half the adjusted gross estate = ½ of $671,800 = $335,900

[a]Denotes items passing under T's will.

Payment of the estate tax

GENERAL RULE   Unless the estate meets one of several conditions, the entire amount of the estate tax is payable when the estate tax return is filed. The due date for the return is nine months after the decedent's date of death. As we shall see, however, several Code sections provide for lengthening the payment period.

The Secretary of the Treasury may extend the payment date for a "reasonable period," defined by Sec. 6161(a)(1) as not more than 12 months. Moreover, if the executor shows "reasonable cause," the Secretary may extend the payment date for a maximum period of 10 years (Sec. 6161(a)(20)).

TABLE **17-4**

ADJUSTED TAXABLE GIFTS

Post-1976 taxable gifts other than those included in gross estate: 1978 taxable gift	$200,000*a*

*a*Included at date of gift value.

sifying partnerships and corporations as closely held businesses. If the value of the closely held business interest exceeds 65 percent of the value of the gross estate less allowable deductions for debts, funeral and administrative expenses, and losses, the executor may elect to pay a portion of the tax in as few as two and as many as 10 annual installments. The first installment is not due until five years after the due date for the return. During the five-year interim, only interest is payable. The portion of the tax that qualifies for installment payment is represented by the ratio of the value of the closely held business interest to the adjusted gross estate (Sec. 6166). The interest rate is only 4 percent on an amount of deferred estate tax not in excess of $345,800 less the amount of the unified credit.

Example: T died in 1981. His gross estate consisted of $100,000 of cash, $400,000 of stock in a closely held corporation, and $120,000 of land. His only deductions were for $20,000 of debts. T was unmarried and had made no lifetime gifts.

T's taxable estate is $600,000, and his estate tax is $145,800, after subtracting the unified credit.

T's estate qualifies for Sec. 6166 because it meets the more than 65 percent test.

$$\frac{400,000}{620,000 - 20,000} > 65\%$$

The fraction of T's estate that may be paid in installments is as follows:

$$\frac{400,000}{600,000} \times \$145,800$$

Section 6166A authorizes installment payments if the value of the closely held business interest is greater than 35 percent of the gross estate or 50 percent of the taxable estate. As many as 10 equal annual installments may be paid. The first installment is due at the time the return is filed. The interest rate imposed on the balance due varies with the prime rate. The portion of the tax eligible for installment payment is the same

as the ratio of the value of the closely held business interest to the value of the gross estate.

Example: Assume the same facts as in the previous example, except that T's stock is worth $250,000 and his land is worth $270,000. His gross estate is still $620,000, his taxable estate is $600,000, and his estate tax is $145,800.

The closely held business interest makes up more than 35 percent of his gross estate.

$$\frac{250,000}{620,000} > 35\%$$

Because his estate meets one of the percentage tests, it qualifies for Sec. 6166A. The portion of T's estate tax that may be paid in installments is as follows:

$$\frac{250,000}{620,000} \times \$145,800$$

STOCK REDEMPTIONS TO PAY DEATH TAXES   As pointed out in another portion of this book (Chapter 5), stock redemptions often trigger dividend income to the stockholder from whom the shares are redeemed. If certain tests are met, however, a redemption to pay death taxes will result in capital gain or capital loss. To be eligible for this special treatment, the value of the decedent's stock must make up more than 50 percent of the value of the decedent's gross estate, reduced by the amount of allowable deductions for debts, funeral and administrative expenses, and losses (Sec. 303 (b)(2)).

Only a certain amount of stock will receive capital gain or loss treatment upon redemption. The maximum amount eligible for such status is an amount equal to (1) federal and state death taxes (including interest) imposed, plus (2) allowable funeral and administrative expenses. Moreover, capital gain or loss classification is available only to the extent that the shareholder from whom the stock is redeemed is required to pay death taxes or funeral or administrative expenses.

TAX PLANNING TO MINIMIZE THE ESTATE TAX BURDEN

Many of the pre-1977 strategies for reducing the amount of the estate tax no longer provide as great an opportunity for tax savings as they did before the passage of the Tax Reform Act of 1976. Gifts are no longer taxed at rates three-quarters as high as the estate tax rates; the rates are now the same. Post-1976 taxable gifts are automatically added to the estate tax base. All gifts made within three years of death automatically make up a part of the gross estate. A gift may no longer be excluded on the grounds that it was not given in contemplation of death. Even gift taxes paid on gifts made within three years of death increase the gross estate. Counterbalancing these changes to some extent, a higher tax base must be reached before any tax is due, and a higher maximum marital deduction is allowed for estates of $500,000 or less.

Opportunities still exist, however, for minimizing estate taxes. One of the most significant strategies is a well-designed, long-term gift program. As long as the gifts to each donee do not exceed the annual exclusion, there will be no additions to the gross estate and no adjusted taxable gifts. If enough donees are selected, and if gifts are made over a substantial number of years, thousands of dollars of property may be passed to others free of transfer tax consequences. If taxable gifts do occur, any post-gift appreciation is removed from the estate tax base, provided the donor survives the gift by more than three years. Moreover, if the donor survives the gift by more than three years, the gift tax paid is removed from the gross estate. An individual's judicious selection of the properties that are to be the subject of his or her lifetime transfers may also improve the chance that his or her estate will qualify for installment payment of the estate taxes. Of course, the individual must own an interest in a closely held business and must survive the transfer by more than

three years. These opportunities for saving transfer taxes should be weighed against the sacrifice of the step-up in basis that would result if the property were retained until death.

SUMMARY

The starting point for calculation of the tax base on which the tentative tax is levied is the valuation of the myriad of property interests included in the gross estate. All items are valued at date of death values or alternate valuation date values. The gross estate is then reduced by debts, losses, and funeral and administrative expenses in order to arrive at the size of the adjusted gross estate, a figure significant for computing the maximum marital deduction. The taxable estate consists of the adjusted gross estate less marital deduction, charitable contribution deduction, and orphans' exclusion. Adjusted taxable gifts are added (at date of gift values) to the taxable estate to arrive at the estate tax base.

A tentative tax is calculated on the estate tax base. This amount is decreased by the unified credit and post-1976 gift taxes paid by the decedent. Four additional credits (the state death tax credit, the credit for pre-1977 gift taxes paid, the credit for tax on prior transfers, and the foreign death tax credit) may reduce the balance due. In general, the estate tax is due when the estate tax return is filed. In certain circumstances, however, the estate may qualify for deferred payment of some or all of the taxes.

PROBLEMS

1. a. Items included in the gross estate are valued as of what date?
    b. In general, for estate tax purposes, at what amount are items valued?
    c. Are there any exceptions to the general valuation rule, which was the answer to part b? If so, explain.
    d. Does the exception, if any, mentioned in part c apply for gift tax purposes also?
2. Kay Kudinsky died August 5, 19X4. Her executor elected date of death valuation. Kay's gross estate included the items listed below. What is the estate tax value of each item?
    a. 100 shares of ABC common stock, traded on August 5 at high of 102, low of 92, and close of 93.
    b. 1,000 shares of Up-N-Down Mutual Fund (an open-end investment company); quotes as of August 5 were bid of 42 and asked of 45.
    c. Life insurance policy on life of Meredith Donald (Kay's sister); face value of $250,000 and replacement cost on August 5 of $74,200.

d. Life insurance policy on Kay's own life; face value of $125,000 and replacement cost of $37,125 immediately prior to Kay's death on August 5.

e. Personal residence at 457 Elm Street; an almost identical residence one block away was sold for $87,000 on July 18.

3. L.D. Lee died February 3, 19X2. His gross estate included the items listed below. His executors elected the alternate valuation date. At what amount will each of the items be valued?

Item	Date of death value	Value on August 3, 19X2	Other information
ZZZ stock	$280,000	$262,000	
MNO stock	127,000	116,000	Sold July 2, 19X2 for $118,000.
Land	75,000	78,000	Sold October 5, 19X2 for $81,000.
BTD stock	35,000	39,000	
Cash dividend on BTD stock	0	720	Declared May 1, 19X2 and payable July 1, 19X2.

4. Assume the gross estate of D is valued at $1,200,000 if date of death valuation is used and $1,420,000 if the alternate valuation date is elected. Why might the executor elect the alternate valuation date?

5. Why did Congress amend the Code to provide for special use valuation?

6. Frank Farmer died October 4, 19X6. His gross estate consisted of the following items:

Cash and stocks $300,000 fair market value
Farm land (1,000 acres) 800,000 fair market value

Frank had no debts.

For the past 25 years Frank had materially participated in farming the land. He willed the land to his daughter Katrina, who plans to continue materially participating in farming.

The following figures are averages for the years 19X1–19X5:

Annual gross cash rent for comparable land in the same locality $58 per acre
Annual real estate taxes for comparable land $2 per acre
Annual effective interest rate for all new loans by Federal Land Bank in this area 11%

a. Does Frank's estate qualify for the special use valuation? If so, at what amount will the farm land be valued if special use valuation is elected? Show your computations.

b. Assume Frank's farm land had a fair market value of $1,200,000. Now answer part a.

7. D died intestate (without a will) in a state in which a law provides that the surviving spouse of intestate decedents receives one-third of the decedent's property. D owned property valued at $3 million. What is the value of his gross estate? In other words, does his gross estate include the $1 million that must pass to his widow according to state law?

8. a. Tillie Taylor died March 5, 1974. On May 3, 1972 she gave stock then worth $400,000 to her daughter. The stock was valued at $620,000 when Tillie died. Does Tillie's gross estate *automatically* include the stock? If the stock is included in Tillie's estate, regardless of whether or not it is automatically included, at what amount is it valued?

b. Same as part a, except Tillie made the gift in 1982 and died in 1984.

c. Same as part b, except Tillie made the gift in 1978.

9. a. In 19X1 Don Davis set up a trust and funded it with $400,000 of assets. He named a bank trustee. The trust instrument provided that the income is payable to Don annually for life. Upon Don's death, the assets are to be divided equally among Don's descendants. Don died in 19X9 at the age of 72. The trust assets were then worth $560,000. What amount, if any, is included in Don's estate?

b. In 19X2 Don transferred title to his personal residence to his daughter Donna. Don continued to live in the residence until his death. He did not pay any rent to Donna. At Don's death in 19X9, the residence was worth $85,000 compared with its $50,000 value in 19X1. What portion, if any, of the value of the residence is included in Don's estate?

c. In 19X2 Don created a trust and funded it with $200,000. The value of the trust fund had risen to $310,000 by the time Don died in 19X9. Don named himself trustee. According to the trust agreement, all the trust income is to be paid out annually for 25 years. The trustee, however, is to decide how much income to pay each year to each of the three beneficiaries—Don's children. Upon termination of the trust, the assets are to be distributed equally among Don's three children or their estates. What portion, if any, of the trust is included in Don's estate?

d. Same as part c, except the trustee is a bank.

e. In 19X3 Don created a revocable trust with a bank trustee. He named his grandchild Ben beneficiary for life. Upon Ben's death, the property is to be distributed equally among Ben's descendants. The trust assets were worth $400,000 when Don died in 19X9. What portion, if any, of the trust assets is included in Don's estate?

10. Ann Anthony died in 19X9. At the time of her death, she was covered by the annuities listed below. Which ones are included in her estate? If there is only a partial inclusion, indicate the amount of the inclusion.

a. An annuity purchased by Ann and payable for the rest of her life only.

b. An annuity purchased by Ann and payable to her for life. Upon the death of Ann, an annuity valued at $15,000 is payable to Ann's sister Gertrude.

c. An annuity purchased by Ann's employer and payable to Ann for life, beginning with the date of her retirement. Upon Ann's death, an annuity valued at $80,000 is payable to Ann's son. The annuity was payable under a qualified plan.

d. Same as part c, except $40,000 is to be paid to Ann's son in a lump sum. The son did not elect to forego the more favorable income tax treatment on the lump-sum distribution.

e. Same as part c, except the employer paid 80 percent and Ann paid 20 percent of the contributions to the plan.

11. a. In 19X1 Tom Hall purchased stock for $40,000 and had it titled in the names of himself and his brother Ron as joint tenants with right of survivorship. Tom died in 19X9, survived by Ron. In 19X9 the stock's value was $88,000. What amount is included in Tom's gross estate?

b. Refer to part a, but assume Ron died, survived by Tom, at a time when the stock was worth $60,000. What amount is included in Ron's gross estate?

c. In 1978 H purchased land for $100,000 and had it titled in the names of H and his wife, W, as joint tenants with right of survivorship. He elected to report the transaction as a gift. H died in 1988, survived by W. The land was then worth $180,000. What amount is included in H's gross estate?

    d.   Same as part c, except H did *not* report the acquisition as a gift.

    e.   Same as part c, except W died, survived by H. At W's date of death, the property was worth $150,000. How much is included in W's estate?

    f.   Refer to part e. What fraction of the land's value will be included in H's estate when he dies subsequent to W's death?

12.   Steve Sokolov died March 15, 1988. He was the beneficiary for life of each of the trusts listed below. Indicate which of the trusts are included in Steve's gross estate. Explain the rationale for your answers.

    a.   A trust created under the will of Steve's mother, who died in 1955. Upon Steve's death the trust assets are to pass to such of Steve's decendants as he directs by his will. Should Steve fail to appoint the trust property, the trust assets are to be distributed to the Smithsonian Institution. Steve willed the property to his twins in equal shares.

    b.   An *inter vivos* trust created in 1960 by Steve's father. The trust agreement authorized Steve to appoint the property to "whomever he so desired." The appointment could be made only by his will. Steve appointed the property to his elderly neighbor Waldo.

    c.   A trust created by Steve in 1963. Upon Steve's death the property is to pass to State University.

    d.   A trust created under the will of Steve's grandmother, who died in 1937. Her will authorized Steve to appoint the property by his will to "whomever he so desired." In default of appointment, the property is to pass to Steve's descendants in equal shares. Steve's will did not mention this trust.

    e.   Same as part b, except Steve's will did not mention the trust property.

13.   Simone Soulé died May 5, 19X2. Immediately after her death, the following life insurance policies were discovered. Which ones are included in her gross estate? Explain the rationale for your answer. For those policies that are included, indicate the value (face value or some other amount) of the inclusion.

    a.   Life of Idaho policy; owner—Simone's sister; beneficiary—Estate of Simone Soulé; purchased by her sister 20 years ago; insured—Simone.

    b.   Inequitable Assurance policy; owner—Simone Soulé; beneficiary—Simone's husband; purchased by Simone 25 years ago; insured—Simone.

    c.   Group-term policy paid for by her employer; owner—Simone Soulé; beneficiary—Simone's husband; policy has been in existence for 15 years; insured—Simone.

    d.   Vagabonds Insurance Company policy; owner—Simone Soulé; beneficiary—Simone Soulé or her estate; purchased by Simone's father 16 years ago and given to Simone as owner 2 years ago; insured—Simone's father.

    e.   Chunk-of-the-Earth Insurance Company policy; owner—Simone's daughter; beneficiary—Simone's granddaughter; purchased by Simone 17 years ago and given to her daughter 2 years ago; insured—Simone Soulé. Simone has paid all the premiums.

14.   What are some examples of incidents of ownership?

15.   H and his wife, W, were residents of Texas, a community-property state. H died, survived by W. At the time of H's death, the couple's community property was valued at $2.6 million. What portion of this property is included in H's gross estate?

16.   Will Giver died November 15, 19X3. At the time he died, he owned property valued at $2 million. His will provided that his surviving spouse was to receive "an amount equal to the maximum estate tax marital deduction." In 19X2, Will transferred $200,000 cash to State University. Assume he had debts of $40,000 but had no funeral or administrative expenses.

    a. Compute his adjusted gross estate.

    b. Compute his taxable estate.

17. a. Tex Tavis died June 5, 19X2. At the time he died, his gross estate was valued at \$1,300,000. He had debts of \$500,000. His funeral and administrative expenses were \$30,000. The administrative expenses will be deducted on his estate tax return.

        Tex's will left \$10,000 to State University. He willed his wife stock valued at \$200,000. His will called for setting up a \$300,000 trust fund from which his widow is to receive the income for life. Upon her death, the trust assets will be distributed to their descendants in equal shares.

        Compute Tex's *adjusted gross estate* and his *taxable estate*.

    b. Same as part a, except Tex willed his surviving spouse property valued at \$420,000. She will receive this property outright. Tex's will did not create any trusts.

18. a. Mary and Mart Miller married in 1972. They had two children. In 1978 Mart died; Mary did not remarry. Mary died in 1984, survived by their two children, who were then 8 and 10 years old. Mary's adjusted gross estate was \$300,000. She willed everything to the two children in equal amounts. Compute Mary's *taxable estate* and her *estate tax balance due*. (Assume she made no lifetime gifts.)

    b. Same as part a, except Mary remarried in 1983. She was survived by her second husband and her two children.

19. a. T died in 1988. He never married. At the time he died, his sole asset was cash of \$800,000. Assume no debts or funeral and administrative expenses. His gift history is as follows:

Date	Amount of taxable gifts	Fair market value of gift property at date of death
Oct. 1977	\$250,000	\$290,000
Oct. 1981	70,000	85,000

        Compute T's estate tax base and his estate tax balance due.

    b. Refer to part a, but assume the second gift was made in 1987 instead of in 1981.

    c. Refer to part a, but assume the first gift was made in 1974 instead of in 1977.

20. In each of the following cases, D died in 1988, survived by her husband. For each case, compute her maximum estate tax marital deduction.

Case	Adjusted gross estate	Post-1976 gifts to D's spouse[a]	Amount of bequests to spouse that qualify for marital deduction[b]	Maximum marital deduction
A	\$800,000	\$ -0-	\$520,000	_____
B	800,000	100,000	425,000	_____
C	800,000	120,000	425,000	_____
D	800,000	220,000	425,000	_____
E	800,000	100,000	425,000	_____

[a]Except for the gift in case E, all gifts were made in 1981. In case E, D made the gift in 1986.
[b]This column indicates the amount that would be deductible as a marital deduction if there were no ceiling on the marital deduction.

21. a. In general, by what date must the estate tax be paid?
    b. Describe any exceptions to this general rule.

22. Otto Shrunk died July 4, 1985, survived by his spouse, Susie, two sons, Ben and Winn, and several grandchildren. He made only one taxable gift during his lifetime: In 1984 he gave Ben stock then worth $253,000. By the time Otto died, the stock had appreciated to $350,000.

    Otto's executor discovered the property listed below. The values shown are values as of July 4, 1985.

a.	Cash in checking account in Otto's name	$60,000
b.	Cash in savings account in Otto's name	30,000
c.	Stock in names of Otto and Winn as joint tenants with right of survivorship. Otto paid for the stock in 1961	10,000
d.	Land in names of Otto and Susie, as joint tenants with right of survivorship. Susie bought the land in 1977 and did *not* elect to treat the transaction as a gift	60,000
e.	Personal residence in Otto's name	150,000
f.	Life insurance on Otto's life; Otto was owner and Susie was beneficiary; face value	300,000
g.	Qualified retirement plan of Otto's employer; the employer made 60 percent of the contributions and Otto made 40 percent; value of annuity payable to Winn	40,000

    When Otto died he owed $10,000 on a two-year note payable to First Bank. Interest at 12 percent was last paid on April 4, 1985. His funeral and administrative expenses were $35,000. Administrative expenses will be deducted on his estate tax return. Excerpts from Otto's will follow: "I leave $2,000 to the National Gallery of Art. I leave the residence to my beloved wife, Susie. The rest of my property I leave to my two sons in equal shares."
    Compute the following:
    (1) Otto's gross estate
    (2) Otto's adjusted gross estate
    (3) Otto's maximum marital deduction
    (4) Otto's taxable estate
    (5) Otto's estate tax base
    (6) Otto's tentative estate tax
    (7) Otto's estate tax balance due

SUPPLEMENTAL PROBLEMS

23. Dee Cedent died January 1, 1979. Her estate tax return was filed September 29, 1979. A major portion of her estate consisted of an interest in a closely held business. Her executor elected under Sec. 6166A to pay the estate tax in 10 equal annual installments.

    On August 5, 1982 the audit of Dee's estate tax return was almost finished. Interest paid to the government with respect to the estate tax being paid in installments has not been deducted on the estate's income tax returns. The interest is an allowable expense of administration per state law. May Dee's estate deduct the interest (payable on the taxes paid in installments) as an administrative expense on the estate tax return? Explain your answer. Include appropriate citations.

24. Hal and Helen Harper were married in 1970. Both had been married previously.

Each had a child by a previous marriage. Hal's child (Herman) was age 26 in 1985. Helen's child (Emily) was age 23 in 1985. Hal died in 1985, survived by Helen, Herman, and Emily.

In April 1974, Helen and Hal each set up a trust funded with stock then worth $400,000. Each trust fund had appreciated to $520,000 by 1985. Each trust was to last 20 years. At the end of the 20th year, corpus and any accumulated income were to be distributed equally between Herman and Emily or their estates.

Hal was named trustee of the trust created by Helen. Helen was named trustee of the trust Hal set up. Each trust provides that the trustee has sole discretion to decide what portion of the trust income or corpus is to be distributed to each of the two beneficiaries (Herman and Emily) each year.

a. What were Hal and Helen trying to accomplish with this "sophisticated" arrangement?

b. With respect to the above transaction, will there be an inclusion in Hal's gross estate? Explain. Cite appropriate authorities.

25. In 1965 Morris Moscowitz purchased a house and lot near Orlando, Florida. It was his practice to live in the house during the months of November through March. The rest of the year, he rented the house to various tenants. In 1975 Morris deeded the house and lot to his adult daughter, Brenda M. Gonzalez. The deed specified, however, that Morris was to have the right to use the residence rent-free each January and February. Brenda rented the house out for the remaining 10 months of the year.

Morris died in 1985, when the house and lot were valued at $84,000. In the year of Morris's death, Brenda rented the property for $700 per month in March, November, and December and for $620 per month for April through October. Comparable properties were rented for $720 per month in January and February of the year of Morris's death.

With respect to the Florida property, what amount, if any, is included in Morris's gross estate? Explain your answer. Cite proper authorities.

26. In 1948 Molly May Guire purchased land costing $10,000. In 1956, when the land was worth $18,000, she deeded it to her two sons (Garwood and Gerald) as joint tenants with right of survivorship. The sons held the land until 1970, when they sold it for $78,000. They divided the sales proceeds equally. Later in 1970, Gerald took his half of the sales proceeds ($39,000) and used that amount to purchase Big Bird Airlines, Inc. stock. He registered the stock in the names of "Gerald Guire and Molly May Guire, joint tenants with right of survivorship." Molly died in 1983, survived by Gerald. At that time the airline stock was worth $58,000.

What portion, if any, of the stock's value is included in Molly's estate?

27. Roscoe Rountree owned a number of acres of land. One month before he died, Roscoe signed an installment land sale contract. The buyer paid 28 percent down (this amount is nonrefundable) and agreed to pay the remainder plus interest in installments. The installments are to be paid over the next 18 years. According to the contract, the deed is to be placed in escrow for the period of the installment payments. If the purchaser defaults on any payments, the seller will have the right to receive all remaining proceeds of the contract.

Roscoe willed all his personal property to his surviving spouse, Rhoda, age 75. He willed his real property to Rudolph, his son. Under state law (of the state in which the real estate is located), the interest in the land became an interest in personal property effective on the date the contract to sell was signed. Under state law, on Roscoe's death, the right to receive the proceeds of the contract vested in

Rhoda. If Rhoda dies before the end of 18 years, her will will control who receives the future installment payments.

Does the right to the proceeds of the installment contract constitute a terminable interest? Will Roscoe's estate be entitled to a marital deduction for the bequest of the right to the proceeds of the installment land sale contract? Explain your answer. Cite appropriate authorities.

28. Mavis Adams transferred ownership of a $500,000 life insurance policy on her life to her husband, Quentin. Quentin died in 1972, survived by Mavis and their daughter Abby Gail. In accordance with Quentin's will, the $500,000 life insurance policy and a number of other assets passed into a testamentary trust. Mavis was named to receive the trust income at least annually for the rest of her life. Upon Mavis's death the trust assets are to pass outright to Abby Gail. Quentin's will named Mavis and Abby Gail cotrustees of the trust.

Quentin's will contained the following provision concerning the testamentary trust: "No trustee shall be answerable to any subsequent beneficiary for anything done or omitted in favor of the income beneficiary, but the income beneficiary may not compel such favorable treatment." The life insurance policy authorized the policy owner (in this case the cotrustees) to receive cash dividends instead of applying the policy dividends toward the payment of premiums or toward the purchase of additional insurance; to cash in the policy for its cash surrender value; to borrow against the loan value of the policy; and to assign the policy as security for loans.

Mavis died in 1986 while serving as cotrustee of the trust. Is the $500,000 life insurance policy included in Mavis's gross estate? Explain your answer. Cite proper authorities. Do you have any belated advice for Mavis?

RETURN PROBLEM

Julio Galleo (aged 61) and his wife Earnestina (aged 63) had lived in Hendersonville, North Carolina, for 20 years at the time of Earnestina's death on December 15, 1981. They were parents of two children, Earnest and Juliette (38-year-old twins). They have four grandchildren (aged 5 through 10). Life-long North Carolina residents, they were married January 1, 1937.

In 1960 Earnestina took $200,000 inherited from her father and bought farm land on which she grew apples. Julio's brother agreed to buy and market all the apples Earnestina's acreage produced. Through 1981 Earnestina continued to sell all the apples from her orchard to Julio's brother.

Earnestina was quite involved in her apple-raising venture. She selected the types of apples to be grown, continually studied methods of increasing orchard production, hired employees, and negotiated sales for the orchard. She even manually worked in the orchard approximately 37 hours a week.

Earnestina's orchard comprised 500 acres. In 1974 Earnestina refinanced the land. At her death, the balance due on the mortgage secured by the land was $100,000. The interest rate on the mortgage is 8 percent. Earnestina last made a mortgage payment on December 1, 1981.

Earnestina's orchard is about 15 miles from Hendersonville. In that locality, the average cash rent per acre is $150. Average property taxes are $25 per acre. An appraiser appraised Earnestina's land at $2,000 per acre. All apples were harvested and sold before Earnestina died.

Earnestina used additional funds to purchase equipment used in the operation of the orchard. An appraiser estimated that the equipment was worth $200,000 at her date of death.

Earnestina and Julio lived in downtown Hendersonville in a nineteenth-century mansion that they purchased and restored. The house and lot are valued at $250,000 total and the household furnishings at $50,000 total. They own the mansion and furnishings as tenants in common.

In 1961 Earnestina and Julio purchased a 50-acre tract of land that had mountain spring water on it. Julio paid $10,000 consideration and Earnestina paid $20,000. The property was titled in the names of Earnestina and Julio, joint tenants with right of survivorship. The fair market value was $90,000 total at Earnestina's date of death.

Other assets discovered are as follows (amounts shown represent date of death values).

(1) Checking account, Hendersonville State Bank, in names of Julio and Earnestina as tenants in common	$8,000
(2) Savings account at Tarheel Savings & Loan in Earnestina's name	4,400
(3) Jeep Wagoneer in Earnestina's name (wholesale value—$5,000, retail value—$7,000)	?
(4) $100,000 life insurance policy on Earnestina's life. Earnestina had incidents of ownership. Beneficiary is Earnestina's estate. Cash surrender value at her date of death was $62,000. Policy No. 1459.	?

Outstanding debts (other than the mortgage mentioned earlier) at Earnestina's date of death were:

Downtown Dress Shoppe, for purchase of various articles of clothing	$870
Accrued salaries for orchard workers	1,250

Her funeral expenses totaled $2,500. Administrative expenses are estimated to be $50,000.

Before her death, Earnestina made the gifts listed below. She *never* elected gift splitting. She claimed the $30,000 exemption as early as possible.

(1) In March 1970, Earnestina transferred to Julio all incidents of ownership in a $25,000 life insurance policy on her life. Julio changed the beneficiary designation to Earnest. The policy was purchased January 1, 1948. Through 1970 she paid the annual premiums of $250. From 1971 to 1981 Julio paid the premiums. In 1970 the value of the gift was $7,000. Policy No. XL427K.

(2) In 1974 Earnestina gave *each* of their two children stock valued at $30,000. At her date of death, the stocks had appreciated to an aggregate value of $150,000.

(3) In 1980 Earnestina gave Juliette turquoise jewelry inherited from her Aunt Minnie in 1960. It was valued at $14,000 when given away and $16,000 at her date of death.

(4) In 1980 Earnestina gave Earnest land, which was worth $400,000 when given away and $420,000 at her date of death.

(5) In 1980 Earnestina gave Julio stocks worth $18,000. They had declined in value to $12,000 by her date of death.

(6) In 1980 she gave First Baptist Church of Hendersonville $5,000 cash.

Pertinent provisions of Earnestina's will are as follows:

To my beloved husband, Julio, I leave my 500 acres of orchard lands and my interest in our home and its furnishings and my automobiles (or other motor vehicles).

The residue of my estate I leave in trust for my children, Juliette and Earnest, for life. Upon the death of the survivor, the property is to be distributed equally among my descendants. Third State Bank is to serve as trustee.

Other information:

Earnestina's estate tax marginal rate is estimated to be higher than her estate's marginal income tax rate. Assume the state estate tax is equal to the maximum state death tax credit. Assume the average annual interest rate for loans by the Federal Land Bank was 11 percent.

After Earnestina's death, Julio began working in the orchards full time. He has no plans to cease raising apples.

Instructions:

Prepare Earnestina's estate tax return. Date of death valuation is elected. Make assumptions (such as Social Security number) that do not affect the tax liability.

the generation-skipping transfer tax

When Nelson Rockefeller died in January 1979, his estate was estimated to be worth $66.5 million.[1] That report hastened to add that the deceased had enjoyed the benefits from a considerably larger treasure-trove estimated at something between $250 and $500 million. No doubt, the general public was reassured that John D., Senior's fortune had not wasted away in the hands of his progeny. For those knowledgeable in tax matters, however, the news story reveals somewhat more. First, the transfer taxes levied by the federal government have not denied successive generations all John D., Senior's bounty. Second, the older Rockefellers evidently received sound tax advice and used generation-skipping arrangements extensively.

What kinds of legal arrangements can account for an estate of only $66.5 million yet enjoyment of a store of wealth possibly as large as $500 million? Suppose that upon the death of John D., Senior, part of his wealth was left in trust with his great-grandchildren, the children of Nelson, the ultimate beneficiaries. Suppose also that Nelson, John D.'s grandson, was given a life estate in the trust property. During life, Nelson would enjoy the income from the property but nothing would be included in his estate because his income interest expires upon his death. Owing to the retained interest rule of Sec. 2036, the trust corpus is not included in Nelson's estate upon his death because Nelson was not the grantor of the trust. The corpus of the trust escapes the estate tax until the deaths of Nelson's children (or grandchildren), who receive outright ownership of the trust property after Nelson's death.

Before 1976, arrangements such as the one described successfully avoided the federal wealth transfer taxes for one or more generations. In this chapter, we shall describe a tax imposed by the Tax Reform Act of 1976 that is designed to curb the use of generation-skipping transfers.

GENERATION-SKIPPING TRANSFERS DEFINED

Congress had been aware of the benefits available to taxpayers through generation-skipping transfers for many years before 1976. This "loophole" attracted considerable attention in the 1960s owing to a statistical study of estate tax returns for the years 1957–59. The study found that:

> Among husbands with estates below $500,000 who established family trusts on their death, 77 percent set up trusts which involved no generation skipping; but among husbands with estates over $2 million who established family trusts, only 25 percent set up trusts which involved no generation skipping and 60 percent made their trust bequests entirely in generation skipping form.[2]

Taxpayers with large estates could meet the financial needs of their children and perhaps their grandchildren by leaving them an income interest only. Direct ownership of the wealth could be delayed for one or more generations, thereby avoiding the transfer tax. For taxpayers with smaller estates, however, an income inter-

[1] *Dallas Morning News,* February 10, 1979, page 1, from wire service reports.

[2] U.S. Treasury Department, *Reform Studies and Proposals,* 91st Congress, 1st Session (U.S. Government Printing Office, 1969) p. 388.

est would not be enough to make the next generation secure.

Armed with these facts, the Treasury proposed in 1969 that Congress levy a tax on generation-skipping transfers. The proposal languished until 1976, when Congress steeled itself to consider general reform of the estate and gift taxes. The law finally adopted, which constitutes Chapter 13 of the Internal Revenue Code, imposes a transfer tax as the wealth passes between each generation that has an interest in or power over the property *as though* such generation owned the property outright. This taxation of an *imaginary* ownership of property involves a number of new terms and concepts.

A simple illustration of how the tax is imposed

Section 2601 provides: "A tax is hereby imposed on every generation-skipping transfer," and thus focuses attention on the definition of a single critical term, *generation-skipping transfer*. Congress has not presumed to tell every taxpayer that he or she must leave his or her wealth to the first succeeding generation. Grandmother may leave her wealth to granddaughter. The fact that the daughter is skipped does not produce a "generation-skipping transfer." If, however, the daughter is given a proscribed interest in or power over the property along with the granddaughter, then a generation-skipping transfer results and the penalty tax is imposed. While this example conveys the general notion behind the tax, some specific terms and their particular statutory meanings must be mastered before the reach of this new tax may be appreciated. Before turning to the technical provisions, a simple example of how the tax is computed will be helpful.

The rules attempt to levy a tax on the property *as though* the skipped generation with an interest in or power over the property had owned it outright.

> *Example:* Assume that grandmother dies in 1982 and leaves her after-tax estate in trust with a life estate to her daughter, D, and the remainder to her granddaughter, GD. When D dies in 1983, her taxable estate is $1.5 million. D has made no lifetime gifts subject to the federal transfer tax and had no interest in other trusts that might be subject to the tax on generation-skipping transfers. At D's death, the value of the property held by the trust in which D held a life estate is $1.45 million.
>
> Note, first, that D is subject to the usual estate tax on the $1.5 million of her own estate. Second, because the trust is terminated, a tax is levied on

the generation-skipping transfer, computed in the following manner:

Daughter's taxable estate	$1,500,000
Value of property involved in generation-skipping transfer, less $250,000 exclusion	$1,200,000
Total transfer base	$2,700,000
Tax on $2.7 million, from the estate tax schedule	$1,131,800
Less: Estate tax on daughter's taxable estate of $1.5 million	555,900
Tax on $1.2 million generation-skipping transfer	$576,000

It can be seen that the tax on the generation-skipping transfer is based on the estate tax rates that would have applied to the property if D had owned it outright. The $576,000 tax is essentially levied against the trust property, not against D's estate, reducing the wealth passing to the granddaughter. We shall discuss the rules governing the computation and payment of the tax later in the chapter. The $250,000 exclusion, which applies to certain transfers to grandchildren, is also explained later.

Generation-skipping trusts and trust equivalents

A *generation-skipping transfer* is defined by Sec. 2611(a) as "any taxable distribution or taxable termination with respect to a generation-skipping trust or trust equivalent." After we have considered what constitutes a generation-skipping trust or trust equivalent, we shall discuss the requirements for a taxable distribution or termination.

A *generation-skipping trust* is "any trust having younger generation beneficiaries ... who are assigned to more than one generation" (Sec. 2611(b)). *Trust equivalents* are arrangements similar to trusts, for example, a life estate and remainder in real estate, or an estate for a term of years in property.

A trust (or equivalent) is not a generation-skipping arrangement unless it has beneficiaries who belong to two or more generations younger than the generation of the grantor of the trust. Thus, the penalty tax applies only to arrangements in which rights to property are divided up among beneficiaries in two or more generations younger than the grantor's generation.

> *Example:* H dies and leaves property in trust with a life estate to W, H's wife, and the re-

mainder to D, H's daughter. The trust does not skip a generation. The beneficiaries do not belong to two or more younger generations. If, on the other hand, D receives a life estate and the remainder is left to GD, H's granddaughter, a generation-skipping trust exists.

Because the beneficiaries in the examples above are lineal descendants of the grantor, the assignment of these descendants to generations poses no problems. Technically, Sec. 2611(c) assigns individuals to generations by reference to the grandparents of the grantor of the trust. This reference point brings in an expanded family unit and permits the assignment of members to generations by counting from the grantor's grandparents. Individuals related to the grantor by marriage are placed in the generation of their descendant spouse. The age of individuals is not important when generation assignments are made by blood relationships.

How are individuals assigned to generations when there is no blood relationship? Suppose a grantor designates his gardener as the life tenant of a trust and the remainder to the son of a friend? Do these two beneficiaries belong to two younger generations? Section 2611(c)(5) provides for arbitrary assignment of such individuals to generations based on their age related to the grantor's age. A beneficiary who is not more than 12½ years younger than the grantor belongs to the grantor's generation. A beneficiary who is more than 12½ years younger than the grantor but not more than 37½ years younger belongs to the first younger generation. Similarly, each younger generation thereafter is spaced at 25-year intervals.

The meaning of the term "beneficiary" is also critical to the definition of a generation-skipping trust. We are concerned only with individuals who are *beneficiaries* who belong to a younger generation. In our examples up to now, we have used life tenants and remaindermen. As used in the statute for this definition, a beneficiary is any person who has a present or future interest in or power over the trust property. Both *interest* and *power* are broadly defined for this purpose. A person has an interest if he or she has a right to receive income or corpus from the trust or if such person is a "permissible recipient of income or corpus" (Sec. 2613(d)). Thus, if the trustee has the right to distribute income over a group, each member of the group has an *interest,* even though income may never in fact be paid to that person. Any income interest, even a percentage or fractional interest or a discretionary interest, falls within this meaning. Further, the holder of a limited power to withdraw corpus has an interest for this purpose and is therefore a beneficiary.

Power means any right to "establish or alter beneficial enjoyment of the corpus or income of the trust" (Sec. 2613(d)(2)). Two important exceptions exist to this broad definition of power. First, a trustee is not a beneficiary of a trust if he or she may appoint trust income or corpus only to beneficiaries designated in the trust instrument, provided the person is not a "related or subordinate trustee." A related or subordinate trustee is a person who might be under the control or influence of the grantor or some beneficiary. Independent trustees such as banks, therefore, are not generally classified as beneficiaries. Under the second exception, a person is not a beneficiary if he or she holds only a power to dispose of the trust's income or corpus to beneficiaries who are lineal descendants of the grantor and who belong to a generation younger than the person holding the power. Thus, a child of the grantor whose only interest or power is the right to assign income and corpus among the grantor's grandchildren does not have a power and is not a beneficiary.

A generation-skipping trust, then, is a trust or trust equivalent with beneficiaries having the requisite interests or powers who belong to two or more generations younger than the generation of the grantor. The tax is levied when such a trust makes a generation-skipping transfer, either a "taxable distribution" or a "taxable termination."

Taxable distributions and terminations

In the classic scheme described early in the chapter, the estate tax is "skipped" upon the death of the intervening generation when the interest in the trust passed to a younger generation. The death of the intervening generation results in a transfer of interest in the generation-skipping trust, and that transfer is a *taxable termination.* Of course, a taxable termination could result from an event other than the death of the intervening generation beneficiary. For example, if the intervening generation has the right to receive income for a fixed period, taxable termination occurs when the income interest expires. Similarly, the tax may be triggered by exercise or nonexercise of a power or the occurrence of some other specific event. In general, a taxable termination occurs if an interest or power of the intervening generation terminates at a time when there are living beneficiaries of a generation younger than the generation of the person holding such power or interest.

Example: S, the son of G, the grantor, enjoys an income interest in a trust until he reaches the age of 50. At that time, the trust corpus is distributed to S's children in equal shares. When S turns 50, there is a taxable transaction. S's interest has expired and the trust property passes to a still younger generation. If, when S reached the age of 50, the life interest were to pass to D, G's daughter, for her life, with the remainder to S's children upon D's death, there is no termination when S reaches 50 years of age. The interest in the property has not yet passed to a generation younger than S and D, and the transfer tax has not yet been skipped. As explained more fully below, the tax is postponed until D's death.

If the new penalty tax were levied only upon terminations, the tax could be easily evaded by making distributions of the trust corpus to the younger generation beneficiaries before the event resulting in termination occurred. Consider the situation in which S has a life interest until age 50, with the corpus to pass to S's children at that time. What if the trust instrument permits the discretionary distribution of corpus to S's children during S's tenancy? Clearly, the corpus could thus be transferred and nothing would be left to be taxed when S becomes 50 years old. Such a distribution of corpus would be a *taxable distribution* and would be occasion for levying the tax.

Only distributions from a generation-skipping trust that are not out of the current income of such trust are taxable distributions. In addition, a distribution to a younger generation beneficiary is taxable only if a beneficiary exists in an older generation at the time of the distribution.

Example: G establishes a trust with income paid to S, G's son, for his life with the remainder to GD, S's daughter. The trustee also has the power to allocate part of the income to D, G's daughter, and may invade the corpus for the benefit of D. First, no generation-skipping transfer occurs if the trustee allocates current income to both S and GD. Assignment of income to the grantor's granddaughter does not postpone the transfer tax on the corpus for a generation. If, however, the trustee invades the trust corpus for GD's benefit, a taxable distribution occurs.

If distributions from corpus and income are made to two or more younger generations in the same year, amounts distributed to the oldest generation are presumed to come first from current income. This rule is essential to avoid a potential abuse.

Example: S, the grantor's son, and GS, S's son, are beneficiaries of a discretionary trust. The trustee distributes the current income of the trust to GS and makes an equal distribution of corpus to S. But for the arbitrary rule, the income distribution to GS is not a taxable distribution and the distribution of corpus to S is not taxable because it does not skip a generation. The law presumes, however, that all distributions to S, the older generation, are from income (to the extent of the current income). The distribution to GS is deemed to come from corpus and is taxable.

Certain terminations and distributions that otherwise would be taxable are specifically excluded from this tax. The most important of these is the $250,000 exclusion for transfers to grandchildren of the grantor.

GRANDCHILD EXCLUSION Congress has exempted from this new tax nominal generation-skipping transfers to the grandchildren of the grantor. The dollar limit on the exemption is $250,000 for each "deemed transferor," the parent of the recipient of the property upon a taxable termination or taxable distribution. The deemed transferor is the parent who is more closely related to the grantor.

Example: H and W have only one child, D. D married S and they have three children, X, Y, and Z. H establishes a trust with life estate for D and the remainder to X, Y, and Z. There is only one $250,000 exclusion on the death of D because there is only one deemed transferor. The same results are obtained if both H and W establish trusts, because there is still only one deemed transferor, D. If the parents of S also establish a trust with X, Y, and Z as beneficiaries, however, two exclusions would emerge because we now have two deemed transferors—D and S.

This exclusion for grandchildren applies to both taxable terminations and taxable distributions. Furthermore, the exclusion apparently applies to every type of interest or power, whether present or future.

OTHER EXCLUSIONS The terms "taxable distribution" and "taxable termination" do not encompass "any transfer to the extent such transfer is subject to the tax imposed by Chapter 11 and 12" (Sec. 2613(a)(4) and (b)(5)). The purpose of the tax on generation-skipping transfers is to impose a tax on transfers that would otherwise escape the gift or estate tax.

If one of these taxes applies to a transfer, the new tax in Chapter 13 has no role to perform.

This exclusion applies in situations in which younger generation beneficiaries hold interests or powers that result in taxable gifts or inclusion in their gross estates when their interests or powers are transferred.

> *Example:* G, grantor, gives D, her daughter, a life estate in a trust and a general power of appointment over the corpus with GD, G's granddaughter, the remainderman if D fails to exercise the power. On D's death, having failed to exercise the power, the transfer to GD is a taxable termination under Chapter 13 and also is included in D's gross estate under Sec. 2041 because of the general power of appointment. Because the transferred wealth is caught by Chapter 11, however, the Chapter 13 tax does not apply.

Finally, an exclusion applies to taxable distributions and terminations that have been subjected at some earlier time to the Chapter 13 tax. This exclusion, of course, extends only to deemed transferors of the same generation. The tax is appropriately levied on the same trust property each time it passes to successively younger generations.

To summarize, Chapter 13 levies a tax on generation-skipping transfers. The events that trigger the tax are taxable distributions from and taxable terminations of generation-skipping trusts or trust equivalents. A generation-skipping trust (or equivalent) is one having beneficiaries in two or more generations that are younger generations than that of the grantor. Now that we have identified the events that give rise to the tax, we shall turn our attention in more detail to the computation and payment of the tax.

COMPUTATION AND PAYMENT OF THE GENERATION-SKIPPING TRANSFER TAX

The simple example of the tax computation earlier in the chapter involved a taxable termination in which, upon the death of the daughter of the grantor, the daughter's life estate in the trust property ended and the property passed directly to the grantor's granddaughter. The tax was computed based on the prior wealth transfers of the daughter. Specifically, the law designates the daughter as the deemed transferor, the person whose total wealth transfers are used as the reference point for computation of the tax on the genera-

tion-skipping transfer. Selection of the daughter is logical because she was the skipped generation. In similar fashion, a *deemed transferor* must be selected for every taxable transfer.

Deemed transferor defined

For most taxable transfers, the deemed transferor is the parent of the transferee who is most closely related by blood to the grantor of the generation-skipping trust. If neither parent is related by blood to the grantor, the parent with the closer "affinity" to the grantor is the deemed transferor. As used here, "affinity" means relationship to the grantor, though the statute uses the word without elaboration. The designation of the transferee's parent as the deemed transferor is reasonable where wealth is passed in direct descent. Typically, the parent of the transferee is the previous beneficiary who would have held the wealth outright except for the generation-skipping device. Nevertheless, designation of the natural parents of the transferee as the deemed transferor, whose history of wealth transfers is used as a basis for the tax, may be purely arbitrary. The transferee's parent may have had no interest in the property and may become the deemed transferor because of a remote relationship to the grantor.

If G leaves property in trust with a life estate to S, his son, and then a life estate to GS, his grandson, with the remainder to GGS, his great-grandson, the tax should be levied upon the death of S and GS as though the property had passed directly to each successive generation. That is, nomination of S and GS as deemed transferors and a computation of a tax upon the death of both S and GS based on total wealth transfers of each makes sense. Consider what may happen, however, when the parent of the transferee is not a descendant of the grantor.

> *Example:* G leaves property in trust with a life estate to N, G's nephew, with the remainder to X, the daughter of M, a long-time household servant of G. Assume that X belongs to a generation younger than N. Upon N's death, X is the transferee and the parent of X, M, becomes the deemed transferor (because as an employee of G, M would have a closer "affinity" to G than would M's spouse). M's history of previous transfers is used to compute the tax, despite the fact that the wealth passes from N, at least in the sense that N was the older generation enjoying the fruits from the property.

Thus, the deemed transferor may be a person who never receives anything directly from the grantor, and the amount of the tax may be totally unrelated to the grantor's wealth or to the wealth of the person who was the beneficiary before the transfer.

One exception exists to the rule that the deemed transferor is the parent of the transferee. The exception applies in situations in which the parent most closely related to the grantor, the person who would otherwise be the deemed transferor, is not a younger generation beneficiary. If an ancestor of the transferee was a beneficiary, this ancestor becomes the deemed transferor. Thus if the transferee's grandfather, but not his father, was a younger generation beneficiary of the generation-skipping trust, the grandparent is the deemed transferor. If no ancestor of the transferee was a younger generation beneficiary, then the parent is the deemed transferor. This exception means that the tax is based on the tax history of the last generation that enjoyed some benefits from the trust property, but only where all beneficiaries are descendants of the grantor.

Remember that we designate a person the deemed transferor *only* as a beginning point for computing the tax. The tax is not levied *on* the deemed transferor.

Amount transferred

In the discussion and examples up to now, we have ignored two troublesome problems. First, we have assumed that the beneficiary of the older generation has an interest in or power over the entire property. When this is true, the amount subject to the tax is clearly the entire fair market value of the property at the time of the generation-skipping transfer. What happens when the older generation beneficiary has an interest in or power over only a part of the trust property? Second, we have assumed that there is only one transferee, or that all transferees had a common parent. As a result, there has been only one deemed transferor. What happens when there are two or more transferees with different parents? The amount transferred to each must be determined before the tax can be computed because there are different deemed transferors.

Note that these difficulties do not arise for taxable distributions. In distributions, there is an observable separation and passage of wealth from the trust to the distributee. We know how much each distributee receives and the tax that should be computed, based on each deemed transferor's past history. For terminations the situation may be less clear.

We shall consider the first of these two problems and begin with a simple situation. Grantor establishes a trust with income to granddaughter GD for life and the remainder to great-granddaughter GGD. Upon the death of GD, GGD comes into possession of the entire corpus, which GD had previously enjoyed. The amount subject to taxation is the entire value, a result that will apply in most situations. But suppose we change the facts and assume that GD's life estate extends only to one-half the income with the remaining half accumulated for and distributed to GGD. Only one-half the trust corpus is transferred on the death of GD and only that amount is subject to the tax. (For postponement of the tax where successive life interests are held by the same generation, see the discussion under "Postponement of the Tax," page **18/9**.) Similarly, if GD had only a special power to appoint one-half the corpus, the lapse of this power on GD's death results in a transfer of only one-half the corpus. The results become less clear if GD has a power to invade the corpus limited to 5 percent of the corpus or $5,000 annually. Logic would dictate that only the amount that GD could have claimed under this power should be subject to the tax, although one could also reason that GD's power extended to the entire corpus.[3] As one might expect, the amount subject to the tax is the entire fair value of the trust corpus except where the interest is clearly limited to something less than the whole property.

We shall now turn to the second problem—identifying the amount transferred to each transferee.

> *Example:* Assume that the grantor establishes a trust with income for life to S and the remainder to grandsons GS_1 and GS_2. If both GS_1 and GS_2 are children of S, no problem arises since they have a common parent who is the deemed transferor and the total value is taxed based on S's transfer tax history. If GS_1 is S's son but GS_2 is the child of D, the grantor's daughter, we have two deemed transferors and the amounts received by GS_1 and GS_2 become important. Because the trust actually terminated, however, the amounts received by each may be determined as a matter of fact.
>
> Extend the example and assume that GS_1 (S's son) and GS_2 (D's son) receive income interests upon the death of S with the remainder interest to the children of GS_1 and GS_2. Assume further that the trustee has the power to allocate income be-

---

[3]The Conference Committee Report, H.R. 1515, 94th Congress, 2nd Session, page 618 (1976) seems to say that the entire corpus is taxable where the right to invade is not limited by a term of years.

tween GS_1 and GS_2 according to some standard specified by G. With different deemed transferors, we need to know how much is transferred to GS_1 and GS_2. In the absence of an actual distribution, the statute provides in Sec. 2613(b)(3) that a distribution is deemed to be made pro rata to the maximum extent the beneficiaries could have participated in an actual distribution. Thus, GS_1 and GS_2 would each be deemed to receive one-half the corpus without regard to the amount each actually receives later.

In the preceding discussion of the amount subject to the tax, we have dealt only with some general rules. We could have selected many more examples that present additional complications. Here, as elsewhere in this chapter, the examples selected are those consistent with an introduction to generation-skipping transfers.

Finally, we should note that Chapter 13 of the Code also provides for an elective alternate valuation date comparable to the rules in Sec. 2032 for the estate tax. The alternate valuation procedures apply to certain taxable terminations and for the same reasons as for the estate tax. Also, a "gift in contemplation of death" rule applies to deemed transferors to eliminate the possibility of reducing taxes through deathbed transfers.

The tax calculation

We shall now briefly summarize how the amount subject to the tax is computed. The tax is levied on generation-skipping transfers, either taxable distributions from or taxable terminations of generation-skipping trusts. Given a taxable transfer, the first step is to determine the gross amount transferred. For taxable distributions, this amount is the fair market value of the distributed property at the date of distribution. For taxable terminations, it is the fair value of the entire corpus, except when the preceding beneficiary has only a clearly defined partial interest or power. Remember that some transfers are exempt from the tax because they are subject to the estate or gift taxes. Second, the gross amount must be allocated between the transferees if more than one transferee exists. Third, the deemed transferor(s) must be identified by reference to the transferee(s). Fourth, the gross amounts allocated to each transferee must be reduced by the exclusions, if any, related to that transferee. The grandchild exclusion is the important one. Finally, certain allowable deductions, discussed below, are subtracted to arrive at the amount subject to the tax.

Recall from an earlier discussion that the law attempts to levy a tax *as though* the deemed transferor had made the transfer directly. Thus, the deemed transferor's previous history of wealth transfers is added to the amount of the generation-skipping transfer. Specifically, the tax base is the sum of the following, determined by reference to the deemed transferor:

1. The current generation-skipping transfer;
2. All previous generation-skipping transfers assigned to the deemed transferor;
3. Taxable gifts made by the deemed transferor after 1976;
4. The taxable estate of the deemed transferor, if he or she died at the same time as or prior to the generation-skipping transfer.

In some situations, the tax base will consist of Item (1) only. For example, when a taxable distribution is made from a trust and the deemed transferor, who is still alive, has made no lifetime taxable gifts and has not been a deemed transferor of a previous generation-skipping transfer, the tax base is the current generation-skipping distribution only. In other words, taxable distributions are taxed as though they were lifetime gifts of the deemed transferor, with all previous gifts taken into consideration in the tax computation.

Item (4) must be added to the base if the death of the deemed transferor results in a taxable termination. Transfers that are both distributions and terminations are treated as terminations for purposes of the calculation. To illustrate, Grantor (G) gives a life estate to A, G's nephew, with the corpus distributed to A's children upon A's death. Although a distribution does occur at A's death, the transfer must be treated as a termination and A's taxable estate included in the base.

A tentative tax is computed on the base, the sum of Items (1) through (4), using the unified rate schedule in Sec. 2001(c). The final tax is this tentative tax reduced by a tax based on the sum of Items (2) through (4). This calculation results in a tax at the highest marginal rates that would have applied to the amount transferred had the deemed transferor passed the wealth directly. A summary of the calculation is:

Sum of Items (1) through (4)	$ XXX
Tax on the above from the unified rate schedule—tentative tax	$ XX
Less: Tax from the unified schedule on Items (2) through (4)	XX
Tax on generation-skipping transfer	$ X

The resulting tax is levied on the generation-skipping trust, not on the deemed transferor. Paying the tax out of the trust property creates no problem for taxable terminations. Just like the beneficiaries of an estate, the transferees receive the wealth that remains after the transfer tax is paid. For taxable distributions, however, the problem is more complicated. If the beneficiary receives a distribution and pays the tax out of the property received, his or her position is the same as a beneficiary in a taxable termination. On the other hand, if the transferee receives the distribution and the trust pays the tax from its remaining assets, the transferee's wealth may not be diminished by the tax. For this reason, Sec. 2613(a)(3) provides that the taxes paid on taxable distributions are also generation-skipping transfers. Thus, the computation of the tax on distributions when the tax is paid from the trust assets evidently involves a simultaneous solution for two amounts: the gross amount transferred and the transfer tax. The several complications that may result from implementation of this rule are beyond our scope here.

DEDUCTIONS ALLOWED   Generally, the tax is based on the gross value of the wealth transferred. Section 2602(c), however, provides for some limited deductions. If transfers qualify as charitable transfers under Sec. 2055 (estate tax charitable deduction) or under Sec. 2522 (gift tax charitable deduction), a deduction is allowed for the generation-skipping tax. Deductions are also allowed for administrative expenses associated with taxable terminations and for expenses related to tax advice for taxable distributions. These deductions are available only for transfers occurring simultaneously with or subsequent to the death of the deemed transferor. The marital deduction for estate tax purposes may be affected by generation-skipping transfers. If the deemed transferor dies at the time of a taxable termination, the deemed transferor's adjusted gross estate, which limits the marital deduction, is increased by the generation-skipping transfer. If the deemed transferor's will provides for a maximum marital deduction, the deduction is increased as a result of the generation-skipping transfer.

CREDITS ALLOWED   Generation-skipping transfers occurring at or after the death of the deemed transferor may be offset by a portion of the unified credit if the entire amount allowed is not needed to offset the gift tax and the estate tax. The unified credit may not be used during life to reduce the tax under Chapter 13, and the credit must be applied first to the gift tax and

estate tax. The tax under Chapter 13 also provides for a credit based on prior transfers similar to that for the estate tax in Sec. 2013. Finally, a credit is allowed for amounts paid to states for generation-skipping taxes (although only California currently levies such a tax). The following example illustrates the tax calculation.

Example: Grantor (G) by will creates a trust with the following beneficiaries: a life estate to D, G's daughter; then life estates to GD and GS, D's daughter and son; then, the remainder to the issue of GD and GS. The trustees also have the power to invade the corpus during the life of D for the benefit of GD and GS. Under this provision, the trustee made an aggregate gross distribution (including the transfer tax) of $850,000 during D's life to GD and GS. Upon D's death, the trust corpus was valued at $1.550 million. D made taxable gifts during her life of $450,000, and her taxable estate was $900,000.

The trust created by G is clearly a generation-skipping trust. Upon D's death, the fruition of GD's and GS's life estates is a taxable termination. Furthermore, the deemed transferor is clearly D, the parent of GD and GS most closely related to the grantor. Note that this transfer is subject to the grandchild exclusion but that only one exclusion of $250,000 is allowed. Finally, assume that there are no other exclusions and no deductions related to this transfer. The tax is computed as follows:

(1)	Gross value of current transfer	$1,550,000
(2)	Prior generation-skipping transfers (less grandchild exclusion)	600,000
(3)	Taxable gifts of deemed transferor	450,000
(4)	Taxable estate of deemed transferor	900,000
	Base for tentative tax	$3,500,000
	Tentative tax—Schedule at Sec. 2001(c)	$1,575,800
	Less: Tax on $1,950,000, the sum of Items (2) through (4)	758,300
	Tax on generation-skipping transfer	$817,500

Upon the deaths of GD and GS, when the remainder is distributed to their children, another taxable transfer will occur. No unified credit is allowed in this instance because, upon D's death, the entire credit would be used first to offset D's estate tax.

Postponement of the tax

Consider the facts in the preceding example and assume that both GD and GS have a life estate in the entire corpus and that no distribution is made to their children until both GD and GS are dead. Do we have a taxable termination when the first dies, survived by the other life tenant? No, the tax is postponed until the last beneficiary in the same generation dies. A different result would occur if GD and GS had distinct separate shares that passed to a younger generation upon the death of each. Note also that postponement of the tax would not change the deemed transferor for purposes of the tax computation.

Postponement rules apply only to terminations. The tax is not levied until the interests or powers of all beneficiaries of the same generation terminate. Furthermore, if a single beneficiary enjoys several interests or powers, the tax is postponed until all are terminated.

Payment of the tax and filing requirements

Rules for payment of tax depend on whether the event is a taxable distribution or a taxable termination. For distributions, the distributee is responsible for filing the return and paying the tax. The return is due 90 days after the end of the tax year of the transfer. For taxable terminations, the trustee is responsible for filing the return and paying the tax. The return is due 90 days after the transfer if the deemed transferor is living or 90 days after the estate tax return is due if the termination results from death of the deemed transferor.

Subject to limitations, the distributee or trustee is personally liable for the tax, although the statute envisions that the tax will be paid from the property. Indeed, the government has a lien on the property until the tax is paid. If the trustee relies on information furnished by the I.R.S. about the marginal tax rates applicable to the transfer, then there is no personal liability for any increased taxes. A distributee has no personal liability beyond the fair market value of the property received.

Rules for payment of the tax are the same as for the gift tax if the deemed transferor is alive at the time of the transfer. If the deemed transferor is deceased,

the estate tax rules apply, except that the extended payments schedules of Sec. 6166 and Sec. 6166A, which apply to closely held businesses, are not available for the Chapter 13 tax.

Effective date

The generation-skipping transfer tax applies generally to generation-skipping transfers made after June 11, 1976. Two grandfather clauses may exempt taxable transfers after that date. First, irrevocable trusts with generation-skipping characteristics in existence on June 11, 1976 are exempt from the tax. This exception, however, does not extend to additions to the corpus of such trusts after the effective date. This exception for irrevocable trusts is consistent with Congressional policy to avoid retroactive punitive changes in the law. Second, wills and revocable trusts in existence on June 11, 1976 are protected in the case of decedents dying before January 1, 1982. This grandfather clause applies only if no amendments are made after June 11, 1976 that create or increase the amount of generation-skipping transfers.

LIVING WITH THE TAX

The tax on generation-skipping transfers is designed to eliminate, or at least to reduce, the effectiveness of a traditional device in estate planning. In this section, we shall discuss some actions that may be taken to avoid or reduce the impact of this new tax.

Keep in mind that the generation-skipping transfer tax is new. Our understanding of how to "plan around it" will grow in the future. What follows is only suggestive of ways and means.

Nothing in these rules penalizes the direct transfer of wealth to grandchildren or great-grandchildren, thereby avoiding transfer taxes on the intervening generations. In the future, the wealthy individual will need to weigh carefully the financial needs of the immediately younger generation against the tax cost of passing wealth to them as opposed to passing it to still younger generations. Direct transfers will be the most common substitute for generation-skipping transfers. As a result, the intervening generations will lose control of the wealth and they will lose the financial security that comes from having an interest in property in generation-skipping trusts. The loss of control may be ameliorated somewhat by making the intervening generations trustees (or co-trustees with a corporate fiduciary). Their powers must be restricted to *managerial* powers if the new tax is to be avoided. For financial security, they must look to the wealth left directly to them, although family affection would give them a moral claim, in dire circumstances, on the wealth passing to the younger generations.

Maximum use should be made of the exclusion for grandchildren. A generation-skipping trust with a corpus of $250,000 for each child of the grantor is clearly in order. While this amount is nominal to quite wealthy families, such a trust would afford the children some security against financial disaster. For only moderately wealthy families, use of the grandchild exclusion may result in substantial savings relative to the total wealth. For example, assume a taxpayer has an estate of $3 million and has four children. Each child also has one or more children. Four generation-skipping trusts with each child as a life tenant pass $1 million to the grandchildren and skip the transfer tax on that amount for one generation.

PROBLEMS

1. In the following cases, Grantor (G) formed a trust in September, 1980, when he was 65 years old. For each arrangement, determine if the trust is a generation-skipping trust. Explain your answers fully.
   a. The trust provides for income for the life of W, G's wife, with the remainder to G's grandchildren. W is 58 years old.
   b. Same as part a, above, except that W is only 28 years old.
   c. The trust provides for income to the wife of G's trusted employee for her life. The wife is 50 years old at the time. The remainder will go to the children of the employee (aged 30 and 31). The beneficiaries are not related to G.
   d. Same facts as part c, except the children of the employee and his wife are aged 20 and 21.
   e. The trust provides a life estate for C, G's brother. The remainder is to C's son, S. C is 50 years old and S is 20 years old.
2. "The tax on generation-skipping transfers, by Congressional intent, is not levied on all transfers that in fact skip one or more generations." Is the preceding statement true or false? Explain.
3. After 1977, Grantor (G) established during his life a trust with the income for life to S, G's son, with the remainder to GD, S's daughter. Wishing to avoid the impact of Chapter 13, G decides to adopt GD, making her his child. Will this scheme work?
4. In the following situations, assume that Grantor (G) establishes an *inter vivos* trust after 1978. For each, determine if the trust is a generation-skipping trust or equivalent.
   a. The trust instrument gives the trustee the power to pay the income of the trust at his discretion to G's grandchildren with the remainder to G's great-grandchildren. Because of the accumulated wealth of G's grandchildren, it is unlikely that the trustee will ever pay out income to them.
   b. The trust instrument gives S, G's son, the right to withdraw a limited amount of corpus. Income of the trust is accumulated until GS, S's son, reaches the age of 30, at which time income and corpus are distributed to GS.
   c. The trust instrument provides that T, a large corporate trustee, will have the power to pay out income at its discretion to G's grandchildren. Equal shares of the trust corpus pass to the grandchildren when the youngest reaches the age of 30.
   d. Same facts as in part c, above, except that T is an employee of G and belongs to the generation just younger than G.
5. In 1979, Grantor (G) creates a trust for the benefit of S, G's son, and for GS, S's

son. The trustee, at its discretion may distribute income to S or GS. After the death of S, provided GS survives, all income is paid to GS. Upon the death of GS, provided S predeceases him, the corpus will be paid to GGS, GS's son. In 1980, the trust had income of $6,000. What is the amount of the taxable distribution(s) in each of the following:

    a. The trustee distributes $6,000 from income in 1980 to GS but distributes nothing to S.

    b. In 1980, the income is accumulated but the trustee distributes $4,000, which is specifically designated as corpus, to GS.

    c. In 1980, the trustee distributes $8,000 to S, nothing to GS.

    d. In 1980, the trustee distributes $4,000 to S and $4,000 to GS. The $4,000 to GS is designated as income.

    e. Assume the same facts as in part d, above, except that the trust instrument provides for discretionary income distributions to GS only (but not to S).

6. G dies in 1983 (after expiration of grandfather clause for the effective date of Chapter 13) and establishes by will a trust with income for life to GD, G's granddaughter, then income for life to GGD, G's great-granddaughter with the remainder to GGD's children. GD dies in 1984. Does this result in a taxable termination? Explain.

7. Assume the same facts as in Problem 6, above, except that the first income interest is to D, G's daughter, then to GD, and so on, and that it is D (not GD) who dies in 1984. Does D's death result in a taxable termination?

8. G dies in 1983 and by will establishes a trust with income for life to S, G's son, and to D, G's daughter. Upon the death of S or D (the last to survive), the remainder goes to GD, G's granddaughter. S dies in 1984, survived by D. Does S's death result in a taxable termination?

9. Herman Henson's will contains the following provisions for two trusts:

Trust A—Corpus of $300,000, which qualifies for the marital deduction, leaving Herman's spouse, Nettie, an income for life and a general power of appointment. If Nettie dies without exercising the power, the corpus of Trust A goes to Trust B.

Trust B—Corpus of $600,000, with a life interest in separate shares to Bob and Jean, Herman's son and daughter. Upon the death of the life tenants, the remainder (by shares) goes to their children in equal shares.

Assume that Herman dies in 1983 and that Nettie dies later without exercising her general power over Trust A.

    a. Is Trust A a generation-skipping trust?

    b. Does a taxable termination occur upon Nettie's death?

    c. Is Trust B a generation-skipping trust?

    d. Does a taxable termination occur upon the deaths of Bob and Jean?

10. What significance attaches to the designation of an individual as the deemed transferor? Explain.

11. In the following independent situations, determine the person who is the "deemed transferor" for each distribution or termination:

    a. Under the terms of a trust, income is to be paid to D, G's daughter, for life, then, upon the death of D, income for the life of GGD, D's granddaughter, with the remainder to the children of GGD. D dies, survived by GGD.

    b. Assume that GGD is the granddaughter of S, who is G's son and D's brother. D dies survived by GGD.

    c. Under the terms of a trust, income is to be paid for life to X, wife of GS, the grantor's grandson. Upon X's death the remainder goes to GGS, the son of GS and X. X dies, survived by GGS.

12. By will, grantor (G) created a trust with the following provisions: a life estate to S, G's son; then a life estate to GS, G's grandson; then, the remainder to GGS, G's great-grandson. During the life of S, the trustees have the power to invade the corpus of the trust for the benefit of GS or GGS. S dies in the current year.

During S's lifetime, the trustee made distributions to GS of $900,000 (including the transfer tax). Upon S's death, the trust corpus was valued at $2,000,000. During his life, S made taxable gifts of $600,000 and had a taxable estate of $1,200,000 at death.

Calculate the amount of the tax under Chapter 13 upon S's death. (Assume that the dates are such as to avoid the phase-in of the 1976 Act.)

PART

SIX

other
business-related
taxes

19

taxes on corporate accumulations

THE ACCUMULATED EARNINGS TAX

Since 1913, corporations, unlike sole proprietorships and partnerships, have been treated as separate taxable entities. In addition, the rate of tax on corporate income has always been lower than the highest marginal rate on individual income. These two factors combined have provided individuals with a powerful incentive to use closely held corporations as a shield against the federal personal income tax.

To illustrate, current corporate tax rates are as low as 17 percent, with a maximum of 46 percent on ordinary income. Individuals, on the other hand, are subject to rates as high as 70 percent on ordinary income. In fact, under the new rate schedules, a married couple filing jointly will pay an effective rate of 18 percent on $25,000 of taxable income, whereas a corporation will pay an effective rate of 17 percent. For all levels of income above $25,000, the effective rate is lower for corporations than for individuals, and the gap widens as income increases. It is easy to see why an individual might look upon the corporate form of business as a device to minimize taxes to the extent that the earnings of the corporation are not needed by the individual for personal living expenses.

Funds accumulated by a corporation could be reinvested without being subjected to the personal income tax, which would apply if the earnings were paid out in dividends. Furthermore, some of the earnings of the corporation may be distributed to stockholders in the form of salaries, which, if reasonable in amount, are deductible to the corporation. Not only is the double taxation of corporate earnings avoided, but the salaries are subject to the 50 percent maximum tax on personal service income.

Originally, Congress sought to prevent the use of corporations as a shield against the individual income tax by taxing the shareholders' ratable share of the corporate income (whether distributed or not) when there was evidence that the corporation had been "formed or fraudulently availed of" for the purpose of escaping the individual income tax by allowing profits to accumulate. This approach was abandoned in 1921 in favor of a penalty tax on the corporation when the "forbidden purpose" was present.

In 1934, Congress became concerned that the accumulated earnings tax was not a sufficient weapon against the use of the corporate rate shelter by wealthy individuals, partly because of the difficulty of establishing the "forbidden purpose." To supplement the existing provision, a second penalty tax was levied on certain closely held corporations with income primarily from passive sources ("personal holding companies"). The purpose was to levy a tax on such companies "without any necessity for proving a purpose of avoiding . . . taxes."[1] In the following sections, we shall discuss the principal features of the accumulated earnings tax.

Determination of vulnerability—
the forbidden purpose

The accumulated earnings tax is intended to discourage the use of the corporation as a device to shield its stockholders from the individual income tax. Thus, Sec. 532(a) imposes the tax on any corporation that is formed or availed of by its shareholders for the purpose of avoiding the personal income tax by permitting cor-

[1] *House Report 704*, 73d Congress, 2d Sess. (1934), p. 12.

porate earnings and profits to accumulate rather than distributing them as dividends. Presumably, a corporation that has no intent to avoid taxes on its shareholders would be exempt from the accumulated earnings tax if "excess" earnings were accumulated for some misguided purpose that could not be explained by a sound business reason. The Supreme Court has held, however, that the forbidden purpose need not be the dominant purpose but only one of the purposes for an unreasonable accumulation.[2]

The regulations list the following factors that are considered in determining whether a tax avoidance purpose is present (Treas. Reg. Sec. 1.533-1(a)(2)):

1. Dealings between the corporation and its shareholders, including loans to shareholders and expenditures of corporate funds for the personal benefit of shareholders;
2. The investment of earnings in assets having no reasonable connection with the corporation's business;
3. The corporation's dividend payment history.

Loans to shareholders and investment of earnings in assets having no connection with the corporation's business are regarded as indicative of ability to pay dividends. While in many cases taxpayers have escaped the tax in spite of such evidence, these factors do help to establish the forbidden motive.

Section 533(a) specifies that earnings permitted to accumulate beyond the reasonable needs of the business shall serve to determine the purpose of avoiding shareholder income taxes, unless the corporation can prove to the contrary by a preponderance of the evidence. If the taxpayer can establish such evidence, it should win the case even though the forbidden purpose of Sec. 532 may have existed. It is rare, however, that a taxpayer successfully rebuts the assumption that tax avoidance was a motive when the accumulations have been found to be unreasonable in amount.

The taxpayer's defense—reasons for accumulation

Assuming that a taxpayer corporation has been accused of allowing excess earnings to accumulate for tax avoidance reasons, what evidence might the corporation put forward as a defense? The corporation must try to establish that reasonable business needs require the accumulations. The regulations list five such needs (Treas. Reg. Sec. 1.537-2(b)):

1. *Expansion of business or replacement of plant.* Many court decisions have held that use of self-financed expansion is acceptable even if long-term borrowing could have been used.[3] Section 537 specifies that reasonable needs may include "reasonably anticipated needs." The critical question is the length of time a taxpayer may anticipate a need before taking action. When delays occur, the taxpayer can often support the claim of accumulation for anticipated needs if the plans have been carried out, in whole or in part, before the case reaches court. Alternatively, the I.R.S. may cite failure to carry out plans as evidence that they were vague and indefinite or not feasible.[4]

2. *Acquisition of a business enterprise through purchasing stock or assets.* There is little question that expansion of a corporation's *existing* business is an allowable reason for accumulating earnings and that this may be accomplished through acquisition of another business enterprise.[5] While the regulations provide that "[t]he business of a corporation is not merely that which it has previously carried on but includes, in general, any line of business which it may undertake" (Treas. Reg. Sec. 1.537-3(a)), expansion into new lines of business is not as clear a basis for accumulation. Corporations that claim to be searching for such acquisition opportunities often have difficulties using this claim as a defense if the proposed acquisitions are in a new line of business. It may be, however, that their difficulties are based not so much on the fact that they are attempting to enter a new business than that their plans are vague and indefinite or that the proposed acquisitions are passive rather than active businesses.[6]

3. *Retirement of bona fide business indebtedness.* Even though the courts have been reluctant to impose their judgment that debt could or should have been used for purposes of expansion or replacement,

---

[2]*The Donruss Co.*, 393 U.S. 297 (1969).

[3]For example, in *Walton Mill, Inc.*, 1972 T.C. Memo, ¶72,025 p. 90, the court noted that "whether to accumulate funds to finance an acquisition or to borrow such funds is a judgment of management and the courts will not substitute their judgment for that of the responsible corporate officials when the record shows the existence of definite, specific, and feasible expansion plans."

[4]In *Alma Piston Company*, 1963 T.C. Memo, ¶63,195, for example, the court noted that [taxpayer's] "plans were specific and clearly feasible as is established by their consummation in 1959." In contrast, the court in *Atlantic Commerce & Shipping Co., Inc.*, 1973 T.C. Memo, ¶73,106, affirmed 500 F2d 937 (2d Cir. 1974), found that "[p]etitioner's failure to ever fully implement its real estate plans in later years is relevant because it sheds some light on the seriousness and specificity of its plans during the years in issue."

[5]See, for example, *Baker & Co., Inc.*, 1943 T.C. Memo, ¶43,436, in which a taxpayer expanded its metal refining and manufacturing business by acquiring other refiners and distributors of its product.

[6]For an excellent discussion, see Gloria L. Case, "Accumulated Earnings Tax Aspects of Business Expansions and Investments," *Tax Law Review*, Vol. 32, 1976, pp. 3–65.

corporations that have incurred debt for legitimate business purposes may justify their need to accumulate funds for debt retirement.[7]

4. *Working capital needs.* Clearly, one reason a corporation accumulates funds is to provide for its investment in working capital. Two cases[8] established judicial recognition of this need and proposed a method of calculating an appropriate amount of accumulation. According to the "Bardahl formula," a company's operating cycle on an annual basis is determined. This is the average length of time it takes to convert inventory into receivables and the receivables into cash, reduced by the average time accounts payable are outstanding. This time (expressed as a percentage of one year) is then multiplied by the sum of cost of goods sold and other expenses excluding taxes and depreciation. The result establishes the corporation's reasonable accumulation to meet working capital needs. Of course, this amount may be increased by other needs, such as replacement of plant and equipment. The following example illustrates the application of the Bardahl formula.

Example: Assume that WC Corporation is trying to establish how much it can reasonably accumulate to meet working capital needs. The following facts have been gathered for the current year:

Cost of goods sold	$300,000
Average inventory	25,000
Inventory turnover (300,000/ 25,000 = 12 times per year = every 30 days)	
Sales	500,000
Average accounts receivable	50,000
Accounts receivable turnover (500,000/50,000 = 10 times per year = every 36 days)	
Purchases	320,000
Average accounts payable	40,000
Accounts payable turnover (320,000/40,000 = 8 times per year = every 45 days)	

Operating cycle:	
Inventory turnover in days	30
Accounts receivable turnover in days	36
Accounts payable turnover in days	(45)
Operating cycle in days	21
Operating cycle as a percentage of one year (21/360)	5.8%
Working capital needs:	
Cost of goods sold	$300,000
Other expenses other than depreciation and taxes	100,000
Annual working capital needs	$400,000
Multiplied by operating cycle as percentage of one year	× 5.8%
Reasonable accumulation to satisfy working capital needs	$ 23,200

A number of cases have modified the Bardahl formula. For example, service firms have been allowed to include depreciation among expenses, and some taxpayers have successfully argued for the use of peak needs rather than average need in the calculation.

5. *Investment in or loans to suppliers or customers.* Relatively few taxpayers have asserted the need to accumulate earnings for this purpose. In one example,[9] the taxpayer, a newspaper publisher, successfully argued that its accumulations were justified partly because it had used funds to purchase stock in a newsprint manufacturer to help assure a source during a period of severe shortage.

Taxpayers have also successfully defended accumulations on a number of other grounds, including reserves for various business risks, contingent liabilities, and plans to relocate.

The *Internal Revenue Manual*[10] provides Audit Guidelines used by agents to determine the possible applicability of the accumulated earnings tax. The guidelines are of particular importance to taxpayers considered vulnerable to the tax, because the accumulated earnings tax is a penalty tax assessed against a corporation by the I.R.S. rather than a self-assessed tax.

Among the factors listed in the manual as favorable to the taxpayer's case are a history of paying dividends, payment of a substantial salary to the principal stockholder–employee of the corporation, public ownership

---

[7]In *Farmers and Merchants Investment Co.,* 1970 T.C. Memo, ¶70,161, for example, the court found that debts were incurred in connection with the taxpayer's business and therefore "the accumulation of surplus to pay the debts would be within the reasonable needs of petitioner's business." Also, in *Sears Oil Co., Inc.,* 359 F.2d 191 (2d Cir. 1966), p. 838, reversing 1965 T.C. Memo, ¶65,039, the court noted that "[s]ection 531 does not ban taxpayer from endeavoring to reduce its borrowing and to become self financing."

[8]*Bardahl Manufacturing Company,* 1965 T.C. Memo, ¶65,200, and *Bardahl International Corp.,* 1966 T.C. Memo, ¶66,182.

[9]*Bremerton Sun Publishing Co.,* 44 T.C. 566(1965).

[10]I.R.S., U.S. Treasury Department, *Internal Revenue Manual,* Exhibit 700-5.

of stock, the use of debt, the need to diversify, documentation of the needs of the business, a low current ratio, and actual entry into an unrelated business. Several of these require comment. First, as mentioned in the introduction to this chapter, paying salaries to avoid the tax may open up another problem for the taxpayer, namely, an assertion that the salaries are unreasonable in amount. Second, while the tax technically may be asserted against publicly held corporations, it is in fact almost always asserted against closely held corporations in which a few people are in control of the dividend policy. Third, the manual notes that "documentation of plans" consists of not just inclusion in corporate minutes but subsequent fulfillment of plans.

Negative indicators

The regulations and the Audit Guidelines also supply the taxpayer with a number of negative indicators. According to the regulations (Treas. Reg. Sec. 1.537-2(c)), "unreasonable" bases for accumulations are loans to shareholders, friends and relatives of shareholders, and to other corporations controlled by the same shareholders when such loans are unrelated to the business of the taxpayer corporation; investment in unrelated properties or securities; and retention to protect against "unrealistic hazards."

The Audit Guidelines list 15 factors favorable to the government. Many are the opposite of those listed as favorable to the taxpayer (for example, a poor dividend history). Some other factors are "vague and indefinite" business needs, investment in uncontrolled subsidiaries, and nonliquid investments of a passive nature. Thus, the taxpayer is provided with many guidelines, both negative and positive, to help determine whether or not the accumulated earnings tax may be imposed.

Computation of the tax

Once the corporation has been found to have accumulated earnings beyond its reasonable needs for tax avoidance reasons, the accumulated earnings tax must be calculated. The base of the tax is defined in Sec. 535(a) as the corporation's "accumulated taxable earnings," which is the taxable income of the corporation for the year or years in question, modified to reflect the corporation's dividend-paying capacity and reduced by the dividends-paid adjustment and the accumulated earnings credit.

The modifications to taxable income, which are found in Sec. 535(b), are the following.

1. Deduction of corporate income taxes;
2. Deduction of charitable contributions in excess of the 5 percent limit;
3. Addition of the special deductions of Secs. 241–250, except for amortization of organizational expenditures as allowed by Sec. 248. The most important addition for most corporations is the 85 percent dividends-received deduction.
4. Addition of the net operating loss deduction of Sec. 172;
5. Deduction of capital losses disallowed by Sec. 1211(a);
6. Deduction of net capital gains (excess of net long-term capital gains over net short-term capital losses), net of applicable taxes.

Once these modifications to taxable income are made, taxable income is reduced by the dividends-paid deduction of Sec. 561. This is the sum of dividends paid during the year plus any dividends paid within the first 2½ months of the following year.

Next, the accumulated earnings credit of Sec. 535(c) is deducted. This credit is currently $150,000 and must be adjusted to reflect accumulations carried over from previous years. The accumulated earnings credit may be larger than $150,000 if the corporation has demonstrated reasonable need to accumulate more. Thus, the accumulated earnings credit is actually the greater of

1. $150,000, less earnings and profits at the end of the previous tax year, reduced by dividends paid in the first 2½ months of the current year, or
2. The reasonable needs of the business, less earnings and profits at the end of the previous tax year, reduced by dividends paid in the first 2½ months of the current tax year.

The balance after deduction of the accumulated earnings credit from modified taxable income is the base of the accumulated earnings tax. The applicable rates are 27½ percent of accumulated taxable income up to $100,000 plus 38½ percent of accumulated taxable income in excess of $100,000.

The following example illustrates the calculation of the accumulated earnings tax:

Example: Assume the I.R.S. has found that AET Corporation has been availed of to shield its shareholders from the individual income tax. In 1979, the corporation had $200,000 of taxable income. The corporation's income for the year included $10,000 of dividends from a domestic corporation and $20,000 of long-term capital gains. Earnings and profits at the beginning of the year were $140,000. AET can establish reasonable need to accumulate $180,000.

AET's accumulated taxable earnings is determined as follows:

Taxable income	$200,000
Less: (1) The corporate income tax at 1979 rates	(69,150)
(2) Excess of NLTCG over NSTCL, reduced by applicable tax ($20,000 − $5,600)	(14,400)
Add: The 85 percent dividends-received deduction	8,500
Modified taxable income	$124,950
Less: Dividends-paid deduction	-0-
Accumulated earnings credit ($180,000 − $140,000)	40,000
Accumulated taxable earnings	$ 84,950
Accumulated earnings tax ($84,950 × 0.275)	$ 23,361

Note that once a corporation's vulnerability to the tax is established, it will continue to be subject to the tax in subsequent years unless it can establish new or increased needs to accumulate. For this reason, cases in which the I.R.S. has asserted the tax against a corporation for only one year are quite rare. Once the corporation has accumulated more than its reasonable needs, the purpose of the tax is to force distribution of further earnings.

THE TAX ON PERSONAL HOLDING COMPANIES

As we mentioned in the introduction to this chapter, Congress established the tax on personal holding companies in 1934 to supplement the accumulated earnings tax. The idea was to make certain companies automatically vulnerable without need to establish the "forbidden purpose." The targets of this legislation were the so-called "incorporated pocketbooks." These corporations typically earned their income from passive sources and were owned by taxpayers in sufficiently high tax brackets to benefit from the corporate rate shelter. The purpose of the tax on personal holding companies is to force such corporations to distribute their earnings as dividends rather than to accumulate them.

Certain corporations are automatically exempted from the personal holding company tax. These include tax-exempt corporations, banks and savings and loan associations, life insurance companies, surety companies, foreign corporations, and small business investment companies.

Determination of vulnerability to the personal holding company tax

Vulnerability to the personal holding company tax is based on a combination of two factors: concentration of ownership and excessive reliance on passive sources of income. Concentration of ownership is present if more than 50 percent of the value of the outstanding stock was owned, directly or indirectly, by five or fewer individuals during the last half of the taxable year (Sec. 542(a)(2)). Excessive reliance on passive sources of income is present if 60 percent or more of the corporation's "adjusted ordinary gross income" is from passive sources (Sec. 542(a)(1)).

Note that the required concentration of ownership automatically exists if the corporation has nine or fewer stockholders. The constructive ownership rules of Sec. 544 apply in determining the concentration of ownership. Under these rules, stock owned by an individual's siblings, spouse, ancestors, or lineal descendants is treated as if owned by the individual. Likewise, stock owned by an individual's partners in a partnership is treated as if owned by the individual. Under the rules of Sec. 544, constructive ownership may also arise from the ownership of options and convertible securities or indirectly through stock owned by a corporation, partnership, trust, or estate in which the individual has an interest.

The result of these complex rules is that most closely held corporations "fail" the concentration of ownership test and therefore cannot avoid the tax on these grounds alone. Thus, the second factor—determining if 60 percent or more of the corporate "adjusted ordinary gross income" is from passive sources—is critical in determining whether or not a corporation is vulnerable to the tax. To do this, we use the following fraction:

$$\frac{\text{Personal holding company income}}{\text{Adjusted ordinary gross income}}$$

If the value of this fraction is 60 percent or more, too much of the corporation's income is from passive sources and the corporation is subject to the personal holding company tax (assuming that the required concentration of ownership exists).

Section 543(b) explains the calculation of the denominator, "adjusted ordinary gross income," as a two-step process. First, "ordinary gross income" is determined by subtracting capital gains and Sec. 1231 gains from gross income (as defined in Sec. 61). Recall that gross income derived from a business is *net* of cost of goods sold (Treas. Reg. Sec. 1.61-3(a)). Potentially, an active corporation with a relatively large cost of goods sold could be vulnerable to the tax. Second, ordinary gross income is "adjusted" for certain receipts and expenditures attributable to income from rents and royalties. These deductions are the following:

1. Depreciation, property taxes, interest, and rent allocable to rental income;
2. Depreciation, depletion, taxes, interest, and rent allocable to mineral royalty income;
3. Certain interest receipts, including interest on condemnation awards, judgments, and tax refunds and interest earned by certain dealers in U.S. securities;
4. Expenses allocable to rents received from a shareholder of the corporation for the use of corporate property when the shareholder owned directly or indirectly 25 percent or more in value of the outstanding stock of the corporation at any time during the taxable year.

The effect of these adjustments is to limit the amount of passive income that may be sheltered in a corporation. This is particularly important when deductions allocable to rental income or to mineral royalty income are quite high. For example, highly mortgaged rental property will shelter little passive income because ordinary gross income is reduced by interest payments on the mortgage.

Once the denominator of our fraction has been determined, then the numerator (sources of passive income) must be determined in order to apply the 60 percent test. The following items (from Sec. 543(a)) comprise the numerator:

1. *Dividends, interest, royalties, and annuities.* Royalties, as used here, refers not to mineral royalties but to receipts for the use of intangible property rights, such as patents and trade names (Treas. Reg. Sec. 1.543-1(b)(3)).
2. *Rents.* Excluded from this category are the type of rents described above involving payments from shareholders for the use of corporate property. Included in this category is adjusted income from rents (the same amount included in the calculation of the denominator). Rents may be excluded from the numerator if they constitute 50 percent or more of the corporation's adjusted ordinary gross income *and* if dividends paid for the taxable year equal or exceed the amount, if any, by which the nonrent personal holding company income (the numerator) exceeds 10 percent of the ordinary gross income. Thus, if a corporation's only source of revenue is rental income, it may avoid personal holding company status. If nonrental personal holding company income is substantial, however, the corporation will be forced to pay some dividends to avoid personal holding company status.

An illustration should help to explain these complex rules.

Example: Assume that Corporation A has two sources of income: $80,000 in rents from an office building and $20,000 in interest income. Deductions allocable to the building amount to $70,000. Thus, ordinary gross income is $100,000, and *adjusted* ordinary gross income (the denominator) is $30,000 ($100,000 − $70,000). Because the adjusted income from rents is $10,000 ($80,000 − $70,000), which is less than 50 percent of adjusted ordinary gross income, Corporation A must include the rents in the numerator as passive income. If deductions allocable to the office building had been $60,000 instead of $70,000, then the adjusted income from rents would have been equal to 50 percent of adjusted ordinary gross income. (Adjusted ordinary gross income would be $100,000 − $60,000 = $40,000; adjusted income from rents would be $80,000 − $60,000 = $20,000.) Under these conditions, rents could be excluded from the numerator *if* dividends paid equaled or exceeded $10,000 (the excess of interest income over 10 percent of ordinary gross income).

3. *Mineral, oil, and gas royalties.* Mineral, oil, and gas royalties, adjusted for allocable deductions, must be included in the numerator unless (1) they amount to 50 percent or more of adjusted ordinary gross income, (2) other passive income is 10 percent or less of ordinary gross income, and (3) the corporation's deductions under Sec. 162 (excluding deductions for compensation for personal service rendered by the shareholders and deductions specifically allowable under sections other than Sec. 162) are at least 15 percent of adjusted ordinary gross income. This last requirement is designed to ensure at least a minimum level of business activity by the corporation.

4. *Copyright royalties.* Copyright royalties are classified as personal holding company income and

must be included in the numerator unless they constitute 50 percent or more of ordinary gross income and several other tests (similar to those applicable to rental and mineral royalty income) are passed. Basically, these tests ensure that publishers and others actively engaged in business will not be classified as personal holding companies.

5. *Produced film rents.* Produced film rents must be included in the numerator unless they constitute 50 percent or more of ordinary gross income. Produced film rents do not include interests acquired after substantial completion of a film. Income from such films must pass the additional tests applied to copyright royalty income in order to be excluded from the numerator.

6. *Rents from use of corporate property by shareholders.* Rents from the use of corporate property by shareholders must be included in the numerator if the shareholder owns (directly or indirectly) 25 percent or more of the corporation's stock at any time during the taxable year and if personal holding company income (other than rents) exceeds 10 percent of ordinary gross income.

7. *Personal service contracts.* Personal service contracts include not only the services of "incorporated talents" but all types of personal services. An "incorporated talent" is a highly paid individual such as a professional athlete who incorporates to shelter earnings from the individual income tax. Income from such contracts is included if some person other than the corporation has the right to designate the individual who is to perform the service and if the designated individual owns, at some time during the taxable year, 25 percent or more of the value of the outstanding stock of the corporation. Proceeds of the sale of such contracts are also included in personal holding company income.

8. *Income from estates and trusts.* Amounts includible in the corporation's income under Subchapter J from estates and trusts are classified as personal holding company income and therefore included in the numerator.

Computation of the personal holding company tax

If personal holding company income from the above eight categories constitutes 60 percent or more of adjusted ordinary gross income, then the corporation is classified as a personal holding company. The personal holding company tax, imposed in addition to the regular corporate income tax, is equal to 70 percent of "undistributed personal holding company income."

Basically, as defined by Sec. 545, *undistributed personal holding company income* is taxable income adjusted to reflect dividend-paying capacity and reduced by the dividends-paid deduction.

The adjustments to taxable income are the following:

1. The federal income tax, excluding the accumulated earnings tax or the personal holding company tax, is deducted.

2. Charitable contributions in excess of the 5 percent limit, up to the limits imposed on individual taxpayers, are deducted.

3. The special deductions for corporations in Secs. 241–250, except for amortization of organization expenditures, must be added back to taxable income. The most important of these is the 85 percent dividends-received deduction.

4. A net operating loss deduction must be added back to taxable income. An exception is provided if the net operating loss originated in the previous year. In that case, the net operating loss may be taken into account in calculating undistributed personal holding company income, but the net operating loss must be calculated without regard to the special deductions of Secs. 241–250 (except amortization of organizational costs).

5. The net capital gain for the year, minus applicable taxes, is deducted.

6. Deductions for expenses under Sec. 162 and depreciation under Sec. 167 must be added back to taxable income to the extent of rent received for the use of the related property, unless the property was rented in an arm's-length transaction entered into with a reasonable expectation of profit.

Taxable income, adjusted according to these rules, is then reduced by the dividends-paid deduction of Sec. 561. This deduction is permitted because the purpose of the personal holding company provisions is to force corporations to distribute earnings to their shareholders.

The dividends-paid deduction is the sum of dividends paid during the taxable year, "consent dividends" for the taxable year, and the "dividend carryover" of Sec. 564. Dividends paid during the taxable year include dividends paid within the first 2½ months of the following year. *Consent dividends,* described in Sec. 565, are, in effect, constructive dividends taxed to the shareholders even though not distributed. The shareholders must sign a consent election before the due date for the corporate return. The *dividend carryover* provision permits a deduction of the excess of dividends paid in the two previous years over adjusted taxable income for those years.

Once a corporation has been classified as a personal holding company, Sec. 547 provides one last opportunity to avoid the tax: The corporation may pay a dividend within 90 days after liability for the personal holding company tax is determined.

The following example illustrates the calculation of the personal holding company tax.

Example: Assume that PHC Corporation, which is owned by three individuals, had the following sources of income during the current year:

Gross profits from retail drugstore	$30,000
Dividends	40,000
Rental income from office above drugstore	12,000
Interest	8,000
Ordinary gross income	$90,000

PHC had $20,000 of general expenses, of which $10,000 were allocable to the rental income. Therefore, adjusted ordinary gross income would be:

Ordinary gross income	$90,000
Less: Expenses allocable to rental income	(10,000)
Adjusted ordinary gross income	$80,000

Personal holding company income:

Dividends	$40,000
Adjusted rentals ($12,000 − $10,000)	2,000
Interest	8,000
Personal holding company income	$50,000

Therefore,

$$\frac{\text{Personal holding company income}}{\text{Adjusted ordinary gross income}} = \frac{50,000}{80,000} = 62.5\%$$

PHC thus fails the source of income test, given that more than 60 percent of its adjusted ordinary gross income is from passive sources.

PHC's undistributed personal holding company income (the base of the personal holding company tax) is calculated as follows:

Gross income	$90,000
Less: General expenses	(20,000)
85% dividends-received deduction	(34,000)
Taxable income	$36,000
Corporate income tax	(6,450)
	$29,550
Plus: Dividends-received deduction	34,000
Undistributed personal holding company income	$63,550
Personal holding company tax (70% of $63,550)	$44,485

CONCLUDING COMMENTS

The tax rate changes of late 1978 increased the attractiveness of the corporation as a rate shelter for high income individuals. Vulnerability to the personal holding company tax is determined by a specific set of rules. Careful planning based on knowledge of the components of the fraction used to apply the 60 percent test can avoid designation as a personal holding company.

Even if a corporation manages to keep its passive income to such a level that it "passes" the 60 percent test, however, it is not necessarily "home free." The accumulated earnings tax must also be taken into account, and vulnerability to this tax cannot be reduced to a formula. Corporations should first be careful to avoid actions indicative of the forbidden purpose (failure to pay dividends, for example). Second, they should be prepared to justify accumulations and, whenever possible, to document these justifications.

PROBLEMS

1. What is the purpose of the accumulated earnings tax?
2. Why did Congress believe it necessary to impose the personal holding company tax?
3. What is the "forbidden purpose" of Sec. 533? What factors do the regulations related to Sec. 533 cite as evidence of this purpose?

4. Sec. 537 refers to "reasonable needs of the business."
   a. Why is this concept important in an accumulated earnings case?
   b. What factors are mentioned in the regulations associated with Sec. 537 as grounds for accumulating earnings and profits?
   c. What factors are mentioned as evidence of excess accumulations?

5. What two factors must be present for a corporation to be classified as a personal holding company?

6. Explain why most closely held corporations fail the concentration of ownership test for the personal holding company tax.

7. What is the effect of capital gains on "adjusted ordinary gross income" and on personal holding company income?

8. What are some of the actions a company may take to avoid personal holding company status?

9. What actions might a personal holding company take to avoid the penalty tax?

10. Jackson Construction Corporation has been in the business of remodeling homes for 10 years. The stock of the corporation is owned by Jim Jackson and his two sons, all of whom work for the corporation. The business has been successful and now has accumulated earnings and profits of $300,000. Jackson and his sons receive modest salaries from the corporation and have never paid themselves any dividends. They have been talking about building a new showroom and warehouse at a cost of at least $250,000 in the "near future." What actions would you suggest the corporation take to avoid an accumulated earnings assessment?

11. Baker Monument Company has $300,000 of accumulated earnings and profits. Sandra Baker, the owner of the corporation's stock, believes she can justify the accumulation for the following reasons:
    a. Next year, a $50,000 note is due at the company's bank.
    b. Baker's annual cost of goods sold has been approximately $120,000 for the past several years. Expenses, other than income taxes and cost of goods sold, amount to roughly $40,000 ($30,000 salary to Sandra Baker and $10,000 depreciation). Inventory turnover is approximately six months, and accounts receivable are normally collected in about three months. Baker's bills are normally paid in one month.
    c. Prices for the stone used by Baker are beginning to rise rapidly. Baker is planning to increase inventories by about 50 percent.
    d. Baker's son will enter college this fall. Baker figures that she will need to withdraw $6,000 per year from the business to pay his expenses.

    Based on these facts, how much of the $300,000 accumulation can Baker justify?

12. Andy Carter runs a successful office supply store as a sole proprietorship. Net income from the store last year was $60,000. Andy's wife earns $30,000 per year as an attorney. The Carters' income from investments (mostly interest) amounts to $10,000 per year. Assume that Andy believes he and his wife could live in the manner to which they have become accustomed if he withdrew $30,000 in salary from the store. Assume also that $30,000 is a "reasonable" salary for the work Andy performs. Calculate income taxes to Andy and his wife, assuming $5,400 of itemized deductions, no dependents, and operation of the business as a sole proprietorship. Calculate total taxes (including the business) if the business were incorporated and determine the savings, if any, to Andy and his wife.

13. Assume that Andy Carter (see Problem 12) operated his office supply store as a corporation for three years, paying no dividends. At the end of the third year, accumulated earnings and profits were $140,000. At the beginning of Year 4, an I.R.S. agent examined Andy's books and records and warned him that an accumulated earnings assessment was probable. Andy can demonstrate a need to ac-

cumulate $70,000. If taxable income to the store in Year 4 is $50,000, how much will be the accumulated taxable income and the accumulated earnings tax for the business?

14. A closely held corporation has been found by a court to be subject to the accumulated earnings tax in 1980. The following data relate to the corporation's 1980 tax year:

Taxable income	$150,000
Dividends received	20,000
Excess charitable contributions	400
Short-term capital loss	5,000
Dividends paid	10,000
Accumulated earnings and profits, beginning of year	130,000
Reasonable needs of the business	90,000

   a. Calculate the corporation's regular income tax liability for 1980.
   b. Calculate the accumulated earnings tax for 1980.
   c. Assume that the corporation could establish reasonable needs for $160,000 rather than $90,000. Now calculate the accumulated earnings tax for 1980.

15. Whipple Properties, Inc., which is owned by five individuals, owns a number of apartment buildings. In 1980, rental income from the buildings was $800,000. Depreciation, interest, and property taxes on the buildings amounted to $770,000. Whipple's other sources of income were $40,000 interest income and a $100,000 Sec. 1231 gain arising from the sale of an apartment building.
   a. Calculate Whipple's ordinary gross income, adjusted ordinary gross income, and personal holding company income.
   b. Calculate Whipple's personal holding company tax, assuming no dividends are paid.

16. Assume the same facts as in Problem 15 except that Whipple's allocable rental expenses were $760,000 instead of $770,000. Will Whipple still be classified as a personal holding company?

17. Assume the same facts as in Problem 15 except that the entire $100,000 gain is subject to Sec. 1250 recapture. Calculate Whipple's ordinary gross income, adjusted ordinary gross income, and personal holding company income. Will Whipple still be classified as a personal holding company?

18. High Rise Office Building, Inc. (owned by one individual) owns one building for which rental income this year was $1,000,000 and allocable rental expenses were $850,000. High Rise also received $150,000 in dividend income. What is the minimum dividend that High Rise must pay in order to avoid personal holding company status? If High Rise pays this dividend, will it be subject to the accumulated earnings tax?

19. Martin Grain Company, owned by four individuals, had the following sources of income this year:

Gross profit from grain business	$50,000
Rental income from an unneeded grain storage facility	15,000
Dividends received	10,000
Interest received	3,500
Long-term capital gain	5,000

Expenses were as follows:

Cost of goods sold, grain business	$40,000
Other expenses, grain business	5,000
Depreciation related to rental income	5,000

   a. Calculate Martin's taxable income and regular federal income tax.

b. Calculate Martin's adjusted ordinary gross income and personal holding company income. Is Martin a personal holding company?

c. Calculate Martin's personal holding company tax, if any.

SUPPLEMENTAL PROBLEMS

20. Two friends formed a partnership and opened a fast-food cashew chicken restaurant, The Oriental Express, in 1980. The partnership signed a long-term lease for the building. After a slow start, the establishment became a local landmark, and the business flourished. In 1982, the partners transferred the business and its assets to a newly formed corporation, The Oriental Express, Inc. Because of their desire to guarantee use of the present location, the corporation offered to purchase the building from the owner. In anticipation of the purchase, the corporation declared no dividends in the years 1982 through 1986, accumulating earnings and profits in excess of $300,000. In 1986, despite the continued efforts of the corporation, the owner informed the shareholders that he had promised to convey the land and building to his son upon the owner's death. At that time, The Oriental Express, Inc., received a notice of deficiency from the Internal Revenue Service for the earnings and profits that had accumulated.

List the issues presented. Outline and briefly discuss the arguments the taxpayer and the I.R.S. will offer in support of their respective positions.

Recommended authority:

I.R.C. Secs. 535(c)(1) and 537(a)(1).

Treas. Reg. Sec. 1.537-1(b).

Senate Report 1622, 83d Congress, 2d Sess. (1954), p. 318.

Smoot Sand & Gravel Corp., 274 F.2d 495 (4th Cir., 1960).

Faber Cement Block Co., 50 T.C. 317 (1968).

21. By 1990, The Oriental Express, Inc. (see Problem 20) had restaurants at 15 locations throughout the Midwest. The two founders of the fast-food dynasty decided to "go public" to ease the burden of financing their dream to expand coast-to-coast and to relieve them of some of the risk. The accumulated earnings in 1990 were reasonable. By 1993, the accumulated earnings had tripled—the result of the founders' desire to avoid individual taxation on any dividends. In 1993, the two original shareholders owned 30 percent of the outstanding shares of common stock. Does the corporation have reason to fear an assessment of the accumulated earnings tax?

Recommended authority:

I.R.C. Sec. 532.

Trico Products Corp. v. *McGowan,* 169 F.2d 343 (2d Cir., 1948).

Alphatype Corp., 38 AFTR2d 6019 (Ct.Cl., 1976).

Golconda Mining Corp., 58 T.C. 139 (1972), *rev'd,* 507 F.2d 594 (9th Cir., 1974).

Rev. Rul. 77-399, 1977-2 C.B. 200.

the Social Security system

Within the limitation of one chapter, we can present many of the interesting and quite controversial aspects of our Social Security system and some economic analysis. One chapter, however, does not permit a detailed analysis of many of the special provisions contained in the various parts of the system.[1]

Our present Social Security system developed from the social and economic problems of the Great Depression of the 1930s. Initially created by the Federal Insurance Contribution Act of 1935 (FICA), it has been changed extensively since then. The system, however, is neither insurance nor is it funded by contributions. In many cases—far too many for the good of the system—Congress has substituted welfare payments for the "insurance" benefits and a harshly regressive double tax system for the contribution funding concept.

THE FUNDING OR "PAY-AS-WE-GO" CONCEPT

As initially enacted, the Social Security system was to be fully funded in an actuarial sense, but most observers believe that this was just Congressional window dressing. Shortly after enactment, the funding concept was eliminated in favor of the "pay-as-we-go" concept. In addition, a contingency balance was created from the "contributions" (FICA taxes) to take care of any

unexpected or unusual demands on the fund. Currently, the fund balance is supposed to approximate one-half the current year's payout. The fund balance is at present about $40 billion, which is far less than the one-half believed to be necessary to retain solvency at all times. Obviously, under a pay-as-we-go system, the annual receipts plus interest earned on the fund balance must equal the benefits paid plus operating expenses not paid by other sources, if the fund balance is to be retained.

The switch from funding to pay-as-we-go may have been fortuitous. Few persons would want Congress controlling a fund with trillions of dollars in it. The fund currently is loaned to the general fund (through the purchase of Treasury securities), and although this produces interest revenue to the fund, it allows Congress to fund greater spending than might otherwise be the case.

SOURCE OF THE REVENUE

One source of revenue for the Social Security system is interest from loans to the general fund of the U.S. government. The principal source, however, is a *tax* (not a contribution) on wages or salaries and self-employment income (if self-employment income is $400 or more for a year). The tax is regressive in that (1) most of the income sources of the wealthy, such as dividends, interest, capital gains, and rents, are not taxed and (2) only wages and self-employment earnings up to a ceiling amount ($25,900 for 1980) are subject to the flat-rate tax. The ceiling is high enough to tax most if not all the income of middle- and lower-income wage earners, but

[1] For perhaps the best and most complete analysis of the many detailed facets of the Social Security system (but before the 1977 amendments), see Robert J. Myers, *Social Security* (Homewood, Ill.: Richard D. Irwin for the Cohan Foundation, 1975). For suggestions on improving the retirement portion of Social Security, see James E. Wheeler, Donald H. Skadden, and B. Kenneth Sanden, *Our Basic Retirement System—Social Security: Suggestions for Improvement* (New York: Federal Tax Division, American Institute of Certified Public Accountants, September, 1978).

low enough to allow much of the salary of upper-income persons to escape this tax. Taxing wages, salaries, and self-employment earnings means that for most low- and middle-income persons, their entire income or nearly all of it is subject to the tax. Table 20-1 shows the scheduled wage base and tax rates for the system from 1978 through 1982.

Note that the aggregate increase (incurred and scheduled) over these four years exceeds the entire tax of the year 1978. It should also be recognized that this is only the employee's half; a like increase would be paid by the employer. In fact, for most large corporate employers in the profit sector this increase only costs them \$583.12 [\$1,079.85 × (1 − 0.46)] because the FICA tax is deductible for the corporate income tax. Therefore, if taxes must be increased, most corporations, except those in the not-for-profit sector, would prefer an increase in Social Security tax to an equal increase in corporate income taxes. For most individuals, however, the tax increase of \$1,079.85 will cost much more, as they will also have to pay income tax on the Social Security tax. Thus, an individual in the 30 percent bracket will pay income tax of \$323.96 (\$1,079.85 × 30%) in addition to the \$1,079.85 FICA tax increase.

We can see, therefore, that the FICA tax is not borne one-half by the employee and one-half by the employer as is commonly assumed. In 1982, after the income tax effects and assuming a 30 percent marginal income tax rate on the employee, an employee will pay \$2,795.91 (\$2,150.70 × 1.30) in FICA tax and income tax on the FICA tax, while a corporate employer in the 46 percent tax bracket will pay only \$1,161.38 [\$2,150.70 × (1 − 0.46)]. Thus, the employee's tax is \$1,634.53 larger (\$2,795.91 − \$1,161.38), or 140.74 percent larger (\$1,634.53/\$1,161.38).

The difference in the FICA tax load will be even greater if the employer can arrange for the employees to be classified as self-employed or independent con-

tractors. Many businesses have been extremely successful in this regard; even the AICPA has had the graders of the CPA exam classified as independent contractors. This classification allows the employer to pay zero FICA tax, while the "self-employed" person pays at the higher self-employment rate. Instead of the system receiving \$3,175.34 (\$1,587.67 × 2) in 1980 on base wages of \$25,900, it would receive only \$2,097.90 (\$25,900 × 8.10%), or \$1,077.44 less, even though the retirement benefits would remain the same.

The flat FICA tax rate is initially paid on the lower of (1) the actual earnings or (2) the ceiling amount by both the employee and the employer at a 6.13 percent rate (for 1979 and 1980). Many economists argue that the worker really pays both halves, one directly through payroll tax deductions and the other indirectly in the form of lower wages for services.

For self-employed persons, the rate for 1979 and 1980 is 8.10 percent. The self-employed rate was originally one and one-half times the employee or employer rate (or three-fourths the combined employee and employer rates). Today the amount is less than three-fourths of the combined rates.

If a person is both an employee and self-employed, the employee rates are applied first. Then, if the taxpayer's wages fall below the ceiling amount, the self-employed rate applies to self-employed earnings but not to exceed the ceiling on taxable sources. Thus, if the ceiling is \$22,900 and a person earns \$20,000 as an employee, only \$2,900 of self-employed net earnings may be taxed at the self-employment rate.

The regressive nature of the flat-rate tax on wages would not be so significant if in fact the taxpayers were buying an insurance policy. When low-income persons buy anything, be it a loaf of bread or an insurance plan, the expenditure is regressive in that it consumes a larger portion of their income than that of wealthy persons to buy the same item. As will be shown later in this chapter, however, many of the benefits from the So-

TABLE **20-1**

PAST, PRESENT, AND SCHEDULED

FUTURE WAGE BASE AND FICA TAX RATES

Year	Base taxable wage	Self-employed rate	Employee and employer rate	Employee's half of FICA	Year-to-year increase in tax
1978	\$17,700	8.10%	6.05%	\$1,070.85	—
1979	22,900	8.10	6.13	1,403.77	\$ 332.92
1980	25,900	8.10	6.13	1,587.67	183.90
1981	29,700	9.20	6.65	1,975.05	387.38
1982	32,100	9.35	6.70	2,150.70	175.65
Four years' total increase					\$1,079.85

cial Security system are really *welfare* payments and welfare should not be financed solely by a tax on a limited amount of wages from labor.

Few persons understand the regressive nature of the FICA tax. Recently, a Congressional advisory panel on Social Security stated,

> Social adequacy is a *welfare objective* in which an individual's benefit amount is determined, not by his contributions, but by (a) appropriate transfer of income *from affluent to needy groups,* ... [emphasis added][2]

Although this consultant panel apparently believed in the welfare aspect of social security, it failed miserably in understanding who pays for it. Can this be a transfer from affluent groups when their primary sources of income such as interest, dividends, capital gains, and rents are not even subject to the tax and when the tax on wages is limited in 1979 to the first $22,900 of these earnings? The answer is obviously *no*. The affluent pay for almost none of the welfare cost of Social Security; The middle-income wage earner, single workers without dependents, and working wives—hardly members of an affluent group—pay by far the greatest amount of this welfare cost.

This is the principal problem with the Social Security system. Welfare is absolutely necessary for our society and its needy individuals, but its cost should come from general tax revenues.

THE MAJOR PARTS OF THE SYSTEM

While we shall concentrate in this chapter on the retirement aspect of Social Security, three other major parts of the system should be mentioned: disability, survivorship, and Medicare. Within the system, each major category has its own fund, except for survivorship, which is included in the retirement fund. Thus, the FICA tax rate, 6.13 percent for employers and employees in 1979, is actually an aggregate of three separate amounts—one for each of the principal funds.

Disability

Before the 1977 amendments to the system, the disability fund was the closest of the three funds to a condition of deficit. Claims for disability under Social

Security have grown rapidly in recent years. The disability benefits (as well as family benefits) are generally available if the covered individual (1) has a disability that is expected to last at least 12 months (or result in death), (2) is unable to work, (3) has been disabled for the prior five months (a waiting period before benefits can start), (4) is under age 65 (at age 65, disability stops and regular retirement begins), and (5) generally, has been fully "insured" under the system.

Survivorship

Upon the death before retirement of a covered worker who is single with no dependents, his or her estate receives a funeral expense check for $255. This is the total amount received, assuming the individual had not collected any disability benefits, from all the worker's years of tax payments. Thus, as an insurance policy, the "premiums" paid in this case (the contribution in the form of taxes) can only be characterized as a "rip-off." A person may pay an *annual* "premium" of as much as $2,807.54 ($22,900 × 0.0613 × 2) for 1979 and receive a total death benefit of $255.

If we assume a married individual who dies before retirement, then the surviving spouse is eligible for survivor's benefits (in addition to the $255 death benefit) when she or he reaches age 60, if ever. If there are dependent children, then the spouse and children receive benefits from the date of the individual's death. When the youngest child reaches age 18 and is no longer eligible, then the benefits stop for the parent unless he or she has reached age 60. When benefits stop because a child is no longer eligible, a hole is created in income support for many widows (and some widowers).

A surviving spouse who also worked and paid FICA taxes may collect retirement benefits based on either his or her own account or on the deceased spouse's account but not both, and not before reaching retirement age. The fact that both spouses have paid taxes on their earnings does not affect this result. This is the equivalent of buying two "insurance" policies and only being able to collect on one of them. Many two-worker families pay the extra cost of the second FICA tax payment with little or no hope of increased benefits. Today, this primarily involves working wives with part-time or even full-time jobs.

As explained later, the amount of the benefits depends primarily on the amount of prior wages subject to tax *and not on the amount of tax paid*. In other words, the tax rate, whether 6 percent or 60 percent, does not affect the benefit computation.

[2] *Report of the Consultant Panel on Social Security to the Congressional Research Service,* Joint Committee Print (Washington, D.C.: U.S. Government Printing Office, 1976), p. 12.

Medicare

Two separate Medicare plans exist: the basic plan and the voluntary supplemental plan. The supplemental plan has a small monthly cost ($8.20 in 1979), which may be deducted from Social Security retirement benefits. For "covered" workers, the basic plan is part of their benefits at age 65. Others may voluntarily enroll in the basic plan. In this case, there is a monthly premium, which was $63 per month in 1979.

The benefits of Medicare are extensive and, when coupled with the voluntary supplemental plan, provide better protection from rising medical costs and more medical services than many, if not most, of these persons enjoyed in their working years.

Retirement

Of the four principal parts of the Social Security system, retirement is the largest in terms of tax receipts and benefits paid. We shall devote much of the remaining portion of this chapter to the retirement part of Social Security.

Basically, retirement may come as early as age 62 with reduced benefits. Retirement age for full benefits is 65, and increased monthly benefits may be received if retirement is postponed to any period after age 65 and up to age 72.

OTHER FEDERAL RETIREMENT SYSTEMS

Other federal retirement systems are military retirement (the largest single item in the defense budget), railroad retirement (a special plan for railroad workers), civil service retirement for federal employees (they are not covered under Social Security), and Congressional retirement (members of Congress are not covered under Social Security nor under the plan for other federal employees). As might be expected, Congressional retirement is reportedly the best of all the federal systems. It is interesting to note that the federal bureaucrats who run the Social Security system do not have to pay the FICA tax.

As we shall demonstrate, federal employees have benefited by their exclusion from the Social Security tax. Representatives and Senators have also benefited by excluding themselves. If Social Security were really a "good deal" for those paying the tax, Congress would most certainly have included itself.

In addition to the noncovered, nontaxed federal employees, all state and local governmental units may elect to be excluded. Some states, such as Ohio, have never elected coverage for their employees. Ohio has a state employee's retirement plan, and Ohio state employees do not have to pay the FICA tax (unless they have second jobs that are under Social Security). The state of Alaska has recently elected to withdraw from the Social Security system.

STATISTICS ON THE GROWTH OF SOCIAL SECURITY

Perhaps nothing in our society (other than precious metals such as gold) has shown greater increases in cost than Social Security. Table 20-2 shows the enormous increases in this tax. The federal budget breaks down the total federal receipts into four basic categories, which are shown for each of three fiscal years in both dollars and percentages of total.

TABLE **20-2**
ACTUAL OR BUDGETED FEDERAL RECEIPTS

	1962 Billions	1962 Percent	1977 Billions	1977 Percent	Budgeted 1981 Billions	Budgeted 1981 Percent
Personal tax and nontax receipts	$ 47.3	45.3	$160.4	44.0	$274.4	45.8
Corporate profits tax accruals	22.9	22.0	58.2	15.9	71.6	11.9
Indirect business tax and nontax accruals	14.2	13.6	24.3	6.7	66.6	11.1
Subtotals	$ 84.4	80.9	$242.9	66.6	$412.6	68.8
"Contributions" for social "insurance"	19.9	19.1	121.8	33.4	187.4	31.2
Totals	$104.3	100.0	$364.7	100.0	$600.0	100.0

SOURCE: U.S. Office of Management and Budget *Special Analyses Budget,* Special Analyses Fiscal Year 1977 and 1980 (Washington, D.C.: U.S. Government Printing Office).

In the 16-year period from 1962 through 1977, the total federal receipts increased to 350 percent ($364.7/$104.3) of the 1962 receipts, reflecting the enormous growth in the federal sector. The budgeted 1981 receipts are more than 575 percent ($600/$104.3) of the 1962 receipts. At the end of this 19-year period, Social Security taxes (including federal unemployment compensation in both years) are 941.7 percent ($187.4/$19.9) of their 1962 total, or almost twice as fast a growth as the 488.9 percent ($412.6/$84.4) change in the other categories of federal receipts.

As a percentage of total federal receipts, approximately one dollar out of every five received in 1962 was from Social Security. By 1977, this ratio was one in three, and has remained at approximately one in three for subsequent years.

Corporate income taxes were bringing in more tax revenue than the Social Security taxes in 1962, but by 1977, the Social Security tax receipts were twice as large as the corporate income tax. This is true even though the revenue from the corporate income tax increased 254 percent ($58.2/$22.9) in this period. The increase in the corporate tax collections has resulted from large increases in corporate earnings. The effective and statutory tax rates applied to these earnings have been declining.

The decrease in effective corporate income tax rates is reflected in the continuous erosion of the corporate income as a percentage of total federal receipts. For the Social Security taxes, however, both the rate of tax and the base on which it is applied have increased. For millions of American taxpayers, and probably for the average American taxpayer, the Social Security tax exceeds the individual income tax. This trend will continue because of the enormous Social Security taxes already enacted.

Although the huge increases in Social Security tax receipts are quite interesting, we are looking only at the revenue side—the expenditure side is equally interesting. In 1962, the system was operating in the black. By 1977, the system was operating in the red; increased expenditures exceeded the 511 percent addition to revenues since 1962. Congress had so greatly increased the benefits from the system that the system was going broke. This led Congress to enact and President Carter to sign the 1977 Social Security Amendments Act, which, beginning in 1979, represents the largest tax increase ever imposed in peacetime. It had been thought that this tax would be sufficient until the turn of the century when the current worker to retiree ratio of 3 to 1 may become 1 to 1. Inflation (if it continues), however, will cause even this tax increase to be insufficient, possibly before 1984.

Congress often gives back to taxpayers part of the increase in income taxes caused by inflation, usually in election years. Using this logic, tax increases will be enacted in nonelection years. Congressional choice of nonelection years for tax increases was quite prevalent in the 1977 Amendments to Social Security, as shown in Table 20-3. Total tax increases in two nonelection years were 100 percent greater than in three Congressional election years.

THE BENEFIT COMPUTATION CONCEPT

If Social Security were a retirement insurance plan, then the retirement benefits should be primarily a function of amounts paid in, length of time these amounts

TABLE **20-3**

INCREASES IN SOCIAL SECURITY TAXES

AS A RESULT OF THE 1977 AMENDMENTS

Total additional taxes due to the 1977 amendments[a] (billions of dollars)	Year	Billions of dollars of increase in taxes from one year to the next	
		Election years	Nonelection years
-0-	1978	-0-	
6.6	1979		6.6
9.8	1980	3.2	
19.8	1981		10.0
24.9	1982	5.1	
Total 61.1	Three election years' total	8.3	
	Two nonelection years' total		16.6
	Average increase	2.77	8.3

[a]Congressional Budget Office, *Aggregate Economic Effects of Changes in Social Security Taxes* (Washington, D.C.: U.S. Government Printing Office, 1978), Table 2, p. 7.

have been "on deposit," and the remaining life expectancy of the retiree (and of his or her spouse, if a joint life retirement option were selected). On the other hand, if Social Security were a welfare plan, then the primary factor in determining the amount to be received should be need. Social Security is largely a welfare system financed by a tax primarily on middle- and low-income labor (but not on poverty-level wage earners with dependent children[3]).

The retirement computation itself was changed somewhat by the 1977 amendments to "eliminate" the (unlikely) possibility of someone receiving more retirement from Social Security than he or she had been earning immediately before retirement.

Coverage requirements for retirement benefits

To be "fully insured" for retirement, a person must have up to 40 quarters of covered employment, but, depending on the year of retirement, full coverage may be obtained with as few as six quarters. "Fully insured" does not mean that you will receive the highest benefit; it simply means you are eligible for benefits when you retire, including the so-called minimum benefit to be discussed later.

For example, an individual who reaches age 62 in 1980 needs only 29 quarters of covered employment. To be eligible, a worker must have one quarter of coverage for each year after 1950 that he or she was *between* the ages of 21 and 62. Thus, reaching age 62 in 1980 means that this person has 29 years (1979 − 1950) between ages 21 and 62 after 1950. A person who needs the maximum of 40 quarters will have to reach age 62 in 1991 or later years; (1990 − 1950 = 40, or age 61 − 21 = 40).

A worker receives one quarter of coverage for each $290 of earnings, but not to exceed four quarters per year. Thus, earnings of $1,160 ($290 × 4) provide four quarters of coverage and cost the employee $71.11 ($1,160 × 6.13%) in FICA tax in 1980. Self-employed persons get four quarters of coverage for $400 of net earnings.

The benefit formula

Retirement benefits are computed by layering the "average indexed monthly earnings." Beginning January 1, 1979, the old seven-strata formula was replaced by the current three-strata formula. For 1979, these strata are as follows (the earnings strata will change in the future in response to increased average earnings):

	Average indexed monthly earnings	Benefit percentage
First	$ 180	90
Next	905	32
Excess over	1,085	15

In the old formula, the highest benefit percentage as of June 1977 was 145.9 percent.

Under the amended three-strata system, the average indexed monthly earnings (from which benefits are computed) may rise, but the benefit percentages remain fixed until retirement. After retirement, the average indexed monthly earnings will remain fixed for the retiree but the benefit percentages are then increased to keep pace with the increases in the consumer price index (CPI). This removes the "double indexing" error that Congress made in the 1972 amendments, which allowed a double adjustment for inflation (on wages and benefit percentage) for some workers.

Within the formula, the average monthly earnings are the *taxed* earnings of each year in the computation period divided by the months in that period. The indexing aspect is achieved by multiplying each prior year's taxable wage by the ratio of the average covered wages of all workers for the test year (two years before the worker reached age 62) to the average covered wages of all workers in the year being indexed. For example, if the average covered wages were $6,000 in 1965 and were $24,000 two years before the retiring worker reached age 62, and if this worker had $4,000 of taxed (covered) wages in 1965 (the year being indexed), the $4,000 would be increased to $16,000 for purposes of calculating the average indexed monthly earnings. Thus, as wages rise, the average indexed monthly earnings of each past year will also increase (but not the amount paid in).

In addition, to prevent a retiree from being pushed into the higher strata and thus into the lower benefit portions of the benefit formula, the three strata will also rise. For example, if covered wages inccrease 20 percent, the three strata will increase by the same percentage. This would change the "average indexed monthly earnings" strata from $180, $905, and over $1,085 to $216, $1,086, and over $1,302.

The welfare aspect

Except for voluntary gifts, welfare may be defined as any benefit received but not earned; thus, it is paid for by others. Former Secretary of Health, Education, and

---

[3]For members of this group, the refundable earned income credit in the income tax fully offsets any Social Security tax, while leaving them eligible for Social Security retirement benefits.

Welfare Wilbur J. Cohen has stated in Congressional testimony that of the *long-range* distributions from the Social Security system, about one-third will not have been paid for by the beneficiaries.[4] With disbursements from the system in excess of $120 billion, the welfare element must exceed $40 billion annually, using Cohen's long-range estimate.

For the short run, the welfare aspect must be even larger. In addition to the possibility of excessively high benefit percentages, the three principal causes of excess benefits over contributions for those receiving benefits are (1) indexing past taxed wages to bring them in line with the recent taxed wage levels, (2) weighting benefit percentages to favor low-wage income persons, and (3) providing a minimum benefit computation to be used whenever it results in greater benefits than the weighting has *already* provided.

The first of these three items has already been discussed, but perhaps another illustration would be helpful. If a person had paid taxes on the ceiling amounts of prior years, the tax would have been much less than currently paid because the base or ceiling amount was lower (for example, $3,600 compared with $22,900) and the rate was lower. Adjusting these prior wages in computing benefits increases the amount of the benefit without increasing the amount of tax paid into the system. Thus, to the extent that this adjustment exceeds the impact of inflation, it will result in welfare benefits.

The "earned income credit" also has an interesting welfare effect. Many very low income wage earners with dependent children, in effect, do not pay any FICA tax. In 1976, Congress enacted as a part of the income tax a refundable earned income credit to offset or eliminate the effect of the Social Security tax on this group of wage earners. Thus, these individuals have their FICA tax refunded on their income tax returns. In effect, they pay zero or reduced FICA taxes and are still entitled to weighted retirement benefits based on their wages and the three-strata formula.

WEIGHTING OF BENEFITS   Obviously, the strata system causes a weighting of retirement benefits heavily in favor of low-income persons or those with low taxable source incomes (wages) in prior years. Thus, using the formula cited on page **20**/6, the monthly retirement benefits of an individual with only $180 average indexed monthly earnings would be $162 ($180 × 90%). For a person with $1,800 of average indexed monthly

earnings, the retirement benefit would be $558.85 ($180 × 90% + $905 × 32% + $715 × 15%), or a benefit of about 31 percent as opposed to a 90 percent benefit in the first example. The individual in the second illustration could have paid 10 times more tax than the first person and would receive a benefit less than three and a half times larger.

Now, suppose the individual in the first case were receiving a million dollars in interest income each year in addition to quite modest wages. Without a needs test being applied, a millionaire receives welfare-weighted benefits. Thus, the system, without a means test, provides welfare to both rich and poor retirees.

It is also interesting to note that FICA rate increases do not have any direct impact on future benefits. In other words, the FICA tax rate could be increased tenfold and, because the benefits are based on taxable wages rather than on amounts paid in, there would be no increase in benefits.

MINIMUM BENEFIT   For covered workers, there is a minimum benefit computation, supposedly to take care of the very low wage earners. Indeed, an individual with low average indexed monthly earnings (below $135) would receive a minimum benefit of $122. This amount was frozen (not to be adjusted for changes in price level) as of January 1, 1979.

Because federal employees, employees of some states, and members of Congress are not covered under Social Security, they may take temporary or part-time jobs (such as traveling barber, yard worker, or greeter at a funeral home) in order to reach the covered status. In past years, if eligibility had been achieved with minimum coverage earnings, the FICA tax paid in for all years would have in effect been recovered in the first month's Social Security "minimum" benefit. According to the Congressional advisory panel on Social Security, "In 1969 one-third of Social Security beneficiaries who were also receiving benefits under another governmental plan were receiving minimum benefits."[5] Of course, many of these persons paid in more than the minimum for coverage, but much if not most of their benefits are unearned and thus constitute welfare. Some former government employees are drawing retirement pay of as much as $2,000 a month and are still receiving the so-called "minimum" Social Security benefit.[6]

[4]Statement of Professor Wilbur J. Cohen, former HEW Secretary, in testimony before the Senate Financial Subcommittee on Social Security as reported in the *Daily Report for Executives* (Bureau of National Affairs), June 16, 1977, p. J-4 (before enactment of the 1977 Amendments).

[5]*Report of the Consultant Panel on Social Security to the Congressional Research Service*, p. 24.
[6]Report to the Congress by the Comptroller General of the United States, *Minimum Social Security Benefit: A Windfall That Should Be Eliminated* (U.S. General Accounting Office, December 10, 1979), p. 16.

Earnings while receiving retirement benefits

President Carter once called our income tax "a disgrace to the human race." He could also have included many aspects of the Social Security tax. Perhaps no part of the Social Security system illustrates this better than the rules regarding work after age 65.

Retired workers between the ages of 65 and 72 (70 after 1981) on Social Security retirement may earn only limited amounts ($4,500 a year for 1979) without incurring a severe penalty. During these retirement years, for each $2 of earnings above the limited amount, $1 of Social Security retirement benefits are removed. In addition, the earnings are subject to the FICA tax and to income taxation.

Example: If a retiree between the ages of 65 and 72 in 1979 received $3,000 in Social Security and earned $8,500 in part-time jobs as her only other source of income, she would have been penalized for the earnings in excess of $4,500 by losing $1 of Social Security retirement for each $2 of earnings above $4,500. In this case, the Social Security retirement benefits would be reduced from $3,000 to $1,000 [$3,000 − ($8,500 − $4,500 × ½)]. In addition, she would have to pay FICA tax on the $8,500 at a rate of 8.10 percent if self-employed ($688.50) or 6.13 percent if not self-employed ($521.05). Also, the individual would have to pay income tax on the $8,500 and would not get a deduction for the FICA tax paid.

Now let us compare this treatment with that received by a retired millionaire.

Example: A millionaire also is to receive $3,000 in Social Security benefits and is the same age as the worker in the prior example. Instead of working, however, our millionaire clips $5 million worth of interest coupons. In this case, the Social Security retirement continues at its full $3,000 amount; he pays no FICA tax and if the interest income is from state and local bonds, there is no federal income tax; indeed, this millionaire is not even required to file an income tax return.

How should one attempt to justify such results? Supposedly, the rules regarding work after age 65 were designed to provide more jobs for younger workers. Is this Congressionally mandated result a reflection of the political power of retired low-income wage earners versus millionaires?

Another problem concerns the application of the earnings test. Recently, the test was changed from a monthly to an annual basis. It is still monthly in the year of retirement.

Example: Assume a company executive retires on January 1 and is paid a $50,000 consulting fee in January for services rendered. He would lose his January Social Security benefits but would receive them for each remaining month in that year (the year of retirement). A $50,000 consulting fee in the following year would cause him to lose all his Social Security retirement for that year.

For retired executives, a new status—"stand-by employee"—has been devised. A stand-by employee is a retired executive (or factory worker) over age 62 who, for a fee of $26,000 ($500 per week) agrees to work. In 1980, if this executive is called to work only 10 weeks, the "earnings" are only $5,000 (10 × $500), although the stand-by employee still receives the total $26,000 fee. Since $5,000 is below the "earnings limitation," this worker is eligible for full Social Security benefits without reduction for excess earnings. Incidentally, only the $5,000 is taxed for FICA purposes, thus saving our "retired executive" additional FICA taxes and of course the corporate employer (often a closely held family corporation) also saves FICA taxes on the $21,000 of stand-by status pay.[7] Allowing this type of form over substance when we take away the entire Social Security of a needy person for excess earnings represents complete destruction of any equity concept.

THE EXCLUSION OF SOCIAL SECURITY BENEFITS

Interestingly enough, Congress provided, in Code Sec. 275(a)(1)(A), that the FICA tax paid directly by the employee is not deductible for income tax purposes. Is it possible that Congress could think about disallowing the deduction of the FICA tax and not consider the tax treatment of the benefits? The Code itself is absolutely silent on the subject. The benefits, therefore, based on a literal reading of the Code, clearly should be taxable under Code Sec. 61, which taxes "all income from whatever source derived." The Treasury Department, however, through an administrative maneuver in 1941, decided not to collect the tax on Social Security income. This position was restated in a revenue ruling in

---

[7] Ernst and Whinney, *Tax Notes,* February 1980, item 6 (pages are not numbered).

1970.[8] Technically, such a ruling is equivalent to legislation, a power that the Treasury Department is not supposed to possess.

How valid is this exclusion of benefits from taxable income? Should anyone want to tax Social Security benefits? The answer, after some analysis, is clearly, yes. To understand this, compare the tax advantage of the exclusion to someone age 65 and receiving, say, $4,300 as his or her Social Security retirement and total income to someone with millions of dollars in interest income plus the same $4,300 in Social Security retirement income. With a zero bracket amount in 1979 of $2,300 and assuming two $1,000 personal exemptions, the first individual's income of $4,300 is already, in effect, excluded; a second exclusion is worthless to the first individual. The exclusion for the second individual is, assuming a 70 percent marginal tax rate, worth $3,010 (70% × $4,300). In other words, persons with only Social Security as retirement income do not benefit at all from the exclusion (although they probably have the most need). The benefit is, instead, in direct relationship to the amount of the non-Social-Security income from taxable sources.

If Social Security benefits were subject to the income tax, the resulting revenue could be used to increase the benefits to those with the most need.

THE SPECTRUM OF DOUBLE TAXATION

When the term "double taxation" is used, virtually everyone immediately thinks about the double taxation of corporate earnings. In reality, there is very little, if any, double tax on corporate earnings.[9] Corporations are often formed for their tax advantages, as can be seen by the proliferation of professional corporations. But double taxation is present, and it is especially severe to the middle-income wage earner. Because Congress prevents a deduction, through Code Sec. 275(a)(1)(A), an income tax is assessed and withheld on the FICA tax already withheld from a worker's wages. This is instantaneous double taxation in the same paycheck; there is no waiting, as there is for a corporation to pay dividends.

To fully appreciate the harshly regressive nature of this tax system, one also needs to understand the basic curve contained in the income tax tables. The curve in Figure 20-1 (page **20/10**) is taken from the single re-

turn table. Note that the curve as determined by the tax rates is *not* a progressive tax curve based on ability to pay. Such a curve would appear as in the top graph in Figure 20-2 (page **20/10**). It is also not a proportionally progressive curve. Such a curve would appear as a diagonal straight line, as shown in the middle graph of Figure 20-2.

Instead of a progressive tax, our income tax curve is a *degressively* progressive one, as shown in the bottom graph of Figure 20-2. Such a slope requires that the *rates of increase* in the tax rates are reduced as income increases. In other words, the rates of tax increase are the heaviest on the lowest taxable incomes. For 1979, a single taxpayer hits the top, or 70 percent, bracket at $108,300 of taxable income; however, with half that amount, or $54,150, the individual would be in the 55 percent bracket. In other words, there are 55 percentage points of tax increase in the first half and only 15 percentage points of increase in the second half. The story, however, gets worse as taxable incomes fall. An individual with only one-tenth of the $108,300 taxable income, or $10,830, is in the 21 percent bracket. Thus, well over one-fourth of the total tax progression takes place in the first 10 percent of the income required to reach the 70 percent bracket. The 1979 tax curve is less degressive than it was for 1978. The curve, however, does not consider the "maximum tax on earned income," the "minimum tax on tax preferences," the effects of the exclusion of 60 percent of capital gains, nor the effects of any of the tax credits.

No economic philosophy can justify a degressive income tax system. Congress has loaded much of the tax burden of this country on the middle-income wage earner through a combination of nondeductible FICA taxes and an income tax structure designed to extract the maximum from this group's earnings. With extensive inflation, this structure demands an increasing share of the wage earner's purchasing power.

It is interesting to note the great length to which Congress goes to encourage savings for retirement through qualified pension plans and individual retirement accounts (IRAs). The I.R.S. recently released data on pension plans for which determination letters were issued in 1978. The following table reflects the dominance of qualified plans:

	Initial qualifications	*Amendments*	*Termination*
Qualified plans	65,684	125,057	15,286
Nonqualified plans	27	33	43

[8] I.T. 3447, 1941 CB 191, and Rev. Rul. 70-217, 1970-1 CB 12.

[9] For an extensive discussion of this, see Dennis Gaffney and James E. Wheeler, "The Double Taxation of Corporate Source Income: Reality or Illusion?" *The Tax Advisor*, September 1977, pp. 516–31.

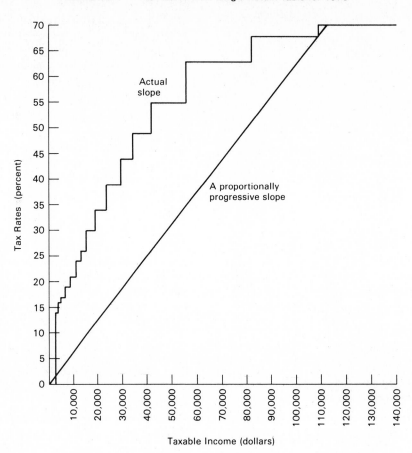

FIGURE **20-1**   Tax Curve from Single Return Table for 1979

In addition, more than 2.5 million individual returns contained IRAs for 1977—an increase of 586,030 over the 1976 figure of 1,948,418.[10] The country's largest retirement plan, however—Social Security—is taxed to the employee as though it were a nonqualified plan. Unlike a qualified or IRA plan, for which contributions are deductible, there is no deduction for Social Security taxes by the employee. For the privilege, apparently, of having the benefits excluded from taxation when received, a worker has to pay income tax on the FICA tax each year of his or her working lifetime at

[10]Data released by the I.R.S., as reported in the *Daily Report for Executives* (Bureau of National Affairs), February 27, 1979, p. G-10.

FIGURE **20-2**   Progressive, Proportionally Progressive, and
Degressive Tax Curves

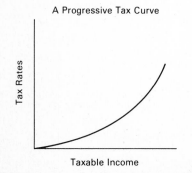

A Progressive Tax Curve

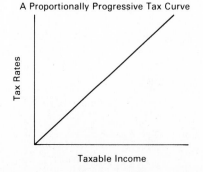

A Proportionally Progressive Tax Curve

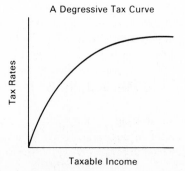

A Degressive Tax Curve

the highest marginal rate on a degressive tax curve. And if this is an individual's only retirement income, it would be tax exempt anyway because of the effects of the zero bracket amount and the personal exemptions.

If, as many economists suggest, the employee pays both halves of the Social Security tax, the employee is much better off on the half paid indirectly in the form of lower wages. By taking lower wages while having the employer pay half the Social Security tax, the employee saves income tax on that half at his or her highest marginal rate. In other words, if it were permitted, an employee could ask an employer to reduce gross wages by the amount of the employee's half of the FICA tax and then to pay the entire FICA tax rather than one-half of it to the government. This would save the income tax on the Social Security tax. Thus, an employee could lower gross wages while increasing take-home pay.

Interestingly enough, however, this technique may be used to reduce FICA taxes but not income taxes.

Example: Suppose a person earned in 1980 exactly the $25,900 "base taxable wage" for Social Security purposes. The employer could then "reduce" the $25,900 by the $1,587.67 of FICA tax to be withheld on that employee and pay the FICA tax rather than withholding it from the employee's pay. For FICA purposes, the taxable wages would then be $24,312.33 ($25,900 − $1,587.67), and at a 0.0613 FICA tax rate, the actual tax is only $1,490.35. This would leave the employee's take-home pay unchanged, but it would save the employer $194.64 [($1,587.67 − $1,490.35) × 2] for both the employer and employee FICA.

This technique would not work for persons whose earnings are well above the "base taxable wage," as it would not reduce their FICA tax, and it does not, for any employee, reduce gross wages for income tax purposes. Thus, while the taxable wage was reduced to $24,312.33 for FICA purposes, it remains at $25,900 for income tax purposes. There is also a long-range disadvantage to the employee in that his or her "average indexed monthly earnings" will be lower and result in lower benefits upon retirement.

SOME ECONOMIC CONSEQUENCES

The shifting of enormous welfare burdens to the labor sector of our economy is certain to have some serious economic consequences. These consequences can be ag-

gravated by also reducing the cost of capital equipment through the investment credit and accelerated depreciation. A balance exists between the use of equipment and the employment of labor. Whenever one becomes more costly, the other can frequently be substituted for it. Thus, automated equipment can reduce the need for labor and the number of jobs. The substitution of equipment for labor or vice versa should occur whenever the marginal cost of one exceeds the other. Our present tax system is increasing the cost of labor through the high cost of welfare paid with FICA tax revenues while the cost of equipment is reduced through tax credits and depreciation. Assuredly, unemployment is the inevitable result unless the economy is expanding rapidly enough to create more jobs than are lost.

While the substitution of capital equipment for labor is a logical consequence, it is not always possible. Many labor-intensive industries, particularly the not-for-profit sectors of our economy, may find themselves paying for more than their fair share of the total cost of government.

Certain units of our economy have more difficulty substituting capital for labor. Universities are a prime example: They are highly labor intensive; often 70 to 80 percent of their budgets are labor costs, and they are in the not-for-profit sector. Because of this, a large increase in FICA taxes is almost twice as difficult for universities to adjust to compared with corporations. Entities subject to the income tax receive a deduction for the employer half of Social Security, which means that for large corporate businesses, 46 percent of the FICA tax increase is immediately refunded in the form of an income tax savings. A university, on the other hand, must absorb or somehow increase its revenues for 100 percent of any FICA tax increase, for there is no offsetting income tax savings of any amount.

The not-for-profit sector of our economy is thus forced to carry more than its fair share of the welfare cost. Because states and local units may opt out of the Social Security system after a two-year wait, the use of FICA taxes to provide benefits far beyond those earned and paid for by the recipients may soon prompt additional states or local units to elect out of the system.

Loading welfare costs onto the FICA tax helps federal employees, members of Congress, the very wealthy, and any state employees not covered under Social Security. In fact, these people do not have to participate in financing this element of the total welfare load, and they then get the chance (which most of them take) to exploit the system through the minimum benefit computation.

PROBLEMS

1. How is the Social Security system funded?
2. What is the primary source of Social Security system revenues?
3. Do Social Security benefits represent one form of transfer from the affluent to the needy? Why or why not?
4. Do employees and employers pay equal amounts in taxes for Social Security? Explain.
5. If, as some economists suggest, employees pay both halves of Social Security, which half is the least costly to the employee?
6. What aspects of the Social Security benefits constitute welfare payments?
7. Why do most corporations prefer increases in Social Security taxes to equal increases in corporate income taxes?
8. What source of federal tax receipts has grown the most since 1962?
9. What source of federal tax receipts has decreased the most in terms of percentage of total federal receipts since 1962?
10. What are the major parts of the Social Security system?
11. What is the largest tax that the average American taxpayer pays?
12. Why are members of Congress and federal employees not included in the Social Security system?
13. What is the "minimum benefit"?
14. How can members of Congress and federal employees obtain coverage under Social Security?
15. How does the earned income credit affect the rate of return to retirees under Social Security?
16. What has "double taxation" to do with Social Security?
17. How is our Social Security system similar to a nonqualified pension plan to an employee (or self-employed person)?
18. What is a degressive progressive tax curve, and what is its purpose?
19. Why does paying for welfare through the Social Security system cause a significant shift of tax burden between the profit and the not-for-profit sectors of our economy?
20. Why might employers want to classify employees as self-employed or independent contractors?
21. Assume Mr. X is an employee of the Double X Corporation and also earns additional compensation by doing plumbing work, as an independent contractor, on weekends. Mr. X's compensation was $24,000 per year in wages, and he consistently earned $5,000 per year as a self-employed plumber.
    a. Compute Mr. X's FICA tax for each year from 1979 through 1981.
    b. If the Double X Corporation were consistently in a 46 percent income tax bracket, what is its annual after-tax outflow for Social Security taxes for Mr. X in years 1979 through 1981?
    c. If Mr. X could be classified in 1980 as a self-employed person rather than an employee, what is the effect in 1980 and 1981 on Mr. X and on the Double X Corporation?
22. A, B, C, and D are all 66 years old in 1979 and retire under Social Security with full coverage. Their "average indexed monthly earnings" were as follows.

	Average indexed monthly earnings	Earnings in retirement year	Dividend income in retirement year
A	$ 100	$6,000	$ -0-
B	200	6,000	-0-
C	950	4,000	10,000
D	1200	-0-	5,000,000

a. Compute the Social Security benefits each individual should receive as retirement benefits in 1979, ignoring adjustment for inflation.

b. If Mr. B had received all his FICA tax back in every year through the refundable earned income credit, what would his Social Security retirement benefits be for 1979?

c. If Mr. A, a retired Congressman, had "average indexed monthly earnings" of only $100 and had a federal pension of $20,000 annually, what would his Social Security retirement benefits be in 1979?

d. In part c, above, would it matter if Mr. A also received $1,000,000 of interest on his foreign bank account?

23. The Decision Corporation can purchase on January 1, 19X1, a new machine that can do the work of four factory workers. Each worker earns $25,000 annually in gross wages. Assume the FICA taxes for 19X1 and the following years equal those for 1978 and the following years. Ignoring present values, determine the price Decision would be willing to pay for the new machine to replace the four employees. Assume the machine has a useful life of five years and that there will be no wage increases.

SEVEN

international taxation

basic concepts in U.S. taxation of international transactions

Taxes imposed by the U.S. government on international transactions must be considered when making many kinds of modern business decisions. U.S. income tax considerations will affect whether a foreign business should be conducted directly by a U.S. corporation, through a foreign branch, through a foreign subsidiary corporation, or through a domestic subsidiary corporation that retains a special tax status. The placement and compensation of U.S. employees in businesses operated outside the United States also require careful consideration of international taxes because, in many cases, such individuals are permitted a number of "special" deductions for excess living costs incurred abroad or are able to exclude part or all of their foreign earned income from their tax returns. In addition, U.S. taxes levied (or the exemption from U.S. taxes permitted) are important in determining the nature and form of a nonresident alien's or foreign corporation's investment, trade, or business activities in the United States.

In all these areas, the tax laws are complex and technical. In this part, we shall discuss the major concepts involved in U.S. taxation of international operations. Many of the more technical provisions within each of these areas are beyond the scope of this book. Our intent in this part is simply to give you a general awareness of the outlines of the U.S. tax laws in the area of international taxation.[1]

---

[1] For more detailed coverage of these materials, see: Michael L. Moore and Ronald N. Bagley, *AICPA Tax Study No. 6* (U.S. Tax Aspects of Doing Business Abroad), (New York: AICPA, 1977); Jon E. Bischel and Robert Feinschreiber, *Fundamentals of International Taxation* (New York: Practicing Law Institute, 1977); or Rufus von Thulen Rhoades and Elliott G. Steinberg, *Income Taxation of Foreign Related Transactions* (New York: Matthew Bender, 1979).

AN OVERVIEW OF THE TAXATION OF INTERNATIONAL TRANSACTIONS

Under the U.S. income tax system, the taxation of international transactions follows a fairly simple general outline. For U.S. citizens, resident aliens, and domestic corporations, all gross income is subject to U.S. income taxation, no matter where the income is earned. Because income earned abroad by a U.S. citizen is also likely to be taxed by the foreign government, significant double taxation of income could occur. To minimize the impact of double taxation, the U.S. tax laws contain the following major provisions:

1. U.S. taxpayers may take a credit against their U.S. tax liability for certain foreign income taxes paid.
2. Bilateral tax treaties between the United States and certain foreign countries reduce the burden of foreign taxes levied on U.S. taxpayers.
3. For U.S. citizens or residents employed abroad by U.S. businesses, some income may be excluded from U.S. taxation or some additional costs incurred in living abroad may be deductible.

We shall explore each of these major provisions more fully in this chapter and in Chapters 22 and 23.

Two instances of special tax treatment of foreign income earned by U.S. corporate taxpayers should be noted. U.S. corporations qualifying as Domestic International Sales Corporations (DISCs) may have as much as 50 percent of their profits that are derived from export-related activities receive a deferral from U.S. taxation (discussed in Chapter 23). In addition, special rules reduce the U.S. income taxes due from both U.S. citizens and domestic corporations that do most of their business in a U.S. possession (discussed in Chapters 22 and 23).

Nonresident alien individuals and foreign corporations are taxed by the United States only on their investment-related, rental, and royalty income earned in the United States and on their worldwide income that is effectively connected with the conduct of a U.S. trade or business. In general, profits earned abroad by a foreign corporation are not subject to U.S. taxation unless the foreign corporation distributes this income to its U.S. shareholders. This tax treatment (taxation only of distributions from foreign corporations) could allow U.S. shareholders to defer significant income through the use of a foreign corporation except for two provisions of the tax law. If the foreign corporation meets the definition of a *controlled foreign corporation* (CFC) or of a *foreign personal holding company* (FPHC), a pro rata share of certain forms of the foreign corporation's income are taxed to its U.S. shareholders in the year in which the foreign corporation earned the income (instead of the year in which the income is distributed).

JURISDICTION TO TAX

Neither international law nor the U.S. constitution limits the ability of the United States to tax income from foreign sources that is earned by persons or business entities coming under the jurisdiction of U.S. laws. The limits that do exist are the result of Congressional decisions based on policy considerations and revenue needs. The income tax burden imposed by these laws varies with the type of taxpayer involved—U.S. citizen, resident alien, nonresident alien, or foreign corporation. In general, all U.S. citizens are taxed on their worldwide income regardless of where they live or where the income originates. For example, a U.S. citizen who owned Mexican property and resided all year in Mexico would still pay U.S. income taxes on his or her rental income derived from the Mexican property. For U.S. citizens who work in foreign countries for extended periods of time, their foreign earnings are fully subject to the U.S. income tax laws, unless some of it may be excluded as explained in Chapter 22. Within the scope of this general rule, numerous provisions of U.S. tax laws may alter the timing of the U.S. tax liability and the applicable tax rates.

As already mentioned, resident aliens are also taxed on their worldwide income, and nonresident aliens and foreign corporations are taxed on their investment-related, rental, and royalty income derived from U.S. activities and on their worldwide income that is considered to be effectively connected with the conduct of a U.S. trade or business. ("Effectively connected" will be defined in greater detail in Chapter 22.) In Chapter 22, we shall discuss in detail the types of income that are taxed to nonresident aliens and foreign corporations and the applicable tax rates for each. Table 21-1 presents a summary of the U.S. taxation of income, based on the type of entity taxed.

SOURCE-OF-INCOME RULES

Each country that taxes international operations differently depending on the location where the income is earned, must devise a series of rules that determines

TABLE **21-1**

U.S. JURISDICTION FOR TAXATION

Taxpayer classification	Income subject to U.S. income taxation
U.S. citizen	Worldwide income
Domestic corporation, trust, or estate	Worldwide income
Resident alien	Worldwide income
Nonresident alien	1. U.S. source investment-related, rental, and royalty income 2. Worldwide income effectively connected with the conduct of a U.S. trade or business
Foreign corporation, trust, or estate	1. U.S. source investment-related, rental, and royalty income 2. Worldwide income effectively connected with the conduct of a U.S. trade or business

the *source* of the income. Under Sec. 61 of the Internal Revenue Code, U.S. citizens and resident aliens are taxed on all income "from whatever source derived," so the source-of-income rules do not affect the total income of such taxpayers. The source-of-income rules, however, do affect the amounts of certain deductions, exclusions, and credits available to these U.S. citizens and resident aliens. In addition, as mentioned above, the total taxable income of nonresident aliens and foreign corporations is greatly affected by the source-of-income rules. The major impact of the rules lies in the following four areas of U.S. taxation:

1. Computation of the foreign tax credit limitation;

2. Determination of the income of foreign corporations and nonresident aliens that is subject to tax;

3. Determination of the income earned in a foreign country or U.S. possession that is eligible for exclusion; and

4. Determination of the need for a U.S. or foreign payer to withhold U.S. income taxes.

Code Secs. 861, 862, and 863 categorize all income as either U.S. source income or foreign source income or—as the Code states—from sources within or without the United States. Remember that these sections only define terms; they do not levy a tax. For example, bond interest paid by a municipality within one of the 50 states is listed as U.S. source income under Sec. 861(a)(1), but such interest is, of course, excluded from U.S. taxation under Sec. 103.

The source-of-income rules are based on types of income. The general source-of-income rules for the major types of income and certain of the more common exceptions are discussed below.

Interest income

The source of any interest income is generally the residence of the obligor—that is, the person who is obligated to pay the interest. Thus, when a U.S. citizen receives an interest payment from a resident of France, the U.S. citizen has derived income from a French source. Interest paid by a U.S. corporation or partnership is generally U.S. source income. Major exceptions to the general rule are:

1. Interest on deposits paid by U.S. banks and savings institutions (including their foreign branches) is foreign source income when paid to a nonresident alien or foreign corporation and the interest is not effectively connected with the corporation's or alien's conduct of a U.S. trade or business. This exception is intended to encourage foreign deposits in U.S. banks and savings institutions.

2. Interest paid by a resident alien or a domestic corporation is foreign source income if less than 20 percent of the payer's gross income for the three years preceding the year of payment was U.S. source income.[2]

3. Interest paid by a foreign corporation is foreign source income unless 50 percent or more of the foreign corporation's gross income for the three years preceding the year of payment was effectively connected with the conduct of a U.S. trade or business. If 50 percent or more was so connected, the interest income must be prorated between U.S. source income and foreign source income. The foreign source portion of the interest income is determined as follows:

$$\text{Interest income} \times \frac{\substack{\text{Total non-U.S.}\\\text{trade or business}\\\text{gross income*}}}{\substack{\text{Total worldwide}\\\text{gross income*}}} = \substack{\text{Foreign source}\\\text{interest income}}$$

*For the three years preceding the year of payment (Sec. 861(a)(1)).

Dividend income

The source of any dividend income is generally the country of incorporation of the firm making the dividend payment. Dividend distributions made by U.S. firms are thus U.S. source income, and dividend distributions made by foreign firms are foreign source income. The three major exceptions to this rule parallel those listed for interest income:

1. A U.S. corporation's dividend distributions are foreign source income if the U.S. corporation derives from U.S. sources less than 20 percent of its gross income for the three years preceding the year of the distribution.

2. A foreign corporation's dividend distributions are prorated between U.S. and foreign source income if the corporation derives 50 percent or more of its gross income for the three taxable years preceding the year of distribution from the conduct of a U.S. trade or business. (If less than 50 percent of the income is derived from the conduct of a U.S. trade or business, then the dividend distribution is entirely foreign source income.)

---

[2]If the corporation has not been in existence for three years, then its entire existence is used to determine whether the 20 percent or 50 percent minimums outlined in Sec. 861 have been met.

3. Dividends paid by a Domestic International Sales Corporation (DISC), which is a U.S. corporation, are foreign source income to the extent they may be attributed to qualified export receipts (Sec. 861(a)(2)). (For further details, see the discussion of DISCs in Chapter 23.)

Foreign corporation dividend distributions that are classified as U.S. source income are eligible for the 85 percent dividends-received deduction under Sec. 245. The portion of such a distribution classified as foreign source income is eligible for the foreign tax credit benefits that are explained below.

Personal services income

In general, compensation for personal services has its source in the location where the services are performed. This means that the employer's nationality, the employer's country of citizenship or residence, and the location in which payment is received are irrelevant. The source of retirement pay is also the place where the employee performed the work. The one exception to this rule applies to nonresident aliens who are temporarily working in the United States. If an alien meets the three qualifications listed below, his or her earnings while in the United States are foreign source income and exempt from U.S. taxation. For income to be exempt, the taxpayer must show that:

1. He or she was temporarily within the United States for a period (or periods) of time that did not exceed 90 days during the taxable year;
2. He or she received $3,000 or less for the services actually performed in the United States; *and*
3. The services were performed for a nonresident alien, a foreign corporation, or a foreign partnership that was not engaged in the conduct of a trade or business in the United States, or for a foreign office or place of business maintained by a U.S. citizen, partnership, or corporation (Sec. 861(a)(3)).

This exception allows foreign businesses to send their employees to the United States on short assignments without having them incur U.S. taxation.

Rents and royalties

The source of rent or royalty payments is determined by the place where the property is located or used. Rents and royalties include payments for the use of such items as real property, machinery or equipment, patents, copyrights, trademarks, and franchises (Sec. 861(a)(4)).

Sale of personal property

The source of income derived from the sale of personal property depends on whether the property is *purchased for resale* or is *produced for sale*. Income from personal property that is purchased for resale generally has its source in the country in which the property is sold.[3] If personal property is produced abroad and sold in the United States, or conversely, is produced in the United States and sold abroad, the income from the sale must be apportioned between the U.S. and foreign sources. These complex allocation rules, which may be found in Treas. Reg. Secs. 1.863-3(b) and 1.863-3(c), are beyond the scope of this book. Of course, goods produced outside the United States and sold abroad would result in the creation of foreign source income.

One question that frequently arises in determining the source of income from the sale of personal property is: Where has the sale actually taken place? The question is simple to answer when sales contracts are signed, goods are delivered, title passes, and the risk of loss on the personal property passes all in one location. Attempts to find the most beneficial tax treatment, however, have resulted in numerous plans to transfer the rights and risks of ownership in one location and arrange for the sale to occur for tax purposes in a location permitting a more favorable tax treatment. The relevant court decisions have relied largely on the standard that the sale occurs where title to the personal property passes from seller to buyer.[4] If the seller keeps *only* the legal title in order to avoid taxes, the tax laws hold that the sale occurs "at the time and place of passage to the buyer of beneficial ownership and the risk of loss" (Treas. Reg. Sec. 1.861-7(c)).

These source rules are in effect for purposes of computing the U.S. income tax. Each country that levies a tax must define the source of income earned in international operations, and source rules may vary greatly among countries. Two different taxing jurisdictions may each treat a single item of income as having its source within their boundaries, causing adverse tax consequences for the taxpayer.

[3]An exception to this general rule is provided for goods purchased for resale within a U.S. possession and sold within the United States. These income amounts are treated under Sec. 863(b)(3) as being partly from U.S. sources and partly from non-U.S. sources.
[4]*Commissioner* v. *Pfaudler Inter-American Corp.*, 330 F.2d 471 (CCA-2, 1964) *aff'g.* 22 TCM 506 (1963); *A.P. Green Export Co.* v. *U.S.*, 284 F.2d 383 (Ct. Cls., 1960); and *Hammond Organ Western Export Corporation* v. *Commissioner*, 327 F.2d 964 (CCA-7, 1964) *aff'g.* 22 TCM 426 (1963).

DEDUCTION RULES

Similar to the taxpayer's need to determine the source of gross income is the need to determine whether deductions reduce the U.S. source income or the foreign source income. The general rules regarding the deductibility or nondeductibility of expenses and allowances are the same for taxpayers operating inside and outside the United States. Special rules exist, however, for determining the origin of a taxpayer's various deductions. In general, expenses, losses, and deductions that are allocable to a specific item or class of gross income are considered to be U.S. source or foreign source, depending on the origin of the related gross income item or items. In addition, a ratable portion of any expenses, losses, or other deductions that may not be allocated to an item or class of gross income is deductible by the taxpayer on a pro rata basis from the U.S. source and foreign source gross income (Secs. 861(b) and 862(b)).

Treasury Regulation Sec. 1.861-8 contains the detailed rules for determining the allocation and apportionment of deductions among the taxpayer's various classes and sources of income. The Sec. 1.861-8 Treasury regulations originally adopted in 1957 were quite simple and were no more than a brief discussion of the need for a taxpayer to allocate his or her deductions between U.S. and foreign source income along with a restatement and amplification of the general allocation principles outlined in Secs. 861-863. Taxpayers used the latitude provided by these regulations to increase or decrease their foreign source income almost at will in order to minimize their total tax liability. The current Sec. 1.861-8 Treasury regulations, which are much more detailed and complex, provide specific rules for allocating certain deductions among the taxpayer's various classes of income and then, when necessary, apportioning the deductions between what are known as "statutory" and "residual" groupings. In addition, specific allocation and apportionment rules are provided for such selected deductions as interest expense, research and development expenditures, and the various home office expenses.

Although the Sec. 1.861-8 Treasury regulations do not specify the types of income classifications to be used, they do indicate that the classes of income may include one or more of the gross income items (or subdivisions thereof) found in Sec. 61. The classes of income selected by a taxpayer should, however, generally be based on the types of deductions that must be allocated. Thus, a taxpayer who provides personal services on a worldwide basis, owns some rental property, and has some royalty income unrelated to his or her per-

sonal service activities probably will select three income classes—one for each of the three types of income.

Definitions

We must define four terms in order to understand the operation of the Sec. 1.861-8 Treasury regulations:

1. *Statutory grouping of gross income.* The *gross income* derived from a specified source or activity that must first be determined in order to arrive at the *taxable income* derived from a specific source or activity under one of the "operative sections" to which the Sec. 1.861-8 Treasury regulations apply[5] is known as the *statutory grouping of gross income.*
2. *Residual grouping of gross income.* The gross income from sources or activities other than those that are included in the statutory grouping is called the *residual grouping of gross income.*
3. *Allocation.* The process of determining the "class of gross income" to which a deduction is related is called *allocation.*
4. *Apportionment.* The process of determining the statutory or residual grouping to which a deduction is related or apportioned is known as *apportionment.*

We may illustrate the application of the statutory and residual grouping concepts by examining the availability of foreign tax credits to a U.S. citizen. Under the Code, foreign tax credits may only be used to offset the portion of the U.S. tax liability that results from foreign source taxable income. Foreign tax credits may not offset any U.S. taxes levied on U.S. source income. In this tax question, the taxpayer's "statutory grouping of gross income" is his or her foreign source gross income that is used to determine the foreign source taxable income. The taxpayer's "residual grouping of gross income" is the remainder of his or her gross income.

Allocation of deductions

The following four deduction classifications are outlined in Treas. Reg. Sec. 1.861-8.

---

[5]Treas. Reg. Sec. 1.861-8(f)(1) defines 17 "operative areas" to which the detailed allocation and apportionment rules apply. Some of these include: determining the taxpayer's foreign tax credit limitation, a Domestic International Sales Corporation's taxable income, a nonresident alien or foreign corporation's taxable income from U.S. or non-U.S. sources or from the conduct of a U.S. trade or business, the exclusion or credit base for Puerto Rican or U.S. possession activities, and the income taxable to the U.S. shareholders of a controlled foreign corporation.

1. *Deductions "definitely related" to a class of gross income.* A deduction is definitely related to a class of gross income, and therefore allocable to the income class, when it is incurred either as a result of, or incident to, an activity from which the class of gross income is derived, or in connection with property from which the class of gross income is derived.

The application of the "definitely related" concept of deductions can be illustrated by the following example. A U.S. company engages in two activities—selling women's slacks in the United States and selected foreign countries and leasing office space in its old office building. The manufacturing costs associated with the slacks sold both inside and outside the United States will be allocated to the company's sales gross income classification. Any operating expenses and depreciation associated with the leasing activity will be allocated to the company's rental gross income classification.

2. *Deductions related to all gross income.* Deductions related to all gross income are allocable to each of the taxpayer's income classes.

3. *Deductions unrelated to any gross income.* No allocation of deductions unrelated to any class of gross income takes place. The seven types of deductions that the regulations include in this classification are: nonbusiness interest, real estate taxes on a personal residence, sales tax on items purchased for personal use, medical expenses, charitable contributions, alimony payments, and the zero bracket amount.

4. *Personal exemptions.* Personal exemptions are neither allocated to a class of income nor apportioned to the statutory or residual groupings (Treas. Reg. Sec. 1.861-8(b)).

General apportionment rules

Three sets of general apportionment rules exist. These rules apply to deductions that are "definitely related" to a class of gross income, related to all gross income, or unrelated to any gross income. In addition, a series of rules exists for specific deduction items including interest, research and development (R & D) expenditures, administrative (stewardship) expenses, supportive expenses, legal and accounting fees and expenses, income taxes, losses on the sale or exchange of property, and net operating loss deductions. Because of the complexity of these specific deduction rules, they are not covered in detail in this text, although we shall present brief discussions of the interest and R & D alloca-

tions. The full explication of these rules may be found in Treas. Reg. Secs. 1.861-8(e)(2)–(8).

Deductions are not required to be apportioned between the statutory and residual groupings when they are definitely related to a class of gross income that is includible in only one of the two groupings. Apportionment is required, however, if the gross income is included in one (or more) statutory groupings and one (or more) residual groupings. The apportionment process must take place in a manner that reflects "to a reasonably close extent" the "factual relationship" between the deduction and the inclusion of the gross income in the statutory and residual groupings. The regulations state that the bases for apportionment may include comparisons of sales units, gross receipts, cost of goods sold, profit contributions, expenses incurred, assets used, time spent, and gross income. The general apportionment rules never indicate that the taxpayer must use the most appropriate base for making the apportionment. Thus, presumably, an apportionment method could be selected that permitted the most favorable results, provided the "factual relationship" between the deduction and the gross income groupings within the class existed (Treas. Reg. Sec. 1.861-8(b)(2)).

Deductions that relate to all gross income are includible in each income class on a pro rata basis. Apportionment between the statutory and residual groupings, once an allocation to an income class has occurred, is based on the "factual relationship" that has been established for that class of income.

Deductions that are unrelated to any gross income are apportioned only between the statutory and residual groupings. The apportionment is based on the relative amounts of gross income in each grouping.

Deductions that are "definitely related" to a class of gross income are allocated to the class even though no gross income is reported in the class for the taxable year, or the amount of the allocated deduction exceeds the income reported in the class. If the allocation or apportionment process uses gross income as the allocation base, gross income must include not only income amounts that are subject to tax, but also income that is exempt or excluded from taxation.

An illustration of the general apportionment rules is presented below:

Example: Elizabeth Watson, a nonresident alien individual from a nontreaty country, is engaged in a number of U.S.-related activities producing the following income:

Type of Income	Amount	Deduction allocation	
		Direct allocation	Indirect allocation
(1) Interest:			
City of Houston, Texas bonds	$ 10,000		$ (1,400)(c)
General Motors Corp. bonds	20,000		(2,800)(c)
(2) Royalty income from the sale in the United States of an art history text	40,000	$(10,000)(a)	(5,600)(c)
(3) Personal services income:			
U.S. trade or business (and U.S. source)	60,000	(20,000)(b)	(8,400)(c)
Non-U.S. trade or business (and foreign source)	120,000	(60,000)(b)	(16,800)(c)
Total	$250,000	$(90,000)	$(35,000)

Type of deductions	Amount
(a) Commission to agent on sale of art history text	$ 10,000
(b) Expenses related to personal services income:	
U.S.	20,000
Non-U.S.	60,000
(c) Expenses related to all classes of income	35,000
	$125,000

Expense items (a) and (b) are directly allocable to the royalty and personal services income, respectively. Within the personal services income class, each subcategory of deductions is apportioned to a specific type of income—U.S. or non-U.S. source. The remaining deductions (item (c)) are allocated to each income class based on the relative amounts of gross income includible in each classification. Even though the income from the City of Houston bonds and non-U.S. personal services is exempt from U.S. taxes, it still receives an "allocation" of its directly related and indirect expenses. Similarly, deductions are allocated to the interest income resulting from holding the General Motors bonds and the royalty income that are both taxed at a 30 percent rate that is applied against gross income. The expenses allocated to this income, like those allocated to the exempt income, do not reduce the U.S. tax liability.

Interest expense

The allocation and apportionment rules relating to interest are based on the presumption that "money is fungible and that interest expense is attributable to all activities and property," regardless of the taxpayer's purpose for incurring the obligation. By adopting this presumption in drafting the regulations, the government realizes that a firm's management has some flexibility as to whether it uses internally generated or externally generated capital to finance its activities and that unless funds are borrowed for a specific purpose, the interest expense relates to the firm's entire activities[6] (Treas. Reg. Sec. 1.861-8(e)(2)(i)).

The following three methods exist for allocating and apportioning post-1976 debt obligation interest expense incurred by taxpayers (other than foreign corporations):

1. *Allocation of interest to specific properties.* Some debts, meeting the *stringent requirements* of the regulations, are related solely to the acquisition of a specific property (Treas. Reg. Sec. 1.861-8(e)(2)(iv)). Interest expense for such debts is allocated to the gross income classification, which includes the income generated by that specific property.

2. *Apportionment of interest based on asset values.* It has been suggested that interest expense is more closely related to the taxpayer's asset holdings than to his or her gross income. Based on that concept, this method apportions interest expense deductions between the statutory group income and the residual group income based on the relative value of the taxpayer's assets that produce the two kinds of income (Treas. Reg. Sec. 1.861-8(e)(2)(v)).

3. *Apportionment of interest based on gross income.* The interest expense deduction is apportioned

---

[6]Treas. Reg. Sec. 1.861-8(e)(2)(iii) excludes nonbusiness interest deductions from these special rules.

between the statutory and residual groupings based on the relative gross income amounts of the two groupings. The minimum apportionment to a grouping using this method, however, is 50 percent of the interest expense that would have been apportioned to the grouping under the "asset value" method (Treas. Reg. Sec. 1.861-8(e)(2)(vi)).

The Sec. 1.861-8 Treasury regulations relating to the interest expense deduction are illustrated below:

Example: Multico, a U.S.-based multinational corporation, incurs $150,000 of interest expense in 19X1. Multico's tax records indicate that in 19X1, $450,000 of gross income originated from U.S. sources, and $50,000 from non-U.S. sources. In addition, assets having a tax book value of $1,000,000 were considered to have a U.S. situs. The only non-U.S. situs assets were investments in foreign branch activities having an adjusted basis of $250,000. The alternate interest deduction apportionments to the statutory (foreign source taxable income) and residual (U.S. source taxable income) groupings based on the available information is presented below.

Asset Method of Apportionment
Statutory Grouping:

$$\frac{\$250,000}{\$1,250,000} \times \$150,000 = \$30,000$$

Residual Grouping:

$$\$150,000 - \$30,000 = \$120,000$$

Gross Income Method of Apportionment
Statutory Grouping:

$$\frac{\$50,000}{\$500,000} \times \$150,000 = \$15,000$$

Residual Grouping:

$$\$150,000 - \$15,000 = \$135,000$$

Multico may choose the apportionment method that is most advantageous in light of its total tax situation.[7]

---

[7]As discussed in a later section of this chapter, Multico would likely wish to increase its foreign source taxable income when calculating its foreign tax credit limitation to increase its available foreign tax credits. In this case, it would select the gross income method of apportionment to reduce the interest expense that was apportioned to foreign source taxable income.

Research and development (R & D) expenditures

The allocation and apportionment of research and development expenditures deductible under Sec. 174 is based on the presumption that these outlays are related to all gross income items (sales, royalties, dividends, and so on) generated within each of the taxpayer's product categories. Research and development expenses may be apportioned among product categories based on sales or on gross income generated by the product categories. General R & D expenditures that may not be identified with any specific product category (or categories), and therefore that may not be allocated on that basis, are considered to apply to all product categories and are apportioned ratably (based on the amount of gross income) to the statutory and residual groupings.

An exception to these general allocation rules applies to outlays made for R & D activities undertaken solely to comply with legal requirements regarding the improvement or marketing of specific products or processes, the results of which cannot be expected to produce more than a minimum amount of gross income outside a single geographic area. Such outlays are considered to be "definitely related" only to the gross income groupings originating within the geographic area for which the outlays are made. An example of such an outlay would be the allocation of the costs incurred for the specific testing required by the U.S. Food and Drug Administration on a drug product to gross income originating from sources within the United States.

THE DOUBLE TAXATION PROBLEM

Every country has resources and revenue needs peculiar to its own economic situation. Accordingly, it is only logical that every country has a unique taxing system to meet its individual policy and revenue goals. Businesses that operate in more than one country face the problem of conducting operations while studying a complex tax picture. It is possible, however, that tax liabilities may be minimized and tax payments may be deferred for considerable periods of time if the tax systems are carefully monitored.

Whenever a business operates in more than one taxing jurisdiction, the possibility exists that some income may be taxed under more than one set of laws. For example, a U.S. corporation manufacturing widgets in France and selling them in that country through its French sales subsidiary will owe tax to the French government based on the subsidiary's income, as well as owe tax to the U.S. government on its worldwide income (including dividend remittances from the French subsidiary). The U.S. tax on the subsidiary's earnings may be deferred, which we shall discuss in Chapter 22, but the income in most cases eventually will be subject to U.S. taxation. Obviously, this double taxation can be a significant problem for multinational firms. Congress, therefore, has devised three principal ways of alleviating the problem:

1. Bilateral tax treaties
2. The foreign tax credit
3. A permanent exemption of certain income from U.S. taxation

We shall discuss in detail below each of the options as implemented by the U.S. government, but be aware that these solutions do not prevent double taxation in all possible situations. In some situations, a taxpayer may still have to pay taxes on a portion of his or her income to more than one country.

TAX TREATIES

A tax treaty is a negotiated agreement between the United States and a foreign country that sets out the rules under which residents of each country are taxed by the other. The first U.S. tax treaty was signed with France in 1932. At latest count, the United States has operating tax treaties with more than 40 countries and territories, and treaties have been signed but not yet ratified with at least half a dozen more.

Tax treaties have two main objectives. First, tax treaties are negotiated to prevent, or at least to minimize, the burden of double taxation that might otherwise occur with international operations. Second, treaties establish cooperation between the taxing authorities of the two treaty countries in the areas of distribution of tax revenue between the countries and in the enforcement of the respective revenue laws. The distribution of tax revenue depends on the allocation of revenues and expenses between portions of an organization in the two countries. The tax treaties contain rules outlining the source of various income and deduction items. In addition, tax treaties outline the powers the two parties to the tax treaties have to reallocate between portions of an organization income and expense items where the organization has failed to comply with the tax laws of the two countries (that is, rules regarding determination of transfer prices). In the area

of enforcement, treaties allow the two countries to exchange information to prevent tax evasion and to settle disputes between taxpayers of one nation and the taxing authorities of the other.

No two tax treaties are exactly alike. Each treaty is negotiated individually to deal with the specific problems that arise when the two countries have different concepts of what is taxable income or different rules concerning the sources of income. Even though each treaty is unique, many provisions are common to most tax treaties. Some common treaty provisions are the following:

1. Every treaty defines exactly what groups of individuals and business entities are covered by the treaty. Generally, treaties apply to individuals and business entities designated as residents of the treaty countries. A treaty country's citizens who reside in a third country, for example, may not be covered by the treaty provisions, while a resident alien residing in one of the treaty countries may be covered.

2. The taxes covered by the treaty are set out. Although for the United States, this generally includes only federal income taxes, some treaties cover both the federal and provincial taxes of the other country.

3. Many treaties include a *nondiscrimination clause.* Basically, nondiscrimination clauses require that the United States not treat nationals of its treaty partners (who reside in the United States) any more severely under its tax laws than it treats U.S. residents, citizens, or domestic corporations under U.S. laws.

4. Most of the treaties include a *savings clause.* The savings clause provides that each treaty country maintains the right to tax its own citizens and residents as if the treaty did not exist. This means that the U.S. income tax liability of a U.S. citizen residing in a treaty country is not reduced by the treaty, but rather the citizen is taxed on worldwide income at the same rates as are other U.S. citizens.

5. Treaties also frequently include a *preservation clause,* which states that the treaty is not to be read to restrict the availability of any deduction, credit, or exemption provided by a country when the tax due to that country is being computed. This clause prevents any inadvertent tax increase from occurring as a result of treaty operations.

The major impact of tax treaties lies in the provisions they make for the taxation of business profits, investment income, and income from personal services earned in the treaty countries. We shall outline each of these provisions on the next page.

Taxation of business profits

Treaties generally provide that business profits earned by a resident or corporation of one treaty country from doing business in the other treaty country will not be taxed by the latter country unless the business is operated through a permanent establishment and the profits are attributable to activities conducted by the permanent establishment. For example, if a resident of the Netherlands sells her merchandise in the United States, the United States does not tax the income from the sales occurring within its boundaries unless the business has a permanent establishment in the United States and the profits are attributable to the permanent establishment. Business profits that are subject to taxation in the source country are generally taxed at that country's full tax rates. These provisions cover only business profits, sometimes called industrial, or commercial, profits. While different treaties define business profits differently, the term frequently excludes such items as dividends, interest, gain from the sale of capital assets, rents, and royalties.

Likewise the definition of the term "permanent establishment" varies from one treaty to the next. In general, it is carefully defined to exclude specific kinds of establishments required to carry on limited activity. For example, the U.S.–Netherlands tax treaty, which is typical of many treaties, specifies that the following business activities do *not* constitute a permanent establishment:

1. Use of facilities to store, display, or deliver the goods of the business.
2. Maintenance of an inventory of goods for the purpose of storage, display, delivery, or processing by another firm.
3. Maintenance of a place of business to purchase goods, to gather information, or to advertise for the business.[8]

Tax treaties commonly say, however, that a permanent establishment exists if an enterprise works through an agent in the treaty country and if that agent has significant authority to bind the parent organization. Such authority is the agent's ability to make contracts for the enterprise if (1) the authority is regularly used and (2) the contracts cover more than just the agent's purchases of goods for the enterprise. This prevents firms from conducting extensive business operations through an agent in order to evade its host country's taxes.

[8]*U.S.–Netherlands Tax Treaty*, Article II.

Taxation of investment income

Without treaty intervention, investment income earned in the United States by nonresident aliens is taxed at a flat rate of 30 percent (discussed in Chapter 22). Treaty provisions allow some investment income to be exempt from U.S. taxation and other investment income to be taxed by the United States at reduced rates. U.S. residents receive reciprocal benefits under the host country's tax laws, and for some taxpayers, these benefits are substantial. A summary of U.S. tax rates for various income forms under selected tax treaties is presented in Table 21-2.

DIVIDENDS   Many countries tax corporate income and also require that taxes be withheld on dividend payments from such income. A 30 percent U.S. withholding tax on U.S. source dividends paid by a U.S. or a foreign corporation to a foreign shareholder is generally required, regardless of where the foreign shareholder lives. Treaties commonly reduce the burden of U.S. withholding taxes from 30 percent to 15 percent for foreign shareholders, with a further reduction to 5 percent when the dividends are paid to a foreign parent corporation. Dividends earned by the recipient in conjunction with a permanent establishment located in the country in which the dividends are earned are usually not eligible for these reduced rates.

INTEREST   Treaties sometimes exempt certain interest income from taxation by the country in which it is earned. U.S. tax treaties commonly provide that the normal 30 percent U.S. withholding tax on interest that is withheld by U.S. obligors is eliminated or is lowered to 15 or 5 percent. Interest earned by the recipient in conjunction with a permanent establishment, like dividend income, is usually not eligible for these reduced withholding tax rates.

RENTS AND ROYALTIES   Treaties generally exempt certain royalty income from taxation by the source country, provided the recipient does not earn the income in conjunction with a permanent establishment located in the source country. Rentals from films and television activities are frequently separated from rental income from real estate, with the former being taxed at rates ranging from 0 to 15 percent. Gross rental income from real estate located in the United States is generally taxed at the withholding rates provided for in the treaty, or, at the taxpayer's election, net income from rental property may be taxed as business profits. Many treaties allow royalty income to be divided into royal-

TABLE 21-2

U.S. WITHHOLDING TAX RATES ON INVESTMENT, ROYALTY, AND ANNUITY INCOME FORMS UNDER SELECTED TAX TREATIES

Income code number	1	2	3	Dividends paid by		6	7	Copyright royalties		10	11
Country of residence of payee	Interest paid by U.S. obligors general rule	Interest on real property mortgage	Interest paid to a controlling foreign corporation	U.S. corporation general rule	U.S. subsidiary to foreign parent corporation[a]	Capital gains	Industrial royalties	Motion pictures and television	Other	Real property income and natural resources royalties	Pensions and annuities
Australia	30	30	30	$15^{b,f}$	$15^{b,f}$	30	30	30	0^f	30	0
Belgium	15^e	15^e	15^e	15^e	15^e	$0^{d,e,g}$	0^e	30	0^e	30	0^c
Canada	15^f	15^f	15^f	$15^{b,f}$	$15^{b,f}$	0^f	15^f	15^f	0^f	15^f	0
France	10^e	10^e	10^e	15^e	$5^{a,e}$	$0^{d,e,g}$	5^e	0^e	0^e	30	0^c
Germany, Fed. Rep. of	0^e	0^e	0^e	15^e	15^e	$0^{d,e,g}$	0^e	0^e	0^e	30	0^c
Japan	10^e	10^e	10^e	15^e	$10^{a,e}$	$0^{d,e,g}$	10^e	10^e	10^e	30	0^c
Netherlands	0^e	0^e	0^e	15^e	$5^{a,e}$	$0^{d,e,g}$	0^e	0^e	0^e	30	0^c
Switzerland	5^f	5^f	5^f	15^f	$5^{a,f}$	30	0^f	0^f	0^f	30	0^c
Union of Soviet Socialist Republics	0^h	30	30	30	30	0^i	0	0	0	30	30
United Kingdom	0^e	0^e	0^e	15^e	$5^{a,e}$	30	0^e	0^e	0^e	30	0^c
Nontreaty countries	30	30	30	30	30	30	30	30	30	30	30

[a]The reduced rate applies to dividends paid by a subsidiary to a foreign parent corporation having the required percentage of stock ownership. In some cases, the income of the subsidiary must meet certain requirements (for example, a certain percentage of its total income must consist of income other than dividends and interest).

[b]The exemption or reduction in rate applies only if the recipient is subject to tax on such income in the country of residence. Otherwise a 30 percent rate applies. In the case of Canada, this requirement applies to intercorporate dividends only.

[c]Exemption does not apply to U.S. Government (federal, state, or local) pensions and annuities; 30 percent rate applies to such pensions and annuities. For Belgium and France includes alimony.

[d]The treaty exemption applicable to U.S. source capital gains includes capital gains under Sec. 871(a)(2) if received by a nonresident alien present in the United States for a period not exceeding 183 days. (182 days for Belgium.)

[e]Under the treaty, the exemption or reduction in rate does not apply if the recipient has a permanent establishment in the United States and the property giving rise to the income is effectively connected with such permanent establishment. Notwithstanding the treaty, if the income is not effectively connected with the conduct of a trade or business in the United States by the recipient, such recipient will be deemed not to have a permanent establishment in the United States.

[f]Under the treaty, the exemption or reduction in rate does not apply if the recipient is engaged in the conduct of a trade or business in the United States through a permanent establishment located in the United States. If the income is not effectively connected with the conduct of a trade or business in the United States by the recipient, however, such recipient will be deemed not to have a permanent establishment in the United States for the purpose of applying the reduced treaty rate to the item of income concerned. (Sec. 894(b)).

[g]Exemption does not apply to gains from the sale of real property; 30 percent rate applies to such sales.

[h]The exemption applies only to interest on credits, loans, and other indebtedness connected with the financing of trade between the United States and the Soviet Union. It does not include interest derived from the conduct of a general banking business.

[i]The exemption only applies to gains from the sale or other disposition of property acquired by gift or inheritance.

SOURCE: I.R.S., *Publication No. 515* (Withholding Tax on Nonresident Aliens and Foreign Corporations), 1979 edition.

ties related to natural resources and royalties from such intangibles as copyrights, designs, and secret processes, with special exemptions or rates applying to each.

CAPITAL GAINS   A number of treaties provide that capital gains other than those derived from the sale of real estate or from the maintenance of a permanent establishment are exempt from tax in the country in which the gains are realized. This exemption, however, does not mean that the country in which the taxpayer resides will also exempt these capital gains from taxation. Under the savings clause, the country of the taxpayer's residence generally will tax the capital gain according to its own law without regard to any treaty provisions.

> *Example:*   Assume that Mr. Jones is a U.S. citizen who sells his interest in a Netherlands business and realizes a capital gain. Even though the U.S.–Netherlands tax treaty provides that these capital gains are exempt from tax by the Netherlands, the United States will tax the gain just as it would have taxed Mr. Jones on any capital gains he earned in the United States during the tax year.

Many treaties specifically state that capital gains are not part of business profits. If they are part of business profits, they generally are not taxed unless the enterprise maintains a permanent establishment in the source country.

Personal services income

Many treaties allow a reciprocal reduction in, or elimination of, taxes on professional or personal services income earned by a resident of one treaty country while temporarily residing in the other treaty country. The time period in the source country that qualifies as a temporary stay is frequently 183 days, with up to two years allowed for persons who teach in a university, college, or other school. Excluded amounts vary from $3,000 to an unlimited amount. Pensions and annuities are also dealt with in treaties. The usual provision is that the country from which the payments are made reserves the right to tax them, but the country in which the recipient resides when the payments are received agrees not to tax these amounts.

FOREIGN TAX CREDITS

The foreign tax credit allows a U.S. taxpayer to reduce the burden of double taxation by paying a combined U.S. and foreign effective tax rate that equals the higher of the applicable U.S. or foreign tax rate.

> *Example:*   Assume that Multico, a domestic corporation, has $10,000 of foreign source income on which $3,000 of foreign taxes have been paid. If Multico's U.S. tax rate is 46 percent, Multico pays U.S. taxes of $1,600 ($4,600 minus a $3,000 foreign tax credit), or a worldwide total of $4,600. If Multico's U.S. tax rate is 46 percent but its foreign tax rate is 50 percent, it pays foreign taxes of $5,000 but pays no U.S. tax on this foreign source income. Multico may also carry back or carry over the excess foreign tax credits of $400 ($5,000 foreign taxes paid minus the $4,600 U.S. tax that would have been levied on the income) to another tax year.[9]

The foreign tax credit does not result in complete avoidance of double taxation for several reasons. First, not all foreign taxes are eligible for foreign tax credit treatment. Some foreign taxes may be neither credited nor deducted, and some foreign taxes are eligible only for the lesser benefits of a deduction (Sec. 164(a)).

A second reason why the foreign tax credit may not prevent double taxation of income is that the source of income rules may differ between the United States and the foreign country. The United States only permits the foreign tax credit to be claimed against the portion of the taxpayer's gross tax liability originating from foreign source taxable income. Thus, even though the United States and a foreign country may tax the same income, a foreign tax credit will be denied if the United States considers a stream of income to be derived from U.S. sources, and the foreign country considers that stream of income as being within their jurisdiction to tax. If the taxpayer has no other foreign source income, the taxpayer may claim only a deduction for foreign taxes paid, provided they fall within one of the classifications of deductible taxes outlined in Sec. 164(a).

An excess foreign tax credit occurs if the amount of creditable foreign taxes paid is greater than the maximum creditable amount allowed by the foreign tax credit limitation. (The calculation of the limitation is described below.) Double taxation may occur if excess foreign tax credits may not be used in the carryback or carryover period. In order for a taxpayer to use excess foreign tax credits, the taxpayer's effective foreign tax rate must fall below the effective U.S. tax rate. Thus, in the above example, for Multico to use the $400 ex-

---

[9]Excess foreign tax credits are defined as the excess of the foreign taxes paid or accrued over the portion of the taxpayer's U.S. tax liability attributable to foreign source taxable income.

cess foreign tax credits in the carryback or carryover period, Multico's foreign tax payments in the carryback or carryover period must be at least $400 less than its gross U.S. tax liability originating from its foreign source taxable income. If the U.S. taxes do not exceed the foreign taxes by at least $400, then part or all of the excess credits are permanently lost to Multico and double taxation results.

Creditable taxes

As mentioned above, not all foreign taxes paid may be credited against U.S. taxes. The only taxes that the taxpayer may choose to credit or deduct are income taxes, war profits taxes, excess profits taxes, and taxes paid "in lieu of an income tax." Other foreign taxes may be deductible but only if they qualify as a business expense, an expense related to the production of income, or a foreign real property tax. Every year, the taxpayer must elect to credit or deduct those taxes that may be credited. A taxpayer choosing to credit any taxes must claim a credit for all taxes that are eligible to be credited for that year. Even if a taxpayer elects to claim a credit for all creditable taxes in a given year, the taxpayer may still deduct those taxes that are not eligible to be claimed as a credit.

In determining the amount of foreign tax that may be credited, the first question to be answered is whether a payment to a foreign government is a tax payment as defined under U.S. laws or whether the payment is made for such items as royalties, licensing fees, penalties, or interest. If the payment is a tax, the next question is whether the tax is assessed on income. The standard to be met is twofold: (1) the foreign tax base must be "income" under the U.S. definition of the term, and (2) the tax must be assessed solely on income and must not be a transactions tax, a sales tax, or a tax levied on the privilege of doing business.[10] In general, an income tax must be based on an amount representing a difference between revenues and expenses. Neither the precise rules for measuring the amount of income nor the timing of income recognition needs to coincide exactly with U.S. laws.[11] The actual decision whether a particular foreign tax qualifies as an income tax is a complex one. Most tax services contain a summary of the I.R.S. promulgations and court cases that have dealt with the creditability of a given foreign tax.[12]

In addition to taxes based on income, a few taxes that are levied as a substitute for an income tax are creditable under the "in lieu of an income tax" provisions of Sec. 903. For a tax to be considered to be levied "in lieu of an income tax," it must satisfy the following three requirements:

1. The foreign country involved must have a general income tax law in effect.
2. The taxpayer must be someone who would be subject to the general income tax if the special "in lieu of" provisions were not in effect.
3. The income tax and the "in lieu of" tax may not both be assessed against income from one activity during a single tax year (Treas. Reg. Sec. 1.903-1(a)).

The "in lieu of" taxes have been used primarily by nations when taxing industries in which the concept of taxable income is difficult to measure, such as in insurance or mining activities.

Taxpayers eligible for the credit

Individuals who are U.S. citizens may claim a foreign tax credit for taxes paid or accrued to a foreign country or a U.S. possession. In addition, a credit may be claimed for the taxpayer's pro rata share of taxes paid or accrued by a partnership in which he or she is a member, a trust or estate of which he or she is a beneficiary, or a controlled foreign corporation on the income of which he or she is taxed under Sec. 962. (See Chapter 22 for a discussion of the taxation of controlled foreign corporations.)

Similarly to U.S. citizens, domestic corporations may claim a foreign tax credit for taxes paid or accrued directly to a foreign country or a U.S. possession (a direct credit). In addition, a domestic corporation may claim a credit for its pro rata share of certain foreign taxes paid by a foreign investee corporation (a deemed paid credit) if it satisfies the minimum stock ownership requirements outlined below. Neither a Subchapter S corporation nor its shareholders may claim a credit for foreign taxes paid by the corporation. The Subchapter S corporation, however, may claim these foreign taxes as a deduction.[13]

Nonresident aliens and foreign corporations may claim a credit for foreign taxes paid or accrued on income that is treated by the U.S. tax laws as effectively connected with the conduct of a U.S. trade or business. Resident aliens may credit taxes paid to U.S. possessions and foreign countries, provided the foreign coun-

[10]Rev. Ruls. 78-61, 1978-1 CB 221; 78-62, 1978-1 CB 226; and 78-63, 1978-1 CB 228. See also Prop. Treas. Reg. Sec. 1.901-2, which attempts to clarify the definition of an income tax.
[11]*Bank of America, N.T.S.A.* v. *U.S.*, 459 F.2d 513 (Ct. Cls., 1972).
[12]For example, see Commerce Clearing House, Inc., *Standard Federal Tax Reporter* (1980), pp. 50,058–50,062.

[13]Rev. Rul. 68-128, 1968-1 CB 381 and Reg. Sec. 1.1378-1.

try of which the resident alien is a citizen allows a similar credit to U.S. citizens residing in that country. Also applicable to resident and nonresident aliens is the pass-through of foreign taxes paid by a partnership in which the alien is a member, or a trust or estate of which the alien is a beneficiary (Secs. 901(b), 901(c), and 906).

The direct credit

The direct foreign tax credit of Sec. 901 generally may be claimed by a taxpayer only if the foreign taxes were legally imposed on him. The courts have considered the taxpayer to be the person upon whom the taxes were imposed if the taxpayer is ultimately liable for the amount of the foreign tax payment. In most cases, the question of ultimate liability may be discerned with little difficulty. The determination may not be as clear, however, when a foreign tax is withheld by a withholding agent. For example, when Krausco, a German corporation, pays a dividend to its shareholders, the German corporation withholds a tax from the dividend and pays only a net dividend to its U.S. shareholders. Krausco then forwards the withheld amounts to the German taxing authorities. If Krausco is acting merely as a withholding agent, then the U.S. shareholders may legally claim a tax credit for the withheld amounts. If, instead, the tax is actually a tax assessed against Krausco itself, and the foreign corporation is ultimately liable for the payment of the tax, then the U.S. shareholders may not credit or deduct the foreign withholding tax. The question of who bears the ultimate liability when a withholding agent is involved has been the subject of a number of court cases and I.R.S. promulgations and occasionally is even specified in tax treaty conventions.[14]

Timing of the credit

Taxpayers who use the accrual method of accounting must claim the foreign tax credit in the year in which it accrues. A cash method of accounting taxpayer may claim foreign taxes as a deduction or a credit in the year in which the tax is paid. Alternatively, the cash method taxpayer may elect to accrue foreign taxes to compute the foreign tax credit (Sec. 905(a)). Two points should be noted. The election to accrue foreign

taxes is not available for a cash method of accounting taxpayer who deducts foreign taxes; it only applies to taxes that are credited. Secondly, this election is a binding one and may not be changed without I.R.S. permission.

An election by a cash method of accounting taxpayer to accrue creditable foreign taxes generally is advantageous because it accelerates by one time period the time at which the credit would otherwise normally be claimed. In addition, such an election eliminates a potential matching problem. Some foreign taxing systems use a system like that found in the United States, which assesses the foreign taxes on one taxable year's income to be paid during the succeeding taxable year. This means a cash method of accounting taxpayer could, in the absence of provisions to the contrary, be required to include foreign source income in one year's U.S. tax return and pay the necessary U.S. taxes but not be able to claim the credit for foreign taxes paid on that income until the following taxable year in which he or she pays the foreign taxes. Because the foreign tax credit is limited each year to the portion of the U.S. tax liability originating from foreign source taxable income, a cash method of accounting taxpayer having occasional foreign transactions could, without this election, have a mismatching of foreign income and foreign tax credits. To reconcile this situation, the taxpayer would have to file an amended tax return for the first year and claim a refund of the overpayment of the U.S. taxes. Accruing the foreign taxes under this election, however, in no way alters the cash method of accounting for other income, deduction, or credit items.

When a foreign tax accrues

A foreign tax accrues when all the events that fix the amount of the liability have occurred under the rules of the foreign jurisdiction.[15] Generally, this means that a foreign tax accrues at the end of the foreign tax year. When a taxpayer's U.S. tax year differs from the tax year used for foreign tax law purposes, the foreign tax does not accrue for foreign tax credit purposes until the U.S. tax year within which the applicable foreign tax year-end falls.[16]

In some situations, foreign income may have been earned but may not be distributed to a U.S. taxpayer because of exchange restrictions or other limitations imposed by a foreign country. When this occurs, the U.S. taxpayer may elect to have the blocked income

---

[14] *Mary Duke Biddle v. U.S.*, 302 U.S. 573 (1938) *aff'g.* 86 F.2d 718 (CCA-2, 1936) and *rev'g.* 91 F.2d 534 (CCA-3, 1937) and *rev'g. and aff'g.* 33 BTA 127 (1935). *Irving Air Chute Co., Inc. v. Commissioner*, 143 F.2d 256 (CCA-2, 1944) *aff'g.* 1 TC 880 (1943); *Singer Manufacturing Co. v. U.S.*, 87 F. Supp. 769 (Ct. Cls., 1950); and Rev. Ruls. 63-51, 1963-1 CB 407 and 74-525, 1974-2 CB 411.

[15] *Dixie Pine Products Co. v. Commissioner*, 320 U.S. 516 (1944) *aff'g.* 134 F.2d 273 (CCA-5, 1943) *aff'g.* 45 BTA 286 (1942).
[16] Rev. Rul. 61-93, 1961-1 CB 390.

excluded from U.S. taxation until the blockage restriction is removed.[17] If the taxpayer elects this exclusion, a credit or deduction may not be claimed for the taxes paid on the blocked income until such time as the income is included in the U.S. tax return (Treas. Reg. Sec. 1.905-1(b)).

Amount of the credit

The amount of the direct credit claimed generally requires that the tax payment made in foreign currency units be translated into U.S. dollars. A cash method of accounting taxpayer translates the tax payment into dollars using the exchange rate in effect at the date of the tax payment. An accrual method of accounting taxpayer, or a cash method of accounting taxpayer electing to accrue taxes, translates the tax liability into dollars using the exchange rate in effect on the last day of the taxable year.[18] If the exchange rate changes between the accrual date and the payment date, then an adjustment to the amount of the foreign tax credit reported on the tax return must be made for the increase or decrease in the translated amount of the taxes. If the taxpayer's tax return has been filed by the payment date, the adjustment is made by filing an amended tax return for the year in question. The increase (or reduction) in the translated amount of the foreign taxes is treated similarly to an additional assessment (or refund) made by the taxing authorities of the foreign country, which also necessitates the filing of an amended tax return[19] (Sec. 905(c)).

Claiming the credit

The foreign tax credit is claimed on the taxpayer's income tax return by filing Form 1116 (for noncorporate taxpayers) or Form 1118 (for corporations). To substantiate the amount of taxes paid, a copy of the paid tax receipt is required. If the credit is based on a tax accrual, a copy of the foreign tax return on which the accrual is based must be attached (Treas. Reg. Sec. 1.905-2(a)(2)). Form 1116 is illustrated on pages **21/24** and **21/25**.

Foreign tax credit limitation

When Congress decided to use a foreign tax credit to reduce the burden of double taxation, it wanted to be certain that the credit could not be used to reduce taxes

[17]Rev. Rul. 74-351, 1974-2 CB 144.
[18]Rev. Rul. 73-491, 1973-2 CB 267.
[19]Rev. Rul. 73-506, 1973-2 CB 268.

assessed on U.S. source income. Therefore, in 1921, Congress instituted a foreign tax credit limitation that sets the maximum foreign tax credit as the portion of the gross U.S. tax liability originating from foreign source income. An example is presented below:

Example: Multico, a domestic corporation, had $10,000 of taxable income from U.S. sources in 19X1; $10,000 of taxable income from foreign sources; and had paid $5,000 of foreign taxes on the foreign source taxable income. Assuming a 46 percent corporate tax rate, Multico would have a gross U.S. tax liability before foreign tax credits of:

Source of income	Taxable income	U.S. tax
United States	$10,000	$4,600
Foreign countries	10,000	4,600
Total	$20,000	$9,200

Without any provision limiting the foreign tax credit, Multico could take a $5,000 credit for its foreign taxes, which would have the effect of reducing its tax on the U.S. source income to $4,200 ($9,200 precredit tax liability minus the $5,000 tax credit).

The effect of the foreign tax credit limitation is to reduce the foreign tax credit that may be taken to the amount of U.S. taxes originating from the foreign source taxable income, which in our example is a $4,600 liability. This limit ensures that the full U.S. tax will be paid on U.S. source income. Thus, the amount of the foreign tax credit that may be claimed in a taxable year is the lesser of the amount of the foreign taxes paid or accrued or the foreign tax credit limitation amount.

Calculation of the limitation

Before the Tax Reform Act of 1976 was passed, taxpayers had two options for computing their foreign tax credit limitation. They could compute a tax credit limitation separately for each foreign country in which they earned income and paid creditable taxes (a per-country limitation), or they could combine their income from all foreign countries and then compute *one* foreign tax credit limitation (an overall limitation). The advantage of the per-country limitation method was that losses from one foreign country would not offset income from other areas in computing the credit limitation and therefore reduce the available foreign tax credit. The Tax Reform Act of 1976 repealed the use of the per-country limitation method for post-taxable 1975 taxable years (with limited exceptions that have now expired).

The overall limitation has the advantage that taxes from countries in which the effective foreign tax rate exceeds the taxpayer's effective U.S. tax rate are combined with taxes from countries in which the effective tax rates are lower than the U.S. tax rate. Therefore, taxes that would have exceeded the limit calculated by using the per-country limitation method (and would require a credit carryback or carryover) may be fully utilized in the current year when the overall limitation method is used. The overall limitation is calculated using the following formula:

$$\text{Overall limitation} = \text{U.S. tax liability} \times \frac{\text{Taxable income from all foreign sources}}{\text{Total worldwide taxable income}}$$

The limiting fraction (foreign source taxable income over worldwide taxable income) can never be greater than one. This simply means that U.S. source losses may not be used to permit the use of a tax credit in excess of the U.S. tax liability.

The U.S. tax liability against which the foreign tax credit may be applied is the taxpayer's gross tax liability. The tax liability computation must include the use of the alternative tax computation but does not include the taxpayer's minimum tax, self-employment tax, personal holding company tax, or the accumulated earnings tax. Individual taxpayers are also required to reduce their gross tax liability by the amounts of any general tax credits (pre-1979 taxable years only) or credits for the elderly claimed (Sec. 904(g)). Special rules are found in Code Sec. 55(c)(2) for applying the foreign tax credit claimed against an individual taxpayer's alternative minimum tax liability.

Note that both foreign source taxable income and worldwide taxable income must be calculated according to U.S. tax accounting principles. Therefore, deductions that are allocated and apportioned to foreign source income under the rules of Treas. Reg. Sec. 1.861-8 must be taken into consideration in computing foreign source taxable income. No reduction in the amount of the creditable taxes is required when income that is subject to the foreign tax laws is exempt from U.S. taxation and excluded from the numerator and denominator of the limiting fraction.

Two additional items must also be remembered in computing taxable income for noncorporate taxpayers. First, individuals, trusts, and estates do not include their personal exemptions in calculating the numerator and denominator of the limiting fraction. Second, the zero bracket amount must be allocated between foreign source and U.S. source income. The numerator of the limiting fraction is reduced by a pro rata portion (based on the relative amounts of U.S. and foreign source gross income) of the zero bracket amount, while the denominator is reduced by the full zero bracket amount (Sec. 904(a)).

The two examples presented below illustrate the application of the foreign tax credit limitation rules.

Example (1): Multico, a domestic corporation, earned taxable income and paid foreign taxes during 19X1 as presented below. Assuming a U.S. corporate tax rate of 46 percent, its foreign tax credit limitation, calculated using the overall limitation method, would be:

Source	Taxable income	Foreign taxes	U.S. tax liability applicable to income
United States	$20,000	-0-	$ 9,200
Country X	5,000	$2,800	2,300
Country Y	6,000	2,200	2,760
	$31,000	$5,000	$14,260

$$\text{Overall limitation} = \$14,260 \times \frac{\$11,000}{\$31,000} = \$5,060$$

Under the overall limitation, the 56 percent Country X effective tax rate [($2,800/$5,000) × 100 = 56%] may be combined with the 36.67 percent Country Y effective tax rate [($2,200/$6,000) × 100 = 36.67%] to produce a 45.45 percent overall effective tax rate [($5,000/$11,000) × 100 = 45.45%]. This permits the full $5,000 of foreign taxes to be creditable because it is less than the portion of Multico's total U.S. tax liability ($5,060) that is attributable to the foreign source taxable income.

Example (2): Court Langefeld, a U.S. citizen, was employed in Country X for part of 19X1. His gross income, deductions, and exemptions for 19X1 were as follows:

U.S. source income	$20,000
Foreign source income	$10,000
Excess itemized deductions	$ 1,600
Personal exemptions	3

Court is married and files a joint tax return with his wife for 19X1. His foreign tax credit limitation for 19X1 is determined as follows:

$$\text{Overall limitation} = \$4,769^a \times \frac{\$10,000 - \$1,133}{\$28,400^b - \$3,400} = \underline{\$1,692}$$

[a]Tax liability based on Married Filing Jointly Tax Table, $28,400 of tax table income, and three personal exemptions.

[b]Taxable income (for foreign tax credit purposes only) equals $20,000 + $10,000 − $1,600 = $28,400.

The numerator of the limiting fraction (foreign source income) is reduced by a pro rata portion (based on gross income) of Langefeld's zero bracket amount.

$$[(\$10,000/\$30,000) \times \$3,400 = \$1,133]$$

The denominator (worldwide taxable income) is reduced by the full amount of the zero bracket amount, or $3,400.

A number of special adjustments apply to the determination of the capital gain income included in the determination of the foreign tax credit limitation. The first adjustment restricts the capital losses included in the limiting fraction so that U.S. source capital losses may not be used by the taxpayer to increase the limiting fraction. To accomplish this, "foreign source capital gain net income"[20] included in the numerator may not exceed the "worldwide capital gain net income" included in the denominator.

The second adjustment adjusts the limiting fraction to compensate for the 28 percent alternative tax rate that may apply to all corporate capital gains. This adjustment requires the "foreign source capital gain net income" included in the numerator to be reduced by 18/46 of the "foreign source net capital gain"[21] and the denominator to be reduced by 18/46 of the "worldwide net capital gain."[22] Foreign source capital losses included in determining worldwide capital gain net income are similarly reduced by 18/46 of the amount by which the U.S. source net capital gain exceeds the worldwide net capital gain.

[20]*Capital gain net income* is defined by Sec. 1222(9) as the excess of capital gains over capital losses.
[21]*Net capital gain* is defined by Sec. 1222(10) as the excess of net long-term capital gains over net short-term capital losses.
[22]The reduction percentage is determined as follows (Sec. 904(a)(2)(A) and (3)(F)):

$$\frac{\begin{array}{c}\text{Highest corporate} - \text{Alternative corporate tax rate on} \\ \text{tax rate (0.46)} \quad \text{capital gains (0.28)}\end{array}}{\text{Highest corporate tax rate (0.46)}} = \frac{0.18}{0.46} = 0.3913$$

The third adjustment is designed to prevent a taxpayer from selling capital assets (or Sec. 1231(b) trade or business property) in a foreign country that exempts capital gains from taxation, or taxes them at a low tax rate, in order to increase the foreign tax credit limitation. Under this adjustment, the gain recognized from the sale of certain personal property (but not real property) that is characterized as a capital asset (or Sec. 1231(b) trade or business property) is converted from a foreign source capital gain to a U.S. source capital gain. This rule requires U.S. source income (rather than foreign source income) to be recognized when:

1. An individual sells or exchanges personal property outside the country (or U.S. possession) of his or her residence; or
2. A corporation sells or exchanges stock of a second corporation in a location other than in the country (or U.S. possession) in which the second corporation derived the majority of its gross income during its three preceding taxable years; or
3. A taxpayer sells personal property (other than stock in a corporation) in a location other than in the country (or U.S. possession) in which it (1) derives the majority of its gross income during the preceding taxable years *or* (2) used the property in the conduct of a trade or business; and
4. The country (or U.S. possession) does not levy an income, war profits, or excess profits tax equal to at least 10 percent of the amount of the recognized gain from the sale or exchange (Sec. 904(b)(3)(C)).

If these requirements are met, then none of the gain is included in the numerator of the limiting fraction, but the entire amount is included in the fraction's denominator.

The two examples presented below illustrate the application of adjustments to the foreign source and worldwide taxable income amounts for capital gains and losses.

Example (1): James Alderman, a U.S. citizen, recognized the following long-term capital gains (and losses) during 19X1:

	Situation		
	No. 1	No. 2	No. 3
Gross gains:			
U.S. source	$ 8,000	$(10,000)	$(10,000)
Foreign source	2,000	15,000	7,500

Total gains or losses (net long-term capital gain[23] or loss)	$10,000	$ 5,000	$ (2,500)
Capital gains or losses included in (after adjustment for LTCG deduction or disallowance of LTCL):			
Numerator	$ 800	$ 2,000	$ (1,250)
Denominator	4,000	2,000	(1,250)

In Situation No. 1, 40 percent (100 percent of the gain minus the 60 percent long-term capital gain deduction) of the foreign source net long-term capital gain of $2,000 is included in the numerator. Similarly, the denominator contains 40 percent of the worldwide net long-term capital gain of $10,000. In Situation No. 2, the numerator and denominator both contain 40 percent of the foreign source net long-term capital gain of $5,000, because the U.S. source losses are permitted to offset part of the foreign source net long-term capital gain when determining both foreign and worldwide taxable income. In Situation No. 3, the foreign source net long-term capital gain of $7,500 included in the limiting fraction's numerator must be reduced (as in Situation No. 2) by the U.S. source net capital loss. As a result of this offsetting process, none of the foreign source capital gains may be included in the numerator of the limiting fraction. The $2,500 of U.S. source long-term capital losses that may be deducted this year [to produce a $1,250 deduction ($2,500 × 0.50 = $1,250)] must reduce both the numerator and denominator of the limiting fraction to prevent the U.S. loss from increasing the foreign tax credit limitation.

Example (2): Multico realized the following ordinary income and long-term capital gains during 19X1:

	Ordinary income	Capital gains	Total
U.S. source	$1,000	-0-	$1,000
Foreign source	-0-	$1,000	1,000
Total	$1,000	$1,000	$2,000

[23]*Net long-term capital gain* is defined as the excess of long-term capital gains over the long-term capital losses. Similarly, *net long-term capital loss* represents the excess of long-term capital losses over long-term capital gains (Sec. 1222(7) and (8)).

Assuming that Multico's tax rates were 46 percent on ordinary income and 28 percent on capital gains, its U.S. tax liability would be $740 [($1,000 × 0.28) + ($1,000 × 0.46)]. Its foreign tax credit limitation would be determined as follows:

$$\text{Foreign tax credit limitation} = \$740 \times \frac{\$1,000 - 0.3913(\$1,000)}{\$2,000 - 0.3913(\$1,000)}$$
$$= \underline{\$280}$$

Special limitations

Three types of foreign source income must be separated from all other types of foreign source income in computing the foreign tax credit limitation. The three kinds of income that must be separated are interest income, DISC dividends, and oil and gas income. The separate interest limitation was instituted to prevent taxpayers from investing excess funds in a low-tax rate nation (other than one in which a trade or business is conducted) in order to increase the foreign tax credit limitation and utilize excess foreign tax credits. The separate oil and gas limitation was enacted in 1975 to prevent excess credits from this income being used by the oil and gas companies to reduce the U.S. taxes due on their non-oil-related income and possibly exempt it entirely from U.S. taxation.

The amount of credit that may be claimed for each of these income classifications is the lesser of the credit limitation determined or the foreign taxes paid or accrued with respect to the income classification. The process of determining these special limitations is outlined below:

1. *Interest income.* A separate overall limitation for all foreign countries is computed for interest income other than:
   a. Interest income derived from the conduct of a trade or business in a foreign country;
   b. Interest income derived from the conduct of a banking or finance business;
   c. Interest income derived from an affiliate in which the taxpayer owns 10 percent or more of the voting stock; and
   d. Interest income received on the disposition of obligations that were acquired as a result of the disposition of a trade or business or the stock of an affiliated corporation (Sec. 904(d)(2)).

2. *DISC dividends.* All taxes deemed paid by a shareholder as a result of receiving a DISC dividend

must be separated from other foreign source income for calculation of the limitation (Sec. 904(d)(1)(B)).

3. *Oil and gas income.* A separate overall limitation is computed for all foreign countries for oil and gas income (Sec. 907(b)).

Excess foreign tax credits within any of the three classifications may not be used to offset U.S. taxes due on any other foreign source taxable income, but must be carried back or forward within the classification. Similarly, excess foreign tax credits or income outside these three classifications may not offset U.S. taxes due on these three income forms.

Carrybacks and carryovers of excess foreign tax credits

In tax years in which the amount of foreign taxes paid or accrued exceeds the amount of the foreign tax credit limitation, a taxpayer has incurred "excess foreign tax credits." These excess credits may be carried back two years and forward five years.

The use of excess foreign tax credits is determined by the following steps:

1. Determine the amount of creditable taxes in the current year.
2. Compute the foreign tax credit limitation.
3. Compare the amounts from Items (1) and (2).
   a. If this year's creditable taxes exceed the foreign tax credit limitation, the taxpayer has "excess credits" that may be carried back and carried forward.
   b. If the limitation exceeds the current year's creditable taxes, the taxpayer has an "excess limitation." Any excess credit amounts from other years that may be carried to this excess limitation year may be used against this excess limitation amount. The excess credits are used on a first-in, first-out (FIFO) basis so that oldest excess credits are used first. Under no condition may the sum of the current year's creditable taxes plus carrybacks and carryovers from other years exceed the current year's foreign tax credit limitation.

A taxpayer may not carry back or carry over excess credits to reduce taxes for a year in which the taxpayer chose to deduct rather than credit foreign income taxes. A taxable year in which a deduction is taken for all foreign taxes paid, however, does count as a full tax-

able year for purposes of determining the carryback and carryover period for any excess credits.[24] The carryback and carryover rules are illustrated in the following example:

Example: Multico, a domestic corporation, has the following history of foreign taxes and foreign tax credit limitations for the period 19X1–19X8:

	Year			
	19X1	*19X2*	*19X3*	*19X4*
Current year foreign taxes paid	$40,000	$50,000	$85,000	$70,000
Foreign tax credit limitation	$45,000	$56,000	$40,000	$75,000
Credit or deduction elected	Credit	Credit	Credit	Credit
Excess credits			$45,000	
Excess limitation	$ 5,000	$ 6,000		$ 5,000

	Year			
	19X5	*19X6*	*19X7*	*19X8*
Current year foreign taxes paid	$50,000	$55,000	$50,000	$62,000
Foreign tax credit limitation	$58,000	$58,000	$60,000	$68,000
Credit or deduction elected	Credit	Credit	Credit	Credit
Excess credits				
Excess limitation	$ 8,000	$ 3,000	$10,000	$ 6,000

The starting point for this analysis is 19X3, when the taxpayer generates an excess credit amount of $45,000. Multico can first carry $5,000 of this excess credit back to year 19X1 and amend its 19X1 return to claim a total foreign tax credit for $45,000—the full limitation amount. Next it carried $6,000 of the excess credit from 19X3 to 19X2 and amends its 19X2 return. Now the taxpayer has used up $11,000 of the 19X3 excess foreign tax credit. The remaining $34,000 ($45,000

---

[24]Nearly all taxpayers who pay foreign taxes claim them as a credit on their tax returns. A deduction may be claimed when, for example, a taxpayer has incurred losses and feels he or she will be unable to use a foreign tax payment as a credit in the current year or one of the carryback or carryover years. The foreign tax deduction will thus provide the taxpayer with an increased net operating loss that may be carried back or forward. Further discussion of this point is beyond the scope of this book and is left for an advanced multinational taxation course.

— $11,000) of excess foreign tax credits may be carried over for as much as five years. Multico will use $5,000 in 19X4, $8,000 in 19X5, $3,000 in 19X6, $10,000 in 19X7, and $6,000 in 19X8. After 19X8, the taxpayer has used $43,000 of its 19X3 excess tax credit, and the remaining $2,000 is lost since the carryover period ends with 19X8.

Special rules exist for carryovers and carrybacks of excess credits incurred in a per-country limitation year to an overall limitation year, and vice versa. These special rules, as well as a series of transitional rules, may apply to taxpayers who were required in 1976 to switch from the per-country limitation method to the overall limitation method and must carry back or carry over credits from a taxable year in which one limitation method was used to a year in which the other method was used (Sec. 904(e)).

Recapture of overall foreign losses

Until 1976, taxpayers who operated overseas and incurred foreign losses could use these losses to reduce the taxes levied on the profits derived from their U.S. activities. Then, when the foreign activities became profitable, they could take advantage of the foreign tax credit provisions to reduce the U.S. taxes due on their foreign source income. To prevent taxpayers from obtaining the benefits of both a loss deduction and the foreign tax credit, beginning in 1976, taxpayers who incur an overall foreign loss are required to recapture this loss when their foreign operations become profitable. The losses are recaptured by treating a portion of these foreign profits as U.S. source income, thereby reducing the foreign tax credit limitation amount.

An overall foreign loss is incurred when foreign source deductions (other than net operating loss deductions, capital loss carrybacks and carryovers, foreign expropriation losses, and casualty and theft losses) exceed foreign source gross income. The amount of this loss that is recaptured in a subsequent taxable year by being treated as U.S. source taxable income is the lesser of:

1. The amount of the original loss minus the portion of the loss recaptured in preceding taxable years; or

2. 50 percent (or more if the taxpayer so chooses) of the taxpayer's foreign source taxable income (Sec. 904(f)(1)).

When a taxpayer sells, exchanges, distributes, or otherwise disposes of property that has been predominately used in a foreign trade or business during a taxable year, the sale triggers the recapture of part or all of the foreign loss, whether or not a gain is required to be recognized on the disposition. The amount of the recapture that is triggered equals the lesser of the amount of the overall foreign loss that was not recaptured during the year of disposition or in a preceding taxable year, or 100 percent of the excess of the fair market value of the property disposed of over its adjusted basis (Sec. 904(f)(3)). Exempted from the definition of a "disposition" is property that is not a material factor in the realization of income by the taxpayer, or a transaction to which the tax attribute carryover rules of Sec. 381(a) apply. Special rules are found in Sec. 907(f)(3) for a foreign oil-related loss.

The conversion of foreign source taxable income to U.S. source income does not reduce the amount of a taxpayer's creditable taxes that were paid or accrued in a year to which the recapture rules apply. The conversion of the income from foreign source to U.S. source does, however, increase the likelihood that these taxes will exceed the foreign tax credit limitation.

Deemed paid foreign tax credit

When a corporation operates overseas through a foreign branch, the parent corporation may, of course, claim the foreign taxes paid by the branch as a direct foreign tax credit to offset the U.S. taxes due on the branch profits. When a corporation operates overseas through a foreign subsidiary, however, the parent corporation is not the taxpayer of record for the foreign taxes paid by the subsidiary and therefore may not claim a direct foreign tax credit for these taxes. If the parent corporation receives dividends from the foreign subsidiary, it must report the dividends as foreign source income but may only claim a direct foreign tax credit for the foreign taxes that are withheld by the subsidiary on the remittance. To reduce the relative advantage of operating overseas through a foreign branch rather than through a foreign subsidiary, Congress in 1918 enacted the deemed paid foreign tax credit provisions, which permit a qualifying investor corporation to claim a pro rata share (based on the amount of dividends received) of the foreign income, war profits, and excess profits taxes that have been paid by its subsidiary.[25]

---

[25]Revenue Act of 1918, Sec. 240(c).

Requirements for claiming a deemed paid foreign tax credit

The following three requirements must be met for a deemed paid foreign tax credit to be claimed:

1. The corporation that makes the dividend payment must be a foreign corporation having foreign source income.

2. A dividend must be paid by the foreign corporation. Payments received from the foreign subsidiary are classified as a dividend or a return of capital based on the U.S. tax laws and not based on the laws under which the foreign subsidiary operates.

3. The domestic corporation must satisfy a series of minimum stock ownership requirements with respect to its investment in the distribuing corporation on the date that the dividend distribution is received. If the minimum stock ownership requirements are satisfied on that date, the deemed paid credit is available for both common and preferred stock distributions that are made out of current or accumulated earnings and profits.

    a. The domestic corporation must own at least 10 percent of the voting stock of the first-tier foreign corporation (Sec. 902(a)).

    b. The first-tier foreign corporation must own at least 10 percent of the voting stock of the second-tier foreign corporation (Sec. 902(b)(1)).

    c. The second-tier foreign corporation must own at least 10 percent of the voting stock of the third-tier foreign corporation (Sec. 902(b)(2)).

    d. In addition, the domestic corporation's indirect ownership interest in the second-tier foreign corporation and third-tier foreign corporation (if applicable) must be at least 5 percent (Sec. 902(b)(3)).

    e. No deemed paid credit is available for dividend distributions made by fourth- or lower-tier foreign subsidiaries.

Figure 21-1 illustrates the minimum stock ownership requirements that must be satisfied in order to claim the deemed paid foreign tax credit.

Calculation of the deemed paid credit

For distributions made before December 31, 1977, there were two possible ways to calculate the deemed paid tax credit. One set of rules applied to distributions made by the special corporate form—the less developed country corporation (LDCC)—and the second to all other foreign corporations. The special rules applying to LDCCs are of historical interest only, and are therefore not discussed.

The deemed paid credit is calculated in the following manner for all dividend distributions received by a

FIGURE 21-1   Minimum Stock Ownership Requirements
for the Sec. 902 Deemed Paid Tax Credit

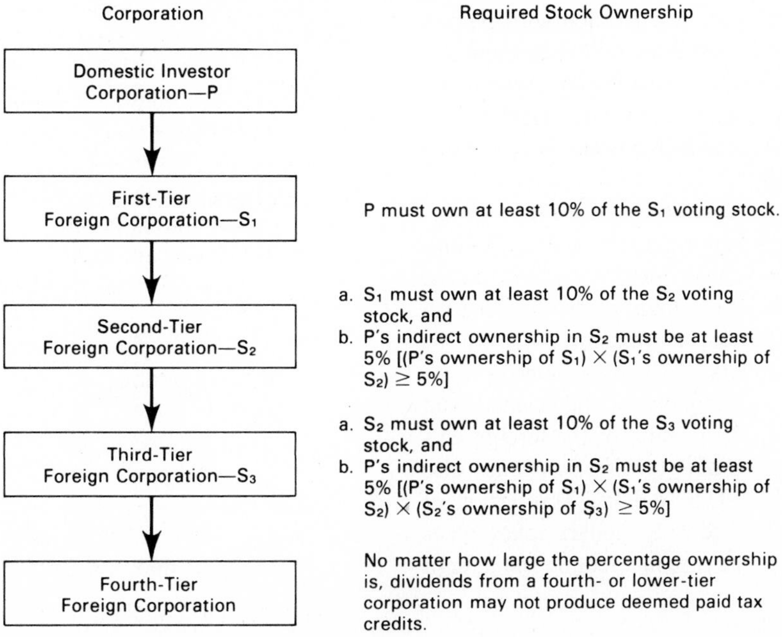

Corporation   Required Stock Ownership

Domestic Investor Corporation—P

First-Tier Foreign Corporation—S_1

    P must own at least 10% of the S_1 voting stock.

Second-Tier Foreign Corporation—S_2

    a. S_1 must own at least 10% of the S_2 voting stock, and
    b. P's indirect ownership in S_2 must be at least 5% [(P's ownership of S_1) $\times$ (S_1's ownership of S_2) $\geq$ 5%]

Third-Tier Foreign Corporation—S_3

    a. S_2 must own at least 10% of the S_3 voting stock, and
    b. P's indirect ownership in S_2 must be at least 5% [(P's ownership of S_1) $\times$ (S_1's ownership of S_2) $\times$ (S_2's ownership of S_3) $\geq$ 5%]

Fourth-Tier Foreign Corporation

    No matter how large the percentage ownership is, dividends from a fourth- or lower-tier corporation may not produce deemed paid tax credits.

qualifying domestic corporation after December 31, 1977 (and all distributions made by non-LDCCs before that date):

$$\begin{array}{l}\text{Deemed paid} \\ \text{foreign tax credit}\end{array} = \begin{array}{c}\text{Percentage ownership of} \\ \text{domestic corporation at} \\ \text{distribution date}\end{array}$$

$$\times \; \frac{\text{Total dividends paid}}{\begin{array}{c}\text{Accumulated profits} \\ \text{minus foreign taxes}\end{array}} \times \begin{array}{c}\text{Foreign taxes paid} \\ \text{or accrued by the} \\ \text{foreign corporation}\end{array}$$

The deemed paid credit is available only if the remittance qualifies as a dividend. A distribution is determined to be a dividend by applying the rules of Sec. 316 to determine if the amount of the remittance was made out of the foreign corporation's current or accumulated earnings and profits (E & P). A special modification to the Sec. 316 rules is found in Sec. 902, which permits a domestic corporation to remit a foreign corporation's earnings back to the United States during the first 60 days of the succeeding taxable year and have them treated as coming out of the E & P of the year in which they were earned. Any distribution made during this 60-day period is considered to be a "throwback" distribution and to come out of the E & P of the preceding taxable year (or years) (Sec. 902(c)(1)). Any distribution made after the first 60 days of the taxable year is considered to come out of the current year's E & P.[26]

The term "accumulated profits" means the foreign corporation's current E & P plus the foreign income taxes paid or accrued by the corporation with respect to the E & P. Because E & P is an annual concept, if a dividend remittance is considered to be made from more than one year's E & P, a separate calculation is required for each year for which the earnings are distributed.

In general, the books and records of the foreign corporation will be maintained in the foreign corporation's local currency. To report the dividend remittance to the U.S. taxing authorities, the amount of the dividend remittance that is includible in gross income must be translated into U.S. dollars. If the distributee is a domestic corporation that is eligible for the deemed paid foreign tax credit, then the amount of the foreign corporation's accumulated profits and foreign taxes also must be translated into U.S. dollars. Translation of each of these amounts into U.S. dollars takes place using the foreign exchange rate in effect on the date of the dividend payment[27] (Treas. Reg. Sec. 1.301-1(b)). Exchange gains and losses on the investment in the foreign corporation are thus recognized for U.S. tax purposes when the earnings are remitted to the United States.

The following two examples illustrate the deemed paid credit calculation:

Example (1): M Corporation, a domestic corporation, owns all the stock of A Corporation, a foreign corporation. A Corporation reported the following 19X1 results:

Corporate profits	$100
Foreign taxes	40
Accumulated profits	100
Dividend to M	30

During 19X1, A remits a $30 dividend payment to M. M is able to claim a $20 deemed paid foreign tax credit with respect to this remittance, based on the following calculation:

$$\begin{array}{l}\text{Deemed} \\ \text{paid credit}\end{array} = 100\% \times \frac{\$30}{\$60} \times \$40 = \underline{\underline{\$20}}$$

(Adapted from Treas. Reg. Sec. 1.902-1(k) Ex. (1))

Example (2): M Corporation, a domestic corporation, owns all the stock of B Corporation, a first-tier foreign corporation incorporated in Country X, which owns all the stock of C Corporation, a second-tier foreign corporation. B and C corporations reported the following profits in 19X1:

First-tier foreign corporation:

B Corp. profits (excluding C Corp. dividends)	$200
C Corp. dividend	90
Foreign taxes	40
Accumulated profits	290
Dividend paid to M	125
Country X taxes withheld by B	12.50

Second-tier foreign corporation:

C Corp. profits	$300
Foreign taxes	120
Accumulated profits	300
Dividend paid to B	90

During 19X1, C makes a $90 dividend remittance to B, and B makes a $125 dividend remittance to

---

[26] Rev. Rul. 69-447, 1969-2 CB 153.

[27] *Bon Ami Co.*, 39 BTA 825 (1939).

M. M is able to claim a $50 deemed paid foreign tax credit with respect to this remittance, which is based on a portion of the taxes paid by both B and C, plus a $12.50 credit for the Country X taxes withheld by B on the remittance. This credit is determined as follows:

Step 1: Foreign Taxes of C Deemed Paid by B:

$$\text{Deemed paid credit} = 100\% \times \frac{\$90}{\$300 - \$120} \times \$120 = \underline{\underline{\$60}}$$

Step 2: Foreign Taxes of B Deemed Paid by Domestic Corporation M:

$$\text{Deemed paid credit} = 100\% \times \frac{\$125}{(\$200 + \$90) - \$40}$$

$$\times (\$40 + \$60) = \underline{\underline{\$50}}$$

Step 3: Foreign Tax Credit Claimed by M:

Deemed paid credit	$50.00
Withholding by B	12.50
Total	$62.50

(Adapted from Treas. Reg. Sec. 1.902-1(k) Ex. (3))

Gross up of a dividend

After the amount of the deemed paid tax credit is calculated, this credit amount must be added to the dividend received in order to report the dividend as income on the U.S. tax return (Sec. 78). For example, a corporate taxpayer that received a $7,000 dividend payment (before reduction for foreign taxes withheld) from its foreign subsidiary, and that calculated that its deemed paid tax credit would be $2,400 on that dividend, includes foreign dividend income of $9,400 ($7,000 plus $2,400) in its gross income. This increase in income for the deemed paid taxes is called a "gross up" of the dividend. Dividends must be grossed up by the full amount of the deemed paid credit, even though part of it may not be used in the current year because of the Sec. 904 foreign tax credit limitation.

Taxes related to international boycott operations

In an attempt to provide an incentive for U.S. taxpayers to refrain from participating in an international boycott, Congress enacted as part of the Tax Reform Act of 1976 a series of provisions repealing the foreign tax credit benefits for foreign taxes paid on income derived from boycott-related operations. In addition, the tax deferral privilege for U.S. shareholders of Controlled Foreign Corporations and Domestic International Sales Corporations is denied for income derived from boycott-related operations (Sec. 999).

REPORTING THE FOREIGN TAX CREDIT

If an individual taxpayer has paid or accrued any creditable foreign taxes during the year, the taxpayer is required to file Form 1116 to support the amount of the credit claimed. The completed Form 1116 on the next page illustrates many of the principles outlined in this chapter.

Form 1116

Department of the Treasury
Internal Revenue Service

Computation of Foreign Tax Credit
Individual, Fiduciary, or Nonresident Alien Individual

For calendar year 19......, or other tax year beginning ...., 19....., and ending ...., 19.....

Attach to Form 1040, 1041, or 1040NR

1979

Name
Harry and Celeste Heinlein

Social security number
123-45-6789

Address (Number and street)
69 Rue Claude Bernard

Employer identification number

City or town, State and ZIP code or country
75005 PARIS FRANCE

This form being completed for credit with respect to:

(*Use a separate Form 1116 for each type of income. See General Instruction J.*)

- [ ] Nonbusiness (section 904(d)) interest income
- [ ] Dividends from a DISC or former DISC
- [ ] Foreign oil related income
- [ ] All other income from sources outside the U.S. (including income from sources within U.S. possessions)

Resident of (Name of country) UNITED STATES

Citizen of (Name of country) UNITED STATES

Schedule A—Taxable Income from Sources Outside the U.S.

2. Gross Income from Sources Outside the U.S.

1. Name of Foreign Country or U.S. Possession (Use a separate line for each)	(a) Dividends	(b) Gross Rents and Royalties	(c) Foreign Source Capital Gain Net Income (See Instruction K)	(d) Wages, Salaries, and Other Employee Compensation	(e) Business or Profession (Sole Proprietorship)	(f) Gross Income from Trusts and Estates	(g) Other (Including Interest) (Attach schedule)	(h) Total (Add columns (a) through (g))
A FRANCE	6000		2000	101,846			150	109,996
B								
C								
D								
E								
F								
G								
Totals (Add lines A through G)	6000		2000	101,846			150	109,996

3. Applicable Deductions and Losses

Directly Allocable Deductions

	(a) Expenses Directly Allocable to Business or Profession	(b) Depreciation and Depletion Directly Allocable to Rent and Royalty Income	(c) Repairs and Other Expenses Directly Allocable to Rent and Royalty Income	(d) Other Expenses Directly Allocable to Specific Income Items (Attach schedule)	(e) Pro rata Share of All Other Deductions Not Directly Applicable (Attach schedule)	(f) Losses from Foreign Sources	(g) Total Applicable Deductions and Losses (Add columns (a) through (f))	4. Taxable Income or (Loss) from Sources Outside the U.S. (before recapture of prior year overall foreign losses) (Column 2(h) less column 3(g))
A	26,552				3105		29,657	80,339
B								
C								
D								
E								
F								
G								
Totals	26,552				3105		29,657	80,339

Schedule B—Foreign Taxes Paid or Accrued

4. Foreign Taxes Paid or Accrued (Attach receipt or copy of return.) (See General Instruction H.)

	1. Credit is claimed for taxes			2. Type of Tax	3. Statute Imposing Tax (Title, number, section, etc.) (Identify in detail)	In Foreign Currency — Tax Withheld at Source on: (a) Dividends	(b) Rents and Royalties	(c) Other Foreign Taxes Paid or Accrued	(d) Conversion Rate (Attach schedule)	In U.S. Dollars — Tax Withheld at Source on: (e) Dividends	(f) Rents and Royalties	(g) Other Foreign Taxes Paid or Accrued	(h) Total Foreign Taxes Paid or Accrued (Add cols. (e), (f), and (g))	5. Reduction for Income Taxes on Income Excluded Under Section 911, Foreign Mineral Income and for Failure to Furnish Returns Required under Section 6038 (Also See General Instruction N)
	☒ Paid	☐ Accrued												
	Date Paid	Date Accrued												
A	12/79			INCOME	INCOME TAX ACT			140,415 FF	$1 U.S. = 4.3 FF			32,655	32,655	NONE
B														
C														
D														
E														
F														
G														
Totals (Add lines A through G)							NONE			NONE	NONE	32,655	32,655	NONE

Schedule C—Computation of Foreign Tax Credit

1 Total foreign taxes paid or accrued (from Schedule B, column 4(h), "Totals" line)	1	32,655
2 Carryback or carryover (attach detailed computation) (see General Instruction L)	2	NONE
3 Reduction for taxes (from Schedule B, column 5, "Totals" line)	3	NONE
4 Total foreign taxes available for credit (Add lines 1 and 2, and subtract line 3 from the result)	4	32,655
5 Taxable income or (loss) from sources outside the U.S. (from Schedule A, column 4, "Totals" line). (If loss, skip lines 6 through 16).	5	80,339
6 Recapture of prior year overall foreign losses (see General Instruction K)	6	NONE
7 Net foreign source taxable income (Subtract line 6 from line 5)	7	80,339
8 Individuals: Enter amount from Form 1040, line 34, or Form 1040NR, line 39. Estates and trusts: Make no entry, skip to line 10	8	87,972
9 Enter $3,400 (joint return or widow(er)), $2,300 (single or head of household), or $1,700 (married filing separate return)	9	3,400
10 Individuals: Subtract line 9 from line 8.—Estates and trusts: Enter on this line your taxable income without the deduction for your exemption	10	84,572
11 Divide line 7 by line 10. (If line 7 is more than line 10, enter the figure "1".)	11	.949949
12 Total U.S. income tax before any credits (see General Instruction D) (MARRIED FILED JOINTLY, TAXABLE INCOME $83,972.)	12	32,623
13 Credit for the elderly	13	ø
14 Subtract line 13 from line 12	14	32,623
15 Limitation on credit (Multiply line 14 by line 11)	15	30,990
16 Foreign tax credit (line 4 or line 15, whichever is smaller)	16	30,990

Schedule D—Summary of Credits from Separate Schedules C

1 Credit with respect to nonbusiness (section 904(d)) interest	1	
2 Credit with respect to dividends from a DISC or former DISC	2	
3 Credit with respect to foreign oil related income	3	
4 Credit with respect to all other income from sources outside the U.S. (including income from sources within U.S. possessions)	4	30,990
5 Total (Add lines 1 through 4)	5	30,990
6 Reduction in credit for international boycott operations (see General Instruction N)	6	NONE
7 Foreign tax credit (Subtract line 6 from line 5). Enter here and on your tax return	7	30,990

☆ U.S. GOVERNMENT PRINTING OFFICE : 1979—O-283-217   23-0916750

PROBLEMS

1. The U.S. tax laws allow different tax treatments depending on the taxpayer's countries of citizenship and residency. What types and sources of income are taxed by the U.S. government for the following taxpayer classifications?
   a. U.S. citizen
   b. Resident alien of the United States
   c. Nonresident alien engaged in the conduct of a U.S. trade or business
   d. Nonresident alien *not* engaged in the conduct of a U.S. trade or business
   e. Domestic corporation
   f. Foreign corporation

2. Determine the source of the interest income for the following payments received in 19X4 by John T. Taxpayer, who is a U.S. citizen unless otherwise indicated.
   a. $1,000 of interest income earned on a deposit with the First National Bank of Detroit. Taxpayer, a nonresident alien, does not engage in the conduct of a U.S. trade or business.
   b. $750 of interest income earned on a deposit with the Paris, France, branch of the First National Bank of Detroit.
   c. $2,500 of interest income paid by DEF Corporation, a domestic corporation that derived 55 percent of its gross income from non-U.S. sources.
   d. The same $2,500 of income earned in part c, except that DEF Corporation earned all its income from foreign sources.
   e. $1,500 of interest income paid by XYZ Corporation. XYZ is a foreign corporation that earned the following income during the period 19X1–19X4:

Year	Worldwide gross income	Income effectively connected with the conduct of a U.S. trade or business
19X1	$150,000	$ 90,000
19X2	250,000	100,000
19X3	400,000	175,000
19X4	500,000	235,000

   f. The same $1,500 of interest income earned in part e, except that the $400,000 of 19X3 gross income included $265,000 of income effectively connected with the conduct of a U.S. trade or business.
   g. $250 of interest paid by Alfredo Diaz, a resident alien of the United States. Nearly all Diaz's income came from U.S. sources.

3. The U.S. tax laws have been used to encourage foreign investments in the United States. One such situation is found in the source-of-income rules relating to interest income. Explain how the application of these rules to U.S. investments made by a nonresident alien accomplishes this purpose.

4. Determine the source of the dividend income for the following payments received in 19X4 by Sally T. Taxpayer, a U.S. citizen.
   a. $5,000 dividend remittance received from a domestic corporation that earns 55 percent of its gross income from non-U.S. sources.
   b. $2,750 dividend remittance received from a foreign corporation that does not engage in the conduct of a U.S. trade or business.
   c. The same $5,000 dividend remittance from part a, except the domestic corporation earns 90 percent of its gross income from non-U.S. sources.
   d. $10,000 dividend remittance received from a foreign corporation that earned the following income during the period 19X1–19X3.

Year	Worldwide gross income	Income effectively connected with the conduct of a U.S. trade or business
19X1	$150,000	$ 90,000
19X2	250,000	100,000
19X3	400,000	175,000
19X4	500,000	235,000

    e. The same $10,000 dividend remittance from part d, except that the $400,000 of 19X3 gross income included $265,000 of income effectively connected with the conduct of a U.S. trade or business.

    f. $25,000 dividend remittance from a domestic corporation that (1) qualified as a Domestic International Sales Corporation in 19X4, and (2) had all its gross receipts considered to be qualified export receipts.

5. Melissa Wainwright III, a citizen and resident of England, was temporarily assigned in 19X1 to the United States for training by her employer, BMI Corporation, a U.S. corporation. Normally, Wainwright is employed in BMI's London sales office. Melissa was present in the United States for a total of six weeks during 19X1. Her compensation while in the United States was $475 per week.

    a. What is the source of Melissa Wainwright's income?

    b. If Wainwright had been paid $600 per week, would your answer change? If so, how?

    c. Suppose in part b Melissa had been paid by the London office during the six weeks in question, and that she had received only $1,000 of her salary while in the United States. Do these new facts change your answer to part b? How?

6. Larry Ochab, a citizen and resident of a nontreaty foreign country, had the following income for 19X1. Determine the source of each of these income forms.

    a. Dividends received of $1,000 from Ford Motor Company, a U.S. corporation that derives 65 percent of its income from U.S. sources.

    b. Interest income of $500 received on Ford Motor Company bonds.

    c. Royalty income of $12,500 (based entirely on sales) derived from the use in the United States of a patent on a microprocessing system by the American Computer Company, Inc.

    d. Interest earned on the following bank accounts:

        1. Savings account with Detroit office of a U.S. bank (not connected with the conduct of a U.S. trade or business), $500.

        2. Account with overseas office of a U.S. bank, $250.

        3. Account with local bank in Mr. Ochab's country of residence, $400.

    e. Rental income of $7,800 received from the leasing of Mr. Ochab's former personal residence in Detroit. Deductible expenses related to the rental income are $4,000.

    f. Book royalties of $10,000 from sale of an art history book in the United States.

    g. Gain on the sale in Detroit of an art work (held for four years) to the Detroit Museum of Art, $5,000.

    h. Dividend income of $1,750 derived from a corporation incorporated in Ochab's country of residence that is not engaged in the conduct of a U.S. trade or business.

    i. Mr. Ochab visited the United States for 75 days this year, selling products to the auto industry as a commission agent for several foreign firms. His commission income totaled $24,000.

7. Karen Spivey, a citizen and resident of a nontreaty foreign country, had the following income for 19X1. Determine the source of each of these forms of income.

a. Salary of $2,500 from a home country law firm that was earned while in the United States for 28 days attending seminars dealing with U.S. taxation. The law firm does not engage in the conduct of a U.S. trade or business.

b. Interest income of $10,000 earned from a land contract on the sale of a U.S. rental property to a U.S. citizen in an earlier year.

c. Royalty income of $25,000 derived from the U.S. showings of a movie. Karen had written the script for the movie, which was filmed outside the United States.

d. Dividend income:
   1. From Braniff Airways, a domestic corporation deriving 60 percent of its income from U.S. sources, $3,000.
   2. From Overseas Industries, a corporation incorporated in Ms. Spivey's country of residence that derives 70 percent of its income from the conduct of a U.S. trade or business, $5,000.

e. Interest income of $750 from funds deposited in a savings account at an office of a U.S. bank located in the foreign country.

f. Rental income of $10,000 derived from a net lease arrangement on a warehouse located in Santa Fe, New Mexico. Expenses in connection with this arrangement were $1,000.

g. Fees of $350 received for a professional presentation made to the California Tax Institute.

h. Capital gain on the sale of the Braniff Airways stocks (held two years) while in New York attending a tax seminar, $15,000.

i. Gain on the sale of land located near Caracas, Venezuela, to a U.S. buyer, $40,000. The property was sold through a U.S. broker while Karen was residing outside the United States.

8. EOC Corporation, a U.S. based multinational corporation, reported the following results for 19X1:

Worldwide taxable income	$10,000,000
U.S. source taxable income	5,000,000
Foreign source taxable income	5,000,000
Foreign income taxes paid or accrued	2,300,000

Before an I.R.S. review of its 19X1 tax return, none of EOC's home office expenses or interest expense was allocated to EOC's overseas activities. After the review, $500,000 of such expenses were reallocated to the overseas activities income under Treas. Reg. Sec. 1.861-8. Determine the effects of such a reallocation on EOC's foreign tax credit limitation, ignoring the rate reductions of Sec. 11(b).

9. Albert Smith is a nonresident alien who engages in various U.S. activities throughout 19X1. The income and deductions from these activities are outlined below.

   Income:

Sales commissions—U.S. (120 days)	$ 50,000
Foreign (245 days)	100,000
Interest: from New York bank account (unrelated to U.S. sales activities)	15,000
Dividend income—General Electric Co.	1,000
French Lingerie, S.A.	2,000
Municipal bond interest income (City of Denver bonds)	10,000
Rental income—New York apartment building	25,000
Royalty income	20,000
Capital gain from sale of painting to Chicago Museum of Art (title passed in Chicago)	2,000

Expenses:

Expenses related to: U.S. sales commissions	15,000
Foreign sales commissions	25,000
Commission paid to leasing agent	4,000
Depreciation on building	6,000
Operating expenses on building	5,000
Loss on sale of apartment building	20,000
Worldwide general and administrative expenses	20,000
Personal exemptions	1

Determine the amount of the deductions that are directly and indirectly allocable to each of the classes of income.

10. SBJ, Inc., a domestic corporation, has a number of foreign branch offices that operate exclusively in foreign countries. SBJ incurs $250,000 of interest expense in 19X1. Its 19X1 gross income by source location and average assets by situs are presented below:

		Assets	
	Gross income	Adjusted basis	Fair market value
U.S. source/situs	$2,500,000	$3,000,000	$5,000,000
Non-U.S. source/situs	2,000,000	2,000,000	2,000,000
Total	$4,500,000	$5,000,000	$7,000,000

All of SBJ's 19X1 interest expense is incurred on funds that are unable to be directly traced to a specific activity. Determine the amount of interest expense that is to be apportioned to SBJ's foreign source taxable income (statutory grouping) and U.S. source taxable income (residual grouping) when determining the foreign tax credit limitation.

11. The United States has entered into a number of bilateral tax treaties. Briefly outline the U.S. objectives behind entering into these agreements.

12. Explain how a tax treaty between the United States and foreign country X affects U.S. taxation of the following individuals:

   a. A U.S. citizen who earns some of his or her salary income in the United States and some in Country X.

   b. A citizen of Country X who is a resident of the United States and earns all of his or her income while physically present in the United States for the entire taxable year.

   c. A citizen of Country X who resides in Country Z (a nontreaty country) and who, because of an assignment by his or her Country Z employer, was physically present for the full year in the United States.

   d. A citizen of Country X whose only U.S. activities are: engaging in the conduct of a U.S. trade or business that has a permanent establishment located in Dime Box, Texas, and an investment in some U.S. stocks that are unrelated to his or her trade or business.

13. In order to claim a foreign tax credit, a taxpayer must first pay a foreign tax levy that the I.R.S. considers to be creditable. What standards are applied to determine if the foreign tax levy is creditable? If the levy is not creditable, what alternative tax treatments are available for the payment under U.S. law?

14. Albert Mitchell is a U.S. citizen who uses the accrual method of accounting. During 19X1 he resided for part of the year in Country X. At year-end, he accrues a Country X income tax liability of 25,000 pira. During 19X1, the ex-

change rate between the U.S. dollar and the pira fluctuated, with the average rate being 2.67 pira = $1 (U.S.). The year-end exchange rate is 2.50 pira = $1 (U.S.).

  a. Determine the translated amount of foreign taxes that are creditable by Albert Mitchell.

  b. Assume that the exchange rate changed to 2.75 pira = $1 (U.S.) on the date the Country X taxes were paid. What action, if any, would be required because of the change in the exchange rate?

  c. Answer part b again, assuming the exchange rate changed to 2.40 pira = $1 (U.S.).

  d. If, in part b, Albert Mitchell used the cash method of accounting instead of the accrual method, determine the translated amount of foreign taxes that could be claimed as a credit.

15. Steve Boyles was employed in both the United States and Venezuela during 19X1. The source of his income and deductible expenses are as follows:

Salary: U.S.	$10,000
Venezuela	50,000
Deductions utilized in determining A.G.I.:	
U.S. sourced	1,000
Venezuelan sourced	12,000
Foreign income taxes	10,500
Personal and dependency exemptions	4

Boyles, who is married and files a joint return with his wife, is unable to itemize his deductions and must utilize the zero bracket amount.

  a. Determine Boyles's gross U.S. tax liability.

  b. Determine Boyles's foreign tax credit limitation.

  c. What happens to the amount of foreign taxes, if any, that Boyles paid in excess of his foreign tax credit limitation?

16. Le Chien, Inc. is the wholly owned French subsidiary of Wolf Corporation, a domestic corporation formed on January 1, 19X1. The two corporations have the following financial positions at the end of 19X5:

	Wolf	Le Chien
Profits (includes gross dividends but not deemed paid foreign tax credits)	$200,000	$65,000
Taxes (before foreign tax credit in U.S.)	87,000	13,000
Gross dividends to U.S. parent		39,000
French withholding taxes on dividends		5,850

Foreign taxes paid and deemed paid by Wolf Corporation and the appropriate foreign tax credit limitation amounts (in dollars) for the years 19X1–19X4 are as follows:

	19X1	19X2	19X3	19X4
Foreign taxes	$4,600	$7,850	$10,500	$14,400
Overall limitation	5,000	8,900	10,650	12,900

Compute the net tax liability of Wolf Corporation for 19X5.

17. JTG Company, a domestic corporation, had the following results from its 19X1 operations.

		Income	Foreign taxes
Manufacturing operations:	U.S.	$200,000	
	German	300,000	$150,000
Long-term capital gain		100,000[a]	-0-
DISC dividend		20,000	1,500[b]
Interest income		30,000[c]	-0-

[a]The gain resulted from the sales of stocks held by JTG in the Bahamas, a country in which it conducted no trade or business activities and that did not levy a tax on the sale.
[b]Deemed paid credit.
[c]Interest earned on funds deposited in a Bahamian bank.

Determine JTG's foreign tax credit for 19X1.

18. GFS Corporation, a domestic corporation, establishes an overseas branch at the beginning of 19X1. The branch activity manufactures and sells electrical products for use in the local market. The operating results for GFS and its branch activity for 19X1–19X4 are presented below.

	(in thousands)			
	19X1	19X2	19X3	19X4
GFS: U.S. gross income	$200	$250	$300	$400
U.S. expenses	75	120	160	225
Branch: Foreign gross income	75	75	150	220
Foreign expenses	100	100	120	140
Foreign income taxes	-0-	-0-	12	32

a. Calculate GFS Corporation's gross U.S. tax liability for 19X3 and 19X4.
b. Calculate GFS Corporation's foreign tax credit for 19X3 and 19X4.
c. What is the amount of any available foreign tax credit carrybacks or carryovers?

19. RAK Corporation is a domestic corporation that engages in overseas activities. During 19X1 it paid or accrued creditable foreign taxes in the amount of $135,000. Its 19X1 results of operations are presented below.

Source	Ordinary income	Short-term capital gain	Long-term capital gain	Total
U.S.	$160,000	-0-	$40,000	$200,000
Foreign	270,000	$10,000	20,000	300,000
Total	$430,000	$10,000	$60,000	$500,000

a. Determine RAK Corporation's gross U.S. tax liability.
b. Determine RAK Corporation's foreign tax credit limitation.
c. What happens to the amount of foreign taxes, if any, that RAK paid or accrued in excess of its foreign tax credit limitation?

20. GLC Corporation, a domestic corporation, owns 80 percent of the stock of NAG Corporation, a foreign corporation. During 19X1, NAG earns $100,000 of pretax profits and pays $40,000 in income taxes to Country I. On December 1, 19X1, NAG paid a $36,000 dividend to its shareholders. The Country I government requires NAG to withhold and remit 15 percent of the dividend payment as an income tax that is levied on nonresident shareholders.

a. How much cash did GLC receive?

b. What is the amount of GLC's deemed paid foreign tax credit?

c. What amount must GLC include in its gross income as a result of the dividend?

d. What is GLC's net increase in its U.S. tax liability as a result of the dividend? (Assume GLC's marginal U.S. tax rate is 46 percent.)

21. JKS Corporation, a domestic corporation, owns 50 percent of the stock of JVB Corporation, a first-tier foreign corporation. JVB, in turn, owns 10 percent of the stock of AXE Corporation, a second-tier foreign corporation. Both corporations are incorporated in Country Z. The following results are reported for JVB and AXE corporations.

JVB Corporation:

Dividend paid to shareholders	$ 50,000
Withholding tax by Country Z on dividend payment to JKS Corp.	2,500
Pretax profits (excluding dividend received from AXE Corp.)	100,000
Country Z income taxes on pretax profits[a]	25,000

AXE Corporation:

Dividend paid to shareholders	$ 20,000
Pretax profits	60,000
Country Z income taxes on pretax profits	30,000

[a]Country Z does not levy a tax on dividends received by a Country Z corporation from a second, Country Z corporation.

Determine the deemed paid credit available to JKS Corporation.

22. X Corporation is a wholly owned French manufacturing subsidiary of Y Corporation, a domestic corporation. Both corporations use the calendar year as their taxable years. On April 1, 19X3, X Corporation pays a $190,000 dividend to Y Corporation. X Corporation has reported the following earnings for the period 19X1–19X3:

Year	Pretax profits	French income taxes
19X3	$200,000	$80,000
19X2	120,000	36,000
19X1	150,000	30,000

a. Compute the deemed-paid foreign tax credit (excluding any foreign tax credit limitations) available to Y Corporation as a result of the dividend remittance.

b. How would your answer to part a change if the dividend had been paid on February 1, 19X3?

23. S Corporation, incorporated in Country X, is a wholly owned manufacturing subsidiary of P Corporation, a domestic corporation. Both corporations use the calendar year as their taxable years. On July 15, 19X2, S Corporation makes a 150,000 quat (Q) remittance to P Corporation. S Corporation reported the following results for 19X1 and 19X2.

Year	Pretax profits (Q's)	Country X taxes (Q's)
19X2	200,000	90,000
19X1	100,000	35,000

The exchange rates for conversion of quats into dollars on selected dates are:

Date	Exchange rate
19X1 Average	5.0:1 (5 Qs = $1 U.S.)
December 31, 19X1	5.2:1
July 15, 19X2	5.5:1
19X2 Average	5.25:1
December 31, 19X1	5.1:1

a. What is the translated amount of the dividend remittance included in P Corporation's gross income?

b. What is the translated amount of the deemed paid foreign tax credit available to P Corporation as a result of the dividend remittance?

c. Assume Country X requires S Corporation to withhold 10 percent of the dividend remittance as an income tax levy on P Corporation. At what exchange rate would this levy be translated for foreign tax credit purposes?

SUPPLEMENTAL PROBLEMS

24. Bobby "Slap Shot" Hall, a resident and citizen of Canada, was employed as a professional hockey player by a U.S. professional hockey club. His salary is paid by the hockey club over a 12-month period, even though the hockey season begins on October 1 and runs until the final league game in mid-April. (Playoff games could extend the season until late May.) Bobby receives a per diem allowance during the period he is in training camp and certain other amounts for playing in exhibition games during the period the training camp is in session. The taxpayer is required by his contract to report to the training camp in good physical condition. To do so, Bobby engages in extensive off-season physical conditioning activities. In addition, the contract prohibits Bobby from playing hockey for any other club. What factors should be considered in determining the source of Bobby "Slap Shot" Hall's salary from the contract?

25. EDB, Inc., a U.S. based manufacturer of small electrical appliances, sells its products both in the United States and in selected foreign countries through its branch sales offices. In 1980, EDB incurred $1,500,000 in R & D expenditures that were deductible under Sec. 174. All the R & D expenditures were incurred in the United States, with $200,000 of the expenses being related to meeting the specific requirements of the U.S. Occupational Safety and Health Administration. The following results were reported by EDB for 1980:

Source	Sales	−	Cost of sales	=	Gross income
U.S.	$10,000,000	−	$5,000,000	=	$5,000,000
Non-U.S.	6,000,000	−	3,600,000	=	2,400,000
Total	$16,000,000	−	$8,600,000	=	$7,400,000

Determine the allocation of the R & D expenditures of the statutory grouping (foreign source taxable income) and the residual grouping (U.S. source taxable income) when determining EDB's foreign tax credit limitation.

26. Locate the provisions in the model U.S. income tax treaty that reference the items listed below. This model treaty was released by the U.S. Treasury Department in 1976 as a guideline for U.S. treaty negotiations.
    1. The persons covered by the treaty
    2. The U.S. taxes covered by the treaty
    3. The savings clause
    4. The nondiscrimination clause
    5. The definition of a permanent establishment
    6. The definition of business profits
    7. The withholding rates applying to nonresident aliens on (a) interest income; (b) dividend income; and (c) book royalties

27. An exemption from U.S. taxation of compensation for personal services is available to nonresident aliens who are employed in the United States for short periods of time. To take advantage of this exemption, an alien must satisfy certain requirements with respect to his or her maximum time in the United States, employer, and total U.S. compensation for such services.
    a. What requirements must be satisfied for an alien who is a resident of a non-treaty country to take advantage of this exemption?
    b. What requirements must be satisfied by aliens residing in the following treaty countries?
       1. Austria
       2. Australia
       3. Canada
       4. Denmark
       5. Switzerland

28. Using one of the tax services, determine whether each of the following taxes are creditable under Sec. 901.
    a. Libyan surtax on petroleum concessions (Libyan Petroleum Law, Article 14(1) (a))
    b. Swiss National Defense Tax
    c. Philippine Islands tax on banks (based on National Internal Revenue Code)
    d. Mexican Tax on Gross Royalty Income (Article 3 of the Ley del impuesto sobre la renta)

29. A U.S. parent corporation owns 100 percent of a foreign subsidiary. It engages in no other foreign activities. The foreign subsidiary has been accumulating profits that Country Y taxes at a 46 percent tax rate. Country Y imposes withholding taxes on dividend remittances at a 15 percent rate. The U.S. parent also provides management services and patents (covering the licensing of a product for production in Country Y) to the subsidiary. The United States–Country Y treaty requires the subsidiary to withhold Country Y taxes on these payments at a 5 percent rate. The treasurer of the U.S. company informs you that she would like to remit some of the foreign subsidiary's accumulated profits to the United States. What are the tax consequences of these remittances?

RETURN PROBLEMS

1. Richard Lee Dibble, a single, U.S. citizen, Social Security number 123-45-6789, was employed in Country X for all of 1979. During this time he reported the following foreign source income and expenses.

Salary	$20,000
Dividends (from a foreign corporation)	4,000
Gross income	$24,000
Expenses attributable to personal services provided in Country X	3,600
A.G.I.	$20,400

Dibble did not have sufficient personal deductions to be able to itemize his deductions. On December 30, 1979 he paid Country X income taxes equal to 8,000 pirogs. The exchange rate between pirogs and the U.S. dollar on December 30, 1979 was 2 pirogs = $1 (U.S.). Complete the Form 1116 that Richard Dibble is required to submit with his 1979 income tax return.

2. Amalgamated Activities, Inc., a domestic corporation, employer identification number 38-1505869, engaged in a variety of overseas activities during 1979. Its results of operations are presented below.

	Country X		Country Y		United States	
Activity	Income	Directly allocable deductions	Income	Directly allocable deductions	Income	Directly allocable deductions
Manufacturing	$200,000	$ 50,000	$350,000	$120,000	$400,000	$200,000
Dividends	40,000		50,000			
Gross-up	10,000		20,000			
Rents	100,000	80,000[a]			100,000	90,000[a]
	$350,000	$130,000	$420,000	$120,000	$500,000	$290,000

[a]25 percent represents depreciation

Other expenses not definitely allocable to any activity are $100,000. Information about Amalgamated's taxes is presented below.

Type of Tax	Country X	Country Y
Income tax on manufacturing and rents	$66,000	$ 90,000
Income taxes withheld on dividends	2,000	7,500
Deemed paid from foreign subsidiary	10,000	20,000
Total	$78,000	$117,500

Complete the Form 1118 that Amalgamated Activities is required to submit with its 1979 income tax return.

22

taxation of U.S. citizens and residents eligible for special overseas benefits, nonresident aliens, and foreign corporations

In this chapter, we shall discuss four groups of tax-payers who are under the jurisdiction of the U.S. income tax system but who are outside the usual tax-paying categories of U.S. citizens who are residents or domestic corporations earning income in the United States. First, we shall examine the options currently available for computing taxes due from a U.S. citizen who resides and works abroad. The special exclusion and deduction benefits available to this taxpayer class are explained along with the necessary conditions for receiving these benefits. Next, we shall analyze U.S. taxation of nonresidents (alien individuals and foreign corporations) who earn one of the forms of income that is taxed under the U.S. income tax system. These two taxpayer categories are taxed on income falling into two classes: (1) income that is "fixed or determinable annual or periodical gains, profits, or income"; and (2) income that is "effectively connected with the conduct of a U.S. trade or business." We shall discuss these income categories in the second part of this chapter along with the income taxes levied on these taxpayers. In the final part of this chapter, we shall review the exclusion available for income derived by qualifying individual taxpayers from sources within a U.S. possession or Puerto Rico.

TAXATION OF U.S. CITIZENS WORKING ABROAD

As a general rule, U.S. citizens, whether they reside in the United States or abroad, must pay U.S. income taxes on their worldwide income. Many U.S. citizens working abroad, however, incur much higher living costs and must be paid higher salaries and allowances by their U.S. employers in order to maintain the same standard of living that they knew when employed in the United States. Under our progressive tax structure, if there were no special tax relief for these citizens, they would be subjected to an increased U.S. tax burden because of their higher income levels, even though their standard of living did not increase. Because U.S. employers generally reimburse U.S. taxpayers for their increased U.S. or foreign tax payments, or both, this higher U.S. tax burden also drives up the cost of sending a U.S. employee overseas and, in many cases, will mean that hiring a local employee will be less costly than sending a U.S. national overseas. An example will illustrate this increased cost.

Example: Watson, a U.S. engineer, earns $30,000 when he works in the United States.

When, in early 19X1, his employer transfers him to Country E, where the cost of living is higher, his employer agrees to a cost-of-living adjustment that increases his pay to $40,000 to compensate him for the higher cost of such necessities as food, clothing, and medical care. In addition, Mr. Watson must pay for his two children to attend a private U.S.-type school in Country E. A modest house in Country E (smaller and less modern than the Watson home in the United States) rents for $2,000 a month. Because Mr. Watson cannot afford this rent on his $40,000 salary, his employer pays the rent. Country E taxes Mr. Watson's salary at a 10 percent rate, so Mr. Watson owes foreign income taxes of $6,400 on his salary and rent [0.10 × ($40,000 + $24,000)]. Mr. Watson's U.S. tax liability would also be based on $64,000 of gross income, which would result in a U.S. tax liability before credits of $19,678.[1] Reducing this amount by Watson's foreign tax credits of $6,400 would leave him with a net U.S. tax liability of $13,278. To enable Watson to maintain his U.S. standard of living, Watson's U.S. employer will also be required to reimburse him for the $6,400 of foreign taxes incurred plus the $8,325 differential between his U.S. tax liability ($13,278) and a hypothetical tax liability ($4,953) based on the $30,000 base salary he would have received had he remained in the United States.[2] The $14,725 tax reimbursement is usually made in the next taxable year, and thus acts to increase Watson's U.S. tax liability for that taxable year. Even though Watson's lifestyle in this situation has remained the same, his employer has incurred an additional $8,325 of U.S. tax costs this year in order to maintain Watson in his overseas position, and will likely incur a larger cost the next year when the tax reimbursement is included in gross income.

Because of this increased tax burden, U.S. firms might be reluctant to send U.S. citizens abroad to occupy management positions when local managers could perform the same task for a lower cost. Alternatively, the result could be a less competitive position for U.S. firms that are unable to substitute less costly foreign employees. Policy makers, however, have been reluctant to see either result and its potential impact on U.S. trade activities. One school of thought holds that U.S. employees abroad are most frequently managers and

executives and it is employees at this level who make most purchasing decisions. Because American managers are most familiar with U.S.-made goods, the belief is they will buy U.S.-made goods and thereby strengthen our balance of payments position. Another school of thought supporting additional tax benefits to the U.S. employee abroad points out that the U.S. firms involved must compete for business with firms from such nations as Japan and Germany, in which expatriates pay no tax (other than the taxes levied in the country where employment occurs) on their foreign earnings. The higher wage expense of U.S. firms employing U.S. citizens and residents could make a significant difference in the firm's overall competitive position. The arguments against providing these additional tax benefits generally center on the lack of equity that exists when special benefits are available to people employed abroad that are unavailable to people employed in the United States, and the fact that no additional tax benefits are provided U.S. citizens who work in high cost of living areas within the United States such as New York City, Alaska, and Hawaii.

Sections 911, 912,[3] and 913 of the Internal Revenue Code provide tax relief for many Americans working abroad. As a matter of policy, Congress generally has chosen to limit the tax relief to U.S. citizens or residents who work abroad for a significant amount of time. To qualify for the tax benefits of Sections 911 and 913, a taxpayer must meet one of two tests. Either the taxpayer must be a bona fide resident of a foreign country or countries for a period that includes a full tax year or the taxpayer must be physically present in a foreign country or countries for at least 510 full days in a period of 18 consecutive months. We shall explain each of the tests more fully in the next two sections.

Bona fide resident of a foreign country

To qualify for the tax benefits available to certain U.S. expatriates, the taxpayer may establish that he or she has been a "bona fide resident of a foreign country or countries for an uninterrupted period which includes an entire taxable year" (Sec. 913(a)(1)). For the expatriate, the question is whether he is a "mere transient or sojourner" in the foreign country (Treas. Reg. Sec. 1.871-2(b)). Whether an individual is a mere transient or sojourner is a question that can be answered only by knowing his intentions about residing in the foreign country. A U.S. taxpayer is not considered a foreign

---

[1] Tax on $60,000 [$64,000 (gross income) − $4,000 (personal exemptions)].
[2] Tax on $26,000 [$30,000 (gross income) − $4,000 (personal exemptions)].

[3] Section 912 permits a civilian officer or employee of the U.S. government that is employed abroad to exclude from gross income certain foreign area allowances or cost-of-living allowances.

resident if the taxpayer is abroad performing a particular job that he or she expects to complete within a relatively short period of time before returning to the United States. If, on the other hand, a taxpayer takes his family and all his possessions with him when he goes to the foreign country on a job that he expects to last until he retires, he is likely to be taxed as a foreign resident. Because the determination of intent is frequently more difficult than these two scenarios indicate, some more objective criteria may be necessary. One of the most important factors used by the courts is the period of time that the U.S. citizen actually stays abroad. A person who stays less than one year tends to be classified as a nonresident, while someone staying longer than one year will tend to be taxed as a bona fide foreign resident. The single factor of the taxpayer's length of stay is *not* determinative, however. Factors that have been considered by the courts as important in determining whether the taxpayer is a resident include:

1. Intention of the taxpayer;
2. Establishment of his or her home temporarily in the foreign country for an indefinite period;
3. Participation in the activities of his or her chosen community on social and cultural levels, identification with the daily lives of the people, and, in general, assimilation into the foreign environment;
4. Physical presence in the foreign country consistent with taxpayer's employment;
5. Nature, extent, and reasons for temporary absences from taxpayer's temporary foreign home;
6. Assumption of economic burdens and payment of taxes to the foreign country;
7. Status of resident contrasted to that of transient or sojourner;
8. Treatment accorded his or her income tax status by employer;
9. Marital status and residence of taxpayer's family;
10. Nature and duration of taxpayer's employment; whether the assignment abroad could be promptly accomplished within a definite or specified time;
11. Good faith in making his or her home abroad; whether for purposes of tax evasion. [*Carol Patton Haggerty,* 32 T.C.M. 788 (1973), at 792.]

To qualify for the expatriate benefits as a foreign resident, the taxpayer must establish not only foreign residency, but also that the foreign residency lasted at least one *full* taxable year. For calendar year taxpayers, this means the period of residency must include at least one complete taxable year beginning January 1 and ending December 31. A taxpayer arriving in a foreign country on January 3, 19X1 and leaving the country on December 30, 19X2, would *not* meet the requirement of being a resident of a foreign country for one entire taxable year, even though he was a resident of the foreign country for 23 months out of a 24-month period.[4] (He would probably qualify, however, under the 510-day physical presence test discussed below.) If our hypothetical taxpayer stayed in the foreign country through December 31, 19X2, he would qualify for the expatriate benefits for both 19X1 and 19X2. In other words, once the full tax year requirement is satisfied, then all the time during which the taxpayer is classified a resident (commencing with when he initially establishes his residency) qualifies for the tax benefits, whether or not he was actually present in the foreign country during all that period of time. A taxpayer may give up residency in one foreign country and establish a new residence in a second foreign country without affecting his or her tax benefits.

Example: On October 8, 19X1, Harry traveled to Europe as an agent of a U.S. manufacturer to begin selling products throughout the continent. Harry's wife and two children joined him on December 10, 19X1, and on that date, they settled in a small apartment in Cannes, France. Before that time, Harry had lived in hotels while selling in various countries. Shortly after his wife and children arrived, Harry rented a home in Cannes intending to remain there for at least one year. In late 19X1, Harry established a sole proprietorship that handled his sales activities for the original U.S. manufacturer as well as a couple of other noncompeting lines. Harry's children began attending the local schools. Harry and his wife became involved in the community life and formed friendships with people of the village while participating in various social and cultural events. Harry established French bank accounts for his business and family. On July 15, 19X3, Harry and his family returned to the United States permanently. The business Harry had started had not worked out as he had planned, so he accepted a new position as advertising manager of a multinational corporation.

Harry, his wife, and his children returned to the United States only twice during their time in France. Each vacation trip lasted 10 days, and

---

[4]Donald F. Dawson, 59 TC 264 (1972).

each time he left France with the intention to return. Harry and his wife made no statement to the local taxing authorities that they were nonresidents, and, in fact, paid French income taxes.

In this situation, Harry is likely to be considered a bona fide foreign resident for part of 19X1, all of 19X2, and part of 19X3, because the intent to stay more than one year generally indicates that he was not a transient while residing in France. In addition, a number of the other factors such as attending local schools, maintaining a residence consistent with the employment, involvement in community life, social events, and cultural events, possessing local bank accounts, paying local income taxes, and intending to return to France after the vacation are in Harry's favor for claiming to be a bona fide foreign resident.

The 510-day "physical presence" test

Use of the bona fide foreign residence test forces the taxpayer to rely on a number of subjective criteria. The 510-day test, however, is an objective test. If the taxpayer is in a foreign country for 510 or more full days out of 18 consecutive months, the tax benefits of Sec. 911 or 913 are available whether or not foreign residence is established. On the other hand, if the taxpayer is on foreign soil for only 509 full days in the 18-month time period, no benefits are received from either Sec. 911 or Sec. 913 unless the taxpayer can establish that he or she is a bona fide foreign resident.

Calculating the 510-day period provides some problems for taxpayers. First, the 510 days must all be "full days," which means the taxpayer must only count days on which he was present in a foreign country for 24 hours from 12:00 midnight to 12:00 midnight. The 510 days need not be consecutive. The taxpayer may return to the United States as often as he chooses as long as he spends 510 full days in a foreign country or countries during the 18-month period.

The 510-day period must be spent in a foreign country or countries, so moving around from one country to another is not precluded. The 510 days begin to count as time in foreign countries as soon as the taxpayer enters any foreign country, even if it is not the country of final destination. Thus, a taxpayer on her way to a job in Paris, France, who first spends a two-week vacation in London, England, begins to count her 510 days on the first full day that she is present in England. Flying over a foreign country also is considered being in a foreign country. If our taxpayer flies over Canada late on the day preceding the day of her arrival

in London, she is able to count the day of her arrival in London as her first full day in a foreign country, as long as she passed over the U.S. border into Canada before midnight (Temp. Treas. Reg. Sec. 5b. 913-2(c)).

The only remaining question for taxpayers is: When does the 18-month period begin? The 18-month period may begin any day of the calendar month. The period ends the day before the corresponding calendar day in the 18th succeeding month or, if there is no corresponding calendar day, with the last day of the 18th succeeding month. The 18-month period may commence before or after the taxpayer's arrival in a foreign country and may terminate before or after the taxpayer's departure. A new 18-month period begins every day after the beginning of the initial 18-month period.[5] Because a taxpayer may count the 18-month period from any day during the foreign stay, the 510-day test may be satisfied during some 18-month periods even if it is not met in other periods.

The calculation of the 510-day test is illustrated in the following example.

Example: Albert Rhoades, a U.S. citizen, arrives in England from New York at 12 noon on April 24, 19X1 (a non-leap-year). He remains in England until 2:00 P.M. on October 25, 19X2 (also a non-leap-year), at which time he departs for the United States for the rest of 19X2. Rhoades is in England for a number of 18-month periods, two of which are March 17, 19X1 through September 16, 19X2 and June 2, 19X1 through December 1, 19X2. The first period is determined by beginning with the first full day in England (April 25, 19X1) and counting forward 510 full days, or until September 16, 19X2. The 18-month period is then determined by backing up 18 full months, or to March 17, 19X1. Thus, Albert's 18-month period begins almost five weeks before his arrival in England. (His special Sec. 913 deductions, however, do not commence until his tax home is located in England.) Similarly, the second 18-month period is determined by taking the beginning of the 510-day time period to be Rhoades's last full day in England, or October 24, 19X2, and counting backward 510 days. Thus, the beginning of Rhoades's 18-month period is June 2, 19X1. The end of this 18-month period is December 1, 19X2, or nearly five weeks after Rhoades's departure from England. (Here also, Rhoades's special Sec. 913 deductions stop

---

[5] Rev. Rul. 56-487, 1956-2 CB 504.

when his tax home ceases to be England and again becomes the United States.)

Once a taxpayer meets either the bona fide foreign residency test or the 510-day physical presence test, he or she is eligible to receive the tax benefits of Secs. 911, 912, and 913. The requirements for receiving the benefits available to expatriates have remained stable, but the tax benefits themselves have been significantly altered twice in recent years—first in 1976 and again in 1978. To understand some of the provisions as they currently exist, it is necessary to be familiar with the major provisions of the pre-1978 laws.

The law prior to 1978

Before the passage of the Tax Reform Act of 1976, tax relief for expatriates was found in Sec. 911 in the form of an annual exclusion of up to $25,000 of foreign source earned income. Provided that the taxpayer qualified for the Sec. 911 benefits as a bona fide foreign resident or under the 510-day physical presence test, the annual exclusion was also available for partial tax years on a daily basis. The maximum $25,000 annual exclusion was available only to taxpayers who had been bona fide foreign residents for three consecutive years, while all other qualified expatriates qualified for a $20,000 annual exclusion. An arbitrary figure, this exclusion amount had no relationship to cost of living differentials between the United States and other countries. It was equally available to expatriates working in areas in which the cost of living was much lower than in the United States and to expatriates who worked in areas with exceedingly high costs of living.

Section 911 as it existed before the Tax Reform Act of 1976 offered two major benefits to U.S. citizens or residents working abroad. First, the exclusion was applied to the income at the highest marginal tax rates, so that the maximum tax savings available to a taxpayer for a full year was generally one-half the exclusion.[6] The second benefit that Sec. 911 offered taxpayers before the Tax Reform Act of 1976 was that the taxes paid to a foreign government on the excluded portion of foreign source earned income could be used as a foreign tax credit. All foreign taxes paid could thus be credited against the U.S. income taxes due on the nonexcluded portion of foreign source income.

Because of the tax advantages that were available with Sec. 911, some policy makers felt the law was an

[6]The maximum value of the exclusion is based on the assumption that the taxpayer is eligible to use the 50 percent maximum tax rate that applies to earned income.

unwarranted windfall for U.S. citizens working abroad. The Tax Reform Act of 1976 significantly changed the Sec. 911 rules so that they are much less advantageous to the expatriate taxpayer for taxable years beginning after December 31, 1975. The exclusion of earned income was reduced to $15,000 for most taxpayers. Two other advantages under the old law were also eliminated. First, the taxpayer could use the exclusion to offset only his or her lowest marginal tax rate income. Second, the taxpayer could no longer use the foreign taxes on excluded income as a foreign tax credit. The new rules, however, provided an additional advantage to a taxpayer in that the taxpayer no longer was required to itemize deductions in order to claim a foreign tax credit. A taxpayer could thus utilize both a standard deduction and a credit for foreign taxes.

The Tax Reform Act of 1976 significantly decreased the advantages of the Sec. 911 exclusion. The enactment of these changes was swiftly followed by an outcry from expatriates and the U.S. firms employing them. The ultimate result of the outcry was the Foreign Earned Income Act of 1978 (FEIA of 1978), which delayed the effective date of the 1976 changes until taxable years beginning after December 31, 1977. As a result, the pre-1976 law was effective for all taxable years beginning before January 1, 1978. For tax years beginning during 1978, taxpayers could choose between the post-Tax Reform Act of 1976 rules or the rules introduced by the FEIA of 1978. For tax years beginning in 1979 and later, the rules promulgated by the FEIA of 1978 are binding.

Foreign Earned Income Act of 1978

The Foreign Earned Income Act of 1978 represents a significant change in the taxation of expatriates. In all but one instance, the tax benefits available have been changed from an exclusion of certain foreign source earned income to a series of deductions for adjusted gross income under Sec. 913. The deductions are tied much more closely to the cost of living level for the area of residence. Taxpayers residing in a high cost of living area may deduct much more than they could exclude under the previous laws, while taxpayers residing in a low cost of living area may receive less benefit than they received from the fixed amount exclusion. In addition to instituting a series of deductions designed to reflect the higher costs of living abroad, the FEIA of 1978 provides other tax benefits to U.S. citizens and residents employed abroad, for example, a suspension of the period in which a taxpayer must reinvest the proceeds from the sale of a principal residence, a liberalization of moving expenses for citizens moving abroad, and an option (available to taxpayers residing in "camps") to elect to exclude the value of meals and lodging plus up to $20,000 of earned income, rather than claiming the excess foreign living expense deductions.

THE SECTION 911 EXCLUSION FOR INDIVIDUALS RESIDING IN CAMPS   The only foreign source income exclusion that remains available for 1979 and subsequent taxable years is the one that may be elected by taxpayers who reside in camps in designated hardship areas. These taxpayers may exclude the value of both meals and lodging provided by their employers under Sec. 119[7] and up to $20,000 more of gross income computed on an annual basis under the amended Sec. 911 rules. The exclusions are available in lieu of the new series of deductions allowed by Sec. 913, and the taxpayer who lives in a camp must choose annually between the Sec. 911 exclusion and the Sec. 913 deductions.

[7]See the first volume of *An Introduction to Taxation*, page 5/18.

To be eligible to make the Sec. 911 election, the taxpayer must reside in a camp in a "hardship area." Section 913(h)(2) defines *hardship area* as any area in which U.S. government employees receive a hardship post differential of 15 percent or more. A listing of qualified hardship areas (by country and location) for 1979 is presented in Figure 22-1. In addition to the post-differential requirement, Sec. 911 specifies three requirements that must be met for an employee's lodging to be considered a "camp." First, the living quarters must be substandard housing provided by or on behalf of the employer because the job site is remote and acceptable housing is not available in the open market. Second, the camp must be located as near as possible to the place where the taxpayer renders services. Third, the housing must be furnished in a common area (or enclave) that is not open to the public and that normally accommodates 10 or more employees (Sec. 911(c)(1)(B)).

A taxpayer who uses the exclusion option may not take any credits or deductions (other than the Sec. 217 moving expense deduction) that relate to the excluded

FIGURE **22-1**

1979 QUALIFIED HARDSHIP AREAS—COUNTRIES AND LOCATIONS

(Unless a beginning or ending date is shown for your area, the location qualified as a hardship area for the entire year. Only the locations listed below qualify as hardship areas.)

Afghanistan (All locations)
Algeria (All locations)
Angola (All locations)
Ascension Island (All locations)
Australia
    Alexandria Station[a]
Bahamas
    Andros Island except Nicolls
        Town[a]
    Hard Bargain, Long Island[a]
    Carter Cay[a]
    Eleuthera Station[a]
    Great Stirrup Cay[a]
    Treasure Cay & Marsh Harbor[a]
Bahrain (All locations)
Bangladesh (All locations)
Belize (All locations)
Benin (All locations)
Bolivia
    All locations, except Cochabamba
    and Santa Cruz
Brazil
    All locations within the states of:
    Acre, Amapa, Amazonas, Cuiaba,
    Goias, Maranhao, Mato Grosso,
    Para, Piaui, Rio Branco, Camamu,
    Bahia[a], and Rio Guarani, Parana[a]
British West Indies
    Antigua Air Station[a]
Bulgaria

All locations except Sofia
Burma (All locations)
Burundi (All locations)
Cameroon (All locations)
Canada
    Northwest Territories
Cape Verde (All locations)
Central African Rep. (All locations)
Chad (All locations)
Chagos Archipelago (All locations)
China (All locations)
Colombia
    All locations within the provinces
    of: Amazonas[a], Arauca[a], Boyaca[a],
    Caqueta[a], Gigante[a], Guainia[a],
    Meta[a], Montelibano[a], Putumayo[a],
    Vaupes[a], Vichada[a]
Congo (All locations)
Cook Islands (All locations)[b]
Costa Rica
    All locations, except San Jose
Cuba
    Havana
Djibouti (All locations)
Dominican Republic
    All locations, except Santo
        Domingo
    (Santo Domingo from 9/13/79 to
        11/17/79)
Ecuador (All locations)

Egypt
    All locations, except Alexandria
    and Cairo
El Salvador
    El Ronco[a]
    San Lorenzo[a]
    San Salvador after 4/21/79
Ethiopia (All locations)
Falkland Islands (All locations)
French West Indies (All locations)
Gabon (All locations)
Gambia (All locations)
Ghana (All locations)
Greenland (All locations)
Guatemala
    All locations, except Guatemala City
Guinea (All locations)
Guinea-Bissau (All locations)
Guyana (All locations)
Haiti (All locations)
Honduras (All locations)
India (All locations)
Indonesia (All locations)
Iran (All locations)
Iraq (All locations)
Israel
    Negev Region Construction Sites after
    4/21/79
Ivory Coast (All locations)
Jordan

FIGURE 22-1 (continued)

All locations, except Amman
Kenya
  Garissa
  Kitale
  Marsabit
  Ngomeni
  Wajir
Korea
  All locations, except Osan AB (including
  Pyongtaek), Pusan, Seoul (including
  ASCOM, Suwon, Kimpo Airfields, Camps
  Eiler, Mercer and Thompson), and
  Chanyan-Myon
Kuwait (All locations)
Laos (All locations)
Lebanon (All locations)
Liberia (All locations)
Libya (All locations)
Madagascar (All locations)
Malaysia
  All locations, except Kuala Lumpur and
  Penang
Maldives
  All locations after 3/10/79
Mali (All locations)
Mauritania (All locations)
Mexico
  Campamento Farallon[a],
  Chichicapan[a]
  Nacozari de Garcia
  Sonora[a]
Midway Islands (All locations)
Morocco
  Ben Guria[a]
  Phos Boucra[a]
Mozambique (All locations)
Nepal (All locations)
New Caledonia

Noumea[a]
Nicaragua (All locations)
Niger (All locations)
Nigeria (All locations)
Oman (All locations)
Pakistan (All locations)
Panama
  All locations, except Panama City,
  Santiago, and Canal Area (Pre-treaty)
Papua New Guinea (All locations)
Paraguay
  All locations, except Asuncion
Peru
  All locations, except Arequipa
  and Lima
Philippines
  All locations, except Baguio City,
  Cagayan de Oro, Cebu, Los
  Banos, Manila (including Cavite),
  San Fernando, La Union, and San
  Pablo
Qatar (All locations)
Romania
  All locations, except Bucharest
Rwanda (All locations)
Saudi Arabia (All locations)
Senegal (All locations)
Seychelles (All locations)
Sierra Leone (All locations)
Sinai Field Mission
Somalia (All locations)
South Africa
  Aggeneys[a]
Southern Rhodesia
  All locations after 10/20/79
Sri Lanka (All locations)
Sudan (All locations)
Surinam

All locations, except Paramaribo
Syria (All locations)
Taiwan
  All locations, except Kaohsiung
  (incl. Tsoying), Taichung (incl.
  Ching Chuan Kang and Ching
  Shui), Tainan and Taipei
Tanzania (All locations)
Thailand
  All locations, except Bangkok
Togo (All locations)
Trust Territory of the Pacific Islands
  (All locations)
Tunisia
  Makthar
Turks and Caicos Island
  Grand Turk Auxiliary Airfield[a]
Turkey
  Afsin-Elbistan[a]
  Diyarbakir-Pirinclik
  Kayseri[a]
  All other locations after
  12/15/79
Uganda
  All locations after 5/5/79
United Arab Emirates (All
  locations)
United Kingdom
  Belfast
  Londonderry[b]
Upper Volta (All locations)
U.S.S.R. (All locations)
Venezuela
  Guri-Compamento[a]
Yemen Arab Republic (All
  locations)
Zaire (All locations)
Zambia (All locations)

[a]These areas were reclassified as hardship areas for all of 1978 after the issuance of the 1978 hardship area list.
[b]These areas will not be listed as hardship areas effective Jan. 1, 1980, because there is not sufficient information to determine the post differential payable after that date.
SOURCE: *I.R.S. Publication No. 54* (Tax Guide for U.S. Citizens Abroad), November 1979, p. 8.

portion of foreign income (Sec. 911(a)). In addition, such a taxpayer is ineligible to claim any benefits under the earned income credit provisions (Sec. 43(c)(1)(C)(i)). An illustration of the use of the camp exclusion is presented in the following example.

Example: Ms. Brown, a single individual, has $40,000 of income earned while she resided in a company-owned camp in a remote area of a foreign country for all of 19X1. The value of the lodging and meals provided by her employer adds another $5,000 to her income. On her $45,000 income she pays foreign taxes of $4,500. Ms. Brown excludes the $5,000 value of her housing under Sec. 119 and also excludes $20,000 of the salary under Sec. 911. Her U.S. income tax before credits is $3,829.[8] Ms. Brown has available a foreign tax credit[9] of $1,417.

[8]Tax on $19,000 [$45,000 − $25,000 (exclusions) − $1,000 (personal exemptions)].
[9]The allowed or creditable tax is equal to:

$$\text{Creditable foreign taxes paid or accrued} - \left[\text{Creditable foreign taxes paid or accrued} \times \frac{\text{U.S. tax liability on excluded income}}{\text{U.S. tax liability on excluded income} + \text{Foreign tax credit limitation}}\right]$$

$$\$1,417 = \left[\$4,500 - \left(\$4,500 \times \frac{\$8,338}{\$8,338 + \$3,829}\right)\right]^{10}$$

leaving her a net U.S. tax liability of $2,412. It should be noted that the $5,000 for meals and lodging is excluded under Sec. 119 rather than Sec. 911, so the Sec. 911 provision that blocks the use of foreign taxes paid on excluded income will not affect the use of the foreign taxes paid on this $5,000.

The $20,000 exclusion is calculated on a daily basis. If a taxpayer resides in a camp for only half a year, his or her maximum exclusion under Sec. 911 is $10,000. In addition, income earned in one year and received in the next taxable year must be excluded under the prior year's $20,000 limit. Income received after the taxable year that follows the year in which services were performed may not be excluded at all (Sec. 911(c)(4)). An illustration will make these rules clearer.

Example: Mr. Kane, a cash method of accounting U.S. citizen, earns the following amounts of income while he is employed during 19X1 and 19X2 in a foreign country and living in a camp in a hardship area.

	19X1	*19X2*	*19X3*
Earnings	$22,000	$15,000	-0-
Amount received	18,000	16,000	$3,000

All the money received in 19X1 represents compensation for services performed that year. The $16,000 received in 19X2 includes $1,000 received for services performed in 19X1. The amount received in 19X3 represents payments for services performed during 19X1. In 19X1 Mr. Kane may exclude from gross income the full $18,000 that he receives. On his 19X2 return, Mr. Kane may exclude the $15,000 he earned in that taxable year. The $1,000 he received in 19X2 that was earned in 19X1 may also be excluded from the gross income of 19X2. When he receives the $3,000 in 19X3 that relates to his 19X1 earnings, Kane is not permitted to exclude any portion of it from his gross

income of 19X3. Even though Kane has only used $19,000 of the available $20,000 exclusion for 19X1 income, this $3,000 was received after the close of the taxable year (19X2) that follows the year in which he earned the income (19X1) and therefore may not be excluded.

THE SECTION 913 DEDUCTIONS FOR EXPENSES OF LIVING ABROAD   Taxpayers who are bona fide residents of foreign countries or who are present in a foreign country for 510 days in an 18-month period are eligible under the provisions of the new Sec. 913 created by the Foreign Earned Income Act of 1978 to deduct the sum of the following amounts:

1. Qualified cost-of-living differential
2. Qualified housing expenses
3. Qualified schooling expenses
4. Qualified home leave travel expenses
5. Qualified hardship area deduction

The total amount deductible under these five categories may not exceed the taxpayer's "Net Foreign Source Earned Income" (Sec. 913(c)(1)). This limiting amount represents foreign source earned income reduced by any Sec. 119 exclusion of meals and lodging, as well as by any deductions allocable to the taxpayer's foreign source earned income. "Allocable deductions" means any deductions (other than the five Sec. 913 deductions listed above) that are properly allocable to the earned income under the allocation and apportionment rules of Treas. Reg. Sec. 1.861-8, discussed in Chapter 21. Examples of allocable deductions are employee business expenses that are related to the foreign source earned income and moving expenses. Allocable deductions do not include the zero bracket amount or non-work-related itemized deductions (Temp. Treas. Reg. Sec. 5b.913-4(a)). For an employee who has lived abroad for the requisite time and who has no employee business expenses, the maximum deduction is the amount of foreign source earned income. The limitation prevents the use of Sec. 913 deductions to reduce income from U.S. sources or to reduce passive foreign source income.

Because these Sec. 913 deductions reduce adjusted gross income (rather than being itemized deductions), taxpayers may deduct the excess costs of living and working abroad without losing the benefit of the zero bracket amount. Unlike the Sec. 911 exclusion, which is an arbitrary amount, these deductions are based in large part on the excess costs the taxpayer could be expected to have incurred. In spite of the theoretical su-

---

[10]Tax on excluded income = The net of: the tax on the sum of taxable income ($19,000) plus net excluded income under Sec. 911 ($20,000) minus the tax on taxable income ($19,000).

$8,330 = $12,167 − $3,837

periority of the deduction system based on excess costs incurred abroad, Congress faced one major hurdle in implementing the system. Administration of the deduction system would be virtually impossible for both the I.R.S. and the taxpayer without a reasonable definition of the *standard* costs of living, housing, and schooling. Without an objective standard cost, deductions based on the excess of costs above that standard could not be defined. The standards established by Sec. 913 are a compromise between economic reality and administrative necessity.

QUALIFIED COST-OF-LIVING DIFFERENTIAL   Before the enactment of Sec. 913, a considerable amount of discussion took place regarding the equity of any general cost-of-living deduction. It was pointed out that residents of the United States who live in areas with a high cost of living are taxed the same as residents of low cost areas. Accordingly, it would be difficult to justify a deduction for U.S. taxpayers abroad who live in areas where the cost of living is the same as or lower than the most expensive areas of the United States. The I.R.S.'s tables (see Figure 22-2) allow a deduction that represents the amount by which the general cost of living in the foreign area in which the taxpayer is located exceeds the highest cost of living for a metropolitan area in the contiguous 48 states. The cost-of-living differential deduction allowed varies depending on the foreign area in which the taxpayer resides, the makeup of the taxpayer's family (spouse and dependents) residing with the taxpayer (or in a qualified second household that is explained below), and the number of days in the tax year during which the taxpayer's tax home[11] was in a particular foreign country. No deduction for a cost-of-living differential is available for any portion of the year during which the taxpayer's meals and lodging are excluded under Sec. 119.

The differential cost of living generally varies depending on the income levels being compared. These differences arise because of different consumption patterns among income levels and the resulting differences in the items that are considered to be part of computing a cost-of-living standard. As a result of these differences, Congress was faced with deciding between designating an income level to be used for the preparation of the tables and having the tables indexed to the taxpayer's income level. Congress chose to set the cost-of-living table to reflect the costs for a family whose income is equal to that of a U.S. employee at GS-14,

grade 1 ($33,010 for early 1980). The table presented in Figure 22-2 is used for all taxpayers for taxable year 1979, regardless of their actual income level. The I.R.S. will revise this table annually to reflect changes in the relative costs of living.

The deduction available for the cost-of-living differential[12] is illustrated in the following example.

Example: Paul O'Dell, who is married and has two children, resided with his family in Norway for all of 19X1 while working for Multico. Paul's base salary from Multico for 19X1 was $25,000. Multico provided him with an additional $12,000 cost-of-living allowance. Based on Norway's "M" Group Code from Figure 22-2, Paul is able to deduct $11,200 as his Sec. 913 qualified cost-of-living differential deduction in determining his adjusted gross income.

QUALIFIED HOUSING EXPENSES   To determine the deductible excess housing costs, the expatriate must subtract a "base housing amount" from actual housing expense. The difference between the amount actually spent for housing and the base housing amount may be deducted when computing the taxpayer's adjusted gross income. This deduction is not available for the portion of the tax year when employer-furnished lodging, other than a qualified second household described below, is excludable under Sec. 119 (Sec. 913(e)(4)). It is also not available for the portion of any tax year during which the employee's tax home is not in a foreign country.

A taxpayer's actual housing expense includes amounts paid during the tax year for rents or for house payments, as well as for other expenses attributable to housing such as insurance and utilities (other than telephone expenses). Housing expenses, however, do not include interest or taxes that may be claimed as itemized deductions. The housing expense also excludes the amount of any depreciation claimed by the taxpayer, reduction in the principal amount of a mortgage that is included in the mortgage payment, and any housing expenses that are considered to be "lavish or extravagant" (Sec. 913(e)(2)).

Calculation of the base housing amount is predicated on the idea that normal housing costs represent approximately one-sixth of earned income net of the

---

[11]Sec. 913(j)(1)(B) defines "tax home" as an individual's home for purposes of determining the deductibility of traveling expenses incurred away from home. This term generally means the taxpayer's household or residence.

[12]The cost-of-living differential deduction in a number of foreign locations is less than the actual amount of cost-of-living differential paid by many U.S. employers. Examples of such locations are generally areas of the world where the cost-of-living is substantially above that found in the United States (for example, Japan, Switzerland, and Saudi Arabia).

FIGURE 22-2

1979 QUALIFIED COST-OF-LIVING DIFFERENTIAL TABLES

TABLE A
GEOGRAPHIC AREAS

(Find the group code that applies to your geographic area and refer to Table B for the cost of living differential for that group code, except group code X where no index is available from the State Department.)

Country	Group code	Country	Group code	Country	Group code	Country	Group code	Country	Group code
Afghanistan	B	Comoros	G	Indonesia	B	Namibia	B	South Africa	A
Albania	X	Congo	J	Iran	B	Nauru	B	Spain	F
Algeria	I	Costa Rica	C	Iraq	F	Nepal	F	Sri Lanka	A
Andorra	I	Cuba	F	Ireland	E	Netherlands	E	Sudan	H
Angola	D	Cyprus	B	Israel	F	Neth. Antilles	D	Surinam	E
Antigua	A	Czechoslovakia	A	Italy	D	New Caledonia	H	Swaziland	A
Argentina	G	Denmark	K	Ivory Coast	M	New Hebrides	D	Sweden	M
Australia	E	Djibouti	H	Jamaica	B	New Zealand	A	Switzerland	M
Austria	M	Dominica	A	Japan	M	Nicaragua	M	Syria	A
Bahamas	G	Dominican Republic	A	Jordan	G	Niger	G	Taiwan	C
Bahrain	J	Ecuador	A	Kenya	D	Nigeria	D	Tanzania	D
Bangladesh	A	Egypt	A	Kiribati	A	Norway	A	Thailand	A
Barbados	C	El Salvador	B	Korea N.	X	Oman	X	Togo	I
Belgium	K	Equatorial Guinea	B	Korea S.	H	Pakistan	H	Tonga	A
Belize	A	Ethiopia	E	Kuwait	I	Panama	A	Trinidad & Tobago	D
Benin	I	Fiji	B	Laos	A	Papua N. Guinea	B	Tr. Terr. of Pac. Is.	A
Bermuda	E	Finland	E	Lebanon	D	Paraguay	B	Tunisia	F
Bhutan	A	France	J	Lesotho	A	Peru	A	Turkey	A
Bolivia	C	French West Indies	L	Liberia	H	Philippines	A	Turks & Caicos Is.	C
Botswana	A	Gabon	N	Libya	N	Poland	A	Tuvalu	A
Brazil	C	Gambia	J	Liechtenstein	M	Portugal	M	Uganda	L
British Virgin Is.	C	Germany E.	L	Luxembourg	K	Qatar	J	United Arab Emirates	J
Brunei	C	Germany W.	L	Madagascar	I	Romania	C	United Kingdom	H
Bulgaria	F	Ghana	L	Malawi	A	Rwanda	I	Upper Volta	K
Burma	D	Greece	D	Malaysia	D	St. Kitts-Nevis	A	Uruguay	A
Burundi	H	Grenada	A	Maldives	A	St. Lucia	D	USSR	I
Cambodia (Kampuchea)	X	Guatemala	B	Mali	J	St. Vincent	A	Vatican City	D
Cameroon	L	Guinea	J	Malta	D	San Marino	A	Venezuela	I
Canada	A	Guinea-Bissau	E	Mauritania	M	Sao Tome & Principe	G	Vietnam	X
Cape Verde	F	Guyana	C	Mauritius	E	Saudi Arabia	J	Western Samoa	B
Cayman Is.	G	Haiti	D	Mexico	J	Senegal	J	Yemen (Aden)	A
Central Afr. Rep.	K	Honduras	A	Monaco	X	Seychelles	F	Yemen (Sana)	H
Chad	M	Hong Kong	C	Mongolia	F	Sierra Leone	X	Yugoslavia	C
Chile	F	Hungary	M	Montserrat	A	Singapore	E	Zaire	P
China	A	Iceland	F	Morocco	K	Solomon Islands	B	Zambia	G
Colombia	A	India	A	Mozambique	A	Somalia	H	Zimbabwe Rhodesia	X

FIGURE **22-2** (continued)

TABLE **B**

COST-OF-LIVING DIFFERENTIAL

Group code	Family size (number of persons)					
	1	2	3	4	5	6 or more
A and B	No cost-of-living differential allowed.					
C	500	600	700	800	800	900
D	1,000	1,100	1,400	1,500	2,300	2,500
E	1,400	1,700	2,100	2,300	3,100	3,300
F	1,900	2,300	2,700	3,000	3,900	4,100
G	2,400	2,800	3,400	3,700	4,700	5,000
H	2,900	3,400	4,100	4,500	5,800	6,100
I	3,500	4,200	5,100	5,500	7,000	7,400
J	4,300	5,100	6,200	6,700	8,500	9,100
K	5,200	6,200	7,500	8,200	10,100	10,700
L	6,200	7,400	8,900	9,700	11,600	12,400
M	7,100	8,500	10,200	11,200	13,200	14,000
N	8,100	9,600	11,600	12,700	14,700	15,700
O	9,100	10,700	13,000	14,200	16,300	17,300
P	10,000	11,900	14,300	15,600		

SOURCE: *I.R.S. Publication No. 54* (Tax Guide for U.S. Citizens Abroad), November 1979, p. 5.

taxpayer's employee-related expenses and any other deductions allowed by Sec. 913 (Sec. 913(e)(3)(A)). To avoid circular mathematical formulas, the actual calculation is performed as follows:

$$\text{Excess housing cost} = \text{Total housing expenses} - \text{Base housing amount}$$

$$\text{Base housing amount} = 20\% \times \left[\begin{array}{c} \text{Total earned income} \end{array} - \left(\begin{array}{c} \text{Total housing expenses} \\ \\ + \begin{array}{c} \text{Non-Sec. 913 deductions allocable against earned income}^a \end{array} + \begin{array}{c} \text{All other Sec. 913 deductions} \end{array} \right) \right]$$

^{a}Examples of such expenses are moving expenses and unreimbursed employee business expenses.

Example: Mr. Johnson earns $40,000 in a foreign country and has $10,000 in total Sec. 913 deductions for the cost-of-living differential, qualified schooling costs, qualified home leave travel expenses, and qualified hardship area deductions during 19X1. In addition, Mr. Johnson paid $15,000 for rent, utilities, and renters' insurance. His base housing amount is $3,000 (20% × [$40,000 − ($10,000 + $15,000)] = $3,000). Therefore, his deductible housing costs are $12,000 ($15,000 − $3,000). Mathematically, this deduction will always be equivalent to one-sixth of earned income minus the sum of all the Sec. 913 deductions (provided no other deduction offsets against earned income exist)(1/6 × [$40,000 − ($10,000 + $12,000)] = $3,000).

(Section 913 provides that deferred compensation is to be taken into account here in the year it is received rather than in the year in which the services are performed that produce the deferred compensation. Special rules are found in Sec. 913 (e)(7) that govern deferred compensation earned in a year in which an excess housing deduction is claimed and deferred to a later year in which no such deduction is claimed.)

The Code allows a taxpayer to deduct his or her *entire* housing costs if the home the taxpayer maintains near the foreign work site is in a hardship area where living conditions are dangerous or unhealthful and a second home is maintained in another location for his or her family. (If no second home is established, then the taxpayer computes the excess housing cost deduction in the normal manner.) Under these conditions, the taxpayer may establish a second living place in another foreign locale for his or her spouse and children and then may deduct the entire cost of the household at the work site (Sec. 913(e)(3)(B)). The deduction calculation for a household maintained for a taxpayer's children and spouse at a second location is discussed below.

QUALIFIED SCHOOLING EXPENSES   For U.S. residents, public schools are freely available and educational costs incurred for private primary and secondary schooling is largely discretionary spending. When U.S. residents move abroad, the cost of private schools for primary and secondary grades becomes a necessary expense. These costs are, in fact, an additional cost of living abroad. Accordingly, Sec. 913(f) allows a deduction for qualified schooling expenses incurred for each dependent from kindergarten through the 12th grade. The deduction for schooling expenses is only available for the portion of the taxable year that the taxpayer's tax home is in a foreign country and only if the taxpayer's spouse and dependents reside at the tax home or a qualifying second residence (Sec. 913(i)(1)(C)).

Under this subsection, schooling expense is defined to include the cost of tuition, fees, books, local transportation, and other expenses required by the school. If a U.S.-type school is available within commuting distance of the taxpayer's foreign home (or qualified second home if one is utilized), the maximum amount that may be deducted is the tuition, fees, books, other required costs, and local transportation costs of going to the *least expensive* nearby U.S.-type school, whether or not the taxpayer's dependents actually attend the nearby school. If there is no U.S.-type school nearby, the qualified schooling expense also includes room and board and the cost of traveling between the school and the foreign tax home. These additional schooling expenses are deductible whether the dependent attends a boarding school located either in the United States or a foreign country (Secs. 913(f)(2)-(4)).

QUALIFIED HOME LEAVE EXPENSE   To induce U.S. employees to work abroad, many employers pay for the employee and his or her family to visit the United States one or more times a year. The amount that the employer pays for these trips is, of course, included in the employee's gross income. Since such trips represent a kind of equalization between foreign and domestic employees, Sec. 913(g) allows the foreign employee to deduct the expenses of the trip home.

The qualified home leave expense is generally the lowest available coach or economy fare (available without advance booking) from the foreign tax home to the employee's present or most recent principal residence in the United States. If no principal U.S. residence exists, or the taxpayer elects to travel to a location in the United States other than his or her principal residence, then the taxpayer may claim a deduction for going to the nearest port of entry. The amounts of such a deduction shall not exceed the cost of traveling between the taxpayers's tax home and his or her principal U.S. residence (Secs. 913(g)(1)-(3)). [The nearest point of entry does not include places in Alaska or Hawaii, unless

the taxpayer so elects (Sec. 913(g)(4).]Costs incurred in going to a non-U.S. location, or in connection with the time spent in the United States, are not deductible. The deduction is available for the actual transportation costs incurred in connection with *one* round trip to the United States for the taxpayer, the taxpayer's spouse, and each dependent for each continuous 12-month period the taxpayer's tax home is in a foreign country. These costs do not include meals and lodging en route to, or after arrival in, the United States. The deduction for home leave expenses may be used by the taxpayer's spouse and dependents only if they live with the taxpayer at the foreign tax home, or if they live in a qualified second household, and the home leave trip originates at one of these two locations. The taxpayer does not need to return to the same foreign location from which he or she departed. Thus, an expatriate may leave a foreign location that is his or her old tax home, return to the United States, and return to a new location that becomes his or her new tax home.

QUALIFIED HARDSHIP AREA DEDUCTION   The Code provides an additional deduction of $5,000 if the taxpayer's tax home is in a hardship area. A hardship area is defined as an area in which U.S. government employees do (or would if they were present) receive a 15 percent or more hardship cost differential and where living conditions are characterized as "extraordinarily difficult" because of an unhealthy environment or because excessive physical hardships exist. The $5,000 is an annual amount and must be computed on a daily basis for taxpayers whose tax home is in a hardship area for less than a full taxable year. A summary of the eligible hardship areas was presented in Figure 22-1 (Sec. 913(h)).

QUALIFIED SECOND HOUSEHOLD DEDUCTION   In addition to the deductions previously explained, Sec. 913 provides special rules when a taxpayer maintains a qualified, separate household for his or her spouse and dependents because the tax home is in an area in which living conditions are adverse. To qualify, the household for the spouse and dependents must be located in a foreign country *but* it need not be in the same country as the tax home. In addition, the tax home must be in a location in which living conditions can be described as "dangerous, unhealthful, or otherwise adverse" (Sec. 913(j)(1)(D)). In general, this provision allows the taxpayer to compute the deductions using the secondary household (instead of the tax home) as the work location. For example, the taxpayer's cost-of-living deduction would be based on the location of the secondary household (rather than on the tax home at the work location) and the taxpayer's family size—including not only those residing in the second household, but the taxpayer as well, provided his meals and lodging are not excluded under Sec. 119.

When a taxpayer maintains a qualifying second home, the basic deduction for qualified housing expenses for the second home is determined by using the general rules that were outlined above.[13] The deduction computation process for the "tax home" at the work location, however, is modified by eliminating the *nondeductible* base housing amount, thereby making all housing costs for this tax home deductible[14] (Sec. 913(i)(1)(B)).

TAX COMPUTATION UNDER SECTION 913   A taxpayer using the benefits of Sec. 913 computes taxable income and tax liability in the same manner as an individual not qualifying for any special overseas benefits. Unlike the exclusion provisions of Sec. 911(a), no deductions or foreign tax credits will be disallowed because the taxpayer elects to use the special "excess living cost" deductions. Like the Sec. 911 computation, the expatriate will be unable to claim the earned income credit (Sec. 43(c)(1)(C)(ii)). Because of the full availability of any possible deductions and credits, a taxpayer who could qualify under both Secs. 911 and 913 by living in a camp located in a hardship area and who pays foreign income taxes at a rate approximately equal to or above the U.S. tax rate, or who has a significant amount of non-Sec. 913-type deductions, probably should compute his or her tax liability under each of these two alternatives. If the Sec. 913 tax liability is lower, a taxpayer may make an annual election for that year not to use the Sec. 911 exclusion and thereby reduce his or her taxes (Sec. 911(d)). Such an annual election will not preclude the use of the Sec. 911 exclusion in a later year.

Other changes for the expatriate

Application of tax law designed for U.S. citizens residing at home to U.S. citizens who move to foreign countries caused some problems. The two most notable problem areas associated with the taxation of the moving process concerned the deduction for moving expenses and the deferral of the gain on the sale of a U.S. residence. Both applicable Code sections were modified

by the FEIA of 1978 to provide greater benefits for the expatriate.

MOVING EXPENSES   When a U.S. taxpayer residing in the United States moves because of a change in job location, many of the taxpayer's moving expenses are deductible for adjusted gross income as set out in the first volume of *An Introduction to Taxation.* Expenses of moves from the United States to a foreign country, or from the foreign country to the United States, which meet the requirements of Sec. 217 concerning changes in job location will also result in deductions for adjusted gross income, even though part of the taxpayer's income is subject to the special benefits of Secs. 911 or 913. Foreign moves, however, are likely to require the taxpayer to maintain temporary living quarters for longer periods of time than a domestic counterpart and therefore to incur greater expenses for temporary living accommodations. The FEIA of 1978 increases the time during which temporary living costs are deductible from 30 days to 90 days and raises the ceiling on the deductible amount from $1,500 to $4,500 (Sec. 217 (h)). These changes apply to all moves between the United States and a foreign country (or from one foreign country to another foreign country to obtain employment) that otherwise qualify under Sec. 217, without regard for the bona fide residence test or the 510-day physical presence test. The FEIA of 1978 also altered the moving expense rules to allow persons retiring to the United States from a foreign work assignment and the survivors of Americans who die while working abroad to deduct moving expenses associated with their return to the United States within six months of the date of death or retirement, subject only to the moving expense limitations for domestic moves (Sec. 217(i)).

SALE OF RESIDENCE   When a taxpayer sells his principal residence, Sec. 1034 permits him not to recognize his gain if he reinvests in a new home within 18 months (24 months if he builds a new house). (See Chapter 24 of the first volume of *An Introduction to Taxation* for a more detailed explanation of Sec. 1034.) For a taxpayer who sells his home and moves overseas, the FEIA of 1978 suspends the time period for reinvesting until the taxpayer or his spouse moves back to the United States. To prevent long-term avoidance of the tax on this gain, the period of time for which the suspension is given may not exceed four years from the date of the sale of the old residence (Sec. 1034(k)).

The application of this deferral privilege is illustrated in the following example.

---

[13]The total housing expenses used in the base housing amount calculation includes the costs for both residences.

[14]When the tax home is not located in the hardship area *and* the taxpayer maintains two non-U.S. homes, the standard qualified housing expense deduction procedures are employed separately for each household.

Example: If Donna Ross sold her residence for a $10,000 gain on July 1, 19X1 and immediately moved overseas, the time for reinvestment of the sales proceeds would be extended. If she returns to the United States on January 1, 19X3, she will begin to count her 18- or 24- month period for reinvestment on January 1, 19X3. If she stays abroad five years (until July 1, 19X6), however, she must reinvest in a principal residence within six months (12 months if she has a home built for her) to avoid recognizing her gain. This occurs because the time period when the clock is not running may not exceed four years.

TAXATION OF NONRESIDENT ALIENS AND FOREIGN CORPORATIONS

Code Secs. 861–896 cover U.S. taxation of nonresident aliens and foreign corporations. In general, these sections establish two classes of income for which the tax treatment is greatly different. The first category of income is U.S. source income, such as dividends, rents, salaries, wages, premiums, annuities, compensations, remunerations, emoluments, or other fixed or determinable annual or periodic gains, profits, and income. This income, which we shall refer to in this book as Type A income, is taxed at a flat rate of 30 percent of the gross amount of the income earned (Secs. 871(a) and 881). The second income category, referred to as Type B income, is income effectively connected with the conduct of a U.S. trade or business, and this type of income is taxed on the net amount at the regular graduated income tax rates (Secs. 871(b) and 882). Depending on the identity of the taxpayer as well as many other factors, capital gains may be totally exempt from taxation, taxed at the 30 percent rate applicable to Type A income, or taxed at rates otherwise applicable to U.S. citizens or domestic corporations.

Resident or nonresident taxpayer

The tax treatment of corporate entities is determined by the country of incorporation. A corporation created or organized under the laws of the United States or one of the 50 states is a domestic corporation and pays tax on its worldwide income (Sec. 7701(a)(4)). All other corporations (including firms incorporated in U.S. possessions) are known as *foreign corporations* and pay taxes as explained below.

The residence of a corporation is not usually an issue in determining its tax consequences. For individuals, however, the question of residence is a prime one. U.S. citizens and foreign citizens who are considered to be U.S. residents are taxed on their worldwide income, but nonresident aliens are taxed generally only on U.S. source Type A income and income effectively connected with the conduct of a U.S. trade or business. The tax consequences of being a nonresident alien rather than a resident alien may be substantial. Figure 22-3 outlines many of these differences.

Like the test for bona fide foreign residence, the test for determining an alien's residence depends on whether the alien is a "mere transient or sojourner" (Treas. Reg. Sec. 1.871-2(b)). The determination is based on the same factors discussed in conjunction with the foreign residence determination for U.S. citizens employed abroad.

An alien who acquires resident alien status remains a resident alien until his or her final departure from the United States. An alien may revoke resident status only by a physical departure from the United States, coupled with an intention to abandon the U.S. residence. Thus, a resident alien who temporarily departs the United States retains resident alien status until he or she engages in an action that indicates an abandonment of the U.S. residence.

During some taxable years, an alien may have a dual tax status—as a nonresident and as a resident. Most commonly, these are the years of the alien's arrival in or departure from the United States. For example, in the year of a resident alien's arrival in the United States, the portion of the year before arrival is a period of nonresidence, and the portion of the year after arrival and establishment of residence is a period of U.S. residence. In these years, the taxpayer must make separate tax computations for the portion of the tax year during which each status is maintained, unless the taxpayer elects to file a joint tax return as a resident alien for the entire taxable year under the provisions of Sec. 6013(g). A further discussion of this election is presented below in conjunction with the calculation of an alien's tax liability.

Gross income

The gross income of a nonresident alien individual or foreign corporation includes only:

1. Amounts derived from sources within the United States not effectively connected with the conduct of a trade or business within the United States, and

2. Amounts effectively connected with the conduct of a trade or business within the United States (Secs. 872(a) and 882(b)).

FIGURE 22-3

COMPARISON OF THE TAX TREATMENT ACCORDED RESIDENT ALIEN AND NONRESIDENT ALIEN INDIVIDUALS UNDER U.S. TAX LAW

	Resident alien	Nonresident alien
1. Income subject to tax under U.S. tax laws	1. Worldwide income regardless of source or type.	1. a. Type A income when U.S. source. b. Type B income regardless of source or type [When a U.S. trade or business is conducted, nontrade or business income other than Type A income and capital gains that are U.S. source is also taxed by the U.S.] c. Worldwide capital gains when effectively connected with the conduct of a U.S. trade or business or U.S. source capital gains when realized by an individual who resides in the U.S. for 183 days or more during the taxable year.
2. Deductions and losses	2. All deductions and personal exemptions that are otherwise available to a U.S. citizen.	2. a. No deductions are permitted to reduce Type A income. b. Deductions are permitted to reduce Type B income and any other income subject to tax because of the conduct of a U.S. trade or business. c. One personal exemption, U.S. source casualty and theft losses, and contributions made to U.S. charities are deductible against Type B income whether or not they are connected with income derived from the taxpayer's conduct of a U.S. trade or business.
3. Tax rates applying to the income	3. Regular graduated tax rates (including alternative tax, income averaging, maximum tax) applicable to U.S. citizen.	3. a. Type A income and nontrade or business capital gains are taxed at a 30 percent rate based on gross income. b. Type B income, trade or business related capital gains, and any other income subject to tax because of the conduct of the U.S. trade or business are taxed at the progressive tax rates otherwise applicable to resident aliens. c. The maximum tax on personal services income provisions are available only if the nonresident alien is married to a U.S. citizen or resident alien and elects to be taxed like a resident alien under Code Sec. 6013(g). d. The income averaging provisions are not available if the individual was a nonresident alien at any time during the computation year or the base period.
4. Foreign tax credit benefits	4. Full foreign tax credit benefits are available under Code Secs. 901–908 unless the alien's home country does not provide similar benefits to U.S. citizens.	4. Foreign tax credits may be claimed only for foreign taxes paid or accrued with respect to income effectively connected with the conduct of a U.S. trade or business (including pass-through of credits from a partnership, trust, or estate).
5. Subchapter S shareholder	5. Resident aliens may own stock in a Subchapter S corporation.	5. Nonresident aliens holding stock of a Subchapter S corporation cause the termination of the election.
6. Controlled Foreign Corporation (CFC) and Foreign Personal Holding Company (FPHC) shareholder	6. Resident aliens are subject to the CFC and FPHC provisions.	6. Nonresident aliens are exempt from the CFC and FPHC provisions.
7. Gift tax	7. Gift tax applies to worldwide gifts at same rates applicable to citizens.	7. An exemption from the gift tax is provided for foreign property and intangible properties (for example, stock and bonds). A maximum rate of 30 percent applies to taxable gifts.
8. Estate tax	8. Estate tax applies to worldwide property at same rates applicable to citizens.	8. Alien's U.S. real property and tangible personal property is subject to the estate tax. A special exemption is provided for deposits and debt obligations producing foreign source interest income, life insurance proceeds received as a result of the death of a nonresident alien, stock and debt obligations of a foreign corporation, and works of art on loan for U.S. exhibition.

At first, all income appears to be included in this list. A careful reading, however, reveals that foreign source income that is not effectively connected with the conduct of a U.S. trade or business is excluded from gross income for a nonresident alien or foreign corporation. Further, Secs. 871 and 882(a) provide that if a foreign taxpayer is not engaged in the conduct of a U.S. trade or business, then some or all of the taxpayer's U.S. source income may also be exempt from taxation.

Virtually all income exclusions available to a U.S. citizen or resident are also available to a nonresident alien or foreign corporation. For example, a foreign taxpayer may exclude gifts and bequests, municipal bond interest, life insurance benefits paid at death, and most other items excludable under Secs. 101–128. One major difference for nonresident alien individuals is the dividends-received exclusion. Each U.S. citizen or resident may exclude up to $100 of dividend income. Nonresident alien individuals, however, may use the dividends-received exclusion only to offset dividends that are considered to be effectively connected with the conduct of a U.S. trade or business (Sec. 116(c)(3)).

In addition to the exclusions available to U.S. citizens and residents, a few additional exclusions are available to nonresident aliens and foreign corporations. For example, income generated by ships documented in foreign countries or by aircraft registered under the laws of a foreign country is excluded, provided that the foreign country grants an equivalent exemption for U.S. citizens and U.S. corporations (Secs. 872(b)(1) and 872(b)(2)). Furthermore, income received by nonresident alien individuals while they are employed by foreign employers and are temporarily in the United States for a cultural exchange program or for special training is excluded from their gross income (Sec. 872(b)(3)). Foreign corporations also have available two relatively minor additional exclusions for earnings derived from railroad rolling stock owned by a foreign corporation and used temporarily in the United States and communications satellite systems (Sec. 883).

Once an income item is identified as part of gross income, foreign corporations and nonresident aliens must carefully identify the type of income that they have in order to compute their taxes.

Type A income

Type A income is taxed to a nonresident alien or foreign corporation only when it is U.S. source income under the rules discussed in Chapter 21. This rule enables certain kinds of income to be tax free to most nonresident aliens and foreign corporations simply by its designation as foreign source income (rather than U.S. source income). For example, when Congress wanted to encourage foreign deposits with U.S. savings institutions, it classified interest on deposits made by these parties with U.S. banking institutions and savings and loan associations as foreign source income and, therefore, exempt from taxation for taxpayers having only Type A income. Similarly, nonresident aliens performing personal services in the United States have foreign source income that is exempt from U.S. taxation if they meet the *de minimus* (of or pertaining to a minimum amount) rules of:

1. Being in the United States no more than 90 days within the taxable year;
2. Earning no more than $3,000 for the services performed in the United States; and
3. Working for a foreign business that is not engaged in the conduct of a U.S. trade or business, or for a foreign branch or office of a U.S. business[15] (Sec. 864(b)(1)).

Numerous other examples can be found of income that might logically be classified as U.S. source income but that Congress has classified as foreign source income and therefore not taxable to the nonresident alien or foreign corporation having only Type A income. As we shall see later, even foreign source income may be taxed to a nonresident alien or foreign corporation, provided the income is effectively connected with the conduct of a U.S. trade or business.

FIXED OR DETERMINABLE ANNUAL OR PERIODICAL INCOME   Nonresident aliens and foreign corporations not engaged in the conduct of a U.S. trade or business pay U.S. taxes only on their Type A income.[16] Sections 871(a) and 881 define Type A income by naming several specific kinds of income, such as interest and dividends, and then describing a class of income as "other fixed or determinable annual or periodical gains, profits, and income." We shall first examine the statutory list of items that are Type A income and then consider the other kinds of income that have been included as Type A income under the phrase "fixed or determinable."

---

[15]Although the performance of personal services is generally considered to be the conduct of a trade or business, Code Sec. 864(b)(1) allows an exemption from providing a trade or business when the nonresident alien satisfies the three requirements indicated. This exemption from the conduct of a trade or business permits the income to be Type A income and exempt from U.S. taxation because of its foreign source.

[16]This discussion does not consider any taxes that may be levied upon the taxpayer by his or her country of citizenship or residence.

ITEMS INCLUDED IN THE STATUTORY LIST   Interest, dividends, rents, salaries, wages, premiums, annuities, compensations, remunerations, and emoluments are the most usual forms of Type A income. While both taxpayers and the I.R.S. generally have been able to readily identify such items of income, a few items need further comment. Dividends received by a foreign corporation distributee (from a domestic distributing corporation) that are unrelated to the conduct of a U.S. trade or business are included in gross income at their fair market value rather than at the lesser of the property's adjusted basis or its fair market value (Sec. 301(b)(1)(D)).

The amount of an annuity that is taxed as Type A income is the difference between the annuity's cost and the payments received, even though a literal reading of Sec. 871 indicates the 30 percent tax is levied on the "amount received."

In addition to the kinds of income named above, Secs. 871 and 881 also provide that a few other items are Type A income if they are not earned in connection with the conduct of a U.S. trade or business. These include several items that may be taxed as capital gains to U.S. citizens and residents, such as certain lump-sum distributions made from a qualified employee pension plan (Sec. 871(a)(1)(B)); a gain on the disposal of timber, coal, or domestic iron where the taxpayer retains an economic interest (Secs. 871(a)(1)(B) and 881(a)(2)); and the portion of the gain on disposal of a corporate bond, note, or indenture that represents original issue discount (Secs. 871(a)(1)(C) and 881(a)(3)). Gains from the sale of such intangible assets as patents, copyrights, secret processes and formulas, goodwill, trademarks, trade brands, and franchises are taxed as Type A income to the extent that payments are contingent on the productivity, use, or disposition of the intangible assets (Secs. 871(a)(1)(D) and 881 (a)(4)). Further, if during a taxable year more than 50 percent of the payments received from the sale of an intangible asset are contingent on the asset's productivity, use, or disposition, then *all* the payments received during that tax year are Type A income (Sec. 871(e)). (Any gain that is not considered to be contingent is ordinarily a capital gain and may possibly be exempt from tax under the capital gains rules discussed below.)

If a nonresident alien individual is physically present in the United States for a total of 183 days or more in a tax year, the amount of the individual's capital gain net income from U.S. sources is subject to tax at a 30 percent rate (Sec. 871(a)(2)). Capital gain net income for the alien represents the amount by which the

capital gains exceed capital losses for those capital transactions having gains and losses allocable to U.S. sources, whether or not they took place while the alien was in the United States. The nonresident alien may neither use the long-term capital gains deduction nor may he or she carry over any capital losses. This exception to the general capital gains exemption does not apply to a foreign corporation.[17]

The major problem with the implementation of the tax on capital gain income revolves around the computation of the number of days the taxpayer was present in the United States. The taxpayer must total all the days he or she is present in the United States during a taxable year to determine if the 183-day requirement has been satisfied. The day the alien enters the United States is not counted, but the day of departure is counted. Unless a nonresident alien has established a fiscal year prior to the year in consideration, the taxpayer must use a calendar year to calculate the 183-day test (Treas. Reg. Sec. 1.871-7(d)(3)).

TYPE A INCOME ITEMS NOT LISTED IN THE CODE   Most of the litigation in the taxation of the Type A income of nonresident aliens and foreign corporations arises from questions about the definition of "other fixed or determinable annual or periodical gains, profits, and income" (Secs. 871(a)(1)(A) and 881(a)(1)). In fact, case history and the regulations indicate that income does not have to be fixed, determinable, annual or periodic to fall within the Type A income classification. If a kind of income is otherwise Type A income, the timing of the receipt of the income does not affect its Type A status (Treas. Reg. Sec. 1.1441-2). For example, interest income is ordinarily Type A income, whether it is received in a series of regular payments or as a lump sum. According to the regulation, a payment of Type A income may be received either annually or periodically (which this regulation defines as being "from time to time, whether or not at regular intervals") (Treas. Reg. Sec. 1.1441-2(a)(2)). In addition to the list of Type A income found in the Code, the courts and the I.R.S. have classified contingent royalty payments, alimony payments, prizes, and awards as Type A income.[18]

For nonresident aliens and foreign corporations not engaged in the conduct of a U.S. trade or business, one exception to the Type A income definition is of major importance: "Income derived from the sale in the United States of property, whether real or personal, is

---

[17]Section 881 exempts from Type A income any capital gain and ordinary income realized by a foreign corporation from dispositions of property that is unrelated to the conduct of a U.S. trade or business.
[18]Rev. Ruls. 65-283, 1965-2 CB 25 and 66-291, 1966-2 CB 279.

not fixed or determinable annual or periodical income" (Treas. Reg. Sec. 1.1441-2(a)(3)). This statement means that with the one exception noted above (the 183-day capital gains rule for nonresident alien individuals), a nonresident alien or a foreign corporation may buy and sell real or personal property in the United States without paying U.S. income taxes. This is true regardless of the volume of sales or the nature of the resulting income (capital gain or ordinary income), provided the taxpayer is not considered to have engaged in the conduct of a U.S. trade or business. This obviously is a major tax advantage for foreign investors and has the result of encouraging foreign investment in U.S. assets.[19]

TAX CALCULATION FOR TAXPAYER WITH ONLY TYPE A INCOME   A taxpayer who has only Type A income and who is not engaged in the conduct of a U.S. trade or business is taxed at a flat 30 percent rate. This 30 percent rate is applied to the gross amount of Type A income with no deductions allowed. If a nonresident alien earns $10,000 in U.S. source dividends and interest, his or her U.S. income tax is $3,000, regardless of how many dollars of expenses were incurred to earn that $10,000. Furthermore, the nonresident alien or foreign corporation not conducting a U.S. trade or business is not allowed any exemptions, itemized deductions, or credits to reduce the U.S. tax bill (Secs. 871(a) and 873(a)). Many of the tax treaties to which the United States is a party reduce the 30 percent tax rate otherwise applicable to Type A income to as low as 5 percent or, in some cases, exempt the income entirely from taxation. (A summary of the rate reductions available to nonresident aliens under selected U.S. tax treaties was presented in Table 21-2.)

The U.S. government generally collects the taxes on Type A income through the use of a withholding system. The person who must withhold the U.S. tax payment is the last U.S. person who actually has control or custody of the funds before they are forwarded to a nonresident alien or foreign corporation. This may be the corporation that is making the dividend payments, or it may be a U.S. agent for the nonresident alien. If this last U.S. person who has custody of the funds (the withholding agent) fails to withhold the

proper amount of U.S. taxes, the withholding agent becomes liable for the taxes due if the foreign taxpayer does not pay (Sec. 1441(a)).

Type B income

Type B income is income that is effectively connected with the conduct of a U.S. trade or business. Income connected with the conduct of a U.S. trade or business is taxed at the regular, graduated individual tax rates, or the corporate tax rates, and all expenses related to the production of that income, which could be deducted by a U.S. citizen or resident, may be deducted by the nonresident alien or foreign corporation. In addition, taxpayers having Type B income may reduce their Type B income by certain casualty losses, charitable contributions, and *one* personal exemption, even though such items might be related to Type A income. Under no circumstances may these deductions be used to reduce the amount of the taxpayer's Type A income.

TRADE OR BUSINESS INCOME   The first question that must be addressed in order to ascertain the amount of Type B income that a foreign taxpayer has is to determine whether the taxpayer's activities constitute a U.S. trade or business.[20] As a general rule, a nonresident alien who owns and operates a business in the United States involving the sale of services, products, merchandise, and so on in the ordinary course of business is considered to be engaged in the conduct of a U.S. trade or business. Similarly, a member of a partnership or a beneficiary of a trust or estate that conducts a U.S. trade or business is also deemed to be conducting a U.S. trade or business (Sec. 875).

Section 864 provides that engaging in a U.S. trade or business includes the performance of personal services within the United States with three limited exceptions. The first exception permits a nonresident alien to work in the United States for 90 days or less in the employ of a nonresident alien individual or a foreign partnership or foreign corporation that itself does *not* engage in the conduct of a U.S. trade or business, provided the alien is not paid more than $3,000 for the U.S. services. A similar exception applies if the alien temporarily works in the United States but is regularly employed outside the United States by a U.S. citizen, resident, or domestic corporation or partnership[21] (Sec.

[19]This tax advantage has been the subject of several criticisms. In response, a number of bills are currently pending before Congress that would either eliminate or restrict the inducement that currently exists through the tax laws for foreign investment in U.S. real property. These bills would generally tax foreign investors on their gains on the disposition of either U.S. real property or a real property holding organization (RPHO). A RPHO is a closely held corporation, trust, or partnership having at least one-half of its interests being U.S. property.

[20]The general rules on whether a taxpayer is engaging in the conduct of a trade or business may be found in the Sec. 355 Treasury Regulations.

[21]Income derived from the performance of personal services is Type A income if received in a taxable year in which the taxpayer did not perform such services in the United States. In this case, such income is taxed at a flat 30 percent rate.

864(b)(1)). The third exception allows a nonresident alien or a foreign corporation to invest in stocks, securities, or commodities through a broker, a commission agent, or an employee without engaging in the conduct of a U.S. trade or business. This investment may be any amount (even though the agent may have the necessary authority to bind the nonresident alien) without creating a U.S. trade or business. Three conditions, however, must be satisfied for this exception to apply:

1. The foreign taxpayer may not be a corporation having its principal office in the United States and its principal business being the trading in stocks or securities for its own account.
2. The foreign taxpayer may not be a dealer in stocks, securities, or commodities.
3. The foreign taxpayer may not at any time during the tax year have a fixed place of business in the United States from which the transactions in stocks, securities, or commodities are directed or carried out (Sec. 864(b)(2)).

A taxpayer who invests in real property located in the United States may not know whether he or she is engaged in the conduct of a U.S. trade or business. How much activity must the foreign owner engage in for the income from such properties to fail to be considered passive income? If the income is passive in nature (Type A income), the owner is taxed at a 30 percent rate on the gross rental income. If the income is effectively connected with the conduct of a U.S. trade or business, the taxpayer pays U.S. taxes at the graduated individual tax rates, or at the corporate tax rates, on "net" income. To relieve this uncertainty, Congress provided the nonresident alien and foreign corporation

with an election so that real estate activity may be taxed as trade or business income, even though the investment is passive (Secs. 871(d) or 882(d)). If the election is made, all real estate income is deemed to be effectively connected with the conduct of a U.S. trade or business. Even though this Sec. 871(d) election conveys trade or business status to the real estate activities, it does not trigger the taxation of the taxpayer's nontrade or business income that falls outside the Type A income classification at the graduated tax rates as would occur if a U.S. trade or business actually was conducted. Further, the election to tax real estate income as trade or business income is binding on all subsequent years unless the I.R.S. agrees to the revocation of the election, and therefore, the taxpayer who makes this election will pay a tax on the capital gains and ordinary income that accrue when the property is sold.[22]

The following example illustrates the foreign taxpayer's choice regarding this election.

Example: Cagnon, Ltd., a foreign corporation incorporated in a non-treaty country, purchases a warehouse in the United States and leases it to a single tenant. The company estimates the expected operating income for the next five years (beginning in 19X1) and the expected gain on the sale of the warehouse at the end of the 5th year as indicated below. By electing to have the real estate income taxed as a U.S. business, a tax savings of nearly $86,000 results through the company's ability to take advantage of the deductions not available with Type A income, even though it does have to pay a tax on the sale of the building.

---

[22]Certain U.S. tax treaties contain provisions permitting the revocation of the election, thereby generally exempting this appreciation from U.S. taxation.

	Year					
	19X1	19X2	19X3	19X4	19X5	Cumulative
Gross income	$70,000	$80,000	$90,000	$100,000	$120,000	$460,000
Expenses	55,000	63,000	71,000	80,000	97,000	366,000
Net income	$15,000	$17,000	$19,000	$ 20,000	$ 23,000	$ 94,000
Gain on sale					$130,000	$130,000
Tax if rental income is Type A income[a]	$21,000	$24,000	$27,000	$ 30,000	$ 36,000[b]	$138,000
Tax if rental income is Type B income[c]	$ 2,550	$ 2,890	$ 3,230	$ 3,400	$ 40,310[d]	$ 52,380

[a]30% × gross income.
[b]There is no tax on a corporation's capital gain that is unrelated to the conduct of a U.S. trade or business.
[c]Net income × corporate tax rates.
[d]Tax on $23,000 ordinary income plus $130,000 Sec. 1231 gain.

EFFECTIVELY CONNECTED INCOME   An even more difficult question to answer is whether income is considered to be effectively connected with the conduct of a U.S. trade or business. The effectively connected distinction was devised to help the foreign taxpayer differentiate between Type A income taxed at the 30 percent rate and trade or business income taxed at the graduated, individual tax rates or the corporate tax rates. To understand the importance of this distinction, it is necessary to know how a taxpayer who is engaged in a U.S. trade or business is taxed. Figure 22-4 illustrates a decision tree summary of the taxation of nonresident alien individuals and foreign corporations. A taxpayer who is engaged in the conduct of a U.S. trade or business during the tax year must categorize income into Type A income, capital gains, income effectively connected with the conduct of a U.S. trade or business, and all other income. The following taxes are applied to the categories:

Income Taxed at 30 Percent or Lower Treaty Rates:
1.   Type A income *not* effectively connected with the conduct of a U.S. trade or business.
2.   Capital gains not considered to be effectively connected with the conduct of a U.S. trade or business *and* not exempt from taxation under the 183-day rule.

Income Taxed at Graduated Rates:
1.   Income that would otherwise be Type A income except that it is effectively connected with the conduct of a U.S. trade or business.
2.   Capital gains effectively connected with the conduct of a U.S. trade or business.
3.   All U.S. source income that is not Type A income or nonbusiness capital gains (whether or not the U.S. source income is effectively connected with the U.S. trade or business).
4.   Foreign source income effectively connected with the conduct of a U.S. trade or business.

Not Subject to U.S. Tax:
1.   Capital gains *not* effectively connected with the conduct of a U.S. trade or business *and* that are exempt from taxation under the 183-day rule.
2.   Foreign source income *not* effectively connected with the conduct of a U.S. trade or business.

From this overview it is apparent that the phrase "effectively connected with the conduct of a U.S. trade or business" serves two functions in the taxing scheme. First, a foreign taxpayer must use the effectively connected tests to identify U.S. source income items that meet the requirements for classification as Type A income or capital gains but that also are related closely to the operations of the U.S. trade or business. These identified items of income are then taxed at the graduated individual rates or the corporate tax rates, rather than with the Type A income or unrelated capital gains. Second, the effectively connected tests are used to identify the foreign source income that is subject to the U.S. income taxation. For U.S. citizens and residents, all foreign source income is taxable. But nonresident aliens and foreign corporations pay U.S. income taxes on foreign source income only when it is effectively connected with the conduct of a U.S. trade or business.

EFFECTIVELY CONNECTED U.S. SOURCE INCOME   Treasury Regulation Sec. 1.864-4 offers two tests for taxpayers to use in deciding whether Type A income or capital gains are effectively connected with the conduct of a U.S. trade or business: the *asset use test* and the *business activity test*. Most U.S. earnings may be easily categorized by taxpayers, but a few kinds of investment or passive income require the use of the tests provided in the regulations.

The asset use test.   The asset use test establishes the rule that an asset and the income it generates is considered to be used in the conduct of a U.S. trade or business when the asset is:

(a)   Held for the principal purpose of promoting the present conduct of the trade or business in the United States, as, for example, in the case of stock acquired and held to assure a constant source of supply for the trade or business, or
(b)   Acquired and held in the ordinary course of the trade or business conducted in the United States, as, for example, in the case of an account or note receivable arising from that trade or business, or
(c)   Otherwise held in a direct relationship to the trade or business conducted in the United States (Treas. Reg. Sec. 1.864-4(c)(2)(ii)).

The final phrase of the regulations requires further amplification. An asset has a direct relationship to the business if:

1.   The asset was purchased with funds generated by that U.S. trade or business;
2.   The income from the assets is retained or invested in that trade or business;
3.   Significant management and control over the asset's investment is exercised by personnel present in

FIGURE 22-4   U.S. Income Taxation of Nonresident Aliens and Foreign Corporations

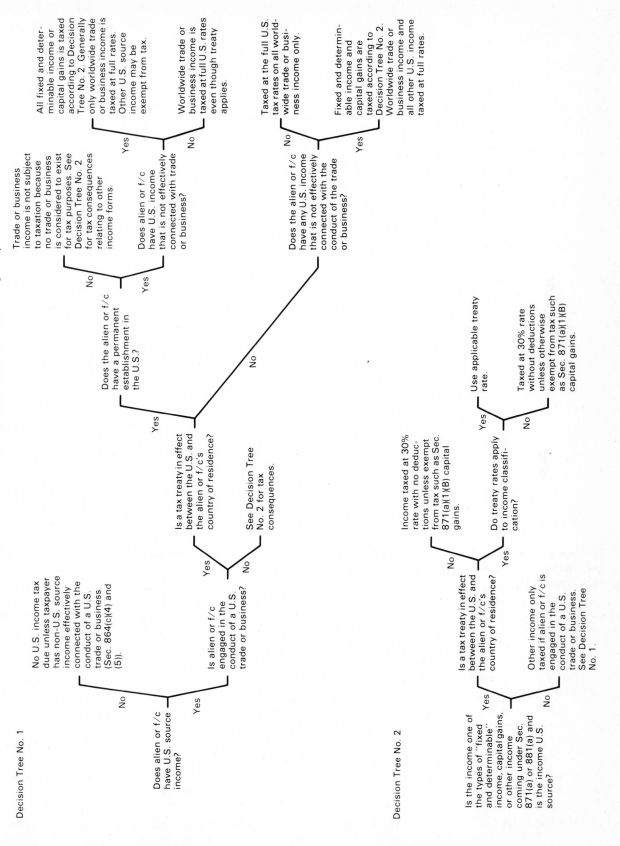

Decision Tree No. 1

Does alien or f/c have U.S. source income?

No → No U.S. income tax due unless taxpayer has non-U.S. source income effectively connected with the conduct of a U.S. trade or business (Sec. 864(c)(4) and (5)).

Yes → Is alien or f/c engaged in the conduct of a U.S. trade or business?

No → Is a tax treaty in effect between the U.S. and the alien or f/c's country of residence?

Yes → See Decision Tree No. 2 for tax consequences.

No → See Decision Tree No. 2 for tax consequences.

Yes → Does the alien or f/c have a permanent establishment in the U.S.?

No → Trade or business income is not subject to taxation because no trade or business is considered to exist for tax purposes. See Decision Tree No. 2 for tax consequences relating to other income forms.

Yes → Does alien or f/c have U.S. income that is not effectively connected with trade or business?

Yes → All fixed and determinable income or capital gains is taxed according to Decision Tree No. 2. Generally only worldwide trade or business income is taxed at full rates. Other U.S. source income may be exempt from tax.

No → Worldwide trade or business income is taxed at full U.S. rates even though treaty applies.

Does the alien or f/c have any U.S. income that is not effectively connected with the conduct of the trade or business?

No → Taxed at the full U.S. tax rates on all worldwide trade or business income only.

Yes → Fixed and determinable income and capital gains are taxed according to Decision Tree No. 2. Worldwide trade or business income and all other U.S. income taxed at full rates.

Decision Tree No. 2

Is the income one of the types of "fixed and determinable" income, capital gains, or other income coming under Sec. 871(a) or 881(a) and is the income U.S. source?

No → Other income only taxed if alien or f/c is engaged in the conduct of a U.S. trade or business. See Decision Tree No. 1.

Yes → Is a tax treaty in effect between the U.S. and the alien or f/c's country of residence?

No → Income taxed at 30% rate with no deductions unless exempt from tax such as Sec. 871(a)(1)(B) capital gains.

Yes → Do treaty rates apply to income classification?

Yes → Use applicable treaty rate.

No → Taxed at 30% rate without deductions unless otherwise exempt from tax such as Sec. 871(a)(1)(B) capital gains.

the United States and actively involved in the conduct of that trade or business; and

4. The asset is held to meet the present needs of the business.

This relationship is illustrated in the following example.

Example: A branch of Rorco, Ltd. sells cameras that are manufactured abroad in a nontreaty country. The U.S. branch operation requires substantial working capital, but the branch occasionally has a temporary excess of funds. These excess funds are usually invested in U.S. government bonds, with the original funds and any income earned on them being used at a later date for working capital. The U.S. government bonds and any income earned on them are considered to be effectively connected with the branch's conduct of a U.S. trade or business. Consider the different result if the same branch of Rorco, Ltd. is accumulating funds in anticipation of expanding its product line. These funds are also invested in U.S. government bonds, but the investment in the bonds and the interest they earn are to be used in the future to expand the product line that Rorco sells through its U.S. branch. These assets and the interest income they generate are not effectively connected with the conduct of the U.S. branch's business because they do not concern a *present need* of the branch. The interest earned from the bonds is considered Type A income and is taxed at a 30 percent rate (or at a lower treaty rate if applicable) (Treas. Reg. Sec. 1.864-4(c)(2)(iv) Ex. (1)).

The business activities test. The second test for determining whether income is effectively connected with the conduct of a U.S. trade or business is: Were the activities of the U.S. business a material factor in the realization of the income? An example will help illustrate the application of this test.

Example: Roxco, Ltd., a foreign corporation, engages in the conduct of a U.S. business through its U.S. branch, which imports and sells machines in the United States. In addition, through its home office, Roxco licenses patents to parties unrelated to its sales activities for use in the United States. The licensing activity is handled through the home office without any participation by the U.S. branch or its employees. Royalties generated by the licensing activity are not effectively connected with the conduct of the U.S. business because the activities of the U.S. branch are not a material factor in the

production of the royalty income. The royalty income, therefore, is Type A income.

One additional test for determining whether income is effectively connected with a U.S. business is simply whether the taxpayer engaged in the conduct of a U.S. trade or business *during* the taxable year in question. If the foreign taxpayer did not conduct a U.S. trade or business at any time during this taxable year, then none of the income is considered to be Type B income. This rule leads to some rather strange results, as the following two examples indicate.

Example 1: Royco, Ltd., a foreign corporation from a nontreaty country, conducts a U.S. business in 19X1 through a New York City sales office, which makes sales that are reported on the installment basis for U.S. tax purposes. In 19X1, Royco's profits from the installment sales are clearly Type B income. Royco closes its U.S. sales offices on December 31, 19X1, and during 19X2 does not engage in the conduct of any other business that may be classified as a U.S. trade or business. Collections that Royco makes during 19X2 on the prior year's installment sales are *not* effectively connected with the conduct of a U.S. trade or business because Royco has not engaged in the conduct of a U.S. trade or business in 19X2. Further, the income from the installment sales is not capital gain nor is it fixed or determinable annual or periodic income. The gain on the installment sales collected in 19X2 will not be subject to U.S. income taxes. Any portion of the installment payment that represents interest is, of course, Type A income taxed at the 30 percent rate (adapted from Treas. Reg. Sec. 1.864-3(b)(1)).

Example 2: Maria Ramirez, a citizen and resident of a nontreaty country, works as a researcher for Multico, a U.S. corporation, during all of 19X1 in Dallas, Texas, and earns $12,000. Maria, a cash method of accounting taxpayer, files her U.S. tax return using the calendar year. Her 19X1 income of $12,000 is taxed as Type B income at the graduated individual tax rates, since her performance of personal services in the United States constitutes the conduct of a U.S. trade or business. In December, 19X1, Maria quits her job and leaves the United States. At no time in 19X2 does she engage in the conduct of a U.S. trade or business. If, instead, she did not receive her final month's paycheck of $1,000 plus a $500 bonus until 19X2, this $1,500 of income is not considered to be effectively connected with the conduct of a U.S. trade or business, since it was received in a year in which she conducted no U.S. business activities. In this situation, however, the $1,500 does not escape U.S. taxation because compensation is defined as Type A income.

EFFECTIVELY CONNECTED FOREIGN SOURCE INCOME

At one time, it was possible for foreign corporations and nonresident aliens to use the United States as a tax haven. Before the enactment in 1966 of the Foreign Investors Tax Act, foreign corporations and nonresident aliens were never taxed on foreign source income.[23] If a corporation's home country did not tax foreign source income, the corporation could establish a U.S. office through which it could conduct its business in still a third country. If properly planned, the sales income escaped worldwide taxation completely. For example, a foreign corporation could have a U.S. sales office through which sales were made to a third country. In this case, the home country would not tax the income, since it was foreign source income; the United States would not tax the income, since the title passed in another country; and the country of final destination would generally not tax the income, since no permanent establishment existed within its borders. It was, at least in part, to prevent this kind of U.S. tax haven activity that Congress chose to tax certain foreign source trade or business income earned by nonresident aliens and foreign corporations.[24]

The foreign source income that is considered effectively connected with a U.S. trade or business is quite narrowly defined. For any foreign source income to be effectively connected with a U.S. business, the following three conditions must be met:

1. The foreign corporation or nonresident alien must conduct a U.S. trade or business during some part of the taxable year.
2. The taxpayer must have an office or fixed place of business in the United States at some time during the taxable year.
3. The U.S. office must be a material factor in the production of the foreign source income (Sec. 864(c)(4)).

We discussed the first of these three requirements earlier. The last two requirements require further explanation.

A fixed place of business. In deciding whether

a foreign taxpayer has a fixed place of business in the United States, a major consideration must be the normal requirements for conducting the kind of business in question. For example, a sales branch of a foreign manufacturer would be likely to have an office and some warehouse space. On the other hand, a foreign taxpayer whose trade is renting out apartments that he owns in the United States might have only an office, or even a corner of the manager's apartment, used to rent the apartments and collect the monthly payments. A fixed place of business may be an office, a factory, a store or sales outlet, a workshop, or a mine, quarry, or other site for extraction of natural resources (Treas. Reg. Sec. 1.864-7(b)(1)). Under certain conditions, the use of a U.S. agent may cause a foreign corporation with no other U.S. facilities to be considered to have a fixed place of business in the United States (Treas. Reg. Sec. 1.864-7(d)).

U.S. office as a material factor. A U.S. office is a material factor in the production of foreign source income only if the office makes a significant contribution to (by being an essential economic element in) the realization of the foreign source income. The fact that the office is not in operation in the United States when the income is realized, however, does not prevent U.S. taxation from occurring, provided the U.S. office is a material factor in the earning process. This rule was necessary to prevent a foreign operation from avoiding taxation simply by closing the U.S. office when a large amount of foreign source income was about to be realized. (Remember, however, that the firm must have had a U.S. office or fixed place of business at some time during the tax year in order for the foreign source income to be subject to U.S. income taxation as Type B income.)

Treasury Regulation Sec. 1.864-6(b) provides that a U.S. office may be a material factor in the production of only three kinds of foreign source income. This means that any *other* kind of foreign source income earned by a nonresident alien or foreign corporation escapes U.S. taxation, no matter how material the U.S. office was in producing the income. The three kinds of foreign source income that may be taxed to foreign taxpayers if a U.S. office is a material factor are:

1. Rents, royalties, and gains from the sale or use of intangible personal property located outside the United States;
2. Foreign source income that is dividends, interest, or gain or loss derived from the sale or exchange of stocks or securities (but only if they are in the business of banking, financing, or trading in stocks or securities for their own account in the United States;

[23] P.L. 89-809, 89th Cong., 2d Sess., Sec. 102(d).
[24] H. Rep. No. 1450, 89th Cong., 2d Sess. (April 26, 1966).

3. Foreign source gain or loss derived from the sale of property held primarily for sale in the ordinary course of the taxpayer's business.

DEDUCTIONS FROM TYPE B INCOME   Section 873 provides that Type B gross income may be reduced by deducting expenses "only if and to the extent that they are connected with income which is effectively connected with the conduct of a trade or business within the United States." Expenses that may be deducted from Type B income must meet two requirements. First, the expense must be a type that is deductible for U.S. taxpayers. Second, deductible expenses must be related to income that is effectively connected with the conduct of a U.S. trade or business. A foreign taxpayer who has both Type A income and Type B income may not generally deduct expenses related to Type A income from Type B income. The amount of the deductible expenses that are determined to be related to the income effectively connected with the conduct of a U.S. trade or business is based on the Treas. Reg. Sec. 1.861-8 allocation and apportionment rules (see Chapter 21).

In addition to expenses that meet the above requirements, a foreign taxpayer having Type B income may deduct three other items, whether or not they are related to income derived from the conduct of a U.S. trade or business. Casualty losses that are deductible under Sec. 165 may be claimed by foreign taxpayers, provided the loss relates to property that is physically located in the United States. Charitable contributions may be deducted by nonresident aliens and foreign corporations within the same limits that apply to U.S. citizens, residents, and domestic corporations.[25] Nonresident aliens in general may claim only one personal exemption, but residents of either Canada or Mexico may claim for U.S. tax purposes all the personal, old age, and blindness exemptions that would otherwise be allowed to a U.S. citizen or resident. Residents of Japan are also permitted under the U.S.–Japan tax treaty to claim additional exemptions, but are restricted to claiming only those that relate to a spouse or children living with them in the United States. A nonresident alien may not elect to use the zero bracket amount but must itemize these "from" A.G.I.-type deductions. This need to itemize the "from" A.G.I. deductions will require the alien to add back the excess of

his or her zero bracket amount over his or her itemized deductions in order to determine taxable income (Sec. 63(e)).

Most of a nonresident alien's expenses that are connected with Type B income are deductions "for" determining A.G.I. Any deductions claimed for nontrade or business casualty and theft losses, charitable contributions, and personal exemptions are deductible "from" the A.G.I. amount, as are any state and local income taxes paid on Type B income.

In making these deductions, one fact must be remembered. These deductions may only reduce Type B income; they may never be applied to reduce the amount of Type A income or taxable capital gains that are unrelated to the conduct of a U.S. trade or business.

Tax computations

Tax computations for taxpayers who have only Type A income are quite different from the computation of taxes due from taxpayers who engage in the conduct of a U.S. trade or business. Figure 22-5 outlines the tax computation processes.

Most of the major credits are available to nonresident aliens and foreign corporations having Type B income. The primary credits available are those for U.S. income taxes that have been withheld and foreign taxes paid on foreign source income that is effectively connected with the conduct of a U.S. trade or business. In addition, the other credits that are available to a U.S. citizen or resident alien are available, although for certain credits (such as the earned income credit) restrictions may be imposed because of the nonresident alien's general inability to join in the filing of a joint tax return.

Foreign corporations use the same tax rate schedule as U.S. corporations for taxing all but their Type A income. A nonresident alien individual uses the single schedule if single, or the schedule for married individuals filing separately if married to another nonresident alien or to a U.S. citizen or nonresident alien and the individual does not elect to be taxed as a resident alien under Sec. 6013(g). If the nonresident alien is married to a U.S. citizen, the couple may elect to file using the schedule for married individuals filing jointly (including the maximum tax provisions). Use of the schedule for married individuals filing jointly requires the nonresident alien spouse to agree to be taxed as a resident alien (Sec. 6013(g)). While there are advantages to using this schedule, this election is normally advisable only if the nonresident alien spouse has lim-

[25]A special rule found in the U.S.–Canada tax treaty permits a Canadian resident to deduct on his or her U.S. tax return contributions made to certain qualified Canadian charitable organizations. This provision runs counter to the rule of Sec. 170(c), which limits the deduction to contributions made to qualified U.S. organizations.

FIGURE **22-5**

Tax Computation for Nonresident Aliens and Foreign Corporations

	Taxpayers Who Have No U.S. Trade or Business	Taxpayers Who Have U.S. Trade or Business
Type A income:	Gross income × 30% (or Lower treaty rate) Tax due on Type A income	Gross income × 30% (or Lower treaty rate) Tax due on Type A income
Nontrade or business capital gains:	No tax unless individual taxpayer who was physically present in U.S. for 183 days or longer. Then: Capital gains − Capital losses (excluding carryovers) = Net capital gain × 30% (or Lower treaty rate) Tax due on capital gains	No tax unless individual taxpayer who was physically present in U.S. for 183 days or longer. Then: Capital gains − Capital losses (excluding carryovers) = Net capital gains × 30% (or Lower treaty rate) Tax due on capital gains
Income effectively connected with the conduct of a U.S. trade or business and all other U.S. source income	None	Gross income (including business capital gains, losses, and carryovers − Deductions for adjusted gross income[a] Adjusted gross income − State and local taxes on effectively connected income − Charitable contributions − Casualty losses − One personal exemption = Taxable income × Applicable graduated rates[b] Tax due on Type B income
Total tax due	Tax due on Type A income + Tax due on capital gains = Gross tax liability	Tax due on Type A income + Tax due on capital gains + Tax due on Type B income = Gross tax liability
Credits	− Credit for taxes withheld = Net tax liability	− Credit for taxes withheld − Foreign tax credits − Other credits available to U.S. citizen or resident = Net tax liability

[a]No such distinction between deductions "for" or "from" A.G.I. exists for a foreign corporation.
[b]To use the graduated rate schedules, this amount must be increased by the amount of the unused zero bracket amount (zero bracket amount minus itemized deductions claimed).

ited amounts of foreign source taxable income because of the taxation of the resident alien's worldwide income.

INCOME EARNED BY INDIVIDUAL TAXPAYERS IN PUERTO RICO AND U.S. POSSESSIONS

For many years Congress has encouraged U.S. business activity in U.S. possessions, and Secs. 931–936 reflect this attitude. These sections provide significant tax benefits to both individuals and corporations doing business in U.S. possession countries. U.S. possessions are American Samoa, Midway Islands, Wake Island, Johnston Island, Jarvis Island, Kingman Reef, Howland Island, Baker Island, Palmyra, and, for Sec. 936 purposes only, Puerto Rico. Although Guam and the Virgin Islands are U.S. possessions, they come under special Code provisions (Secs. 934 and 935), which are beyond the scope of this book. The sections that concern taxation of individuals—Secs. 931 and 933—are discussed here, while the corporate tax benefits of Sec. 936 are discussed in Chapter 23.

Section 931 is the major tax provision for individuals doing business in possessions other than Puerto Rico, Guam, and the Virgin Islands. This section provides that individuals who meet the requirements listed below will, with a few exceptions, be taxed only on income from U.S. sources, and both possession source income and all other foreign source income will be excluded from U.S. taxation. In order to receive these benefits, an individual must be a U.S. citizen and must satisfy two tests for the applicable portion of the three-year period ending with the close of the taxable year in question. The two tests are:

1. 80 percent or more of gross income for the three-year period must be derived from within a U.S. possession, *and*

2. 50 percent or more of gross income for the three-year period must be derived from the active conduct of a trade or business in a U.S. possession. The active conduct of a trade or business includes working as an employee, as an agent, or for oneself. Dividend income derived from the active conduct of a trade or business does not count as qualifying income even if the shareholder/taxpayer manages the corporation.

The time period for which the test must be met is referred to in the Code and regulations as "the three-year period immediately preceding the close of the taxable year (or for such part of such period immediately preceding the close of such taxable year as may be applicable)" (Sec. 931(a)(1)). Revenue Ruling 69-481 has interpreted the phrase "such part . . . as may be applicable" to mean only the portion of the three-year period during which the individual was employed in a possession.[26] Therefore, if an individual spends only six months in a possession, he or she qualifies for the Sec. 931 benefits if 80 percent of the income for that six-month period is derived from within the possession and at least 50 percent of the income during the six-month period is derived from the active conduct of a trade or business.

Under Sec. 931, only three kinds of income remain taxable to individuals who pass the two tests outlined. All U.S. source income is, of course, taxable. In addition, any income that is physically received in the United States is subject to taxation whether or not the income's source is within the United States. Thus, a taxpayer who works in American Samoa for several months but receives her last salary check from her Samoan work in the United States after she returns may not exclude the amount of income that she received at

her U.S. address. The third kind of income that may not be excluded under this section is wages paid to employees of the U.S. government or any of its agencies (Sec. 931(h)).

Computation of taxable income under Sec. 931 differs significantly from the computation when there is no U.S. possession source income. Using Sec. 931, a U.S. citizen may claim only those deductions that are related to U.S. source income under the Treas. Reg. Sec. 1.861-8 rules outlined earlier plus the following three deductions:

1. Losses connected with a transaction entered into for profit (but not connected with the conduct of a trade or business) that are deductible under Sec. 165(c)(2). These losses may be deducted only if the profit on the transaction would have been taxable to the taxpayer.

2. Casualty or theft loss deductions deductible under Sec. 165(c)(3) and incurred on nontrade or business property located within the United States.

3. Charitable contribution deduction (Sec. 931 (d)(2)).

The zero bracket amount may not be utilized, and taxable income must be adjusted so that *only* the amount of these three itemized deductions enter into the computation of the tax liability. The U.S. citizen using Sec. 931 is also limited to claiming only one personal exemption. In addition, neither the earned income credit nor a foreign tax credit that relates to excluded income may be claimed (Secs. 931(g) and 43(c)(1)(C)).

As a result of these limitations, some individuals may choose not to use Sec. 931. The following example illustrates the possible advantage of not using Sec. 931.

Example: Mr. Lee, a U.S. citizen, works in the United States from January 1, 19X1 to October 31, 19X1 and earns $20,000. On November 1, 19X1, he is transferred to Wake Island and earns $4,000 there by the end of the year. His total itemized deductions attributable to U.S. source income are $1,000. Mr. Lee has a wife and two children. If we compare his tax table income under each of two alternatives, we can see that he should choose not to use Sec. 931.

	Using Sec. 931	Without Sec. 931
Gross income:		
U.S. source	$20,000	$20,000
U.S. possession source	-0-	4,000

	Using Sec. 931	Without Sec. 931
Less:		
Personal exemptions	(1,000)	(4,000)
Plus:		
Unused zero bracket		
amount		
($3,400 − $1,000)	+ 2,400	-0-
Tax table income	$21,400	$20,000

Further differences may also occur because, without using Sec. 931, Mr. Lee may use a foreign tax credit for taxes paid to a foreign country or U.S. possession.

Section 933 provides that a U.S. citizen or resident alien who has been a bona fide resident of Puerto Rico for an entire taxable year may exclude from gross income all income derived from Puerto Rican sources. Because residents of Puerto Rico are not covered under Sec. 931, the special section provides the only tax relief for these residents. This section allows the taxpayer to exclude only the income derived from Puerto Rican sources and not the income from (1) other non-U.S. source activities, or (2) services performed as an employee of the United States or any of its agencies. The taxpayer is not permitted to claim any deductions related to income excluded under Sec. 933, except for personal exemption(s) claimed under Sec. 151.

REPORTING THE EXEMPTION OF, OR DEDUCTION FROM, INCOME EARNED ABROAD

A taxpayer residing abroad uses Form 2555 to report the special tax benefits of Secs. 911 and 913. Form 2555, which is reproduced in Figure 22-6, illustrates many of the concepts outlined in our discussion. In the following example, using selected tax return information, we shall illustrate the determination of these benefits for a hypothetical taxpayer.

Example: Harry Heinlein and his family moved to Paris, France, in January 1978. The Heinleins departed Austin, Texas at 4:05 P.M. on January 6, 1978 and arrived in Paris at 11:07 A.M. on January 7, 1978. Mr. Heinlein was a systems analyst employed by the Very Public Corporation (VPC) in its Paris office. Harry elected to use the physical presence test in computing his earned income exclusion for 1978.

Harry left Paris at 9:00 P.M. on Friday, March 2, 1979, and arrived in Austin Saturday afternoon.

He worked five days in Austin before departing for Paris on Friday evening, March 9, 1979. Harry and his family moved back to the United States on Friday, December 14, 1979. Harry remained on vacation in the United States (while being paid by his employer) through the end of 1979. Heinlein has paid his moving expenses and will be reimbursed by his employer in January 1980. The Heinleins' only other trip to the United States was a two-week home leave visit from Friday, August 17, 1979 through August 31, 1979. Harry continued to draw salary during this period but did not perform any services for his employer.

Mr. and Mrs. Heinlein have the following income and expenses for 1979:

Income:

Compensation paid by VPC	
(assume 240 possible	
working days in 1979):	
Salary	$60,000
Fringe benefits:	
Accident & health insurance plan	700
Group-term life insurance (50K)	300
Group legal services	150
Total compensation	$61,150
Allowances paid by VPC (for portion	
of year residing in France):	
Educational allowance	$ 7,000
Home leave allowance	9,000
Housing allowance	13,000
Cost-of-living allowance	14,000
Total allowances	$43,000

Expenses:

Moving expenses:		
Furniture		$ 6,000
Travel to Austin		2,500
Temporary living costs		1,750
Home leave expenses:		
Air fare to U.S.	$1,000	
Other items	2,800	3,800
Rental of housing		8,000
Utilities		1,200
Renter's insurance		450
Tuition at The American School of Paris		
(U.S. school)		7,500
Books for The American School of Paris		500
Transportation to and from school		1,200

Harry Heinlein's Form 2555 for 1979 is illustrated in Figure 22-6.

FIGURE 22-6   Exemption of, or Deduction from, Income Earned Abroad

Form **2555** Department of the Treasury Internal Revenue Service	**Deduction from, or Exclusion of, Income Earned Abroad** ▶ See separate instructions. ▶ Attach to Form 1040. For the year January 1–December 31, 1979, or other tax year beginning ...., 1979, ending ...., 19.......	**1979** 31

This Form is to be Used Only by United States Citizens and Resident Aliens

Name of taxpayer Harry and Celeste Heinlein	Social security number 123 : 45 : 6789

Foreign address (including Country) 69 Rue Claude Bernard, 75005 PARIS FRANCE	Your occupation Systems Analyst

Name of employer ▶ VERY PUBLIC CORPORATION

Employer's address	U.S. ▶ 1730 N.W. 68th TERRACE, GAINESVILLE, FLA. 32605
	Foreign ▶ 1130 RUE CHARLES DE GAULLE, 75005 PARIS FRANCE

Employer is (check } ☐ A foreign entity   ☒ A U.S. company
any that apply) } ☐ A foreign affiliate of a U.S. company   ☐ Self   ☐ Other (specify) ▶

Give the latest year for which you filed a U.S. income tax return ▶ 1978	Service Center where filed ▶ PHILADELPHIA, PA.

Enter earlier years you claimed deduction from, or exclusion of, income earned abroad under section 911 or 913 ▶ 1978

Check the status under which you claim deduction from, } or exclusion of, income earned from services abroad }	☐ Bona fide residence. ☒ Physical presence.	Are you a U.S. citizen? ☒ Yes ☐ No

Complete all items in either Part I or Part II. If an item does not apply, write "DOES NOT APPLY." Failure to submit required information may result in disallowance of the claimed deduction or exclusion.

Part I   To be Completed for Bona Fide Residence Only (See Instruction 8)

1 List the countries where you have lived and the dates of residence during your 1978 and 1979 tax years ....

.... Bona fide residence began (date) ...., ended (date) ....

2 Kind of living quarters in foreign country ▶ ☐ Purchased house ☐ Rented house or apartment ☐ Rented room ☐ Quarters furnished by employer

3 Did any of your family live with you abroad during any part of the tax year? . . . . ☐ Yes ☐ No

If "Yes," who and for what period? ▶ ....

4 (a) Have you made a statement to the authorities of the foreign country you claim bona fide residence in that you are not a resident of that country? . . . . ☐ Yes ☐ No

(b) Are you required to pay income tax to the country you claim bona fide residence in? . . . . ☐ Yes ☐ No

If you made a statement to the authorities of the foreign country that you are not a resident, and the country holds you are not subject to its income tax, you do not qualify for this status. (See Instruction 8(c).)

5 Complete the following for days present in the U.S. or its possessions during the tax year:

Date arrived in U.S.	Date departed from U.S.	Number of days in U.S. on business	Amount earned in U.S. on business (Attach statement showing computation.) ¹	Date arrived in U.S.	Date departed from U.S.	Number of days in U.S. on business	Amount earned in U.S. on business (Attach statement showing computation.) ¹

¹ Do not include this income in Part III. Report on Form 1040.

6 (a) State any contractual terms or other conditions relating to the length of your employment abroad ....

....

(b) State the type of visa you entered the foreign country under ....

(c) Did your visa contain any limitations as to the length of your stay or employment in a foreign country? . . ☐ Yes ☐ No

If "Yes," attach explanation.

(d) Did you maintain a home in the U.S. while residing abroad? . . . . ☐ Yes ☐ No

If "Yes," show address of your home, whether it was rented, and the names and relationships of the occupants ....

Part II   To be Completed for Physical Presence Only (See Instruction 9)

7 The 18-month period that the test of physical presence in foreign countries is based on is from 6 15 78 through 12 14 79

8 Enter your principal country of employment during your tax year ▶ ....

9 Enter all travel abroad during the 18-month period that the test is based on, except travel between foreign countries that did not involve travel on or over international waters for 24 hours or more. If the last entry is an arrival in a foreign country, enter the number of full days to the end of 18-month period. If you have no travel to report during the period, write in the schedule that you were physically present in a foreign country or countries during the entire 18-month period.

Name of country (Including U.S.)	Date arrived		Date departed		Full days present in country	Number of days in U.S. on business	Amount earned in U.S. on business (Attach statement showing computation.) ²
FRANCE	6-15-1978	12:00 MIDNIGHT	3-2-1979	9:00 PM	260		
U.S.	3-3-1979	7:00 AM	3-10-1979	5:00 PM		5	$1,250.00
FRANCE	3-11-1979	8:00 AM	8-17-1979	NOON	158		
U.S.	8-17-1979	10:00 PM	8-31-1979	7:00 AM		Ø	NONE (HOME LEAVE)
FRANCE	8-31-1979	9:00 PM	12-14-1979	NOON	104		

² Do not include this income in Part III. Report on Form 1040.

| U.S. | 12-14-1979 | 11:00 PM | NONE | — | | | NONE |

c70—283-155-1

Part III To be Completed by All Taxpayers

10 Enter below all, including noncash remuneration, income from sources outside the United States earned during 1979. (See Instructions 7, 10(b), 10(c), and 10(d).) Is part of the income (such as bonuses) for services performed in 1979, but received in another tax year? . . . . ☐ Yes ☒ No
If "Yes," see Instructions 10(a) and 10(e).

Report all income received during 1979 on your Form 1040 regardless of when the services were performed. *If you received all or part of your income in foreign currency, translate its exchange value into terms of U.S. dollars at the rates prevailing at the time you actually or constructively received the income. Do not report income shown in Part I, line 5, on this schedule.*

Earned Income for Personal Services Rendered in Foreign Countries During 1979	Exchange rates used	Amount (In U.S. dollars)
11 Total wages, salaries, bonuses, commissions, etc., earned this year	$1(U.S.)=4.3F	$60,000
12 Pensions and annuities (see Instruction 10(d))		
13 Allowable share of income for personal services rendered this year (see Instructions 7 and 10(a)):		
(a) In a business (including farming) or profession (attach Schedule C or F (Form 1040)) .		
(b) In a partnership (give name, address, and nature of income)		
14 Noncash remuneration (market value of property or facilities furnished by employer—attach statement showing how determined):		
(a) Home (lodging)		
(b) Meals		
(c) Car		
(d) Other property or facilities (specify)		
15 Other foreign earned income (specify)		
16 Allowances, reimbursements, or expenses paid on your behalf for services rendered this year:		
(a) Cost of living	$1(U.S.)=4.3F	$4,000
(b) Overseas differential		
(c) Family		
(d) Education	$1(U.S.)=4.3F	7,000
(e) Home leave	1(U.S.)=4.3F	9,000
(f) Quarters	1(U.S.)=4.3F	13,000
(g) For any other purpose (specify) LESS: U.S. source income attributable to work days in the U.S. (See attached schedule)		(1,250)
(h) Total allowances, reimbursements, etc. Add lines 16(a) through line 16(g)		
17 Total earned income from foreign sources (add lines 11 through 15 and line 16(h))		101,750
18 (a) Value of meals and lodging included in income above which are excludable under section 119. (See Instruction 10(c))		
(b) Net earned income from foreign sources (subtract line 18(a) from line 17) . . . . ▶		101,750

19 Did you maintain a separate foreign residence for your family due to adverse living conditions at your tax home? ☐ Yes ☒ No
If "Yes," give city and country of the separate foreign residence. Also show number of days during your tax year that you maintained a second household at that address
20 List your tax home(s) during your tax year PARIS, FRANCE (1/1/79 – 12/14/79)
Did you change your tax home at any time during your tax year? . . . . ☒ Yes ☐ No
Note: *If you answered "Yes" to either 19 or 20 above, see Instructions 11, 15, and 17 before completing this form.*
21 Did you live in a camp located in a hardship area for the convenience of your employer? . . . . ☐ Yes ☐ No
(See Instruction 18 for a description of what is considered a camp.)
If "Yes," you may elect (a) or (b) below. If "No," you may claim (b) below.
(a) You may exclude from gross income the amount of $20,000 (prorated on a daily basis for days you lived in a camp). See Part V.
(b) You may claim the deduction for excess foreign living expenses. See Part IV.

Part IV To be Completed by Taxpayers Claiming the Deduction for Excess Foreign Living Expenses

Qualified Schooling Expense (See Instruction 12)

22 Complete the following for each dependent child for whom you claim a schooling expense deduction:

Name of dependent child	Age	Address (including country) of school attended	Schooling expenses claimed
John Lawrence Heinlein	13	American School of Paris 211 Rue de Ste. Bernard 75005 PARIS, FRANCE	$9,200

23 Total qualified schooling expenses. Enter here and on lines 31(b) and 36 . . . . ▶ | $9,200

Qualified Home Leave Transportation Expense (See Instruction 13)

24 Enter total number of trips for which you are claiming a deduction. Count each trip by you, your spouse, and your dependents as a separate trip ▶ **1** . Total expense for all trips; also enter on lines 31(c) and 37 . . ▶ | $1,000

Qualified Hardship Area Amount (See Instruction 14)

25 Name of hardship area .... Date tax home was established .... ended ....

26 Maximum amount . . . . | $ 5,000.00

27 Number of days that you qualified during the tax year . . . .

28 Percentage applicable (divide the number of days on line 27 by 365) . . . . | %

29 Allowable amount (multiply the amount on line 26 by the percent on line 28). Also enter on lines 31(d) and 38 . . . . . ▶ | $ NONE

Qualified Housing Expenses (See Instruction 16)

30 Expenses paid or incurred for housing at your tax home during the year. (If you maintained a qualified second household, see Instruction 17 for additional information) . . . . | $9,650

31 Figure your base housing amount as follows. Enter:

(a) Earned income from all sources (see Instruction 16) . . . . . . | 103,000

(b) Qualified schooling expenses (from line 23) . . . . . . | 9,200

(c) Qualified home leave transportation expenses (from line 24) . . . | 1,000

(d) Qualified hardship area amount (from line 29) . . . . . . | NONE

*(e) Qualified cost-of-living differential (from tables—see Instruction 15) | 8461

(f) Housing expenses from line 30 . . . . | 9,650

(g) Total expenses (add lines 31(b) through 31(f)) . . . . | 28,311

(h) Subtract line 31(g) from line 31(a) . . . . | 74,689

(i) Base housing amount: Enter 20% (⅕) of line 31(h) . . . . | $ 14,938

32 Subtract line 31(i) from line 30. If less than zero, enter zero . . . . | NONE

33 If you maintained a qualified second household, enter earned income as modified by Instruction 17(b)(i). Otherwise, omit line 33 and enter zero on line 34(e) . . . .

34 Amount from line 31(g) . . . .

(a) Housing expenses for qualified second household . . . . . .

(b) Add line 34 and line 34(a) . . . .

(c) Subtract line 34(b) from line 33. If less than zero, enter zero . . . . .

(d) Base housing amount for second household; enter 20% (⅕) of line 34(c) . . . . .

(e) Subtract line 34(d) from line 34(a) . . . .

35 Total qualified housing expenses. If you maintained a qualified second household and your tax home was in a hardship area, enter total of amounts on lines 30 and 34(e). Otherwise, enter the total of lines 32 and 34(e). Also enter on line 40 . . . . ▶ | NONE

Summary of Excess Foreign Living Expenses

36 Qualified schooling expenses from line 23 . . . . | $9,200

37 Qualified home leave transportation expenses from line 24 . . . . | 1,000

38 Qualified hardship area amount from line 29 . . . . | NONE

39 Qualified cost-of-living differential from line 31(e) . . . . | 8,461

40 Qualified housing expenses from line 35 . . . . | NONE

41 Total expenses (add lines 36 through 40) . . . . | 18,661

42 Limitation:

(a) Total earned income from foreign sources (from Part III, line 18(b)) . . . . . | $101,750

(b) Adjustments allocable to income from foreign sources (see Instruction 11(b)) . . . .

(c) Net earned income from foreign sources (subtract line 42(b) from line 42(a)). If less than zero, enter zero . . . . | $ 101,750

43 Deduction for excess foreign living expenses. Enter the amount from line 41 or 42(c), whichever is smaller. Also enter this amount on Form 1040, line 24, and label it as "Expense from Form 2555" . . . . ▶ | $ 18,661

$$ * \ \$8,900 \times \frac{347}{365} = \$8,461 $$

Part V To be Completed by Taxpayers Claiming the Exclusion of
Income Earned in a Hardship Area Camp (See Instruction 18)

44 Complete the following for days you lived in a hardship area during the tax year:			Full days you lived in hardship area	Number of days during your residence that area qualified
Name of hardship area	Date arrived	Date departed		

45 Total number of full qualifying days in all hardship areas. (Enter here and on line 47 below.) . . . . . ▶   NONE

46 Maximum exclusion $20,000.00

47 Number of days that you qualified for exclusion during the tax year (from line 45 above) . .

48 Percentage applicable (divide the number of days on line 47 by 365) . . . .   %

49 Maximum allowable exclusion (multiply the amount on line 46 by the percent on line 48) . . . . . ▶ $ NONE

50 Enter the exclusion from line 49 or the amount you earned during the days you qualified, whichever is smaller . . . .

51 Deductions allocable to excluded income. (See Instruction 18(c) and attach a schedule.) . . . .

52 Subtract line 51 from line 50. Enter here and in parenthesis on Form 1040, line 21, and label it "Exclusion from Form 2555". (On Form 1040, subtract the amount from your income to arrive at **Total income** on line 22.) . ▶   NONE

PROBLEMS

1. The tax laws before the Foreign Earned Income Act of 1978 provided for an annual exclusion of $15,000 of foreign earned income. For most Americans overseas, this exclusion has been replaced by a series of special deductions. What are the advantages of the new deductions over a flat rate exclusion?

2. The Foreign Earned Income Act (FEIA) of 1978 marked a major change in U.S. tax policy toward earned income derived from the performance of services overseas. Compare the tax exemption benefits for foreign earned income before and after the FEIA.

3. Mary Kitchens accepted a job in Italy and arrived in Rome at 6:01 A.M. on January 1, 1979. She returned to the United States for two weeks, from July 15, 1979 (date of departure) to July 28, 1979 (date of return) because of a death in the family. She then stayed in Italy until May 15, 1980, at which time she returned to the United States and stayed for 22 days arriving back in Italy on June 5, 1980. She worked in Italy until September 9, 1980, when she returned to the United States permanently.

   Calculate the maximum number of days Mary qualifies for the Sec. 913 benefits under the 510-day physical presence rule for 1979 and 1980.

4. Andrew Joyce is an employee of Amalgamated Aircraft Corporation. He was transferred from the United States to a foreign country on March 15, 19X1 to work on a five-year service contract to repair planes purchased by the local government from Amalgamated. The position provides Joyce with a fine salary and fringe benefits, which include a two-month annual leave with pay and transportation for his family back to the United States. Joyce and his family return to the United States for home leave on April 1, 19X2 and return to the foreign country on May 31, 19X2. Because of political unrest, Joyce and his family are forced to leave the foreign country on November 25, 19X2. Does Joyce qualify for the Sec. 913 benefits?

5. Andrew Cauthen, a U.S. citizen, is a bona fide resident of Peru for the period April 1, 1979 through September 30, 1981. Cauthen resides in a camp located in a hardship area during that entire period, except for a two-week vacation each year. Cauthen receives a salary of $3,500 per month for each month of the period in question. In addition, he receives meals and lodging during that period in the amount of $750 per month that are excludable under Sec. 119. Determine the amount of income that Cauthen may exclude during his period in Peru.

6. Albert Jackson, a single U.S. citizen, has been a bona fide resident of Brazil since his arrival on July 15, 19X1. Jackson has resided in a camp located in a hardship area from July 15, 19X1 through the end of 19X2, except for a 10-day vacation period during each three-month period. These vacation periods have been spent outside the United States. Jackson is paid $4,000 per month while in Brazil. He also receives meals and lodging, valued at $1,000 per month, which are excludable under Sec. 119. Jackson's Brazilian income taxes are $3,000. Calculate Jackson's net U.S. tax liability for 19X2.

7. Which of the following locations qualifies as a hardship area for taxable year 1979?
   a. Tokyo, Japan
   b. New Delhi, India
   c. Lagos, Nigeria
   d. Jeddah, Saudi Arabia
   e. Belfast, Northern Ireland

8. Determine the qualified cost of living differential for taxable year 1979 for each of the following individuals who are "bona fide foreign residents."

   a. John Jones, who with his three dependents resided for the full taxable year in Oslo, Norway.

   b. Mary Smith, who with her six-year old dependent daughter was a resident of Tokyo from August 18 through December 31.

   c. Albert Jenkins, a single individual, who resided in a construction camp in Venezuela and elected to exclude his earned income, meals, and lodging under Secs. 911 and 119.

   d. Bev Mellinger, a single individual, who was employed for the full taxable year in Toronto, Canada.

   e. John Jones in part a, who worked and lived in Bahrain but because of adverse living conditions maintained a second residence for himself and his family of four in London.

9. Mark Rogers, who is married and has two children, has been a bona fide resident of Japan for the entire 1979 taxable year. He earned the following income for services he performed in Japan: salary, $50,000; cost-of-living allowance, $32,000; educational allowance, $11,800; home leave travel allowance, $4,000; housing allowance, $30,000; and an overseas premium of $7,500. Compute Mark Rogers's qualified housing expense deduction if his actual housing costs were $38,000, his educational expense deductions were $12,000, and his home leave expenses were $4,000.

10. The Sec. 217 moving expense deduction rules are applied differently to moves within the United States and moves from the United States to a foreign country. What are the differences between the two sets of rules?

11. Pursuant to an overseas transfer, Ronny Gardiner sold his personal residence and incurred various moving expenses. The residence, which has an adjusted basis of $30,000, was sold on January 1, 19X1 for $47,500. Selling costs of $2,500 were incurred in connection with the sale. Determine the last date on which Mr. Gardiner must purchase a replacement residence in order to defer his gain under Sec. 1034 in the following independent situations.

    a. Mr. Gardiner moves overseas on January 1, 19X1 and remains there until March 1, 19X3.

    b. Mr. Gardiner moves overseas on January 1, 19X1 and remains there until June 1, 19X4.

    c. Mr. Gardiner moves overseas on November 1, 19X0 and remains there until June 1, 19X3.

    d. Mr. Gardiner moves overseas on April 1, 19X1 and remains there until December 24, 19X9.

12. Abe Akers, a U.S. citizen and coach of the Tokyo Redbirds, Tokyo's entry in the new Continental Football League, has resided in Tokyo for all of 19X3. Abe's income and deductions for 19X3 are outlined below. Abe has lived in Tokyo, with his family, since the beginning of the Redbirds' training camp on July 6, 19X1, except for one short vacation trip with his family back to the United States in 19X3. Assume all of the Redbirds games are played in Japan or Europe. Abe filed his 19X1 and 19X2 returns claiming that he was a bona fide resident of Japan.

    Income:

Base salary	$40,000
Overseas premium	6,000
Cost-of-living allowance	25,500
Housing allowance	30,000

Education allowance	10,500
Home leave travel allowance	11,000
19X2 tax reimbursement from employer	26,000
Premiums on group term life insurance ($50,000 face amount policy)	370
Interest from U.S. bank account	4,000

Deductions:

Schooling at U.S. school (two children)	10,500
Home leave: Travel to U.S.	7,500
Other expenses	3,500
Housing expenses (rental of home)	35,500
Itemized deductions (before reduction for zero bracket amount)	2,500
Personal and dependent exemptions	4

Compute Abe Akers' taxable income for 19X3.

13. Maria Konokpa, a Canadian citizen, is temporarily in the United States as a nonresident alien in 19X1. During early 19X1, she decides that she wants to remain in the United States permanently and takes steps to establish residency (that is, she obtains a visa permitting permanent residence). Assuming that Maria is determined to be a U.S. resident as of April 1, 19X1, how is she taxed on the income she earns in 19X1?

14. Brian Winters, a British citizen, engages in the activities outlined below during 19X1. For each of these independent situations, indicate whether Brian is considered to be engaging in the conduct of a U.S. trade or business.
    a. Brian earns $7,500 while in the United States for 45 days performing sales activities for a foreign corporation. The foreign corporation is not considered to be engaged in the conduct of a U.S. trade or business.
    b. Assume the same facts as in part a, except that Brian earns only $2,750.
    c. Brian earns $12,500 in dividend income and $17,500 in capital gains from buying and selling stocks through a stockbroker located in New York City. He does not maintain a U.S. office.
    d. Brian earns $90,000 in gross rental income, which is offset by $74,000 in expenses, from a 28-unit apartment complex that he owns in Los Angeles.
    e. Brian earns $25,000 from his interest in a partnership. The partnership is engaged in the conduct of a U.S. trade or business.

15. Linda McKenzie, a nonresident alien from Ireland, incurs the following deductions in five independent situations. Determine the amount of these deductions that she may claim for U.S. tax purposes.
    a. $5,000 of interest expense that relates to borrowings used to purchase stocks that produced $15,000 of U.S. source dividend income. Linda does not conduct a U.S. trade or business.
    b. $1,000 charitable contribution to the United Way. Linda earned $25,000 for performing services while in the United States.
    c. $2,500 in deductions related to the rental of her former residence in Florida. Linda does not engage in the conduct of a U.S. trade or business but earned $6,000 from the rental of the residence.
    d. Assume the same facts as in part c, except that included in the deductions is a $500 casualty loss related to the residence.
    e. Would your answer to part d change if Linda had also earned $10,000 from performing services in the United States?

16. Determine the U.S. tax liability of Larry Ochab in Problem 6, Chapter 21, ignoring the benefits of any U.S. tax treaties. Assume that Mr. Ochab's tax rate on any U.S. trade or business income is 60 percent.

17. Determine the tax liability of Karen Spivey in Problem 7, Chapter 21, ignoring the benefits of any U.S. tax treaties. Assume that Ms. Spivey's tax rate on any U.S. trade or business income is 40 percent.

18. Mr. His, a nonresident alien, owns a secret formula (having a nominal adjusted basis) for DIET DRINK, which Multico, a U.S.-based multinational corporation wants to acquire. Multico offers to pay Mr. His either:

    (1) $100,000 in the current year as full payment for the formula.
    (2) $8,000 per year for each of the next 10 years plus 1 percent of Multico's gross margin from the sales of DIET DRINK.

Discuss the tax ramifications to Mr. His of each of the offers.

19. Foreign source income is taxable to a nonresident alien only when it is effectively connected with the conduct of a U.S. trade or business. What requirements must be satisfied for this taxation to occur?

20. A nonresident alien is permitted to make an election under Sec. 6013(g) to be taxed as a resident alien. List the income tax advantages and disadvantages of such an election.

21. Frank Smith is an accountant who went to work on Johnston Island for a private construction company on August 15, 19X1 and remained there until the end of 19X1. During the period August 15 to December 31, 19X1, Smith earned the following income:

Possessions source wages	$4,950
Other income:	
U.S. source dividends	600
Foreign source dividends	150
Possessions source interest	325
U.S. source interest	125
Total income	$6,150

All Smith's income was received on Johnston Island.

a. Does Smith qualify for the benefits of Sec. 931?

b. Determine Smith's exempt income for the period August 15 to December 31.

22. Oliver White was employed by a contractor in American Samoa, beginning on June 16, 19X1 and ending December 31, 19X2. During this time, White earned the following income:

	19X1	19X2
Samoan wages	$15,200	$32,000
U.S. source capital gain	800	10,000
U.S. dividends	600	4,000
Samoan interest	1,000	2,000
Foreign interest	-0-	750
Total income	$17,600	$48,750

All White's income was received in American Samoa except the U.S. dividends, which the domestic corporation automatically reinvested in additional shares of its stock.

   a. Does White qualify for the benefits of Sec. 931 for 19X1? for 19X2?
   b. Determine White's exempt income for 19X1 and 19X2.
23. Compare the eligibility requirements and benefits for Code Secs. 911, 913, and 931.

SUPPLEMENTAL PROBLEMS

24. Spike "Spitball" Weaver, an aging baseball player left the United States in 19X1 to play professional ball in Japan. Spike told his friends that he planned to play ball in Japan as long as he was able and then return to the United States to manage a ball club. Spike bought a home in Tokyo, but continued his church affiliation and country club memberships in the United States. Spike's wife moved with him to Japan, but their only daughter continued to attend the University of Chicago. Both Spike and his wife attempted to learn Japanese. Neither of them attained fluency, but Spike's wife was able to translate her recipes into Japanese so their cook would be able to prepare American food.

    During 19X3 Spike made two trips back to the United States. The first trip lasted four weeks and was related to a job offer of managing a minor league club. The second trip was with his wife and lasted three months. During this time, the Weavers attended their daughter's graduation and took a vacation in California.

    Is Spike eligible to claim the benefits of Sec. 913 during 19X3?

25. Andrea Jones has lived abroad for a number of years as a bona fide foreign resident. Determine what portion of the income from an overseas activity in each of the following independent situations is foreign source earned income (and thus can be offset by the special Sec. 913 deductions).

    (a) Andrea, an American artist, gave her paintings to galleries on consignment. The galleries remit the amount received from the sale of the painting less their commission. Andrea earned $40,000 from the sale of the paintings during 19X1.

    (b) Andrea received slot machine payoffs of $60,000. The payoffs resulted from her skill in "fixing" the slot machines to produce an abnormally high payoff rate.

    (c) Andrea ran a horse farm as a sole proprietorship. Capital is a "material income producing factor" in the earning of her profits. During 19X1 Andrea earned $150,000 from the horse farm.

26. The United States taxes a U.S. citizen on worldwide income even though the citizen may reside abroad. In 1977, 237[27] individuals gave up their U.S. citizenships. Some of these people may have taken this action for tax purposes. What situations or tax factors would lead an individual to renounce U.S. citizenship? What protection does the U.S. government have to prevent the avoidance of U.S. taxation of income or profits, gifts and property held at death? *Hint:* See Secs. 877 (income taxes), 2107 (estate tax), and 2511 (gift tax).

27. Ole Andersen, a resident alien, is a Swedish citizen. During 19X1 Andersen resided in California for the entire year and made alimony payments in the amount of $10,000 to his ex-wife. The ex-wife is a Swedish citizen and has no U.S. business or investment activities. The alimony payments are made from a special bank account that Andersen maintains in a Swedish bank for his earnings from Swedish investments.

---

[27] According to *The Journal of Taxation,* June 1978, p. 382.

a. Is Andersen's ex-wife subject to U.S. taxation on the alimony income?
b. Is Andersen required to withhold U.S. income taxes under Sec. 1441(a) from his alimony payments to his ex-wife?
c. Assume U.S. taxes are due in this situation but that Andersen fails to withhold them. Who is liable for the taxes?

28. Determine the tax liability of Larry Ochab in Problem 6, Chapter 21, assuming that he is a resident of the following treaty countries:
a. The Netherlands
b. Canada

29. Determine the tax liability of Karen Spivey in Problem 7, Chapter 21, assuming that she is a resident of the following treaty countries:
a. The Netherlands
b. Canada

RETURN PROBLEM

1. On December 28, 1977 Robert Baxter and his wife and four children were transferred to Jeddah, Saudi Arabia, where they immediately established residence. Robert's base salary for 1979 is $48,000. He received the following additional pay for his overseas work during 1979:

Overseas cost-of-living bonus	$11,500
Housing paid for by employer (four-bedroom apartment three miles from office)	36,000
Meals (cost of hiring cook and maid as well as for food purchased)	12,000
Tuition at Jeddah Preparatory, a British School (four children at $2,800 each)	11,200
Home leave allowance	15,000
Total allowances	$85,700

Mr. Baxter indicated that during 1979 the costs of maintaining his family in Saudi Arabia were as follows:

Actual housing costs (including rent and renter's insurance)	$36,500
Education—the children were enrolled at the Parents' Cooperative School, an American School whose tuition the firm was willing to pay (rather than at the British school).	16,000
In addition, the following costs were incurred: Transportation via bus for children (in Jeddah)	540
Books	320
Home leave costs—round-trip air fare for family of six is approximately $9,000 (from Jeddah to the Baxter's home in Austin, Texas)	16,075
Utilities	6,000

During 1979 the Baxters spent 14 days (August 6–19) in the United States on home leave. In addition, they spent 14 days (March 2–15) on vacation in Europe. Saudi income taxes during 1979 were $17,500.

Complete a Form 2555 for the Baxters. Assume that the Baxters filed their 1977 and 1978 returns claiming that Robert was a bona fide resident.

taxation of U.S. firms doing business abroad

When a U.S. corporation decides to expand into international operations, the expansion may be accomplished in a number of ways. The U.S. corporation may export items directly from its existing facilities; it may open a foreign branch of the domestic firm; it may form a domestic subsidiary through which the export operations are carried on; or it may form a foreign subsidiary operation.[1] Numerous factors, such as the nature of the business to be conducted, management's experience with foreign markets, the depth of the management team (that is, the size of the management pool), the relative costs of the business alternatives, and the availability of outside capital must be considered in making the business choice. In addition, the tax effects of the various alternatives must be considered. While it is true that a U.S. corporation is generally taxed on its worldwide income, the form in which foreign operations are undertaken may affect the timing of the U.S. tax and, in a few cases, even reduce the total amount of U.S. taxes paid. Some forms of foreign operations result in immediate U.S. taxation; some result in deferral of U.S. taxes on the foreign operations; and some result in permanent savings of U.S. taxes. In this chapter, we

shall discuss the various alternatives and the tax effects of each alternative.

DIRECT EXPORTS

When a U.S. business begins to develop a foreign market, direct exportation from the domestic parent through its own sales force or foreign agents may be the best way to "test the water." In this way, the development of the foreign market and of executive expertise in international operations may proceed with caution within an existing business operation.

Income from such foreign operations is taxed by the United States in the year the income is earned. Foreign earnings or losses are combined with income from the corporation's domestic operations. When the foreign operations generate losses, such losses may be used immediately to offset income from domestic operations, but these losses may have to be "recaptured" in later years when the foreign operations become profitable. (The recapture provisions operate through the foreign tax credit procedures; see the discussion in Chapter 21.) Whether or not the foreign operations are taxed in the foreign country that is the destination of the exports depends, of course, on that country's tax laws. In countries with which the United States has tax treaties, the sales probably will not be taxed by the foreign country unless the U.S. firm has a permanent establishment in that country. If the foreign country does tax the income generated by foreign operations, the U.S. corporation may claim a foreign tax credit for these taxes to offset some or all of the U.S. taxes due.

---

[1] As an alternative to engaging directly in international operations, a taxpayer might license or sell rights to a product for a given geographic area to a foreign business entity. Generally, the royalties or sales proceeds received would be subject to full U.S. taxation at the ordinary income or capital gains rates otherwise applicable. Gains realized by a domestic corporation from the sale or exchange of a patent, for example, to a "controlled" foreign corporation are an exception to the regular capital gain rules and are taxed as ordinary income under Sec. 1249. No further discussion of these alternatives is presented because we do not consider these activities to be "directly engaging" in international operations.

DOMESTIC SUBSIDIARIES

One nontax problem that arises when foreign operations are handled by a domestic corporation (or its branch) is that all the corporate assets are liable to the foreign creditors. One way for the domestic corporation to minimize this problem is to form a domestic subsidiary to operate overseas. Such a subsidiary effectively insulates the parent corporation's assets from foreign creditors and leaves only those assets that are part of the foreign activities subject to liabilities arising from the foreign business. The tax benefits resulting from foreign losses are retained under this arrangement, because the domestic parent corporation and its domestic subsidiary may join in filing a consolidated tax return. In the same way, domestic losses incurred by the parent corporation may be used to reduce U.S. taxes levied on foreign profits.

DOMESTIC INTERNATIONAL SALES CORPORATIONS

One form of domestic subsidiary that has been given a significant tax advantage is the Domestic International Sales Corporation (DISC). Congress designed this domestic corporation to encourage export activities by U.S. producers largely in order to achieve a more favorable balance of payments position. To qualify for the substantial tax benefits, a corporation must be a domestic corporation primarily engaged in exporting, it must meet certain statutory requirements, and its shareholders must have elected to be taxed under the DISC rules. DISC profits are not taxed to the DISC, and only a portion of the DISC profits are taxed to its shareholders in the year the profits are earned. Special pricing rules allow DISCs to maximize their profits and, therefore, maximize tax deferrals. Certain shareholders may use the tax-deferred profits in the form of loans from the DISC. Taxes on DISC profits are deferred indefinitely, as long as the untaxed income is not distributed, the shareholders do not sell their stock, and the DISC does not fail to qualify under the statutory tests described below.

Qualification as a DISC

Many complex requirements must be satisfied to attain and retain DISC status. We shall briefly describe the requirements here, but full details are beyond the scope of this book. Seven of the requirements concern the structure of the domestic firm and its operation and

must be met each taxable year. These seven requirements are the following:

1. The DISC must be a domestic corporation. Incorporation in a U.S. possession or a foreign country is not allowed (Sec. 992(a)(1)).
2. Only one class of DISC stock may be outstanding. This limitation exists because DISC earnings are taxed to the shareholders and not to the DISC itself. Therefore, the existence of more than a single class of stock could complicate the division of earnings to the shareholders (Sec. 992(a)(1)(C)).
3. The par value or stated value of outstanding stock must total at least $2,500 on each day of the taxable year. This allows the DISC structure to be used with only minimal capitalization (Sec. 992(a)(1)(C)).
4. The DISC must have a separate bank account in its own name on each day of the taxable year (Treas. Reg. Sec. 1.992-1(a)(6)).
5. The DISC must maintain separate books and records (Treas. Reg. Sec. 1.992-1(a)(7)).
6. The domestic corporation must elect to be treated as a DISC, and all its shareholders at the time that the corporation itself revokes the election or until the corporation first elects to be taxed as a DISC must consent to the election. Once the original election is made, it is retained until the corporation itself revokes the election or until the corporation fails to meet the DISC qualifications for five consecutive years. Failure to meet a DISC requirement in any one year may result in the corporation being taxed as a regular corporation for that one taxable year. The failure to qualify as a DISC for the taxable year also triggers the taxation of the tax-deferred DISC income in the same fashion as if the DISC election had been revoked (see page **23/9**). Even if this happens, the DISC election itself continues, so that in the following year the corporation may again be taxed as a DISC, and obtain the tax deferral for up to 50 percent of its profits, if it satisfies the various DISC requirements (Secs. 992(a)(1)(D) and 992(b)).
7. The corporation may not be one of the organizations that Sec. 992(d) lists as ineligible to be treated as a DISC, such as Sec. 501(c)(3) tax-exempt organizations, personal holding companies, banks, insurance companies, regulated investment companies, and Subchapter S corporations.

In addition to these seven structural requirements, a DISC must satisfy two other operational requirements annually. These two requirements are objective tests designed to ensure that the benefits of DISC taxation are applied only to firms that are engaging almost entirely in export operations.

8. 95 percent or more of the adjusted basis of all the DISC's assets held at the close of the taxable year must be considered to be "qualified export assets."

9. 95 percent or more of the DISC's gross receipts must be considered to be "qualified export receipts" (Secs. 992(a)(1)(A) and (B)).

Each of these requirements requires additional explanation.

QUALIFIED EXPORT ASSETS TEST   At the end of each taxable year, 95 percent or more of the adjusted basis of all the assets owned by the DISC must consist of qualified export assets. The term *qualified export assets* is defined in Sec. 993(b) to include a wide variety of export assets and export-related investments. Qualified export assets include the following.

1. *Export property of the DISC.* Export property is the inventory that the DISC holds and intends to export. Such inventory may be counted as qualified export assets only if: (a) it was grown or manufactured in the United States by a party other than the DISC, (b) it is intended for direct use or consumption outside the United States, and (c) not more than 50 percent of the property's fair market value is attributable to imported components. Although a DISC may not manufacture a product for export, it may perform limited assembly or packaging of the product. These qualifications are consistent with the Congressional intent of providing a mechanism for encouraging the export of U.S.-made goods (Sec. 993(c)).

2. *Support facilities of the DISC.* Assets used in connection with the sale, lease, rental, storage, handling, transportation, packaging, assembly or servicing of export property, the performance of architectural or engineering services on foreign construction projects, or the performance of managerial services related to the production of qualified export receipts by a second DISC are themselves qualified export assets.

3. *Certain trade receivables.* Accounts receivable and other debt instruments generated by the DISC are qualified export assets if they result from such transactions as the sale, lease, or servicing of export property, as well as the sale or lease of qualified export assets (other than export property).

4. *Working capital.* Reasonable amounts of working capital necessary to operate the DISC in the form of money, bank deposits, and temporary instruments all represent qualified export assets.

5. *Certain U.S. bank deposits.* Deposits in U.S. banks that exceed the reasonable working capital needs of the DISC may be considered qualified export assets if they are invested within a reasonable period of time in other qualified export assets. This provision allows the DISC some flexibility in its financial management so that large cash payments received at year-end will not cause the corporation to fail the qualified assets test.

6. *Stock or securities of a related foreign export corporation.* Section 993(e) specifies three kinds of related foreign corporations, the stock or securities of which are acceptable investments. Host country investment rules may require a nonresident corporation such as a DISC to operate or own property only through a local corporation.

7. *Obligations issued or guaranteed by the Export-Import Bank* (Eximbank), *the Foreign Credit Insurance Association* (FCIA), *or the Private Export Funding Corporation* (PEFCO). These obligations were included among qualified export assets to provide investments for a DISC's accumulated earnings. The Eximbank obligations, however, are rarely available, and the FCIA has never issued any qualifying obligations. The PEFCO obligations frequently have been used as DISC investments.

8. *Producers' loans.* A DISC itself may not manufacture goods for export, but the DISC may lend its accumulated earnings to a "producer" of export goods without endangering its DISC status. The producer may be an unrelated entity or it may be a related entity, such as one of the DISC's shareholders. When the DISC makes a producer's loan to a major shareholder, this action permits the shareholder to use the DISC's funds without a taxable event (such as a dividend) occurring. The DISC-associated tax deferral continues for the entire time that the shareholder has use of the funds (Sec. 993(b)).

For the producer's loan benefits to apply, a number of requirements must be met (Sec. 993(d)). Each loan must be designated a producer's loan when made, a note or other evidence of indebtedness must exist, and the loan's stated maturity must not exceed five years. The maximum amount of producers' loans that a DISC may make equals the amount of the DISC's undistributed tax-deferred profits. If a loan qualifies as a producer's loan when it is made, it continues to qualify until its maturity (Sec. 993(d)).

QUALIFIED EXPORT RECEIPTS TEST   To retain DISC tax benefits, the domestic corporation must demonstrate each year that 95 percent of its gross receipts are *qualified export receipts*. Like the test for qualified export assets, the test for qualified export receipts is intended to ensure that the DISC benefits are not used to shelter non-export-related income. Within the class of export-related receipts, Congress has allowed the DISC substantial flexibility.

Most of the qualified export receipts are directly related to income generated by the qualified export assets described above. Section 993(a) describes eight categories of receipts that are considered to be qualified export receipts:

1. Gross receipts from the sale, exchange, or other disposition of export property by the DISC, or by any principal for whom the DISC acts as a commission agent.
2. Gross receipts from the lease or rental of export property when such property is to be used by the lessee outside the United States.
3. Receipts earned for services within or without the United States that are related and subsidiary to a sale (including commission sales) or lease of export property in 1 or 2, above.
4. Gross receipts from the sale, exchange, or other disposition of qualified export assets (other than export property).
5. Actual or constructive dividends from a related foreign export corporation.
6. Interest on all obligations qualifying as qualified export assets. Some interest-generating assets are trade receivables, producers' loans, and Eximbank, FCIA, and PEFCO obligations.
7. Receipts from the performance within or without the United States of engineering or architectural services for construction projects that are located or proposed for location outside the United States.
8. Receipts from the performance by a DISC of managerial services for a second, unrelated DISC (Sec. 993(a)(1)).

Failure to meet the DISC qualifications tests

A domestic corporation may be taxed as a DISC only if it has filed a valid election to be taxed as a DISC and it meets all the qualifications described above. Congress recognized, however, that the gross receipts test or the assets test could be violated by a corporation even if its activities were predominantly those that the DISC legislation was designed to encourage. As a result, Sec. 992(c) has provided a mechanism through which firms failing one or both of these tests may re-

tain DISC status, and thereby avoid taxation of current profits and the tax-deferred profits of prior years, by making a deficiency distribution if the failure was due to a "reasonable cause."

If the corporation fails the gross receipts test, it may retain its DISC status by making a deficiency distribution equal to the entire amount of taxable income resulting from transactions giving rise to nonqualified export receipts. The rules require that *all* taxable income from nonqualified transactions be distributed and not just the taxable income that is attributed to nonqualified export receipts in excess of the 5 percent amount that is generally permitted. For purposes of this deficiency distribution, taxable income consists of gross receipts minus the sum of the cost of goods sold and any expenses that are allocated or apportioned to this sale under the rules of Treas. Reg. Sec. 1.861-8. Expenses such as accounting services that may not be allocated to a class of income, including the nonqualified receipts, may not be deducted to arrive at taxable income (Treas. Reg. Sec. 1.992-3(b)(2)).

If the corporation fails the assets test, it may retain its DISC status by making a distribution equal to the fair market value of all its assets that are not qualified export assets. The amount of the distribution is based on the nonqualified asset's fair market value at the end of the DISC's taxable year. Thus, a DISC having a January 31 end to its taxable year would apply the gross assets test by comparing the total adjusted basis of its qualified export assets to the total adjusted basis of all its assets. If the adjusted basis of the qualified assets is at least 95 percent of the adjusted basis of all assets, the test is met and no deficiency distribution is necessary. If the adjusted basis of nonqualified assets exceeds 5 percent of the adjusted basis of all assets, a deficiency distribution must be made equal to or exceeding the fair market value of all the nonqualified assets that the DISC owned on January 31. Note also that the deficiency distribution is the full fair market value of all nonqualifying assets and is not just the fair market value of assets that exceeded the permissible 5 percent amount of nonqualifying assets (Treas. Reg. Sec. 1.992-3(b)(3)).

Deficiency distributions are allowed only when a reasonable cause existed for the corporation to fail the original test. The regulations provide, however, that the corporation is deemed to have reasonable cause for failing the test if 70 percent of its gross receipts are qualified export receipts and 70 percent of its gross assets are qualified export assets and the corporation makes a deficiency distribution within 8½ months after its year-end (Treas. Reg. Sec. 1.992-3(d)).

Types of DISCs

A number of different types of DISCs exist. The most common DISC sells export property and is either a "sales DISC" or a "commission DISC." A *sales DISC* is a qualifying domestic corporation that purchases export property and resells it either to a third-party purchaser or to a related foreign export corporation. A *commission DISC* is treated as an agent of a related or unrelated producer corporation and receives a commission on its sales of the export property. Other forms of DISCs may be engaged in leasing or rental activities, performing architectural or engineering services, or performing managerial services for another DISC.

A DISC is not required to perform any functions to receive a portion of the profits created by the export sales.[2] The DISC may have its own sales force, perform significant services, and bill and collect from its customers independently; on the other hand, the DISC may perform no services at all and may be only a "paper DISC" controlled by its producer parent. If the DISC uses one of the special pricing methods outlined below, no reallocation of profits under Sec. 482 between the DISC and its shareholder–producer may occur, no matter how few services are actually performed by the DISC.

COMPUTING DISC INCOME   Because DISC income receives preferential tax treatment, a manufacturer with a wholly owned DISC would like to shift as much income as possible to the DISC. Section 482 may become operative, however, when related parties deal with each other. Under Sec. 482, transfer prices between related firms must be essentially the same prices that would occur in an arm's-length transaction. This would effectively preclude shifting income between the producer and the DISC and would restrict the DISC's income to the profits that it "earned." Two special pricing rules for DISCs, however, avoid many of the complexities and uncertainties associated with Sec. 482 and, in many cases, allow the producer to shift some of the production profits to the DISC. These special rules apply only to transfers between a related producer or producers and a DISC if: (1) the transfer gives rise to qualified export receipts, and (2) a producer's agreement exists between the DISC and the related producer detailing the pricing method to be employed. If the transfer gives rise to nonqualified export receipts or no agreement exists, the Sec. 482 arm's-length pricing rules govern the calculation of the transfer price from

[2]Rev. Rul. 72-166, 1972-1 CB 220.

the producer to the DISC. The two pricing rules, the "4 percent of gross receipts method" and the "50-50 combined taxable income method," are also available at the taxpayer's option. These special pricing rules are explained below.

Neither of the special pricing rules actually computes a transfer price. Instead, the rules establish the maximum amount of taxable income that is attributable to a DISC, and then permits a transfer price between the producer and the DISC to be established that results in the calculated amount of taxable income plus a reimbursement to the DISC for costs incurred by or allocated to it. This approach allows enough flexibility so that the tax results are the same whether the DISC is a sales DISC or a commission DISC. The actual calculation of the transfer price may be best understood by studying the following brief outlines of the taxable income calculation for the two types of DISC.

Sales DISC

	Transfer price
Less:	Cost of goods sold
Less:	DISC expenses attributable to sales
Less:	Export promotion expenses
Equals:	Taxable income

Commission DISC

	Commission to be charged by the DISC
Less:	DISC expenses attributable to sales
Less:	Export promotion expenses
Equals:	Taxable income

For a sales DISC, the transfer price to be calculated is the amount charged by the related producer to the DISC for the export property that was sold. For a commission DISC, the transfer price to be calculated is the commission charged by the DISC to the related producer. Once taxable income for the DISC is determined under one of the special pricing rules explained below, the transfer price or commission charge may be readily calculated. Each of these pricing rules may be applied on a transaction-by-transaction basis, or based on a product group or product line grouping, or for all qualifying transactions, according to the option that maximizes the DISC's profits.

4 PERCENT OF GROSS RECEIPTS RULE   The maximum taxable income under the 4 percent of gross receipts rule equals 4 percent of the DISC's qualified export re-

ceipts from the sale plus 10 percent of its export promotion expenses attributable to those receipts (Sec. 994(a)(1)). Export promotion expenses are expenses incurred by the DISC to "advance the sale, lease, or other distribution of export property," such as expenses for market studies, advertising, sales commissions, warehousing, other selling expenses, packaging, and even general and administrative costs for billing customers (Treas. Reg. Sec. 1.994-1(f)(1)).

Calculation of the taxable income and the transfer price under this rule is illustrated in the following two examples.

Example 1, Sales DISC: J and S Corporations are both domestic corporations. J Corporation sells its products to its wholly owned sales DISC, S Corporation. In 19X1, J produces 100 units of ex-port property at a total cost of $5,000, which J transfers to S. S sells the 100 units to a third party for $10,000 and incurs $1,000 of administrative expenses and $2,300 of export promotion expenses.

S's maximum taxable income is calculated as follows:

	4% × Gross receipts ($10,000)	= $400
Plus:	10% × Export promotion expenses ($2,300)	= 230
Equals:	S's maximum taxable income	$630

The transfer price from J to S (or cost of goods sold for the sales DISC S) is:

$$\text{Gross receipts} - \left(\begin{array}{c}\text{DISC taxable income}\end{array} + \text{DISC expenses} + \begin{array}{c}\text{Export promotion expenses}\end{array}\right) = \text{Transfer price}$$

$$\$10,000 - (\$630 + \$1,000 + \$2,300) = \$6,070$$

This transfer price results in J recognizing $1,070 in taxable income [$6,070 (transfer price) − $5,000 (J's total costs)].

Example 2, Commission DISC: J and S Corporations are domestic corporations. J sells its products abroad through its wholly owned commission DISC, S Corporation. In 19X1, J produces 100 units of export property at a total cost of $5,000. S arranges a sale of the 100 units for $10,000 and incurs $1,000 of administrative expenses and export promotion expenses of $2,300. S's maximum taxable income is calculated as follows:

	4% × Gross receipts ($10,000)	= $400
Plus:	10% × Export promotion expenses ($2,300)	= 230
Equals:	S's maximum taxable income	$630

The commission charged to J in this case is:

$$\begin{array}{c}\text{DISC taxable income}\end{array} + \text{DISC expenses} + \begin{array}{c}\text{Export promotion expenses}\end{array} = \begin{array}{c}\text{Commission charged}\end{array}$$

$$\$630 + \$1,000 + \$2,300 = \$3,930$$

J's profit on the sale is the same using the commission DISC as it was when the sales DISC was used—$1,070 [$10,000 − ($5,000 + $3,930)].

THE 50-50 COMBINED TAXABLE INCOME METHOD The 50-50 combined taxable income method also sets a taxable income for the DISC and then determines the transfer price necessary to achieve that taxable income. The taxable income under this rule equals the sum of (1) 50 percent of the combined taxable income of the DISC and its related supplier that may be attributed to the sale of the export property that was transferred, and (2) 10 percent of the export promotion expenses attributable to such receipts. The combined taxable income of the DISC and the related supplier is the difference between the gross receipts from the sale of the export property and the combined expenses of the two corporations. The expenses include expenses that are directly attributable to these sales, such as direct selling costs and export promotion expenses, as well as a ratable portion of expenses that are not directly related to any class of income (Treas. Reg. Sec. 1.861-8).

Calculations of transfer prices for sales DISCs and commission DISCs are illustrated using the same J and S Corporations and information as in the above examples.

Example 1, Sales DISC: Assume the same facts as in Example 1, above.

Calculation of Combined Taxable Income:

Gross receipts		$10,000
Less: J's cost of goods sold	$5,000	
Less: S's administrative expenses	1,000	
Less: S's export promotion expenses	2,300	8,300
Equals: Combined taxable income		$ 1,700

Calculation of DISC Taxable Income:

50% × Combined taxable income ($1,700)		$ 850
Plus: 10% × Export promotion expenses ($2,300)		230
Equals: DISC taxable income		$ 1,080

The transfer price from J to S is now determined to be $5,620 [$10,000 − ($1,080 + $1,000 + $2,300)] using the 50-50 combined taxable income pricing method. This pricing method increases the DISC's taxable income by $450 from that obtained under the 4 percent method (from $630 to $1,080), and consequently the resulting tax benefits obtained from making the DISC election are increased.

Example 2, Commission DISC: Assume the same facts as in Example 2, above. Calculation of combined taxable income and DISC taxable income proceeds as in the preceding example. The maximum amount of commission chargeable by S when using the 50-50 combined taxable income pricing method is determined (from the formula illustrated for a commission DISC in Example 2, above) to be $4,380 ($1,080 + $1,000 + $2,300). As with the sales DISC, the commission DISC's taxable income has increased by $450 to $1,080.

The regulations limit the transfer price that may be used after application of these special pricing rules. Under these rules, the transfer price may not cause the DISC's taxable income to exceed the combined taxable income of the producer and the DISC, thereby forcing the producer to recognize a "loss" on the transaction (Treas. Reg. Sec. 1.994-1(e)).

In addition to the "full costing" pricing rules outlined above, a set of marginal costing pricing rules are found in Treas. Reg. Sec. 1.994-2, which may be used

when a DISC is "seeking to establish or maintain a foreign market" for a product or service in a year, and may provide a larger tax deferral than does full costing.

Taxation of DISC profits

A DISC is exempt from the corporate income tax (Sec. 991). The shareholders of a DISC must recognize certain amounts of DISC income each year, whether or not they receive any actual distributions. The amount of dividends each shareholder recognizes is the sum of any deemed distributions made by the DISC and actual distributions received that are not considered to be a distribution of previously taxed DISC income.

TAXATION OF A CONTINUING DISC For a corporation that continues to qualify as a DISC, seven kinds of deemed distributions are taxable as ordinary income to its shareholders to the extent of current earnings and profits.[3] These deemed distributions are:

1. Gross interest income derived from producers' loans. This type of distribution prevents the producer from deducting the interest expense and the DISC from deferring part of the payment from taxation.
2. Gain on the sale of nonqualified export assets acquired in a nontaxable exchange to the extent of the lesser of the recognized gain or the gain deferred at the time the DISC acquired the property. This provision prevents a DISC from acquiring nonqualified export assets in a nontaxable exchange and then selling the assets so that part of the preacquisition gain escapes current taxation.
3. Gain on the sale of qualified export assets (other than export property) acquired in a nontaxable exchange to the extent of the lesser of the recognized gain or the portion of the gain existing at the time of the DISC's acquisition of the property that would have been recognized as ordinary income had such property been sold.
4. Fifty percent of the taxable income that is attributable to sales of military property including arms, munitions, and implements of war. The remaining 50 percent of this income is included with DISC taxable income in determining the deemed distribution in item 6, with the result that three-fourths or more of military sales income is taxed currently.
5. The portion of DISC taxable income attributable to a base amount of qualified export receipts.

---

[3]Distributions made because of producer's investments (Item 7) may be made up to the amount of the current and accumulated earnings and profits.

6. One-half the DISC's taxable income in excess of the deemed distributions made in items 1–5.

7. The amount of any foreign investment made by producers that is attributable to producers' loans made by the DISC.

8. An amount equal to any illegal bribe or kickback paid by the DISC, as well as a portion of the DISC taxable income related to any international boycotts in which the DISC has participated (Secs. 995(b) and 995(d)).

When Congress was debating the Tax Reform Act of 1976, at which time DISC taxation was modified, it decided that it wanted the tax deferral benefits to accrue only to DISCs that were expanding their export trade. Accordingly, the law now taxes the shareholder *fully* on profits originating from a base amount of the DISC's qualified export receipts but taxes only *one-half* the profits originating from export gross receipts in excess of the base amount (items 5 and 6 above). The distribution attributable to base period receipts is calculated using the following formula:

$$\begin{matrix} \text{Adjusted} \\ \text{taxable} \\ \text{income} \end{matrix} \times \dfrac{0.67 \times \begin{matrix}\text{Average base period} \\ \text{export gross receipts}\end{matrix}}{\text{Current export gross receipts}} = \begin{matrix}\text{Deemed} \\ \text{distribution} \\ \text{attributable} \\ \text{to base} \\ \text{period} \\ \text{receipts}\end{matrix}$$

The DISC's adjusted taxable income represents DISC taxable income minus the four items that were deemed distributed in items 1 through 4, above. Export gross receipts (EGR) means *only* those qualified export receipts derived from the following: the sale, exchange, or lease of export property; the performance of services related and subsidiary to the sale, exchange, or leasing of export property; the performance of certain engineering and architectural services; and the performance of managerial services for other DISCs. Excluded from this amount is one-half of such receipts attributable to military property sales. Average base period EGR is the simple average of such receipts for a four-year base period. The base period for this calculation is the 4th, 5th, 6th, and 7th years preceding the current tax year. As a result of these procedures, the entire amount of DISC taxable income attributable to these base period export gross receipts plus one-half the DISC taxable income remaining after reduction for (a) the base period distribution and (b) any distributions considered to have been made in items 1–4 is deemed to be distributed to the shareholder.

The following example illustrates the calculation of the DISC income taxable to the shareholder.

Example: Multico is a domestic corporation that retains DISC status for taxable year 19X7. Multico has derived the following taxable income:

1. Producers' loans interest	$ 2,000
2. Gain on sale of manufacturing machine acquired in a Sec. 351 exchange	800
3. Gain on sale of warehouse acquired in Sec. 351 nontaxable exchange —all Sec. 1250 income	5,000
4. Taxable income from sale of guns	8,000
5. Other DISC taxable income	173,000
Total DISC taxable income	$188,800

Current year DISC export *gross* receipts are equal to $400,000. All such receipts are considered to be qualified. The average base period export gross receipts for the period 19X1–19X4 equaled $240,000. The following deemed distributions are required of Multico:

1. Producer's loan interest	$ 2,000
2. Gain on sale of machine	800
3. Sec. 1250 recapture on sale of warehouse	5,000
4. One-half of taxable income from military sales	4,000
5. Attributable to base period export gross receipts[4]	71,154
6. One-half of DISC taxable income not included in above[5]	52,923
Total deemed distribution	$135,877

Because of the base period rules and the special provisions, only 28 percent of the DISC profits may be deferred from taxation here rather than the 50 percent theoretical maximum. Had the level of base period export gross receipts been lower, the portion of deferred profits could have approached the theoretical 50 percent amount.

---

[4]$71,154 = $177,000 \times \dfrac{(0.67 \times \$240,000)}{\$400,000}$

Adjusted taxable income = $188,800 − ($2,000 + $800 + $5,000 + $4,000) = $177,000

[5]$1/2 \times [\$188,800 − (\$2,000 + \$800 + \$5,000 + \$4,000 + \$71,154)] = \$52,923$

A special exemption exists for the base period distribution rules when a DISC's adjusted taxable income is $100,000 or less. A DISC having adjusted taxable income between $100,000 and $150,000 receives a partial exemption from the need to make a distribution under these rules.

ACTUAL DISC DISTRIBUTIONS   The DISC distribution scheme somewhat resembles that used for the Subchapter S Corporation. Three "tiers" of earnings and profits exist, which are:

1. *Previously taxed income.* The amount of the DISC's constructive dividend distributions from prior years ordered within the tier by taxable years.
2. *Accumulated DISC income.* The amount of the DISC earnings and profits for a taxable year reduced by the amount of any constructive dividend distributions.
3. *Other earnings and profits.* The amount of any earnings and profits not included in tiers 1 and 2. Generally, this includes only earnings and profits accumulated during taxable years in which the DISC election was not in effect. Dividends from this earnings and profits tier are the only ones eligible for a dividends-received deduction under Sec. 243 (Sec. 996(a)(1) and (f)).

The sequencing of the reduction of the earnings and profits balance for various types of adjustments is as follows:

Adjustment	Sequencing of tiers
1. Ordinary distribution	1, 2, 3
2. Qualifying distribution	2, 3, 1[6]
3. Losses	3, 2, 1 (Secs. 996(a) and (b))

The balance of one tier is reduced to zero before adjustments are made to subsequent tiers. Actual distributions made at any time during the taxable year are treated as being made subsequent to any deemed distributions for the taxable year. Thus, as long as actual distributions made in a year do not exceed the deemed distributions for that year, such distributions are treated as coming out of previously taxed income. Qualifying distributions, however, are treated as being made after the deemed distributions but before the "regular" actual distributions (Sec. 996(c)).

DISC dividends are treated as foreign source income to the extent they are attributable to qualified export receipts (other than interest on producer's loans and gains from the sale or exchange of qualified export assets other than export property) (Sec. 861(a)(2)(D)). As such, foreign taxes attributable to these distributions are creditable.

ADJUSTMENT TO BASIS   Deemed distributions increase the adjusted basis of the shareholder's DISC stock. Actual distributions made out of previously taxed income reduce the adjusted basis for the stock. Distributions made after the adjusted basis of the shareholder's stock has been reduced to zero are treated as gain realized from the sale or exchange of the DISC stock (Sec. 996(e)).

TAXATION WHEN THE DISC TERMINATES   When a DISC terminates its election either willingly or by failing to meet the DISC requirements for five consecutive years, the shareholders are taxed on their pro rata share of the DISC's accumulated earnings.[7] The earnings subject to taxation include only the DISC income on which taxation has been deferred. Because this amount may be quite large and has likely been accumulated over several years' time, taxation in one year would subject the shareholders to a significant tax burden. To ease the burden, the DISC's shareholders may spread the taxation of this income over the number of years equal to two times the number of immediately preceding years during which the corporation has retained DISC status, but not more than 10 years. For example, if a corporation loses its DISC status for a taxable year, after having retained it for the three preceding years, then the accumulated DISC income is taxable over a six-year period (2 x 3 years = 6 years).[8] If DISC status had been retained for the seven preceding taxable years, then such income would be taxable over a 10-year period. Such deemed distributions commence on the last day of the taxable year following the year of disqualification and continue for the requisite time period. Thus, if in the first example above, the DISC election was lost in 19X0, the accumulated DISC earnings would be taxed during the years 19X1–19X6. None of these earnings would, however, be taxed in 19X0.

---

[6]Special rules apply to qualifying distributions made to satisfy the gross receipts test. One-half of such a distribution reduces earnings and profits according to the rules for a qualifying distribution; the remainder follows the rules for an ordinary distribution.

[7]The tax-deferred DISC profits may also be constructively distributed when the DISC election is not in effect for a taxable year because of a failure by the corporation to satisfy one or more of the DISC requirements.

[8]This income is subject to taxation only if the DISC fails to make the necessary deficiency distribution under Sec. 992(c) to retain the DISC tax treatment for the taxable year in question.

TAXATION WHEN SHARES ARE SOLD If there were no special tax consequences on the sale of DISC stock, a shareholder would be able to convert his or her ordinary income into capital gains merely by selling the DISC stock rather than receiving actual distributions. To ensure that the shareholder recognizes ordinary income, Sec. 995(c) provides that all or part of the gain on the sale of DISC stock is taxed as ordinary income. The amount taxed as ordinary income is the lesser of (1) the recognized gain from the sale of the DISC shares or (2) the shareholder's pro rata share of tax-deferred DISC earnings (accumulated DISC income). Any gain on the sale of the DISC shares that exceeds the amount of tax-deferred income is taxed as gain from the sale of stock.

A FOREIGN BRANCH

A U.S. producer choosing to establish facilities abroad may establish a foreign branch operation. A *foreign branch* is an office or establishment of a domestic entity that operates in a foreign country. Establishment of a foreign branch of a domestic parent is, in many ways, quite similar to conducting foreign operations directly. Because a branch is treated for U.S. tax purposes as the same entity as the domestic corporation, gains and losses flow through and are taxed with all other income of the domestic home office in the year the income is earned. Foreign losses may be used immediately to offset domestic profits, but the losses may be "recaptured" in the future when foreign operations are profitable. Even though the recapture provisions may apply, use of the foreign branch losses to offset domestic profits does provide a tax benefit that is unavailable when a foreign subsidiary corporation is used.

If a branch is located in a tax treaty country, its operations generally are taxed locally only if the branch maintains a permanent establishment in that country. If the branch is located in a nontreaty country, local taxation of the foreign income depends on that country's tax laws. Since payments from a branch to its home office are not dividends, the branch form of operations often avoids any withholding taxes that the host country may impose on dividends. A few countries, however, such as Canada, levy an additional tax on remitted branch profits in lieu of the withholding tax.

Another tax advantage of the branch form of operation is that property may be transferred from the domestic operation to the branch without triggering the taxation of appreciation in the property's value. When property is transferred to a foreign corporation, Sec.

367 requires that the taxpayer obtain an advance ruling and include in gross income any appreciation that attaches to certain "tainted" assets (see page **23**/22). Transfer within a single corporation, such as from a domestic office to a foreign branch, does not trigger a tax.

While both direct exporting and branch activity provide some tax benefits, their biggest tax disadvantage is that U.S. taxes on foreign income are not deferred at all. Tax deferral is a frequently sought tax objective because its effect is to give the taxpayer an interest-free loan, equal to the amount of the U.S. taxes that are otherwise due, for the deferral period. If the taxpayer can delay paying taxes to the U.S. taxing authorities, the taxpayer can invest these funds and earn income on them during the deferral period. Because of the operation of the foreign tax credit, however, deferral of U.S. taxation on foreign source income is advantageous only when the foreign effective tax rate is less than the U.S. tax rate. If the effective foreign tax rate equals or exceeds the effective U.S. tax rate, the foreign tax credit eliminates the U.S. tax due and may provide excess foreign tax credits that may offset U.S. taxes currently due on other foreign source income or that may be carried to other years.

POSSESSIONS CORPORATIONS

Domestic corporations doing business in Puerto Rico or in one of the U.S. possessions[9] are taxed on their worldwide income but may claim a special tax credit under Sec. 936. This credit is available whether or not any tax is paid to the possession, and therefore, the special credit has the effect of exempting certain income from U.S. taxation.

The Sec. 936 requirements for corporations are quite similar to the Sec. 931 exclusion provisions (discussed in Chapter 22) available for individuals. In fact, two of the requirements are identical in wording to the Sec. 931 provisions. Section 936 requires that:

1. At least 80 percent of the domestic corporation's gross income for the three-year period immediately preceding the close of the taxable year (or for such part of the three-year period immediately preceding the close of the taxable year as may be applicable) was derived from within a U.S. possession;

2. At least 50 percent of the domestic corporation's gross income for the three-year period immedi-

---

[9]U.S. possessions are defined for purposes of Sec. 936 as Puerto Rico, American Samoa, Guam, Johnston Island, Midway Island, and Wake Island (Treas. Reg. Sec. 1.931-1(a)(1) and Sec. 936(d)(1)).

ately preceding the close of the taxable year (or shorter period, if applicable) was derived from the active conduct of a trade or business in a U.S. possession;

3. The domestic corporation elects to use Sec. 936;

4. The domestic corporation is not a DISC, a former DISC, and did not own stock in a DISC, or a former DISC, during the taxable year (Secs. 936(a)(1), (a)(2), and (f)).

The amount of the Sec. 936 credit is computed as follows:

$$\text{Sec. 936 credit} = \text{Allowed U.S. taxes} \times \frac{\text{Sec. 936 taxable income}}{\text{Worldwide taxable income}}$$

"Allowed U.S. taxes" for this formula is the amount of U.S. income taxes on worldwide taxable income, excluding any of the following taxes that may have been incurred:

1. Minimum tax
2. Accumulated earnings tax
3. Personal holding company tax
4. Taxes levied on recoveries of foreign expropriation losses

Section 936 taxable income is the taxable income from non-U.S. sources derived from: (1) the active conduct of a trade or business in a U.S. possession, (2) the sale or exchange of substantially all the assets used in the conduct of such a trade or business, and (3) qualified possession source investment income. Any gross income that is received by the domestic corporation in the United States (whether from U.S. or non-U.S. sources) will *not* qualify as Sec. 936 taxable income. Qualified possession source investment income is investment income that has its source within a possession in which the domestic corporation actively conducts a trade or business, providing that the corporation can establish that the funds that were invested were derived from their business activities within the same possession. Thus, a U.S. corporation that conducts a business in Puerto Rico may invest its Puerto Rican earnings in a savings account in that country and the interest from the savings account will be qualified possession source investment income. If the Puerto Rican earnings were invested in American Samoa, the interest would not be qualified possession source investment income because the earnings were not invested in the possession in which they were earned.

A number of factors must be considered in deciding whether to use the Sec. 936 credit. First, for an initial 10-year period, the election may be revoked only with I.R.S. consent. After that time it may be revoked for any taxable year without I.R.S. consent. Second, the taxpayer may not claim any deductions or foreign tax credits with respect to income subject to the Sec. 936 credit provisions nor may the taxpayer join in the filing of a consolidated tax return. Thus, a taxpayer's ability to use operating losses and excess foreign tax credits may be restricted. Dividends paid by a corporation electing the Sec. 936 credit, however, are eligible for the 85 or 100 percent dividends-received deduction.

Calculation of the Sec. 936 credit is illustrated in the following example.

Example: Domco, a domestic corporation, engages in the conduct of a Puerto Rican business. Domco had the following results for 19X1:

Type of Income: Manufacturing operations:

Source of income	Place of receipt by Domco	Taxable income
Puerto Rico	Puerto Rico	$355,000
Puerto Rico	United States	15,000
United States	United States	60,000
	Subtotal	$430,000

Investment income:

Source of income	Place of receipt by Domco	Taxable income
Puerto Rico	Puerto Rico	$ 85,000
United States	United States	10,000
	Subtotal	$ 95,000
	Total Taxable Income	$525,000

Assuming Domco is eligible for the credit, its Sec. 936 credit is determined as follows:

Gross U.S. tax liability on $525,000 = $222,250

$$\text{Sec. 936 credit} = \text{Gross U.S. tax liability } (\$222,250) \times \frac{\text{Qualifying taxable income } (\$355,000 + \$85,000)}{\text{Worldwide taxable income } (\$525,000)}$$

$$= \$186,267$$

Net U.S. tax liability = $222,250 − $186,267 = $35,983

Domco is thus required to pay U.S. corporate income taxes at its 42.33 percent overall effective tax rate only on the $85,000 of income that is received in the United States.[10]

WESTERN HEMISPHERE TRADE CORPORATIONS

For taxable years ending before January 1, 1980, a special deduction (and permanent exemption from U.S. taxation) was available for domestic corporations that derived most of their gross income from non-U.S. sources and that conducted nearly all their trade or business activities in the Western Hemisphere (Sec. 921(a)). Section 922 provided a special deduction equal to a certain fraction of the Western Hemisphere Trade Corporation's (WHTC's) taxable income. For most pre-1976 taxable years, this special deduction equaled 14/48ths of the WHTC's taxable income. The WHTC provisions were phased out by the Tax Reform Act of 1976 over the period 1976–1979 and are no longer available to taxpayers (Sec. 922(b)).

NONSPECIAL TAX STATUS FOREIGN CORPORATIONS

A U.S. individual or corporation may decide to do business abroad by buying shares in a foreign corporation or by forming a new foreign corporation. Unless the foreign business falls under the definition of a controlled foreign corporation (CFC), or a foreign personal holding company (FPHC), each of which is discussed below, the U.S. taxation of the investment is, in general, quite simple. The tax on the foreign corporation's earnings is deferred until such time as the U.S. investor receives a share of those earnings as a dividend. When a dividend from a foreign corporation is received by a U.S. corporation (but generally *not* by a U.S. individual), the U.S. corporation may claim a deemed paid credit for foreign taxes paid on the earnings (see Chapter 21). In these cases the U.S. investor corporation will not be able to claim a dividends-received deduction, but the result is not likely to be double taxation on the distributed income since the foreign corporation generally has paid no previous U.S. taxes on its income. The foreign corporation's losses may not be used to offset the U.S. parent's earnings unless the

subsidiary belongs to a limited class of Mexican or Canadian subsidiaries permitted to join in the filing of a consolidated tax return (Sec. 1504(d)). Sale or exchange of the foreign corporation stock is ordinarily treated as the disposition of a capital asset and triggers the recognition of a capital gain or loss.

FOREIGN PERSONAL HOLDING COMPANIES (FPHC)

The use of a separate corporate entity and the corporation tax structure has long been seen by individual taxpayers as a potential tax-saving device. The combination of the corporation's favorable tax structure and the potential deferral and savings of a foreign corporation makes the foreign personal holding company (FPHC) an almost irresistible tax-planning tool. Congress understood these consequences quite as well as the taxpayers, and accordingly, in 1937 it enacted the FPHC provisions that are now contained in Secs. 551–558. These sections provide that U.S. citizens and residents who own stock in a foreign personal holding company must report their pro rata share of the entity's undistributed FPHC income. The FPHC income is treated as a constructive dividend, distributed to the U.S. person, and which is immediately reinvested in the holding company's capital.

A foreign personal holding company exists only if the following three requirements are met:

1. The corporation must be a foreign corporation that is not of a type exempt from the Subpart F provisions[11] (Secs. 951–964).
2. In the first year a corporation qualifies as a foreign personal holding company, 60 percent or more of its gross income must be FPHC income. In subsequent years, only 50 percent of its gross income must be FPHC income.
3. At some time during the corporation's tax year, more than 50 percent of the value (not the voting power) of the outstanding stock must be owned directly, indirectly, or constructively by five or fewer individuals who are U.S. citizens or residents (Sec. 552).

Items of FPHC income include dividends, interest, royalties, annuities, net gains on stocks and securities transactions, certain net gains from commodities trades, trust or estate income (as well as the gain on

---

[10]$\frac{\$222,250}{\$525,000} \times 100\% = 42.33\%.$

[11]Organizations exempt from Subpart F are corporations exempt from tax under Sec. 501 and certain foreign banking corporations.

the sale of an interest in an estate or trust), income from personal service contracts where the individual to perform the services can be designated by the purchaser, income from the use of a foreign personal holding company's property by certain 25 percent shareholders, and rents (Sec. 553(a)). Rents are FPHC income unless they represent 50 percent or more of the corporation's gross income (Sec. 553(a)(7)). These income items are quite similar to those classified as personal holding company income for a domestic corporation under Sec. 543 (see Chapter 19). It should be noted that the U.S. shareholder is not taxed on his or her pro rata share of the kinds of FPHC income listed above but rather is taxed on his or her share of undistributed FPHC income. Undistributed FPHC income is defined by Sec. 556(b) as the corporation's total taxable income reduced by the amount of dividends paid, taxes paid, and certain other adjustment items.

The provisions of the FPHC sections and the Subpart F provisions described below are mutually exclusive. If a U.S. shareholder is taxed currently on certain income forms under the Subpart F income provisions of the CFC rules, the taxpayer is not again taxed on such income forms in the same year under the foreign personal holding company rules. He or she may have to recognize otherwise excluded income earned by a CFC that qualifies as an FPHC, however, when it is invested in U.S. property that is taxable under Sec. 951 (a)(1)(B).[12]

CONTROLLED FOREIGN CORPORATIONS

Before the administration of John F. Kennedy, multinational firms used the tax deferrals available to foreign corporations to minimize their total tax on foreign operations. Following the usual scenario, a domestic corporation formed a foreign corporation in a country having little or no income taxes levied on transactions occurring outside the country of incorporation. These tax-haven foreign corporations would then send salespeople to other countries from the tax-haven base. Orders could be forwarded by the foreign corporation to the domestic corporation, with the goods being sent to the foreign corporation for distribution to the customer, or the orders could be sent directly to the parent corpo-

ration, which shipped the goods directly to the customer, with only the billing and clerical details being handled by the foreign corporation. With this procedure, earnings accrued to the foreign subsidiary, but they were not taxed to the domestic parent until they were paid out as dividends. The foreign subsidiary could even invest such earnings in U.S. property without any U.S. tax assessment. The foreign subsidiary paid little if any local tax, because the sales activity did not occur in the host country. The sales transactions themselves caused little if any taxation since few countries tax business activity occurring without a permanent establishment located within the country.

Subpart F of the Internal Revenue Code (Secs. 951–964) was enacted as part of the Revenue Act of 1962 largely to prevent this form of tax avoidance. In part, the "Subpart F income" provisions of Sec. 952 (to be described below) assess a tax on the U.S. shareholders of certain foreign corporations (but not on the foreign corporations themselves) engaging in transactions from a foreign base company in an activity like that described above that generates foreign base company income (see Figure 23-1). Three other types of profits are also taxed currently under the "Subpart F income" rules, even though they may not be connected with a base company activity. Two of these profit forms result from specific activities conducted by the foreign corporation and include any profits derived (1) from the insurance of U.S. risks and (2) from foreign boycott-related activities. The third type of currently taxed earnings occurs because the foreign corporation makes prohibited payments. The deferral privilege available to U.S. shareholders is lost for an amount of foreign profits equal to any illegal bribes, kickbacks, or other payments made by the foreign corporation. In addition, the Subpart F provisions levy a tax on these U.S. shareholders when the foreign corporation increases its investments in U.S. property (Sec. 956), or when it withdraws Subpart F income (that has been deferred from current taxation under one of the exceptions to the Subpart F rules) from investments in (1) "qualified" shipping investments; (2) less developed countries; or (3) export trade assets. Details of each of the various income forms are illustrated below.

Definition of controlled foreign corporation

THE 50 PERCENT VOTING POWER TEST   Most foreign corporations are organized in such a way that they do not fall under the terms of Subpart F because Subpart F applies only if a foreign corporation is a Controlled Foreign Corporation (CFC). A CFC is a foreign corpo-

[12]*Estate of Leonard E. Whitlock* v. *Commissioner,* 547 F.2d 506 (CCA-10, 1977) *rev'g.* and *aff'g.* 59 TC 490 (1973). A comparison of the FPHC provisions and the CFC provisions may be found in: W. Allen Barnett, "Effects of Differences Between Provisions Covering Foreign PHCs and CFCs," *Journal of Taxation,* October 1974, pp. 236–38.

FIGURE **23-1**   Amount of Income of a Controlled Foreign Corporation
Ordinarily Included in Gross Income of U.S. Shareholders

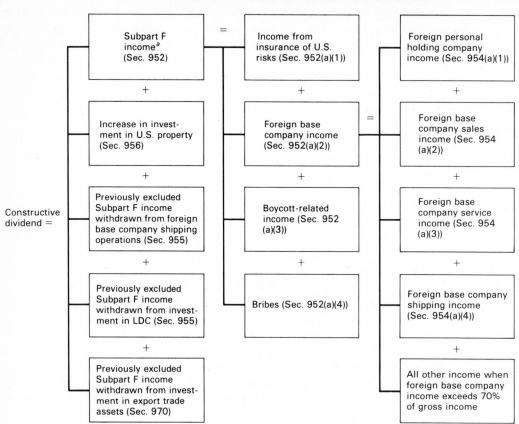

a Subpart F Income does *not* include:
1. Foreign base company income if it is less than 10 percent of gross income.
2. Foreign base company shipping income reinvested in qualified investments in "foreign base company shipping operations."
3. U.S. source income of the CFC that is effectively connected with the conduct of a U.S. trade or business.
4. Blocked foreign income.
5. Income earned by a corporation that the I.R.S. is satisfied was not organized to reduce taxes.

ration having more than 50 percent of its voting stock held by "U.S. shareholders." Thus, a French corporation owned equally by a U.S. corporation and an unrelated Swiss corporation is not a CFC since "U.S. shareholders" do not possess more than one-half the voting power of the firm. Notice that the test is whether more than one-half the *voting power* is held and not whether one-half the *value* of the stock is held. If only one class of voting stock is outstanding, this test is straightforward. If more than one class of voting stock is outstanding, the test is basically one of determining whether the "U.S. shareholders" may elect more than one-half the board of directors.

The application of the CFC voting requirements to a foreign corporation having more than one class of stock may be seen in the following example.

Example: Forco, a foreign corporation, has two classes of stock outstanding. Class A stock has 50

shares outstanding and a majority of its voting power may elect six directors. Class B stock has 100 shares outstanding, and a majority of its voting power may elect the remaining four directors. Each share of stock has one vote in directorship elections. Mr. Sims, a U.S. citizen, owns 31 shares of Class A stock, while all the remaining Class A shares and all the Class B shares are owned by unrelated foreign persons. By virtue of owning a majority (31 shares) of the Class A stock, Mr. Sims is classified as a U.S. shareholder because he may elect 6 of 10 directors. Forco qualifies as a CFC, even though Mr. Sims does not own more than one-half the outstanding voting stock (Treas. Reg. Sec. 1.957-1(c) Example (2)).

The voting power test is not a mechanical test. Paper arrangements to shift voting control from U.S. shareholders will not be recognized by the I.R.S. if the

U.S. shareholders actually maintain the ability to exercise voting control. If expressed or implied arrangements exist so that U.S. shareholders who do not have nominal control actually do exercise control, the foreign corporation may still be treated as a CFC[13] (Treas. Reg. Sec. 1.957-1(b)).

U.S. SHAREHOLDERS   The voting power test must be met by U.S. shareholders if the foreign corporation is to be designated a CFC. A U.S. shareholder is a "U.S. person" who owns directly, indirectly, or constructively 10 percent or more of the total combined voting power of all classes of stock entitled to vote in the foreign corporation (Sec. 951(b)). Therefore, if a foreign corporation is owned by 11 U.S. individuals, who each own 9 percent of the single class of stock, the corporation has *no* U.S. shareholders and, thus, cannot be a CFC. For purposes of this definition, a U.S. person is an individual citizen or resident of the United States, a domestic partnership, a domestic corporation, or a domestic trust or estate (Sec. 957(d)).

STOCK OWNERSHIP RULES   To calculate the ownership percentages for the 50 percent test of CFC status and the 10 percent test for U.S. shareholder status, the indirect and constructive ownership rules of Sec. 958 must be applied. The indirect stock ownership rules of Sec. 958(a) attribute to a U.S. person any stock ownership in a foreign corporation that the U.S. person owns indirectly through a second foreign corporation, a foreign partnership, a foreign estate, or a foreign trust. The stock is considered to be owned in proportion to the U.S. person's proportionate ownership or beneficial interest. These rules are so structured to prevent their application in a chain of ownership beyond the first U.S. person. The ownership of a foreign corporation's stock by a domestic corporation thus may not be attributed by the indirect ownership rules to the domestic corporation's shareholders (Sec. 958(a)(2)).

Section 958(b) incorporates the corporate attribution rules of Sec. 318 (see Chapter 5) and provides some modifications to the rules. The major modifications to the Sec. 318 attribution rules under the Sec. 958(b) constructive ownership rules are explained below:

(a)   *Family attribution.* A nonresident alien family member's stock is not attributed to a resident alien or citizen.

(b)   *Attribution from a partnership, estate, trust, or corporation.*

(1)   Stock owned by a corporation in a second corporation is generally considered under Sec. 318 to be owned by the investor corporation's shareholders in proportion to their ownership of the investor corporation's stock. For the CFC rules, only shareholders who own 10 percent or more of the investor corporation's stock will have any stock ownership attributed to them under this rule.

(2)   If a partnership, estate, trust, or corporation owns directly or indirectly more than 50 percent of the stock of a corporation, it is considered to own *all* the stock of the corporation.

(c)   *Attribution to a partnership, estate, trust, or corporation.* Attribution of shares held by a non-U.S. person to a partnership, estate, trust, or corporation for reattribution to a U.S. person is not permitted.

When different amounts of stock ownership occur under both the indirect and constructive ownership rules, the U.S. shareholder is considered to own the greater of the two levels of ownership. Double counting of stock ownership by the same shareholder, or among shareholders when applying the 50 percent test, is not permitted. Stock may be considered owned by two or more persons for purposes of the U.S. shareholder test.

The following two examples illustrate these attribution rules.

Example 1:   Mr. Smith, a U.S. citizen, owns 9 percent of Forco, a foreign corporation, and 10 percent of Domco, a domestic corporation. Mr. Jones, a U.S. person, owns 32 percent of Forco. Domco itself owns 10 percent of Forco directly. Is Mr. Smith a U.S. shareholder?

Yes, he owns 9 percent directly and 1 percent (10 percent of 10 percent) indirectly through his ownership of Domco. If all other shareholders are foreign persons, is Forco a CFC? Yes, Forco is 51 percent owned by three U.S. shareholders: Mr. Smith owns 9 percent; Domco owns 10 percent; and Mr. Jones owns 32 percent. Notice that Mr. Smith's ownership is only 9 percent for purposes of applying the 50 percent test since the 1 percent he owns indirectly (or constructively) through Domco may not be counted twice (Treas. Reg. Sec. 1.958-2(f) Example (2)).

Example 2:   Mr. Kase owns 20 percent of the stock of Forco, a foreign corporation, and Forco owns 60 percent of the stock of Forco-S, a second foreign corporation. How much of Forco-S stock is

[13]*Garlock, Inc,* v. *Commissioner,* 489 F.2d 197 (CCA-2, 1974) *aff'g.* 58 TC 423 (1972); *Hans P. Kraus* v. *Commissioner,* 490 F.2d 898 (CCA-2, 1974) *aff'g.* 59 TC 681 (1973); *Koehring Co.* v. *Commissioner,* 583 F.2d 313 (CCA-7, 1978) *aff'g.* 433 F.Supp. 929 (DC- Wis., 1977).

Mr. Kase considered to own? Indirectly, Mr. Kase is considered to own 12 percent of Forco-S (20 percent of 60 percent). Because of the (b)(2) rule, above, Forco's ownership of Forco-S is increased from 60 percent to 100 percent for the constructive ownership rules. Therefore, Mr. Kase constructively owns 20 percent of Forco-S (20 percent of 100 percent) for computing the tests for CFC status and U.S. shareholder status.

Gross income of U.S. shareholders

Section 951 provides that U.S. shareholders must include in their income the sum of their pro rata share of the increase of the foreign corporation's earnings invested in U.S. property, Subpart F income, and previously excluded Subpart F income withdrawn from investments in shipping operations, from investments in less developed countries, or from investments in export trade assets. Each of these types of income is discussed in the sections that follow.

INVESTMENT IN U.S. PROPERTY   A U.S. shareholder who controls a foreign corporation may also be able to control its business operations, including the method and timing of distributions of earnings. Before the Revenue Act of 1962, some shareholders had their controlled foreign corporations either invest corporate funds directly in assets located in the United States or make loans to the shareholder instead of paying dividends. In many cases, the U.S. shareholder effectively received use of the foreign corporation's earnings without paying either the U.S. tax that would have been levied had a dividend been received or a foreign withholding tax.

To prevent tax avoidance through such methods, the Subpart F provisions require the U.S. shareholder to include in his income his pro rata share of the increase in earnings of the foreign corporation that are invested in U.S. property at the close of the taxable year to the extent that the earnings would have been taxed as a dividend if they had been distributed. Earnings invested in U.S. property are taxed currently, even if they were generated by foreign earnings that were not covered by Subpart F and, therefore, would not have been taxed currently without the U.S. investment.

For purposes of this section, U.S. property includes tangible property located in the United States, an obligation of a U.S. person, and any patent, copyright, invention, model, design, secret formula, or process that is acquired or developed by the CFC for use in the United States. Stock or obligations of domestic corporations are U.S. property only if the domestic corporation itself is a U.S. shareholder, or if any U.S. shareholder of the CFC owns 25 percent or more of the voting power of the domestic corporation. To encourage foreign deposits in U.S. banks, Congress has stated that obligations of the United States and U.S. bank deposits are not to be considered U.S. property (Sec. 956(b)). The amount of the investment in U.S. property is the adjusted basis of the U.S. property reduced by any liability to which the property is subject (Sec. 956(a)(3)).

To compute the U.S. shareholder's income inclusion because of CFC investments in U.S. property, we must determine the increase in the investment in U.S. property that would have been characterized as a dividend if it had been paid out. The first step is to compare the amount of the investment in U.S. property at the end of the current year with the foreign corporation's current and accumulated earnings and profits that have not been subject to taxation under the investment in U.S. property rules. Second, the amount of investment from the preceding year-end that could have been treated as a dividend must be reduced by the amount of any distributions to the shareholders during the current tax year that were made tax free to the U.S. shareholders because they consisted of amounts previously taxed to the shareholders under the investment in U.S. property provisions. The difference between the amount determined for the current year-end and the amount determined for the preceding year-end (reduced by subsequent tax-free distributions) represents the increase in earnings invested in U.S. property. Any portion of this increase that has been previously taxed as Subpart F income is exempt from U.S. taxation. (Because of this exemption, any earnings that have been taxed as Subpart F income generally may be invested in U.S. property without incurring any additional U.S. tax consequences.) Each U.S. shareholder is then taxed on his or her pro rata share of the increase in earnings invested in U.S. property in excess of this exempt amount.

An example will help clarify the process:

Example: Multico, a domestic corporation, owns 60 percent of the only class of Multico-X stock. Multico-X is a CFC that was incorporated in Country X on January 1, 19X1. At the end of 19X4, Multico-X had an investment in U.S. property of $150,000—all of which would constitute a dividend if distributed. At the end of 19X4, Multico-X's current and accumulated earnings and profits was $150,000. During 19X5, Multico-X accrued $200,000 of earnings and profits, of which $50,000 was taxed as Subpart F income, and increased its investment in U.S. property to $250,000. The portion of the 19X5 increase in investment in U.S. property that is currently taxable to Multico is determined as follows:

Aggregate investment in U.S. property on December 31, 19X5		$250,000
Current and accumulated E & P on December 31, 19X5 ($150,000 + $200,000 = $350,000)		$350,000
Amount of earnings invested in U.S. property that would constitute a dividend if distributed		$250,000
Less: December 31, 19X4 investment in U.S. property that would constitute a dividend	$150,000	
Less: Distributions of earnings previously invested in U.S. property and taxed to the U.S. shareholder	-0-	150,000
Increase in earnings invested in U.S. property		$100,000

Because $50,000 of the $100,000 was already subject to tax under the Subpart F rules, however, only the $50,000 portion of this increase that is untaxed by Subpart F is taxable. Multico's pro rata share of this amount is $30,000 (0.60 × $50,000 = $30,000).

SUBPART F INCOME   Subpart F income comprises income from the insurance of U.S. risks, foreign base company income (FBCI), boycott-related income, and an amount equivalent to the bribes paid by the foreign corporation (Sec. 952(a)). Each of the four kinds of Subpart F income is explained below.

An exception to the current taxation of Subpart F income occurs when the CFC itself is taxed on its "tainted" earnings. If the CFC pays the U.S. taxes on "tainted" U.S. source income at the full U.S. corporate tax rates because it is effectively connected with the conduct of a U.S. trade or business, the U.S. shareholder does not have to include the "tainted" income in

the determination of Subpart F income. If this "tainted" U.S. source income is exempt from U.S. taxation, or is taxed at a reduced rate because of treaty provisions, the U.S. shareholder must include such income as part of Subpart F income (Sec. 952(b)).

1. Insurance of U.S. risks.   Before the enactment of the Revenue Act of 1962, domestic corporations could save taxes by establishing a foreign insurance subsidiary. If the domestic corporation simply chose to self-insure, no amounts were deductible except for casualty losses. If, however, the domestic corporation set up a foreign insurance subsidiary, the domestic company could deduct its premiums, and the affiliated foreign corporation paid no U.S. tax on its income. Section 953 now requires a U.S. shareholder of a CFC to include the income derived from the insurance of U.S. risks in the shareholder's own tax return. To avoid compliance problems for CFCs that insure very few U.S. risks, a 5 percent *de minimus* rule was included in the law (Sec. 953(a)). Under this rule, if the premiums from coverage of U.S. risks are no more than 5 percent of total premiums received by the CFC in a taxable year, the U.S. shareholders do not have to recognize any of the income derived from the insurance of U.S. risks. Income from the insurance of U.S. risks includes premiums for property insurance on U.S. property, premiums for liability insurance coverage for U.S. activities, premiums for life and health insurance on a U.S. resident, and premiums for insurance issued as part of an artificial arrangement for tax avoidance. These artificial arrangements usually involve a CFC that insures non-U.S. risks in return for a non-CFC issuing insurance with substantially the same premiums on U.S. risks. This indirect coverage is deemed to be a U.S. risk and, therefore, is subject to taxation under the CFC rules (Sec. 953(a)).

2. Foreign base company income (FBCI). Foreign base company income comprises four kinds of income: foreign personal holding company income, foreign base company sales income, foreign base company services income, and foreign base company shipping income. Each of these four kinds of income is discussed below. Having income in these four categories, however, does not always result in a tax to the U.S. shareholder. Three exceptions exist to inclusions of these income types as Subpart F income: the 10-70 rule, the rule for foreign corporations not availed of to reduce taxes, and the aforementioned rule for U.S. source income that is derived from the conduct of a U.S. trade or business.

(a) Foreign personal holding company income. Foreign personal holding company income may be earned either by a CFC or by a foreign personal hold-

ing company (FPHC). The rules set out in Secs. 551–558, which determine if a foreign corporation is a foreign personal holding company, were briefly explained earlier in this chapter (see pages **23**/12–13). A CFC may have FPHC income without meeting all the qualifications for being a foreign personal holding company. The FPHC income of these CFCs is taxed as Subpart F income. However, if the U.S. shareholder is subject to tax under the FPHC provisions, the FPHC income is *not* taxed again under the Subpart F provisions.

For Subpart F purposes, FPHC income generally uses the definition found in Sec. 553 as modified by Sec. 954. The major modification excludes from Subpart F taxation certain transactions among related persons that otherwise would generate FPHC income. Rents and royalties received from related persons[14] are not FPHC income if they are for the use of property within the CFC's country of incorporation. Dividends and interest are not FPHC income if they are received from related persons created or organized in the CFC's country of incorporation and those related persons have a substantial part of their assets involved in a trade or business in that same country (Secs. 954(c)(3) and (4)).

Rents generally are included in the definition of FPHC income used for Subpart F purposes without regard to the 50 percent exception found in the FPHC rules. In addition to the related party exception indicated above, rents and royalties received by a CFC from an unrelated party are excluded from the FPHC income definition if connected with the CFC's active conduct of a trade or business (Sec. 954(c)(2) and (3)).

(b) Foreign base company sales income.   Foreign base company sales income is the fees and profits that result from the sale or purchase of personal property when a related party is involved in a transaction in which the property in question was both manufactured or produced *and* sold for use outside the CFC's country of incorporation. Specifically, four kinds of transactions may generate foreign base company sales income:

1.   The purchase of personal property from a related person and its resale to *any* person;
2.   The sale of personal property to *any* person on behalf of a related person;

3.   The purchase of personal property from *any* person and its resale to a related person;
4.   The purchase of personal property from *any* person on behalf of a related person (Sec. 954(d)).

Foreign base company sales income is *not* produced if the product sold is (1) manufactured in the CFC's country of incorporation, (2) sold for *use* in the CFC's country of incorporation, or (3) manufactured by the CFC itself. All three of these exceptions are concerned with the tax avoidance strategy that the Subpart F rules tried to eliminate. If any of these three exceptions are applicable, such a tax avoidance strategy is deemed not to be in use.

Manufacturing or production of property is defined by the Subpart F rules as involving a substantial transformation of the product. Whenever component parts are involved, the CFC's direct labor and overhead must account for 20 percent or more of the product's total cost of goods sold in order for manufacturing to be deemed to have taken place (Treas. Reg. Sec. 1.954-3(a)(4)).

(c) Foreign base company services income.   Without the foreign base company services income provision, a CFC could be used in numerous situations to shift income from a domestic parent corporation or another CFC without the income being taxed under Subpart F. For example, the domestic parent corporation could make sales but have the CFC contract for all services, such as installations, warranty repairs, and maintenance. If the CFC were organized in a tax-haven country and performed the services outside its base country, generally little if any tax would be levied on the services income. The inclusion of foreign base company services income as part of Subpart F income, however, prevents this tax avoidance.

Foreign base company service income comprises compensation, fees or commissions for the performance of certain service activities, such as "technical, managerial, engineering, architectural, scientific, skilled, industrial, commercial or like services" (Treas. Reg. Sec. 1.954-4(a)). Examples of services that may fall into these categories are the installation and maintenance services on machinery, drilling of oil wells, and construction of dams, highways, and buildings.

The income from such service activities will be taxed under Subpart F only if they are both (1) performed for or on behalf of a related person and (2) are performed outside the country in which the CFC is created or organized (Sec. 954(e)). In general, for purposes of determining whether foreign base company services income exists, the services are considered to be

---

[14]A related person is: (1) any individual, partnership, trust, or estate that controls the CFC; (2) any corporation that controls, or is controlled by the CFC; or (3) any corporation that is controlled by the same person or persons who control the CFC (Sec. 954(d)(3)). Control is defined as direct, indirect, or constructive ownership of more than 50 percent of the CFC's total combined voting power.

performed in the place where the person performing the services is physically located at the time. When services are performed in more than one country, the income must be apportioned between the countries, based on the time spent in each country as well as on the relative value of services performed (Treas. Reg. Sec. 1.954-4(c)).

(d) Foreign base company shipping income. Foreign base company shipping income is income derived by the CFC from the use of any aircraft or vessel in foreign commerce, and income derived from the hiring or leasing of such a vessel for use in foreign commerce by another person. In addition, foreign base company shipping income includes income derived from services performed for a person who is the owner, lessor, or operator of an aircraft or vessel used in foreign commerce that is directly related to shipping—for example, cargo handling, terminal services, maintenance and repairs, pilot and crew training, and services of a booking or managing agent. Also included in the foreign base company shipping income definition are incidental services related to shipping activities that are performed by the operator of the aircraft or vessel for unrelated persons. Such incidental services include services for passengers or consignors (for example, rental of staterooms and berths); services for passengers aboard the vessel (for example, barbershop and other service facilities); and demurrage, dispatch, and dead freight. Gains on the sale or exchange of an aircraft or vessel used in these activities are also foreign base company shipping income (Sec. 954(f)). Shipping income that arises from the use of an aircraft or vessel between two points within the foreign country in which the CFC is created *and* in which the aircraft or vessel is registered is excluded from Subpart F income (Sec. 954(b)(7)).

Section 955(g) provides that a CFC may avoid recognizing foreign base company shipping income by increasing its investment in "qualified foreign base company shipping operations" (as defined by Sec. 955(b)) by the amount of the year's "tainted" shipping earnings. This provision simply allows a CFC to defer its tax on foreign base company shipping operations as long as earnings are used to increase shipping operations. Whenever qualified investment in shipping operations is reduced, this tax deferral ends and a pro rata portion of the amount of the decrease is taxed to the U.S. shareholders (Sec. 955(a)).

(e) Exceptions to foreign base company income. In general, the foreign base company income taxable under Subpart F is simply the sum of foreign personal holding company income, foreign base company sales income, foreign base company services income, and foreign base company shipping income. Three major exceptions to this generalization, however, must be considered by the CFC shareholder. The first exception for U.S. trade or business income derived by the CFC was explained above. The remaining two exceptions are explained below.

The second exception is known as the "10-70 rule." The 10-70 rule provides that if the CFC's foreign base company income represents less than 10 percent of its total gross income, then no part of the CFC's income is treated as foreign base company income. This allows a company with very little of the tax avoidance behavior at which these sections are aimed to defer all its income for U.S. tax purposes. At the other end of the spectrum, if the CFC's foreign base company income represents more than 70 percent of its total gross income for a tax year, then all the CFC's income is treated as foreign base company income (Sec. 954(b)(3)). Only if the CFC's foreign base company income is between 10 and 70 percent of total gross income is the actual amount of foreign base company income taxed under Subpart F.

The third exception to the foreign base company income rules provides that an income item earned by the CFC is exempt from the foreign base company income rules if the CFC, or its U.S. shareholder, can demonstrate that the foreign corporation was not availed of to reduce taxes (Sec. 954(b)(4)). Avoidance of the foreign base company rules through the use of the Sec. 954(b)(4) exception is illustrated in the following example.

> *Example:* Rurco, a CFC, was organized in Ruritania to control and manage a group of Ruritanian radio and television stations. Each station was a wholly owned subsidiary. Ruritania modified its laws and required that a controlling interest in all communications corporations be owned by Ruritania's citizens. Accordingly, Rurco sold a 51 percent interest in each subsidiary to Ruritanian citizens. The gain Rurco realized on this sale of stock would not be Subpart F income (foreign personal holding company income) because neither the formation of the CFC nor the sale transaction was undertaken in any way to reduce taxes.

3. Boycott-related income. In the mid-1970s, considerable concern existed that some foreign countries were requiring participation in boycotts against particular other nations as a requirement for doing business. Because of this concern, the Tax Reform Act of 1976 imposed economic penalties for participation in boycotts. One of these penalties is an addition to Subpart F income for boycott-related income. *Boycott-related income* is defined by Sec. 952(a)(3) as the lesser of the CFC's actual income earned from boycott-related activities or:

$$\left[\begin{array}{ccc} \text{All} & \text{Income recognized by} & \text{Income taxed as} \\ \text{CFC} - & \text{the U.S. shareholder} - & \text{connected with} \\ \text{income} & \text{under other CFC} & \text{a U.S. trade or} \\ & \text{provisions} & \text{business} \end{array}\right]$$

$$\times \begin{array}{c} \text{International} \\ \text{boycott} \\ \text{factor} \end{array} = \begin{array}{c} \text{Boycott} \\ \text{related} \\ \text{income} \end{array}$$

The *international boycott factor* is a fraction, the numerator of which represents operations in or related to countries that are associated with an international boycott and the denominator of which represents worldwide operations. Operations are defined in terms of purchases made, sales made, and payroll paid by the corporation (Sec. 999(c)).

    4. Bribes. During the mid-1970s, numerous companies admitted to paying bribes, kickbacks, and other illegal payments to foreign governments through their foreign corporations. Under the Tax Reform Act of 1976, an amount equal to the sum of all bribes, kickbacks, and other illegal payments paid by, or on behalf of, a CFC is to be included in a company's Subpart F income. The tainted payments included in Subpart F income represent amounts paid to any official, employee, or agent of a government that are considered nondeductible under Sec. 162(c) (Sec. 952(a)(4)). Thus, the end result of making these payments is that the deferral privilege is lost for a portion of the CFC's profits equal to the amount of these illegal payments.

DEDUCTIONS RELATED TO SUBPART F INCOME   The foreign base company income rules permit the gross income recognized as a result of tainted transactions to be reduced by any deductions allocated and apportioned to the income under the Sec. 1.861-8 regulations described earlier. These same rules also apply to tainted insurance income, boycott-related income, bribe-related income, and excluded U.S. trade or business income (Treas. Reg. Sec. 1.861-8(f)(1)(v) and (vi)(J), (K), and (L)).

PREVIOUSLY EXCLUDED INCOME   U.S. shareholders of a CFC must include in gross income their share of two types of previously excluded income, along with their share of the increased investments in U.S. property and

Subpart F income.[15] As explained above, foreign base company shipping income may be excluded from foreign base company income if investments in foreign base company shipping operations are increased. When investments in foreign base company shipping operations are withdrawn, this previously excluded income is taxed (Sec. 955(a)(2)).

    Before the Tax Reduction Act of 1975, a CFC could defer certain Subpart F income generated by making investments in a group of nations designated as "less developed countries."[16] The Tax Reduction Act of 1975 repealed these provisions. Amounts that had been invested in less developed countries while the prior law was in effect, however, remained excluded from the Subpart F income definition as long as the investments were not reduced. Accordingly, withdrawal of investments in these less developed countries will result in taxation of the withdrawn amounts (Sec. 951(a)(1)(A)(ii)).

Blocked income

Section 964(b) permits a U.S. shareholder to avoid recognizing a Sec. 951 constructive distribution for any of the income forms taxable under the Subpart F provisions if the U.S. shareholders can show that the earnings could not have been distributed by the CFC because of currency or other restrictions imposed by a foreign country. Such restrictions generally have to run throughout the 90 days preceding and the 60 days following the end of the CFC's taxable year. The income becomes taxable to the U.S. shareholder in the year the restriction is removed.

Distributions from a CFC

U.S. shareholders are taxed on their pro rata share of the types of CFC income described above only when the foreign corporation retains CFC status for at least 30 days during its taxable year. If this requirement is met, each U.S. shareholder who owns stock on the last day of the CFC's taxable year must include his or her pro rata share of these income forms in gross income as a deemed distribution (Sec. 951(a)(1)). In addition,

[15]An export trade corporation was a CFC that sold certain U.S.-produced products in foreign countries. Its Subpart F income could be reduced by the portion of its income that was characterized as export trade income and was invested in export trade assets (Sec. 970(a)). No additional CFCs have been able to qualify as export trade corporations since 1971 because of the enactment of the DISC rules, but withdrawals of Subpart F income excluded from taxation earlier because of investment in export trade assets has triggered limited recognition of income by a limited number of U.S. shareholders since that date.

[16]The Less Developed Countries are listed in Treas. Reg. Sec. 1.955-4(b).

such U.S. shareholders may have to include some part of certain actual distributions made by the CFC in their income. Since year-end ownership is required, a U.S. shareholder may avoid taxation on a year's worth of Subpart F earnings merely by selling stock before year-end. For U.S. shareholders at year-end, the CFC income to be recognized is calculated as follows:

$$
\begin{array}{c}
\text{Pro rata} \\
\text{share of} \\
\text{Subpart F} \\
\text{income for} \\
\text{a U.S.} \\
\text{shareholder}
\end{array}
=
\begin{array}{c}
\text{Subpart F} \\
\text{income}
\end{array}
\times
\begin{array}{c}
\text{Percent of} \\
\text{stock directly} \\
\text{owned by} \\
\text{U.S.} \\
\text{shareholders}
\end{array}
\times
\begin{array}{c}
\text{Portion of} \\
\text{year} \\
\text{(in days)} \\
\text{CFC status} \\
\text{was retained}
\end{array}
$$

This income recognition process is illustrated in the following example.

> *Example:* Tomco, a foreign corporation, met the CFC requirements for 91 days during 19X1. During the year, Tomco earned $425,000 of Subpart F income. Mr. Sini owns 400 of the 900 outstanding shares of the CFC. Mr. Sini must recognize Subpart F income of $47,093, calculated as follows:

$$
\$47,093 = \$425,000 \times \frac{400 \text{ shares}}{900 \text{ shares}} \times \frac{91 \text{ days}}{365 \text{ days}}
$$

Similar limitations exist for recognizing income from earnings invested in U.S. property and previously excluded Subpart F income withdrawn from investments in shipping operations and less developed countries.

Actual distributions made to a U.S. shareholder are taxed only if they are made from current or accumulated earnings that have not been taxed under Sec. 951 in either the current taxable year or a preceding taxable year. The distributions are deemed to be paid from the most recently accumulated earnings and profits (E & P) within the following tiers:

1. Earnings and profits that are attributable to earnings invested in U.S. property.[17]
2. Earnings and profits previously taxed as Subpart F income.
3. Other earnings and profits.

Distributions are considered to be made entirely from within an E & P tier until the tier is completely exhausted. Accordingly, actual distributions are taxed

only if they exceed the sum of the first two E & P accounts.

Under Sec. 960, corporate shareholders are allowed to take a deemed paid foreign tax credit for taxes paid by the CFC that relate to the constructive distributions. When an actual distribution of previously taxed income takes place, it is excluded from current taxation by Sec. 959. An additional credit is granted for any foreign taxes withheld by the CFC on the amount of this excluded distribution (Sec. 960(b)).

An individual U.S. shareholder may elect to be taxed as a domestic corporation on the deemed distributions from CFCs or be taxed at the individual income tax rates. The domestic corporation election allows the individual to be taxed on the deemed distribution at corporate rates and to claim the deemed paid foreign tax credit that is otherwise available only to corporations. A later actual distribution of this income is not excluded under Sec. 959 but causes the shareholder to owe an additional tax at the regular individual rates on the amount of the distribution in excess of the net tax the individual paid as a "corporation." The final effect of this election is simply to defer the CFC income from taxation at the higher individual rates until an actual distribution is made (Secs. 962(a) and (d)).

Basis adjustment

Income that is included in the shareholder's gross income increases the shareholder's basis in the CFC's stock. Distributions of previously taxed income that are excluded under Sec. 959 reduce the basis of the CFC's stock (Sec. 961).

Disposition of CFC stock

Some of the appreciation in the value of CFC stock is attributable to earnings of the foreign corporation that have never been subject to U.S. taxes. If the earnings had been distributed to the shareholder, they would have been taxed as dividend income to the extent of the foreign corporation's E & P. When the dividend payout is less than the full amount of the E & P, some of the gain on a subsequent sale will be attributable to these untaxed earnings. Section 1248 provides that gain realized on the sale or exchange of qualifying stock is treated as a dividend to the extent that the gain on the sale or exchange transaction is attributable to earnings and profits that were accumulated (1) in a taxable year after December 31, 1962, (2) during a time period that the stock sold or exchanged was held by the U.S. per-

---

[17]Earnings that have been taxed as Subpart F income may be invested in U.S. property without incurring any additional tax liability because this action only results in E & P being shifted from tier 2 to tier 1.

son, and (3) while the foreign corporation retained CFC status. Any gain that exceeds this amount is ordinarily taxed at capital gains rates (Sec. 1248(a)).

Section 1248 only applies to certain kinds of sales and exchanges of CFC stock that would otherwise ultimately result in gain taxed at capital gain rates including: an outright sale of the stock, a Sec. 331 distribution in complete or partial liquidation of the CFC, a Sec. 302 distribution in redemption of CFC stock, a dividend distribution of CFC stock by a domestic corporation (unless the distribution is to a second domestic corporation), and sale of the CFC stock pursuant to a Sec. 337 12-month liquidation. Transactions that are not covered by Sec. 1248 are taxed according to the normal sale or exchange rules.

Section 1248 applies only to a U.S. person who, within five years of the date of the stock sale or exchange, owned 10 percent or more of the total combined voting power of the foreign corporation's stock at a time when the foreign corporation retained CFC status. This means that the foreign corporation does not have to be a CFC on the date of the sale or exchange for Sec. 1248 to apply. Any U.S. person who satisfies this requirement must recognize as dividend income his or her pro rata share (based on the number of shares sold or exchanged) of the CFC's E & P accumulated during each day of *each* post-December 31, 1962 taxable year on which the stock was held while CFC status was retained. Dividend income is recognized for all times during this holding period, even periods during which the taxpayer's holdings fall below the 10 percent ownership minimum.

The rules for application of Sec. 1248 quickly become too complex to be covered by this book. A simple example, however, will serve to illustrate the impact of Sec. 1248 on the U.S. person.

Example: On January 1, 19X1, Multico, a domestic corporation, purchased a block of 100 shares of the 500 outstanding shares of Beta Corporation, a CFC, and on January 1, 19X2, it purchased an additional 100 shares. On May 26, 19X3, Multico sells the stock to a third party for a $65,000 gain. Multico has never had to recognize any Subpart F income with respect to its investments in Beta. Beta uses the calendar year as its taxable year and does not own stock in any lower-tier foreign corporations. Beta's E & P and foreign taxes for the period 19X1 to 19X3 and the E & P and foreign taxes attributable to the stock sold or exchanged are as follows.

Year	Total		Attributable to shares sold	
	E & P	Foreign taxes	E & P	Foreign taxes
19X1	$ 40,000	$ 8,000	$ 8,000	$ 1,600
19X2	75,000	25,000	30,000	10,000
19X3	125,000	50,000	20,000	8,000

During 19X1 and 19X2, the E & P and foreign taxes attributable to the stock sold are based solely on Multico's 20 and 40 percent ownership position, respectively. For the year of sale, Multico's share of the E & P is still 40 percent, but only for the portion of the taxable year it held the stock (146/365 of the year). This results in $58,000 of dividend income being recognized and eligible for the Sec. 902 deemed paid foreign tax credit. The remaining $7,000 of gain is taxed at capital gains rates.

For an individual, the tax under Sec. 1248 is limited to the amount of tax that would have been paid had the individual invested in a domestic corporation that conducted the foreign operations directly. A hypothetical tax liability is calculated for the amount of Sec. 1248 dividend income at the regular corporate tax rates minus a direct foreign tax credit for taxes paid by the foreign corporation. The amount of the gain on the sale or exchange that exceeds the hypothetical U.S. corporate income tax is taxed at the individual's capital gain rates. The individual's tax liability is limited to the sum of these two separate tax liabilities (Sec. 1248(b)).

SECTION 367

The transfer of property involving a foreign corporation that comes under the Sec. 351 tax-free corporate formation rules, the tax-free liquidation rules, and the tax-free corporate division or reorganization rules all come under the special requirements of Sec. 367, which may cause the transaction not to be totally tax free. The transfer of property to a foreign corporation is one of a series of transfers labeled "outbound transfers" that requires the transferor to obtain a favorable ruling from the I.R.S. within 183 days of the commencement of the transaction for the gain on the transaction to go unrecognized. This ruling granted by the I.R.S. generally requires the transferor to recognize the amount of any unrealized appreciation or income with respect to certain "tainted" assets transferred to the foreign corporation that would have been recognized if a sale had taken place. Tainted assets include stocks and securities, intangible assets, inventory, and assets generally intended to be sold or exchanged by the foreign corporation. Transfers of property into the United States or transfers of property between foreign corporations occurring in one of these tax-free transactions do not require the taxpayer to obtain a ruling from the I.R.S. In many cases, such as in the case of a tax-free

liquidation of a foreign corporation, the transaction triggers the recognition of the taxpayer's pro rata share of the dividend income that would otherwise be recognized under Sec. 1248(a). The remainder of the taxpayer's unrealized gain or loss on the transaction is required to be deferred. The regulations under Sec. 367 indicate the types of transfers triggering the recognition of this income, and the amount of the income that is to be recognized.

PROBLEMS

1. As of February 1979, 10,978 DISC elections had been made. What are some of the tax advantages that make these corporate forms so popular?
2. Which of the following events will prevent a corporation from retaining DISC status for a taxable year?
   a. Being incorporated in a foreign country.
   b. Having multiple classes of stock outstanding.
   c. Making loans to a related supplier equal in amount to its untaxed profits.
   d. Revoking its DISC election during the first 90 days of the taxable year.
   e. Having more than 5 percent of its gross receipts being other than qualified export receipts.
   f. Having more than 5 percent of its assets being other than qualified export assets.
3. Which of the following properties, when owned by a DISC, qualifies as a "qualified export asset"?
   a. Inventory held for sale to foreign customers.
   b. Accounts receivables resulting from the sale of export property.
   c. Stock of a related manufacturing corporation.
   d. Working capital.
   e. Obligations issued by the Export-Import bank.
   f. Inventory held for sale to U.S. customers.
4. Which of the following receipts, when received by a DISC, qualifies as "qualified export receipts"?
   a. Producers' loan interest.
   b. Sales of inventory to a foreign purchaser for use outside the United States.
   c. Sales of inventory to a foreign purchaser for ultimate use in the United States.
   d. Dividends received from a related foreign export corporation.
   e. Proceeds from the sale of a qualified export asset (other than export property).
   f. Proceeds from the sale of an asset that is not a qualified export asset.
5. a. GAC Corporation elects to be taxed as a DISC in 19X1. At year-end, GAC holds assets having an adjusted basis of $200,000 (and a market value of $260,000). Included among these assets is a 27-foot sailboat having a $22,500 adjusted basis (and a market value of $24,000), which is not a qualified export asset. What actions must GAC take to preserve its DISC status in 19X1?
   b. BSM Corporation elects to be taxed as a DISC in 19X1. Its total gross receipts for 19X1 are $1,000,000. One transaction resulted in the receipt of

$125,000 of nonqualified export receipts. The costs of sales and other indirect expenses attributable to this sale were $80,000 and $20,000, respectively. What actions must BSM take to preserve its DISC status in 19X1?

6. EXPO-DISC is a domestic corporation that elected DISC status beginning in 19X1. It is 100 percent owned by EXPO, Inc., its related supplier. During 19X1, EXPO-DISC sold 100 units of Wham-Bang to foreign purchasers at $100 per unit. EXPO-DISC's per unit costs are as follows: arm's-length price for transfer of Wham-Bang by EXPO, $65; export promotion expenses, $15; other expenses incurred by EXPO-DISC, $10. EXPO's per unit costs for manufacturing Wham-Bang are $50.
   a. What is EXPO-DISC's maximum amount of profit?
   b. What is the per unit transfer price for Wham-Bang, assuming EXPO-DISC reports the maximum possible profits?
   c. What is the maximum per unit commission that EXPO-DISC would earn as a commission DISC if it reports the maximum possible profit?
   d. What is EXPO's total profit if the transfer price in part b is used?

7. Assume the same facts as in Problem 6, except that EXPO's per unit costs for manufacturing Wham-Bang are $70 (instead of $50) and its arm's-length transfer price is $75 (instead of $65).
   a. What is the maximum amount of profit for EXPO-DISC?
   b. What is the per unit transfer price for Wham-Bang, assuming EXPO-DISC reports the maximum possible profits?
   c. What is the per unit maximum commission that EXPO-DISC would earn as a commission DISC if it reported the maximum possible profit?
   d. What is EXPO's total profit if the transfer price in part b is used?

8. ABC Corporation, a domestic corporation, is owned by a single U.S. shareholder. ABC made its initial DISC election in 1973. Its taxable income for 1980 is $400,000. ABC made no cash distributions to its owners during 1980. Included in ABC's gross receipts are: interest from producer's loans, $40,000; and Sec. 1231 gain on the sale of a nonqualified export asset, $10,000. (A gain of $8,000 was permitted to be deferred under Sec. 351 when the asset was transferred to the DISC.) ABC's export gross receipts for the period 1973–1980 are as follows:

	Export gross receipts	
Year	Foreign	U.S.
1980	$1,000	$25
1979	750	30
1978	520	20
1977	410	10
1976	208	8
1975	103	3
1974	52	2
1973	41	1

Determine the taxability of the DISC's 1980 taxable income.

9. 8-Ball Corporation elected DISC status for 19X1, at which time it had $10,000 of earnings and profits (E & P). During the period 19X1–19X3, 8-Ball accrued profits of $120,000, of which $70,000 was constructively distributed to its sole shareholder, individual A. No actual distributions were made during this time. During 19X4, 8-Ball reported taxable income of $150,000, constructive distributions of $90,000, and actual distributions of $200,000.
   a. Determine the taxability of 8-Ball's 19X4 earnings and distributions.

b. What is the largest possible tax-free cash distribution that 8-Ball may make?

c. Assuming all of 8-Ball's receipts were qualified export receipts, what is the source of these distributions for foreign tax credit purposes?

10. X Corporation, a domestic corporation, elects to be taxed as a DISC commencing in 19X1. During the period 19X1–19X5, X has 100 shares of stock outstanding, of which 40 shares were continuously owned by B Corporation. On January 1, 19X6, B Corporation sells its 40 shares to a third party for $200,000. B originally paid $6,000 for the shares. X's earnings and profits balances as of December 31, 19X5 are as follows: previously taxed income, $300,000; accumulated DISC income, $250,000; other earnings and profits, $0. X has never paid any dividends. Determine the amount and character of B's gain.

11. Gamma Corporation elected to be treated as a DISC beginning with 19X1. It remains qualified as a DISC for taxable years 19X1 through 19X4. On January 1, 19X5, it revokes its DISC election and is disqualified as a DISC. On January 1, 19X5, Gamma's accumulated DISC income amount was $64,000.

a. In what taxable years will Gamma's shareholders receive a constructive distribution as a result of the disqualification?

b. What is the amount of each constructive distribution?

c. How would your answers to parts a and b change if Gamma had accumulated the $64,000 during the period 19X1–19X6?

12. Omega Corporation, a domestic corporation, is eligible to elect the benefits of the Sec. 936 possessions tax credit. The taxable income derived in which of the following independent situations may be exempted from taxation by the Sec. 936 credit? Assume all funds are received in Puerto Rico unless otherwise indicated.

a. Manufacturing profits from the production and sale of a product in Puerto Rico.

b. The profits in part a, except that they are collected by the corporation's New York office.

c. Dividend income received from an investment in a foreign corporation.

d. Manufacturing profits derived from the production and sale of goods by a branch facility located in South America.

e. Interest income derived from bonds issued by an unrelated Puerto Rican corporation.

f. Interest income derived from deposits in a Virgin Islands bank account.

13. ABC Corporation, a domestic corporation, engages in the conduct of a Puerto Rican business, with the following results:

(1) Income from Manufacturing Operations

Source	Place of receipt	Gross income	Allowable expenses
Puerto Rico	Puerto Rico	$250,000	$120,000
Puerto Rico	United States	25,000	10,000
Foreign Country	Puerto Rico	60,000	24,000
Subtotal		$335,000	$154,000

(2) Investment Income

Source	Place of receipt	Gross income	Allowable expenses
Puerto Rico	Puerto Rico	$ 85,000	$ -0-
Puerto Rico	United States	35,000	-0-
Subtotal		$120,000	$ -0-
Total		$455,000	$154,000

a. Is ABC Corporation eligible for the Sec. 936 credit benefits?

b. Determine the amount of ABC's Sec. 936 credit.

c. Assume that $18,000 in foreign taxes were paid with respect to the foreign source manufacturing income. Are any of these taxes eligible to be claimed as a credit or a deduction?

14. XYZ, Ltd., a Bermuda corporation, is owned equally by three U.S. citizens and one Bermuda citizen at all times during 19X1. In 19X1, the corporation earned $300,000 of dividend income, $80,000 of long-term capital gains, and incurred $30,000 of expenses as a result of investments in foreign stocks. None of the income is considered to have been derived from the conduct of a U.S. trade or business. XYZ pays a $50,000 cash dividend during 19X1 out of its profits. How much income must each of the U.S. citizens recognize as a result of its investment in XYZ?

15. Tax commentators for a number of years have debated the merits of the deferral privilege for earnings derived from direct foreign investments. Discuss the pros and cons of the deferral privilege.

16. XYZ Corporation establishes a foreign sales subsidiary, X-Sales, to handle its Country X sales activity. XYZ sells a product to X-Sales for $250 that it in turn sells to Country X customers for $300. The product costs XYZ $200 to produce.

a. What is the value (additional funds for reinvestment that are available) to XYZ of the deferral privilege if the Country X tax rate is 35 percent and the U.S. tax rate is 46 percent?

b. How would your answer to part a change if Country X did not levy a corporate income tax?

c. How would your answer to part a change if Country X did not levy a corporate income tax and XYZ Corporation sells the product to X-Sales for its cost, $200?

17. ABC Corporation is considering expanding its activities overseas by building plants in foreign countries to conduct manufacturing operations on products that are currently produced and sold domestically. Because of the additional start-up costs of the new facilities and the costs to enter the new market, ABC anticipates annual overseas losses of $500,000 for each of the next three years. ABC's controller asks you whether a foreign branch or foreign subsidiary should be used. What would you advise her regarding the tax aspects of such an action?

18. In the following independent situations, determine whether or not the foreign corporation, having a single class of stock outstanding, is characterized as a CFC.

a. The foreign corporation's stock is owned 12 percent by A, 8 percent by B, 31 percent by C, and 49 percent by D. A, B, C, and D are unrelated individuals. A, B, and C are U.S. citizens, and D is a nonresident alien.

b. Would your answer to part a change if B were A's son?

c. The foreign corporation's stock is owned 6 percent by A, 8 percent by B, 37 percent by C, and 49 percent by X. A, B, and C are unrelated U.S. citizens. X is a foreign corporation that is owned equally by A and B.

d. The foreign corporation's stock is owned 7 percent by A, 7 percent by B, and 40 percent by C. A and B are equal owners of P, a domestic corporation that does not own any stock in the foreign corporation. The remainder of the foreign corporation's stock is owned by foreign individuals. A, B, and C are U.S. citizens.

19. Sunco, a domestic corporation, owns all the stock of SunSub, a CFC. SunSub reported the following gross income, expenses, and net income for 19X1:

	Gross income	Allocable expenses	Taxable income
Foreign base company sales income	$250,000	$137,500	$112,500
Foreign base company services income	50,000	37,500	12,500
Foreign personal holding company (FPHC) income	100,000	42,500	57,500
Insurance of U.S. risks	7,000	1,000	6,000
Insurance of non-U.S. risks	150,000	50,000	100,000
Other gross income	143,000	60,000	83,000
Total	$700,000	$328,500	$371,500

a. What amount of Subpart F income must Sunco recognize in 19X1?

b. Would your answer change if FPHC income were $200,000 (rather than $100,000) and other gross income were $43,000?

c. Assume that SunSub's country of incorporation imposes a restriction that currency may not be exported without a license. Would your answer to part a change if SunSub could obtain a license to remit only $100,000 of profits?

20. Watkins Corporation, a publicly held domestic corporation, owns 60 percent of the outstanding stock of Wombat, Ltd., a U.K. corporation. For the year ended December 31, 19X4, Wombat reported the following gross income:

Foreign base company sales income	$22,000
Foreign base company services income	10,000
Dividends from investment in French corporation (Wombat owns 5 percent of the stock)	6,000
Interest from investment in Swedish bonds	4,000
Dividends from wholly owned U.K. subsidiary that conducts U.K. manufacturing activities	15,000
Rental income earned from leasing London office space to U.K. subsidiary	7,500
Other income	45,000

Determine Watkins's Subpart F income, assuming Wombat does not engage in the conduct of a U.S. trade or business.

21. WRS Corporation, a domestic corporation, owns all the stock of MCL Corporation, a CFC. During 19X1, MCL Corporation engages in a number of sales and manufacturing activities, both within and without its country of incorporation, Country X. Which of the following transactions produces foreign base company sales income?

a. MCL purchases a product from WRS and sells it to unrelated parties within Country X.

b. Assume MCL sells the product in part a for use in Country Y.

c. MCL manufactures a product and sells it to unrelated parties for use in Country Y.

d. MCL purchases a product from an unrelated supplier and sells it for use in Country Y.

e. MCL purchases an unfinished product from WRS, performs certain activities to finish the product, and sells the product for use in Country Y. MCL's direct labor and overhead account for 30 percent of its total cost of sales.

f. Assume MCL makes the sale in part d to a related purchaser.

22. RLS Corporation, a domestic corporation, owns all the stock of LES, Ltd., a CFC incorporated in Canada. During 19X1, LES, Ltd. earns $20,000 of Subpart F income, accrues $50,000 of earnings and profits (E & P), and distributes $10,000 to RLS. LES has no pre-19X1 E & P.

  a. What income is required to be recognized by RLS in 19X1, based on its investment in LES?

  b. What are the E & P balances (amounts and types) of LES, Ltd. at the end of 19X1?

  c. Suppose LES distributed $25,000 to RLS in 19X2, a taxable year in which it neither accrued E & P nor incurred an E & P deficit. What portion of the distribution (if any) is taxable?

  d. Suppose that in part c LES had invested the $25,000 in U.S. property instead of making the distribution. What portion of the distribution is taxable?

23. EJW, a domestic corporation, paid $75,000 for 800 of the 1,000 shares of Zeta Corporation stock when the corporation was formed on January 1, 19X1. Zeta, a foreign corporation, is characterized as a CFC at all times during 19X1 and 19X2. During these years, Zeta reports $12,500 and $7,500, respectively, of pre-tax profits, all of which represent Subpart F income. Zeta pays foreign taxes at a rate equal to 20 percent of its pretax profits. During 19X3, a taxable year in which no Subpart F income is reported, Zeta makes a distribution of $8,000 to EJW.

  a. Determine the taxability of the 19X3 distribution to EJW.

  b. What is the basis of the Zeta stock on January 1, 19X2, January 1, 19X3, and January 1, 19X4?

  c. What is the maximum amount that may be distributed tax free to EJW during 19X3?

24. Alpha Corporation, a domestic corporation, acquired for $400,000 all the stock of XYZ, Ltd., a foreign corporation on January 31, 19X1. Alpha sold the XYZ stock on December 1, 19X4 for $1,250,000. During the period of time Alpha owned the stock, XYZ reported the following earnings and profits and foreign taxes:

Year	Earnings & profits	Foreign taxes
19X1	$100,000	$ 50,000
19X2	125,000	60,000
19X3	175,000	100,000
19X4	225,000	125,000

  a. Determine the amount and character of Alpha's gain.

  b. If Alpha instead had sold the stock for $800,000, determine the amount and character of Alpha's gain.

  c. What amount of deemed paid foreign tax credit may Alpha claim with respect to the dividend in part a?

SUPPLEMENTAL PROBLEMS

25. A number of European nations have charged that the U.S. special corporation form known as a DISC constitutes a tax subsidy on exports and violates the anti-subsidy provisions of the General Agreement on Tariffs and Trade (GATT). Do

the DISC provisions create a tax subsidy by providing a special permanent exemption from taxation for these export profits that is not available for similar profits earned by a U.S. corporation's foreign branch sales activity?

26. The Revenue Act of 1971 provided that the Treasury shall annually present an "analysis of the operation and effect" of the portions of the act that authorize the creation of DISCs. Examine the most recent DISC Annual Report[18] and answer the following questions:
    a. How many DISC elections have been made?
    b. What geographical regions have accounted for the most DISC export receipts?
    c. What product classifications have accounted for the most DISC export receipts?
    d. What assets represent the largest portion of a typical DISC's balance sheet?
    e. What is the total amount of DISC net income, constructive distributions, and tax-deferred income for the most recent year?

27. EXPO-DISC is a domestic corporation that elected DISC status commencing in 19X1. It is 100 percent owned by EXPO, Inc., its related supplier. During 19X1, EXPO-DISC reported the following sales activity for its Wham-Bang product:

		U.S. sales		Foreign sales
Units		100		100
Per unit revenues and costs:				
Sales price		$100		$100
Cost of goods sold:				
Direct costs	$50		$50	
Overhead	10		10	
Export promotion expenses			15	
Other expenses of: EXPO-DISC			10	
EXPO	10		___	
Total costs		(70)		(85)
Profit		$ 30		$ 15

An arm's-length transfer price for the transfer of goods to EXPO-DISC for resale to foreign buyers would be $90.
    a. What is the maximum per unit amount of profit for EXPO-DISC under both the full costing and marginal costing alternatives?
    b. What is the per unit transfer price for the Wham-Bang, assuming EXPO-DISC reports the maximum possible profits?
    c. What is EXPO's total profit if the transfer price in part b is used?

28. The enactment of Sec. 1248 as part of the Revenue Act of 1962 was intended to tax the earnings of controlled foreign subsidiaries at full U.S. tax rates by considering a portion of a gain (otherwise taxable at capital gains rates) to be dividend income. Most taxpayers usually would prefer to have the earnings realized as capital gains. Explain why a domestic corporation might prefer to have the gain characterized as dividend income.

[18]U.S., Department of the Treasury, *The Operation and Effect of the Domestic International Sales Corporation Legislation: 1977 Annual Report* (Washington, D.C.: U.S. Government Printing Office, April 1979).

29. Amalgamated Manufacturing Company, a domestic corporation, is planning on establishing its operations in France. In order to establish these operations it needs to transfer on July 1, 19X4, the following assets to its wholly owned, newly formed French manufacturing corporation.

Assets	Adjusted basis	Fair market value
(1) Cash	$100,000	$100,000
(2) Inventory of raw materials	40,000	75,000
(3) Patents relating to a product to be sold in France	5,000	25,000
(4) Patents relating to a product to be sold in the U.S.	10,000	60,000
(5) Stock of a wholly owned French sales subsidiary having accumulated E & P of $100,000 (and foreign taxes paid of $40,000). This stock has been held since the formation of the subsidiary on January 1, 19X1.	5,000	125,000
(6) Machine (Depreciation previously claimed is $7,500)	10,000	6,000

a. Indicate the amount and type of income that must be recognized in order to secure a favorable ruling on the creation of the French subsidiary. (*Hint:* See Rev. Proc. 68-23, 1968-1 CB 821.)

b. Failure to obtain the favorable ruling results in what negative tax consequences?

30. JVB Corporation, a domestic corporation, acquires all the stock of Birdsly, S.A., a controlled foreign corporation on January 1, 19X1 for $100,000. JVB decides to liquidate Birdsly on July 1, 19X6. At the time of liquidation, Birdsly will have accumulated earnings and profits of $240,000, of which $60,000 have been taxed to JVB under Sec. 951. JVB will receive assets having a fair market value of $1,000,000 (its adjusted basis is $350,000) and liabilities in the amount of $200,000.

a. What is JVB's realized gain on the liquidation?

b. Must any of the gain be recognized? If so, what is its character?

c. What is JVB's basis in the Birdsly assets?

appendix
a

Unified Rate Schedule for Estate, Gift, and Generation-skipping Transfer Taxes
(Effective date: 1977 and later.)

If the amount with respect to which the tentative tax to be computed is:	The tentative tax is:
Not over $10,000	18 percent of such amount.
Over $10,000 but not over $20,000	$1,800, plus 20 percent of the excess of such amount over $10,000.
Over $20,000 but not over $40,000	$3,800, plus 22 percent of the excess of such amount over $20,000.
Over $40,000 but not over $60,000	$8,200, plus 24 percent of the excess of such amount over $40,000.
Over $60,000 but not over $80,000	$13,000, plus 26 percent of the excess of such amount over $60,000.
Over $80,000 but not over $100,000	$18,200, plus 28 percent of the excess of such amount over $80,000.
Over $100,000 but not over $150,000	$23,800, plus 30 percent of the excess of such amount over $100,000.
Over $150,000 but not over $250,000	$38,800, plus 32 percent of the excess of such amount over $150,000.
Over $250,000 but not over $500,000	$70,800, plus 34 percent of the excess of such amount over $250,000.
Over $500,000 but not over $750,000	$155,800, plus 37 percent of the excess of such amount over $500,000.
Over $750,000 but not over $1,000,000	$248,300, plus 39 percent of the excess of such amount over $750,000.
Over $1,000,000 but not over $1,250,000	$345,800, plus 41 percent of the excess of such amount over $1,000,000.
Over $1,250,000 but not over $1,500,000	$448,300, plus 43 percent of the excess of such amount over $1,250,000.
Over $1,500,000 but not over $2,000,000	$555,800, plus 45 percent of the excess of such amount over $1,500,000.
Over $2,000,000 but not over $2,500,000	$780,800, plus 49 percent of the excess of such amount over $2,000,000.
Over $2,500,000 but not over $3,000,000	$1,025,800, plus 53 percent of the excess of such amount over $2,500,000.
Over $3,000,000 but not over $3,500,000	$1,290,800, plus 57 percent of the excess of such amount over $3,000,000.
Over 3,500,000 but not over $4,000,000	$1,575,800, plus 61 percent of the excess of such amount over $3,500,000.
Over $4,000,000 but not over $4,500,000	$1,880,800, plus 65 percent of the excess of such amount over $4,000,000.
Over $4,500,000 but not over $5,000,000	$2,205,800, plus 69 percent of the excess of such amount over $4,500,000.
Over $5,000,000	$2,550,800, plus 70 percent of the excess of such amount over $5,000,000.

appendix
b

TABLE A (1). TABLE, SINGLE LIFE MALE, 6 PERCENT, SHOWING THE PRESENT WORTH OF AN ANNUITY, OF A LIFE INTEREST, AND OF A REMAINDER INTEREST

(1) Age	(2) Annuity	(3) Life estate	(4) Remainder	(1) Age	(2) Annuity	(3) Life estate	(4) Remainder
0	15.6176	0.93705	0.06295	56	10.0777	0.60466	0.39534
1	16.0362	.96217	.03783	57	9.8552	.59131	.40869
2	16.0283	.96170	.03830	58	9.6297	.57778	.42222
3	16.0089	.96053	.03947	59	9.4028	.56417	.43583
4	15.9841	.95905	.04095	60	9.1753	.55052	.44948
5	15.9553	.95732	.04268	61	8.9478	.53687	.46313
6	15.9233	.95540	.04460	62	8.7202	.52321	.47679
7	15.8885	.95331	.04669	63	8.4924	.50954	.49046
8	15.8508	.95105	.04895	64	8.2642	.49585	.50415
9	15.8101	.94861	.05139	65	8.0353	.48212	.51788
10	15.7663	.94598	.05402	66	7.8060	.46836	.53164
11	15.7194	.94316	.05684	67	7.5763	.45458	.54542
12	15.6698	.94019	.05981	68	7.3462	.44077	.55923
13	15.6180	.93708	.06292	69	7.1149	.42689	.57311
14	15.5651	.93391	.06609	70	6.8823	.41294	.58706
15	15.5115	.93069	.06931	71	6.6481	.39889	.60111
16	15.4576	.92746	.07254	72	6.4123	.38474	.61526
17	15.4031	.92419	.07581	73	6.1752	.37051	.62949
18	15.3481	.92089	.07911	74	5.9373	.35624	.64376
19	15.2918	.91751	.08249	75	5.6990	.34194	.65806
20	15.2339	.91403	.08597	76	5.4602	.32761	.67239
21	15.1744	91046	.08954	77	5.2211	.31327	.68673
22	15.1130	.90678	.09328	78	4.9825	.29895	.70105
23	15.0487	.90292	.09702	79	4.7469	.28481	.71519
24	14.9807	.89884	.10116	80	4.5164	.27098	.72902
25	14.9075	.89445	.10555	81	4.2955	.25773	.74227
26	14.8287	.88972	.11028	82	4.0879	.24527	.75473
27	14.7442	.88465	.11535	83	3.8924	.23354	.76646
28	14.6542	.87925	.12075	84	3.7029	.22217	.77783
29	14.5588	.87353	.12647	85	3.5117	.21070	.78930
30	14.4584	.86750	.13250	86	3.3259	.19955	.80045
31	14.3528	.86117	.13883	87	3.1450	.18820	.81130
32	14.2418	.85451	.14549	88	2.9703	.17872	.82178
33	14.1254	.84752	.15248	89	2.8052	.16831	.83169
34	14.0034	.84020	.15980	90	2.6536	.15922	.84078
35	13.8758	.83255	.16745	91	2.5162	.15097	.84903
36	13.7425	.82455	.17545	92	2.3917	.14350	.85650
37	13.6036	.81622	.18378	93	2.2801	.13681	.86319
38	13.4591	.80755	.19245	94	2.1802	.13081	.86919
39	13.3090	.79854	.20146	95	2.0891	.12535	.87465
40	13.1538	.78923	.21077	96	1.9997	.11998	.88002
41	12.9934	.77960	.22040	97	1.9145	.11487	.88513
42	12.8279	.76967	.23033	98	1.8331	.10999	.89001
43	12.6574	.75944	.24056	99	1.7554	.10532	.89468
44	12.4819	.74891	.25109	100	1.6812	.10087	.89913
45	12.3013	.73808	.26192	101	1.6101	.09661	.90339
46	12.1158	.72695	.27305	102	1.5416	.09250	.90750
47	11.9253	.71552	.28448	103	1.4744	.08846	.91154
48	11.7308	.70385	.29615	104	1.4065	.08439	.91561
49	11.5330	.69198	.30802	105	1.3334	.08000	.92000
50	11.3329	.67997	.32003	106	1.2452	.07471	.92529
51	11.1308	.66785	.33215	107	1.1196	.06718	.93282
52	10.9267	.65560	.34440	108	.9043	.05426	.94574
53	10.7200	.64320	.35680	109	.4717	.02830	.97170
54	10.5100	.63060	.36940				
55	10.2960	.61776	.38224				

*Source: Treas. Reg. Sec. 20.2031-10(e).

TABLE A (2). **TABLE, SINGLE LIFE FEMALE, 6 PERCENT, SHOWING THE PRESENT WORTH**
OF AN ANNUITY, OF A LIFE INTEREST, AND OF A REMAINDER INTEREST

(1) Age	(2) Annuity	(3) Life estate	(4) Remainder	(1) Age	(2) Annuity	(3) Life estate	(4) Remainder
0	15.8972	0.95383	0.04617	55	11.6432	0.69859	0.30141
1	16.2284	.97370	.02630	56	11.4353	.68612	.31388
2	16.2287	.97372	.02628	57	11.2200	.67320	.32680
3	16.2180	.97308	.02692	58	10.9980	.65988	.34012
4	16.2029	.97217	.02783	59	10.7703	.64622	.35378
5	16.1850	.97110	.02890	60	10.5376	.63226	.36774
6	16.1648	.96989	.03011	61	10.3005	.61803	.38197
7	16.1421	.96853	.03147	62	10.0587	.60352	.39648
8	16.1172	.96703	.03297	63	9.8118	.58871	.41129
9	16.0901	.96541	.03459	64	9.5592	.57355	.42645
10	16.0608	.96365	.03635	65	9.3005	.55803	.44197
11	16.0293	.96176	.03824	66	9.0352	.54211	.45789
12	15.9958	.95975	.04025	67	8.7639	.52583	.47417
13	15.9607	.95764	.04236	68	8.4874	.50924	.49076
14	15.9239	.95543	.04457	69	8.2068	.49241	.50759
15	15.8856	.95314	.04686	70	7.9234	.47540	.52460
16	15.8460	.95076	.04924	71	7.6371	.45823	.54177
17	15.8048	.94829	.05171	72	7.3480	.44088	.55912
18	15.7620	.94572	.05428	73	7.0568	.42341	.57659
19	15.7172	.94303	.05697	74	6.7645	.40587	.59413
20	15.6701	.94021	.05979	75	6.4721	.38833	.61167
21	15.6207	.93724	.06276	76	6.1788	.37073	.62927
22	15.5687	.93412	.06588	77	5.8845	.35307	.64693
23	15.5141	.93085	.06915	78	5.5910	.33546	.66454
24	15.4565	.92739	.07261	79	5.3018	.31811	.68189
25	15.3959	.92375	.07625	80	5.0195	.30117	.69883
26	15.3322	.91993	.08007	81	4.7482	.28489	.71511
27	15.2652	.91591	.08409	82	4.4892	.26935	.73065
28	15.1946	.91168	.08832	83	4.2398	.25439	.74561
29	15.1208	.90725	.09275	84	3.9927	.23956	.76044
30	15.0432	.90259	.09741	85	3.7401	.22441	.77559
31	14.9622	.89773	.10227	86	3.5016	.21010	.78990
32	14.8775	.89265	.10735	87	3.2790	.19674	.80326
33	14.7888	.88733	.11267	88	3.0719	.18431	.81569
34	14.6960	.88176	.11824	89	2.8808	.17285	.82715
35	14.5989	.87593	.12407	90	2.7068	.16241	.83759
36	14.4975	.86985	.13015	91	2.5502	.15301	.84699
37	14.3915	.86349	.13651	92	2.4116	.14470	.85530
38	14.2811	.85687	.14313	93	2.2901	.13741	.86259
39	14.1663	.84998	.15002	94	2.1839	.13103	.86897
40	14.0468	.84281	.15719	95	2.0891	.12535	.87465
41	13.9227	.83536	.16464	96	1.9997	.11998	.88002
42	13.7940	.82764	.17236	97	1.9145	.11487	.88513
43	13.6604	.81962	.18038	98	1.8331	.10999	.89001
44	13.5219	.81131	.18869	99	1.7554	.10532	.89468
45	13.3781	.80269	.19731	100	1.6812	.10087	.89913
46	13.2290	.79374	.20626	101	1.6101	.09661	.90339
47	13.0746	.73448	.21552	102	1.5416	.09250	.90750
48	12.9147	.77488	.22512	103	1.4744	.08846	.91154
49	12.7496	.76498	.23502	104	1.4065	.08439	.91561
50	12.5793	.75476	.24524	105	1.3334	.08000	.92000
51	12.4039	.74423	.25577	106	1.2452	.07471	.92529
52	12.2232	.73339	.26661	107	1.1196	.06718	.93282
53	12.0367	.72220	.27780	108	.9043	.05426	.94574
54	11.8436	.71062	.28938	109	.4717	.02830	.97170

TABLE B. TABLE SHOWING THE PRESENT WORTH AT 6 PERCENT OF AN ANNUITY FOR A TERM CERTAIN, OF AN INCOME INTEREST FOR A TERM CERTAIN, AND OF A REMAINDER INTEREST POSTPONED FOR A TERM CERTAIN.

(1) Number of years	(2) Annuity	(3) Term certain	(4) Remainder	(1) Number of years	(2) Annuity	(3) Term certain	(4) Remainder
1	0.9434	0.056604	0.943396	31	13.9291	0.835745	0.164255
2	1.8334	.110004	.889996	32	14.0840	.845043	.154957
3	2.6730	.160381	.839619	33	14.2302	.853814	.146186
4	3.4651	.207906	.792094	34	14.3681	.862088	.137912
5	4.2124	.252742	.747258	35	14.4982	.869895	.130105
6	4.9173	.295039	.704961	36	14.6210	.877259	.122741
7	5.5824	.334943	.665057	37	14.7368	.884207	.115793
8	6.2098	.372588	.627412	38	14.8460	.890761	.109239
9	6.8017	.408102	.591898	39	14.9491	.896944	.103056
10	7.3601	.441605	.558395	40	15.0463	.902778	.097222
11	7.8869	.473212	.526788	41	15.1380	.908281	.091719
12	8.3838	.503031	.496969	42	15.2245	.913473	.086527
13	8.8527	.531161	.468839	43	15.3062	.918370	.081630
14	9.2950	.557699	.442301	44	15.3832	.922991	.077009
15	9.7122	.582735	.417265	45	15.4558	.927350	.072650
16	10.1059	.606354	.393646	46	15.5244	.931462	.068538
17	10.4773	.628636	.371364	47	15.5890	.935342	.064658
18	10.8276	.649656	.350344	48	15.6500	.939002	.060998
19	11.1581	.669487	.330513	49	15.7076	.942454	.057546
20	11.4699	.688195	.311805	50	15.7619	.945712	.054288
21	11.7641	.705845	.294155	51	15.8131	.948785	.051215
22	12.0416	.722495	.277505	52	15.8614	.951684	.048316
23	12.3034	.738203	.261797	53	15.9070	.954418	.045582
24	12.5504	.753021	.246979	54	15.9500	.956999	.043001
25	12.7834	.767001	.232999	55	15.9905	.959433	.040567
26	13.0032	.780190	.219810	56	16.0288	.961729	.038271
27	13.2105	.792632	.207368	57	16.0649	.963895	.036105
28	13.4062	.804370	.195630	58	16.0990	.965939	.034061
29	13.5907	.815443	.184557	59	16.1311	.967867	.032133
30	13.7648	.825890	.174110	60	16.1614	.969686	.030314

glossary

Entries marked with an asterisk (*) are taken from Henry Campbell Black, *Black's Law Dictionary,* Revised Fourth Edition (St. Paul, Minn.: West Publishing Co., 1968).

Account (of Proceedings)   A detailed statement of the fiduciary's acts and proceedings in connection with an estate, rendered by the fiduciary under oath to the court and to the persons interested in the estate. (Ch. 13)

Accumulated DISC Income   The portion of the DISC's earnings and profits that have gone untaxed and have been permitted to accumulate. (Ch. 23)

Accumulated Earnings Credit   An amount deducted from taxable income to help determine the accumulated taxable income of a corporation, upon which the accumulated earnings tax is imposed. The accumulated earnings credit represents the reasonable needs of the business, with a few modifications and exceptions. (See I.R.C. Sec. 535.) *See also* Accumulated Earnings Tax, Accumulated Taxable Income, and Reasonable Needs of the Business. (Ch. 19)

Accumulated Earnings Tax   A tax imposed on the accumulated taxable income of a corporation. This tax penalizes the unwarranted accumulation of a corporation's earnings and encourages distributions to its shareholders. (See I.R.C. Secs. 531–537.) *See also* Accumulated Taxable Income. (Ch. 19)

Accumulated Profits   A foreign corporation's current earnings and profits (E & P) plus the foreign income

taxes paid or accrued by the corporation with respect to the E & P. Accumulated profit is an annual concept, and a separate balance is maintained for each of the foreign corporation's taxable years. (Ch. 21)

Accumulated Taxable Income   The amount upon which the accumulated earnings tax is imposed. The accumulated taxable income is a modification of the taxable income of a corporation; it is further adjusted by the dividends-paid deduction and the accumulated earnings credit. (See I.R.C. Sec. 535.) *See also* Accumulated Earnings Credit, and Accumulated Earnings Tax. (Ch. 19)

Acquisitive Reorganization   A type of reorganization in which the assets or stock of one (or more) corporations are acquired by a second corporation. This type of reorganization may fall within the Type A, B, C, D, or F reorganization classifications. *See also* Type A, B, C, D, and F reorganizations. (Ch. 7)

Adjusted Basis   The initial basis of property increased or decreased as required by specific Code provisions; for example, capital improvements increase the initial basis, and deductions for depreciation and/or depletion decrease the initial basis. (Ch. 4)

Adjusted Ordinary Gross Income   An amount used to determine whether a corporation is a personal holding

company subject to the personal holding company tax. Adjusted ordinary gross income is derived by deducting from the gross income of a corporation all capital gains, Sec. 1231 gains, and specified expenses. If personal holding company income is equal to or greater than 60 percent of adjusted ordinary gross income, the corporation may be a personal holding company. (See I.R.C. Sec. 543(b).) *See also* Personal Holding Company. (Ch. 19)

Administration   The management of a decedent's estate, including the marshaling of assets, the payment of expenses, debts, and charges, the payment or the delivery of legacies, and the rendition of an account. (Ch. 13)

Administration Expenses   Fiduciary commissions, attorneys' and accountants' fees, and other expenses of administering an estate or trust. (Ch. 13)

Administrator   A fiduciary appointed by a probate court to administer the estate of an intestate decedent. (Ch. 13)

Affiliated Corporations   Two or more parent–subsidiary corporations, the ownership of which is distributed in a manner detailed in Sec. 1504(a). This distinction is important because the group is eligible to make an election to file a consolidated corporate federal income tax return. (Ch. 4)

Affiliated Group   One or more chains of includible corporations connected through stock ownership with a common parent corporation (which is also an includible corporation) that meets the stock ownership minimums of Sec. 1504(a). *See also* Includible Corporation. (Ch. 8)

After-the-Facts Research   Research applicable to facts that have already transpired. *See also* Tax Compliance. (Ch. 1)

Aggregate Theory   A theory that treats a partnership not as a separate entity but as an aggregate of individual partners. This theory supports numerous partnership tax provisions, including the provision that permits partnership income to be reported on the partners' tax returns. (Ch. 10)

A.G.I.   Adjusted gross income, as defined in Sec. 62. (Ch. 4)

Allocation   The process of determining the class of gross income to which a deduction is related. (Ch. 21)

Alternate Value   For estate tax purposes, the value of the gross estate six months after the date of death, unless disposed of in fewer than six months when the value is determined as of the date of disposition. (Ch. 13)

Amount Realized   The sum of (1) the cash received, (2) the fair market value of any noncash property received, and (3) the amount of any debt transferred to another taxpayer in an external transaction. (Ch. 4)

Apportionment   The process of determining the statutory or residual grouping to which a deduction is related or apportioned. *See also* Statutory Grouping and Residual Grouping. (Ch. 21)

Assignee   A person who owns an interest in a partnership but has not been accepted into the partnership as a full partner. An assignee is generally treated as a partner for federal income tax purposes. (Ch. 10)

Association   An organization that is not a corporation under state law but that will be taxed as a corporation under the federal income tax laws. Associations have a predominance of corporate characteristics. A limited partnership is susceptible to classification as an association. (Ch. 12)

At-risk Limitation   A limitation of the amount a partner may deduct on his or her personal tax return to the partner's at-risk investment in the partnership. A partner's interest is generally considered at risk to the extent of the cash and the adjusted basis of property contributed by the partner to the partnership. The partner may also be at risk to the extent of his or her share of partnership's liabilities. (Ch. 12)

Attribution of Stock Ownership   The tax laws in a variety of situations will attribute the stock owned by or for an entity (for example, a corporation, partnership, estate, or trust) to certain individuals (for example, shareholders, partners, or beneficiaries). Alternatively, stock owned by or for these same individuals may be attributed to one of the various entity forms. Stock ownership may also be attributed among certain family members so that, for example, a parent may be considered to constructively own stock held by one of his or her children. Different attribution rules may apply to different situations. For example, the attribution rules found in Sec. 318 apply generally to the Subchapter C area, the attribution rules of Sec. 544 apply to personal holding companies, while the Sec. 318 attribution rules (as modified by Sec. 958) apply to the controlled foreign corporations. (Ch. 23)

Base Housing Amount   The nondeductible portion of an expatriate's actual housing expenses. This amount is 20 percent times the net of total earned income minus the sum of (1) total housing expenses, (2) non-Sec. 913 deductions allocable against earned income, and (3) all Sec. 913 deductions other than the qualified housing expenses (Sec. 913(e)(3)(A)). Special rules apply when the expatriate maintains a qualified second home. (Ch. 22)

Basis   A technical tax term that, in a general sense, is a measure of the previously taxed capital base that a taxpayer may recover without the need to recognize any additional amount of gain on the sale, exchange, or other disposition of property. The specific rules that determine basis vary for purchased property (Sec. 1012), property received as a gift (Sec. 1015), inherited property (Sec. 1014), and property acquired in a nontaxable exchange (various sections, for example, Sec. 358.) *See also* Adjusted Basis. (Ch. 4)

Before-the-Facts Research   Research in conjunction with a business transaction that has yet to unfold. *See also* Tax Planning. (Ch. 1)

Beneficiary   (a) One who inherits a share or part of a decedent's estate; or (b) one who takes the beneficial interest under a trust. (For income beneficiary, *see* Life Tenant.) (Ch. 13)

Bequest   A gift of personal property by will. Synonymous with "legacy." (Ch. 13)

Blocked Income   Foreign earnings that are unable to be remitted to the United States because of currency or other restrictions or limitations imposed under the laws of any foreign country. (Ch. 23)

Bona Fide Foreign Resident   A U.S. citizen or resident alien who is considered to be a resident of a foreign country for a particular time period. In general, the same standards are applied under the U.S. tax laws to determine whether an individual is a bona fide foreign resident as are used to determine whether an alien is a resident or nonresident of the United States. (Ch. 22)

Bottom-line Income   The partnership income after adjustment for items that are required to be reported separately by Sec. 702. The term derives its name from the fact that it is the bottom line on the first page of the partnership tax return (Form 1065). (Ch. 11)

Brother–Sister Controlled Groups   Two or more corporations where (1) five (or fewer) shareholders own at least 80 percent of the total combined voting power of all classes of stock entitled to vote or at least 80 percent of the total value of shares of all classes of stock of each corporation *and* (2) more than 50 percent of the total combined voting power of all classes of stock entitled to vote or at least 50 percent of the total value of shares of stock of each corporation represents "identical ownership" by the five (or fewer) persons identified above. A brother–sister controlled group may not be an affiliated group and elect to file a consolidated return. (Ch. 8)

Built-in Deductions   Those deductions or losses of a corporation that are recognized in a consolidated return year, or which are recognized in a separate return year and carried over in the form of a net operating loss or a net capital loss to the consolidated return year, but which are economically accrued in a separate return limitation year. *See also* Separate Return Limitation Year (SRLY). (Ch. 8)

Camp Lodging that: (1) is substandard; (2) is provided by or on behalf of the employer for the convenience of the employee because the taxpayer renders services in a remote area where satisfactory housing is not available on the open market; (3) is located as near as practicable to the work site of the taxpayer; (4) is furnished in a common area or enclave that is not open to the public for lodging or accommodations; and (5) normally accommodates 10 or more persons who are either employees of the taxpayer's employer or other employees performing services at the taxpayer's work site. (Ch. 22)

Capital Gain Net Income The excess of gains from sales or exchanges of capital assets over the losses from such sales or exchanges. (Ch. 7)

Carryover Basis Occurs when the basis of the property received by the transferee is the same as the basis of the property to the transferor, increased, perhaps, by the amount of gain recognized by the transferor. (Ch. 10)

Centralized Management One of the four corporate attributes that help determine whether a partnership should be taxed as a partnership or as an association (corporation). Centralized management exists when any person or group of persons has continuing exclusive authority to make independent management decisions without being required to seek continuing approval of these decisions from the owners of the business. (Ch. 12)

Citizen A person who retains citizenship in a particular country. Citizenship may be acquired either (1) by being born in or (2) by satisfying certain requirements set forth by the government of the country in which citizenship is claimed. An individual's country of citizenship may be different from his or her country of residence. (Ch. 21)

Closely Held Corporation An imprecise phrase referring to any corporation in which a large share—

usually more than 50 percent—of the common stock is owned either by one person or by a closely related group of persons. (Ch. 4)

Code Unless otherwise specified, Code (or Internal Revenue Code) refers to the Internal Revenue Code of 1954 as amended to date. Technically, this is also known as Title 26 of the United States Code. (Ch. 2)

Combined Taxable Income The excess of the gross receipts of the DISC arising from a sale of export property (as defined by Sec. 993(f)) over the total costs of the DISC and related supplier that relate to such gross receipts (Treas. Reg. Sec. 1.994-1(c)(6)). *See also* "Fifty-Fifty" Combined Taxable Income Pricing Method. (Ch. 23)

Commission The compensation provided to a fiduciary by law. (Ch. 13)

Commission DISC A DISC that acts as an agent of a related or unrelated producer and receives a commission on its sales of the export property. *See also* Paper DISC. (Ch. 23)

Common Parent Corporation The corporation in an affiliated group through which one or more chains of includible corporations is connected. The common parent corporation is required to own 80 percent or more of the voting power of all classes of stock *and* 80 percent or more of each class of nonvoting stock of at least one of the other includible corporations. *See also* Subsidiary Corporation. (Ch. 8)

Complex Trusts For income tax purposes, all trusts other than "simple" trusts. (Ch. 14)

Conduit Concept The tax principle that permits various partnership tax items to be reported on each partner's personal tax returns. (Ch. 11)

Consolidated Net Capital Gain or Loss For any consolidated return year, the sum of: (1) the aggregate of the capital gains and losses of the members of the affiliated groups, (2) the consolidated Sec. 1231 net gain for the year, and (3) the consolidated net capital loss carryovers or carrybacks to such year. Excluded are any gains and losses from deferred intercompany transactions. *See also* Consolidated Section 1231 Net Gain or Loss. (Ch. 8)

Consolidated Net Operating Loss The net operating loss reported by an affiliated group during a consolidated

return year. These losses may be carried back or over to other consolidated return years and, subject to certain restrictions or limitations, carried back or over to other separate return years. *See also* Separate Return Limitation Year (SRLY) and Consolidated Return Change of Ownership (CRCO). (Ch. 8)

Consolidated Return Change of Ownership (CRCO) A CRCO occurs in any taxable year of the common parent corporation to which a tax attribute is carried (for example, a net operating loss) if, at the end of the year of change, a more than 50 percentage point increase in the stock owned by the 10 (or fewer) shareholders owning the greatest percentage of the fair market value of such stock has occurred since the beginning of the taxable year, or the beginning of the preceding taxable year, as a result of a purchase transaction or a decrease in the amount of the common parent corporation's stock that is outstanding. The occurrence of a CRCO limits the usability of certain carryovers (but not carrybacks) to the contributions of the "old members" of the affiliated group. *See also* Old Members. (Ch. 8)

Consolidated Return Year A taxable year for which a consolidated tax return is filed, or is required to be filed, by an affiliated group of corporations. (Ch. 8)

Consolidated Section 1231 Net Gain or Loss The aggregate of the Sec. 1231 gains and losses for the consolidated return year for all members of the affiliated group. Gains and losses from casualty and theft occurrences are included only if the aggregate of these amounts reported for all group members results in a net gain being reported. Excluded are any gains and losses from deferred intercompany transactions. *See also* Consolidated Net Capital Gain or Loss. (Ch. 8)

Consolidated Taxable Income The taxable income of the affiliated group that is reported when a consolidated tax return is filed. The rules for computing consolidated taxable income are found in Treas. Reg. Sec. 1.1502-11. (Ch. 8)

Consolidation A newly created corporation, known as the acquiring corporation, uses its stock (and perhaps some of its cash and/or securities) to acquire the stock of two or more corporations, known as the acquired corporations. Each of the acquired corporations is then liquidated. The newly created corporation thus acquires all of the acquired corporations' assets and liabilities before causing these corporations to go out of existence. *See also* Type A Reorganization. (Ch. 7)

Continuity of Life One of the four corporate attributes that help determine whether a partnership should be taxed as a partnership or as an association (corporation). This attribute exists if the death, insanity, bankruptcy, retirement, resignation, or expulsion of any member will not cause the partnership to dissolve. (Ch. 12)

Controlled Foreign Corporation (CFC) Any foreign corporation for which more than 50 percent of the total combined voting power of all classes of its stock entitled to vote is directly, indirectly, or constructively owned by U.S. shareholders on any day of its taxable year. Special rules exist for defining CFCs that are engaged in insurance activities. *See also* U.S. Shareholder. (Ch. 21)

Controlled Group of Corporations A group of corporations that satisfies either the parent–subsidiary controlled group definition of Sec. 1563(a)(1) or the brother–sister controlled group definition of Sec. 1563(a)(2). A controlled group of corporations is limited in its ability to use certain tax attributes, such as: the reduced tax rate benefits of Sec. 11(b); the $150,000 accumulated earnings credit; and the $25,000 small business deduction for life insurance companies. *See also* Parent–Subsidiary Controlled Group and Brother–Sister Controlled Group. (Ch. 8)

Controlled Group of Corporations Two or more corporations, the ownership of which is distributed in any one of the ways detailed in Sec. 1563(a). This distinction is important because the controlled group of corporations collectively will be treated for federal income tax purposes as a single corporate entity. (Ch. 4)

Corporate Division Arrangements by which the owners of a single corporate entity divide up their investments among two or more corporate entities. These arrangements usually take the form of a spin-off, a split-off, or a split-up that comes under the purview of Secs. 355 and 356. *See also* Spin-off, Split-off, and Split-up. (Ch. 7)

Corporation A legal entity created under the laws of either a state or the U.S. (federal) government, which entity is regarded as having an existence that is distinct from that of its owners and which is further characterized by continuity of life, centralization of management, limited liability, and free transferability of ownership. (Ch. 4)

Corpus *See* Principal. (Ch. 13)

Court Decisions The written decisions of a court that announce how the court ruled in a disagreement between two parties. In tax disagreements, one party is usually a government agency or a representative of that agency. The written decision usually contains a summary of the disagreement(s) before the court, an enumeration of the issues as determined by the court, a conclusion, and the reasoning for that conclusion as found by the court. (Ch. 2)

Creditable Tax A foreign tax levy that may be claimed as a credit by a taxpayer against a U.S. tax liability. Such taxes are restricted to income taxes, war profits taxes, and excess profits taxes or a tax levied "in lieu of an income tax." (Ch. 21)

Curtesy The estate to which by common law a man is entitled, on the death of his wife, in the lands or tenements of which she was seized in possession or fee-simple or in tail during her coverture, provided they have had lawful issue born alive which might have been capable of inheriting the estate.* (Ch. 17)

Decedent A deceased person whose estate is being administered. (Ch. 13)

Decree An official order of a probate court. (Ch. 13)

Deduction for Distributions to Beneficiaries The deduction allowed on a fiduciary income tax return for income currently paid, credited, or required to be distributed to beneficiaries of estates and trusts. (Ch. 13)

Deemed Transferor The individual who is "deemed" to have made a taxable transfer from a generation-skipping trust to a younger generation beneficiary. Generally, the deemed transferor is the parent of the transferee who is more closely related by blood to the grantor. (Ch. 18)

Deferral Privilege The ability of a U.S. citizen, resident alien, or domestic corporation to defer from current taxation its pro rata share of the earnings of a foreign investee corporation until the earnings have been distributed as a dividend. Exceptions to the deferral privilege exist for a U.S. investor's share of certain earnings of a controlled foreign corporation or a foreign personal holding company. *See also* Controlled Foreign Corporation and Foreign Personal Holding Company. (Ch. 21)

Deferred Intercompany Transaction An intercompany transaction that involves: a sale or exchange of property, the performance of services where the acquiring party capitalizes the amount of the outlay for the services, and any other transaction involving an expenditure that is capitalized by the acquiring party. *See also* Intercompany Transaction and Other Intercompany Transaction. (Ch. 8)

Domestic International Sales Corporation (DISC) A domestic corporation that conducts export-related activities and that is exempt from the corporate income tax. A DISC's shareholders are taxed on constructive distributions of a portion of the DISC's profits in the year in which these profits are earned, and on actual distributions of the portion of the DISC's profits that were able to be deferred from taxation in the year in which they were earned. These special rules permit up to 50 percent of the DISC's profits to be exempted from taxation at the shareholder level in the year in which they are earned. (Ch. 23)

Domestic Partnership Any partnership created or organized in the United States or under the law of the United States or any state. *See also* Foreign Partnership. (Ch. 23)

Donee The recipient of a gift. (Ch. 13)

Donor For gift tax purposes, the person who makes a gift. (Ch. 13)

Dower The life estate to which every married woman is entitled on death of her husband, intestate, or in case she dissents from his will, one-third in value of all lands of which husband was beneficially seized in law or in

fact, at any time during coverture.*
(Ch. 17)

Deficiency Distribution A distribution that is made by a DISC that has failed the gross receipts test and/or assets test in order to prevent the taxation of the current year's profits and the tax-deferred profits of prior years (the accumulated DISC income) to the DISC's shareholders. If the gross receipts test is failed, then all taxable income derived from transactions producing nonqualified export receipts must be distributed. If the assets test is failed, then a distribution at least equal to the fair market value of all assets that are not qualified export assets must take place (Sec. 992(c)). (Ch. 23)

Devise A gift of real property under a will. (Ch. 13)

Devisee The person to whom a legacy is given. (Chs. 13,15)

Direct Foreign Tax Credit A credit available under Sec. 901 for a foreign tax levy that is directly imposed upon the taxpayer. This direct imposition of the tax may be either through an actual tax payment made by the taxpayer or through the withholding of the foreign tax amount from a payment made by a foreign payor. (Ch. 21)

DISC Incremental Rules Special rules that in 1976 added a new category of DISC dividends that are deemed distributed to its shareholders. These incremental rules thus permit a smaller amount of DISC taxable income to be subject to the deferral privileges. In addition to the one-half of DISC taxable income that is otherwise deemed to be distributed, the incremental rules cause an additional amount of DISC taxable income to be deemed distributed. The portion of this remaining DISC income that is deemed distributed under the incremental rules depends on the relationship between the current year's export gross receipts and the average of export gross receipts for a four-year base period (Secs. 995(a)(1)(E) and (e)). (Ch. 23)

Distributable Net Income For fiduciary income tax purposes, the taxable income of the estate or trust for any taxable year, computed with certain modifications. (Ch. 13)

Distributive Share A partner's share of partnership income, gain, loss, deduction, or credit. Each partner's distributive share is determined in accordance with the partner's interest in the partnership (determined by taking into account all facts and circumstances). (Ch. 11)

Dividend Any nonliquidating distribution of assets by a corporation to its shareholders, in their role as shareholders, to the extent of the distributing corporation's current or accumulated earnings and profits. (Ch. 4)

Divisive Reorganization A type of reorganization in which a single corporation is divided up into two or more corporations, one of which may be the original corporation. Also known as a Type D Reorganization, this type of reorganization comes under the rules of Sec. 368(a)(1)(D). *See also* Type D Reorganization, Spin-off, Split-off, and Split-up. (Ch. 7)

Domestic Corporation A corporation created or organized in the United States or under the law of the United States or any state. *See also* Foreign Corporation. (Chs. 8, 21)

Earned Income Wages, salaries, or professional fees and other amounts received as compensation for personal services actually rendered. This term, however, does not include that part of the compensation derived by the taxpayer for personal services rendered by him or her to a corporation that represents a distribution of earnings and profits. For Sec. 911 purposes only, a taxpayer's reasonable allowance for compensation is not permitted to exceed 30 percent of the taxpayer's share of an unincorporated entity's net profits when personal services and capital are both material income-producing factors. For all other purposes (such as Sec. 1348), this limitation is a "reasonable compensation" for the services actually rendered. (Ch. 22)

Effectively Connected with the Conduct of a U.S. Trade or Business Income or capital gains of a nonresident alien or foreign corporation that are related to the alien or corporation's conduct of a U.S. trade or business. To be effectively connected with the conduct of a U.S. trade or business, either the "asset use test" or "business activity test" must be satisfied. In the first test, both the asset and the income it generates must be used in the conduct of a U.S. trade or business. In the second test, the activities of the trade or business must be a material factor in the realization of the income. Any income of an alien or foreign corporation that is considered to be effectively connected with the conduct of a U.S. trade or business is taxed at the full U.S. tax rates that would apply to a citizen or domestic corporation. (Ch. 21)

Entity Theory The concept that treats the partnership and its partners as separate entities. For example, under the entity theory, a partner may recognize gain on the sale of property to the partnership. (Ch. 10)

Exchange Rate The relationship between one unit of foreign currency and one U.S. dollar. Thus, if one U.S. dollar is the equivalent of five foreign currency units (FCs), the relationship could be expressed as $1(U.S.) = 0.20(FC)$. Alternatively, the relationship could be expressed as 5(FC):1(U.S.$). (Ch. 21)

Executor The fiduciary nominated by the testator in his or her will to administer the estate thereunder, except insofar as it is to be held in trust, according to law. (Ch. 13)

Excess Loss Account (ELA) The negative investment account balance associated with one group member's ownership of stock issued by a second group member (subsidiary corporation). The ELA is created because of the downward investment account adjustments (other than those related to distributions) required by Treas. Reg. Sec. 1.1502-32(b) (for example, earnings and profits deficits incurred by a subsidiary in a consolidated return year or a net operating loss incurred in a prior taxable year but that could not be absorbed until the current year). A disposition of part or all of the stock of the subsidiary corporation may require the investor group member to include the ELA balance in its gross income. (Ch. 8)

Expatriate A U.S. citizen or resident alien who is employed in a foreign country for an extended period of time. As such, the individual in most cases will be eligible for the special benefits of Secs. 911 and 913 for part or all of his or her overseas employment. (Ch. 22)

Export Promotion Expenses Any expenses incurred to advance the distribution or sale of export property for use, consumption, or distribution outside the United States. Excluded from this definition are such expenses as income taxes, interest expense, bad debt expense, and any manufacturing or assembly costs. (Ch. 23)

Export Property Property that is (1) manufactured, produced, grown, or extracted in the United States by a person other than a DISC and (2) held primarily for sale, lease, or rental, in the ordinary course of trade or business, by, or to, a DISC, for direct use, consumption, or disposition outside the United States. In applying this rule, the property may not have more than 50 percent of its fair market value attributable to articles that were imported into the United States *nor* may the property be one of the excluded export property types listed in Sec. 993(c)(2). (Ch. 23)

Export Trade Assets Export trade assets (defined in Sec. 971(c)) are assets used primarily in the production of export trade income. Increases in the amount of the CFC's investment in these assets will reduce the amount of the foreign base company sales income taxed to its U.S. shareholders. As DISCs have become more widely used, and these export trade asset investments have been reduced, the U.S. shareholders are being taxed under Sec. 970(b) on the Subpart F income that has previously been excluded from taxation because of the increased investments in export trade assets. *See also* Foreign Base Company Sales Income and Export Trade Corporation (ETC). (Ch. 23)

Export Trade Corporation (ETC) A controlled foreign corporation that engaged primarily in export activities for a domestic corporation. Any corporation that was an ETC for any taxable year beginning before November 1, 1971, may continue to be an ETC and claim the exclusion from foreign base company income for an amount equal to the increased investments in export trade assets. No new corporations may qualify as an ETC after October 31, 1971. The ETCs are being replaced by the DISCs, and special tax provisions govern the conversion of an ETC into

a DISC. *See also* Export Trade Assets. (Ch. 23)

External Transaction Any transaction involving more than one taxable entity. (Ch. 4)

Family Partnership A partnership owned by members of the same family. Such partnerships are subject to certain special rules found in Sec. 704(e) and the related regulations. (Ch. 12)

Fiduciary A person occupying a position of trust, for example, executor, administrator, or trustee. (Ch. 13)

Fiduciary Income Tax Return The income tax return (Form 1041) filed by the fiduciary of an estate or trust. (Ch. 13)

"Fifty-Fifty" Combined Taxable Income Pricing Method One of three special pricing methods that may be used for transactions between a DISC and a related supplier that ultimately produces qualified export receipts. When this pricing method is used, DISC taxable income may not exceed 50 percent of the combined taxable income of the DISC and the related supplier plus 10 percent of the export promotions expenses of the DISC, that are attributable to the qualified export receipts (Sec. 994(a)(2)). *See also* Four Percent of Gross Receipts Pricing Method and Marginal Costing Pricing Rules. (Ch. 23)

First-tier Foreign Corporation Any foreign corporation in which a U.S. investor maintains a direct investment. In order to claim a deemed paid foreign tax credit for taxes paid by a first-tier foreign corporation, a domestic corporation must own stock possessing at least 10 percent of the foreign corporation's voting stock on the distribution date. *See also* Lower-tier Foreign Corporation. (Ch. 21)

Foreign Base Company Income (FBCI) One of the components of Subpart F income. FBCI is made up of five components: Foreign Personal Holding Company Income, Foreign Base Company Sales Income, Foreign Base Company Service Income, Foreign Base Company Shipping Income, and all other income when FBCI exceeds 70 percent of gross income (Sec. 952(a)(2)). *See also* Foreign Personal Holding Company Income, Foreign Base Company Sales Income, Foreign

Base Company Services Income, and Foreign Base Company Shipping Income. (Ch. 23)

Foreign Base Company Sales Income Fees and profits derived by a controlled foreign corporation that result from the sale or purchase of personal property when a related party is involved in a transaction in which the property in question was both manufactured and sold for use outside the CFC's country of incorporation (Sec. 954(a)(2)). (Ch. 23)

Foreign Base Company Service Income Income from service activities derived by a controlled foreign corporation that are (1) performed for or on behalf of a related person and (2) performed outside the country in which the CFC is created or organized (Sec. 954(a)(3)). (Ch. 23)

Foreign Base Company Shipping Income Income derived by a controlled foreign corporation from the use of any aircraft or vessel in foreign commerce, and income derived from the hiring or leasing of such a vessel for use in foreign commerce by another person. Also included in this definition is income derived from certain services that are related to shipping activities (Sec. 954(a)(4)). (Ch. 23)

Foreign Branch An office or establishment of a domestic entity that operates in a foreign country. This branch activity generally is a branch office, or a branch factory, that is related to a similar type of domestic activity. Foreign branch profits and losses are included as part of the U.S. taxpayer's taxable income annually, rather than being exempt from taxation until distributed, as is the case with the earnings of a foreign investee corporation. (Ch. 23)

Foreign Corporation A legal entity created under the laws of a foreign government, which entity is regarded as having an existence that is distinct from that of its owners and which generally shares the other legal characteristics common to domestic corporations. *See also* Domestic Corporation. (Chs. 4, 8, 21)

Foreign Country For tax purposes, any country other than the United States or one of the U.S. possessions. *See also* U.S. Possession. (Ch. 21)

Foreign Estate Any estate the income of which, from non-U.S. sources, which is not effectively connected with the conduct of a trade or business in the United States, is not includible in gross income under Subtitle A (Secs. 1–1564). (Ch. 21)

Foreign Export Corporation   A foreign corporation whose stock is owned by a DISC and that is used to conduct sales or other types of export activities in a foreign country. The three types of foreign export corporations are foreign international sales corporations, real property holding companies, and associated foreign corporations (Sec. 993(e)). These special foreign corporate forms are generally used because host country investment rules require a nonresident corporation, such as a DISC, to operate or own property only through a local corporation. (Ch. 23)

Foreign Partnership   Any partnership that does not satisfy the requirements for being a domestic partnership. *See also* Domestic Partnership. (Ch. 21)

Foreign Personal Holding Company (FPHC)   Any foreign corporation that has (1) 60 percent or more of its gross income for the taxable year being foreign personal holding company income *and* (2) more than 50 percent in value of its outstanding stock being directly, indirectly, or constructively owned by or for five or fewer individuals who are U.S. citizens or residents. The 60 percent minimum level for gross income to achieve FPHC status is reduced to 50 percent after the initial year during which FPHC status is retained. A FPHC's shareholders, who are U.S. citizens, U.S. residents, domestic corporations, domestic partnerships, or an estate or trust having non-U.S. source income, will be taxed on their pro rata share of undistributed foreign personal holding company income. (Ch. 23)

Foreign Personal Holding Company Income (FPHCI)   An income form earned by either a foreign personal holding company or a controlled foreign corporation. The specific income definitions for each of the two areas are basically the same, but they do contain a number of technical differences. Income items that are FPHCI include dividends, interest, royalties, annuities, net gains on stocks and securities transactions, certain gains from commodities trades, trust or estate income, compensation earned from certain personal services contracts, and rental income (Sec. 553). (Ch. 23)

Foreign Source Income   Any type of income that is considered to originate from outside the United States under the rules of Secs. 861–863. *See also* U.S. Source Income. (Ch. 21)

Foreign Tax Credit   A tax credit that is available to U.S. persons and certain nonresident aliens and foreign corporations for income, war profits, or excess profits taxes paid to a foreign country or a U.S. possession. *See also* Foreign Country and U.S. Possession. (Ch. 21)

Foreign Tax Credit Limitation   A restriction placed on a taxpayer's ability to claim a foreign tax credit that limits the credit to the portion of the taxpayer's tax liability that is attributable to foreign source taxable income. Four separate foreign tax credit limitations are actually computed. These include limitations for interest income, DISC dividends, oil and gas income, and all other forms of foreign source income. (Ch. 21)

Foreign Trust   Any trust the income of which, from non-U.S. sources, which is not effectively connected with the conduct of a trade or business in the United States, is not includible in gross income under Subtitle A (Secs. 1–1564). (Ch. 21)

Four Percent of Gross Receipts Pricing Method   One of three special pricing methods that may be used for transactions between a DISC and a related supplier that ultimately produce qualified export receipts. When this pricing method is used, DISC taxable income may not exceed 4 percent of the qualified export receipts on the sale of the export property by the DISC plus 10 percent of the export promotion expenses of the DISC attributable to such receipts (Sec. 994(a)(1)). *See also* "Fifty-Fifty" Combined Taxable Income Pricing Method and Marginal Costing Pricing Rules. (Ch. 23)

Free Transferability of Interest   One of four corporate attributes that help determine whether a partnership should be taxed as a partnership or as an association (corporation). This attribute exists if most of the partners have the unrestricted right to transfer their partnership interest to another. (Ch. 12)

Gain Realized   The excess of (1) the amount realized over (2) the adjusted basis of an asset surrendered in an external transaction. (Ch. 4)

General Legacy   A pecuniary legacy payable out of the general assets of an estate. (Ch. 13)

General Partner   A partner who has personal liability for the debts of the partnership. A general partner usually participates in the management of the partnership. (Ch. 12)

General Partnership   A partnership whose members are all general partners. (Ch. 12)

Generation-skipping Transfer   Any taxable distribution from or taxable termination of a generation-skipping trust or trust equivalent. (Ch. 18)

Generation-skipping Trust   A trust that has younger-generation beneficiaries who are assigned to more than one generation. (Ch. 18)

Gift   Property or property rights or interests gratuitously passed on to another, whether the transfer is in trust or otherwise, direct or indirect. (Ch. 13)

Grandchild Exclusion   The exclusion permitted for generation-skipping transfers when the prohibited skipped generation consists of the grantor's children and the next younger beneficiaries are the grantor's grandchildren. The exclusion is $250,000 for each child of the grantor who is a deemed transferor. (Ch. 18)

Grantor   The person who establishes a trust, either while alive (*inter vivos* trust) or through will on death (testamentary trust). (Ch. 13)

Grantor Trust   For income tax purposes, a trust under which the settlor (grantor) retains substantial ownership. The income from such a trust is includible in the owner's annual income for tax purposes. (Ch. 14)

Gross Up   The process of increasing a domestic corporation's gross income for the amount of any deemed paid foreign tax credit available (before foreign tax credit limitations) from first- or lower-tier foreign corporations. (Ch. 21)

Guaranteed Payment   Certain payments made by a partnership to a partner. Guaranteed payments must be compensation for the partner's services or for the use of the partner's capital. They must not be determined by reference to the partnership income. (Ch. 11)

Hardship Area Any foreign place designated by the Secretary of State as a hardship post where extraordinarily difficult living conditions, notably unhealthful conditions or excessive physical hardships, exist and for which a post differential of 15 percent or more is provided under Sec. 5925 of Title 5, U.S.C., or would be provided if officers and employees of the U.S. government were present at that place. Hardship areas are periodically designated by the I.R.S. for part or all of each taxable year. (Ch. 22)

Heir A person who inherits or is entitled to inherit the property of another. Also, the person appointed by law to succeed to the estate in case of intestacy. (Chs. 13, 15)

Home Leave A trip provided by the taxpayer's employer for the taxpayer and his or her family from the location of the foreign assignment back to the United States or, under certain circumstances, to an alternative foreign location. This trip is generally provided to enable the employee to transact personal business or handle family matters in the United States. (Ch. 22)

Inbound Transfer An exchange coming under the rules of Secs. 332, 351, 354, 355, 356, or 361, whereby assets are transferred into the United States. An advance ruling is not required in this type of transfer, as is the case with an outbound transfer. However, the Sec. 367 Treasury Regulations may require that the U.S. shareholders recognize income under the rules of Sec. 1248 to prevent the earnings of a controlled foreign corporation that have been previously exempted from U.S. taxation under the deferral privilege from permanently escaping U.S. taxation. *See also* Outbound Transfer. (Ch. 23)

Includible Corporation A corporation that is eligible to be a member of an affiliated group and is not excluded from participating in the consolidated return election by Sec. 1504(b). (Ch. 8)

Incorporation Transaction The initial financial transaction between a corporation and its shareholders in which the shareholders exchange cash, other property, and/or personal services for the corporation's stocks and/or securities. (Ch. 4)

Indirect (Deemed Paid) Foreign Tax Credit A credit available to a domestic corporation under Sec. 902 for a foreign tax levy that has been paid by a foreign investee corporation. The credit is only available when a dividend payment has been made by the foreign investee corporation to a domestic investor corporation. The amount of the deemed paid credit equals:

$$\begin{aligned}&\text{Deemed Paid}\\&\text{Foreign Tax} = \begin{array}{c}\text{Percentage}\\\text{Ownership}\\\text{of Domestic}\\\text{Corporation}\\\text{at Distribution}\\\text{Date}\end{array}\\&\text{Credit}\end{aligned}$$

$$\times \frac{\text{Total Dividends Paid}}{\begin{array}{c}\text{Accumulated}\\\text{Profits minus}\\\text{Foreign Taxes}\end{array}} \times \begin{array}{c}\text{Foreign Taxes}\\\text{Paid or}\\\text{Accrued by}\\\text{the Foreign}\\\text{Corporation}\end{array}$$

The deemed paid credit may also be claimed for certain constructive distributions under the Controlled Foreign Corporation (CFC) rules of Secs. 951 and 960 and gains on the sale of the stock of a CFC under Sec. 1248. *See also* Controlled Foreign Corporation. (Ch. 21)

Initial Inventory Amount The intercompany profit amount for a group member's separate return year that immediately precedes the affiliated group's initial consolidated return year. *See also* Intercompany Profit Amount. (Ch. 8)

Intercompany Profit Amount The amount of intercompany profits that have arisen with respect to goods that are included in the inventories of other group members at the close of the selling group member's taxable year. (Ch. 8)

Intercompany Transaction A transaction during a consolidated return year between corporations that are members of the same affiliated group immediately after the transaction. Excluded from this definition are (1) certain distributions made by one group member to a second group member with respect to the distributing corporation's stock and (2) the sale, exchange, or worthlessness of obligations of a group member that are held by a second group member. (Ch. 8)

Internal Transaction Any transaction involving only one taxable entity. (Ch. 4)

International Boycott Factor This term is a fraction, the numerator of which reflects boycotting operations in or related to a group of countries associated in carrying out an international boycott and the denominator of which reflects worldwide operations (other than those occurring in the United States) (Secs. 999(c)(1) and (3)). (Ch. 21)

Inter Vivos Between the living, for example, an *inter vivos* gift, that of a living settlor. (Ch. 13)

Inter Vivos Trust A gift of property by a living settlor to a trustee for the uses and purposes set forth in the trust instrument. (Ch. 13)

Intestate Without making a will. A person is said to die intestate when he or she dies without making a will.* (Ch. 17)

Investments in U.S. Property Investments made by a controlled foreign corporation (CFC) in certain forms of U.S. properties (defined by Sec. 956(b)(1)) that result in a constructive distribution by the CFC at year-end to its U.S. shareholders. The distribution amount equals the portion of such an investment that would have constituted a dividend if an actual distribution had occurred. Thus, to the extent that the CFC's investment is in a U.S. asset that is an exception to the "U.S. property" definition (under Sec. 956(b)(2)), or would not constitute a dividend (for example, made out of previously taxed earnings), no current taxation will occur to U.S. shareholders. (Ch. 23)

Joint Tenancy with Right of Survivorship An estate in fee-simple, fee-tail, for life, for years, or at will, arising by purchase or grant to two or more persons. The grand incident of joint tenancy is survivorship, by which the entire tenancy on the decease of any joint tenant remains to the survivors, and at length to the last survivor.* (Ch. 16)

Legacy A gift of personal property under a will (a bequest). (Ch. 13)

Legatee The person to whom a legacy is given. (Chs. 13, 15)

Less Developed Country One of a group of foreign countries, territories, and possessions that was designated by the president of the United States as eligible to receive certain special benefits under the U.S. tax laws (Secs. 902, 951, and 1248) and trade laws. (Ch. 21)

Less Developed Country Corporation (LDCC) A foreign corporation that derived most of its income from the conduct of a trade or business in a less developed country or from owning majority control in a corporation or corporations that conducted such business activities. The U.S. owners of an LDCC were at one time eligible for special benefits under the deemed paid foreign tax credit rules (Sec. 902), the Subpart F rules (Sec. 951), and the sale or exchange of stock in a controlled foreign corporation rules (Sec. 1248). (Ch. 21)

Life Estate The title of the interest owned by the life tenant (income beneficiary). The duration of a life estate is limited to the life of the party holding it or of some other person. (Chs. 13, 16)

Life Tenant One who holds an estate in lands for the period of his or her own life or that of another person.* (Ch. 16)

Life Tenant The person who receives the income from a legal life estate or from a trust fund during his or her own life or that of another person (income beneficiary). (Ch. 13)

Limited Partner A partner whose liability to partnership creditors is limited to his or her investment in the partnership. A limited partner is not permitted to participate in the management of the partnership. (Ch. 12)

Limited Partnership A partnership consisting of at least one general partner and one limited partner. (Ch. 12)

Liquidating Distribution A distribution that liquidates the partner's entire interest in the partnership. (Ch. 12)

Liquidation/Reincorporation Transaction A type of transaction that attempts to combine the capital gains treatment accorded the liquidation of an existing corporation under Sec. 331 and the nonrecognition of gain or loss permitted under Sec. 351 when transferring assets to a newly created corporation, in order to withdraw excess funds from a corporation as a capital gain while continuing the existing business activities. A second

advantage may be obtained by stepping up the basis of the operating assets that are transferred to the new corporation to their market value. (Ch. 7)

Litigation The process of subjecting a disagreement between the I.R.S. and a taxpayer to adjudication before a court. (Ch. 2)

Loss Realized The excess of the adjusted basis of a property surrendered in an external transaction over the amount realized. (Ch. 4)

Lower-tier Foreign Corporation Any foreign corporation in which a U.S. investor maintains an indirect investment. A deemed paid foreign tax credit is only available for foreign taxes paid by foreign corporations that are considered to be second- or third-tier foreign corporations. In order to claim a deemed paid foreign tax credit for taxes paid by a second-tier foreign corporation (or third-tier foreign corporation), the first-tier foreign corporation (or second-tier foreign corporation) must directly own at least 10 percent of the voting stock of the second-tier foreign corporation (or third-tier foreign corporation) and the domestic corporation's indirect ownership of voting stock in the second-tier foreign corporation (or third-tier foreign corporation) must be at least 5 percent. *See also* First-tier Foreign Corporation. (Ch. 21)

Marginal Costing Pricing Rules The special marginal costing pricing rules may be used for transactions between a DISC and a related supplier that ultimately produce qualified export receipts—provided the DISC is treated for its taxable year as seeking to establish or maintain a foreign market for sales of an item, product, or product line of export property. As such, the "fifty-fifty" combined taxable income pricing method is applied to a combined taxable income figure that is based on marginal costing amounts for cost of goods sold, rather than the full costing amounts used otherwise (Treas. Reg. Sec. 1.994-2). (Ch. 23)

Member A corporation (including the common parent corporation) that is included in an affiliated group. (Ch. 8)

Merger A corporation, known as the acquiring corporation, acquires the stock of one or more other corpora-

tions, known as the acquired corporation(s), and then proceeds to liquidate the acquired corporation(s). The acquiring corporation thus indirectly acquires all of the acquired corporation's assets and liabilities before causing the acquired corporation to go out of existence. *See also* Type A Reorganization. (Ch. 7)

Net Capital Gain The excess of the net long-term capital gain for the taxable year over the net short-term capital loss for such year. (Ch. 21)

Nonacquisitive Reorganization A type of reorganization that involves either (1) a change in the capital structure of a single corporation that itself remains in existence, or (2) a change in the identity, form, or place of incorporation of a single corporation, whereby the "new" corporation represents a continuation of a corporation that itself goes out of existence. This type of reorganization may fall within the Type E or F reorganization classifications. *See also* Type E and Type F Reorganizations. (Ch. 7)

Nondiscrimination Clause A clause in a tax treaty that requires one nation not to treat nationals of its treaty partner (who reside in the first nation) any more severely under its tax laws than it treats its own citizens, residents, or corporations. (Ch. 21)

Nonrecourse Debt Liabilities for which neither the general nor the limited partners have any personal liability. In other words, the creditor may not look to the personal assets of the limited or general partners for satisfaction of the debt. (Ch. 12)

Nonresident Alien A citizen of a foreign country who is temporarily residing within the United States, or is conducting certain business-related activities that come under the purview of the U.S. tax laws while residing in a foreign country. A nonresident alien is generally taxed under the U.S. tax laws only on his or her U.S.-source investment income and worldwide income that is considered to be "effectively connected with the conduct of a U.S. trade or business." (Ch. 21)

Nontaxable Transaction Any transaction the results of which will *not* be recognized for federal income tax purposes. (Ch. 4)

Old Members   Corporations that were members of the affiliated group immediately preceding the first day of the taxable year in which a consolidated return change of ownership (CRCO) occurred. Special rules exist if the affiliated group did not exist before the year in which the CRCO occurred. (Ch. 8)

Operative Section or Area   One of 17 areas of the Internal Revenue Code to which the Sec. 1.861-8 Treasury Regulation rules for allocating and apportioning deductions apply. Examples of such areas are the determination of a taxpayer's foreign tax credit limitation, a Domestic International Sales Corporation's taxable income, and a U.S. shareholder's constructive dividend distribution from a controlled foreign corporation. (Ch. 21)

Optional Adjustment to Basis   A provision that permits the transferee of a partnership interest to increase or decrease the adjusted basis of partnership assets to reflect the purchase price paid for the assets. An optional adjustment to basis may also be made by the partnership when assets are distributed to a partner. This adjustment reflects the difference between the partner's basis in the partnership and the adjusted basis of the assets distributed to the partners. (Ch. 11)

Organization Expenditures   Amounts spent in creating a partnership that are chargeable to a capital account and that would be amortizable if the partnership had an ascertainable life. Such costs include legal fees incurred in establishing the partnership and fees paid to the state in which the partnership is organized. (Ch. 10)

Other Intercompany Transaction   Any intercompany transaction that does not fall within the category of a deferred intercompany transaction (for example, interest paid by one group member or funds loaned to it by a second group member). *See also* Intercompany Transaction and Deferred Intercompany Transaction. (Ch. 8)

Outbound Transfer   A transfer of property (other than stock or securities of a foreign corporation that is a party to the exchange or reorganization) from a U.S. person to a foreign corporation in an exchange described in Secs. 332, 351, 354, 355, 356, or 361. In order to consider the foreign corporation to be a corporation for purposes of applying the aforementioned Code Sections, the U.S. person engaging in the transfer must request a ruling within 183 days after the beginning of the transfer. This request must establish that the exchange is not in pursuance of a plan having tax avoidance as one of its principal purposes. In some instances, approval of the ruling request will depend on the U.S. person agreeing to recognize certain amounts of previously unrealized income or gain, otherwise known as a "toll charge." (Ch. 23)

Overall Foreign Loss   A situation in which foreign source deductions (other than net operating loss deductions, capital loss carrybacks and carryovers, foreign expropriation losses, and casualty and theft losses) exceed foreign source income. This loss is "recaptured" in a later taxable year when the taxpayer earns a profit from his or her foreign activities. The recapture process treats part or all of the foreign profits as U.S. source income, thereby making it ineligible for the foreign tax credit benefits. (Ch. 21)

Paper DISC   A DISC that performs limited or no services and that generally exists only to receive a portion of the profits that are generated by its parent corporation on its export activities. In these cases, the parent corporation is usually the producer of the goods that are "sold" by the DISC on a commission basis. The use of a "paper DISC" can shelter part or all of the producer's profits on the export transaction from current taxation. (Ch. 23)

Parent–Subsidiary Controlled Group   One or more chains of corporations connected through stock ownership to a common parent corporation that satisfy the minimum stock ownership requirements of Sec. 1563(a)(1). The parent–subsidiary controlled group may or may not be characterized as an affiliated group. The inclusion of a group in both definitions depends upon whether the entire group of corporations (1) satisfies both the stock ownership rules of Sec. 1563(d)(1) for controlled groups and the Sec. 1504(a) rules for affiliated groups *and* (2) are component members of the controlled group (as defined by Sec. 1563(b)) and includible corporations (as defined by Sec. 1504(b)). *See also* Includible Corporations. (Ch. 8)

Partially Liquidating Distribution   A distribution that reduces the partner's interest in partnership capital or profits but does not liquidate the partner's entire partnership interest. (Ch. 12)

Partner   A member of a partnership. For tax purposes, a partner may be a general partner, a limited partner, or an assignee of either a general or a limited partner's interest. (Ch. 10)

Partnership   A syndicate, group, pool, joint venture, or other unincorporated organization through or by means of which any business, financial operation, or venture is carried on, and that is not, within the meaning of this title, a corporation, trust, or estate (Sec. 761(a)). (Ch. 10)

Party to a Reorganization   A corporation resulting from the reorganization, or both corporations in a reorganization transaction in which one of the corporations acquires the stock or assets of the second corporation. (Ch. 7)

Permanent Establishment   Generally defined within the tax treaties to which the U.S. is a party as the minimum facility level required in one of the two countries to trigger taxation of a nonresident alien's profits from the conduct of a trade or business in that country. In the U.S.–Canadian tax treaty, for example, a permanent establishment is defined as including "branches, mines and oil wells, farms, timberlands, plantations, factories, workshops, warehouses, offices, agencies, and other fixed places of business of an enterprise." (Ch. 21)

Personal Holding Company   A corporation that satisfies two requirements: At any time during the last half of the year more than 50 percent of the value of the outstanding stock must be owned, directly or indirectly, by five or fewer individuals, and at least 60 percent of its adjusted ordinary gross income must be personal holding company income. A 70 percent personal holding company tax is imposed on the undistributed personal holding company income of a corporation that qualifies as a personal holding company. (See I.R.C. Secs.

541–547.) *See also* Adjusted Ordinary Gross Income, Personal Holding Company Income, and Undistributed Personal Holding Company Income. (Ch. 19)

Personal Holding Company Income The portion of the adjusted ordinary gross income that consists of "passive income" as established in Sec. 543. Personal holding company income includes, in general, dividends; interest; annuities; mineral, oil, gas, and copyright royalties; rents; produced film rents; income from personal service contracts; distributions from estates and trusts; and income from the use of corporate property by shareholders. The amount of personal holding company income relative to adjusted ordinary gross income is relevant in determining whether a corporation is a personal holding company subject to the 70 percent penalty tax. (See I.R.C. Sec. 543.) *See also* Adjusted Ordinary Gross Income and Personal Holding Company. (Ch. 19)

Possessions Corporation A domestic corporation that, for the preceding three taxable years, derives at least 80 percent of its gross income from within a U.S. possession *and* at least 50 percent of its gross income from the active conduct of a trade or business in a U.S. possession. A possessions corporation is eligible to elect the Sec. 936 Possessions Corporation Tax Credit, which eliminates the domestic corporation's U.S. tax liability on taxable income derived from (1) the conduct of a trade or business in a U.S. possession, (2) the sale of such a trade or business, or (3) qualified possession source investment income. (Ch. 23)

Preservation Clause A clause in a tax treaty that states that the treaty is not to be read to restrict the availability of any deduction, credit, or exemption provided by a country when the tax due that country is being computed. (Ch. 21)

Principal The property making up the estate or fund that has been set aside in trust, or from which income is expected to accrue (corpus). (Ch. 13)

Probate Proof of the genuineness and due execution of a will. (Ch. 13)

Probate Court The court that administers justice in all matters relating to decedents and estates. (Ch. 13)

Producer's Loan A loan of accumulated DISC income to a producer of export property that has been designated a "producer's loan" by the DISC. The producer may be related to the DISC (for example, its controlling shareholder) or may be an unrelated party. A producer's loan permits the controlling shareholder of a DISC to utilize the tax-deferred profits without triggering a taxable event (such as a dividend). (Ch. 23)

Qualified Export Asset An asset classification that applies to a DISC. The adjusted basis of a DISC's qualified export assets at the close of its taxable year must exceed 95 percent of the adjusted basis of all its assets. Assets that fit within this category include export property of the DISC, support facilities of the DISC, trade receivables, working capital, U.S. bank deposits, producer's loans, and certain stocks, securities, and other obligations (Sec. 993(b)). *See also* Export Property. (Ch. 23).

Qualified Export Receipts Export receipts that receive favorable treatment under the DISC rules. At least 95 percent of a DISC's gross receipts for a taxable year must be qualified export receipts in order for DISC status to be retained. Receipts that fit within this category primarily include those from the sale or exchange of export property by the DISC, the leasing or rental of export property outside the United States, services performed that are related and subsidiary to a sale of export property, the sale of qualified export assets (other than export property), dividends from a related foreign export corporation, and interest earned from qualified export assets (Sec. 993(a)). (Ch. 23)

Reasonable Needs of the Business The accumulation of earnings to meet the "reasonable needs of the business" constitutes the major defense against assessment of the accumulated earnings tax. Reasonable needs of the business may be reasonably anticipated future needs, certain stock redemptions, business expansion and plant replacement, working capital, retirement of indebtedness, and acquisition of a business enterprise by

the purchase of its stock or assets. (See I.R.C. Secs. 535, 537, Treas. Reg. Secs. 1.537-1, -2, -3.) *See also* Accumulated Earnings Credit, Accumulated Earnings Tax, and Accumulated Taxable Income. (Ch. 19)

Regional Conferee An employee of the Internal Revenue Service who is responsible for representing the government in administrative proceedings with taxpayers. A conferee is usually trained as an attorney and has authority to reach compromise settlements. In effect, a conferee tries to arbitrate disagreements between an I.R.S. revenue agent and a taxpayer that arose during an audit of the taxpayer's return. (Ch. 2)

Remainder (or Remainder Interest) An estate limited to take effect and be enjoyed after another estate is determined [terminated].* (Ch. 16)

Remainderman The person who is entitled to receive the principal (corpus) of an estate upon the termination of the intervening life estate or estates. (Chs. 13, 16)

Resident Alien A citizen of a foreign country who has established residency in the United States. Resident alien status continues indefinitely until the individual takes an action to relinquish such status. A resident alien is taxed under the U.S. tax laws on his or her worldwide income. (Ch. 21)

Residual Grouping The gross income from sources or activities other than those that are part of the statutory grouping. *See also* Statutory Grouping. (Ch. 21)

Residuary Legacy A gift of all the property of the testator not otherwise effectually disposed of by will. (Ch. 13)

Retroactive Allocation An allocation of partnership loss, deduction, income, gain, or credit to a partner who was not a partner at the time the loss, deduction, income, gain, or credit was incurred by the partnership. These allocations have been curtailed by a 1976 amendment to Sec. 706(c)(2)(B). (Ch. 11)

Reverse Acquisition A transaction (defined in Treas. Reg. Sec. 1.1502-1(d)(3)) whereby assets or stock of the common parent corporation of one affiliated group are acquired by the common parent corporation of a second affiliated group. In this type of transaction, however, the shareholders of the acquired affiliated group's parent corporation end up owning a majority of the stock of the acquiring affiliated group's parent corporation. In this situation, the acquired affiliated group is considered to remain in existence. The acquiring affiliated group goes out of existence, with its members becoming members of the surviving, acquired affiliated group. The common parent corporation for the acquiring group, however, becomes the common parent corporation for the enlarged, surviving affiliated group. (Ch. 8)

Revenue Agent An employee of the Internal Revenue Service whose assigned duty is to establish the accuracy of tax returns filed by taxpayers. In this capacity, a revenue agent examines underlying documents used to prepare the return and files a revenue agent's report (RAR) of the findings. (Ch. 2)

Reversionary Interest An interest in the reversion of lands or other property. A right to the future enjoyment of property currently in the possession or occupation of another. Unlike a remainder interest, a reversionary interest is an interest of the person who transferred the property. (Ch. 16)

Sales DISC A DISC that purchases export property from either a related or unrelated producer and resells it either to a third-party purchaser or to a related foreign export corporation. *See also* Paper DISC. (Ch. 23)

Savings Clause A clause in a tax treaty that provides that each treaty country maintains the right to tax its own citizens and residents as if the treaty did not exist. (Ch. 21)

Section 306 Stock Noncommon stock that is received by a shareholder that is partially or totally exempt from taxation at the shareholder level because of the rules of Sec. 305(a). Section 306 stock may also be (1) noncommon stock that is received partially or totally tax free as a result of a corporate reorganization or corporate division or (2) stock that has a substituted basis in the hands of the shareholder that references the basis of Sec. 306 stock. The sale or exchange of Sec. 306 stock may result in ordinary income and/or capital gains being recognized by the exchanging shareholder. (Ch. 7)

Section 368(c) Control Ownership of 80 percent of the total combined voting power of all classes of stock entitled to vote and 80 percent of the total number of shares of each additional class of stock. The 80 percent test is applied separately to each class of nonvoting stock. (Ch. 7)

Section 482 A Code provision that permits the Internal Revenue Service to "distribute, apportion, or allocate gross income, deductions, credits, or allowances" between or among commonly controlled organizations if such an action is necessary to prevent the evasion of taxes or to clearly reflect income. This power permits the I.R.S. to place a "controlled taxpayer" in a similar tax position with an "uncontrolled taxpayer," by determining, according to the standard of the uncontrolled taxpayer the "true taxable income" that has been derived from the property and business of the controlled taxpayer. "True taxable income" represents the amount of income that would be reported by two independent parties dealing at arm's length with one another. (Ch. 8)

Section 736(a) Payments Ordinary income payments made by a partnership to a retiring partner or to the successor in interest of a deceased partner. (Ch. 12)

Section 736(b) Payments Capital-gain-producing payments made by a partnership to a retiring partner or to the successor in interest of a deceased partner. (Ch. 12)

Section 751 Assets Unrealized receivables and substantially appreciated inventory. When a partnership interest is sold, any gain attributable to the receipt of non-Section 751 assets in exchange for Sec. 751 assets is taxed as ordinary income. Section 751 assets may also create ordinary income when assets are distributed to a partner in either a partially or completely liquidating distribution. (Ch. 11)

Security A debt instrument, such as a bond or note, that when issued by a corporation is of a nature that permits the deferral of gain under the rules of Secs. 351 and 354. In general, these are debt instruments that permit the holder to retain a continuing creditor interest in the business entity, rather than being of a short-term nature and representing a "near-cash" item. In general, a debt instrument will not be

a security if its duration is less than five years, although time is but one of a series of factors used to determine if a debt instrument is a security. (Ch. 7)

Separate Return Limitation Year (SRLY) Any separate return year of a member or a predecessor of a member unless the year falls within the exceptions of Treas. Reg. Sec. 1.1502-1(f). Certain losses, deductions, and credits incurred or earned in a separate return limitation year (for example, net operating losses, capital losses, and investment tax credits) are limited in their use as a carryback or carryover in consolidated return years. (Ch. 8)

Separate Return Year A taxable year of a corporation for which the corporation files a separate income tax return or for which it joins in the filing of a consolidated tax return with an affiliated group different from the one it is affiliated with in the current year. (Ch. 8)

Separate Taxable Income The taxable income of a member of an affiliated group that is combined with similar amounts from the other group members in the initial step of the determination of the affiliated group's consolidated taxable income. This amount is computed under the rules of Treas. Reg. Sec. 1.1502-12 as if the group member were filing a separate tax return, except for a series of adjustments generally relating to intercompany transactions and items reported on a consolidated basis by the affiliated group. *See also* Consolidated Taxable Income. (Ch. 8)

Settlor The person who makes a gift to an *inter vivos* trust. (Ch. 13)

Simple Trust For income tax purposes, a trust that requires that income, as defined by the governing instrument or by local law, be distributed currently to the beneficiaries other than charities. (Ch. 13)

Special Allocation An allocation of partnership income, gain, loss, deduction, or credit that differs from the partner's distributive share for most items of income, gain, loss, deduction, or credit. A special allocation will be honored for tax purposes only if it has substantial economic effect. (Ch. 11)

Specific Legacy A testamentary gift of a special item in a decedent's estate that may be identified with particularity. (Ch. 13)

Spin-off   A transaction that involves the transfer by the distributing corporation of part of its assets (and possibly some liabilities) to one or more controlled corporations, followed by the distribution of the necessary amount of the controlled corporation's stocks and securities to the distributing corporation's shareholders and security holders. (Ch. 7)

Split-off   A transaction that involves the transfer by the distributing corporation of part of its assets (and possibily some liabilities) to one or more controlled corporations, followed by the exchange of part or all of the controlled corporation's stocks and securities held by the distributing corporation for part or all of the distributing corporation's outstanding stocks and securities. (Ch. 7)

Split-up   A transaction that involves the transfer by the distributing corporation of all of its assets to two or more controlled corporations whose stocks and securities are then exchanged by the distributing corporation for all of its outstanding stocks and securities. The transferor (or distributing) corporation is then liquidated, and the two or more former subsidiary corporations carry on the transferor corporation's business activities. (Ch. 7)

Statutory Grouping   The gross income derived from a specific source or activity that must first be determined in order to arrive at the taxable income derived from a specific source or activity under one of the operative sections to which the Sec. 1.861-8 Treasury Regulations apply. *See also* Residual Grouping and Operative Section. (Ch. 21)

Subchapter S Corporation   A corporation given special tax treatment according to the provisions of Subchapter S of the Code. (Chs. 4, 9)

Subpart F   Sections 951–964 of the Internal Revenue Code. (Ch. 23)

Subpart F Income   Income of a controlled foreign corporation (CFC) that is constructively distributed on a pro rata basis to the CFC's U.S. shareholders under Sec. 951(a)(2) in the year in which it is earned. Subpart F income is made up of four components: (1) income from the insurance of U.S. risks; (2) foreign base company income; (3) boycott-related income; and (4) an amount equal to the bribes and illegal

kickbacks paid by or for the CFC. This last category of Subpart F income eliminates the deferral privilege for a portion of the CFC's profits equal to the amount of its illegal bribe or kickback payments. *See also* Deferral Privilege and Foreign Base Company Income. (Ch. 23)

Subsidiary Corporation   A corporation, other than the common parent corporation, that is a member of an affiliated group. *See also* Common Parent Corporation. (Ch. 8)

Substantial Economic Effect   The requirement that any special allocation of partnership income, gain, loss, deduction, or credit must affect (1) the dollar amount of the partner's share of partnership income or loss independently of tax consequences, and (2) the partner's cash flow when his or her partnership interest is liquidated. (Ch. 11)

Substituted Basis   The basis when the basis of the property received by a transferor is the same as the basis of the property transferred by the transferor. (Ch. 10)

Syndication Expenditures   Costs incurred in selling partnership interests. Examples of syndication expenditures are commissions, professional fees, and printing costs incurred in selling such interests. (Ch. 10)

Taxable Distribution   A distribution from the corpus of a generation-skipping trust, made to a younger generation beneficiary, that skips a generation. (Ch. 18)

Taxable Termination   The termination of the interest in or power over a generation-skipping trust of a beneficiary when an interest in the trust passes to an individual who belongs to a generation younger than that of the individual whose interest or power terminates. (Ch. 18)

Tax Advisor   A person who is professionally trained to offer advice in all areas of the federal, state, and local tax laws. Usually a certified public accountant or a lawyer, the person will most likely have progressed beyond the staff assistant level. In an accounting firm, a tax advisor has usually achieved the level of senior staff accountant. (Ch. 1)

Tax Compliance   Tax work performed by trained professionals that focuses

on complying with the existing rules and requirements of the tax laws after the results of a business decision are known. This usually involves the preparation of tax returns and dealing with the I.R.S. regarding administrative proceedings to explain the treatment of specific items in the return. (Ch. 1)

Tax Home   An individual's home for purposes of determining the deductibility of traveling expenses incurred while away from home. Generally, tax home means the taxpayer's household or residence. (Ch. 22)

Tax Planning   Tax work performed by trained professionals that focuses on the development of a tax plan before the various steps of a business decision have begun. Planning before-the-facts allows the sequence of events to be structured in such a way as to produce the most favorable tax results. (Ch. 3)

Tax Researcher   A person who is professionally trained to perform research to assist in tax planning or compliance work. The person may consult such resource materials as the Internal Revenue Code, the Treasury Regulations, tax services, court decisions, and various editorial sources to reach a conclusion with respect to a previously determined issue. Basic research is frequently performed by staff professionals who have not yet reached senior standing. (Ch. 1)

Tax-Shelter Partnerships   Partnerships designed to provide partners with a positive cash flow and a negative taxable income during the initial years of the shelter's operation. Loss incurred by the partnership shelters the income earned by the partners outside the partnership. (Ch. 12)

Tax Statutes   The laws that govern the payment of taxes. Such laws are enacted by an appropriate representative government (such as the U.S. Congress, a state legislature, or a city council) to collect taxes. (Ch. 2)

Tax Treaty   A bilateral agreement between two nations that determines the tax treatment for certain specified transactions. Tax treaties usually apply only to individuals, corporations, or other parties that are considered to be residents of one of the two treaty countries. (Ch. 21)

Tenancy by the Entirety   Created by a conveyance to husband and wife, whereupon each becomes seized and possessed of the entire estate and after the death of one the survivor takes the whole. Available only to husband and wife. The grand characteristic that distinguishes it from a joint tenancy is that it may be terminated only by joint action of husband and wife during their lives, while "joint tenancy" may be terminated by one tenant's conveyance of his or her interest.* (Ch. 16)

Tenancy in Common The holding of an estate in land by different persons under different titles, but there must be unity of possession and each must have the right to occupy the whole in common with his cotenants. A tenancy in common may exist in personalty as well as realty.* (Ch. 16)

Term for Years (Term Certain Interest) An interest whose duration is limited to a certain amount of time, such as 15 years, at the end of which the property will pass to another.* (Ch. 16)

Testament A will. (Ch. 13)

Testamentary Trust A legacy or devise of property to a trustee for the uses and purposes set forth in the will. (Ch. 13)

Testate (adj.) Deceased, leaving a valid will. (Ch. 13)

Testator (Testatrix) The maker of a will. (Ch. 13)

Thirty-day Rule Two rules permitting a subsidiary corporation (1) to be excluded from being a group member for a taxable year or (2) to be included as a group member for a full taxable year. The rule may be elected to exclude a corporation from an affiliated group if it was a group member for 30 or fewer days during a consolidated return year. Alternatively, if a corporation joins an affiliated group in the first 30 days of its taxable year, it may elect to be a member of the affiliated group for its full taxable year. (Ch. 8)

Transaction Any significant change in the form or the substance of any property or property right. (Ch. 4)

Trustee The fiduciary nominated by the testator or settlor or appointed by the court to administer the trust property. (Ch. 13)

Type A Income Investment-related income, capital gains, and certain other types of income that are *not* effectively connected with the conduct of a U.S. trade or business. The usual forms of Type A income are interest,

dividends, rents, salaries, wages, premiums, annuities, compensations, remunerations, alimony, certain forms of capital gain income, and emoluments. These forms of income are usually taxed at a 30 percent rate (with no deductions permitted) or at a lower tax rate permitted under a tax treaty. *See also* Type B Income and Income Effectively Connected with the Conduct of a U.S. Trade or Business. (Ch. 22)

Type A Reorganization A reorganization transaction that is structured as either a merger or a consolidation and that satisfies the corporation laws of the United States, a state, or the District of Columbia. This type of reorganization comes under the rules of Sec. 368(a)(1)(A). *See also* Merger and Consolidation. (Ch. 7)

Type B Income Any type of income that is considered to be effectively connected with the conduct of a U.S. trade or business. Such income is taxed at the full U.S. tax rates that are applicable to U.S. citizens, residents, or domestic corporations. *See also* Type A Income and Income Effectively Connected with the Conduct of a U.S. Trade or Business. (Ch. 22)

Type B Reorganization An exchange transaction involving the acquisition by one corporation, known as the acquiring corporation, of the stock of a second corporation, known as the acquired corporation, in such a way that the acquiring corporation has control (defined by Sec. 368(c)) of the acquired corporation immediately after the exchange. This "stock-for-stock" reorganization comes under the rules of Sec. 368(a)(1)(B). *See also* Section 368(c) Control. (Ch. 7)

Type C Reorganization A reorganization transaction that results in the acquisition by one corporation, known as the acquiring corporation, of substantially all of the assets of a second corporation, known as the acquired corporation. After the reorganization transaction, the acquired corporation may be liquidated or remain in existence to either hold the stock received in the reorganization or conduct a new trade or business. This "asset-for-stock" reorganization comes under the rules of Sec. 368(a)(1)(C). (Ch. 7)

Type D Reorganization A

reorganization that involves the transfer by a corporation of either part or all of its assets to one or more corporations that immediately after the transfer are controlled by the transferor corporation, by one or more of its shareholders, or a combination thereof. In addition, the stocks and securities of the controlled corporation must be distributed by the transferor corporation in a tax-free transaction coming under Secs. 354, 355, or 356. The Type D reorganization may be either a divisive or acquisitive type of reorganization, and comes under the rules of Sec. 368(a)(1)(D). (Ch. 7)

Type E Reorganization A reorganization that involves a recapitalization of an existing corporation. Such a transaction, which falls under the rules of Sec. 368(a)(1)(E), usually involves the reshuffling of the capital structure within the framework of an existing corporation, rather than any increase or decrease in the amount of the corporation's assets. (Ch. 7)

Type F Reorganization A reorganization that involves a "mere change in identity, form, or place of organization." This type of transaction, which falls under the rules of Sec. 368(a)(1)(F), ordinarily results in the continuation of one or more existing corporations in a new corporate shell with substantially all of the owners of the old corporate entities participating in the new venture. (Ch. 7)

Undistributed Foreign Personal Holding Company Income (UFPHCI) The taxable income of the foreign personal holding company (adjusted by Sec. 556(b)) to provide deductions for federal income taxes, excess charitable contributions, and so on, and to disallow any special deductions claimed under Secs. 241–250 (other than Sec. 248). This UFPHCI amount is then constructively distributed to each of the foreign personal holding company's U.S. shareholders. (Ch. 23)

Undistributed Personal Holding Company Income The amount upon which the personal holding company tax is imposed. The undistributed personal holding company income is derived by making certain adjustments to the taxable income of the personal holding company. (See I.R.C. Sec. 545.) *See* *also* Personal Holding Company. (Ch. 19)

Uniform Limited Partnership Act A model set of limited partnership statutes developed by the National Commissioners on Uniform Laws. The purpose of the Act was to create uniformity among states in the statutes governing limited partnership transactions. The Act has been adopted in whole or in part by most states. (Ch. 12)

Uniform Partnership Act A model set of partnership statutes developed by the National Commissioners on Uniform Laws. The purpose of the Act was to create uniformity among states in the statutes governing general partnership transactions. The Act has been adopted in whole or in part by most states. (Ch. 12)

Unrecovered Inventory Amount For a consolidated return year, the lesser of the group member's intercompany profit amount for the taxable year or its initial inventory amount. *See also* Intercompany Profit Amount and Initial Inventory Amount. (Ch. 8)

U.S. Possession Any of a number of specially designated geographical areas that are under the control of the U.S. government. Sections 931–936 permit special tax benefits for U.S. citizens and domestic corporations deriving most of their income from a U.S. possession. Although the definition of a U.S. possession will vary among tax provisions, it generally includes American Samoa, Midway Islands, Palmyra, Johnston Island, Kingman Reef, Wake Island, Howland Island, Baker Island, Jarvis Island, the Virgin Islands, Puerto Rico, Guam, and the Northern Marianna Islands. Puerto Rico is defined for tax purposes as a U.S. possession even though it is technically a U.S. territory. (Ch. 22)

U.S. Shareholder For controlled foreign corporation purposes, any U.S. person (defined by Sec. 957(d)) who directly, indirectly, or constructively owns at least 10 percent of the total combined voting power of all classes of stock entitled to vote of the foreign corporation (Sec. 951(b)). (Ch. 21)

U.S. Source Income Any type of income that is considered to originate from within the United States under the rules of Secs. 861–863. *See also* Foreign Source Income. (Ch. 21)

Western Hemisphere Trade Corporation (WHTC) A domestic corporation that derived nearly all its income from the active conduct of exporting activities in the Western Hemisphere. Before 1976, a WHTC received a special deduction equal to 14/48ths of its taxable income. Phased out over the period 1976–1979, this special deduction is no longer available (Sec. 921). (Ch. 23)

Will A proper disposition of property made in the form and manner prescribed by law, by a competent testator who is free from fraud, duress, and undue influence, which takes effect upon the death of the maker. (Ch. 13)

Younger Generation Beneficiary An individual who has an interest in or a power over a trust and who belongs to a generation younger than the generation of the grantor of the trust. For this purpose, a person has an interest if he or she is a permissible recipient of income or corpus from the trust. A person has a power over a trust if he or she has any right to establish or alter beneficial enjoyment of the corpus or income of the trust. (Ch. 18)

index of cases cited

index

A 0
B 1
C 2
D 3
E 4
F 5
G 6
H 7
I 8
J 9